The Family Guide to

MOVIES
ON VIDEO

The Family Guide to

THE MORAL AND ENTERTAINMENT VALUES OF 5,000 MOVIES ON TV AND VIDEOCASSETTE

Edited by Henry Herx and Tony Zaza

CROSSROAD • NEW YORK

1988

The Crossroad Publishing Company
370 Lexington Avenue, New York, NY 10017

Printed in the United States of America

Library of Congress Cataloging-in-Publication Data

The Family guide to movies on video : the moral and entertainment
value of 5,000 movies on TV and videocassette / edited by Henry
Herx.
    p.   cm.
Prepared under the auspices of the United States Catholic
Conference.
    ISBN 0-8245-0816-5   ISBN 0-8245-0817-3 (pbk.)
    1. Motion pictures—Reviews. 2. Motion pictures—Moral and
ethical aspects. 3. Video recordings—Catalogs. I. Herx, Henry.
II. United States Catholic Conference.
PN1995.F26   1988
791.43'75—dc 19   88-1398
                                  CIP

Introduction

The Reason for This Work

Old movies never die; most don't even fade away. Their screen after-life lingers on, and for many actually increases, through the electronic media of television, cable and videocassette. Hollywood movies today make more money in these forms of home video than they do in movie theaters. Even more important is the fact that they are seen by considerably larger numbers of viewers at home than by the patrons of movie theaters.

This has created something of a consumer problem for the home viewer, because the information and publicity that surrounds the theatrical release of a movie is no longer available by the time it appears on the home screen. The usual television listings in newspapers are simply inadequate for making an informed decision about whether or not the movie is worth several hours of anyone's time. Yet most Americans have to make up their minds based on the title, year of release, a hint of the plot situation, the names of a couple of actors and perhaps a few words or a symbol indicating the fact that it's anything from a classic to a clunker.

This is not much better than reading tea leaves. There are some books which provide plot summaries of and observations on many of the theatrical features in circulation, but they are mainly written for those who take movies seriously as a form of popular culture and want to know where a particular movie fits within the history of the motion picture medium.

Parents, of course, have other concerns in searching out the value and appropriateness of a movie for members of their family. It is the intention of this guide to provide concerned parents with sufficient information about the moral dimension of story and treatment, age suitability and the artistic and entertainment quality of each of the movies listed in the following pages.

How to Use the Guide

Contained within are descriptions and evaluations of virtually all motion pictures in national release to American theaters during the years 1966–87. A number of films released prior to 1966 are also included, especially those that have particular relevance—good, bad and indifferent—for family viewing.

Each movie capsule consists usually of two sentences, the first of which summarizes the plot or theme of the picture, and the second provides an evaluation of its relative merits as entertainment or enrichment and its suitability for various age groups.

Following each entry are the symbols used by two rating groups, the first being that of the United States Catholic Conference Department of Communication (USCC) followed within parentheses by that of the Motion Picture Association of America (MPAA). The USCC classifications indicate moral suitability as well as appropriateness for children, adolescents and adults. The MPAA ratings are divided according to age suitability.

USCC CLASSIFICATIONS

A-I—general patronage
A-II—adults and adolescents
A-III—adults
A-IV—adults, with reservations (this refers to certain movies which are not morally offensive in themselves but do require some analysis and explanation to avoid mistaken interpretations and false conclusions)
O—morally offensive

MPAA RATINGS

G—general audiences, all ages admitted
PG—parental guidance suggested, some material may not be suitable for children
PG-13—parents are strongly cautioned to give special guidance for attendance of children under 13, some material may be inappropriate for young children
R—restricted, under 17 requires accompanying parent or adult guardian
X—no one under 17 admitted (age limit may vary in certain areas)

In addition to the above, the MPAA in its first years used the symbol GP and later M for what today has become the PG category. However, the MPAA does not allow the automatic substitution of the present PG rating for these two former rating symbols unless it has officially changed these original designations. Consequently, though perhaps confusing, GP and M are used where appropriate.

Because MPAA ratings are changed occasionally, it was thought advisable to indicate such changes by a slash mark, with the rating following the slash being the present rating. For example, (R/PG) indicates that a movie was originally rated as restricted but has since been changed to the parental guidance category.

Such changes may indicate that the distributor has cut the scenes responsible for the R rating or that scenes which had previously been thought inappropriate for young viewers have subsequently been thought a decision parents should make. Since such ratings apply only to the version being shown in theaters, it is important for parents to realize that the video version may contain material that once had been removed. In fact, some videos even state that they have scenes not in the original theatrical version.

Finally, the rating system has an appeal process by which a group of industry representatives can over-rule the rating administration. Though this happens rarely, it was thought worth indicating those instances when the appeal process changed the rating. This is indicated by the original MPAA rating, then a slash and the new rating followed by the word "appeal," for example, (R/PG appeal).

ABBREVIATIONS

nr—not rated (movies that have been released without applying for a rating from the MPAA)

br—before ratings (movies released before the MPAA classification system began in October 1968)

The Reason for Ratings

Many people like good movies but don't like taking chances on bad ones. This book tries to take the chance out of selecting movie fare, especially for those concerned about the quality of the screen experience for themselves and, even more, for those that depend upon their guidance. Youngsters are the most vulnerable to current screen fare and need some assistance in selecting movies that help them grow without false values and wrong ideas.

This didn't used to be a problem. The American movie industry was born in the last part of the 19th century as a mass medium of entertainment. During World War I, it grew to international stature and Hollywood dominated the screens of the world until World War II. Hollywood became synonymous with the movies.

The genius of American movies was their appeal to the entire family. For the most part they were simple stories well-told, and they were relatively inexpensive fare easily affordable for most and, they became a regular habit.

The post-war world changed that by making the home television screen the easiest way for people to see popular entertainment, including movies. In the 1950s, Hollywood tried to fight back by introducing 3-D devices and the wide screen. Neither brought back the family audience.

In the 1960s, movie producers and exhibitors turned to adult material that television, their chief competitor, would not allow on the home screen. In order to do this, however, the MPAA realized they would have to advise viewers, especially parents, that certain movies were not for youngsters. This resulted in the MPAA Rating Administration replacing the MPAA Production Code which had carefully regulated the content of Hollywood movies.

The MPAA ratings are determined by officials of the Rating Administration in Los Angeles and were initiated in October of 1968.

USCC Movie Classifications

The USCC Department of Communication classification system is an outgrowth of a program that began in 1934 with the founding of the National Legion of Decency and its initiation of moral ratings in 1936. Over the years, various modifications have been implemented in trying to reflect the development of movies from primarily escapist entertainment to their gradual emergence as also a medium of serious artistic expression.

The classifications are the result of a consensus process involving the staff of the department and a group of outside consultants who contribute their recommendations as to the moral considerations and values or lack thereof to be found in the movies that they screen. This volunteer group is today an ecumenical one, representative of the general moviegoing community, non-Catholic as well as Catholic.

Though the classifications serve busy parents as an instant means of identifying the age suitability and moral quality of a particular movie, they are only labels to be applied in terms of the level of maturity of their own youngsters. The capsule comments attempt to provide enough information to enable parents to decide for themselves what is suitable for their family's screen fare.

In 1964 the department's staff began writing reviews of the best of the new releases, and since 1969 all movies have been reviewed as well as classified. This volume represents the work of the many individuals, both staff and consultants, who contributed their moral judgments, aesthetic sensibilities and considerable writing talents to the task of movie evaluation. The present format makes their work readily accessible to any seeking guidance about past movies.

Particularly helpful in the long process of editing, typing and proofing of copy were Dorothy Farley, O.P., Stephanie Stefko and Marjorie Valleau, and their perseverance, as well as that of an already overburdened department staff, is gratefully acknowledged.

HENRY HERX

A

Aaron Loves Angela (1976) The story of a teenage romance between a black youth (Kevin Hooks) and a Puerto Rican girl (Irene Cara) is told in a lifeless movie that tries to get too much mileage out of the charm of its two young principals. Director Gordon Parks Jr.'s absurdly melodramatic conclusion involves violence between a brutal but soft-hearted heroin pusher (Robert Hooks) and some syndicate types. O (R)

Abby (1975) Low-budget, black version of "The Exorcist" in which God and the Devil clash, this time in the form of a young woman (Carol Speed) possessed by a demon unleashed by her archaeologist father-in-law (William Marshall) who, fortunately, also happens to be a clergyman. Directed by William Girdler, it has all the defects and excesses of the original plus a few of its own. Exploitative sex and violence. O (R)

Abdication, The (1974) Having relinquished the Swedish throne for various religious reasons, Queen Christina (Liv Ullmann) arrives in Rome to prostrate herself before Pope Alexander VII. Suspecting a Protestant plot to discredit the church, a cardinal (Peter Finch) is appointed to examine the ex-queen and his interrogation forms the bulk of the movie. It is a test the movie thoroughly fails, despite director Anthony Harvey's efforts to breathe fire into a tired historical drama with little historicity and less drama. A-III (PG)

Abductors, The (1972) Using local New Jersey talent and a story line that Mickey Spillane would have thrown in the waste-basket, writer-director Don Schain pits sexy, sadistic private eye Ginger (Cheri Caffaro) against a seedy gang who abduct young women, instruct them in the finer points of depravity and then sell them to needy executives around the country. Trash with violence and nudity. O (R)

Abe Lincoln in Illinois (1940) Raymond Massey stars as Honest Abe and Ruth Gordon plays Mary Todd in this well-acted drama based on the Pulitzer Prize-winning Robert Sherwood play. Directed by John Cromwell, the movie's emphasis is upon the development of Lincoln's character and his compassionate confrontation with adversity. A-I (br)

Abominable Dr. Phibes, The (1971) Horror movie featuring superb Art Deco sets and the campy good humor of Vincent Price as the gruesome doctor (of both medicine and theology) but an unnecessarily ugly story about Phibes' taking revenge for his wife's death by following the pattern of the ten plagues found in Exodus. Despite a certain whacky unreality running through the whole exercise, director Robert Fuest uses some full close-ups that seem a little strong for anyone but the devoted horror fan. A-III (PG)

About Last Night (1986) Romance set against the vulgar background of the singles scene where the immaturity and insecurities of two young professionals (Demi Moore and Rob Lowe) doom to failure their struggle to form a lasting bond. Played for comedy by director Edward Zwick, the movie is socially, emotionally and morally uninformed about the nature of a truly loving relationship. Rough language and nudity in a sexual context. O (R)

Absence of Malice (1981) Ambitious Miami reporter (Sally Field) is duped into reporting false information on the son of an organized crime figure (Paul Newman). Though director Sydney Pollack slickly stacks the deck against the news media, the movie does succeed in raising serious issues about media responsibility and public opinion. Incidental details include suicide, abortion and an illicit sexual relationship. A-II (PG)

Absent-Minded Professor, The (1961) Mildly amusing Disney comedy with Fred MacMurray as a daffy science professor who discovers a potion that lets people and objects defy the laws of gravity. The resulting silliness might best be appreciated by the very young. A-I (G)

Absolute Beginners (1986) Youth-oriented musical drama starring David Bowie as an ad man selling materialism to adolescents, represented by a teenage song-and-dance team (Eddie O'Connell and Patsy Kensit). British production directed by Julien Temple links the euphoria of young people in the late l960s with the birth of a youth subculture and consumer market. Mainly, however, it celebrates lack of conscience and good judgment as the substance of adolescence. An intense scene of violence and a confused perspective on adolescent sexuality. A-III (PG-l3)

Accident (1967) Cryptic Harold Pinter script begins with an auto crash killing the young man engaged to an Oxford coed, after which the events and forces contributing to the "accident" are presented in flashback, including the rivalry of two dons for the woman student's affection. Director Joseph Losey and an excellent cast use the sparse dialogue and strained situations to give clues to the violence developing beneath the tranquil surface of academic life. Adult situation and treatment. A-III (br)

Ace Eli and Rodger of the Skies (1973) Cliff Robertson and Eric Shea play a father-son team of Kansas barnstormers in the early 1920s who are flying away from the tragic death of the woman in their life. For Eli, his wife's death triggers a streak of womanizing while for his 11-year-old son, the loss of a mother brings out a raunchy maturity and wisdom far surpassing that of his father but also the search for a new mother-figure. Director Bill Sampson's failed drama is a confusing and confused, largely unmotivated concoction of scenes alternately nostalgic, crude, cruel, near-perverse and sappy. A-III (PG)

Ace High (1969) Revenge with a humorous twist is the theme of this low-budget Italian Western starring Eli Wallach as a bug-ridden, baby-sitting Greek bandit. Director Giuseppe Colizzi's action is slapdash but unflagging enough to compensate for rough dubbing, poor color and ragged editing. Stylized violence. A-II (M)

Across 110th Street (1972) Anthony Quinn plays a tough old-time cop compelled for political reasons to work with a black new-breed policeman (Yaphet Kotto) in tracking down the three blacks who ripped off a syndicate-controlled, black-managed Harlem numbers bank. Unfortunately, director Barry Shear develops neither the broader implications of the story's social conflicts nor the potentially interesting personality clash of his principals, apparently too involved with the mechanics of all the violence that is so grossly in evidence. O (R)

Across the Great Divide (1977) Two orphans on the pioneer trail to Oregon in 1876 are guided through the perils of frontier America by a charming gambler (Robert Logan). Directed by Robert Raffill, it provides a familiar mixture of

11

attractive characters, photogenic animals and gorgeous scenery. The slick use of these wholesome elements at the expense of any realism may strike some viewers as rather calculated but that does not lessen its value as fantasy entertainment for family audiences. A-I (G)

Act of Aggression (1975) French vigilante movie about a man (Jean-Louis Trintignant) whose wife and daughter have been brutally raped and murdered, apparently by vicious bikers, and his lust both for revenge and for his wife's sister (Catherine Deneuve). Director Gerard Pires never grapples seriously with the vendetta theme but concentrates instead on the romance, employing some nudity and kinky sexuality. O (R)

Act of Vengeance (1974) Exploitative melodrama about rape and the efforts of five victims, led by Joann Harris, to entrap their assailant, a sadist with a penchant for singing "Jingle Bells." Director Robert Kelljan seems less concerned about showing the degradation and humiliation of rape as an act of violence against women than as using an anti-rape theme as an excuse for displaying naked bodies as sex objects. O (R)

Act of the Heart, The (1970) Sensitive but flawed Canadian drama about a young woman (Genevieve Bujold) whose love for a priest (Donald Sutherland) results in his leaving the ministry but his subsequent disillusionment with the world leads her to burn herself to death. Until this grisly conclusion, the movie had been a perceptive study of character and feeling in which director Paul Almond explored issues of loneliness and the search for self and meaning in the contemporary world. Inadequately motivated, the violent act of self-immolation is a major miscalculation in what otherwise is a gentle story of idealism and love. A-IV (GP)

Activist, The (1969) Amateurish semi-documentary account of several months in the life of a Berkley student who is a dedicated militant in the protest movement. Directed by Art and Jo Napoleon, the best thing about this fictional reconstruction is some actual newsreel footage of campus demonstrations. Lengthy and explicit love-making scene lacks any dramatic purpose or justification. O (X)

Adalen '31 (1969) Swedish production re-creates a 1931 labor strike by focusing on the lives of individual workers involved in the struggle for subsistance. The political conflict and social commentary are crystal clear, but remarkably unobtrusive amid the vignettes of daily life in a small town during hard times. When scab workers arrive, a peaceful demonstration ends in violence and death. Using a mixture of romantic fiction and economic realities, director Bo Widerburg successfully combines social awareness with lyric beauty. Brief nudity and casual acceptance of abortion. A-IV (X)

Adam at 6 A.M. (1970) West Coast college professor (Michael Douglas), searching for the values of heartland America, spends a summer doing construction work in Missouri, decides to settle down and marry a local belle (Lee Purcell) but then realizes that life in the Midwest will be no less conformist than that of the world from which he has fled. Director Robert Scheerer employs a number of easy stereotypes to characterize America's geographic and cultural polarities, but beneath the movie's slick surface is a profoundly cynical commentary upon the country's heritage and the values of its people. A-IV (GP)

Adding Machine, The (1969) An office worker (Milo O'Shea), saddled with a nagging wife (Phyllis Diller), has fantasies of an affair with his pretty assistant (Billie Whitelaw). When he kills his boss and a sentence of death is carried out, he ultimately winds up in a hell of adding machines. Adapted by producer-director Jerome Epstein from a 1930's Elmer Rice play, the stagey result speaks less about the contemporary onslaught of automation and economic disparity than it does of a very dated kind of ideological indignation. A-III (PG)

Adelaide (1969) Director Jean-Daniel Simon has been unable to elevate this pulp story of a widow whose new husband continues to carry on an affair with her teenage daughter. Static and introverted atmosphere, incomprehensible plot development and determined underplaying by Ingrid Thulin and Jean Sorel supply no motivation for the senseless actions of the story's characters. O (R)

Adieu Philippine (1973) French production about a young man awaiting his army call-up who begins a flirtation with two girls who are intimate friends, a situation left unresolved by the boy's departure but with the sense of embarking on a new, more mature phase of life. Directed by Jacques Rozier, this 1961 movie is a mosaic of scenes, beautifully photographed and evocative of the carefree romanticism of youth, carefully knit together by the juke-box music of the period. Without a traditional narrative, however, its appeal is mainly to those who enjoy watching a well-crafted film. A-III (nr)

Adios, Sabata (1971) Routine Italian Western with bounty hunter Yul Brynner polishing off great gobs of humanity in his relentless pursuit of a Mexican revolutionary and a share of Maximilian's gold. Taken seriously, all this violence would be alarming, but played tongue-in-cheek under Frank Kramer's direction, it's a comic fantasy for those who enjoy such action programs. A-II (GP)

Adrift (1971) Czechoslovakian production about a fisherman who rescues a beautiful woman from drowning and his gradual disintegration (told in flashbacks mixing reality with fantasy) driven by desire for the girl (Paula Pritchett) who has become a member of his household. Although not entirely successful in its fancy time sequences, director Jan Kadar's leisurely pace builds steadily towards his powerful conclusion concerning man's vulnerability to temptation. The erotic element of the film is a necessary one counterbalanced by the very human portrayals of the fisherman and his wife (Rade Markovic and Milena Dravic). A-IV (R)

Adventure of Sherlock Holmes' Smarter Brother, The (1975) Gene Wilder directs as well as stars in a fairly conventional romantic comedy except for his eclectic choice of comedy styles, including some heavy-handed vulgarities. Instead of satirizing mystery movies, the plot is a disconnected series of complications about a stolen document that is at last recovered by chance rather than by ratiocination. The movie's intermittent amusement is marred by some spectacularly tasteless visuals, double entendres and a love scene that goes beyond comic intentions. O (PG)

Adventurers, The (1970) One man's experiences from childhood to early middle age in a revolutionary South American country are the focus of this long, sprawling soap opera based on

Harold Robbins' novel and directed by Lewis Gilbert. Motivation is frequently sacrificed for plot elements featuring brutality, pillage, rape, sadism, voyeurism, nudity, lesbianism and adultery. O (R)

Adventures In Babysitting (1987) Teenage babysitter (Elizabeth Shue) and her wards suffer through an evening of harrowing escapades while trying to rescue their runaway friend stranded in a downtown Chicago bus station. Flawed seriocomic tale deals with real urban dangers in a treatment made irresponsibly light and mundane by writer-director Chris Columbus. Some violence, sexual innuendo and profanity mar this trite diversion aimed at youngsters. A-III (PG-13)

Adventures of Buckaroo Banzai, The (1984) Director W.D. Richter's sci-fi spoof is about a punk-rock, space-age neurosurgeon (Peter Weller) who stumbles into the eighth dimension where he learns of an alien plot to destroy the world. How all this happens or, indeed, what happens is not very clear. It's comic book fantasy for people who are content to watch a lot of action and strange characters without asking too many questions. Very stylized violence. A-II (PG)

Adventures of Bullwhip Griffin, The (1967) Roddy McDowall deadpans for gold in the Wild West with Suzanne Pleshette along for romantic interest. The plot broadly spoofs Gold Rush days with director James Neilson getting the most from its collection of jokes and sight gags. Karl Malden, Arthur Haydn and Mike Mazurki help make this pleasant comedy one of the better efforts by the Disney studios. A-I (br)

Adventures of Mark Twain, The (1986) Combining elements of the author's life and times with excerpts from his writings, this animated fantasy will engage youngsters while providing older viewers with some insights into Twain's complex character. Will Vinton's use of clay animation, with fully-modeled characters in imaginative sets, is a visual treat. Several scenes may be frightening for the very young but otherwise unusually fine family entertainment. A-I (G)

Adventures of the Wilderness Family, The (1975) Los Angeles family, fed up with the problems of urban life, leave it all behind to set up housekeeping in a remote section of the Rocky Mountains. What follows is predictable, but director Stewart Raffill tells it with a disarming combination of artlessness and professional competence. Good wild life adventure. A-I (G)

Adversary, The (1973) Indian production directed by Satyajit Ray tells the story of a former student who has high hopes of achieving more than a dead-end job but, when he falls in love, becomes a rural drug salesman, resigned to becoming part of the faceless Indian masses. Set in Calcutta, a city drowning in its mass of humanity, Ray's protagonist is society itself and the failure of the present system to humanize the process of industrialized urbanization. Ray's blending of human sensibility with a passion for social justice makes this an unusually important work. A-III (nr)

Africa — Texas Style (1967) Texas cowboys are hired to herd wild animals on the plains of Kenya because domestic cattle are turning the land into a dust bowl. The idea of switching from cattle ranching to game ranching is an intriguing one that director Andrew Marton keeps moving with old-fashioned Western action in exotic African settings. Good family entertainment. A-I (nr)

Africa Addio (1967) Cruelty, violence, blood, gore and human indignity are highlighted in director Gualtiero Jacopetti's Italian documentary which claims that its aim is to enlighten viewers concerning the "birth pangs" of emerging African nations. Exploitation of serious subject. O (R)

Africa Blood and Guts (see: "Africa Addio")

African Elephant, The (1971) Simon Trevor, a former African guide and game warden turned wildlife filmmaker, has made an in-depth birth-to-death documentary on the world's largest and strongest land mammal. Achieving its aims with beauty, sensitivity and intelligence, the movie conveys an experience of the land, the surrounding wildlife and the environment in which the elephant exists. Unlike many such movies, the violence which is so much a part of the wild is given a rationale and thoroughly integrated into the whole. Parents in search of suitable movies for children will find it a healthy, broadening experience for even their youngest. A-I (G)

African Queen, The (1951) Director John Huston's tale of high romantic adventure set in Africa during World War I features Katherine Hepburn as a prim missionary who enlists the aid of rough riverboat captain Humphrey Bogart in escaping capture by German forces. Sharing a harrowing voyage down a wild jungle river, they gradually develop a relationship that changes both their lives -- for the better. Wartime violence. A-II (br)

African Safari (1969) Interesting and exciting documentary excursion into Central and East Africa with beautiful photography of the area's wild life and native customs. Directed and photographed by Ron E. Shanin, it is a rewarding experience both for young people and sophisticated moviegoers. A few graphically violent animal sequences. A-II (G)

After Hours (1985) A bored yuppie (Griffin Dunne) from Manhattan's fashionable East Side ventures into a dangerous part of town to meet an eccentric date (Rosanna Arquette) only to encounter a series of life-threatening misadventures before escaping back to the safety of his own turf in the dawn's early light. Director Martin Scorsese's black comedy lacks satiric bite, preferring instead to wring laughs out of mental instability and bizarre sexual practices. Sophomoric nihilism and some brief nudity. A-IV (R)

After the Fox (1966) Scriptwriter Neil Simon and director Vittorio de Sica collaborated on this surprisingly flat and frequently overdone comedy revolving around a bungling ex-convict (Peter Sellers) who hatches a preposterous scheme to steal the fortune in gold that he has been hired to smuggle into Italy. There are some mildly vulgar jokes but they offend only one's sense of humor. A-II (br)

Against All Odds (1984) Los Angeles bookie and entrepreneur (James Wood) sends his buddy, an aging pro football star (Jeff Bridges), to find his runaway mistress (Rachel Ward). Director Taylor Hackford tries to build up a suspenseful and sinister mood but spends too much time developing the improbable romance that develops between fugitive and tracker. Hair-raising Sunset Boulevard chase scene, violence, graphic sex scenes and rough language. O (R)

Agatha (1979) Agatha Christie's never-explained 11-day disappearance in December 1926 provides the basis for director Michael Apted's romantic mystery starring Vanessa Redgrave as the shy and retiring writer who strikes up a fragile and tender relationship with dapper journalist Dustin Hoffman. Rich in period atmosphere but muddled conclusion and mature theme and treatment. A-III (PG)

Age of Consent (1970) Australian production about an artist (James Mason) who retreats to an island to be alone but discovers it is already inhabited by a local child of nature (Helen Mirren) who has trouble keeping her shift on. When her gin-soaked grandmother obligingly falls off a cliff, the artist and his new model are free to romp artistically and amorously. Michael Powell directs a sorry little diversion that bogs down somewhere between Lolita and Paul Gaughin. O (R)

Agent from H.A.R.M. (1966) Mediocre spy melodrama about an American secret agent (Mark Richman) assigned to keep a defecting foreign scientist from being grabbed by Iron Curtain operatives (led by heavy Martin Kosleck). Directed by Gerd Oswald, the formula is marred by heavy-handed violence and sexual suggestiveness. O (br)

Agent on Ice (1986) Dreary little melodrama about the separate efforts of the C.I.A. and a crime syndicate to kill a double-agent (Tom Ormeny) who knows too much. Director Clark Worswick's effort lacks suspense and drive but offers excessive amounts of bloodshed and stereotyping of Italian Americans. O (R)

Agnes of God (1985) A psychiatrist (Jane Fonda) sent to a cloistered convent to evaluate the mental stability of a novice (Meg Tilly) accused of strangling her newborn baby provokes the determined opposition of the nun's superior (Anne Bancroft). With the psychiatrist looking for a rational explanation and the mother superior hoping for a supernatural one, director Norman Jewison's movie straddles the fence in a dramatically fraudulent conclusion. Although this pretentious and shallow movie is not meant to be anti-religious, some may be offended by its use of a religious setting. A-IV (PG-13)

Aguirre, the Wrath of God (1977) Ponderous and plodding German production by avant-garde director Werner Herzog about gold-seeking, power-hungry conquistadores in 16th-century Peru. Klaus Kinski in the title role looks so vicious that one grows increasingly impatient with his failure to do anything interesting. Occasional violence, particularly a beheading. A-III (nr)

Airplane (1980) This aviation-disaster spoof offers a sprinkling of bright and funny gags. If you don't like one, wait a minute and another will be along. Directed by Jim Abrahams, the comedy is moderately entertaining for those who don't mind an excess of silliness and a certain amount of crudity. A-III (PG)

Airplane II: The Sequel (1982) For those who liked the jokes in the original, here they are again, although many fewer and much farther between this time around under Ken Finkleman's direction. What was of questionable taste in the first movie, however, has now crossed the line into the downright offensive, including quite a bit of nudity. O (PG)

Airport (1970) Screen version of Arthur Hailey's best-seller in which the fate of passengers and crew of an airborne 707 are in the hands of a mad bomber (Van Heflin). Director George Seaton's lumbering Hollywood blockbuster revels in its all-star cast of stereotyped characters and surface melodrama. Adult situations. A-III (G)

Airport 1975 (1974) This time disaster takes the form of a private plane piloted by Dana Andrews who suffers a heart attack and crashes into a 747's cockpit, leaving chief stewardess Karen Black in command and responsible for landing the plane via radio instructions. On board is the usual all-star cast and a ground rescue team led by Charlton Heston and George Kennedy. Directed by Jack Smight, it has some entertaining thrills that will have viewers reaching to fasten their seatbelts. A-II (PG)

Airport 77 (1977) The third edition of the series has to do with a huge 747 crashing into the ocean, trapping a host of major stars in its watertight fuselage. It's all pretty silly but entertaining enough under Jerry Jameson's direction. Restrained violence and some mild profanity. A-II (PG)

A.K.A. Cassius Clay (1970) Documentary on the career of Muhammed Ali, also known as (a.k.a.) Cassius Clay, from his first interest in boxing at the age of 12 to involvement with the Black Muslims and the draft controversy. Fight fans may enjoy several of the clips from some now-classic bouts, but William Cayton's direction is amateurish and superficial, leaving many loose ends and unanswered questions. A-II (GP)

Alamo, The (1960) John Wayne, who also directed and produced, stars as Davy Crockett in a movie about the heroic stand of the Texans at the Alamo against the Mexicans under Santa Ana. Patriotic entertainment but somewhat deficient in historical accuracy and ethnic stereotyping. A-I (br)

Alamo Bay (1985) On the Texas Gulf Coast in 1979, Vietnamese refugees working as shrimp fishermen arouse the animosity of local citizens who feel their livelihood is being taken away from them. Director Louis Malle wastes some good material by bogging down in a melodramatic plot involving adultery and shallow characterizations. Violence and some nudity. A-III (R)

Alex and the Gypsy (1976) Seriocomic story of an autumnal romance between a bail-bondsman (Jack Lemmon) and a gypsy (Genevieve Bujold) has problems of character motivation and a highly improbable ending. Although director John Korty has brought a strong sense of value and human dignity to what could have been sordid situation, there is a rather extended sexual scene that is both graphic and boorish. O (R/PG)

Alex in Wonderland (1971) The only character of interest in this movie about the cinematic and familial hang-ups and private fantasies of a youngish, modish director (Donald Sutherland) is his rather ordinary, sweet and appealing wife (Ellen Burstyn) who can't understand what her husband's problem is all about and won't pretend to be awed by its manufactured profundity. Director Paul Mazursky's self-indulgent effort, with themes and images borrowed from Fellini, wastes itself on condemning such easy targets as Hollywood and Los Angeles' pollution while praising sexual liberation and the peoples' revolution. O (R)

Alf 'n' Family (1972) Screen version of the popular British television series, which was Americanized as "All in the Family," stars Warren Mitchell as Alf, the simple but ridiculously opinionated bigot. By movie's end, Alf is an isolated, pathetic man barely tolerated by his wife (Dandy Nichols) and married daughter. Though justly deserving his fate, it is to the credit of Norman Cohen's direction of Johnny Speight's script that we feel pity for the old reprobate. Comedy of insult with a bit of rough language. A-III (PG)

Alfie (1966) A modern rake (Michael Caine) who regards women only as sexual objects is brought to the realization that his way of life is empty and sterile. Caine brilliantly interprets the title role with deadpan expression, flip Cockney dialogue and occasionally addresses the audience directly in a film directed by Lewis Gilbert and adapted by Bill Naughton from his own play. Although the treatment includes a series of sexual escapades, this British production largely succeeds as a contemporary morality play. A-IV (PG)

Alfred the Great (1969) This elaborate British production re-creates ninth-century England when a youthful prince, later king, rallied the feuding, demoralized Saxon tribes against their common enemy, the Vikings. The barbarism of the period, only slightly leavened by an imperfectly realized brand of Christianity, is handled with some human credibility. Clive Donner's direction is marked by striking visual effects and well controlled, though necessarily bloody, battle scenes. A-III (PG)

Alfredo, Alfredo (1973) Mildly entertaining, occasionally quite funny Italian sex farce directed by Pietro Germi, about a shy bank clerk (Dustin Hoffman) whose desperate attempts to avoid marriage to a predatory woman (Stefania Sandrelli) fail and his troubles begin. There are enough character bits pointing up the foibles, battles and games that go on between the sexes to entertain those whose tastes do not run deep. A-III (R)

Alice Doesn't Live Here Anymore (1975) A widow (Ellen Burstyn) takes her young son (Alfred Lutter) on a sojourn across the Southwest trying to pursue her dream of a singing career but winds up as a waitress in a greasy spoon where she is courted by a local rancher (Kris Kristofferson). Director Martin Scorsese's somewhat ambiguous and ambivalent picture of a single parent in a contemporary American landscape offers some interesting insights on women in a male chauvenistic society. Though some may be distressed by certain tawdry situations and rough language, the movie achieves its purpose of looking at its subject without too much sentimentality or idealization. A-IV (PG)

Alice in Wonderland (1951) Disney animated version of the Lewis Carroll classic about a schoolgirl who daydreams her way through a fantasy world of strange creatures and odd personages, such as the White Rabbit, the Madhatter and the Cheshire Cat, is whimsical entertainment for the entire family, especially youngsters unfamiliar with the original. A-I (G)

Alice of Wonderland in Paris (1966) Animated movie by Gene Deitch on the further adventures of Alice incorporating children's stories written by Ludwig Bemelmans, James Thurber, Eve Titus and Crockett Johnson, and featuring the voices of Carl Reiner, Norma Macmillan and Howard Morris. Youngsters will enjoy the stories and the animation is passable. A-I (br)

Alice's Restaurant (1969) Based on the popular song by Arlo Guthrie, the movie loosely follows various events alluded to in its lyrics, a kind of personal odyssey in which Guthrie plays himself. Although not a very cohesive work, director Arthur Penn succeeds best in satiric bits done in the style and spirit of the song. Despite its stylistic lapses, the result is a balanced film, presenting the life of flower children neither as dismal nor utopian, but as human. Adult themes. A-III (PG)

Alien (1979) Science-fiction thriller about a deep space freighter whose crew is ravaged by a hungry alien intruder which causes havoc on the long voyage home. Director Ridley Scott goes in for lots of noise and flashing lights rather than characterization and the slick enterprise depends more on shock than on suspense. Considerable gore, graphic violence and foul language make this unsuitable for youngsters. A-III (R)

Aliens (1986) Sigourney Weaver returns in a sequel as the maternalistic superheroine who singlehandedly battles an egg-laden alien to prevent its infesting the galaxy with slimy creatures from hyperspace. Director James Cameron balances his affinity for moody sets and special sound and visual effects with a satirical reversal of roles in which a woman dominates the inept and witless bravado of macho males. Stylized violence and excessive sexually derived profanity. A-IV (R)

All American Boy, The (1973) Jon Voight stars as a boxer with great expectations in this precious, pretentious little exercise in destroying the myth of the small-town-boy-making-good. Directed by Charles Eastman, this reverse Horatio Alger story, with its poorly staged boxing scenes and amorous goings-on, is sprinkled with helpings of gratuitous nudity and truly foul language. O (R)

All Neat in Black Stockings (1969) Without too much imagination or subtlety, this British import centers on the amorous adventures of a young, irresponsible window cleaner (Victor Henry) and his buddy (Jack Shepherd) with whom he shares everything, including the woman he marries. While the visuals and dialogue rarely become offensive, the entire situation as developed in this film can hardly be considered wholesome adult entertainment. O (R)

All Night Long (1981) After being demoted from the executive ranks to manager of an all-night drugstore, a married man (Gene Hackman) finds himself being pursued by a seductive married housewife (Barbra Streisand). Streisand and Hackman are both good, and director Jean-Claude Tramont's movie has its moments, but it is basically shallow and mean-spirited rather than amusing. Casual acceptance of adultery. O (R)

All of Me (1984) Steve Martin plays a lawyer who becomes the host for the soul of a recently deceased client, a rich crank played by Lily Tomlin. Martin gives a bravura slapstick performance in trying to liberate himself of the possession, but director Carl Reiner's sense of humor is largely oriented to the sexual, with some needlessly crude dialogue. A-III (PG)

All Screwed Up (1976) Italian tragicomedy about the plight of a group of workers from the agrarian South who come to bustling, industrial Milan to seek a better life but wind up worse off than before. Director Lina Wertmuller's vision is pessimistic but pulsates with the vigor of life and a concern and affection for its characters. Earthy treatment of sex and ambiguous view of prostitution and abortion. A-IV (PG)

All That Jazz (1980) The story of an egotistical, womanizing Broadway director-choreographer who drives himself quite literally to death while rehearsing a new musical. Director Bob Fosse's semi-autobiographical movie stars Roy Scheider who gives a fine performance demonstrating the pitfalls of living in the fast lane, obsessed with one's work while using drugs, sex, alcohol and jazz to heal the pain. The nihilistic mood, and some lewd dance parodies, are wholly self-indulgent. O (R)

All the Loving Couples (1969) This extended stag film has its serious moments contemplating the morality and psychological ramifications of wife-swapping. Gross handling of the subject in graphic exploitation terms negates whatever serious intentions it may have had. O (X)

All the President's Men (1976) The investigation by two "Washington Post" reporters (Dustin Hoffman and Robert Redford) of the facts behind the 1974 Watergate break-in has been dramatized with restraint and objectivity. Director Alan Pakula's deliberately low-keyed, well-acted and comprehensive account of a political scandal emphasizes the painstaking work involved in investigative journalism. Though it uses a few coarse words in a realistic context, the movie is one that most teenagers would benefit from seeing. A-III (R/PG appeal)

All the Right Moves (1983) The hopes of a high school senior (Tom Cruise) to escape the poverty of his blighted factory town by getting a college athletic scholarship seemed doomed by a clash with his football coach (Craig T. Nelson). Although the situation is realistic enough, director Michael Chapman's shallow treatment lacks any moral perspective, especially in its depiction of the youth's relationship with his girlfriend. Graphic bedroom scene and a casual attitude toward abortion. O (R)

All the Right Noises (1971) Dull British production about a theatrical lighting technician (Tom Bell) who succumbs to the charms of a lovely actress (Olivia Hussey) and seems quite content to divide his attentions between her and his pretty wife (Judy Carne) until the predictable complications ensue. Director Gerry O'Hara competently records this story of adultery without weighing any moral issues so that the result is more a clinical report than a thoughtful, moving drama. A-III (GP)

All the Way, Boys (1974) Italian action comedy featuring the hi-jinks and misadventures of the "Trinity" boys (Terence Hill and Bud Spencer), this time as bush pilots in the Amazon where they fly in supplies for emerald-mining outposts and their gradual friendship with one particularly touched prospector (Cyril Cusack). Directed by Giuseppe Colizzi, the clumsy dubbing and sloppy editing seem only to enhance the modest fun offered by a chaotic plot, some whimsical mayhem and the cheerful mugging of its principals. A-II (PG)

All Things Bright and Beautiful (1979) Genial family film about the work of a dedicated veterinarian (John Alderton) practicing in the Yorkshire countryside prior to the onset of World War II. Director Eric Till concentrates on the details of healing at the expense of characterization. Graphic depiction of the birth of a calf may be too intense for some youngsters. A-I (G)

All This and World War II (1977) Tasteless, misconceived documentary that reduces the newsreel footage of six years of agony that was the Second World War to a mindless light show for rock enthusiasts grooving to Beatle's music. Director Susan Winslow spares viewers a magical, mystery tour of Dachau, but not much else in a production so inane as to be beneath contempt. Wartime actualities. A-III (PG)

All Together Now (1970) Low-budget peep show narrated by a blonde corpse (Cileste Eslar) recounting how her experimentation with lesbianism and autoeroticism drove her to suicide. Written and directed by William Louis Allan, the monochromic sex scenes photographed on closet-sized sets will stifle viewers more than shock them. O (nr)

All the Marbles (1981) Peter Falk plays the manager of a tag team of women wrestlers (Vicki Frederick and Laurene Landon) who battle in dinky arenas across the country on the way to the championship match in Reno. Directed by Robert Aldrich, the vulgar, slipshod story wavers between the farcical and the serious. Sadistic violence of the wrestling sequences, exploitative nudity and general air of sleazy amorality. O (R)

Allan Quartermain and the Lost City of Gold (1987) Richard Chamberlain's overacting as the soldier of fortune and Gary Nelson's direction make this action-adventure yarn play with comic-book superficiality. Like "Indiana Jones," this dramatically silly jungle adventure offers youngsters only laughable mock-heroics and exotic sets. Stylized violence. A-II (PG)

Alligator (1981) Director Lewis Teague and writer John Sayles have taken the old chestnut about the baby alligator that grows to monstrous proportions after being flushed down into the sewer system and turned it into a moderately entertaining thriller with some tongue-in-cheek asides. Although the creature has a selective appetite, devouring villains for the most part, such violent actions are graphically depicted. A-III (R)

Almost Perfect Affair, An (1979) American filmmaker (Keith Caradine) brings his movie to Cannes, is held up by customs officials and has an affair with the helpful wife (Monica Vitti) of a movie producer (Raf Vallone). Toothless satire from director Michael Ritchie gets bogged down in private conceits leaving only industry jokes and a carnival atmosphere in which adultery is condoned. O (PG)

Almost Summer (1978) Dull and sophomoric comedy about a class election at a Southern California high school. Director Martin Davidson presents the school's suffocatingly materialistic and amoral environment in uncritical fashion. Gratuitous nudity and offensive jokes at the expense of the disabled. O (PG)

Almost You (1985) Manhattan couple (Brooke Adams and Griffin Dunne) have everything and are so miserable that the husband contemplates running off with his wife's physical therapist (Karen Young). Adam Brooks directs a trivial and boring effort. Rough language and adultery figures in the plot. A-III (R)

Aloha, Bobby and Rose (1975) Director Floyd Mutrux chronicles the tragic love affair between a tousled-haired auto mechanic (Paul Le Mat) and a starry-eyed, unwed mother (Diane Hull) apparently intending an object lesson in the dangers of too much law and order and too little justice. The message is not expressed at all convincingly in the contrived ending of this inept, low-budget melodrama whose chief merit is the acting of the principals in creating characters for whom one feels real concern. A-III (PG)

Alpha Beta (1976) Screen version of E.A. Whitehead's two-character play about a couple (Albert Finney and Rachel Roberts) who feel trapped by marriage, a theme developed with wit and compassion. Although superbly acted and quite affecting, as a movie it suffers from being a straightforward recording of the play. Adult themes. A-III (nr)

Alphabet Murders, The (1966) Tony Randall badly mangles the role of Hercule Poirot, Agatha Christie's dapper Belgian detective, who is investigating a case in which a murderer is killing his victims, apparently in alphabetical order. British production directed by Frank Tashlin, the effort to add comedy to the mystery falls flat and badly hurts the rest of the movie. A-II (br)

Alphaville (1966) A secret agent (Eddie Constantine) in a future science-fiction world accomplishes his mission of destruction. Jean-Luc Godard directs his own script with imaginative visual gusto, ably abetted by Raoul Coutard's camerawork. The French production is enjoyable both as a spy spoof and as a satire on humanity threatened by the machine. Stylized violence and implied sexual affair. A-III (br)

Altered States (1981) The talents of director Ken Russell and writer Paddy Chayefsky have joined in this story about a scientist (William Hurt) who, in trying to find the essence of being, takes a hallucinogen and regresses into a primeval form. He is rescued from total chromosomal metamorphosis by his wife (Blair Brown) who proves that love conquers all. Rather than exploring the spiritual self-realization the character sought, the emphasis is on the physical and sexual, with instances of nudity. O (R)

Alvarez Kelly (1966) This Civil War film involves a cowboy (William Holden) supplying beef for the Union Army being forced by a Confederate officer (Richard Widmark) to steal the herd for the South. There is plenty of violent action in this colorful production, but director Edward Dmytryk has a hard time keeping all the motivations straight. A-III (br)

Alvin Purple (1974) Australian sex comedy about a young man (Graeme Blundell) who is absolutely irresistible to women, a malady that takes him through a series of predictable paces from high-school lecher, to waterbed salesman extraordinaire, to star therapist in a sex clinic. Tim Burstall directs in cheerfully inept style, apparently unaware that his sophomoric premise is more boring than it is humorous or titillating. O (R)

Amadeus (1984) Director Milos Forman's gaudy evocation of the great age of the Baroque features Tom Hulce in the title role of the young, brash, often vulgar Wolfgang Amadeus Mozart. Dramatic intensity is below the level of the Peter Shaffer play but the movie exquisitely details the pain and anguish of Mozart's spiritual and physical assassin, Salieri (F. Murray Abraham) driven by an overwhelming sense of divine injustice and abandonment. A-II (PG)

Amarcord (1974) Director Federico Fellini recalls his youth in the little seaside village of Rimini through a seemingly plotless series of recollections and fantasies, held together by a genially bombastic host-narrator-historian (Luigi Rossi) who provides social and historical commentary on events that typified life during the Fascist 1930s. Fellini is in full control of these various episodes which have a powerful and warming effect as the artist looks back with mellow affection, compassion and humor on experiences that shaped his creative life. In celebrating the dreams and schemes, petty and grandiose, of the ordinary folk of this little town, Fellini reminds us of our own past and our own humanity. Though there is some bawdy earthiness, it is a thoroughly humane work, seeing everything but judging no one. A-IV (R)

Amateur, The (1982) CIA technician John Savage forces the agency to train him as a field operative so that he can go behind the Iron Curtain to avenge his girlfriend's murder by terrorists. Director Charles Jarrott weaves a complex spy thriller which is not saved from mediocrity by the fine performances of Marthe Keller and Christopher Plummer in supporting roles. Stylized violence. A-III (R)

Amazing Grace (1974) Comedy with fine black performers, notably Moms Mabley as an earthmother type who sets out, with the help of retired train conductor Slappy White, to bring Baltimore politician Moses Gunn back to the straight and narrow path. Though there are cameo appearances by such oldtimers as Stepin' Fetchit and Butterfly McQueen, director Stan Lathan keeps his camera mainly on Moms' rolling of the eyes, toothless grins and ceaseless line of hilarious homespun patter. Entertaining, frequently quite funny and occasionally moving general audience pleaser. A-I (G)

Amazing Grace and Chuck (1987) Little League baseball player (Joshua Zuehlke) and a pro-basketball star (Alex English) join in a protest against nuclear weapons. When the basketball star is suspiciously killed in a mid-air explosion, his death precipitates a U.S.-Soviet accord on disarmament. Director Mike Newell provides a strained example of how the altruistic actions of the individual can make a difference. Given the complexity of world affairs, the movie may be more confusing than inspiring for youngsters. A-II (PG)

Amazon Women on the Moon (1987) Tasteless compilation of comic skits and parodies of TV fare presented by John Landis. Irreverent satire, excessive gratuitous nudity and rough language are low points of this sophomoric joke fest whose huge cameo cast is its only remarkable feature. O (R)

Ambush Bay (1966) Slack World War II action movie with a group of Marines (Hugh O'Brien, Mickey Rooney, James Mitchum) battling on a Pacific island under Ron Winston's direction offers nothing new to the wartime violence formula. A-III (br)

Ambushers, The (1968) Dean Martin stars as Matt Helm in a mindless spy spoof that has an almost non-existent plot and is full of devices from other and better movies. Directed by Henry Levin, the effort is little more than a device for spewing out a succession of smutty jokes and sexual encounters reducing women to objects. O (br)

America at the Movies (1976) The American Film Institute put together a bicentennial mosaic of some 92 excerpts from 83 American movies but the result fails to convey much of significance about our nation and way of life. Although the overall tone of the compilation is innocuous, it contains a few instances of strong language and a frank depiction of sex. A-III (PG)

American Anthem (1986) Shallow tale about a teenage athlete (Mitch Gaylord) who, demoralized after his arm is broken during a violent argument between his parents, finds romance and renews his competitive spirit. Olympic gold-medalist Gaylord can't overcome the emotional limitations of a script that plays like a gymnastic music video. Acceptance of casual sex. A-III (PG-13)

American Dream, An (1966) In this generally inept screen adaptation of the Norman Mailer novel, Stuart Whitman plays an ex-war hero who becomes a muckraking TV commentator. When his exposes are not making trouble for others, personal problems with his wife, mistress and a supposedly "accidental" death come to the fore. Directed by Robert Gist, the treatment of some unappealing adult themes is offensive. O (br)

American Dreamer (1984) Director Rick Rosenthal's miserably failed comedy about an Ohio housewife (JoBeth Williams) who wins a trip to Paris and, after suffering a blow to the head, carries on like a female James Bond. Because of its ringing endorsement of adultery, the movie languishes in the realm of soap-opera fantasy derisively stereotyping women. O (PG)

American Flyers (1985) Two brothers (Kevin Costner and David Grant), one with a fatal brain disorder, enter a high-speed bicycle race to face the grueling competition together one last time. A well-acted but mundane tearjerker directed by John Badham. Vulgar language and some casual sex. A-III (PG-13)

American Friend, The (1977) Murky psychological thriller in which a shadowy American (Dennis Hopper) is asked by a French gangster to murder an American criminal but winds up getting a German to do the job instead. Although German director Wim Wenders is sensitive to the cultural milieu of his characters and there is some tension in certain scenes, the narrative fails to generate suspense and ultimately becomes trite and dull. Stylized violence. A-II (nr)

American Game, The (1979) Documentary contrasts the lifestyles, motivations and family ties of two high school basketball stars, a black from Brooklyn and a white from Hoosier country. Producer Anthony Jones follows the young men through a crucial decision-making period detailing the uncertainties and pressures of winning and losing in sports and in the game of life. Spotted with some rough locker room language, but still worth the attention of teenagers facing similar problems. A-II (PG)

American Gigolo (1980) Richard Gere plays a man who lives off women and Lauren Hutton is a politician's wife who falls for him, but his world collapses when he's accused of murder. Written and directed by Paul Schrader, this is a silly and pretentious movie with much nudity, graphic sexuality and a quite muddled moral stance. O (R)

American Graffiti (1973) It's the last, long, California night of the summer of 1962 and for two recent grads (Richard Dreyfuss and Ron Howard) jetting away to college in the morning, it's a last chance to taste the innocent fantasies of a teenage world about to be lost, perhaps forever. A high school lifetime is packed into this one, hugely eventful evening and, despite the bemused smiles of its star-crossed lovers, the mood is ultimately sobering. This delightful comedy from director George Lucas not only captures the signs of former times but comments on them with both eloquence and incisiveness. A-III (PG)

American Hot Wax (1978) Nostalgic rock 'n' roll musical focusing upon a few days in the life of 1950's disc jockey Alan Freed (Tim McIntire) before his last big show at the Brooklyn Paramount in 1959. The work, directed by Floyd Mutrux, will appeal to those who like the music and stars of the time. Occasional vulgarities. A-III (PG)

American Justice (1986) Corrupt border police enslave illegal Mexican aliens in a movie that begins as an exploration of the problems of illegal aliens and ends in a blood bath between good and bad lawmen. Excessive violence, some nudity and rough language add to the unpleasantries in the desert. O (R)

American Pop (1981) Animated feature by Ralph Bakshi presents a history of American popular music through the story of an immigrant family from the turn of the century to the present, with the great-grandson gaining fame as a rock star. Interesting concept but the story lacks dramatic focus and many of the characters are unappealing, if not repulsive. Depiction of some sleazy environments and the use of drugs. A-III (R)

American Tail, An (1986) A family of Jewish mice emigrate from Russia to America in 1885 in search of a new life free of Cossack cats but become separated during a storm at sea. While searching for his parents in New York, a young mouse finds adventure and the meaning of the Statue of Liberty. Director Don Bluth uses Disney-style full animation in meticulous, loving detail on a story that may delight youngsters but which some parents might find a bit too saccharine. A-I (G)

American Werewolf in London, An (1981) Trashy, sardonically muddled horror show by writer-director John Landis attempts to combine comedy and fright with a dash of steamy sex. The result is a squalid mess. Contains violence and explicit sex. O (R)

American Wilderness (1973) Little more than a collection of self-congratulatory home movies taken during the past decade or so by an Oregon sportsman named Art Dubs. Although it has a down-home folksiness, there are many other fine outdoor adventure documentaries that offer family viewers better camerawork and information on wildlife than this narrowly conceived, often poorly photographed movie. A-I (G)

Americanization of Emily, The (1964) Attached to an American military headquarters, a British volunteer (Julie Andrews) learns fast as a megalomaniacal admiral (Melvyn Douglas) tries to make a hero of himself, while his aide (James Garner) tries to take advantage of her and others. The conclusion to director Arthur Hiller's cynical look at life in World War II England is Emily's own compromise of her virtue and previously unimpeachable character. O (br)

Americathon (1979) With America about to go bankrupt in this dismal comedy directed by Neil Israel, a massive telethon is held to rescue the national finances. Besides being unfunny, the movie employs objectionable language and graphic depictions of misconduct. O (PG)

Amin — The Rise and Fall (1981) Amateurish and exploitative account of the Uganda dictator's bloody career in a Kenyan production directed by Sahrad Patel. Posing as socio-political document, it offers little more than sensationalism through a disreputable mix of violence and sex. O (R)

Amityville Horror, The (1979) The anemic plot of this tepid horror movie about a suburban couple whose house is possessed by some demonic force doesn't allow for much in the way of a satisfactory resolution. Director Stuart Rosenberg's garish special effects are relatively restrained but his superficial treatment of the story's religious dimension is ludicrous. A-III (R)

Amityville II: The Possession (1982) Set in a period previous to that of the original, director Damiano Damiani's sequel features Burt Young in a partly haunted-house story and a partly wretched remake of "The Exorcist," highlighted by a ludicrously inept depiction of the religious rite of exorcism. Excessive violence and nudity. O (R)

Amityville 3-D (1983)   The third in this dreary series features Tony Roberts as a writer who moves into the demonic house, confident he's gotten a real bargain. This silly mess is probably all the worse for viewers aggravated by the headache from the 3-D glasses. Absurd, spurious violence. A-III (PG)

Amsterdam Kill, The (1978)   Robert Mitchum plays a disgraced but incorruptible ex-narcotics agent who finds himself caught in a bloody struggle among rival Chinese drug dealers in Hong Kong and Amsterdam. Director Robert Clouse's plot seems no more than a string of action sequences, none of which are very exciting, let alone entertaining. Stylized violence and high body count. A-III (R)

Amy (1981)   This warm and amiable Disney movie, set in the early 1900s, tells the story of a determined young woman (Jenny Agutter) who leaves her wealthy but unloving husband (Chris Robinson) to teach at a school for the deaf. Director Vincent McEveety does well in developing the contrast between personal and social commitment in a film that is ideal for children except for the marital estrangement in the plot. A-II (G)

Anais Observed (1974)   Anais Nin was both participant in and observer of the avant-garde scene between the world wars. Robert Snyder's feature documentary reveals all the paradox implicit in her work of self-absorption bordering on the narcissistic, combined with a warm and encouraging interest in relating to others (as with some awed students who visit her). The viewer will have to judge, however, how valuable are her aesthetic judgments and personal philosophy. A-III (nr)

And Hope to Die (1972)   In a considerably shortened version of a French production directed by Rene Clement (originally entitled "The Race of the Hare Across the Fields"), the plot itself seems to have gone the way of the Cheshire Cat. What remains are a series of interesting but capricious scenes involving a gang of colorful cut-throats (Robert Ryan, Jean-Louis Trintignant, Lea Massari and Aldo Ray) that finally culminates in a "kidnapping" from police headquarters in the middle of Montreal. If Clement's intention was to liken this kind of adult entertainment to childhood games, something is missing in the translation. A-III (PG)

...And Justice for All (1979)   Al Pacino stars as an honest but abrasive anti-establishment lawyer who is blackmailed into defending a "law and order" judge (John Forsythe) accused of rape. A heavyhanded and muddled potboiler directed by Norman Jewison. Foul language and sexual promiscuity. O (R)

And Now for Something Completely Different (1972)   This random sampling of skits from "Monty Python's Flying Circus," the BBC zany comedy series, offers some distinctly British humor ranging from social satire and black comedy to broad slapstick and sexual jokes, most notably at the expense of homosexuals. Under director Ian MacNaughton, the young cast come over as a quite likeable group of performers, which helps when jokes fall flat. Best of all, however, are Terry Gilliam's animated pieces linking the skits but also standing on their own as contemporary graphic humor. However, it is comedy not for all tastes. A-IV (PG)

And Now Miguel (1966)   An engaging portrayal of a year in the life of a small boy (Pat Cardi) in New Mexico whose only wish is to become a shepherd like his father (Michael Ansara). Produced by Robert B. Radnitz and based on Joseph Krumgold's prize-winning novel, the film emphasizes the strength of Hispanic family life rooted in mutual love and respect. The natural beauty of the terrain and the naturalistic acting of the cast convey a satisfying sense of reality to this story of a pastoral family. A-I (br)

And Now My Love (1975)   French production using the history of Europe from World War I to the present as the backdrop to a love story tracing, in almost surrealistic fashion, the heritages and key events in the lives of a young Jewish heiress (Marthe Keller) and an ex-convict turned film director (Charles Denner). Beautifully produced and directed by Claude Lelouch, history is interestingly put at the service of love and there is no denying that the optimism of his romantic fable makes one feel good even though aware that its selective view of the past is being used only to make a romantic trifle seem more consequential than it really is. A-III (PG)

And Now the Screaming Starts (1973)   British horror movie directed by Roy Ward Baker offers no more than average example in this 18th-century tale of inherited guilt from a diabolically-inspired family curse. Good production values and special effects and the cast includes horror veterans Peter Cushing, Patrick Magee and Herbert Lom. A number of the plot elements involve rape and other forms of brutality but their treatment is restrained. A-III (R)

And Soon the Darkness (1971)   Two pretty English lasses (Pamela Franklin and Michele Dotrice) on a bicycle tour of France have a row and Dotrice disappears on the site of an unsolved grisly sex-murder leaving Franklin to search for her friend while eluding the crazed killer. British thriller directed by Robert Fuest takes her up and down any number of verdant but blind alleys, establishing everyone she meets as a prime suspect, but even the pretty French countryside cannot compensate for the overall disappointment in the climax. A-III (GP)

And There Came a Man (1968)   Part documentary and part re-enactment, this screen biography of Pope John XXIII features Rod Steiger as narrator and stand-in for the person of the title. The Italian production is best in its unpretentious re-created scenes of Pope John's early boyhood but director Ermanno Olmi is less successful in depicting his clerical career. A-I (br)

Anderson Platoon, The (1968)   French documentary about the Vietnam War centers not on the issues of the war but on a few weeks in the lives of an airmobile unit under Lt. Joseph B. Anderson fighting in the Central Highlands. Directed by Pierre Schoendorffer, its focus on these men helps give a human perspective to the reality of combat, something the screen too often glamorizes. A-II (br)

Anderson Tapes, The (1971)   Director Sidney Lumet almost succeeds in splicing together an exciting, perfect heist narrative and an ironic statement about electronic eavesdropping, public and private. Sean Connery masterminds the robbery of an entire luxury apartment building but all those he recruits for the job are already under surveillance by various law agencies, none of whom has a full picture of what is going on. Adult material with occasional violence that some may find excessive. A-IV (PG)

Andromeda Strain, The (1971) When a New Mexico hamlet is wiped out by extraterrestrial microbes, a team of top medical specialists try to find a way to destroy the deadly bacteria before it destroys the human race. Despite some overdone special effects and unnecessary plot complications, director Robert Wise's screen version of Michael Crichton's best-seller is gripping and its impact is sharp. A-II (G)

Andy Warhol's Dracula (1975) In this variation on the Dracula theme, the ever-thirsty Count must live on "virgin's blood," as it is rendered in one of the dreadful accents abounding here. Besides the accents, there's no lack of other offensive elements in director Paul Morrissey's campy efforts in trying to make perversion seem hilarious. O (X/R)

Andy Warhol's Frankenstein (1974) Written and directed by Warhol's alter ego, Paul Morrissey, this version emphasizes the fatal and the perverse aspects of the Mary Shelley original, ever escalating the campy hijinks for shock value. If one isn't offended by the gross nudity and kinky sex combinations, perhaps the gory charnel scraps flying all over the place will. O (X/R)

Angel (1984) Advertised as "High school honor student by day, Hollywood hooker by night" is all one needs to know about this dismal effort by director Robert Vincent O'Neil to tell the story of a young prostitute (Donna Wilkes) who helps a detective catch a psychopathic killer. Nudity, graphic sex and violence. O (R)

Angel, Angel Down We Go (1969) An 18-year-old virgin (Holly Near), desperate to lose that state, is helped out by a rock singer (Jordon Christopher) who also gives sexual aid to her wealthy mother and father and then destroys them all. Blaming a corrupt society for the depicted immoral activity, director Robert Thom's presentation tries to smooth over the guilt feelings of viewers slightly ashamed at their own voyeurism. Promiscuity and several insulting references to religion. O (R)

Angel Heart (1987) Director Alan Parker's bloody, often disgusting depiction of one man's grappling with the devil and the consequences of his refusal to face the evil within him forms the core of this parable about a private eye (Mickey Rourke) hired to find a missing person only to discover it is a missing soul. Graphic mix of sex and violence in a demonic setting, nudity and vivid results of dismemberment. O (R)

Angel in My Pocket, An (1968) A newly ordained minister (Andy Griffith) comes to serve his first congregation in a small Kansas town when he immediately becomes involved in the feud between two families that has wrecked the ministry of all his predecessors. Directed by Alan Rafkin, the comedy is broad and mindless, the characters stereotypes and the sugary situations enough to give some viewers diabetes. A-I (G)

Angel Levine, The (1970) A devout old Jewish tailor (Zero Mostel) living in poverty in Harlem seems to have his prayers answered when·a black man (Harry Belafonte) arrives claiming to be an angel who can help, but only if the tailor has faith in him. Though some viewers may find the tailor's wavering between belief and disbelief growing tiresomely repetitive, others will see it as the point of director Jan Kadar's brilliant allegory asserting people's need for belief and commitment for the

sake of human survival. A-III (GP)

Angel Unchained (1970) Routine motorcycle melodrama about a biker (Don Stroud) who leaves his cycling buddies to join a commune but when its peaceful members are harassed by the local cowboys he calls on his old friends to help even out the odds in the big showdown. Director Lee Madden's contrived plot provides the opportunity for some hard-hitting brawls, a touch of sex, an abundance of beer and pot and, of course, plenty of daredevil bike riding. A-III (GP)

Angels Die Hard (1970) Unenlightened motorcycle movie about a gang of bikers who invade a small town, brutally torment the locals and linger nearby to do it again. Underdeveloped conflicts center around the sheriff's blustering threats to shoot them down, especially since his teenage daughter is keen on joining them. Director Richard Compton leans to admiring shots of the gang riding the road but the coarse customs and cruelty of these outlaw heroes far outweigh any suggestions of their benevolent humanity. O (R)

Angi Vera (1980) A marvelously subtle and complex Hungarian production set in 1948, the early days of the Communist regime, a tragic and confused era full of idealism and opportunism. Veronica Papp gives a flawless performance in the title role as a young woman with a talent for survival who is sent by the Party to a political training center where she has an affair that could threaten her future. Director Pal Gabor shows that human nature has a way of infiltrating the most resistant of ideologies. Adult situations and politically complex themes. A-III (nr)

Angry Harvest (1986) Set in a Polish village during World War II, a simple but devout farmer abuses the trust of a Jewish refugee he is sheltering by his lust for her. In the Polish production, director Agnieszka Holland offers a compelling portrait of a man whose loneliness undermines his basic moral character resulting in betrayal and death. In this context, several brief scenes of partial nudity and simulated sex are anything but titillating. A-IV (nr)

Animal Crackers (1930) In this Marx Brothers comedy, Groucho plays Captain Geoffrey T. Spaulding, the inveterate African explorer and improbable guest of honor at a party given by Margaret Dumont to unveil a valuable painting which is stolen and replaced by not one but two bogus ones. Chico and Harpo are on the scene to provide the music, Lillian Roth sings and Zeppo, the fourth brother, plays Groucho's private secretary. Directed by Victor Heerman, the coarseness and vulgarity of the early Marx Brothers comedies may not appeal to everyone's tastes, but their zany verbal and physical assaults on conventions of every kind continue to be one of the hallmarks of screen comedy. A-II (G)

Animal House (see: "National Lampoon's Animal House")

Animals Are Beautiful People (1975) Wildlife documentary filmed in a vast tract of desert, swamp and mountains in Southwest Africa with an exotic variety of animal species. Director Jamie Uys provides some humorous as well as fascinating moments, marred slightly by a Disney-style anthropomorphic slant and what some might detect as a paternalistic attitude toward blacks. A-I (G)

Ann and Eve (1970) Swedish story of a jaded journalist (Gio Petre) who takes a young innocent

(Marie Liljedahl) on a vacation to a Yugoslav resort where she is initiated into a predictable series of sexual adventures around town. Arne Mattsson directs the lurid melodrama with clinical coldness toward the characters who meander through arbitrary situations. Excessive nudity. O (nr)

Anne of the Thousand Days (1969) Screen version of Maxwell Anderson's play about the romance between Henry VIII (Richard Burton) and Anne Boleyn (Genevieve Bujold). Directed by Charles Jarrott, the story centers on all the dynastic complications that motivated Henry's break with Rome and his six-year pursuit of Anne. Though the action is limited, the acting is impressive, especially that of Anthony Quayle as Cardinal Wolsey. For those who are not history buffs, there is plenty of royal pageantry, colorful costumes and well-preserved castles. In dealing with the period and its characters, there is some blood-letting and sexual candor. A-III (PG)

Annie (1982) Although John Huston's direction of the screen version of the popular stage musical is somewhat cynical and definitely disappointing, it does preserve much of the exotic ambiance of the comic strip about the little orphan (Aileen Quinn) and Daddy Warbucks (Albert Finney). With awkward dance numbers, some coarse dialogue and Carol Burnett's mean-spirited characterization, the movie's appeal is somewhat limited beyond uncritical viewers. A-III (PG)

Annie Hall (1977) Director Woody Allen's romantic comedy about an on-again, off-again relationship between a Jewish comedian from New York (Allen) and a WASP from the Midwest (Diane Keaton). Although the movie is frequently very funny and has a touch of humanity lacking in Allen's earlier work, it falls far short of its more ambitious intention of making a serious statement about human relationships. Some rough language and much humor derived from sexual matters. A-III (PG)

Anniversary, The (1968) Bette Davis overacts dreadfully as a dreadful mother who rules the lives of every member of the family. Director Roy Ward Baker's comedy of the outrageous fails in satirizing the evils of momism because it lacks compassion and its unhealthy humor is frequently tasteless. O (br)

Anonymous Venetian, The (1971) A young musician (Tony Musante) calls his estranged wife (Florinda Bolkan) to Venice and they spend their day revisiting scenes that once brought them happiness until the wife learns that, like the city, he and their marriage are dying. Italian production directed by Enrico Maria Salerno, it is a tragically lyric travelogue through the canals and streets of a great city which by day's end slowly sinks into the sea, surrounded by the pollution and technology of modern times. With a little less sentimentality, its story of the fragility of human love and man-made beauty might have been more credible. A-III (GP)

Another Man, Another Chance (1977) French director Claude Lelouch's romantic sagebrush drama about a widowed veterinarian (James Caan) who falls in love with a charming widowed photographer (Genevieve Bujold). Despite the movie's striking photography and excellent acting, Lelouch's calculatedly relaxed style of characterization and glossy romanticism do not lend themselves well to the more austere mood of a Western. Brief violence in a scene of rape. A-III (PG)

Antonio Das Mortes (1970) Brazilian folk epic

about a gunman hired by a feudal landlord to eliminate the leaders of a peasant rebellion in the hills and how the hired assassin eventually joins the rebels himself. Using a gaudy color photography that suits his strange story and setting, director Glauber Rocha intermingles black and Indian rituals and ceremonies with Christian saints and symbols to create a world of bizarre superstitions and revolutionary fervor. It is an episodic movie of unusual power and beauty that some tastes may find too exotic. A-III (nr)

Any Wednesday (1966) Jaded successful businessman (Jason Robards) is a good husband six days of the week but Wednesday is reserved for a young lady (Jane Fonda) until his wife (Rosemary Murphy) forces a showdown and his lady friend finds the man of her dreams (Dean Jones). Under Robert Ellis Miller's direction, it's a lively, sappy, broad comedy with some serious overtones about the pain of infidelity. A-III (br)

Any Which Way You Can (1980) An auto repairman and free-lance streetfighter (Clint Eastwood) finds happiness with a skittish prostitute (Sondra Locke). Director Buddy Van Horn's salute to machismo presents an abundance of violence and an atmosphere of sleazy immorality. O (br)

Anyone Can Play (1968) Failed Italian sex farce with Ursula Andress, Virna Lisi and Jean-Pierre Cassel tends to condone adultery. Clumsily directed by Luigi Zampa, its emphasis is on sexual titillation. O (br)

Anzio (1968) Huge, sprawling World War II epic about the Allied invasion at Anzio in southern Italy with Robert Mitchum, Peter Falk and Robert Ryan in the thick of combat. Directed by Edward Dmytryk, the movie is graphic in its depiction of the grim images of battle, with appropriately harsh action and language. A-III (PG)

Apache Uprising (1966) Routine Western directed by R.G. Springsteen with Rory Calhoun using his six-guns to fight off rampaging Indians while Arthur Kennedy and Richard Arlen do their bit in hastening the departure of the vanishing American. Of interest only to the Rory Calhoun fan club. A-II (br)

Apartment, The (1960) Director Billy Wilder's comedy satire about the corporate rise and moral near-downfall of a garden variety office manager whose sudden success in climbing the company ladder comes from loaning out his bachelor apartment to philandering executives. His falling in love with one of their girl friends (Shirley MacLaine) leads to the usual moral comeuppances for all involved but Wilder and his talented cast devise startling ways of arriving at the obvious, obligatory conclusion. A-III (br)

Apocalypse Now (1979) Director Francis Ford Coppola's uneven attempt to transpose Joseph Conrad's "Heart of Darkness" to Vietnam stars Martin Sheen as an intelligence officer sent into Cambodia to kill a renegade Special Forces officer (Marlon Brando) who has set up a private domain. Much ambiguous and unresolved soul-searching in between several brilliant battle sequences but Robert Duvall steals the show as a gung-ho helicopter commander. Rough language and graphic violence. A-IV (R)

Appaloosa, The (1966) Marlon Brando stars as a would-be rancher whose prize horse is stolen by Mexican bandits (led by John Saxon). British director Sidney J. Furie follows the action conventions of the Western but pays more attention to colorful camerawork than to developing character motivation. The result is a picture with lots of atmosphere but little human interest. Assorted stylized violence. A-II (br)

Apple Dumpling Gang, The (1975) Western comedy about three little orphans left with a gold mine who con suave gambler Bill Bixby into a marriage of convenience with stage coach driver Susan Clark to protect them from greedy townspeople and bungling robbers Don Knotts and Tim Conway. Norman Tokar directs a standard Disney family entertainment. A-I (G)

Apple Dumpling Gang Rides Again, The (1979) Inept outlaws (Don Knotts and Tim Conway) try to go straight with predictably disastrous results in this Disney sequel. Directed by Vincent McEveety, the comedy is not helped much by a bland romantic subplot (Tim Matheson and Elyssa Davalos) but the humor is carried by the manic efforts of a frenzied marshal (Kenneth Mars) to get the zany pair. A-I (G)

Appointment, The (1968) Romantic melodrama about a successful lawyer (Omar Sharif) who comes to suspect that his wife (Anouk Aimee) was once a prostitute and, when he tries to find out the truth, tragedy results. Directed by Sidney Lumet, the silly tale of a strange jealousy cannot sustain its length and comes to an unsatisfying conclusion. A-III (br)

Apprenticeship of Duddy Kravitz, The (1974) Superior Canadian drama about an ambitious young man (Richard Dreyfuss), growing up in a Jewish ghetto in Montreal, who discovers that making money is not all there is to life. Directed by Ted Kotcheff, the moral problems and mistaken goals of youth are convincingly presented in terms of Duddy's relationships with family and those he meets along the way. More than the story of one man's greed, it is also the chronicle of a ghetto, finely evoking a detailed and realistic world whose humanity transcends any ethnic group, making all the more universal its picture of human self-centeredness. Some crude religious and sexual references used within a purposeful context. A-IV (R)

April Fool's Day (1986) Group of wealthy college students, acting like retarded adolescents, spend a weekend playing deadly tricks on each other at an island estate. Director Fred Walton treats the women involved solely as sexual objects and the dialogue is preoccupied with profanity, sexual innuendoes and off-color jokes. Accepts sexual promiscuity as a natural part of youthful behavior. O (R)

April Fools, The (1969) Director Stuart Rosenberg's comedy-drama involves a New York stockbroker (Jack Lemmon) and a jet-set beauty (Catherine Deneuve) who start a 24-hour romance by flying off to Paris and forsaking their own shallow previous marriages. The underlying seriousness of the film's healthy criticism of the "good" life creates definite moral problems and a credibility gap for its glib resolution, especially when set beside the film's slapstick routines and the unlikely liaison between the central characters. O (PG)

Arabella (1969) Italian comedy set in the 1920s tells the story of a young Roman aristocrat (Virna Lisi) who tries to help her grandmother (Margaret Rutherford) out of financial difficulties by fleecing various victims (all played by Terry Thomas). Whether director Mauro Bolognini means to satirize the Italian tax laws or indict Italian manners

and morals, his farcical complications strain frantically and often repulsively for laughs that seldom materialize. A-III (PG)

Arabesque (1966) Muddled thriller in which an American exchange professor at Oxford (Gregory Peck) gets involved with several sets of Arab spies, one of whom (Sophia Loren) keeps shifting sides. Directed by Stanley Donen, villains and villainy abound, there's eye-catching violence and sexy romance but it's all surface and no substance. A-III (br)

Arabian Adventure (1979) British fantasy is a thrilling flying carpet adventure about a prince on a mission to foil the evil ambitions of sinister sorcerer Christopher Lee. Directed by Kevin Connor, the brisk costume and special effects vehicle is devoid of violence or trite romanticism. Pleasant escapist fare for young and old. A-I (G)

Arch, The (1972) Hong Kong production presenting a doomed tale of unrequited passion in which a widow, true to the memory of her dead husband and her social position, refuses the love of a handsome captain, but then allows her daughter to marry him. The movie's deliberate, timeless creation of mood has been broken up with freeze-frames and some heavy-handed montages by its woman director, Shu Shuen. It is an oriental curio which may best be left to the romantically inclined. A-II (nr)

Aristocats, The (1970) Directed by Wolfgang Reitherman, the first animated feature from the Disney studio since Disney's death in 1966 tells the adventures of a family of felines who, after being made the heir of their millionaire mistress, are catnapped and ditched in the country but then rescued by a pair of bumbling hounds, a couple of giggling geese, a rodent named Roquefort and an alley cat named O'Malley. Enhanced by the voices of Eva Gabor, Phil Harris, Hermione Baddeley and Sterling Holloway, with five songs thrown in for good measure, the result, while not purr-fect, is plentifully good. A-I (G)

Arizona Bushwackers (1967) Routine Western directed by Lesley Selander in which a Confederate agent (Howard Keel) stops a renegade (Scott Brady) from selling a cache of rebel guns to the Indians and the movie concludes happily with the end of the Civil War. A-I (br)

Armed and Dangerous (1986) Posing as social spoof, this failed slapstick movie concerns security guards (John Candy and Eugene Levy) who fight organized crime by being more aggressive and anti-social than the criminals. Violent and destructive imagery sprinkled with profanity and sexual sight gags that fail as burlesque. A-III (PG-13)

Arnold (1973) At least half of this creaky horror-comedy takes place in a fog-bound graveyard, and all of it centers around a well-heeled, well-preserved cadaver (in the title role). The gimmick derives from a condition in the deceased's will that his wife (Stella Stevens), who married him hastily just after his demise, has to keep him near her for the rest of her life, a condition that leads to a number of murders and other preposterous goings-on. All director George Fenady can do with this bizarre material is to play it for laughs and these do come at reasonably close intervals. A-III (PG)

Around the World Under the Sea (1966) Producer-director Andrew Marton's underseas adventure with scientists (Lloyd Bridges, David McCallum, Brian Kelly, Shirley Eaton) setting earthquake warning devices on the ocean floor and meeting monsters of the deep should appeal to most youngsters. A-I (br)

Around the World in 80 Days (1956) Mike Todd's lavish production of the Jules Verne classic about an English armchair adventurer (David Niven) who makes a bet that he can circle the globe within 80 days and sets off with his valet (Cantinflas) to prove it. Michael Anderson's direction makes the most of the cultural splendor of the late Victorian period, visits just about every scenic locale worth a postcard and offers an all-star marathon of cameo appearances. The result is a wonderful romp that is great fun for all. A-I (G)

Arrangement, The (1969) Director Elia Kazan's screen version of his own novel suffers less from being ambitious than from its pretentiousness. Kirk Douglas plays a man who attempts suicide because his life has been a sham, a series of "arrangements" in business as well as with mistress (Faye Dunaway) and wife (Deborah Kerr). Among the many flaws in this failed work, the greatest is its reduction of personal crises to predominantly sexual conflicts and involvements. Rough language and some coy nudity. O (R)

Arrivederci, Baby! (1966) Dull, tasteless and vulgar vehicle for Tony Curtis clownishly playing a con man who marries and murders a series of wealthy women. Written, produced and directed by Ken Hughes, the attempts at humor fall flat making the proceedings all the more vulgar and pointless. O (br)

Arruza (1972) Documentary by Budd Boetticher on the final years of the legendary Mexican bullfighter, Carlos Arruza. Narrated by Anthony Quinn, it fails to explore the make-up of the man, presenting instead a cold, distant portrait of the torero seen totally from the outside. What will impress most viewers, however, is only the foolish, cruel and debasing side of this contest between man and beast. A-II (PG)

Arthur (1981) A rich and spoiled young man named Arthur (Dudley Moore), who spends his days and nights drinking to excess and pursuing all sorts of women, falls in love with a waitress (Liza Minnelli). Director Steve Gordon tries to distill humor from the playboy's sexual weaknesses and from his indecision about meaningful commitment but most of the humor comes from John Gielgud's performance as the snobbish, harsh-tongued valet. Adult situations. A-III (PG)

Arthur Rubenstein — Love of Life (1975) Extraordinary documentary about one of the world's greatest piano virtuosos is concerned not only with music but also with humanity. Directed by Francois Reichenbach, it captures the artist and the man at age 82 and is equally important as a commentary on classical music as it is a testament to a rare human being. Of far greater appeal than the specialized art audience. A-I (nr)

Ash Wednesday (1973) Dowdy middle-aged matron (Elizabeth Taylor), on the verge of losing her successfull lawyer husband (Henry Fonda) to a younger woman, undergoes body sculpture in a posh European clinic but it will take Liz a good deal longer than the audience to figure out that no amount of face-lifting will change Henry's mind. Director Larry Peerce elicits solid performances from a good cast and the plot moves along smoothly through a series of plush settings but it is no more than a well-made but uninvolving melodrama without any perspective upon the actions and motivations of its characters and their lifestyle. A-III (R)

Assassination (1987) Through his experience and cunning, a Secret Service agent (Charles Bronson) protects the wife (Jill Ireland) of the President of the United States from assassination. Directed by Peter Hunt, the movie is relatively restrained in its violence and sexual treatment. A-III (PG-13)

Assassination Bureau, The (1969) British tongue-in-cheek comedy set in the early 1900s about an international organization of killers-for-hire that is commissioned by a neophyte reporter (Diana Rigg) to kill their own leader (Oliver Reed). Good cast, marvellous settings but Basil Dearden's direction is rather uncertain in its mixture of slapstick and satire. Comic violence. A-III (M)

Assassination of Trotsky, The (1972) The death of the magnetic Russian revolutionary in his Mexican exile in 1924 is portrayed not from the political angle but the human, centering on the two protagonists -- the sympathetic victim (Richard Burton) and the shadowy assassin (Alain Delon) who clearly exhibits classic symptoms of psychological disturbance that his infiltration of the closely-guarded Trotsky compound is simply not credible. Despite this central dramatic flaw, director Joseph Losey has fashioned a fascinating movie that succeeds in placing its figures into an historical time and place. A-III (R)

Assault on a Queen (1966) Navy veterans (Frank Sinatra and Richard Conte) raise a sunken U-boat and use it to hi-jack and rob the Queen Mary in mid-ocean. Directed by Jack Donahue, it's routine escapist entertainment with the bad guys getting their just desserts and the good guys escaping, but without the loot. A-II (br)

Assignment K (1968) Masquerading as a toy tycoon, a British agent (Stephen Boyd) matches wits with enemy spies and counterspies in rich and exotic European settings. Director Val Guest's weak spy melodrama is cluttered with plot complications whose only purpose is to afford changes of glamorous locales and chic costumes. Moderate violence. A-III (br)

Assignment to Kill (1968) Private detective (Patrick O'Neal) works his way up the ladder in an organization headed by a mobster who sinks his own ships to collect the insurance. Threadbare plot directed by Sheldon Reynolds but with much action and many dead bodies. A-III (br)

Asylum (1971) British production of four psychological horror tales by Robert Bloch that are tied together by being set in an insane asylum run by Patrick Magee and the gimmick of a puzzle to be unraveled by the end of the last episode. Director Roy Ward Baker provides a few mild chills, a handful of ironic chuckles and a couple of nifty twists at the conclusion. A-II (PG)

At Any Price (1970) Poor Italian caper movie about a retiring curator of the Vatican museums (Walter Pidgeon) who, though blind, gathers a group of willing and unwilling professional accomplices to carry out the intricate heist of Vatican treasures. Directed by Emilio Miraglia, it is little more than a series of highly improbable, unmotivated and badly dubbed escapades. A-II (PG)

At Close Range (1986) In director James Foley's harrowing, fact-based tale of youth corrupted by the seductive powers of evil, a son (Sean Penn) blindly follows his menacing, ruthless father (Christopher Walken) as he steals, murders and betrays without remorse. Some brief nudity, profanity and intense moments of violence. A-IV (R)

At Long Last Love (1975) Tedious, boring musical about a New York millionaire (Burt Reynolds) who becomes romantically involved with a musical comedy star (Madeline Kahn) and, then, with a bankrupt society girl (Cybill Shepherd). Director Peter Bogdanovich has mastered the form of the 1930's Hollywood musicals but not their spirit, drive nor buoyant style. The miscast principals savage some lesser songs by Cole Porter. Permissive attitude toward casual sex. A-III (G)

At the Earth's Core (1976) Director Kevin Connor's low-budget science fiction movie about finding a lost world of prehistoric creatures far beneath the earth's surface falls considerably short of its modest entertainment goals. Considerable special effects violence and monsters. A-II (PG)

Atlantic City (1981) Aging, opportunistic con man (Burt Lancaster) living in poverty in Atlantic City, becomes involved with a young woman (Susan Sarandon) and after her husband is killed in a heroin shipment, he is left with the proceeds from the sale. Director Louis Malle powerfully evokes the seedy side of casino life, as well as a portrait of a small-time loser who takes one last shot at the big time and thinks he can succeed. Some violence, scenes of drug dealing and brief nudity. A-III (R)

Atragon (1964) Standard Japanese science fiction fantasy about an evil underseas empire whose plans to rule the world are stopped by the underwaters battleship of the title. Director Inoshiro Honda manages some nifty special effects in this kiddie matinee story. A-I (br)

Attack on the Iron Coast (1968) Routine World War II action movie about the training of an elite British commando force (led by Lloyd Bridges) and their raid on German positions in France. Director Paul Wendkos adds nothing new to the old story of brave men who give their lives for their country. A-I (br)

Attica (1974) Documentary recounting the tragic events that took place in the 1971 New York prison revolt at Attica (43 dead, 200 wounded) from the point of view of the inmates, using footage shot inside the prison before and during the National Guard's attack, TV coverage of the state's official investigations as well as its own interviews with participants. Directed by Cinda Firestone, it takes a clear advocacy position toward prison reform to insure no future Atticas. A-III (nr)

Au Hasard, Balthazar (1970) French production centering on a donkey as a device to tie together a series of vignettes of human injustice. In this unusual and challenging work, director Robert Bresson presents a view of selfishness and inhumanity that is unrelenting in its condemnation of evil. As austere and as uncompromising as any film he has made, it will be hard going for those unacquainted with his previous explorations of the human condition. A-III (nr)

Audrey Rose (1977) Slow-moving, low-voltage thriller about an 11-year-old girl who becomes an object of contention between a man (Anthony Hopkins) who claims that she is the reincarnation of his dead daughter and her shocked parents (Marsha Mason and John Beck). Although director Robert Wise's movie concerns the spiritual dimension of human existence, its poorly developed theme of reincarnation is confusing and youngsters may be discomfited by some graphic scenes of the young girl's acute anguish. A-III (PG)

Author, Author (1982) Armenian-American playwright (Al Pacino), left by his wife (Tuesday Weld) with five children on his hands, finds another woman (Dyan Cannon) to help him get through it all. While pleasant enough, director Arthur Hiller's romantic comedy is not especially funny and offers an intemperate moral outlook, viewing adultery and divorce as an inevitable part of self-development. A-III (PG)

Autumn Afternoon, An (1973) Japanese production about the transient joys of family life and the loneliness of parents after children leave home. Its story is of a widower (Chishu Ryu) who realizes that if his daughter devotes any more of her time to him, it will ruin her life. With his encouragement she eventually marries and after the wedding, the father returns home to the form of loneliness he has anticipated throughout the movie. Directed by Yasujiro Ozu, it is a movie rich in the rhythm of life, the warmth of humanity and the web of relationships that sustain any individual. A-I (nr)

Autumn Sonata (1978) Ingmar Bergman's bleak examination of a middle-aged woman (Liv Ullmann) and her relationship with her mother (Ingrid Bergman). What results is a film long on talk and short on characterization and dramatic action. Fine acting throughout, but the mother-daughter conflict may be too depressing for young people. A-III (PG)

Avalanche (1978) Scorning all ecological considerations, an entrepreneur (Rock Hudson) builds a luxurious ski resort on a Colorado mountainside, hoping to impress his estranged wife (Mia Farrow) enough to effect a reconciliation. With ludicrous dialogue and shallow characterizations, director Corey Allen's run-of-the-mill disaster movie deserves to be buried in the avalanche that follows. Nudity and suggestive sexual behavior. O (PG)

Avalanche Express (1979) Cold War thriller in which C.I.A. agents (Lee Marvin and Linda Evans) try to spirit a defecting head of Soviet intelligence (Robert Shaw) out of Italy by train. Noisy ambushes, counter-spy intrigue and conventional violence lets the steam out of the plot. Director Mark Robson's last film lacks humor and genuine excitement using its climactic avalanche sequence midway, derailing most of the attempts at tension that follow. A-II (PG)

Avanti! (1972) American businessman (Jack Lemmon), in attempting to bring his father's remains back to the U.S. after the old man's death in an auto accident at an Italian resort, falls for the woman (Juliet Mills) his father has been meeting there for the last 10 years. Director Billy Wilder bludgeons the situation with some rather unfunny black humor, a good deal of vulgarity, much rough language and a bit of gratuitous nudity. O (R)

Awakening, The (1980) The mummy of a dead Egyptian queen tries to fulfill an ancient prophecy with devastating consequences for the family of the archeologist (Charlton Heston) who opened her tomb. The best asset of director Mike Newell's plodding horror story is the location photography of the Valley of the Kings. Implications of incest and some gore. A-III (R)

B

Baby Blue Marine (1976) World War II boot-camp washout (Jan-Michael Vincent) pretends to be a Marine Ranger and is received as a hero in a small Colorado town. When a waitress (Glynnis O'Connor) falls for him, he has to prove his courage. Although the story is abundantly sentimental, director John Hancock warmly evokes the people and the period, the acting is good and the result is a fairly entertaining movie. A-II (PG)

Baby Love (1969) Psychotic teenager (Linda Hayden) is taken into a wealthy London home where she proceeds to destroy each member of the family out of resentment against the father who had had an affair with her own mother (Diana Dors). Alistair Reid directs the British production as if it were a manual on sexual pathology ranging from attempted rape to lesbianism, with plenty of nudity and little concern for characterization, consistent motivation or common sense. O (R)

Baby Maker, The (1970) Barbara Hershey plays a freethinking hippie who agrees to bear a child for a couple who want a baby at least half theirs (the wife is infertile). Writer-director James Bridges provides an ending in which the wife is now insecure about her husband's affection, the husband has fallen for the girl and she realizes she wants to keep the child after all. Because the basic immorality of the arrangement is never addressed, their various disappointments seem hollow and crass. O (R)

Baby, It's You (1983) Bright daughter of a Jewish doctor (Rosanna Arquette) and the son of working-class Catholic parents (Vincent Spano) fall in love when they're high school seniors in Camden, N.J., in the late 1960s. Director John Sayles's perceptive, compassionate, if uneven, movie is made memorable by an absolutely pitch-perfect performance by Arquette and very good acting by Spano. Some needlessly graphic sex scenes and nudity. O (R)

Baby: Secret of the Lost Legend (1985) American couple (William Katt and Sean Young) exploring in Africa discover a cute baby brontosaurus which they later reunite with mama from whom it had been separated by some villains. Directed by B.W.L. Norton, it's a pleasant enough adventure tale for most age groups. A violent battle scene and some mild vulgarity. A-II (PG)

Bachelor Party (1984) Prospective bridegroom Tom Hanks has a tasteless time with crude friends in director Neil Israel's sex farce full of gross, unfunny jokes, exploitive nudity and demeaning raps about women. O (R)

Back Roads (1981) A prostitute (Sally Field) and a cheerful down-and-outer (Tommy Lee Jones) hit the road for California, and in the course of their misadventure, fall in love. Under Martin Ritt's direction the performances are appealing but the basic narrative has an air of sentimental romanticism. Its soapy mix of sexuality and occasional violence is disappointingly emphasized. A-III (R)

Back to the Beach (1987) Frankie Avalon and Annette Funicello return to the seashore and discover that the chaste relationships of the 1950s have evolved into the sexual alliances of the 1980s. Fanciful nostalgic trip from director Lyndall Hobbs is consistently upbeat, but accepting of the plot's implied premarital sex while offhandedly affirming the virtues of enduring marriage and fidelity. A-III (PG)

Back to School (1986) Rodney Dangerfield provides his special brand of uncouth humor in this story about a self-made millionaire who returns to college to help his son but finds that there are some things money can't buy. Alan Metter's direction keeps things moving in a somewhat tame sophomoric comedy about higher education. Brief instance of nudity and a bit of foul language. A-III (PG-13)

Back to the Future (1985) Above-average entertainment about a teenager (Michael J. Fox) who is transported back through time and obliged to serve as matchmaker for his parents or face retroactive non-existence. A major problem is that his mother-to-be finds him far more attractive than she does his father-to-be. Directed by Robert Zemeckis, it is funny and clever with a bit of genuine sentiment, that unfortunately is marred by casual profanity, the depiction of violence as manly and, though there is no depiction of it, an implicit acceptance of sexual promiscuity as standard teenage behavior. A-III (PG)

Backtrack (1969) Standard Western directed by Earl Bellamy in which a cowboy on his way to Mexico to buy some cattle gets involved with a trio of Texas Rangers in a desperate battle with Mexican bandits. Stylized violence. A-II (G)

Bad Boys (1983) Sean Penn stars as a vicious young criminal sent to a reformatory in this brutal exploitation movie trying to pass itself off as socially significant. The uninspired direction of Richard Rosenthal of a cliche-littered script owes little to real life and everything to some five decades of Hollywood prison movies. Bereft of moral or social perspective, it places a heavy emphasis on violence and vengeance within the gruesome context of prison life. O (R)

Bad Company (1969) French production composed of two dramatic variations on a single theme: loneliness is only masked by the companionship of equally lonely pals. Director Jean Eustache skillfully communicates the desperate bravado which hides the gnawing uncertainties of the immature youths in these two stories. Viewers may be put off by the movie's drab documentary style and some gross sexual language but none will be unmoved by the pathetic nature of these young lives. A-IV (nr)

Bad Company (1972) Clean-cut Pennsylvanian youth (Barry Brown), fleeing conscription during the Civil War, joins up with a youthful band of Missouri toughs (led by Jeff Bridges) and as they make their way West, he becomes as adept as any of them at robbing banks and killing hombres. Directed by Robert Benton, its morality tale is not very profound but the period piece is beautifully mounted and painstakingly detailed. One wonders, however, if all the cursing and updated sex talk is really credible for teenagers in 1862. A-IV (PG)

Bad Man's River (1973) Tame Italian Western with Gina Lollobrigida as a shady lady whose hobby is bilking amorous males (among them, Lee Van Cleef and James Mason) of whatever they're worth. Director Gene Martin stages a lot of forgettable action involving a sheriff's posse, a horde of revolutionary banditos and the Mexican Army. Waste of time. A-III (PG)

Bad Medicine (1985) Misfit American students (led by Steve Guttenberg and Julie Hagerty) attend a bogus medical school in Central America. Director Harvey Miller's movie fails both as social satire and as broad comedy, offering little more than some insulting humor pointed at Hispanic stereotypes along with bad jokes about incest and drug abuse. O (PG)

Bad News Bears, The (1976) Walter Matthau stars as a former minor leaguer who takes over a hopelessly misdirected and inept Little League baseball team and makes it a winner. Under Michael Ritchie's direction, the children are cute but used to communicate a cynical, albeit humorous, critique of middle-class values. Profanity, especially from the mouths of children, not exemplary imagemaking. O (PG)

Bad News Bears Go to Japan, The (1978) The third and least accomplished in the series celebrating the exploits of the inept but lovable and cunning Little League team features Tony Curtis as a somewhat unsavory promoter who hopes to exploit the exhibition game he sets up for the Bears in Tokyo. Director John Berry keeps the language pretty much under control but Curtis's visit to a Geisha house is sexually suggestive. A-III (PG)

Bad News Bears in Breaking Training, The (1977) An estranged father (William Devane) of one of the team's players takes the Bears to the Astrodome for a taste of Big League atmosphere but the film's language is anything but tasteful. Director Michael Pressman's sequel, like the original, is too cynical in its view of human foibles to provide solid family entertainment. A-III (PG)

Bad Timing: A Sensual Obsession (1980) Director Nicolas Roeg's coldly somber account of obsessive love in modern Vienna stars Art Garfunkel as a smug, domineering psychiatrist and Theresa Russell (whose performance gives the movie the only life it has) as an unstable American woman. Some very explicit sex scenes. O (X/R)

Badge 373 (1973) New York City detective (Robert Duvall), suspended from the force pending an investigation into the death of a Puerto Rican drug pusher, becomes a one-man crime-stopper. Director Howard Koch places his violent action in the slums and dives of the big city, showing in gritty detail racism, graft, greed and venality on every human level. Add constant coarse language and seamy situations, and the result is a cynical view of humanity. O (R)

Badlands (1974) Fact-based story of a drifter (Martin Sheen) who takes his teenage sweetheart (Sissy Spacek) on a bizarre shooting spree across South Dakota and Montana in the 1950s. Director Terrence Malik presents a panoramic view of American life and myths, looking at the reality and the fiction behind the American Dream from the perspective of two archetypal characters. It is a dark and troubling vision with senseless violence at its core. A-III (PG)

Ballad of Cable Hogue, The (1970) Going to some absurd extremes is director Robert Altman's off-beat, turn-of-the-century Western about a man's last stand against the machine and the alienation that comes with it. Some violence, bawdiness and profanity undercut Jason Robards' warmly credible performance. O (R)

Ballad of Gregorio Cortez, The (1983) Fact-based movie tells the story of Gregorio Cortez, an Hispanic-American (Edward James Olmos), who in 1901 in Gonzales, Texas, shoots a sheriff when a mistake made by an interpreter turns a question into a threat. He flees for the Mexican border, pursued by a huge posse led by Texas Rangers, but surrenders when he learns that his wife and children are being held in prison. Director Robert M. Young's sensitive, restrained, beautifully photographed movie does justice to both sides in this clash of cultures. There is brief, if graphic, violence. A-II (PG)

Ballad of Josie (1967) Director Andrew McLaglen's plotless Western stars dungareed Doris

Day and offers little else. The form of a ballad is simple and episodic whereas the movie, unfortunately, is merely simple-minded and fragmented. A-I (br)

Ballad of Orin, The (1979) Japanese movie, set in the early part of this century, in which a blind girl raised by blind women becomes a social outcast after being raped, until she is befriended by an army deserter, the only person not to take advantage of her. Director Masahiro Shinoda uses the lyric tale as a vehicle of social criticism directed against Japanese militarism and the inferior status of women. Several restrained scenes of sexual activity. A-III (nr)

Ballad of a Soldier (1960) A 19-year-old soldier, on a six-day furlough, makes his way home through the war-torn Russian countryside, encountering a variety of people, each with his or her own unique experience of World War II. Director Grigori Chukhrai avoids the blatant Soviet propaganda of previous Russian exports while fashioning a warm and humanistic tribute to the integrity and goodness of ordinary people. A-II (br)

Baltimore Bullet (1980) Moderately funny comedy about a master pool hustler (James Coburn) who takes on a young protégé (Bruce Boxleitner) in order to fulfill the veteran's dream of getting revenge on the greatest pool sharpster of them all (Omar Sharif). Sexual scenes played in a leering and demeaning manner make this Robert Ellis Miller directed road show with Ronee Blakley unsuitably vulgar. O (PG)

Bambi (1942) One of Walt Disney's most enchanting animated features, the movie conveys the simplicity, charm and excitement of Felix Salten's novel, especially through the appeal of Thumper, Flower and all the others who inhabit Bambi's forest world. The story's colorful development, most notably the forest fire sequence, is imaginative enough for viewers of every age. A-I (br)

Bambina (1976) Insensitive Italian comedy about a con artist who tries to exploit a retarded teenage girl but who winds up marrying her instead. Vestiges of humanism and serious intent are overridden by distasteful treatment of mental retardation. O (R)

Bamboo Gods and Iron Men (1974) Honeymooning in the Orient, a black American couple (James Iglehart and Shirley Washington) get mixed up with a ruthless gang. The inept Philippine production, clumsily directed by Cesar Gallardo, spices up its dreary martial arts violence with a massage parlor sequence. O (R)

Bamse (1970) Swedish import about a young man who falls in love with his dead father's mistress (Grynet Molvig) but she does not reciprocate his affections. The situation is far from being morally or psychologically healthy, but it is handled with restraint and artistic sensitivity. A-III (GP)

Bananas (1971) Woody Allen's patchwork comedy is loosely tied to a Latin American revolution which serves as the excuse for the standard fare of tasteless insult and irreverence, chock full of gratuitous nonsense dragged in seemingly because there was still a little film in the camera. As those familiar with Allen's approach might expect, religious orthodoxy comes in for its share of ecumenical jibes that many will find needlessly offensive. O (GP)

Bandolero (1968) Uneven Western starring

Jimmy Stewart and Dean Martin as brothers who redeem their shady past but who finally redeem themselves in a battle against Mexican bandits. Directed by Andrew V. McLaglen, the characterizations are interesting, women are treated in a positive fashion and the humor is sly and refreshing. Some vulgar language and violent climax. A-III (G)

Bang Bang Gang, The (1972) Relentlessly brutal, sex-obsessed exploitation movie directed by one Van Guylder, which details the rural escapades of two amateur gangster couples in the 1920s. O (X/R)

Bang, Bang, You're Dead (1966) Standard espionage story directed by Don Sharp in which an American (Tony Randall) gets swept away by romance and intrigue in Morocco. Stylized violence and a bedroom scene. A-III (br)

Bang the Drum Slowly (1973) Director John Hancock's humorous and touching portrait of a young baseball player who wants to play one last season before he dies made Robert De Niro a name to remember. Michael Moriarty co-starred as the best friend who shares his hopes and pains. Realistic but sensitive treatment of terminal illness. A-II (PG)

Bank Shot (1974) George C. Scott plays a safecracker sprung from jail in order to use his unique skills to direct a bank robbery. Director Gower Champion's fast-paced comedy is a satire on the criminal mind but its theme may give youngsters the wrong impression that crime pays. A-III (PG)

Banning (1967) Director Don Winston's story of corruption among the operators and affluent members of a California golf club overdoes the plot elements of vice and greed. O (br)

Barbarella (1968) French production about the misadventures of a vulnerable earth woman (Jane Fonda) facing various perils in a science-fiction world where evil has the upper hand. In a movie which is part comic strip and part Marquis de Sade, director Roger Vadim concentrates on the kinky and the unwholesome in this French production. Sexist theme and brief nudity. O (PG)

Barbarosa (1982) Country-western singer Willie Nelson plays the title role of a grizzled outlaw who is an unwilling participant in a 30-year old feud with the aristocratic Mexican family into which he married. Gilbert Roland is the patriarch who keeps sending out young men to kill him and Gary Busey is the young farmer with whom he teams and who ultimately receives Barbarosa's mantle. Offbeat concept, mediocre script, but Nelson's performance is fine. Australian director Frank Schepsi's American debut contains restrained violence. A-II (PG)

Barefoot Executive, The (1971) The title character in this Disney spoof is a chimpanzee with an uncanny taste for quality TV programs. An ambitious office boy (Kurt Russell) uses the talents of his monkey friend to become the boy wonder of network programming. The movie is really stolen by dead-panning Wally Cox and a building-ledge sequence as well-timed and suspenseful as Harold Lloyd's silent comedies. A-I (G)

Barefoot in the Park (1967) Young married couple (Jane Fonda and Robert Redford) live in a five-flight walk-up which leads to a number of amorous mix-ups. Directed by Gene Saks, Neil Simon's adaptation of his own Broadway hit, offers surefire broad comedy with strong supporting cast (Mildred Natwick and Charles Boyer). A-III (br)

Baron Blood (1972) Italian horror movie about an evil medieval baron whose American descendent (Elke Sommer) rejuvenates him to continue his evil doings in the form of an invalid millionaire (Joseph Cotton). Director Mario Bava stresses a fine assortment of torture machines but the story is a perfectly forgettable bit of nonsense. A-III (PG)

Barquero (1970) Uneven Western directed by Gordon Douglas about a ferryman (Lee Van Cleef) who takes on a horde of bandits who want to use and then destroy his barge to delay their pursuers. It proceeds as a battle of wits with some caustic dialogue, amusing characterizations and occasional violence and sexual references. A-III (GP)

Barren Lives (1969) Brazilian production set in an arid area of the interior where in 1940 a poor family looks for a place to settle and live like human beings instead of like migrant laborers the world over. Stark and unrelieved, filled with the accusing silence of the destitute, this work by director Nelson Pereira dos Santos visualizes a powerful sermon on social justice and the dignity of the human person. A-II (nr)

Barry Lyndon (1975) Delicate screen adaptation of William Makepeace Thackeray's novel about the manners and morals of 18th-century Europe is pictorially exquisite and has an appropriately elaborate musical score. Director Stanley Kubrick pays more attention to setting and mood than to the human dimensions that are part of its story of an ambitious young man (Ryan O'Neal) trying to rise to social prominence. Mature themes. A-III (PG)

Bartleby (1972) Adaptation of Herman Melville's short novel about a perplexed accountant (Paul Scofield) who can neither get his pallid clerk (John McEnery) to do the work desired, nor can he bring himself to fire him. Director Anthony Friedmann's austere movie is faithful to the spirit, if not the flavor, of the original and the acting is superb. However, the decision to update the period the present can only be labeled an interesting failure. A-II (nr)

Basic Training (1986) This totally offensive sex farce posing as political satire has the look and sense of a badly re-edited, X-rated home videocassette. O (R)

Batman (1966) Movie version of the TV series based on the comic book characters of the Masked Marvel (Adam West) and the Boy Wonder (Burt Ward) have them battling the United Nations. Directed by Leslie H. Martinson, the very young will find the action exciting and those over 12 may be amused by the movie's consciously heavy-handed and seriocomic approach to the story. A-I (br)

Batteries Not Included (1987) Failed fantasy about a group of tenement dwellers, headed by an old couple (Jessica Tandy and Hume Cronyn), who are being terrorized by thugs in the pay of a greedy real estate developer until two miniature spaceships come to their rescue. Directed by Matthew Robbins, the alien reproducing metalworks are cute and there are some whimsical special effects, but the fantasy level of this urban melodrama never gets very far off the ground. Some scenes of intense menace and realistic violence. A-II (PG)

Battle Beneath the Earth (1968) Low-budget adventure fantasy directed by Montgomery Tully in which maverick Chinese Reds, undermining the United States with a network of tunnels containing atomic bombs, are stopped by a unit of Marines led by Kerwin Mathews. Stylized violence. A-II (br)

Battle Beyond the Stars (1980)   Young volunteer Richard Thomas goes on a hunt to hire mercenaries to defend a planet threatened with conquest by an intergalactic tyrant. Scripted by John Sayles and directed by Jimmy T. Murakami with some style and humor, it is a moderately entertaining science fiction action fantasy. Many sexually oriented jokes. A-III (PG)

Battle Command (1976)   Old-fashioned war movie of uncertain origin—all the soldiers seem to be Italian no matter what their uniforms—done on a limited budget and with an appalling lack of skill. A-II (PG)

Battle for the Planet of the Apes (1973)   Final sequel to the series with Roddy McDowell heading up the ape cast and John Huston as a campy sort of simian Moses. Directed by J. Lee Thompson, the most entertaining sequences are excerpts from the previous movies used as the background of the story. A-II (G)

Battle of Algiers, The (1967)   The 1954-58 Algerian struggle for independence from French rule is re-created in this French production directed by Gillo Pontecorvo. Sympathetic to the rebels, yet compromising neither the facts nor the personalities involved, the film's documentary-like authenticity is achieved without resort to actual newsreel footage. It is a remarkable look at the process of revolutionary terror and counter-terror that victimizes ordinary citizens on both sides. A-II (br)

Battle of Britain (1969)   With the fall of France in 1940, Great Britain stood alone against the might of the German air force. The movie pays tribute to the smaller number of British fighter pilots who, in the months that followed, downed so many planes that the Luftwaffe was unable to mount its massive raids. Laurence Olivier, Michael Redgrave and Trevor Howard star in this huge and impressive British production directed by Guy Hamilton. Wartime violence. A-I (G)

Battle of Chile, The (1978)   Documentary on the 1973 overthrow of the Allende government, it shows in painstaking detail the growing agony of a society on the verge of civil war and the inevitable brutal usurpation of power by the military. Assembled from footage smuggled out of Chile and edited in Cuba under the direction of Patricio Guzman, it is a partisan account but one does not have to accept its Marxist politics in examining for oneself the visual record of events showing how the elected government of a constitutional democracy was subverted and overthrown. Some violent actualities. A-III (nr)

Battle of El Alamein, The (1971)   Italian-French shoot-em-up World War II movie seen from the Axis point-of-view in which Rommel (Robert Hossein) loses to the superior British forces of Field Marshall Montgomery (Michael Rennie). Directed by Calvin Jackson, it's not strong on characterization but it does have a sturdy string of exciting battle sequences. A-II (GP)

Battle of Neretva (1971)   Yugoslavian production about the 1943 victory of Tito's Partisans over the German Army re-creates the horror of a ferocious battle and is a tribute to their sacrifices enacted by a large international cast. Directed by Veljko Bulajic, the work is developed with little dramatic punctuation and evokes only mild sympathy and audience identification with the events it portrays. A-II (G)

Battle of Okinawa (1973)   Japanese re-creation of the ferocious, last-ditch defense of the island of Okinawa by its undermanned garrison. Directed by Kihachi Okamoto, it has a semi-documentary objectivity that distances viewers from the considerable amount of special-effects battle gore and mass suicide by part of the civilian population. A-II (nr)

Battle of the Amazons (1973)   Extremely low-budget sexploiter, directed by Alfonso Brescia, features scantily attired, man-hating Amazons in an endless round of battles, sadistic rituals, stylized orgies and gruesome torture scenes. O (R)

Battle of the Bulge, The (1965)   Henry Fonda, Robert Shaw and Robert Ryan star in a big-budget re-creation of the last, desperate German offensive against American forces in December 1944. In an ambitious, wide-ranging epic, director Ken Annakin tries to turn one of the most brutal battles of World War II into star-studded entertainment. Wartime violence. A-I (nr)

Battlestar Galactica (1979)   A fleet of survivors of an alien attack travel through deep space in search of a refuge they call Earth. Lorne Greene is at the helm of the flagship avoiding the dreaded Cylons in this compilation of episodes from the television series. As directed by Richard A. Colla, the only peril is its worshipful portrayal of the military in contrast to a foolish civil government. A-I (PG)

Bawdy Adventures of Tom Jones, The (1976)   Dull and unimaginative adaptation of a stage musical based on the Henry Fielding novel. More boring than bawdy, director Cliff Owens has made a sexual burlesque of the original with much sexual innuendo and some partial nudity. O (R)

Baxter! (1973)   British story of a London youngster with a speech defect (Scott Jacoby) who is crushed when his parents ignore his limited speech improvement but his speech therapist (Patricia Neal) stands by him. Director Lionel Jefferies treats his sentimental melodrama with crisp dispatch, some gentle humor and fine performances. It's a bit too serious for the small but others may find it quite rewarding entertainment. A-II (PG)

Beach Red (1967)   Directed by and starring Cornel Wilde, the movie attempts to explore the inhumanity of war in the story of a World War II assault on a Pacific island, but it fails by its repetitious emphasis on the realistic details of carnage and its degrading treatment of women in flashbacks. O (br)

Bear and the Doll, The (1971)   Rather flat French farce about radio cellist (Jean-Pierre Cassel) preoccupied with providing for a young son and four nieces and apparently the only man in France not willing to fall instantly at Brigitte Bardot's adorable feet. Directed by Michele Deville, there are some amusing moments in this adult comedy but the two principals seem impossibly mismatched. A-III (GP)

Bears and I, The (1974)   A Vietnam veteran (Patrick Wayne) trying to find peace on a remote Indian reservation, unknowingly breaks a tribal taboo when he starts raising three bear cubs whose mother has been killed by a poacher. Disney outdoor adventure directed by Vincent McEveety should please the younger set with its wilderness background and the cute antics of the baby cubs. A-I (G)

Beast in the Cellar, The (1971)   Pair of dotty spinsters (Beryl Reid and Flora Robson) brick up their draft-age brother in the cellar rather than see him sent off to the Western Front. Director James Kelly's horror movie has its scary moments, but far too much is given over to the doting sisters trying to rationalize their past errors in rearing their now-mad sibling. Sordid seduction-murder scene. A-III (R)

Beast Must Die, The (1974) British thriller in which a millionaire (Calvin Lockhart) invites some guests (Peter Cushing, Tom Chadbon, Michael Bambon) to spend a weekend at his remote country estate where everything is wired for sight and sound because the host knows that one of them will turn into a beast on the night of the full moon. Directed by Paul Annett, the updated werewolf tale offers some novelty and a fair amount of trumped up horror and gore for fans of this kind of thing. A-III (PG)

Beast of Blood (1970) Philippine horror movie in which a scientist (John Ashley), searching Blood Island for the crazed creature that shipwrecked him, discovers a mad surgeon (Eddie Garcia) experimenting on human head transplants. Directed by Eddie Romero, the spurting blood, slicing blades and a rape scene will upset the squeamish. O (GP)

Beast of the Yellow Night (1972) Stonefaced John Ashley and toothy Mary Wilcox team up for some terrible acting and a spot of torrid lovemaking in a preposterous tale of a vicious army deserter who sells his soul to the devil in a Southeast Asian jungle. Director Eddie Romero packages his low-budget Philippine production of soap-opera sex and disgusting gore with plenty of static dialogue. O (R)

Beat Street (1984) Skimpy plot, involving the aspirations of young blacks and Hispanics in the Bronx, loosely holds together a series of production numbers, many of which involve break dancing. Director Stan Lathan's lavish production fails because of its pretension and high gloss. Some rough language now and again but the movie is innocuous for the most part. A-II (PG)

Beau Geste (1968) The French Foreign Legion becomes the refuge for two English brothers (Dean Stockwell and Doug McClure) after the apparent theft of a family jewel worth a fortune. Well-done re-make of classic adventure story, the movie is restrained in its treatment of military brutality and the violence inherent to a desert uprising. A-I (br)

Beautiful Swindlers, The (1967) Cheap European production consists of three stories on the theme of foolish older men being taken advantage of by young seductive women. Sexually exploitative. O (br)

Bed and Board (1971) Continuing French saga of Antoine Doinel (Jean-Pierre-Leaud) who, still somewhat delinquent and fumbling, marries his sweetheart (Claude Jade) and gets through the first year of marital adjustment: a change of jobs, the coming of their first child and a test of conjugal fidelity. Director Francois Truffaut has etched a sensitive, compassionate, humorous and exquisitely tasteful picture of the maturation of love and marriage. Whether one has seen the previous two films in the trilogy or not, this will delight, amuse and captivate the imagination. A-III (GP)

Bed-Sitting Room, The (1969) Three years after World War III, which took place in less than two-and-a-half minutes, 20-odd survivors wander around the bizarre remains of London, including such grotesques as Sir Ralph Richardson, turning, quite literally, into a bed-sitting room. Director Richard Lester's screen version of playwright Spike Milligan's surrealistic farce is meant to be a commentary on the horrors of war and middle-class morality but the result is merely a disappointing jumble of British wit and rude humor. A-III (M)

Bedazzled (1968) A shy short-order cook (Dudley Moore) in love with a waitress (Eleanor Moore) sells his soul to a satanic figure (Peter Cook) for seven wishes which turn out hilariously different from what was intended. Director Stanley Donen has reshaped the Faust legend to the cut of contemporary man, though the lust sequence gets a bit too sinful and another satirizing the image of nuns may seem more distasteful than funny. A-IV (br)

Bedford Incident (1965) An American destroyer and a Russian submarine are antagonists in the creation of an international incident. Richard Widmark as the destroyer's captain is ably assisted by Sidney Poitier, Martin Balsam and Wally Cox under James Hills' capable direction. A-II (br)

Bedknobs and Broomsticks (1971) In an English seaside village during World War II, a would-be witch (Angela Lansbury) invokes an army of spectral warriors to rout 20th-century German invaders and takes some trips with three children on her big brass bed. Director Robert Stevenson keeps this Disney musical moving merrily and emphasizes the smiling high spirits of the youngsters. A-I (G)

Bedroom Mazurka (1972) Stale Danish pastry serves up coy breast-and-buttocks nudity with some unintentional humor. A mazurka, by the way, is a spirited Danish folk dance which has nothing to do with this total waste of energy. O (X/R)

Bedroom Window, The (1987) Steve Guttenberg plays a young, carefree executive whose affair with his boss's wife (Isabelle Huppert) ends in her death when a killer-rapist they tried to bring to justice is freed. Director Curtis Hanson's treatment of an engaging, convoluted plot includes brief instances of nudity, profanity and violence but the themes of dishonesty and betrayal are decidedly for mature audiences. A-III (R)

Been Down So Long It Looks Like Up to Me (1971) Episodic melodrama directed by Jeff Young about a college drop-out (Barry Primus) who, disenchanted by his odyssey in the real world, returns to college to mock everything it stands for, take drugs and have sex. It's a bad trip. O (R)

Before Winter Comes (1969) A Russian deserter (Topol) becomes the right-hand man of a British officer (David Niven) responsible for the care of refugees in an Austrian outpost after World War II. Director J. Lee Thompson focuses on the officer's dilemma of following orders to the letter or bending a little to help these displaced persons whose problems are convincingly detailed. A decent little film but one of the problems is a woman (Anna Karina) who can't say no to anyone in uniform. A-III (PG)

Beguiled, The (1971) Civil War story in which a wounded Union soldier (Clint Eastwood) takes refuge in a Southern school for ladies whom he must keep beguiled or risk being turned over to the Confederates. Directed by Don Siegel, this murky gothic horror story ends with the captive paying dearly for his ingratitude towards his captors' sick brand of Southern hospitality. In addition to the implied sexual situation, there is an explicit seduction followed by a gruesome amputation scene. A-IV (R)

Being There (1980)   Slender and austere comic tale directed by Hal Ashby from the screenplay by Jerzy Kosinski about a middle-aged, television-addicted gardener (Peter Sellers) who becomes a national celebrity when the rich and powerful mistake his slow-wittedness and ignorance for profound intelligence. This sardonic commentary about values in the television age has a seduction scene with Shirley MacLaine which places it in the adult category. A-III (PG)

Belated Flowers (1972)   Russian director Abram Room has taken a very early, uncharacteristically romantic story by Chekhov and made a simple but moving tale of doomed lovers. Room has fashioned a stylish set piece in which every artifice is used to establish and maintain a lyric mood of idealized romance. A-III (nr)

Believe in Me (1971)   Michael Sarrazin plays a promising young intern who gets hooked on amphetamines and Jacqueline Bisset is the girl he takes down the primrose path. Directed by Stuart Hagman, the story is one long TV hospital soap opera but this one features a number of slow-motion love scenes. O (R)

Believers, The (1987)   Martin Sheen is a detective who saves his son from a ritual death at the hands of a New York City cultist group who derive power from human sacrifices. Director John Schlesinger's flawed, superficial treatment of a serious subject is marred further by graphic shots of naked corpses, bloody animal entrails, some killings and a violent suicide. A-III (R)

Bell Jar, The (1979)   Dreary, painful adaptation of the Sylvia Plath autobiography detailing a seemingly well-adjusted college girl's mental breakdown after the death of her father and her rude encounters with the realities of the New York publishing world. Director Larry Peerce resorts to extensive use of nudity groping for the muddled sexual basis of the tragic heroine's problems. O (R)

Belle de Jour (1968)   The marital frigidity of a wealthy Parisian housewife (Catherine Deneuve) is traced to a religiously-induced sense of guilt over a childhood incident which she seeks to expiate by working in a brothel. In this coldly elegant French production, director Luis Bunuel has some surrealistic fun with such themes as sexual perversity among the affluent, middle-class conservative values and traditional concepts of religion. Degrading view of sexuality. O (br)

Ben (1972)   Ben (a rat) moves in with a musician-puppeteer (Lee Harcourt Montgomery) who, though he is recuperating from open heart surgery, exhausts himself trying to protect his new friend from unsympathetic adults. Director Phil Karlson passes the cheese to animal trainer Moe Di Sesso to generate some sympathy for the little fur balls who kill just about everyone but their friendly host. Stylized violence. A-II (PG)

Ben Hur (1959)   Director William Wyler's classic Hollywood epic about a Jewish prince (Charlton Heston in the title role), betrayed by his boyhood Roman friend (Stephen Boyd), but who finally achieves retribution after suffering many miseries. The conventional melodrama of the narrative is transformed by the grand scale of the spectacle whose highlight is the chariot race with stunts rigged by Yakima Canutt. The principals, moreover, manage to stand out as individuals among all the film's myriad cliches and stereotypes. A-I (G)

Beneath the Planet of the Apes (1970)   Lame sequel has astronaut (James Franciscus) reaching the bombed-out earth where the ape people are warring with the subterranean remnants of the human race, a skinless colony of people who worship "the Holy Bomb" and these deformed humans destroy the planet in the final scene. Directed by Ted Post, it lacks the wit, excitement and ingenuity of the original's warning to war-mongering, damage-prone humanity. A-III (G)

Ben-Gurion Remembers (1973)   Israeli documentary on the 25th anniversary of the embattled state of Israel pays tribute to the unique role played by David Ben-Gurion in its founding. Directed by Simon Hesers, it is a warm, personal portrait of a man not usually known for his congeniality, intermingling documentary footage and reminiscences with friends who today comprise the leadership of the country. A-I (nr)

Benjamin (1968)   Though the French production directed by Michel Deville is a handsomely mounted period piece, this movie about the initiation of an innocent young man (Pierre Clementi) into the depraved society of 18th-century aristocrats concentrates on sexual suggestiveness and titillation at the expense of any meaningful comment. O (X)

Benji (1974)   Tough little mongrel maintains his independence by begging food only from people who attach no strings and ultimately becomes the hero of his small town by foiling some kidnappers. Directed by Joe Camp, it is light, wholesome entertainment with enough tension and false leads to keep children on the edge of the seats as the little dog toughs it out and wins on his own. A-I (G)

Berserk (1967)   Lurid story of a series of gruesome murders in a circus run by Joan Crawford is directed by Jim O'Connolly. Macabre atmosphere and violence. A-III (br)

Best Defense (1984)   Supremely unfunny vehicle for the irreverent humor of comedian Eddie Murphy involves the development of a supertank for the military. Director Willard Huyck tries desperately to revive the brain-dead comedy by resorting to graphic sex and tasteless jokes about sex and the Third World. O (R)

Best Friends (1975)   Low-budget road picture about two discharged soldiers making their way home in a camper accompanied by their girl friends. Whenever the action drags, a bit of violence or sexual exploitation is brought in. O (R)

Best Friends (1982)   Burt Reynolds and Goldie Hawn play a happy Hollywood couple, a screenwriting team, who seem to have everything going for them until they put it all in jeopardy by deciding to get married. Director Norman Jewison offers a somewhat cynical comedy about the institution of marriage without insight into the values it represents. A-III (PG)

Best House in London, The (1969)   A mansion in Victorian London, donated for the worthy purpose of serving as a residence for the rehabilitation of wayward girls, is soon turned into a high class bordello by a notorious profligate (David Hemmings). Directed by Philip Saville, this witless, tasteless satire on the hypocrisy of the Victorian Age is excessive in its use of nudity and sexual references. O (X)

Best Little Whorehouse in Texas, The (1982) Broadway musical about a Texas brothel threatened by a clean-up campaign has been made into a vehicle for Burt Reynolds and Dolly Parton. The characterizations and country music are so lackluster that the virtues of the original must remain a mystery to anyone who has not seen it. Director Colin Higgins resorts to quite a bit of nudity and several fairly graphic bedroom scenes. O (R)

Best of Times, The (1986) Slack comedy about middle-aged out-of-shape losers (Robin Williams and Kurt Russell) who get a second chance to replay the big football game they lost as high school seniors. Starting with some wry, tongue-in-cheek humor, director Roger Spottiswoode lets the comic situation go downhill and the quest of grown men for their lost youth grows ever more tiresome. Much rough language, some sexual innuendo and a passing reference to locker room drugs. O (PG-13)

Best Way, The (1978) From France comes a drab and pale little film devoted to the theme of sexual ambivalence. Director Charles Miller loosely sets the drama in a boys camp in 1960, but provides undeveloped characters in a story about a sexual confrontation between two counselors (Patrick Dewaere and Patrick Bouchitey). Occasional nudity. O (nr)

Betrayal (1983) Screen version of Harold Pinter's play about a love triangle is a pretentious and anemic exercise which hints at profundities that lie too deep for words, but never delivers the goods. The British production under the direction of David Jones squanders a talented cast (Patricia Hodge, Jeremy Irons and Ben Kingsley). Single instance of obscene language. A-III (R)

Betsy, The (1978) Supremely trashy novel by Harold Robbins, adapted into a supremely trashy movie about the obsession for power, sex and wealth among the upper echelon of the automobile industry (Laurence Olivier, Robert Duvall and Katherine Ross). Director Daniel Petrie's potboiler contains nudity and is lacking completely in moral perspective. O (R)

Better a Widow (1968) Weak Italian romantic comedy directed by Duccio Tessari about the daughter (Virna Lisi) of a Sicilian Mafia Don and an Englishman (Peter McEnery) who has come to build an oil refinery. Light treatment of murder and sex. A-III (PG)

Better Off Dead (1985) This crass comedy about teenage suicide has the gall to aim itself at teenage audiences and, indeed, proclaims all the verities of the genre, including the portrayal of parents as congenital idiots. Terribly inappropriate theme as well as jocular view of drug abuse. O (PG)

Betty Blue (1986) A French import that tries to visualize the various moods of a love affair that goes from delirious heights of passion to depths of despair. By emphasizing the carnal aspects of the affair with endless amorous interludes and naked embraces, director Jean-Jacques Beinex fails to create a sense of intimacy and compassion for his characters (Beatrice Dalle and Jean-Hugues Anglade). Excessive amounts of nudity and sexual simulations. O (nr)

Between Miracles (1980) Nino Manfredi directs and stars in this dull and insipid film about a not-too-bright young man who as a boy was saved from death by an apparent miracle, raised in a monastery, and then has difficulty coping with the problems he finds in the world outside. Some sexual situations. A-III (nr)

Between the Lines (1977) Rather aimless comedy-drama about the youthful staff of a once

radical Boston newspaper attempting to come to terms with changing times. Though director Joan Micklin Silver gets some good acting from a young cast (John Herd, Stephen Collins and Jill Eikenberry), the movie comes off as nothing more than a slick, run-of-the mill Hollywood production emphasizing nudity and sexual innuendo. O (R)

Beverly Hills Cop (1984) For those who like the comedic crassness of Eddie Murphy, there's plenty of it in his role as a supercool Detroit detective whose quest for justice in the shooting of a friend takes him to Los Angeles where he bears the brunt of prejudice. Murphy's streetwise charm and cunning overcome a script infused with rough language and director Martin Brest's reliance upon violence, some brutality and awkward stereotyping. A-III (R)

Beverly Hills Cop II (1987) Tiresome vanity production directed by Tony Scott features Eddie Murphy as the clever Detroit cop who helps his California friends break up a gang of thieves and gunrunners. Unfunny, vulgar sight gags, rampant profanity, topless dancers, brutality and violence are fused with extended demolition derby-style chase sequences. O (R)

Beware My Brethren (1972) Beware indeed of this annoying British movie which tells of a fanatical evangelist (Patrick Magee) and his merciless influence upon a pathetically devout diabetic (Ann Todd) and her emotionally unstable son (Tony Beckley). Such things as rape, baptizing in blood and crucifying are treated in detail by director Robert Hartford-Davis', disgusting little shocker that is an insult to moral sensibilities. O (R)

Beware! The Blob (see: "Son of Blob")

Beyond and Back (1978) This movie presents itself as a serious, scientific examination of certain alleged happenings that seem to indicate that there is life after death. The result, however, proves to be utterly uncritical in its treatment of data and many of its conclusions are not merely absurd but at variance with some traditional religious beliefs. Its realistic depiction of death experiences may be too strong for the very young. A-III (G)

Beyond Control (1971) German import in which a pair of young men and their girl friends rob banks during the 1930s supposedly as a form of anti-Nazi protest is not only suffocatingly inept but made thoroughly offensive as well by splicing in some sex exploitation footage (shot entirely from the neck down). O (R)

Beyond Love and Evil (1971) French sex exploitation movie directed by Jacques Scandelari about the woodland villa of an evil count where a seemingly endless parade of perversity and cruelty take place. O (X)

Beyond the Door (1975) Cheap horror movie directed by Oliver Hellman is an inept, tasteless attempt to combine "Rosemary's Baby" and "The Exorcist." O (R)

Beyond the Fog (see: "Horror on Snape Island")

Beyond the Law (1968) Novelist Norman Mailer's self-indulgent home movie about brutality in a New York City police station is offensive in its almost jocular use of violence and its coarse and obscene language. O (nr)

Beyond the Limit (1983) Director John Mackenzie's screen version of the Graham Greene novel, "The Honorary Consul," is a plodding, uninspired effort given some merit only by Michael Caine's performance as the hapless diplomat in an Argentine backwater, whom an inept band of revolutionaries kidnap by mistake. Another mistake is Richard Gere as Greene's introspective protagonist. Extensive nudity in the context of an adulterous affair. O (R)

Beyond the Poseidon Adventure (1979) Tugboat captain Michael Caine (aided and abetted by Karl Malden and Sally Field) try to salvage the Poseidon, moments after the climactic rescue of the previous disaster film. Producer-director Irwin Allen supplies only vacuous plot, dialogue and resolution in a boring adventure yarn. A-II (PG)

Beyond the Reef (1981) This is a South Pacific idyll about a Polynesian lad and his pet shark who helps him win the love of a rich man's daughter, despite interference from her greedy brother and unscrupulous land developers. Directed by Frank C. Clark, it's an amateurish little movie, save for some remarkable underwater photography and a school of apparently trained sharks. Some partial nudity and permissive attitude toward the lover's affair. A-III (PG)

Beyond the Valley of the Dolls (1970) Director Russ Meyers' unfunny spoof of Hollywood lacks story, stars and appeal. Boring as it may be, it abounds in unhealthy fantasies of sex, with some nudity, and violence. O (X)

Beyond Therapy (1987) Based on the Christopher Durang play, Robert Altman's emotionally anemic romance tries to find humor in the failures of modern psychoanalysis and in the flaws of a sexually confused cast (Jeff Goldblum, Julie Hagerty, Glenda Jackson, Tom Conti and Christopher Guest). Shallow insights pervade the movie which relies totally upon sexual innuendo, negative stereotypes and some vulgar language for interest. O (R)

Bible, The (1966) Six episodes from Genesis (Creation, Adam and Eve, Cain and Abel, Noah, the Tower of Babel and Abraham) are pictured as literally as they were written, largely leaving their interpretation to the viewer. John Huston directs, narrates and plays the part of Noah in this reverent but entertaining spectacular. George C. Scott as Abraham takes acting honors among a cast including Ava Gardner, Richard Harris, Ulla Bergryd and Michael Parks. A-I (br)

Big Bird Cage, The (1972) Poorly-made Philippine movie directed by Jack Hill in which a woman (Pam Grier) smuggles her boyfriend into a women's prison camp in order to foment a rebellion. Much nudity, savagery and raw language. O (R)

Big Bounce, The (1969) Young drifter (Ryan O'Neal) becomes deeply involved with a supposedly lovable psychotic (Leigh Taylor-Young) whose desire for thrills eventually drives him away, but only after she has committed murder. Directed by Alex March, the heavy-handed melodrama is totally unconvincing. Several ludicrous nude scenes and much coarse language used so self-consciously as to emphasize its offensiveness. O (R/PG)

Big Bus, The (1976) A parody of disaster movies, it follows the misadventures of a nuclear-powered bus on its maiden run non-stop from New York to Denver. The gags work about 30 percent of the time, not too bad an average for this type of film, and director James Frawley keeps a light touch on the often heavy-handed proceedings. Innocent, mostly sophomoric humor except for several sexual references. A-III (PG)

Big Chill, The (1983) Seven old friends (William Hurt, Kevin Kline, Glenn Close among them) from college days in the 1960s are reunited by the suicide of the most brilliant of their number. After the funeral they spend the weekend together soul-searching and, to some degree, mourning their lost innocence. Director Lawrence Kasdan indicates no political awareness on the part of his characters despite their supposed sophistication and the result is an entertaining but shallow and contrived work. Brief nudity, rough language and a benign attitude toward adultery. A-III (R)

Big City, The (1967) From India comes this unassuming but dignified story of the problems that occur when a young mother must work in the city to help support her family. Director Satyajit Ray generates considerable human warmth out of a simple situation of ordinary family life. While the conclusion doesn't exactly follow and audience involvement may wear thin at times, Ray has captured the universal qualities of this Bengali family whom many will find worth a visit. A-II (br)

Big Cube, The (1969) Lana Turner is sent over the psychic edge by George Chakiris who has been spiking her medicine with LSD in order to control her fortune when she is declared incompetent. Director Tito Davison's low-budget melodrama shot in Mexico splices in some scenes of over-age hippies cutting up at drug parties. O (PG)

Big Doll House, The (1971) Low-budget Philippine sex melodrama directed by Jack Hill about a bunch of desperate women prison inmates (Judy Brown, Roberta Collins, Pam Grier) is full of innuendo as heavy as the passionate breathing on the sound track. O (R)

Big Easy, The (1987) Quirky romance about a Cajun detective (Dennis Quaid) and an assistant district attorney (Ellen Barkin) who weather a conflict of interests and the low moral atmosphere of New Orleans to solve a drug-related crime. Director Jim McBride's nervously stylistic movie stays light and often dopey despite some gruesome flashes of murder victims, a shot of topless dancers and an explicit, albeit fumbling, lovemaking scene. A-III (R)

Big Enough and Old Enough (1968) Family of Mexican migrant workers runs afoul of a motorcycle gang in this wretched movie directed by Joseph Prieto. Rape, mental and physical violence, sexually suggestive dialogue and visuals and coarse language. O (br)

Big Fix, The (1978) A Los Angeles private eye (Richard Dreyfuss), a former 1960's campus radical, is now cynical, disenchanted and divorced, scraping a living out of minor gumshoe jobs. When an old college friend (Susan Anspach) asks him to investigate a smear campaign against a political reformer, he is drawn back into the idealism of his youth. Director Jeremy Paul Kagan has made an entertaining though convoluted detective thriller that benefits greatly from the vitality of Dreyfuss' performance. Some of its humor and its less than adequate treatment of the political and moral issues it deals with make it mature fare. A-III (PG)

Big Gundown, The (1968) In this Italian-made Western, snickering ex-lawman (Lee Van Cleef) aids in tracking down a shifty Mexican (Tomas Millian) accused of rape and murder but, discovering his quarry's innocence, he then joins with him to punish the real culprits. Director Sergio Sollima's formula plot is simply an excuse to string together chases and places for the hero to exhibit his brutal brand of six-gun justice. Particularly objectionable in this film is sadistic violence and perversion perpetrated by and upon women. O (R)

Big Hand for the Little Lady, A (1986) An outstanding cast (Henry Fonda, Joanne Woodward, Jason Robards, Burgess Meredith, Paul Ford and Kevin McCarthy) are uniformly excellent in playing out the most comical and colorful poker game in the Old West. Director Fielder Cook places emphasis on the personalities, and the plot's ingenious bluffing makes for fascinating entertainment even without the clever surprise ending. A-II (br)

Big Jake (1971) John Wayne Western in which he and his two grown sons (Patrick Wayne and Christopher Mitchum) trail the gang who kidnapped his grandson, with occasional pauses for bloodshed, to a Mexican village where they take on villain Richard Boone and his band of eight cutthroats. Directed by George Sherman, it's a rather old-fashioned kind of shoot-em-up, except some of the violence is overdone. A-III (GP)

Big Mo (see: "Maurie")

Big Mouth, The (1967) Working from what seems an almost totally improvised script, director Jerry Lewis takes a bank clerk (Jerry Lewis) who happens to look exactly like a gangster (Jerry Lewis) through a tediously meandering story line. The look-alike gimmick sets up encounters with a hotel manager, a lunatic who thinks he's an FBI agent, a group of smugglers, amusement parlor police, cruel Orientals and so on until its frantic conclusion. For Jerry Lewis fans. A-I (br)

Big Red One, The (1980) Director Samuel Fuller's attempt to honor the bravery of the U.S. Army in World War II has sadly resulted in an episodic and tedious work. Lee Marvin seems to be sleepwalking through his pivotal role as the sergeant in charge of a special infantry unit. Instead of conveying the sacrifice and futility of war, it doesn't get much beyond obnoxious characterizations of some of the G.I.s who fought it. Wartime violence and incidental vulgarities. A-III (PG)

Big Sleep, The (1978) In a remake of the 1946 Howard Hawks-Raymond Chandler private eye classic, writer-director Michael Winner makes a disastrous mistake by taking the hard-boiled yet soft-edged detective Philip Marlowe out of his era and environment and plunking him down in contemporary London. This cultural dislocation only adds further confusion to the story's flurry of killings, eccentric cast of characters, and incredibly complex plot. Under the circumstances, Robert Mitchum has no chance of competing with Humphrey Bogart's performance as Marlowe in the original. Violence, brutality and some nudity. O (R)

Big T.N.T. Show, The (1966) Concert film directed by Larry Peerce and featuring such performers as Roger Miller, Ray Charles, Joan Baez, Donavan, The Byrds, Petula Clark, Ike & Tina Turner and Bo Diddley. Mixed bag of positive, wholesome songs and tribal chants whose lyrics are understandable only by rock cultists. A-II (br)

Big Trouble (1986) A zany pair of con artists (Peter Falk and Beverly D'Angelo) force a broker (Alan Arkin) to become their unwilling accomplice in an insurance fraud until a detective (Charles Durning) nails the pair. Director John Cassavetes elicits amiable performances in this witty but slight farce. Some rough language and brief nudity. A-III (R)

Big Trouble in Little China (1986) Kurt Russell reveals a comic flair for mock heroics in an action-fantasy about a 2000-year-old Chinese wizard who is determined to kidnap and marry the green-eyed girl friend of one of Russell's pals. John Carpenter directs this martial-arts frolic in a movie teeming with special effects. Much profanity and sadistic violence. A-III (PG-13)

Big Wednesday (1978) Three young surfer fanatics spend their time boozing, fighting and womanizing in director John Milius' vulgar glorification of the male bond, arrested in the adolescence of the beach-bum culture of the past, offering viewers little save scenes of nature's grandeur. O (PG)

Biggest Bundle of Them All (1967) Comic crime melodrama directed by Ken Annakin about the kidnapping of an American gangster relies excessively on sexual innuendo. O (br)

Billion Dollar Brain (1968) Filmed on location in Finland, the third in the British spy-with-horn-rimmed-glasses series starring Michael Caine as Harry Palmer goes gimmicky, humorless and even offensive with some graphic love-making. Almost nothing of the original Palmer character is recognizable but the glasses, as Caine stumbles stolidly through acres of snow on a mission involving bio-warfare and a Texas millionaire's giant computer. Director Ken Russell's elaborate satire on obsessive anti-Communist types is clear enough, but that's about all that is in this brainless film. Violence and sexual scenes. O (br)

Billy Jack (1971) Simple-minded story of the conflict between a redneck town and a school for runaway teenagers located on an Arizona Indian reservation where the title hero (Tom Laughlin who also directed) champions the area's oppressed Indians, Mexicans, blacks and school's youngsters by fighting violence with violence. Besides the violent proceedings are a rape, brief nudity and rough language. O (GP)

Billy the Kid Vs. Dracula (1966) Director William Beaudine's low-budget attempt to graft the Western and horror movie strains results in a silly hybrid that youngsters might possibly sit through but anyone of the age of reason will find beyond endurance. A-I (br)

Billy Two Hats (1974) Two smalltime bank robbers (Gregory Peck and Desi Arnaz Jr.) are on the run from a racist, Indian-hating marshall (Jack Warden) and his deputy (David Huddleston). Directed by Ted Kotcheff, the two friends in crime become symbolic reference points for the death of the Old West with the passing of the buffalo and the advent of the railroad. One very violent sequence. A-III (PG)

Bingo Long Traveling All-Stars and Motor Kings, The (1976) Warmly nostalgic comedy about a black baseball team barnstorming through the Midwest during the Depression summer of 1939, an era when black players were barred from the major leagues. Starring Billy Dee Williams, James Earl Jones, and Richard Pryor as top players who start hamming it up in the style of the Harlem Globe Trotters to make their victories against white teams go down easier. Director John Badham's movie looks back at the way it was, good and bad, without finding villains or making excuses. Good entertainment but coarse language and a brothel vignette unfortunately limit its appeal. A-III (PG)

Birch Interval (1976) Charming and affecting

movie produced by Robert B. Radnitz, about a pre-teen New York City girl (Susan McClung) who in 1947 confronts the emerging complexities of adult life when she is sent to stay with her grandfather (Eddie Albert) and uncle (Rip Torn) in a tranquil Amish community in Pennsylvania. Director Delbert Mann treats the marital problems of the uncle delicately while depicting in close detail Amish country life. Episodic and a little slow-moving, the movie nonetheless is a refreshing view of family matters that parents and their teenagers might benefit from discussing. A-II (PG)

Bird with the Crystal Plumage, The (1970) Failed Italian thriller in which a passer-by (Tony Musante) saves a woman (Eva Renzi) from the black-cloaked knifer and then finds himself and his sleep-in girlfriend (Suzy Kendall) the target of the ripper. Directed by Dario Argento, the loose ends and false clues are so apparent that the state of terrifying suspense so necessary to such a film is never fully realized. A-III (GP)

Birds Do It (1966) Harmless comedy directed by Andrew Marton in which Tab Hunter plays a secret agent trying to get from Soupy Sales, who he mistakes for a scientist, a secret ionizer that enables people to fly. Innocuous story which young children may find amusing. A-I (br)

Birds Do It, Bees Do It (1974) Documentary focuses on how living things make other living things from the world of microbes to that of human beings. Very graphic in depicting the mating of birds, bees, and just about everything else. For adults and older teens. A-III (R/PG)

Birds In Peru (1968) French melodrama written and directed by Romain Gary in which a nymphomaniac (Jean Seberg) spends the night with four lovers on a Peruvian beach where each year flocks of birds come to die. Graphic treatment of sex scenes. O (X)

Birds, the Bees and the Italians, The (1967) Director Pietro Germi's biting satire on Italian hypocrisy may prove offensive to some viewers because its story concerns adultery and because of coarse language. A-IV (br)

Birdy (1984) Vietnam vet (Matthew Modine) left virtually catatonic by a battlefield wound dreams about his past and his boyhood desire to be a bird while a friend (Nicolas Cage) tries to bring him back to reality in the grim confines of an Army hospital. Director Alan Parker gets lost in sketchy characterizations and great globs of tedious monologues that seem pointless, especially recollections of youthful sexual encounters with graphic nudity. O (R)

Birthday Party, The (1969) Good adaptation of Harold Pinter's play about two overnight guests (Patrick Magee and Sydney Tafler) who entertain the permanent lodger (Robert Shaw) with disastrous consequences. Director William Friedkin succeeds in conveying the play's never explained mood of fear that pervades the menacing rooms of the house and the acting is superb. Mature themes. A-III (G)

Biscuit Eater, The (1972) A couple of kids (Johnny Whitaker and George Spell) train a rejected bird dog for the regional championships which, if it wins, will make Johnny's dad (Earl Holliman) look bad in the eyes of his boss (Lew Ayres). Director Vincent McEveety's version of the James Street classic will appeal mainly to the elementary school set since it follows the Disney

formula of animals exceeding humans in intelligence. A-I (G)

Bite the Bullet (1975) Muddled Western directed by Richard Brooks dealing with a 700-mile horse race shortly after the turn of the century. Its hero (Gene Hackman) gives a coolly reasoned critique of the cruel stupidity of the race and its win-at-all-costs spirit but not long afterwards, he himself joins in and submits his horse to the brutal ordeal. Stylized violence. A-III (PG)

Bittersweet Love (1977) A couple (Meredith Baxter Birney and Scott Hylands) fall in love but only after getting married and her pregnancy is well advanced do they discover that they have the same father (Robert Lansing). Director David Miller takes a glossy soap-opera approach to the theme of incest in a cloying and tedious film that raises issues about abortion and divorce without much insight. A-III (PG)

B.J. Lang Presents (1972) Only Mickey Rooney's hardiest fans may be able to endure a picture in which their idol rants and rages mercilessly as a movie director driven insane by fantasies of former glory. Director Yabo Yablonsky revels in flashy camera tricks, strobe lighting and sound effects in a pointless exercise in horror. A-III (R)

Black and White in Color (1977) Extremely subtle and probing French comedy set in West Africa at the start of World War I, it tells the story of what happens when a small French settlement decides to attack a nearby German post. In looking at the human factors that lead to war, director Jean-Jacques Annaud avoids sentiment entirely, spares no one in this cast of characters and delivers an outrageous challenging and extremely funny anti-war film. Wartime violence and brief, incidental nudity. A-III (PG)

Black Beauty (1971) British version of the classic tale of a boy (Mark Lester) and his horse comes to the screen under the direction of James Hill. It is lovely to look at but, unfortunately, it is flawed by stilted scripting and wooden performances which, one hopes, will not spoil it for younger audiences. A-I (G)

Black Belly of the Tarantula, The (1972) Confusing Italian murder mystery directed by Paolo Cavara in which a sultry female voice sighs on the sound-track while a hooded psychotic stalks inadequately clad women and commits a series of excessively graphic crimes. O (R)

Black Belt Jones (1974) Black kung-fu movie with Jim Kelly and Gloria Hendry fighting to keep their school of self-defense in the Watts area of L.A. from falling into the hands of the Mafia. Director Robert Clouse goes in for a lot of clowning and sight gags leading to a sudsy climax in a car-wash gone berserk, an approach which makes the movie fairly tolerable despite its deep-down mindlessness and brutality. A-III (R)

Black Bird, The (1976) Unfunny spoof of "The Maltese Falcon" private eye classic with George Segal playing Sam Spade Jr. and Stephane Audran as the femme fatale who has not quite mastered the American idiom. Director David Giler strains hard for laughs, even trying for some religious parody, but nothing works. The language is frequently blasphemous. O (PG)

Black Caesar (1973) Black crime movie in which Fred Williamson takes over a Harlem-South Bronx crime syndicate by acquiring pay-off ledgers incriminating New York politicians. Written, produced and directed by Larry Cohen, it trades exclusively in ruthless violence, sex and street language. O (R)

Black Cauldron, The (1985) In this delightful fantasy epic, a peasant boy must prevent the evil Horned King from gaining possession of a black cauldron capable of producing an army of supernatural warriors. Along the way he learns about love, loyalty, courage and the importance of friendship over power. A new Disney animated adventure especially suitable for young viewers. A-I (PG)

Black Christmas (1975) Nasty Canadian horror movie directed by Bob Clark follows the exploits of a maniac who terrorizes a sorority house over the Christmas holidays. The incoherent script attempts to bridge the gap between the gruesome murder of coeds with obscene telephone calls that are disgusting. O (R)

Black Eye (1974) Black private eye Fred Williamson is searching Los Angeles for an antique cane stuffed with heroin and for a missing girl who is reportedly being held in a commune of Jesus freaks. Jack Arnold's direction is fast-paced, but muddying the waters is a sub-plot involving a bisexual relationship between our hero, his girl friend (Teresa Graves) and her girl friend (Rosemary Forsyth). Routine violence. A-IV (PG)

Black Girl (1972) Uneven drama of a black American family, portrays the tensions and conflicts, the misplaced love and bitterness, that stem from a kind of collective familial sense of inferiority. Directed by Ossie Davis, the movie seems largely aimed against its own members, particularly those who attempt to break the mold and escape the family's self-imposed cultural limitations. A-III (PG)

Black Godfather, The (1974) Low-budget black exploitation movie with heavy doses of unrelieved brutality and shrill racism. Written, produced and directed by John Evans, it offers a low view of humanity in general and of black life in particular. O (R)

Black Gunn (1973) Black crime movie features Jim Brown as a posh nightclub owner drawn into a confrontation with the mob when they kill his younger brother for knocking off a numbers parlor. Directed by Robert Hartford-Davis, the story provides ample opportunities for violence of every description, some casual sex and coarse language. O (R)

Black Hole, The (1980) Disney science fiction movie with some fine special effects and a mediocre plot about a maverick scientist (Maximilian Schell) and his mysterious space laboratory. Unfortunately, director Gary Nelson has made the experience no more intriguing than a ride at Disneyland. Incidental violence. A-II (PG)

Black Jesus (1971) Awkward Italian production about a black African revolutionary (Woody Strode) who tries to maintain a peaceful course in the midst of leading an energetic revolution. Director Valerio Zurlini's narrative suffers from interminable, badly-dubbed dialogue, an agonizingly slow pace and a mechanical plot devise drawing rather simplistic and superficial parallels to the passion of Jesus. Some brutal violence. A-III (GP)

Black Mama (1976) A black woman raising her child in a Los Angeles ghetto is gradually radicalized by her experiences in just trying to survive. Although director Haile Gerima uses an impressionistic style, alternating between objective reality and subjective fantasy, its message is clear that the dehumanizing conditions of poverty and racism are intolerable. A-III (nr)

Black Mama, White Mama (1973) Philippine story of two women (Pam Grier and Margaret Markhov) who escape from a prison camp handcuffed together. Director Eddie Romero, no stranger to this kind of thing, features lots of whipping, stripping and degradation. O (R)

Black Marble, The (1980) Joseph Wambaugh adapted his own novel for this movie about the romance that develops between two police officers (Paula Prentiss and Robert Foxworth). Director Harold Becker succeeds with some fine characterizations and valid emotions but fails to integrate a major subplot involving a hapless, bungling dognapper (Harry Dean Stanton). The film's decent edge is blunted by some violence and an acceptance of a premarital relationship. A-III (PG)

Black Moon (1975) French surrealistic fantasy in which a young girl (Cathryn Harrison), fleeing a bloody civil war between men and women combatants, finds refuge in an isolated country house in which live a bedridden old woman (Therese Gieshe), a brother and sister (Joe Dallesandro and Alexandra Stewart) and a band of children. While battles rage round the estate, the girl is preoccupied with her bizarre surroundings which include a talking unicorn, crying flowers, and an enormous rat named Humphrey. Director Louis Malle is less concerned with the theme of innocence than with the modern preoccupation with death and sex. Mature themes. A-IV (R)

Black Moon Rising (1987) Seething raw sexuality and toughness, Tommy Lee Jones slithers through this implausible drama from director Harley Cokliss as a thief hired to obtain some tax court evidence. He hides his findings in a prototype racing car which is then stolen. The casual sex, brutal beatings and hair-raising stunts he puts up with to retrieve the data are not worth the viewing time. O (R)

Black on White (1969) Exploitation movie directed by Tinto Brass about the sex fantasies of a white woman pursued through London by a black man. Much nudity and graphic sex. O (nr)

Black Pearl, The (1977) A young lad (Mario Custodio) in a small Mexican village whose livelihood depends upon pearl-diving is taught to respect the power of the sea by an old Indian (Gilbert Roland). Produced in Mexico and directed by Saul Swimmer, the movie's greatest strength lies in its beautiful natural setting and in its depiction of a youngster coming to terms with his religious beliefs and his doubts about himself. The very young may find the scenes with a sea monster quite scary. A-II (PG)

Black Peter (1971) Czechoslovakian movie of a 17-year-old boy (Ladislav Jakim) growing up with all the anguished diffidence of adolescence in his dealings with parents and friends, his first job and his shy curiosity about girls. The first feature of director Milos Forman, made in 1964, it is a string of small gems crystallizing the final, wonderfully hazy days of uncommitted youth the world over. A-III (nr)

Black Rodeo (1972) Documentary about a contingent of black cowboys who bring a Wild West show to New York which serves to make people aware of the black contribution to the heritage of the American West. Directed by Jeff Kanew and narrated by Woody Strode, the result has some expert slow-motion photography and a soundtrack full of pop songs commenting ironically on the action in the arena. A-I (G)

Black Samson (1974) Familiar story of black versus white in the struggle over inner-city turf, though the hero this time is a rather whimsical ghetto bar owner (Rockne Tarkington) who wants to keep his Los Angeles neighborhood drug-and-crime-free. Directed by Charles Bail, it wastes its potential by taking the predictable, brutal path leading to the inevitable bloodbath climax. Violence, rough language and numerous glimpses of the casual nudity in a topless bar. O (R)

Black Six, The (1974) Black motorcycle movie with Gene Washington as the leader of a bike pack of Vietnam War veterans who seem to find nothing but trouble wherever they go. Excessive violence and rough language. O (R)

Black Stallion, The (1979) Strikingly visualized tale about the magical relationship between a youngster (Kelly Reno) and the horse he finds shipwrecked on a deserted island becomes a beautiful metaphor for the force of youthful ambition taming the raw power of nature. Directed by Carroll Ballard from the Walter Farley story, the drama is the perfect children's movie—unsentimental, gripping and good stimulation for the young imagination. A-I (G)

Black Stallion Returns, The (1983) Uninspired sequel directed by Robert Dalva in which the stallion's original owners spirit it back to Morocco while its present master (teenaged Kelly Reno) pursues them, making his way across the desert to reclaim his beloved horse. The climax, of course, is a horse race but perhaps the dullest ever committed to film. Corny, muddled and a bore. A-I (PG)

Black Starlet (1976) A serious topic, the exploitation of women, is handled ineptly and is not above incorporating a bit of what it pretends to decry. O (R)

Black Sunday (1977) Palestinian extremist group plots to commit a terrorist atrocity at the Super Bowl while Israeli agent (Robert Shaw) tries frantically to avert it. Director John Frankenheimer's thriller is exciting enough but it unfortunately exploits some larger issues for the sake of entertainment. Some intense violence. A-III (R)

Black Thursday (1974) On July 16, 1942, Paris police rounded up 13,000 Jews for deportation to Nazi concentration camps, from which all but 30 failed to return after the war. Director Michael Mitrani has reconstructed in semi-documentary style that terrible Black Thursday, using as his script the account of a young student who attempted to save those he could. A-III (nr)

Black Widow (1987) Debra Winger and Theresa Russell square off in a confrontation of cunning and guile when a Justice Department data analyst (Winger) tries to put an end to the series of seductions and murders of wealthy men by a mysterious and deadly woman (Russell). The double-bluff conclusion is as flawed as the sensually toned melodrama which has a brief instance of nudity and a decidedly adult treatment by director Bob Rafelson. A-III (R)

Black Windmill, The (1974) Above average British thriller about an espionage agent (Michael Caine) whose son has been kidnapped by enemy agents and, in trying to get him back, he is suspected of being a double agent by his superior (Donald Pleasence). Directed by Don Siegel, the highly charged movie's rapid pace and sharp

action gloss over the obvious holes and inconsistencies in the plot but the real interest is in Caine's characterization and a conclusion that for once is not cynical but rather optimistic. A-III (PG)

Blackbeard's Ghost (1968) A Disney comedy in which some elderly New England ladies are saved from eviction through the invisible machinations of pirate Blackbeard (Peter Ustinov) who helps the inept local school track team win a meet and a big sum of money. Director Robert Stevenson's simple-minded slapstick and special effects provide laughs, but the team's coach (Dean Jones), after being thoroughly ridiculed for objecting to Blackbeard's tactics, gets into the act himself. The impression that uncritical youngsters might get from all this is that cheating is O.K. if you can't win honestly. A-II (G)

Blacula (1972) African prince (William Marshall), seeking Dracula's signature on a petition abolishing slavery is instead bitten by the Transylvanian count, entombed in the cellar and liberated two centuries later by a pair of swishy interior decorators whereupon he begins teething on the town. Director Bill Crain provides a few genuine thrills on the horror side but, for the most part, the movie tries to have some simple fun with its horror premise. A-II (PG)

Blade Runner (1982) Science fiction thriller about a private eye (Harrison Ford) whose job is to hunt down and dispose of out-of-control humanoids. His work gets complicated when he falls in love with an advanced prototype who doesn't know she's not human (Sean Young). Director Ridley Scott's moody atmosphere and futuristic sets evoke an ecologically fouled and spiritually demoralized metropolis, but the disappointing script meanders listlessly. Excessive violence and partial nudity. O (R)

Blame It on Rio (1984) Businessman (Michael Caine) yields to the seduction of the daughter of his best friend (Joseph Bologna) who is depending upon him to help trap the daughter's lover. Director Stanley Donen's misguided celebration of male sexual fantasies tries to milk humor from a promiscuous situation and its use of partial nudity. O (R)

Blast Off (see: "Those Fantastic Flying Fools")

Blazing Saddles (1974) Vulgar and broad satire on Westerns has not so much a plot as a series of wacky situations and comic stereotypes, including black sheriff Cleavon Little, rail baron Harvey Korman and bar room singer Madeline Kahn. Directed by Mel Brooks, it offers some funny moments but the overall tone of its humor runs solidly toward the coarse, the smutty and the scatological. O (R)

Bless the Beasts and Children (1971) Failed melodrama about a handful of adolescent misfits wanting to set free a herd of captive buffalo. Directed by Stanley Kramer, the obvious aim was to deal with man's inhumanity to wildlife and youth but the result is a heavy-handed succession of mini-soap operas that wrench the emotions without any semblance of insight. Some rough language. A-III (GP)

Blind Date (1987) Bruce Willis goes on a blind date with Kim Basinger but forgets to keep her away from alcohol. The consequences are traditional slapstick sequences of reckless abandon and funny sight gags in this romance from director Blake Edwards. Jealous ex-boy friend John Larroquette supplies most of the genuine humor, but

Basinger shows some flare for the zany. Brief nudity, casual treatment of alcoholism and some rough language are adult fare. A-III (PG-13)

Blind Dead, The (1973) Spanish-Portuguese horror movie in which three young people, camping amidst the ruins of a medieval monastery, fall prey to the vampire spectres of 12th-century Crusaders. Directed by Amando De Ossorio, the story is silly and the horror is minimal. Some sexual innuendo and spilling of blood. A- III (PG)

Blindfold (1966) Complicated espionage story directed by Philip Dunne starts in Central Park where a psychiatrist (Rock Hudson) is approached by a G-man and asked to treat a top government scientist but when he does, enemy agents and the patient's sister (Claudia Cardinale) get on his trail. Moderately entertaining with some mildly romantic interludes. A-II (br)

Blindman (1972) Italian Western in which the hobo hero of the title (Tony Anthony) is robbed of the 50 women he is delivering to a Texas mining camp by two hairy bandits (Ringo Starr and Lloyd Batista) who have other plans for them. Time and again senseless slaughter follows sadistic torture as blindman and badmen match wits under Ferdinando Baldi's routine direction. Most objectionable is its presentation of women as objects to be abused. O (R)

Bliss (1986) An advertising executive (Barry Otto) dreams that he has died and gone to hell but, when shocked out of this nightmare, he tries to change his already hellish and misdirected life. Directed by Ray Lawrence, this Australian import has difficulty finding a balance between social commentary and sex farce. Nudity and some profanity. O (R)

Bliss of Mrs. Blossom, The (1968) Shirley MacLaine plays a housewife with a devoted and hard-working husband (Richard Attenborough) while keeping a male admirer (James Booth) hidden in the attic. Whether or not this is the romantic daydream of all housewives, it does have a comic potential that this ménage-à-trois fantasy plays with until the situation wears thin and then falls flat because of an over-inflated script. Though director Joe McGrath's broadly exaggerated treatment keeps the questionable shenanigans within the bounds of good taste, the basic material will not appeal to everyone. A-III (PG)

Blood and Lace (1971) Orphanage operator (Gloria Grahame) has runaways killed by a cleaver-wielding lunatic (Len Lesser) and stashed in the freezer, lest she lose the monthly state subsidy for each orphan. That's only the plot premise of director Philip Gilbert's movie which goes on to add some sexual titillation to its low-budget bloody horror formula. O (GP)

Blood Beach (1981) A nasty-looking creature devours bathers before they can even get their feet wet, sucking them down into the sand, in this mindless, wholly inept little horror movie directed and written by Jeffrey Bloom. Excessive violence. O (R)

Blood Feud (1980) Fascist Italy is the setting for director Lina Wertmuller's serio-comic melodrama about a vengeance-crazed widow (Sophia Loren) who enlists the aid of her two lovers (Marcello Mastroianni and Giancarlo Giannini) to avenge the murder of her husband. Considering the talents involved, the result is a disappointing but ambitious failure. Violence, a frank approach to sex and the complex social, religious and politi-cal background serve as sources for the movie's satiric drive. A-IV (R)

Blood from the Mummy's Tomb (1972) Mild British horror tale taken from a Bram Stoker novel about a professor (Andrew Keir) who gives his daughter (Valerie Leon) a ruby ring pilfered from the hand of an ancient Egyptian princess, who returns to take her revenge. Directed by Seth Holt, it plays the game rather well and is worth exploring for a few chuckles, if not chills. A-II (PG)

Blood Mania (1971) Wealthy surgeon's daughter (Maria De Aragon) administers a heart stimulant to speed up her father's death which opens the door to other crimes of passion and greed. Between acts of violence, there are some bouts of nude lovemaking that place this pathetically sensational melodrama directed by Robert O'Neil in the sticky mire of the sex-violence formula. O (R)

Blood of Dracula's Castle (1969) Vampire couple (Paula Raymond and Alex D'Arcy) keep a collection of young women guests manacled in the cellar of a deserted desert castle where they have taken residence until a new owner (Robert Dix) arrives and tries to evict them. Directed by Al Adamson, the only horrifying aspect of this synthetic foolishness is seeing a fine character actor, John Carradine, playing a moon-baying butler. A-II (M)

Blood of the Condor (1973) Bolivian documentary investigating charges that a Peace Corps medical clinic had been sterilizing Indian women who came for treatment without telling them what they were doing. Director Jorge Sanjines places the report in the context of Indian culture and politics and has made a quite sophisticated film out of a direct and simple story. A-III (nr)

Blood on Satan's Claw, The (1971) Failed British chiller set in bucolic 16th-century England where an unsuspecting plowman unearths the remains of a devil who comes to life and, with the aid of a seductive local recruit (Linda Hayden), manages to terrify the local yokels. Directed by Piers Haggard, the movie has its gory moments but it is severely undercut by a clumsy emphasis on the sexual side of witchcraft. O (R)

Blood Queen (see: "Little Mother")

Blood Simple (1985) A young wife (Frances McDormand) runs away from her Texas saloon owner husband (Dan Hedaya) who hires a seedy private detective (M. Emmet Walsh) to kill both her and her lover. Joel and Ethan Coen's cleverly plotted, well-acted tale of love, hate and vengeance in which nothing works out as the hapless characters intended, proves to be a work of somber, quirky brilliance, with glints of black humor. Some bloody violence subordinated to plot and characterizations. A-IV (R)

Blood Thirst (1972) Low-budget Philippine horror import about an American detective (Robert Winston) called to Manila to investigate a series of murdered women found drained of blood. Producer-director Newt Arnold handles the standard nonsense with the fast economy of a black-and-white movie and nary a gown is shed nor a vein slit before the camera pulls away. A-III (GP)

Bloodbrothers (1978) The tension between father (Tony Lo Bianco) and son (Richard Gere) are at the core of this movie about a tightly knit, Italian American working-class family living in the Bronx which is under siege from other ethnic groups. The father and his brother (Paul Sorvino) bestow all their hopes for the future on the young lad but he is not sure that he wants to follow in their footsteps. Director Robert Mulligan's work has a certain amount of raw power but it is far too melodramatic and lacking in ethnic authenticity to be able to deal convincingly with the important moral and social issues it raises. Excessive profanity and an uncritical attitude toward sexual promiscuity. O (R)

Bloodline (1979) Audrey Hepburn, surrounded by a host of veteran actors, inherits control of a vast pharmaceutical empire and becomes the target of a killer. Director Terence Young's treatment of the story adapted from Sidney Sheldon's best seller reeks of sexual exploitation, sadistic violence and a sleep-inducing plotline. O (R)

Bloodsuckers (1972) British horror movie about a vampire cult in the ruins of ancient Greece and an Oxford professor (Patrick Mower) who believes that vampirism is a remedy for impotency. Directed by Robert Hartford-Davis, there is some stunning photography of Greece but the disjointed plot doesn't hold together. Some graphic shots of body mutilations and nudity. O (R)

Bloodthirsty Butchers (1970) Poor British horror movie about a Fleet Street barber who shaves patrons too closely, his sadistic assistant who separates their components with his cleaver, and a baker's wife who sells assorted anatomic pies. The real victims are the viewers partaking of this low-budget exercise in sex and cruelty. O (R)

Bloody Mama (1970) Sordid crime melodrama about the 1930's Ma Barker gang with Shelley Winters in the title role. Directed by Roger Corman, the character is presented as a psychopath and the treatment includes excessive violence and the vagaries of sexual appetites. O (R)

Blow Out (1981) A movie soundman (John Travolta) records an auto accident, rescues a young woman (Nancy Allen) and then attempts to bring to light an assassination plot. Director Brian De Palma's thriller is short on suspense and long on sadism, employs ludicrously self-conscious techniques and offers a shamelessly confused moral outlook. Mixture of violence and nudity in a sexual context. O (R)

Blow-Up (1967) In this British production, director Michaelangelo Antonioni takes on the themes of alienation in modern society and the uncertain relationship between illusion and reality in a story about an egocentric man (David Hemmings) who becomes indirectly involved in a murder. His cold and impersonal film, however, is unconvincing in its pessimistic vision of modern life. Nudity in a sexual context. O (br)

Blue (1968) A failed Western in which Terence Stamp stars as the adopted blue-eyed gringo son of a Mexican bandit chief (Ricardo Montalban). The son sides with the American settlers against his former comrades but is torn between the two cultures for the duration of this muddled movie. Beautiful landscapes but English director Sylvio Narizzano offers only a superficial development of a complex theme. Winked-at bedroom encounter. A-III (br)

Blue Bird, The (1976) Filmed in Leningrad, this American-Soviet co-production presents Maurice Maeterlinck's children's classic about two peasant youngsters searching for the blue bird that will bring health and happiness to the sick daughter of a neighboring family. George Cukor directs this intermittently beautiful but ultimately earthbound musical fantasy whose songs thankfully pass almost unnoticed. The child actors, (Todd Lookinland and Patsy Kensit) are fine which cannot be said of the adult cast (Elizabeth Taylor, Jane Fonda, Ava Gardner, Cicely Tyson). Ponderous but innocuous entertainment. A-I (G)

Blue City (1986) A sour and violent story depicting vigilante ambitions on the part of a wayward adolescent (Judd Nelson) who returns home to discover his dad has been murdered. Under Michelle Manning's direction, Nelson and co-star Ally Sheedy give wretched performances as they mix violence, casual sex and sexually-derived profanity in this blue movie. O (R)

Blue Collar (1978) Screenwriter Paul Schrader's directing debut looks at the frustrations of three Detroit auto workers (Harvey Keitel, Richard Pryor and Yaphet Kotto), trapped in a grueling environment while being taken advantage of by their union and management. A dim failed work, it exploits such serious issues as factory conditions, union corruption, management oppression, economic distress and marital tensions, rather than explore them in some coherent and intelligent fashion. Crass cynicism and harsh language. O (R)

Blue Country (1978) The setting for this French comedy is a gorgeous bucolic valley into which comes a little stream of expatriates from the city in search of a more humane existence. What they find is that the natives are themselves longing for the easy life of the city. Unfortunately, writer-director Jean-Charles Tacchella has burdened his delightful cast and comic anecdotal style with the weight of a seriously flawed broadside against the institution of marriage. O (PG)

Blue Lagoon, The (1980) Two marooned children (Brooke Shields and Christopher Atkins) grow through puberty to the discovery of sex and parenthood on a deserted island paradise. Director Randal Kleiser exploits teen sexuality with cute, peek-a-boo nudity and the only innocence on the screen is its unawareness of the realities of life in the tropics. O (R)

Blue Max (1966) Saga of a German flying ace (George Peppard) toward the end of World War I details his exploits in sky as well as on the ground with the wife (Ursula Andress) of a general (James Mason) who has turned him into a hero. Directed by John Guillermin, the movie soars with the scenes of biplanes in action but falters on the earthbound melodramatic problems of its characters. Two excessively explicit scenes of lovemaking. O (br)

Blue Thunder (1983) Tough, dedicated police helicopter pilot (Roy Scheider) and his callow but brainy sidekick (Daniel Stern) thwart the efforts of some sinister government types to use real people in testing a super-helicopter designed to put down urban riots. The unbelievable plot, however, serves only as a pretext for some slam-bang aerial action in a callous and cynical movie directed by John Badham. Much violence and utterly gratuitous nude sequence. O (R)

Blue Velvet (1986) Adolescent (Kyle MacLachlan) confronts the lighter but mostly darker sides of sexual desire in a small town when he comes across a severed human ear in a field and is drawn into a web of sadistic sex and eroticism. Director David Lynch's sinister fable of sex and violence in small-town America leaves only a vivid after-image of decadence and brutality. O (R)

Blue Water, White Death (1971) Wildlife filmmaker Peter Gimbel sets out to find and photograph the magnificent Great White shark in its natural surroundings of the open sea. Apart from the menacing sharks themselves, Gimbel's documentary dwells on a number of other forms of sea life and offers some ecological observations on the approaching extinction of the whale. Some terrifying moments with attacking sharks. A-II (G)

Bluebeard (1972) Richard Burton stars as the infamous lady-killer in a dull version of the story set in pre-Nazi Germany. Some of his victims (Raquel Welch, Virna Lisi, Nathalie Delon) play it for snickers while others play it very straight. Directed by Edward Dmytryk, the movie doesn't succeed either as spoof or as melodrama. Restrained violence and much coy nudity. O (R)

Blues Brothers, The (1980) Two blues singers (John Belushi and Dan Aykroyd) try to raise money for an orphanage by putting a band together and playing some concert dates. The plot is interspersed with scenes of wholesale destruction and frenzied chases which are spectacularly unfunny and uninvolving. Some good musical portions from Cab Calloway and Ray Charles, but not enough depth from director John Landis to save this zany comedy from milking cheap laughs from rough language and crude situations. A-III (R)

Blues for Lovers (1966) Well-intentioned but weak melodrama directed by Paul Henreid about how a little blind boy with an over-protective widow gets comfort and help from blind musician Ray Charles (playing himself). The mother's illicit relationship with a boy friend makes it mature fare. A-III (br)

Blume in Love (1973) Beverly Hills divorce lawyer (George Segal), who loses his wife (Susan Anspach) when she catches him committing adultery, tries desperately to win her back in this uneven, sometimes amusing, romantic comedy directed by Paul Mazursky. Some casual nudity and harsh language. A-III (R)

Boardwalk (1979) Aging Brighton Beach Jewish couple (Lee Strasberg and Ruth Gordon) suffer through the deterioration of their health and of their neighborhood in this inept and heavy-handed moral tale from director Stephen Verona. Although some serious issues are presented, the conclusion is crude and melodramatic, overbaked with violence and a frank treatment of sex. A-III (nr)

Boat Is Full, The (1981) A desperate party of Jewish refugees arrives in Switzerland vainly seeking asylum from Nazi persecution. An outstanding Swiss production written and directed by Markus Imhoof, it is a convincing and quite moving depiction of the plight of these refugees and the various attitudes of the Swiss toward them. A richly human treatment of a grim but important subject. A-II (PG)

Boatniks, The (1970) Typical Disney romp follows the slapstick misadventures of a bumbling Coast Guard officer (Robert Morse) and a master jewel thief (Phil Silvers) trying to leave the country with the loot. There's a seasoning of innocuous adult humor to interest the parents watching with their youngsters. A-I (G)

Bob & Carol & Ted & Alice (1969) When Bob & Carol (Robert Culp and Natalie Wood) introduce their friends Ted & Alice (Elliott Gould and Dyan Cannon) to the new freedom of being honest about their feelings, it is only a question of time before the two couples go to bed together. Director Paul Mazursky's modern morality tale about the new

morality spoofs much that deserves spoofing but ultimately fails because it exploits the many opportunities for comic titillation worked into the obvious script. Excessive nudity and sexual references. O (R)

Bobbie and the Outlaw (1976) Inane and brutal western from director Mark Lester about a band of robbers whose antics seem designed as an obvious attempt to grind out a cheap Bonnie and Clyde copy, replete with excessive violence and some nudity. O (R)

Bobby Deerfield (1977) Plodding romantic melodrama directed by Sydney Pollack about a famous racing car driver (Al Pacino) and his relationship with an Italian aristocrat (Marthe Keller) who is dying of an incurable disease. Scenic, sentimental and predictable, the film's theme and brief nudity make it mature fare. A-III (PG)

Bobo, The (1967) Penniless clown with two guitars but no voice (Peter Sellers) aims at becoming Spain's first singing matador but he must first seduce a girl-about-town (Brett Ekland) in three days if he is to get a contract. Director Robert Parrish's dreary comedy is neither moving nor hilarious and it was aiming at both. Sexual innuendo. A-III (br)

Body, The (1971) With an impressive list of technical advisers, doctors, scientists, and educators, producer Tony Garnett and director Roy Battersby have set about a visual exploration of the fabric and functions, inside and out, of the human body. While their intentions may be pure, the explicit nature of the sexual material has no place in a movie theater and its use either in classroom or home is highly questionable. O (X)

Body Beneath, The (1971) Venerable British family of vampires, threatened by an infusion of bad blood and local harassment, decides to emigrate to America. The movie suffers from an infusion of bad acting, ludicrous scripting and an over-generous display of sex, gore and psychedelic nonsense. O (nr)

Body Double (1984) Director Brian De Palma's attempt at concocting an imitation Hitchcock thriller once again combines voyeurism and violence directed at women. Hitchcock might have been cruel but he was clever, while De Palma is only cruel and banal. A self-indulgent travesty with an unnecessary detailed depiction of the vicious murder of a woman and excessive use of nudity. O (R)

Body Heat (1981) Passing through a small Florida town, a smalltime lawyer (William Hurt) tarries to pursue a married woman (Kathleen Turner), who persuades him to rid her of an unwanted and very wealthy husband. Written and directed by Lawrence Kasdan, its a labored imitation of a dark romantic melodrama of the 1940s, with the only modern touch being its extensive and explicit depiction of sex. O (R)

Body Rock (1984) Middling youth movie directed by Marcelo Epstein about a youngster (Lorenzo Lamas) who turns his back on friendships to pursue a career as a dance club disc jockey. Focus is on the hormonal rather than the moral. A-III (PG-13)

Bofors Gun, The (1968) British adaptation of John McGrath's play about a long night of guard duty in a munitions depot during which a fanatic Irish rebel-poet (Nicol Williamson) turns his rage on an ineffectual upper-class superior (David Warner) in an increasingly nightmarish situation.

Director Jack Gold builds the growing antagonism between the two characters to the busting point. Harrowing tension and barracks language. A-IV (nr)

Bolshoi Ballet 67 (1966) Using the framework of a tour through the school of this famous troupe, the documentary affords a privileged view of the discipline and training that develops its leading dancers after years of effort. Much of the movie consists of performances including the spectacular "Paganini" and the colorful "Bolero." A-I (br)

Bombay Talkie (1970) Western pulp author (Jennifer Kendal) visits India, falls in love first with a screenwriter and then with a young film star but, constantly trailing misery in her wake, she completely ruins both their lives. Directed by James Ivory, the plot is low-key and conventional, with interest lying in the psychological development of the relationships and the unique setting. A-III (GP)

Bon Voyage, Charlie Brown (And Don't Come Back!) (1980) This fourth animated feature starring Charlie Brown and his friends, brings them to France as exchange students where they find themselves quartered in a spooky chateau. Written by Charles Schulz, the comic strip's creator, and directed by Bill Melendez, the movie is pretty thin fare, talky and episodic, but youngster and Peanuts fans will love it. A-I (G)

Bone (1974) Beverly Hills household of a used car tycoon (Andrew Duggan) and his repressed wife (Joyce Van Patten) is invaded by a black rapist (Yaphet Kotto) in a movie that apparently intended to show the hypocrisies of the affluent and contemporary American racial attitudes. Incoherently written and badly directed by Larry Cohen, all it shows is human ugliness. O (R)

Bonjour Amour (1978) Shy, studious high school lad falls in love with a 17-year-old shopgirl and despite objections from his parents, he tries to run away with her. French director Roger Andrieux is handicapped by a script that oversimplifies and romanticizes the serious problem of irresponsible teenage sexuality. O (nr)

Bonnie and Clyde (1968) Warren Beatty's production stars himself and Faye Dunaway, with supporting cast of Gene Hackman, Estelle Parsons and Michael J. Pollard, in a vivid and strikingly real re-creation of the treadmill existence of the Barrow Gang, ill-fated bank robbers of the Depression. Director Arthur Penn brings a human perspective to the gang's wildly distorted legend and their senselessly violent deaths which leaves viewers to ponder the brutal frontier ethic of American justice. Scenes of strong violence. A-IV (br)

Bonnie's Kids (1972) Lurid crime melodrama about deceitful, promiscuous sisters (Tiffany Bolling and Robin Mattson) who flee their shanty town after killing their lecherous stepfather, become models and end as pawns in a big robbery. Writer-director Arthur Marks bases much of the plot on sexual jealousies from which stem this story of murder and suicide. O (R)

Book of Numbers (1973) Pair of fast-talking slickers (Raymond St. Jacques and Philip Michael Thomas) set up a wildly successful numbers game in a small but monumentally venal Tennessee town, much to the chagrin of some local criminals. Also directed by St. Jacques, some bitter lessons in free enterprise and the futility of bucking the system are put over with lots of broad slapstick and sight gags. Some violence, a suggestive sex scene

and rough language. A-III (R)

Boom (1968) Screen version of Tennessee Williams' play in which a wealthy woman (Elizabeth Taylor) who is terminally ill is visited by the Angel of Death (Richard Burton) in her posh Mediterranean villa. Director Joseph Losey fails to give life to what is essentially a play of not very profound ideas. Mature themes with excessively crude sexual references. O (br)

Boot Hill (1973) Flat Italian Western about a pair of adventurers (Terence Hill and Bud Spencer) who help some Colorado miners fight a corrupt boss (Victor Buono). Unfortunately, rather than try to make any sense out of the story, director Giuseppe Colizzi relies mostly on his cast's acrobatic antics and close-ups of their snickering faces. Some violence. A-II (GP)

Bora Bora (1970) Sex exploitation movie in which a husband pursues his wife to the South Seas where they engage in various affairs before reuniting for a happy ending that has no redeeming value. Except for the Polynesian setting, the movie is truly boring, boring. O (R)

Border, The (1982) A member of the Border Patrol (Jack Nicholson) is appalled by the corruption of his fellow officers but then begins himself to take small bribes from poor Mexicans because of his spendthrift wife (Valerie Perrine). Thoroughly muddled in both intentions and structure, director Tony Richardson keeps the narrative limping along until the sustained burst of improbable violence that concludes it. Also profanity and some brief nudity. A-III (R)

Born Again (1978) Based on Chuck Colson's book about his years in the Nixon White House, his trial, his prison term and conversion to fundamentalist Christianity, director Irving Rapper's well-intentioned but inadequate movie fails to move, much less convince, because it equates religious conviction with sentimentality. The result is both an insult to those who take religion seriously and an occasion for contempt to those who look down on any form of belief as intellectually indefensible. A-III (PG)

Born American (1986) Absurdly implausible action-adventure yarn about three college lads who, while vacationing in the Arctic, cross into the Soviet Union for a lark. Imprisoned and brutalized by Soviet guards, one of these All-American boys turns into a mini-Rambo visiting death and destruction on their tormentors. Profanity, graphic torture sequences, excessive violence and an imbecilic perspective on international relations. O (R)

Born Black (to White Parents) (1972) German-Italian attempt at soft-core titillation whose title refers to a black child born of Caucasian parents, the result of a sperm transfer, not by promiscuity. O (R)

Born Free (1966) African game warden and his wife (Bill Travers and Virginia McKenna) teach Elsa, their grown-up pet lion, how to survive in the jungle rather than confined in a zoo. A splendid wildlife film, directed by James Hill, viewers will relish the natural beauty of the game preserve and a warm husband-and-wife portrayal but none of this stops Elsa from stealing the picture. A-I (br)

Born to Win (1971) Czech director Ivan Passer's first American movie concerns a Times Square junkie (George Segal) who becomes involved with a woman (Karen Black) after stealing her car but, despite her help and his dreams of breaking his habit, he is a born loser. Though occasionally funny, too many scenes are played simply for their sexual content and the sensationalism of the drug counter-culture. O (R)

Born Wild (1968)   Sordid melodrama directed by Maury Dexter about the conflict engendered by the bigoted treatment of Mexican-American students in a Southern California high school is excessive in its sensationalized treatment of sex and violence. O (PG)

Borsalino (1970)   French gangster story set in 1930 Marseilles (the Chicago of its day) follows the rise of two petty crooks (Jean-Paul Belmondo and Alain Delon) until they control the city's rackets and are targets for other ambitious criminals. Directed by Jacques Deray, the point is not so much the story as it is the relationship between the two men and the evocation of the mood and feeling of life in the 1930s. A-III (GP)

Boss Nigger (1975)   Fred Williamson, co-producer and star of this most recent ripoff of Kurosawa's samurai epic, "Yojimbo," surrounds himself here with a set of supposed actors even more inept then he, with a fine disregard for race, creed, color or natural ability. Gratuitous violence and sex limit this to uncritical adults. A-III (PG)

Boston Strangler, The (1968)   Fact-based movie about a sex murderer who terrorizes a city and the investigation which resulted in his capture. Director Richard Fleischer treats the case in plodding semi-documentary style, devoting the first half to the women victims and the last to the compulsive killer (Tony Curtis). Though well-intentioned, its graphic detailing of these brutal sex crimes is needless and offensive. O (R)

Bostonians, The (1984)   Interesting adaptation of the Henry James novel about a strong woman (Vanessa Redgrave), a domineering male (Christopher Reeve) and an innocent young woman (Madeleine Potter) whom both are trying to influence. Director James Ivory gets some notable performances, though Potter lacks the magnetism to be the focal point for the ensuing struggle between feminist and chauvinist, but it does succeed in conveying 19th-century American attitudes about sexual roles. A-III (nr)

Boulevard Nights (1979)   Inner-city Hispanic brothers strive for contrasting ideals. One wants a better life, the other wants gang supremacy. Director Michael Pressman's superficial examination of the macho rituals of gang violence and drug dependence in the Mexican-American community generates bogus excitement, relying too heavily upon their graphic depiction. O (R)

Bound for Glory (1977)   Screen biography of folk singer Woody Guthrie (David Carradine), based on his 1943 autobiography, showing his odyssey among the Depression's dispossessed from Oklahoma farmers to California migrant workers and how the songs he wrote and sang about them led to a national radio career. The outstanding achievement of director Hal Ashby's dramatization is its faithful re-creation of the Depression years and Guthrie's sense of social justice. Restrained depiction of promiscuity. A-III (PG)

Bounty, The (1984)   Revisionist account of the mutiny aboard the "HMS Bounty" portrays Lt. William Bligh (Anthony Hopkins) as a flawed hero and Fletcher Christian (Mel Gibson) as an unstable young man bewitched by a Tahitian beauty. Roger Donaldson directs with intelligence and visual flare but despite fine acting, no real sparks ignite the drama because of a weak script. Extensive

Polynesian nudity. A-IV (PG)

Boxcar Bertha (1972)   Trashy melodrama about a former labor unionizer turned bank robber (David Carridine), his woman companion of the title (Barbara Hershey) and some drifters (Barry Primus and Bernie Casey) picked up along the way. Directed by Martin Scorsese, the movie rumbles along through a tacky morass of redneck police and hired railroad thugs, pausing only for a shotgun blast in the chest here or a frolic in the buff there. There is a climactic massacre that leaves Carradine nailed cruciform to the side of a boxcar. O (R)

Boy and His Dog, A (1976)   A not very bright boy (Don Johnson) and his extremely intelligent dog try to survive in a post-nuclear holocaust world. The two, moreover, can communicate telepathically with one another until the inevitable love triangle is introduced (Susan Benton). The acting, including the dog's is very good, but it is questionable that the violence and sex add to this black comedy from director L.Q. Jones based upon the Harlan Ellison novella. A-IV (R)

Boy, Did I Get a Wrong Number (1966)   Hopeless comedy directed by George Marshall in which a real-estate operator (Bob Hope) lets a movie actress (Elke Sommer) hide out from the studio in an unsold estate causing all kinds of implausible complications with his wife (Marjorie Lord) and maid (Phyllis Diller). Sexual innuendo. A-III (br)

Boy Friend, The (1972)   British spoof of 1930's Hollywood backstage musicals with Twiggy as the understudy who becomes the star. Writer-producer-director Ken Russell had the genius to turn Sandy Wilson's romantic musical set in the 1920s into an extravaganza of Busby Berkeley production numbers. Pure old-fashioned escapist musical done on a lavish scale, though a bit too long for the youngsters. A-I (G)

Boy In Blue, The (1986)   Based on the life of a legendary Canadian scull racing champion, the movie not only lacks a romantic vision but features a wholly anachronistic portrayal by Nicolas Cage in what becomes a teenage macho study of false pride and determination in 1870's America. Moronic teen romance and brief nudity. A-III (R)

Boy Named Charlie Brown, A (1969)   First animated movie version of the Peanuts comic strip characters created by George Schulz centers on Charlie Brown's obsession with failure as he enters a national spelling bee contest. The animation team under director Bill Melendez has been completely faithful to the stylized world of the comic strip in giving movement and voice to the small fry characters. Refreshing but meaningful amusement for both youngsters and grown-ups. A-I (G)

Boy of Two Worlds (1970)   After the death of his parents, a West Indian boy is sent to live with his maiden aunt in a small Danish village. When she dies, he runs away and lives in the forest rather than stay in an orphanage. All ends happily in a very engaging children's movie directed by Astrid and Bjare Henning-Jensen that will also interest adults. A-I (G)

Boy Ten Feet Tall, A (1965)   Orphaned boy journeys alone across the length of Africa to find an aunt and matures considerably during the course of his adventures. Directed by Alexander Mackendrick, the story is slight but very appealing, especially for youngsters. A-I (G)

Boy Who Could Fly, The (1986)   A teenage girl befriends an autistic boy and tries to help him overcome his muteness in a tender and sensitive fable about the importance of friendship for those growing up in a socially inflexible environment. Nick Castle directs this unpretentious, life-affirming movie that uses brief but effective special-effects fantasy to provide some good-natured fun for youngsters. A-I (PG)

Boy Who Cried Werewolf, The (1973) Inept semi-horror movie about a youngster (Scott Sealey) whose father (Kerwin Matthews) is bitten by a werewolf near the family's secluded summer cabin but no one will listen as the locals are decimated in traditional fashion. Lethargically directed by Nathan Juran, it may frighten youngsters insecure in their parental relationships, but lycanthropy lovers can only lament this travesty of a cherished movie myth. A-II (PG)

Boys from Brazil, The (1978) Fanatical Nazi war criminal (Gregory Peck) oversees the care and feeding of some Hitler clones born in Brazil and distributed throughout the world. Laurence Olivier plays his opponent, an aging Jewish Nazi hunter. Some good acting but, for the most part, director Franklin Schaffner achieves only an overwrought melodrama with a large dose of graphic, sadistic violence. A-III (R)

Boys in Company C, The (1978) Directed by Sidney J. Furie with a cast of unknown actors, this muddled movie about a company of young Marines in boot camp and subsequent combat in Vietnam focuses on drugs, atrocities, greed and cynicism. Veering from slapstick to supposedly real emotion, the movie uses foul language, bereft of any significant context, while failing to give any moral or political dimension to the drama. O (R)

Boys in the Band, The (1970) Screen version of a stage play about a birthday party attended by eight homosexual and one heterosexual college friends. Directed by William Friedkin, it is a gripping, frighteningly honest view of human relationships and the introverted homosexual psyche with all its anxiety, bitterness, depression and solitude. A-IV (R)

Boys Next Door, The (1986) Two socially-disadvantaged youths, about to graduate from high school and take on dull factory jobs, vent their frustrations and anxieties in a series of brutal encounters with innocent strangers who have the misfortune to cross their path. Director Penelope Spheeri's exploration of the dark side of maladjusted youth exploits only the violent consequences of alienation without a compassionate insight into adolescent behavior. Excessive use of brutality and foul language. O (R)

Boys of Paul Street, The (1969) Hungarian movie in which two bands of school-boys vie for possession of a vacant lot in 1902 Budapest but the outcome of their skirmishes proves as disillusioning to them as the battles they will fight a few years later in World War I. Director Zoltan Fabri's nostalgic production re-creates the historical period as well as the innocent earnestness with which the boys regard their secret societies and strange rituals. Good family fare. A-I (G)

Brain, The (1969) French comedy in which a master criminal (David Niven), whose brain is so large he has trouble keeping his head erect, comes up with a million dollar scheme that becomes an international cops-and-robbers chase. Director Gerard Oury has made an old-fashioned romp with a couple of good laughs, but many scenes are over-extended and full of cliches. Comic violence. A-II (G)

Brainstorm (1983) Some dedicated scientists invent a device to enable one person to experience another's thoughts and sensations, but some nasty military types try to take it over for their own purposes. Directed by Douglas Trumbull, starring Natalie Wood and Christopher Walken, the movie is more interested in its special effects than in developing the human dimensions of its characters. Brief but graphic sex scene. A-III (PG)

Brand X (1970) Taylor Mead stars in an underground movie satirizing TV programming with a self-conscious grab bag of humorous improvisations. Some of the skits are indeed witty but the majority are crude, tasteless, vulgar and indeed indecent. O (nr)

Brannigan (1975) John Wayne, violating civil rights at home and abroad, plays a police officer sent to England to extradite a hood with whom he has a personal score to settle. British production directed by Douglas Hickox focuses on Wayne's character as contemptuous of all legal restraint, an attitude in which he is joined ultimately by his London counterpart (Richard Attenborough). Heman violence. A-III (PG)

Brass Target (1979) Yarn blurring the border between history and fiction about a failed attempt to assassinate General Patton (George Kennedy) who wants to retrieve the German gold highranking American staff officers have hijacked. John Hough's direction smothers suspense but inflates the violence making the movie unsuitable for youngsters. A-III (PG)

Brazen Women of Balzac, The (1971) The only thing brazen about this coarse German-made exploitation movie which portrays sexual activities in a villa overlooking the Rhine is the way its importers have edited in several yards of sexually explicit footage to compete with porno products. O (R)

Brazil (1986) This production combines the failed utopian vision of "Blade Runner" with the whimsical outlook of the Monty Python comedy troupe in a playful, expressionistic fantasy of a madcap totalitarian England where nothing works. Director Terry Gilliam's mix of mirth and menace proclaims the futility of the hero's slapstick struggle to combat conformity and complacency with romantic love. A-III (R)

Bread and Chocolate (1978) In this tragicomedy from director Franco Brusati, Nino Manfredi plays an Italian immigrant worker desperately trying to make a go of it in Switzerland so that he can bring home some money to his family. Light social satire contrasting unfeeling bourgeois with passionate working-class loser, it resorts to some indecent exposure and a gratuitous incident in which a priest is involved in a bizarre murder. O (nr)

Breaker, Breaker (1977) An amateurish little movie directed by Don Hulette about a martial arts master and trucker (Chuck Norris) who cleans out a nest of thugs and criminals with the help of a fleet of trucks called in by CB radio. Considerable violence and some rough language. A-III (PG)

Breakfast Club, The (1985) Five teenagers spend a Saturday detention in their school library. After much abrasive interchange and a little marijuana, they become downright chummy when they realize they share common attitudes about adult authority figures, drugs and sex. Under John Hughes' direction the movie lacks any critical perspective, seeming to justify anti-social behavior, casual sex and the concept of drugs as a harmless escape, if not a liberating experience. O (R)

Breakheart Pass (1976) This Charles Bronson vehicle is an interesting Western that is part mystery and part suspense. Although the action takes place mostly on a train, outside is the world of the U.S. cavalry vs. the Indians. The movie's production values and Tom Gries' direction are tops, but there is some brutal violence. A-III (PG)

Breakin' (1984) Director Joel Silberg's quickie movie cashing in on the break-dancing craze is innocuous, light entertainment. A classical dancer, going nowhere as a waitress (Lucinda Dickey), joins up with break dancers Adolfo "Shabba-Doo" Quinones and Michael "Bongaloo Shrimp" Chambers, and the three conquer the prejudice of the dance establishment and make it to Broadway. There is some charm in its unpretentiousness but little, if any, style. A-II (PG)

Breakin' 2: Electric Boogaloo (1985) Breakdancing sequel is this time a case of "putting on a show of our own" in the old Judy Garland-Mickey Rooney tradition. The necessary ingredient is the dancing, with the plot being only the occasion for it. The performers are pleasantly exuberant and the whole exercise is innocuous. A-II (PG)

Breaking Away (1979) Light comedy chronicling a summer in the lives of four teenagers in mid-America who are determined to stay together despite community and hometown college pressures to the contrary. Director Peter Yates reveals a depth and feeling for character in this exploration of youthful determination which concludes with a vivid bike race. A-II (PG)

Breaking Glass (1981) Brian Gibson directs an offbeat movie that takes a hard look at British society and the empire of pop music. It gets a bit too slick and sentimental at the end, but despite its defects it's fairly entertaining and provocative, thanks in large part to the talent of actress-singer-composer Hazel O'Connor. Restrained portrayal of the seamy side of life. A-III (PG)

Breaking Point, The (1976) Bo Svenson plays the abused, honest citizen tracked by the hoods against whom he testified in this typically brutal and mindless variation on the revenge theme. Canadian director Bob Clark's viewers are subjected to an assault of violence, maiming and a brutal rape. O (R)

Breakout (1975) Down-on-his-luck pilot (Charles Bronson) contracts to fly a wrongly accused American out of a Mexican prison and finds himself involved with a rogue CIA operation. Directed by Tom Gries, it's an old-fashioned adventure yarn with the emphasis on action rather than violence, except for a grisly depiction of a villain being killed by an airplane propeller. A-III (PG)

Breathless (1983) Remake of Jean-Luc Godard's 1963 movie about a petty criminal betrayed by love is a self-indulgent exercise in graphic sex and sentimentality. Neither of the two lovers (Richard Gere and Valerie Kaprisky) shows sufficient humanity to stake a claim on our interest but, to be fair, both are constantly upstaged by a blaring rock score and the slick, flashy, altogether shallow technique of director Jim McBride. O (R)

Breezy (1973) May-December romance blooms when divorced L.A. realtor (William Holden) finds a 17-year-old flower child (Kay Lenz) on his doorstep, and soon they are off romping together until, of course, he meets her friends and she his.

Directed by Clint Eastwood, the romantic twaddle makes frequent use of nudity and pointless profanity. O (R)

Brewster McCloud (1971) Failed allegory about a fallen angel (Sally Kellerman) who inspires a boy (Bud Cort) to fly under the power of his own homemade wings. Director Robert Altman manages to wring spirited performances from a fine supporting cast but not from his principals and the result is a confused narrative with only flashes of humor and satire, much of it bawdy but toothless. A-III (R)

Brewster's Millions (1985) Richard Pryor stars in another remake of the venerable chestnut about a man who inherits a vast fortune on the condition that he squander a modest one. Under Walter Hill's direction, it's funny enough and fairly good entertainment, though the present version introduces too many needless complications. Some vulgar language. A-II (PG)

Bride, The (1985) In this freely adapted remake of "Bride of Frankenstein," the mad doctor (rock star Sting) decides to keep for himself the mate (Jennifer Beals) he has fashioned for his creature (Clancy Brown). Unfortunately, director Franc Roddam is unable to bring this fine-looking but inert movie to life. Innocuous save for a brief sequence involving nudity. A-III (PG-13)

Bride Wore Black, The (1968) Superior murder thriller starring Jeanne Moreau as a revenge-obsessed bride who sets out to kill the five men responsible for her bridegroom's death. Directed by Francois Truffaut, the French production is an exercise in suspense of the Hitchcock variety. Restrained violence. A-III (br)

Brides of Fu Manchu, The (1966) This time the Oriental master criminal (Christopher Lee) plans to conquer the world by forcing kidnapped scientists to develop a weapon utilizing intensified sound waves to destroy selected targets. Directed by Don Sharp, the action features mild violence and sexual innuendo. A-II (br)

Bridge at Remagen, The (1969) While the Germans try to destroy the last bridge across the Rhine in World War II, an American unit (led by George Segal) races to capture it. Director John Guillerman does well in building the tension and suspense inherent in the situation but the human level of the relationships between the soldiers comes across as affected and shallow. Much wartime violence and strong language. A-III (PG)

Bridge Too Far, A (1977) Director Richard Attenborough's epic re-creation of the tragic Allied offensive code-named Market Garden details the fate of the massive paratroop force dropped behind German lines in Holland during World War II. The excellent all-star cast includes Dirk Bogarde, Anthony Hopkins, Laurence Olivier, Robert Redford, Ryan O'Neal, Gene Hackman and Elliot Gould. Although the violence is unusually graphic, the movie has value as an historical dramatization that has tried to be faithful to the facts. A-III (PG)

Brief Season (1971) Pia Degermark and Christoper Jones play a pair of Roman dropouts desperately having a go at life by bedding down, joyriding in the woods and buying expensive gifts before taking their own lives. Director Renato Castellani's attempt to make alienation seem glamorous reduces everything to the most boring and inane level. A-III (R/GP)

Brief Vacation, A (1975) Italian portrait of a

woman (Florinda Bolkan), her health broken from overworking to support three children and several relatives, who is sent to a sanitarium to regain her strength. There she has a brief affair with a younger man, but he comes from another class and her life remains unchanged. Director Vittorio de Sica contents himself with a realistic portrayal of a complex human being, letting viewers draw their own conclusions about the larger social implications in his story of the plight of the poor. Mature themes. A-III (PG)

Brighton Beach Memoirs (1986) Screen adaptation of Neil Simon's lighthearted play about a Jewish adolescent (Jonathan Silverman) coming of age in 1937 Brooklyn. Director Gene Saks recreates the look and atmosphere of pre-World War II America and its traditional family values while finding humor in the young lad's struggle with the onset of puberty. Some discussion of masturbation, adolescent sexuality and a sight gag featuring a nude postcard. A-III (PG-13)

Brighty of the Grand Canyon (1967) Brighty, a brave burro with a natural instinct for distinguishing between good people and bad, helps track down the killer of an old prospector. Written and directed by Norman Foster, based on a book by Marguerite Henry, the outdoors adventure offers some dandy suspense as well as glorious photography of Arizona's Grand Canyon country. No violent visuals. A-I (br)

Bring Me the Head of Alfredo Garcia (1974) Down-at-the-heels American (Warren Oates) takes the grisly job of tracking down a man and delivering his head but in the process has to kill more and more people until he becomes mad with bloodlust. Director Sam Peckinpah turns the story into a sordid essay on the pornography of violence. O (R)

Brink's Job, The (1978) Director William Friedkin focuses on the crooks (Peter Falk, Peter Boyle and Allen Goorwitz) involved in a spectacular 1950 robbery in Boston, providing a fascinating picture of the underside of society in a particular time and place. Laced with wry humor, the movie has almost no violence, the language is relatively restrained, but there is moral ambiguity in its somewhat romanticized view of criminal life. A-III (PG)

Britannia Hospital (1983) Crude, muddled British satire about a hospital celebrating its 500th anniversary and whose preparations for a visit from the Queen become reduced to chaos as various factions within and without clash. Director Lindsay Anderson obviously intends the clash of special interest groups as a metaphor of the condition of Britain herself and the world in general. Violence, nudity and a general air of cynical amorality. O (R)

Broadcast News (1987) News producer (Holly Hunter) in the Washington bureau of a TV network finds herself drawn away from a hardworking reporter whom she admires (Albert Brooks) by an off-again, on-again attraction to a handsome but unprofessional reporter (William Hurt) being groomed as network news anchor. Written, produced and directed by James L. Brooks, the romantic comedy is often quite funny and also worthwhile in its satiric portrait of television news being more concerned with image and packaging than with the news story itself. Permissive attitude toward casual sex, several explicit sexual references and some rough language. A-IV

(R)

Broadway Danny Rose (1984) Director Woody Allen's nostalgic essay on showbiz self-deception is a droll and almost provincial tribute to the smalltime theatrical agents who, like Danny Rose (Allen), labor with scant hope of monetary reward for some fourth-rate talent. The plot, revolving around reviving the career of a has-been singer (Nick Apollo Forte) only to be betrayed at the point of success, is thin and only mildly amusing. Some Italian stereotyping. A-III (PG)

Broken Mirrors (1987) Dutch import directed by feminist Marleen Gorris examines the ruthless and abusive relationships between men and women as viewed by two women who try to free themselves from the spiritual suffocation of working in an Amsterdam brothel. As a lesson for women to escape victimization, the amateurish production resorts too often to extreme and explicit examples of injustice, sadistic brutality and abuse. Foul language and brief nudity are intermittent. O (nr)

Bronco Billy (1980) Clint Eastwood directs and stars in an offbeat movie about a former shoe salesman from New Jersey who puts together a modest but competent Wild West Show with other dreamers and misfits like himself. An amiable and relaxed comedy marred by one brutal fight sequence. A-III (PG)

Bronco Bullfrog (1972) British story of a young worker who falls in love with an underage girl, but its principal intent is to describe a deadening environment which has already condemned him to a life without hope. Directed by Barney Platt-Mills, the 1969 semi-documentary is an honest portrayal of young people's alienation from the modern world. There are subtitles for those who can't catch the Cockney dialogue. A-III (nr)

Brood, The (1979) Canadian movie in which a mentally disturbed woman (Samantha Eggar) generates such intense hatred that she gives birth to children of rage who go out and murder the objects of her enmity. Directed by David Cronenberg, some good acting is overwhelmed by blood and gore, building to an even more bloody conclusion. O (R)

Brother Carl (1972) Study of four tortured individuals (Gunnel Lindblom, Genevieve Page, Laurent Terzieff and Keve Hjelm) who for no apparent reason torment themselves and one another. Director Susan Sontag's effort falls flat because, lacking an understandable human context, it is too abstract to evoke an emotional response from viewers. A-IV (nr)

Brother from Another Planet, The (1984) Black extra-terrestrial crashes to Earth and finds sanctuary in Harlem from two bounty hunters determined to find and return him to his home planet. Moderately entertaining social satire from writer-director John Sayles has some profanity and a relatively restrained sexual scene. A-III (nr)

Brother John (1971) World traveler and studious observer of humanity (Sidney Poitier) returns to Alabama for his sister's funeral, becomes involved with a minister's daughter (Beverly Todd), her jealous friends (Lincoln Kilpatrick and Paul Winfield) and an ambitious politician (Bradford Dillman). Ineptly directed by James Goldstone with ludicrous close-ups, faulty emphasis on inane action and insensitivity to his small-town locale, the movie's intention to make the title character some sort of apocalyptic figure vaporizes as he departs on a Trailways bus. A-III (GP)

Brother of the Wind (1975) Kindly old mountain dweller raises four cuddly, frisky wolf cubs amid the scenic splendor of the Canadian Rockies. Short on plot but long on shots of nature, the movie introduces the quartet to a variety of wildlife and, alas, a snowmobile, shotgun-wielding hunter. Though younger children might be frightened by a few scenes depicting hunting and killing in the wild, the beauty of the scenery and the intimate glimpses of wildlife make it a pleasant experience for all. A-I (G)

Brother Sun, Sister Moon (1973) Director Franco Zeffirelli's version of the oft-told story of Francis of Assisi (Graham Faulkner) treats him as secular saint and social heretic, emphasizing parallels between his age and our own. The strength of the movie lies in its rich visualization of the natural beauties of the Umbrian hills and the Romanesque architecture of medieval Assisi. While the lush and lavish production has nothing to do with the Franciscan spirit of poverty and simplicity, it is a pictorially beautiful movie which succeeds quite well in celebrating nature and the quest for finding more to life than accumulating material goods. A-II (PG)

Brother, Can You Spare A Dime (1975) Slapdash documentary supposedly dealing with the hard times of the Depression is not so much edited as spliced together. The vulgarity captured belongs not to the 1930s, but to the people who produced it. A-II (PG)

Brotherhood, The (1969) When a Mafia member (Kirk Douglas) kills one of the crime bosses (Luther Adler), he flees to Sicily and the mob sends his younger brother (Alex Cord) to kill him. Directed by Martin Ritt, the core of the movie is the contrast between the older brother's reverence for tradition and the younger one's ambitious pragmatism. Some graphic violence. A-III (M)

Brotherhood of Satan (1971) Coven of devil worshippers (led by Strother Martin) in their quest for eternal youth abduct 13 children while killing their parents in bizarre, bloody fashion that confounds a dimwitted sheriff (L.Q. Jones) as their bodies accumulate in the local ice house. Director Bernard McEveety ladles out his witchcraft murders with remarkable ineptitude. Visual gore and a conclusion in which evil triumphs over good. A-III (GP)

Brotherly Love (1970) Peter O'Toole gives an outstanding performance as a Scottish lord caught up in a longstanding and unhealthy relationship with his sister (Susannah York), but the story fails to come alive. Directed by J. Lee Thompson, the movie's unexplained motivations, the slow pacing and unpleasant characterizations contribute to a sense of disinterest in what is happening. A-IV (R)

Brothers (1977) Fictionalized and highly romanticized account of the friendship between imprisoned radical George Jackson (Bernie Casey) and Communist intellectual and philosophy professor Angela Davis (Vonetta McGee). Although the movie directed by Arthur Barron is obviously sympathetic towards its central characters, it offers intelligent and compassionate insights into the agony of prison life. Rough language, violence and borders on justifying political terrorism. A-III (R)

Brubaker (1980) Henry Brubaker (Robert Redford) is a prison warden and reformer who goes inside a prison disguised as a convict to find out what is wrong with the system. Director Stuart

Rosenberg's fact-based movie is uncompromising and harrowingly realistic with graphic and implied violence, a brief scene of nudity and much profanity. A-III (R)

Brute and the Beast, The (1969) Formula Italian Western in which a cowboy (Franco Nero) returns to his home town, finds it dominated by a petty land baron's band of gunfighters and proceeds to right the wrongs done his family and friends. Directed by Lucio Fulci, some four dozen men, women and children are killed as the unimaginative story unfolds. Much stylized violence and brutality. A-III (M)

B.S., I Love You (1971) Young advertising hustler (Peter Kastner) stumbles into high position by making it with both mother and daughter. Director Steven Hillard concentrates upon the sexual aspects of the narrative portrayed in a series of supposedly humorous, but terribly tasteless scenes. O (R)

Buck and the Preacher (1972) Sidney Poitier plays guide and wagon master for a group of freed slaves moving West after the Civil War but they face wild Indians and a gang of outlaws. Also directed by Poitier, it is little more than a standard shoot-'em-up, though Harry Belafonte's cunningly exaggerated performance as an opportunist-preacher with a six-shooter in his Bible adds some much needed humor. A-III (GP)

Buck Rogers in the 25th Century (1979) An American astronaut (Gil Gerard) gets caught in a time warp and flashes forward 500 years just in time to save Earth from evil invaders sent by a sensuous but immature princess (Pamela Hensley). Director Daniel Haller's gadget-ridden, lighthearted space adventure has a few mild double entendres, but is reasonably diverting pulp for sci-fi fans. A-II (PG)

Buckskin (1968) Formula Western directed by A.C. Lyles about a marshal (Barry Sullivan) who thwarts the plans of a crook (Wendell Corey) to force out the homesteaders and sell their land to the railroad. Restrained gunplay. A-I (br)

Bucktown (1975) Vicious, mindless black exploitation movie, the first half of which offers racism and violence (Fred Williamson and friends wiping out the corrupt white police force of a southern sin city) and the second half dealing solely with violence (black against black). Director Arthur Marks ends it in a bloody, drawn-out fist fight, witnessed by a little boy, who chortles the movie's last line about how happy he is to be a man. Ugh. O (R)

Buddy Buddy (1981) Ill-conceived attempt by director Billy Wilder and writer I.A.L. Diamond to turn a mediocre French farce about the chance meeting of a ruthless hit man and a suicidal cuckold into a vehicle for Walter Matthau and Jack Lemmon. The result is achingly unfunny, vulgarly sentimental and generally tasteless. Profanity and incidental nudity. O (R)

Buddy Holly Story, The (1978) Straight-forward screen biography of one of the pioneers of rock 'n' roll music, from his initial success in 1956 to his death in a plane crash three years later at the age of 22. The script by Robert Gittler is extremely competent as is Steve Rash's direction. The movie's best feature, however, is the genial singing and acting of Gary Busey in the title role. A-III (PG)

Buddy System, The (1984) Unwed mother (Susan Sarandon) is brought together with a would-be novelist working as a security guard (Richard

Dreyfuss) by her 9-year-old son (Wil Wheaton). Although director Glenn Jordan takes a long time to set up a rather obvious situation, the rest is a gentle romantic comedy, with some sensitive and perceptive moments. Vulgar language and a benign view of a premarital relationship. A-III (PG)

Buffalo Bill and the Indians Or Sitting Bull's History Lesson (1976) Starting with the fact that Chief Sitting Bull once toured with Buffalo Bill's Wild West Show, director Robert Altman proceeds to show Buffalo Bill (Paul Newman) as a mere braggart with no real accomplishments in contrast to the unfailingly noble and heroic Indian chief. The movie is entertaining enough, with some flashes of brilliance and humor, but strikes few genuine sparks in its repetitious debunking of the Western myth. Coarse language. A-III (PG)

Bug (1975) Bradford Dillman, playing a variant of that hoary staple of horror movies, the mad scientist, brings to the role hyperbolic histrionics. Director Jeannot Szwarc's unsubtle special effects are much more likely to provoke nausea than terror and the degree to which the film steps over the line in its depiction of brutal, degrading incidents should cause parents serious concern. O (PG)

Bugs Bunny's 3rd Movie: 1001 Rabbit Tales (1982) A compilation of vintage theatrical "Merry Melodies-Looney Tunes" cartoons bridged by some new material which isn't nearly as good. Stringing together a 90-minute feature of such cartoon shorts will be too much of a good thing for some, especially youngsters. Cartoon violence. A-I (G)

Bugs Bunny/Road Runner (1979) Feature-length compilation of vintage Warner Brothers' cartoons created by Chuck Jones has some new material featuring a retired Bugs and the typical Road Runner brand of cartoon violence that some parents may find unsuitable for their very young children. A-I (G)

Bugsy Malone (1976) Director Alan Parker's unique musical is a crime melodrama spoof done with a cast whose average age is twelve. Unique, however, does not mean good. Jodie Foster gives the only redeeming performance, the music is at best inoffensive, the humor consistently misfires and some may note a touch of sexual ambivalence in moppets posturing as adults. A-I (G)

Bullet for Pretty Boy, A (1970) Bloody account of the life of 1930's gangster Pretty Boy Floyd (Fabian Forte) who commits some daring crimes and is eventually gunned down in a violent shoot-out. Directed by Larry Buchanan, it is of minimal interest. A-III (PG)

Bullet for the General, A (1969) Italian Western directed by Damiano Damiani consists of a series of wanton killings and excessive brutality. O (br)

Bullies (1986) A city family moves to a rural town in British Columbia only to be terrorized by a clan of demented toughs. A nasty little Canadian production, directed by suspense-terror specialist Paul Lynch, the movie ends in a crescendo of vengeance and retribution as the family's teenage son kills all the bullies. Profanity, promiscuity, rape, brutality, murder and other assorted acts of violence. O (R)

Bullit (1968) When an underworld informer is killed while in the protective custody of a San Francisco police detective (Steve McQueen), he sets up a ruse in order to smoke out those responsi-

ble. Under the direction of Peter Yates, the action thriller displays a convincing degree of realism thanks to close attention to police work details, harrowing car chases through city streets and McQueen's tight-lipped performance. Some graphic violence and sexual references. A-III (PG)

Bunny Lake Is Missing (1965) Suspenseful thriller about a child who appears to have been abducted but who, in fact, may never have existed. Otto Preminger directs Keir Dullea and Carol Lynley as a properly mysterious couple with Laurence Olivier as a quietly effective London policeman. Mature themes. A-III (br)

Bunny O'Hare (1971) Disguised as hippies, a pair of mature citizens (Bette Davis and Ernest Borgnine) pull off a series of bank robberies under Gerd Oswald's unimaginative direction. Their antics supply the frame-work for some heavy-handed, pseudo-satiric statements on everything from a migrant worker's savings and police intelligence to psychiatry and youthful protestors. A-III (GP)

Buona Sera, Mrs. Campbell (1969) American air force unit has a reunion in the Italian village where it had been stationed in World War II and three of the group learn that each has been supporting a local "widow" (Gina Lollobrigida) who told each that he is the father of her daughter (Janet Margolin). The complications that make up this situation comedy are fairly predictable but writer-director Melvin Frank comes up with a lively mixture of satire and sight-gags making the most of the comic possibilities in an inherently serious plot. Adult humor. A-III (PG)

Burglar (1987) Whoopi Goldberg is a cat burglar implicated in a murder which she has to solve in order to stay out of jail. The unflattering vanity production directed by Hugh Wilson offers little chance for Goldberg's talent to sparkle. Instead it is buried under false and demeaning stereotyping of women, brief nudity and mild profanity. A-III (R)

Burglars, The (1972) French crime caper with Jean-Paul Belmondo stealing a cool million in emeralds and then playing cat-and-mouse games with Omar Sharif, a sadistic cop who uses Dyan Cannon and her striptease club as one way of persuading Belmondo to share the gems with him. Director Henri Verneuil opts for speed over suspense and the beautiful scenery on the Greek island of Corfu helps him get away with a preposterous script. A-III (PG)

Burn! (1970) Complex Italian dramatization of a 19th-century revolution that takes place on a Caribbean island where the conflict centers on a British agent (Marlon Brando) and the black leader (Evaristo Marquez) he creates and then has to destroy. Directed by Gillo Pontecorvo, there are some uncomfortable modern parallels in the movie's vivid statement that violence only begets more violence. A-III (GP)

Burnt Offerings (1976) Inept horror movie about a family living in a haunted house in which the odds are hopelessly stacked aganist the best efforts of Oliver Reed, Bette Davis and Karen Black to survive the proceedings. In trying to inject some interest in this rather nasty business, director Dan Curtis relies heavily on visual shock. A-III (PG)

Bus Is Coming, The (1971) Black Vietnam veteran (Mike Simms) returns home to discover that his brother has been murdered by a racist policeman, gets caught between a black militant group and redneck cops and eventually becomes the moderate spokesman for his people. Directed by Wendell James Franklin, the movie manages to avoid a simplistic approach to its subject matter. A-II (GP)

Bushbabies, The (see: "The Bushbaby")

Bushbaby, The (1970) Young girl (Margaret Brooks) leaves the ship taking her back to England in order to return her pet monkey to an East African jungle and winds up trekking through the hinterland with a faithful black (Lou Gosset) to escape the police who suspect that he has kidnapped her. Though not explicit, the movie's attitude towards the black natives is condescending, making it less suitable as family entertainment. A-I (G)

Buster and Billie (1974) The story of a high school romance in a sleepy Georgia town in 1948 in which the boy (Jan-Michael Vincent) gives up his sweetheart (Pamela Sue Martin) when he falls in love with a girl from the wrong side of the tracks (Joan Goodfellow). Director Daniel Petrie's sappy and predictable movie has a feel for the era, the locale and the people but indulges in an excess of violence and nudity. O (R)

Bustin' Loose (1981) Richard Pryor and Cicely Tyson star in this frumpy comedy about an ex-con forced into taking a group of developmentally disabled youths and their teacher across the country in a decrepit bus. Scripted by Pryor and directed by Oz Scott, the result is outrageously sentimental with a few laughs and some rough language. A-II (R)

Busting (1974) Two honest L.A. vice squad cops (Elliott Gould and Robert Blake) attempt to nail a crime boss (Allen Garfield) but eventually accept the inevitability of defeat under a corrupt system of justice. Director Peter Hyams throws in some comedy but too much violence, nudity and profanity. O (R)

Butch and Sundance: The Early Days (1979) Buddy movie directed by Richard Lester features William Katt and Tom Berenger as the not very dynamic duo stuck in a lifeless series of comedically-failed situations involving their bumbling quest for notoriety. Sparce vulgar language and violence is less objectionable than the film's romanticization of the lawless, irresponsible lifestyle. A-III (PG)

Butch Cassidy and the Sundance Kid (1969) Stylish seriocomic Western set at the end of the outlaw era follows the dissolution of the notorious Wild Bunch gang as Butch (Paul Newman) and the Kid (Robert Redford) realize that civilization has overtaken their profession and head for the Bolivian frontier. Director George Roy Hill brings off the action scenes with gusto and the proper amount of humor but balanced by enough realistic scenes to show that, beneath the surface of the laughter and the silly mishaps, these men are killers whose actions have serious consequences. Much stylized violence. A-III (PG)

Butcher, The (see: "Le Boucher")

Buttercup Chain, The (1971) Four crazy, mixed-up kids (Hywel Bennett, Jane Asher, Sven-Bertil Taube and Leigh Taylor-Young), resort to a thoroughgoing and deliberate demonstration of the various illicit pairings that lead to regret, tragedy and moral awakening. Director Robert Ellis Miller's clumsy treatment lets the movie run amok in pseudo-serious tangles that only emphasize the sexual misadventures. O (R)

Butterflies Are Free (1972) Good screen version of Leonard Gershe's play about a blind youth (Edward Albert), the cheerfully amoral kook in the apartment next door (Goldie Hawn) who becomes emotionally attached to him and his over-protective but ultimately very wise and sensible mother (Eileen Heckart). Director Milton Katselas keeps the romantic melodrama moving along quite nicely, the acting is quite good and the clash between the new morality and the old is treated very gently. A-III (PG)

Butterfly (1982) This is the story of a scheming and manipulative girl who uses seduction as a weapon, in this frivolous and inept screen version of the grim James M. Cain novel about incest...or supposed incest. With Pia Zadora in the lead role and Stacey Keach and Orson Wells who fail to rise above director Matt Cimber's offhanded material. Some nudity and a general air of sleazy amorality. O (R)

Butterfly, The (1971) Scandinavian sexploiter about a streetwalker (Anna Kristina) fluttering around various clients sent her way by director Alexis Neve. O (R)

By the Blood of Others (1978) A French production about an escaped maniac who hold a woman and her younger daughter hostage while demanding that he be sent the prettiest girl in town. The melodramatic situation turns into a static problem play as the mayor (Bernard Blier) and other townspeople debate what to do until action is taken by the mayor's daughter (Mariangela Melato). Some fine acting and interesting observations about people under crisis, but not enough to compensate for the flat and predictable script and a brutal rape scene. A-III (nr)

Bye Bye Braverman (1968) In a serio-comic drama, four Jewish friends (George Segal, Joseph Wiseman, Jack Warden and Sorrell Booke) spend an afternoon trying to find the funeral of Braverman, their mutual friend. In concentrating on the mourner's attitudes, hopes and fears, director Sidney Lumet misses more than he scores in a flawed film that culminates in a graveyard soliloquy seeking to find some kind of meaning in an alien universe. A-III (br)

C

Cabaret (1972) Bouncy Liza Minnelli stars as an exploited and exploiting American showgirl performing in a decadent Berlin cabaret circa 1930. Showing a nation headed toward moral and political bankruptcy in a spirited musical format results in an entertainment with several levels of meaning given sharp ironic bite by director Bob Fosse. Themes of Nazi brutality, twisted sexual relationships and a bizarre nightclub setting provide some challenging fare for grown-ups. A-III (PG)

Cactus Flower, The (1969) Screen adaptation of the Broadway version of a French comedy about a prosperous Manhattan dentist (Walter Matthau) caught between a dizzy young girlfriend (Goldie Hawn) and his devoted but staid receptionist (Ingrid Bergman) who ultimately blooms like the prickly cactus on her desk. Director Gene Saks adds proper comic timing to the absurd complications of the lightweight romance but it is the comic vitality of a talented cast that makes it enjoyable. A-III (PG)

Cactus in the Snow (1972) Movie entirely devoted to the attempts of an Army private (Richard Thomas) to have his first sexual experience with a teenager (Mary Layne) he has met on a weekend pass. Directed by Martin Zweiback, the movie is quite explicit about contraceptive devices and even resorts to having the soldier tutored by a prostitute. With crude sexual references throughout, it is reprehensible to aim this at young audiences. O (R/GP appeal)

Caddie (1981)   Australian domestic drama about a young wife (Helen Morse) who walks out on her brutal and adulterous husband and makes a living for herself and her two young children by working as a barmaid in Sydney during the Great Depression. Morse gives a winning performance and director Donald Crombie's period re-creation is finely detailed but the story is listless and lacks dramatic force. A-III (nr)

Caddyshack (1980)   Bill Murray and Chevy Chase cavort in this buffoonish slapstick comedy about a caddy's summer adventures at a loony country club. Director Harold Ramis counts on an assortment of obnoxious characters, lewd jokes and brief nudity to energize a sophomoric plot. O (R)

Cafe Express (1981)   Nino Manfredi plays a Sicilian selling coffee on a train contrary to the rules of the railroad with the action taking place in the course of one night's run. Italian comedy directed by Nanni Loy has its moments but is no more than a vignette and the balance between the comic and the tragic falters. Earthy dialogue and a comic sexual incident. A-III (nr)

Caged Men Plus One Woman (1972)   The various manifestations of homosexuality in prison provide sensational subject matter for Edward J. Forsyth's movie about an incredibly ignorant victim (Ross Stephanson) who just as incredibly wreaks bloody revenge on his tormentors inside as well as on the girl friend outside who had betrayed him. O (R)

Cahill, U.S. Marshal (1973)   John Wayne stars in a contemporary Western about an overworked peace officer whose two neglected sons are involved in a robbery he is investigating. When Wayne decides to make his pursuit of the criminals into an object lesson for his sons, director Andrew V. McLaglen's movie seems to condone the use of guns in the hands of the young. Worse than the violence is what youngsters may make of the story's muddled morality. A-III (PG)

Cal (1984)   Set against the background of the present conflict in Northern Ireland is the story of a doomed love affair between the widow (Helen Mirren) of a slain policeman and a shy, sensitive young man (John Lynch) who was inadvertently involved in her husband's death. Director Pat O'Connor has fashioned a nuanced morality tale of human beings caught in a divided world but there is some use of nudity and a fairly graphic love scene . A-IV (R)

Calamity Jane (1953)   Doris Day plays the legendary Wild West sharpshooter who must change her tomboy attitudes in order to catch the eye of Wild Bill Hickock (Howard Keel) in this uneven but lively musical. Director David Butler tempers an ultimately subservient image of women with Day's charm and singing abilities. A-II (br)

California Split (1974)   Magazine writer (George Segal) befriends a small-time hustler (Elliott Gould) whose wild antics intrigue but this leads him deeper and deeper into the gambling underworld of dumb call girls, tough losers, impatient bookies, sleazy bars, and hole-in-the-wall

games. Director Robert Altman's off-beat comedy ends with Segal's realization that he, unlike Gould, doesn't really care about winning, suggesting that with this knowledge, his obsession to gamble has been exorcised. Questionable attitude toward casual sex. A-IV (R)

California Suite (1978)   Screen version of Neil Simon's play integrates the original's four one-acters into a single narrative with a good cast, including Jane Fonda, Alan Alda, Maggie Smith and Michael Caine. Although not a completely successful adaptation from the stage, director Herbert Ross's movie is good fun for the most part and sometimes unexpectedly moving. Mature themes. A-III (PG)

Caligula (1981)   The R-rated version of the X-rated original is no less a dreary exploitation movie awash with sex and violence. Directed by Tinto Brass, it brings not a trace of insight to the historical figures of the Roman Empire or to this period of history. O (R)

Call Me Bwana (1963)   Generally funny but mindless Bob Hope comedy about a space scientist (Hope) who is easily distracted by the feminine wiles of a foreign agent (Anita Ekberg) from his mission of retrieving a space capsule that has landed in the African jungle. Directed by Gordon Douglas, it consists of typical Hope one-liners and double-entendres. A-II (br)

Camelot (1967)   Director Joshua Logan's screen version of the Broadway musical on King Arthur's legend offers the charming Lerner and Loewe score and lyrics, a grand cast (Richard Harris, Vanessa Redgrave, Franco Nero and David Hemmings) and luxurious fantasy settings. Emphasizing the human implications of the legend rather than its romanticism, the musical shows that power is not strength and that compassion is not weakness. Never has adultery carried so large a penalty—the downfall of Camelot. A-II (br)

Cameraman, The (1928)   Buster Keaton plays a newsreel cameraman sent to Chinatown where he finds himself in the middle of a chaotic Tong War. Still hilarious today, the mark of his genius in physical comedy is present in almost every frame of the picture. It was his last silent feature and the last movie in which he was in complete control. A-I (br)

Camila (1985)   The daughter of a wealthy family in 19th-century Argentina falls in love with a Jesuit priest in this tragic love story with modern political implications. In this Argentinian production, director Maria Luisa Bemberg deals with difficult historical matters as well as the sacrilegious character of the love affair. Powerful but problematic, with one brief but excessively graphic love scene. A-IV (nr)

Camille 2000 (1969)   In updating Dumas' tubercular heroine, director Radley Metzger has changed the flighty and unstable Camille into an amoral jet-setter who fills her days with hip slang, liquor, drugs and sex. The plot is no more than a flimsy structure for scenes replete with nudity, joyless orgies and 20th-century guilt-ridden anxieties. O (R)

Camouflage (1981)   Meditative essay on the corruptive nature of any bureaucratic system and the destructive games people play in seeming to conform to what is expected of them. The Polish production's success lies in an intelligent script and perceptive direction by Krzysztof Zanussi. Several sexual situations. A-III (nr)

Can Hieronymus Merkin Ever Forget Mercy Humppe and Find True Happiness? (1969) Writer-director Anthony Newley plays a star entertainer making a movie about his career and using fragmented and surrealistic techniques both for the film and the film-within-the-film. Apparently an attempt to make a statement about the artist's quest for identity, the result is an incoherent failure, floundering in excesses of explicit sexual adventures and moral relativism that leave viewers with little to share other than the character's lack of self-knowledge and the director's lack of ability to control his material. O (X/R)

Can't Buy Me Love (1987) Suburban nerd (Patrick Dempsey) pays a popular cheerleader (Amanda Peterson) to date him for a month in director Steve Rash's comic exploration of teen mores which condemns in-crowd conformism and self-deception but passively conveys a permissive attitude toward adolescent sex. A-III (PG-13)

Cancel My Reservations (1972) Bob Hope plays the henpecked half of a husband-wife TV talk-show team who falls victim to a gang of murderous Arizona land-grabbers. Wife Eva Marie Saint races to Hope's rescue and ultimately learns that a woman's place is in the home. Director Paul Bogart strikes out with tired gags and dated topical humor. A-II (G)

Candidate for a Killing (1972) Itinerant sportsman (John Richardson) is used by a businessman (Fernando Rey) in a scheme to extort gold from the Congo and becomes a target for assassins as he races around Europe accompanied by a questionable ally (Anita Ekberg). Director Sidney Pink pads his picture with silly conversations and irrelevant interludes, many of them of a teasing sexual nature. O (R)

Candidate, The (1972) Robert Redford stars in the title role as a California lawyer who finds himself in the middle of a hot race for U.S. Senator. Director Michael Ritchie, working with an excellent cast and a literate script, has constructed a fast-paced, cool and very slick movie about the process of electing a candidate for major office. How power politics and the hard sell work, as seen from the inside, is all laid bare in this realistic and frequently quite funny political satire. A-III (PG)

Candleshoe (1978) Jodie Foster plays a Los Angeles juvenile delinquent whom confidence man Leo McKern uses to hoodwink wealthy Helen Hayes into thinking is her long-lost granddaughter. Standard Disney fare from director Norman Tokar that tends towards slapstick rather than anything more gentle and satisfying. A-I (G)

Candy (1969) Screen version of the Southern-Hoffenberg novel about the travail of a threatened virgin (Ewa Aulin) is no more than a gross sex farce that reinforces all the behavioral patterns it supposedly satirizes. Christian Marquand directs a big-name cast with a sensitivity only for the vulgar remark, the suggestive sequence and the explicitly titillating. O (R)

Candy Tangerine Man, The (1975) Black exploitation movie makes a hero out of a vicious black procurer and serves up the sex and violence that is the standard of the genre. O (R)

Cannibal Girls (1973) The title refers to three beauties in a remote Canadian town whose diner serves beefy portions of male travelers whom they have seduced and slaughtered. Director Ivan Reitman's low-budget movie romps in sex and gore to no entertaining end. O (R)

Cannon for Cordoba (1970) George Peppard, leader of an undisciplined platoon in Pershing's Mexican expedition, is responsible for the loss of cannon and supplies, and subsequently must recapture or destroy them. Directed by Paul Wendkos, the far-fetched adventure is seasoned with torture and violence, in ludicrous fashion. A-III (R/GP)

Cannonball Run, The (1981) Banal and tedious cross-country car race movie with Burt Reynolds and Farrah Fawcett, directed by ex-stunt coordinator Hal Needham. Some vulgarity and sexual innuendo. A-III (PG)

Cannonball Run II (1984) Sequel with Burt Reynolds and friends is a sort of cinematic People magazine-on-wheels. Stuntman Hal Needham's direction of this demolition-derby comedy is geared toward dangerous auto stunts and off-color jokes. A-III (PG)

Can't Stop the Music (1980) This vehicle for The Village People, a disco singing group, is a high-energy, low-IQ, 100-percent synthetic product. Directed by Nancy Walker, the silly comedy about the music publishing and recording business is marked by sexual situations and jokes as well as a homosexual sheen coloring most of the production numbers. A-III (PG)

Caper of the Golden Bulls, The (1967) Stephen Boyd and Yvette Mimieux star in a hokey caper movie about a jewel robbery. Directed by Russell Rouse and set in Pamplona, Spain, the only point of interest is the bullring and its environs. Some violence. A-III (br)

Capone (1975) The rise of Al Capone (Ben Gazzara) from Brooklyn street mug to Chicago's top mobster is depicted with excessive resort to violence and sexual displays. Directed by Steve Carver, the movie is a sleazy, slapdash effort. O (R)

Capricious Summer (1968) In this Czechoslovakian production set in a small country village between the world wars, three aging friends make fools of themselves over a young woman in a traveling circus and, by summer's end, they realize that their courting days are over. Director Jiri Menzel captures the elegaic mood of period and character with a tolerance of human foibles. Adult situations. A-III (br)

Capricorn One (1978) Three astronauts are persuaded by a NASA official (Hal Holbrook) to fake a landing on Mars to save the threatened space program but a hot-shot reporter (Elliott Gould) eventually saves the day. Director Peter Hyams has come up with a solid if unspectacular entertainment with some clever twists. A-II (PG)

Captain Apache (1971) Poor Western about an Indian scout for the U.S. Cavalry who becomes the unwilling victim of a plot to fake an uprising that will see the Indians cruelly exiled to uninhabitable territory. Director Alexander Singer's message of brotherhood is as subtle as his battle sequences. Stylized violence and sexual innuendo. A-III (GP)

Captain Kronos: Vampire Hunter (1974) Classy British horror import in which the itinerant Kronos (Horst Janson) is called to a rid a village of a vampire who has been putting the bite on local maidens which he accomplishes with his able hunchback assistant (John Cater). Director Brian Clemens maintains the proper chilling atmosphere for hair-raising encounters with the hooded fiend who comes to a grisly end. Stylized violence and sexual implications. A-III (R)

Captain Nemo and the Underwater City (1970) Jules Verne's Nemo (Robert Ryan) rescues a group of landlubbers (Nanette Newman, Bill Fraser, Kenneth Connor and Chuck Connors) on condition that they not attempt an escape from his self-sufficient city 20,000 leagues under the sea. Directed by James Hill, the special effects, the underwater city and the dramatic complications are intriguing enough to engross a child's imagination in this generally pleasing utopian, anti-war fantasy. A-I (G)

Captive (see: "Two")

Car, The (1977) In a new and not at all entertaining twist to the possession theme, an evil spirit takes over a huge car and terrorizes a Southwestern town. Directed by Elliot Silverstein, everything about the movie is embarrassingly bad, save for the special effects of Albert Whitlock. Some violence and a lot of stupidity. A-III (PG)

Car Wash (1976) Director Michael Schultz's touching, sometimes extremely funny movie follows the course of a day at an inner city car wash where the employees keep a jive rhythm to their work and to their joking. Richard Pryor, Ivan Dixon, the Pointer Sisters and George Carlin supply the wit and energy in this comic tale of streetwise survival. Some rough language, sexual innuendo and casual acceptance of drug use. A-III (PG)

Caravans (1978) A young State Department official (Michael Sarrazin) in 1948 Iran is ordered to locate a missing American (Jennifer O'Neill) reportedly in the mountainous domain of a nomad chief (Anthony Quinn). Directed by James Faro, the effort is a silly misfire, with rambling and unfocused plot line, atrocious dialogue and lead-footed pacing. A bloody execution as well as a sequence involving a homosexual dancer make it mature fare. A-III (PG)

Carbon Copy (1981) Successful business man (George Segal) marries the boss' shrewish daughter (Susan St. James) but finds his snug, affluent nest disrupted when a black youth (Denzel Washington) shows up one day claiming to be his illegitimate son. Director Michael Schultz's crude and heavyhanded comedy attempts to get laughs by some cheap shots at religion, not excluding a dose of male chauvinism. Strong language and two rather distasteful bedroom scenes. A-III (PG)

Cardinal, The (1963) Otto Preminger directs an adaptation of the Henry M. Robinson novel about an American priest (Tom Tryon) from the time of his ordination to his nomination as a cardinal. As a dramatization of the humanity of the Catholic priesthood, presented amidst a heritage of liturgical splendor and realized with some sensitive performances, the production is absorbing entertainment. Some issues may be confusing for those unfamiliar with Catholic theology and practices. A-III (br)

Care Bears Adventures in Wonderland, The (1987) Vastly superior sequel to failed original, the Canadian animated feature is a lively, colorful, complexly designed and orchestrated travelogue through Wonderland with the Bears and a little girl named Alice who must save the kingdom from a power-hungry wizard. Director Raymond Jafelice holds even adult interest with his fast cuts and engaging fantasy characters. A-I (G)

Care Bears Movie, The (1985) The Care Bears are sweet little pastel-colored creatures who inhabit a saccharine world called Care-a-Lot. Unless they teach the earth to care, Care-a-Lot will fall into ruin. Only very young children will care very much about this sentimental, mediocre effort. A-I (G)

Careful He Might Hear You (1984) Sensitive, extremely well-acted Australian movie about a 1930's custody fight between two sisters over the six-year-old son of a third sister who died in childbirth. Director Carl Schultz has done well with showing the effect of all this upon the boy, partly in a less-than-wholesome attraction of a woman for a young child. A-III (PG)

Carey Treatment, The (1972) Hip California doctor (James Coburn) comes to a conservative Boston hospital where he uncovers the murder of the chief-of-staff's daughter and the disappearance of large amounts of hospital drugs. Director Blake Edwards employs a good deal of rather self-conscious vulgarity and profanity but worse is its casual attitude toward abortion and marital commitments. O (PG)

Carnal Knowledge (1971) Producer-director Mike Nichols and screenwriter Jules Feiffer collaborate on a movie with three episodes spanning two decades (late 1940s to late 1960s) in the lives of two men (Jack Nicholson and Art Garfunkel), tracing their non-maturation from sex-starved college students to sex-saturated, middle-aged men in professional life. It is a feeble morality play which preaches once again, with pathetic exploitation, that the wages of sin is impotence. Brief nudity and rough language. A-IV (R)

Carny (1980) Set against the background of a traveling carnival is a triangle theme involving a teenage runaway (Jody Foster), a clown (Gary Busey) and his best friend (Robbie Robertson). The theme, however, is undeveloped because director Robert Kaylor is more interested in documenting carnival life, especially its seamy side with generous amounts of violence, sex and rough language. O (R)

Carrie (1976) A repressed high school student (Sissy Spacek) discovers that she has telekinetic powers which she uses at the senior prom to wreak a bloody revenge on taunting classmates and her religious fanatic mother. Director Brian De Palma's horror movie is too ludicrous and overdrawn to scare, but succeeds in the shock value of its callous, unhealthy mix of nudity and violence. O (R)

Carry It On (1970) Documentary on an anti-Vietnam draft resister, David Harris, sentenced to a three-year term in federal prison focuses on his last meeting with his wife, folk singer Joan Baez, and then on her activities with the anti-war movement. Robert Jones, Christopher Knight and James Coyne have assembled a very moving and effective statement against war. A-III (GP)

Carry On Camping (1972) Rude British send-up of summer campers employs such familiar funsters as Sidney James, Kenneth Williams and Joan Sims. Director Gerald Thomas has assembled a grab-bag of comic skits but too often strains for double entendres and vulgar sexual shenanigans to carry the day. O (R)

Carry On Doctor (1972) Director Gerald Thomas commits his comic cronies (Sidney James, Frankie Howard, Kenneth Williams, Hattie Jacques, Barbara Windsor and Jim Dale) to a hospital, but the operation results in the same old monkey business. There is a generous share of double entendres, but the ribaldry is fairly tame. A-III

(PG)
Carry On Henry VIII (1972)   The latest offering in this series from director Gerald Thomas concerns two previously undiscovered wives of King Henry and their topsy-turvy effect on the beleaguered monarch and his court. Coarse language and blatant double entendres. O (GP)

Casa Assassinada, A (1974)   Brazilian story of an eccentric family of shabby aristocrats living on a crumbling, neglected plantation into which comes a woman who throws the entire household into turmoil and finally violence. Director Paulo Cesar Saraceni's study of creeping moral and mental deterioration is heavily melodramatic but visually powerful in its images of the simultaneous fecundity and decay of the jungle surroundings. Explicit sex scene in a story which otherwise unfolds through indirection. A-IV (nr)

Case of the Naves Brothers, The (1972)   Brazilian director Lutz Sergio Person tells the fact-based story of two peasant brothers sentenced in 1938 for an apparent murder but even when the supposed victim resurfaced several years later, it was not until 1963 that the brothers were released on parole. The story of a miscarriage of justice contains all too graphic depictions of torture. A-III (nr)

Casey's Shadow (1978)   An irascible but basically good-hearted Cajun horse trainer (Walter Matthau) has to make an agonizing decision whether or not to run a horse with an injured leg in a race that could mean fame and fortune for him and his three sons. Director Martin Ritt captures the colorful world of quarter-horse racing in the Southwest but the movie's benign attitude toward the trainer's moral failings and the frequent use of profanity make it mature fare. A-III (PG)

Cassandra Crossing, The (1977)   George Pan Cosmatos directs a disaster epic about a train load of international stars (including Sophia Loren, Burt Lancaster, Richard Harris and Ava Gardner), a crowd of extras and a lovable Basset hound who are exposed to a lethal germ, a decaying bridge and a witless, only fitfully exciting storyline. Extremely violent conclusion and some rough language. A-III (R)

Cast a Giant Shadow (1966)   Standard Hollywood biography of David (Mickey) Marcus, New York lawyer and World War II hero, who helped whip the young Israeli army into shape. Written and directed by Melville Shavelson, the dramatization is at times painfully stilted but for the most part human and likable. Extramarital attachment and wartime violence. A-III (br)

Castaway Cowboy, The (1974)   James Garner plays a shanghaied Texas cowboy who jumps ship in Hawaii and is persuaded by potato-farm widow Vera Miles to stay around long enough to teach her lazy, fun-loving islanders how to round up the wild cattle which are trampling and eating her farm out of business. Disney director Vincent McEveety makes the most of the sunny story, the location scenery and a good cast but adults may find it less than riveting. A-I (G)

Castle, The (1969)   German adaptation of Franz Kafka's unfinished novel about a land surveyor (Maximilian Schell) trying to report for a job assignment but frustrated by an absurdist bureaucracy and a dehumanized populace. Director Rudolf Noelte's production is strangely flat, despite its effective use of photography, settings and peasant faces to convey a mood of grim

eerieness. Perhaps in our era, faceless bureaucracy has become too facile and cliched a target. A-III (nr)

Castle Keep (1969)   Screen version of novelist William Eastlake's surrealistic satire on the absurdity of war is set in a Gothic chateau with its priceless art treasures where an American major (Burt Lancaster) and a company of infantrymen prepare to make a stand against the German army's offensive at Bastogne. Regrettably, director Sydney Pollack fails to incorporate a convincing human and moral dimension to counterbalance the senseless heroics and casual sexual relationships that result. O (R)

Castle of Fu Manchu, The (1973)   With weapons developed by kidnapped scientists, Fu (Christopher Lee) broadcasts his intention to rule the world but Scotland Yard sleuth Nayland Smith (Richard Greene) manages to come to the rescue. Directed by Jess Franco, this is not accomplished until the screen has been deluged with flimsy skirmishes, unsynchronized voices and stock footage of a sinking ship, a bursting dam and an exploding house. Fooey. A-II (PG)

Cat, The (1966)   Poorly done outdoor adventure story of a boy who gets lost on a camping trip and who is saved by a mountain lion who befriends him. Directed by Ellis Kadison, it would only be of interest to the very young and the gullible. A-I (br)

Cat and Mouse (1970)   German adaptation of the Gunter Grass novel about a young man's groping for maturity under the Nazi regime, and his subjective way of facing reality and his own handicaps. Directed with precision and style by Hans-jurgen Pohland, it is of interest for what it shows of the period but also has some insights for those working with adolescents. A-III (nr)

Cat and Mouse (1978)   Unorthodox police inspector (Serge Reggiani) is baffled by what appears to be a millionaire's murder and theft of his art collection but as the case progresses nothing is quite what it seems and the viewer is never exactly sure where the abundance of clues will lead. Written and directed by Claude Lelouch, the mystery comedy is both intelligent and playful, especially with its offbeat cast of characters acted with style by the likes of Michele Morgan and Philippe Leotard. A-III (nr)

Cat from Outer Space, The (1978)   A stricken spaceship piloted by a very sophisticated cat lands on earth for repairs and is aided by an odd assortment of friendly scientists (Ken Berry, Sandy Duncan and McLean Stevenson) to get airborne again despite interference from the military (Henry Morgan) and the charms of an earth cat named Lulubelle. Surviving Norman Tokar's unsubtle direction, it proves better than average Disney fare. A-I (G)

Cat O'Nine Tails, The (1971)   Italian director Dario Argento's B-grade murder mystery centers on a series of killings in a medical research center which are eventually unraveled by newspaper reporters (James Francisus and Karl Malden). The assorted graphic murders and death agonies are utterly pointless, as are the sex interludes with Catherine Spaak and a ludicrous encounter in a gay nightclub. O (GP)

Cat People (1982)   Very loosely based on Val Lewton's 1942 horror classic, this one is tediously explicit in showing the tribulations of a brother and sister (Malcolm McDowell and Nastassia Kinski)

51

who turn into black panthers at odd moments and must kill to regain their human form. Paul Schrader's direction offers clumsy, heavyhanded doses of blood and gore, graphic sex and nudity. O (R)

Catch My Soul (1974) Uneven rock opera version of Shakespeare's "Othello" turns the wicked Iago (Lance Le Gault) into the devil incarnate dressed as a hippie and the noble Moor (Richie Havens) is now a pacifist preacher who heads a hippie commune. The score by Havens and Tony Joe White is quite good but Jack Good's script ranges from the sublime to the ridiculous in its mixture of Shakespearean imagery, Biblical diction and contemporary argot. Directed by Patrick McGoohan and photographed by Conrad Hall, the New Mexico locations are an impressive backdrop for the opera but the contemporary rarely meshes smoothly with the classic. A-III (PG)

Catch 22 (1970) Screen version of Joseph Heller's black comedy about a bomber squadron in Italy during World War II and its troubled airman, Yossarian (Alan Arkin). Although skillfully done under Mike Nichols' direction, it is more pretentious than profound in its statement that war is madness. Brief nudity and some graphic depiction of wartime casualties. A-IV (R)

Catherine & Co. (1976) French production about an English prostitute, played with nauseating coyness by Jane Birkin, who decides to incorporate herself as a business enterprise. Thoroughly unfunny and offensive sex comedy directed by Michael Boisrond. O (R)

Catlow (1971) Flip outlaw (Yul Brynner) shoots his way across the Southwest and part of Mexico with a quixotic marshal (Richard Crenna) in hot pursuit. Directed by Sam Wanamaker, action rather than plot is all this meandering, serio-comic Western shoot-'em-up has to offer. Stylized violence. A-III (GP)

Cat's Eye (1985) Three episodes that are an unstable blend of suspense, violence and black humor linked together tenuously by the presence of the same cat in each. Directed by Lewis Teague from a screenplay by horror writer Stephen King, these are moderately entertaining with relatively restrained violence. A-II (PG-13)

Cattle Annie and Little Britches (1981) Two teenage girls (Amanda Plummer and Diane Lane) join a once famous outlaw gang (led by Burt Lancaster) and inspire its aging members to live up to their reputation. Director Lamont Johnson's contrived Western does not measure up to its whimsical intentions and takes a benign view of immorality of various sorts, including sexual. A-III (PG)

Cauldron of Blood (1971) Far-fetched, unscary would-be chiller about a mad housewife (Viveca Lindfors) who won't tell her blind sculptor-hubby (Boris Karloff) the source of the skeletons she supplies for him to use as models for his lifelike statues. A bubbly vat of acid has the title role. Directed by Edward Mann, it is pure hokum, but innocuous enough for hardy, undemanding adults. A-III (GP)

Caveman (1981) Prehistoric slapstick comedy with Ringo Starr, John Matuszak and Barbara Bach has at least the virtue of being unpretentious yet garners few laughs along the way. Director Carl Gottlieb's sense of humor is only for those whose weakness for buffoonery and vulgarity borders on total insensibility. A-III (PG)

C.C. and Company (1970) Ann-Margret acts

bored and Joe Namath doesn't act at all in this aimless, trashy motorcycle melodrama directed by Seymour Robbie. Exploitative sex scenes. O (R/PG)

Cease Fire (1985) A Vietnam veteran has difficulty adjusting to civilian life because of the traumatic effect of his war experiences. Good acting by Don Johnson and Lisa Blount but the film itself is superficial and not very moving. Some rough language and use of narcotics. A-III (R)

Celebration at Big Sur (1971) Lackluster documentary about a rock/folk music festival at California's Big Sur with performances by Joan Baez, Joni Mitchell, Crosby Stills Nash & Young, John B. Sebastian and, best of all, Dorothy Morrison and the Combs Sisters. The inevitable shots of casual nudity and drug-taking are brief, but they are there almost as tokens of the music scene which, in itself, is very sad indeed. A-III (GP)

Ceremony, The (1974) With this chronicle of an influential family that spans from 1946 to the present, director Nagisa Oshima has taken the measure of the Japanese upper-class and found it wanting. His picture of the convoluted relationships within this archetypal family stresses the unthinking ritualistic approach to life which was harmful in the past and even more dangerous today. Violence. A-III (nr)

Cesar and Rosalie (1972) French romance about a liberated woman (Romy Schneider) who divides her time between her young daughter, her current lover (Yves Montand) and her first love (Sami Frey) just returned from America but, in the end, she leaves them both. Directed by Claude Sautet, the movie is a fine character study of middle-aged people and their feelings about life, though some may find the implied sexual relationships offensive. A-IV (R)

Chain Gang Women (1972) Two convicts (Michael Stearns and Robert Lott) escape from a Georgia prison farm and two women provide them with places of refuge and plenty of sexual satisfaction. Directed by Lee Frost and Wes Bishop, the women's complicity hardly justifies the title but, in any event, its sex and violence is excessive. O (R)

Chaingang Girls (see: "Sweet Sugar")

Chairman, The (1969) A scientist (Gregory Peck) goes to Red China to steal a secret formula at the urging of Western military intelligence who implant a pill-sized transmitter in his skull. J. Lee Thompson directs an entertaining secret agent melodrama that is mildly suspenseful yet also raises hypothetical questions about U.S. cold war policies and procedures. Adult situations. A-III (PG)

Challenge to Be Free (1976) Mike Mazurki plays a trapper who accidentally shoots a policeman and leads a posse on a two-month chase through the depths of an Alaskan winter. A family film directed by Tay Garnett, the flimsy plot is no more than a pretext for showing the austere, rugged beauty of Alaska and a number of photogenic animals that children will love. A-I (G)

Challenges, The (1973) Three-part Spanish movie, knit together by using American actor, Dean Selmier, in three separate roles, each as an outsider doomed to disaster in a foreign land, simply doesn't go very far with its basic theme of alienation. The interplay between cultures and people is a fascinating subject but each segment is treated with disappointing shallowness by its director (Claudio Guerin, Jose Luis Egea and Victor Erice). Violence. A-III (GP)

Chamber of Horrors (1966) Hy Averback directs a weak murder mystery with wax museum setting and a cast including Cornel Wilde, Wildred Hyde-White and Patrice Wymore. Stylized violence and a sequence set in a brothel. A-III (br)

Champ, The (1979) Over-the-hill boxing champ (Jon Voight) tries a comeback for the sake of his adoring son (Ricky Schroder) in director Franco Zeffirelli's romanticized remake of the 1931 classic. Racetrack atmosphere and Voight's performance are more interesting than the melodramatic plot, but the boxing sequences may be too brutally intense for younger teens. A-II (PG)

Champagne Murders, The (1967) Uneven French murder mystery about a jaded playboy (Maurice Ronet) who is being made to believe that he has murdered several women in drunken blackouts. Director Claude Chabrol is more interested in showing upper-class corruption than working out the details of a rather complicated plot. Scenes of immorality and decadence tend to be excessive for their purpose. O (br)

Chandler (1971) Private eye (Warren Oates) falls in love with the French woman (Leslie Caron) he's been hired to follow in a ruse concocted by government agents to flush an underworld biggie out of the shadows. Director Paul Magwood's confused, convoluted plot is a poor imitation of a Raymond Chandler mystery. Stylized violence. A-III (GP)

Change of Habit (1969) Three coy nuns don civilian clothes to work in a Spanish Harlem ghetto clinic run by Doctor Elvis Presley who, unaware of the convent's experimental program, naturally falls in love with one of them (Mary Tyler Moore). William Graham directs with plenty of sentimentality, cliches and stereotypes of the 1940's variety that some modern nuns may not appreciate. A-II (G)

Change of Mind (1969) A white district attorney in a Southern town who is dying of cancer survives by means of a medical operation transplanting his brain into the healthy body of a black accident victim (Raymond St. Jacques). Though burdened with stereotypes, cliches and a far-fetched premise, director Robert Stevens achieves an allegory with some insights into how race affects people's perceptions and actions. Some adult situations and dialogue limit it to mature audiences. A-III (R)

Change of Seasons, A (1980) Shirley Mac-Laine plays a loving wife who, shocked to learn that her husband (Anthony Hopkins) is having an affair vith a woman young enough to be their daughter (Bo Derek), jumps into an affair with a younger man (Michael Brandon). This pretentious, meandering, excruciatingly cute effort, directed by Richard Lang and written by Erich Segal, features extravagant nudity and lack of any positive moral perspective. O (R)

Changeling, The (1980) An unusually subtle and intelligent haunted house melodrama starring George C. Scott as the man who rents a huge, isolated old mansion where soon the fun begins with strange noises, eerie manifestations and a seance that reveals the secret of the house. Directed by Peter Medak, its mood of horror and flashes of violence are remarkably restrained, though there is a scene depicting the cruel murder of a child. A-III (R)

Changes (1969) A college student (Kent Lane) leaves home looking for a more authentic meaning to his life than he has experienced from his parents and passes through a series of relationships in his quest for self-identity. Writer-director Hall Bartlett's restatement of the problems and inner conflicts confronting youth in an affluent American society is well-intentioned but abounds in cliches both in its romantic visuals and probes of adult hypocrisies. A-III (PG)

Chaplin Revue, The (1972) Three silent featurettes written, directed and starring Charles Chaplin for First National were originally released as "A Dog's Life" (April 1918), "Shoulder Arms" (October 1918) and "The Pilgrim" (1923). This sampler of films from what may have been Chaplin's most inventive period helps to explain better than anything else why he will endure in the memory of the movie public. A-I (G)

Chappaqua (1967) In an autobiographical semi-documentary featuring himself, Conrad Rooks chronicles his treatment for drug dependence in a private hospital abroad. Disjointed montage of images convey the nightmarish existence of an addict in the physical agony of withdrawal. A-III (br)

Chapter Two (1979) A successful writer (James Caan) marries an actress (Marsha Mason) but the memory of his dead wife threatens their happiness in this adaptation of a Neil Simon play. Under Robert Moore's direction, the one-liners are still funny but the attempt to deal with more serious material is beset with problems, chief of which is the lack of dramatic action. Attempted adultery figures in a subplot, though it is far from being condoned. A-III (PG)

Charade (1963) Black romantic comedy about a rich widow (Audrey Hepburn) who is hounded by criminals (James Coburn and Walter Matthau) and seeks help from a mysterious, debonair stranger (Cary Grant) whom she must learn to trust. Director Stanley Donen makes exquisite use of the Parisian locales and Henry Mancini's memorable score. A-II (br)

Charge of the Light Brigade, The (1968) Heavy-handed account of the 1853-56 British campaign against the Russian forces in the Crimea, set in the context of the power politics and social inequalities of the Victorian age. Director Tony Richardson fails to keep the scale of the spectacle from reducing the stature of its characters, thereby wasting a large and talented cast. Anti-war violence. A-III (br)

Chariots of Fire (1981) Two young Englishmen (Ben Cross and Ian Charleson) overcome quite different obstacles to win gold medals at the Paris Olympics of 1924. One is a Jew determined to beat the anti-Semitic establishment at its own game and the other is a devout Scot who runs for the glory of God. Directed by Hugh Hudson, it is a richly entertaining and highly inspiring movie for the whole family. Several coarse words. A-I (PG)

Chariots of the Gods? (1974) Eric von Daniken's account of the mammoth constructions of prehistory, from the pyramids to Easter Island, relates their creation to spacemen from more highly developed planets than Earth. The mysteries of man's past are many and awesome, but this pseudo-documentary sheds little light on them. A-I (G)

Charles—Dead or Alive (1972) Swiss movie in which a successful businessman (Francois Simon) decides one day that he hates his daily routine and goes off to think about his future. His son, frantic about the welfare of the business and afraid of publicity, hires a detective to locate his father and then commits him to an insane asylum. Director Alain Tanner's story about a mid-life crisis is also a criticism of Swiss conformity but done in such a light-hearted and gently human way that it is first-rate entertainment and not just a social lesson. Mature themes. A-III (nr)

Charles and Lucie (1980) Uneven French sentimental comedy about a middle-aged Parisian couple whom swindlers leave penniless and on the run from the police in the picturesque south of France. What follows is a series of comic misadventures and absurd encounters that director Nelly Kaplan handles somewhat haphazardly in a mixture of farce, satire and whimsey. Holding the film together are the marvellous performances of Ginette Garcin and Daniel Ceccaldi as the struggling couple who steadfastly face adversity with a comic dignity that is in the best tradition of screen comedy. A-III (nr)

Charley and the Angel (1973) After Fred MacMurry is informed by angel Harry Morgan that he has only a short time on earth, he changes his ways and becomes a dedicated family man. Director Vince McEveety handles the Disney Depression Era story with a suitably light touch that allows Harry Morgan a maximum amount of fun while emphasizing the positive messages of the story. A-I (G)

Charley Varrick (1973) Unusual, action-packed and curiously disturbing film about a seemingly ordinary individual (Walter Matthau) who supplements his income as a cropduster pilot by robbing small-town banks on his mornings off. When he happens to rob a bank used by gangsters, he winds up being chased by the mob as well as the police. Director Don Siegel's movie is tense and occasionally quite brutal, with an undercurrent of amorality in the dog-eat-dog atmosphere of the underworld. A-III (PG)

Charley-One-Eye (1973) Fugitive black soldier (Richard Roundtree) makes his way across the Mexican desert in 1866 in the company of a lame, half-breed Indian (Roy Thinnes), occasionally bothered by Mexican bandits and a bounty hunter (Nigel Davenport). Directed by Don Chaffey, the movie is shallow, ponderous and considerably violent. A-III (R)

Charlie Bubbles (1968) Seriocomic think piece about a sensitive, generous, popular writer of romantic novels who discovers that success is more trouble than its worth but can't go back again. Though some may not care for the movie's non-narrative style and may even find Charlie's boredom contagious, others will find it thoughtful and provocative. Directed by Albert Finney, who also plays the lead, there is a fine supporting cast (Billie Whitelaw, Colin Blakely and Liza Minnelli). Adult situations. A-III (br)

Charlie Chan and the Curse of the Dragon Queen (1981) Called out of retirement to help the San Fancisco police solve a series of bizarre murders, Charlie Chan (Peter Ustinov) trades leaden aphorisms with a dotty in-law, her daffy servants and a cloddish Number One grandson. Ineptly directed by Clive Donner, this witless farce relies on vulgarity and profanity for laughs. A-III (PG)

Charlie, the Lonesome Cougar (1967) Disney wildlife documentary featuring an agile cougar named Charlie who has outgrown the northwoods lumber camp where he was raised and finds happiness with a female cougar in a nearby game preserve. Charlie is a very photogenic animal but his "adventures" are on the cute side and begin to wear thin. A-I (br)

Charlotte's Web (1973) E.B. White's classic fable has been turned into a charming Hanna-Barbera animated musical about a little pig named Wilbur who develops from runt of the litter to full-grown county fair champ with the help of his friends, most notably the spider of the title. Directed by Charles A. Nichols, it is good family viewing. A-I (G)

Charly (1968) Mentally retarded adult (Cliff Robertson) becomes a genius during a medical experiment that has only one drawback, and it's a heartbreaker. A somewhat sentimental adaptation of Daniel Keyes' short story, "Flowers for Algernon," the intriguing plot is delicately handled by director Ralph Nelson and given dramatic impact by the range of Robertson's performance in the title role. Mature treatment of romantic subplot. A-III (br)

Charro! (1969) Elvis Presley sings only one song, and that off-camera, in a silly Western vehicle about a gang of outlaws and a golden cannon in Old Mexico. Directed by Charles Marquis Warren, it contains stylized violence, a bit of sadism and some dubious entendres. A-III (G)

Charulata (1974) Director Satyajit Ray's story is of a wife neglected by her husband's total commitment to his work. As the film ends with a freeze-frame of the couple reaching for each other, the picture reaches far beyond the boundaries of Ray's native Bengal. A-II (nr)

Chase, The (1966) When an escaped convict (Robert Redford) makes his way home, the entire community dissolves in outbreaks of hate and violence, putting local sheriff (Marlon Brando) on the spot in trying to uphold the law. An outstanding cast flounders in a murky political allegory directed by Arthur Penn from Lillian Hellman's adaptation of Horton Foote's play. Confused treatment of significant themes, including racism, greed, lust, alcoholism and religious fanaticism. A-III (br)

Chase for the Golden Needles, The (see: "Golden Needles")

Chastity (1969) Produced by Sonny and starring Cher, the movie intends to be a personal statement about dropping out and searching for identity and true relationships, here depicted in time-honored trial-and-error fashion. Directed by Alessio De Paola, it unfortunately suffers from a lack of sophistication and insight as well as the severe technical limitations that are common in small budget films. A-IV (R)

Chato's Land (1972) Failed Western about a half-breed Indian (Charles Bronson) who is goaded into killing a brutish sheriff and becomes the object of an intense manhunt led by an ex-Confederate officer (Jack Palance) which ends in the parched Indian country of the title. Directed by Michael Winner, the problem is that once the movie gets into the groove of steady killing, it becomes both tedious and glaring in its cumulative brutality. A-III (PG)

Che! (1969) Dramatization of different points of view on the life and career of Ernesto (Che) Guevara (Omar Sharif), the Argentinian who was the theoretician and moving spirit behind Cuban revolutionary Fidel Castro (Jack Palance). Directed by Richard Fleischer, it's a boring and lifeless illustrated lecture, devoid of the passion, politics, urgency and conflict that might have involved viewers in potentially interesting and significant political realities. A-II (PG)

Cheap Detective, The (1978) Overdone parody of the private-eye melodramas of the 1940s with Peter Falk as a Humphrey Bogart-like detective searching for the murderer of his partner, smashing a smuggling ring led by John Houseman doing a Sidney Greenstreet interpretation and helping a Free French agent gain passage to Oakland. Robert Moore directs a Neil Simon script lacking in wit and invention, sporting tired jokes and some sexually derived humor. A-III (PG)

Cheaper to Keep Her (1981) A divorce lawyer (Tovah Feldshuh), concerned about late alimony payments, hires a private investigator (Mac Davis) who is newly divorced himself in a dreadfully acted, determinedly vulgar attempt by director Ken Annakin at romantic comedy. The humor, when not lewd, comes at the expense of homosexuals and Hispanics. O (R)

Checkered Flag or Crash (1977) Joe Don Baker plays a driver in a 1000-mile road race in the Philippines, with Susan Sarandon as an intrepid photographer-journalist. Directed by Alan Gibson, it is mindless even by the modest standards of racing movies and exhibits a disregard for human life. A-III (PG)

Cheech and Chong's Next Movie (1980) Second movie with the comedy team of Cheech and Chong (Cheech Marin and Thomas Chong) assaults the audience with drugs, foul language, crude sexual references and a plot that goes nowhere. Directed by Chong. O (R)

Cheech and Chong's Nice Dreams (1981) The dopey duo this time out are entrepreneurs dealing marijuana from an ice cream truck which leads to the usual rambling misadventures with drugs and sex. O (R)

Cheech and Chong's "The Corsican Brothers" (1984) Cheech and Chong take the plot of the venerable old swashbuckler and bedeck it with their usual slapstick gags, though this time they avoid drugs and nudity. Directed by Thomas Chong, however, it's all very unfunny, especially its gross sexual humor. O (R)

Cher Victor (1976) French black comedy to which director Robin Davis brings a hard-edged sensibility in a story of two old men for whom petty quarrels turn into a vendetta that ends in tragedy. Bernard Blier and Jacques Dufilho, two great character actors, give a performance worth seeing as the geriatric odd couple who are locked in a symbiotic relationship neither can break. The movie is amusing yet underneath lurks the truth that the frailties of old age await each viewer. A-III (nr)

Cherry, Harry and Raquel (1970) Marijuana operation in the Arizona desert is interfered with by a pesky Indian. Sex exploitation job directed by Russ Meyer with extensive nudity and perverse acts. O (X/R)

Chess Players, The (1978) Indian director Satyajit Ray tells a 19th-century story of British encroachments on a small Moslem kingdom in the north of India, using as his focus two idle aristocrats who pass their days in playing chess, oblivious of the danger that threatens their land and its poet-king. Based on an actual incident and told with some humor and much irony, the film suffers from being overly talky and stagy. Its greatest asset for American viewers is its careful re-creation of a vanished era. A-II (nr)

Cheyenne Autumn (1964) Western epic of Indian courage in the face of the white man's neglect and broken promises. Director John Ford's rugged locales match the grandeur of the story, even though the narrative sometimes falters. A-I (br)

Cheyenne Social Club, The (1970) Jimmy Stewart, a cowboy with moral inhibitions, inherits a brothel but his ownership of the building depends on the ladies remaining there. Sidekick Henry Fonda jumps in and out of ladies beds while Stewart stammers his way through an excruciatingly silly seduction scene (complete with maid in transparent blouse). An exercise in off-color humor directed by Gene Kelly, the result lacks wit, taste and interest. O (GP)

Chicago 70 (1970) Witty anti-establishment satire intertwines the Chicago conspiracy trial of Bobby Seale and Abbie Hoffman with Lewis Carroll's "Alice in Wonderland." Director Kerry Feltham photographed the stage play as performed by the Toronto Workshop, with its bizarre, colorful costumes and a minimum of props in a black limbo setting. Mature themes. A-III (nr)

Chicken Chronicles, The (1977) Obnoxious youth-oriented comedy set in the late 1960s about a self-indulgent Beverly Hills high school senior determined to get his girl friend into bed. Though avoiding nudity, director Francis Simon's treatment of sex, drugs and alcohol is exploitative. O (PG)

Child's Play (1972) Failed screen version of Robert Marasco's play about the tragedy of evil that grows from the school rivalry between a paranoid Latin teacher (James Mason) and a jovial paternalistic English teacher (Robert Preston) who has come to hate him. The only mystery is why director Sidney Lumet weakened what was originally a straight chiller by throwing in all kinds of sidelong glances, creaky doors, murky corridors and unsubtle theatrical effects. A-III (PG)

Childhood II (1973) Group encounter sessions held in the nude because, we are told, without clothes people can be more honest and open with one another. Martin J. Spinelli's documentary indicates that this technique is as inadequate as most other shortcuts to mental health. O (nr)

Children, The (1980) An orange, radioactive cloud turns a group of children into nasty creatures bent upon murder in director Max Kalmanowicz' cheap, amateurish horror movie that overdoes the blood and gore. O (R)

Children of a Lesser God (1986) A deaf girl (Marlee Matlin) who has resigned herself to a life of solitude and mediocrity painfully comes to accept the love and admiration of a professor (William Hurt) at the school for the deaf where she works as a janitor. A well-acted sentimental love story, its potential insights into the problems of interpersonal communication are undercut by director Randa Haines' concentration on the sexual aspects of the lovers' relationship. Nudity and harsh language. A-III (R)

Children of Rage (1975) Set in 1968, after the disastrous Arab losses in the Six Day War, this movie tries to explain why the Palestinians adopted the desperate policy of terrorism in their fight against the state of Israel. An embarrassingly amateurish production directed by Arthur Allan Seidelman, its failure to do so in any coherent fashion can only serve to exacerbate the feelings of both sides. Violence. A-III (PG)

Children of the Corn (1984) Some nasty kids, in the sway of some demonic power, slaughter all the adults in a Midwestern town where a doctor and his wife (Peter Horton and Linda Hamilton) chance to stop on an auto trip. Fritz Kiersch directs this dull, predictable horror movie adapted from a story by Stephen King. Violence. A-III (R)

Children of Theatre Street, The (1978) American documentary on the famous ballet school in Leningrad that produced Nijinsky and whose more recent graduates include Nureyev, Makarova and Baryshnikov. Directed by Robert Dornhelm and narrated by Princess Grace of Monaco, it offers some lovely, if fragmented, ballet sequences and some fine views of Peter the Great's city but the narrative tends to be bland and repetitive, pursuing its subject in rather aimless fashion. A-I (nr)

Chilly Scenes of Winter (see: "Head Over Heels")

China Girl (1987) Interracial teen romance blooms amid a climate of gang warfare in New York's Chinatown and Little Italy. Director Abel Ferrara emphasizes action and setting over characterization and an understanding of ethnic loyalties and traditions of prejudice that rule the lives of two generations of Chinese and Italians. Bloody violence, a love-making scene and profanity abound. O (R)

China Is Near (1968) Italian satire on the country's politics and morals centers on a man's campaign for office in a small town where everything revolves around sex, politics and religion. Marco Bellocchio's confusing direction lacks a clear enough viewpoint to support its heavyhanded and at times offensive treatment. A-IV (br)

China Syndrome, The (1979) Director James Bridges' prophetic drama suspensefully deals with nuclear safety issues in a movie featuring Jack Lemmon as an executive and Jane Fonda as a news reporter whose consciences won't let them conceal the imminent danger of a nuclear meltdown at a power plant. Thoughtful entertainment. A-II (PG)

Chinatown (1974) Jack Nicholson plays a private eye trying to unravel a murder and a civic scandal in the Los Angeles of the 1930s. Faye Dunaway is a mysterious, frightened woman and Roman Polanski, who also directed, plays one of the heavies. A superior entertainment altogether adult in its theme of social and personal corruption, especially its implication of incest. A-IV (R)

Chinese Connection, The (1973) Martial arts movie with Bruce Lee revenging the murder of his beloved teacher. In the end, the hero goes to jail for his murderous deeds, affording him one last snickering kick at the audience as he's led away. Director Lo Wei employs excessive violence and a totally irrelevant striptease by a geisha girl. O (R)

Chipmunk Adventure, The (1987) Animated feature plays like a musical revue of pop tunes as Alvin and his Chipmunk friends sing and race around the world with their female cousins, the Chipettes, in hot-air balloons inadvertently delivering stolen diamonds for their wicked human guardians. Director Janice Karman's charming, lighthearted diversion for the younger set includes a sweet song about motherhood and the critters' comical conversation. A-I (G)

Chisum (1970) Boisterous, good old-fashioned Western stars John Wayne as cattle baron John Chisum, who figured prominently in the bloody Lincoln County cattle wars involving the likes of Pat Garrett and Billy the Kid. Directed by Andrew V. McLaglen with the usual oversimplification of moral issues in the taming of the West, the movie will appeal to those who like action at the expense of historical accuracy. A-I (G)

Chitty Chitty Bang Bang (1968) Widowed inventor (Dick Van Dyke) takes his two children and girl friend (Sally Ann Howes) on a magical mystery tour of the imagination involving an evil baron (Gert Frobe), a cavernous castle in the air, the rescue of imprisoned children and the strange flying car of the title. Though adults may be disappointed by the indifferent lyrics and lackluster special effects of this musical fantasy directed by Ken Hughes, there is still more than enough good fun for the young and uncritical. A-I (G)

Chloe in the Afternoon (1972) French drama about a married man (Bernard Verley) with a wonderful wife (Francoise Verley), lovely daughter, secure job and serene life who is drawn into intimacy with a sensuous woman (Zouzou) that takes him to the brink of actual infidelity. The final episode in director Eric Rohmer's series of "Six Moral Tales" is an elegant, sophisticated story of a smug, self-absorbed man who viewers will have to decide was strong enough to resist temptation or simply not nervy enough to indulge it. Restrained nudity. A-III (R)

Choirboys, The (1977) The screen adaptation of Joseph Wambaugh's novel seems to imply that Los Angeles would be a relatively peaceful city if it could only get rid of its corrupt, drunken, violent, perverted and vicious police force. Scriptwriter Christopher Knopf has thrown together a pointless series of clumsy, presumably black-comedy sketches of police antics which director Robert Aldrich treats in cynical, leering fashion. Excessive profanity. O (R)

Choke Canyon (1986) Cowboy-scientist (Stephen Collins) fights for his rights against big business, foils the flying hit man (Bo Swenson) sent to silence him, exposes the effort to turn his canyon lab into a toxic waste site, saves his horse, gets the girl and manages to complete his experiment turning sound waves into energy. Supposedly about integrity and personal initiative, the story gets derailed by juvenile action scenes, pyrotechnics, romance and a small bit of rough language. A-II (PG)

C.H.O.M.P.S. (1979) Young engineer (Wesley Eure) invents the perfect home protection device—a robot watchdog—and wins the hand of the boss' cute daughter despite the machinations of some inept industrial spies. This weak little comedy from Hanna-Barbera might be of passing interest to very young children if its producers had not seen fit to add a sizable amount of vulgar language. A-II (PG/G)

Choose Me (1984) Smug, irritating little comedy-drama about a man (Keith Carradine) who gets involved with three very talkative women who are supported by their lovers in Los Angeles. He suffers, but viewers suffer more. Directed by Alan Rudolph, it has a benign view of sexual amorality. O (R)

Chorus Line, A (1985) Screen version of the hit stage musical provides a close-up view of backstage fears and emotions at a Broadway audition. Directed by Richard Attenborough, the film tries too hard to translate the theatrical experience to the big screen. Discussion of adult sexual themes. A-IV (PG-13)

Chosen Survivors (1974) Group of people (Bradford Dillman, Jackie Cooper, Diana Muldaur, Barbara Babcock, Alex Cord and a handful of others) are thrown together in a self-contained underground environment and told that they are the only survivors of a nuclear holocaust. Their problems begin, however, when vampire bats start invading the ventilating system. Directed by Sutton Rolley, it is a scary movie psychologically, especially if bats are not quite your dish. A-III (PG)

Chosen, The (1978) Italian production about an industrial magnate (Kirk Douglas) building a super nuclear power plant in a Third World country who learns that one of the major backers of the project is the devil and that the Antichrist waiting to take over is none other than his own son (Simon Ward). Director Alberto De Martino's supernatural slash-'em, crunch-'em movie is abysmal drivel exploiting nudity and gory violence. O (R)

Chosen, The (1982) Set in Brooklyn during and immediately after World War II, different views of life and religious faith confront two Jewish teenagers (Robby Benson and Barry Miller), one the son of a revered Hassidic rabbi (Rod Steiger), the other the son of a secular scholar (Maximilian Schell). Directed by Jeremy Paul Kagan, the only shortcoming in the screen adaptation of the Chaim Potok novel is a certain lack of dramatic tension. A-II (PG)

Christa (1971) Swedish story about a woman (Birte Tove) looking for someone with whom she'd be sexually compatible and who would make a nice father for her illegitimate son. Producer-director Jack O'Connell seems interested only in putting as much of his actress on display as the law allows. O (R)

Christian Licorice Store, The (1971) Beau Bridges plays a California tennis pro whose descent into the nether world of casual sex with proper Hollywood strangers and into TV product endorsements affords neither food for thought nor dramatic morsels to chew. When he winds up killing himself, it is simply stupid, not tragic. Director James Frawley's slick, shallow work is all style and no substance. O (GP)

Christian the Lion (1977) George Adamson, whose story was dramatized in "Born Free," again becomes involved with the task of rehabilitating a tame lion cub to survive in the perils of its natural African habitat. Assisting in this real-life adventure are the stars of "Born Free," Virginia McKenna and Bill Travers who co-directed the film with James Hill. Beautifully photographed in Kenyan game preserve, it is an engrossing picture of wildlife and worthwhile family fare. A-I (G)

Christine (1983) Adaptation of Stephen King's novel about a 1959 car that kills people either for the sheer fun of it or because they're rude to its teenage owner (Keith Gordon) who rescued it from a junkyard and restored it to pristine splendor. Director John Carpenter's plodding, mediocre movie has foul language, sex, violence and an unwholesome view of family life. O (R)

Christine Jorgensen Story, The (1970) The story of a sex change operation certainly has a place in medical annals, but whether it's a proper subject for a movie, except perhaps in a documentary, is another matter. Directed by Irving

Rapper, the result is neither entertaining nor illuminating. A-IV (R)

Christmas Story, A (1983) Adapted from Jean Shepherd's novel, "In God We Trust, All Others Pay Cash," this is a nostalgic re-creation of what it was like to be a boy (Peter Billingsley) yearning for a genuine Red Ryder air rifle for Christmas in the Midwest of the 1940s. Director Bob Clark gets some good performances (Darren McGavin and Melinda Dillon as the understanding parents) and the result is a warm celebration of a more innocent, less sophisticated America. A-II (PG)

Christmas Tree, The (1969) Wealthy widower (William Holden), told that his only child is dying of leukemia, lavishes all his attention on the boy during his final months. Director Terence Young treats the subject of death with a good deal of sense and sensibility and by focusing on the son's acceptance of his terminal condition, infuses the film with vitality (and even some humor) instead of the static and fruitless sentiment that is common in such films. A-II (G)

Chrome and Hot Leather (1971) When the girl friend of a Green Beret (Tony Young) is accidentally killed by a motorcycle gang, he and three of his Green Beret comrades set out to avenge her death. Directed by Lee Frost, the routine biker movie contains occasional and relatively restrained sex and violence. A-III (GP)

Chronicle of Anna Magdalena Bach, The (1969) Unusual concert performance film with brief dramatic scenes from the life of the 18th-century composer connecting the musical presentations. Directed by Jean-Marie Straub, the German production is static, with almost no camera movement, but the ornate settings and elaborate costuming contribute to a rare musical experience in this performance of works by Johann Sebastian Bach. A-I (nr)

Chu Chu and the Philly Flash (1981) Alan Arkin and Carol Burnett struggle desperately for laughs in director David Lowell Rich's contrived mishmash of a comedy about a pan-handler and failed show girl who find secret government documents. Some profanity. A-III (PG)

Chubasco (1968) Story of the regeneration of a rebellious young man (Christopher Jones) through hard work with a tuna fisherman (Joe De Santis) and the love of a young woman (Susan Strasberg) who marries him despite her father's (Richard Egan) objections. Writer-director Allen H. Miner has given fresh life to an old plot by selecting San Diego's tuna fleet as its setting and utilizing to the full the excitement and dangers of deep sea tuna fishing. A-II (br)

C.H.U.D. (1984) Run-of-the-mill horror movie about monsters created by toxic waste. Ineptly directed by Douglas Cheek, it contains violence and gore. A-III (R)

Chuka (1967) Slack Western directed by Gordon Douglas about a lone gunfighter (Rod Taylor) who arrives at an Army fort filled with misfit soldiers just before it is attacked by starving Indians. Much violence and some sexual innuendo. A-III (br)

Ciao! Manhattan (1973) John Palmer and David Weisman have fashioned a semi-documentary about the sorry life of Edie Sedgwick, a New York society girl who in 1965, at age 28, overdosed on pills. The result proves sophomoric and smart-alecky, with not a little exploitation of the girl's debilitated state of mind and scarred, siliconed body. O (R)

Cinderella (1949) Disney animated feature has the traditional elements of pumpkin coach and glass slipper but adds a pair of mice, Jaq and Gus-Gus, a mean old cat, Lucifer, and a daffy fairy godmother. Good visual fun for all the family. A-I (G)

Cinderella Liberty (1973) A sailor (James Caan) becomes involved with a bar-girl (Marsha Mason) and her young son who understandably acts surly towards his mother's night-time visitor. Caan and Mason establish a stable arrangement of sorts but this unusual family unit is brought to the brink of ruin by various sappy plot devices. Director Mark Rydell coats the transparent soap opera with heartbreak, misery, pathos and, of course, a happy ending. Much foul language and some nudity. O (R)

Cindy and Donna (1971) The title duo are a pair of teeny-bopper sisters who use their Southern California environment to pollute the screen with any number of crude displays. With adulterous sots as parents, it's a picture of family to be avoided at all costs. O (X/R)

Circle of Deceit (1982) German production directed by Volker Schlondorff follows the random wanderings of a journalist through the horrors of strife-torn Beirut, Lebanon. Although some of the terrible madness of urban civil warfare is apparent, there is little clear thinking or real drama in a movie marred by an extremely explicit bedroom scene. O (R)

Circle of Iron (1979) Ambitious but botched recounting of the adventures of a mythic hero (David Carradine) on a Far Eastern journey toward enlightenment. In homage to marial arts king Bruce Lee, director Richard Moore's action adventure relies too heavily on stylized violence and a ridiculously inappropriate sex scene which reflects the movie's overall inversion of the values its hero seeks. O (R)

Circus, The (1928) Charles Chaplin wrote, directed, produced, and starred in this silent feature for which he has written a musical score as well as a song for the sound version. Charlie, on the run from the police, hides in the circus and becomes a prop man but inadvertently proves funnier than the clowns. He falls in love with the bareback rider (Merna Kennedy) but she loves the high-wire artist and the circus goes on leaving Charlie walking off alone. Admittedly not his best, it is nevertheless a real gem of comic invention and sympathetic understanding of human nature and the human condition. A-I (G)

Cisco Pike (1971) Kris Kristofferson plays a faded flower child forced by narcotics detective Gene Hackman to re-enter the drug-dealing world he hoped was all in the past. Directed by Bill Norton, there are some kinky sex scenes and meanderings through the California drug scene. O (R)

Citizens Band (see: "Handle with Care")

City Heat (1984) Police detective (Clint Eastwood) and a private eye (Burt Reynolds) talk rudely to each other whenever their paths cross during the course of a mob war in Depression-era Kansas City. Director Richard Benjamin apparently means these exchanges to be terribly funny, but they're not. Amidst all the shooting, carnage and violence, the in-joke nature of the two macho stars becomes quite wearing. A-III (PG)

City Lights (1931) Produced, written and directed by Charles Chaplin, in which he stars as the Little Tramp, the plot involves his love for a blind girl (Virginia Cherrill) with the classic fade out when, sight restored, she sees him for the first time. Continuing Chaplin's cheerful bout with all manner of adversity in the big city, it was the first of his movies to use sound effects, though not spoken dialogue. A-I (G)

City of Women (1981) Italian director Federico Fellini offers a heavy-handed analysis of the male ego threatened by feminist demands for sexual equality in a story about an aging Lothario (Marcello Mastroianni) and his erotic daydreams. There are touches of the old Fellini magic, but his penchant for the grotesque has grown wearisome, his imagery repetitious and his studio artifice annoyingly obvious. O (R)

City on Fire (1979) One of the most disastrous disaster movies ever made, the title tells the entire plot. The Canadian production directed by Alvin Rakoff is unbelievably dull and pedestrian. Violence involving fire victims. A-III (R)

Clair de Femme (1980) A recent widower (Yves Montand) and a woman (Romy Schneider) who has just lost her daughter in an auto accident and her husband to insanity, meet and a love affair ensues, apparently meant to be the salvation of both. The melancholy romance is directed by Costa-Gavras in pretentious and tedious fashion, wasting the talents of those involved in this French production. Treatment of sex makes this adult fare. A-III (PG)

Claire's Knee (1971) Amusing but cerebral French drama in which a middle-aged diplomat (Jean-Claude Brialy) is introduced to a young woman (Laurence de Monaghan) and becomes disconcertingly obsessed with her knee. Director Eric Rohmer's fifth in his series of "Six Moral Tales" is a droll study of a rather pompous man's self-deception in trying to rationalize his fixation in a movie of literate conversations about everything from love to philosophy. A-III (GP)

Clambake (1967) In order to know whether he is liked more for his money than himself, a tycoon's son (Elvis Presley) switches identities with a penniless water-ski instructor (Will Hutchins). Directed by Arthur Nadel, the results are entirely predictable, with Elvis singing a few subdued ballads and driving in a speed boat race that is the movie's highlight. A-I (br)

Clan of the Cave Bear, The (1986) Based on Jean Auel's popular novel about prehistoric times, this movie plods along with its band of dull-witted Neanderthals who raise an orphaned Cro-Magnon child Ayla. Except for the scenery, not much happens until Ayla grows intelligent enough to leave the clan to its caves. Several scenes of simulated sex and some violence. O (R)

Clash of the Titans (1981) Greek mythology plays second fiddle to a whole medley of not especially enthralling special effects in director Desmond Davis' languid and hopelessly episodic reworking of the Perseus-Andromeda legend. The immense talents of Laurence Olivier, Burgess Meredith, Claire Bloom, Sian Phillips and Flora Robson are helpless in this mess of a movie. Incidental nudity. A-III (PG)

Class (1983) Jacqueline Bisset plays a woman who has an affair with a teenage boy (Andrew McCarthy), later discovering that he is her son's (Rob Lowe) best friend. Director Lewis John Carlino can't decide whether to play the contrived, ill-considered effort as romantic comedy, slapstick farce or serious drama. The result settles for adolescent vulgarity and the sensationalism of graphic sex. O (R)

Class of '44 (1973) Director Paul Bogart's quarter-baked sequel to the half-baked "Summer of '42" takes two of the adolescent boys of the earlier movie into college and one into the Marines. When it is not being either sentimental or tasteless (sex on campus), it is something like an old Henry Aldrich comedy. A-III (PG)

Class of Miss MacMichael, The (1979) Dedicated, embattled teacher (Glenda Jackson) struggles with a classroom of maladjusted youngsters and an incompetent headmaster (Oliver Reed). Director Silvio Narizzano can't decide on either a serious or farcical mood for this British story whose flow of obscenities and depiction of sexual misbehavior are objectionable. O (R)

Class of '74 (1973) Three aggressive college coeds teach a fourth how to dispel memories of harsh parents and develop into a sexually liberated woman. Directed by Arthur Marks and Mack Bing, the low-budget package grossly exploits its intended young audience. O (R)

Claudine (1974) Diahann Carroll stars as a welfare mother of six, with James Earl Jones as a sanitation man who likes being her lover but who cannot cope with the idea of becoming her husband. Directed by John Berry, it is an interesting and at times dramatically compelling attempt to create a compassionate, realistic picture of black city life tempered with both humor and bitterness. Some raunchy humor with street vocabulary to match. A-III (PG)

Clay Pigeon (1971) Returned Vietnam war hero (Tom Stern) resents a ruthless narcotics agent (Telly Savalas) setting him up in order to nab L.A.'s top dope dealer, especially when it causes the death of some of the vet's playmates. Also produced and directed by Stern, the result is full of pretense and good intentions, but empty of real achievement. Though against hard drugs, it is in favor of soft ones. Some nudity and rough language. O (R)

Cleopatra (1972) Japanese cartoon for adults retells the story of the Egyptian queen but its main interest is in the mangled pronunciations of historical names and observing the color scheme used for the animation. Directed by Osamu Tezula and Eilichi Yamamoto, the movie's sexual appeal centers mostly in topless cartoon characters and a few mildly erotic abstractions. O (nr)

Cleopatra Jones (1973) Black adventuress (towering Tamara Dobson) is used by the U.S. Government to shake up the illegal drug traffic worldwide but most of the action unfolds in the L. A. Watts neighborhood as Cleo carries out a personal vendetta. Directed by Jack Starrett, the movie goes down pretty easily as light, action-packed adult entertainment. A-III (PG)

Cleopatra Jones and the Casino of Gold (1975) Tamara Dobson, tall, black and beautiful, is the main ingredient of a plot whose chief villain is the Dragon Lady (Stella Stevens). Directed by Chuck Bail, it features extravagant violence with a bit of sexual exploitation thrown in for bad measure. O (R)

Climax, The (1967) Italian satire about a polygamist (Ugo Tognazzi), happily married to three women and raising three sets of families. Equally devoted to each, he dies of sheer exhaustion. Deftly directed by Pietro Germi, the black comedy pushes a rather silly male sex fantasy to its absurd conclusion. A-III (nr)

Cloak and Dagger (1946) Midwestern professor (Gary Cooper) is sent to Switzerland during World War II to spy on German attempts to develop an atomic bomb. With Lilli Palmer as the love interest, director Fritz Lang almost succeeds in making something more than another espionage thriller, though Ring Lardner Jr.'s screenplay offers little more than wartime intrigue. A-II (br)

Cloak and Dagger (1984) Lonely young boy (Henry Thomas) escapes from reality by playing superspy, but when reality obtrudes and he witnesses a murder, nobody will believe him—except the killers. Directed by Richard Franklin, it's well-acted, fastpaced escapist fare but its violent situation makes it questionable entertainment for pre-teens. A-II (PG)

Clockmaker, The (1976) A good-hearted, middle-aged clockmaker (Philippe Noiret) is visited one morning by a police inspector (Jean Rochefort) and told that his son is wanted for murder. Though the father has never understood his son, he stands by him at the trial and afterwards. Bertrand Tavernier directs what is essentially a character study of the father without any sentimentality, yet with sufficient quiet charm and convincing performances to earn one's interest. A-II (nr)

Clockwise (1986) British import about a headmaster (John Cleese) whose neurotic obsession with punctuality makes him suffer inordinately through a series of complications impeding his attempt to arrive at a headmasters' convention in time to deliver his presidential address. Dry wit, gentle humor and general silliness pervade a farce illustrating the futility of a rigid approach to life. A-II (PG)

Clockwork Orange (1972) Produced, directed, and written by Stanley Kubrick, the urban scene of the 1962 Anthony Burgess novel is ruled by day by the forces of law and order, and by punk teenagers like Alex (Malcolm McDowell), the central character, and his pals by night. The Kubrick-Burgess message about the human right to a free will is not very new or startling, and only Burgess' marvelous language, and Kubrick's grandiose style have made it seem at all fresh and significant. Excessive violence and nudity in a sexual context. O (X/R)

Cloportes (1966) Uneven French gangster movie in which a Paris underworld character (Lino Ventura) takes his revenge on those who left him in the lurch during a robbery. Directed by Pierre Granier-Deferre, the acting is superior but its treatment of the criminal world and its liberal use of nudity are excessive. O (br)

Close Encounters of the Third Kind (1977) Richard Dreyfuss stars in director Steven Spielberg's epic about UFOs and the humanistic, hopeful and, for some, religious theme of mankind's close encounter with an extragalactic lifeform. The scenes involving simple person-to-person relationships may be somewhat flat but the movie boasts some dazzling special effects and is tinged with a feeling of awe rare in science fiction works. Some effects might frighten the very young. A-II (PG)

Closely Watched Trains (1968) Czechoslovakian director Jiri Menzel's story about a young man's blundering search for maturity seems to imply that the transition to manhood cannot be made without the experience of sex. A-IV (br)

Clowns, The (1971) Federico Fellini directs a highly imaginative documentary about the disappearance of laughter and fantasy in modern life, but it concentrates on the tradition of the circus and various kinds of clowns, citing them as sources of his own cinematic inspiration. Most viewers will find more than enough to satisfy their curiosity about the subject and will be abundantly entertained as well. A-I (G)

Club Paradise (1986) Robin Williams and numerous other comics try to create some fun and frolic in the Jamaican sun. The mild satire of the Club Med scene features Jimmy Cliff, his music and predictable drug and sex references which do very little for the funny bone. A-III (PG-13)

Clue (1985) Parker Brothers' board game comes to life in a mildly entertaining screen version that is being circulated with three different endings. Although for some it will be nostalgic fun, slapstick comedy prevails. A-II (PG)

C'mon, Let's Live a Little (1966) Silly college campus musical about a country yokel (Bobby Vee) and the dean's lovely daughter (Jackie De Shannon). Directed by David Butler, nothing much happens, but there is enough innocent romance to appeal to some teenagers. A-II (br)

Coal Miner's Daughter (1980) Sissy Spacek, who does all her own singing, gives a warm and utterly winning performance as Loretta Lynn. In this semi-biographical story, director Michael Apted depicts her life from poverty and obscurity in the Kentucky hills to undreamed of riches and success. Tommy Lee Jones plays Loretta's husband who escorts her along the rocky road to stardom. Frank language about sex and a wedding night sequence would rule out younger children. A-II (PG)

Coast to Coast (1980) Mediocre chase comedy with Dyan Cannon and Robert Blake as an odd couple—she's a runaway from a mental institution and he's a hard-luck trucker—who make their way across the country pursued by various characters with hostile intentions. Directed by Joseph Sargent, the slapstick grows tedious and often abrasive. Some rough language. A-III (PG)

Cobra (1986) Sylvester Stallone as the ace crime-stopper of the Los Angeles Police Department single-handedly blows away an army of cultist serial murderers in director George Cosmatos' excessively violent treatment to the vigilante spirit. O (R)

Cobra, The (1968) Failed adventure melodrama directed by Mario Sequi about an American agent (Dana Andrews) fighting an Oriental drug-smuggling ring. Fairly heavy violence and sexual innuendo. A-III (br)

Coca-Cola Kid, The (1985) American whiz-kid trouble-shooter (Eric Roberts) for Coca-Cola arrives in Australia determined to boost sales but is stymied by one small town that is content with its own local soft drink. In visiting its manufacturer, the American discovers a competitor who is every bit as fanatical as himself. Directed by Dusan Makavejev, the movie begins with some satiric promise but becomes unglued midway and spins off in several different directions. Despite some good acting and clever touches, it's a disappointing failure. Some nudity and a needlessly graphic bedroom scene. O (nr)

Cockeyed Cowboys of Calico County, The (1970) Lumbering blacksmith (Dan Blocker) in a small Western town is bilked when he sends for a mail-order bride and sympathetic townsfolk (Mickey Rooney, Jim Backus, Wally Cox, Stubby Kaye) enlist the aid of a local dance hall girl (Nanette Fabray) to take her place. Director Tony

Leader's silly charade ends in true love. Youngsters may enjoy the Western setting and broad acting. A-I (G)

Cocoon (1985) Three old Rover Boys, young at heart, become young in body as well when they take a dip in a swimming pool being used as a rejuvenating force by some genial extraterrestrials. Good acting from some veterans, especially Don Ameche, but the plot premise is weakly contrived and the view of rejuvenation banally condescending. Directed by Ron Howard, the movie reinforces the stereotypes of old age as sexless and of women as passive. Some locker room humor and an emphasis upon the sexual aspect of rejuvenation. A-II (PG-13)

Code of Silence (1985) Chuck Norris stars as a Chicago detective who uses his martial arts skills to combat evil. Directed by Andy Davis, it's fairly standard action fare, though a cut above Norris' earlier efforts. Violence and profanity. A-III (R)

Coffy (1973) Black exploitation picture of a woman (Pam Grier) who seeks revenge on the drug pushers who turned her little sister into a catatonic hospital patient. Her weapons range from sawed-off shotguns to her full-blown figure, which lets the sex and violence crowds have it both ways. Directed by Jack Hill, it is a low-grade exploitation piece. O (R)

Cold Turkey (1971) Led by the local minister (Dick Van Dyke), a small town in Iowa decides to take up a cigarette adman (Bob Newhart) on his offer of $25 million if the townspeople stop smoking for 30 days. Director Norman Lear obviously intended the movie as a satire on rural America, Madison Avenue and all points in between, but its slight sense of humor is overworked to the point of tedium. Vulgar language, tasteless sexual references and the portrayal of the clergy as venal and self-serving. A-III (GP)

Color Me Dead (1969) Australian production about a man (Tom Tryon) who becomes unwittingly involved in a uranium swindle and is then given a dose of slow-working poison, a plot device allowing him to spend the rest of the movie looking for his own murderer. Director Eddie Davis' remake of "D.O.A." (1949) is slow-moving and not very inventive but at least the unfamiliar Australian locales give it some interest. Permissive attitude toward sex and a nightclub striptease make it mature fare. A-III (R)

Color Purple, The (1985) Steven Spielberg's glossy screen version of Alice Walker's Pulitzer Prize-winning novel about a young black woman (Whoopi Goldberg) growing up in a rural Georgia between the two world wars. The screen adaptation lacks cohesion and unwittingly reinforces damaging racial and sexual stereotypes. O (PG-13)

Color of Money, The (1986) An aging poolroom pro (Paul Newman) is obsessed with turning a young pool player (Tom Cruise) into a champion. Directed by Martin Scorsese, this disappointing sequel to "The Hustler" lets its conflict of personal integrity vs. the lure of money get lost in the clash of male egos. Brief nudity and extensive profanity. A-III (R)

Colossus: The Forbin Project (see: "The Forbin Project")

Coma (1978) Screen version of Robin Cook's novel about a spunky Boston doctor (Genevieve Bujold) who uncovers a murderous scheme involving trafficking in human organs. Michael Crichton directs a suspenseful, well-acted drama with a relatively sophisticated plot and some rather graphic operating room scenes, incidental nudity and the casual treatment of an affair. A-III (PG)

Come Back Charleston Blue (1972) Raymond St. Jacques and Godfrey Cambridge repeat their "Cotton Comes to Harlem" roles as two detectives in a caper movie about a black gang's attempt to wrest control of the Harlem drug traffic from white mobsters. Under Mark Warrren's direction, there is a good deal of violence and killing but enough authentic references to ghetto life to cloak the escapist action fantasy with a pathos that was probably not intended. A-III (PG)

Come Have Coffee with Us (1973) Italian black comedy about a middle-aged man (Ugo Tognazzi) who decides to settle down and marries an aging, grotesque heiress. His virile prowess eventually extends to her two equally unattractive sisters but, when the maid catches his eye, nature strikes him down in an ending that is both fitting and hilarious. Directed by Alberto Lattuada, the rise and fall of this figure of smug satisfaction will not please those who object to earthy humor. A-IV (nr)

Come Play with Me (see: "Grazie Zia")

Come Spy with Me (1967) Failed spy spoof directed by Marshall Stone about an agent (Troy Donahue) in the Caribbean who joins a scuba diving contest as a blind while he investigates several murders. Stylized violence and mild sexual innuendo. A-II (br)

Comedians, The (1967) Multi-leveled tragicomedy about a man (Richard Burton) who finds himself involved in a plot to overthrow a ruthless dictatorship in Haiti. Strong cast (Alec Guinness, Peter Ustinov, Elizabeth Taylor), thoughtful script by Graham Greene from his own novel and assured direction by Peter Glenville result in a powerful movie about personal commitment in the context of political injustice. Some violence and brutality. A-III (br)

Comes a Horseman (1978) Somber, slow-moving Western set in 1945, when a small rancher (Jane Fonda) stands up to the encroachments of a cattle baron (Jason Robards) by enlisting the help of a discharged serviceman (James Caan). The best parts of director Alan J. Pakula's movie are its Colorado setting and the depiction of the warming relationship between Fonda and Caan, but the film's violence and the nature of their relationship rule out younger viewers. A-III (PG)

Cometogether (1971) Made in Italy by Saul Swimmer, the story of an offbeat ménage à trois is a compendium of bad production techniques that serve only to emphasize the sordid characters and relationships without satisfying those voyeurs who expect the visuals to exploit the potential of the subject matter. O (R)

Comfort and Joy (1984) The melancholy-comic chronicle of the worst Christmas week ever spent by an aging Scottish disc jockey (Bill Peterson) who, deserted by his mistress, throws himself into his work and becomes involved as mediator in a local ice cream war. Directed by Bill Forsyth, there's not much of interest here except for the Glasgow locale. A-II (PG)

Comic, The (1969) Although this Dick Van Dyke movie is about a silent screen comedian, it is not a comedy. Van Dyke's performance as Billy Bright incorporates some unamusing parodies of physical comedy from the slapstick era, but Carl Reiner's direction lacks any sense of nostalgia or even sentimentality in what is essentially a maudlin presentation of Bright's various problems with alcohol and women. A-III (PG)

Coming Apart (1969) Rip Torn plays a psychiatrist who uses a hidden camera to record his own disintegration through a series of sexual encounters with neurotic women. The characters, however grotesque, are recognizably human rather than sex fantasy objects but director Milton Moses Ginsberg hopelessly dilutes any potential insights into psychological anguish and need by indulging in sheer sensationalism. O (nr)

Coming Home (1978) When a Marine captain (Bruce Dern) is assigned to Vietnam in 1968, his wife (Jane Fonda) volunteers to work in a veteran's hospital where she falls in love with a paraplegic Vietnam casualty (Jon Voight). Good performances by Fonda and Voight and fine camerawork by Haskell Wexler, but director Hal Ashby's movie lacks the political sophistication to examine the war issue and concentrates instead only on the theme of romantic love. Brief nudity in a sexual context and acceptance of adultery. O (R)

Commando (1985) When the daughter of a retired Army martial arts expert (Arnold Schwarzenegger) is kidnapped by a Latin American strongman to force him to assassinate a political rival, he turns, instead, to assassinating the kidnapper's entire army. Mark Lester's direction has a certain leavening of comic book humor, but it won't seem especially funny unless you happen to think there is something intrinsically amusing about sudden death. Unrelenting celebration of violence. O (R)

Committee, The (1969) Stage revue featuring the antics of eight young West Coast comics was videotaped during a performance and the results were then transferred to color film. Produced and directed by Del Jack, the program consists of 18 sometimes lively skits, often spiked with adult language, that concentrate on exposing the foibles of everyday life, especially of young couples, married and unmarried. Though there are some good laughs, it's for those who appreciate satire even when it misses. A-III (GP)

Companeros (1972) Italian-Spanish-German production shot mostly in English and set in turn-of-the-century Mexico finds Franco Nero running guns during the revolution. Director Sergio Corbucci clutters the story with plenty of loudly-staged massacres and a bit of sexual innuendo. A-III (R)

Company of Killers (1970) Van Johnson heads a special police squad trained for unusual assignments, while Ray Milland sets the wheels in motion for a murder to help his financial designs. Routine crime melodrama directed by Jerry Thorpe contains mild doses of violence, sex and some ambiguous religious themes. AII (G)

Competition, The (1980) Rival concert pianists (Richard Dreyfuss and Amy Irving) fall in love but have problems because of his sense of insecurity in a romantic melodrama written and directed by Joel Oliansky. Despite good performances, it is but mediocre entertainment marred by crude sexual references and a graphic bedroom scene. O (PG)

Compromising Positions (1985) A former journalist (Susan Sarandon), caught up in the investigation into the murder of a womanizing dentist (Joe Mantegna), does some snooping on her own and comes into conflict with the detective in charge (Raul Julia). Director Frank Perry's shal-

61

low, contrived and unpleasant comedy-mystery leans heavily on crude, sexually oriented humor. A-III (R)

Computer Wore Tennis Shoes, The (1970) Typical Disney comedy in which none-too-bright college student (Kurt Russell) accidentally has his brain computerized and becomes an intellectual phenomenon who by chance threatens the operations of a racketeer (Cesar Romero). Director Robert Butler's movie is a zany, very superficial comedy intended to amuse youngsters. A-I (G)

Conan the Barbarian (1982) Based on a pulp hero's violent exploits in savage prehistoric times, the movie's preliterate narrative ponderously details how the slow-witted Conan (Arnold Schwarzenegger) revenges the slaughter of his parents. John Milius directs with heavy emphasis on brutality, violence and some graphic sex. O (R)

Conan the Destroyer (1984) Director Richard Fleischer's sequel may be more polished and less gory than the original, but with Arnold Schwarzenegger again in the title role the result is still nothing more than a lead-footed, muscle-bound costume epic with an extremely high violence quotient. O (PG)

Concert for Bangladesh (1972) Saul Swimmer's documentary record of a landmark benefit concert in New York's Madison Square Garden features the performances of Bob Dylan, Billy Preston, Eric Clapton, Leon Russell, Ravi Shankar and Ringo Starr to name a few of those who appeared. A-I (G)

Concorde—Airport '79, The (1979) Another in the series of airport movies with the usual multitude of disasters and film stars (Alain Delon, Susan Blakely, Robert Wagner, et. al.) who can do nothing with the script's ineptness. Directed by David Lowell Rich, it contains harsh language and casual love affairs. O (PG)

Concrete Jungle, The (1982) Low-budget women-in-prison melodrama is directed by Tom De Simone as another exploitative sex-and-violence movie. Much nudity. O (R)

Conduct Unbecoming (1975) Set on India's Northwest Frontier in 1878, the honor of the regiment is at stake when a flirtatious widow (Suzannah York) accuses a young subaltern (James Faulkner) of assaulting her. With an idealist (Michael York) appointed to defend him, the movie turns from larger issues of conflicting claims of duty and loyalty and becomes no more than a whodunit of only moderate ingenuity. Directed by Michael Anderson, the movie offers a very talented cast, magnificent locales and exotic costumes but only mediocre drama. A-III (PG)

Confession, The (1970) Dramatic re-creation of the 1951 Czechoslovakian Purge Trials in which 14 dedicated Party members were convicted of high treason, to which all confessed though none were involved in any kind of political plot. Director Costa-Gavras focuses on one of them (Yves Montand), showing the process by which the man's idealistic faith in the Party was used against him in obtaining his confession. A-III (GP)

Confessions of Tom Harris (1972) The story of a tough mob enforcer (Don Murray) whose chance encounter with a woman (Linda Evans) led to his religious conversion at her father's commune for the spiritual and physical rehabilitation of alcoholics. Murray also wrote and produced, but neither he nor co-directors John Derek and David Nelson seem capable of capturing the spiritual

malaise or, for that matter, the religious convictions of the characters in their drama. The result is a series of incidents, ranging all the way from a rape to a symbolic re-creation of the Last Supper, which convey little of human or religious significance. A-III (PG)

Confessions of a Police Captain (1972) Italian story of corruption in high places features a police official (Martin Balsam) who will use any method, including assassination, to get rid of crooks, and a young prosecutor (Franco Nero) who is an honest but ineffectual bureaucrat. Directed by Damiano Damiani, the result is little more than a pot boiler with considerable violence. A-III (PG)

Confessions of a Window Cleaner (1974) Infantile sex comedy with a pimply young apprentice window-washer (Robin Askwith) as he makes his predictable rounds of suburban London. Witless sniggering and leering sex. O (R)

Conformist, The (1971) Italian movie about a man (Jean-Louis Trintignant) who joins the Fascist party and is eventually entrusted with a mission to kill one of his former university professors who is now causing trouble for the regime. Director Bernardo Bertolucci's portrait of a man who goes along with those in authority is frighteningly real and much more dangerous than any political fanatic. The central theme of the movie is a cautionary one for any politically threatened society though it has powerful scenes of violence and sexual inferences including that of homosexuality. A-IV (R)

Confrontation (1976) In 1936 a Jewish medical student assassinated the leader of the Nazi Party in Switzerland, an event and an era that this Swiss production has succeeded in re-creating with vivid force. Directed by Rolf Lyssy, the movie does not defend political murder but poses the kind of moral problems individuals must face in a time when injustice is an accepted national policy. A-III (nr)

Conqueror Worm, The (1968) Inept British horror movie about a 17th-century witchhunter (Vincent Price) who combines his delight in human suffering with the profits he makes out of his trade. Directed by Michael Reeves, it offers little more than a series of sadistic episodes. O (br)

Conquest of the Planet of the Apes (1972) This fourth attempt at reworking the same material marks the fatal deterioration of a series that had some good moments. This time around all the apes on earth are abject slaves until a new Moses (Roddy McDowell) leads them in revolt against their cruel masters. Under J. Lee Thompson's direction there is too much violence for youngsters who might otherwise buy this stale stuff but it won't satisfy anyone else. A-III (PG)

Conrack (1974) Jon Voight gives a convincingly exuberant performance as the idealistic white teacher who comes to a remote sea island off the coast of South Carolina to teach the island's black children. The problems he encounters in adjusting to the island's timeless way of life, in reaching his students with useful knowledge and in dealing with suspicious adults and cranky school officials form the core of an unusual and often moving work. Director Martin Ritt does well with a movie that is enjoyable, funny, sad, poignant, full of hope and real feeling for people. A-II (PG)

Contest Girl, The (1966) Superficial British movie debunking beauty contests tells the story of a newspaper editor (Ian Hendry) teaching a nobody

(Janette Scott) the tricks of the beauty game. Produced and directed by Val Guest, the movie and its moral are skin deep. Suggestive costuming and some sexual innuendo. A-III (br)

Continental Divide (1981)   A hotshot Chicago newspaperman (John Belushi) and an ornithologist who studies eagles in the Rockies (Blair Brown) fall in love, though both are lost outside of their chosen habitat. The attempt to resurrect a 1940's type of romantic comedy comes to grief because of Lawrence Kasdan's lackluster script and Michael Apted's uncertain direction. Winks at premarital sex and some brief nudity. A-III (PG)

Conversation, The (1974)   Intricate story about the world of electronic eavesdropping in which a colorless professional bugger (Gene Hackman) is hired to spy on a young couple but then finds himself being spied upon. Directed by Francis Ford Coppola, it is beautifully acted, meticulously paced and of interest because it looks at some of the ambiguities and shades of responsibility in the subterranean area of electronic snooping as practiced by anonymous professionals for hire. Some violence. A-III (PG)

Convoy (1978)   Kris Kristofferson plays a free-spirited trucker who finds himself turned into a folk hero when he leads a group of fellow truckers across state lines in protest against police harassment. Ali MacGraw goes along for the ride. Director Sam Peckinpah lends some visual energy to an otherwise muddled, pretentious and often quite ludicrous movie displaying casual sex and a sophomoric disregard for the law. O (PG)

Coogan's Bluff (1968)   Arizona deputy (Clint Eastwood) runs amok in Manhattan while tracking down an escaped prisoner. Action director Don Siegel emphasizes sex and sadism in a plot based on the premise that law enforcement should not be bound by constitutional restraints. Excessive violence and sex. O (br)

Cool Breeze (1972)   Black exploitation movie traces the generally downhill course of a gang of thieves (Thalmus Rasulala, Raymond St. Jacques, Jim Watkins and Lincoln Kilpatrick). Written and directed by Barry Pollack, it has atrocious dialogue covering every racial stereotype and gripe in the book, flashy violence, gratuitous nudity and a particularly offensive attitutde toward black women. O (R)

Cool Hand Luke (1967)   Paul Newman stars as an independent loner imprisoned in a brutal Southern penal farm who gains the respect of his fellow inmates for standing up to the guards' degrading treatment and cruel punishments. Director Stuart Rosenberg transforms Luke from a pathetic victim of systematic injustice into a symbol of the rebellious spirit that refuses to accept the legitimacy of power. Excellent drama, with well-timed humor relieving the grim situation and a memorable performance by Newman. A few scenes of brutality that some might consider overly realistic. A-IV (br)

Cool Ones, The (1967)   Once-popular singing idol (Gil Peterson) tries to stage a comeback but his struggles are complicated by a budding romance that his manager (Roddy McDowall) threatens to ruin. Director Gene Nelson contributes much ado about nothing. A-I (br)

Cooley High (1975)   Director Michael Schultz' story of young blacks, graduating seniors, in Chicago in the mid-1960s, has some good acting (Glynn Turman and Lawrence-Hilton Jacobs) and

flashes of honesty and insight about ghetto life but its narrative is by turns clumsy and pretentious. More seriously, sexual promisicuity is either played largely for laughs, despite the hurt looks on the faces of the girls cast aside, or, in the case of its hero, given lyrical treatment hard to condone in a work aimed at a young audience. O (PG)

Coonskin (1975)   Ralph Bakshi's animated feature with some live action tells the story of three southern blacks (a rabbit, bear and fox) who go to Harlem, take over the rackets and vanquish a corrupt white policeman and a gross Mafia don's brood of murderous homosexual sons. Though it has some effective scenes of indignation at the squalor and hopelessness of ghetto life, the satire places heavy emphasis upon violent action, brutal caricature and a heavy-handed use of sex. O (R)

Cop, The (1971)   In order to avenge the death of a fellow policeman, an honest cop (Michel Bouquet) takes the law into his own hands, becoming as ruthless as the gangsters he hunts. Director Yves Boisset has made a fast-moving action film, hard-edged in violence, but with all elements completely integrated in expressing his theme of moral and social corruption. A-IV (GP)

Cop-Out (1968)   Failed British murder mystery directed by Pierre Rouve has a generation-gap story of alcoholic lawyer (James Mason) whose neglect of his daughter (Geraldine Chaplin) leads to her joining the wrong crowd. Muddled story line fails to integrate several sexually suggestive sequences and a near rape. O (br)

Cops and Robbers (1973)   Nifty comedy about two New York policemen (Joe Bologna and Cliff Gorman) who hatch the perfect crime in a scheme to steal and sell $10 million in bearer bonds to the Mafia. Director Aram Avakian breaks up the humor by building in some taut sequences showing the risks and demands of day-to-day police work in a big city environment, keeping the viewer from asking the sort of logical questions that might puncture the plot. Stylized violence. A-III (PG)

Corky (1973)   Amateur hotshot speedster (Robert Blake) wants to make the big-time as a professional driver but from the very first scene, when he beats out another car at a stoplight, endangering wife, children, and best friend, it is obvious this is the story of a loser. Directed by Leonard Horn, the track footage has class, the Southern locales and people are evoked quite well and Blake's performance as a man whose delusions lead to inevitable self-destruction is first-rate. A-III (PG)

Cornbread, Earl and Me (1975)   When a black youth (Keith Wilkes) is shot accidentally by two policemen, one black and one white, the city administration engages in a coverup but a lawyer (Moses Gunn), hired by the parents, clears their son's name. Directed by Joe Manduke, the movie deals well with the complexity of black-white relations and has a fine, convincing cast. Mature treatment. A-III (PG)

Corpse Grinders, The (1972)   Felines feeding on a new brand of cat food made from grain, exhumed corpses and freshly dispatched winos acquire a desire to attack their slovenly mistresses. Producer-director-editor Ted V. Mikels has made his dumb little movie in dim, closet-size settings which render transparent any horror that the disgusting plot and mangy characters might suggest. A-III (R)

Corruption (1968)   Routine British thriller directed by Robert Hartford-Davis about a mad doctor (Peter Cushing) who murders women for their pituitary gland in a vain effort to restore the burned flesh of his beloved (Sue Lloyd). Graphic violence. A-III (br)

Corvette Summer (1978) Innocent California high school senior (Mark Hamill) goes to Las Vegas to track down a car stolen from his shop class but things get very complicated once there. Boy meets aspiring hooker (Annie Potts), boy loses girl and regains his former ideals. Director Matthew Robbins' movie shows a much too benign acceptance of the affair between the two youngsters. O (PG)

Cotton Club, The (1985) Big splashy celebration of the famous white-owned, black-talent nightclub that flourished in Harlem in the 1920s and 1930s has some entertaining moments, but it lacks emotional power and fails to mesh its two diverse elements: gangsters and show business. Directed by Francis Coppola with Richard Gere and Gregory Hines heading a good cast, the movie contains some very graphic violence and two restrained bedroom scenes. A-III (R)

Cotton Comes to Harlem (1970) In a high-powered action story focusing on a big-time con game up in Harlem, two bumbling-but-uncanny detectives (Godfrey Cambridge and Raymond St. Jacques) unmask the fraud being worked by a back-to-Africa preacher (Calvin Lockhart). Directed by Ossie Davis, the dialogue and visuals are harsh and raunchy, with a lot of black racial humor and much gore to round things out. A-IV (R)

Cougar Country (1972) Semi-documentary on the life and hard times of a young cougar in the Great American Northwest makes a fine wildlife story, especially the earlier sequences showing the young animal learning to cope with life within its natural habitat. The going gets a little tougher when the grown cougar has to outwit human invaders of its domain. For the young and curious and all who enjoy the world of nature. A-I (G)

Count Yorba, Vampire (1970) Fairly old-fashioned kind of horror movie with an involving, almost believable plot, underplayed stereotypes of good and innocent vs. evil and ghoulish, plus a very effective ending. Director Bob Kelljan suggests more than he shows of the story's sex, blood and violence. A-III (G)

Countdown (1968) Exciting visual exploration of the frantic behind-the-scenes activity surrounding a space launch. James Caan stars as the NASA astronaut whose life as a scientist spaceman is complicated by domestic troubles. Directed by Robert Altman, the location photography in the Houston ground control center and at Cape Kennedy overshadow the otherwise routine drama. A-I (br)

Countdown at Kusini (1976) Directed by Ossie Davis and filmed in Nigeria, the movie's theme of struggle against neo-colonialism in Africa is never treated seriously and leads to no new insights into the old story of exploitation. Its muddled structure and melodramatic plot, however, wreck havoc with its credibility and do little to further the black image on the screen. A-III (PG)

Counterfeit Constable, The (1966) Droll British comedy directed by Robert Dhery about a Frenchman (Dhery) in England on the run from a publicity-seeking actress (Diana Dors), the police and his fiancee. Mild sexual innuendo. A-II (br)

Counterfeit Killer (1968) Routine story of counterfeiters and treasury agents directed by Josef Leytes and with Jack Lord as the undercover man

who infiltrates the gang and Shirley Knight as the waitress who falls in love with him. Fairly graphic violence. A-III (br)

Counterpoint (1968) The fate of an entire symphony orchestra lies in the balance when a German general (Maximilian Schell) insists that they perform a concert and their conductor (Charlton Heston) refuses. Directed by Ralph Nelson, the World War II meldodrama's only merit is its classical music soundtrack. Wartime violence. A-II (br)

Countess Dracula (1972) Aging countess (Ingrid Pitt) discovers quite by accident that her youth is revived by quick dips in virgin's blood. Directed by Peter Sasdy, the horror aspect is lost in a story line in which almost every relationship turns about the anticipation of a nude sexual encounter. O (R/PG)

Countess from Hong Kong, A (1967) The last movie directed by Charlie Chaplin is unfortunately an over-produced, heavy-handed romantic comedy about an impoverished countess (Sophia Loren) who tries to get into the U.S. by stowing away in the stateroom of an American diplomat (miscast Marlon Brando). There are some laughs, mainly from Margaret Rutherford and Patrick Cargill. Sexual inferences. A-III (br)

Country (1984) An Iowa family (Jessica Lange and Sam Shepard) trying to hold on to their farm while burdened with the interest due on massive government loans extended in more prosperous times. Nicely directed by Richard Pearce, it may be a little too predictable and its heroine a bit too courageous and noble, but it's an admirable achievement nevertheless. The only reservation for pre-teens is some humorous by-play occasioned by a contraceptive. A-II (PG)

Country Boy (1966) Randy Boone of TV's "The Virginian" stars in a story of grass roots patriotism. Scenario and catchy country-western songs by Paul Crabtree. A-I (br)

Country Music (1972) Marty Robbins' company put together what is essentially a feature-length commercial for his kind of music. Directed by Robert Hinkle, the best that can be said for it as a movie is that there is a certain fascination in its naive artlessness as well as its unconscious humor. A-I (G)

Country Music Daughter (see: "New Girl in Town")

Coup de Grace (1978) Sober but rather dull German movie about the entangled passions of three German aristocrats set against the chaotic background of post-World War I Latvia. Starring Margarethe von Trotta and Matthias Habich, director Volker Schlondorff's tale of unrequited love and its wasteful consequences is for the patient and mature. A-III (nr)

Coup de Tete (1980) French comedy about a maverick soccer player (Patrick Dewaere) who wins the big match and becomes the hero of his home town which once scorned him as a feckless ne'er-do-well but which now is ready to believe that his conviction for rape was a miscarriage of justice. Though the acting is good and director Jean-Jacques Annaud's flair for satire occasionally hits home, the rape's central place in the plot makes for heavy going in a comedy. A-IV (nr)

Cousin Angelica (1977) A middle-aged man (Jose Luis Lopez Vazquez) returns to the village where he had been a boy during the Spanish Civil War and his recollections help explain his alienation as an adult. Carlos Saura directs the Spanish production with controlled intensity, making the individual's story credible but also using it to show the Spanish character and culture at war with itself. A-III (nr)

Cousin, Cousine (1976) A married man and a married woman (Victor Lanoux and Marie-Christine Barrault) meet at their relative's wedding that makes them cousins and are immediately drawn to each other. The story of marital infidelity that results is an amusing, malicious trifle which has more to do with wish fulfillment than reality. Under the good-humored surface of this French production directed by Jean-Charles Tachella is a pervading acceptance of adultery. Some nudity. O (R)

Covenant with Death, A (1966) Suspenseful drama about an innocent man (Earl Holliman), wrongfully convicted of a crime and sentenced to death, whose fight for his life results in the death of another and a dilemma for a small-town judge (George Maharis). Director Lamont Johnson's lackluster production lets an intriguing moral-ethical-legal premise get lost in side issues. Casual love affair condoning seduction. O (br)

Cover Me Babe (1970) Bad movie about a student filmmaker (Robert Forster) whose wrongheaded ideas about moviemaking alienate his co-workers, girl friend (Sondra Locke) and department instructor (Robert Fields). Directed by Noel Black, the movie suffers many of the faults it seems to be criticizing, including an exploitative emphasis on sex. O (R/PG)

Cowards (1970) Draft-age youth (John Ross), pondering the alternatives to imminent induction, moves in with his girl friend (Susan Sparling) and takes part in a raid to destroy draft files. Writer-producer-director Simon Nuchtern makes light of the moral issues, preferring instead to anchor his hero in absolute confrontations with an overloaded anti-war tract disseminated by supporting characters. A-IV (nr)

Cowboys, The (1972) When the local cowpokes join the Gold Rush to California, a tough old rancher (John Wayne) resorts to hiring some schoolboys (ages 9 to 15) to drive his cattle to the railhead, teaching them the dangerous craft of cow-punching along the trail. In a traditionally violent finale, the young adolescents slaughter a gang of cattle rustlers who have brutally murdered the rancher (one of the rare roles in which Wayne is not invincible). Well directed by Mark Rydell but definitely not for the youngsters or the squeamish. A-III (GP)

Crackers (1984) Donald Sutherland plays the ringleader of an inept band of San Francisco characters who devise an elaborate plot to break into their local pawnshop and repay its cranky owner (Jack Warden) by cracking open his safe. Director Louis Malle spends more time trying to find some new angles on the old caper formula than on character development, a miscalculation that results in a flat, lackluster comedy with some sexual situations and a benign view of petty crime. A-III (PG)

Crazies, The (1973) Backwoods Pennsylvanians go wild when their water supply is contaminated by Army chemicals and they react viciously when troops are sent in to pacify them. Directed by George A. Romero, the title belongs to the moviegoers who would sit through this frantic, inconclusive, blood-spurting exercise in silly mayhem. A-III (R)

Crazy Joe (1974) Peter Boyle plays the late Joe Gallo, a maverick Brooklyn mobster who paid for his crimes with his life, thanks to the mob's rough system of instant justice. Director Carlo Lizzani's movie is grade-A trash in its pretensions on the "noble savage" theme and the dialogue is ridiculous. Worthless, especially in view of its misguided sense of morality. O (R)

Crazy Quilt (1966) Burgess Meredith narrates this offbeat attempt at spanning the whole life of a married couple who have completely different outlooks on life. Producer-director John Korty's use of realistic images in unpretentious, semi-documentary style greatly enhances the movie's keen perceptions of human relationships. Mature themes. A-III (br)

Crazy World of Julius Vrooder, The (1974) Vietnam veteran (Timothy Bottoms) is a genially demented soul in a California psychiatric hospital who continues to live out war game fantasies until a comely nurse (Barbara Seagull Hershey) solves his problems by applying large doses of affection. Directed by Arthur Hiller, it's all attractively packaged nonsense but glazed with a gooey sweetness that may thrust some viewers into diabetic comas. Some rough language. A-III (PG)

Crazy World of Laurel and Hardy, The (1969) Compilation of highlights from the comedy team's many shorts and features from 1927 through the 1940s. The boys are still irresistable as their simpleminded logic reduces a seemingly rational universe to complete absurdity. Short on narration, the excerpts emphasize their two-reelers, most notably "The Music Box," their only Academy Award-winner. Though their work still plays on television, they are seen to best advantage on the big screen. A-I (nr)

Creator (1985) Harry (Peter O'Toole), the hero of this sentimental comedy-drama directed by Ivan Passer, is a Nobel laureate widely believed by his jealous rivals to be a bit over the hill. Constantly talking about God and the Big Picture, Harry is obsessed with, among other things, finding a way to clone his dead wife. Though it deals with ideals, the movie undercuts them by its lack of discipline and its tendency to veer off into excess, especially scenes involving nudity and graphic sexuality. O (R)

Creature with the Blue Hand (1972) Murky German mystery based on an Edgar Wallace novel in which a man (Klaus Kinski) is unjustly committed to an insane asylum, then allowed to escape so that he might be blamed for a series of murders. Director Alfred Vohrer employs rats and serpents, secret passageways and poisoned potions, stodgy police inspectors and shadowy villains in a fast-paced tale that cares little for clarifying motives amidst all the dark doings. A-III (GP)

Creatures the World Forgot (1971) British story of the struggle between twin brothers for leadership of a prehistoric band of nomads and the love of primitive pin-up girl Julie Ege. It's entirely forgettable entertainment from director Don Chaffey, but there is enough violence and buttock-and-bosom shots for parents to strongly discourage their youngsters from seeing. A-III (GP)

Creepers (1985) Maniac terrorizes a Swiss girls' school in this inept Italian horror movie written and directed by Dario Argento. Profusion of blood and gore. O (R)

Creeping Flesh, The (1973) Fair British horror

movie about Victorian brothers (Peter Cushing and Christopher Lee) who find the bones of a giant human skeleton that grow flesh when they get wet and their trying to cash in on their discovery results in a predictable ending. Directed by Freddie Francis, horror buffs will find this adequate fare for a rainy day. A-III (PG)

Creepshow (1982) Screenwriter Stephen King and director George Romero join forces in this omnibus of five horror stories, each featuring an abundance of disgusting gore. Although an undercurrent of humor runs through each story, there is a nasty edge to the movie, especially in its depiction of graphic violence. O (R)

Creepshow 2 (1987) Producer-writer George Romero resurrects the pulp horror form in this group of three tales based on Stephen King ghost stories. Light on fright and nudity but heavy on sadistic violence, the moral lessons of the gory fables are bogus and not worth the viewing effort. O (R)

Crescendo (1972) British melodrama in which a writer (Stefanie Powers) researching the life of a famous composer is invited by his widow (Margaretta Scott) to visit her estate and soon discovers herself in the middle of some very kinky goings-on involving sex and drugs. Unfortunately, director Alan Gibson never manages to work up much interest in the proceedings, let alone the intensity of the title in the disappointing climax. A-III (R/PG)

Cria! (1977) Fragile 9-year-old (Ana Torrent) lives with her ultraconservative family in a big house in Madrid where she mourns the death of her mother and ponders the actions of the adults around her. In attempting to present a child's view of the world, Spanish director Carlos Saura shows that while childhood is not all oblivious innocence, children do have a resilience enabling them to bounce back from all but the most traumatic experience. Brief non-erotic nudity. A-III (nr)

Cries and Whispers (1973) Director Ingmar Bergman presents an anguished study of four women, each representing a different aspect of woman as victim. Harriet Anderson plays a spinster deprived of love from the time she was a child; Ingrid Thulin has been destroyed by marriage and five children who mean nothing to her; Liv Ullmann is the empty-headed coquette who must attract everyone but who can be faithful to none; and Kari Sylwan who is the simple, uneducated maid who is the only one capable of an active, outgoing love. It is filled with emotional insights but it takes a dark view of human nature in an alienated world. A-IV (R)

Crime and Passion (1976) A dark and murky murder comedy filmed in Austria about an unscrupulous financier (Omar Sharif) who encourages his assistant (Karen Black) to marry one of the world's richest men so she can bail him out when his speculations go bust. Director Ivan Passer loses control of his plot quite early on and never recovers. Attempted cuteness about sex throughout and some nudity. O (R)

Crimebusters (1979) Terence Hill and Bud Spencer play rough-and-tumble vigilantes who enjoy beating up crooks and so they join the police force and continue on their merry way. Director Enzo Barboni's Italian spoof of American crime melodrama is tediously violent and vulgar in service of heavy-handed social satire. A-III (PG)

Crimes of Passion (1984) Director Ken Russell's sordid and squalid melodrama about a prostitute (Kathleen Turner), a sexually frustrated married man (John Lauglin) and a crazed minister (Anthony Perkins) leads to little but graphic sex and violence. O (R)

Crimes of the Heart (1986) Mutual love and acceptance keep three sisters (Sissy Spacek, Diane Keaton and Jessica Lange) together and help them survive their personal problems in this adaptation of Beth Henley's play. Bruce Beresford's direction elicits performances of insight, tenderness and forgiveness. Casual attitude toward infidelity and some crude language. A-III (PG-13)

Crimson Cult (1970) Noteworthy only as Boris Karloff's last major screen appearance, the weak British horror movie concerns a local expert in witchcraft (Karloff) who investigates the mysterious disappearance of a young man. Directed by Vernon Sewell, the plot elements involve ancient cults, witch-burning ceremonies, strange dreams and a brief love affair. A-III (PG)

Critical Condition (1987) Richard Pryor is the failed con man who tries to plead insanity to avoid going to prison where he's sure to be killed by the mobsters with whom he inadvertently got busted when undercover cops caught them making a deal. Director Michael Apted's keen social satire contrasts the insane patients and the insane administrators of the institution. Although the language is vulgar and incessantly harsh, its message about personal and professional integrity is significant. A-III (R)

Critters (1986) Small, fuzzy space aliens invade a small farm community and terrorize a captive family of four who ultimately vanquish the hungry little beasts with the help of two space bounty hunters. The critters might give young children the jitters as they grow and ferociously bite everything in sight, and there is subtitled profanity in an otherwise mildy amusing sci-fi movie. A-II (PG-13)

Crocodile Dundee (1986) Central premise of this Australian comedy is the clash of cultures when a wild and woolly crocodile hunter from Down Under (Paul Hogan) visits New York City accompanied by an attractive journalist (Linda Kozlowski) assigned to do a human interest story on the Crocodile Man. Director Peter Faiman is more concerned about fashioning a vehicle showcasing Hogan's charming mannerisms than about achieving the lighthearted romance the movie pretends to be. Mild satire of some of the seamier sides of urban life. A-II (PG-13)

Cromwell (1970) Alec Guinness and Richard Harris star as king and commoner in the British Civil War of 1640-49. Director Ken Hughes succeeds in telescoping the wide reaches of the action into a manageable sequence of events centering on the two principals. The lavish historical spectacle, the issues it raises and the competence of its performances make interesting viewing, especially for those studying its history in school. A-I (G)

Crook, The (see: "Simon the Swiss")

Cross and the Switchblade, The (1970) Fact-based dramatization about David Wilkerson, a Protestant minister from rural Pennsylvania, who converted two rival Harlem gangs by the power of his personal dedication and forceful preaching. Directed by Don Murray and starring Pat Boone, it is honest and sincere in its message that the cure for drugs, slums and youthful rebellion is to be found in the simple acceptance of religious faith. A-II

(GP)
Cross Creek (1983)   Screen biography of author Marjorie Kinnan Rawlings ("The Yearling") begins in 1928 when Rawlings (Mary Steenburgen) walks out on an unhappy marriage and drives to the tiny settlement of Cross Creek, Florida, where she finds herself as a writer. Directed by Martin Ritt, the movie vividly evokes the period and place, has solid acting and is centered in a compassionate regard for human values. A-II (PG)

Cross My Heart (1987)   Blatant sex comedy about two young singles (Annette O'Toole and Martin Short) who wind up in bed on their third date. Directed by Armyan Bernstein, there are some comic moments but the seduction and sex scenes are heavy-handed and sour. Nudity, simulated sex and rough language. O (R)

Cross of Iron (1977)   World War II movie about a hardened yet humane German Army sergeant (James Coburn) who finds himself fighting not only the Russians but his glory-hungry company commander (Maximilian Schell) as well. Though Sam Peckinpah directs the action with convincing authenticity, the movie proves little more than a sophomoric celebration of nihilism and the bond that shared hardship forges between males. Much violence, some nudity and brutality in a sexual context. O (R)

Crossed Swords (1978)   Director Richard Fleischer's version of Mark Twain's "The Prince and the Pauper" wisely exploits its potential for romance and spectacle. Starring Mark Lester in the dual role of the street urchin who trades places with the Prince of Wales, the story provides sound lessons in trust and loyalty. Well-mounted historical production and good performances from a fine cast (George C. Scott, Rex Harrison, Charlton Heston and Oliver Reed) but there is some graphic violence. A-II (PG)

Crossplot (1970)   Harried ad agency executive (Roger Moore) is romantically involved with a model (Claudie Lang) who knows too much about a forthcoming assassination planned by her aunt, Martha Hyer. Shallow but diverting intrigue with a lot of fast action, a dash of violence and nudity, some beautiful photography of the English countryside and a few good laughs. A-III (PG)

Crossroads (1986)   This musically-inclined teen romance relates the story of an aspiring adolescent music student who frees an old blues musician from confinement in a nursing home and helps him win back his soul from the Devil. Walter Hill's musical allegory about determination and growing up is weakened by rough language and a permissive attitude toward casual adolescent sex. A-III (R)

Crucible of Horror (1971)   Eerie British horror item about a sadistic father (Michael Gough) whose pretty daughter (Sharon Gurney) and long-suffering wife (Yvonne Mitchell) hatch a scheme to be rid of the old man. Director Viktors Ritelis keeps the proceedings taut until the last 20 minutes when it becomes just another routine chiller. A-III (GP)

Cruising (1980)   Al Pacino plays an undercover cop assigned to find a killer who preys upon homosexuals in New York City's sado-masochistic underground. Murky, muddled movie from director William Friedkin depicts a series of gory murders, male nudity and bizarre sexual practices without a single redeeming bit of humanity anywhere to be found. O (R)

Cry Blood, Apache (1971)   Irate Indian stalks the gold-seeking murderers of his family who also abducted his sister and only Jody McCrea, who protects the girl from the lecherous prospectors, will survive his revenge. Directed by Jack Starrett, it's a terribly tedious little Western with failed pretensions of being something more. Some nasty violence. A-III (R)

Cry Freedom (1987)   The story of Steve Biko (Denzel Washington), a black South African leader who died in 1977 from police mistreatment, is told by Donald Woods (Kevin Kline), a white editor who had to escape from his native land to reveal the truth of what had occurred. Director Richard Attenborough's large-scale dramatization re-creates an authentic picture of the enormity of South Africa's racist policy of apartheid and effectively conveys the need for racial harmony in effecting social and political changes in that tragic land. A-II (PG)

Cry of the Banshee (1970)   Mild-mannered medieval witch hunter (Vincent Price) is cursed by an old hag for having killed some of her young followers and his own children begin to die as the curse runs its course. Directed by Gordon Hessler, the movie relies on graphic shock effects, with blood and gore, torture, promiscuity, nudity and a casual disrespect for life. O (GP)

Cry of the Wild (1974)   Fascinating documentary study of the elusive Arctic wolf, as well as an interesting chronicle of Bill Mason's adventures in photographing these wild creatures. Spending months alone in the Arctic, his perseverance and ingenuity has resulted in some stunning wildlife footage. Its raw picture of hunting and carnage in the wild, and also its matter-of-fact presentation of courting and birth in a wolf pack, suggest it is not for young children unless they see it with their parents. A-II (PG)

Cry Rape (1975)   German movie shot on a low budget with three characters and a single setting in a sensationalized story of sex and brutality. O (R)

Cry Uncle! (1971)   Paunchy New York private detective (Allen Garfield) fornicates his way through half the ranks of the city's netherworld of streetwalkers and porno actresses whilst tracking down a murderous, blackmailing filmmaker. Director John Avildsen apparently intended this to be funny though it is anything but amusing. O (R)

Cuba (1980)   Sean Connery plays a soldier of fortune who arrives in 1959 to help the Baptista regime in it's struggle against Castro's rebels. Connery meets a former love (Brooke Adams), now happily married, and their rekindled relationship provides some unresolved conflict working against director Richard Lester's remarkable evocation of period and setting. Adventure romance contains violence and a desultory striptease in a half-empty night club. A-III (R)

Cujo (1983)   Stephen King's script of his own horror story about a vicious dog that goes on a rampage and eventually threatens a mother (Dee Wallace) and her young son trapped in their car. Lewis Teague directs the mediocre horror movie which has some considerable blood and gore. A-III (R)

Cul-De-Sac (1966)   British thugs threaten a man (Donald Pleasance) and his wife (Francoise Dorleac) in a pointless exercise in terror directed by Roman Polanski. Perverse violence and sex. O (br)

Culpepper Cattle Co., The (1972)   Gary Grimes signs on as the cook's helper for a particularly gritty cattle drive way out in the Old West.

Directed by Dick Richards, the movie reaches a climax of sorts when Grimes and a couple of trigger-happy cowhands decide to make their stand protecting some Quaker squatters, but this degenerates into a pointless bloodbath, making Grimes' final renunciation of the gun a hollow act. A-III (PG)

Curious Female, The (1970) Sex exploitation movie using a frame device of 25th-century voyeurs watching a 20th-century sex exploitation movie. That's as imaginative as it gets. O (R)

Curse of the Vampires (1970) Family honor, religious piety and a romantic love story provide the diverting background of this low-budget Philippine horror movie. Unfortunately, its plot about the father of a noble family who cannot preserve the secret that his mother is a vampire is alternately confusing and unintentionally amusing. A-II (GP)

Custer of the West (1968) Epic-sized Western reduces both the legend of the general (Robert Shaw) and the history of the times to postage stamp dimensions. Filmed in Spain and directed by Robert Siodmak, the re-creation rings as hollow as the motivations of the various characters. Stylized violence. A-II (G)

Cutter and Bone (1981) Bitter, crippled Vietnam veteran (John Heard), despite objections from his neglected wife (Lisa Eichorn), teams up with his best friend (Jeff Bridges), an aging and feckless beach boy, in a quixotic, obsessive attempt to smoke out a fat-cat oil magnate whom they believe to be responsible for the brutal murder of a teenage girl. Director Ivan Passer's uneven thriller contains strong language, violence and a frank depiction of sex. A-III (R)

D

Daddy's Gone A-Hunting (1969) Urban thriller in which a wife (Carol White) and her husband (Paul Burke) are terrorized by her manic ex-boyfriend (Scott Hylands) who seeks revenge for the child that years before she had aborted without his consent. Director Mark Robson manages to work up a little tension in a rather thin story of people living in fear which, together with some silly but non-prurient bits of nudity, make it mature fare. A-III (PG)

Dagmar's Hot Pants, Inc. (1971) Copenhagen prostitute (Diana Kjaer) retires to marry the doctor she has been working to put through medical school. Vernon Becker directs a crash course in boredom with special emphasis on bare female anatomy. O (X/R)

Daisy Miller (1974) Good adaptation of the Henry James story about a rich American (Cloris Leachman) touring Europe with her spoiled son (James McMurty) and impetuous daughter (Cybill Shepard). Directed by Peter Bogdanovich, the slight story is a gentle probe of the American character, but what makes the movie so charming and absorbing is the director's care in visualizing the mannered style of a past age. A-II (G)

Damien—Omen II (1978) Sequel follows Damien the Antichrist (Jonathan Scott-Taylor), now 13 and living with wealthy Chicago aunt and uncle (Lee Grant and William Holden), as the special effects department disposes of everyone who can reveal his secret. Directed with some intelligence by Don Taylor, the horror movie contains some gory violence and a dubious use of scripture. O (R)

Damnation Alley (1977) The survivors of a nuclear holocaust trek across a devastated America in search of a haven in this muddled and unexciting disaster film directed by Jack Smight and starring Jan-Michael Vincent, Dominique Sanda, and George Peppard. Some violence. A-III (PG)

Damned, The (1969) Using the story of a corrupt aristocratic family (Dirk Bogarde, Ingrid Thulin and Helmut Berger) whose immense wealth derives from steel and armaments, director Luchino Visconti has fashioned a picture of the moral decadence within German society that made possible the rise of Hitler. The result has the primitive force of a Wagnerian opera in its mixture of fury and spectacle portraying the obscene lusts not only of the flesh, but of power and greed. Scenes of sexual perversity (incest, child molestation, homosexuality) are repulsive and anti-erotic, all part of a fabric that includes the obscenities of mass murder and unlimited violence on the part of those who ruled totalitarian Germany. Many will find this picture of evil a disquieting experience. A-IV (R)

Dance of Death (1979) Claustrophobic rendering of Strindberg's play about an embittered army captain (Laurence Olivier) commander of a remote and unimportant fortress off the coast of Sweden and his love/hate relationship with his wife (Geraldine McEwan). Director David Giles preserves the relentless pessimism of the play which expresses the dreary results of the couple's inability to find the grace of reconciliation. A-III (G/PG)

Dandy in Aspic (1968) A British secret agent (Laurence Harvey) also happens to be a Soviet double agent but has become expendable to both sides. Directed by Anthony Mann the film is marked by interesting Berlin locales wasted on a confused plot that gets lost in its own web of intrigue. Stylized violence. A-III (br)

Danger: Diabolik! (1968) Based on a European comic strip for adults, this campy Italian import features a cold, humorless thief and escape artist (John Philip Law) who confounds the police with his elaborate ploys and gadgetry. Its attitudes toward authority are cynical rather than satiric and many scenes are sexually suggestive. O (br)

Dangerously Close (1986) Director Albert Pyun's hard-edged depiction of a high school breeding ground for Rambo-styled vigilantes is a disturbing look at what some fear may be a contemporary trend. Starring and co-written by John Stockwell, the drama has no message but its observation of the dread and menace caused by adolescent "law and order" fascists is a cautionary tale. Some violence, brutality and profanity. A-III (R)

Daniel (1983) Fictional treatment of the execution of Julius and Ethel Rosenberg for treason in the 1950s and its effect on their son (Timothy Hutton) as he grows into adulthood in the 1960s, determined to learn the truth about his parents' trial and their guilt or innocence. Sidney Lumet directs a well-intentioned but murky treatment of political events and personal relationships treated in a rather simplistic and romantic manner. It succeeds best, however, in showing the continuity of social justice issues and movements over the last half century. Graphic electrocution scene. A-III (R)

Danny (1979) A little girl (Rebecca Page) acquires a horse, nurses it back to health and then rides it to victory over the nasty and spoiled little rich girl who formerly abused it. Director Gene Feldman's simple tale about the positive effects of caring should appeal to a family audience wishing to sensitize youngsters to the virtues of gentility and compassion. A-I (G)

Danton (1984) Polish director Andrzej Wajda has made a stark and powerful film about the conflict between two leading figures of the French Revolution, the cold ideologue Robespierre (Wojciech Pszoniak) and the warm, passionate humanist Danton (Gerard Depardieu). The dubbed French production is essentially an intimate drama, revolving around the personality of its two protagonists. Although no prior knowledge of the intricacies of this revolutionary period is required, those who want to appreciate all the nuances of the situation may be motivated to do some reading in the history of the time. Some graphic violence. A-II (PG)

Daredevil, The (1972) George Montgomery plays an aging, amoral dirt-track race driver forced by the mob to run heroin shipments across Florida and Terry Moore is the local school teacher who tries to reclaim him. Directed by Robert W. Stringer, the story and action are so inept that some will find it unintentionally entertaining. Some rough language. A-III (PG)

Daring Game (1967) Bubbly underwater action-adventure movie starring Lloyd Bridges, Nico Minardos and Joan Blackman who don rubber suits and flippers in an attempt to rescue a man held prisoner on a desert isle by a banana-Republic dictator. Director Laslo Benedek pumps up the action in attempting to supply some mediocre fun for all. A-I (br)

Dark Crystal, The (1983) Muppet masters Jim Henson and Frank Oz join in directing a Tolkien-like fairy tale about the restoration of a shattered crystal to wholeness which will bring about a never-ending reign of justice and peace. Although its story of good versus evil is a bit thin, the inventiveness of the puppetry and special effects is magical. Some scary moments for the very young. A-I (PG)

Dark of the Night (1986) Lightweight Gothic tale about a woman (Heather Bolton) whose life is saved by the ghost of the former owner of her recently purchased vintage Jaguar. Directed by Gaylene Preston, the New Zealand import plays like a children's mystery devoid of any visual shocks and only mild suspense. A-I (nr)

Dark of the Sun (1967) Sleazy but gripping action-adventure melodrama about the efforts of mercenary soldiers Rod Taylor and Jim Brown to retrieve a fortune in uncut diamonds from their Congo employer's jungle outpost that has fallen into the hands of bloodthirsty rebels. British production directed by Jack Cardiff emphasizes gory slayings, tortures and some sexual situations. O (PG)

Dark Places (1974) British horror movie about a man (Robert Hardy) who inherits the creepy estate of a wealthy maniac and then must defend it against outsiders (Joan Collins, Christopher Lee, and Herbert Lom) looking for the fortune stashed somewhere in the house. Directed by Don Sharp, the dark places are spooky enough for the undemanding horror buff. A dollop of blood and gore and some subtle sex. A-III (PG)

Darker Than Amber (1970) Adaptation of a John MacDonald mystery with Rod Taylor as Travis McGee up to his neck in a tangle of brutal murders that begin when he falls in love with a woman (Suzy Kendall) he tries to protect from killers. Directed by Robert Clouse, the violence and brutality goes beyond bounds of taste and restraint, as do some sex scenes. O (R/GP)

Darling (1965) Realistic British examination of the emptiness that characterizes the purposeless lives of the jet set. Directed by John Schlesinger with unrelenting honesty, the episodic movie follows the rise of a young woman (Julie Christie) through a series of affairs until she marries a wealthy prince whose palace becomes a sterile prison. A-IV (br)

Darling Lili (1970) Uneven musical comedy set in World War I about a London music hall entertainer (Julie Andrews) who feigns romance with an Allied pilot (Rock Hudson) in order to ferret military secrets for the Germans. Produced and directed by Blake Edwards, Andrews' charming performance and the lavish re-creation of the period's rickety automobiles and biplane aircraft are generally pleasing but some love-making scenes and a couple of strip tease numbers place it in the adult category. A-III (G)

Darwin Adventure, The (1972) Jack Couffer directs an historical dramatization of the events that led to Charles Darwin (Nicholas Clay) writing "Origin of Species" with loving attention to the world of nature but little feel for the human conflicts and emotional crises aroused by the scientist's theories. A-II (G)

D.A.R.Y.L. (1985) Sci-fi version of Pinocchio in which government scientists experimenting with artificial intelligence develop a robot that is like a boy in almost every respect. Some nasty higher-ups decide to put an end to the project when the robot transforms into a living boy with loving foster parents. Predictable story line but director Simon Wincer maintains interest and save for a few ill-considered vulgar expletives, it would have been quite suitable for young children. A-II (PG)

Das Boot (1982) Authentic World War II movie about the final cruise of a German submarine in the North Atlantic in the days when U-boats were the terror of Allied convoys. Director Wolfgang Petersen emphasizes the claustrophobic conditions of serving on a sub as well as its dangers, the photography and acting are first rate and the haggard face of the captain (Jurgen Prochnow) is likely to haunt the viewer for some time. For all its virtues as a war movie, the moral dilemma of serving one of the worst causes in history is treated only indirectly. Sexual references and crude language abound in this all-male environment. A-III (R)

Date with an Angel (1987) Plodding romantic comedy about a young man with a brain tumor (Michael E. Knight) who alienates his fiancee (Phoebe Cates) when he rescues an angel with a broken wing (Emmanuelle Beart). Writer-director Tom McLoughlin turns what might have been a lightweight, bouncy comedy into a leaden, earthbound fantasy. Some sexual innuendo, brief nudity and verbal vulgarities. A-III (PG)

Daughter, The (1970) Low-budget sex exploitation movie in which a daughter discovers that her moralizing mother is a sexual hypocrite and gets back at mom by experimenting wildly with all sorts of kinky sex practices. O (nr)

Daughters of Darkness (1971) Delphine Seyrig plays a glamorous 300-year-old vampire in a very bizarre but very stylish horror fantasy directed by Harry Kumel. The Belgian production is a nightmarish study in mood and atmosphere with contemporary settings used to brilliant effect but its explicit treatment of the sexual perversity usually only implicit in such horror movies is offensive. O (R)

Daughters of Satan (1972) Philippine devil cult huff-and-puff their way through a ritual murder of the reincarnated Inquisitor responsible for the burning of three witches in 1592. Innocent of any coherence of plot, acting (Tom Selleck, Barra Grant, Tani Phelps Guthrie) or direction (Hollingsworth Morse), the movie carries the burden of several gratuitous scenes featuring sadism and nudity. O (R)

Dawn of the Dead (1979) Survivors of a previous night of the living dead are now besieged in a shopping mall. George Romero's camp pulp yarn has metaphorical pretensions as social satire but essentially what's on the screen, peppered with rough language, is a relentless exploitation of gore and violence and the repulsive effects of violence. O (R)

Day for Night (1973) Director Francois Truffaut presents an amusing day-to-day diary of how a melodrama gets filmed in a studio on the French Riviera and himself plays the role of the director battling production difficulties while trying to deal with various complications in the (mostly love) lives of his cast (Jacqueline Bisset, Jean-Pierre Leaud, Valentina Cortese and Jean-Pierre Aumont). It not only has some charming comedy, but it provides viewers with a real insight into how movies are made. A-III (PG)

Day in the Death of Joe Egg, A (1972) Intense drama about the parents (Alan Bates and Janet Suzman) of a hopelessly retarded, spastic 12-year-old raises issues of abortion and euthanasia but is hardly a propaganda piece for either faction. Directed by Peter Medak, the ambiguities of its characters and situation are left unresolved and casual moviegoers are likely to find it a difficult, draining and confusing experience. A-IV (R)

Day James Dean Died, The (see: "24 Hours of the Rebel")

Day of Anger (1969) Routine Italian Western about a gunman (Lee Van Cleef) and his hero-worshipping young assistant (Giuliano Gemna) who take over a small town by blackmailing its leading citizens. Directed by Tonino Valeri, bullets fly quite readily but the violence is controlled. A-III (PG)

Day of the Animals (1977) A depletion in the atmosphere's ozone layer provokes Rocky Mountain wildlife into a wholesale attack upon humans. There is some elemental terror and suspense in this silly plot premise but director William Girdler quickly depletes the suspension of disbelief by ineptly staging the resulting violence, including an attempted rape. A-III (PG)

Day of the Dead (1985) Director-writer George Romero's third low-budget zombie chiller provides a loathsome and unimaginative mix of violence, blood, gore and some sexual references demeaning to women. O (nr)

Day of the Dolphin, The (1973) Dedicated scientist George C. Scott, privately funded and working in secret, has begun teaching a dolphin to talk. What he doesn't know is that he and the dolphin are being used by a mysterious clique of powerful officials in an assassination attempt.

Director Mike Nichols' melodramatic plot about the corruption of the innocent is only intermittently interesting but at least the movie serves as a reminder of the accelerated dangers of modern science. A-II (PG)

Day of the Evil Gun (1968) Routine but interesting Western stars Glenn Ford as a long-lost rancher who returns home to find that his wife and child have been carried off by Apaches but that she was about to marry a neighbor anyway. Search for them he must, though, and director Jerry Thorpe packs the ensuing adventures with action, suspense and some stylized violence. A-II (G)

Day of the Jackal, The (1973) Screen version of Frederick Forsyth's novel stars Edward Fox as a professional assassin hired by a rightist group of military officers to murder the President of France. Directed by Fred Zinnemann, this superbly crafted thriller succeeds not only as a gripping action movie but also as a serious probe into a theme of political expediency and amorality. A-III (PG)

Day of the Locust, The (1975) Aspiring artist (William Atherton) plumbs the emotional depths of the glittering Hollywood of the 1930s in director John Schlesinger's adaptation of the Nathaniel West novel about the superficial values and exploitive relationships that bind the Tinseltown community together. Karen Black is one of the victims who works as an extra and is obsessed by the dream of future stardom. Provoking at times, but ultimately a disappointing melodrama, with unnecessarily graphic violence. A-IV (R)

Day That Shook the World, The (1977) Yugoslavian re-creation of the 1914 assassination of the Archduke Ferdinand and his wife (Christopher Plummer and Florinda Bolkan) at Sarajevo, the tragic incident that triggered World War I. Director Veliko Bulajic captures the period atmosphere and historical background but fails to bring its characters to life, the result being merely a colorful but unmoving pageant. Excessively graphic torture sequence. A-IV (R)

Day the Fish Came Out, The (1967) When dying fish surface around a small Aegean island teeming with tourists, it's the result of an accidently jettisoned nuclear weapon contaminating its waters and world doom is forecast. Michael Cacoyannis wrote, produced and directed this satiric morality play starring Candace Bergen and Tom Courteney that tries to do too many things and none of them well. Some sexual references concerning homosexuality. A-III (br)

Daydreamer, The (1966) A little boy runs away from home and has a series of adventures, most of them taking place in his imagination. Jules Bass directs a part-animation, part live-action children's entertainment combining the biblical concept of Paradise with the fancy of Hans Christian Anderson and the result adds up to a diverting fantasy. A-I (br)

Daydreamer, The (1976) French comedy starring Pierre Richard (who also wrote and directed) as an eager but completely absent-minded art director for an advertising agency, where his wacky ideas prove so sensationally successful that they finally arouse the public to violence. In satirizing the vagaries of a consumer society, Richard's talent for remaining oblivious to all the chaos caused by his innocent eccentricities is in the best tradition of visual comedy. Minor romantic complications. A-III (PG)

Days and Nights in the Forest (1973) Indian movie about four men on holiday in a large forest preserve where they meet a number of interesting individuals, not least, two women of wit and intelligence. Director Satyajit Ray's character study offers very little of dramatic action but it is fascinating to observe the interplay of characters who are as authentic as our own circle of friends. A-II (nr)

Days of Heaven (1978) In a drama set in 1916, a Chicago mill worker (Richard Gere), his common-law wife (Brooke Adams) and his kid sister (Linda Manz) work their way West as migrant farm laborers until they are hired by a wealthy Texas wheat grower (Sam Shepherd). Directed by Terrence Malick, there is unfortunately not much in the characterizations or the plot's passionless romantic triangle to match the grandeur of Nelson Alemendros' camerawork and its visual homage to the land and those who work in it. A-III (PG)

D.C. Cab (1983) Fifth-rate taxi company on the verge of extinction suddenly shapes up and plays a heroic role in foiling a kidnapping. Cast includes Gary Busey, Adam Baldwin and Mr. T. Badly written and directed by Joel Schumacher, this vulgar comedy is dreary and unfunny, with foul language and some nudity. O (R)

De Sade (1969) The aging Marquis de Sade (Keir Dullea), in between bouts of prison and the insane asylum, returns to the decaying family mansion where he recalls significant events in his life. Instead of providing any insight into the relationships and misfortunes that formed his character, director Cy Enfield's kindergarten Freud lacks even a thread of intelligibility or coherence. Numerous orgy sequences and a leering depiction of sadism. O (R)

Dead, The (1987) Screen version of a story in James Joyce's "The Dubliners" is a small but beautifully crafted mood piece about a party on Epiphany in 1904 Dublin. After the party, a wife (Anjelica Huston) tells her husband about the death of a boy who loved her when she was a girl and this sets the husband (Donal McCann) to reflecting on the transitory nature of love, life and the world. Director John Huston's warm evocation of the story's characters is helped by the excellent performances of a mostly Irish cast. A few indelicate words and some mature references. A-II (PG)

Dead Are Alive, The (1972) Muddled European thriller about a series of murders occurring around the Etruscan excavations of an archaeologist (Alex Cord) who has some enemies (Samantha Eggar and John Marley). Director Armando Crispino's treatment of the story's abundant sex and violence can only be described as neo-paleolithic. O (R)

Dead Heat on a Merry-Go-Round (1966) Crass ex-con (James Coburn) engineers a bank robbery at the Los Angeles airport timed to coincide with the arrival of the Soviet premier. Directed by Bernard Girard, the emphasis is less on the crime aspects than on depicting its amoral hero who not only gets the loot but ditches his girl friend. Some violence. A-III (br)

Dead Men Don't Wear Plaid (1982) Steve Martin playing a 1940's private eye cavorts with famous stars of the period, thanks to some clever editing of footage from old Hollywood detective movies. Affectionate and moderately entertaining spoof directed by Carl Reiner, it's a one-joke movie, but the joke holds up fairly well. Some sexually oriented jokes. A-III (PG)

Dead of Summer (1971) Wealthy neurotic American (Jean Seberg), in a desolate Moroccan city beset by sweltering heat and a howling sandstorm, spends the day in her elegant apartment (with broken air conditioner) making various attempts to communicate with others. Director Nelo Risi's boring existential study has several needlessly extended erotic sequences. O (R)

Dead of Winter (1987) Aspiring actress becomes the pawn in a blackmail attempt which proves fatal to her captors and to the rich woman who's the target of their extortion. Director Arthur Penn's unconvincing thriller features Mary Steenburgen in a triple role. Unnecessarily explicit violence at the conclusion makes the film unsuitable for youngsters. A-III (R)

Dead Run (1969) Petty German pickpocket steals some secret government papers and becomes the target for undercover agents all over Europe. Humdrum foreign intrigue melodrama starring Peter Lawford and directed by Christian-Jacque, it's only saving feature is that it does not take itself seriously. Scenes of violence and torture and one featuring a strip tease. O (R)

Dead Zone (1983) Good screen version of the Stephen King novel about a man (Christopher Walken) who awakens after being in a coma for five years to discover that he has the gift of second sight enabling him to tell things of the future and past of anyone with whom he comes into physical contact. Such a gift has its drawbacks, of course, and director David Cronenberg does well in exploring them. More a psychological suspense thriller than a horror film, its strong supporting cast includes Brooke Adams, Tom Skerrit and Herbert Lom. Passably entertaining for a mature audience. A-III (R)

Deadfall (1968) Convoluted tale about a cat burglar (Michael Caine) who, linking up with a married couple of jewel thieves (Eric Portman and Giavanna Ralli), falls in love with the wife which is all right with the husband because he's a homosexual but, than again, maybe he's really her father. Obscure British production directed by Bryan Forbes fails both as action thriller and psychological drama with its implications of incest and homosexual relationships. O (br)

Deadlier Than the Male (1967) Bulldog Drummond detective adventure starring Richard Johnson on the trail of a pretty pair of female assassins (Elke Sommer and Sylvia Koscina) whose specialty is murdering key executives involved in business mergers. Dim-witted British production directed by Ralph Thomas, it offers a frothy mixture of sex and violence adding up to some very distasteful entertainment. O (br)

Deadline (1987) Reporter assigned to Beirut (Christopher Walken) not only loses his big story but gets caught between warring factions and has to flee for his life. Directed by Nathaniel Gutman, the personal story gets lost in the chaos and confusion of the war-torn city whose violence is depicted in realistic, stomach-churning fashion. Much bloody violence with vivid and gruesome scenes of the dead and dying. A-IV (R)

Deadly Affair, The (1967) Screen version of a John Le Carre novel about an aging government agent (James Mason) who, just before retirement, discovers he must carry out one last investigation that probably will shatter whatever small security he has left in life. Director Sidney Lumet gets fine performances from a cast which includes Simone

Signoret, Harriet Andersson and Harry Andrews in this taut British spy thriller for grown-ups. A-III (br)

Deadly Fathoms (1973) Documentary explores the graveyard of sunken ships that were involved in the 23 atomic bomb tests in South Pacific waters near the atoll of Bikini. Despite a no-nonsense narration by Rod Serling, these grotesque monuments to the nuclear age often only serve the purposes of an underseas adventure directed by Michael Harris. A-I (G)

Deadly Friend (1986) A strange but mild-mannered horror movie about a teenager who brings his girlfriend back to life by implanting a computer chip in her brain. She thereupon kills her abusive father and the nasty old lady next door. Director Wes Craven makes little of this or anything else in a dull and pedestrian tale. Restrained violence. A-II (R)

Deadly Hero (1976) After killing an unarmed man (James Earl Jones) who has been terrorizing a cultured musician (Diahn Williams), a violence-prone New York policeman (Don Murray) becomes enraged when his career is put in jeopardy by her telling the truth. Director Ivan Nagy gets convincing performances and evokes the gritty atmosphere of the big city, but his creative energies flag midway and it becomes little more than another woman-stalked-by-terror movie relying on violence and the sexual menace it generates. O (R)

Deadly Trackers, The (1973) Excessively violent story of Western revenge in which a sheriff (Richard Harris) sees his family murdered by a band of outlaws, follows them to Mexico and kills them one by one, until a Mexican sheriff, upholding law and order, kills the American sheriff. Directed by Barry Shear, much of the movie is devoted to bloody fights and shootouts as well as expounding a simplistic notion of law and justice. O (PG)

Deadly Trap, The (1972) Frank Langella and Faye Dunaway play an uneasily married couple living in Paris and troubled by a series of peculiar occurrences that culminate in the disappearance of their two children. Badly failed French suspense thriller directed by Rene Clement, the plight of the two young children might be distressing for some pre-teens. A-II (PG)

Deaf Smith and Johnny Ears (1973) Italian Western filmed in sunny Spain and set in frontier Texas where Anthony Quinn and Franco Nero spend most of their time preventing a particularly nefarious Mexican general from taking over the Southwest. Director Paolo Cavara provides numerous fistfights, shootouts, rattling Gatling guns and lots of explosions, with an occasional visit to the local bordello. A-III (PG)

Deal of the Century (1983) Chevy Chase and Gregory Hines play traveling salesmen selling bargain-basement weaponry to Third World governments and those who are trying to overthrow them. It might have worked as a satire on the illicit arms trade but as a straight slapstick comedy, it is merely disappointing and only sporadically funny. Directed by William Friedkin, it is marred by some outrageous stereotyping of Hispanics, both in Latin America and in this country. A-III (PG)

Dealing: Or The Berkeley-To-Boston Forty-Brick Lost-Bag Blues (1972) Harvard law student (Robert F. Lyons) flies out to Berkeley to pick up a marijuana shipment for the campus pusher

(John Lithgow) and meets a liberated woman (Barbara Hershey) but they run into a corrupt cop (Charles Durning). Directed by Paul Williams, the supposed comedy views pot as amusing and contains nudity and rough language. O (R)

Dear Detective (1978) Two former college classmates, now in their mid-40's, bump into each other (quite literally) and discover that he's still a bachelor (Philippe Noiret) and she's divorced (Annie Girardot). The main source of humor in this French comedy directed by Philippe de Broca is how their romance is complicated by each other's professions—he's a college professor and she's a police inspector. Cheerful little comedy with two charming, talented performers. Some Gallic wit about the war between the sexes and brief partial nudity. A-III (PG)

Dear John (1966) Swedish movie written and directed by Lars Magnus Lindgren is intended to explore the beginnings of a meaningful love relationship through a couple's physical experience of sex. It deals only superficially with the human dimension of its characters and never gets much beyond the physical. Graphic portrayal of sexual activity. O (br)

Death Before Dishonor (1987) Trite, almost propagandistic account of hostilities between Arab terrorists and U.S. Marines assigned to protect a U.S. Embassy in a small Middle Eastern country. Fred Dryer is a clone of Clint Eastwood's "Heartbreak Ridge" gunnery sergeant in this failed drama replete with harsh language, violence and explicit brutality. O (R)

Death by Hanging (1974) Japanese movie made in 1968 presents a scathing attack on capital punishment with the sub-theme of Japanese racist attitudes towards Koreans. Directed by Nagisa Oshima, its originality in structure and technique takes chances in combining documentary and dramatic styles but is unusually successful in making an exciting movie on a most provocative subject. A-III (nr)

Death Collector (1976) Crime syndicate melodrama about a rash but engaging young hoodlum (Joseph Cortese) who refuses to stay in line and suffers the ultimate penalty. Aided by some talented actors, director Ralph De Vito's effort, for all it's low-budget defects, has a tough sense of reality and some intelligence but resorts to excessive violence and some nudity. O (R)

Death Hunt (1981) Lee Marvin plays a grizzled Mountie tracking Charles Bronson, a wrongly accused fugitive, in the 1930's Canadian backwoods, both men aware that they are the last of the old breed upon whom civilization is fast closing in. Routine outdoor melodrama directed by Peter R. Hunt with some rough language and violence. A-III (R)

Death in Venice (1971) Fine adaptation of the Thomas Mann novel in which an artist (Dirk Bogarde), in the twilight of his career and unwilling to chance personal encounters with others, is taken with the beauty of a golden-haired youth, setting off within him an unresolved conflict between mind and body. Directed by Luchino Visconti, it is a movie of character and mood rather than of plot, with the interior drama being much more significant than any external actions. A-III (GP)

Death of a Bureaucrat (1979) Cuban director Tomas Gutierrez Alea fashions a satire on the hypocrisy of government bureaucracy. A widow must retrieve the work card buried with her husband in order to receive her pension. Black comedy with wry moments but a bit too sardonic and cynical for some tastes. A-III (nr)

Death of a Hooker (see: "Who Killed Mary What's'ername")

Death of a Jew (1973) Captured Israeli agent (Assaf Dayan) is befriended by an old Arab policeman (Akim Tamiroff), a promising situation which goes nowhere except to a very predictable conclusion. The 1970 Israeli production is a well-intentioned parable on the brotherhood of man but it is without a shred of insight into people or politics and the direction of Denys de la Patalliere is hopelessly lackluster. A-III (PG)

Death of an Angel (1986) This unconvincing drama attempts to contrast a rationalistic vs. charismatic approach to matters of faith. An Episcopal priest (Bonnie Bedelia) confronts her doubts about her own religious belief and the integrity of a seemingly dishonest faith healer (Nick Mancuso) patronized by poor, destitute and crippled Mexican peasants. In addition to several instances of harsh language, writer-director Petro Popescu offers several scenes of needless sadistic brutality and ambiguous sexual references. O (PG)

Death of a Gunfighter (1969) Western town trying to attract Eastern industry wants to get rid of its tough, old-fashioned sheriff (Richard Widmark) but he won't resign. So, in the interest of civic progress, the town fathers decide to have him gunned down. Though given little to do, Lena Horne as a madam who marries the sheriff is a real asset. This period of transition for the Old West makes an interesting setting for a movie that under Allen Smithee's direction is only fitfully successful either as Western or as social document. Adult material and violence. A-III (PG)

Death of Tarzan, The (1968) This Czechoslovakian version of the Tarzan legend has the ape-man return to Europe in order to make its point that human society can be more predatory than that of the jungle. A dark comedy directed by Jaroslav Balik, it nevertheless demonstrates that love is a more basic part of human nature than greed or violence. A-II (br)

Death on the Nile (1978) An heiress (Lois Chilez) is murdered on a honeymoon cruise up the Nile and Hercule Poirot (Peter Ustinov), Agatha Christie's Belgian sleuth, is on hand to interrogate such suspects as Bette Davis, Angela Lansbury, Maggie Smith, Mia Farrow and George Kennedy. Directed by John Guillermin, it is an intricately plotted whodunit that plays the game fairly in laying out clues to challenge the mystery fan. A lavishly produced 1930's period piece with exotic Egyptian locales, it's solid escapist entertainment for those who don't mind rather graphic depictions of murder. A-III (PG)

Death Race 2000 (1975) Satire about the American passion for violence and speed set against the background of a transcontinental auto race in the year 2000 when America is ruled by a dictatorship whose main method of control is the bread and circus device. Director Paul Bartel exploits what supposedly he is satirizing, including an unneeded sampling of sex and nudity. O (R)

Death Rides a Horse (1969) After a gruesome opening in which a small boy watches his whole family brutalized and killed by outlaws, director Giulio Petroni's Italian Western moderates the violence as it follows the pursuit of the killers by the boy (John Phillip Law) 15 years later. While it's somewhat lower on the violence scale than many others of the genre, it also registers fairly low on the scale of originality. A-III (M)

Death Ship (1980) George Kennedy and other unfortunates perform in a witless story about a Nazi ghost ship that roams the Atlantic ramming passenger ships and seeking the blood of the survivors to keep its ghoulish act going. Besides considerable gore and violence, director Alvin Rakoff's horror movie trades upon memories of the Holocaust to give substance to it's cheap and grisly thrills. O (R)

Death Valley (1982) Homicidal maniac (Steve McHattie) menaces a young boy (Peter Billingsley) in a terribly inept thriller that starts out like "Kramer vs. Kramer" and ends up like "The Texas Chainsaw Massacre." Directed by Dick Richards, it trafficks in explicit violence, bloodshed and nudity. O (R)

Death Wish (1974) New York executive (Charles Bronson) sets about avenging the vicious assaults upon his wife and daughter by systematically doing away with the criminal population of the city. Director Michael Winner treats his judge-and-jury actions as if they were an admirable example of civic consciousness. Objectionable are not only the movie's incessantly bloody visuals but even more so its dangerous vigilante message. O (R)

Death Wish II (1982) Charles Bronson reprises his role of the decent citizen turned murderous vigilante in a sequel utterly condoning unlawful actions. Directed by Michael Winner with graphic violence, including sexual violence. O (R)

Death Wish III (1985) Urban vigilante Charles Bronson again mows down felons in this third outing directed by Michael Winner with a variation on the theme increasing the body count to the point of utter absurdity. Unremitting and exploitative violence, including sexual violence. O (R)

Deathmaster (1972) Stale story of a vampire (Robert Quarry) who employs brainless hippies to bring victims (Bill Ewing and Brenda Dickson) to his isolated beach mansion. Lifelessly directed by Ray Danton, the movie indulges in some raw dialogue and a bit of coy nudity. A-III (PG)

Deathtrap (1982) A washed-up playwright (Michael Caine) contemplates murdering an up-and-coming one (Christopher Reeve) and stealing his play in this competent if uninspired movie version of Ira Levin's Broadway comedy-thriller. Though it drags and its ending is weak, director Sidney Lumet gets first-rate performances from a cast including Dyan Cannon and Irene Worth. Rough language. A-III (PG)

Debut, The (1971) Quiet little Russian comedy about a young woman worker who is selected to play Joan of Arc in a movie production and her affair with a married man. Director Gleb Pantilov gently contrasts proletarian life and attitudes with those of the official class of state artists and functionaries. A-III (nr)

Decameron, The (1971) Italian director Pier Paolo Pasolini's adaptation of some tales from Boccaccio's 14th-century volume of 100 stories is faithful to the original in burlesquing religious beliefs and practices in favor of the joys of the natural life, especially those relating to sex and greed. Though splendid in its robust evocation of Renaissance Italy, its explicit visualizations of sexual encounters is seriously offensive. O (X)

Decline and Fall of a Birdwatcher (1969) Delightful screen version of Evelyn Waugh's 1928 novel about a naive school teacher (Robin Phillips) who becomes involved with the elegant Lady Margot Beste-Chetwynde (Genevieve Page) and her vice ring and winds up taking the rap for her and going to prison. Director John Krish has caught the satirically solemn flavor of the original and his fine British cast never cracks a smile in carrying on with Waugh's outrageous lampooning of English high and low life. Stylish comedy even for those who don't usually like British humor. A-III (PG)

Deep, The (1977) Screen version of Peter Benchley's novel about an unmarried couple (Jacqueline Bisset and Nick Nolte) whose scuba diving on a Bermuda vacation leads to sunken treasure and the help of a salvage expert (Robert Shaw) in outwitting a crew of black villains (led by Louis Gosset). Simpleminded but clunky melodrama directed by Peter Yates, it has at least the Bermuda scenery and underwater photography to recommend it. Otherwise it makes much of a blissful premarital relationship, stereotypes blacks as threats, offers a particularly brutal fight scene and mixes an abundance of highly calculated titillation with sexual menace. O (PG)

Deep End (1971) London adolescent (John Moulder-Brown) gets a job in a public bathhouse, becomes involved with one of the girl attendants (Jane Asher) and ruins his life and hers. Directed by Jerzy Skolimowski, the seedy environment is of more interest than the human characters within it. Some bizarre, graphic sex scenes. O (R)

Deep in the Heart (1984) A rape victim (Karen Young) gains vengeance upon the rapist (Clayton Day), an amoral but respectable attorney who is a gun enthusiast, by learning how to use a pistol and then turning this symbol of male dominance against him. Directed by Tony Garnett, this British production relies on exploitative violence and nudity. O (R)

Deep Red (1976) David Hemmings stars in a badly acted, worse dubbed Italian horror movie in which director Dario Argento devotes most of his attention to depicting a series of gory, sadistic murders. O (R)

Deep Throat (1972) This is the first thoroughly hardcore porno feature to receive a sophisticated national promotion campaign, enabling it to reach beyond the porno theater circuit. It is not about cough remedies. O (X)

Deep Thrust—The Hand of Death (1973) Mindless Hong Kong Kung Fu story about a woman's revenge on the man who seduced her sister. Directed by Heang Feng, it is explicit in its physical violence almost to the point of nausea. O (R)

Deer Hunter, The (1979) Three small-town steel-workers (Robert De Niro, Christopher Walken and John Savage) have their mettle tested by the horrors of Vietnam in director Michael Cimino's harsh evocation of the effects of war on friendship and spirit. Somewhat racist and chauvinistic treatment and the film's brutal and intense moments of violence play on gut emotions overriding any serious intent to explore the painful tragedy of Vietnam. O (R)

Defector, The (1966) Muddled espionage story about an American scientist (Montgomery Clift) recruited as a CIA spy and an East German scientist (Hardy Kruger) recruited by the Reds to get him to defect. Directed by Raoul Levy, the plot has some gaping holes and the Cold War politics are heavy-handed. Mild violence and romance. A-II (br)

Defiance (1980) Young merchant seaman (Jan-Michael Vincent) leads the terrorized residents of a New York ghetto neighborhood in a vigilante assault on their tormentors. The oft-told tale, directed by John Flynn, is run-of-the-mill entertainment with some graphic violence. A-III (PG)

Degree of Murder (1969) German crime melodrama about a waitress who casually recruits two young men to help her dispose of the body of an ex-lover she has just as casually, though accidentally, killed. Director Volker Schlondorff's study of unfeeling, amoral youth emphasizes the matter-of-fact hedonism of the three as they enjoy themselves while going about their grisly errand. The treatment of these incidents is excessively graphic and undermines whatever serious intentions the movie may have had. O (R)

Deliverance (1972) Screen version of the James Dickey novel about four Atlanta businessmen (Burt Reynolds, Jon Voight, Ned Beatty and Ronny Cox) who decide to spend a weekend canoeing down a hazardous mountain river on a wilderness journey that turns into a nightmare. Director John Boorman's powerful and absorbing adventure piece tries fitfully to provide some insights on masculinity, civilization and nature. Those deciding to take the trip should be prepared for some harrowing violence and a brutal homosexual assault. A-IV (R)

Delta Force (1986) Lee Marvin and Chuck Norris replay the 1985 Lebanese hijacking of an American airliner in a fictional account portraying a U.S. Army Special Forces team successfully routing Arab terrorists while rescuing every American hostage. Excessive violence, unacceptably justified by patriotic fervor, runs consistently throughout the film. O (R)

Delusions of Grandeur (1975) Set in 17th-century Spain, this costume drama from director Gerard Oury stars Louis De Funes whose frenetic zest carries the comedy about avarice and pride. As the dismissed minister of finance for the Spanish king, he concocts an absurd plot whereby his valet (Yves Montand) is to make compromising advances to the beautiful queen. Innocent, light farce in French with English subtitles. A-II (PG)

Demon (1977) Inept thriller about a New York detective (Tony Lo Bianco) trying to solve the mystery behind an outbreak of random murders in which the killers say that God told them to do it. Directed by Larry Cohen, the movie is marked by violence, nudity and a tawdry use of religious references. O (R)

Demon Seed (1977) Proteus IV, a thinking computer, focuses on the problem of giving its mind a body and propagating itself with the unwilling assistance of the wife (Julie Christie) of its creator (Fritz Weaver). The special effects are exceptional but director Donald Cammell's treatment dwells on the vulnerability of a helpless woman, in the degrading context of its depiction of procreation via computer. Brief nudity and some profanity. O (R)

Demons (1974) Masterless samurai, duped by a woman out of the money he needs to redeem his honor, sets out on a rampage of violence to revenge himself on everyone associated with his betrayer. Directed by Toshio Matsumoto, its theme is the senseless wastefulness of any code of "honor" based on revenge. Stylized violence. A-III (R)

Deranged (1974)   Robert Blossom plays an aging Mama's boy in a sick study of incestuous necrophilia, with Cosette Lee as the late object of his present affection, and a host of unknowns filling in as his erstwhile victims. Directed by Jeff Gillen, the grisly movie lives up to its title. O (R)

Derby (1971)   Documentary by Robert Kaylor on the Roller Derby in Dayton, Ohio, focuses on the players, the hopefuls and the fans. Though it contains some unexpected humor and pathos, the violence and crude appeal of the sport is what it's all about. A-III (R/GP)

Dersu Uzala (1978)   Russian production about the friendship that grows between a turn-of-the-century explorer in Siberia and his guide, an aging Tungus hunter whose name gives the film its title. Japanese director Akira Kurosawa concentrates on evoking the vast remoteness of the Siberian wilderness, a world the Russian finds forbidding but one in which the hunter is perfectly at home. Finely acted, beautifully photographed, it is an admiring portrait of a man living in harmony with nature and with his fellow hunters. A-I (G)

Desert Bloom (1986)   An idealistic young girl (Annabeth Gish) runs away from her family she has tried to keep together when she sees her father (Jon Voight) making a drunken pass at her visiting aunt (Ellen Barkin). Set in Las Vegas during the 1950s era of atomic testing, the movie by first-time director Eugene Coor expresses the adaptability and resilience of a compassionate teenager's growing maturity as she returns to try to bring her troubled parents back together. Brief scene of domestic violence. A-II (PG)

Desert Hearts (1986)   Awaiting the finalizing of her divorce at a ranch near Reno, Nev., a 1950's professional woman creates a new self-image during a sexual relationship with a younger woman. Director Donna Deitch's very personal romantic vision treats homosexuality as basically a matter of sexual preference and sex as the fundamental basis for a meaningful commitment between the film's main characters. Lengthy nude scene. O (R)

Deserter U.S.A. (1969)   Swedish production about U.S. servicemen who defected during the Vietnam War to take refuge in Sweden is atrociously acted by the deserters themselves staging "typical" situations. Written and directed by Lars Lambert and Olle Sjogren, the pseudo-documentary's anti-American, anti-establishment bias is excessively heavy-handed and its production values are barely adequate. O (nr)

Deserter, The (1971)   Cynical Western about the U.S. Cavalry's recruiting an Indian-hating deserter (Bekim Fehmiu) to lead a raid against an Apache stronghold. Mediocre Italian production directed by Burt Kennedy, the movie exploits its subject for the sake of brutish violence. O (GP)

Despair (1979)   Expatriate White Russian (Dirk Bogarde) living in Berlin prior to Hitler's takeover, grows in madness and desperation, eventually killing a stranger and trying to change his identity. Portrait of a fragmented psyche from director Rainer Werner Fassbinder based on the Vladimir Nabokov novel also delves deeply and graphically into the anti-hero's sexual perversities. O (nr)

Desperados, The (1969)   Substandard Western about an outlaw family fathered by a mad, Bible-quoting parson (Jack Palance) who vows vengeance against his son (Vince Edwards) when he decides to go straight. Under Henry Levin's direction, everyone concerned looks embarrassingly ridiculous in a movie that emphasizes violence and toys with nudity, suggestive costuming, prostitutes and a little aberrant sex thrown in for good measure. O (M)

Desperate Characters (1971)   Middle-class, childless couple (Shirley MacLaine and Kenneth Mars) live comfortably in New York City until urban realities of crime and vandalism begin to unravel their sense of security. Written and directed by Frank D. Gilroy, there is a hollow staginess about this affluent but loveless couple that makes it difficult to share their plight. Graphic, violent and, yes, desperate bedroom scene. A-IV (R)

Desperate Ones, The (1968)   Uneven melodrama about two Polish brothers (Maximilian Schell and Raf Vallone) who escape from a Siberian labor camp during World War II and, as they make for the Afghanistan border, elude the NKVD, survive the elements and have improbable love affairs. Directed by Alexander Ramati, it has some good moments but its sentiments are too often cloying. A-III (br)

Desperately Seeking Susan (1985)   A New Jersey housewife (Rosanna Arquette) exchanges identities with a Manhattan playgirl (Madonna) in this screwball comedy directed by Susan Seidelman. Bright at moments but for the most part limp. Benign view of adultery and some exploitation of nudity. O (PG-13)

Destroy All Monsters (1969)   It is 1999 and such monsters as Godzilla and Rodan have been exiled to Monsterland in remote Oceania from which they are unleashed by space aliens who want to make Earth their new home. Director Ishiro Honda's model work and special effects are unconvincing but fun for those who liked earlier editions of these Japanese monster movies. A-I (G)

Destructors, The (1974)   Drug-syndicate thriller about a Paris-based U.S. narcotics agent (Anthony Quinn) who goes outside the law to nab the heads of rival syndicates (Michael Caine and James Mason). Directed by Robert Parrish, it is for those who like escapist action entertainment. Some violence in an amoral atmosphere. A-III (PG)

Detective, The (1954)   British adaptation of the adventures of G.K. Chesteron's amateur sleuth, Father Brown. Directed by Robert Hamer and with Alec Guinness in the title role, the movie offers a dandy mystery and some intelligent entertainment. A-I (br)

Detective, The (1968)   Tough but honest New York cop (Frank Sinatra) has a number of problems, including railroading an innocent psychotic into the electric chair and a bad marriage to a nymphomaniac (Lee Remick). Gordon Douglas' flat-footed direction bludgeons home its condemnation of big city crime and corruption, mostly through rather lurid depictions of homosexual practices and much crude language. O (br)

Detective Belli (1971)   Failed Italian crime melodrama in which crooked Rome cop (Franco Nero) supplements his paycheck by keeping the precocious son of a rich lawyer (Aldolfo Celli) out of harm's way. The plot is jumbled enough without director Romolo Guerreri adding to the confusion with jump cuts, flashy zooms and ragged editing. Stylized violence and brief nudity. A-III (R)

Detour (1969)   Touching Bulgarian story of a chance meeting of two former lovers who had had a brief affair 17 years before when they were idealistic college students. Their nostalgic remembrances are told succinctly and with restraint, while their renewed affections and awkward present situations are handled sympathetically and with grace. A-III (PG)

Detroit 9000 (1973) The title is the signal used by the Detroit police force to indicate an officer in need of assistance and the predictable story is of a cop (Alex Rocco) who doesn't want any assistance, let alone that of the black partner (Hari Rhodes) assigned him. Director Arthur Marks handles the action and supertough dialogue quite well, although the constant grittiness of both is eventually enervating. Excessive violence and brief nudity. O (R)

Devil and Max Devlin, The (1980) Sour owner of a rundown apartment house (Elliott Gould) plummets into hell after being struck by a bus while in pursuit of a jogger behind in his rent. Fiendishly unfunny fantasy has Satan's left-hand man (Bill Cosby) offer him a deal to escape damnation if he delivers the souls of three young people. Disney movie directed by Steven Hill Stern gives Cosby next to nothing to do and Gould, especially charmless here, has far too much. Some mild vulgarity. A-II (PG)

Devil by the Tail (1969) Breezy, exhuberant French comedy about a once-noble family who maintain their ancient chateau by running it as a hotel, helped by the local garage mechanic's disabling passing automobiles, one of which belongs to a bank robber (Yves Montand) whose loot could permanently solve the family's financial woes. Directed by Philippe de Broca, the plot weaves in and out of comic situations with amazing speed and vivacity. Its amoral and unscrupulous stereotyped characters are in the great tradition of frothy farce. Adult situations. A-III (PG)

Devil Doll (1936) Using a deceased scientist's discovery for shrinking animals and people to fountain-pen size, Lionel Barrymore seeks revenge on his former banking partners who framed him and sent him to prison. Director Todd Browning's horror classic offers a fine cast in a good story supported by some ingenious special effects. A-II (br)

Devil in Love, The (1968) An Italian comedy in which a devil (Vittorio Gassman), sent by Satan to provoke war between Renaissance Florence and the Papal States, falls in love with a princess and loses his diabolical powers. Directed by Ettore Scola, the movie has a sniggering script with a lascivious, overacted central character and nasty jabs at religious figures. Sexually suggestive situations and dialogue. O (br)

Devil in Miss Jones, The (1973) Hardcore porno item boasting limitless artistic pretensions and lush photography, but otherwise as totally degrading to watch as it must have been to enact. O (X)

Devil is a Woman, The (1975) Italian potboiler with Glenda Jackson as the mother superior of what seems to be a cross between a medieval monastery and an early 1960's Italian Holiday Inn. Director Damiano Damiani postulates institutional religion as a repressive force that stifles any sense of self-determination. Not only is the movie hopelessly adrift in depicting religious belief and practice, but its sexual implications are offensive. O (R)

Devil Rider (1971) Low-budget motorcycle movie about a biker gang hanging around Miami Beach and terrorizing two sisters and those who try

to help them. Director Brad F. Grinter exploits an amateur cast with an emphasis on brutality and leering sex. O (R)

Devil within Her, The (1976) After many mysterious complications, a pregnant woman (Joan Collins) gives birth to a murderous baby in a clumsy, repulsive British horror movie directed by Peter Sasdy. Gore and nudity. O (R)

Devil's Bride, The (1968) Adequate British horror movie in which Christopher Lee is the hero in fighting a sect of devil worshippers. Directed by Terence Fisher, there is a lot of hokum about black magic but the forces of good are more than equal to those of darkness. Mild violence. A-II (br)

Devil's Brigade, The (1968) World War II movie based on the training and battle experiences in Italy of the Special Service Force, the forerunner of the Green Berets. William Holden stars in the rather routine men-in-battle epic directed by Andrew V. McLaglen showing the hard work that prepares soldiers for the stress and grimness of combat. Wartime violence. A-III (br)

Devil's Eight, The (1969) A federal agent (Christopher George) springs a group of convicts (led by Ross Hagan) from a Southern prison and cowers them into helping him crack a whiskey-running operation. Producer-director Burt Topper manages to mix questions of law enforcement, racial justice and the hippie philosophy together with scenes of violent action, fast cars and suggestions of promiscuity without any sense of priorities, taste or judgment. O (M)

Devil's Rain (1975) Routine horror movie stars Ernest Borgnine who gives an embarrassingly broad performance in his central role as a satanic recruiter. Director Robert Fuest's gimmick of having most of the cast melt away at the end is in keeping with his lack of interest in the logical and religious nuances of the subject in favor of simple gory visuals. A-III (PG)

Devil's Widow, The (see: "Tam Lin")

Devils, The (1971) Failed British adaptation of the Aldous Huxley novel about the demonic possession of a 17th-century French convent (led by Vanessa Redgrave) and the burning of a local priest (Oliver Reed) for his alleged commerce with the devil. Director Ken Russell's attempts to shock with scenes such as nuns cavorting at the altar in the nude are pathetic both in their imagination and in their execution. O (X/R)

Diamonds (1975) Dull jewel-heist caper with an ex-con (Richard Roundtree) and girl friend (Barbara Seagull Hershey) being recruited by a wealthy London jeweler (Robert Shaw) to break into a mammoth jewelry exchange in Jerusalem. Director Menahem Golan succeeds much better as an Israeli travelogue than as crime melodrama with fleeting nudity and crude language. A-III (PG)

Diamonds Are Forever (1971) This time James Bond's antagonist is intent on cornering the world diamond market in order to finance still worse villainy. British production directed Guy Hamilton lacks the wit and wizardry with which the 007 series began and everything about this entry seems tired including Sean Connery's performance. Usual stylized violence and sexual byplay. A-III (GP)

Diary of a Country Priest (1951) Director Robert Bresson's classic adaptation of the Georges Bernanos novel is a study in anguish, doubt and frustrated zeal set in the bleak Normandy countryside where a dedicated priest tries to revitalize a run-down parish but is regarded with suspicion by the locals. The diary format serves to evoke the interior life of a lonely soul who accepts his trials and ultimately finds peace within himself. The subtitled French production presents aspects of religious faith and human responses that make it ideal for study and discussion. A-II (br)

Diary of a Mad Housewife (1970) Attractive Manhattan housewife (Carrie Snodgrass in a fine performance) rebels against her frustrating domestic life with an egotistical, social-climbing lawyer husband (Richard Benjamin) by acquiring a lover (Frank Langella) who proves an equally unenlightened male chauvinist. Director Frank Perry's exercise in women's liberation issues is ultimately unsatisfying in its melodramatic conclusion with the mental breakdown of its affluent but unfulfilled housewife-victim. Some harsh language and brief nudity. A-IV (R)

Diary of a Schizophrenic Girl (1970) Disappointing dramatization of the recovery of a mentally disturbed patient (Ghislaine D'Orsay) through the ministrations of a woman therapist (Margarita Lozano). Director Nelo Risi's plodding study spends too much time documenting the background and course of illness rather than on the cure. A-III (GP)

Diary of a Shinjuku Burglar (1973) Pretentious Japanese movie uses a young couple's confusion about their sexual identity to supposedly mirror the conflicting realities of the Tokyo student district of Shinjuku. Director Nagisa Oshima uses a number of confusing techniques that don't reflect much of anything for American viewers. Several very graphic sex sequences. O (nr)

Diary of Forbidden Dreams (see "What?")

Did You Hear the One about the Traveling Saleslady? (1968) A corny, cliche-ridden vehicle for comedienne Phyllis Diller who plays a player-piano peddler in a Missouri town circa 1910. Tedious. A-I (br)

Die Laughing (1980) Young cabdriver (Robby Benson who also worked on the screenplay), accused of murdering a famous nuclear scientist, tries to clear himself with the aid of his girl friend (Linda Grovenor) and a monkey. Directed by Jeff Werner, the lame comedy-mystery is mediocre entertainment in every respect. Violence. A-III (PG)

Die, Monster, Die (1966) Weak British horror movie directed by Daniel Haller with Boris Karloff playing a sort of contemporary wizard. Mild violence. A-II (br)

Different Story, A (1978) Failed romantic comedy in which boy meets girl (Perry King and Meg Foster) and, though both are homosexual, they settle down to a happily married life, complete with baby. Directed by Paul Aaron, there are few amusing lines and a good performance from Foster, but its rough language and a nude sequence are excessive. O (R/PG)

Digby, the Biggest Dog in the World (1974) British children's fantasy in which a lonely boy (Richard Beaumont) loses his dog when it consumes a secret growth chemical, expands to the size of three elephants and terrorizes the countryside. Director Joseph McGrath makes the most of a good cast of zanies (Jim Dale, Spike Milligan, Milo O'Shea and Victor Spinetti) who come to the lad's rescue in a shaggy dog story that relies on funny dialogue and comic gesture rather than transparent special effects. For the kids but most parents will

get some enjoyment too. A-I (G)

Dillinger (1973) The crime odyssey of John Dillinger (Warren Oates) through the 1930's Midwest is paralleled with the obsession of FBI agent Melvin Purvis (Ben Johnson) to capture the fear of criminals and the respect of the public. Written and directed by John Milius, the acting and period settings are very good and the special effects are appropriately brutal and eye-catching. Although extremely violent, one should emerge from the experience a little more reflective about our national fascination with guns. A-IV (R)

Diner (1982) Low-keyed, humane and often very funny movie about several young men whose favorite hangout is a diner in 1959 Baltimore. Now in their early twenties, they still want to cling to the carefree life of high school days. Writer-director Barry Levinson has come up with an offbeat and entertaining piece which in its modest way is also a worthwhile one. A major portion of the dialogue is concerned with sex and there is a sequence involving a lewd practical joke. A-III (R)

Dionysus in '69 (1970) Filmed performance of an experimental play loosely based on Euripides depends mainly on its own uninhibited eroticism and the unrestrained participation of the audience. Director Brian De Palma records the proceedings in wave after wave of split-screen nakedness and orgiastic behavior that has little to do with art but seems more related to cheap exploitation. O (nr)

Dirt Gang, The (1972) Rampaging biker gang invades a Western movie set and proceeds to terrorize and otherwise debauch the movie makers until a movie stuntman (Michael Forest) pummels the gang's leader to death in a bike duel. Directed by Jerry Jameson, its combination of sex and violence is grossly offensive. O (R)

Dirty Dancing (1987) Coming-of-age story set in the 1960s about a middle-class girl (Jennifer Grey) and a local dancer (Patrick Swayze) who teaches her a few bold new steps. Director Emile Ardolino's lightweight effort at evoking the teen scene of a generation ago uses an ill-conceived plot contrivance about an abortion, brief nudity and an acceptance of casual sex. A-III (PG-13)

Dirty Dingus Magee (1970) Western spoof with Frank Sinatra in the title role as an outlaw involved with a town whose mayor (Anne Jackson) is also a madam whose brothel business thrives on a cavalry clientele and to keep them around she orders the sheriff (George Kennedy) to incite an Indian uprising. Director Burt Kennedy has a field day altering allegiances in a mad cacophony of discordant sequences that are juvenile in their attempts to ridicule the Old West and tiresome in their constant leering. Boisterous, bawdy and dumb. A-III (GP)

Dirty Dozen, The (1967) World War II story about a free-wheeling officer (Lee Marvin) and the dozen army convicts he trains to destroy the headquarters of the German General Staff. Directed by Robert Aldrich, the movie is savage in its violence, yet raises questions about authorized brutality. A-IV (br)

Dirty Game, The (1966) Jumbled European-produced espionage movie with Henry Fonda, Vittorio Gassman, Robert Ryan and three directors (Terence Young, Christian-Jaque and Carlo Lizzani). Some violence and sexual innuendo. A-III (br)

Dirty Hands (1976) Silly, convoluted plot about a wife (Romy Schneider) who plots with her lover to murder drunken, maudlin husband (Rod Steiger in a self-indulgent performance). French production written and directed by Claude Chabrol is a sordid little story of marital infidelity and contains some nudity. O (R)

Dirty Harry (1971) Clint Eastwood stars as a hard-boiled detective of the San Francisco homicide squad who takes the law into his own hands when a psychotic killer is released on a technicality. Director Don Siegel keeps the action tightly-wound and fast-paced but his cynical superhero is basically irresponsible in endangering the lives of innocent people in his personal crusade against criminals. Harry is clearly dangerous and so is a movie which evades the complex legal problems and moral issues of vigilante justice. Sadistic brutality and graphic violence. O (R)

Dirty Little Billy (1973) The story of how and why Billy the Kid (Michael J. Pollard) began his life of crime is told by director Stan Dragoti by making him the victim of the times and circumstances, an idea neither very new nor very stimulating and, at any rate, goes nowhere. Contains a barrage of gritty, peripheral sex and violence. A-IV (R)

Dirty Mary, Crazy Larry (1974) Peter Fonda and Adam Roarke extort big money from supermarket executive Roddy McDowall, pick up Susan George, and destroy every car is sight while trying to escape with the cash. Directed by John Hough, it is thin action entertainment with an abundance of rough language. A-III (PG)

Dirty O'Neil (1974) Small-town policeman (Morgan Paull) finds his job less challenging than trying to bed the area's entire female population until three thugs come to town and sodomize his steady girl friend. Directors Howard Freen and Lewis Teague start with a sex farce that ends in sordid, sickening violence. O (R)

Dirty Outlaws, The (1972) Pallid Italian Western directed by Franco Rossetti tells the story of a desperado (Chip Corman) who seeks gold and discovers that his heart is made of it. Some fairly benign violence. A-III (R)

Dirty Tricks (1981) Harvard history professor (Elliott Gould) and a television newswoman (Kate Jackson) are the unwitting targets of gangsters and government men in this inane comedy-thriller directed by Alvin Rakoff. Some leering humor. A-III (PG)

Dirtymouth (1971) At the time of his death, controversial comedian Lenny Bruce was the center of a legal storm that has far-reaching implications about the freedom of expression in modern society. Viewers of Herbert Altman's documentary will get little insight into the man and, more importantly, will come away without any perspective on his times. The failure exploits an already tragic career. O (nr)

Discreet Charm of the Bourgeoisie, The (1972) Director Luis Bunuel's surrealistic satire on the lives of the very rich presents an incredibly complicated series of events, such as dreamers dreaming of other dreamers, that grows more satisfying as the narrative becomes more outrageously illogical. The central recurring situation is that of six wealthy friends (Fernando Rey, Delphine Seyrig, Stephane Audran, Bulle Ogier, Jean-Pierre Cassel and Michel Piccoli) about to sit down to dinner but always being interrupted by something which prevents them from being able to proceed with the meal. The movie is meant to be enjoyed as something as playful as the title itself. A-III (PG)

Disorderlies (1987) The Fat Boys, a rap music group, star as health-care interns who unwittingly foil inept nephew Anthony Geary's plot to do in his wealthy uncle (Ralph Bellamy). Director Michael Schultz's not-exactly uplifting comedy relies on pure physical slapstick brought off amiably by the funky boys and is marred only by some midly crude language and a brief nude swimming scene. A-II (PG)

Distance (1976) Black sergeant (Paul Benjamin), on a Georgia army post in 1956, becomes estranged from his German wife (Eija Pokkinen), a woman desperately trying to save her marriage and her own sense of worth. With good acting, strong characterizations and period authenticity, Anthony Lover directs a meaningful story of alienation, but the fragile web of relationships that had been developing so well is finally overwhelmed by a needlessly melodramatic climax. Adult situations. A-III (R)

Distant Thunder (1975) Indian production about a young Brahman couple whose quiet, secure lives in a small Bengali village are disrupted and their modest expectations destroyed in the terrible famine of 1943 when more than five million people starved to death. Showing the gradual breakdown of village society as rice shortages and hunger grow, director Satyajit Ray makes the viewer share his compassion and anger for the fate of those anonymous victims of a catastrophe caused by World War II. Moving but unsentimental, it is also a cogent parable for our own times. A-II (nr)

Diva (1982) Bright French production recounting the adventures of a romantic 18-year-old postman (Frederic Andrei), obsessed with an opera diva (Wilhelmenia Wiggins Fernandez), but when he records her performance at a concert, his tape gets mixed up with one incriminating some gangsters and the chase is on through the streets and subways of Paris. Jean-Jacques Beineix directs a diverting tongue-in-cheek thriller that's an all-style, no-substance entertainment. Violence and brief nudity. A-III (R)

Divine Mr. J., The (1974) Thoroughly mindless, abysmally inept, yawningly unfunny attempt to satirize the New Testament. Cast as a Flatbush-accented Virgin Mary, Bette Midler appears to be totally without any redeeming talent, a condition afflicting the rest of the cast in this low satire. O (R)

Divine Nymph, The (1979) Italian study of upper-class decadence after World War I from director Giuseppe Patroni Griffi tells the story of an insensitive woman (Laura Antonelli) who drives one lover (Terence Stamp) to suicide and another (Marcello Mastroianni) to join the Fascists. The theme of the destructive force of thwarted passion is given surface treatment as is the unclothed figure of its heroine. O (nr)

Divorce American Style (1967) Dick Van Dyke and Debbie Reynolds have to decide whether to call it a day after 17 years of marriage and one of separation in their divorce-riddled California community. Producer-writer Norman Lear and director Bud Yorkin have come up with an entertaining satire that touches all the bases: the senseless rift, the well-meant advice, the legal razzle-dazzle, the shuffled offspring, the social plight of disconnected spouse, the financial bite. Well paced and occasionally very funny, it's a good try that largely succeeds. A-III (br)

Doberman Gang, The (1972) Enterprising gang (Byron Mabe, Julie Parrish and Hal Reed) use a pack of doberman pinscher attack dogs in an intricate, highly-orchestrated bank robbery. Director Byron Chudnow's inventive low-budget heist movie depends on an element of terror that attack dogs provide and has some mild love-making scenes. A-III (PG/G)

Doc (1971) Stacy Keach stars as legendary gun-fighter and gambler Doc Holliday. Director Frank Perry's re-creation of an oft-told tale attempts to turn the events leading up to the gunfight at the O.K. Corral into some sort of allegory about American involvement in Vietnam and the movie collapses under the weight of its pretensions. Considerable violence. A-III (PG)

Doctor and the Devils, The (1985) An often-too-gleefully gruesome dramatization of a famous 19th-century case involving a prominent surgeon (Timothy Dalton) who refuses to inquire into the source of the cadavers furnished him for his lectures in anatomy. Though well-directed by Freddie Francis, with an exceptionally literate script by Ronald Harwood based on a Dylan Thomas scenario plumbing its theme of ends and means. Violent, sordid environment and brief nudity. A-III (R)

Doctor Death: Seeker Of Souls (1973) John Considine plays the dastardly doctor who specializes in giving a new lease on life to the ailing by finding a body into which his client's soul can be liberated. Directed by Eddie Saeta, it is so witless in plot and execution that its bloody excesses become equally meaningless and boring. A-III (R)

Doctor Detroit (1983) A mild-mannered but oddball English professor (Dan Aykroyd) assumes the role of Doctor Detroit, a real bad gangster, in order to protect four prostitutes who have been abandoned by their pimp (Howard Hesseman). The shuttle back and forth between the two identities is the basis for most of the comedy, but under Michael Pressman's direction the laughs are infrequent and mild at best. Sexually oriented humor, brief shots from a pornographic movie and a benign view of drug use. O (R)

Doctor Dolittle (1967) Gentle, turn-of-the-century musical fantasy about an eccentric animal doctor's adventures searching for the Great Pink Sea Snail. Rex Harrison stars as the doctor who can talk to animals in an attractive but slow-moving production directed by Richard Fleischer. Movie musical purists may be disappointed in Leslie Bricusse's uninspired screenplay, music and lyrics but others, especially children, may be charmed. A-I (br)

Doctor Faustus (1968) British adaptation of Christopher Marlowe's classic drama about the German university professor (Richard Burton) who sells his soul to the devil for knowledge, power and a woman (Elizabeth Taylor). Directed by Burton and Nevill Coghill, the result is something of a witch's brew of scenes depicting the emptiness of the world, the flesh and the devil. Brief nudity. A-III (br)

Doctor Glas (1969) In late 19th-century Stockholm, a physician (Per Oscarsson) sexually obsessed with a young woman (Lone Hertz) poisons her much older minister husband (Ulf Palme) but his undetected crime gains him nothing except a life of increasing loneliness and frustration. One may admire the icy precision of Oscarsson's performance and director Mai Zetterling's restrained

treatment of the material but it remains no more than a repugnant case history with little in the way of human insight, significance or even dramatic involvement. O (M)

Doctor, You've Got to Be Kidding (1966) Glamorized treatment of teenage pregnancy in director Peter Tewksbury's vacuous movie starring Sandra Dee and George Hamilton is offensive, especially considering the juvenile audience to which it is directed. O (br)

Doctor Zhivago (1965) Boris Pasternak's novel has been turned into an epic of the Russian Revolution and its effect upon fictional characters (Julie Christie, Omar Sharif, Alec Guinness) who struggle to survive in difficult times. Director David Lean uses the vast canvas of the Revolution as a backdrop for Robert Bolt's script which focuses on the disruption of individual lives and values under the pressure of external events. A-II (GP)

Doctors' Wives (1971) Dyan Cannon and Richard Crenna star in an adult soap opera about doctors in a posh California medical clinic who dally with the nurses while their wives find diversion elsewhere. A colleague's fatal heart attack provides the necessary scandal and shame to motivate everyone back into their proper and respective beds. Ploddingly directed by George Schaefer, the shenanigans are mostly off-camera and recounted in euphemistic dialogue. Gruesome open-heart surgical sequence but the movie itself has no heart or any real emotion for that matter. O (R)

Dog Day Afternoon (1975) Al Pacino stars as a hapless Brooklyn bank robber whose plans go awry when the police arrive before he and an accomplice can flee. A taut, well-acted drama with comic overtones, director Sidney Lumet is consistently entertaining in his treatment of this fact-based incident, but the bisexual character of the hero (who needed money for his partner's sex-change operation), the rough language and the disquieting look at the seamy side of life limit its appeal. A-IV (R)

Dog of Flanders (1959) In a turn-of-the-century Antwerp suburb, an old man (Donald Crisp) and his small grandson (David Ladd) rescue a dog left to die at the roadside. Produced by Robert B. Radnitz and directed by James B. Clark, the movie shows how unselfish love and understanding bring happiness even under conditions of dire poverty. Fine family fare. A-I (br)

Dogpound Shuffle (1975) Tap-dancing vagrant (Ron Moody) teams up with an itinerant harmonica player (David Soul) in order to make enough money to retrieve his impounded dog. Director Jeffrey Bloom's frequently moving study of the interaction between the two has an affirmative, spunky quality marred by an unnecessarily bloody fight scene and a few expletives. A-II (PG)

Dogs of War, The (1981) Screen version of Frederick Forsyth's novel about mercenaries (headed by Christopher Walken) hired to oust a bloody West African tyrant in order to replace him with a man just as bad but one who will be more amenable to foreign business interests. Though the movie lacks sympathetic and well-defined central characters, the narrative's action is handled quite well by director John Irvin. The result is an interesting melodrama with serious but ambiguous implications and some graphic violence. A-III (R)

Dolemite (1975) Black exploitation movie about an army of women Kung Fu killers features violence, sex and an army of non-actors. Its production values are on a par with a badly done home movie. O (R)

Doll's House, A (1973) Director Patrick Garland interprets Ibsen's play as anything but a repudiation of the married state. Fine cast (Claire Bloom, Anthony Hopkins, Ralph Richardson) conveys those qualities of maturity, compassion, and respect for the integrity of the individual without which human growth and fulfillment in marriage is impossible. It is a film for women who yearn to be emancipated, for women who have been and for men who have wondered why Women's Lib was even necessary. A-II (G)

$ (Dollars) (1971) Richard Brooks wrote and directed this only occasionally amusing Hamburg bank heist action drama that features Warren Beatty as the brains of the bank's security system and Goldie Hawn as his brainless, high-priced hooker accomplice. Unfortunately Brooks' fascination with electronic gadgetry impedes the pace of the action which creaks along too implausibly to maintain much interest. Short on comedy and high on ugly twists and brutal turns, the movie has large doses of nudity, sexual innuendo and crude language. O (R)

Domino Principle, The (1977) Gene Hackman plays a convict recruited by a powerful and mysterious group to carry out an assassination whose intended victim apparently is the President of the United States. Director Stanley Kramer disappointingly fails to deal with the political paranoia of our times in any significant fashion, settling instead for another pointless and simple-minded melodrama with violence. A-III (R)

Don Giovanni (1979) Great voices and sumptuously romantic Italian landscapes predominate in director Joseph Losey's screen version of the Mozart opera about a jilted woman (Kiri Te Kanawa) obsessed with her husband's damnation. Realistic treatment of the Don's compulsive sexuality takes on Marxist significance as a reflection of the conflict of the old regime with the working class. A cultural artifact whose romantic vision of adultery requires a mature perspective. A-IV (nr)

Don Is Dead, The (1973) Crime godfather (Anthony Quinn) suffers a heart attack, triggering a power struggle to fill the vacuum. Directed by Richard Fleischer, it is a dull, mindless variation on a theme. Excessive violence. O (R)

Don Quixote (1973) A performance by the Australian Ballet Company of the Cervantes classic, co-directed by Rudolph Nureyev and Robert Helpmann, with Helpmann in the title role and Nureyev dancing that of the young Basilio. A-I (G)

Don't Cry with Your Mouth Full (1975) Pastoral symphony about a not very eventful summer spent by a family in the South of France is lovely to look at but drama consists of more than holding a mirror up to reality. The only element of tension is the older teenage daughter's impending loss of virginity, but even this is not exploited and nothing is allowed to get beneath the shimmering surface of things. Beautiful, human, naturalistic but disappointing. A-IV (nr)

Don't Drink the Water (1969) Hapless Newark caterer (Jackie Gleason) tours Europe with wife (Estelle Parsons) and daughter (Joan Delaney), but in the process their plane is hijacked to Vulgaria, an Iron Curtain country, where the family is mistaken for American spies. Written by Woody Allen and directed by Howard Morris, the comedy's brightest moments come during the credits when the family is preparing for the trip which itself proves less than memorable. Obligatory, but tastelessly handled, romance between the daughter and the American ambassador's son (Ted Bessell) brings the whole affair to its inevitable happy conclusion. A-III (G)

Don't Go in the House (1980) When a little boy whose mother burns him as punishment for being naughty grows up, he doesn't want to set the world on fire, only mama and every other woman who reminds him of her. Starring Dan Grimaldi and directed by Joseph Ellison, it's a grisly piece of trash exploiting violence and nudity. O (R)

Don't Just Stand There (1968) Brainless comedy in which two Americans (Mary Tyler Moore and Robert Wagner) in Paris deal with the problems caused by an authoress who has gone on a pleasure cruise leaving the last chapter of her new sex novel unwritten. Directed by Ron Winston, the plot complications don't make much sense and, even if they did, they are not very amusing. Excessive sexual innuendo. O (br)

Don't Look Back (1967) Feature documentary on folk singer Bob Dylan produced by D.A. Pennebaker during Dylan's 1965 concert tour of England. Filming the singer in performance and off stage, the documentary records his expression of the doubts, depressions and joys of his generation without comment or explanation. Some crude language. A-II (br)

Don't Look Now (1969) Zany slapstick World War II comedy done with style by Terry Thomas, Bourvil and Louis de Funes about the confused attempts of the crew of a downed British bomber to escape from Occupied France. Written and directed by Gerard Oury, the comedy routines and sight gags may not be entirely new but they are done imaginatively and with verve by three great film clowns. The period supplies suspense and is never used to make wartime look like a lark. The Disney release provides superior entertainment for audiences of all ages. A-I (G)

Don't Look Now (1973) English couple (Donald Sutherland and Julie Christie), distraught about the drowning of their only child, attempt to regain their emotional balance as he helps restore a crumbling church in Venice. Sutherland's gift of second sight is pivotal to both their dead child and their deteriorating marriage in this psychic potboiler directed by Nicholas Roeg with moody, atmospheric photography. Extended scene of explicit lovemaking. O (R)

Don't Make Waves (1967) California beach-blanket movie geared towards the easy-living teenage set revolving around the attempts of undernourished Tony Curtis to woo shapely Sharon Tate away from her muscle-bound surfer boyfriends. Directed by Alexander Mackendrick, the movie's light-headed attitudes towards teenage sexuality make it somewhat tainted fare, especially for impressionable viewers. O (br)

Don't Open the Window (1976) Italian-Spanish horror movie set in England, starring Arthur Kennedy affecting a thick Irish accent while the rest of the cast of characters are dubbed with very British accents. Unpretentious and fairly competent production, but mainly preoccupied with setting up scenes of gore. O (R)

Don't Raise the Bridge, Lower the River (1968) Jerry Lewis stars in and directs a British-made comedy about a semi-shady promoter who likes to do things the hard way. Most of the humor is typical Lewis farce, with some really funny sight (and sound) gags, as well as some slack stretches. Gap-toothed Terry-Thomas, Bernard Cribbins and some other British comedy pros lend some extra spark. A-II (G)

Dona Flor and Her Two Husbands (1978) Brazilian sex fantasy about a remarried widow visited by the ghost of her first mate is interesting chiefly for its exotic locales and characters. Directed by Bruno Barreto, the slight Boccaccio-like anecdote employs several graphic sex scenes. O (nr)

Dorian Gray (1971) Italian adaptation of the Oscar Wilde story about a young man (Helmut Berger) who watches a painting of himself take on the spiritual decay of his soul while his physical exterior remains unblemished. Director Massimo Dallamano treats the story's perversions, ranging from sodomy to murder, in such coy fashion that its hero's many vices are as lackluster as they are corrupting. O (R)

Dossier 51 (1979) Tediously subjective melodrama about a minor French diplomat harrassed by all the technique and technology an intelligence agency can bring to bear against him. Director Michel Deville's deliberate but failed attempts at humor and extensive use of nudity make the unexciting plot even more mindless. O (nr)

Double Con, The (see: "Trick Baby")

Double Man, The (1968) Routine spy thriller about a CIA agent (Yul Brynner) who ventures to the Swiss Alps to investigate his son's murder which, it turns out, was set up to lure him into a trap so that a look-alike (also played by Brynner) can take his place and infiltrate the U.S. intelligence network. British production directed by Franklin Schaffner, its intriguing premise had promise which is left largely unrealized. A-I (br)

Double Ransom (see: "The Terrorists")

Double Trouble (1967) Elvis Presley vehicle casts the singer as a nightclub entertainer playing London and pleasantly plagued by pretty, lovestruck fan Annette Day. Directed by Norman Taurog, the plot includes a parental attempt to break up the romance, a spate of spies and nine well-swiveled song numbers. A-II (br)

Dove, The (1974) Fact-based odyssey of a 16-year-old (Joseph Bottoms) who sets out to sail around the world in a 23-foot sloop of the title until he meets an Australian girl (Deborah Raffin) and decides to marry but she convinces him to complete his journey first. Directed by Charles Jarrott and beautifully photographed by Sven Nyquist, the entertaining adventure would appeal to youngsters but the moral ambiguities of the early stages of the Bottoms-Raffin relationship warrant labeling it as adult fare. A-III (PG)

Down and Dirty (1979) Director Ettore Scola's Italian farce stars Nino Manfredi as a drunken, lecherous patriarch of an extended family of poverty-striken streetfolk trying to grab the insurance money he received after the loss of an eye. Irreverent, unkind attempt to derive comedy from human degradation, frustration and ignorance replete with sexual references. O (nr)

Down and Out in Beverly Hills (1986) Nick Nolte portrays a supertramp who relieves everyone's misery in a jaded and spoiled Beverly Hills household. Director Paul Mazursky's movie is an overly simplified tale of manners and morals poking fun at the tribulations of a suddenly rich family headed by Richard Dreyfuss and Bette Midler. Its farcical treatment of sex as a remedy for all ills marks it as a misguided burlesque, carefully avoiding any sense of conviction or consequence. O (R)

Down by Law (1986) This lighthearted comedy begins with a breezy introduction to three likeable but corrupt residents of Louisiana's bayou country. The friendship and humorous camaraderie which develops after they are wrongfully sent to jail propels them to escape detention and try to start new and more rewarding lives for themselves. Some profanity and nudity. A-III (R)

Down the Ancient Stairs (1975) Italian movie set in an insane asylum in the 1930s whose lecherous director (Marcello Mastroianni) gets his comeuppance from a new, no-nonsense assistant (Francoise Fabian). Director Mauro Bolognini draws a half-hearted parallel between the madness inside the asylum and the madness of an Italy rapt in Fascist frenzy but he covers its flaws by baring a good deal of flesh. O (R)

Downhill Racer (1969) Robert Redford plays a surly American skier with enough recklessness and skill to challenge the best Europeans but is unwilling to listen to his team's tough, long-suffering coach (admirably played by Gene Hackman) in preparing for the big skiing competition. Though the personal drama follows the formula of such sports movies, director Michael Ritchie concentrates on providing a vivid overview of a dangerous and photogenic sport and the fallible people who compete in it for the psychological rewards that some find worth all its rigors and traumatic nervous strain. A-III (PG)

Dr. Frankenstein on Campus (1971) Contemporary namesake of the legendary scientist is a college student who doesn't fit in very well with the rest of the campus scene. Director Gilbert W. Taylor's attempt to update a classic story flounders in scenes more suited to sex exploitation movies than to the horror genre. O (R)

Dr. Jekyll and Sister Hyde (1972) British horror movie directed by Roy Ward Baker features Ralph Bates as Jekyll and Martine Beswick as his alter ego-ess. It is at its best when it slyly rings the changes on the 19th-century story but it offers a lot of just-beneath-the-surface sexual ambience. A-III (PG)

Dr. Phibes Rises Again (1972) Vincent Price as Phibes is still trying to bring his beautiful wife back to life while he fends off Robert Quarry's devious attempts to locate the elixir of life beneath an Egyptian mountain. Directed by Robert Fuest, much of the fun comes from Phibes' ingenious manner of dispatching his enemies against Brian Eatwell's amusing art deco sets. Restrained violence. A-II (PG)

Dr. Strangelove or: How I Learned to Stop Worrying and Love the Bomb (1964) Peter Sellers is President of the United States, as well as the mad doctor of the title, when a fanatical general (Sterling Hayden) launches a nuclear bomber strike on the U.S.S.R. Director Stanley Kubrick's black comedy shows the absurdity of a world quaking under the threat of annihilation by its own artifacts. It may not be everyone's cup of tea, but sifting the leaves remains a provocative challenge even today. A-IV (GP)

Dr. Who and the Daleks (1966) Derived from the British TV science fiction series, the movie shows how the good Doctor (Peter Cushing) stops the Daleks, a tribe of mutants, from using their robot army to destroy their neighbors, the peaceful

Thais people. Directed by Gordon Flemyng, the fantasy with all its colorful gadgetry will please the children and Dr. Who fans. A-I (br)

Dracula (1979) Clever British version of the horror story features Frank Langella re-creating his Broadway role as the ruthless vampire romantically obsessed with the daughter of a madhouse caretaker (Kate Nelligan). Director John Badham's ill-considered use of violence directed against seemingly willing female victims and the gory and bloody killings of the Count's henchmen make the movie an exercise in excess. O (R)

Dracula A.D. 1972 (1972) Fairly mild British horror movie in which the vampire count (Christopher Lee) returns to settle a score with the descendant (Peter Cushing) of the man who last put Dracula to sleep back in the 1870s. Director Alan Gibson holds attention with some gaudy twists and turns in the modern setting and with the usual amount of gory effects. A-III (PG)

Dracula Has Risen from the Grave (1969) When Dracula (Christopher Lee) is accidentally unentombed from a frozen mountain stream, he proceeds to take his revenge on the cleric (Rupert Davies) who exorcised his castle and barred its doors with a large cross. British production directed by Freddie Francis, this version of the old horror tale takes a much more sensual approach to the vampire's blood-lust and its young hero (Barry Andrews) is an outspoken atheist. Graphic blood and gore. A-III (G)

Dracula, Prince of Darkness (1966) Routine British vampire movie directed by Terence Fisher with Christopher Lee as the revived Count preying on unwary visitors to his castle. Mild violence. A-II (br)

Dragnet (1987) Dan Aykroyd plays police sergeant Friday, with Tom Hanks as his sidekick. Together they foil a group of PAGANs (People Against Goodness and Normalcy) headed by a minister (Christopher Plummer) wishing to take over Los Angeles. Sarcastic putdowns of virginity, anti-pornography, government and personal integrity, combined with vulgar sexual gestures, rough language and brief nudity provide little genuine humor in director Tom Mankiewicz's updated spoof of the popular 1960s television show. O (PG-13)

Dragon Files, The (1975) Martial arts story of a police inspector (Jimmy Wang Yu) in pursuit of the chief drug dealer in the Far East. It's all an excuse, of course, for running the gamut of Kung Fu brutality with some incidental interracial romance thrown in for good measure. Once again, however, the cardboard violence is vicious and the police are as reprehensible as the criminals. O (R)

Dragonfly (1976) Released from a mental institution where he was committed at age 13, a young man (Beau Bridges) is helped by a sympathetic woman (Susan Sarandon) to find out the truth about his past and the mother (Mildred Dunnock) he fears he has killed. Well-acted and sensitively directed by Gilbert Cates, the movie has much to recommend it, in spite of an uneven script and an overwrought conclusion that leaves some significant loose ends. Heavy-handed seduction scene. A-III (PG)

Dragonslayer (1981) Sorceror's apprentice (Peter MacNicol) has to do battle with a fierce dragon terrorizing a distant kingdom to fulfill the promise of his dead master (Ralph Richardson). Above average Disney production directed by

Matthew Robbins starts well but unravels in the latter third of the story, with showy special effects diminishing the simple human elements of romance and gallantry. Extremely jarring and unsettling sequence of a gory death, several other scenes of violence and very brief nudity. A-III (PG)

Draughtsman's Contract, The (1983) Mannered and pretentious period piece set in late 17th-century England, depicts an artist (Anthony Higgins) and the lady of a manor (Janet Suzman) caught up in a web of evil and hostility. Written and directed by Peter Greenway, the period re-creation is stylish but its too clever plot eventually becomes boring, undone by its carelessness and its airs. Considerable male nudity and a general air of amorality. O (R)

Dream City (1977) A troubled artist and his wife are invited to join a utopian community hidden in a remote area of Africa but upon arrival, find that they are prisoners in an asylum run by the mad inmates. German production directed by Johannes Schaaf, this allegory on society and human nature is stunning to the eye but leaves the heart and imagination untouched. Several scenes are given a voyeuristic emphasis. O (R)

Dream Lover (1986) Psychological thriller starring Christy McNichol as a young girl tormented by a recurring nightmare in which she repeatedly stabs an intruder and potential rapist. Under a dream state induced to cure her, she envisions her own rape, the stabbing of her father and an unsuccessful leap off a 40-story building. Needless repetition of excessively violent acts. O (R)

Dream of Kings, A (1969) Uneven screen version of the Harry Mark Petrakis novel about a Greek American (Anthony Quinn in a larger-than-life performance) who, desperate for the money to take his terminally ill son to Greece to be cured by breathing the air of their noble ancestors, is caught cheating at dice and is brutally beaten. But his pride and dreams are saved by his long-suffering wife (Irene Papas). Daniel Mann's direction puts more emphasis on character study than on Chicago's Greek community but the result has vitality and compassion for human struggle and endurance. A-III (R)

Dream of Passion (1978) Aging international star (Melina Mercouri), back in her native Greece to play Medea, finds herself drawn to an American (Ellen Burstyn) imprisoned for killing her three children in revenge for her husband's infidelity. Director Jules Dassin's muddled attempt to give a modern slant to the Medea theme suffers from some dreadful acting (save for Burstyn), fatuous dialogue and a general mood of self-indulgence. Some rough language and violent emotions. A-III (R)

Dreamchild (1985) A lovely movie full of genuine sentiment based upon the 1932 trip of 80-year-old Alice Hargreaves (Coral Browne)—the same Alice who inspired Lewis Carroll (Ian Holm) 70 years before—to New York City to celebrate the centenary of the author's birth. The trip unlocks a flood of memories in the old woman's mind as she recalls the past with a wisdom that comes only with age. Directed by Gavin Millar, the movie makes evident that the writer's love for the little girl, though kept within proper bounds, was more intense than it should have been. A-II (PG)

Dreamer (1979) Unranked amateur (Tim Matheson) becomes national bowling champ in director Noel Nosseck's insignificant little film about athletic determination. Implication of premarital sex further mars a bland plot and second-rate performances. A-III (PG)

Dreamer, The (1970) Israeli story of a vague young handyman working in an old age home who, after a love affair with a woman visitor, decides he is happier with the old folks. It is a beautifully photographed, quiet paced study in loneliness, with gentle human and some winning emotions, but it lacks any sort of dramatic depth or narrative interest. A-III (R)

Dreams of Glass (1969) Trite and banal romance between a rather irresponsible California youth (John Denos) and a charming Japanese girl (Caroline Barrett) whose trysting place in an abandoned warehouse is wrecked one day by a group of young thugs. Lacking a story with substance, director Robert Clouse relies on stylish camera-work and luscious photography. Visually beautiful but emotionally vapid. A-III (PG)

Dreamscape (1984) Absurd melodrama with a hero (Dennis Quaid) who enters the nightmares of disturbed people and performs instant repairs on their wounded psyches. Pulp fantasy movie directed by Joseph Ruben. A torrid but relatively restrained love scene. A-III (PG-13)

Dressed to Kill (1980) Young prostitute (Nancy Allen) witnesses the brutal murder of a woman (Angie Dickinson) and, with the help of the woman's son (Keith Gordon), searches for the killer, a transvestite in a blond wig. An urbane psychiatrist (Michael Caine) is also part of the mix. Director Brian De Palma's suspense thriller, with its slipshod story line, flat dialogue and paper-thin characters, is an empty, sterile exercise in fantasy sex and violence directed against women. O (R)

Dresser, The (1983) Albert Finney and Tom Courtenay score twin triumphs in a splendid adaptation of the play by Ronald Harwood on the symbiotic relationship between a vain, doddering Shakespearean actor (Finney) and his dresser (Courtenay). The main portion of the action takes place during a performance of "King Lear" given in the midst of an air raid in the darkest days of World War II. Peter Yates's direction helps greatly to make this an inspired adaptation of a stage play though for some tastes it may be too theatrical. A-II (PG)

Drive, He Said (1971) Self-indulgent story of a college basketball star (William Tepper) who divides his time between working out in the gym and the front seat of his car with the wife (Karen Black) of the drama prof (Robert Towne). Directed by Jack Nicholson, it is a mindless exercise in sexual explicitness and rough language. O (X/R)

Drive-In (1976) Star-crossed teenagers, youth-gangs, inept armed robbers, nasty children and a variety of other characters converge upon a Texas drive-in to see a movie called "Disaster '76." Under Rod Amateau's direction, the results are sometimes amusing, but more often unfunny with some back-seat romancing and use of marijuana. A-III (PG)

Driver, The (1978) In this somber crime movie, Ryan O'Neal plays a criminal who specializes in driving getaway cars and Bruce Dern is an obsessed detective out to get him even if he has to break the law to do it. Written and directed by Walter Hill, the confrontations between policeman and criminal lack any deeper resonances than that of other routine melodramas. Violence. A-III (R)

Driver's Seat, The (1975) Uneven adaptation of Muriel Spark's story is a mood piece about a psychotic spinster (Elizabeth Taylor) who travels to the South of Italy to seek her lover-murderer. Director Giuseppe Patroni Griffi complicates the narrative by intercutting past and future scenes with the present and the result offers little insight into the characters' motives and actions. Its themes of alienation, the elusiveness of reality and the relationship between sexuality and violence will appeal only to a limited audience. A-IV (R)

Drowning Pool, The (1975) Uninspired adaptation of a Ross MacDonald mystery with Paul Newman as the low-key private eye hired by frightened, rich Joanne Woodward. Director Stuart Rosenberg does better conveying the local flavor of New Orleans than he does stirring the plot's distasteful gumbo of corrupt police, sadistic oil men, blackmail and genteel depravity. The treatment of sexual elements in the story is marred by some ill-considered attempts at comic relief and by the use of a very young actress in an especially distasteful role. O (PG)

Drum (1976) Like "Mandingo," its sequel is an unsavory stew of sex and brutality that makes a ludicrous attempt to seem an earnest exploration into the evils of slavery. Directed by Steve Carver, it is a totally crass exploitation movie. O (R)

Duck, You Sucker! (1972) Director Sergio Leone spins out another of his endless, blood-drenched Western epics, this one telling how Rod Steiger and James Coburn win the Mexican Revolution. The story is far too long to hold up either its story line or the viewer's sagging attention. Much preposterous violence. A-III (PG)

Duel at Diablo (1966) Sidney Poitier, James Garner and Bibi Andersson star in a Western rife with brutal killings and wife-kidnapping by Apache Indians, with Dennis Weaver as a vengeful husband who cannot forgive his wife for surviving her ordeal. Director Ralph Nelson disguises his movie's shortcomings with a complicated plot and larger-than-life characters but can't hide its violent excesses. O (br)

Duellists, The (1978) Screen version of a Joseph Conrad story about two hussar officers in Napoleon's army (Keith Carradine and Harvey Keitel) who fight a series of duels over two decades. Director Ridley Scott excels in his re-creation of the settings, costumes and general flavor of the era and does well with a delightful supporting cast (notably Albert Finney and Diana Quick). These virtues cannot compensate, however, for a large hole at the center of the story due to inept performances by the two principals. Violence. A-III (PG)

Duet for Cannibals (1969) Young man and his girl friend become involved with a fantasy-ridden political activist and his unstable wife in a relationship that becomes sexually bizarre and potentially murderous. Writer Susan Sontag's debut as a director is an interesting failure in its black-and-white variations on a theme of the corruption of innocence. A-IV (nr)

Duet for One (1987) Brilliant, world-renowned concert violinist (Julie Andrews) struggles to overcome the anger and depression she feels when her talents are diminished by multiple sclerosis. Frightened by the realization of her mortality, she finds consolation in her psychiatrist (Max Von Sydow) only after two adulterous affairs and a failed suicide attempt. Director Andrei Konchalovsky stresses righteous indignation as a life-sustaining virtue over spiritual renewal. Alan Bates co-stars in this morbid and morally muddled melodrama. Brief nudity. O (R)

Duffy (1968)   James Coburn plays a pop-erotic artist living in Tangiers who becomes involved in a complicated piracy plot with relatives of wealthy James Mason who has a few surprises in store for those trying to rob him. Instead of a sophisticated comedy, director Robert Parrish has come up with a shallow, low-grade bore whose sexual references are occasionally offensive. O (PG)

Dulcima (1972)   Rustic British movie traces the relationship between a cunning country lass (Carol White) who moves in as a "housekeeper" for a wealthy, much older farmer (John Mills) but the arrival of a handsome newcomer results in a shocking finale. Director Frank Nesbitt keeps things admirably subdued, although he is uncompromising in terms of the earthy language and lusty pursuits of his isolated characters. A-III (PG)

Dumbo (1941)   In this classic Disney animated feature, a baby elephant with over-sized ears, the laughing stock of the entire circus troupe to which he belongs, is befriended by a sympathetic mouse. What happens to the diminutive pachyderm shows children how self-respect and self-confidence can be gained by making the most of one's imagination and inventive initiative. A-I (G)

Dune (1984)   Screen version of Frank Herbert's science fiction trilogy about four factions struggling for control of a desert planet and its wonderous spice has been turned into a dark, quirky movie. Much of this adaptation is incomprehensible to anyone who has not read the original and director David Lynch's action sequences are badly staged. Some vulgarity and graphic violence. A-III (PG-13)

Dungeonmaster (1985)   Dreadful hodgepodge of a movie, with no less than seven directors, about a computer wizard who must overcome a series of challenges of the sort found in the game that gives this clunker its title. Sadistic violence. O (PG-13)

Dunwich Horror, The (1970)   Young warlock (Dean Stockwell), despite the warnings of his grandfather (Sam Jaffe), strives to conjure up some devil-monsters from the underworld but is foiled by a professor of witchcraft (Ed Begley). Director Daniel Haller's weak horror movie has some sexually suggestive scenes. O (M)

Dusty and Sweets McGee (1971)   Semi-documentary by Floyd Mutrux on the tragic lives of drug addicts and pushers parades the dehumanizing effect, the withdrawals and death which drugs produce. The result is a talk piece which poses tough questions about real people but gets nowhere in what ultimately proves to be a surface examination of substantive matters. A-IV (R)

Dutchess and the Dirt-Water Fox, The (1976)   Western comedy about a bumbling gambler (George Segal) and a dance hall girl (Goldie Hawn) whose avarice brings them together in a series of cliched chases and misadventures. Director Melvin Frank's mostly unfunny effort collapses under the weight of incessant visual and verbal vulgarities, double entendres and some crude satire at the expense of Mormons and Jews. O (PG)

Dynamite Chicken (1972)   Director Ernie Pintoff's low-budget collection of skits on pot smoking, campus rebellion, Madison Avenue hucksterism, nudity, LBJ, Lenny Bruce and other dated topical items, is merely trite and self-consciously offensive. O (R)

E

Eagle Has Landed, The (1977)   Director John Sturges' lethargic adventure yarn based on the fictional premise involving a German plot to kidnap Winston Churchill during World War II. is a conventional spy melodrama. Michael Caine, Robert Duvall and Donald Sutherland star in the suspenser which is marred by some graphic violence, sexual byplay and profanity. A-III (PG)

Eagle in a Cage (1971)   Exiled after Waterloo on the barren isle of St. Helena in the middle of the South Atlantic, Napoleon wages an unequal contest of will with the English garrison and its overbearing commander. Director Fielder Cook's direction simply reflects the strength and weakness of an uneven script, though it does capitalize on the grandeur of the Yugoslavian location where it was filmed. A-III (GP)

Early Spring (1974)   Japanese study of a man's alienation from job and home until a series of events jolt him out of his benumbed apathy and he decides to make the best of things. Directed in 1956 by Yasujiro Ozu, the movie conveys the density of feeling and the richness of relationships that make up ordinary life. A-II (nr)

Earth Is Our Sinful Song, The (1975)   Director Rauni Mollberg's extraordinary picture of life in a Finnish Lapland village tells the story of a father's ill-considered act of vengeance provoked by the pregnancy of his unmarried daughter. The story taking place beneath the awesome, brooding northern sky has the authenticity of a documentary but also the power of drama about lust and love, passion and remorse. Some sexual scenes that are graphic but not titillating and some violence that is brutal but not gratuitous. Some may find this picture of another, more elemental culture disturbing. A-IV (R)

Earthling, The (1981)   Dying man (William Holden) teaches a lost orphan (Ricky Schroder) how to survive in the wilds of the Australian bush in this import from director Peter Collinson. The photography of Don McAlpine is outstanding with its lavish scenic splendor, but the story's stilted dialogue and sketchy characterizations make for a long sit. Mild profanity and threatening wild animals. A-II (PG)

Earthquake (1974)   Moderately entertaining disaster spectacle of Los Angeles before, during, and after a cataclysmic earthquake. Directed by Mark Robson, Charlton Heston stars but is outclassed by the special effects. Unfortunately, in an attempt to include something for everyone, there is a seduction here, an attempted rape there, and a certain amount of strong language. A-III (PG)

Easy Money (1983)   Happily married lout (Rodney Dangerfield), given to drinking, gambling, philandering and narcotics, is forced to clean up his act when wealthy mother-in-law (Geraldine Fitzgerald) leaves him a fortune on condition that he reforms completely. This dreary, witless failed comedy, directed by James Signoredli and written by Dangerfield and half a dozen others, passes off some nudity, obscenity and a benign attitude towards drugs as supposedly harmless gags. O (R)

Easy Rider (1969)   Two drifters (Peter Fonda and Dennis Hopper), with a wad of cash from a drug transaction, motorcycle through the American Southwest on their way to New Orleans to celebrate. Along the way they encounter a disparate variety of American life, meet a small-town

ACLU lawyer (Jack Nicholson in a fine performance) and wind up murdered for being different. Also directed by Hopper, the journey may lead nowhere but its use of the natural landscape brings beauty and lyricism to a work exploring the American Dream and its promise of individual freedom. A thoughtful, provocative movie, it is marred by some graphic violence, a foggy mixture of sex and religion and a benign view of drugs. A-IV (R)

Eat My Dust (1976) Ron Howard stars in a brainless romp, a kind of live-action Roadrunner cartoon, about some youngsters obsessed with fast cars. Directed by Charles Griffith, it is an inane vision of youth culture and glorifies a dangerous pastime. A-III (PG)

Eboli (1980) The political exile of Italian anti-Fascist writer and artist Carlo Levi is the subject of director Francesco Rosi's warmly human dramatization. Though it does convey some of the complexities of Levi's social, political and artistic concerns, it is more interested in the man and his place in the context of the times. Serious subject matter and complex background might be confusing for young viewers. A-III (PG)

Echo Park (1986) In a rare unglamorous view of Los Angeles, an aspiring actress (Susan Dey) who is a single parent finds security and devotion with a down-to-earth younger man (Tom Hulce). The gritty drama contrasts blind ambition and false illusions with the rewards of patience and kindness. Director Robert Dornhelm's harshly realistic but truthful treatment counterbalances a sexually explicit nude scene, some foul language and violence. A-IV (R)

Echoes of a Summer (1976) Young girl (Jodie Foster) dying of a heart defect who conveys stoic acceptance of her condition and provides the inspiration for her family to deal gracefully with impending tragedy. Good cast with Lois Nettleton as the mother, Geraldine Fitzgerald as the tutor, and Richard Harris, who also co-produced, as the father. Director Don Taylor is a bit heavy-handed but the sentiment is genuine. A-II (PG)

Eddie and the Cruisers (1983) A reporter (Ellen Barkin) investigates the fate of a 1960's rock group whose sudden disappearance raises questions about the apparent suicide of its lead singer (Michael Pare). Director Martin Davidson, hampered by a mediocre script, fails to create any visual or narrative interest. Mildly vulgar dialogue. A-II (PG)

Educating Rita (1983) This British production adapted from Willy Russell's play and directed by Lewis Gilbert stars Michael Caine as a disillusioned, drunken professor of English in Dublin who becomes involved with a spunky housewife (Julie Walters) determined to get an education. The Pygmalion relationship has some charm but Walter's characterization is somewhat crude and ethnically stereotyped. A-III (PG)

Education of Sonny Carson, The (1974) Screen biography of a black militant (Rony Clanton), graduating from the Brooklyn ghetto to reform school and prison, embittered by the brutal cops and uncaring parole officials. Directed by Michael Campus, this attempt to show a world of racial injustice suffers from an onslaught of foul language, disjointed episodes, jarring switches in movie styles and an excessively prolonged scene of a merciless beating by a racist cop. O (R)

Edvard Munch (1976) Written and directed by Peter Watkins, this is the story of the Norwegian artist Edvard Munch (1863-1944), who, as one of the founders of Expressionism, has had a great influence upon the direction of contemporary art. Watkins interweaves three main strands of narrative: the historical, the intellectual, and the personal. Beautifully photographed, with the feel of a semi-documentary, the movie's treatment of the tormented life of this artist is at times intense, but diffused by the cultural context. A-II (nr)

Effect of Gamma Rays on Man-in-the-Moon Marigolds, The (1972) Joanne Woodward stars in the screen version of Paul Zindel's play about a desperate middle-aged mother living in an urban hovel, abandoned by her husband and struggling to raise two teenaged daughters (Nell Potts and Roberta Wallach). Producer-director Paul Newman's ambitious but flawed exploration into the labyrinthian workings of the human heart is largely redeemed by Woodward's superb performance. A-III (PG)

Effi Briest (1977) Tragedy based on Theodor Fontane's 19th-century romantic novel about a 17-year-old girl, married to a middle-aged Prussian official, who makes the mistake of having an affair, ultimately leading to her destruction. Directed by Rainer Werner Fassbinder, the German production is a haunting black-and-white evocation of a bygone age with some insight into the morals of the times. A-III (nr)

Eiger Sanction, The (1975) An art professor (Clint Eastwood who also directed) moonlights as an assassin for an intelligence outfit run by a former Nazi. The movie is exploitative in its treatment of sexual promiscuity and brutality. O (R)

8 Million Ways to Die (1986) In this heartless murder mystery, Jeff Bridges plays a reformed alcoholic ex-cop who breaks up a drug ring as he finds a prostitute's killer. Violence, ethnic stereotyping, extreme amounts of profanity and some nudity. O (R)

84 Charing Cross Road (1987) Screen version of New Yorker Helene Hanff's autobiography telling of her 20-year transatlantic correspondence with a London bookseller, starting with an inquiry about some rare books in 1949 and ending with his death in 1969. Though they never meet, the book seller (Anthony Hopkins) and the book lover (Anne Bancroft) come sharply into focus through letters sharing their mutual love of literature and other cultural matters. Director David Jones does extremely well in conveying the spiritual meeting of minds underlying their long-distance friendship. This uplifting celebration of kind and gentle souls may be above the heads of the very young, but they would benefit from seeing it with their parents. A-I (PG)

80 Steps to Jonah (1969) Young drifter (Wayne Newton), innocently implicated in a car theft, takes refuge in a camp for blind children where he finds commitment and a new purpose in life. Romance and exoneration follow in director Gerd Oswald's simple, somewhat sentimental tale of spiritual renewal that has special appeal for youngsters. A-I (G)

El Condor (1970) Big, bold Jim Brown joins up with skinny, mean Lee Van Cleef in this gory Western about getting Maximilian's vast gold horde out of El Condor, which is guarded by cruel Patrick O'Neal. Director John Guillermin rightfully pays little attention to the shoddy script but, unfortunately, devotes his energies to heavy-handed violence and sex scenes. O (R)

El Dorado (1967) Western sheriff (Robert Mitchum), immobilized by drinking, is helped by his old partner (John Wayne), who suffers occasional spinal spasms, in fighting off a band of cut-throats terrorizing the town. Produced and directed by Howard Hawks, the movie has a good mixture of action, farcical situations and unconventional treatment to keep things moving at a good clip. Stylized violence. A-III (br)

El Greco (1966) Mel Ferrer and Rosanna Schiaffino star in a very melodramatic romance based loosely on the life of the 16th-century Spanish painter. European production directed by Luciano Salce features beautiful location photography but art is secondary to a presentation of the artist's tempestuous romance with a high-born lady. A-III (br)

El Norte (1984) Fleeing a terrorist attack in which their father was killed and their mother kidnapped, two Guatemalan teenagers head towards "El Norte," that is, the United States, where they hope to begin a new life free from fear and exploitation. The journey has its own terrors, of course, but they do reach Los Angeles, get jobs and have a taste of the good life they have dreamed about before one becomes seriously ill and the other is deported as an illegal alien. Director Gregory Nava has made a splendid film about the dignity of human beings, with some good-natured humor keeping matters from getting too solemn. Subtitles aplenty with much of the dialogue in Spanish and Mayan. Several scenes of intense violence. A-III (R)

El Super (1979) Unpretentious and affecting film about a former Havana bus conductor (Raymundo Hidalgo-Gato) struggling to get through his 10th New York winter as a building superintendent, supported by his loving wife (Zully Montero) but troubled by their promiscuous, drug-taking daughter (Elizabeth Pena). Directed by Leon Ichaso and Orlando Jimenez-Leal, the slice-of-life portrait is brightened by wit and humor. It bridges the gap between North American and Latin cultures with low-budget ingenuity and cultural integrity. A-II (nr)

El Topo (1971) Argentinian director Alexandro Jodorowsky presents the story of a man's spiritual journey through life and the contradictions that arise between physical and moral power. The form is the time-honored Western with its gunfighters, open landscapes, and frontier towns. But in addition to using the Western conventions, the film also employs religious imagery, and sections of the Bible serve as its ideological frame of reference. Some will find its images of violence, sexuality and venality to be unsettling, if not offensive. A-IV (nr)

Eldridge Cleaver (1970) William Klein's documentary on political refugee Cleaver, an American whose radical ideas are uncongenial to the majority of his fellow citizens, uses the rhetoric of violence in presenting his views on revolution. Viewers will make their own judgment about the validity of his statements according to their knowledge and experience. A-IV (nr)

Electra Glide in Blue (1973) Ironic slice-of-life movie about a motorcycle cop (Robert Blake) in a small Southwestern town who revels in his splendid uniform and rugged equipment but yearns for the status he might have as a detective. A short stint with the local marshall (Mitch Ryan) cures him of that and a botched twist ending leaves a bad aftertaste. Embarrassingly pretentious but empty movie, painfully directed by James Guercio, it contains violence, rough language and sexual references. A-III (PG)

Electric Dreams (1984) Bland, innocuous British romantic comedy from director Steve Barron about a computer which falls in love with a woman. Youth-oriented movie features Lenny von Dohlen, Virginia Madsen and Bud Cort who manage to cavort in bed together, but this is implied rather than depicted. A-III (PG)

Electric Horseman, The (1979) Television reporter (Jane Fonda) teams up with over-the-hill rodeo star (Robert Redford) to save a gallant racehorse from commercial exploitation. Low voltage but cheerful and unassuming movie directed by Sydney Pollack. Treatment of the romantic involvement between the two principals makes it mature viewing fare. A-III (PG)

Eleni (1985) A New York newspaper reporter (John Malkovich), born in Greece, returns to his native land to find the man responsible for the execution of his mother (Kate Nelligan) in the Greek Civil War 30 years earlier. Despite the emotional power intrinsic to its fact-based subject, director Peter Yates has made a flat and unmoving movie, due largely to a pedestrian script and miscasting. Some scenes of wartime violence. A-II (PG)

Elephant Called Slowly, An (1971) Director James Hill offers a rambling account of a return visit by Bill Travers and Virginia McKenna, the stars of "Born Free," to a Kenyan game preserve where they are befriended by a baby elephant. Nothing much happens, but this album of wildlife is so low-keyed and innocent that parents, especially accompanied by their youngsters, will find it a pleasant, relaxing experience. A-I (G)

Elephant Man, The (1980) Touching fact-based portrait of an impoverished man deformed by a rare disease who is rescued by a doctor from a London freak show only to become the curiosity of fashionable Victorian society. Directed by David Lynch with evocative black-and-white photography, it features a fine performance by Anthony Hopkins as the concerned physician who rehabilitates the outcast (John Hurt under great wads of make-up). Some intense scenes of brutality. A-III (PG)

11 Harrowhouse (1974) Routine caper movie in which jewel thieves (Charles Grodin and Candice Bergen) get some inside help from a dissident employee (James Mason). Director Aram Avakian does make the most of his London setting and especially the metallic glint of the sophisticated detection devices in the basement of the diamond exchange. A-II (PG)

Elvira Madigan (1967) Romantic 19th-century tale of a cavalry officer and a young circus performer who run away to the Danish countryside for a summer's idyll but, as the chill of fall sets in, realize their future is doomed. Director Bo Widerberg's sensitive, straight-forward version of a popular Swedish legend is lushly beautiful with a darkly somber ending. A-III (br)

Elvis on Tour (1972) Pierre Adidge's documentary of a 15-day concert tour by Elvis Presley reveals nothing new about the man behind the legend but devotees of the legend will find it entertaining enough. A-I (G)

Elvis: That's the Way It Is (1970) Documentary profile of rock 'n' roll superstar Elvis Presley beginning with the rehearsals and exhausting preparations for a gala opening night performance at the International Hotel in Las Vegas. The performance itself is a winner giving fans of old swivel hips 30 songs to savor. Director Denis Sanders captures the quality of the man as performer and conveys that special Elvis magic that is part put-on and part solid singing conviction. A-II (G)

Embalmer, The (1972)   Ensconced in a sunken monastery beneath a fancy hotel in Venice, a psychotic frogman enshrines the beautiful women he has abducted and drowned in the canal until he tries to nab a lovely tourist who has caught the eye of a handsome reporter staying at the hotel. Dino Travella directs this failed 1966 Italian thriller with absolutely no imagination, but a few red herrings mildly seasoned with sexual innuendo. A-III (PG)

Embryo (1976)   Scientist (Rock Hudson) injects a human embryo with a drug that speeds growth to save the baby of a woman who has committed suicide. The result is a young girl (Barbara Carrera) with a photographic memory that creates terrifying results. Director Ralph Nelson's sci-fi horror story contains graphic, but brief, nudity and a shockingly violent conclusion. O (PG)

Emerald Forest, The (1985)   An American father (Powers Booth) searches the Amazonian jungle for 10 years until he finds the son who was kidnapped by Indians. The boy, however, now a teenager, has no desire to return to civilization. Under John Boorman's direction, the exotic setting provides some interest to this simplistic and melodramatic story of noble and ignoble savages and the ravages wrought on nature by commercial exploitation. Passable entertainment but strictly for mature audiences because of a great deal of nudity and some rather graphic violence. A-IV (R)

Emigrants, The (1972)   Superb Swedish production starring Liv Ullmann and Max Von Sydow about a young couple who leave their native land in the early 19th century to find a new home in Minnesota. Directed by Jan Troell, the re-creation of the era is finely detailed and the acting is first rate. A-II (PG)

Emil and the Detectives (1964)   A group of boys play detective and thwart the plans of a trio of comically sinister bank robbers in West Berlin. Disney production directed by Peter Tewksbury may please the young and uncritical. A-I (br)

Emitai (1972)   Fact-based Senegalese movie about a small village whose men are conscripted by France during World War II but, when they refuse a year later to give up all their rice, the remaining villagers are massacred. Directed by Ousmane Sembene, much of the story is told solely through its expressive images, and these visuals are the great strength of the movie. The title is the name of one of the tribe's gods who represents the passage from one stage of life to a new and better one. Stylized violence. A-II (nr)

Emmanuelle (1975)   French sex exploitation movie about a young woman's forays into the steamy regions of tropical sex in Thailand. O (X/R/X)

Emperor of the North (1973)   Brutal, altogether unsubtle drama about a clash between a hobo (Lee Marvin) and a sadistic train guard (Ernest Borgnine) set in the era of the Great Depression. It captures some of the mood of the 1930s, with out-of-work men living in hobo camps and riding the rails, but this is only used as the context for director Robert Aldrich's myopic vision of the male mystique and the cult of violence. A-IV (PG)

Empire of the Sun (1987)   Adventure saga of a young British lad (Christian Bale) who has to learn how to survive on his own after he is separated from his parents when the Japanese capture Shanghai and intern him for the duration of World War II. Director Steven Spielberg uses a large-scale action canvas to tell with some feeling and conviction the story of a youth growing up in the midst of wartime inhumanity. Some fairly intense scenes of war's violence and the brutality of the internment camp as well as a scene showing the boy's curiosity about sex. A-II (PG)

Empire Strikes Back, The (1980)   Gallant intergalactic rebels led by Luke Skywalker (Mark Hamill), Hans Solo (Harrison Ford) and Princess Leia (Carrie Fisher) and lovable android companions continue the fight against the evil Empire aided by Yoda, a remarkable creature who safeguards the Force and teaches moderation in all things. Some intense fight sequences punctuate director Irvin Kershner's sci-fi fantasy action. A-II (PG)

End, The (1978)   Except for the buffoonery of Dom Deluise, this is a painfully unfunny Burt Reynolds comedy about how not to commit suicide. Also directed by Reynolds, it contains an explicit love scene, some highly insulting ethnic jokes and disrespectful treatment of a religious rite. O (R)

End of a Priest (1970)   Seriocomic Czechoslovakian tale about villagers rehearsing for a play during which the sexton becomes saintly playing the role of a priest and the teacher becomes an unimaginative buffoon in the role of mayor. The movie's theme is not the conflict between church and state but the difference between doing good and talking about it. Though it has a moral, director Evald Schorm is mainly concerned with its characters and the high comedy of the absurd. A-III (nr)

End of the Game, The (1976)   Screen version of a Friedrich Duerrenmatt novel about a Swiss detective (Martin Ritt) who is obsessed with bringing to belated justice a former friend (Robert Shaw), now possessed of immense wealth and power, who 30 years earlier had killed a young woman. Director Maximilian Schell elicits strong performances from the cast, which also includes Jacqueline Bisset and Jon Voight, in this convincing crime melodrama about retribution and redemption. A-III PG)

End of the Road (1970)   Screen version of John Barth's novel about a catatonic (Stacy Keach) who falls into the hands of a mad doctor (James Earl Jones) practicing multi-media shock treatment on his insane patients. Directed by Aram Avakian, vignettes of perversion, sadism, masochism and fetishism are woven into a story of adultery and exploitation, ending in a gross abortion sequence. O (X)

Endangered Species (1982)   Ex-cop from New York City (Robert Urich) settles in Colorado to find peace and quiet but, instead, becomes involved in a bizarre case of cattle mutilations. Director Alan Rudolph manages to obscure a theme about chemical warfare by focusing upon the romance between the local sheriff (Jobeth Williams) and the boorish, foul-mouthed ex-cop. Some violence, nudity and rough language. A-III (R)

Endless Love (1981) Glossy fantasy about teen-age love takes an inexplicable turn when the boy (Martin Hewitt) sets fire to the house in which the girl (Brooke Shields) and her family are sleeping. Directed by Franco Zeffirelli, the lovemaking scenes and needless nudity dissolve all pretense of sensitivity. O (R)

Endless Summer, The (1966) Two young experts (Robert August and Mike Hinson) travel to Africa, New Zealand, Tahiti and Hawaii in search for the perfect wave. Producer-director Bruce Brown pictures the pleasures of surfing with enthusiasm and humor. A-I (br)

Enemy Mine (1985) In a science fiction parable about the solidarity of intelligent life forms, a human (Dennis Quaid) and a reptilian alien (Louis Gossett, Jr.), enemies from warring star systems, find themselves marooned on an uninhabited planet where they must work together or perish. Plodding script by Edward Khmara and leaden direction by Wolfgang Petersen make the premise more silly than it might have been. Violence and a confusing sequence involving the reptilian reproductive process. A-III (PG-13)

Enforcer, The (1977) Clint Eastwood again plays Dirty Harry, the sadistic San Francisco policeman who, with a female partner (Tyne Daly) in tow, is on the job tracking down an underground terrorist group. Director James Fargo's crime melodrama has scant concern for plot consistency but just enough realism for its excessive violence to be offensive. O (R)

England Made Me (1973) British screen version of the Graham Greene novel about a crooked Swedish tycoon (Peter Finch) and an ineffectual loser (Michael York) who gets in his way. By changing the locale from Depression Sweden to Hitler's Germany, director Peter Duffell focuses more on Nazi villainy than on the individual problems of the characters. The drama rejects the confused morality of its characters but lacks the sense of guilt that characterized Green's moral universe. A-IV (PG)

Enigma (1983) French-British production has an agent (Martin Sheen) sent on a perilous mission behind the Iron Curtain in this stodgy thriller directed by Jeannot Szwarc. Supporting cast, headed by Brigitte Fossey and Sam Neil, can do nothing to lift it above the conventional and mediocre. Some violence, brief nudity and a general air of moral ambiguity. A-III (PG)

Enough Rope (1966) French adaptation of a Patricia Highsmith mystery about a wife-killer (Gert Frobe), a man who would like to kill his wife (Maurice Ronet) and a police inspector (Robert Hossein) who gives them enough rope to wrap up his case. Directed by Claude Autant-Lara, the plot is intriguing in bringing together two strangers-in-crime, but the inspector's extra-legal methods are questionable. Mature themes. A-III (br)

Enter Laughing (1967) Autobiography based on comedian Carl Reiners first break into show biz. Reni Santoni is somewhat bland as the young comic but Elaine May creates an outlandishly laughable neurotic and Michael J. Pollard adds a fine folksy touch to the laughter. Also directed by Reiner, viewers will exit, if not laughing, at least smiling. A-I (br)

Enter the Dragon (1973) Domestic martial arts exercise with Bruce Lee, Jim Kelly, and John Saxton as secret agents out to get the goods on a dope and prostitution ring by taking part in a Kung Fu competition staged by the gang. Directed by Robert Clouse, the complications are simply an endless repetition of brutal beatings, undifferentiated by the participant's race, creed or sex. O (R)

Entertaining Mr. Sloane (1970) British screen version of Joe Orton's black comedy about an unscrupulous young man (Peter McEnery) being wooed and won simultaneously by a pathetic aging doxy (Beryl Reid) and her fastidious brother (Harry Andrews). Director Douglas Hickox gets too close to the corruption of human nature without the distancing of laughter that was intended, leaving most viewers incredulous about the film's surface reality and unconcerned about any inner meaning that might be there. A-IV (nr)

Equinox (1971) The forces of good and evil emerge to do battle, this time in an inept and highly ludicrous story of devils and monsters and invisible castles. Directed by Jack Woods, this cornball exercise in fright and horror has phony special effects that could only scare the very young. A-II (PG)

Equinox Flower (1977) Gentle Japanese domestic comedy about a father's foolish concerns over his daughter's marriage. Directed in 1958 by Yusujiro Ozu, the story is infused with his loving brand of insight into character and situation that transcends national boundaries. A-II (nr)

Equus (1977) Director Sidney Lumet has brought Peter Shaffer's play to the screen with Richard Burton as the psychiatrist who treats a 17-year-old boy (Peter Firth) accused of blinding six horses. The tedium is made bearable only by Burton's presence and the work of a fine supporting cast. The fearful punishment that heterosexuality takes, the violence of the blinding, and the nude scene are unwarranted and insensitive. O (R)

Ernest Goes to Camp (1987) TV commerical legend Jim Varney plays the slap-happy goon of the title who bears the brunt of juvenile pranks and the callous villainy of some land developers in director John R. Cherry III's lame, often violently slapstick comedy set in a children's summer camp. Ex-football star Lyle Alzado's convincingly brutal beating of the Chaplin-like clown and Ernest's numerous pratfalls are too realistic to be funny. A-III (PG)

Erotic Three, The (see: "Scratch Harry")

Eroticon (1972) Barnard L. Sackett's sex exploitation movie interviews free love advocates, illustrating their views with hard-core pornographic footage and smutty songs. O (X)

Escape Artist, The (1982) Teen-ager (Griffin O'Neal), trying to measure up to his dead father's reputation as a magician, puts his lock-picking and wallet-lifting skills to good use in exposing a ring of corrupt politicians. Director Caleb Deschanel's offbeat adventure story has a rather underdeveloped plot but what makes it worth seeing is O'Neal's precocious performance as the plucky youngster who beats an adult world at its own shady game. A-II (PG)

Escape from Alcatraz (1979) Clint Eastwood stars as a convict who attempts the impossible in a taut prison drama about one man's struggle to free himself from the conflicts and brutalities of the one-time island fortress known as the Siberia of prisons. Don Siegel's direction is grim but compelling. Some graphic violence. A-III (PG)

Escape from New York (1981) Futuristic fantasy written and directed by John Carpenter imagines the island of Manhattan as a prison for incorrigible criminals who have taken captive the U.S. President (Donald Pleasence) and a seedy, cynical war hero (Kurt Russell) is sent in to bring him out. It's a clunker with excessive violence, brutality and sexual innuendo. A-III (R)

Escape from the Planet of the Apes (1971) Third in the series features Roddy McDowall and Kim Hunter as the upright apes from the future who whisk through the time barrier to land in the USA of today. The chaos resulting from mankind's inhumanity to apes provides a so-so adventure that ends in tragedy but hope for the future in the birth of a baby ape. The appeal of director Don Taylor's movie is less in its ragged story than in its creation of an imaginative situation and the zesty performances of its two leads. A-I (G)

Escape to Athena (1979) Mediocre World War II movie has to do with a raid on a Nazi communications station in the Mediterranean led by some old familiar faces (Roger Moore, Telly Savalas, Elliott Gould and David Niven). British production directed by George Pan Cosmatos, it has considerable violence and a few brothel scenes. A-III (PG)

Escape to Nowhere (1974) French spy thriller about a physicist (Lino Ventura) who is fleeing for his life from Soviet agents and whose only chance of survival is to trade a Soviet spy for his life. Director Claude Pinoteau has given new life to the old conventions of suspense, with menace and threat everywhere and the most ordinary places concealing potential dangers. A-II (PG)

Escape to the Sun (1972) Heavy, melodramatic escape adventure about a pair of Soviet Jews who hijack an Aeroflot jetliner to land at an abandoned airstrip and pick up a group of Jews hiding nearby. Director Menahem Golan's story is grim in outlook and execution, especially a long torture sequence, and its political implications require mature perspective and sensitivity. A-III (PG)

Escape to Witch Mountain (1975) Above average Disney adventure about two orphans with supernatural powers who become runaways sought by a greedy millionaire, muddled police, gangsters who think they are witches and even their own mysterious relatives from another solar system. Younger children will love the fantasy of kids having powers adults don't but parents may wish that director John Hough had put a little more zest in the action. A-I (G)

E.T. the Extra-Terrestrial (1982) Ugly-duckling fable in which a boy (Henry Thomas) befriends a stranded alien creature from outer space and helps him return to his home. Director Steven Spielberg fashions an inspiring image of youthful innocence and courage in a story that some may find overly sentimental. Nevertheless, the childlike fantasy conveys some genuine emotion and a message of trust and peace that the family might enjoy sharing. A-I (PG)

Eugenie (1970) Sex exploitation movie about a woman (Marie Liljedahl) who journeys into perversions perpetrated by satanists for the sex and violence trade. O (X)

Europeans, The (1979) Screen version of the Henry James novel is a quiet comedy of manners about the unsettling effect of their European cousins (Lee Remick and Robin Ellis) upon the Wentworths, a proper Bostonian family. Though pleasant enough to watch, director James Ivory's moderately entertaining period piece lacks a sense of vitality and the feel for life that is to be found in

the original. A-II (nr)

Evel Knievel (1971) Dramatization with George Hamilton playing a real-life character whose story this slapdash movie purports to be from growing up in Butte, Montana, and getting started on the motorcycle circuit to preparing for his impossible jump over 19 cars. Director Marvin Chomsky's portrayal of a man driven by the desire to forever outdo himself in order to fend off personal insecurities has a passing interest, but Evel's amiable antics do not completely redeem the immaturity of his feelings about death or the cynical attitude of those fans who watch hoping for the worst. A-III (GP)

Even Dwarfs Started Small (1972) Pretentious German movie in which the head of some kind of correctional institution is forced to barricade himself inside his office while crude male and female midget inmates wreak havoc upon the facilities and one another. Director Werner Herzog has come up with a visually striking, emotionally disturbing, curiosity piece which will tax the patience of most viewers. A-IV (nr)

Evening with the Royal Ballet, An (1965) Filmed on stage at the Royal Opera House in London, the work features Margot Fonteyn and Rudolph Nureyev in the performance of four ballets and two encores. Directed by Anthony Asquith and Anthony Havelock-Allan, it is a record of a prime ballet event marred only by static camerawork. A-I (br)

Event, An (1970) Yugoslavian adaptation of a short story by Chekhov relates a simple, tragic tale of a little boy and his grandfather who take a horse to the market and are waylaid on their return. Directed by Vatroslav Mimica, the hauntingly beautiful photography and credible acting of the small cast help make this small but terrible event an emotional experience of universal dimension. A-III (nr)

Events (1970) Feeble sex exploitation movie about a filmmaker making a stag movie to finance a serious movie. Director Fred Baker exploits a group of non-actors cavorting in graphic sexual excess. O (nr)

Every Bastard a King (1970) Israeli movie set during the Six Day War is a contrived potboiler about an American journalist (William Berger) trying to understand the new society of Israel. Director Uri Zohar's title refers to the Israeli's spirit of democracy, but the movie itself manages to turn an interesting subject into a mediocre and incredibly muddled melodrama. A-III (GP)

Every Little Crook and Nanny (1972) The nanny of the title (Lynn Redgrave) revenges the loss of her dancing school by kidnapping the young son of the crime boss responsible (Victor Mature). Director Cy Howard plays the situation comedy for dumb, at times coarse, laughs. A-III (PG)

Every Time We Say Goodbye (1986) Iowa minister's son (Tom Hanks) joins the British Royal Air Force during World War II, meets a Jewish Hispanic girl living in Palestine and convinces her to wait for him to return after the war. The overdone, glossy romance has some positive value in exploring the meaning of full commitment required for marriage. Bedroom scene and some violence. A-III (PG-13)

Every Which Way But Loose (1979) Clint Eastwood stars as a footloose trucker and barroom brawler who falls in love with a fickle country-western singer (Sondra Locke). Supporting characters includes an orangutan and Ruth Gordon as a foul-mouthed old lady whose antics and vocabulary are supposed to be funny. Director James Fargo's slipshod movie features unremitting violence and sick humor. O (PG)

Everything You Always Wanted to Know About Sex But Were Afraid to Ask (1972) Writer-director Woody Allen's take-off on Dr. David Reuben's book and the curiosity that made it a best-seller does better debunking sex obsessions than sex itself. The result is an uneven jumble of sketches, most of which go on too long, and range from the witty to the perverse, from hilarious sight gags to crudely offensive material. O (R)

Evil That Men Do, The (1984) Soldier-of-fortune (Charles Bronson) is hired to kill a political despot. Director Lee J. Thompson's violent action vehicle is set against the background of an oppressive regime in Central America, but sidesteps any serious political commentary in favor of the usual excessively brutal melodrama. O (R)

Evil Under the Sun (1982) Hercule Poirot (Peter Ustinov) is the thoughtful sleuth on a mission in the Adriatic in this fairly amusing adaptation of the Agatha Christie story. Director Guy Hamilton's British production turns the mystery into a travelogue which, lacking suspense, allows a talented cast free reign. The dialogue contains a few double entendres meant as witty insults. A-II (PG)

Excalibur (1981) Long and lavish retelling of the legendary story of King Arthur (Nigel Terry) and his tutor Merlin (Nicol Williamson) is distinguished by an earnest sincerity and by its impressive settings, visual effects and cinematography. The treatment emphasizes the folk magic elements of the legend rather than its early Christian origin. In striving for effect, however, director John Boorman overdoes the sex and violence. O (R)

Executioner, The (1970) British spy thriller about an agent (George Peppard) who suspects a top level government security leak and takes it upon himself to execute the person he believes responsible. Director Sam Wanamaker emphasizes gray areas of conscience and morality in a setting of violence and intrigue but the plot is unnecessarily complicated and lacking in subtlety, sympathy and credibility. A-III (GP)

Executive Action (1973) Failed political thriller about a conspiracy of right-wing millionaires who are behind the assassination of President John F. Kennedy neglects to offer any coherent, convincing demonstration of its fictional premise. Director David Miller wastes a good cast (Robert Ryan, Burt Lancaster and Will Geer) in a static movie that is disturbing only in its inability to stir even pathos for the fallen President. A-III (PG)

Exorcist, The (1974) Screen version of the William Blatty novel about the demonic possession of a young girl (Linda Blair) and two priests (Jason Miller and Max von Sydow) who try to exorcize the devil from her. Directed by William Friedkin, the movie is on shaky ground theologically and its special effects are horrific but it is exciting horror fantasy for those with strong stomachs. Its violence and obscenity as well as the powerful effect its subject matter and special effects could have on young viewers makes it strictly adult fare. A-IV (R)

Exorcist II: The Heretic (1977) It is four years later and Reagan (Linda Blair), still bothered by a demon, is in the care of a psychiatrist (Louise Fletcher) and gets some help from a priest (Richard Burton) assigned to investigate the case. Director John Boorman's crass sequel, through simple ineptitude or outright ignorance, manages to denigrate a whole range of religious values. Some violence and profanity. O (R)

Explorers, The (1985) Three 12-year-old boys, inspired by dreams, rig up their own spaceship and have some unusual close encounters. Moderately entertaining, but too much time is spent on the preliminaries with the outer-space payoff not packing the punch that it was meant to, namely some kind of profound lesson that lies beyond the cinematic vocabulary of director Joe Dante. Some profanity in the mouths of the young space cadets. A-II (PG)

Explosion (1970) Canadian movie about a disturbed youth (Gordon Thomson) whose anti-Vietnam views supposedly cause him to rape a woman, flee to Canada and join a local hippie (Don Stroud) on an orgy of sex and violence through British Columbia. Director Jules Bricken's one-dimensional melodrama is hopelessly confused with flashbacks and fantasy sequences that rely for interest on bloodshed and nudity. O (R/GP)

Exposed (1983) Wisconsin farm girl (Nastassia Kinski) becomes a hot New York model and falls for a concert violinist (Rudolf Nureyev) who turns out to be a notorious terrorist tracking down his mother's murderer (Harvey Keitel). Director James Toback's shallow and silly vehicle exploits serious issues in an attempt to appear chic and witty. Excessive graphic sexuality. O (R)

Exterminating Angel, The (1967) A number of wealthy party guests find that after a long night in the home of their host, they are unable to leave, held by some mysterious force. In the days that follow, their veneer of politeness disintegrates until raw ego shows through. When finally released from each other's presence, they gather in a church to celebrate their deliverance only to discover themselves once again unable to leave. Director Luis Bunuel's 1962 surrealistic satire amusingly suggests that hell is other people. A-III (br)

Exterminator, The (see: "The Inheritor")

Extraordinary Seaman, The (1969) World War II action fantasy in which a captain in the Royal Navy (David Niven) who died in 1914 is granted a celestial reprieve to vindicate an inglorious death by taking on the Japanese Navy with his dilapidated island steamer. Director John Frankenheimer fails in an embarrasssingly bad effort to keep this seagoing bomb afloat. A-II (G)

Extreme Close-Up (1973) Researching a story on electronic surveillance techniques, a reporter (James McMullan) becomes obsessed with the easily obtainable gadgets of the trade and their potential for invading the private lives of innocent people. Director Jeannot Szwarc uses Michael Crichton's screenplay simply as a vehicle for spying upon the sexual escapades of a rather dull group of characters. O (R)

Extreme Prejudice (1987) Nick Nolte plays a bulletproof Texas Ranger poised to stamp out a drug traffic kingpin (Powers Boothe) with the aid of a ruthless commando group made up of legally dead Vietnam vets headed by a double-crossing major (Michael Ironside). Director Walter Hill's lengthy sequences of excessively brutal gunplay and some nudity mark this as a conventional blood-and-guts timewaster. O (R)

Extremities (1986) A woman (Farrah Fawcett) is the target of a sadistic rapist (James Russo) whom she manages to restrain and molest in turn. Film plays upon the vulnerability of women in a man's world and suggests that fighting back is an essential survival tactic. It concludes somewhat weakly that justice must be tempered with mercy in spite of possible further endangerment. Instead of being thought-provoking, the film brutalizes the viewer with explicit scenes of sadism, violence and foul language. O (R)

Eye for an Eye, An (1966) Routine Western directed by Michael Moore in which a former bounty hunter (Robert Lansing) teams with a young bounty hunter (Pat Wayne) to take revenge on the villains who brutally murdered his wife and son. Stylized violence and the revenge is accomplished through self-defense. A-II (br)

Eye of the Cat (1969) San Francisco mansion full of cats is the setting for the story of two nephews (Michael Sarrazin and Tim Henry) scheming to eliminate a rich, but ailing aunt (Eleanor Parker) and each other in order to inherit her fortune. Director David Lowell Rich manipulates the cats for shock and suspense effect but not enough to cover the gaping holes in the plot. Some violence and sexual implications. A-III (PG)

Eye of the Devil (1967) The head of an aristocratic French family (David Niven) journeys to his ancestral chateau to offer himself as a victim in a religious rite practiced by his forbears. Under the direction of J. Lee Thompson, the performances of Niven and Deborah Kerr compensate for a plot that often strains credibility. A-III (br)

Eye of the Needle (1981) Mediocre British screen version of Ken Follet's World War II thriller in which a coldly proficient German spy (Donald Sutherland) becomes distracted from his mission when he encounters a love-starved woman (Kate Nelligan) on a bleak island off the coast of Scotland. Directed by Richard Marquand, the unabsorbing melodrama combines a conventional espionage plot with a needlessly explicit depiction of a love affair. O (R)

Eyes of a Stranger (1981) Sadistic rapist-murderer (John DiSanti) stalks the blind adolescent sister (Jennifer Jason Leigh) of a television reporter (Lauren Tewes) in this sleazy, amateurish horror movie. Director Ken Wiederhorn's suspense thriller forfeits finesse in favor of stomach-churning violence and nudity. O (R)

Eyes of Laura Mars, The (1978) Failed thriller about a series of brutal murders that happen exactly as seen in the premonitions of a top New York fashion photographer (Faye Dunaway). The shallow, slick, kinky movie directed by Irvin Kershner leeringly exploits sex and violence. O (R)

Eyewitness (1981) A young janitor (William Hurt) falls in love with a television reporter (Sigourney Weaver) whom he has never met and, when she asks him questions about a murder committed in his building, he pretends to know more about the crime than he actually does. Director Peter Yates' romantic mystery succeeds better in terms of characterization of the young couple than its muddled attempts at suspense. Some violence and a rather graphic bedroom scene. A-III (R)

F

Face to Face (1976) Stockholm psychiatrist (Liv Ullmann) discovers that she must heal herself

when she suffers from a nervous breakdown in director Ingmar Bergman's clinical investigation into the realm of the feminine psyche. Ullmann's magnificent performance conveys the failure of psychiatry as a remedy to the disappointments and contradictions of her guilt-ridden life. The movie includes some harrowing scenes, including an attempted rape, but the emphasis is on the interior journey to peace of soul. A-III (R)

Faces (1968) Director John Cassavetes intense study of the marital crisis of a middle-aged, middle-class couple (Gena Rowlands and John Marley) who discover that divorce isn't the answer to their personal emptiness and despairing search for meaning in life. Troubling, sardonic, somewhat depressing treatment of a mature theme that is part of so many contemporary relationships. Some rough language, sexual innuendo and a suicide attempt. A-IV (br)

Faces of Love (1978) A movie director (Jean-Louis Trintignant) tries to win back his ex-wife (Delphine Seyrig) by starring her in an adaptation of Chekhov's "The Three Sisters" (with Lea Massari and Valerie Mairesse as the other leads). Swiss director Michael Soutter wastes a talented cast with what is in effect a shallow exercise in psychodrama. A-III (nr)

Fail Safe (1964) A mechanical failure makes impossible the recall of nuclear bombers headed for Russia in a movie questioning the ability of humans to control their inventions. Sidney Lumet directs Henry Fonda, Dan O'Herlihy and various machines with mounting suspense. A-II (br)

Falcon and the Snowman, The (1985) Some boyhood friends, now young men (Timothy Hutton and Sean Penn), sell secret data to the Soviets. How all this happened and why is an engrossing and very well-acted story but director John Schlesinger has left too many loose ends and tends to sentimentalize these treasonous actions as mistaken idealism. Brief nudity, some drug use and ambivalent treatment of a complex subject. A-III (R)

Falling in Love (1984) Two train commuters (Robert De Niro and Meryl Streep) fall in love, have a secret affair and part, never resolving their true feelings and their commitments to others. Although the story is essentially about adultery, the whole enterprise is so lacking in substance that moral principles hardly seem relevant. Director Ulu Grosbard fails to convey adequately the moral dilemma which was meant to be the core of the film's romantic theme. A-II (PG-13)

Falling in Love Again (1980) Elliott Gould plays the middle-aged owner of a Beverly Hills garment store who spends his time in nostalgic daydreams about his Bronx origins much to the chagrin of his wife (Susannah York) in this contrived and determinedly simple-minded little movie written and directed by Steven Paul. A bedroom sequence and a certain moral ambiguity makes this mature fare. A-III (PG)

Fame (1980) Irene Cara and several other talented youngsters from various ethnic and racial backgrounds learn the showbiz ropes studying in New York City's High School for the Performing Arts. Following them from audition to graduation, director Alan Parker's movie is a vibrant showcase for physical prowess not the least of which is demonstrated in some scenes involving nudity in a sexual context. Permissive sexual attitudes and irreverent treatment of religion overshadow the film's portrait of youngsters expressing their creativity and striving for professionalism. O (R)

Family, The (1987) Interesting Italian production recounting the lives of several generations of a family inhabiting an elegant apartment in Rome from the turn of the century to the present. Directed by Ettore Scola, the family portrait recalled by an aging man (Vittorio Gassman) is limited to the domestic life within the rooms of the apartment over the years. Many will find its fragmentary vignettes of personal drama surprisingly remote and lacking in emotional involvement. Some mature themes. A-III (PG)

Family Game, The (1984) Japanese director Yoshimitsu Morita fashions a gentle and noble comedy of family life and incisively chronicles their problems and how they resolve them. For those willing to read subtitles, the film will be an enjoyable as well as rewarding experience of the universality of family themes. A-II (nr)

Family Honor (1973) New York cop (Anthony Page) seeks revenge on the policemen who set up his father, also a member of the force, for opposing their taking payoffs from mobsters. Director Clark Worswick's crime movie is remarkable only in its consistent mediocrity which follows a predictable course of killings, drug traffic, warehouse confrontations and corruption in high places. Some Italian Americans may be offended by ethnic stereotyping. A-III (R)

Family Plot (1976) Director Alfred Hitchcock turns in a below-par thriller about the efforts of a not-quite-bogus medium (Barbara Harris) and her not-too-bright boy friend (Bruce Dern) to match wits with a pair of diabolically clever kidnappers (William Devane and Karen Black). The movie is peppered with profanity and unwitty double entendres, perhaps meant to inject some life into a slack picture. A-III (PG)

Family Way, The (1967) The lives of a young married couple (Hywell Bennett and Hayley Mills) are frought with problems, including the groom's temporary inability to consummate their union. The groom's well-meaning but domineering father (John Mills) stands in his son's way but it is the strengths of family life that save the day. Directed by Roy Boulting with musical score by Paul McCartney. A-IV (br)

Fan, The (1981) Young psychopath (Michael Biehn) stalks a glamorous star (Lauren Bacall) with whom he has become obsessed, striking with a razor at those whom he believes are preventing her from seeing him. Bacall is very good, but here she lends her presence and talent to a cheap, exploitative movie by director Ed Bianchi who seems obsessed with delivering brutal visual shocks. Extremely graphic violence. O (R)

Fandango (1985) It's May 1971, and five new-minted Texas college graduates go off on a car trip to the Mexican border in search of their lost youth—fleeing Vietnam, marriage, regular jobs and other fearful spectres. Written and directed by Kevin Reynolds, the movie is sporadically amusing but more often sentimental, self-indulgent and tedious. Some brief nudity meant to be comic. A-II (PG)

Fando and Lis (1970) In an allegorical search for eternal happiness, Sergio Klainer and Diana Mariscal journey through a rocky, garbage-strewn landscape where a grotesque assortment of nightmarish characters confront them with sex and perversions. Scripted by Fernando Arrabal, directed by Alexandro Jodorowsky and filmed in Mexico, the bizarre narrative lacks coherence and is exploitative in its treatment of sex and violence. O (nr)

Fanny and Alexander (1983) Directed by Ingmar Bergman, this autobiographical mood piece set at Christmas in 1907 examines family ties through the eyes of a 10-year-old boy. Replete with the themes of earlier films, the period drama has none of the depth and perception of Bergman at his best but does offer the spectacle of a lavish re-creation. Scatological and sexually-derived humor and some brief nudity set the naturalistic tone of this decidedly mature tale of Swedish provincial life. A-IV (R)

Fanny Hill (1969) Swedish exploitation movie directed by Mac Ahlberg about an inexperienced country girl (Diana Kjaer) who comes to the big city to find a job. The situation is used as the premise for a series of crudely explicit sexual encounters. O (R)

Fantasia (1940) Walt Disney's only excursion into the world of the fine arts presents eight selections of classical music, including Dukas' "Sorcerers Apprentice" with Mickey Mouse and a bucket brigade of brooms, Stravinsky's "Rite of Spring" with its massive, earth-bound images and the macabre vision of Musorgsky's "Night on Bald Mountain." Using different approaches and animation styles for each separate section, it was not only Disney's most ambitious undertaking but it remains an enjoyably creative introduction to fine music, especially for youngsters. A-I (G)

Fantastic Animation Festival (1977) Compilation consisting of 16 award-winning animated films. The majority are solidly entertaining, especially two featuring the clay figures of Will Vinton. For youngsters, it's a chance to view other approaches to the art of frame-by-frame moviemaking in contrast to Saturday morning cartoon fare. A-II (PG)

Fantastic Planet (1973) Lovely, haunting animated feature set in the far distant future where humans have become miniscule vermin in a world of purple reptilian giants who periodically exterminate the humans just as people today routinely exterminate rodents and roaches. For adults, this unusual picture, the creation of Rene Laloux and a Franco-Czech production team, can be a fascinating experience, heightened by its surrealistic imagery and eerie electronic soundtrack. Youngsters, however, might be disturbed by the occasional brutalities and the type of nudity associated with tribes living in a savage state. A-III (R/PG)

Fantastic Voyage (1966) The miniaturization of a medical team to the size of a molecule and their injection into a stroke patient's bloodstream is the only possible way to save the life of an important scientist. Director Richard Fleischer's incredible plot premise yields rich dividends in the form of exacting special effects re-creating the surreal world within the human body. A-I (br)

Fantomas (1966) Gimmicky French-Italian superhero story about a master of disguise who battles all manner of Parisian criminals is directed by Andre Hanebelle in the melodramatic style of the old Saturday matinee adventure serials. Innocuous escapist fare. A-I (br)

Far from the Madding Crowd (1967) Excellent British screen version of Thomas Hardy's romantic melodrama of early Victorian country life with Julie Christie being pursued by Peter Finch, Terence Stamp and Alan Bates. Director John Schlesinger avoids the pitfalls of the formula blockbuster and comes up with a superbly realistic, atmospheric production filmed entirely on location in Hardy's Dorset. A-II (br)

Farenheit 451 (1966)   A fireman (Oskar Werner) reforms his book-burning ways in this adaptation of Ray Bradbury's science fiction novel about a society that forbids the printed word. First rate performances by Julie Christie in a dual role as two women in the fireman's life and Cyril Cusack as a smiling fanatic help sustain the dream-like reality of director Francois Truffaut's allegorical fantasy. A-II (br)

Farewell, My Lovely (1975)   Hulking ex-convict (Jack O'Halloran) hires private investigator Philip Marlowe (Robert Mitchum) to find his girl friend, though she hasn't bothered to write while he served a seven year sentence for bank robbery. Director Dick Richards' version of the Raymond Chandler mystery is skillfully crafted and Mitchum gives an outstanding performance. A-III (R) Some violence and incidental nudity. A-III (R)

Farewell Uncle Tom (1972)   Gualtiero Jacopetti and Franco Prosperi have been responsible for a long and dismayingly popular series of pseudo-documentaries but this time their subject is an historical one, slavery in the United States. Their voyeuristic treatment of the subject is simply vicarious flesh-peddling and the concluding section, specially prepared for the American version of this Italian film, can only deepen racial misunderstanding. O (X)

Farmer, The (1977)   Revenge story of a World War II veteran (Gary Conway) has arty pretensions but not a spark of intelligence. Mechanically directed by David Berlatsky, it is excessively brutal and sexually degrading. O (R)

Fast Break (1979)   Very funny movie about a new basketball coach (Gabe Kaplan) who recruits a motley collection of youths to give an obscure college a winning season. Directed by Jack Smight, it contains some rough language and several mildly suggestive sexual scenes. A-III (PG)

Fast Charlie...The Moonbeam Rider (1979)   Failed period road comedy about a World War I vet (David Carradine) who enlists the aid of some of his old buddies to help him enter a transcontinental motorcycle race. Director Steve Carver's thin story is amiable but not very funny. Permissive attitude toward casual sex. A-III (PG)

Fast Forward (1985)   Some bright and talented teenagers from Sandusky, Ohio, go to New York to win a dance contest without bothering to inform their parents. The poor kids have to hang on for a month or so before they make it to the top. Mediocre entertainment, disappointingly directed by Sidney Poitier. Some vulgar language, nose-thumbing at parental authority and teenage drinking presented as humorous. A-III (PG)

Fast Talking (1986)   A modern artful dodger lies, cheats and steals his way out of high school and into the brave new world of self-sufficiency in reaction to flawed family, alienated friends and a social order which offers little positive encouragement. But it's hard to accept the amiable, resourceful teenager as someone incapable of finding positive options. The film points to the moral and political inadequacies of adult society but in less than constructive fashion. A-III (nr)

Fast Times at Ridgemont High (1982)   Director Amy Heckerling's examination of teen mores in the suburban jungle of shopping malls,

discos and the playing fields of Southern California has some insights. However, for the most part it is a crass, insensitive and superficial movie with an unsettling nastiness lurking just beneath its pleasant surface. Some extremely graphic nudity and a scene of adolescents discussing oral sex. O (X/R)

Fat City (1972)   Complex character study of two boxers, one a has-been (Stacy Keach) and the other a youth of 19 (Jeff Bridges) whose prospects on the B-grade California boxing circuit are at best uncertain. Director John Huston's theme of wasted lives and loves and the hopes of youth for affluence and success (the ironic meaning of the title) are evocative but unsatisfying in terms of the dramatic whole. Well-staged, realistic fight sequences. A-III (PG)

Fata Morgana (1974)   German director Werner Herzog's interior journey to Africa is a stunning portrait of the North African landscape where people are transformed into fragments of an alien, dreamlike world. For those adventurous enough to take a trip without the security of guideposts, it will most likely prove a consciousness-expanding experience. A-III (nr)

Fatal Attraction (1987)   Predatory, happily-married lawyer (Michael Douglas) has a fling with a compulsive admirer (Glenn Close) and both suffer the dangerous consequences. Director Adrian Lyne's fatalistic romance begins as a moral tale and ends as melodramatic bloodbath. Several graphic love-making scenes and rough language and violence dominate. O (R)

Fathom (1967)   Mindless spy intrigue with Raquel Welch being pursued by plane, by boat, by harpoonist and by bull (both figuratively and literally). Directed by Leslie Martinson, the star vehicle becomes tiresome long before the ending. A-II (br)

Fatso (1980)   Actress Anne Bancroft fails to convey much sincerity or intelligence in her directorial debut. Her comedy stars Dom DeLuise as a compulsive eater who is so shocked by the early death of an obese cousin that he determines to lose weight. The humor is weighted down, however, by foul language and silly sight-gags in a social satire which provides little insight into a serious malady. A-III (PG)

Fear, The (1967)   Greek movie directed by Costas Manoussakis centers on a retarded youth's morbid preoccupation with sex and is offensive because of its explicit treatment of erotic activities. O (br)

Fear Eats the Soul—Ali (1974)   German movie in which a 60-year-old cleaning woman meets a young Moroccan mechanic, and out of mutual loneliness and a desperate need for some special other person, they marry and encounter the same rejection and discrimination suffered by minorities everywhere. Directed by Rainer Werner Fassbinder, the story is simply told and yet is profoundly human and affecting in its picture of two ordinary people persecuted by a hypocritical society. A-IV (nr)

Fear Is the Key (1973)   Adaptation of Alistair MacLean thriller about an ex-salvage operator (Barry Newman) who, by reason of a wild and complex chain of events, finds himself in the palatial home of an oil heiress (Suzy Kendall) and given the task of dredging up a sunken treasure. Director Michael Tuchner's wildly improbable melodrama in which nothing is what it seems is moderately entertaining, mercifully short on sex and violence but awfully hard to swallow. A-II (PG)

Fear No Evil (1981) Bright but popular high school student is possessed by the devil in this inept horror film written and directed by Frank Laloggia. Excessive violence, nudity and exploitation of religious themes. O (R)

Fearless Frank (1969) The Second City gang have put together a super-spoof of crime movies with some digs at sex and religion. Jon Voight plays Frank, a Superman character flying through the air and fighting evil wherever it rears its ugly head. Director Philip Kaufman's campy, superficial adult comedy is of limited quality and appeal. A-III (G)

Fearless Vampire Killers, The (1967) Offbeat horror spoof in which an old scholar of the occult (Jack McGowran) and his young assistant (Polanski) seek out a vampire's castle in the hills of Transylvania, using the tools of garlic, the cross and a wooden stake in their research but the vampires are released to spread throughout the world. Also directed by Polanski, it is imitation camp at best, all very short on humor, long on blood-drinking and sexual innuendo. A-III (br)

Fedora (1979) Down-on-his-luck Hollywood producer (William Holden) journeys to the Greek island of Corfu to persuade a legendary actress (Marthe Keller) to come out of retirement and play the lead in his movie. German production directed by Billy Wilder is a failed curiosity piece about the old and the new wave of moviemakers. Some adult situations. A-III (PG)

Fellini Satyricon (1970) Federico Fellini's self-indulgent vision of ancient Rome presents not a story but a series of sequences juxtaposed with little or no cause and effect relationship. Buried beneath its array of imagery ranging from the sensuous and opulent to the grotesque and orgiastic are such unconnected themes as youth's search for fulfillment, the destruction of the artist by his patrons and the collapse of a society burdened by the luxury of wealth. Though an extraordinary visual experience, it is disappointing in its lack of structure, logic and viewer engagement. Many scenes of sex and violence. A-IV (R)

Fellini's Casanova (1977) Director Federico Fellini's first English-language production concentrates on the sordid details of the sexual legend surrounding Giacomo Casanova without concern for any human dimensions of the worldly lover. Technically brilliant but lacking emotion, it is an empty work. Some nudity and consistently gross and perverse imagery becomes tedious and excessive. O (R)

Fellini's Roma (1972) Director Federico Fellini's imaginary tour of Rome is founded on an indulgent nostalgia for the 1930s and 1940s as against the city's present-day traffic jams, tourist traps and imported lifestyles. His dramatic re-creations of the past are at times heavy-handed (the pathetic contrast between cheap and high-class bordellos) or coy (an ecclesiastical fashion show) but, for the most part, they are fond and playful evocations of a Rome that no longer exists except in memory. Some grotesque images may be troubling. A-IV (R)

Female Animal, The (1970) Biographical account of a young woman (Arlene Tiger) who became a prostitute because of family and social pressures. Its gross treatment of basically immoral situations nullifies whatever social value it may have intended. O (nr)

Female Bunch, The (1972) Drugs, sex and sadism are the routine for a group of women at a remote ranch where some lustful admirers (Russ Tamblyn and Lon Chaney, Jr.) become tortured victims of the gang. Sex exploitation Western directed by Al Adamson and John Cardos. O (R)

Female Response, The (1972) Sex exploitation story of a newspaper lovelorn columnist (Raina Barrett) exploring the sex life of five women. Voyeuristic trash directed by Tim Kincaid. O (R)

Femme de Personne (1986) In a French production directed by Christopher Frank, four women try to work out their individual problems in relationships with stereotyped males in an over-long drama whose message is that men are a lost cause and that women must sustain and support themselves. Promiscuity and infidelity are treated as positive strategies for women's survival in an alienating world of insensitive men. Some nudity. O (nr)

Ferris Bueller's Day Off (1986) Director John Hughes turns in a lighthearted spoof about a teenager (Matthew Broderick) who has made a science out of truancy because he likes to take a break now and then to observe the world around him. The cheerfully implausible plot serves as the catalyst in changing the attitudes of his sister and best friend. Some vulgar language. A-II (PG-13)

Fever Heat (1968) Low-budget melodrama about a former stock-car racer (Nick Adams) who becomes romantically involved with the widow (Jeannine Riley) of a racer and she overcomes her fear of the dirt track. Director Russell S. Doughten Jr. does better with the world of racing than with the development of the personal relations of his characters. A-II (br)

Fever Pitch (1985) Sportswriter (Ryan O'Neal) addicted to gambling is sent to Las Vegas to do a story about compulsive gamblers. A well-intentioned drama about the evils of gambling that, unfortunately, becomes dull and repetitive, with a neat upbeat ending that undercuts the seriousness of the problem. Brief nudity and vulgar language. A-III (R)

Ffolkes (1980) Eccentric soldier of fortune (Roger Moore) and his crack team of underwater commandos are recruited by Her Majesty's Government to battle a sinister duo (Anthony Perkins and Michael Parks) and their dastardly gang of hijackers. Moore is in top form in director Andrew V. McLaglan's thriller which, unfortunately, has somewhat more graphic violence than necessary. A-III (PG)

Fiddler on the Roof (1971) Fine family entertainment awaits in a screen adaptation of the Broadway musical about Tevye (Topol), a milk seller in a Czarist-era Russian village whose life of Jewish Orthodoxy is filled with joy and sadness but always buoyed by the human spirit and eternal hope. Struggling in a time of cultural and political flux to find suitable husbands for his three dowry-less daughters, Tevye has more than his share of earthly challenges. But his faith and hope and sheer love of life and humankind keep him and the family going. Norman Jewison's direction does full justice to an appealing musical whose book is by Joseph Stein, music by Jerry Bock and lyrics by Sheldon Harnick. A-I (G)

Fiendish Plot of Dr. Fu Manchu, The (1980) Peter Sellers, in his last movie, plays both the diabolical 168-year-old Fu Manchu and his now-retired nemesis, Nayland Smith of Scotland Yard. Seller's forte as a character actor is not supported by any comic imagination behind either the clumsy script or the flat direction of Piers Haggard. Some vulgar expletives and a mildly suggestive striptease. A-II (PG)

Fifth Floor, The (1980)   A young woman (Diane Hull) is wrongly committed to an institution for the insane in this exploitation movie directed by Howard Avedis. Contains much nudity and violence. O (R)

5th Musketeer, The (1979)   Uninspired Austrian remake of the 1939 American movie, "The Man in the Iron Mask," stars a miscast Beau Bridges in the dual role of Louis XIV and his twin brother, with aged musketeers Jose Ferrer, Cornel Wilde, Alan Hale Jr. and Lloyd Bridges assuring that the good twin ascends the throne. Director Ken Annakin's lackluster adventure includes some adult situations. A-III (PG)

52 Pick-up (1986)   A wealthy industrialist and unfaithful husband (Roy Scheider), who dabbles in the sleazy underworld of drugs and sex, is taped in a liaison with a young girl that implicates him in her subsequent murder. The demand for blackmail motivates him to use his money to set the killers against themselves. The nasty peep-show ambiance of the proceedings, directed by John Frankenheimer, wallows in brutish violence, nudity, drugs and profanity. O (R)

Fighting Back (1982)   Inner-city Italian American (Tom Skerrit) organizes his neighbors to fight crime. Despite a muddled homage to the complexity of big city problems and an attempt to give some sort of moral perspective, the end result is the usual formula of simplistic violence as the way to solve all problems. Director Lewis Teague's movie is too morally confused to avoid giving the impression of extolling the virtues of vigilantism. Abundant violence. O (R)

Fighting Prince of Donegal, The (1966)   Young Irish prince tries to unite his country against the occupation by soldiers of Queen Elizabeth. Directed by Michael O'Herlihy, this Walt Disney production is an unpretentious action piece with adequate acting by its young leads, Peter McEnery and Susan Hampshire, and Gordon Jackson excels in the villainy department. A-I (br)

Figures in a Landscape (1971)   Enigmatic chase movie begins with two escaped prisoners (Robert Shaw and Malcolm McDowell), hands bound, fleeing across a desolate Spanish countryside, pursued by a helicopter that occasionally shoots at them. Director Joseph Losey never explains who the fugitives are, nor from whom they are fleeing, in a movie that has only a middle, an unexplained antagonism between the principals and a landscape in which both figures and viewers become lost. A-III (GP)

File of the Golden Goose (1969)   Yul Brynner portrays a tough, determined American CIA agent trying to infiltrate a British counterfeiting gang. Director Sam Wanamaker's rather pedestrian British spy thriller contains some rather gruesome killings, coarse language and homosexual references of questionable taste. A-III (PG)

Fillmore (1972)   Documentary record of the final days and closing night at Fillmore West, the pioneering San Francisco rock house, showing rock producer Bill Graham in action, for instance, haggling with the managers of groups he wants to perform in the farewell concert. Those who do include Jefferson Airplane, Santana, Quicksilver, New Riders of the Purple Sage and Hot Tuna. Director Richard T. Heffron has not only captured some of the bittersweet moments of a memorable event, but has made an enlightening work about the rock world. Scatter-shot profanity in an otherwise wholesome and entertaining movie. A-III (R)

Film Portrait (1974)   The year before his death in 1972, Jerome Hill put together this picture which consists of his reflections on the magic of cinema and on how his own life got so intimately bound up with it. Definitely for film students but the casual moviegoer may also enjoy it because it's an interesting look at an individual taking stock of his life's work and finding it, on the whole, something still filled with wonder. A-I (nr)

Final Chapter—Walking Tall (1977)   Like the previous two movies about Tennessee Sheriff Buford Pusser and his fight against crime in McNairy County, Tennessee, director Jack Starrett's version is crude and simplistic in its good guys vs. bad guys approach. Bo Svenson in the Pusser role is a sensitive and appealing performer with a fine presence which, unfortunately, is wasted in the rigors of excessive violence and bloodshed. O (R)

Final Comedown, The (1972)   Black exploitation movie with Billy Dee Williams as a young man on his way to death and destruction is a quite simple story cluttered unnecessarily by a raft of flashbacks. Written, produced and directed by Oscar Williams, the movie pits the violence of ghetto blacks against the fears of middle-class whites and relies on prejudice and stereotype for effect. Relentless stream of vile epithets and a generous helping of gratuitous nudity. O (R)

Final Conflict, The (1981)   Lackluster concluding episode in "The Omen" trilogy with the now adult Damien (Sam Neill) growing desperate as his days as the Antichrist are drawing to an end. Graham Baker's plodding direction of Andrew Birkin's witless script strings together a boring series of scenes with gory violence. a touch of sadomasochistic sex and absurd theological allusions. O (R)

Final Countdown, The (1980)   The premise of this film is clever even if a bit too reminiscent of "Twilight Zone" type television drama. Kirk Douglas, Martin Sheen and James Farentino are aboard the "U.S.S. Nimitz" when it slips through a time warp in the year 1980 and reappears at Pearl Harbor in December 1941. It is a clever premise but the most interesting aspect of director Don Taylor's drama is the aircraft carrier herself, which, photographed in detail, constitutes an overwhelming presence. Some brief, but intense violence. A-II (PG)

Final Crash, The (see: "Steelyard Blues")

Final Option (1983)   Elite anti-terrorist unit battles fanatical peace activists who take over an embassy in an extremely violent and simplistic melodrama directed by Ian Sharp from a screenplay by Reginald Rose. Mediocre entertainment with cardboard characters tries to justify excessive gunplay and brutal retribution for political crimes. A-III (R)

Find a Place to Die (1973)   Routine Italian Western about a disgraced Texas Ranger (Jeffery Hunter) who tries to regain his honor by helping a widow (Pascale Petit) recover the gold stolen by the outlaws who murdered her husband. Director Hugo Fregonese's movie is notable only as the last performance of Hunter before his untimely death at age 40. Some brutal violence. A-III (R)

Finders Keepers (1984) Director Richard Lester's attempt at screwball comedy concerns a variety of characters (of which only David Wayne has a sense of comedy) trying to get their hands on a stolen $5 million in the course of a transcontinental train ride. The failed comedy revels in tastelessness, foul language and an offensively unfunny sexual sequence. O (R)

Fine Madness, A (1966) Sean Connery stars in a quaintly stereotyped role as an eccentric, romantically inclined Irish poet who is totally out of place in normal society. Unfortunately, director Irvin Kershner's movie places its emphasis on his promiscuity which undercuts what might in other circumstances have been a very funny adult satire. O (br)

Fine Mess, A (1986) When two friends (Ted Danson and Howie Mandel) win big money on a crooked horse race, they find themselves being chased by looney Mafia thugs (Stuart Margolin and Richard Mulligan) as well as the promiscuous wife (Maria Conchita Alonzo) of the Mafia boss (Paul Sorvino). Writer-director Blake Edwards turns the slapstick comedy into a burlesque of the sexual-tease variety. The result provides an unwholesome acceptance of social and sexual irresponsibility, largely in scenes of an adulterous affair. O (PG)

Fine Pair, A (1969) Square New York police detective (Rock Hudson) gets involved with a fey crook (Claudia Cardinale) and after innumerable plot complications they wind up as a couple of lighthearted jewel thieves. Director Francesco Maselli's romance gets overly serious in its treatment of the supposedly idyllic love affair of the unprincipled principals, completely out of keeping with the movie's humorous intentions. O (PG)

Finest Hours, The (1964) British documentary on the life and times of Winston Churchill presents an overview of his accomplishments and defeats as statesman, orator, author, soldier and painter. Narrated by Orson Welles and good selection of photographs and newsreel footage. A-I (br)

Fingers (1978) Crude, pretentious crime melodrama with Harvey Keitel as a would-be concert pianist who supports himself by collecting bad debts for his loan-shark father (Michael V. Gazzo), and hotly pursues a blank-eyed young woman (Tisa Farrow). Directed by James Toback, the resulting confrontations, including random sex and violence, make no sense at all. O (R)

Finian's Rainbow (1968) Screen version of a 1940's Broadway musical is a variation on the girl-meets-boy plot, with a cantankerous father (Fred Astaire) and a lonely leprechaun (Tommy Steele) thrown in for good measure. Director Francis Ford Coppola brings off an enjoyable entertainment, not quite the lighthearted romantic fantasy that it might have been, but something that is pleasant to watch and, more especially, to listen to. A-I (br)

Fire and Ice (1983) Animated feature created by Ralph Bakshi about a war between good and evil wizards—the good one's weapon is fire, the bad one's is ice—displays in abundant detail Bakshi's obsession with grotesque sex and extravagant violence. All the more disheartening is to see such material appearing in a format traditionally reserved for family entertainment. O (PG)

Fire and Ice (1987) Series of spectacular stunts on skis, bobsleds, wind sleds and skateboards are strung together by the flimsy device of a Canadian skier (John Eaves) searching for the girl of his dreams (Olympic skier Suzy Chaffee). German production photographed and directed by Willy Bogner offers plenty of winter feats with a pounding rock score and the limited dramatic talent of his principals. Some brief nudity in a bedroom scene. A-III (PG)

Fire with Fire (1986) Awkward teen romance with a bright and pretty convent schoolgirl (Virginia Madsen) being consumed by love for a boy (Craig Sheffer) from a nearby juvenile offenders' work camp. Directed by Duncan Gibbons, the plot of teenagers against a passionless adult world is dramatically unjustified. Instances of profanity and violence as well as scene of sexual gropings in a graveyard. A-III (PG-13)

Fire Within, The (1969) Taut, well-constructed and thoroughly engrossing French movie records two days in the life of an alcoholic ex-playboy (Maurice Ronet) desperately searching for security, understanding and meaning in his life. Director Louis Malle's 1963 drama presents a stinging indictment of upper middle-class life in a work whose theme is one of soul-searching despair. A-III (nr)

Fireball 500 (1966) Frankie Avalon plays a tough stock-car racer with Fabian Forte as his chief rival for the high racing stakes and for the dimpled hand of sweet Annette Funicello as well. William Asher directs this dumb, garden variety teenage vehicle which has everything that used to happen in those beach-blanket-bingo movies of the early 1960s, except that instead of bikinis the bouncing babes are wearing abbreviated racing duds. The giggles and inane songs are the same, though. A-III (br)

Firecreek (1968) Henry Fonda terrorizes the town where Jimmy Stewart is sheriff in a Western reminiscent of the showdown situation immortalized in "High Noon" but it lacks that movie's punch. Director Vincent McEveety can't make up his mind whether the climactic shootout is a good thing or not so best not waste your time. Stylized violence. A-II (br)

Firefox (1982) Clint Eastwood stars as an American pilot traumatized by his Vietnam experiences who sneaks into the Soviet Union and steals a secret superplane. Also directed by Eastwood, the action movie is plodding and unexciting but does feature some graphic violence. A-III (PG)

Fireman's Ball, The (1968) Unpretentious Czechoslovakian comedy deals with the foibles of average people in the story of a small-town fire brigade's annual ball. Disorganized and inept, the brigade bungles through in the face of stolen raffle prizes, an embarrassing beauty contest and finally a real fire where the ball continues as if nothing had happened. Directed by Milos Forman, the film is done with such good humor and loving care that the viewer cannot help but enjoy its affirmation that people are good no matter how silly or stupid they may act. Some mature material. A-III (br)

Firepower (1979) Retired hit man (James Coburn) is recruited by the Justice Department to kidnap a crooked financier from his Caribbean sanctuary and bring him back to stand trial in the States. The lavishly mounted British production has lots of lovely scenery but director Michael Winner's trite melodrama overdoses on heavy-handed action and violence, made even more repugnant by its sleazy moral outlook. O (R)

Firestarter (1984) Screen version of Stephen

King horror story about a little girl (Drew Barrymore) who is kidnapped by a secret government agency which wants to use her psychokinetic power to make things burst into flames. Martin Sheen and George C. Scott make an interesting contrast in villains but director Mark Lester's treatment of the premise is more absurd than frightening. Youngsters, however, may be negatively influenced by and even delight in the film's theme of a child's revenge against a cruel adult world. A-III (R)

Firewalker (1986) Simple but plodding action-adventure yarn about a woman (Melody Anderson) who hires two soldiers-of-fortune (Chuck Norris and Louis Gossett, Jr.) to hunt for ancient Mayan treasure in Central America. J. Lee Thompson's direction is amiable but slack in its treatment of the usual assortment of villains and plot complications. Stylized, almost slapstick, violence. A-II (PG)

First Blood (1982) Sylvester Stallone plays John Rambo, a disillusioned Vietnam veteran who reacts to police brutality in a small northwestern town by waging a one-man war against the local police force and the National Guard. Though Ted Kotcheff's direction is effective in fashioning a quite brutal action melodrama, it offers nothing of substance about the plight of the Vietnam veteran. Violence and rough language. A-III (R)

First Charge of the Machete (1974) In 1868, Cuban nationalists declared their independence from the Spanish colonial regime and defeated the army sent against it by using machetes in hand-to-hand combat. Manuel Octovio Gomez re-creates this patriotic episode as if it were a documentary filmed as the events occurred, interviewing participants of both sides and using high-contrast photography to effect a period feeling. A-II (nr)

First Circle, The (1973) Screen adaptation of Russian author Aleksandr Solzhenitsyn's account of the spiritual and physical torments of a political prisoner under Stalinist oppression is a deeply felt one, but its meaning never gets beyond the literal level of story and dialogue. Director Alexander Ford's graphic depictions of sadistic brutalization and sexual degradation needlessly depart from the rest of the movie's stylized visualization of prison camp oppression. A-IV (R)

First Deadly Sin, The (1980) Frank Sinatra stars as an aging New York detective in pursuit of a deranged killer while worrying about his bedridden wife (Faye Dunaway). Brian G. Hutton directs a deeply flawed but entertaining enough crime melodrama with some gratuitous violence. A-III (R)

First Family (1981) Awkward, unfunny comedy starring Bob Newhart, Madeline Kahn and Gilda Radner as the U.S. presidential family. Buck Henry directs with total reliance upon humor derived from vulgar language and crude sight gags, combined with a few implicitly racist scenes. O (R)

First Love (1970) Romanticized German tale of fantasy and imagination in which a young lad falls in love with a slightly older flirt who has moved in next door, only to find out that his father (Maximilian Schell) is sleeping with the girl. Also directed by Schell, the movie concentrates on atmosphere and mood with bucolic settings and lush photography but its lack of plot and shallow substance will leave most viewers yawning. A-III (R)

First Love (1977) College student (William Katt) looking for a lasting relationship catches a rich coed (Susan Dey), loses her to a married man, gets her back but then doesn't want her any more because the "magic" is gone. Director Joan Darling's overripe soap opera of instant gratification takes itself so seriously that it would be laughable if its nudity, simulated intercourse and coarse language were not so offensive. O (R)

First Men in the Moon (1964) Eccentric scientist (Edward Judd) and two reluctant companions reach the moon in a homemade rocket in this adaptation of an H.G. Wells yarn. British production directed by Nathan Juran, it is an entertaining combination of satirical comedy and fairly serious science fiction. A-I (br)

First Monday in October (1981) Walter Matthau and Jill Clayburgh star in this drama about the first woman appointed to the U.S. Supreme Court. On the surface director Ronald Neame's movie deals with liberal-conservative conflicts but essentially demonstrates that women have the same problems as men in dealing with the complex and often unfair American justice system. A pornography case involves a needless nude insert and mature line of dialogue. A-III (R)

First Nudie Musical, The (1977) Shoddy production about a producer who is inspired to put on a pornographic musical to save his seedy company from ruin. Directors Mark Haggard and Bruce Kimmel emphasize sophomoric vulgarities and exploit nudity. O (R)

First Position (1973) Inside look at the training of ballet students in which the real test is whether they have sufficient talent and determination to devote their lives to the pursuit of artistic perfection. Produced and directed by William Richert, the documentary succeeds admirably in conveying the hard work that goes into the learning of any art and the self-doubts of students as they look to the future. A-II (nr)

First Time, The (1969) Empty-headed movie based on the supposition that the average American boy yearns to visit a house of prostitution and that listening to teenagers talk naively about sex is amusing. Directed by James Neilson, the treatment of characters and situation lacks any sensitivity or insight, and the movie is slapped together so badly as to give the impression of being an amateur production. O (M)

First Time, The (1978) Easygoing, highly indulgent memoir about a 16-year-old boy's first sexual encounter gives some warm and positive details of French family life but the view of sex presented here is morally wanting. Directed by Claude Berri, the movie is further marred by offensive dialogue and graphic depictions of sexual behavior. O (X)

First Turn-On, The (1984) Exploitation film about a female guide and four teenage male campers who become trapped in a cave and pass the time describing their first sexual experiences. Nudity in a sexual context. O (R)

Firstborn (1984) Divorced mother (Terri Garr) falls for a brutish loser (Peter Weller) who moves in and precipitates domestic violence with resentful teenage sons. Trite melodrama directed by Michael Apted tries to be a cautionary tale about distraught women making desperate commitments to men before knowing anything about them. Brutality rules out youngsters. A-III (PG-13)

Fish Hawk (1980) The story of the friendship between a farmer's young son (Charlie Fields) and the lone Indian (Will Sampson) living in a white community in the Ozarks at the turn of the century is an unremarkable but pleasant and unpretentious entertainment directed by Donald Shebib. The acting is excellent and the outdoor adventures of the two principals will appeal to younger children. A-I (G)

Fish That Saved Pittsburgh, The (1979) Dreadfully inept comedy about the rejuvenation of a basketball franchise through applied astrology, with Stockard Channing as the team astrologer, has been thrown together in slapdash fashion by director Gilbert Moses. Several instances of vulgar language. A-II (PG)

F.I.S.T. (1978) Sylvester Stallone stars in a deeply flawed, highly romanticized saga of the labor movement, which draws heavily upon the history of the Teamsters Union and the rise and fall of James Hoffa. Director Norman Jewison works on a large canvas telling a story that begins with hope and ends in corruption. The violence along the way is set in the context of a well-intentioned theme of social justice. A-III (PG)

Fistful of Dollars, A (1967) The spaghetti Western that launched Clint Eastwood's meteoric career as the squinting, black-hatted, cheroot-chomping gunslinger known as The Man with No Name who hires himself out to one side or the other, and occasionally both at once, in the settling of a border dispute. Directed with style by Sergio Leone, the action is swift, the violence plentiful and the vengeance all Clint's. O (br)

Fistful of Dynamite (see: "Duck, You Sucker!")

Fists of Fury (1973) Kung-fu artist Bruce Lee takes on a gang of Bangkok dope smugglers, dispatching them with axes and clubs, and in countless stabbings and slashings with knives and swords. Viewers will gasp at the gore more than at the hero's prowess in this inept action movie written and directed by Lo Wei. Excessive violence and nudity in a brothel scene. O (R)

Fists of the Double K (1973) Karate and kung fu are among the lethal means of killing people in this worthless action movie whose violence is bloody and interminable, interrupted only by some sex scenes by way of an attempted rape of a blind girl and a homosexual baddie. O (R)

Fitzwilly (1967) Breezy variation of the Robin Hood theme with a canny butler (Dick Van Dyke) running a thievery racket with other domestics in order to keep up the household of his once rich New York employer (Dame Edith Evans). Directed by Delbert Mann, it has its amusing moments but, in spite of a comment on the dishonesty of bilking insurance companies, it still implies that what people don't know won't hurt them. A-III (br)

Five Bloody Graves (1971) Violent Western in which foolhardy Robert Dix, trailing the Yaqui warrior who slaughtered his wife, encounters sneaky Indians, stubborn homesteaders, stranded stagecoach passengers, wily gunrunners and a half-breed renegade—all of whom dispatch one another before several suns have set. Women are not exempt from bullets or arrows, and producer-director Al Adamson treats one rape-murder in an especially cruel manner. O (R/GP)

Five Card Stud (1968) Mediocre Western mystery pits Dean Martin as a fast-talking, fast-loving gambler against Robert Mitchum as a hellfire preacher who also carries a gun. Director Henry Hathaway spins a simple story of retribution motivated by the lynching of a card cheat but the identity of the revengeful killer is fairly obvious.

Gory violence, sexual innuendo and a questionable use of religion. A-III (PG)

Five Days One Summer (1982) Produced and directed by Fred Zinnemann, this is the story of a 1930's romance set against the stunning background of the Swiss Alps where a man and his niece (Sean Connery and Betsy Brantley) try to pass themselves off as husband and wife during a skiing vacation. The well-crafted movie has very good acting and acknowledges in no-nonsense fashion, the existence of good and evil. Several love scenes handled with much restraint. A-II (PG)

Five Easy Pieces (1970) Jack Nicholson gives an outstanding performance as a young man who has lost his sense of identity and is wasting his life searching and unsatisfied. Directed with precision by Bob Rafelson, the movie's best scene is when Nicholson breaks down and confesses his loneliness to his stroke-victim father. The movie's moral ambiguity makes it more suitable for serious viewing rather than casual entertainment. A-III (R)

5 Fingers of Death (1973) Hong Kong martial arts movie directed by Cheng Chang Ho shows the training of a young disciple of a kung fu master and their problems with thugs from a rival school. The atrocious dubbing of this thin effort makes the action seem at first to be played for laughs but it proves, unfortunately, to be deadly serious. Acrobatic violence. A-III (R)

Five Man Army (1970) Peter Graves plays the leader of an odd collection of renegades whom he has brought together to rob a shipment of gold from the Mexican government at the turn of the century. Substandard Western directed by Don Taylor has a lumpy double-cross plot that fails to bridge the credibility gap. Some of the violence gets a bit gruesome in spots. A-III (PG)

Five Million Years to Earth (1968) Above-average British science fiction movie in which workers digging a London subway extension find skeletons and an indestructible spacecraft with a prehistoric secret that threatens the entire human race until a brave scientist (James Donald) discovers the origins and meaning of the craft. With good acting, dialogue and special effects, director Roy Ward Baker's unpretentious effort sustains interest and an air of plausibility. Mild violence. A-II (br)

Five on the Black Hand Side (1973) Good screen version of a play by Charlie L. Russell tells a simple but humorous story of the varying effect black awareness has on a middle-class family living in Los Angeles. Under the direction of Oscar Williams, the performances are warm and engaging, with Clarice Taylor and Leonard Jackson as the parents and Glynn Turman, Bonnie Banfield and D'Urville Martin as their grown children. The ultimate message is one of positive respect for oneself and others, which in turn leads to a sense of solidarity and community. A-III (G/PG)

Fixer, The (1968) Set during a time of pogroms in Czarist Russia, the movie tells the story of a simple carpenter (Alan Bates) who is falsely accused of the ritual murder of a young boy. The man's stubborn refusal to confess to the crime makes his case internationally famous and the country which holds him prisoner must force his confession in order to save its good name. Director John Frankenheimer's intense but thought-provoking adaptation of the Bernard Malamud novel confronts viewers with a universal theme of intolerance and abuse of power. Solid fare for adults and older adolescents. A-III (PG)

Flame and the Fire (1966) French documentary about the Stone Age lives of primitive tribes in remote areas of South America, Africa and the Pacific. Directed by Pierre Dominique Gaisseau, it is not sensationalistic but some of its elements may prove distasteful or shocking to sensitive viewers. A-IV (br)

Flaming Frontier, The (1968) Ludicrous German Western directed by Alfred Vohrer based on the Old Shatterhand character created by Karl May appears here as Old Surehand (Stewart Granger) who tries to keep peace between the Indians and frontier settlers. Mild violence. A-I (G)

Flamingo Kid, The (1985) Brooklyn youth of 18 (Matt Dillon) gains some maturity in the summer of 1963 while working at an affluent Long Island beach club, an experience that confirms his blue-collar father's traditional values over those of the would-be rich and famous. Director Garry Marshall's work is slickly fashioned but contrived and superficial. Sympathetic depiction of sexual promiscuity. O (PG-13)

Flanagan (1985) Middle-aged out-of-work actor (Philip Bosco), burdened with family and personal problems, is forced to drive a taxi while he struggles along trying to be ready to seize the big chance when it comes his way. Directed and co-scripted by Scott Goldstein, it's an interesting, often moving little film, though the script is too episodic and the happy ending is several shades too improbable. Mature treatment of the hero's marital problems and some rough language. A-III (R)

Flap (1970) Anthony Quinn plays Flapping Eagle in a serio-comic attempt to decry the mistreatment and indifference endured by today's Native Americans. Flap fights police prejudice and highway construction in trying to preserve his people's cultural heritage but, regrettably, the movie fails to confront far deeper issues of discrimination and, indeed, stereotypes Indians as deceitful, debauched (by Madam Shelley Winters and her girls) and destructive daredevils. British director Carol Reed's movie is an embarrassment that will seem funny only to the most ill-informed viewer. A-III (GP)

Flareup (1969) Shallow chase film with little suspense and much trite characterization stars James Stacey as a mentally unbalanced, jealous husband who thinks go-go dancer Raquel Welch has broken up his marriage. Directed by James Neilson, the movie's bumbling treatment of violence, nudity, drugs and homosexuality only further encumber an already weak film. O (PG)

Flash of Green, A (1985) Reporter in a small Florida town lets himself be drawn into the orbit of a corrupt politician intent on enriching himself in fronting for an ecologically destructive resort development. An interesting, very well-acted but flawed movie based on a John D. MacDonald novel and directed by Victor Nunez. Violence and a fairly graphic bedroom scene. A-III (nr)

Flashdance (1983) Director Adrian Lyne romanticizes the rags-to-riches story of a working-class female (Jennifer Beals) who overcomes hardships to fulfill her dreams of becoming a professional dancer. Blatantly exploiting female anatomy, the musical tries to overcome the commercial sexism with a love story about self-reliance. Some nudity. O (R)

Flashpoint (1984) Two Border Patrol officers (Kris Kristofferson and Treat Williams) in a remote part of Texas find themselves the targets of ruthless covert agents after they discover a jeep long buried in the desert. Director Bill Tannen's moderately entertaining action adventure has restrained violence, but because of its somber mood and extremely rough language, it is not for younger viewers. A-III (R)

Flavor of Green Tea over Rice (1973) Japanese drama shows the changes in the traditional view of marriage during the post-war era in the story of a woman's passage from indifference to rebellion and finally to a new appreciation of herself and her husband. Director Yasujiro Ozu's movie, made in 1952, is another of his quiet studies of family life, very intimate and warm with the special quality of humanity that Ozu manages to evoke from his characters. A-I (nr)

Flea in Her Ear, A (1968) Dull French bed-sitting room farce in which Rex Harrison and Rosemary Harris lead a parade of comically malcontent marrieds who get themselves into an essentially innocent tangle of mistaken identities and intentions that result in much door-slamming, sneaking around corners and hallway chases at a disreputable Paris hotel. Directed by Jacques Charon, the proceedings are energetic but lack the sense of timing and pace required for farce. A-III (PG)

Flesh Gordon (1974) Witless spoof on both the old Flash Gordon and Buck Rogers serials and the new porno movies. Sophomorically smutty humor, nudity, rough language and cheap thrills. O (X/R)

Fletch (1985) This is a vehicle for comedian Chevy Chase to showcase several disguises and display his somewhat limited talent for accents. He plays a reporter trying to break a drug case with everybody against him, even his editors. Chase fans should enjoy this, but others are less likely to. The humor runs heavily to the vulgar side, with the emphasis on the scatological and the anatomical. A-II (PG)

Flight of the Doves (1971) Young brother and sister (Jack Wild and Helen Raye) escape the crushing rule of their stepfather (William Rushton) in gray Britain for their dear granny (Dorothy McGuire) in green Ireland. Learning that the children are heirs to a large fortune, they are pursued by a menacing uncle (Ron Moody) who intends to dispose of them and claim the money for himself. Director Ralph Nelson, steering clear of the scary potential of the situation, produces a fancy, frothy entertainment package, stuffed with colorful set pieces, songs and sentimentality. The confection may be too sweet for adults, but young children will especially enjoy Moody's magic tricks and bag of disguises. A-I (G)

Flight of the Eagle, The (1983) Swedish director Jan Troell's fact-based drama illustrates an ill-fated attempt to reach the North Pole by a group of explorers (Max Von Sydow, Goran Stangertz and Sverre Anker Ousdal) making use of a hydrogen balloon. Though beautifully photographed and well-told, the somber nature of the story and the intensity of its treatment make it inappropriate for younger viewers. A-II (G)

Flight of the Navigator (1986) A youngster (Joey Kramer) gets trapped in a time warp when he's transported to and from a distant world in the blink of an eye. Although he has not aged, he has been away from his family eight years and must decide if this is really home. The alien spacecraft which transported him figures prominently and humorously in this good-natured and unpretentious family movie directed by Randal Kleiser. A-I (PG)

Flight of the Phoenix (1966)   Uneven disaster movie in which an airplane with the usual motley collection of male passengers crashes in the Arabian desert somewhere off course and without a working radio. Their only chance of survival is to build a new plane from the wreckage of the old, which leads to friction between the pilot (James Stewart) and the German aircraft-designer who proposes to do it. Directed by Robert Aldrich, the situation is overly extended but provides enough suspense and excitement to please most old and young adventure fans. A-I (br)

Flim-Flam Man, The (1967)   Aging confidence man (George C. Scott) tutors a young Army deserter (Michael Sarrazin) in the subtle art of capitalizing on the greed of his fellow man as the unlikely pair go on some genuinely hilarious adventures across the Kentucky countryside. Scott plays the role with carefree flamboyance and glimpses of the pathos that is part of a drifter's loneliness, and Sarrazin is appealing as the AWOL farm boy who is finally brought to his senses by pretty Sue Lyon. Directed by Irvin Kershner, it has beautiful location photography, first rate dialogue and a uniformly capable supporting cast that help make the movie enjoyable for all but the very young. A-II (br)

Float Like a Butterfly, Sting Like a Bee (1970)   Though boxing fans may be disappointed at the sparsity of ring action in this documentary on Muhammad Ali (aka Cassius Clay), it succeeds in being objective and entertaining while exploring the racial ramifications of Ali's success and notoriety, as well as providing insight into his life and character. A-III (nr)

Flowers in the Attic (1987)   Failed suspense thriller about four youngsters locked in the upper story of a remote mansion where their lives are endangered by unknown hands. Writer-director Jeffrey Bloom's heavy-handed treatment of the situation becomes boringly repetitive long before the movie's grisly resolution. Mature themes and some violence. A-III (PG-13)

Fly, The (1986)   Tender romance fades quickly when a biological experiment intermixing human and insect genes fails. The result is a mutant in the form of a sexually-powerful human fly (Jeff Goldblum) who gets some compassion from his lover (Geena Davis) but his condition, like director David Cronenberg's beauty-and-the-beast allegory, degenerates into an unhealthy mix of sex, brutality and disgustingly grotesque imagery. Explicit sexual scenes, nudity and some profanity. O (R)

Flying Matchmaker, The (1970)   Israeli musical comedy set in a 19th-century East European Jewish community with a busy matchmaker promoting happy weddings but silly confusion runs rampant when an impersonator of a prospective groom shows up. Directed by Mordechai Navon, the colorful production stars Mike Burstein, Lillian Lux and Pesach Burstein but the poorly dubbed comedy grows a bit tedious for those unaccustomed to its conventions. A-II (G)

FM (1978)   Lightweight, derivative comedy about a popular radio station which is taken over by its disc jockeys because they refuse to contaminate their music with unsuitable commercials. Under John A. Alonzo's direction, the characters are uninteresting and the jokes feeble. Some highly suggestive dialogue. A-III (PG)

Fog, The (1980)   Victims of a century-old shipwreck caused by a false beacon stalk the descendants of their murderers under the cover of a lethal fog. Director John Carpenter's listless and heavy-handed thriller has little intelligence and much violence. A-III (R)

Follow Me (1969)   Three American youths travel the globe in search of the perfect surfing wave in a movie that lacks any wit or style. Director Gene McCabe's material is so repetitious that one has time to question the young surfers' value system and sense of social consciousness. A-II (G)

Follow Me, Boys! (1966)   Disney family movie with Fred MacMurray as a small-town Scoutmaster who devotes his life to helping the boys in his troop. Director Norman Tokar emphasizes the ideals of Scouting, has the period atmosphere of a generation ago and benefits from the capable acting of Lillian Gish and Charles Ruggles. Though a sentimental formula picture, it has more than enough spirited action to keep most viewer's interest. A-I (G)

Follow That Bird (1985)   In this first Sesame Street movie, a do-gooder type persuades Big Bird that he should be living with his own feathered kind and places him with the Dodo family in the distant Midwest. Pining for home, Big Bird heads East and immediately becomes the innocent object of a birdhunt. In Sesame Street style, the movie maintains a gentle, whimsical spirit rather than going for the big laughs. As such it will succeed best with younger children and least well with teenagers. A-I (G)

Food of the Gods, The (1976)   Directed by Bert I. Gordon and loosely based on a H.G. Wells story, the gross science fiction movie delights in gore and vicious attacks by giant rats and insects on hapless explorers (Marjoe Gortner and Pamela Franklin). Excessive violence. O (R)

Fool for Love (1986)   Under Robert Altman's direction, Sam Shepard's adaptation of his own play about a brutalizing love-hate relationship between kissing cousins (Shepard and Kim Basinger) is unremittingly violent, both physically and psychologically. Sexual coarseness in dialogue and unresolved ambiguity of a theme of incest. O (R)

Fool Killer, The (1969)   Young runaway (Edward Albert) escaping from severe foster parents meets a brooding war veteran (Tony Perkins) bitter about his own excessively strict religious upbringing, but his youth comes to find a home while the man is doomed to wandering. Although the comparatively lighthearted atmosphere of the first part of movie does not prepare the viewer for the darker tone of the later sequences, director Servando Gonzalez keeps the story consistently interesting. A-II (nr)

Foolin' Around (1980)   Failed update of 1930s screwball comedy has a callow college freshman (Gary Busey) falling for an heiress (Annette O'Toole) and ruining her engagement to a boorish sophisticate. Directed by Richard Heffron, the slapstick overwhelms the few funny moments while an implication of pre-marital sex and some rough language rule out younger viewers. A-III (PG)

Fools (1970)   Aging actor tired of being typed in low-budget horror movies (Jason Robards) and a rich girl drifting away from her status-seeking spouse (Katharine Ross) traipse around San Francisco feebly attempting to forget life's frustrations by hopping into bed half a dozen times. Directed by Tom Gries, the movie is singularly devoid of any feelings for humanity that might justify one's interest in the intimate affairs of the neurotic pair. O (GP)

Fools' Parade (1971) With money earned in prison, lovable ex-cons James Stewart, Strother Martin and Kurt Russell want to set up a general store but mean prison captain George Kennedy wants their dollars and their lives. Perhaps director Andrew McLaglen intended a cornball-campy spoof but the result is a disappointing chase melodrama that is sometimes silly but only occasionally funny. Some violence and sexual references. A-III (GP)

Footloose (1984) A city boy (Kevin Bacon), brought to live in a small Bible Belt town which has an ordinance against dancing in public places, promptly gets in trouble with the local preacher (John Lithgow) over seeing his daughter (Lori Singer), but eventually wins over the town. Director Herbert Ross tries to give the story line as much weight as the dazzling scenes of acrobatic dancing, but the simplistic script's treatment of issues is woefully inadequate. A-III (PG)

For a Few Dollars More (1967) Spaghetti Western directed by Sergio Leone with Clint Eastwood playing the cheroot-smoking Man with No Name and Lee Van Cleef, garbed all in black, as his not-to-be-trusted partner. Clint squints, Lee snarls and dozens of Mexican banditos bite the dust in a routine shoot-em-up involving Clint's vengeance for a double-cross. A-III (br)

For Better, For Worse (see: "Zandy's Bride")

For Love of Ivy (1968) Sidney Poitier plays a slick gambler who falls in love with a beautiful but ambitious maid (Abbey Lincoln) but what might have been an interesting romantic comedy is confounded by the overabundance of phony plot complications. As directed by Daniel Mann, whatever message the movie might have intended is lost in its glossy upper-class setting, pop songs and a pair of "hip" youngsters. Mature themes. A-III (G)

For Pete's Sake (1974) Barbra Streisand vehicle about a Brooklyn housewife who borrows money to speculate on the commodities market in order to finance her husband's college diploma and then gets into trouble with a succession of unsavory characters who pressure her to pay back the loan. Director Peter Yates lets the promising comedy turn sour and not even a final hilarious chase sequence can save it. Some grim twists and bizarre plot turns, including the housewife taking a job as a part-time prostitute. A-III (PG)

For Singles Only (1968) Living in a swinging Southern California hotel for unmarrieds, a serious but poor graduate student (John Saxon) bets that he can seduce a high-principled coed (Mary Anne Mobley). She goes along because winning the bet will pay off his overdue tuition bills and then really cooperates because they are in love and are going to get married anyway. Directed by Arthur Dreifuss, the witless movie lacks any human texture or intelligence. Justifies premarital sex. O (br)

For the Love of Benji (1977) Extremely entertaining sequel with the lovable canine hero, this time on vacation in Greece, becoming the unwitting central figure in an international oil conspiracy and the chase is on through the streets and byways of picturesque Athens. Director Joe Camp's lively adventure is surefire entertainment

for younger children and it goes down easily for parents as well. A-I (G)

For Your Eyes Only (1981) Uninspired, derivative James Bond spy adventure has to do with the retrieval of a top-secret device in sunken British spy ship, but the flimsy plot is only a pretext to string together a dozen or so spectacular stunt sequences. Roger Moore is in good form, as are several of the disposable women who are a fixture in the Bond fantasy world. Director John Glen administers the usual violence and overdoes an underwater sequence exploiting nudity. O (PG)

Forbin Project, The (1970) An enormous self-sustaining and unjammable computer complex coordinating all U.S. military defenses locates a Soviet counterpart and together they plan a benevolent world dictatorship guaranteeing peace and a better way of life for the peoples of the world at the expense of their freedom. A kind of horror film with contemporary allusions, director Joseph Sargent's movie has moments of genuine interest in its depiction of a modern electronic Frankenstein controlling humanity's fate but incapable of any human emotion or spiritual growth. Mild bedroom sequence. A-III (GP)

Force of One, A (1980) Run-of-the-mill melodrama about how karate champ Chuck Norris breaks up a narcotics ring. Justice triumphs by means of the martial arts instead of superior firepower with the violence being skillfully choreographed and kept in check by director Paul Aaron. A-II (PG)

Force 10 from Navarone (1979) Penny-ante sequel to "The Guns of Navarone" follows the mission of two American Rangers (Robert Shaw and Edward Fox) in Yugoslavia to blow up a bridge before the Germans can use it to attack the Partisans. Director Guy Hamilton's limp war movie is filled with cliches and occasional graphic violence. A-III (PG)

Forever Young, Forever Free (see: "Lollipop")

Fort Apache, the Bronx (1981) Paul Newman stars as a tough but compassionate police officer striving to do his job in a precinct that has the highest crime rate in New York City. Director Dan Petrie's standard urban melodrama is marked by excellent acting and fine cinematography but, though it has occasional insights, it tends to exploit a serious and tragic subject. Some tough scenes involving sex and violence. A-IV (R)

Fortune, The (1975) Jack Nicholson and Warren Beatty play a bumbling pair of 1920's con men and would-be murderers who try to do in heiress Stockard Channing. Director Mike Nichols' comedy is contrived, clumsy and only intermittently funny. Some sexual innuendo. A-III (PG)

Fortune and Men's Eyes (1971) Jailed on a minor narcotics rap, a young man (Wendell Burton) in fear of homosexual assault by the other prisoners lets a prison tough (Zooey Hall) protect him in return for exclusive rights to his body and eventually he himself becomes one of the brutalizers that he had once so feared. Directed by Harvey Hart, the movie examines homosexuality in prison not only as a sexual release but as a means of wielding power. The treatment, however, is heavy-handed to the point of exploiting an important subject. O (R)

Fortune Cookie, The (1966) Shyster lawyer (Walter Matthau) gets brother-in-law (Jack Lemmon) to feign injuries in hopes of a million dollar settlement. Directed by Billy Wilder, the situation is at first amusing but grows increasingly cynical and mean-spirited. Vulgar language and low morals. A-III (br)

Forty Carats (1973) Very slight romantic comedy about a 40-year-old divorcee (Liv Ullmann) who falls in love with a man (Edward Albert) half her age during a holiday in Greece. Directed by Milton Katselas, it's lighthearted and entertaining enough, thanks primarily to gorgeous Hellenic scenery and Ullmann's bright performance. A-III (PG)

48 Hrs. (1982) San Francisco police detective (Nick Nolte) frees a convict (Eddie Murphy) on a 48-hour pass in order to get his help tracking down some vicious killers. Directed by Walter Hill, it is a crude, repulsive movie filled with entirely disagreeable characters who indulge in extreme violence, vulgar sight gags and rough language. O (R)

Foul Play (1978) Goldie Hawn and Chevy Chase are teamed in this comic melodrama about a feisty librarian and a police detective who foil a plot to assassinate the pope during a visit to San Francisco. Colin Higgins directs an above-average comedy that is frequently very funny but yet maintains enough tension to be enjoyable as a thriller too. Some crude language and a casual attitude toward premarital sex. A-III (PG)

Fountain of Love, The (1970) German sex farce about a little town which has a spring that bolsters the virility of all who bathe in it. The mayor's attempt to keep people from using it succeeds as badly as a meandering plot sprinkled with voyeurism and nudity. O (R)

4 Clowns (1970) Robert Youngson's compilation deals with the art of visual comedy as shown in the work of four of its leading buffoons: Charley Chase, Buster Keaton, Stan Laurel and Oliver Hardy. The selection of excerpts is fine, the narration is helpful and the silent comedy is timeless. A-I (G)

Four Deuces, The (1975) Apparently intended as a spoof, this clunker about gangland warfare during Prohibition gets its laughs all in the wrong places. Director William H. Busnell, Jr., directs the lavish period sets better than he does his floundering cast and there is nothing funny about the movie's violent brutality and view of women as sex objects. A misdeal from the title on. O (R)

Four Flies on Grey Velvet (1972) Italian director Dario Argento pursues his usual theme of homicidal paranoia in a story about a rock drummer (Michael Brandon) who, fearing his life is in danger, sends his raspy wife (Mimsy Farmer) out of town, seeks help from a bohemian friend (Bud Spencer), hires an effeminate private eye (Jean-Pierre Marielle) and hops into the bathtub with his visiting cousin (Francine Racette). If anyone cares, there is unsettling violence, coarse language, illicit sex and a cast of unwholesome characters. O (PG)

Four Friends (1981) Young immigrant from Yugoslavia (Craig Wasson) comes of age in 1960's Indiana in Steve Tesich's uneven semi-autobiographical screenplay directed by Arthur Penn. Few effective moments are evident in this often outrageously sentimental melodrama which tries to evoke something of significance about the era and the Midwest. Permissive attitude toward adolescent sex and some brief nudity. A-III (R)

491 (1967) Spurious Swedish movie uses a rehabilitation program for incorrigible boys as an excuse for a parade of sadism, violence, vandalism and sexual perversity. O (br)

Four Musketeers, The (1975) Oliver Reed, Raquel Welsh, Richard Chamberlain and Faye Dunaway star in director Richard Lester's sequel to his previous movie based on the Dumas novel. The style is halfway between spoof and in earnest with both pratfalls and bloodshed. The uneasy mix makes for rather uncertain entertainment and the violence makes it questionable fare for younger viewers. A-III (PG)

Four Nights of a Dreamer (1972) French adaptation of a Dostoevsky story about a lonely artist in need of someone to personify his ideals of beauty. He saves a young woman from suicide and they meet for the next three nights to talk but on the last night, the lover she thought untrue returns to claim her. The artist is again a solitary dreamer but now he has an ideal based upon reality. Directed by Robert Bresson, adults will find this a tender and loving film, and a warm, if predictable, exercise in romantic fantasy. A-III (nr)

Four Seasons, The (1981) Three couples (Alan Alda and Carol Burnett; Len Cariou and Sandy Dennis; Jack Weston and Rita Moreno) maintain a friendship despite various ups and downs, most having to do with marital problems. Written and directed by Alda, the entertaining but superficial comedy tries to elicit some sense of the complacency of middle-aged, middle-class suburban lifestyles. Mature subject matter, some crude gags and profanity. A-III (PG)

Four Times That Night (1972) Footloose guy (Brett Halsey) picks up a poodle walker (Daniela Giordano) in the park one afternoon, and the next morning fabricates conflicting reports—she for her mother, he for his barroom buddies—about how they spent their evening together. A third version is supplied by the apartment house superintendent. Director Mario Bava's purported comedy, with an emphasis on nudity and perversions, is merely one more sex exploitation movie. O (R)

Fox (1976) German melodrama directed by Rainer Werner Fassbinder tells of the rise and fall of a naive worker (played by Fassbinder himself) who is exploited by the bourgeoisie and then discarded when no longer useful. It's the old Hollywood story of the corruption of an innocent by the power placed within the context of the homosexual world. Devoid of any kind of sexual sensationalism, the movie is more about the evils of capitalism than about homosexuality. A-IV (nr)

Fox and the Hound, The (1981) A fox and hound raised as friends have to confront the consequences of the roles assigned them by humans and nature in this Disney animated feature directed by Art Stevens, Ted Berman and Richard Rich. Based on the book by Daniel P. Mannix, should make pleasant entertainment for the young, though its sentimentality and cloying cuteness will put off older and more demanding viewers. A-I (G)

Foxes (1980) Director Adrian Lyne's grim, depressing tale of four teenage girls (Jodie Foster, Marilyn Kagan, Cherie Currie and Kandice Stroh) left to their own devices amid the urban and moral squalor of Los Angeles. Fairly interesting, but the viewer stops caring about a third of the way through. Rough language and a superficial depiction of adult and youthful decadence. A-III (R)

Foxy Brown (1974) Pam Grier busts up a ring of ghetto drug dealers out of revenge in a movie directed by Jack Hill with more foul language, more horrible violence (rape and castration) and an even wider variety of sexual kinkiness than is usual for this kind of black exploitation movie. O (R)

Fragment of Fear (1971) When his aunt (Flora Robson) turns up strangled in the ancient ruins of Pompeii, a reformed drug addict (David Hemmings) resolves to track down her killer. Director Richard C. Sarafian initiates a crackling good study of the effect of the past on the present of a recovering addict but those interested in it as a mystery thriller will be infuriated at its abrupt surprise ending. A-II (GP)

Fragrance of Wild Flowers, The (1979) Yugoslavian movie in which a successful actor gets fed up with life, takes up residence on a friend's river barge and winds up being celebrated by the media as a fashionable rebel, more in demand than ever. The alienation theme is a familiar one but director Srdjan Karnovic handles it with incisive human detail and, amidst all the ironies, some warmly gentle humor. A-III (nr)

Framed (1975) Wronged man (Joe Don Baker) comes out of prison to wreak a quite literal bloody vengeance upon his oppressors. Directed by Phil Karlson, it is a vicious movie that goes all out in its depiction of brutal violence, especially against women. O (R)

Frances (1984) Impassioned film biography of Frances Farmer, the 1930's Hollywood starlet who bucked the system, got involved with alcohol, drugs and strange men and whose mother had her placed in a mental institution where she was abused, raped and received a lobotomy. Jessica Lange's fine performance makes this sincere, non-exploitative but rather plodding and episodic movie worth seeing. Director Graeme Clifford's depiction of Frances' suffering and fate is so unremittingly cruel, that the movie will be too harsh for many viewers. A-IV (R)

Frankenstein and the Monster from Hell (1974) Peter Cushing again assumes the role of the mad doctor who, with his assistant (Shane Briant) assembles a creature from assorted parts they collect at the insane asylum in which they are residents. Directed by Terence Fisher, the gore is both sickening and sick. O (R)

Frankenstein Must Be Destroyed (1970) Mediocre British installment in the Frankenstein saga with the mad doctor (Peter Cushing) fanatically intent on perfecting his experiments in brain transplants. Directed by Terence Fisher, the macabre setting and atmosphere are good but the gore, with heads being lopped off and blood splattering freely, is less effective than the earlier convention of suggesting such shock effects. A-III (PG)

Frankie and Johnny (1966) Elvis Presley vehicle with plenty of rock-'n'-roll music, fist-swinging action and cutsie-poo romance. Allegedly based on the famous folk ballad, Presley plays a two-timing but ultimately redemptive riverboat gambler with Donna Douglas as his tired-but-true love, Frankie. Directed by Frederick de Cordova, it's lightweight fun. A-II (br)

Fraternity Row (1977) Shallow and sentimental look at fraternity life in the mid-1950s in a story about an idealistic young man who becomes a pledge at a prestigious college fraternity and runs afoul of a sadistic bully. Director Thomas J. Tobin takes an uncritical view of the frat system on American campuses. Some sexual references. A-III (PG)

Fraternity Vacation (1985) Frat nerds place a wager on who will seduce Britt Ekland first.

Directed by James Frawley, this "Animal House" clone offers nothing but the usual nudity and gross, vulgar humor. O (R)

Fraulein Doktor (1969) World War I German spy (Suzy Kendall) engineers the sinking of Lord Kitchener's ship, steals a poison gas formula from a French scientist (Capucine) and supervises the theft of the master battle plan from Allied headquarters in Belgium. Alberto Lattuada directs the movie in an almost documentary style that encourages a suspension of disbelief. Though uneven and deliberately devoid of emotional involvement, its events are often grimly absorbing and hard to dismiss. A-III (M)

Freaks (1932) Tod Browning, a director specializing in the field of horror and the grotesque, centered this story around a group of circus freaks who take in a normal woman in need of refuge but who betrays them. Browning endows the movie with an unusual sympathetic quality in not exploiting the deformities and monstrous appearance of his characters. The result is a unique film of the horror genre, a real classic of its kind, that is not easily forgotten by even the most sophisticated cinema-addict. A-II (nr)

Freaky Friday (1977) Mother and teenage daughter (Barbara Harris and Jodie Foster) vehemently wish to trade places for a single day, only to have the wish granted to their mutual discomfiture. Gary Nelson directs a typical Disney slapstick comedy bolstered by good performances in the leads. A-I (G)

Free Woman, A (1974) German drama of a woman (Margarethe von Trotta) struggling for self-identity and fulfillment following her divorce and bitter court battle for custody of her little boy. Directed by Volker Schlondorff, it seethes with a restrained anger that leads to occasionally brutal characterizations of male stereotypes but avoids the pitfalls of exploiting women in the process. A-III (nr)

Freebie and the Bean (1974) Two freewheeling San Francisco cops career dangerously around the city to protect a mobster they plan to arrest when the time is ripe for a promotion. In director Richard Rush's failed comedy, Bean (Alan Arkin) and Freebie (James Caan) are gun-crazy psychopaths who enjoy indulging their penchant for foul language, ethnic slurs, kinky sex and beating up hapless individuals whenever they get a chance. O (R)

Freedom to Love (1970) Presented in the form of a serious examination of sexual freedom, interspersed with some shallow commentary, the movie is merely a poor excuse to present scenes of graphic sex and nudity. O (nr)

French Connection, The (1971) Tough, unorthodox New York detective Popeye Doyle (Gene Hackman) and his partner (Roy Scheider) track down a massive heroin cache in this tense, exciting, very violent look at the darker side of law enforcement. Director William Friedkin makes excellent use of New York City locations in giving his fast-paced story the grimy look of reality and the acting of the leads is first-rate. The violent action and language are in the context of a sobering, perhaps shocking, portrayal of the kill-or-be-killed undercover world of cops and dope dealers. A-IV (R)

French Connection II (1975) Gene Hackman repeats his role as fanatical detective Popeye Doyle in a sequel set in France and directed by John

Frankenheimer. Not nearly as successful as its predecessor, the movie is marred by its ambivalent attitude towards Doyle's ruthless methods, some strong violence and rough language. A-IV (R)

French Conspiracy, The (1973) Dramatic recreation of the events in a political scandal that rocked the French government in the late 1960s when Ben Barka, a Moroccan revolutionary exile, was kidnapped in France with the apparent complicity and cooperation of some French officials. Directed by Yves Boisset, the result is not an espionage thriller, but rather a careful exposition of the intelligence community that operates beneath the surface of modern governments. Stars Gian-Maria Volonte, Michael Piccoli, and Jean-Louis Trintignant. A-II (PG)

French Cousins, The (see: "From Ear to Ear")

French Detective, The (1979) Gallic version of an American police thriller features a tough cop (Lino Ventura) and his young assistant (Patrick Dewaere) who encounter a dishonest political machine while investigating a murder. Director Pierre Granier-Deferre spends too much time on philosophical exchanges between his policemen but its abuse of citizen's rights are familiar enough to American moviegoers. There is enough violence and moral ambiguity to make it adult fare. A-III (nr)

French Lessons (1986) Producer David Puttnam's somewhat anachronistic romance details the first sexual experience of a British exchange student in Paris. Jane Snowden gives a sensitive portrayal of the youth experimenting in adult responsibilities but the dialogue is so awful and the script so woefully inadequate that the movie never achieves any credibility. O (PG)

French Lieutenant's Woman, The (1981) Scriptwriter Harold Pinter's adaptation of the John Fowles' novel uses a movie-within-a-movie gimmick so that the story of a wealthy gentleman's pursuit of a mysterious governess in the Victorian Age also becomes a tale of two performers carrying on an adulterous affair in the present. Meryl Streep and Jeremy Irons play the dual roles of the lovers. Director Karel Reisz' result is interesting, but too pretentious and humorless for its own good. Rather graphic bedroom scene. A-III (R)

French Postcards (1979) Lighthearted but aimless movie about a trio of American students in Paris (Miles Chapin, Blanche Baker and David Marshall Grant) and their various amorous misadventures. Director Willard Huyck's episodic, listless and anti-intellectual effort seeks unearned viewer sympathy for feckless youths whose acting ability seems more suited to amateur night at the fraternity house. The movie's implicit endorsement of sexual promiscuity makes it unacceptable entertainment. O (PG)

French Provincial (1976) Interesting French melodrama about a seamstress (Jeanne Moreau) who marries into a bourgeois family in the South of France and becomes the one who holds it together from the early 1930s to the 1970s. Director Andre Techine integrates the episodic family chronicle within the larger frame of the changes taking place within France during that period. A-III (nr)

French Way, The (see: "Love at the Top")

Frenzy (1972) Alfred Hitchcock's masterful suspense thriller focuses on a deranged strangler preying on women in contemporary London. The central character is an innocent man (Jon Finch) whose careless way of living implicates him as the serial murderer who dispatches his victims by means of a characteristic necktie, with accompanying perverse violence. The suspense is built on whether the wrong man will be punished for the crimes, something which is not resolved until the very last moment. Though of the same caliber as Hitchcock's best works, it lamentably resorts to some very explicit violence and brief nudity. A-IV (R)

Friday Foster (1976) Director Arthur Marks wastes some talented performers (Yaphet Kotto, Godfrey Cambridge, Eartha Kitt and Pam Grier) in a black exploitation number adapted from a comic strip but without whatever depth and subtlety the original may have had. Excessive sex and violence. O (R)

Friday the 13th (1980) Homicidal maniac menaces teenagers at a summer camp. Crude, mindless exploitation cheapie directed by Sean S. Cunningham with much blood and violence and graphic sex scenes. O (R)

Friday the 13th, Part II (1981) Disgusting horror sequel with the homicidal maniac once more stalking slow-witted camp counselors who have sex on their minds rather than self-preservation. Wholly uninspired direction and script are by Steve Miner and Ron Kurz, with the usual unhealthy mix of nudity and graphic violence. O (R)

Friday the 13th, Part III (1982) The 3-D version directed by Steve Miner is no better than its predecessors in the blood and gore department. O (R)

Friday the 13th—The Final Chapter (1984) Freddie the ghoulish maniac is on the loose again as director Joseph Zito fills the screen with the usual gore and violence mixed with crude language and much nudity. O (R)

Friday the 13th, Part V—A New Beginning (1985) Directed by Danny Steinmann, this time out Freddie the maniac stalks a home for disturbed children. Violent, gory horror flick whose only goal is to shock. O (R)

Friday the 13th, Part VI: Jason Lives (1986) The demonic killer is brought back from the dead via a lightning bolt to torment, terrorize and molest the descendants of his killers. This excessively violent sequel, written and directed by Tom McLoughlin, consists of little more than a succession of bloody slaughter scenes with a little explicit sex between minors thrown in for good measure. O (R)

Friend of the Family (1965) Weak French comedy directed by Robert Thomas about a toy inventor (Pierre Dux) and his wife (Danielle Darrieux) whose serenity is upset by a rival manufacturer (Jean Gabin) and his interest in their teenage daughter (Sylvie Vartan). A-III (br)

Friendly Persuasion (1956) Screen version of Jessamyn West's novel about a Quaker household (Cary Cooper, Dorothy McGuire and Tony Perkins) at the time of the Civil War. Director William Wyler's lyric treatment of family life and human relationships build to the conflict between the hard realities of war and the pacifist Quaker way of life. Still a warm and loving classic staple of family entertainment. A-I (br)

Friends (1971) Soapy, sappy sudser about two unhappy teens (Sean Bury and Anicee Alvina) running away from cruel homes who meet in the Paris Zoo and flee to a seaside refuge where instead of being friends they become lovers and parents in the pseudo-lyrical style of director Lewis Gilbert.

The explicitness of their barely post-pubescent sexual awakening is not only offensive but a saddening exploitation of minors in the name of box-office romance. O (R)

Friends of Eddie Coyle, The (1973) Solid adaptation of a George V. Higgins' novel about a tired, smalltime Boston crook (Robert Mitchum), who wants to retire on one last job but gets caught in the middle of con men, cops and criminals, and tries desperately to find an out. Directed by Peter Yates, the story is given a fine, naturalistic treatment, tough and complex, but tight. The powerful effect of the conclusion is achieved through the movie's careful accumulation of detail, though some may be unwilling to wait for the final turn of events because of the harsh and uncompromising depiction of criminal life. A-III (R)

Fright Night (1985) This horror movie attempts to evoke chills in a quite ordinary setting when a high school youth (William Ragsdale) becomes convinced that his new neighbor (Chris Sarandon) is a vampire. A major problem with writer-director Tom Holland's approach is its uncertain tone in veering between straight horror and a spoof of horror movies. The conclusion is dominated by gory pull-out-all-the-stops special effects. Benign view of extramarital sex. O (R)

Fringe Dwellers, The (1987) Insightful portrait of a young Australian aborigine girl's coming of age while struggling to break the cycle of poverty and oppression that crushes youthful ambition and enthusiasm. The contrived plot supplies an abrupt solution to a complex series of social and moral problems, but the overall perspective of director Bruce Beresford's movie provides an uplifting vision of community values and strong family ties. A-III (PG)

Frisco Kid, The (1979) A rabbi (Gene Wilder), sent cross-country on horseback during the Gold Rush to head a congregation in San Francisco, endures many misadventures that are potentially hilarious but prove only mildly funny in execution. Harrison Ford as the badman who brings him cross-country unscathed, makes the long journey as enjoyable as the material allows. Contains some hard-edged violence and profanity. A-III (PG)

Fritz the Cat (1972) Foul-mouthed comic book feline has been brought to the screen in an animated feature that lacks not only a clever script but a sense of humor. Under director Ralph Bakshi's slapdash direction, all attempts at satire regularly succumb to sexual sordidness, putting Fritz and his friends in the same category as the humans who toil in porno pictures. O (X)

Frogs (1972) Harmless looking frogs and toads send an army of snakes, leeches, snapping turtles and alligators to invade the home of Ray Milland on his swampy tropical island. Instead of playing the silly horror fantasy for laughs, director George McGowen tries for gasps in scene upon grisly scene with a transparent ecology message about nature taking its revenge. A-III (PG)

From Beyond the Grave (1976) British horror movie composed of four tales linked together by the device of a sinister antique shop and its affable proprietor (Peter Cushing). Director Kevin Connor can't improve upon the weak script, but he gets some fine performances (Ian Bannen, Donald Pleasance and Margaret Leighton as an eccentric medium right out of Noel Coward). The blood flows a little too freely in one of the stories but, other than that, it's a relatively mild litte chiller.

A-III (PG)
From Ear to Ear (1971) Tawdry French import offers a psycho-sexual thriller about two bisexual women who taunt a deeply disturbed wife into a drug-induced orgy that ends in murder. Director Louis Soulanes uses velvety amber photography to induce a mood of ennui and shrill music to suggest suspense, but its graphic sensationalism puts it in the sex exploitation category. O (X)

From Noon Till Three (1976) Seriocomic Western about an outlaw (Charles Bronson) whose sexual dalliance with a zany widow (Jill Ireland) blossoms into true love. The cast's wooden performance, the script's utter banalities and Frank Gilroy's inept direction obscure the theme of mistaken identities and half-truths becoming the basis for a legend. Excessive sex scenes. O (PG)

From the Hip (1987) Law clerk (Judd Nelson) uses deceit and bravado to advance his career, but when he is given an unwinnable murder case, his defense of a psychotic literature professor (John Hurt) brings about a change of heart and conscience. Bob Clark directs this optimistic yuppie portrait with care and wit. Some vulgar language and a brief outburst of courtroom violence. A-II (PG)

From the Life of the Marionettes (1980) Disappointing exploration of the homicidal psyche details the killing and sexual violation of a prostitute by a sullen businessman. Director Ingmar Bergman's narrative is devoted to flashbacks and flashforwards that supposedly shed some light on what caused this irrational act. Darkly clinical and emotionally sterile, the movie is obscure and troubling. Extensive nudity. O (R)

From the Mixed Up Files of Mrs. Basil E. Frankweiler (1973) Two youngsters (Sally Prager and Johnny Doran) run away from home and choose to live in New York City's Metropolitan Museum of Art which leads to their dealings with a rich recluse (Ingrid Bergman) in whose files they learn a lesson in human integrity. Directed by Fielder Cook, it is a well-intentioned but disappointing family movie in which few things work the way they are supposed to, though young children may enjoy some of the midnight wanderings through the museum. A-I (G)

Front, The (1976) Tragicomedy set during the early 1950s about a born loser (Woody Allen) who fronts for blacklisted writers by submitting their work under his name until he himself is turned by a blacklisted actor (Zero Mostel) whose subsequent suicide is story's turning point. Many of those associated with the movie, including director Martin Ritt and writer Walter Bernstein, were themselves blacklisted during that period. It is an interesting look at a tragic era but the drama and humor do not mix easily. Some rough language and comic sexual references. A-III (PG)

Front Page, The (1974) New edition of the Charles MacArthur-Ben Hecht play about tough Chicago newspapermen in the 1920s pits Jack Lemmon as the ace reporter against Walter Matthau as his wily editor. Directed by Billy Wilder, there is plenty of sharp, fast comedy straight out of the original, but nicely put over by a fine cast and a few neat touches of the director. Some, however, will be put off by the constant stream of pressroom profanity. A-III (R/PG appeal)

Frozen Dead (1967) Failed horror movie about a good-bad scientist (Dana Andrews) who thaws out former Nazi military leaders after their 25 years of deep freeze existence. Ineptly directed by Herbert J. Leder, its story of suspended animation and revivification is stupid but innocuous. A-I (br)

F.T.A. (1972)   Filmed record of performers Jane Fonda, Donald Sutherland and troupe staging a series of anti-war shows outside military bases in the U.S. and in the Pacific. The group as a whole looks rather sappy but the show's politics, which is what it is all about, is as worthy of a platform as those of Bob Hope's Christmas troupe. A-III (nr)

Fuego (1969)   Argentinian story of a nympho-maniac (Isabel Sarli) features a cliche-ridden plot, atrocious acting and a low level of technical competence. Written, produced and directed by Armando Bo, it is aimed squarely at the sex exploitation market. O (nr)

Full Life, A (1972)   Japanese movie whose title indicates the goal that a young woman (Ineko Arima) sets for herself after leaving her worthless husband. Nothing very dramatic happens in director Susumu Hani's 1962 work, but the accumulation of small details of life in a large urban complex makes the woman's realization that she needs friends and social commitment seem quite real. A-III (nr)

Full Metal Jacket (1987)   Director Stanley Kubrick's moody essay on the dehumanizing effects of basic training and combat during the Vietnam era traces the transformation of a typical Marine Corps recruit from observer to participant. Sexual come-ons by hookers, graphic bloodshed and excessive profanity provide the realistic texture for the expression of diminishing spiritual sensitivity and moral ambiguity. A-IV (R)

Fun with Dick and Jane (1977)   Leaden comedy about an upwardly mobile suburban couple (Jane Fonda and George Segal) who suddenly find their direction reversed when the husband loses his job as an aerospace executive. After trying welfare and foodstamps, they take to armed robbery and succeed beyond all measure. Apparently director Ted Kotcheff was aiming at satire, a task too formidable for the modest talents involved. Besides the movie's general insensitivity to genuine social ills, it employs coarse language and a tasteless bathroom scene. O (PG)

Funeral in Berlin (1967)   In a sequel to the "Ipcress File," Michael Caine returns as the disreputable British intelligence agent, Harry Palmer. The plot's intermingling of German, Russian, British and Israeli spies defies synopsis but the action is plentiful and exciting. The British production directed by Guy Hamilton succeeds in brilliantly contrasting the ways of life in East and West Berlin. A winner for those who enjoy undercover work. Restrained violence. A-III (br)

Funeral Parade of Roses (1973)   Failed Japanese experimental work by Toshio Matsumoto is a mishmash of scenes filmed at a gay bar in Tokyo. Never have fragmented images of eroticism and bloodshed looked more boring than those concocted here in a venture that adds nothing to our understanding of human nature. O (nr)

Funhouse (1981)   A monster stalks four extremely dim young people trapped in a carnival funhouse in a loathsome horror movie written and directed by Tobe Hooper. More likely to sicken than frighten, the film exploits sex and violence in grotesque and ugly ways. O (R)

Funniest Man in the World, The (1970)   Douglas Fairbanks Jr. narrates a documentary on Charlie Chaplin's early career as shown through excerpts from his work at the Keystone, Essanay and Mutual studios and makes a good introduction to the comic art of silent comedy. Chaplin's admirers, however, may wince at the way some of his movies have been chopped up and comic routines presented out of context in a compilation assembled by Vernon P. Becker. A-I (nr)

Funny Girl (1968)   Barbra Streisand musical is a sentimental treatment of certain aspects of the life of Fanny Brice, the Ziegfield Follies queen whose marriage to a gambler (Omar Sharif) fails in spite of their love. Director William Wyler turns Streisand's movie debut into a personal triumph. A-II (G)

Funny Lady (1975)   Barbra Streisand musical comedy in which she brings some depth to her portrayal of the maturing Fanny Brice trapped by her love for a professional gambler (Omar Sharif) and her attraction to a gambler (James Caan) without losing any of her zest in interpreting the Billy Rose songs and elaborate dance routines. Directed by Herbert Ross, the serious moments tend to drag, but the comic ones are hilarious, and the verve and nostalgia of the revue help to conceal a flawed plot. Basic plot situations and some of the dialogue are adult fare. A-III (PG)

Funny Thing Happened on the Way to the Forum, A (1966)   Wacky and ribald Broadway hit about a cunning slave (Zero Mostel) in ancient Rome who has great fun in exploiting a series of mistaken identities and in misinterpreting various orders in an effort to gain his freedom. Director Richard Lester keeps the humor swift and visual, backed by such fine screen clowns as Buster Keaton, Phil Silvers, Jack Gilford and Michael Hordern in a crisp and stylish musical burlesque of ageless low comedy routines. A-III (br)

Funnyman (1971)   Photographer-director John Korty applies his sensitivity and compassion to create a sort of fictional documentary about a young coffee-house comic (perfectly played by Peter Bonerz) who aspires to more intellectual work as a writer-actor and is forever feeling disappointed with himself. Matter-of-fact acceptance of casual sex and some lingering shots of an artist's nude model are questionable elements in an otherwise perceptive study of a talented young man's aspirations. A-IV (nr)

Further Adventures of the Wilderness Family, The (1979)   A sequel to the 1976 film about a family who leaves Los Angeles to live in the Rocky Mountains. This time Dad (Robert Logan) is caught in an avalanche and jumped by a cougar, however, the main crisis involves Mom, who is coming down with double-pneumonia and visited by a nasty pack of wolves. None of these perils are treated realistically by director Frank Zuniga, however, and even the younger children should be able to bear up and even enjoy them. A-I (G)

Fury, The (1978)   Kirk Douglas plays a man who tries to rescue his son from a sinister government agency that wants to use the boy's psychic powers for its own ends. Director Brian De Palma's crude, heavy-handed melodrama wallows in violence and gore. O (R)

Futureworld (1976)   Sequel to "Westworld" takes viewers back among those rambunctious robots. The plot gimmick this time is a scheme to replace world leaders with robots but enterprising journalists Peter Fonda and Blythe Danner foil the bad guys. Under Richard T. Heffron's direction, it's all pretty silly but mildly diverting entertainment, thanks mostly to Danner's decidedly non-robotized performance. Some scenes involving sexually-programmed robots. A-III (PG)

Futz (1969) Filmed performance by New York's La Mama Repertory Troupe of a play by Rochelle Owens about a farmer who is murdered by the community because, failing to find human love, he loves his pig. Supposedly an allegory about freedom and personal responsibility, its deliberately shocking and disgusting elements are less intolerable than its pretentious air of self-righteousness. O (nr)

Fuzz (1972) Police satire about the bumbling crime-fighting antics of writer Ed McBain's mythical 87th Precinct in Boston where detective Burt Reynolds and subordinates Jack Weston, Tom Skerritt and Raquel Welch as a policewoman decoy fail to take seriously Yul Brynner's extortion demands. Their inept performances are about as laughable as director Richard Colla's inept comedy ever gets. Viewers who find murder, attempted rape and the burning of helpless hobos less than hilarious may wish to take a pass on this one. A-III (PG)

F/X (1986) Tough suspense thriller concerning a movie special-effects expert (Bryan Brown) asked by a government agency to stage a fake killing but then finds himself hunted by the police for murder and shot at by unknown assassins. The plot is full of holes but director Robert Mandel rivets attention on the action's twists and turns. There is some intense violence but because the movie is about the trickery of special effects, the fake blood and gore is unlikely to offend most adult moviegoers. A-IV (R)

G

Gable and Lombard (1976) Nostalgic love story about two famous Hollywood stars (James Brolin and Jill Clayburgh) is a slick but embarrassingly bad job of story-telling by British director Sidney J. Furie. Sympathetic and romanticized presentation of infidelity. O (R)

Gaily, Gaily (1969) Ben Hecht, swaddled in adolescent innocence, makes his way to Chicago in 1910 and director Norman Jewison milks his autobiographical recollections into a nostalgic portrait capturing both the naivete of the young man and the corruption of the times. Illuminating satire stars Brian Keith, Beau Bridges and Hume Cronyn. A-III (M)

Galaxina (1981) Low-budget, tediously sophomoric spoof of science fiction films stars Dorothy R. Stratten in the title role. Directed by William Sachs, Stratten is made the target for an unrelenting series of sexually suggestive remarks. A-III (R)

Galileo (1975) Producer Ely Landau's screen version of the Bertolt Brecht play about the 16th-century scientist (Topol) and his confrontation with the church and with his own conscience comes across brilliantly. Directed by Joseph Losey, the work presents Galileo not as a hero but as a loving portrait of a great man who becomes the victim of ordinary creature comforts. A-III (PG)

Gallipoli (1981) Enthusiastic young Australians (Mel Gibson and Mark Lee) enlist for service in World War I and soon have their romantic notions of the war as a glorious and noble adventure dissolved. Director Peter Weir contrasts naive patriotism with youthful idealism in this superbly

rendered period drama. Intense battle scenes and a depiction of a brothel. A-III (PG)

Gambit (1966) Shirley MacLaine and Michael Caine set out to steal a priceless sculpture from wily Herbert Lom in the familiar plot about a perfect crime gone wrong. Director Ronald Neame comes up with a couple of new twists and some fine acting to distinguish it from a host of other romantic thrillers. A-I (br)

Gambler, The (1974) Static story of a compulsive gambler (James Caan) who betrays his bookies (Paul Sorvino and Carmine Caridi), his too-forgiving mother (Jacqueline Brookes), his doting grandfather (Morris Carnovsky) and his lovely girl friend (Lauren Hutton) as he degrades himself on the path to self-destruction. Directed by Karel Reisz, the story is obvious from the beginning and there is no attempt to make the viewer care a whit about the characters and their problems. A-III (R)

Game Is Over, The (1967) French adaptation of an Emile Zola novel about a woman (Jane Fonda), married to a ruthless business man (Michel Piccoli), falls fatefully in love with her husband's son (Peter McEnery). Directed by Roger Vadim, the movie's emphasis on nudity and eroticism is excessive. O (br)

Games (1967) Mediocre thriller about a bored couple (James Caan and Katharine Ross) and a mysterious stranger (Simone Signoret) who introduces them to some macabre games that end in murder. Directed by Curtis Harrington, some viewers will feel cheated by the twist ending which explains the illogical situations which precede it. Mature themes and stylized violence. A-III (br)

Games, The (1970) Ponderous Olympic marathon movie tracing the personal stories of various competitors, including an obnoxious American long-distance runner (Ryan O'Neal), his British counterpart (Michael Crawford), an exploited Australian aborigine (Athol Compton) and a patriotic Czech runner (Charles Aznavor). Forgettable British production directed by Michael Winner, it goes on and on to no point. Some sexual references. A-III (G)

Gandhi (1982) Superb portrait of India's great political and spiritual leader in a performance by Ben Kingsley which is so authoritative, yet so sensitive that any flaws in the movie fade into insignificance. Director Richard Attenborough's epic-scale production is used effectively to re-create Gandhi's life and times, especially the way in which he used non-violence and hunger strikes to bring together the diverse peoples of India and unify them as a nation. Though its scenes of violence are not for children, the movie's vision of justice and peace is for everyone else, especially young people. A-II (PG)

Gang That Couldn't Shoot Straight, The (1972) Failed screen version of Jimmy Breslin's novel about a bunch of inept South Brooklyn hoods bent on "takin' ovah da territory" features ethnic humor that tends to give credence to the efforts of the Italian-American Anti-Defamation League. So inept are director James Goldstone's satirical irreverences that an adult perspective seems to be a basic requirement for viewing. A-III (PG)

Gang's All Here, The (1943) Wartime musical extravaganza in which a nightclub singer (Alice Faye) falls in love with a soldier (James Ellison) who happens to be engaged to someone else. Directed by Busby Berkeley, things work out happily between the big musical numbers, including

Carmen Miranda's "The Lady in the Tutti Frutti Hat." Innocent but dated fun. A-I (br)

Ganja & Hess (1973) Mindless horror movie about an anthropologist who is addicted to human blood and a beautiful young woman who is both smitten and bitten by the evil doctor. The story never gets much beyond this, though director Bill Gunn adds a number of silly sex interludes suggesting even more unhealthy goings-on than plasma addiction. O (R)

Garbo Talks (1984) Sentimental comedy about a loving son (Ron Silver) who spares no effort to fulfill the wish of his dying mother (Anne Bancroft) to meet Greta Garbo. Directed by Sidney Lumet, it is modestly entertaining, but a little hard to take unless you share the Garbo mystique and don't mind watching a callous depiction of the collapse of a marriage. A-III (PG-13)

Garden of Delights, The (1971) Spanish director Carlos Saura has fashioned a quietly haunting, surreal black comedy about an aristocratic Madrid family perverted by greed. The story focuses on the aged family patriarch (Jose Luis Lopez Vasquez), struggling to regain his faculties after an auto accident, and is an insightful study of a man coming to terms with the deceit and selfishness of loved ones. A-III (GP)

Garden of the Finzi-Continis (1972) Director Vittorio De Sica's drama about the effects of Fascist anti-Semitism on the Jewish community in a small Italian town tells the story of a poor Jewish college student (Lino Capolicchio) who loves the beautiful daughter (Dominique Sanda) of a wealthy Jewish family. Structured as a somber nostalgic romance in which old class divisions prove stronger than racial bonds, the movie develops into a disturbing elegy for the loss of human dignity. A-III (R)

Gardens of Stone (1987) Director Francis Coppola's mildly nostalgic and insightful vision of the military as family contrasts the beliefs and aspirations of a decorated combat vet (James Caan) with those of a raw recruit (D.B. Sweeney) assigned to his Old Guard Arlington National Cemetary unit during the difficult Vietnam War years. Tragic story of the meaning of military service has some rough language and sexual situations which mark it for mature audiences. A-III (R)

Gas-s-s-s (1970) When the country's over-30 generation is wiped out by an accident with experimental nerve gas, a group of the under-30 crowd go for a cross-country romp, encountering demented cowboys, motorcycle freaks, a paramilitary football squad, a teenage brain surgeon, and so on and on. Director Roger Corman's silly, disjointed fantasy ends in a harmonious youth celebration, long before which most viewers will have sought some fresh air. Some adult material. A-III (PG)

Gate, The (1987) Modern fairy tale for the younger set about the dangers of toying with the darker side. Pre-teens accidentally unleash suburban demons while parents are away and need a heavy-metal album, courage and pure hearts to chase them back through the "gate" from which they escaped. Director Tibor Takacs provides some mild scares in a simple good vs. evil tale. A-II (PG-13)

Gator (1976) Burt Reynolds stars in and directs this story of an undercover agent's attempt to send the Mr. Big of a corrupt Southern county to prison. Mediocre entertainment at best, the movie veers in mood from slapstick to melodrama to soap opera

and back again. Violence. A-III (PG)

Gauntlet, The (1977) Not-too-bright Phoenix police officer (Clint Eastwood) goes to Las Vegas to extradite a convicted prostitute (Sandra Locke) only to discover that both of them have been marked for death. Eastwood also directed the shoddy, violent movie which is little more than a pretext for an extravagant display of gunplay, a steady stream of verbal obscenities and a bit of sex and nudity. O (R)

Gay Deceivers (1969) Young men pose as homosexuals to avoid military induction but the charade backfires when they have to convince parents, girl friends and teachers that they are straight. Stereotyped characters may offend members of the gay community while the instances of nudity and lovemaking add little to director Bruce Kessler's muddled social satire. A-IV (R)

Generation (1969) Hippie (Pete Duel) and little rich girl (Kim Darby) move in together in Greenwich Village and decide to have a baby by natural childbirth. Anti-establishment comedy based on William Goodhart's play doesn't have the sharp edges of the original but preserves its wit and charm thanks to director George Schaefer's toned-down treatment. A-III (PG)

Gentle Giant (1967) Engaging but less than credible adventure yarn about a young boy (Clint Howard) who rescues a bear cub in the Florida Everglades and raises him into a 650-pound house pet. Dennis Weaver is the boy's put-upon but understanding dad with Ralph Meeker as an antagonist of sorts. Directed by James Neilson, the problems of the situation are all very predictable but they are still fun, especially for the youngsters. A-I (br)

George! (1973) The title character is a Saint Bernard whose clumsy exuberance embarrasses one and all, until he and his guardian (Marshall Thompson) rescue each other from an avalanche in the Swiss Alps. Director Wallace C. Bennett concentrates on the gorgeous Alpine locales, providing some distraction for audiences who may tire of watching actors engage in pratfalls for the benefit of a dopey, if loveable dog. A-I (G)

Georgia, Georgia (1972) Written by Maya Angelou and directed by Stig Bjorkman, this story of a beautiful black singer on tour in Sweden quickly lapses into a romantic interracial interlude between the singer (Diana Sands) and a photographer (Dirk Benedict). Clumsy insertion of coy material focusing on the homosexual appetites of the singer's manager and a jarring climax that shocks but without providing an adequate resolution. A-IV (R)

Georgy Girl (1966) Tragicomedy of a warm-hearted, awkward young woman (Lynn Redgrave) who tries to make a life of her own after her friends (Alan Bates and Charlotte Rampling) break up and leave her to care for their neglected child. Under Silvio Narizzano's direction, Redgrave brings warmth and credibility to the title role, with James Mason adding a wry, slightly self-mocking performance as the aging millionaire who has long pursued her. Frank treatment of sexual matters. A-IV (br)

Get Carter (1971) Violent British crime melodrama in which Michael Caine plays a gangland killer-enforcer whose investigation into his brother's death finds him in and out of danger, bed and dens of rival gangsters. Directed by Mike Hodges, the movie's principle is kill or be killed in coldly brutal, cruel style, varied only by scenes of graphic sex and nudity. O (R)

Get Charlie Tully (1977) Tedious British comedy directed by Cliff Owen about two con men who, after bilking a foreign industrialist, find themselves on the run from the mob. A plot gimmick about the numbers of a secret Swiss account tattooed where anyone familiar with this kind of British humor can probably guess is the occasion for a good deal of female nudity. O (PG)

Get Out Your Handkerchiefs (1979) Very uneven French comedy in which a not-too-bright but good-natured husband (Gerard Depardieu) is willing to go to any lengths to cure his wife (Carole Laure) of a galloping case of boredom, even to propositioning a stranger (Patrick Dewaere) on her behalf. While entertaining a few clever moments, director Bertrand Blier's attempts to sustain the one-joke affair are more frantic that successful and its nudity and sexual immorality are seriously offensive. O (R)

Get to Know Your Rabbit (1972) Inane sex farce features Tom Smothers as a high-powered corporate dropout who turns road magician and lover to a veritable parade of naked females. Director Brian De Palma's self-indulgent comedy is an utterly sophomoric burlesque posing as a spoof of conventional society. O (R)

Getaway, The (1972) Released from prison through the connivance of a crooked politician, Steve McQueen has to return the favor by robbing a bank and sharing the proceeds. When the heist goes bad, McQueen and Ali McGraw skip town with the law in hot pursuit. The movie, however, goes nowhere under Sam Peckinpah's heavy-handed direction which resorts to some fairly ugly violence and a little sex. A-IV (PG)

Getting Straight (1970) Superficial survey of some elements of campus unrest in the story of a graduate student (Elliott Gould) and his encounters with sloganeering students, black militants, self-satisfied professors, insensitive administrators, bloodthirsty riot police, promiscuity, narcotics use, draft-dodging, profanity. Directed by Richard Rush, the movie exploits serious social issues, without any attempt to put them in context or provide a perspective for trying to understand them. O (R)

Getting of Wisdom, The (1980) Spirited Australian girl (Susannah Fowle) at a stuffy academy for young women in turn-of-the-century Sydney gives teachers, classmates, long-suffering mother and various other people a run for the money before she settles down and graduates with honors. Unfortunately, director Bruce Beresford's heroine remains unlikable and self-absorbed from first to last, making the result less than engaging entertainment. A-II (nr)

Ghetto Freaks (1972) Young people preach to each other, between rounds of dancing and heavy drug-taking, about the joyful simplicity of urban communal life. It ends in a nude psychedelic orgy sufficiently explicit to relegate the movie to the exploitational junk pile. O (R)

Ghidrah, the Three-Headed Monster (1965) Japanese rubber-suited monsters threaten miniatures of Tokyo in a standard fantasy thriller directed by Inoshiro Honda. Stylized violence. A-II (br)

Ghost and Mr. Chicken, The (1966) Don Knotts comedy vehicle in which he spends a night in a haunted house is ineptly directed by Alan Rafkin. A-I (br)

Ghost Story (1981) Fred Astaire, Melvyn Douglas, Douglas Fairbanks, Jr., John Houseman and Patricia Neal appear in director John Irvin's lavishly produced but intellectually impoverished film version of Peter Straub's novel about a vengeful spirit (an extremely fleshy spirit) stalking four old codgers who sent her to the bottom of a Vermont pond 50 years before. Ectoplasmic nudity and graphic spooky sexuality. O (R)

Ghostbusters (1984) Three parapsychologists (Bill Murray, Dan Aykroyd, and Harold Ramis), bounced from Columbia University because of the dubious nature of their research, go into private practice as ghost exterminators and find that all hell is about to break loose, quite literally. There are some very funny moments, largely due to Murray, but director Ivan Reitman lets the spectacular special effects begin to dominate midway and the humor fades. Some adult ribald jokes. A-III (PG)

Ghosts Italian Style (1969) Italian romantic comedy about newlyweds trying to save their sputtering marriage by living rent-free in a decaying baroque mansion haunted by a womanizing Count. Sophia Loren and Vittorio Gassman turn social satire into farce as director Renato Castellani tries to make something out of a story about false impressions and mistaken identities. A-III (G)

Ghoulies (1985) Shameless, thoroughly inept ripoff of "Gremlins." Directed by Luca Bercovici, it has some brief partial nudity and gore but not too much in the way of real violence. A-III (PG-13)

Giant (1956) Inarticulate cowhand (James Dean) strikes it rich in the Texas oilfields in director George Stevens' sentimental but stylish adaptation of the Edna Ferber novel about 1950's oil-rich parents (Elizabeth Taylor and Rock Hudson) and their idealistic offspring (Dennis Hopper). Children may find it of only intermittent interest. A-I (G)

Gilda Live (1980) Concert film by director Mike Nichols of comedienne Gilda Radner's Broadway stage show should appeal to fans of "Saturday Night Live," but leave others flat. Most of the amusing moments come from Don Novello as Father Guido Sarducci. Some rough language and Norvello's occasional (and highly original) ventures into theology make this mature fare. A-III (R)

Gimme Shelter (1970) Straightforword documentary gives an honest picture of what it was like to tour America with the Rolling Stones rock group and their notorious Altamont Speedway free concert where a fan was beaten to death by a member of the Hell's Angels. Directed by David Maysles, Albert Maysles and Charlotte Zwerin, it is a disturbing picture of the dark side of the American Dream. A-IV (R)

Ginger (1971) Cheri Caffaro plays the female private eye of the title who has a yen for sadistic revenge. Her methods range from castration to outright murder as she disrobes and dispatches a nasty band of sex merchants. Directed by Don Schain, it is another tired sex and violence exploitation movie. O (R)

Ginger and Fred (1986) Ginger (Giulietta Masina) and Fred (Marcello Mastroianni), a former vaudeville team who imitated Hollywood's Rogers and Astaire, are invited to perform in a Christmas television special. In this Italian production about the disappointments of old age and the commercialization of contemporary life, director Federico

Fellini pays homage to performers important in his career, while at the same time indulging his penchant for visual cascades of freakish humanity. Some earthy proverbs about sex and several ambiguous references to religion. A-III (PG-13)

Girl and the General, The (1967) Muddled Italian movie set in World War I in which an Austrian general (Rod Steiger) is captured by an Italian private (Umberto Orsini) and a peasant waif (Virna Lisi). Directed by Pasquale Festa Campanile, it has wartime violence and brief nudity. A-III (br)

Girl from Petrovka, The (1974) Romance between a Russian woman (Goldie Hawn) and an American journalist (Hal Holbrook) based in Moscow blossoms into true love but she is picked up by the police while on an errand of mercy and sentenced to prison. Directed by Robert Ellis Miller, the story is thin and watery and treated in ponderously sentimental style. Some ludicrously inappropriate nudity. A-III (PG)

Girl Getters, The (1966) British look at contemporary society through the eyes of young rebels without goals. Michael Winner's direction of Peter Draper's episodic script captures something of the cynical innocence of its subject. A-III (br)

Girl in Blue, The (1974) David Selby crisscrosses picturesque Ontario looking for the blue-clad girl (Maud Adams) he encountered long ago. He also lives with his girl friend (Gay Rowan) just in case the girl in blue never materializes. Directed by George Kaczender, the hackneyed exercise in romantic sentimentality is so slight and silly that even the occasional expletive and glimpse of nudity seems innocuous. A-III (nr)

Girl on a Motorcycle, The (1968) The woman of the title (Marianne Faithfull) relives her past as she speeds down the highway early one morning to meet her lover and her fate. Failing to come to grips with the motivation of the character's past actions, director Jack Cardiff understandably concentrates on the travelogue aspects of a ride through the beautiful French and German countryside. Frequent and explicit depictions of scenes of physical intimacy are dramatically as well as morally unjustified. O (X/R)

Girl Who Couldn't Say No, The (1969) Bland Italian comedy of a young surgeon (George Segal) who frequently falls in and out of love with an energetic Virna Lisi who's a soft touch for distressed persons. Directed by Franco Brusati, its permissive attitude toward sex is treated farcically but with excessive detail. O (PG)

Girl Who Knew Too Much, The (1969) Mystery story about a hired gun (Adam West) caught between the love for a slain crime boss' girl (Nancy Kwan) and his job of uncovering a Communist plot to take over the syndicate. Director Francis D. Lyon features a full-length strip-tease to enliven the dull, but brutally violent proceedings. O (R)

Girlfriends (1978) Director Claudia Weill's contrasting portrait of two New York women and the measures they take to find romance and commitment. Realistic treatment of sex and use of profanity override what little sensitivity and insight the film conveys. O (PG)

Girls Are for Loving (1973) In this latest chapter in the apparently ceaseless adventures of Ginger, our heroine breaks up a nasty extortion-kidnapping plot in high places and low. Once again Cheri Caffaro and writer-director Don Schain outdo themselves as the perfect husband-wife team

of voyeur and exhibitionist working the sexploitation-action flick market. O (R)

Girls Just Want to Have Fun (1985) Standard teen movie in which two plucky, clean-cut kids (Sarah Jessica Parker and Lee Montgomery) win a dance contest. Competent but mediocre light entertainment. A-II (PG)

Girly (see: "Mumsy, Nanny, Sonny and Girly")

Give 'Em Hell, Harry (1976) James Whitmore gives his interpretation of Harry Truman in a film recording of his one-man performance in the Samuel Gallu play. Directed by Steve Binder, Whitmore brings a passion, a conviction and a dauntless energy that engenders some understanding for the man and his controversial political career. The language is sometimes rough, but it is in the service of honest emotions. A-II (PG)

Give Her the Moon (1970) Unpretentious French comedy in which an American industrialist is so determined to get a French maid (Marthe Keller) that he transports her entire village to New York where culture shock becomes amusingly apparent. Though there is some romance, director Philippe de Broca concentrates on the contrasting lifestyles with some gentle satire of both. It's an old-fashioned escapist movie that may be lost on the young. A-II (G)

Gizmo (1980) Howard Smith's delightfully zany little film uses newsreels from the 1920s and 1930s to chronicle the dogged if flawed ingenuity of a host of inventors whose creations did not become household words. Very entertaining. A-I (G)

Glacier Fox, The (1979) Outstanding Japanese wildlife documentary, narrated by Arthur Hill, presents the story of a glacier fox, his mate and their five pups who live on the Okhotsk Sea coast of Hokkaido, a region blasted in winter by frigid winds that blow down from Siberia. Directed by Koreyoski Kurahara, the photography is stunning as it captures the intrinsic drama and humor in the life cycle of this fox family. Though it does not shy from some of the grimmer aspects of life in the wild, there are no visuals that might prove too strong for younger children, making it perfectly suited for the whole family. A-I (G)

Glass Bottom Boat, The (1966) A secretary (Doris Day) and a scientific genius (Rod Taylor) get involved with each other and assorted spies, gadgets and contrivances. The comedy has a number of good sight gags, some clever situations and a fine supporting cast. As put together by director Frank Tashlin, it adds up to a lot of fun. A-II (br)

Glass Houses (1972) Broken family seeks self-revelation through group encounter therapy at a California spa. Director Alexander Singer's ill-conceived satire features Jennifer O'Neil as a mistress and Deirdre Lenihan as the daughter of a business type who contend for his sexual attention. Most viewers will experience a gagging sensation rather than a catharsis. O (R)

Glass Sphinx (1968) Inept European production directed by Luigi Scattini about an archaeological expedition led by Robert Taylor in searching the Egyptian desert for a lost tomb containing the art treasure of the title. Some violence and sexual innuendo. A-III (br)

Glen and Randa (1971) After a thermonuclear apocalypse has destroyed contemporary civilization, two lost innocents (Steven Curry and Shelly Plimpton) live like primitive natives among the debris of Howard Johnson restaurants and deserted superhighways. Director Jim McBride's failed allegory about the primacy of animal passions becomes pretentious in execution and offensive in treatment, employing crude sex scenes and frontal nudity. O (X/R)

Gloria (1980)   Independent filmmaker John Cassavetes tries to transport a 1930s crime melodrama to the 1980 streets of New York in the story of a middle-aged gun moll (Gena Rowland), retired from the mob, who suddenly finds herself responsible for a young boy marked for death by her old gang. The movie's strength lies in the extraordinary performance of Rowland, which more than makes up for some of the narrative's incoherence. A-III (PG)

Glory Boy (1971)   World War II vet (Michael Moriarty) returns to the family farm with two of his buddies (William Devane and Mitchell Ryan) with the intention of proving to his patriotic father (Arthur Kennedy) that there is no glory on the battlefield but things get out of hand. Director Edwin Sherin's movie about the dehumanizing effects of war goes to excess in depicting rape and murder and its use of nudity and foul language. O (R)

Gnome-Mobile, The (1967)   A lumber baron takes his two grandchildren to one of his forests, discovers some lonely gnomes and helps them find another gnome-infested forest. Walter Brennan is excellent in a dual role as the kindly grandfather and a waspish, irascible little old man. Robert Stevenson directs the colorful Walt Disney fantasy whose good humor and many finely executed special effects will divert just as many adults as children. A-I (G)

Go Tell the Spartans (1978)   Burt Lancaster plays an overaged major who commands a small American cadre working with a motley collection of regular Vietnamese troops, mercenaries and militia in the hostile countryside during the early days of the Vietnam involvement. Director Ted Post handles the action sequences extremely well and, as a whole, the movie is intelligent, well-acted and moving. Violence and rough language, but conveys the contradictions and pathos of the Vietnam struggle. A-IV (R)

Goal! (1967)   Good sports documentary highlights the skill and endurance of the champion soccer teams which vied for the 1966 World Cup in England. Octavio Senoret's production does well in showing the differences in the style of play of the 16 countries represented and Nigel Patrick's narration helps explain the worldwide popularity of a sport in which no substitutions are allowed during the game. A-I (br)

Goat Horn, The (1974)   Bulgarian folk tale set during the time of Turkish rule when a goatherd raises his daughter as if she were a boy so that she will never be the victim, as was her mother, of the lust of their despotic master. Though it all ends badly, director Metodi Andonov conveys the sense of powerlessness of a subject people, not through dialogue, but through small details showing the daily life of the period. A-IV (nr)

Go-Between, The (1971)   British period romance features Michael Redgrave reminiscing about his childhood role as the innocent messenger between lovers (Julie Christie and Alan Bates) who are separated by the gulf of social class. Director Joseph Losey handles with sensitivity the boy's growing awareness of the nature of the couple's relationship and how, on his 13th birthday, he is directly confronted with the physical realities of adult life. A-III (PG)

Gobots, Battle of the Rock Lords (1986)   This animated action-adventure movie features constant combat between humanoids, robots and other silicon-based life forms, perpetuating the exploitation of the pre-teen market. Parents should consider the merits of further exposure of the very young to increased levels of hostility depicted in this movie. A-II (G)

God Forgives, I Don't (1969)   Professional gambler (Terence Hill) tracks down a notorious outlaw for personal reasons rather then to bring him to justice. Directed by Giuseppe Colizzi, the tale of a personal vendetta has little action or sense, but maintains an atmosphere throughout of brutality and needless violence. O (M)

Godfather, The (1972)   Blockbuster screen version of the Mario Puzo novel about a Mafia family's rise, decline and resurgence in the murderous world of New York racketeering. Marlon Brando plays the aging but indomitable Don with James Caan and Al Pacino as leading family members. Francis Ford Coppola's direction is a study in control and pacing with all the right touches in establishing the proper 1940s ambience. The murders are plentiful and gruesome and very little is spared in detailing the intricacies of mob life. A-III (R)

Godfather, Part II, The (1974)   Lacking the original's grace, majesty and energy, the sequel follows the rise to power of a crime boss (Robert De Niro) and the subsequent use of that power by his son (Al Pacino). Produced and directed by Francis Ford Coppola, the unmanageably complex scenario shifts interminably from Lake Tahoe to the Kefauver hearings, from the lower East Side to the Florida base of a crime kingpin. The effect is unsettling and there is much graphic violence. A-III (R)

Gods and the Dead, The (1972)   Brazilian turn-of-the-century drama about cocoa plantation owners who try to destroy each other with the ultimate survivor being a peasant who discovers that, just as he has been victimized by the owners, so too they were victimized by international business interests. Director Ruy Guerra's movie about the unequal distribution of wealth is filled with poetic imagery of the struggle for social justice. A-III (nr)

Gods Must Be Crazy, The (1983)   An African bushman discovers a discarded Coke bottle and, after it causes dissension among his people, undertakes a trek to throw it off the edge of the world, but in the course of the journey he runs into some very peculiar civilized people. Director Jamie Uys' simple comedy-adventure explores amiably the cultural differences between industrial society and ritualized tribal folkways. Some violence. A-II (PG)

Gods of the Plague (1977)   German crime melodrama made in 1969 about a young gangster who teams up with a killer for another robbery but is betrayed by one of his girl friends. Director Rainer Werner Fassbinder overdoes the murky underworld atmosphere, in which violence needs no motivation or justification, and the film has little point other than as an exercise in criminal brutality. O (nr)

Godsend, The (1980)   Foundling with a nasty disposition knocks off, one by one, the natural children of her foster parents, who seem to be inordinately slow to get the drift. Director Gabrielle Beaumont's tepid British thriller has little to recommend it and, though all of its violence is off-camera, it creates a foreboding atmosphere and features a rather graphic birth scene. A-III (R)

Godson, The (1972) Chilling psychological study of a lonely criminal (Alain Delon) whose life is held in a delicate balance between the gang and the law. French director Jean-Pierre Melville unfolds this lone wolf's struggle to survive police pursuits, the distrust of his gangland associates and the false sympathy of a woman in a restrained and highly visual manner without the violent excesses associated with gangster films. A-II (PG)

Godspell (1973) Sparkling screen version of musical based loosely on the Gospel according to Matthew, featuring an off-Broadway cast with Victor Garber as the Christ figure and David Haskell as both John the Baptist and Judas. What makes the movie so high-spirited is director David Green's turning the entire city of New York into a giant stage set, with its buildings, streets and parks all strikingly used for great effect. The parables are presented in imaginative skits, many of which serve as springboards for the irresistible tunes, such as "Day by Day" and "God Save the People!," that made the play so popular. A-I (G)

Godzilla 1985 (1985) You can't keep a good monster down and Japan's favorite has risen again, along with his old pal Raymond Burr, in a fairly competent new version. Godzilla fans everywhere should have reason to be happy with the results, though all the crashing and banging might frighten young children. A-II (PG)

Godzilla Vs. the Smog Monster (1972) Godzilla tangles with a smog monster that bloats itself on factory and automobile wastes, and succeeds in frustrating its ambition to feed on the sacred fumes of Mt. Fuji. Wry social satire on pollution from director Yoshimitu Banno whose use of blurry, grainy, anemic color photography here is for once thematically motivated. A-I (GP/G)

Godzilla's Revenge (1971) Young boy's conversation with Godzilla (who is in retirement on Monster Island) and also with his son teach him a few tricks which help thwart a pair of bank robbers who are hiding near his home. Director Ishiro Honda resurrects his collection of monsters for another round of campy adventures. A-I (G)

Goin' All the Way (1982) Shoddy exploitation movie about the sexual yearnings of some high school students, not one of whom looks a day under 25. Directed by Robert Freedman with crass vulgarity, abundant nudity and graphic sexuality. O (R)

Goin' Down the Road (1970) Canadian movie in which two Nova Scotians come to Toronto in search of a better life but soon find themselves back on the highway, a little less likely of ever finding their place in the world. Directed by Donald Shebib, it is best in its celebration of the city and its environs, but its young people (Doug McGrath, Paul Bradley and Jane Eastwood) are so sincere and earnest in their idealism that they almost overcome the handicap of stereotyped roles. A-III (R/GP)

Goin' South (1978) Jack Nicholson directs his own performance as a raffish outlaw who is saved from hanging when a young woman (Mary Steenburgen) agrees to marry him. Her sole interest is a hired hand to help her work a supposedly exhausted gold mine, but, naturally, romance blooms in the desert air. Moderately entertaining comedy Western with some sexually oriented humor. A-III (PG)

Going Ape! (1981) Three orangutans provide the madcap antics in director Jeremy Joe Kronsberg's inept and witless situation comedy about a young man (Tony Danza) who inherits a fortune with the requirement that he care for the apes. Danny De Vito helps him protect the beasts from a greedy zoological society that also tries to get the dough. Much vulgarity and frequent profanity. A-III (PG)

Going Berserk (1983) Collection of skits loosely joined together by the gimmick of having television comic John Candy handcuffed to an escaped convict. Written and directed by David Steinberg, the farce offers little other than much foul language and some gross sexually oriented humor. O (R)

Going Home (1971) Jan-Michael Vincent plays a man who as a young child saw his father (Robert Mitchum) kill his mother in a drunken rage and now seeks to avenge her by raping the paroled father's new bride-to-be (Brenda Vaccaro). Producer-director Herbert Leonard's failed drama deals in the cliches of abnormal psychology without any serious analysis of characters and their actions nor is there any meaningful resolution of its muddled plot. Some violence. A-III (GP)

Going in Style (1980) Three oldsters on pension (George Burns, Art Carney, and Lee Strasberg), fed up with feeding pigeons in a Queens park, decide to rob a Manhattan bank. Only George Burns' fine performance makes director Martin Brest's flat and uninspired geriatric farce at all worth watching. Some rough language and its benign view of the crime. A-III (PG)

Going Places (1974) Pair of petty thieves (Gerard Depardieu and Patrick Dewaere) graduate to auto theft, kidnapping and assault as they wander aimlessly through the French countryside, with a sex encounter of some sort at every stop. Directed by Bertrand Blier, the movie's amoral view of life is conveyed in gross language and even grosser, occasionally degrading images. O (R)

Gold (1974) Though its plot is a rather tiresome affair about the manipulations of an international gold syndicate, this large-scale disaster movie offers an exotic catastrophe (the flooding of an entire gold mining area), fresh South African locations and some gripping action sequences and spectacular special effects. Director Peter Hunt, however, fights a losing battle against an inept script. Some double entendres and an illicit romance make it inappropriate for youngsters. A-III (PG)

Golden Calf, The (1974) The stratagems of a confidence man (Sergei Yursky) in the Soviet Union of the late 1920s backfire with slapstick regularity and when one of his schemes finally brings in a million rubles, he learns that money does not buy happiness and returns to his con games. Directed by Mikhail Shveitser, it is an amusing change of pace from the usual socialist realism of Soviet cinema. A-I (nr)

Golden Child, The (1986) A private detective (Eddie Murphy) is charged with rescuing from evil kidnappers a Tibetan toddler, revered by a cult as their sacred leader. A tiresome Murphy vehicle, more irreverent than funny, replete with some unwholesome seduction humor, many indecent expressions and other harsh language as well as much violent action and gruesome images. O (PG-13)

Golden Needles (1974) Fair adventure movie in which Elizabeth Ashley, acting for aging millionaire Burgess Meredith, hires Joe Don Baker to obtain an Oriental statuette whose seven gold needles are said to be able to restore youth and virility to its possessor. Directed by Robert Clouse, there are some generous helpings of kung fu and karate fights and enough love scenes to put it in the adult class, but otherwise it is an escapist movie that doesn't take itself seriously. A-III (PG)

Golden Raiders, The (see: "Escape to Athena")

Golden Seal, The (1983) Isolated by a storm, a lonely boy (Torquil Campbell) living on an island in the Aleutians befriends a mother seal and protects it from family and poachers. There is a lot of profanity, including some dark pearls from the mouth of our young hero, and a bit of violence. A-II (PG)

Golden Voyage of Sinbad, The (1974) John Phillip Law as Sinbad sails off to find the Fountain of Destiny, harassed by a variety of demons and other nasty types conjured up by Ray Harryhausen's imaginative special effects. Director Gordon Hessler's lighthearted and entertaining adventure movie brings a treat for youngsters and those adults who wish to recapture some of the magic of childhood. A-I (G)

Goldengirl (1979) Muddled potboiler about the merchandizing of an Olympic sprinter (Susan Anton) by a promoter (James Coburn) who discovers that her scientist father (Curt Jurgens) has been giving her periodic injections of a dangerous growth hormone. Directed by Joseph Sargent, the movie is against the commercialization of sports and the manipulation of human beings, but it compromises this by exploiting the sheer spectacle of the Olympics and Miss Anton herself. A number of rather crude sexual references. O (PG)

Gone With The Wind (1939) Epic historical romance spanning 20 years in the troubled lives of its southern heroine (Vivian Leigh), the man she loves (Leslie Howard) and the man she marries (Clark Gable). Produced by David O. Selznick and directed by Victor Fleming, the movie re-creates not the history but the myth of the Old South and its destruction in the Civil War and Reconstruction. Though it treats blacks in the stereotyped manner of its time, it is sympathetic towards its black characters, especially Hattie McDaniel who received an Academy Award for her performance. A-II (G)

Gong Show Movie, The (1980) Chuck Barris' television game show featuring out-takes too deplorable to show on television form the basis for this monument to bad taste and witless vulgarity. O (R)

Good Father, The (1987) Middle-aged executive, troubled and resentful because of his broken marriage, uses his anger and a male-dominated legal system to pressure an unhappy friend into divorce and a child custody battle in Mike Newell's somber drama. Anthony Hopkins' statement about lost idealism is conveyed with quiet rage as he rejects the feminism he once championed and seeks vengeance vicariously through the court battle of another, gaining only a greater sense of remorse. A-II (R)

Good Guys Wear Black (1979) Mediocre action adventure directed by Ted Post concerns the vengeful exploits of the leader (Chuck Norris) of an elite unit that was betrayed and almost wiped out in the last days of the Vietnam War. Standard violence and sexual hijinks in the service of eye-for-an-eye justice. A-III (PG)

Good Guys and the Bad Guys, The (1969) Aging marshal Robert Mitchum joins forces with aging outlaw George Kennedy to thwart a train robbery in this tongue-in-cheek tribute to the senior side of the generation gap. Director Burt Kennedy's entertaining, energetic Western spoofs the New West of inept bad men, greedy politicians and complacent townspeople. Its aging stars' heroics are more slapstick than swashbuckling. A-III (PG)

Good Morning, Babylon (1987) The Taviani brothers take us on an operatic tour of the early days of Hollywood as two Italian brothers learn that creativity and passion don't last as long as movies and cathedrals. This homage to the silent era and celebration of brotherhood and paternal obligations has some brief nudity, but is, otherwise, emotionally and visually engaging. A-III (PG-13)

Good Morning, Vietnam (1987) Robin Williams stars as a wacky U.S. Armed Forces radio disc jockey brought to boost troop morale in 1965 Vietnam but his unmilitary sense of humor brings him into conflict with those in charge of the station. Directed by Barry Levinson, the serio-comic movie has some hilarious routines but also considerable raunchy sexual humor, rough language and irreverances, only somewhat redeemed by being placed within the context of the obscenity of war. A-IV (R)

Good Times (1967) Sonny and Cher star as themselves in a spoofy, puffy vehicle allowing them to try out various types of Hollywood roles and generally have a lot of fun fooling around in fancy costumes on colorful sets. Directed by William Friedkin, it's a cheerful, unassuming little movie. A-I (br)

Good Wife, The (1987) Seemingly faithful and modest wife (Rachel Ward) tries to overcome a sexual crisis in her marriage by having an affair with her brother-in-law and succumbing to the temptations of an aggresive stranger (Sam Neill). Bryan Brown is the unexciting lumberjack who suffers through his wife's sexual odyssey with the hope of putting their marriage back together. Director Ken Cameron makes it trashy with too many simulated sex scenes and a confused moral perspective. O (R)

Good, the Bad, and the Ugly, The (1968) Typically cynical, brutal Spaghetti Western with Clint Eastwood, Lee Van Cleef and Eli Wallach looking for some stolen gold at the time of the Civil War. Directed with some class by Sergio Leone, the movie's good is overwhelmed by the bad and the ugly. O (br)

Goodbye, Columbus (1969) Uncompromising screen version of Philip Roth's novel about the generation gap in early 1960s America in a story about an affluent Jewish family whose daughter (Ali MacGraw) is pursued by an ambitious young man (Richard Benjamin). The conflicting social and generational attitudes result in general disillusionment for almost everyone involved. Directed by Larry Peerce, the young couple's sexual relationship is treated quite frankly. A-IV (R/PG)

Goodbye Gemini (1970) Surrounded with an aura of evil and perversion, maladjusted twins (Judy Geeson and Martin Potter) take up residence in a London fantasy world of their own making and become involved in a series of senseless and promiscuous escapades ending in murder. Director

Alan Gibson's foul black comedy is replete with rape and other violence, nudity and implied incest. O (R)

Goodbye Girl, The (1977) Aspiring actor from Chicago (Richard Dreyfuss) sublets a New York apartment from a friend and finds it already furnished with a 33-year-old divorcee (Marsha Mason) and her 10-year-old daughter (Quinn Cummings). Neil Simon's romantic comedy, directed by Herbert Ross, is pleasant and entertaining, though unfortunately flawed by occasional vulgarities and the acceptance of premarital sex. O (PG)

Goodbye, Mr. Chips (1969) Musical version of the James Hilton novel with Peter O'Toole as the distracted, unbending schoolmaster who is set upon, conquered and finally humanized by a hoydenish music hall performer (Petula Clark). Director Herbert Ross shifts the focus from the academic to the happy marriage of such unlikely opposites. Leslie Bricusse's songs are pleasantly unobtrusive in the enjoyable old-fashioned romance, that some will find quite moving. Youngsters, however, are more likely to find it sentimental and over-long. A-I (G)

Goodbye, Norma Jean (1976) Director Larry Buchanan's obsessive exploitation of the speculative and sordid details of Marilyn Monroe's rise to stardom is a dreadful little film trading on tabloid sensationalism, sexual intimacies and demeaning images of women. O (R)

Goonies, The (1985) A gang of kids search for pirate treasure to save their homes from foreclosure. A scaled-down version of "Indiana Jones" aimed squarely at children, but many parents will have reservations about exposing their pre-teens to the vulgar expletives that pepper the dialogue, supposedly as all part of the fun. A-II (PG)

Gordon's War (1973) Former Green Beret captain (Paul Winfield) declares war on Harlem drug pushers with the help of three other Vietnam vets (Carl Lee, Tony King and David Dowling). It is unfortunate that the movie dishes up so much unrelenting street violence, frank nudity and unconscious acceptance of the hero as righteous avenger, because director Ossie Davis obviously has a moral point to make about the social evil of substance addiction. O (R)

Gorky Park (1983) Disappointing adaptation of the Martin Cruz novel about murder in Moscow with William Hurt playing the honest, apolitical detective in charge of the investigation but his listless, mannered portrayal proves deadening. Director Michael Apted reduces Cruz's ingenious story to a run-of-the-mill mystery with a brief but graphic love scene, some violence and several gruesome sequences involving corpses. A-IV (R)

Gospel According to St. Matthew, The (1966) Straight-forward Italian dramatization of the evangelist's account of the life of Jesus and his message. It succeeds exceptionally well in placing the viewer within the Gospel events, avoiding the artificiality of most biblical movie epics. Director Pier Paolo Pasolini is completely faithful to the text while employing the visual imagination necessary for his realistic interpretation. A-I (br)

Gospel According to Vic, The (1987) Tom Conti is a schoolmaster teaching learning-impaired children in a school in Scotland. Pride and public opinion lead him to believe that he's a miracle worker, but he slowly discovers that his special gifts of love, courage and generosity are so rare that they are often mistaken for divine providence. Some profanity and implied sex impose upon an otherwise thoroughly gentle and uplifting story. A-III (PG-13)

Gospel Road (1973) Produced by Johnny Cash and filmed in locales around Jerusalem, the movie is a very personal and sincere interpretation of the public ministry of Jesus Christ. Directed by Robert Elfstrom (who is often seen as the Christ figure), it avoids for the most part a literal portrayal of the events of the New Testament and wisely opts for a symbolic visualization. Cash appears as on-screen narrator as well as vocalist backed by a country-folk musical score and the result reflects, better than most, the spirit of the Gospels. A-I (G)

Gotcha (1985) A college boy (Anthony Edwards), eager to rid himself of his virginity, vacations in Europe, meets an agreeable older woman but becomes the target of real bullets instead of the liquid air-gun pellets used in a campus game called "gotcha." Director Jeff Kanew's sophomoric fantasy is neither funny nor exciting. Benign view of sexual promiscuity. O (PG-13)

Gothic (1987) Director Ken Russell's muddled exploration of the nightmarish roots of creativity is set during a Victorian era weekend visit by poet Percy Shelley and fiancee Mary to the weird villa of Lord Byron. This grotesque vision of the darker side of the imagination features an unpleasant mix of nudity in a sexual context, images of death, deprivation and degeneracy. O (R)

Grace Quigley (1985) Aged widow (Katharine Hepburn) hires a professional hitman (Nick Nolte) to do her in and then becomes his agent. A satiric comedy that went dreadfully wrong, despite the efforts of director Anthony Harvey and talented cast. Because of the movie's ineptness and its lack of satiric point, the view of suicide is more benign than not. O (PG)

Graduate, The (1968) Director Mike Nichols' tale of an innocent in a corrupt world tells of the seduction of an aimless middle-class young man (Dustin Hoffman) by a suburban housewife (Anne Bancroft) and his redemption by his love for her daughter (Katherine Ross). Some viewers will question its treatment of adultery and use of some strong language. A-IV (br)

Grand Prix (1967) Large-scale production takes viewers around the 10 courses of Europe's Grand Prix auto-racing circuit that conveys in almost documentary fashion the experience of racing. Director John Frankenheimer interweaves the story of four drivers (Yves Montand, James Garner, Brian Bedford and Antonio Sabata) but is less successful with their off-track romances. A-III (br)

Grand Slam (1968) European production in which a retired teacher (Edward G. Robinson) plans the complex robbery of a Brazilian diamond firm during the time of the Rio Carnival and with some inside assistance (Janet Leigh). Tautly directed by Giuliano Montaldo, crime does not pay but a seduction scene is not for youngsters. A-III (br)

Grasshopper, The (1970) Small-town Canadian girl Jacqueline Bisset comes to Los Angeles for romance but ends up as a show girl who becomes an executive's mistress and then a prostitute. Director Jerry Paris' sordid and pessimistic melodrama resorts to frequent use of nudity. O (R)

Gravy Train, The (1974) Pair of brothers from the hills of West Virginia (Stacy Keach and Frederic Forrest) join in a complex armored-car robbery only to be ripped off by the caper's mastermind (Barry Primus). What follows is a downhill race against time to intercept the loot before it is sold to a fence. Director Jack Starrett has an eye for pell-mell action and an ear for racy backwoods expletives and witticisms. But the killings and cursing, plus a gratuitous massage parlor visit, tends to put a sour edge on the action. A-IV (R)

Gray Lady Down (1978) Reconditioned nuclear submarine on a shakedown cruise is struck by a freighter and sinks into a deep sea canyon from which the Navy tries to rescue the survivors. Charlton Heston, as the sub commander, and Stacy Keach, as the officer in charge of the operation, are properly taut-jawed and grimly heroic, while for variety's sake, David Carradine is relaxed and cheerfully heroic as the pilot of a small experimental submarine. Director David Greene plumbs the depths and comes up with some fairly good entertainment. A-II (PG)

Grayeagle (1978) A dying Indian chief commissions a warrior to kidnap a supposed white woman who is in fact his daughter so that he might see her before he dies. Not even the presence of Ben Johnson helps this embarrassingly bad Western written, produced and directed by Charles B. Pierce (who also does some dreadful acting in it). Violence and some partial nudity make it a tall tale for adults. A-III (PG)

Grazie Zia (1969) Ironic Italian fable about a rich young psychopath (Lou Castel) who torments his attractive aunt (Lisa Gastoni), a doctor trying to cure his affliction. Director Salvatore Samperi reduces the theme of good and evil to an unrelenting series of sexual games and perverse role-reversals ending in self-destruction. O (PG)

Grease (1978) Nostalgic 1950s musical romance in which John Travolta plays the leader of a slick-haired, leather-jacketed gang, and Olivia Newton-John is a sweet high school transfer student from Australia whose attraction for him transforms her into a tough, sensual leather groupie. Though director Randal Kleiser plays it for simpleminded fun, the teen fantasy glamorizes negative role models and is preoccupied with sex in its dialogue and lyrics. O (PG)

Grease 2 (1982) Taking up where the original musical left off, an English youth (Maxwell Caulfield) enrolls at Rydel High School and learns to ride a motorcycle to impress his girlfriend (Michelle Pfeiffer). Set in the 1960s, director Patricia Birch's movie is bland and synthetic but its gaping moral vacuum, emphasis on conformity at all costs and sexual innuendo in the lyrics make it unsuitable for younger viewers. A-III (PG)

Greased Lightning (1977) The usually comic Richard Pryor gives an extremely restrained and effective performance as a stock car racer in the Deep South who has to overcome racial prejudice to succeed. Despite director Michael Schultz's blunting of the story's conflict and tension by inappropriate humor, Pryor's charm and skill along with an excellent supporting cast provide some buoyant and entertaining moments. A-II (PG)

Greaser's Palace (1972) Director Robert Downey's wacky fable juxtaposes the Old Movie West with the Second Coming of Christ (by parachute), a comic concept that deteriorates into a meandering string of sight gags. Those who find nothing funny in religious irreverence should be warned that this is definitely not their movie. Some explicit sexual and scatological references are excessive. O (nr)

Great Bank Hoax, The (1979) Fine but ill-used cast headed by Ned Beatty, Burgess Meredith and Michael Murphy is unable to get anything but a mild chuckle or two from this leaden-paced, awkward comedy about an attempt to cover up an embezzlement by staging a mock robbery. Director Joseph Jacoby adds an adult flavor to the jokes and slapstick situations. A-III (PG)

Great Bank Robbery, The (1969) Sophomoric Western spoof stars Zero Mostel and Kim Novak as the Rev. Pious Blue and Sister Lyda who try to save a small Western town from themselves as well as from some bandits. Directed by Hy Averback, a seduction sequence, a tasteless comic nude scene and double-entendre sermonizing are not for youngsters, and probably most adults. A-III (PG)

Great Battle, The (1974) Inept Soviet dramatization depicting the bitter and dramatic siege of the Russian city of Kursk by German forces in 1943. The badly-dubbed movie has little interest either historically or dramatically, and its scenes of carnage are not for young children. A-II (PG)

Great Catherine (1969) Chaotic flight-of-fancy based on George Bernard Shaw's bedroom farce opposes Peter O'Toole, as a British Dragoon, and Jeanne Moreau, as the 18th-century Russian Empress. Director Gordon Flemyng manages to erode Shaw's fragile, pungent satire of pompous British aristocracy and unbridled Russian passion with slapstick humor, frantic chases and crude caricatures. A-III (G)

Great Dictator, The (1940) In this satirical indictment of Hitlerian totalitarianism, writer-producer-director Charles Chaplin plays dual roles as Hynkel, the mini-moustachioed dictator of Tomania and as the Little Fellow in the form of a Jewish barber. As his lady love, Paulette Goddard shines luminously, even when she's banging storm troopers over the head with her frying pan. Because of its subject and themes, the movie is less likely to engage the interest of the very young. A-II (G)

Great Escape, The (1963) Thrilling rendition of a fact-based story about an elaborate escape of Allied prisoners from a German P.O.W. camp during World War II. Steve McQueen is the most ambitious of a group which includes Henry Fonda, Kirk Douglas, Richard Attenborough and James Garner as they plot a mass escape that results in a fascinating and highly entertaining suspense gripper. With John Sturges directing, it all builds to a stunning, sobering climax that both tugs at the heart and keeps it racing. A-I (br)

Great Gatsby, The (1974) Lavish but disappointing screen versioin of F. Scott Fitzgerald's novel about the fatally ill-matched love of a millionaire (Robert Redford) for another man's wife (Mia Farrow). Director Jack Clayton's lush production gives more attention to the movie's set design and costuming than to Francis Ford Coppola's very literate but frequently literal adaptation. The result is beautiful to watch but proves an empty experience. Mature themes. A-III (PG)

Great McGonagall, The (1975) Spike Milligan directs and stars in an offbeat movie about a poor 19th-century Scottish weaver who late in life gives up everything to write truly atrocious poetry and dies unknown and impoverished. Milligan's comedy lacks the anarchistic zest of his glory days on BBC radio and only occasionally reflects the mad-

115

cap fancy of simpler times. A brief nude dance only compounds the movie's many problems. O (nr)

Great Mouse Detective, The (1986) This Disney feature-length animated adventure concerns a tiny girl mouse who seeks the aid of Basil of Baker Street, a wise and worldly detective who foils the wicked plans of the evil Ratigan (don't call him a rat) and frees her captive papa mouse. Less enchanting than one might expect, but it has the traditional Disney care for characterization. A-I (G)

Great Muppet Caper, The (1981) Jim Henson directs his incomparable cast of muppets as wise-cracking Kermit and song-and-dance lady Miss Piggy lead the troupe off to England to thwart Charles Grodin's plan to rob fashion queen Diana Rigg of her jewels. Great silly fun for adults and children. A-I (G)

Great Northfield, Minnesota Raid, The (1972) Western melodrama about one of the last great robberies before the onset of the machine age contrasts the non-violent, philosophical Cole Younger (Cliff Robertson) and the murderous, Bible-spouting Jesse James (Robert Duvall). Director Philip Kaufman's mix of character study and a demythologizing of the frontier experience has many good moments but is flawed and derivative. Graphic violence and some incidental nudity. A-III (PG)

Great Race, The (1956) Slapstick potpourri of sight gags and broad characterizations abound in an automobile race from New York to Paris whose chief competitors are Tony Curtis and Jack Lemmon. Blake Edwards directs his low comedy farce in high comedy style. A-I (br)

Great Santini, The (1980) Solid portrait of a gung-ho but aging Marine fighter pilot (Robert Duvall) who, having no war to fight in 1962, brings his own war home to cause conflict with his wife (Blythe Danner), and especially his teenage son (Michael O'Keefe). Though flawed with some heavy melodrama and a contrived resolution, director John Lewis Carlino's story of family life has much heart, strong values, warm humor and three marvellous performances to more than compensate. Some rough language and the intensity of emotional family conflict. A-II (PG)

Great Scout and Cathouse Thursday, The (1976) Lee Marvin plays a veteran scout out to avenge a swindle worked on him by former partner Robert Culp, but in the process he falls in love with a young prostitute. Director Don Taylor's Western spoof is tedious, unfunny, occasionally brutal and unremittingly vulgar in its attempts at bawdy hijinks. O (PG)

Great Spy Chase, The (1966) Flat French spy spoof directed by Georges Lautner in which the world's leading secret agents pursue the blonde widow (Mireille Darc) of a manufacturer who left her his papers on a devastating new weapon. Much sexual innuendo. A-III (br)

Great Texas Dynamite Chase, The (1977) Two young women carry out a bank-robbing spree and live happily ever after. Despite oafish attempts at tongue-in-cheek satire, director Michael Pressman's farce sinks into gratuitous sex and violence with degrading female stereotypes. O (R)

Great Train Robbery, The (1979) Sean Connery stars as a debonair Victorian con man who carries off the first high-speed train robbery in history with the aid of accomplished locksmith

Donald Sutherland and girlfriend Lesley Anne Down. British production boasts hair-raising hijinks and an impressive re-creation of the period by director-writer Michael Crichton. There is a fair amount of lighthearted double-entendres and an acceptance of less than virtuous behavior. A-III (PG)

Great Waldo Pepper, The (1975) Robert Redford stars as a 1920s stunt pilot who realizes his fantasy of meeting a great German ace in air combat. Director George Roy Hill's movie is rather flat but its aerial photography of the great old biplanes is entertainment enough. Some strong language. A-III (PG)

Great Wall, A (1986) Gentle but keenly observed comedy of cultural collision when a Chinese-American family visits relatives in Peking in the first American feature produced in mainland China. Directed by Peter Wang, the movie provides an entertaining and informative dissection of the humorous pitfalls of stereotyping. A-I (PG)

Great Waltz, The (1972) Failed musical extravaganza tracing the life and times of 19th-century German composer Johann Strauss, Jr., from when he first eclipsed his father as the most popular songwriter of Old Vienna, through the middle period when Strauss chased skirts and the muse with equal fervor, to his moment of triumph when he presented "On the Beautiful Blue Danube" at the 1872 Boston World Peace Jubilee. Horst Bucholz as Strauss looks like he is ready to gag on a steady diet of producer-writer-director Andrew L. Stone's preposterous dialogue. And the audience might gag on the saccharine treatment of this controversial composer's life. A-II (G)

Great White Hope, The (1970) Fictionalized but hardly sanitized story based on the life of prizefighter and onetime heavyweight champion of the world, Jack Johnson, here named Jack Jefferson. Set in the early decades of the century, the narrative traces the swift rise and sudden, prolonged fall of the giant black boxer who taunted the racial attitudes of the time. The role is played with burning intensity by James Earl Jones who is at first defiant, then wounded and finally outcast. Directed by Martin Ritt, the movie is hardly reassuring in its social indictment and is full of bitterness and stinging material, both visual and verbal. It is a strong film that should be approached with clear eyes and an open mind. A-III (GP)

Greatest, The (1977) Entertaining but rather flat and patched together film version of Muhammad Ali's autobiography with Ali playing himself. Director Tom Gries' dramatization seems to have simplified a great deal, and the effect is to show the heavyweight boxing champion with no warts at all. Ring violence and religious stereotyping. A-III (PG)

Greatest Story Ever Told, The (1965) While it is obviously not the greatest movie ever made, director George Stevens' vision of the Gospel story presents a consistent, traditional view of Christ as the God Incarnate. The movie, despite its epic Hollywood scale, is well-acted, tastefully and realistically written, beautifully photographed and Max von Sydow's believable portrayal of the Christ is the most essential element in its success. A-I (br)

Greek Tycoon (1978) Tabloid melodrama in which a Greek shipping magnate (Anthony Quinn) woos and wins the chic widow (Jacqueline Bisset) of an assassinated president of the United States. Directed by J. Lee Thompson, the movie is trashy to the core in its shameless trafficking in actual events viewed through the distorting glass of malicious gossip and innuendo, compounded by rough language and a graphic nude scene. O (R)

Green Berets, The (1968) John Wayne stars in and co-directs (with Ray Kellogg) this ghastly commercial for U.S. involvement in Vietnam. Based on the popular Robin Moore novel, the movie follows Wayne and his green-bereted force as they slaughter wave upon wave of slant-eyed commies. Racial stereotyping and wartime violence depicted in much the same manner as the old Hollywood World War II movies set in the Pacific. A-III (G)

Green Room, The (1979) French director Francois Truffaut's adaptation of two short stories by Henry James is a philosophical meditation on the subject of death and the transcendence of the human spirit. Truffaut himself plays the World War I soldier who returns safely from the trenches to find that his wife has died. A masterful exercise in the cinema of atmosphere and characterization, but some may find the hero's obsession with death morbid. A-III (PG)

Green Slime, The (1969) A big mushroom from outer space plays the title role, with support from earthlings Robert Horton and Richard Jaeckel. Forgettable Japanese sci-fi production directed by Kinji Fukasaku. A-I (G)

Green Wall, The (1972) Young couple have carved out a homestead in the jungle of Peru's interior, fighting the lush vegetation for each acre of arable land. When their young son is bitten by a poisonous snake, the movie becomes a race to get the vaccine that will save the child, underlining the isolation of every frontier community. Writer-director Armando Robles Godoy has constructed his script around that one fateful day, with flashbacks filling out the story. Discreet lovemaking scene. A-III (R)

Greetings (1968) Brian De Palma directs a way-out satire on draft-dodgers, computer dating and other aspects of 1960s society. The effort is sometimes humorous but when wit fails, it turns to sex, nudity and tasteless situations. O (X)

Gregory's Girl (1982) A charming movie about the travails of adolescence in urban Scotland. Written and directed by Bill Forsyth, it retains to the end its capacity to surprise with its daffy, yet at times touching incongruity. A-II (PG)

Gremlins (1984) Bouncy, but often repulsively dark comedy about nasty little creatures spawned by a cute, furry little monster (Hoyt Axton) buys for his son (Zach Galligan). A strained moral tale about the consequences of not following directions, the fantasy directed by Joe Dante is steeped in fierce, violent, savage sight gags which lead to mindless mischief, mayhem and murder. A-III (PG)

Grey Fox, The (1983) Stagecoach robber (Richard Farnsworth), released after 30 years in prison into a world without stagecoaches, heads for Canada and starts robbing trains. Leisurely directed by Philip Borsos, the beautiful locales and some fine acting obscures the Canadian production's basically anti-social theme. A-III (PG)

Grey Gardens (1976) Documentary about two women, an aging mother and a middle-aged daughter, once wealthy but who now live as recluses in a crumbling mansion in an exclusive community which wants them out. Directed by Albert and David Maysles, the often moving, often

troubling portrait of rugged individualism invades their privacy but presents them as noble and heroic women who refuse to compromise their ideals to the standards of society. A-III (PG)

Greyfriars Bobby (1961) Disney movie about a 19th-century dog in Scotland whose faithfulness in staying by his master's grave in an Edinburgh cemetary make him a town legend. Director Don Chaffey's fine cast (Donald Crisp, Alex MacKenzie, Laurence Naismith, Gordon Jackson) and solid staging make it superior family entertainment that young children especially will enjoy. A-I (br)

Greystoke: The Legend of Tarzan, Lord of the Apes (1984) Director Hugh Hudson's visually stunning, extremely intelligent, well-acted retelling of the Edgar Rice Burroughs popular classic about a boy raised by apes and returned to civilization only to recoil from its moral savagery. The violence in the jungle sequences is very strong stuff, and there is also a brief bedroom sequence and some male nudity. A-III (PG)

Grimm's Fairy Tales for Adults (1971) Pretentious sex fantasy with two impotent bumpkins seeking their fortune in the deep woods where they have encounters with Snow White, Sleeping Beauty and Cinderella. Director Rolf Thiele allays his own subsconscious anxieties by lacing the uncouth undoings with gory details in a German-produced strudel full of raw and rotten apples. O (nr)

Grissom Gang, The (1971) Perverse tale of a poor little rich girl (Kim Darby) who finds true love with one of her kidnappers (Scott Wilson) in director Robert Aldrich's excessively violent movie set in Prohibition-era Kansas City. O (R)

Grizzly (1976) Inept action thriller about a 15-foot grizzly bear attacking unwary campers in a national park. Starring Christopher George and directed by William Girdler, it is no more than a tedious exercise in special-effects mayhem, totally inappropriate for youngsters. A-III (PG)

Grizzly Adams (see: "The Life and Times of Grizzly Adams")

Groove Tube, The (1974) Satirical skits spoofing the state of television programming by imagining what it would be like if there were no sacred cows and the predominant color were blue. Directed by Ken Shapiro, the result is wild satire, mad slapstick and, as might be expected, adolescent smut, gross scatological humor and a garden variety of tastelessness. O (X/R)

Groundstar Conspiracy, The (1972) Mediocre espionage thriller about a plot to sabotage an important government nuclear research center focuses mainly on George Peppard's ruthless, amoral methods of flushing out the traitor at the top. Directed by Lamont Johnson, the movie's hazy philosophical-political attitudes, as well as a romantic sub-plot, are not for the immature. A-III (PG)

Group, The (1966) Screen version of the Mary McCarthy novel about the private lives of eight Vassar girls capitalizes on the comeliness of its principals, particularly Candice Bergen, Elizabeth Hartman and Joanna Pettet, to the detriment of real dramatic interest and human values. Lumpily directed by Sidney Lumet, the screen adaptation emphasizes the young ladies' sexual proclivities as they pursue husbands and careers in the 1930s. O (br)

Groupies (1970) Director Ron Dorfman's movie about the idolization of pop musicians by the young seems less a documentary than a put on with the kids acting up for the camera in amateur fashion. It is exploitation masked as celebration of the uninhibited, irresponsible lifestyles of the rock music subculture. O (X)

Guernica (1976) Fernando Arrabal's movie presents a surrealistic history of the Spanish Civil War, making grotesques out of the Nationalists and idealizing the Republicans. It is basically a series of theatrical set pieces whose best images are filled with pain, sadness and longing but the imagery frequently operates on the level of shocking violence and anti-religious references. O (nr)

Guess What We Learned in School Today? (1971) Pretending to parody puritanical attitudes toward the sex education of the young in affluent suburbia, director John G. Avildsen's satire teaches its paltry lessons mainly with redundant nudity and protracted promiscuity. The movie's various sex-obsessed caricatures are embodied by passable unknown performers. O (R)

Guess Who's Coming to Dinner (1967) Pat comedy starring Spencer Tracy and Katharine Hepburn as parents of a daughter (Katharine Houghton) who is planning to marry a distinguished black doctor (Sidney Poitier). Directed by Stanley Kramer, the movie has some good comic moments and by showing the efforts of both families to cope with the racial issue and the generation gap, it achieves a dimension of truth. A-II (br)

Gulliver's Travels (1939) Max Fleischer's animated version of Swift's story of the shipwrecked Englishman who is washed ashore in Lilliput, the land of the small. The adaptation goes over well with youngsters, it has some good bits of comic invention and the songs are not bad. A-I (br)

Gulliver's Travels Beyond the Moon (1966) Young children will like this Japanese-produced but western-geared animated feature about a little boy, a puppy dog and a tin soldier who join forces with old Lemuel Gulliver on an adventuresome trip by spaceship to the distant star of Hope. Charming and worthwhile. A-I (br)

Gumball Rally, The (1976) Mindless cross-country car race featuring a cast of characters led by Michael Sarrazin. Stunt coordinator-turned-director Chuck Bail tries some leering sex at the pit-stops. O (PG)

Gumshoe (1972) British movie in which Albert Finney plays a man who imagines himself as a hard-boiled private eye of the Raymond Chandler and Dashiell Hammett school and these fantasies get him involved in a nasty but highly implausible case of gun-running and murder. Directed by Stephen Frears, the movie is fun at first, but it lacks a solid plot and therefore bogs down very quickly in its non-stop allusions to old detective movies. Violence and sexual innuendo. A-III (GP)

Gunfight, A (1971) Retired gunfighters Kirk Douglas and Johnny Cash have little more to look forward to than an inevitable showdown with each other or with a younger, faster gun so they stage their own final shootout. Director Lamont Johnson aiming at audience participation in the outcome settles for heavy symbolism spotted with some rough language and a brief nude scene. A-III (PG)

Gung Ho (1986) Michael Keaton stars in this comedy about the reluctance of U.S. workers to accept the standards of performance imposed upon them when a Japanese management team takes over a defunct auto manufacturing plant in a small Pennsylvania town. Offering a multitude of stale one-liners and sight gags, the script seems some-

what insensitive in the stereotyping of Japanese businessmen as obsessively concerned with efficiency and saving face. Failed comedy with low humor, harsh language and ethnic stereotyping. A-III (PG-13)

Gunn (1967) Seamy, occasionally brutal feature based on the once-popular "Peter Gunn" TV detective series, with Craig Stevens impeccable as ever in the title role. It's a minor effort from director Blake Edwards, offering little more than routine private eye segments, a passel of cameo appearances by screen stars and an unoriginal twist ending. Excessive violence and sexual situations. O (br)

Gunpoint (1965) Substandard Western directed by Earl Bellamy in which Audie Murphy plays a lawman chasing an outlaw band. Stylized violence. A-I (br)

Guns for San Sebastian (1968) Mexican rebel (Anthony Quinn), mistaken for the priest expected by the inhabitants of a village ravaged by Indians and bandits, teaches them how to fight back and drive off the marauders. Directed by Henri Verneuil, the 18th-century setting is beautifully evoked but the story is somewhat far-fetched and on the sentimental side. Stylized violence. A-II (br)

Guns of a Stranger (1973) Boring Western in which Marty Robbins plays a straight-shooter who comes to the rescue of a damsel-in-distress (Dovie Beams) whose boozy grandfather (Chill Wills) is about to lose his ranch to a cattle baron (William Foster). Robert Hinkle directs Robbins who is a singer but no cowboy, and certainly no actor. A-I (G)

Guns of August, The (1965) Based on Barbara Tuchman's study of how World War I started, this documentary popularizes the scholarly story of diplomatic blunders and political miscalculations. Director Nathan Kroll and his film researchers have accumulated a mass of familiar and unfamiliar footage on the outbreak of the war, presented in a straight-forward, factual manner. A-I (br)

Guns of the Magnificent Seven (1969) Mercenaries try to outwit superior forces in this sequel set in revolutionary Mexico. Plot operates on the level of gunfights rather than coherent story, with George Kennedy trying hard but simply not the taciturn strong-man type. Best is the historical background which director Paul Wendkos occasionally brings in. A-II (G)

Guru, The (1969) English pop singer (Michael York) journeys to Bombay to learn to play the sitar where his teacher (Uptal Dutt) tries but fails to convert him to the spiritual values of the East. Rita Tushingham plays a wandering hippie fleeing Western materialism. Director James Ivory's uneven story is essentially a study in contradictions, with humorous overtones, between two cultures and their outlook on life. A-II (G)

Guru, the Mad Monk (1971) The title character is a maniacal chaplain of a prison island where Central Europe sends its prisoners to be tortured and executed. The film's blood and sex diversions are complicated with a silly vampire and a hodgepodge of religious symbolism offensive to all faiths. O (nr)

Gus (1976) Above average Disney comedy about a mule who kicks field goals. Vincent McEveety directs the lively, fast-moving entertainment, especially suitable for children. A-I (G)

Guyana: Cult of the Damned (1980) Dull fact-based dramatization of the 1978 Jonestown tragedy in which 900 followers of the Reverend James Jones went to their death with their deranged leader. Stuart Whitman stars as the false prophet in director Rene Cardona, Jr.'s Mexican production which is not as sensational as it might have been but neither does it have the least merit. A scene featuring nudity and another involving physical punishment are gratuitous and offensive. O (R)

Gypsy Girl (1966) Slight British story of a retarded girl (Hayley Mills), fatherless and neglected by her alcoholic mother, whose tragic young life is changed when a handsome gypsy pays attention to her and she learns what it means to be loved. Directed by John Mills, it is a well-done study of the simplicity of childlike people. The girl's prolonged sadness and her fights with her mother make it inappropriate for young children. A-II (br)

Gypsy Moths, The (1969) Burt Lancaster, Gene Hackman and Deborah Kerr star in an unusual action movie about a rough-and-tough team who make a living as sky-divers performing at state fairs across the Midwest. Director John Frankenheimer's aerial photography, especially the actual dive sequences, is absolutely breathtaking, but the dramatic portions unfolding on terra firma, having to do with the personal lives and problems of the divers, lack credibility. A-III (R)

H

Hagbard and Signe (1968) Scandanavian medieval romance based on the Romeo and Juliet theme is set against the stunning landscape of Iceland. Though there is much that is compelling and authentic in director Gabriel Axel's beautifully-crafted movie, its treatment is regrettably marred by excessive nudity and graphic depictions of brutality. O (br)

Hail, Hero (1969) Generation gap movie about a college drop-out (Michael Douglas) who returns to the ranch to announce to his indifferent parents that he's joining the Army. Character portrait from director David Miller conveys an overly optimistic embodiment of joyous vitality and spiritual awareness. Disjointed comments about family ties, first love, prejudice and war. A-III (M)

Hail! Mafia (1966) Forgettable crime melodrama directed by Raoul Levy about a paid killer involved in a gang war. Violence. A-III (br)

Hail Mary (1985) The Gospel account of the Incarnation and Virgin Birth is updated to present-day Switzerland in this French production. Though seriously intended, director Jean-Luc Godard's movie is not only tedious and disjointed, but its extensive use of nudity and extremely rough language in a context so sacred to Christians will be offensive to many. O (nr)

Hail to the Chief (1973) Occasionally hilarious, more often sophomoric spoof of Presidential politics stars Dan Resin as the nation's Chief Executive who is more than slightly demented about stamping out dissent in the land. Directed by Fred Levinson, there are some sterling gags of sight and sound but also a malicious sense of humor in regard to American politics. A-III (PG)

Hair (1979) Key Broadway musical of the 1960s was as much a slick exploitation of the flower children phenomenon as it was a celebration of it. Director Milos Forman's 1970's screen version keeps intact its virtues, including its measure of sincerity, and its defects, including its large dose of showbiz phoniness. For the most part, Forman does not romanticize his characters (John Savage, Treat Williams, Beverly D'Angelo, Charlotte Rae), though there are huge, lavish dance numbers and a restrained depiction of scenes with drugs, promiscuity, nudity and some rough language. A-IV (PG)

Half a Sixpence (1968) Director George Sidney's expanded version of the stage musical stars Tommy Steele as an exuberant dancing, singing draper's clerk who pledges his love to a girl of his own background, Ann (Julia Foster), inherits a fortune, nearly marries a society girl and goes back to faithful Ann, a bit sadder and wiser. Though overlong and somewhat lacking in variety, its handsome sets and soft lens photography give the movie an Edwardian storybook quality that most viewers should find delightful. A-I (br)

Half Moon Street (1986) Intelligent and attractive woman (Sigourney Weaver) supplements her meager salary as a London researcher by working as a part-time prostitute for upper-class clients. When one of them (Michael Caine) falls in love with her, she finds herself in the middle of a Middle Eastern power struggle that nearly costs her her life. Director Bob Swaim's routine tale of scandal among the British power elite apparently intends to show how badly women were exploited but it only does more of the same. Violence, nudity and simulated sex. O (R)

Hallelujah, I'm a Bum (1933) Fine musical comedy about the Depression stars Al Jolson as the Mayor of Central Park, a bum respected by every tramp in New York City until he falls in love and gets a regular job. Directed by Lewis Milestone, the movie is one of a kind in providing a socially-conscious rather than escapist Hollywood musical. A-III (nr)

Halloween (1978) Criminally insane patient escapes to his hometown on Halloween, the 15th anniversary of the brutal murder for which he was locked up, and becomes a deadly menace to unsuspecting babysitters in director John Carpenter's low-budget horror show. Mixture of some nudity with much violence. O (R)

Halloween II (1981) The further adventures of the homicidal maniac and his relentless pursuit of babysitter Jamie Lee Curtis. Directed by Rick Rosenthal, it is just as bad as the original with its nauseating violence, sadism, tastelessness and general senselessness. O (R)

Halloween III: Season of the Witch (1982) Director Tommy Lee Wallace's sequel uses a plot about a fiendish toy manufacturer (Dan O'Herlihy), intent upon giving the tots of America a Halloween to remember, as an excuse for trotting out the usual sickening special-effects violence and gore as well as some nudity. O (R)

Halls of Anger (1970) Sixty white students are bused to a large, all-black high school where the lid is kept on by a disciplinarian who happens to be a former athlete (Calvin Lockhart). Director Paul Bogart handles the desegregation issue with some authenticity but resorts to typical cliches and easy solutions. Much violence and brief nudity. A-III (PG)

Hamburger...The Motion Picture (1986) Former football star Dick Butkus is the harsh and talkative coach teaching management techniques to trainees at a special college dedicated to Lyman Funk's All Bull Buster Burgers. What begins as social satire upon callous commercialism quickly collapses into an unfunny sex farce with profanity, nudity and violence. O (R)

Hamlet (1969) Director Tony Richardson's intimate rendering of the Shakespearean tragedy emphasizes personal confrontations, heroic solitude and star Nicol Williamson's penchant for caustic repartee. Some omissions lose the spirit of the original text but this boisterous version still provides a poignant portrait of a man's search for truth. A-II (G)

Hammer (1972) Black exploitation movie about an ex-dockworker (Fred Williamson) who becomes a boxer but when the mob wants him to take a dive, he takes them on and lays them out. Directed by Bruce Clark, the production values are good and the violence is toned down but it suffers from weak characterization and too-familiar story line. Some raw sex scenes and rough language. O (R)

Hammer of God, The (1973) Mindless martial arts movie about Japanese karate fighters who slaughter students of a Chinese kung-fu school, but a survivor bolsters himself with iron fist techniques and takes revenge on the baddies. Usual amount of violence except for a savage rape of a woman who has nothing to do with the story. O (R)

Hammerhead (1968) An American soldier of fortune (Vince Edwards) and his companion (Judy Geeson) spend most of their time tracking down an international spy posing as an art collector (Robert Vaughn). Sluggish espionage melodrama directed by David Miller. Nasty violence and sexually suggestive treatment. O (R)

Hammersmith Is Out (1972) Sluggish variation on the Faust legend in which a psycho-ward attendant (Beau Bridges) is promised strength, wealth and a hashhouse waitress (Elizabeth Taylor) if he will let an inmate (Richard Burton) escape. From there it is a murderous journey to the upper reaches of corruption in a movie directed by Peter Ustinov with a total lack of wit and vigor. Some graphic sex and violence and much crude language. O (R)

Hammett (1983) Mediocre melodrama about Dashiell Hammett (Frederic Forrest), the creator of Sam Spade, getting started as a writer in 1928 San Francisco but becoming sidetracked by a murder case in which he absorbs the same kind of punishment that would later appear in his hard-boiled detective stories. Directed by Wim Wenders, the result proves to be a pretentious, sentimental and uninspired tribute to old Hollywood murder mysteries, and at times borders on self-parody. Some vulgar expletives and some violence. A-II (PG)

Hand, The (1981) Successful cartoonist (Michael Caine) loses his drawing hand in a freak accident and then imagines that the severed hand, never recovered, is pursuing him and threatening those who arouse his anger, especially his restless wife (Andrea Marcovicci). Director Oliver Stone achieves some scary effects, but it's otherwise a gloomy, depressing story with cardboard characters. Some graphic sex and violence. O (R)

Hand in Hand (1960) A British movie about the childhood friendship between a Catholic boy and a Jewish girl who discover that God is everywhere, watching over everyone. Directed by Philip Leacock, it is a fine little film, especially for family audiences. A-I (br)

Handle with Care (1977) Good-natured, warm-hearted little comedy set in a small California town where a Citizens Band radio enthusiast (Paul Le Mat) dashes about rescuing people and doing other good deeds, though not always with the approval of his pensive girl friend (Candy Clark). Director Jonathan Demme contrives an ending that tries to pull all his diverse story elements together but it's forced and out of keeping with the relaxed mood of the rest of the movie. A sub-plot about a bigamous trucker and his two wives is adult fare. A-III (PG)

Hands of the Ripper (1972) A pioneer psycho-analyst (Eric Porter) tries to cure the daughter of Jack the Ripper (Angharad Rees) who has inherited her father's tendency to slash things in moments of stress. Fairly well done British horror movie, but too violent for younger viewers. A-III (R)

Hang 'em High (1968) Vigorous Western starring Clint Eastwood as a former lawman who journeys into the Nebraska Territory where he is promptly hanged—but not high enough to keep him from coming back to enforce a rough version of justice on the range. Directed by Ted Post, the result is clever without being campy and, unusual for an action-packed Eastwood vehicle, without too much violence. A-III (M)

Hangar 18 (1981) Within the title edifice are the remains of a wrecked flying saucer kept undercover as part of a government cover-up in this anemic little movie directed by James Conway and starring Darren McGavin and Robert Vaughn. Some incidental violence. A-II (PG)

Hanky Panky (1982) Limp and tedious comedy-adventure in which a mild-mannered architect from Chicago (Gene Wilder) finds himself suspected of murder and pursued by all sorts of hostile people, among them a mystery woman (Gilda Radner). Directed by Sidney Poitier, the poor effort contains a scene involving the beating and murder of a woman and some strong language. A-III (PG)

Hannah and Her Sisters (1986) Writer-director Woody Allen's disappointing treatment of infidelity and adultery in the lives of three sisters (Mia Farrow, Dianne Wiest and Barbara Hershey). Although it shows the struggle and disappointments of people searching for a better life, it romanticizes amoral behavior and dishonesty as a natural consequence of contemporary urban lifestyles. A-IV (PG-13)

Hannibal Brooks (1969) British World War II P.O.W. (Oliver Reed) escapes in the company of an elephant to Switzerland. Director Michael Winner's pacifist fable resorts to some large-scale but graphically restrained guerrilla warfare to conclude the escape but preserves the lighthearted adventure motif of this generally amiable satire. A-II (M)

Hannie Caulder (1972) A rancher's wife (Raquel Welch) learns to take justice and a six-shooter into her own hands after being raped and widowed by three bumbling bandits (Strother Martin, Ernest Borgnine and Jack Elam). Director Burt Kennedy's erratic Western focuses on a simple-minded and unquestioned theme of vengeance. Exploitative rape sequence, bloody violence and coarse language. O (R)

Hanoi Hilton, The (1987) Michael Moriarty is the Christ-like crucified leader of a group of U.S. POWs tortured by callous North Vietnamese until their release at the end of the war. Canadian director Lionel Chetwynd intends this as a tribute to their uncommon bravery but manages to convey an insidious jingoistic notion that duty to country is equal to Christian virtue. Profanity, male nudity and scenes of brutality and torture are more prominent than religious references. O (R)

Hanover Street (1979)   Dashing American bomber pilot (Harrison Ford) falls in love with a married woman (Lesley-Anne-Down) during a 1943 London air raid, they have an affair and then he winds up on a secret mission in France with her nice-guy husband (Christopher Plummer). Written and directed by Peter Hyams, it is an inept attempt to make an old-fashioned wartime romance without the skill or intelligence to evoke any genuine emotions or feelings. Though it does not condone adultery, its glossy and graphic treatment of it is offensive. O (PG)

Happiest Millionaire, The (1967)   Musical biography of Anthony J. Drexel Biddle (Fred McMurray), an eccentric turn-of-the-century millionaire who kept alligators as pets, collected prizefighters and alternated a family program of physical fitness with hymn-singing. Directed by Norman Tokar, it has all the usual Disney staples: some innocent romance, a sentimental view of family life and amusing animals. It is, however, overlong and the music by Richard and Robert Sherman is undistinguished. A-I (br)

Happiness (1934)   Soviet silent slapstick comedy about a peasant misfit who is put in the Czarist army but after the Revolution returns home to what is now part of a collective farm where he is as much of a misfit as ever. Directed by Alexandre Medvedkine, the action has the zany absurdity that is universal to visual comedy, though the ending is predictably didactic as the peasant learns that happiness is working for the common good. Some earthy humor. A-III (nr)

Happiness Cage, The (1972)   Army private (Christopher Walken) receives some experimental brain wave treatment to control his schizophrenic behavior, administered by a neurosurgeon (Joss Ackland) who is trying to learn how to rehabilitate undesirables. Directing an adaptation of Dennis Reardon's play, Bernard Girard fails to provide enough information or human feeling about the scientific conditioning process to make the movie anything more than an old-fashioned horror movie. Patients rant and curse periodically. A-III (PG)

Happy Birthday Gemini (1980)   Screen version of Albert Innaurato's play about a poor Italian-American youth (Alan Rosenberg) who receives a surprise visit on his 21st birthday from two wealthy classmates, a brother and sister, but he thinks he loves the brother more than he does the sister. Directed by Richard Benner, the youth's sexual ambivalence is used as the hook upon which to hang all sorts of vignettes of working-class life but the movie is loud, messy and overacted. Lacks any moral perspective on the sexual identity question, and features crude ethnic stereotypes, vulgarity and profanity. O (R)

Happy Birthday to Me (1981)   Simple-minded Canadian horror movie about a disturbed student (Melissa Sue Anderson) at an exclusive school whose friends start disappearing. The climax is her birthday party, at which they all show up rather the worse for wear. Directed by J. Lee Thompson, it is senselessly nauseating in its gore and violence. O (R)

Happy Birthday, Wanda June (1971)   Screen version of the Kurt Vonnegut, Jr., play in which an explorer (Rod Steiger), presumed dead after disappearing in the Amazon jungles eight years before, returns home to discover that his wife (Susannah York) is about to marry a doctor (George Grizzard). Director Mark Robson's stagebound adaptation is a muddled black comedy about the destructive he-man image of masculinity, the nature of aggression and the status of women. Though there are some amusing bits, they do not add up to a coherent whole and the number of verbal obscenities becomes needlessly excessive. O (R)

Happy Ending, The (1970)   The movie begins with a disillusioned couple (John Forsythe and Jean Simmons) out of love on the morning of their 16th wedding anniversary and, after various complications, concludes with the wife asking whether, if her husband had to do it over again, he would marry her. Directed by Richard Brooks, it is as unenlightening as it sounds and more than a little cliched. A-III (PG)

Happy Hooker, The (1975)   Lynn Redgrave struggles gamely to give some life and glamour to the essentially sordid trade of prostitution. Though there are some humorous touches and a minimum of offensive graphics and vulgar speech, director Nicholas Sgarro's movie fails to justify its existence as either art or entertainment. O (R)

Happy Mother's Day...Love, George (1973)   A young lad (Ron Howard) searching for his unknown father comes to a New England fishing village inhabited by a bizarre set of characters (Cloris Leachman, Patricia Neal and Tessa Dahl). Ineptly directed by Darren McGavin, the film's gory violence, supposedly motivated by sexual repression, is an unsavory fantasy. O (PG)

Happy New Year (1973)   French comedy about a pair of jewel thieves (Lino Ventura and Charles Gerard) who meticulously plan a heist on New Year's Eve, set it in action and have it fail because one of them falls completely for the charming owner (Francoise Fabian) of an antique shop next door. Director Claude Lelouch succeeds in presenting a crime caper in a human context that has some moral weight to it. A-III (PG)

Hard Contract (1969)   Hired gun James Coburn gets amorously sidetracked by Lee Remick on his way to murder three people in Europe. He has a change of heart but struggles with his own lack of sensitivity. Talkathon by director-writer S.Lee Pogostin questions how much authority figures are responsible for society's dehumanization. A-IV (R)

Hard Ride, The (1971)   Vietnam vet (Robert Fuller) escorts home the body of his black buddy who had wanted his motorcycle pals to be present at his funeral but, in trying to fulfill this request, he is killed in a bikers' brawl and is buried with his friend. Directed by Burt Topper, the movie mutes the usual sex and violence to make the point that being a road bum is a senseless way of life. A-III (GP)

Hard Times (1975)   Tough loner (Charles Bronson), down on his luck during the Depression, picks up money by street fighting, an elemental no-holds-barred kind of contest whose payoff comes from the bets wagered. Director Walter Hill gets the period right and does well with the New Orleans locales, but the movie has no pretensions to being anything but good pulp fiction and it succeeds on this level. Some brutal fighting scenes. A-III (R/PG)

Hard to Hold (1984)   A rock star (Rick Springfield) falls madly in love with a sophisticated lady (Janet Eilber) whom he meets in a traffic accident.

Director Larry Peerce's listless, awkward movie features bad acting by all concerned. A benign view of sex outside of marriage and some rough language are adult fare. A-III (PG)

Hard Traveling (1986) Dan Bessie directs a grim, fact-based story of the Depression years about a down-and-out farmer convicted of murder. Although this movie offers a depressing vision of social injustices and their causes, its sensitive portrayals and strong period details lessen its pessimistic outlook. A-III (PG)

Hardbodies (1984) California smut-in-the-sun movie about three middle-aged lechers who engage a teen-age lothario (Grant Cramer) to instruct them in the art of seduction. Badly directed by Mark Griffiths, it features abundant nudity, graphic sex and utter disregard of every moral consideration. O (R)

Hardcore (1979) Deeply committed Christian from the Midwest (George C. Scott) hires a Los Angeles detective (Peter Boyle) to find his 15-year-old daughter who has disappeared while attending a religious youth convention in California. When she turns up in a porno film, Scott is plunged into the pornographic underworld trying to find her. Writer-director Paul Schrader's movie deals with a serious subject, but on the whole is crude and simplistic, its characters shallow and its melodramatic resolution unbelievable. Nudity and frequent rough language. O (R)

Harder They Come, The (1973) The movie, in English but frequently subtitled because of the thickly accented Jamaican speech, stars Jimmy Cliff as a country boy come to Kingston town seeking fame and fortune and winding up with the wrong sort of the one and none of the other. Directed by Perry Henzell, the result is a fast-paced picture full of color and action, sometimes violent and harsh, occasionally confusing, but constantly bursting with energy and interest. A-III (R)

Hardly Working (1981) Jerry Lewis directs as well as stars in the role of an out-of-work circus clown who tries to hold down a string of varied jobs, ranging from chef to postman, with predictably disastrous results. As usual in his comedies, there are some genuinely funny moments, but otherwise this is for diehard Lewis fans only. Some mild and incidental profanity. A-II PG)

Harlan County, U.S.A (1977) Documentary filmed during a bitter 13-month coal strike in eastern Kentucky examines the origins of the strike, the working and living conditions of the miners and their families and the violence that erupts between the pickets and the strikebreakers. Though flawed by a clumsy narrative structure that is sometimes confusing, filmmaker Barbara Kopple's stirring picture of the still-unfinished struggle for labor justice has the raw power of reality and the passion of the worker's cause. A-II (PG)

Harold and Maude (1971) Bud Cort plays an immature youth who finds a sympathetic older woman to help him grow up in the person of an eccentric woman bordering on 80 (Ruth Gordon). Cort is a neurotic smothered by the love of his mother (Vivian Pickles) upon whom he takes his revenge by acting out all kinds of elaborate fake suicides. Hal Ashby directs with a good photographer's eye, but his emphasis on the cute is out of place. A-III (PG)

Harper (1966) Paul Newman stars as a hard-boiled private eye hired to track down a missing

millionaire and his various leads include Lauren Bacall, Shelley Winters, Robert Wagner and Julie Harris. Director Jack Smight's mystery thriller has an intricate plot that sustains interest, solid performances by a good cast and a satisfying pay-off. Restrained violence. A-III (br)

Harper Valley P.T.A. (1979) When the hypocritical board of a small-town P.T.A. sends a nasty letter to a fun-loving widow (Barbara Eden), scolding her for her behavior and threatening to expel her daughter from junior high school, they get much more than they bargained for. Based upon a hit song of the late 1960s, this unsophisticated comedy is standard drive-in fare, though the actors add an enjoyable zest to the proceedings. Some vulgar and risque humor. A-III (PG)

Harrad Experiment, The (1973) James Whitmore plays the dean of an experimental coed college at which a controlled group experience in premarital sex is the major item of the curriculum. Directed by Ted Post, the movie has much unintentional comedy but it's message of sexual indulgence as primal cure for all attitudinal problems comes off as such sentimental hogwash that only the most naive college freshman will be deceived. Some nudity. O (R)

Harrad Summer (1974) Those boring, sexually liberated students from Harrad are adrift for the summer and two couples travel together as a quartet, keeping their respective journals as summer homework. Directed by Steven H. Stern, the result is low-grade exploitation that will disappoint the voyeur trade and put everyone else to sleep. O (R/PG)

Harry and Son (1984) Meant to be a warmhearted comedy that tugs at the heartstrings, this woeful misfire about a laid-off construction worker (Paul Newman, who also produced, directed and did the screenplay) and his sensitive son (Robby Benson) is painful to sit through. Not the least oppressive element is Benson's insufferably cloying acting style. Aside from some rough language, the movie would be entirely innocuous if the filmmakers had not tried to get some comic mileage out of a sexually liberated secretary bestowing her favors on the heroes. O (PG)

Harry and the Hendersons (1987) When John Lithgow and family come across a bigfoot primal creature they name Harry, they try to protect him from the media, the police and a French-Canadian hunter while, along the way, learning a bit about the human links to the animal kingdom. Director William Dear's Northwestern fantasy tale has some violent auto chases but otherwise is a mild-mannered presentation of family values and the virtues of teamwork. A-II (PG)

Harry and Tonto (1974) Art Carney stars as Harry, the 72-year-old retired teacher who, after being evicted from his New York apartment, takes to the road with his cat Tonto, sees different aspects of contemporary American life and reaches California to continue his struggle alone. Written, produced and directed by Paul Mazursky, the subtle, sensitive, bittersweet comedy about old age and loneliness is marred only by the needless inclusion of many vulgarisms that may not be suitable for the young. A-III (R)

Harry and Walter Go to New York (1976) James Caan is crafty Harry and Elliott Gould is guileless Walter, two safecrackers so inept that, according to gentleman safecracker Michael Caine, "they would require practice to become oafs." But that doesn't stop them from trying to beat Caine to the biggest safe of them all, with the competent assistance of Diane Keaton. Director Mark Rydell's slack, tepid gaslight-era comedy has overcooked a satirical breast fetish scene and some crude verbal gags. A-III (PG)

Harry in Your Pocket (1973) James Coburn fills the title role as a pickpocket working some of the Northwest's most photogenic watering places in collusion with Walter Pidgeon and Trish Van Devere. Directed by Bruce Geller, it misses as an offbeat crime movie but does offer lovely travelogue footage of the posh resorts visited by the gang, and some silly romantic sex and hip humor. A-III (PG)

Hatchet for the Honeymoon (1973) Spanish-Italian movie about a bridal wear designer (Stephen Forsyth) who cannot bear to see his young models leave to get married because at age 12, the poor paranoiac hacked up his mother when she remarried, and ever since — well, never mind. Badly directed by Mario Bava, the bloodier frames have been chopped from the picture, leaving only a stuffy sexual aura to put adults to sleep. A-III (GP)

Haunted Honeymoon (1986) Light and uneventful horror spoof written and directed by Gene Wilder with silly performances by Wilder, Gilda Radner and Dom DeLuise as radio actors. When Wilder develops a strange malady, some of his friends try to frighten him out of it during his honeymoon at his aunt's weird mansion. Slapstick violence and a bit of rough language. A-II (PG)

Haunting of Julia, The (1981) Mia Farrow, playing a grief-stricken mother who has just lost her young daughter in a tragic accident, moves into an old house which comes completely furnished, including just the kind of unholy secret one would expect to find in this kind of place and this kind of movie. Director Richard Loncraine's muddled and tedious movie utterly lacks the inner logic that a good ghost story must have. Some violence. A-III (R)

Hawaii (1966) Big, boring movie based on the sweeping epic by James A. Michener concentrates on the struggle between missionary Max von Sydow and the islands' pagan way of life. Von Sydow does as well as possible in his one-dimensional role of religious fanatic, while Julie Andrews is patient and long-suffering and Jocelyne Le Garde is delightful as the Hawaiian ruler. Though the spectacular re-creates its locale convincingly, it romanticizes the natives and vilifies the missionaries. Some nudity and harrowing childbirth scene. A-III (br)

Hawaiians, The (1970) Readers of James A. Michener's sweeping novel, "Hawaii," will be disappointed that almost none of its spirit and style has survived in this sequel. Its witless, wordy screenplay avoids every opportunity for action in telling the potentially lively story of the lusty sea captain (Charlton Heston) who brought the pineapple to Hawaii. Though at times showing a nice sense of place, the lethargic direction of Tom Gries fails to do much with his cast. Silly nude bathing scene. O (GP)

Hawks and the Sparrows, The (1967) Italian movie about the human journey on the road of life is a simple but strikingly photographed allegory in two acts which reject both Christian and Communist ideologies in favor of a very earth-bound vision of humanity. Director Pier Paolo Pasolini offers a sketchy probe rather than a finished statement and it is an interesting challenge for seasoned moviegoers. A-IV (br)

Hawmps (1976) The Army's attempt to replace horses with camels in the rugged terrain of the Southwest was ended by the Civil War and the railroad. Director Joe Camp's comic version of that attempt does have its occasional moments but the humor never gets beyond the level of silliness. The camels steal every scene they're in, and only character actor Jack Elam comes close to out-mugging them. Children will find it fun, but parents may wish for a little less slapstick. A-I (G)

Hazel's People (1978) When a New York hippie goes to rural Pennsylvania for the burial of a student activist friend, he finds himself at home with the simple, anti-materialistic people of the local Mennonite community, but finally leaves to find his own way. What the film lacks in moviemaking polish, it makes up for in sincerity, photogenic locale and superb performances by Pat Hingle and Geraldine Page. A-II (PG)

He Knows You're Alone (1980) Psychotic killer of young brides-to-be is the focus of director Armand Mastroianni's low-budget exploitation thriller. Physical and psychological violence, sexual titillation and occasional profanity. O (R)

He Who Must Die (1957) French drama adapted from the Nikos Kazantzakis novel about the inevitable fate of some Greek refugees in a Turkish occupied village. Whether seen as religious allegory or political tract, director Jules Dassin has made an emotionally arresting motion picture. A-III (br)

Head (1968) Flashy vehicle for the Monkees musical group (Peter Tork, Davy Jones, Mickey Dolenz and Michael Nesmith) juxtaposes a nonsical melange of scenes against a background chromatically and acoustically gone berserk. Directed by Robert Rafelson, the Monkees themselves are simply four ordinary young men trying to imitate the Beatles but without the British group's spontaneity and sense of fun. Some tasteless spoofs. A-II (G)

Head Over Heels (1979) Minor bureaucrat (John Heard) has had a brief affair with a married woman (Mary Beth Hurt) but, when she returns to her husband, he is obsessed to win her back. Directed by Joan Micklin Silver, the story is told in a series of flashbacks interspersed with scenes of the poor fellow's cheerless present life. All in all, it is a deadly dull affair. A-III (PG)

Hearse, The (1980) Supernatural thriller starring Trish Van Devere who is recovering from a nervous breakdown and haunted by visions of a hearse. Directed by George Bowers, there is some graphic violence and devil worship figures in the plot. A-III (PG)

Heart Beat (1980) Anemic screen biography of 1950's writer Jack Kerouac (John Heard) focuses on his friendship with fellow Beat Generation figures, Neal and Carolyn Cassady (Sissy Spacek and Nick Nolte). John Byrum's simplistic script and direction waste good performances and suggest nothing of the force and passion that must have driven Kerouac. Some use of nudity and a muddled moral outlook. O (R)

Heart Is a Lonely Hunter, The (1968) Sensitive adaptation of a Carson McCullers story about a deaf-mute (Alan Arkin), his frustrations in trying to help others and his friendship with a teenager (Sondra Locke) which is simply not enough to compensate for his isolated world of utter silence. Director Robert Ellis Miller successfully treads the line between sentiment and sentimentality. A-II (br)

Heart Like a Wheel (1983) Fact-based story of Shirley Muldowny who overcame prejudice in a man's profession to achieve success as a racing car driver, but her career triumphs cost heartbreak and bitterness in her personal life. With Bonnie Bedelia giving a wonderful performance in the role, director Jonathan Kaplan catches the human level of the story in moving and poignant fashion. Because adultery figures in the plot, it is not for younger viewers. A-III (PG)

Heart of Glass (1978) German movie about a town of glass blowers in the 18th century who find their livelihood threatened when the secret of a unique scarlet glass dies with a master craftsman. Werner Herzog directs a muddled parable so ponderous and dense, so inane in story line and dialogue that the whole enterprise lies beyond parody. A-III (nr)

Heartbeeps (1981) Dreadful futuristic comedy about two robots who fall in love and run off together is an endless one-joke situation with no place to go. Andy Kaufman and Bernadette Peters have an impossible task as the romantic robots, and the banality of John Hill's script is underscored by the ineptness of Allan Arkush's direction. To be avoided at all costs. A-I (PG)

Heartbreak Kid, The (1973) Adult comedy about an immature Jewish bridegroom (Charles Grodin) who is stung by a WASP (Cybill Shepherd) on his Miami Beach honeymoon with his ill-fated bride (Jeannie Berlin) is a marvelous but uneven combination of strengths, especially those of Elaine May's deft direction. The movie bristles with telling barbs about contemporary life, some of which are merely entertaining, but many of which are truly enlightening and occasionally frightening. A-III (PG)

Heartbreak Ridge (1986) Flag-waving portrait of a Marine sergeant (Clint Eastwood who also directed), a hardened veteran whose last assignment before retirement is to train a reconnaissance troop for combat. His brutal methods and end-justifies-the-means philosophy supposedly prepare his troop for victory in Grenada. Violent combat footage, scenes of dramatic brutality and excessive profanity and vulgar language. O (R)

Heartbreakers (1985) Two friends (Peter Coyote and Nick Mancuso) in the throes of midlife crisis share everything, even their girlfriends. Shallow, unsympathetic characterizations under the direction of Bobby Roth. Nudity and a graphic sex scene. O (R)

Heartburn (1986) Meryl Streep and Jack Nicholson are professionals whose marriage dissolves over his infidelity. Director Mike Nichols' essentially pessimistic view of the contemporary state of romance in the 1980s implies more than it expresses but focuses amiably on the plight of women who must find options to the American male's fear of commitment and responsibility. Adult theme, harsh language and sexual innuendo. A-III (R)

Heartland (1981) Poor widow (Conchata Ferrell) takes her 7-year-old daughter to Wyoming in the first decade of the century where she has signed on as housekeeper of a dour and laconic Scotsman (Rip Torn) on a remote ranch. During the long months of a hard and terrible winter, they realize that life would be better together and the rancher proposes marriage. Director Richard Pearce's optimistic conclusion doesn't seem justified by the couple's poor circumstances, but this low-budget effort is unusually effective both in its emotional force and fine performances by Ferrell and Torn. Extremely realistic birth sequence and some scenes of slaughtering farm animals are inappropriate for younger viewers. A-II (PG)

Hearts and Minds (1975) Documentary on the Vietnam War avoids the political realities that polarized U.S. public opinion about the conflict and presents instead a painful picture of American soldiers lost in a moral quagmire. Director Peter Davis has compiled a selective history of the war as a visceral experience which may touch some hearts and open some minds about the moral paradox that Vietnam represented for our nation. Graphic scenes of battlefield and civilian casualties and some explicit scenes of prostitution. A-IV (R)

Hearts of the West (1975) Would-be writer of Westerns (Jeff Bridges) gets a job in 1930's Hollywood as a cowboy extra but on his rise to stardom he has to dodge some crooks who are out to recover the loot he took by mistake. Director Howard Zieff's old-fashioned narrative makes an enjoyable comedy of character and situation, though for a film based on the innocence of its young hero, the needless scene of a stag party with a stripper interrupts the fun and makes it adult fare. A-III (PG)

Heat (1972) Sylvia Miles, Joe Dallesandro and Andrea Feldman play characters living on the fringes of Hollywood and using sex to help their careers or assuage their loneliness. Director Paul Morrissey has made the "Sunset Boulevard" of independent cinema but his characters here drown in a heavily-convoluted and sexually explicit narrative. O (R)

Heat (1987) An extremely dull and pointless exercise in violent self-defense as Burt Reynolds, playing a compulsive gambler, slays the son of a crime boss and his hired thugs who are bent upon revenge for a previously murderous encounter. Contrasts two kinds of revenge, both equally demented. O (R)

Heaven Can Wait (1978) Charming remake of the 1941 classic "Here Comes Mr. Jordan" in which Warren Beatty plays a past-his-prime quarterback who dies prematurely and comes back to earth (thanks to the bungling of angel James Mason) as an eccentric millionaire who has been done in by his wife (Dyan Cannon) and her lover (Charles Grodin). In his new body he enlists the aid of his former coach (Jack Warden) to help him get back in shape, and also falls in love with an Englishwoman (Julie Christie). Directed by Beatty and Buck Henry, the entertainment succeeds in being very innocent and yet wise and funny. A-II (PG)

Heaven Help Us (1985) The adventures of four desperate misfits in a Catholic boys' school in Brooklyn in 1965. Though Catholic education of the era does take its lumps, the underlying feeling is one of affection. Written by Charles Purpura and directed by Michael Dinner, the movie is flawed, especially with regard to its fragmented story line, but the overall result is moderately entertaining. Some rough language and sexually oriented humor. A-III (R)

Heaven with a Gun (1969) Glenn Ford plays a gunslinging preacher who mediates between feuding ranchers and sheepherders, punctuating his sermons with gunplay. Director Lee Katzin trades on the family-type Western to introduce a sexually-oriented saloon encounter, a graphic rape scene and a brief but totally gratuitous nude scene. A-III (M)

Heaven's Gate (1980) Bloated Western written and directed by Michael Cimino takes up the familiar theme of ranchers versus settlers and is set in late 19th-century Wyoming with lavish and exhausting attention to period authenticity. However, the characters are shallow, the story lacks dramatic force and the whole thing becomes a pretentious bore. Extravagant nudity in one bedroom scene and lacks any moral frame of reference. O (R)

Heavenly Bodies (1985) Canadian movie directed by Lawrence Dane in which rival aerobic academies face off in a winner-take-all marathon workout. This "Flashdance" clone is so vapid, banal and brainlessly cheerful that it makes the original look like a somber work of art. Excessive sex and nudity and some foul language. O (R)

Heavenly Kid, The (1985) Feeble effort telling of a teenager who had been killed in the early 1950s and sent back to Earth in the 1980s to earn his wings by helping a gawky teen to become a success with the girls. Written and directed by Gary Medoway, the movie is contrived, clumsy, not very funny and manipulatively sentimental. A-III (PG-13)

Heavy Metal (1981) Feature-length cartoon made in a variety of styles and backed by the music of various rock groups offers six science fiction tales loosely tied together by the appearance of a malevolent green sphere of death and destruction. The animation is far more imaginative than the narratives themselves, which never rise above the elemental level of pulp comic books. Abundance of cartoon sex and violence. O (R)

Heavy Traffic (1973) Director Ralph Bakshi and producer Steve Krantz's animated feature about black and white love in the gritty streets of New York is infantile in technique and scabrous in theme and image. The film seems to have set out to offend just about everybody, and has generally succeeded with a constant flow of racial, ethnic, sexual and religious slurs. O (X/R)

Heidi's Song (1982) Hanna-Barbera's animated, musical version of the popular story about an orphan girl who brings cheer into the life of her grandfather, a crippled child and all sorts of other people, is an entertaining film for younger children. A nightmare sequence in which Heidi is menaced by rats might be rather scary for the very young. A-I (G)

Helga (1968) German sex education motion picture is too superficial for adults, too detailed for adolescents and has no place in movie theaters. It might have use in a classroom or the home where parents could put the material in a moral context. A-IV (br)

Hell Boats (1970) Routine World War II story about an American (James Franciscus) in the British navy whose difficult mission is to destroy a German base on Sicily which has proven impenetrable from the sea and the air. The focus is on the American's relationship to the men under his command and a romantic involvement with his superior's wife but, though the acting leaves a bit to be desired, action buffs should be pleased with the special effects. A-III (PG)

Hell in the Pacific (1968) Two enemy soldiers (Lee Marvin and Toshiro Mifune), marooned on a Pacific island during World War II, struggle against each other until they form a tentative friendship and begin building a raft together. Directed by John Boorman, the cast of two are not only contrasts in culture but also in acting styles and this helps make very watchable what is essentially an allegory on the nature of aggression and the will to survive. A-II (G)

Hell Up in Harlem (1974) Fred Williamson fights his way to the top as a black mobster before turning onto the straight and narrow and becoming a family man of sorts. Larry Cohen's writing and direction are third-rate and the acting of Williamson and cast is even worse. Excessive violence. O (R)

Hell with Heroes, The (1968) Cynical World War II veteran (Rod Taylor) needing cash to bail out the air freight business he started in Algeria, gets involved with a black marketeer (Harry Guardino) and then falls for the criminal's mistress (Claudia Cardinale). Directed by Joseph Sargent, the entirely predictable melodrama has some excessive brutality and sexually suggestive scenes. O (br)

Hell's Angels on Wheels (1967) Overly violent motorcycle gang movie directed by Richard Rush exploits sex and brutality for their own sake. O (br)

Hell's Angels 69 (1969) Two wealthy playboys (Tom Stern and Jeremey Slate) infiltrate the Hell's Angels gang in order to use them as a diversionary front to pull off a casino heist. Biker girl (Conny Van Dyke) upsets the plan and the rather dull climax of director Lee Madden's cycle flick is a bumpy cross-country chase ending in death. Notable only in that the real Hell's Angels tried a stint at acting. A-III (M)

Hell's Belles (1969) A young roughhewn, stoic rancher (Jeremy Slate) sets out alone to retrieve his valuable bike and the girl (Jocelyn Lane) swapped for it, from the lawless gang that stole it. Director Maury Dexter's motorcycle epic features violent action and a moral theme, but the film is too steeped in adolescent rat-pack thinking. A-III (M)

Hell's Bloody Devils (1971) The title characters are beefy motorcyclists in the pay of a German counterfeiter who has a deal with Las Vegas mobsters to help finance a worldwide resurgence of Nazism. Director Al Adamson tosses into this noxious mix some FBI agents, wily blondes and a Jewish woman searching for the war criminal who executed her parents. Much violence and gratuitous sex. O (GP)

Hellfighters (1968) John Wayne heads an oil well firefighting team whose highly dangerous profession take them worldwide at a moment's notice but his worries are about his daughter (Katherine Ross) whose marriage is in danger of winding up like that of his estranged wife (Vera Miles). Directed by Andrew McLaglen, the marital comparisons are strained and of less interest than the grand pyrotechnics of flaming oil wells and vintage Wayne action, including the expected but totally irrelevant barroom brawl. A-II (G)

Hello Again (1987) Failed romantic comedy about a housewife (Shelley Long) brought back from the dead by an occult incantation of her sister (Judith Ivey) to find that her husband is now married to her best friend. Frank Perry's pedestrian direction of a rather dull and unimaginative script provides few laughs and almost no romance. Some sexual innuendo, vulgar situations and coarse language. A-III (PG)

Hello Dolly! (1969) Zesty New York Jewish widow and matchmaker (Barbra Streisand) gets emotionally involved with a rich client (Walter Matthau). Lavish musical extravaganza is a vehicle for Streisand's melodious talents staged and directed by Gene Kelly with exhilarating, albeit synthetic, Hollywood effervescence. Thornton Wilder's play is memorably infused with Jerry Herman's music. A-I (G)

Hello Down There (1969) An Ivan Tors production with plenty of marine life to entertain the kiddies, the adventure yarn situates a family with three teenagers complete with guitars in an experimental undersea house to sample living on the ocean floor and save their father's job. Plot centers around how the youngsters will get their music published while down under. A-I (G)

Hello-Goodbye (1970) Languid European triangle features Curt Jurgens as a baron with a love for antique autos, Genevieve Gilles as a baroness with a roving eye and Michael Crawford as a lover of ladies and fine cars. Millions were spent on the cars, sets and costumes but not a penny's worth of action, dialogue or characterization to break up the sheer boredom. Director Jean Negulesco's agonizing pace makes both the inept acting and slack moral values all the more apparent. O (PG)

Hellstrom Chronicle, The (1971) Odd mixture of fascinating yet unsettling documentary footage of insect life in all its forms, from kindly moths and lady-bugs to deadly fire ants and black widow spiders. Unfortunately, director Walon Green's movie uses scare tactics in arguing that the world is on the brink of an ecological disaster from which insects will emerge as the dominant form of life. Though the information is neither startling nor precise, the insect footage is stunning. A-II (G)

Hennessy (1975) Routine thriller about an Irishman (Rod Steiger) who decides to blow up Parliament after seeing his family killed by the British, but trying to stop him are a brutal British police officer (Richard Johnson) and an Irish widow tired of all the bloodshed (Lee Remick). Director Don Sharp works every conceivable variation on the chase, but the thrills aren't there and the result is quite ordinary melodrama. A-III (PG)

Henry VIII and His Six Wives (1974) Keith Mitchell gives a memorable performance in a role that spans Henry's entire reign from the boyish energy of the young king to the quiet suffering of an amorous man betrayed by age and disease. Director Waris Hussein turns the historical events into personal drama, with each of the wives getting their fair share of attention, and the result proves as satisfying for the average viewer as for the specialist in Tudor history. A-II (PG)

Her and She and Him (1970) Boring French sex exploitation movie about a young woman student, her lesbian lover and the male companion of a homosexual painter, all four of whom offer endless apologies for their devious behavior while engaging in boudoir episodes under the direction of Max Pecas. O (R)

Herbie Goes Bananas (1980) The little car with a personality takes a Caribbean cruise to Panama this time, where it and its young owners become involved with villains looting ancient ruins. Director Vincent McEveety's effort is dismal, the Disney production is sub-standard and it is hard to see how children would like it any more than their parents. Sprinkling of double-entendres, presumably for adults accompanying their tots. A-I (G)

Herbie Goes to Monte Carlo (1977) Disney's "Love Bug" Volkswagen with a personality makes a comeback to win the TransFrance car race, a feat complicated by a diamond theft and his falling in love with a sleek sports car. Director Vincent McEveety makes the mildly amusing fantasy with the two cars much easier to take than the human actors (Dean Jones, Don Knotts and Julie Sommars). Strictly for the kids. A-I (G)

Herbie Rides Again (1974) Sequel to "The Love Bug" with Herbie the lovable Volkswagen back not as a race car but as the well-kept companion of eccentric dowager Helen Hayes who is trying to keep her home from being bulldozed by snarling land developer Keenan Wynn. Directed by Robert Stevenson, it's all lots of witless fun in the standard Disney vein. A-I (G)

Hercules (1983) Lou Ferrigno, better known as the Incredible Hulk, brings his massive pectorals to the role of the classic strongman, but not even Ferrigno's muscles can hoist John Thompson's languid direction and Lewis Coates's silly script out of the slough of mediocrity. Some mild violence. A-II (PG)

Here Comes Every Body (1973) British filmmaker John Whitmore photographed a week's worth of encounter therapy at California's Esalen Institute where participants are encouraged to remove their clothing as part of the treatment. The mostly young group grope frantically and vituperate fiercely but seem to be acting more for the camera than to learn anything about themselves. Exploitative nudity. O (nr)

Here We Go Round the Mulberry Bush (1968) British sex comedy in which a 17-year-old lad (Barry Evans) wants to to be initiated into the mysteries of sex, gets involved with a string of girls who are easily available, but when he gets the one pure girl who is not, she turns out to be no better than the rest. Directed by Clive Donner, the predictable course of the story tries to hide behind overdone optical effects and its humor tends toward the sordid. Unnecessary prolonged nude sequence. O (br)

Here's Your Life (1969) Exceptional seriocomic coming-of-age Swedish movie about an idealistic youth's (Eddie Axberg) experiences, beautifully evoked with period and location details, shortly before World War I. Director Jan Troell's gentle, warm and sincere drama reveals the youthful search for the spiritual significance of life, sex and brotherhood. Brief nudity in a sexual situation. A-III (PG)

Hero, The (1972) Richard Harris stars as an aging footballer with feet of clay who is befriended by a 10-year-old runaway (Kim Burfield). Produced in Israel, the banality of the script by Wolf Mankowitz is exceeded only by the ineptness of its direction by Harris. A-II (PG)

Hero Ain't Nothin' But a Sandwich, A (1978) Benjie (Larry B. Scott) is a black 13-year-old living with his mother (Cicely Tyson) and grandmother (Helen Martin) in a Los Angeles ghetto and his inability to accept his mother's lover (Paul Winfield) leads to school problems, the wrong companions and drug addiction. Produced by Robert Radnitz and directed by Ralph Nelson, the movie deals realistically with the ghetto environment whose problems go far beyond those of drugs, but it does so from a perspective of hope and human potential. Some coarse street language and the depiction of Benjie shooting heroin and the agony of withdrawal. Good for parents to see with their older children and discuss afterwards. A-III (R/PG appeal)

Hero at Large (1980) Disarming romantic comedy about a struggling young actor (John Ritter) who, returning from a job still dressed in a superhero costume, routs a pair of thugs robbing a grocery, becomes a media celebrity and is then exploited by a smooth public relations man (Bert Convy). Director Martin Davidson's contrived story runs out of invention about two-thirds of the way through but it has the prime assest of Ritter's warm appeal in the role and Anne Archer is extremely likable as the disdainful neighbor eventually won over by his charm and decency. Despite its melodramatic ending, the comedy has a generous amount of good humor and the romance is unabashedly sentimental. Occasional burst of rough language. A-II (PG)

Heroes (1977) Henry Winkler plays a mentally disturbed Vietnam War veteran who treks cross-country with Sally Field to meet old buddies and set up a worm farm. Director Jeremy Paul Kagan tries for seriocomic social relevance but manages only some underdeveloped ideas about the psychic toll wrought by war. Violent fight scene makes this less suitable for youngsters. A-III (PG)

Heroes of Telemark, The (1966) Norwegian resistance fighters (Kirk Douglas, Richard Harris and Ulla Jacobson) try to stop the Nazis from developing the atom bomb. Director Anthony Mann accomplishes a lot with the action scenes but the story line keeps getting in the way. Stylized violence. A-II (br)

Hester Street (1975) Lively tale of Jewish immigrant life in New York's Lower East Side just before the turn of the century tells of the conflict between a husband (Steven Keats) who wants to forget all traces of his origins and his wife (Carol Kane) who refuses to abandon the Russian Jewish traditions in which she was raised. Directed by Joan Micklin Silver, it is a film to be seen as a piece of Americana but also to be savored for the many brilliant little scenes that comprise a pulsating mosaic of the immigrant experience shared by so many Americans of diverse national origins. A-III (PG)

Hex (1973) Motorcycle gang led by Keith Carradine fall upon a little Nevada town on their way to California but are decimated by two comely farm girls (Hilarie Thompson and Tina Herazo). The year is 1919 and the girls are daughters of an Indian medicine man whose legacy to them is the power of witchcraft. Directed by Leo Garen, the unintentionally comic proceedings are distinguished only by its attempt to an erotic atmosphere which is as silly as it is unnecessary. O (PG)

Hey Good Looking (1982) Animated feature by Ralph Bakshi about juvenile gang warfare in Brooklyn in the 1950s is extremely ugly and distasteful. It has an unremitting emphasis upon sex and violence. O (R)

Hi, Mom! (1970) After failing as a porno-filmmaker, a serious young lad (Robert De Niro) finds success as an urban guerrilla. Director Brian De Palma's movie is a put-on put-down of present American customs and culture. However, its clumsy satirization of contemporary fads and fashions will also outrage the moral sense of some of its viewers. O (R)

Hickey and Boggs (1972) When Los Angeles private-eyes Bill Cosby and Robert Culp take a simple case of finding a missing person, they are soon embroiled in a sticky mess involving murder, a fortune in stolen currency, Chicago bank robbers, the Mafia, brutal cops and black militants. Also directed by Culp, the movie starts promisingly enough but soon bogs down in plot complications and ends on a bitter, hopeless note. Hard-edged look at the tribulations of crime-fighting, it is extremely violent. A-IV (PG)

Hidden, The (1987) An alien inhabits the bodies of a series of individuals, turning them into homicidal maniacs until it is finally stopped by a good alien (Kyle MacLachian) and a Los Angeles detective (Michael Nouri). Jack Sholder directs all the mayhem with mindless gusto. Excessive violence, brief nudity and rough language. O (R)

Hide in Plain Sight (1980) Taut, fact-based story about a divorced factory worker (James Caan) whose two small children disappear when the government gives a new identity to his ex-wife's new husband who has turned state's witness against the mob. Also directed by Caan, the emphasis is upon characterization rather than action and the acting is uniformly convincing. The measure of its success is its ability to convey an authentic sense of reality with but the most sparing use of violence and rough language. A-II (PG)

Hiding Place, The (1975) Interesting story of two Dutch Christians, Corrie and Betsie ten Boom, who gave shelter to Jews during the Nazi occupation but, when discovered, one of them (Julie Harris) was sent to her death in Ravensbruck, while her sister (Jeannette Clift) was released by mistake. Produced by Billy Graham's World Wide Pictures and directed by James F. Collier, the movie is quite well done, though the script belabors the theological questions raised by the evil of fascism to the point of becoming preachy. Harsh violence. A-III (PG)

High Anxiety (1978) Mel Brooks spoof of suspense thrillers has Brooks as the new director of the Institute for the Very, Very Nervous, the unwitting target of a staff (Harvey Korman and Cloris Leachman) who want him out of the way so they can continue to rip off wealthy patients. Though dedicated to Hitchcock, the entirely predictable plot consists of one liners, outrageous slapstick and a mixture of sexual and tasteless humor that some may find offensive. A-IV (PG)

High Commissioner, The (1968) Entertaining crime melodrama in which Rod Taylor plays an Australian policeman sent to London to arrest his country's leading diplomat (Christopher Plummer) for murder but thwarts a plot to assassinate him instead. Directed by Ralph Thomas, the action holds one's attention, the acting is more than adequate and it accomplishes its purpose of painless diversion. Stylized violence. A-III (br)

High Plains Drifter (1973) Clint Eastwood directs and stars in a pretentious, if not perverse tale of a stranger with no name who destroys a town for its cowardly collaboration in the murder of a marshal opposing the local mining company's appropriation of federal land. Eastwood's celebration of sadistic vengeance applied by an individual outside the law features repeated graphic brutalities and a sexist attitude toward women, in particular the male fantasy that women cannot fail to respond to rape. In short, an utterly despicable movie. O (R)

High Risk (1981)   American adventurers (James Brolin, Bruce Davison and Cleavon Little) meddle in the affairs of a Latin American drug ring in a trite melodrama directed by Stewart Raffill. Excessive violence. O (R)

High Road to China (1983)   Spoiled rich girl Bess Armstrong, 1920s vintage, hires hard-drinking, disillusioned World War I ace Tom Selleck to fly her from Turkey to China to find her father (Wilford Brimley) who has disappeared in the midst of a civil war. Jack Weston is good as Selleck's mechanic-sidekick and Brian Blessed scores as a vividly nasty war lord. Director Brian G. Hutton's consistently entertaining adventure movie does not rely upon sex and extravagant violence to keep the viewers interest. A-II (PG)

High Street (1977)   Belgian movie of the Holocaust which has the haunting central figure of a woman (Annie Cordy) whose Jewish husband was taken one night to the camps and their child killed in the confusion. Twenty years later, living in a Brussels slum and regarded as a harmless eccentric, she awaits her husband's return, irrationally screaming profanities at passersby, until an expatriate American artist (Mort Shuman) befriends her and shares her plight with the world. Told simply but with emotional directness, director Andre Ernotte's powerful indictment of people's unconcern for the suffering of others is an eloquent reminder of the indifference that made the Nazi camps a tragic part of human history. A-III (nr)

High, Wild and Free (1968)   Fairly interesting documentary about fishing and hunting in British Columbia and Alaska with sportsman Gordon Eastman as the guide. Also directed and narrated by Eastman, the emphasis is on the beauty of nature, conservation and ecology. A-I (br)

High Wind in Jamaica, A (1965)   Some children fall into the hands of pirates (Anthony Quinn and James Coburn) who see to it that they are unharmed in the hazardous events that follow. Director Alexander Mackendrick's exciting adventure is an excursion into the uncertain world of childish logic but the action is too intense for younger children. A-II (br)

Highlander (1986)   Action adventure fable of good conquering evil offers a positive hero (Christopher Lambert) as one of group of immortals who must battle to the death throughout history until only one survives. Director Russell Mulcahy's mix of action and diverse period settings lift the movie somewhat above the average for this kind of escapist fantasy. Some foul language, brief nudity and several less than realistic decapitations. A-III (R)

Hill, The (1965)   World War II British military prison is the setting for a story of human injustice with Sean Connery as a prisoner who bucks the system and Harry Andrews as the chief warder. Sidney Lumet directs a tightly-wound script that is a brutal, agonizing experience, yet a meaningful one. A-IV (br)

Hills Have Eyes, The (1977)   Amateurish little horror about a family on a trip who are attacked by some very nasty people but whom they eventually beat at their own game. Director Wes Craven overdoes the blood and gore. O (R)

Hindenburg, The (1975)   Based upon the ill-fated last voyage of the famous German zeppelin in May 1937, the movie half-heartedly proposes that the disaster was caused by anti-Nazi sabotage.

Director Robert Wise's thin plot and its Grand Hotel collection of passengers is of less interest than the majestic airship in flight (the special effects are quite effective). The final tragedy is too intense for youngsters. A-II (PG)

Hired Hand, The (1971)   Offbeat, sensitive and quiet little Western directed by and starring Peter Fonda. The tale of a young man turning away from his life as a drifter in order to return to the wife, child and farm he deserted years before is probably too slow for most Western fans. But those who stick with it will find the movie rewarding in the way it attempts to sort out human values and relationships. Warren Oates as Fonda's sidekick gives a subtle performance and figures in a gentle resolution that follows a climactic outburst of frontier violence. A-III (GP)

Hireling, The (1973)   Superb British screen version of the L.P. Hartley novel about a high-born lady (Sarah Miles) recovering from a breakdown who hires a brooding World War I veteran (Robert Shaw) to drive her to her mother's house in Bath. Thus begins a slow and somber character study which under the painstaking direction of Alan Bridges results in a painful awareness of the tragic limitations of a class-conscious society. Mature themes. A-III (PG)

History of the Blue Movie, A (1970)   Blurry 16mm stag films are not only hard on the eyes but quite deadening to the spirit, especially when accompanied by dreary, pseudo-sociological commentary. Alex de Renzy's compilation is really nothing more than a long advertisement for the more technically proficient pornography that he is in the business of putting out. O (nr)

History Of The World, Part I (see: "Mel Brooks' History of the World, Part I")

Hit! (1973)   Billy Dee Williams plays a hard-nosed federal agent whose daughter's death from an overdose determines him to mastermind a plot to exterminate the entire drug syndicate of Marseilles. Director Sidney J. Furie's movie uses all the essential story devices of the traditional detective movie but needlessly laced with casual sex, nudity and rough language. O (R)

Hit Man (1973)   Bernie Casey plays a hood stalking the killer of his brother through some of the seamier sites of East Los Angeles where his quest takes him into the arms of some of the ghetto's most unliberated but libidinous ladies. George Armitage's sharp direction is well above black exploitation standards but it is squandered in a plot featuring graphic sex and super-graphic violence. O (R)

Hitcher, The (1986)   Homicidal maniac (Rutger Hauer) terrorizes a teenage driver (C. Thomas Howell) who has unwisely given him a lift one rainy night on a lonely southwestern highway. Director Robert Harmon makes excessive use of violence and scenes of bloodshed to propel the narrative to its gory conclusion. O (R)

Hitchhikers, The (1973)   Pregnant runaway (Misty Rowe) finds happiness with a group of hippies who subsist by seducing and robbing lonely motorcyclists. Its a bum trip of sex and violence from low-budget filmmakers Ferd and Beverly Sebastian. O (R)

Hitler: The Last Ten Days (1973)   The paradox of this movie directed by Ennio de Concini is that, while it is very well made and has an excellent performance by Alec Guinness as Hitler, it misses the boat historically by getting all the details right but without giving them the meaning of their context. The result is a faithful but impossibly constricted dramatization which reduces a genuine monster to a figure of morbid curiosity and becomes little more than a footnote to a much more complex and significant chapter of human history. A-II (PG)

Hoa-Binh (1971) Low-key French drama about life in a Vietnamese village as seen through the eyes of an 11-year-old boy. The child, who has never known a day of peace, loses his sick mother to death, and all that keeps the boy going is his hope that some day he and his sister will be reunited with their father who is presumed to have joined the Viet Cong. Directed by Raoul Coutard, it is a film of compassion and not polemics. A-II (GP)

Hold On (1966) Mindless youth film directed by Arthur Lubin about a rock music group is utterly innocuous and eminently forgettable. A-I (br)

Hollywood Babylon (1972) Director Van Guylder's movie uses a few photos and brief footage of famous silent movie personalities, then dresses up actors of no ability to resemble them and stages re-enactments of their reputed escapades. Wallowing in explicit sex sequences, it is solely of prurient interest. O (nr)

Hollywood Blue (1971) Crude compilation of hard-core pornographic footage interspersed with sidewalk interviews of people giving their opinion of the social value of such movies. Sheer exploitation. O (nr)

Hollywood Horror House (1975) Miriam Hopkins plays an aging, former movie star whose reveries are interrupted by a psychopathic visitor (John David Garfield) to her remote Beverly Hills estate. Thoroughly B-grade film with sex and violence directed against women. O (R)

Hollywood Knights (1980) Writer-director Floyd Mutrux's vulgar attempt at slapstick comedy recounts the misadventures of a cretinous Beverly Hills car club on Halloween night. Its crudity and graphic sexuality are seriously offensive. O (R)

Hollywood Shuffle (1987) Writer-producer-director Robert Townsend provides satirical comment on black stereotyping in the movie business while contrasting career aspirations with his character's sense of dignity. The low-budget feature is informed social satire with limited scope but right-minded intention of racial self-reflection. Much profanity treated within the context of streetwise social conventions of the environment. AII (R)

Holocaust 2000 (see: "The Chosen")

Holy Outlaw, The (1971) Documentary about Daniel Berrigan, Jesuit priest, poet and pacifist, examines the man's personal witness against human indifference and the horror of war. Filmmakers Don Lenzer and Lee Lockwood rely mainly on interviews with Father Berrigan, members of his family, close friends and his religious superior, during a four-month period when the FBI was seeking to arrest him. A-II (nr)

Homage to Chagall: The Colours of Love (1977) Documentary on the occasion of Marc Chagall's 90th birthday pays tribute both to the beauty of his art and the humanity of the artist. With a script based upon Chagall's own writing and featuring hundreds of his paintings, murals and stained-glass windows, director Harry Rasky searches for the vision that inspired their creation, a quest helped immensely by a remarkable interview with Chagall himself. A-I (nr)

Hombre (1967) White man living as an Apache (Paul Newman) is on an ambushed stagecoach with people he neither likes not trusts and who neither like nor trust him but, in the course of a struggle for survival, he wins their admiration. Directed by Martin Ritt, its story of injustice is brutal in spots but it serves a purpose in this above average Western. A-II (br)

Home and the World, The (1985) Indian director Satyajit Ray's screen version of Nobel laureate Rabindranath Tagore's novel set in 1907 Bengal centers on a triangle involving a wealthy and idealistic landowner, his willful and naive wife, and his best friend, a charismatic revolutionary who has feet of clay. Though static and talky, it provides a fascinating glimpse into a bygone era and aspects of human nature that are universal. A-II (nr)

Home Movies (1980) Failed attempt at a screwball comedy about a high school student (Keith Gordon) who tries to become something more than "an extra in my own life" by turning it into a film about himself with the help of an instructor (Kirk Douglas). Director Brian De Palma's embarrassingly bad movie achieves the level of an almost unwatchable student film exercise. Sexual nature of some of the gags is adult fare. A-III (PG)

Home of the Brave (1986) In a concert performance, composer-director Laurie Anderson offers a musical diversion for the cultivated few who appreciate Far Eastern-inspired pointilist melody, Dadist minimalism and the poetry of alienation. Musically and visually dull, the concert does not demonstrate the potential of its all-digital sound track. A-II (nr)

Homebodies (1974) Handful of oldsters living in a creaking Cincinnati tenement doomed to be torn down rebel against the wrecker's ball, first by sabotaging the encroaching construction sites, then by taking more direct guerrilla actions that culminate in murder. Thanks to a sprightly set of aging character actors (Paula Trueman, Frances Fuller, Peter Brocco), it is a gripping and macabre little slice of black comedy. Director Larry Yust's ending is as grisly as it is illogical, yet its theme that the lives of old people, like those quaint Victorian houses, are all too often wasted in the face of "progress" remains to haunt the viewer. A-III (PG)

Homer (1970) Midwest farm boy (Don Scardino) likes to swill cheap wine, spark his girl (Tisa Farrow), smoke a little pot and bug his dad by refusing to get a haircut and staging a one-man anti-war demonstration outside the local VFW Hall. Before mercifully ending the picture by running away, Scardino manages to sing or listen to enough songs to fill a soundtrack album, which seems about all that director John Trent has on his mind. A-III (PG)

Honey Pot, The (1967) Pretending to be dying, a bachelor (Rex Harrison) summons three women (Susan Hayward, Edie Adams and Capucine) from his past and says that one of them will become his sole heir. Intricate plot twists and a murder in his Venetian palace reveal his real motives. Typically witty, urbane performance by Harrison, who also manages to make the cynical and crafty bachelor a touching figure as well. Written and directed by Joseph L. Mankiewicz, the movie's mixture of satire and suspense doesn't quite jell but will please sophisticated tastes. A-III (br)

Honeycomb (1972) Spanish psychological study of a young wife (Geraldine Chaplin) who is emotionally still a child and of her middle-aged husband (Per Oscarsson) whose chief interest is business. Directed by Carlos Saura, the story takes place over the course of a weekend during which their suppressed marital discontents emerge through dreams, fantasies and murderous games in a destructive pattern worthy of an abnormal psychology textbook. Intense psychological and some physical violence. A-IV (PG)

Honeymoon Killers, The (1970) Fact-based story of a professional gigolo and the 200-pound nurse he loves as they bilk and kill off a number of female victims responding to lonely hearts club letters. Without any real distinction on the part of the actors (Tony LoBianco and Shirley Stoler) or director (Leonard Kastle), the movie quickly descends into a quagmire of sick, morbidly sexual and violent situations, offensive both in theme and treatment. O (R)

Honeysuckle Rose (1980) Boring romantic triangle involves a singing star (Willie Nelson), his wife (Dyan Cannon) and a young musician (Amy Irving). The three principals give good performances but are up against a trite script, uninspired direction (Jerry Schatzberg) and poor editing. Coarse language, the use of marijuana and an adult theme. A-III (PG)

Hong Kong Cat, The (see: "Karado, the Hong Kong Cat")

Honkers, The (1972) James Coburn, free spirit and sometime rodeo performer, returns to sometime wife Lois Nettleton and son Ted Eccles in between one-night stands. Directed by Steve Ihnat, the movie gives no reason why viewers should be expected to sympathize with an aging adolescent loser who is incapable of making responsible decisions or understanding their consequences. A-III (GP)

Honky (1972) Black teenager (Brenda Sykes) and a white classmate (John Neilson) fall in love, cut class to hustle some pot, crack up daddy's flashy car and split for the Coast where the girl is raped and the boy beaten to a pulp. Director William A. Graham's story of adolescent folly is a shallow dramatic effort with a matching moral sensibility in its treatment of drugs and sex, teen irresponsibility and parental unresponsiveness. O (R)

Honky Tonk Freeway (1981) Converging on a small Florida town which is trying to effect its own exit ramp from a new superhighway are a dozen or so uninteresting motorists, including some New York bank robbers, a would-be writer, a cocaine-sniffing hitchhiker, a Kentucky waitress and other vacationers. Director John Schlesinger's failed satire of American road culture is an incoherent hodge-podge of silly sight gags and insulting sterotypes. A number of scenes involve casual sex. O (PG)

Honkytonk Man (1982) Hard-living, hard-drinking honkytonk singer-composer (Clint Eastwood), accompanied by his 14-year-old nephew (played by Kyle Eastwood, Eastwood's own son), goes to an audition in Nashville for the Grand Old Opry. A brink-of-death recording session insures supposedly a measure of posthumous glory. Also directed by Eastwood, there are some good moments, but most of it suffers from self-indulgence. Not only does the hero go to bed with a 16-year-old girl, but he pays a prostitute to introduce his nephew to sex. O (R)

Hook, Line & Sinker (1969) Informed by his doctor that he has only a few months to live, Jerry Lewis embarks on a trip around the world in order to indulge his favorite sport—fishing. Director George Marshall's alleged comedy also involves his wife (Anne Francis) and doctor (Peter Lawford) attempting to cash in on the peripatetic fisherman's large insurance policy by pulling a switcheroo in the local morgue. Unfunny stuff. A-II (G)

Hooker's Revenge (see: "They Call Her One Eye")

Hooper (1978) Aging Hollywood stuntman (Burt Reynolds) faces competition from a young newcomer (Jan-Michael Vincent) who is seeking to displace him, just as he had done to a top stuntman (Brian Keith) 20 years earlier. Directed by former stuntman Hal Needham, the movie is little more than a succession of stunts (barroom fights, car crashes, helicopter jumps, chariot races and so on) set within a film-within-a-film being directed by Robert Klein. Bawdy humor and rough language seem to jusify the reckless endangerment of life for profit. O (PG)

Hoosiers (1987) Dedicated but dictatorial coach (Gene Hackman) leads a small town high school basketball team to the 1952 Indiana state championship while effecting some attitude adjustments in the community and rebuilding his self-esteem along the way. Director David Anspaugh's film recalls and celebrates a vanishing American rural ethic where integrity is everything and winning is the spice of life. Brief instances of mildly vulgar language and a courtside scuffle. A-I (PG)

Hopscotch (1980) When a veteran CIA agent (Walter Matthau) is demoted by his incompetent superior (Ned Beatty), he goes underground to write an expose of international covert operations, trying to stay one step ahead of liquidation by the world's spy organizations. Matthau is in top form as the maverick agent and Glenda Jackson is fine as his helpful friend in a highly entertaining chase thriller directed by Ronald Neame. It has intelligence and wit, but also some rough language. A-III (R)

Hornet's Nest (1970) Trapped behind enemy lines in Italy during World War II, rugged Marine Rock Hudson assembles a rag-tag army of kids too young to join the Resistance but old enough to smell blood, Hollywood-style. Phil Karlson directs an improbable and confused war adventure movie that resorts to several rape scenes and excessive gore, made all the more gruesome by using youngsters in violent, foul-mouthed roles. O (M)

Horoscope (1970) Slow-paced Yugoslavian movie about some aimless young men in a sweltering small town on the Adriatic who for want of anything better try to seduce a pretty new shopkeeper with tragic results. Without becoming overly moralistic, director Boro Draskovic provides an engrossing vignette of youth trapped in a wasteland of inactivity. A-IV (nr)

Horror House (1970) When Frankie Avalon leads a group of youths in exploring an old house, one of them is killed and the audience is led to believe that the psychopath responsible is the lover of one of the girls, but Frankie finally unmasks the mental case. Directed by Michael Armstrong, there's lots of tension, plenty of false alarms and a couple of bloody murders. A-III (PG)

Horror of Blackwood Castle, The (1973) German murder mystery spoof about a retired ship's captain (Otto Stern) whose apparent demise brings daughter and former crew members to search for pirated jewels. Directed by Alfred Vohrer, its good fun with an intricate, fast-moving plot, a bushel of snakes and scary props, at least three surprise endings and a batch of frisky characters. A-II (PG)

Horror of Frankenstein (1971) When the monster finally appears in this fresh reworking of the Mary Shelley classic, he is considerably less frightening than his creator (Ralph Bates) whose total lack of human feeling is chilling. Directed by Jimmy Sangster with understated black humor, whose tone is established by Dennis Price as a discreet grave robber, this proves to be witty, literate and a cut above the usual horror fare. A-III (R)

Horror of the Blood Monsters (1971) After arriving by plastic rocketship on a planet remarkably like Earth, astronaut John Carradine tussles with the Tubertons, fang-toothed archetypal vampires. Meanwhile, mission controllers Robert Dix and Vicki Volante take time out to engage in electronically controlled love-making. Producer-director Al Adamson has slapped together a flimsy science-fiction adventure that is not worth anybody's traveling time. A-III (GP)

Horror on Snape Island (1972) Archaeological expedition searches a long-abandoned island off the English coast for a Phoenician burial site after some youths are found there slaughtered by ancient weapons. Unfortunately, British writer-director Jim O'Connolly, unable to sustain much suspense with his story, settles for a tacky mixture of nudity and mayhem. O (R)

Horse in the Gray Flannel Suit, The (1968) Weak Disney comedy about the problems of a widowed advertising man (Dean Jones) in finding ideas for his client, a horse for his daughter and a romance for himself. Directed by Norman Tokar, there is some colorful photography and trained horses but parents will likely find it a long sit. A-I (G)

Horsemen, The (1971) Failed adventure movie filmed in the mountains of Afghanistan about a man who is driven to prove his bravery but in the process loses his leg and ultimately his pride. Directed by John Frankenheimer, the narrative is incongruous and its movie stars (Omar Sharif, Leigh Taylor-Young, Jack Palance) are ridiculously out of place among the rugged mountain tribesmen. What it offers is plenty of violent action and feats of horsemanship. A-III (GP)

Hospital, The (1971) Uneven black comedy about a series of deaths in a big-city hospital whose chief of surgery (George C. Scott) begins to suspect that what is going on is not simply gross medical incompetence but the work of a madman on the loose. Brilliantly written by Paddy Chayefsky and well directed by Arthur Hiller, some of the situations are hilarious, but the feeling is one of giddiness, followed by the bite of terror. Language and uncompromising situations make it for adult patients only. A-III (GP)

Hot Box, The (1972) Philippine production in which four foul-mouthed nurses become tortured objects of lust, first at the hands of jungle revolutionaries who kidnap them, then at the hands of government troops who rescue them. Director Joe Viola simply alternates scenes of nudity with displays of bloodshed. O (R)

Hot Dog...The Movie (1984) Featuring Patrick Houser and Tracy Smith, this Animal House-on-skis is about a rivalry between clean-cut but lecherous American skiers and some sneaky and unsportsmanlike Europeans. Director Peter Mar-

kle's mindless diversion features action on the slopes by day and in hot tubs by night. Graphic sex and nudity. O (R)

Hot Lead and Cold Feet (1978) Poor Disney Western satire in which twin brothers of markedly different character (both played by Jim Dale) inherit a vast fortune with the stipulation that they engage in a winner-take-all competition. The talented Dale does as well as he can with the script's slapstick cliches and the support offered by Karen Valentine, Don Knotts and Jack Elam. But not even children are likely to enjoy director Robert Butler's effort very much; the very young won't understand the jokes and the older children won't find them very funny. A-I (G)

Hot Millions (1968) Deft British comedy in which an embezzler (Peter Ustinov) takes revenge on the computer system which caused his previous imprisonment by setting up phony companies for which he has programmed the computer to make regular payments. Aiding and abetting the comedy are Maggie Smith, Karl Malden and Bob Newhart, with director Eric Till contributing some fine comic visuals and gags. Mild romantic complications. A-II (G)

Hot Pants Holiday (1971) Harried New York housewife (Tudi Wiggins) on holiday in the Caribbean shares lust with native sex symbol (Christopher St. John) but after a voodoo ceremony as inept as it is lewd, housewife discovers that her native is two-timing her. Directed by Edward Mann, there are no surprises here. O (X/R)

Hot Pursuit (1987) Weak attempt to build romance around the madcap efforts of a college student (John Cusack) to catch up to his girlfriend's vacationing family stretches credibility. Director Steve Lisberger's contemporary comedy adventure set in the West Indies has some ambiguities about drugs, premarital sex and heroism which are further obscured by improbable plot devices and concluding gunplay. A-III (PG-13)

Hot Rock, The (1972) Lighthearted caper movie in which four bumbling crooks (Robert Redford, George Segal, Ron Leibman and Paul Sand) are hired by an African diplomat (Moses Gunn) to steal a huge uncut diamond that was taken from his country and now resides inside a heavily guarded display case in the Brooklyn Museum. Directed by Peter Yates, the fast-paced entertainment has a number of intriguing twists but Gunn and Zero Mostel steal the picture in their supporting roles. A-II (GP)

Hot Rod Action (1969) Feature documentary celebrating America's penchant for speed and danger uses footage from Indianapolis, Daytona and other speedways without commentary or narrative structure. For racing car buffs and anthropologists. A-I (G)

Hot Stuff (1979) Routine comedy directed by Dom DeLuise, who also has the leading role, about a police burglary task force who set up a phony fencing ring to ensnare thieves and run afoul of the Mafia. Some adult humor and an abundance of profanity. A-III (PG)

Hotel (1967) Screen version of Arthur Hailey's novel about a New Orleans hotel famous for its old-fashioned hospitality but losing money and facing a take-over. Richard Quine directs an old-fashioned melodrama using the hotel as the site for dramatic events in the lives of those staying there. Standing out among the large cast of stars are Melvyn Douglas as the aristocratic hotel owner and

Karl Malden as a sneak thief. Escapist entertainment with some adult situations. A-III (br)

Hotel New Hampshire (1984) Eccentric New England family (Natassja Kinski, Jodie Foster, Beau Bridges and Rob Lowe) jokes and cavorts in the face of human mortality in this glib and shallow adaptation of the John Irving novel adapted and directed by Tony Richardson. A kind of absurdist "You Can't Take It with You," it affects a benign view of all sorts of sexual activity, including incest. O (R)

Hotel Paradiso (1966) British bedroom farce set in Paris at the turn of the century has a fine cast (Alec Guinness, Gina Lollobrigida, Robert Morley and Akim Tamiroff) and a plot filled with mistaken identities and broad characterizations. Unfortunately, Peter Glenville's direction lacks the fast pace and timing required by this sort of comedy. A-III (br)

Hound of the Baskervilles, The (1939) The first and one of the best in a series of adaptations of the cases of Sir Arthur Conan Doyle's Victorian detective featuring Basil Rathbone in the role of Sherlock Holmes with Nigel Bruce as Dr. Watson. Directed by Sidney Lanfield, the story has mysterious murders on the moors, a baying hound, old cemetery ruins, ancestral curses, eccentric neighbors, a young couple in love and an escaped convict on the prowl. Engrossing and entertaining thriller, but a little scary for young children. A-II (nr)

Hour of the Gun (1967) Standard Western about Marshal Wyatt Earp (James Garner) defending Tombstone against the Clantons (led by Robert Ryan) in the famed gunfight at the O.K. Corral. After the bloody shoot-out, Earp begins taking the law into his own hands until Doc Holliday (Jason Robards) straightens him out. John Sturges directs with a steady hand for convincing action sequences. A-II (br)

House (1986) Director Sean Cunningham's parody of "Poltergeist" has some fun and fright in the story of a divorced novelist (William Katt) rescuing his captive son from angry spirits which infest his grandmother's house. Unfortunately, there is excessive gore and harsh language in Vietnam War flashbacks that flow, intermittently, from the hero's memory. O (R)

House II: The Second Story (1987) Inventive fantasy with touches of horror in which Arye Gross digs up his ancestor Royal Dano, kept alive for a century by a magical skull. Director Ethan Wiley takes the funhouse approach which wrecks more terror upon the cast than on the young audience which the movie's weirdness is certain to engage. Brief violence, ghoulish faces and silly female stereotypes. A-II (PG-13)

House by the Lake, The (1977) Four hoodlums terrorize a couple in an isolated villa only to have the woman (Brenda Vaccaro) wreak revenge on each of them. Canadian exploitation movie directed by William Fruet focuses on rape and bloodletting. O (R)

House Calls (1978) Walter Matthau plays a doctor who enthusiastically pursues women after the death of his wife, only to get his comeuppance from an independent-minded divorcee (Glenda Jackson). Director Howard Zieff's tepid little comedy looks like a slipshod re-working of "Cactus Flower" and is thoroughly adult in theme and dialogue. A-III (PG)

House of Cards (1968) Handsome, footloose American tutor (George Peppard) is up against

fanatical Algerian ex-patriots. Good wins over evil despite conventional mystery-melodrama trimmings from director John Guillermin who uses the commonplace as a source of horror. Attractively lush Parisian milieu, some spurts of violence and gratuitous, though silly attempts at sexual titillation. A-III (G)

House of Dark Shadows (1970) Movie version of a daytime television series about a family of vampires features Jonathan Frid re-creating his role of Barnabas, the 175-year-old owner of the spooky Collinwood estate, with Joan Bennett and Grayson Hall as residents. The melodrama often slips into a mire of gushing blood and gore directed by Dan Curtis for the fantasies of die-hard horror fans. Others are likely to be repulsed. A-III (PG)

House of Exorcism (1976) Playing the role of a suave butler in a sinister mansion is Telly Savalas, who seems to be making it up as he goes along, in a standard Italian Gothic horror filled with gore and nudity, and innocent of the least trace of taste or wit. O (R)

House of Missing Girls, The (1972) French movie with Anna Gael as a salesgirl who freely exhibits her own contours in a sordid adventure which has her fleeing a band of abusive slavers and finding refuge with a hermit-like musician. Jean-Francois Davy directs the English-dubbed exploitation import. O (R)

House of Whipcord (1974) British sex exploitation movie about a woman (Penny Irving) who is kidnapped and held prisoner by some demented types who torment and degrade. Director Pete Walker's flimsy story is only an excuse for an unhealthy fantasy of sex and violence. O (R)

House on Chelouche Street, The (1974) Israeli movie about a widow (Gila Almagor) in 1946 Tel Aviv who decides to remarry to give her family some security, but her adolescent son (Ophir Shalitan) resents her choice, has a brief affair with an older woman (Michal Bat-Adam) and learns something about adult responsibilities. Written and directed by Moshe Mizrahi, it proves an engaging and interesting portrayal of human problems and makeshift solutions in a time of great turmoil. A-III (PG)

House That Dripped Blood, The (1971) Four tired tales of the preternatural are linked by the weak device of a haunted house that supposedly influences the behavior of its inhabitants. British director Peter Duffell fails to develop the least sense of dread and the only surprise is that the screenplay is by veteran horror writer Robert Bloch. A-II (GP)

House That Screamed, The (1971) Lilli Palmer plays the turn-of-the-century proprietress of a French finishing school for wealthy girls and, while her 15-year-old son (John Moulder-Brown) persues the girls, they persue the local deliveryman. The promiscuous pursuits at the school are finally relieved by several bloody murders but, by then, director Narciso Ibanez Serrador's attempts at horror are lost in a sophomoric sex teaser. O (GP)

Housewife (see: "Bone")

How Do I Love Thee? (1970) Long-suffering, Bible-thumping wife (Maureen O'Hara) desires only to instill a fear of God in her college professor son (Rick Lenz) and to pray for the conversion of her atheist husband (Jackie Gleason) who is fooling around with a client (Shelley Winters). Director Michael Gordon, failing to elicit any depth or purposeful narrative, settles for prolonged and vacuous discussions of religion, remarkably tasteless sexual innuendo and a generally witless sense of the comic. O (PG)

How Funny Can Sex Be? (1976) Tedious Italian sex farce starring Giancarlo Giannini in a series of six ribald stories that under Dino Risi's direction vie with one another in lack of wit and general tastelessness and features considerable nudity. O (R)

How I Won the War (1967) Unusual British anti-war movie ridicules the military concept of war as a noble game and debunks the cliches and slogans of belligerents. Michael Crawford stars as an inexperienced lieutenant assigned to build an advanced cricket field in World War II North Africa, with John Lennon as the compliant everyman of the unit which deserts at the Rhine. Directed with comic ingenuity by Richard Lester, its pacifist view of war may be controversial but it is neither anti-religious nor anti-patriotic, and it merits attention and reflection. Stylized violence. A-II (br)

How Sweet It Is! (1968) James Garner and Debbie Reynolds star in a comedy-melodrama about a crazy, mixed-up American family sightseeing in Europe. Basically a happy couple, in the midst of complications caused by their son and his girlfriend, they find themselves on the brink of extra-curricular flirtations. Forgettable froth directed by Jerry Paris. A-III (br)

How Tasty Was My Little Frenchman (1973) Brazilian movie set in the early colonial times when a Frenchman is taken captive by a cannibal tribe and is held for execution at an upcoming festival. The final horror (and key to the title) in this black comedy is the cheerful smile of the young girl who has been his native wife as she prepares to eat her alloted portion of his dead body. Director Nelson Pereira Dos Santos does not romanticize nor sentimentalize the savages or the Europeans, but neither does his movie miss the joy of life that exists in every culture. Scenes of nudity in this semi-ethnographic movie are without any sense of sexual exploitation. A-IV (nr)

How to Beat the High Cost of Living (1980) Three housewives (Susan Saint James, Jane Curtin and Jessica Lange) conspire to replenish their depleted finances by stealing the money displayed in a huge plastic ball in a shopping center promotion. Director Robert Scheerer's comedy has some tart humor, but is pretty mediocre going and sometimes mean-spirited to boot. Adult humor and situations. A-III (PG)

How to Commit Marriage (1969) When the daughter of real estate agent (Bob Hope) and his wife of 19 years (Jane Wyman) learns that her parents are about to be divorced, she goes off to live out of wedlock with the son of a cynical agent for rock groups (Jackie Gleason). How everyone, including Gleason and his girlfriend Tina Louise, is eventually legally united or reunited might have been the basis for some good satire but director Norman Panama treats both his characters and the institution of marriage in a consistently grotesque and sleazy fashion. Though there are a few scattered laughs, this is not a funny picture. O (PG)

How to Frame a Figg (1971) Dimwitted City Hall clerk (Don Knotts) accidentally uncovers some shady dealings by the boys in the back room who promote him to a high-pay, no-sweat job, but eventually he figures out why and then blows the whistle on the corrupt officials. The comedy's humor revolves around the inane personality of Knotts, as well as around the farfetched situations he bumbles into and out of. Alan Rafkin directs the appropriately juvenile script as if it were an extended TV sitcom. A-I (G)

How to Save a Marriage...and Ruin Your Life (1968) Eli Wallach and Anne Jackson play an adulterous couple under investigation by bachelor Dean Martin who mistakenly identifies Stella Stevens as Wallach's compliant girlfriend in a divorce action. Fielder Cook directs a not-so-funny marriage-go-round comedy that goes cheerfully around in circles leading nowhere. A-III (br)

How to Seduce a Woman (1974) Witless one-joke sex comedy with Angus Duncan is ineptly directed by Charles Martin. O (R)

How to Steal a Million (1966) Audrey Hepburn as the daughter of art forger Hugh Griffith desperately tries to steal his bogus masterpiece from a museum exhibit before it can be revealed as a fraud. Peter O'Toole stages the caper, foils art dealer Charles Boyer, and wins the hand of the fair lady from Eli Wallach. William Wyler directs the romantic comedy with sophisticated elegance. A-I (br)

How to Succeed in Business Without Really Trying (1967) Robert Morse and Rudy Vallee whoop it up at the World Wide Wicket Company in an adaptation of the Broadway musical about an ex-window-washer's schemes to reach the top of a big corporation in the shortest possible time. Director David Swift's sharp, witty spoof retains most of the original's running gags and Frank Loesser music. A-II (br)

Howard the Duck (1986) This caustic, cynical and malevolent fantasy-adventure features a fully costumed duck from outer space trying to find his way home after having been accidentally transported to a hostile Earth. Director Willard Huyck fills the screen with too much vulgarity, violent destruction and sadistic humor to make the movie of interest to any sensitive earthling. O (PG)

Howling, The (1981) Trashy but flashy horror movie written by John Sayles and directed by Joe Dante in which a television newswoman (Dee Wallace) finds herself in dire straits when her companions at a psychiatric retreat turn out to be a pack of werewolves. The special effects by Rob Bottin are remarkable, but not enough to justify what is essentially a sex-and-violence exploitation movie. O (R)

Huckleberry Finn (1974) Sugary musical version of the Twain classic, with script and lyrics written by the Sherman Brothers, features Jeff East in the title role and Paul Winfield as Jim. Directed by J. Lee Thompson, it contains a clutter of supremely forgettable musical numbers, entirely misses the book's point and adds up only to a minor children's matinee entry. A-I (G)

Hugs and Kisses (1968) Swedish movie about a triangular relationship that develops between a woman, her husband and his bumbling friend. Written and directed by Jonas Cornell, the fragmentary story and its seriocomic incidents are at best ambiguous in developing a theme about human relationships. Unnecessarily graphic nude sequence. O (br)

Human Factor, The (1975) When the family of a computer expert (George Kennedy) at a NATO base in Naples is murdered by international terrorists, he tracks down the villains and slaughters them in an orgy of violence. Despite the title and Kennedy's efforts to give his role some human dimension, Edward Dmytryk directs his story of vigilante vengeance with little feeling for any of its characters. O (R)

Human Factor, The (1980) Nicol Williamson plays a quiet family man, working for British Intelligence but also leaking information to the Russians, who has a crisis of conscience that causes him to risk everything. Also with Richard Attenborough and Derek Jacobi, the performances are excellent and Tom Stoppard's too literal adaptation of the Graham Greene novel and Otto Preminger's plodding direction results in a movie that entertains, but does not excite or have the moral complexity of the original. Suggestive nightclub dance scene. A-III (R)

Human Revolution, The (1974) Japanese dramatization of the 1930's beginnings and beliefs of the Nichiren Shoshu Academy (a Buddhist sect numbering some 20 million adherents). Directed by Toshiro Masuda, it is a handsome and intelligent production whose philosophical rather than religious message is that the world can only become better through the inner change of each individual. A-II (G)

Humanoids from the Deep (1980) Meddling scientists tampering with genetic laws turn some prehistoric creatures, who are minding their own business at the bottom of the sea, into sex maniacs. Directed by Barbara Peeters, this penny-ante dreadful contains excessive violence and nudity. O (R)

Hunger, The (1983) Catherine Deneuve and David Bowie play vampires whose love has stood the test of time until he, after dining on punk rockers, begins to die and she falls in love with the doctor (Susan Sarandon) called in to try to save him. Director Tony Scott's relentlessly slick and shallow movie consists of elegant surroundings and extravagant doses of blood and gore, nudity, graphic sexuality and not one bit of plausibility. O (R)

Hunger for Love (1973) Brazilian drama presents a socio-psychological survey of contemporary values in the story of a young man who decides to run away with the wife of his best friend. Directed in 1969 by Nelson Pereira Dos Santos, the beautifully-crafted movie will appeal most to those interested in themes of social justice. A-III (nr)

Hunt, The (1967) Spanish movie in which three old friends spend a day hunting rabbits while the pressure of resentments caused by changed fortunes grows in each until the occasion culminates in senseless tragedy. Director Carlos Saura's veiled political allegory about the Spanish Civil War makes a subtle anti-fascist statement. A-III (br)

Hunter, The (1980) Steve McQueen plays a modern-day bounty hunter hired by bail bondsmen to bring back clients who have jumped bail. Though McQueen is very good, director Buzz Kulik's action movie is put together in slipshod fashion with an excess of plot threads that never come together. Good deal of violence. A-III (PG)

Hunting Party, The (1971) Repulsive Western about a wife (Candice Bergen) kidnapped by a sex-crazed outlaw (Oliver Reed) and pursued by bloodlusting husband (Gene Hackman). Directed by Don Medford, its depiction of sex and nudity is mild in comparison to its graphic presentation of senseless violence and sadistic brutalities. O (R)

Hunting Scenes (1970) German movie about a young man who becomes the object of ridicule in his small village when a rumor starts that he is a homosexual and he kills someone in a vain attempt to escape his persecutors. Writer-director Peter Fleischmann's story is not about homosexuality but about a tightly-knit community whose fear of those who are different unite them, and may be seen as referring to Hitler's popular support. A-III (nr)

Hurricane (1979) Listless, mediocre remake of the 1937 John Ford movie about ill-fated South Sea lovers (Mia Farrow and Dayton Ka'Ne) was filmed in Bora Bora but the spectacle of the climactic hurricane does not measure up to the Hollywood original. Director Jan Troell's melodramatic script and its shallow characterizations waste a good cast including Jason Robards, Max Von Sydow and Trevor Howard. Erotic dance sequences and distasteful pre-marriage ritual. O (PG)

Hurry Sundown (1967) Michael Caine plays a Cockney-accented cracker and Jane is his somewhat bruised Georgia peach. Director Otto Preminger's superficial depiction of social, marital and racial unrest in a small Southern town during the 1940s is patronizing in its treatment of racial attitudes and also demeaning in its approach to sex. O (br)

Hurry Up, or I'll Be 30 (1973) Young man in Brooklyn (John Lefkowitz), crushed by thoughts that he is almost 30, tries vainly to break out of his sterile life-style. Director Joseph Jacoby's generally sappy narrative involves George's frustrating job in his father's small print shop and his brief affair with an aspiring Broadway actress (Linda DeCoff). Entirely predictable movie about boring people, the occasional nudity is totally gratuitous. O (R/GP)

Husbands (1970) Long Island commuters (John Cassavetes, Ben Gazzara and Peter Falk) attend the burial of a mutual friend suddenly carried off by a coronary, and their own sense of mortality becomes both the catalyst and context for the drunken antics, middle-aged frustrations and inarticulate revelations that follow. For all of its excesses, from a lavatory vomiting scene to a crude sex romp in a London hotel, director John Cassavetes injects a compassion for his male misfits that redeems many of the glaring faults in his treatment of the proceedings. A-III (PG)

Hustle (1975) Los Angeles detective (Burt Reynolds), whose mistress is an expensive call girl (Catherine Deneuve), finds nothing but corruption in places high and low during his investigation of a young girl's death. Director Robert Aldrich's muddled movie is not above purveying a bit of the corruption it seems to be decrying. Excessive sex and violence. O (R)

I

I Am a Dancer (1973) Pierre Jourdan's documentary records Rudolf Nureyev as he rehearses, in performance and working with promising novices. John Percival has written a reverent, rather adulatory, narration for the movie which is pleasantly read by Bryan Forbes. A-I (nr)

I Am Curious (Blue) (1970) The Blue version is just as boring as its Yellow predecessor. Though it contains fewer erotic sequences, its social and political subject matter is as intemperate, irrelevant and uninteresting to an American audience as previously. O (nr)

I Am Curious (Yellow) (1969) Failed social commentary by Swedish director Vilgot Sjoman tries to find a metaphorical link between the ills of Swedish society and the sexual problems of a young woman. The theme of smug complacency boils over into a sensationalized exploitation of nudity. O (X)

I Am the Cheese (1983) Story of an adolescent's identity crisis adapted from the novel by Robert Cormier presents a rather bleak and depressing portrait of the hurt child under psychiatric care. Director Robert Jiras has some insight into ways children might deal with the loss of parents but it is not a movie youngsters will find engaging. A-II (PG)

I Could Never Have Sex with Any Man Who Has So Little Regard for My Husband (1973) Dreary, psuedo-sophisticated sex comedy written by Dan Greenburg and directed by Robert McCarty is set on a rainy Martha's Vinyard where Carmine Caridi, Cynthia Harris, Andrew Duncan and Lynne Lipton play strip hide-and-seek while they wait for the weather to clear. Monogamy wins in the end but till then, it's a low comedy exercise in sexual brinkmanship. A-III (R)

I Drink Your Blood (1971) Low-budget horror movie exploiting the hippie and drug scene begins with some phony occult rites and ends in a ridiculous rabies epidemic. Directed by David Durston, it is devoid of style and notable only for the way in which it proceeds to turn trash into garbage. O (X/R)

I Eat Your Skin (1971) Routine horror movie is set on a mysterious island with voodoo ceremonies, secret medical experiments and roaming zombies. It has all been done before and with much more dash than writer-producer-director Del Tenney has been able to come up with, though the zombie make-up does add a little craft to tiresome proceedings. A-III (GP)

I Escaped from Devil's Island (1973) Held prisoner in the forbidding French penal colony circa 1918, Jim Brown and Christopher George are brutalized by sadistic guards until they flee through shark-infested waters and the teeming jungle. Director William Witney's tough and sweaty movie has excessive violence and a lengthy nude scene. O (R)

I.F. Stone's Weekly (1973) Fine documentary by Jerry Bruck, Jr., is primarily a study of Stone as a reporter's reporter, whose labors have made him an ebullient force in contemporary jounalism. Not least of the film's virtues is its rare picture of a man who thoroughly enjoys what he does for a living and even feels a little guilty that he gets paid for it. A-II (nr)

I Love My Wife (1971) Selfish, overgrown adolescent surgeon (Elliott Gould) spends increasing amounts of time with his mistresses while ignoring his wife (Brenda Vaccaro) who had put him through medical school and whom he loves deep down inside. Director Mel Stuart indulges Gould's shaggy-panda style which generates the barest number of painful laughs and a great deal of embarrassment at his frantic sex life. O (R)

I Love You (1982) Vapid and pretentious Brazilian movie about two bored members of the privileged class (Sonia Braga and Paulo Cesar Perelo) acting out their fantasies at tedious length in a luxurious Rio high rise. Director Arnaldo Jabor presumes to deal with politics in sexual terms but succeeds only in producing a boring exercise in softcore pornography. O (R)

I Love You, Alice B. Toklas (1968) Peter Sellers plays a Beverly Hills attorney drawn by love into the hippie lifestyle in what begins as an amusing satirical farce harpooning both the establishment as well as the counter-culture. Directed by Hy Averback, it eventually turns into a sex comedy with graphic sexual scenes, hash parties and coarse language. O (R)

I Love You, I Kill You (1972) German movie set in the future where there is a village existing only to maintain a game preserve for the ruling class and whose inhabitants are kept happy by popping pills. Written and directed by Uwe Brandner, the movie operates on many levels of love-hate relationships, but it is primarily a political parable about fascism and freedom. For those who have the inclination to interpret its languid, dreamlike visuals, it is a demanding exercise but worth the experience. A-IV (nr)

I Love You, Rosa (1973) Israeli movie about an 11-year-old boy who wants to marry his brother's widow (Michal Bat-Adam) and as he grows older and more insistent, she finally has to take him seriously. Writer-director Moshe Mizrahi's story is set in late 19th-century Jerusalem and is told with a charmingly poetic, humorously sentimental glow that romantics will find hard to resist, though it does indulge in some nudity, crude dialogue and has a casual attitude about premarital sex. A-IV (nr)

I Married You for Fun (1969) Monica Vitti displays comic flair as the "kooky" swinging wife of a young man from an absurdly stuffy background in this Italian sex farce posing as a satire on marriage. Director Luciano Salce opens with a suicide attempt and goes on to employ a decadent orgy scene and nudity in a sexual context. O (X)

I Never Promised You a Rose Garden (1977) The parents of a teenage schizophrenic (Kathleen Quinlan) reluctantly place her in a mental institution. Quinlan and Bibi Andersson as the psychiatrist give superb performances in this drama of mental illness directed by Anthony Page. The too realistic depiction of the teenager's fantasy world and some brief nudity are sufficiently graphic to be inappropriate for youngsters. A-III (R)

I Never Sang for My Father (1970) Gilbert Cates directs a solid adaptation of the Robert Anderson play about a grown son (Gene Hackman) who is forced to come to some decision about how to care for his aging father (Melvyn Douglas). Both give remarkable performances filled with compassion and understanding and their scenes together are charged with the love and hate that simultaneously bind them together and make them strangers. It would be fine for adolescents save for a rather frank bedroom scene. A-III (GP)

I Ought to Be in Pictures (1982) Superficial seriocomic Neil Simon story about a teen (Dinah Manoff) who reunites with the father (Walter Matthau) who had deserted her in order to become a Hollywood writer. Directed by Herbert Ross, the movie tries to make light of an adulterous, misguided character, and says very little of import about parent-child relations. Because of a brief scene involving nudity and the father's dealings with a mistress (Ann-Margaret), it is mature fare. A-III (PG)

I, the Jury (1982) Gross remake of the 1953 Mickey Spillane private eye melodrama features Armand Assante as the sullen Mike Hammer out to avenge a dead friend by smashing a rogue CIA operation which uses a sex clinic as a front. Director Richard T. Heffron makes unbridled use of a repulsive mix of sex and violence. O (R)

I Walk the Line (1970) Taking its title from a bittersweet Johnny Cash country-western song, the movie concerns a redneck Tennessee sheriff (a miscast Gregory Peck) and his romance with a moonshiner's daughter (Tuesday Weld). Director John Frankenheimer reduces the story to a series of heavy, melodramatic surface strokes, avoiding the issues of life's social and moral complexities, resulting in a movie without any substance. A-III (GP)

I Wanna Hold Your Hand (1978) Three New Jersey high school girls enact an elaborate scheme to get to see their heroes (the Beatles) on the day the singing group is to appear on the Ed Sullivan Show in 1964. Director Robert Zemecki's farcical style, rough language and a tasteless scene with a prostitute make it a decidedly adult comedy. A-III (PG)

I Want What I Want (1972) Anne Heywood playing both the before and after role in the story of a transsexual struggles sincerely, if not quite convincingly. Directed by John Dexter, the result is wanting in such basics as dramatic interest and literacy, as well as depth in the psychological, medical and moral areas it opens up. A-III (R)

I Will, I Will...For Now (1976) Limp sex farce about sexually-based marital problems stars Elliott Gould and Diane Keaton. Directed by Norman Panama, the movie's tasteless humor is structured as a parody of a sex manual with vulgar jokes and negative female stereotypes. O (R)

I'll Never Forget What's'isname (1968) Failed British melodrama about an advertising whiz (Oliver Reed) who, disillusioned with success, an unsatisfying marriage and two mistresses, decides to throw it all up and return to making an honest living but learns one can't recapture a lost innocence. Directed by Michael Winner, there is some satirical goring of TV commercials and the emptiness of affluence, but the plot goes nowhere and ends in cynicism. Excessive gory violence and graphic sex scenes. O (br)

I'm Dancing as Fast as I Can (1982) Disappointing movie version of television producer Barbara Gordon's account of her struggle to overcome an addiction to tranquilizers. Jill Clayburgh's characterization casts little light upon why she is so driven to drugs, the result being an unnerving melodrama rather than anything deeper. Director Jack Hofsiss details the horrors of quitting "cold turkey" and uses violence and rough language to realistic effect. A-III (R)

Ice (1970) Writer-director Robert Kramer has made a fictional movie with a documentary look about shadowy revolutionary groups joining together to plan and then carry out a regional show of force in preparation for a nationwide uprising. Though its surface realities seem to have little connection with any actual violence of radical groups, it does offer a chilling picture of the fantasies engendered in those frustrated by their hopes for social change. A-IV (nr)

Ice Castles (1979) When a talented young skater (Lynn-Holly Johnson) training for the Olympics is blinded in an accident, her father (Tom Skerritt) and boy friend (Robby Benson) persuade her to resume her career. Director Donald Wrye gets good performances in this mildly inspirational tale but the movie is undone by

frequent rough language and its sympathetic attitude towards premarital sex on the part of its teenage heroine. O (PG)

Ice Pirates, The (1984) Lackluster science fiction story about the hijacking of spaceships that supply ice to waterless planets tries but fails to get by as a spoof. Directed by Stewart Raffill and starring Robert Urich and Mary Crosby, it has some sexually oriented humor, a relatively mild bedroom sequence and an air of pervasive vulgarity. A-III (PG)

Ice Station Zebra (1968) Uneven screen version of an Alistair MacLean thriller in which a nuclear submarine captain (Rock Hudson) is ordered to bring a British spy (Patrick McGoohan), a friendly Russian (Ernest Borgnine) and a detachment of Marines to an Arctic weather station where a Russian surveillance satellite has landed, but the Russians are already enroute. Directed by John Sturges, there are double agents and a Cold War show-down to keep up adult interest and plenty of adventure for the youngsters. A-I (G)

Iceman (1984) Talented Australian director Fred Schepisi has too little to work with in a script by Chip Proser and John Drimmer about an Arctic expedition revivifying a frozen Neanderthal man (John Lone). There is a running argument betweeen a scientist-humanist (Timothy Hutton) and a more clinical type (Lindsay Crouse) as to what to do with him, but it fails to generate enough heat to thaw out anything. Some mild vulgarities. A-II (PG)

Icy Breasts (1975) French suspense movie set on the Riviera in winter when a hack writer (Claude Brasseur) sees a striking blonde (Mireille Darc) with a hurt, gamin-like quality, and sets out in pursuit but is stopped by her lawyer (Alain Delon) who tells him she is unstable and a murderess. Director Georges Lautner has made a taut, spare thriller with talented performers and luxurious settings. Some brief nudity which the context makes far from erotic. A-IV (R)

Identification Marks: None (1969) Impressionistic Polish drama about a youth waiting to enter military service. Directed by Jerzy Skolimowski, the movie poetically evokes the confusions and personal conflicts of young people in a bleak, repressive society. A-III (nr)

Idi Amin Dada (1976) Self-portrait of the Ugandan leader shows Amin as a dangerous dictator perhaps more effectively than if director Barbet Schroeder had been permitted to make his own objective documentary. Its display of the ruler's gross self-indulgence in the midst of such an impoverished nation is of value for future historians, if not contemporary viewers. A-II (nr)

Idol, The (1966) Self-centered American art student in England (Michael Parks), pursued by his friend's girl friend, is more interested in seducing his pal's mother (Jennifer Jones). Director Daniel Petrie fails to make clear why anyone would find his confused, boorish hero of the slightest interest, let alone appeal. Adult themes and treatment. A-III (br)

Idolmaker, The (1980) Ray Sharkey turns in a fine performance as a Svengali-like manager who turns two marginally talented youngsters (Peter Gallagher and Paul Land) into rock stars in the early 1960s. Although the picture runs out of energy and interest about two-thirds of the way through, director Taylor Hackford's portrait of the power-hungry is superior entertainment up till then. Some sexual references. A-III (PG)

If (1969) British schoolboys (among them, Malcolm McDowell) rebel against the abuses of a social and educational system out-of-step with their yearnings and fantasies for a life of freedom from unenlightened authority. Director Lindsay Anderson's complex fable half-heartedly accepts violence as a means to social change and uses nudity as a symbol of liberation. A-IV (X/R)

If Ever I See You Again (1978) Self-indulgent story about a hugely successful commercial songwriter (Joe Brooks) who after 12 years rediscovers, loses and, at movie's end, wins his college sweetheart (Shelley Hack) while echoes of "Venite Adoremus" are heard on the sound track. Also directed by Brooks, it is so gloppy it makes "Love Story" look like a Tolstoy novel. Some scenes, by suggestion at least, are adult. A-III (PG)

If He Hollers, Let Him Go (1968) Black auto mechanic (Raymond St. Jacques), wrongly convicted of a capital crime, escapes prison and saves the life of a wealthy woman (Dana Wynter) who offers all the financial aid necessary to prove his innocence. Written, produced and directed by Charles Martin, its story of racism and injustice is little more than a cheap exploitation of explicit sex and brutality. O (R)

If I Had a Gun (1973) The setting is a small rural village in Slovakia, the state created after the Nazi occupation of Czechoslovakia, during the last years of World War II. The central figure is a young boy living through the normal problems of early adolescence, which are compounded by the extraordinary conditions of wartime. Director Stephen Uher does not sentimentalize his subject but suggests that the effect of violence upon the young is the most terrible heritage that the adult world has to bestow. A-III (nr)

If It's Tuesday, This Must Be Belgium (1969) Drip-dry comedy about American tourist stereotypes, camera and luggage ladened, on an economy tour of Europe. Both the people and the places make easy targets for director Mel Stuart to poke fun at. Less funny is a romantic complication involving tourist Suzanne Pleshette who tries a fling with grabby guide Ian McShane. A-III (G)

If You Could See What I Hear (1982) Based upon the college experiences of blind singer-entertainer Tom Sullivan (Marc Singer), this muddled movie offers both crude slapstick and pathos with very little in between. Sullivan's pursuit of women and an off-again, on-again religious dimension is conveyed in a crude, insensitive manner by director Eric Till. A-III (PG)

If You Don't Stop It... (1975) Montage of ancient dirty jokes acted out and trying to pass itself off as a movie. Often enough, it is merely vulgar, an aspect not nearly as offensive as its cynical exploitation of female nudity. O (R)

Illustrated Man, The (1969) Failed attempt to tie in three unrelated tales with the story of a man (Rod Steiger) whose body is covered from head to foot with tatooes in which others see their future. Directed by Jack Smight, the movie wavers between horror, thriller and science fiction with unsatisfying results. Some violence and brief nudity. A-III (PG)

Ilsa, Harem Keeper of the Oil Sheiks (1976) The moral cretins who brought "Ilsa, She-Wolf of the SS" to the screen offer another sex exploitation movie with the same low-budget production values. O (R)

Images (1972) Psychological thriller in which events are seen through the eyes and mind of a troubled woman (Susannah York) and leaving, until the final shot, the audience to determine which of her perceptions are real and which imaginary. Director Robert Altman demonstrates a technical mastery of his medium, a willingness to take chances in achieving an effect and a talent for eliciting strong performances from his actors. Mature themes. A-III (R)

Immortal Bachelor, The (1980) Claudia Cardinale serves on the jury trying the case of a charwoman (Monica Vitti) on trial for murdering her philandering husband. Vitti's defense is that she could not possibly murder a man who was unequaled among lovers. Director Marcello Fondato's mood of artificiality undercuts the social satire while his emphasis upon marital infidelity makes this adult fare. A-III (PG)

Immortal Story (1969) Orson Welles directs as well as stars in this solemn tale about a merchant baron's grotesque obsession with transforming pretense into reality. Jeanne Moreau appears in a cameo in this haunting, elusively obscure fable about the futility of wealth and power to provide fulfillment. A-III (nr)

Impasse (1969) Salvage company owner (Burt Reynolds) reassembles four members of an Army detail which had buried a fortune in gold bullion in the tunnels of Corregidor just before its surrender to the Japanese. What could have been an interesting action melodrama in Philippine locales is ruined by a confused screenplay, formula characters and the unsavory cynicism with which director Richard Benedict treats a love affair that eventually causes failure for the entire operation. Some violence, coarse language and a rather graphic lovemaking scene. O (M)

Impossible on Saturday (1966) Mediocre French import. A-II (br)

Impossible Years (1969) Sappy situation comedy about a university professor (David Niven), a supposed authority on teenage behavior, who is unaware that his own teenage daughter (Christina Ferrare) is secretly married (to Chad Everett). The girl's permissive standards of conduct become the source of irreverent generation gap humor which director Michael Gordon plays badly as adult farce. A-III (G)

Improper Channels (1981) Alan Arkin stars as a screwball architect who is unjustly accused of child abuse when his five-year-old daughter hits her head and a social worker misjudges the situation. Canadian production directed by Eric Till elicits a few comic moments but refuses to deal with the real questions of domestic violence and children's rights. A-II (PG)

Impulse (1984) Young couple (Meg Tilly and Tim Matheson) return to her home town to find that everyone has gone berserk, indulging in bloody violence and promiscuous sex. Director Graham Baker's horror movie is as ridiculous as it is vicious. O (R)

Impure Thoughts (1987) Four recently deceased friends are reunited in purgatory and reminisce about their 1960s Catholic upbringing. Some mildly irreverent humor is offset by director Michael Simpson's exploration of religious values and family life. Some crude language and sexual references. A-III (PG)

In Celebration (1975) British adaptation of the David Storey play about three sons (Alan Bates,

James Bolam and Brian Cox) who return home to a coal-mining town to celebrate their parents' 40th wedding anniversary. Director Lindsay Anderson's incisive portrait of family relations and each individual's struggle to cope with the bonds of the past is emotionally powerful and will deeply involve most viewers. Mature themes. A-III (PG)

In Cold Blood (1967) Meaningful screen version of Truman Capote's non-fiction novel about the senseless 1959 slaying of a Kansas family and the apprehension and hanging of their killers (Robert Blake and Scott Wilson). Director Robert Brooks takes a semi-documentary approach in re-creating these events with shattering realism but with compassion and a notable lack of sensationalism. It also explores the backgrounds and the motivations of the two criminals as well as scrutinizes the practice of capital punishment. Strong stuff but the experience is thought-provoking. A-III (br)

In Enemy Country (1968) Limp World War II spy thriller about the exploits of a French intelligence agent (Tony Franciosa) behind German lines. The mediocre effort is directed by Harry Keller with no moral considerations beyond that of all is fair in love and war. Some violence and sexual situations. A-III (br)

In God We Trust (1980) Marty Feldman's inept and hugely unfunny comedy, intended as a satire on the exploitation of people in the name of religion, displays a tasteless, irreverent, crude mocking of religious beliefs. O (PG)

In Praise of Older Women (1979) Hopelessly episodic, shallow and sexually exploitative Canadian movie about a young Hungarian emigre (Tom Berenger) and his amorous adventures with the likes of Karen Black and Susan Strasberg. Directed by George Kaczender, events never stray far from the bedroom. O (R)

In Search of Gregory (1970) British female Don Quixote fantasy set in the 20th century centers on a young woman (Julie Christie) who is told by her wealthy father (Adolfo Celi) and neurotic brother (Peter Hurt) about a young man (Michael Sarrazin) who will bring romance and fulfillment into her life. Directed by Peter Wood, the story is so murky and its execution so undisciplined that its moral about not taking fantasy for reality becomes bogged down in its own tedium, making the occasional nudity and brother-sister incest theme even more offensive than they might have been. O (PG)

In Search of Historic Jesus (1980) Pseudo-documentary by Henning G. Schellerup moves from a summary of the life of Jesus to a detailed examination of the significance of the Shroud of Turin, believed by many to be Jesus' burial cloth. Ludicrous dramatizations and dubious embellishments of the Gospel story suggest parental discretion in exposing youngsters to such a grab-bag selection of material, no matter how orthodox it is in regard to Christian doctrine. A-I (G)

In Search of Noah's Ark (1977) Semi-documentary sets out to prove the literal truth of the biblical account of the Flood, basing its case largely on conjecture and hypothesis. Directed by James Conway, its inept dramatization of the building and stocking of the Ark makes it appear ridiculous and undercuts the religious significance of the biblical story. A-I (G)

In the Heat of the Night (1967) One steamy night, an industrialist is murdered in Sparta, Mississippi, and the local police chief (Rod Steiger) has to rely on the scientific experience of a black homicide expert (Sidney Poitier) who is passing through town. Though the movie begins with a very suggestive sex scene, the superior acting of the two principals and the sure hand of director Norman Jewison turn a rather muddled detective plot into a balanced and significant expression of the complex racial, legal and intellectual prejudice permeating many areas of American life. A-III (br)

In the Name of the Father (1974) Italian drama about a boys' school run by a corrupt religious order into which comes a new teacher (Yves Beneyton), a man of efficiency, pragmatism and scientific bent, who dedicates himself to reforming the old ways and introducing a new regime. Director Marco Bellocchio's talent is everywhere in evidence, though his political allegory about fascism will probably seem to viewers with little knowledge of Italian culture as a rather strange and tedious fable. A-III (nr)

In the Realm of the Senses (1977) Japanese director Nagisa Oshima's study of perverse sex and its consequences is a tale of a former prostitute working as a maid whose affair with the owner of an inn culminates in her killing him and mutilating his body in horrbile fashion. Pretentious mix of violence and ertoticism. O (nr)

In the Shadow of Kilimanjaro (1986) Gritty wildlife adventure, based on an actual event at a game preserve in Kenya during a severe drought, turns into a gruesome carnage as thousands of starving baboons attack humans. Timothy Bottoms and John Rhys-Davies are featured in the bloody rampage, which relies too heavily on visual shock, including gory scenes of dismemberment. A-III (R)

In the Year of the Pig (1969) Emile de Antonio's documentary recounts the political history of Vietnam from French colonial days to the American military involvement. Less an anti-war tract than a lucid examination of the complex political realities that have made Vietnam an American tragedy, it's a valuable document worthy of retrospective scrutiny. A-II (nr)

Inadmissible Evidence (1968) Mid-life crisis of a successful London lawyer (Nicol Williamson) triggers fears of an unsure future and concerns about failures of the past, especially his relations with women. Director Anthony Page's adaptation of the John Osborne play is claustrophobic and introspective but it is Williamson's tortured performance that makes it worth seeing. A-IV (br)

Inchon (1982) Expensively staged but wretched retelling of General Douglas MacArthur's amphibious victory in the early stages of the Korean War. Though Laurence Olivier plays MacArthur, supported by an international star cast, director Terence Young can't overcome the poor script, leaving only wartime melodrama and pyrotechnics for interest. A-III (PG)

Incident, The (1967) Dynamic social drama about a group of passengers riding the New York subway late at night and being terrorized by two hoodlums (Tony Musante and Martin Sheen). Tautly directed by Larry Peerce, it is not a pleasant story, but gripping and thought-provoking. A-IV (br)

Incorrigible (1980) French director Philippe De Broca's wan comedy in which a hyperactive flimflam artist (Jean-Paul Belmondo) meets his match in a lovely and quick-witted social worker (Genevieve Bujold). The dash and charm of these two actors are the saving grace of the movie. Some sexual references. A-III (nr)

Incredible Journey, The (1969) Fact-based Walt Disney story of a 250-mile trek through the Canadian wilds undertaken by an English bulldog, a Labrador retriever and a Siamese cat to rejoin their owner who had left them with friends while on vacation. Director Fletcher Markle allots most of the time to his four-footed actors which prove more engaging than the human characterizations and an over-cute narration. A-I (G)

Incredible Sarah, The (1976) Pop bio of French actress Sarah Bernhardt (Glenda Jackson) lacks the warmth or stateliness that might have conveyed the magnetism of the reputedly great performer. Incredibly misdirected by Richard Fleischer and filmed in England with little sense of the misfortune in her life and career. A-II (PG)

Incredible Shrinking Woman, The (1981) Lily Tomlin plays a harried suburban housewife and mother who suddenly finds that she is shrinking due to an allergy from all the chemical additives in her household products. Strained allegorical slapstick comedy directed by Joel Schumacher falls far short of satire despite its jibes at consumerism and its consequences. Mild sexual innuendo. A-III (PG)

Incredible Two-Headed Transplant, The (1971) Disappointed medical student (Bruce Dern) grafts the head of a homicidal maniac onto the shoulders of a retarded brute and the maniac takes over, escapes and is not caught until he has committed half a dozen murders. Director Anthony Lanza's low-budget horror movie supplies only a few grisly laughs here and there. A-III (GP)

Independence Day (1983) Small-town girl (Kathleen Quinlan) yearns for success as a photographer in Los Angeles and must choose between love and ambition. Director Robert Mandel's predictable story has a subplot of wife abuse but only Quinlan's vibrant performance is of interest. There is a love affair and a relatively sympathetic depiction of suicide. A-III (R)

Indian Paint (1965) Naive, sometime dramatically inept account of the testing of an adolescent Indian brave (Johnny Crawford). Directed by Norman Foster, the movie's chief interest is in its authentic native lore and insights into the honorable values of another culture. A-I (br)

Indiana Jones and the Temple of Doom (1984) Director Steven Spielberg's sequel to "The Raiders of the Lost Ark" has Indiana (Harrison Ford), with the help of a chorus girl (Kate Capshaw) and a Chinese war orphan (Short Round), rescue a stone from a nasty Indian sect and return it to its rightful owners. Non-stop stunts take precedence above all else, making it entertaining for action fans but the comic book violence is a little intense, especially one sequence involving the removal of a human heart. A-III (PG)

Infinite Tenderness, An (1973) French documentary on the world of a brain-damaged, physically-handicapped child confined to a wheel chair, unable to speak but trying desperately to communicate with his nurse and the other children in the hospital. It chronicles his friendship with another youngster even more crippled than himself, their joy in being together, their little spats and, finally, the termination of their friendship by death. Directed by Pierre Jallaud, it is a remarkable achievement, treating its subject creatively yet with complete integrity. There is no commentary, no dialogue, only the natural sounds of the children and their environment. A-II (nr)

Inga (1968) Swedish sex exploitation import directed by Joseph W. Arnbo details the initiation of a young girl (Marie Liljedahl) into a life of promiscuity. O (R)

Inheritor, The (1973) Slick French mystery adventure in which a ne'er-do-well playboy (Jean-Paul Belmondo) investigates the circumstances of his industrialist father's death and his search leads to some dark secrets in his own family as well as to the top leadership of Europe's industrial giants. Director Philippe Labro takes some elegant jabs at high society and the swaggering Belmondo has some discreet fun with the ladies. A-III (PG)

In-Laws, The (1979) Prominent New York dentist (Alan Arkin) and a seedy CIA agent (Peter Falk) are brought together when their children are engaged and the hapless dentist finds himself unexpectedly plunged into a wild adventure in a corrupt Central American dictatorship. Directed by Arthur Hiller, the pairing of Arkin and Falk is bright and the comedy frequently hilarious. Some comic violence and a few mild vulgarities. A-II (PG)

Innerspace (1987) Martin Short is the victim of industrial espionage as he tries to safely return the miniaturized capsule floating through his body and piloted by Dennis Quaid to the lab which created it. Madcap comedy from director Joe Dante falls short of large laughs but has some genuinely charming, albeit dumb, moments of clean fun. A-II (PG)

Innocence Unprotected (1971) Yugoslavian director Dusan Makavejev's 1968 work is a documentary about the making of the first Serbian talking feature (done in 1942 under the nose of the Nazis). The central figure is acrobatic strongman Dragoljub Aleksic, a national hero whose feats of strength have to be seen to be believed. Makavejev captures the warmth and vitality of the 1942 filmmakers so that his movie becomes a commentary on society's changing values with a nostalgia for the innocence that is missing from our own "enlightened" times. A-II (nr)

Innocent, The (1979) Italian director Luchino Visconti's last movie tells of a turn-of-the-century Roman aristocrat (Giancarlo Giannini) who makes no secret of his infidelities to his wife (Laura Antonelli) until she pursues an affair of her own which has tragic consequences. Although the feel for the period and place is assured, the suicide of a major character is completely unmotivated. Extravagant, at times ludicrously so, use of nudity. O (R)

Innocent Bystanders (1973) Substandard British spy movie in which an aging agent (Stanley Baker), in order to save his job, has to find a scientist escaped from a Siberia camp before other agents bring him in. Peter Collinson's awkward direction highlights the story's violence, sadism and cynical view of humanity. Particularly distasteful is a just off-screen torture sequence involving Geraldine Chaplin. O (PG)

Inserts (1976) There are fitful glints of serious intent amid the dreary chaos of this vulgar, pretentious movie about a once-brilliant Hollywood director (Richard Dreyfuss) reduced to making stag movies. Though Dreyfuss gives a convincing portrayal of a man bored with himself, director John Byrum has made nothing of consequence out of the movie's vulgarities and considerable nudity. O (X)

Inside Daisy Clover (1966) Cute 15-year-old starlet (Natalie Wood) is exploited by suave 1930s Hollywood producer (Christopher Plummer). Though it has its moments, director Robert Mulligan's oft-told story of the empty lives of media stars is itself empty, if not dull. Mature themes. A-III (br)

Inside Moves (1980) Director Richard Donner's melodrama is set in a neighborhood bar patronized by men who have physical disabilities but who team up to help each other. Crippled John Savage regains his love of life and helps a buddy (David Morse) go on to play pro basketball. Some rough language and crude sexual references mar an otherwise articulate story about regaining one's self-esteem. A-III (R/PG appeal)

Inspector Clouseau (1968) Miscast Alan Arkin gamely plays the role Peter Sellers made his own but is let down by an unfunny script and lethargic direction by Bud Yorkin. Those with a taste for simple pratfalls may find some amusement in this crime comedy. A-III (G)

Interiors (1978) Written and directed by Woody Allen, the plot involves three sisters (Diane Keaton, Marybeth Hurt and Kristin Griffith), their mother (Geraldine Page), their father (E.G. Marshall) and his new wife (Maureen Stapleton). Save for the last named, all the rest of the characters are locked in their narcissistic prisons, the exquisite interiors Allen strives mightily to explore, but the dense theme often leaves the viewer staring into space rather than focusing on the profound. The claustrophobic and pessimistic movie communicates a sense of nihilistic ennui. A-IV (PG)

Interlude (1968) Married orchestra conductor (Oskar Werner) conducts both the Royal Philharmonic and an affair with a London reporter half his age (Barbara Ferris). Director Kevin Billington's romantic tearjerker treats adultery as a bittersweet affair. A-III (br)

International Velvet (1978) Lavishly produced and entertaining sequel to the 1944 movie has Velvet (Nanette Newman) living with a writer (Christopher Plummer) and her newly-orphaned niece from America (Tatum O'Neal) who goes on to win the gold medal in the Olympic equestrian competition. Directed by Bryan Forbes, there is a little violence and the unmarried state of the two adults raises questions of propriety for younger viewers. A-II (PG)

Interplay (1970) By the time the long-suffering heroine of this clumsy movie has tried and rejected group sex in affluent suburbia, the hapless viewer has been subjected to a series of immoralities as boring as they are unconvincing. Directed by Albert T. Viola, it is an inept exploitation of contemporary moral confusion. O (X/R)

Interval (1973) Sentimental romance with Merle Oberon as an unattached woman traveling through an amber-colored Yucatan while fending off any number of mature males who become enchanted with her ageless beauty, one of whom (Robert Wolders) finally catches up with her. Aside from some quite pleasant travelogue footage of Mayan ruins, director Daniel Mann's movie is so trite as to be an embarrassment, and all the gauze over the close-up camera lens and the fireworks at climactic moments of passion only serve to emphasize its dated soap opera origins. A-III (PG)

Intimate Lighting (1969) A Prague cellist together with his girl friend returns to his home-town for a few days and stays with a childhood chum and his family. Director Ivan Passer's loving portrait of Czech life, culture and people is done with affection and earthy humor. A-III (nr)

Into the Night (1985) A man (Jeff Goldblum), bored with such problems as insomnia and an unfaithful wife, finds life noticeably more exciting when a beautiful woman (Michelle Pfeiffer) dives into his car with a quartet of assassins in hot pursuit. Crude, unimaginative effort from director John Landis with excessive violence and nudity. O (R)

Invaders from Mars (1986) Inferior remake of the 1953 original about a little boy (Hunter Carson) who tries to warn his parents that their neighbors are being taken over by Martians. Director Tobe Hooper concentrates on the period settings to the detriment of some talented performers (Laraine Newman and Timothy Bottoms). Although the movie resorts to bullets as the answer to a communication problem, the movie is light enough for family entertainment. A-I (PG)

Invasion of the Blood Farmers (1973) Moronic movie about descendants of an ancient Druid cult who depopulate a rural area of upstate New York searching for the perfect specimen whose transfused blood would revive their catatonic queen. Director Ed Adlum's low-budget horror involves a cast of amateurs in excessively gory murders and tortures, with some teasing sexual allusions. O (GP)

Invasion of the Body Snatchers (1979) Mediocre remake of the 1956 thriller in which aliens from outer space take over the identity of earthlings through a pod producing a double of the sleeping victim. Its basic failing is director Philip Kaufman's inability to turn the banal pod people into villains worth rooting against. Donald Sutherland and Brooke Adams try to stem the tide but Kevin McCarthy and Dana Wynter did it better in the low-budget, yet more imaginative original. Some excessive scenes of blood and gore and gratuitous nudity. O (PG)

Invasion U.S.A. (1985) Group of Soviet terrorists sneaks ashore at Miami Beach and proceeds to wreck havoc until stopped by karate champion Chuck Norris and director Joseph Vito's simple-minded script. Unremitting violence. O (R)

Investigation of a Citizen Above Suspicion (1970) Italian drama of a police chief (Gian Maria Volonte) who murders his girl friend (Florinda Bolkan), then leaves a trail of evidence that inescapably reveals his identity. Director Elio Petri's narrative interweaves the investigation of the crime with flashbacks establishing its motivation. The engrossing thriller has many implications about the role of authority in maintaining an ordered society but some may find its realistic scenes of sex and violence rather unsettling. A-IV (R)

Invitation, The (1975) Pleasant little Swiss movie about a shy, awkward bachelor (Michel Robin) who invites his fellow office workers to a Sunday afternoon gathering at his rather plush home. Though everyone gets a little drunk, nothing much really happens in director Claude Goretta's adroitly precise celebration of ordinary people and their mundane foibles. A-III (nr)

Ipcress File, The (1965) Story of spy and counter-spy that amuses as it confuses, deglamorizing the business of undercover work to some extent with humor while the story moves by tricky plot twists, some of which do not bear later examination. Michael Caine is excellent as the uncertain hero and director Sidney Furie holds everything together with a lightly satiric touch. A-II (br)

Iphigenia (1977) Greek adaptation of Euripides' play faithfully retells the story of King Agamemnon (Costa Kazakos) who is told to sacrifice his daughter, Iphigenia (Tatiana Papamoskou), in order to assure safe passage for his fleet to Troy. Considering the difficulties inherent in bringing Greek tragedy to the screen—not just translating one art form to another but overcoming the cultural diversities of two millenia—producer-director Michael Cacoyannis' work represents a considerable accomplishment. Mature theme and some incidental nudity. A-III (nr)

Iron Eagle (1986) Taking seriously his high school commencement speech about accepting adult responsibilities, Air Force brat (Jason Gedrick) steals a Phantom jet fighter and, with a little help (Lou Gossett, Jr.), blasts his way through an unfriendly Arab country to free his captive father. Self-righteous adolescent fantasy directed by Sidney J. Furie justifies excessive violence in the service of youthful idealism. Negative role model and extremely foul language. O (R)

Irreconcilable Differences (1984) Pre-teen girl (Drew Barrymore) sues to be free of her parents (Ryan O'Neal and Shelley Long) who have been driven to distraction by life in the Hollywood fast lane. Some parents may be chagrined over the legal and emotional precedent of the child rights issue, but director Charles Shyer can't choose whether this is light comedy or fairly serious drama. Very brief nudity in a comic context. A-III (PG)

Is Paris Burning? (1966) Rene Clement directs this epic tribute to the French people who fought valiantly to save their city from the senseless destruction ordered by Hitler. In concentrating on the sweep of events rather than on the many individuals involved, the movie is convincing history but fails as human drama. Wartime violence. A-I (br)

Is There Sex After Death? (1971) Writer-director Alan Abel plays a sexologist who, when not attending local patients, roams the country asking pointed questions of people on the street. A few familiar personalities contribute risque routines or scatological interviews but for the most part the porno parade is strictly amateur night. O (X/R)

Isabel (1968) French Canadian story of a young woman (Genevieve Bujold) who returns to a stifling back country environment upon the death of her mother and finds herself unable to escape from her strange family whose history is tied to the land. Written, produced and directed by Paul Amond, it has plenty of lushly beautiful country scenes but its moody, sinister interiors with their turgid, murky implications of incest do not add up to a satisfying experience. A-III (br)

Isadora (see: "The Loves of Isadora")

Ishtar (1987) Warren Beatty and Dustin Hoffman play failed songwriters who find themselves pawns in a dangerously ironic game of international intrigue in director Elaine May's failed buddy comedy set in the Moroccan desert. Essentially a story about the saving grace of brotherly love, the exotic romantic adventure has some rough language, brief slapstick violence and a momentary flash of nudity. A-II (PG-13)

Island, The (1980) Clumsy, brutish thriller about a writer (Michael Caine) and his young son who inadvertently come across the descendents of 16th-century pirates still plying their bloodthirsty trade in the shelter of the Bermuda Triangle. Director Michael Ritchie's fantasy veers wildly between the cruel, ridiculous and downright nasty. Excessive violence, some nudity and profanity. O (R)

Island at the Top of the World, The (1974) Disney version of an Ian Cameron novel about an American archaeologist (David Hartman) and a British adventurer (Donald Sinden) who journey to the Arctic where they discover a tropical island atop a polar ice cap inhabited by the descendents of the Vikings. Directed by Robert Stevenson, it is burdened by a ragged screenplay, some lackluster special effects and many atrocious performances. Harmless family fun, but it could have been so much better. A-I (G)

Island of the Blue Dolphins (1964) The poignant dramatization of the devotion a young Indian girl (Celia Kaye) to her brother and to the wildlife of a small island can be a delightful lesson for children. Produced by Robert B. Radnitz and directed by James B. Clark, the movie captures the wondrous beauty of nature and the creatures that inhabit it. A-I (br)

Island of Dr. Moreau, The (1977) Second screen version of H.G. Wells' novel about a scientist's obsession to turn animals into human beings starts out promisingly enough with a shipwrecked engineer (Michael York) finding himself on a remote Pacific island presided over by a kind but somewhat sinister doctor (Burt Lancaster). Once Moreau's secret is out, however, director Don Taylor's movie degenerates into rather clumsy and ineffective melodrama with considerable violence and bloodshed. The 1933 version with Charles Laughton is the one to see. A-III (PG)

Island of the Burning Damned (1971) Standard British science fiction programmer with Christopher Lee and Peter Cushing combating extraterrestrial beings who invade a country inn. Director Terence Fisher engenders as much suspense as possible with invaders who resemble nothing so much as bubbling, crawling neon pancakes. A-III (GP)

Islands in the Stream (1977) George C. Scott stars as an expatriate American living in the Bahamas who is jolted out of his self-pitying sense of failure as a man and as an artist by the demands of World War II. Franklin Schaffner has directed this adaptation of the posthumous Ernest Hemingway novel with considerable success in focusing upon the interior world of the central character, the prototypical Hemingway hero acting with style under pressure. A-II (PG)

It Happened Here (1966) Imagining what life might have been like if Hitler had succeeded in invading Great Britain is shown in the story of a nurse who is drawn into collaboration with the puppet regime under the German Occupation. Directed by Kevin Brownlow and Andrew Mollo, it is an interesting inquiry into the nature of Nazi totalitarianism, with some scenes of brutality that, though not vivid, are extremely realistic and not for children. A-II (br)

It Lives Again (1978) Cheap and shoddy horror movie about an epidemic of monstrous infants who kill with superhuman force. Director Larry Cohen's blood-and-gore thriller is excessive not only in its concept but also its graphic visuals. O

(R)
It Lives by Night (1974)   When a honeymooning couple (Steward Moss and Marianne McAndrew) run into a bat while frolicking in a Western cave and the husband is bitten, he goes around by night killing people, including the local tourist trade. Directed by Jerry Jameson, it is an innocuous bottom-drawer horror movie but a love scene and some grisly gore make it inappropriate fare for the youngsters. A-III (PG)

It Only Happens to Others (1971)   Written and directed by Nadine Trintignant, this is a very personal movie about the loss of a child (the Trintignant's lost their child when Jean-Louis was filming "Z"). With Marcello Mastroianni and Catherine Deneuve playing the grieving parents, the result is a movie that seems to mourn over the loss of a sweet, precious toy rather than for a human life. The director seems to have kept her own feelings private while distracting viewers with both the luminous personalities of her players and the glossy plastic backgrounds against which they emote. A-III (GP)

It's Alive (1977)   Thoroughly nauseating movie in which a newborn baby turns out to be a bloodthirsty monster who kills some 20 people before the police stop it. Director Larry Cohen is most interested in using gore and graphic brutality for shock value alone. O (PG)

It's My Turn (1980)   Jill Clayburgh plays an intelligent independent woman who meets an outgoing man (Michael Douglas) and knows enough to dump the man she has been living with (Charles Grodin). Director Claudia Weill's attempt at a Tracy-Hepburn romantic comedy lacks the essential chemistry between the principals and its delineation of sexual as well as feminist themes requires a mature perspective. Some rough language. A-III (R)

It's Showtime (1976)   Compilation of excerpts from Hollywood movies whose stars were four-footed, furry, winged or other varieties of the animal kingdom. The clips have charming appeal in their lively and nostalgic remembrance of a time when movies were perhaps less sophisticated, but definitely more fun. Good family viewing. A-I (G)

It's Your Thing (1970)   Produced by brothers Ronald, Rudolph and O'Kelly Isley who also topline the marquee and perform the title number, the movie records a June evening in 1969 when New York's Yankee Stadium shook with the Gospel singers and pop groups who strut and stomp inexhaustibly. Jackie "Moms" Mabley steals the show with a heartfelt interpretation of "Abraham, Martin and John." Some revealing costumes as well as suggestive lyrics and movements. A-III (G)

Italian Connection, The (1973)   German-Italian B-grade gangster movie about a Milan pimp (Mario Adorf) who has been set up by the mob as scapegoat for a missing shipment of heroin sought by two American hit men (Henry Silva and Woody Strode) and the result is endless mayhem and violence. Director Fernando Di Leo punctuates the physical action with lots of sex and nudity. O (R)

Italian Job, The (1969)   Tongue-in-cheek spoof of heist thrillers follows the hijacking of $4 million in gold as it is being transferred from the Turin airport to bank by staging the world's most spectacular traffic jam. Michael Caine organizes the job for mastermind Noel Coward who operates from an English prison. Before director Peter Collinson brings it all to a close with a maniacal, hair-raising

auto chase, there's some good visual satire and a lot of busy acting to make up for the loose ends in the plot. A-II (G)

Italiano Brave Gente (1965)   The plight of Italian soldiers fighting on the Russian front during World War II is portrayed in the fate of four individuals, with Peter Falk and Arthur Kennedy as part of an impressive international cast. Director Giuseppe De Santis' large-scale epic manages to retain some feeling for the human pain of war. Fairly intense battle scenes. A-III (br)

J

Jabberwocky (1977)   British farce inspired by some lines of Lewis Carroll and shaped by the comic spirit of the Monty Python gang tells of a medieval country bumpkin (Michael Palin) who suffers all manner of indignities until he finally becomes a hero by slaying a monster. Directed by Terry Gilliam, much of the humor is of the British bathroom variety, with some comic gore and brief nudity adding up to a movie less offbeat than it is offensive. O (PG)

Jack Frost (1966)   Russian version of the Cinderella story with wicked stepmother, beautiful maid and handsome prince set in a wintry countryside and told with charm. Adults will enjoy the gorgeous scenery, colorful costuming and doll-like performances even if they don't appreciate the old fairy tale as much as the youngsters do. A-I (br)

Jack and the Beanstalk (1976)   Japanese animated musical version of the childhood classic. Its songs are insipid and the animation rather primitive, still it moves along at a lively enough pace and may amuse younger children. A-I (G)

Jack of Diamonds (1967)   Mild suspense thriller about a suave international jewel thief (George Hamilton) who plans a big haul at a posh Bavarian ski resort lodging Zsa Zsa Gabor, Carroll Baker, Lilli Palmer and their jewelry boxes but meets a rival in pretty Marie Laforet who's equally adept at light-fingering the ice. Directed by Don Taylor, it's diverting if familiar entertainment. A-II (br)

Jackson County Jail (1976)   While driving cross-country to a new job, a young woman (Yvette Mimieux) is raped by a small-town sheriff whom she kills in self-defense and then flees with an accused murderer (Tommy Lee Jones). Director Michael Miller conveys with some care and sensitivity a fugitive's view of ruthless authority and the rape scene, though intense, is treated as a repugnant act of violence. A-IV (R)

Jacob the Liar (1977)   East German movie about some Polish Jews forced to serve the Nazis as laborers whose spirits are kept up by reports on advancing Allied troops by one of their number who pretends to have a secret radio. Under Frank Beyer's direction, the acting of Vlastimil Brodsky in the title role helps redeem a somewhat thin story line, though its theme of hope born of invention has universal appeal. Stylized violence. A-II (nr)

Jacqueline Susann's Once Is Not Enough (1975)   Kirk Douglas stars as a washed-up movie producer who marries rich Alexis Smith so he can continue providing motherless daughter Deborah Raffin with a luxurious lifestyle, even though he realizes that his new wife is having a lesbian affair with Melina Mercouri who is sleeping with George Hamilton. Directed by Guy Green, the movie is simple-minded trash whose formula is to reduce every human relationship to its genital components. O (R)

Jacques Brel Is Alive and Well and Living in Paris (1975) Lively, freewheeling collage of bittersweet romantic songs written and composed by Brel makes a charming piece of cabaret entertainment. Directed by Denis Heroux, it has a good cast, including Elly Stone, Mort Schuman, Joe Masiell and, of course, Jacques Brel. A-III (PG)

Jagged Edge (1985) Woman attorney (Glenn Close), defending a client (Jeff Bridges) accused of murdering his wife, begins to fall in love with him while becoming increasingly convinced of his guilt. Director Richard Marquand tries for Hitchcock style suspense but the plot line is implausible and the ending disappointing. Graphic violence, foul language and nudity. O (R)

Jail, The (1974) Documentary, originally aired on public television, takes viewers within the walls of San Francisco County Jail to experience the daily life of the inmates and guards. Filmmakers Michael Anderson, Paul Jacobs, Saul Landau and Bill Yahraus have collaborated in an effort to show that even in a relatively humane prison, keeping people locked away behind bars is an inhuman condition. A-III (nr)

Jail Bait (1977) German movie about a 14-year-old girl who has an affair with a 19-year-old boy, gets pregnant and persuades the boy to kill her father for trying to keep them apart. Director Rainer Werner Fassbinder's unsavory tale about adolescent relationships and middle-class hypocrisy is seriously marred by excessive nudity. O (nr)

Jake Speed (1986) Self-indulgent action-adventure yarn in which a deadpan, not-too-perfect hero (Wayne Crawford) saves a college coed (Karen Kopins) from white slavers. Filmed in Zimbabwe, director Andrew Lane's pulp drama lacks comedic flair which might have saved its stodgy characterizations. Comic book violence. A-II (PG)

Jamilya (1972) Lyric Russian movie evoking the life of a peasant village during World War II in which a 12-year-old parts with his childhood as he witnesses his sister-in-law's clandestine affair with a convalescent soldier and their subsequent flight from her ruthless husband. Director Irina Poplavskaya paints her celluloid picture in predominantly sepia tones reflecting the primitive locale and a people whose personal emotions are habitually overshadowed by communal devotion to duty. A-III (nr)

Janis (1975) Documentary on blues singer Janis Joplin is less a coherent chronicle of a life or a pop music era than an assemblage of available footage, some of it quite elegant, but much rough-edged film clips people were willing to let directors Howard Alk and Seaton Findlay use in their musical portrait. The segments don't add up to a whole person (none of the personal problems that contributed to her death of a drug overdose in 1970 are broached), but it does have some of her finest numbers as seen in performance. Some rough language. A-III (R)

Jaws (1975) Solid thriller about a killer shark first establishes the monster's reality by the effect of its attacks on the tourist trade of a seaside community and then becomes the all-out battle of three men (Roy Scheider, Robert Shaw and Richard Dreyfuss) against a malignant force of nature. Aided by good acting and superior special effects,

Steven Spielberg directs the hunt and killing of the monster with sustained and riveting dramatic intensity. Graphic scenes of the shark attacks may be far too strong for younger viewers. A-III (PG)

Jaws 2 (1978) Roy Scheider re-creates his role of an embattled sheriff pitted against a great white shark in this dull sequel directed by Jeannot Szwarc. Violence, teenage promiscuity and vulgar language. A-III (PG)

Jaws 3-D (1983) This second sequel to the big blockbuster only demonstrates there is a world of difference between technology and creativity. The 3-D effects are really rather effective in a grisly sort of way but the movie itself is slow-moving, talky and generally dull. The big fish inspires little fear, the plot inspires little excitement and director Joe Alves tries to rescue his mediocre effort by emphasizing the violence. A-III (PG)

Jaws: The Revenge (1987) The great white shark tries to eat up the remainder of the Brody family but can't get past Mom (Lorraine Gary). Failed attempt by director Joseph Sargent to milk the suspense and shock of Steven Spielberg's original offers only mild scares for the small fry and dull, repetitive bloody visual effects. A-II (PG-13)

Jazz Singer, The (1980) Neil Diamond stars as the cantor's son who pursues a career in show business, with Laurence Olivier as his grieving father and Lucie Arnez as the woman who promotes the son's career. Director Richard Fleischer's dim, sentimental tearjerker has more cliches than either the 1927 or 1953 versions. A-III (PG)

J.C. (1971) Strange biker movie about an itinerant preacher (William F. McGaha) whose motorcycling congregation share his rootless, searching way of life and return with him to his Alabama home town. Its redneck sheriff (Slim Pickens) torments them and the story quickly resolves itself by violent confrontations ending in death. Also produced and directed by McGaha, the movie may strike some as an interesting parable about an outcast heralding peace, while others will dismiss it as glamorizing an irresponsible vision of life. A-IV (R)

J.D.'s Revenge (1976) The vengeful spirit of a slain hoodlum takes control of a clean-cut black law student who becomes a vicious sadist. Director Arthur Marks' tale of demon possession is a tiresome and disagreeable affair revolving around sex and violence. O (R)

Je T'Aime, Je T'Aime (1972) French movie about a failed suicide (Claude Rich) who agrees to participate in a scientific experiment aimed at sending him one year into the past where he becomes lost in the labyrinth of bits and pieces of his life, centering mostly around the tragic love affair which led to his attempted suicide. Director Alain Resnais dazzles viewers with mental gymnastics and some uncharacteristic humor but this excursion into the memories of a man who has no future is only a minor exercise by a major director marking time. A-II (nr)

Jennifer (1978) Mediocre thriller about a poor girl (Lisa Pelikan) in a posh private school on a scholarship who gets her revenge on the vicious and snobbish girls persecuting her by using her family training in snake-handling. John Gavin and Nina Foch in supporting roles lend whatever dignity there is to director Brice Mack's low-budget effort whose violence makes it adult fare. A-III (PG)

Jennifer on My Mind (1971) Pretentious story

starts with the death of a young woman (Tippy Walker) and then proceeds through flashbacks and tape-recordings to chronicle the life of cute pot-smokers and heroin-shooters. Director Noel Black has rendered something that would have been merely boring as straightforward narrative into something insipid and absurd. Its most serious flaw is a total absence of any perspective, moral or otherwise. A-III (R)

Jenny (1969) Marlo Thomas stars in the title role as a patient, intelligent, resolute girl who intends to keep her baby even though born out of wedlock. She meets and marries Alan Alda, a self-centered filmmaker trying to avoid the draft. Director George Bloomfield's superficial melodrama reverses itself and manages to demonstrate how familiarity slowly leads to mutual respect and responsibility, and ultimately a deep regard and tender affection. A-III (PG)

Jeremiah Johnson (1972) Robert Redford stars in the story of a mountain man from his arrival in the foothills of the Rockies, through his development over several years into a self-sufficient trapper, then as family man and, finally, Crow Indian fighter of legendary proportions. Director Sydney Pollack's story offers the awesome natural spectacle of the mountain locales, the swift frontier violence and action, the intense cultural conflict and interesting characters rendered without the burdens of sentimentality and contrivance. Stylized violence. A-II (GP)

Jeremy (1973) Robby Benson stars in the title role as a shy New York high school sophomore who finds true love with a pretty senior transfer student (Glynnis O'Conner) but they are parted when her father gets his old job back in Detroit. Directed by Arthur Barron, the slickly sentimental tearjerker is so phony in its contrivances that it should make any self-respecting teenager retch. A-III (PG)

Jerk, The (1980) Steve Martin plays a poor sharecropper who goes from rags to riches in a dreary, relentlessly vulgar and foul-mouthed comedy directed by Carl Reiner. Sexual innuendo and racial stereotyping. O (R)

Jerusalem File, The (1972) Idealistic American student (Bruce Davison), against the advice of his college professor (Nicol Williamson) and an Israeli intelligence officer (Donald Pleasence), sets up a tragic meeting between some moderate Arab nationalists and a group of Israeli students. Director John Flynn handles the mechanics of the espionage caper adequately enough but cannot disguise what ultimately is a naive, unnecessarily muddled narrative. A-III (PG)

Jesse James Meets Frankenstein's Daughter (1966) Laughable horror movie in a Western setting and ineptly directed by William Beaudine with an amateur cast. A-II (br)

Jesus (1979) Originally intended for educational purposes, this screen version of the Gospel of St. Luke is more a picture album illustrating the Good News Bible translation than a creative attempt to use the power of the film medium. Directed by Peter Sykes, the presentation is more likely to provoke boredom than stir admiration among young viewers. A-I (G)

Jesus Christ Superstar (1973) Screen version of the Andrew Lloyd Webber and Tim Rice musical adds a completely new dimension and drive to the music by virtue of a cinematography that enhances the original songs but also threatens to overwhelm them. Director Norman Jewison presents a visual recording, with optical embellishment, of a performance of the rock opera based on the last days of Christ's life on earth, ending in his crucifixion. Entertaining as musical theater, it can also be seen as a sincere if naive effort to tell the story of Jesus in contemporary musical and ethical terms. Some scenes require a mature perspective. A-III (G)

Jewel of the Nile, The (1985) Jack and Joan (Michael Douglas and Kathleen Turner) take off in their yacht for the Middle East to rescue a special kind of "jewel" in this disappointing sequel to "Romancing the Stone." The zest of adventure has faded and even the comic touches seem forced in a ponderous plot with endless chase sequences and little suspense. Some mature subject matter and mild vulgarity. A-III (PG)

Jewish Gauchos, The (1976) Entertaining Argentinian movie about a group of Jewish refugees from pogroms in Czarist Russia who settle in the ranchlands of Argentina. A nostalgic version of immigrant history not too far different from our own, it tells the story of how these Jewish gringos become gauchos with robust action, comedy and romance, helped by some lovely songs sung by Ginamaria Hildalgo. Restrained but intense scene of violence. A-II (PG)

Jigsaw Man, The (1984) Laurence Olivier, Michael Caine and Susan George are wasted in a dismal spy movie pitting a Soviet double agent against British Intelligence. Director Terence Young fails to make all the intrigue and plot contrivances of the slightest interest. A-II (PG)

Jim, the World's Greatest (see: "Story of a Teenager")

Jimi Hendrix (1974) Documentary on pop singer Hendrix who died tragically in 1971, ending at age 27 his meteoric rise in the glittering constellation of rock music. An unusual and occasionally profound work assembled by Joe Boyd from mostly familiar footage of Hendrix performances interspersed with interviews and reminiscences of people who were close to him. Some rough language and crude gestures. A-III (R)

Jinxed (1982) Unhappy wife (Bette Midler) of a seedy gambler (Rip Torn) teams up with a blackjack dealer (Ken Wahl) to get rid of her unwanted husband whom the dealer believes is a jinx. Director Don Siegel's attempt at black comedy is an embarrassing, unqualified disaster resorting to vulgarity and profanity as sources of humor. A-III (R)

Jo Jo Dancer, Your Life Is Calling (1986) Richard Pryor directs as well as stars in a tragi-comic story of a comedian on his deathbed, reliving his past, assessing what went wrong and finally affirming the value of his life. Pryor takes some chances, with what many will see as autobiographical material, as he exposes the hurt and anger that was the source of the comedian's personalized brand of humor. Excessive harsh language and some nudity, but utilized as an authentic reflection of the environment in which the action takes place. A-IV (R)

Joanna (1968) Pretentious British movie about a 19-year-old innocent (Genevieve Waite) who comes to London to live with her grandmother and study art but the wrong friends and the urban lifestyle lead her astray. Directed by Michael Sarne, the movie is supposedly about the need for an authentic value system but its graphic sex scenes are excessive. O (R)

Jock Petersen (1975) Australian sex exploitation movie directed by Tim Burstall is distinguished only by some pretty travelogue footage of Quantas-land. O (R)

Joe (1970) Low-budget look at a blue-collar worker (Peter Boyle) whose hatred of hippies leads him to join in the search of an executive (Dennis Patrick) for his lost daughter and in their forays into the youth subculture, they participate in orgies of promiscuity and pot-smoking with tragic results. Written by Norman Wexler and directed by John G. Avildsen, the movie deals with the conflict between rebellious youth and conventional society in terms of stereotypes, yet Boyle's performance as a bigoted hard-hat has a three-dimensional quality. A-IV (R)

Joe and Maxi (1980) Documentary made by Maxi Cohen about her father, Joe, who during the filming learned he was dying of cancer. The result is utterly lacking in style and point of view, raising only questions of the propriety in continuing a project which the dying man insists be stopped. Perhaps it has some educational use in classroom discussions of death and family relationships. A-II (nr)

Joe Hill (1971) Turn-of-the-century labor saga of an itinerant union organizer for the International Workers of the World (I.W.W. or more commonly, the Wobblies), about whom little is known except that he wrote a number of songs popular in the labor movement. Swedish director Bo Widerberg has taken this almost mythical character and fleshed out a personality that is more poetic than real, yet Tommy Berggren's appealing performance as Joe makes credible his dedication to society's unfortunate and downtrodden. A-II (GP)

Joe Kidd (1972) Predictable Western in which an Eastern landgrabber (Robert Duvall), needing to get rid of the Mexican American (John Saxon) standing in the way of his scheme, hires a shiftless gunman (Clint Eastwood) who eventually gets around to seeing that justice is done his way. Directed by John Sturges, the justice-of-the-gun theme is distanced by the Western myth and can be dismissed as simple fantasy. A-III (PG)

John and Mary (1969) Dud melodrama focusing on the relationship between two young singles (Mia Farrow and Dustin Hoffman) after they spend the night together. Director Peter Yates' essay on sexual morality in a liberated age raises questions about love and commitment but capitalizes on nudity and bogs down in endless discussions about sex. O (R/PG)

Johnny Cash: The Man, His World, His Music (1970) Documentary follows Cash on his tours, at home and behind the scenes in warm, intimate sessions with friends and admirers. There is plenty of music for the fans, and its above average production values contribute to an enjoyable and entertaining movie. Some passages of dialogue are not for youngsters. A-II (GP)

Johnny Dangerously (1984) Michael Keaton stars as a man who turns to crime in order to pay for his mother's multiple medical crises. Director Amy Heckerling's spoof of 1930s gangster movies, with Keaton doing a take-off on James Cagney, is defeated by an unfunny script emphasizing vulgar language and sexual situations. A-III (PG-13)

Johnny Got His Gun (1971) Dalton Trumbo directs his own adaptation of his 1938 novel about the hideous ironies of war, specifically the limbless,

faceless, senseless but conscious trunk which is all that remains of a World War I soldier (Timothy Bottoms). The story of an innocent sent out by his elders to make the world safe for democracy is told in straightforward, homey flashback scenes with a warmth and poignance that makes ordinary American life wonderously appealing. It is remarkable for its achievement as a disturbing moral statement about the immorality of war, though many will turn away from its uncompromising treatment. A-IV (R/GP)

Johnny Minotaur (1971) Sojourning on Crete with the intention of making a movie about the myth of the Minotaur, surrealist poet and painter Charles Henri Ford evidently became preoccupied with the shiftless lifestyle of some young Greeks he retained to help with his project. The result is an amateur movie documenting homosexual diversions in graphic detail. O (nr)

Johnny Nobody (1965) Unusual British mystery about a priest (Nigel Patrick) who becomes an amateur sleuth when a writer is murdered in front of him and his entire congregation. Also directed by Patrick, the plot has some some suspenseful twists and the star is quite credible as a clergyman. A-II (br)

Johnny Reno (1966) Low-budget Western ineptly directed by R.G. Springsteen about a sheriff (Dana Andrews) trying to keep a prisoner from being lynched by the townspeople. Stylized violence. A-II (br)

Johnny Tiger (1965) Set in Florida Everglade country is the story of a half-breed Seminole Indian (Chad Everett) and a teacher (Robert Taylor) who tries to help him in a mediocre melodrama directed by Paul Wendkos. Some violence and mature themes. A-III (br)

Joke, The (1970) Czechoslovakian story of a man (Josef Somr), sent to prison and his career ruined for holding political ideas that 20 years later have become fashionable, determines to take revenge on those mouthing the new line as glibly as they had the old. Director Jiromil Jires infused his 1966 movie with a sense of quiet outrage, a sour and acerbic protest against the intolerance of the past and a warning for the present. A-III (nr)

Joke of Destiny, A (1984) Director Lina Wertmuller's satire on modern life and Italian politics is a disappointing misfire. Plodding and heavy-handed, the movie's comic invention fails badly after a brilliant opening. Adult situations. A-III (PG)

Joker, The (1967) British comedy about two brothers (Michael Crawford and Oliver Reed) who concoct a scheme to steal the crown jewels from the Tower of London, but the zany lark gets out of control when one brother double-crosses the other. Director Michael Winner keeps the plot boiling all the time, not in the least concerned that there are a number of gaping holes in it. Viewers who like fast-paced humor won't mind either, especially with the picturesque London setting. A-II (br)

Jonah Who Will Be 25 in the Year 2000 (1976) Whimsical, very talky and coolly-detached movie from Swiss director Alain Tanner about the effects of today's sexual and political upheavals on the lifestyles of several young adults. Its focus is on the future and, as its title implies, it is fundamentally optimistic about people and their ability to survive. Some frank talk about sexual relationships and brief nudity. A-IV (nr)

Jonathan (1973) German horror movie about an

isolated area where Dracula maintains a reign of terror until a student leads the villagers in a raid driving the vampire hordes to their destruction in the sea. Writer-director Hans W. Geissendorfer's plot is secondary to its theme that total helplessness leads ultimately to revolt. Highly stylized but graphic images of the bizarre and the demonic. A-IV (nr)

Jonathan Livingston Seagull (1973) Richard Bach's pretentious little fable about a seagull who makes a number of discoveries, personal and cosmic, has been turned into a big pretentious movie. Director Hall Bartlett's reverential treatment of Bach's jumbled bits and scraps of mystical adages only highlights the weaknesses of the source, an effect helped not at all by the drone of Neil Diamond's uninspired ballads. A-I (G)

Joni (1982) Fact-based story of Joni Eareckson, a talented athlete who breaks her neck a month after graduation from high school and is doomed to a wheelchair for the rest of her life. Director James F. Collier details her fight to rebuild her life and the central part played by her religious conversion. Inspiring and often deeply moving, it is made quite special by Eareckson's performance as herself. Restrained but realistic hospital scenes. A-I (G)

Jory (1972) Dim Western with Robby Benson in the title role as a 15-year-old who witnesses his father's murder, avenges it, repeats the pattern for a friend and gets involved in a range war before riding off into the sunset. Directed by Jorge Fons, the tale of a youth coming to renounce violence by first bathing in blood is familiar to the point of being trite as well as poorly done. Stylized violence. A-II (PG)

Joseph Andrews (1977) Failed British adaptation of Henry Fielding's 18th-century farce about a virtuous servant lad (Peter Firth) beset by lustful females (Ann-Margret among them). Director Tony Richardson offers little more than a tedious and distasteful exercise in period lechery with gratuitous nudity and rough language. O (R)

Joshua Then and Now (1985) Jewish writer (James Woods) from Montreal finds true love in London with a woman (Gabrielle Lazure) who comes from one of Montreal's first families but, upon returning to Canada, their happy marriage threatens to come apart under pressure of their quite different social and religious backgrounds. Directed by Ted Kotcheff, it is an entertaining if uneven and often awkward movie that occasionally presents some serious ideas in provocative fashion. Extremely crude and vulgar language and situations, including brief nudity. A-IV (R)

Journey into the Beyond (1977) Shoddy documentary which purports to be a serious inquiry into life after death is little more than tabloid exploitation of footage that is by turns tedious and revolting. O (R)

Journey of Natty Gann, The (1985) Courageous young girl (Meredith Salenger) searches for her father on a dangerous but wondrous trek cross-country, accompanied by a protective drifter (John Cusack) amidst the political unrest, social upheaval and economic hardship of the 1930's Depression. Though unabashedly sentimental, this Disney movie under the direction of Jeremy Kagan is enjoyable family entertainment, filled with life-affirming people and situations. A-I (PG)

Journey Through Rosebud (1972) Well-intentioned but inept movie about an Indian tribe's refusal to accept U.S. government restrictions on their hunting rights involves a draft dodger (Kristoffer Tabori) who unwittingly causes the suicide of the tribe's demoralized leader (Robert Forster). Written by Albert Ruben and directed by Tom Greis, the movie's attempt to explore the causes of the Indians' bitter behavior gets lost in a welter of history, psychology and contemporary sociology that most will find difficult to unravel. A-III (GP)

Journey Through the Past (1974) Basically a home movie for the fans of rock superstar Neil Young, vaguely structured and larded with interview clips and lots of musical numbers recalling Young's early work with other groups. Its scenes showing his relationship with a screen actress are of dubious taste if not morality. A-IV (R)

Journey to Shiloh (1967) Seven young Texans join the Confederate Army to take part in what they believe will be a grand and glorious adventure, but soon become disillusioned with the war and all but one (James Caan) are killed at the bloody Battle of Shiloh. Directed by William Hale, the melodramatic story is carelessly patched together and ineptly told, especially the badly handled battle action. Violence and a bedroom scene. A-III (br)

Journey to the Far Side of the Sun (1969) Sci-fi melodrama about a deep-space journey to explore a newly discovered planet. Theme contends with dangers of space-age technology. Above average attempt to probe the vast mysteries of new worlds from director Robert Parrish. A-II (G)

Jovita (1970) Polish story of illusion and ennui about a young long distance runner who meets a girl at a masquerade party and, in his attempts to find her again, makes a few self-discoveries along the way. Directed Janusz Morgenstern, the simple romance has a bit of athletics and classical music but is chiefly of interest as one of the last performances of its star, Zbigniew Cybulski. A-III (nr)

Judex (1966) French-Italian action melodrama about a daredevil champion of justice (Channing Pollack) who fights crime in the era just before World War I. Directed by Georges Franju, it will appeal to those who enjoy the innocent adventures of the superheroes of yesteryear. Stylized violence. A-II (br)

Judith (1966) Sophia Loren plays a concentration camp refugee in Palestine after the war who joins an anti-Arab group in order get revenge on her ex-husband (Hans Verner), a former Nazi now working for the Arabs. Directed by Daniel Mann, it is melodramatic hokum, though some may enjoy its picturesque locales and a supporting cast including Peter Finch and Jack Hawkins. Restrained violence. A-II (br)

Judo Saga (1972) Japanese movie about the moral discipline necessary for a student of judo to best the rival followers of jujitsu is set in 1882 when Japan was emerging from feudalism under the Meiji restoration and contrasts the changes of the period with the constant values of a moral code. Directed by Akira Kurosawa in 1943, his first movie already reveals the characteristic narrative style that so distinguishes his later, internationally popular works. A-I (nr)

Juggernaut (1974) Demolition expert Richard Harris tries to disarm seven bombs placed by a madman aboard Omar Sharif's luxury liner carrying some 1200 passengers. Director Richard Lester deftly turns a routine thriller into a grand, fast and suspenseful entertainment. A-II (PG)

Julia (1977) Recollections by writer Lillian Hellman (Jane Fonda) of her friendship with Julia (Vanessa Redgrave), an extraordinary English-woman whose struggle to help Jews and anti-Nazis flee Hitler's Germany ends in tragedy. Directed by Fred Zinnemann, it is rather slow-moving but its good acting and stress on human dignity in the face of inhumanity compensate for its dramatic flaws. A-II (PG)

Juliet of the Spirits (1965) Federico Fellini's first movie in color centers on a middle-aged woman (Giulietta Masina) trying to take stock of her life by sorting through her problems, memories and illusions. Fellini's imaginative imgery and Masina's aging gamin make the reveries and evocations a delight to the eye and the spirit. Ambiguous treatment of mature themes. A-IV (br)

Juliette De Sade (1970) Sex exploitation movie about a young girl's desires to be initiated into a life of unrestricted sex and crime. The plot, dialogue and acting are of poor quality, with no other aim than titillation. O (R)

Julius Caesar (1970) Failed version of Shakespeare's tragedy directed by Stuart Burge with awkward staging, uniformly poor performances (Charlton Heston as Antony and Jason Robards as Brutus) and gauche Roman costuming right out of an Italian muscle movie. Even a desperate teacher, willing to try anything to motivate English students, had best beware this slack effort. A-III (PG)

Jumpin' Jack Flash (1986) Whoopi Goldberg plays a compassionate but fiercely independent computer operator who saves the life of a British intelligence agent trapped in an Iron Curtain country when she communicates with him via computer terminal. Director Penny Marshall's raucous but lighthearted spoof of the spy genre is chilled by an extraordinary amount of sexually derived expletives. A-III (R)

Jun (1980) Japanese movie about a maladjusted Tokyo worker who gives vent to his frustrations by molesting women on crowded commuter trains. Written and directed by Hiroto Yokoyama, its pretentious vision of urban alienation becomes a heavy-handed display of graphic sexual excesses. O (nr)

Jungle Book, The (1967) Rudyard Kipling's adventures of Mowgli, a boy-child reared by obliging wolves in the jungles of India, has been freely but nicely adapted in this animated feature in Disney's best traditions. Using contemporary humor and the voices of Phil Harris as Baloo, a lovable bear, George Sanders as Shere Khan, a suave, menacing tiger and Sterling Holloway as an opportunistic python, the movie will amuse everyone in the household. A-I (G)

Junior Bonner (1972) Aging cowboy Steve McQueen has one big challenge left to meet in the form of a brahma bull that nearly killed him last time around. The film is stolen, however, by Robert Preston as Junior's wild Pa and Ida Lupino as his heartbroken, long-suffering but tough Ma in their superb and emotionally wrenching scenes together. Unlike some of his violent Westerns, director Sam Peckinpah has here devoted his talents to constructing a well-balanced, well-paced and well-acted rodeo movie. A-II (PG)

Jupiter Menace (1983) Narrated by George Kennedy with a straight face, this is one of those psuedo-scientific, quasi-religious documentaries which forecasts the end of the world. It may scare the wits out of those not inclined to take it all with several grains of salt, but then, fear is sometimes good for the soul. A-II (PG)

Just Before Nightfall (1975) French psychological melodrama in which an ordinary man (Michel Bouquet) murders his mistress and then, overcome by guilt, decides to confess but his wife (Stephane Audran) takes steps to prevent him from disgracing the family name. Director Claude Chabrol tells his story of conscience and middle-class morality with one ironic twist after another, confronting viewers with an ambiguous conclusion that implicitly indicts the emptiness of materialistc values. Brief nudity. A-IV (PG)

Just Between Friends (1986) Marital infidelity is the starting point for a seriocomic treatment of the relationship between a naive housewife and an independent career woman. When the man in their lives is killed in an accident, the wife (Mary Tyler Moore) discovers his affair with her friend (Christine Lahti) who is now pregnant with his child. The women ultimately find grounds for reconciliation and mutual support after the baby's birth. Directed by Allan Burns and the sitcom format and soap-opera characterizations offer little inspiration and less justification for a frivolous handling of a serious theme. A-III (PG-13)

Just Like at Home (1979) Hungarian director Marta Meszaros explores the relationship between a precocious 11-year-old girl (Zsuzsa Czinkoczy) and a rash and bedeviled man in his 30s. A flawed but nonetheless absorbing movie, it conveys the somber texture of life in contemporary Hungary. Mature themes. A-III (nr)

Just One of the Guys (1985) An ambitious high school girl (Joyce Hyser) who wants to be a journalist decides that no one takes her work seriously because she's too pretty and so she disguises herself as a boy. Director Lisa Gottlieb's plodding, mediocre comedy has a heavy emphasis on vulgarity and sexually oriented humor. Worse, outright promiscuity is portrayed as perfectly normal. O (PG-13)

Just Tell Me What You Want (1980) Long-time mistress (Ali McGraw) of a greedy tycoon (Alan King) tries to break away by marrying a New York playwright (Peter Weller) and the tycoon's devious efforts to get her back provide the thrust for most of the plot in a sour and vulgar comedy directed by Sidney Lumet. Though it has a lot of action, it has little purpose and no heart. Condones immoral actions and features foul language. O (R)

Just the Way You Are (1984) Crippled musician (Kristy McNichol) goes to bed with a succession of men at home and in the course of a vacation at a Swiss ski resort where she hides her affliction with a plaster cast. Directed by Edouard Molinaro, the dull and listless attempt at light romance takes an entirely benign view of the heroine's promiscuous behavior. O (PG)

Just You and Me, Kid (1979) Retired comedian (George Burns) finds a teenage girl (Brooke Shields) in the trunk of his vintage Pierce-Arrow clad in nothing but an old inner tube. Neither the plot explanation nor the attempts at humor are convincing in director Leonard Stern's generation-gap bore which has some brief laughs from John Schuck and Andrea Howard as nosey neighbors. Some violence and strong language. A-II (PG)

Justine (1969) The last days of the British involvement in Egypt frame this complicated story featuring Anouk Aimee as the somber, crafty medium of the title, Michael York as a spineless schoolmaster and Anna Karina as the tubercular dancer he comes to love. Director George Cukor uses the city of Alexandria to convey the social and moral decadence of the late 1930s. Graphic rendering of homosexuality and excessive use of nudity. O (R)

J.W. Coop (1972) Cliff Robertson plays a rugged rodeo champ fresh out of prison after serving 10 years for forging a check and raring to get back on the circuit to catch up with his life and the times. Also written, produced and directed by Robertson, the success story may be a bit long in the telling but its picture of a man who grits his teeth and gets on with the job of regaining a hold on life provides reasonably intelligent entertainment. Questionable romantic entanglement. A-III (GP)

K

Kaleidoscope (1966) Warren Beatty and Susannah York star in a sophisticated comedy-thriller having to do with the big con games of a gambler on the loose in London and on the Continent. Beatty is miscast as a suave playboy but the largely British cast is excellent, the plot is complicated but director Jack Smight keeps it diverting enough for those who like this kind of derring-do. Moderate violence. A-III (br)

Kama Sutra (1971) Exploitation movie using the Hindu sexual manual as an excuse for graphic sex scenes and frequently ludicrous commentary. O (X/R)

Kamouraska (1975) French-Canadian movie set in the early 19th century in which a passionate and headstrong young woman (Genevieve Bujold) marries the boorish master of a remote estate (Philippe Leotard), leaves him to return to civilization and has a romance with a doctor (Richard Jordan) that ends in murder. Directed by Claude Jutra, the movie captures a vanished era, has excellent acting and the beauty of its settings but its story of hot passion in a cold climate is heavily melodramatic. Some incidental nudity and scenes of questionable taste. A-IV (R)

Kansas City Bomber (1972) Raquel Welch plays a top skater on the Roller Derby scene with Kevin McCarthy as the team owner trying to promote a bigger and better franchise. Burdened with some unconvincing, if decorative, performances, director Jerrold Freedman's inept and shallow melodrama manages to make the Roller Derby look boring. Some rough language. A-III (PG)

Kaos (1986) Comprised of four fables of Italian peasant life drawn from Luigi Pirandello's short stories, this Italian production by the Taviani brothers offers a range of sensitive characterizations expressing simple but profound truths. Each segment is a self-contained tale on a social, political or moral theme. Visually rich and dramatically provocative, the film's life-affirming narrative is well worth its running time of over three hours. A brief shot of partial nudity and a gruesome shot of a decapitated head punctuate an otherwise pastoral vision. A-III (R)

Karado, the Hong Kong Cat (1973) Martial arts champion returns to the island of his birth and finds himself between two opposing factions. Nonstop violent encounters in which everything from chain whips to revolvers come into play, as well as some sex scenes. O (R)

Karate Kid, The (1984) High school student (Ralph Macchio) learns about life, friendship and karate from a kindly Japanese-American gardener (Pat Morita) who shows him how to deal with the bullies tormenting him. Directed by John G. Avildsen, the movie is made extremely appealing by the performances of Morita and Macchio despite its message that violence solves all ills. Parents should be sure that their youngsters realize karate is considerably more lethal than depicted here. A-II (PG)

Karate Kid Part II, The (1986) Repeating his role in the sequel, Pat Morita gives a winning performance as the martial arts teacher who brings his young student (Ralph Macchio) to Okinawa in a gentle story re-affirming the importance of devotion, loyalty and the sweet-and-sour of life as seen from the perspective of old age. Unabashedly moralistic without being didactic, it is high-spirited, engaging entertainment. A-I (PG)

Katerina Izmailova (1969) Russian production of Shostakovich's opera features the performance of Galina Vishnevskaya, first soprana of the Bolshoi. Director Mikhail Shapiro provides a fluid rendering of tragic lovers who resort to murder to preserve their relationship but imprisoned in Siberia, love gradually turns, through mutual recriminations and the man's infidelity, into hatred. Dreary moral tale in Russian with English subtitles. A-III (nr)

Kaya, I'll Kill You (1969) Yugoslavian import conveys the simplicity of life in a pre-war Croatian village and the terror which is unleashed by the emergence of its own home-town fascists inebriated by power. Symbolic narrative set in exotic locales and directed by Vatroslav Mimica makes obscure points about the nature of violence and militarism. A-III (nr)

Kazablan (1974) Israeli musical pits the Sephardim against Ashkenazim in the Jaffa slums of Tel Aviv, telling the story of two lovers from different sides of the ethnic gap. Director Menahen Golan's economy-sized extravaganza of dancing and singing has some natural charm and its salty taunting and gesture is submerged in its theme of finding one's heart by relaxing one's prejudices. A-III (PG)

Keep, The (1983) Nazi unit guarding an ancient fortress in Romania runs into some odd events in this arty, pretentious and thoroughly muddled drama of the supernatural written and directed by Michael Mann, and starring Scott Glenn and Ian McKellan. Vicious rape scene and some graphic sex. O (R)

Keep On Rockin' (1974) Documentary of the 1969 Toronto Rock and Roll Revival features performances by Chuck Berry, Little Richard, Jerry Lee Lewis and Bo Didley. Made by D.A. Pennebaker, the film captures the infectious energy of the performers, and the drive of their music. A-II (PG)

Keetje Tippel (1976) Dutch drama about a 19th-century woman, forced by her mother into prostitution to support the family, who learns from a middle-class lover how to act and dress like a lady, and eventually marries a wealthy social reformer. Director Paul Verhoeven's masterful depiction of the terrible poverty of the working class and their first stirrings of revolt are overshadowed by obsessive detailing and graphic treatment of sexual encounters. O (nr)

Kelly's Heroes (1970) Clint Eastwood and Telly Savalas lead a group of U.S. soldiers (including Don Rickles and Donald Sutherland) 30 miles behind German lines to pull off a gold heist. Directed by Brian Hutton, the movie's premise is that all Germans are stupid, that American pragmatism is invincible and that the realities and deadly rituals of warfare make engrossing entertainment. A-III (PG)

Kentucky Fried Movie, The (1977) Unfunny collection of sketches spoofing television and movies, especially movie trailers. Director John Landis finds vulgarity a proper source of humor but even on a simple slapstick level his satire is often tasteless and sexually exploitive. O (R)

Kes (1970) British movie set in a small, drab Yorkshire coal mining town tells the story of a lonely, sullen boy (David Bradley) whose life is momentarily given meaning by his experience in raising and training a baby kestrel, a European falcon. Directed by Ken Loach, the movie is a compassionate study of the blighted conditions and brutalizing life of this youth which in its final scenes indicates the possibility of his rising above his environment. Fine experience for adults and older adolescents. A-III (PG)

Key Exchange (1985) Young novelist (Ben Masters), unsure of his feelings about a young woman (Brooke Adams), joins a friend (Dan Jenny), whose wife deserted him, in prowling the singles bar jungle before the inevitable happy ending. A very slight sex farce with little wit or charm, directed by Barnet Kellman. Nudity, graphic depiction of sex, benign view of adultery and fornication. O (R)

Khartoum (1966) Exciting action adventure with modern overtones about the British involvement in the Sudan during the 19th-century pits the Empire's most famous general (Charlton Heston) against the ferocious leader of the desert tribes (Laurence Olivier). Directed by Basil Dearden, the movie has the sweep of history and some good characterizations. Stylized violence. A-III (br)

Kid Blue (1973) Petty outlaw (Dennis Hopper) gives up on crime to make his way honestly in the little Texas town of Dime Box, whose single industry is a ceramic novelty factory, finds honesty hard work and decides to rob the factory pay-roll. James Frawley's direction makes the most of the comic potential of an uneven script which stretches to make contemporary references to everything from the drug culture to the plight of the American Indian. Brief but explicit seduction scene. A-III (PG)

Kid Rodelo (1966) Passable melodrama about a drifter (Don Murray) who is forced to protect a young woman (Janet Leigh) from a rough band of former convicts who are looking for gold. Director Richard Carlson moderates the violence in favor of the action adventure. A-II (br)

Kidnapping of the President, The (1980) South American terrorist (Miguel Fernandes), laden with dynamite, handcuffs himself to the President of the United States (Hal Holbrook) but the villains are no match for the head of the Secret Service (William Shatner). Canadian director George Mendeluk's routine suspense thriller features unnecessarily graphic violence in the opening sequence. A-III (PG)

Kids Are Alright, The (1979) Performance and interview film featuring the antics and music of the British rock group, The Who. Director Jeff Stein's poorly organized documentary is marked by very little revelation, some vulgar language and sexual references. A-III (PG)

Kill a Dragon (1967) Run-of-the-mill action adventure movie set in the Orient with contrived plot and unbelievable scenes of bravado. Directed by Michael Moore, it follows a predictable course of sex and violence. A-III (br)

Kill and Kill Again (1981) Martial arts master (James Ryan) is hired to rescue a scientist from the clutches of a villain who wants to control the world in this slapdash, simple-minded melodrama produced in South Africa. Directed by Ivan Hall, the movie's violence is far less fierce than the accompanying grunts and groans. A-III (PG)

Kill Them All and Come Back Alone (1970) Italian Western in which Chuck Conners heads a band of Confederate renegades out to steal gold from a Yankee mining camp. Director Enzo G. Castellari lets the killings run their course until only anti-hero Conners remains. Extreme violence. O (R)

Killer Elite, The (1975) James Caan and Robert Duvall give fine performances as professional assassins working for a secret government agency in a suspense drama directed by Sam Peckinpah. Though flawed and lapsing into melodrama at times, the film raises questions of undercover agencies. Some brutal violence. A-III (PG)

Killer Force (1976) Peter Fonda plays the leader of a raid on the vaults of a diamond mine in South Africa and after much muddlement escapes with the loot. Directed by Val Guest, the plot twists in this movie are so arbitrary that they are not worth following. Excessive gory violence. O (R)

Killer Grizzly (see: "Grizzly")

Killing Fields, The (1984) Powerful and visually overwhelming movie about the friendship of an American correspondent (Sam Waterston) and his Cambodian assistant (Haing S. Ngor) set against the background of the fall of Cambodia and the slaughter of millions by the Khmer Rouge. Director Roland Joffe's fact-based story makes an extraordinary human document. Graphically realistic but not overdone scenes of carnage. A-II (R)

Killing Game, The (1968) Pretentious French murder mystery directed by Alain Jessua has excessive nudity. O (br)

Killing of a Chinese Bookie, The (1976) Owner of a cheap nightclub (Ben Gazzara) undertakes a murder to pay off the gambling debt he owes gangsters. Director John Cassavetes' quest for authenticity and spontaneity takes an indecorous turn down a blind alley at the end of which one becomes sandbagged by sex and violence in a tedious drama that doesn't ring true. O (R)

Killing of Sister George, The (1969) British story about a fading soap-opera actress (Beryl Reid) whose lover (Susannah York) has been seduced by another woman (Coral Browne). Director Robert Aldrich fails to treat lesbianism with any depth, opting instead for heavy-handed melodrama and a rather clinical demonstration of lovemaking with ample peek-a-boo nudity. O (X/R)

Kim (1950) Errol Flynn, Dean Stockwell and Paul Lukas star in this adaptation of the Rudyard Kipling story about an English boy orphaned in 19th-century India. Director Victor Saville manages to give some sense of authenticity to the geographic, social and political texture of an adventure which focuses on themes of honesty and social justice. A-I (br)

King and Country (1966) The court martial and execution of a British deserter during World War I is the grim story told by this impressive indictment of war and its injustices. Tom Courtenay is the passive and withdrawn victim of the military system and Dirk Bogarde plays his sincere but ineffectual defense counsel. Director Joseph Losey's anti-war statement at times stretches for symbols but its sense of moral outrage is perfectly clear. A-III (br)

King David (1985) For half its length, this is a superb biblical film in which the sex, violence and pageantry usually emphasized in this genre do not obscure the central theme of God's intervention in humanity's messy affairs. However, the last half of director Bruce Beresford's work seems badly truncated which, together with a miscast Richard Gere in the title role, make it a severely flawed film, but nonetheless one worth seeing. There is some nudity and considerable violence, but they are subordinated to the theme and not exploitive. A-III (PG-13)

King in New York, A (1957) Produced, written, and directed by Charles Chaplin, the movie is a rather mild satire of the 1950's witch hunts and black listings, as well as some of the foibles in American life. It is a less than profound work but a reminder of a past political hysteria that barred a great comedian from working in America. A-I (G)

King Kong (1977) The Empire State Building and Fay Wray are in no danger of being outdone by the World Trade Towers and Jessica Lange in a moderately entertaining but uninspired remake of the 1933 classic. Director John Guillerman's lack of creative energy contrasts unfavorably with the naive vigor of the original. Some semi-nudity and graphic violence. A-III (PG)

King Kong Escapes (1968) Japanese monster movie directed by Inoshiro Honda has a modern setting but unwisely goes out of its way to try to duplicate a number of sequences from the 1933 original and comes up looking somehat ludicrous. For the undemanding only. A-I (G)

King Kong Lives (1986) After an open-heart operation revives his comatose state, Kong returns to find a mate, father a child and be killed in a better-safe-than-sorry military action. Needlessly detailed and extended scenes of bloodshed, both of the heart operation and fight sequences, and a very suggestive sexual encounter. A-III (PG-13)

King Lear (1971) Director Peter Brook's adaptation of Shakespeare's tragedy is a brilliant, stunning production, almost overwhelmingly powerful, owing to the combined strengths of the bold direction and the brilliance of a cast boasting Paul Scofield as Lear, Irene Worth as Goneril, and Alan Webb as Gloucester. It stands as one of the screen's most striking homages to the Bard of Avon. A-II (GP)

King Murray (1969) Semi-documentary centers on Murray King, an over-bearing, loud-mouthed Long Island insurance agent who caters exclusively to a wealthy clientele. Director Jonathan Gordon's fictionalized reenactment follows King through business deals, lunch breaks and finally a Las Vegas excursion replete with obscene stories and the typical vulgarities of character the film suggests go hand-in-hand with a dehumanizing profession. O (nr)

King of Comedy (1983) Robert De Niro plays an aspiring standup comedian who kidnaps a famous talk show host (Jerry Lewis) in order to obtain an appearance on his show. Director Martin Scorsese transforms an act of desperation into a

black comedy in an offbeat and menacing study of a social misfit. Attempted seduction scene is done with restraint. A-III (PG)

King of Hearts, The (1967) Seriocomic French commentary on the insanity of war makes its point in the story of a sane British soldier (Alan Bates) who happens upon a World War I town taken over by an asylum of lunatics after the townspeople have fled. Directed by Philippe De Broca, its awkward composite of realism and fantasy just barely manages to avoid both sheer comedy and fresh insight. A-III (br)

King of Marvin Gardens, The (1972) Jack Nicholson and Bruce Dern play two brothers who get together for a reunion in wintry Atlantic City to muse about their problems and wander around the near-deserted resort with girl friends (Ellen Burstyn and Julia Anne Robinson) in tow. Directed by Bob Rafelson, nothing much happens but the setting and situation seem to suggest that life is a game, and a fixed one at that. Several sexual scenes. A-IV (R)

King of the Grizzlies (1970) Disney adventure about a 1300-hundred pound mountain bear who roams the Canadian Rockies and his friend, a young Cree Indian of the bear clan, who must choose between his sympathy for the animal and his position as foreman of a cattle ranch. Ron Kelly directs with fine wildlife footage with a mildly dramatic story suitable for youngsters. A-I (G)

King of the Gypsies (1978) Young New York Gypsy (Eric Roberts) is appointed king of the clan by his grandfather (Sterling Hayden), passing over his father (Judd Hirsch) who hires two men to kill him. Sven Nykvist's beautifully photographed vision of a little-known world directed by Frank Pierson conveys a wholly negative portrait of Gypsy life characterized by rough language and brutal violence. O (R)

King of the Mountain (1981) Banal and pretentious movie whose anemic plot concerns the empty-headed romance between a woman singer and a young mechanic who loves to race his Porsche down a treacherous California road. Director Noel Nosseck celebrates the teen obsession with death-defying speed and takes a permissive attitude toward casual sex. A-III (PG)

King, Queen, Knave (1975) Gawky, naive nephew (John Moulder-Brown) is initiated into the ways of love by his earthy aunt (Gina Lollobrigida) while his urbane uncle (David Niven) tends to his own affairs. Director Jerzy Skolimowski turns Vladimir Nabokov's novel into a sex farce lacking in humanity and humor. O (R)

King Rat (1965) Japanese prisoner-of-war camp with George Segal as the American opportunist of the title and James Fox as the British officer who tries to befriend him. Director Bryan Forbes' story of the human spirit under duress does not gloss over the rigors of captivity and its depiction of degradation is strong fare. A-III (br)

King Solomon's Mines (1950) Rousing good version of the H. Rider Haggard adventure saga about an English woman (Deborah Kerr) who hires a guide (Stewart Granger) to search for her lost brother (Richard Carlson) in the African jungle where they also find fabulous diamond mines. Directed by Compton Bennett and Andrew Marton, the picturesque sights and colorful action make this a first-rate family safari. A-I (br)

King Solomon's Mines (1985) Richard Chamberlain stars in an extremely silly action-adventure spoof of the search for King Solomon's fabled diamond mines. Directed by J. Lee Thompson, the movie is not only exceedingly violent but also has unacceptable racial attitudes. O (PG-13)

Kingdom in the Clouds (1971) Rumanian fairy tale about a young man who goes in search of a fabulous kingdom where no one ever grows old, survives various tests on the way and at last wins the hand of the princess of the deathless kingdom. Adequately directed by Elisabeta Bostan, it has colorful characters in picturesque locales that will satisfy younger members of the audience. A-I (G)

Kingdom of the Spiders (1978) Complacent community in Arizona finds itself suddenly besieged by a horde of hungry mutant tarantulas. Director John Cardos's camp chiller features William Shatner and Tiffany Bolling trying to stop the revolt-of-nature nightmare in a fairly routine but mindless entertainment for the undemanding. A-II (PG)

Kings of the Road (1976) German story about a movie projector repairman and a hitchhiker who share their dissatisfaction with contemporary life and search for some way to change things. Director Wim Wenders's exploration of alienation reaches towards positive affirmation about the future. Some matter-of-fact nudity and a scene depicting a bodily function that would affront some viewers. A-IV (nr)

Kipnapped (1972) British adaptation of the Robert Louis Stevenson story of the young David Balfour (Lawrence Douglas) who is rescued from the villainy of his uncle (Donald Pleasence) by Alan Breck (Michael Caine), the heroic Stuart who opposes English rule over Scotland. Directed by Delbert Mann, it is still a classic children's adventure story, though there is some violence that might disturb young children. A-II (G)

Kiss Me Goodbye (1982) Dull, plodding remake of a popular Brazilian sex farce in which an about-to-be-married widow (Sally Field) is haunted by the ghost of her dead husband (James Caan) who tries to scare off the fiance (Jeff Bridges). Directed by Robert Mulligan, the situation is so poorly contrived as to be embarrassing. Restrained sex scene. A-III (PG)

Kiss of the Spider Woman (1985) Brazilian political prisoner (Raul Julia) shares a cell with a relatively flamboyant homosexual (William Hurt) who helps both of them pass the time by giving detailed descriptions of old Hollywood movies. Much musing about politics and sex, about verities of love and of betrayal, but there is not enough intelligence and wit in the script to carry off the high purpose that Argentinian director Hector Babenco obviously had in mind. Mature subject matter. A-IV (R)

Kiss the Girls and Make Them Die (1966) Failed Italian spy spoof about a CIA agent (Michael Connors) on the trail of a power-mad industrialist (Raf Vallone) who has developed a satellite which can render the entire world sterile. Directed by Henry Levin, the result is largely unamusing and mildly sexually suggestive. A-III (br)

Kiss the Other Sheik (1968) Italian sex farce about a husband (Marcello Mastroianni) who sets out to sell his wife to a rich sheik but she winds up selling him into a homosexual harem. Director Luciano Salce's heavy-handed treatment is flat and extremely vulgar. O (PG)

Klansman, The (1974) Adaptation of William Bradford Huie's novel about white-garbed fanatics set upon preserving racial purity by stopping a voter registration rally. Director Terence Young and his cast (Richard Burton, Lee Marvin and O.J. Simpson) can do nothing with a dated scenario placed in a contemporary setting. It is an irresponsible premise for a repellent motion picture that makes rape, castration, murder and racist terror into spectator sports. O (R)

Klute (1971) Taut thriller about a savvy yet pathetic call girl (Jane Fonda) and an unruffled, methodical private eye (Donald Sutherland), whose lives intersect when he comes to New York to search for a missing friend and uncovers a sadistic murderer (Charles Cioffi). Director Alan J. Pakula takes a serious, unflinching view of his characters, their actions and the dark world they inhabit. Challenging subject matter but not treated exploitatively. A-IV (R)

Knife in the Head (1980) Swiss drama in which a totally apolitical scientist (Bruno Gans) becomes the political pawn of leftists and police while recovering from a police gunshot wound which has left him an amnesiac. Director Reinhard Hauff focuses on the man's lonely struggle to regain his identity and personality in an alienated world. Violence and frank treatment of sex. A-IV (nr)

Knightriders (1981) Writer-director George A. Romero's lengthy and overambitious attempt to re-create the Arthurian legend in the saga of a troupe of daredevils who joust on motorcycles instead of horses. The idea is promising and the acting is appealing enough, but the plot is simple-minded at best, with too little action and too much gratuitous sex. O (R)

Kona Coast (1968) Lurid melodrama with Richard Boone playing a brutally vengeful father out to crush the dope peddlers responsible for his daughter's death. The lush Hawaiian setting is the movie's only asset as director Lamont Johnson's treatment of drug trafficking lacks substance and credibility. Tends to condone taking the law violently into one's own hands. O (br)

Kotch (1971) Walter Matthau captures to perfection the eccentric but loveable grandfather who adores children and befriends an unwed teenage mother (Deborah Winters) when his son (Charles Aldman) places him in an old age home. Directed by Jack Lemmon, it's an old-fashioned sentimental melodrama, full of warmth and fun, but avoids some of the serious implications of the situation. A-III (GP)

Krakatoa, East of Java (1969) Lavish disaster movie built around the 1883 eruption of a small volcanic island in the Dutch East Indies features the skipper (Maximilian Schell) of a vessel searching for sunken treasure but also transporting a gang of convicts to an island prison. Directed by Bernard L. Kowalski, the grand scale of the eruption is awesome on the big screen but the cliche-studded story that precedes it is a yawner. Its terribly melodramatic dialogue and some romantic liaisons make it less appropriate for youngsters. A-II (G)

Kramer vs. Kramer (1979) Superficial treatment of child custody battle between angry wife (Meryl Streep) and resentful husband (Dustin Hoffman). Director Robert Benton conveys the tragedy of divorce by putting the emphasis on the father's attempts at parenting but neglects the child's perspective. Some harsh language and a sex scene witnessed by the young child. A-IV (PG)

Kremlin Letter, The (1970) Screen version of Noel Behn's spy novel about a scramble among the world's intelligence agencies to obtain a letter outlining U.S. policy in case of war between Russia and Red China. Director John Huston has fashioned a complex, action-packed and occasionally very cruel and violent Cold War thriller whose twists and turns leave nearly all its characters, which include Patrick O'Neal, Richard Boone, Nigel Green, Dean Jagger, and George Sanders, either murdered or revealed as double or even triple agents. A-III (PG)

Krull (1983) Director Peter Yates cannot quite bring into focus his tale of a mythical land, an enchanted weapon and an evil monster. There are too many characters (a cyclops, a wizard, a spider-woman, a magician, a seer, etc.), too many illogical jumps in the plot and the familiar quest to save a damsel in distress has been done better before by others. A-II (PG)

Krush Groove (1985) Backstage saga of the rap music scene, featuring some dynamic young performers under the direction of Michael Schultz. Disarming and energetic, the movie nevertheless suffers from a weak story line and the very specialized nature of music that is for rap fans only. Some vulgar language. A-II (R)

Kwaidan (1966) Japanese fantasy composed of three ghost stories set in the days of the samurai will engross, if not enthrall viewers. Directed by Masaki Kobayashi, the narratives are so simple, direct and carefully-paced that one is lulled into acceptance of their eerie logic. The stories are by Lafcadio Hearn, an American who went to live in Japan at the turn of the century and wrote many stories based upon their legends and the movie helps one see why he found their culture so fascinating. A-II (br)

L

La Bamba (1987) Pop biographical homage to teenage rock singer Ritchie Valens (Lou Diamond Phillips). Director Luis Valdez sets Valens meteoric success and tragic death against the poverty and oppression of the barrios of Southern California and ethnic bias of middle-class suburbia. Effective study of Valens' struggle against cultural stereotyping and his relationship with his wayward brother (Esai Morales). Scenes of domestic violence, a brief instance of nudity and some profanity are overcome by the film's overall inspirational tone and depiction of positive youthful aspirations. A-II (PG-13)

La Boheme (1965) Puccini's opera as performed on stage by the La Scala Opera company with musical direction by Herbert Von Karajan and stage direction by Franco Zeffirelli. The singing apparently was recorded separately with the result that the excitement associated with a live performance is missing. A-II (br)

La Bonne Soupe (1966) This French movie's graphic portrayal of the details of prostitution is offensive. O (br)

La Cage Aux Folles (1979) Transvestite nightclub owner (Ugo Tognazzi) lives with the club revue star Zaza (Michel Serrault), a situation he wishes to conceal from his son who returns to announce his marriage to the daughter of a sanctimonious town official. A comedy of deceptions and misconceptions, this French farce directed by Edouard Molinaro uses homosexuality as the context for poking fun at moralistic hypocrites, flamboyant transvestites and society in general. A-IV (R)

La Cage Aux Folles II (1981) Sequel to the popular French comedy about a homosexual couple isn't up to the original. But thanks to Ugo Tognazzi and Michel Serrault, re-creating their original roles, director Edouard Molinaro's movie has some diverting moments before getting bogged down in an improbable plot that has the heroes becoming involved in a counterespionage operation. A-IV (R)

La Chamade (1969) Bland, menage-a-trois melodrama with Catherine Deneuve as mistress to both wealthy greying Michel Piccoli and young, handsome and not-so-wealthy Roger Van Hool. Adapted from a Francoise Sagan novel and directed by Alain Cavalier, there is little to recommend in its frothy cliches, stock characters and passionless bedroom scenes but its moral meaning is clear: such vapid relationships are unfulfilling and provide no real meaning or stability to one's life. A-IV (R)

La Chienne (1976) A drab accountant and henpecked husband (Michel Simon) falls hopelessly in love with a crass prostitute who is only interested in getting every cent he has. A familiar story of passion and ruin, the 1931 French production is of interest chiefly for Simon's rich performance and as an example of the early sound work of director Jean Renoir. A-III (nr)

La Collectionneuse (1971) French story of a stuffy young wastrel (Patrick Bauchau) who meets an attractive woman (Haydee Politoff) staying at his friend's country estate, becomes totally infatuated but, in the end, through a quirk of fate and not entirely of his own volition, he rejects her. Director Eric Rohmer's third in his series of "Six Moral Tales" presents a picture of a not very sypathetic male chauvinist who has to rationalize the woman's lack of interest in him. A-III (nr)

La Femme Infidele (1969) French director Claude Chabrol manages to generate suspense with many layers of tension, ambiguity and passion seething under a placid surface. Here he examines the apparently happy suburban marriage of insurance man Michel Bouquet and wife Stephane Audran but the husband's growing suspicions of his wife's infidelity are confirmed and he confronts and kills the other man (Maurice Ronet). Though Chabrol's style is coolly detached, viewers will be caught up in an inquiry into the human potential for evil. A-III (R)

La Fuga (1966) Italian dramatization of the psychiatric treatment of a disturbed 27-year-old wife whose marital problems are related to latent lesbian tendencies. Directed by Paolo Spinola, the effort is well-intentioned but the graphic treatment of several sexual scenes is excessively explicit. O (br)

La Mandragola (1966) Italian adaptation of a Machiavellian satire whose theme is adultery and whose treatment is steeped in prurience and cynicism is unrelieved by any redeeming qualities. O (br)

La Prisonniere (1969) French import about a woman who finds herself first intrigued by, and then hopelessly attracted to an art dealer (Laurent Terzieff) who proves to be a sadistic voyeur incapable of love. Director Henri-Georges Clouzot affects a detached, noncommital attitude toward his subject, forcing viewers to share the voyeurism which his characters are experiencing. O (nr)

La Rupture (1975) Contrived French mystery about a woman (Stephane Audran) seeking a divorce from her deranged husband in order to protect herself and her child without realizing that her rich father-in-law (Michel Bouquet) will stop at nothing to get custody of his grandson. Director Claude Chabrol has used the theme of social decadence and moral corruption to better effect in other movies but this one is little more than an interesting exercise in the modern gothic imagination. A-III (nr)

La Salamandre (1972) Engrossing Swiss drama about the collaboration between a journalist and a fiction writer on a television play based on a recent case of a young woman's shooting of a relative but when they finally meet her (Bulle Ogier) she is too chameleon-like for them to continue the project. Director Alain Tanner's story seems on the surface an amusing anecdote about whether imagination or fact reveals the truth better but underneath is the question of survival in a destructive post-industrial society where by movie's end it is clear that the woman has made the most progress toward self-liberation. Mature themes and treatment. A-III (nr)

La Vie De Chateau (1967) Set in Normandy just before D-Day, the story is about a wealthy orchard farmer (Philippe Noiret), his lively wife (Catherine Deneuve), a lovelorn leader of the Resistance (Henri Garein) and a detachment of German soldiers quartered there. Some haphazard heroics take place on the beautiful old estate before it finally becomes the landing point for Allied paratroopers. A-II (br)

La Visita (1966) Middle-aged spinster (Sandro Milo) uses the personal columns to arrange a meeting with a seemingly eligible suitor (Francois Perier). The day they spend together is both amusing and touching as they come to discover the truth about their personalities. Director Antonio Pietrangeli's seriocomic tale is minor but deftly played. A-III (br)

Labyrinth (1986) Menagerie of muppet goblins and related little folk tries to defer a young girl from solving the puzzle of the labyrinth and saving her infant brother from the snare of the Goblin King (David Bowie). Directed by Muppet-master Jim Henson, the movie is a colorful but overlong intricate visual romp for the young. Some bathroom humor. A-I (PG)

Lacemaker, The (1977) The heroine of Swiss director Claude Goretta's film is an 18-year-old Parisian (Isabelle Huppert) who falls in love with wealthy, educated gentleman (Ives Beneyton) and their relationship results in her mental breakdown. It's a carefully etched melodrama about class consciousness, false impressions and male irresponsibility. A-IV (nr)

Lacombe, Lucien (1974) Excellent French World War II drama about a 17-year-old farm boy (Pierre Blaise) who wants to join the Resistance but, when he is turned down as too young and irresponsible, joins the French collaborators of the local German police. Directed by Louis Malle, the movie succeeds admirably as a chilling story of an immature youth but it also adds considerable insight to our knowledge of the history of this period. A-II (nr)

Ladies and Gentlemen, the Rolling Stones (1975) Pop concert documentary with Mick Jagger and crew at their slightly satanic but self-parodying best. Directed by former ad man Rollin Binzer, it is bright, swift and irresistable for adult rock fans. A-III (PG)

Lady and the Tramp (1955) Walt Disney's animated feature about a cute little cocker spaniel in a Victorian family who loses her place in the couple's affections with the birth of their first child but who is reinstated through the efforts of a freedom-loving mongrel. The cast of lovable dog characters and some delightful songs by Peggy Lee still appeal to youngsters. A-I (G)

Lady Caroline Lamb (1973) Robert Bolt wrote and directed this vehicle for Sarah Miles about a high-born but promiscuous lady who consorts with poets and other male playthings during the early 19th century. Miles' non-acting is complemented by Richard Chamberlain's non-limping parody of Byron, and the sincere efforts of Jon Finch as her stoical husband Willie cannot offset the movie's overall absurdity. Brief nudity. A-III (PG)

Lady Chatterley's Lover (1982) French director Just Jaeckin's skin-deep adaptation of the D.H. Lawrence novel, with Sylvia Kristel and Nicholas Clay, is a dulling exercise in commercial eroticism. Graphic sex. O (R)

Lady Frankenstein (1972) When her fanatic father (Joseph Cotton) dies at the hands of the demented creature he created, his daughter (Sara Bey) vows to create a perfect superman to destroy her father's murderer. Unfortunately in this Italian penny-dreadful directed by Mel Welles, she has to seduce her subjects for surgery and graphic sex sequences only detract from the blood-drenched horror fantasy. O (R)

Lady Ice (1973) Middling diamond heist caper in which an insurance investigator (Donald Sutherland) gets involved with a diamond fence (Jennifer O'Neill) and a hard-bitten U.S. Justice Department agent (Robert Duvall) who adds a bit of class but his scenes get lost in the shuffle. Directed by Tom Gries, the complex, and at times, confusing plot doesn't add up to much. A-II (PG)

Lady in Cement (1968) Frank Sinatra gets involved in the murder of a woman in the title but director Gordon Douglas provides neither credibility nor atmosphere in the rambling, loosely plotted proceedings that create an ersatz excitement only by resorting to brutal violence and some sleazy sexual distractions. O (R/PG)

Lady in the Car with Glasses and a Gun, The (1970) Failed mystery thriller in which Samantha Eggar takes a holiday drive in the South of France and, after a number of puzzling incidents happen to her, she discovers a body in the trunk of the car she got from her boss (sinister Oliver Reed). Director Anatole Litvak goes overboard trying to create some suspense but the result of all his efforts is no more than pure cleverness and empty contrivance. Some adult mayhem. A-III (R)

Lady Jane (1986) The innocence and altruism of youth are contrasted with the deceit and treachery of the adult world in this period drama about the religious power struggle following the reign of King Henry VIII. Its romantic treatment of adult themes contains a brief scene of nudity and a brutal scene of flogging. A-III (PG-13)

Lady L (1966) Tasteless British comedy set in 1920's Europe stars Sophia Loren and under Peter Ustinov's direction is excessive in its sexual emphasis. O (br)

Lady Liberty (1972) When Sophia Loren flies into JFK Airport to rejoin her fiance, she has a 20-pound mortadella sausage under her arm and the crisis this causes at Customs promises one of those coarse peasant comedies the Italians do so well. Unfortunately, director Mario Monticelli presents a freak show of grisly New York stereotypes in a cynical blend of contempt, distrust and generally low opinion of humanity. A-IV (PG)

Lady of Monza, The (1970) Sordid Italian melodrama supposedly based on a 17th-century incident in which the lover of a Spanish nun was beheaded and she was walled up alive. Directed by Eriprando Visconti, the movie's production values are as minimal as its ludicrous nude love scenes. O (R)

Lady on the Tracks, The (1968) Czechoslovakian musical fantasy about a lady streetcar driver in Prague (Jirina Bohdalova) who mounts a campaign for women's rights when she discovers her husband's love affair. Directed by Ladislav Rychman, its musical numbers are done in 1930's Hollywood style and the result is a warm and humorous tale of one woman's dreams of glory. A-II (br)

Lady Sings the Blues (1972) Diana Ross stars as Billie Holiday in a screen biography that reduces the famous singer's life to a series of cliches and soap opera theatrics. A very good performance by Ross can't save director Sidney J. Furie's failed movie. Rough language and sordid situations. A-IV (R)

Lady Yakuza (1974) Japanese gangster movie in which a young woman (Junko Fuji) takes over the leadership of a gang after her father's murder and ultimately is able to avenge his death. Directed by Kosaku Yamashita, there is plenty of violence but used within a context of group loyalty and personal friendship. A-III (nr)

Ladyhawke (1985) Medieval sword-and-sorcery epic looks beautiful but tells a silly story of a curse which changes two true lovers into a hawk (Michelle Pfeiffer) and a wolf (Rutger Hauer). Directed by Richard Donner, it is rife with bad dialogue, bad acting and anachronisms. Aside from some violent swordplay, it is innocuous. A-II (PG-13)

L'Amour (1973) Andy Warhol's counterculture denizens flutter around Paris in this generally vapid put-on which Warhol co-directed with Paul Morrissey. In tune with Warhol's philosophy, the camerawork is grainy, the color is anemic and the parade of verbal and visual vulgarities is constant. O (R)

Lancelot of the Lake (1975) French director Robert Bresson takes the Arthurian legend and interprets it in austere realistic fashion, focusing on the decline of the Knights of the Round Table after their failure in the quest of the Grail. His treatment purges the legend of its magic and romance, searching for some historical substance which for some will have more interest than the story. Some realistic violence. A-III (nr)

Land Raiders (1970) Telly Savalas plays a loud, overbearing rancher who stirs up trouble with a local Indian tribe, is discovered to have killed his brother's girl and gets his just desserts when the Indians go on the warpath. Directed by Nathan Juran, it's a poorly done Western with some gory violence and sexual references. A-III (PG)

Land That Time Forgot, The (1975) Doug McClure, John McEnery and Susan Penhaligon are among the survivors of a World War I U-boat attack who find themselves in a strange land filled with prehistoric beasts. Routine British fantasy adventure directed by Kevin Connor. Restrained violence. A-II (PG)

Landlord, The (1970) Rich young man (Beau Bridges) becomes a ghetto landlord in some vague hope that by renovating a decaying Brooklyn brownstone, tenanted by justly suspicious blacks, he can rebuild his empty life. Directed by Hal Ashby, the seriocomic drama has some good performances (Diana Sands and Lou Gossett) and lyric photography but lacks depth and coherence. Interesting failure with some mature themes. A-IV (R/PG)

Landscape after Battle (1978) Polish drama directed by Andrzej Wajda is a compilation of short stories by Tadeusz Borowski, survivor of Auschwitz and suicide victim. Some brief nudity, but the somberness of the theme makes this a movie for mature viewers. A-III (nr)

Language of Love (1971) Swedish exploitation import is a crudely done series of demonstrations of sexual techniques that will offend any who consider sex a private human expression of love rather than a perfectable mechanical task. O (nr)

Las Vegas Hillbillys (1966) Ferlin Husky comes out of the hills and gains success in Las Vegas in a mindless story directed by Arthur C. Pierce. A-I (br)

Lassiter (1984) Tom Selleck stars as a womanizing detective forced to become a spy in this espionage thriller directed by Roger Young and set in London just before World War II. Lauren Hutton is the German Mata Hari with a kinky appetite for blood, sex and brutality. Violence and nudity. O (R)

Last Adventure, The (1968) Episodic French movie about the comradeship between two men (Alain Delon and Lino Ventura) and a young woman (Joanna Shimkus) with the trio winding up on a dangerous search for sunken treasure. Directed by Robert Enrico, the emphasis is less on their adventures than on the qualities of loyalty and respect that keep the three together. A-II (br)

Last American Hero, The (1973) Story of champion stock-car driver Junior Johnson (Jeff Bridges) who evolved from running corn whiskey over the backroads of North Carolina to earning $100,000 a year racing cars. Directed by Lamont Johnson, the movie's gritty atmosphere is evoked beautifully, supported by a fine cast (Art Lund, Geraldine Fitzgerald, Gary Busey and Ned Beatty). A-III (PG)

Last Days of Man on Earth, The (1977) Failed British satire set against the background of a post-nuclear disaster in which a group of scientists led by a ruthless woman (Jenny Runacre) force a brilliant young man to help them in an attempt to create a new breed of superhumans. Directed by Robert Fuest, the exotic settings are far more interesting than the action occuring in them. Excessive nudity. O (R)

Last Detail, The (1974) Career sailors (Jack Nicholson and Otis Young), assigned to escort a young seaman (Randy Quaid) to the Marine brig, stop off along the way to give him a last fling, which proves to be his first. Directed by Hal Ashby, it is fairly consistent but very coarse adult entertainment. Brothel scene with brief nudity and unrelenting flow of rough language are part of the movie's apparent definition of manliness. A-IV (R)

Last Dragon, The (1985) A kind of black Kung Fu movie that doesn't take itself too seriously.

Although it has a banal story line about a good martial arts expert vanquishing a nasty one, director Michael Schultz is helped out by lively high-spirited performers. Some restrained violence and vulgar language. A-II (PG-13)

Last Embrace (1979) Florid melodrama directed by Jonathan Demme about a government agent (Roy Scheider) who has a mental breakdown after his wife is killed in a shootout in which he inadvertently involved her. A mysterious graduate student (Janet Margolin) is somehow involved in a flimsy plot loaded with red herrings. Generous doses of brutality and sexual scenes. O (R)

Last Escape, The (1970) Stuart Whitman leads an Allied operation in the final months of World War II to smuggle a leading rocket scientist out of war-scarred Germany while the Russians are attempting to do the same. Director Walter Grauman compensates for an obvious script and wooden acting by a lot of wartime action scenes with remarkably little bloodshed. A-II (G)

Last Flight of Noah's Ark (1980) Elliott Gould agrees to fly missionary Genevieve Bujold and a menagerie of domestic animals to a South Pacific island but, when the plane crash lands, they discover two child stowaways (Ricky Schroder and Tammy Lauren). Directed by Charles Jarrott, the Disney production is disarming and has a light-hearted grace that is irresistible. Appealing fare for young and old. A-I (G)

Last Grenade, The (1970) British agent Stanley Baker tramps up and down the hills bordering Hong Kong in pursuit of Alex Cord, a grinning sadist working for the other side. Director Gordon Flemyng's chase story, in which an adulterous affair plays a part, doesn't make much sense and the movie is a dud. A-III (M)

Last Hard Men, The (1976) Ugly, distasteful Western about an escaped convict (James Coburn) who is determined to get revenge upon the retired sheriff (Charlton Heston) who put him in jail. Coburn manages to be interesting and Michael Parks contributes a few bright moments, but all director Andrew V. McLaglen's movie really has on its mind is the usual rape and other brutalities that go with simple-minded debasements of the Western myth. O (R)

Last House on the Left, The (1972) Two teenagers (Lucy Grantham and Sandra Cassel) are kidnapped, tormented, raped and slaughtered while a foolish sheriff bungles his investigation and the parents of one girl take their own brutal revenge. Written and directed by Wes Craven, this lurid movie indulges in gore, sex and profanity. O (R)

Last Married Couple in America, The (1980) George Segal and Natalie Wood begin to doubt the validity of their own relationship when the marriages of all their friends shatter around them. Directed by Gilbert Cates, it is a clumsy, shapeless affair, poorly scripted and badly acted. Some nudity and a great deal of foul language. O (R)

Last Metro, The (1981) Uninvolving wartime melodrama directed by Francois Truffaut about a harried actress-theater manager (Catherine Deneuve) who tries to keep her theater open and her Jewish husband (Heinz Bennent) hidden during the German Occupation of Paris. It is a romantic and sophisticated production lacking depth and passion. Adultery figures in the plot. A-III (PG)

Last Movie, The (1971) Failed story about the bizarre and tragic effects a movie company has on

a community of primitive Peruvian Indians whose village they use as a location. Directed by Dennis Hopper, who also stars, the movie's concept is an intriguing one that, unfortunately, is not realized in a work totally out of control with incredible lapses of logic and jumbled time sequences. Graphic scenes of sexual encounters and a demeaning attitude toward Indian culture and religious beliefs. O (R)

Last of Sheila, The (1973) Film producer (James Coburn) invites some friends (Richard Benjamin, Joan Hackett, Dyan Cannon, James Mason, Raquel Welch and Ian McShane) for a week's cruise in the Mediterranean celebrating the first anniversary of the hit-and-run killing of his wife, whose name graces both the yacht and the movie's title. Director Herbert Ross is so busy being slick and clever in his parody of Hollywood types, that he creates an elaborate hoax rather than a plausible whodunit. A-III (PG)

Last of the Mobile Hot-Shots (1970) Failed screen version of a play by Tennessee Williams presents a muddled and superficially symbolic story of Southern racial attitudes involving James Coburn, Robert Hooks and Lynn Redgrave. Directed by Sidney Lumet, this talky affair has an excess of crude dialogue and several unnecessarily explicit sex scenes in the flashbacks. O (X/R)

Last of the Red Hot Lovers (1972) Failed screen version of the Neil Simon comedy about a man (Alan Arkin) who uses his unsuspecting mother's apartment for sex in the afternoon. Directed by Gene Saks, it tries desperately to be amusing but, except for the occasional one-liner, it is boring when it's not irritating in its search for euphemisms for sin. A-III (PG)

Last Picture Show, The (1971) Bleak picture of life in a dust-stricken and culturally depressed little town in 1951 Texas. Director Peter Bogdanovich captures brilliantly the banal details of time and place but they have more interest in themselves than the drama which unfolds in the foreground. The town's inhabitants are presented as a hopeless lot whose only interests are sexual experimentation (treated quite graphically) and the pursuit of TV soap-opera and quiz-show fantasies. There's more to life than that, even in a small town. Brief nudity. O (PG)

Last Rebel, The (1971) Joe Namath smirks his way through a puerile Western as an ex-Confederate adventurer who shoots up a few rivals, hustles some local pool sharks and makes merry with ladies high and low. Director Denys McCoy's movie has crude language, stylized violence and brief nudity, but its major offense is being so witless and dull that an adult will find it hard to sit through. A-III (GP)

Last Remake of Beau Geste, The (1977) Witless and boring spoof of a classic adventure movie stars Ann-Margret and Michael York who are less embarrassing to watch than the struggle of a cast of comedians in the clutches of a dreary script. Director Marty Feldman relies almost solely on vulgar sight gags and crude humor to keep the French Foreign Legion afloat. A-III (PG)

Last Resort (1986) Charles Grodin takes his movie family on an island resort vacation in this failed satire about the crude excesses of the travel business. The sex maniacs who run the resort manage to corrupt the middle-class values of mom, dad and the kids in this unfunny farce obsessed with crude sexual innuendo and sight gags, the drug-and-booze culture and profanity. O (R)

Last Romantic Lover, The (1979) French sex farce begins with a male beauty contest sponsored by a women's magazine and ends with the runner-up romancing the supposedly liberated woman editor with such old-fashioned techniques as tenderness. The movie is directed by Just Jaeklin with all the gloss and glamour that he learned as a fashion photographer. Except for some partial nudity, it is a throwback to an earlier age of sexual comedy that feminists may find more objectionable than moralists. O (R)

Last Run, The (1971) George C. Scott plays an old-time professional getaway driver hired to break-out a young convict (Tony Musante) and he handles all the ensuing ambushes, chases and double-crosses with credible assurance. Directed by Richard Fleischer, the flawed narrative is of less interest than Scott's bravura performance. Some violence and sexual references. A-III (GP)

Last Safari, The (1967) Mediocre British adventure directed by Henry Hathaway with Stewart Granger as a safari guide. The original version featured extensive nudity which was edited out of the American release. A-I (br)

Last Shot You Hear, The (1969) Unintriguing thriller dealing with a renowned marriage counselor (Hugh Marlowe) who, after refusing to give his wife a divorce, is murdered by her lover. Director Gordon Hessler's movie concludes fatuously attempting to elicit sympathy for the murderers. O (PG)

Last Starfighter, The (1984) High school senior (Lance Guest), a whiz at electronic games, finds himself defending the frontiers of the universe against ruthless space invaders in a touching, romantic, humorous fantasy from director Nick Castle. Some of the violence might be too much for younger viewers. A-II (PG)

Last Summer (1969) Suntanned teenagers (Richard Thomas, Bruce Davison and Barbara Hershey) exploring adolescent limits of mutual trust and confidence and the tragic destruction of a self-possessed young girl (Kathy Burns) form the background and structure of the movie. Director Frank Perry's vision of upper-class youths contending with their curiosity about each other's physique and psyche features a terrifying rape sequence in which the antics and silliness in the first part of the film turn to dread. Though its use of nudity is questionable, this journey of sorts into self-discovery is a provocative examination of physical and spiritual maturation. A-IV (X/R/GP/R)

Last Tango in Paris (1973) Middle-aged man (Marlon Brando), numb with despair at the suicide of his wife, happens upon a woman (Maria Schneider) inspecting a vacant apartment, and they immediately engage in sex. She returns again and again to the apartment for further encounters but when he eventually proposes marriage, she runs away and in pursuing her he is killed. Directed by Bernardo Bertolucci, the romantic twaddle about tortured, alienated people adds up to very little and the sex scenes, while not pornographic are needlessly extended and explicit. O (X/R/X)

Last Tycoon, The (1976) Uninspired film version of the unfinished F. Scott Fitzgerald novel about an Irving Thalberg-like producer (Robert De Niro) who slowly works himself to death. Despite the handsomely mounted production, director Elia Kazan runs out of creative ideas of what to do with

a cast (Robert Mitchum, Jeanne Moreau and Tony Curtis) seemingly adrift in the setting. Occasional rough language and an overextended nude sequence. A-IV (PG)

Last Unicorn, The (1982) Animated feature about the last unicorn (voice of Mia Farrow) which goes off in a quest to find out what happened to the others of her kind. The voice-over talent (Alan Arkin, Angela Lansbury, Keenan Wynn, Christopher Lee and Tammy Grimes) is superb and the plot itself is likeable enough. Though the animation is not very imaginative, younger children will find it pleasant fantasy. A-I (G)

Last Valley, The (1971) Omar Sharif plays a man of letters fleeing the 17th-century wars of religion and nationalism in the Germanies who takes refuge in an out-of-the-way, untouched village but soon it is also found by a band of freebooters (led by Michael Caine). Written, produced and directed by James Clavell, it is of more historical than dramatic interest and its scenes of mass slaughter and individual cruelty coupled with the moral ambiguities of life under duress make it decidedly mature fare. A-III (GP)

Last Waltz, The (1978) This is a cinematic record of the last concert given by a rock group called The Band. Supplemented by interview footage and some numbers shot in a studio, director Martin Scorsese has put it all together extremely well, but its appeal is obviously limited to rock fans for the most part. Some coarse language and an amoral attitude on the part of some of the performers. A-III (PG)

Last Wave, The (1979) Serious and reserved Australian lawyer (Richard Chamberlain) defends four aborigines accused of tribal murder but a mysterious tribal seer divines that the lawyer is the precursor of some cycle-ending event of cataclysmic proportions. Director Peter Weir's movie strongly evokes a sense of the aborigine's transcendental link with nature in stark contrast to the sterile materialistic environment of the city in which the trial takes place. A-III (PG)

Last of the Renegades (1966) Routine European-made Western directed by Harald Rinl is an old-fashioned cowboy and Indian movie with Lex Barker and Anthony Steel trying to avert an Indian war while both pursue the same Indian maiden (Karin Dor). Stylized violence. A-I (br)

Last of the Secret Agents?, The (1966) Stupid undercover spoof directed by Norman Abbott features the tiresome slapstick antics of comics Marty Allen and Steve Rossi. Overemphasis on the sexually suggestive. O (br)

Late Autumn (1973) Fine Japanese drama made in 1961 about a young woman who rejects marriage because she does not wish to leave her widowed mother alone but the mother tricks her into getting engaged. Director Yasujiro Ozu lightens the mood with some gentle humor, especially pointed at insufferable male smugness in a society in which women are dependent upon men. A-I (nr)

Late Great Planet Earth, The (1979) Screen version of a book proving the imminent destruction of earth using prophecies from the Old and New Testament is a mishmash of interviews with experts of greater and lesser authority, portentous narration and stock newsreel footage, with a touch of pseudo-biblical drama thrown in. Its distorted idea of the nature and purpose of biblical prophecy makes it unsuited to young and impressionable viewers. A-III (PG)

Late Liz, The (1973) Anne Baxter plays a hard-drinking woman who sifts through multiple marriages and attempted suicide before salvation into her through the guidance of a local clergyman. Directed by Dick Ross, its rather bogus sentimentality and adult situations make it adult fare. A-III (GP)

Late Show, The (1977) Art Carney as the aging private eye (who spends most of his time watching old movies on television) feels compelled to solve the murder of his old partner (Howard Duff) who shows up on his doorstep with a fatal bullet wound. Lily Tomlin teams up in the sleuthing and the result is an above average crime entertainment directed by Robert Benton. Occasional violence and crude language. A-III (PG)

Late Spring (1972) Japanese story of a dutiful daughter who refuses to leave her widowed father until he finally is forced to trick her into marriage. Director Yasujiro Ozu's 1949 movie is a lyric study of the abiding strength of family life and relationships, warmly told and universal in its values. A-I (nr)

Latitude Zero (1970) Japanese science fiction movie with Joseph Cotton and Cesar Romero pitted against each other as the classic counterparts of good and evil. Directed by Inoshiro Honda, an underwater outing in the Jules Verne vein, grotesque monsters, and some excellent miniature work make it a must for sci-fi fans. A couple of grisly scenes are inappropriate for small children. A-II (PG)

Laughing Policeman, The (1973) Detective thriller about a brutal mass murder on a San Francisco bus that veteran detective Walter Matthau pursues because his partner is one of those killed and the clues point to a previous unsolved murder case. There's the basis for a good yarn here, but director Stuart Rosenberg puts too much emphasis on violence, crude language and an exploration of the city's tawdry side. O (R)

Laughter in the Dark (1969) British drama about a man of some intelligence and breeding being destroyed by his infatuation for an unscrupulous schemer. The performance of Nicol Williamson, as the titled art dealer victimized by a dreadful cinema usherette (Anna Karina) is skillful, and Tony Richardson's direction evidences serious intentions, but the cumulative effect is merely ludicrous with more than a little nudity and explicit depiction of sex. O (X)

Laurel and Hardy's Laughing Twenties (1966) Retropective look back at the great comedy team of Stan Laurel and Oliver Hardy in a collection of excerpts from their silent two-reelers. The narrative is helpful and the sight gags irresistible. A-I (br)

Law and Disorder (1974) A taxi driver (Carrol O'Connor) and a hairdresser (Ernest Borgnine) form a number of their New York neighbors into an auxiliary police force to put a stop to an invasion of muggers, thieves and exhibitionists. Directed by Ivan Passer, there is some sharp satire on contemporary urban crime and middle-class frustrations. Some intense violence, very rough language and a number of embarrassing sexual references. A-IV (R)

Lawman (1971) Straight-shooting marshal Burt Lancaster attempts to round up seven murder suspects in a town where long-time sheriff Robert Ryan has learned to compromise with local cattle baron Lee J. Cobb. The situation results in bloodshed with justice depending upon the fastest, surest gun. Director Michael Winner seems to have pretentions about examining what or who is the law but the conclusion solves nothing. Stylized violence and bloodshed. A-III (GP)

Lawrence of Arabia (1962) Set within the frame of a grand adventure is an interesting study of a 20th-century mythic hero, T.E. Lawrence (Peter O'Toole), whose World War I exploits in leading the Arabs against the Turks made his literary works popular in the 1920s. Director David Lean focuses on the diverse aspects of the man with a suitable ambiguity true to the mystery that still surrounds this figure. Bloody wartime battles and implication of a homosexual incident. A-II (G)

Lawyer, The (1970) Routine crime melodrama in which a hotshot lawyer (Barry Newman) races around California in his beat-up camper trying to get his client, philandering Dr. Jack Harrison (Robert Colbert), off the hook for murdering his wife. Directed by Sidney J. Furie, it contains frequent nudity and crude dialogue. O (R)

Le Beau Mariage (1982) French comedy of manners and morals from director Eric Rohmer proves to be an amusing yet perceptive exploration of courtship rituals and mating practices not far different from our own. Its young heroine (Beatrice Romano), fed up with the complications of her affair with a married man, decides to get married and sets out to find her own husband. The result is a comedy of situations seen from a feminine perspective. A-III (PG)

Le Boucher (1972) Excellent psychological thriller about a schoolteacher (Stephane Audran) and the butcher of the title (Jean Yanne) who live in a small French village where a series of insane murders have taken place. Written and directed by Claude Chabrol, the script is marvellously tight and disciplined and the characterizations have an unusually solid psychological foundation. There are some shocks but they are done with all the authority of the old master, Hitchcock himself. A-III (GP)

Le Chat (1975) French study of a couple (Simone Signoret and Jean Gabin) who have been married for 25 years but whose ardor has cooled and turned to rancor. Directed by Pierre Granier-Deferre, the script is one of unrelieved bleakness, yet the two principals invest their roles with a rich human dimension as two imperfect individuals who stubbornly go on, fueled by hate, but they sometimes remember love. A-III (nr)

Le Depart (1968) Belgian story of an assistant hairdresser (Jean-Pierre Leaud) who is so obsessed with the idea of entering an upcoming motor rally that he neglects his girl friend in trying to find a suitable car. Director Jerzy Skolimowski treats his self-indulgent youth with stinging humor but also with some sympathy. A-III (br)

Le Magnifique (1976) Jean-Paul Belmondo stars in a failed satire of superspy adventures of the James Bond variety. Forgettable French production directed by Phillipe de Broca. A-III (nr)

Le Mans (1971) Steve McQueen combines his acting and racing skills in a convincing portrait of a driver in the famed Le Mans competition in France. Directed by Lee H. Katzin, the drama is on the track and racing fans will find much satisfaction in the authenticity of the driving and in the beauty of the machines A-I (G)

Le Petit Theatre de Jean Renoir (1969) Three short nostalgic sketches present a Christmas fantasy, a wildly funny opera-bouffe and a tribute to the French game of boules. A charming interlude, sung by Jeanne Moreau, complements this homage to life by director Jean Renoir who introduces each of his tales with an unpretentious explanation of his reasons for bringing it to life on film. Lovely, quaint and sentimental by turn, but with some mature themes. A-III (nr)

Le Retour D'Afrique (1973) Swiss drama about a young couple who decide to join a friend in Africa to help fashion a better world. After a final farewell party, a telegram arrives from their friend telling them not to come and that the explanation is in the mail. Awaiting the letter in their empty flat, they begin to confront themselves and their relationship to society. Director Alain Tanner's theme of real change coming only from within is a bit pretentious and stilted, yet it does raise questions about coping in a post-industrial society. A-III (nr)

Le Sex Shop (1973) Unfunny French sex farce about the owner of a failing book store (Claude Berri) who opens a shop selling erotic books and related mechanical contraptions and then becomes obsessed with his merchandise and starts experimenting. Also written and directed by Berri, what might have been a satire on contemporary sexual mores itself becomes obsessed with the subject and the explicit nature of its treatment is at best tasteless and at worst grossly offensive. O (X/R)

Le Trio Infernal (1974) Failed French black comedy depicting the moral bankruptcy of society following World War I, the plot details the murder-for-profit of two German sisters (Romy Schneider and Mascha Gomska) by a French war hero (Michel Piccoli). Directed by Francis Girod, what begins as a Gallic sex farce soon becomes mired in details of ghoulish dismemberments and bizarre sex. O (nr)

Leadbelly (1976) Screen biography tracing the troubled life of neglected Huddie Ledbetter, legendary black folk singer and master of the twelve-string guitar whose work became part of the post-World War II folk renaissance. Director Gordon Parks downplays the racial themes in favor of a musical tribute while eliciting a colorfully authentic performance from Roger E. Mosley as Huddie. A-III (PG)

Learning Tree, The (1969) Director Gordon Park's lifeless cinematic version of his autobiographical novel is a highly romantic, colorful recreation of a black adolescent's coming-of-age in a mixed atmosphere of gentleness and violence, honesty, hypocrisy and bigotry. The result has more a sense of a photographic essay than of a realistic portrait of the rural black experience. A-III (PG)

Leather Boys, The (1966) British story of a failed marriage with Rita Tushingham as a teenager who weds to escape her appalling home, Colin Campbell as the immature husband and Dudley Suttton as his calculating friend. Though the episodic story is loosely motivated, the acting is first-rate and Sidney Furie's direction has the ring of authenticity. A-III (br)

Legacy (1976) Middle-aged woman (Joan Hotchkis) is too busy to notice that she is on the verge of a breakdown in director Karen Arthur's attempt to turn a myriad of feminist themes into a movie. Her treatment of a woman's repressed sexuality and guilt feelings about her life might have some use for women's discussion groups but not as a popular entertainment. O (R)

Legacy, The (1979) Inferior horror movie of the satanic, let's-make-a-deal sub-genre depicts the misadventures of a bright, unmarried young couple (Katharine Ross and Sam Elliot) in a Gothic English manor. Directed by Richard Marquand, the story is extremely silly and excessively gory. O (R)

Legal Eagles (1986) Robert Redford tries his best to be funny, charming and resourceful as the lawyer whose political ambitions get sidetracked when two women, a lawyer (Debra Winger) and her client (Daryl Hannah), implicate him in an art fraud that turns into a murder case. Director Ivan Reitman's shallow comedy is marred by female stereotyping and casual sex. A-III (PG)

Legend (1986) Director Ridley Scott's sumptuous fairy tale contrasts exceptionally cruel evil with extraordinarily sweet innocence in a quest to redeem a frozen world from the control of the Lord of Darkness. Tom Cruise is the hero who vanquishes the devil (Tim Curry) in an astonishing visual delight but some instances of grotesque imagery, especially the Lord of Darkness may frighten very young children. A-II (PG)

Legend of Billy Jean, The (1985) Four teenagers unwittingly become outlawed folk heroes. The value system represented is so confused that the movie is inappropriate for its intended adolescent audience. Some vulgar language. A-III (PG-13)

Legend of Boggy Creek, The (1973) Little town in Arkansas is bothered by a hairy monster, with a dubious footprint or two as evidence of its existence. In the fictionalized speculations about the monster's attacks, an actor made up with a lot of hair is photographed from the rear and sides in shadowy condition; he is as skillful at evading pursuing dogs and townsmen as he is the camera. A-I (G)

Legend of Hell House, The (1973) Good British horror movie in which a skeptical physicist (Clive Revill), his wife (Gayle Hunnicutt) and two mediums (Pamela Franklin and Roddy McDowell) attempt to unravel the source of the ghastly murders that occurred when a previous group of scientists attempted to penetrate the mysteries of a deserted gothic mansion on the outskirts of London. Directed by John Hough, it has plenty of atmosphere, not a little suspense but also some intense violence and a suggestion of perverse sexuality. A-III (PG)

Legend of Lylah Clare, The (1968) Sudsy, sentimental soap opera in which a young starlet (Kim Novak) is coached by a has-been movie director (Peter Finch) who exhibits untoward interest in her that leads to tragedy. Directed by Robert Aldrich, it's a clunker with sexually suggestive scenes. O (R)

Legend of Nigger Charley, The (1972) Runaway slaves (Fred Williamson, D'Urville Martin and Don Pedro Colley) are pursued by a bloodthirsty slave-tracker (Keith Prentice). Directed by Martin Goldman, the mindless action movie indulges in some foul language and incidental nudity. A-IV (PG)

Legend of the Lone Ranger, The (1981) Klinton Spilsbury plays the masked champion of justice who, with the aid of Tonto (Michael Horse), rescues President Grant (Jason Robards) from the clutches of a badman (Christoper Lloyd). While moderately entertaining, director William A. Fraker's Western has considerable violence and occasional rough language. A-III (PG)

Lenny (1974) Screen version of Julian Barry's

play about comic Lenny Bruce's problems with drugs and obscenity prosecution of his routines takes a semi-documentary stance by way of interviews with Bruce's widow, mother, agent and others. Bob Fosse has directed an intelligent, complex and often disturbing film, with Dustin Hoffman extraordinarily fine in the title role. No viewer should be surprised to hear a good deal of crude language. A-IV (R)

Leo and Lorrie (1980)   A young actor and actress (Danny Most and Linda Purl), struggling for fame in television, fall in love, and encourage and console each other in this featherweight romantic comedy directed by Jerry Paris. The unabashed approval of unmarried co-habitation has enough substance to be morally offensive. O (PG)

Leo the Last (1970)   The title character (Marcello Mastroianni), the last of an exiled European royal line, lives in the elegant family mansion in the heart of London's West Indian ghetto. When Leo realizes that the family fortune depends entirely on the rental income from these ghetto flats, he leads a peasant's revolt to blow up his mansion. The final frames show those who took part milling aimlessly around the rubble, wondering along with the audience what purpose director John Boorman's symbolic gesture served. Several relatively graphic sex scenes. A-IV (R)

Lepke (1975)   Crime melodrama about a top Jewish member (Tony Curtis) of Murder Incorporated who has the unenviable distinction of being the only upper-echelon gang leader to suffer capital punishment. Directed by Menahem Golan, the problem of working up sympathy for a ruthless criminal, though a dedicated family man, is not surmounted by the talents involved. The treatment is restrained except for one excessive scene combining both sexuality and violence. O (R)

Les Biches (1968)   Corruption is the theme of this subtle French production about the complicated relationship between a man and two women. Director Claude Chabrol is above all a moralist in telling the story of an innocent artist destroyed by the lavish excesses of wealthy society. Its context is psychologically ambiguous and seemingly amoral and it ends in an outburst of madness. Chabrol's work raises questions about life rather than resolves them and for this reason will not be very satisfying for the casual filmgoer. Others, however, will find it a thoughtful experience. A-IV (br)

Les Enfants Terribles (1975)   Jean Cocteau's story about the perennial revolt of youth against all that established society represents was brought to the screen in 1950 by director Jean-Pierre Melville. A remarkable achievement in many ways, some of its themes of alienation and self-destruction are troubling and even anarchistic but serve as a reminder that life is not as tidy and rational as one might wish. A-IV (nr)

Les Gauloises Bleues (1968)   While his wife is giving birth in the hospital, the husband (Jean-Pierre Kalfon) waits, his thoughts of his own unhappy childhood and troubles as a young man. Written and directed by Michel Cournot, the surrealistic flow of these memories reflect the man's insecurity about himself and his relations with others, but many viewers will be put off by the obscurity of much of it. A-III (G)

Les Violons du Bal (1974)   French director Michel Drach has constructed a film-within-a-film dealing with the various problems he encountered in making a feature based upon his World War II memories of a Jewish childhood. The essential merit of this work lies in its strong evocation of the love uniting a family caught up in the terrors of the Nazi era. It succeeds admirably as a fragmentary remembrance of a child's struggling to cope with events beyond his comprehension. A-III (nr)

Less Than Zero (1987)   Failed cautionary tale about the terrible consequences of the drug scene for three bright high school students in an affluent California community. Director Marek Kanievska spends most of his energies depicting the high gloss drug scene so that none of the main three earn viewer sympathy or interest. Several excessive scenes of simulated sex and a pervasive atmosphere of the sordid depths of the drug culture. O (R)

Let It Be (1970)   Filmed practice session of The Beatles as they rehearse various songs and clown around a bit. Directed by Michael Lindsay-Hogg in semi-documentary fashion with no real focal point or direction, but does give an interesting and informal low-key look behind the scenes. A-I (G)

Let Joy Reign Supreme (1976)   French director Betrand Tavernier details the abuses of the aristocratic regime that led to the French Revolution. Philippe Noiret, Jean Rochefort and Jean Pierre Marielle tend to get lost in a narrative preoccupied with noblemen's debauchery and clergymen's corruption in a manner closer to the excesses of sex farce than historical drama. O (nr)

Let the Good Times Roll (1973)   Director Sid Levin's documentary shows the story of the Golden Age of Rock, and does it with a dazzling array of stars and an extraordinary balance of intelligence, artistry and warm good humor. Stars Chuck Berry, Little Richard, Fats Domino, Chubby Checker, Bill Haley and the Comets and Bo Diddley. A-II (PG)

Lethal Weapon (1987)   Mel Gibson is a deadly effective Los Angeles cop almost psychotically ruthless in getting his job done. He's teamed with a veteran policeman (Danny Glover) whose family is threatened by drug dealers headed by a former Vietnam Special Forces and CIA operative. Gibson's square-jawed version of a legalized Rambo and Richard Donner's powerfully frenetic direction festers with excessive violence, brutality and profanity. O (R)

Let's Do It Again (1975)   Sidney Poitier (who also directed) and Bill Cosby play two lodge brothers from Atlanta who, in order to get money for a new meeting hall, get involved in a prize fight and the gangsters who go with it. Once the situation is set up, the comedy begins to flag and the gags become repetitious. It would be fine for children except for two sequences involving illicit lovemaking and an off-color verbal exchange. A-III (PG)

Let's Kill Uncle (1966)   Offbeat British thriller about a young boy (Pat Cardi) who finds out his uncle (Nigel Green) is plotting to murder him and so contrives with his girl friend (Mary Badham) to kill uncle. Produced and directed by William Castle, Green is excellent in the preposterous situation but children may find the suspense a bit too intense. A-II (br)

Let's Scare Jessica to Death (1971)   Zohra Lampert plays a young woman who goes to a remote farmhouse to recover from a nervous breakdown only to find herself beset with eerie voices from beyond the grave. Unpretentious little horror movie directed with some intelligence by John Hancock. Some instances of sudden, graphic

159

violence. A-III (GP)

Let's Talk about Men (1976) Italian director Lina Wertmuller's 1965 movie with four vignettes depicting the foibles of the male gender is a moderately entertaining parable with Nino Manfredi playing five roles that humorously contrast definitions of manhood. A-III (PG)

Letter to Brezhnev (1986) Two tough working-class girls in Liverpool search for romance and a way out of the narrow confines of their dull lives. This uncompromisingly realistic but lighthearted slice-of-life comedy, directed by Chris Bernard, features Peter Firth as a Russian sailor who provides a possible new direction for one of the girls (Alexandra Pigg). Harsh language and sexual innuendo. A-III (R)

Lianna (1983) Young wife (Linda Griffiths) falls in love with another woman (Jane Hallaren) and impulsively abandons her philandering husband and two children only to find that she has traded one set of problems for another. Written, produced and directed by John Sayles, it is a sensitive account of a lesbian relationship but lacks any but the most rudimentary of moral perspectives. Graphic and unnecessarily extended love-making sequence. O (R)

Liberation of L.B. Jones, The (1970) Melodrama about the determined efforts of an upright black undertaker (Roscoe Lee Browne) to get a divorce from his unfaithful wife whose lover happens to be the white deputy of the little Tennessee town in which they live. Though perhaps overlong and cluttered with subplots, director William Wyler tells his story of racial justice in straightforward and dignified fashion. A-III (R)

Libertine, The (1969) Young widow (Catherine Spaak) avenges her late husband's sexual indulgences by experimenting with a host of graphically portrayed sadistic perversions. Posing as a spoof of exploitation films, this Italian sex farce from director Pasquale Festa-Campanile succumbs to the same indecent cliche it has chosen to mock. O (X)

Libido: The Urge to Love (see: "The Sensuous Teenager")

Lickerish Quartet, The (1970) Producer-director Radley Metzger's dreary sex melodrama is set in a decaying Italian castle occupied by a decadent husband, wife and son who spend their time watching porno movies and having sex with a house guest (Silvana Venturelli). O (R)

Lies My Father Told Me (1975) Warm, lyric picture of a boy's growing up in Montreal's Jewish ghetto with a careful exploration of the customs and values of a ritualistic culture. Directed by Jan Kadar, it is a delicate poem about being Jewish and, at the same time, about being human. Some sexual elements make it mature fare. A-III (PG)

Life and Times of Grizzly Adams, The (1976) Dan Haggerty stars as a late 19th-century trapper who lived with and befriended the animals of the Rocky Mountains. Directed by Richard Friedenberg, the movie is less a story than an occasion to show sun-drenched photography of picturesque landscapes and frolicsome animals that will appeal to very small children and undemanding adults. A-I (G)

Life and Times of Judge Roy Bean, The (1972) Director John Huston has a great deal of fun with this seriocomic tale of frontier justice as administered by the legendary "hanging judge" of Vinegaroon, Texas (Paul Newman). Some viewers, how-

ever, may not be as readily amused by its loud, coarse and bawdy humor or repetitive use of fantasy violence. A-III (PG)

Life at the Top (1966) Laurence Harvey continues his callow progress in a sequel to "Room at the Top." Directed by Ted Kotcheff, the movie's realistic treatment of his groping for some kind of personal integrity in a rootless and corrupting society will seem excessive to some. A-IV (br)

Life, Love, Death (1969) French director Claude Lelouch examines the apprehension, trial and execution of a murderer (Amidou). The drama indicts capital punishment suggesting that it dehumanizes those who demand it, and especially, those who carry it out. Coldly intellectual, his treatment responsibly distances the viewer from a subject easily sensationalized. A-III (R)

Life, Loves, and Operas of Giusepppi Verdi, The (1974) Mediocre European dramatization of Verdi's career with Tito Gobbi and Mario Del Monaco appearing in excerpts from his major works. The production is lavish, the personal dimension is not interesting but the music is for all who love opera. A-I (nr)

Life of Brian (1979) Monty Python movie about a hapless fellow named Brian, a contemporary of Jesus, who is mistaken for the Messiah and eventually crucified by the Romans. The nihilistic, anything-for-laughs thrust of director Terry Jones's comedy deliberately exploits much that is sacred to Christian and Jewish religious tradition. Especially offensive is the mocking parody of the crucifixion scene. O (R)

Life Study (1973) Low-budget feature directed by Michael Nebbia tells the story of a girl chasing a reluctant boy encompasses 30 years of screen cliches done with such awkward sincerity as to evoke laughter in all the wrong spots. A-IV (nr)

Lifeforce (1985) Vampires from outer space wreak havoc in director Tobe Hooper's disjointed sci-fi end of the world movie which tries to sell itself by exploiting sex, nudity and gore. O (R)

Lifeguard (1976) This is a paean to arrested adolescence, an uninspired soap opera on the beach. Director Daniel Petrie's bland, morally insensitive account of the growing pains of a 32-year-old lifeguard (Sam Elliot) is sheer male romanticism with a dash of nudity. A-III (PG)

Light at the Edge of the World, The (1971) Brutal adaptation of a Jules Verne story about a lighthouse keeper (Kirk Douglas) whose rock-ribbed Cape Horn isle is invaded by blood-thirsty pirates (under Yul Brynner) who, after impaling Douglas' co-workers, hack apart the hapless passengers aboard the first ship they manage to drive upon the rocks. Samantha Eggar is preserved, however, for a series of fates worse than death. Produced by Douglas and directed by Kevin Billington, it's literal visualizations of violence are excessive. O (GP)

Light of Day (1987) A brother-sister music team (Michael J. Fox and Joan Jett) have their self-centered attitudes toward life changed when faced with the death of their mother (Gena Rowlands). Awkward but naturalistic portraits of misdirected young adults in this film spotted with rough language are somewhat elevated by Rowlands' exquisite cameo performance. A-III (PG-13)

Lightship, The (1986) Obscure drama centered in a contest of wills between a Coast Guard skipper (Klaus Maria Brandauer) and a Southern con man (Robert Duvall) who needs the skipper's boat to make a getaway. Aiming at a parable about freedom and determination, the movie has a dark and foreboding air, some explicitly violent murders and some harsh language as it builds up to an abrupt and muddled conclusion. A-III (PG-13)

Lily in Love (1985) Stage actor (Christopher Plummer) disguises himself to get the romantic movie role for which his screenwriter wife (Maggie Smith) thinks he's entirely unsuited and she begins falling in love with her husband's new persona. Witty, sophisticated comedy from Hungarian director Karoly Makk, it's a game of who's playing a trick on whom. A-II (PG-13)

Limbo (1972) Sincere tearjerker based on the stateside emotional and financial hardships of a group of Vietnam POW-MIA wives (Kathleen Nolan, Katherine Justice and Kate Jackson). Despite its obvious melodrama, director Mark Robson makes the situation ring true much of the time by showing the human side of women trying to keep their family and emotional lives intact without any certainty about their husbands or the future. Nolan's performance, strong yet vulnerable, is worth seeing. Mature themes. A-III (PG)

Limelight (1952) Written, produced and directed by Charles Chaplin, the story is about a World War I music hall comic (Chaplin) who helps a ballerina (Claire Bloom) but its importance resides in the light it casts on Chaplin as an artist and a man. It is deeply steeped with Victorian sentimentality and is centered in a naive belief in nature's goodness, something modern audiences will have to conjure with but something which is sincere, deeply felt and enduring. Well worth seeing. A-II (G)

Limit, The (1972) Yaphet Kotto gets in over his head as writer, director, and star in a film about a Los Angeles cop having trouble justifying his job and the special demands it makes on him because he is black. As a director, Kotto is unable to overcome the insurmountable problems of an underdeveloped script and an obviously bargain-basement budget. Some mature themes. A-III (PG)

L'Immortelle (1969) Director Alain Robbe-Grillet's existential love story set in Istanbul about a man who dies trying to unravel the mystery behind the woman he loved and lost in a car accident. Narrative unfolds jumping back and forth in time and space in an attempt to make a cinematic (and philosophical) comment upon the nature of illusion and reality. An exercise for film buffs and poets. A-III (nr)

Lincoln Conspiracy, The (1977) Revisionist account of Lincoln's assassination alleges that Secretary of War Stanton and other high officials were involved in the plot directed at the President. As history, the movie relies upon still questionable documentation. As entertainment, director James L. Conway's stiff, instructive treatment would be more suited to a slide lecture. A-II (G)

Lion Has Seven Heads, The (1974) Brazilian production about African neo-colonialism and revolution told not in narrative form but through a series of highly stylized scenes conveying various forms of social, economic and ideological exploitation. Directed by Glauber Rocha, one may object to some of the excesses in imagery, but there is no question it does contribute a sense of the revolutionary ferment in underdeveloped parts of the world. A-IV (nr)

Lion in Winter, The (1968) Toward the end of her life, Eleanor of Aquitane (Katharine Hepburn) engaged in a running duel with her husband, Henry II of England (Peter O'Toole), over which of their sons should ascend the throne. Director Anthony Harvey does not allow history to get in the way of the principals whose performances make absorbing entertainment. Adult themes. A-III (PG)

Lion of the Desert (1981) Director Moustapha Akkad's homage to Libyan hero, Omar Mukhtar (Anthony Quinn), who defied Mussolini's forces for 20 years until his capture and execution in 1931. Some of the desert battle scenes and those involving Italian reprisals are both extremely violent and poorly staged. A-III (PG)

Lion's Love (1969) French director Agnes Varda's homage to and criticism of the Hollywood ethos is little more than a series of cameos with show business types and pop art personalities who seem terribly phony trying to act genuine. The amoral lifestyle espoused by its principals severely limits the movie's appeal and acceptability. O (nr)

Lipstick (1976) Lamont Johnson directs this tawdry melodrama in which a woman (Margaux Hemingway), after being raped by a man who is freed and later attacks her younger sister (Mariel Hemingway), takes justice into her own hands. Exploitation of serious social problems offers only violence and brutality instead of insight. O (R)

Liquidator, The (1966) British spy thriller directed by Jack Cardiff about a tough intelligence agent (Rod Taylor) assigned to liquidate a number of folks the agency considers to be security risks. One of them is Jill St. John, and this complicates things, much to boss Trevor Howard's dismay. Routine action movie with stylized violence. A-III (br)

Listen, Let's Make Love (1969) Inept Italian soap opera directed by Ferdinando Scarfiotti purports to describe the pitfalls and insecurity of a young gigolo enmeshed in the opulent decadence of Milanese society. Excessive sexual depictions. O (R)

Lisztomania (1975) Ken Russell directs an extravagant tribute to composer Franz Liszt whom he presents as a 19th-century pop star (Roger Daltrey) whose concerts are mobbed by shrieking teenage girls who teeter on the verge of hysteria whenever his fingers touch the piano keys. Though there is much here that is good, funny and on-target, the movie flounders in excesses of every variety, most frequently sexual. O (R)

Little Ark, The (1972) Director James B. Clark tells the story of two children (Philip Frame and Genevieve Ambas) who are separated from their parents during the 1953 floods in northern Holland. It has an intelligent message about human community but the children face some intense dangers best left unexperienced by small children. A-II (G)

Little Big Man (1970) Dustin Hoffman as the sole survivor of Custer's Last Stand relives the story of his life and times on the frontier. Although not tightly conceived or executed, director Arthur Penn's large canvas provides a major overview of the Old West and its conflicts between Indians and pioneers. A-III (GP)

Little Cigars (1973) Sadistically abused woman (Angel Tompkins) takes refuge with a group of midgets in a traveling side show where she runs an aphrodisiac candy bar, while having an affair with the head midget (Billy Curtis). Directed by Chris

161

Christenberry, it is an utterly cruel and tasteless movie, with the worst big-woman, little-man joke ever devised. O (PG)

Little Darlings (1980) Silly but nasty little movie wasting the talents of young Kristy McNichol and Tatum O'Neal in a story that has to do with a group of girls at a summer camp making a bet that places loss of virginity into the category of a competitive sport. Besides some distasteful visuals and offensive language, director Ronald F. Maxwell's movie condones immoral behavior despite some moralistic hedging at the end. O (R)

Little Drummer Girl, The (1984) Lackluster screen adaptation of the John Le Carre novel about an actress (Diane Keaton) recruited by Israeli agents to trap a terrorist. Director George Roy Hill appears unconcerned for politics, characterization or moral details. Considerable violence, some nudity and rough language. A-III (R)

Little Fauss and Big Halsy (1970) Routine motorcycle-racing movie that dotes upon the idiosyncracies of one of its stars (Michael J. Pollard) and the good looks and sexual prowess of the other (Robert Redford). Sidney J. Furie directs an undistinguished clunker which has a permissive attitude toward casual sex. A-IV (R)

Little Girl Who Lives Down the Lane, The (1977) Jodie Foster plays a mysterious, self-sufficient 13-year-old in a Maine village who is befriended by a teenage boy (Scott Jacoby) and threatened by an unstable adult (Martin Sheen) because she has something to hide. Pat, unbelievable Canadian melodrama directed by Nicholas Gessner, the movie condones teenage promiscuity and makes an adolescent the object of sexual titillation. O (PG)

Little Miss Marker (1980) Adaptation of the Damon Runyon story about a six-year-old (Sara Stimpson) who is left as security (a marker) for a bet with a bookie (Walter Matthau). Although director Walter Bernstein's reliance upon one-liners keeps the movie lively and his treatment of the romance between Matthau and Julie Andrews is light, the original 1934 version remains unequalled by this remake. Occasional rough language. A-II (PG)

Little Mother (1973) Exploitative fictional life of Eva Peron hypothesizes a woman's rise to power in Argentinian politics through the use of her body and various forms of murder, torture and brutality. Director Radley Metzger's ridiculous sexual obsessions will satisfy neither voyeurs nor students of Latin American politics. O (R)

Little Murders (1971) Screen version of Jules Feiffer's black comedy about an apathetic man (Elliott Gould) who is awakened to a need for personal relationships by an aggressive young woman (Marcia Rodd) but when she is senselessly murdered by a sniper, he joins in the insanity that surrounds him. Directed by Alan Arkin, the film's object apparently is to sensitize its audience to the alienation of urban life by shocking it with sudden violence and a barrage of profanity. Viewers willing to undergo such an experience will find enough insights to justify the approach. A-IV (R/PG)

Little Night Music, A (1978) Screen version of the Broadway musical about ill-matched spouses and lovers who sort out their differences and find happiness in the course of a turn-of-the-century summer night. Harold Prince's uninspired direction and some unfortunate casting (Elizabeth Taylor is sadly unsuited to the central role of the

charming and magnetic Desiree) cause what should have been a light and airy sophistication to become rather earthbound. The situations and dialogue make it mature viewing fare. A-III (PG)

Little Prince, The (1974) Screen version of the Alan Jay Lerner and Frederick Loewe musical made from Antoine de Saint Exupery's classic fable about a planet-hopping child prince (Steven Warner) who relates his adventures to a crash-landed pilot (Richard Kiley). Directed by Stanley Donen, the story ends with a gentle let-down that may bring a wee tear to the eye of the very young but, overall, it is warm and upbeat, with engaging acting, pleasant music and clever dancing. A-I (G)

Little Romance, A (1979) Romantic comedy about two teenagers in Paris, an American girl (Diane Lane) and a French boy, who run away to Venice to kiss under the Bridge of Sighs in fulfillment of a legend told to them by a romantic pickpocket (Laurence Olivier). Director George Roy Hill's treatment of adolescent love is affectionately tender with only two risque asides about human anatomy conveyed in the context of honest curiosity. A-II (PG)

Little Sex, A (1982) Romantic comedy about a newly married young man (Tim Matheson) who has trouble remaining faithful to his wife (Kate Kapshaw). Director Bruce Paltrow's nearsighted sexual soap opera offers a sniggery bit of irreverent cynicism. O (R)

Little Shop of Horrors (1986) The wit and charm of the stage musical's black comedy about a carnivorous plant has been mistaken for the theater of cruelty. Director Frank Oz concentrates on literal depictions of the plant's feeding sessions and use of foul language, the sadism and masochism of various characters, including Steve Martin in a madcap cameo, and constant references, both visual and verbal, to killing and brutality. O (PG-13)

Little Treasure (1985) An erotic dancer (Margot Kidder) and a down-on-his-luck ex-seminarian (Ted Danson) team up in Mexico to find the loot from a Depression-era bank robbery her father had buried there. Alan Sharp wrote and directed a morality tale with serious overtones but not enough substance, despite some good acting and dialogue. Dance sequence involving nudity and some rough language. A-IV (R)

Littlest Horse Thieves, The (1977) Directed by Charles Jarrott this Disney production is set in England around 1909 in a coal mining town in Yorkshire. Three children (Andrew Harrison, Chloe Franks, and Benjie Bolgar) try to save the ponies who haul the coal from the mines and who are about to be taken to the slaughterhouse and replaced by machinery. There is an ingenious twist, however, which provides a happy ending, though with a bittersweet touch. A-I (G)

Live a Little, Love a Little (1968) Elvis Presley puts some new twists into his 28th screen effort, directed by Norman Taurog, his 9th collaboration with Presley. The gyrations are vintage swivel hips but there's an attempt to update the stock dialogue and situations with the introduction of double entendre and sexual titillation. A-III (PG)

Live a Little, Steal a Lot (1975) Failed crime melodrama about the petty thief, Murph the Surf (Don Stroud), who stole the Star of India from New York's Museum of Natural History is a yawner. Directed by Marvin Chomsky, it tries to glamorize its immature hero and the peek-a-boo sex is dreary going. O (PG)

Live and Let Die (1973) James Bond (Roger Moore) takes on hokey mixture of Harlem hoods (led by Yaphet Kotto) and Caribbean voodoo worshippers, all eager to chop him up before he blows the whistle on their plan to saturate the U.S. with heroin. Directed by Guy Hamilton, the plot is preposterous, the humor more tasteless than spicy and the special effects department works overtime to hold the spectator's flagging attention. A-III (PG)

Live for Life (1967) Long rambling story about the late maturing of a French photographer (Yves Montand) and his wife (Annie Giradot) after his affair with a model (Candice Bergen). Director Claude Lelouch sustains interest in a superficial, sentimental story with beautiful photography, locales, music and talented actors. A-III (br)

Living Daylights, The (1987) Timothy Dalton plays the new, more altruistic James Bond who foils an arms and drug-dealing scheme by KGB bigwig Jeroen Krabbe and ruthless dealer Joe Don Baker. Mellow treatment of spy triller by director John Glen includes a conventional romance with agent Maryam d'Abo and violence toned down to a level more acceptable for adults and mature teens. A-II (PG)

Living Free (1972) Sequel to Joy Adamson's "Born Free" tells of her attempts to rescue a trio of Elsa's orphaned lion cubs. Many adults will find their patience in short supply as Adamson (Susan Hampshire) and her gamekeeper-husband (Nigel Davenport) pursue their silly and sentimental ends in the name of humanitarianism while the cubs damage property and endanger themselves. Children, however, will only see cute wildlife antics. A-I (G)

Lizard in a Woman's Skin (1971) Italian clunker about a detective (Stanley Baker) investigating a series of murders finds the clues pointing towards a psychotic woman (Florinda Bolkan). Director Lugio Fulci's treatment of the heroine's real and imagined sexual perversions and the grisly representation of several murder victims are exploitative. O (R)

Local Hero (1983) Hotshot young executive (Peter Riegert), comes to buy up a remote Scottish village to turn it into an oil refinery and goes native, while the natives themselves pant after the millions he is prepared to deliver over to them. Director Bill Forsyth's delightful comedy keeps taking strange but enjoyable turns and the prevailing mood is low-keyed zany. Some adult humor. A-II (PG)

Lock Up Your Daughters (1969) Musical farce about three sex-starved sailors is a blend of two British Restoration comedies with their stock characters and scenes cluttering its ribald scenario of permissive "wenching." Christopher Plummer stars and Peter Coe directs the slapstick action and humor at the level of TV sitcom spiced with nudity and sexual jokes. O (R)

Logan's Run (1976) Futuristic social order is a hedonistic paradise except that its citizens are automatically exterminated at age 30. Instead of submitting, Michael York and Jenny Agutter make a run for it, pursued by zealous policeman Richard Jordan. Director Michael Anderson's rather simple-minded sci-fi chase movie is made moderately entertaining by its sets, special effects and the talents of its three principals. Some incidental nudity and disappointing downbeat conclusion.

A-III (PG)

Lola (1971) Charles Bronson, terribly miscast as an aging American writer living in Britain, is smitten with a 16-year-old girl (Susan George) and marries her with predictable results. Directed by Richard Donner, the story has some interest but ultimately fails on the dramatic levels of coherence and acting. A-III (GP)

Lola Montes (1969) Heavily romantic treatment of the life of the 19th-century's most famous courtesan (Martine Carol) and her romance with King Ludwig of Bavaria (Anton Walbrook). Produced in 1955, director Max Ophul's visually masterful and lavish evocation of the Age of Romanticism plays down the heroine's amorality and paints, instead, a compassionate portrait of a pathetic and tragic figure who ends as a circus attraction for the curious. A-IV (nr)

Lollipop (1976) Ailing white orphan (Norman Knox) from a Catholic mission in South Africa flees from his Afrikaner grandmother to the hills where he nearly freezes to death. Director Ashley Lazarus tells a poignant tale about racial prejudices and interracial brotherhood, somewhat sentimentalizing his stereotyped characters, yet for many reasons, it is rewarding fare for young viewers. A-I (G)

Lollipop Cover (1966) Retired prizefighter (Don Gordon) and a 9-year-old girl (Carol Selfinger) help each other come to terms with their problems. The low-budget production is directed by Everett Chambers and the fine acting of the principals helps keep the slight but uplifting story convincing. A-II (br)

Lolly-Madonna XXX (1973) Two neighboring Tennessee mountain families (headed by Rod Steiger and Robert Ryan) engage in a modern-day Hatfield-McCoy feud over a piece of pasture land and an innocent passer-by (Season Hubley) is held captive by one clan who thinks she belongs to the other. Directed by Richard C. Sarafian, the self-indulgent movie seems only interested in graphic displays of violence, including rape and the threat of rape. O (R/PG)

Lone Wolf McQuade (1983) Martial arts star Chuck Norris plays a modern Texas Ranger out to get a nasty arms smuggler (David Carradine) with Barbara Carrera on hand to look sultry and utter her share of the sappy dialogue. There is considerable violence, though treated by director Steve Carver in rather stylized and unrealistic fashion. A-III (PG)

Lonely Guy, The (1984) Steve Martin plays a writer of greeting-card verses, thrown out by his lover and wandering in Central Park where he meets Charles Grodin who initiates him into the Lonely Guy fraternity. Director Arthur Hiller's comedy has sparse humor, stemming mainly from the encounters between Martin and Grodin. Some mild sexual humor. A-III (PG)

Lonely Lady (1983) Screen version of Harold Robbins' novel stars Pia Zadora as a young writer who cannot find happiness as she wins fame and fortune in Hollywood. Crass, sleazy vanity production directed by Peter Sasdy has graphic sex scenes and much nudity. O (R)

Lonely Passion of Judith Hearne, The (1987) Disappointing movie version of the 1955 Brian Moore novel about a middle-aged Dublin spinster (Maggie Smith) who mistakes a gentleman's attentions as romantically intended and suffers a nervous breakdown when she discovers the truth.

Elegantly directed by Jack Clayton, the novel's religious dimension is underdeveloped and the spinster becomes a pathetic figure of sheer desperation. Some sexual scenes involving a teen-aged maid. A-III (R)

Lonesome Cowboys (1969) Minimal Western spoof from pop artist Andy Warhol treats its homosexual characters with repellent cruelty and is little more than an adolescent peep-show exhibition of sexual acts. O (nr)

Long Ago, Tomorrow (1971) British love story of a man (Malcolm McDowell), paralyzed from a soccer injury, and a quiet, attractive polio victim (Nanette Newman) who reside in a nursing home for the disabled. Director Bryan Forbes' story of their determination to marry in spite of their limitations is cut short by her death but the movie handles a delicate subject with great sensitivity. A-III (GP)

Long Day's Dying, The (1968) British World War II drama about three soldiers (David Hemmings, Tom Bell and Tony Beckley) trying to get back to their lines with a German prisoner. Directed by Peter Collinson, the realistic brutality used in this anti-war movie to convey the horror of war will strike some as excessive. A-IV (br)

Long Duel, The (1967) British India is the setting for this stiff-upper-lip story starring Trevor Howard as a non-conformist official who wants to treat even an outlaw native chief (Yul Brynner) with man-to-man justice. British production directed by Ken Annakin is routine escapist affair. A-II (br)

Long Good Friday, The (1982) Tough British gangster movie in which Bob Hoskins gives a remarkable performance as a London gang-lord done in by his own pride. Director John Mackenzie invests his brutal underworld story with grim but intelligent realism that some will find unnerving. Some intense scenes of violence. A-IV (R)

Long Goodbye, The (1973) Raymond Chandler's private eye, Philip Marlowe (Elliott Gould), by helping a friend out of a jam, finds himself picked up by the police and booked as an accessory to murder and left to sort through a tangle of murder, deception, robbery, suicide and double-crossing. Directed by Robert Altman, the action is handled quite well as is the tacky atmosphere, but Marlowe and his moralities are hopelessly confused. Some rough language and brief nudity. A-IV (R)

Long Ride from Hell, A (1970) Steve Reeves stars in an Italian Western as a man bent on revenge for a horse theft and the death of his brother. Directed by Alex Burks, the movie makes up in blood and sadism what it lacks in wit and talent. O (R)

Long Ride Home, The (1967) Vicious psychological triangle set at the end of the Civil War pitting Union officer Glenn Ford against Confederate counterpart George Hamilton with Inger Stevens in the middle. Dwarfed by the magnificence of its Grand Canyon locations, the characters lack human interest and director Phil Karlson's movie ends up somewhere between muddled comment on the brutality of war at best and distorted, misguided melodrama at worst. A-III (br)

Long Riders, The (1980) Slow-paced, somber Western starring the Carradine, Keach and Quaid brothers re-enacting the James and Younger gangs' disastrous raid on the bank in Northfield, Minnesota. Though it has its moments, director Walter Hill's effort is a little too pretentious to be really entertaining or enlightening. Some graphic violence and a realistic bordello scene. A-IV (R)

Longest Yard, The (1974) Burt Reynolds stars as an imprisoned ex-pro quarterback who leads a team of fellow convicts against a team made up of guards. Directed by Robert Aldrich, the movie has a careless, slapped-together look and relies heavily on violence and foul language. A-III (R)

Looker (1981) Beverly Hills plastic surgeon (Albert Finney) uncovers a plot by a conglomerate (headed by James Coburn) to hypnotize television viewers into buying products advertised in commercials. The scheme involves the murder of several actresses who are turned into computerized images. Writer-director Michael Crichton's confused story substitutes superficiality for social satire and flashiness for mystery. Some violence and brief nudity. A-III (PG)

Lookin' to Get Out (1982) Two luckless gamblers (Jon Voight and Burt Young) in debt to gangsters flee New York for Las Vegas where they stake a down-on-his-luck gambling whiz (Burt Remsen) to one last try at the jackpot. Director Hal Ashby's movie written by Voight is a total disaster, utterly lacking in charm, with unremitting vulgar language, some brief nudity and a benign view of the easy sex to be had in a resort. A-III (R)

Looking for Mr. Goodbar (1977) Director Richard Brooks' harrowing account of some of the consequences of the sexual revolution stars Diane Keaton as a wildly self-destructive young single on the prowl for love and commitment. Drama tries to evoke the moral confusion that pervades the lives of young people caught up in the liberated lifestyles of the 1970s but says little about the options open to them. Details of the singles drug and sex scene including a graphic rape and murder hammer home the obvious. O (R)

Looking Glass War, The (1970) Failed screen version of John Le Carre's story of a Polish national (Christopher Jones) who jumps ship in Britain and is promised asylum by a group of British intelligence agents (led by Ralph Richardson) who cynically plan to use him for their own espionage ploys. Directed by Frank R. Pierson, the adaptation misses the interest and suspense of the original by bogging down in unmotivated and barely credible incidents, including his affair with a German woman (Pia Degermark). A-III (PG)

Looking Up (1977) Documentary directed by Linda Yellen offers a fragmented chronicle of the lives of three generations of a Jewish family seeking upward mobility and success in America. Although used to establish character, there are instances of vulgar language that may offend some viewers. A-III (PG)

Looney Looney Looney Bugs Bunny Movie, The (1981) Compilation of vintage Warner Brothers cartoon shorts with some new material. The art work and the style of the animation are light years removed from the crude fare offered a new generation watching Saturday morning television. A-I (G)

Loot (1972) British black comedy by Joe Orton in which a mortician-bank robber (Hywel Bennett), his adoring pal (Roy Holder), the pal's freshly widowed father (Milo O'Shea), the dead wife's piously amoral nurse (Lee Remick) and a batty Scotland Yard inspector (Richard Attenborough) get mixed together in a tacky Brighton hotel with a fresh but rapidly stiffening corpse. Directed by Silvio Narizzano, the result is flat, chewy but indigestible. O (R/PG)

Lord Jim (1965) Screen version of Joseph Conrad's novel about courage and cowardice in the story of the Far Eastern adventures of its flawed hero (Peter O'Toole). Directed by Richard Brooks, the result is only a superficial and disjointed pageant, though handsomely photographed and containing many effective individual scenes. A-II (br)

Lord Love a Duck (1966) Uneven black comedy about high school kids in Southern California that tries to offer some biting commentary on the meaningless lives of a certain segment of contemporary society. Starring Roddy McDowall and Tuesday Weld, there are some good laughs at the expense of ready targets but George Axelrod's direction is frank and adult in terms of treatment and dialogue, including a plot complication involving hypnosis to regulate the love lives of students. A-IV (br)

Lord of the Rings, The (1978) Ralph Bakshi's animated film version of the J.R.R. Tolkien epic of Middle Earth deals with the darker side of the trilogy. Since the monsters, and not the Hobbits, make a stronger impression, parents may want to think twice about their smaller children seeing this often frightening film. A-II (PG)

Lords of Discipline, The (1983) David Keith stars as a decent young cadet at a Southern military academy who tries to stop the hazing of a black freshman by a brutal clique trying to force him to quit the academy. Director Franc Roddam uses some fairly graphic violence and very rough language in depicting the ravages of prejudice and abuse of power. A-III (R)

Lords of Flatbush, The (1974) Small saga of leather-jacketed kids coming of age in Brooklyn in the late 1950s. Co-directed by Stephen F. Verona and Martin Davidson, it is not very probing but it does have some good performances by Perry Kind, Sylvester Stallone and Henry Winkler as well as offering considerably more humanity and substance than most such nostalgia films. Some graphic depiction of sexual encounters and crude language. A-III (PG)

Losers, The (1970) Motorcycle gang goes to Vietnam and they blast their way into a Viet Cong stronghold to rescue a CIA official. Director Jack Starrett's action movie is appalling in its excessive bloodshed, glamorized violence, cheap moralizing and phony patriotism. O (R)

Lost and Found (1979) George Segal, a widowed professor of English at a second-rate university, meets sharp-tongued divorcee Glenda Jackson while on a sabbatical in Europe. They marry, return to the States, only to have everything fall apart. Melvin Frank's uninspired direction doesn't help the offhanded message that commitment dulls romance. A few vulgar turns of dialogue and some cynical humor concerning marriage. A-III (PG)

Lost Boys, The (1987) Strained parable of the evils of drugs and sex couched in a story about a gang of teenage vampires headed by Kiefer Sutherland trying to get the new kid in town (Jason Patric) to join them. Director Joel Schumacher leaves it up to pre-teens to foil the pack via the gruesomely violent, albeit traditionally effective, stake-in-the-heart bit. A-III (R)

Lost Command, The (1966) French paratroopers retaliate by atrocity and torture against the terrorists whom they are fighting in Algeria.

Directed by Mark Robson, the politics may be muddled but the acting is good (Anthony Quinn and Alain Delon) and the action well-staged with realistic violence. A-III (br)

Lost Continent, The (1968) British horror movie in which a ship, beleagured in the Saragasso Sea, finds a centuries-old Spanish galleon whose strange occupants (Hildegard Knef, Daryl Read and Eddie Powell) are the descendents of the original crew and passengers. Director Michael Carreras offers a senseless mix of threatening violence and sexual innuendo. A-III (br)

Lost Flight, The (1971) Innocuous little melodrama about a planeful of people marooned on a remote South Sea island as a result of engine failure. Gallant pilot Lloyd Bridges tries to maintain peace among his passengers while awaiting rescue from various plot contrivances under the uninspired direction of Leonard J. Horn. A-II (G)

Lost Honor of Katharina Blum, The (1976) Written and directed by Volker Schlondorff and Margarethe von Trotta, this is a plodding adaptation of Heinrich Boll's 1974 novel about an ordinary citizen (Angela Winkler) who is victimized by the police and the press because they mistakenly believe she is part of a terrorist group. The movie overall makes it too easy to condemn police excesses while not clearly defining its complex political theme. A-III (PG)

Lost Horizon (1937) Director-producer Frank Capra's classic yarn about a British consul (Ronald Coleman) who is kidnapped and brought to Shangri-La, a thriving utopian community in the High Himalayas, as the chosen successor of its dying leader (Sam Jaffe). Re-released in 1986 in its original form, its picture of an ideal society whose people live in peace and harmony has as much meaning for the troubled world of today as it did for audiences on the eve of World War II. A-I (br)

Lost Horizon (1973) Producer Ross Hunter's mammoth, lavish musical version of the 1937 Frank Capra classic is an enormous dud. Director Charles Jarrott wastes a fine cast and good story in a welter of forgettable Burt Bacharch-Hal David tunes. Charles Boyer as the ancient High Lama wisely succumbs midway. A-I (G)

Lost in America (1985) Slight comedy about a Yuppie couple (Albert Brooks and Julie Hagerty) who buy a Winnebago and go off in search of America when he's fired instead of promoted at the ad agency. Also written and directed by Brooks, their misadventures lead to no greater insight than his going back to the ad game, though viewers will see the emptiness of their materialistic values. Several instances of profanity. A-II (R)

Lost Man, The (1969) A decent man (Sidney Poitier) engages in robbery to get money needed for the families of jailed black militants. Director Robert Alan Aurthur's movie refuses to grapple with the real issues posed by the black movement yielding only a mixed-up story of revolution born of despair and an ethic based on the end justifying the means. A-III (PG)

Love (1973) Hungarian drama about the wife (Mari Torocsik) of a man imprisoned by the Stalinist regime who tries to keep her aged mother-in-law (Lili Darvas) from learning the truth about her son's absence. Director Karoly Makk's work is simple, unpretentious and quite honest in its celebration of such sentiments as love, fidelity and sacrifice. A-I (nr)

Love and Anarchy (1974) Seriocomic Italian story of an anarchist (Giancarlo Giannini) who decides to avenge a friend murdered by Fascists by journeying to Rome to assassinate Mussolini, staying with a prostitute (Mariangela Melato) whose life has been ruined by Blackshirts. Directed by Lina Wertmuller, the movie's vulgar humor clashes uneasily with the serious tragedy being played out. Some ribald bordello scenes are certainly not glamorized and anything but attractive. A-IV (R)

Love and Death (1975) Ambitious and delightful spoof of Russian literature with Woody Allen turning his wit on the most turgid aspects of Dostoevski and Tolstoy, mocking both the characters and the heavy philosophy. It's a rather rarefied comedy trying perhaps a little too hard to be naughty and nice, funny and ferocious. Given the context and some knowledge of the subject of the satire, it should not offend mature viewers. A-III (PG)

Love and Marriage (1966) Italian movie presents a quartet of stories making fun of marital fidelity. O (br)

Love and Money (1982) Silver magnate (Klaus Kinski) hires a troubleshooter (Ray Sharkey) to persuade a Latin American dictator (Armand Assante) to give back his mines. Scripted by Sharkey and directed by James Toback, it's a dreadful little movie with the depth of a television pilot. Prolonged and extravagant sex scenes. O (R)

Love and Pain and the Whole Damn Thing (1973) Aging, ailing, inhibited English spinster (Maggie Smith) meets an inarticulate young American (Timothy Bottoms) on a bus tour of Spain and the summer friendship turns into a love affair. Director Alan J. Pakula succeeds with poignant comic sequences as the unlikely pair get to know each other but the romantic ending turns the movie into routine soap opera. A-III (R/PG)

Love at First Bite (1979) Dracula (George Hamilton) comes to New York and falls in love with a glamorous model (Susan St. James) in this uneven, essentially one-joke comedy directed by Stan Dragoti. Several graphic lovemaking scenes and blacks are made the butt of some jokes. O (PG)

Love at the Top (1975) Frothy, stylish French comedy that bounces from slapstick to vitriolic satire in telling the story of a young man (Jean-Louis Trintignant) climbing the ladder of success by exploiting a long line of women. Director Michel Deville has his tongue firmly in cheek but some viewers may find the darkness of the comedy too bleak, the general amorality of the characters offensive and the casual nudity too pervasive. A-IV (R)

Love Bug, The (1969) Disney comedy about a sentient Volkswagon named Herbie who adopts a has-been, egotistic racing driver (Dean Jones) and drives him to victory and the altar (with Michele Lee). Mildly diverting fantasy from director Robert Stevenson but it's mostly for the kids. A-I (G)

Love Child (1982) Amy Madigan makes an impressive screen debut as Terry Jean Moore, a troubled, unloved teen-ager who undergoes a remarkable transformation by learning to love. Thrown into prison, she becomes pregnant by a prison guard (Beau Bridges) and fights for her right to keep her baby. The film is worth seeing for Miss Madigan's performance. Director Larry Peerce's fact-based somewhat sentimental drama

has a relatively graphic scene involving sex and nudity. A-IV (R)

Love Clinic, The (1971) The title says it all in this hardcore pornography which apparently is also circulating in a softcore porno version. O (nr)

Love Doctors, The (1971) These doctors run a friendly neighborhood sex laboratory where they conduct clinical sex experiments involving various combinations of men, women, and machines. Thoroughly cheap and offensive. O (X/R appeal)

Love God?, The (1969) Leaden comedy in which the editor (Don Knotts) of a bankrupt bird-watching magazine becomes a sex symbol when tricked into selling his fourth class mailing permit to a publisher of pornography. Director Nat Hiken makes up in tastelessness what the satire lacks in wit, making obscenity legislation, civil liberties and public morality all seem as silly as the movie itself. A-III (M)

Love in Our Time (1969) Psuedo-documentary purports to explore contemporary sexual mores in Britian by examining the cases of eight volunteer couples. Director Elkan Allen employs graphic re-enactments of marital problems which focus on cruel and unusual sex acts. O (X)

Love Is a Funny Thing (1970) French romance about a film composer (Jean-Paul Belmondo) and a film actress (Annie Giradot) who meet on a Hollywood set and initiate a casual affair. The actress admits the situation to her husband in Paris, not knowing that for the composer it's all a game and she is being taken for a ride. Directed by Claude Lelouch, there's some funny spoofing of Hollywood, but the story moves too slowly in parts and the characterzations too facile to be either effective or affecting. A-III (PG)

Love Letters (1984) Jamie Lee Curtis plays a disc jockey who becomes involved in an obsessive affair with a married man. She is inspired to risk all for love, it seems, by the discovery of some old letters that indicate that her dead mother also had a great love in her life. Contrived, sentimental film directed by Amy Jones has extensive nudity and graphic sexuality. O (R)

Love Machine, The (1971) Screen version of Jacqueline Susann's raunchy novel about highpowered sex and corporate intrigue is just as raunchy with John Phillip Law as the ruthless young executive, Robert Ryan as his corporate head, David Hemmings as his swishy confidant and Dyan Cannon as only one of the innumerable mistresses who help him earn his mechanical nickname. Directed by Jack Haley Jr., it is laughably stupid and banal, qualities that only partially relieve the boredom. O (R)

Love Object, The (1971) Graphic demonstration of what a pretty but basically untalented young woman must do in order to get her start in the New York Theater. The producers have recruited Kim Pope, a pretty but basically untalented young woman who seems to know what she must do in order to get into movies. O (R)

Love on the Run (1979) Francois Truffaut's fifth film about Antoine (Jean-Pierre Leaud), now feckless and boring at age 33, in the midst of an affair and about to get a divorce from his wife (Claude Jade). Shallow and vapid exercise in middle-age melodrama whose point seems to be the inevitability of divorce. A-III (nr)

Love Songs (1986) French drama about a woman (Catherine Deneuve) who balances the responsibilities of motherhood with her biological needs by sexually exploiting a younger man (Chris Lambert) whom she coldly leaves when she decides to go back to her husband. Directed by Elie Chouraqui, the movie treats infidelity not as a moral issue but rather as a device to explore some muddled ideas about the nature of the family bond from a feminist perspective. Justifies casual sex. O (nr)

Love Story (1970) Supersuds screen version of Erich Segal's romantic melodrama about a rich youth (Ryan O'Neal) and rough-talking baker's daughter (Ali MacGraw) whose Harvard-Radcliffe courtship and marriage survive their social and cultural differences until her early death from some sort of dread ailment. Director Arthur Hiller manipulates viewer emotions skillfully and shamelessly in a sentimental, old-fashioned tear-jerker, updated with some rude language. A-III (GP)

Love Under 17 (1973) German exploitation import directed by Wolfgang von Schiber combines roving reporter interviews with softcore episodes of young women seeking to satisfy their sexual appetites. O (R)

Lovely Way to Die, A (1968) B-grade thriller concerning an ex-cop (Kirk Douglas) hired by a district attorney (Eli Wallach) as a bodyguard for a New York socialite (Sylvia Koscina) accused of murdering her husband. Directed by David Lowell Rich, the proceedings are crudely violent and sexually suggestive. O (br)

Lovers and Other Strangers (1970) Seriocomic view of love and marriage told through a series of vignettes of the unhappy experiences of those taking part in the wedding of a young couple (Michael Brandon and Bonnie Bedelia). Directed by Cy Howard, the bittersweet currents that underlie the slick, surface witticisms seem to suggest that even as characters deny their love for one another, they share something deeper than a sexual attraction. A-IV (R/GP)

Loves and Times of Scaramouche, The (1976) Moronic Italian slapstick comedy directed by Enzo Castellari with Michael Sarrazin in the title role as a farcical rogue whose sexual exploits, primarily with Ursula Andress, are embroiled in the intrigues of Napoleon's court. Exploitative nudity. O (PG)

Loves of a Blonde (1966) Czechoslovakian movie about the lesson in life that a shy young girl learns from her first disillusioning experience with romance. Director Milos Forman's otherwise sensitive treatment indulges in an unnecessarily graphic seduction sequence. O (br)

Loves of Isadora, The (1969) Spectacular and poignant dramatization of the life of Isadora Duncan, one of modern dance's daring pioneers and free spirits. Director Karel Reisz focuses on the colorful (and ultimately tragic) career of the artist, with special emphasis on her vigorous and unorthodox romantic life. Vanessa Redgrave carries the title role and her dancing is surprisingly graceful and appealing. Some sexually frank dialogue and suggestive visuals. A-III (PG)

Lovesick (1983) Dudley Moore plays a married psychiatrist on Manhattan's Upper East Side who falls in love with a patient (Elizabeth McGovern), which isn't a problem because his wife is having an affair with a deranged painter. Predictable and unfunny romantic comedy directed by Marshall Brickman takes a benign view of adultery. A-III (PG)

Lovin' Molly (1974) Adaptation of the Larry McMurtry Western novel in which the earth

mother of the title (Blythe Danner), who lives and loves with the same abandon, gives her favors freely to two men (Anthony Perkins and Beau Bridges) before and after her marriage to a third. Director Sidney Lumet focuses most on her two lovers, thus leaving a good deal of Molly's motivation obscure, at best. Some nudity and much earthy language. A-IV (R)

Loving (1970) Flawed but interesting study of a commercial illustrator (George Segal) who fancies the ladies and himself as an artist condemned to drawing trucks and who finally goes overboard when, during the course of a party, he is monitored on closed circuit television making love to a neighbor's wife. Directed by Irvin Kershner, the movie succeeds best in placing its aimless hero in the context of affluent, materialistic suburbia. Needlessly extended sex scene. O (R)

Loving Couples (1980) Director Jack Smight's comedy about mate swapping, featuring James Coburn, Shirley MacLaine, Susan Sarandon and Stephen Collins, is only intermittently funny. Though it is innocuous for the most part, its implication that such behavior can have a therapeutic effect on a marriage is objectionable. O (PG)

Lt. Robin Crusoe, U.S.N. (1966) Dick Van Dyke stars as a navy pilot marooned on a Pacific Island in this mindless Disney comedy directed by Byron Paul without the slightest subtlety of any sort. A-I (br)

Lucas (1986) Bright 14-year-old boy nearly kills himself trying to impress his best and only friend, a 16-year-old girl who is attracted instead to one of the school's football stars. This teen drama offers thoughtful and sensitive characterizations and insightful depiction of high school socializing. Its gentle tone is slightly jarred by some foul language and locker room hijinks. A-II (PG-13)

Lucia (1974) Unusual Cuban movie with three different stories told from the perspective of three different women in three entirely distinct styles are united by the theme of Cuban revolutions in 1895 against the colonial Spanish rulers, in 1933 against the dictator Machado and finally the Castro revolution in the 1960s. Director Humberto Solas demonstrates not only technical virtuosity but his real accomplishment is in the vigor with which he expresses the humanity of his characters. Some shocking brutalities and some confusing historical material. A-IV (nr)

Lucky Lady (1976) Failed crime melodrama spoof in which smalltime 1920's bootleggers (Gene Hackman, Burt Reynolds and Liza Minelli), at war with rival mobsters and the U.S. Coast Guard, find time to engage in some kinky sex. Director Stanley Donen seems to have choreographed all the action to a musical whose songs have been edited out. Much sexual innuendo and frequent profanity. O (PG)

Lucky Luciano (1974) Francesco Rosi's dramatization of the most wily of America's wily Mafiosi never manages to bring the facts of Luciano's life into focus, especially with Gian Maria Volonte's detached performance in the title role. The result is a disjointed and confusing portrait of a complex figure, ineffective as a movie entertainment and as history. Stylized violence and profanity. A-III (R)

Ludwig (1973) Director Luchino Visconti presents the story of the mad German ruler (Helmut Berger) of the 19th-century Austrian Reich as a companion piece to his depiction of the madness of the Third Reich in "The Damned". Severed from any political or social purpose, the work is a pointless exercise in pictorial opulence and rococo style, with questionable implications that latent homosexuality was the reason for Ludwig's problems. A-IV (R/PG)

Lulu the Tool (1975)   Italian dramatization of a political theme illustrating the dehumanization of a worker (Gian Maria Volonte) being driven mad by his assembly-line job. Director Elio Petri's movie is a cry of moral outrage, a reminder that people are more than machines. There is strong material in its depiction of economic injustice, particularly brutish living conditions, with some vulgar language and a pathetic seduction scene some may find offensive. A-IV (nr)

Lumiere (1976)   Subtle French exploration of the varieties of femininity as mirrored by four actresses (Jeanne Moreau, Lucia Bose, Francine Rachette and Caroline Cartier) who share their insecurities about men, career and family. Written and directed by Jeanne Moreau, the psycho-social portrait exudes a cool detachment concerning adult themes of love, seduction, suicide and ambition. A-III (R)

Luna (1979)   Italian director Bernardo Bertolucci treats the subject of incest in the story of a recently widowed opera star (Jill Clayburgh) who drags her 15-year-old son (Matthew Barry) off on an Italian tour. A sullen, self-indulgent movie, it is an unmitigated disaster for all involved. Some violence and graphic sexual scenes. O (R)

Lupo! (1971)   Israeli comedy revolving around an honest, earthy man who acts from the heart without attention to protocol or official regulations, thereby embarrassing his daughter and friends. It is a refreshingly entertaining, low-key comedy with quiet humor and some charm. A-II (G)

Lust for a Vampire (1971)   Teacher Ralph Bates eyes comely student Yutte Stensgaard at a finishing school for young ladies but she has only fangs for him. This film is at best a teasing corruption of the vampire genre, introducing some graphic situations of casual nudity and a touch of lesbianism. O (R)

Lust in the Dust (1985)   Director Paul Bartel's attempt at a satirical Western is relentlessly tasteless and unfunny. Among other things, its crude humor is directed at women and religious groups. O (R)

Luv (1968)   Uneven, occasionally tasteless screen version of Murray Schisgal's Broadway comedy about the marital mixups of a New York couple (Peter Falk and Elaine May) and a talkative loser (Jack Lemmon). Director Clive Donner tries everything from burlesque to satire but is unable to elicit much more than stock reactions from its stock situations about love and marriage. A-IV (br)

M

MacArthur (1977)   Gregory Peck plays the title role in this sprawling screen biography of World War II hero General Douglas MacArthur, giving equal time to both sides of his public image as ruthless egotist and noble patriot but without providing any key to the real man. Capable if unspectacular dramatization directed by Joseph Sargent, it's basically a one-man show with the lesser roles devoid of substance. Restrained wartime violence. A-II (PG)

MacKenna's Gold (1969)   Gregory Peck stars as a former prospector, now marshall, forced by outlaw Omar Sharif to lead his gang to a hidden Valley of Gold sacred to the Indians but which Peck insists doesn't exist. Interminable complications set in as gold fever corrupts all in a story of cruelty, betrayal and vengeance. J. Lee Thompson directs an episodic work whose theme of universal greed is morally unappealing and dramatically boring. Frequent violence and brief nudity. O (M)

Macaroni (1985)   Breezy Italian comedy in which an uptight American (Jack Lemmon) on a business trip to Naples is confronted by the brother (Marcello Mastroianni) of a woman with whom the American had a wartime romance and, in the process of fulfilling the forgotten woman's expectations, the two men become friends. Under Ettore Scola's deft direction, the cheerful proceedings result in a charming little slice of Neapolitan life. Mildly profane language. A-III (PG)

Macbeth (1972)   One of Shakespeare's most violent dramas has been visualized on the screen in an extremely realistic manner, turning the tragedy's verbal imagery of evil acts and brutal deeds into a real-life horror show that is neither convincing as human experience nor dramatically necessary. Yet director Roman Polanski's version of the play does have its virtues in being faithful to the text, in creating the primitive time period in Welsh and Northumberland locations and in a very capable supporting cast for the unfortunately miscast leads (Jon Finch in the title role and Francesca Annis as Lady Macbeth). A mixed-bag with some graphic violence and brief nudity. A-IV (R)

Machine Gun McCain (1970)   Paroled convict John Cassavetes pulls off a one-man heist of a Las Vegas gambling casino and is subsequently tracked down by the Syndicate who disapprove of such private initatives. Mediocre Italian production directed by Giuliano Montaldo with cast mostly from Italian B-grade movies. Some violence and ethnic stereotyping. A-III (PG)

Macho Callahan (1970)   After a gutsy escape from a grisly Confederate prison, outlaw David Janssen kills the husband of Jean Seberg who puts up a reward and then hunts him down herself. She finds him irresistible but their relationship is finally terminated when his past and the bounty hunters catch up with him. Bernard L. Kowalski misdirects a twisted exercise in brutality and violent sex. O (R)

Mack, The (1973)   Black exploitation movie about an ex-con (Max Julien) who claws his way to the top in the mink coat, customized limo world of a big-time ghetto pimp in Detroit. Directed by Michael Campus, the shoddy production views prostitution as an economic necessity. Excessive violence and sexual references. O (R)

Mackintosh & T.J. (1976)   Returning to the screen after an absence of more than 20 years, Roy Rogers is back in the saddle as a washed-up rodeo cowboy of stern moral principles who befriends a young boy (Clay O'Brien in a good performance). Amiable, old-fashioned Western entertainment directed by Marvin J. Chomsky, it has an absurd sub-plot involving a sex maniac but nothing that would be too strong for most teenagers. A-II (PG)

Mackintosh Man, The (1973)   Paul Newman stars in a suspense thriller about a plan to capture a master spy who is a British politician. Though directed by John Huston and filmed on quite enchanting Irish and Maltese locations, it is no more than routine spy fare until the climax which emphasizes the indistinguishable morality of spies, whatever their allegiance. A-III (PG)

Macon County Line (1974) Cluttered suspense thriller about brothers (Alan and Jesse Vint) driving through the South during the 1950s with a hitchhiker (Cheryl Waters) who find themselves wrongly accused of murdering the wife of a county deputy (Max Baer) and flee for their lives from his bloody rampage. Director Richard Compton supplies the gritty effects but writer-producer Baer is responsible for the bizarre twist ending to this tangled tale, supposedly based on a true incident. Excessive violence and exploitative nudity. O (R)

Macunaima (1972) Brazilian satire about a modern Don Quixote who rambles through a series of often-contradictory adventures which take him from primitive jungle to industrialized metropolis and back again. Told in crude but colorful folkloric style, with a melange of symbolic characters and unrelated episodes, the point of it all seems to be that poor nations destroy themselves in their quest for commercial growth. Written and directed by Joaquim Pedro de Andrade, the movie might be likened to the theater of the absurd but some casual nudity and lewd sight gags prove more offensive than humorous. O (nr)

Mad Adventures of 'Rabbi' Jacob, The (1974) Madcap is the word for this zany French production which begins on New York's Lower East Side from which Rabbi Jacob departs for Paris to attend the bar mitzvah of a favored nephew. What happens after that is a delightful, non-stop romp with Louis de Funes as an idiotic anti-Semite whose prejudices lead him into, among other things, a bubblegum vat and a rabbinical disguise. Under the deceptively casual direction of Gerard Oury, bigotry is thoroughly ridiculed with very controlled and funny slapstick humor. The result is a comedy that the whole family can enjoy. A-I (G)

Mad Dog (1976) Writer-director Philippe Mora's ragged account of the career of a 19th-century Australian outlaw (Dennis Hopper) squanders a good re-creation of the era because of its incoherent narrative, undue attention to the effects of violence and some brief nudity. O (R)

Mad Dogs and Englishmen (1971) Performance documentary of 1970 American tour by Joe Cocker's musical group. Director Pierre Adidge also spends some time documenting the communal lifestyle of Cocker's troupe as a warmly sympathetic, but doubtless for many, shockingly irresponsible experiment in human relations. Rather graphic description of a sexual encounter by a groupie, some flashes of nudity, as well as the musicians' nonconformist lifestyle require an adult perspective. A-III (nr)

Mad Max (1980) Australian action melodrama set in the near future when the world has lurched a little further towards chaos and nomadic motorcyclists and a brutal police force fight it out on desert roads. Mel Gibson stars as the decent cop who tries to fight within the system until his wife and daughter are brutally killed and he goes on a bloody rampage. Director George Miller stages the action sequences quite impressively, but characterizations count for nothing and the poor dubbing of American voices is distracting. Excessively graphic violence. O (R)

Mad Max Beyond Thunderdome (1985) Solitary, two-fisted roamer of the post-Armageddon Australian Outback, Mad Max (Mel Gibson) chances upon a backward settlement where he is forced to fight in its arena (the Thunderdome), goes on to becomes a hero figure for a tribe of lost children and then has a final showdown with the settlers, involving the usual collection of bizarre vehicles. With the backgrounds showing the appalling consequence of nuclear holocaust, there is more than a touch of solemnity to the proceedings. Directed by George Miller and George Ogilvie, it's all rather violent, but not excessively so, and action fans will find it fairly intelligent entertainment. A-III (PG-13)

Mad Room, The (1969) After having killed their parents, two children committed to a home for the mentally insane are released as teenagers (Barbara Sammeth and Michael Burns) in the custody of their older sister who lives with her disagreeable, unsuspecting employer. The outcome of this psychological thriller is predictably dire but writer-director Bernard Girard's disappointing adaptation of a real chiller, "Ladies in Retirement," is clumsy and only infrequently establishes the required mood of suspense. Restrained violence. A-III (M)

Madame Rosa (1978) Memorable performance by Simone Signoret as an aging former prostitute and survivor of Auschwitz who makes a living of sorts by running a foster home for the children of prostitutes in her sixth-floor walkup in a rundown Parisian neighborhood. As her health deteriorates, she develops a relationship of need with a 14-year-old Algerian boy (Samy Ben Youb). French production directed by Moshe Mizrahi, its Arab-Jewish jokes quickly wear thin and its evocation of the horror of Auschwitz and persecution is far too superficial. Mature theme and atmosphere. A-III (PG)

Maddalena (1971) Italian soap opera about a passionate woman (Lisa Gastoni) and her destructive love for a priest (Eric Woofe) contents itself with wallowing in extensive nudity, pulp psychology and phoney pathos. Talented Polish director Jerry Kawalerowicz has turned a potentially interesting theme into a boring feature that has little to offer but sensationalism. O (R)

Made for Each Other (1971) Italian boy and Jewish girl find each other at a group therapy session and shout and fight their way across the city into matrimony. The film's few virtues and many faults are all attributable to Renee Taylor and Joseph Bologna, who both wrote and star in what one may assume is something of a real-life experience. As directed by Robert B. Bean, the movie's contrast of ethnic value systems and traditions provides some humor but cloaks its lack of depth in some puerile sentimentality. A-III (PG)

Made in Heaven (1987) Failed romantic fantasy about a youth (Timothy Hutton) who dies and goes to heaven, falls in love with an unborn soul (Kelly McGillis) and then pursues her when she is sent to earth. Director Alan Rudolph's fantasy lacks imagination and the romance lacks any appeal or interest. Some restrained love scenes and rough language. A-III (PG)

Made in Italy (1967) Series of semi-documentary vignettes of Italian life, exploring such topics as work, women, customs, the family, politics and religion. The episodes, which feature some leading Italian and French performers, are directed by Nanni Loy with humor, affection and pathos. Standout is Anna Magnani as a mother determined to get her family across an auto-jammed highway, a triumph both hilarious and moving. Older adolescents might enjoy this beautifully photographed, very human work. A-III (br)

Mademoiselle (1966) Lurid French movie about a woman who uses her sexuality for evil ends. O (br)

Madhouse (1974) Undistinguished horror melodrama but some fun because its story line is about a faded horror movie star (Vincent Price) whose attempts to get a leading part in a new TV horror series are thwarted by a fellow actor (Peter Cushing) who starts killing off Price's friends and leaving evidence implicating Price as the murderer. Directed by Jim Clark, the plot is a jumble, not helped much by the inclusion of a number of clips from old horror movies, but there are enough grisly murders for the horror trade. A-III (PG)

Madigan (1968) Fast-moving crime thriller featuring Richard Widmark and Harry Guardino as New York City detectives who spend a couple of frenzied days trying to redeem themselves by recapturing the psychotic killer they let escape. Vividly directed by Donald Siegel, the focus is on the details of routine police work rather than on resolving its numerous plot complications and moral ambiguities. Some tough violence. A-III (br)

Madigan's Millions (1969) Botched comedy with Dustin Hoffman playing a bumbling U.S. treasury agent sent to locate a million dollars smuggled into Italy by deported gangster Cesar Romero. Ineptly directed by Stanley Preger, the silly plot has a few amusing moments but the rest is woefully unfunny. A-II (G)

Mado (1978) Long, rambling tale of a pure-of-heart prostitute (Ottavia Piccolo) whose devotion to her working-class friends and lack of greed are a constant reproach to her most enamored patron, a wealthy businessman (Michel Piccoli). The inconsequential French comedy directed by Claude Sautet gets muddled in corrupt business deals but has the good sense to drop them for a country outing, a driving rainstorm, and huge quantities of mud in some dim metaphorical resolution. Sexual situations and some gratuitous nudity. O (nr)

Madron (1971) Low-budget Western about an Indian fighter (Richard Boone) who rescues a nun (Leslie Caron) left for dead by Apaches after a stagecoach attack. Together they wend their way through the desert, fighting off Indians and outlaws, until eventually Sister lets her hair down and seems to anticipate a love scene that never fully materializes. As directed by Jerry Hopper, the principals play their sharply contrasting roles with an undeserved verve and the ultimate discretions of the silly script render the movie an innocuous exercise. Some violence and tasteless treatment of religious elements. A-III (GP)

Madwoman of Chaillot, The (1969) Katharine Hepburn, Richard Chamberlain and Danny Kaye play slighty daft Parisian idealists who rally the poor and simple of the city to foil an insane plot to destroy Paris for the sake of oil deposits deep beneath its streets. Director Bryan Forbes has made a beautiful-looking but sluggish screen version of the delightful Jean Giradoux play in which the mad are really sane and the supposed sane are quite mad. Disappointing but has plenty of good moments. A-III (G)

Mafia (1969) Italian crime melodrama with Lee J. Cobb as the head of the local syndicate controlling a Sicilian town where an uncooperative businessman is murdered and the husband of Claudia Cardinale disappears. The efforts of the local police to solve the crimes are thwarted in an involved plot sluggishly directed by Damiano Damiani. Violence. A-III (M)

Magic (1978) Anthony Hopkins stars in this dull and brutal melodrama about an unbalanced ventriloquist who tends to get into arguments with his dummy. Burgess Meredith plays his manager who inadvertently sets off a series of tragic events for all concerned, including Ann-Margaret as an unhappily married woman. Director Richard Attenborough falls far short of the modest goal of making an entertaining thriller. Violence, a bedroom sequence and a sympathetic attitude towards adultery. O (R)

Magic Christian, The (1969) Screen version of Terry Southern's novel about a wealthy tycoon (Peter Sellers) who sets out to prove that money means everything and everyone has his price. Directed by Joseph McGrath, this spoof of all things establishment has some humorous situations but the satirical intent of the movie is largely unrealized. Some purple patches of homosexual innuendo, nudity and off-color language. O (PG)

Magic Flute, The (1975) Director Ingmar Bergman presents this opera by Wolfgang Amadeus Mozart as an actual performance on a cramped 18th-century stage, boldly taking viewers into a world of illusion, stagecraft and mystery. Originally produced for Swedish television, its stress on the theatricality of Mozart's fairy-tale operatics is to the advantage of a pretty silly libretto. Bergman's austere yet ingratiating visual style suitably complements Mozart's beautifully intricate music. It is a classic that might serve as a good introduction to opera for young people, though parents should be aware that it contains some sexual allusions and a brief close-up of an erotic drawing. A-III (G)

Magic Garden of Stanley Sweetheart, The (1970) Exploitative melodrama about a college student (Don Johnson) who gradually retreats from reality as he becomes dependent upon sex and drugs. Director Leonard Horn stages an interminable series of explicit sexual encounters and pot parties without providing the least insight into the youth's problems or reasons for his downward climb into sexual aberrations and drugged lethargy. O (R)

Magic of Lassie, The (1978) The celebrated collie returns to foil the bad guy (Parnell Roberts) in his attempt to steal James Stewart's ranch. Good production of a standard plot and solid supporting cast includes Mickey Rooney and Alice Faye. Though director Don Chaffey elevates Lassie's human qualities to new heights of absurdity, younger viewers will take much delight in the adventures of this canine movie legend. A-I (G)

Magic of the Kite, The (1971) Children's adventure movie, with beautiful location photography in France and China, follows the odyssey of a young lad and his little sister in search of the owner of a magic kite. The imaginative French production (dubbed in English) features flying bedsteads, a colorful Chinese magician and two charming youngsters, presented with enough flair and fantasy to captivate the small fry. A-I (G)

Magician of Lublin (1979) Failed screen version of the Issac Bashevis Singer novel about an irreligious, woman-chasing, Jewish magician (Alan Arkin) in turn-of-the-century Poland who convinces a Warsaw theater manager (Lou Jacobi) that he can fly but then squanders the money he receives on a countess (Louise Fletcher). Director Menachem Golan's crude and plodding effort misses the religious theme of the original and Arkin is badly miscast as the magnetic, erotic and ultimately spiritually tormented hero. Some extravagant nudity and graphic sexuality. O (R)

Magnificent Seven Ride!, The (1972) After his wife is kidnapped, raped and murdered, Lee Van Cleef sets out to find those responsible and, when the trail leads to a large and vicious band of renegades, he gathers his old comrades, the Magnificent Seven, five of whom are in prison. Director George McCowan's sequel is a standard Western, though the climactic showdown, as might be expected, is violent in the extreme. A-III (PG)

Magnum Force (1973) Clint Eastwood returns as San Francisco detective "Dirty Harry" Callahan, this time taking on a group of renegade rookie cops who are systematically murdering the city's mobsters. Harry stops them by taking the law into his own hands, though viewers may have difficulty distinguishing between his brand of fascism and theirs. Ted Post directs an irresponsible movie celebrating the vigilante spirit. Graphic violence and incidental sexual references. O (R)

Magus, The (1968) British teacher (Michael Caine), escaping the marrriage plans of his mistress (Anna Karina), comes to a Greek island where he happens upon a practitioner of the occult (Anthony Quinn). As the young teacher becomes sexually involved with one of the magician's followers (Candice Bergen), the movie shifts from reality to self-indulgent fantasy. Director Guy Green's screen version of the John Fowles novel is not only pretentious but hopelessly muddled and ultimately senseless. Explicit sex and nudity. O (PG)

Mahanagar (see: "The Big City")

Mahler (1976) British production about the Austrian composer constructed out of a series of recollections triggered in Mahler's mind by his triumphant return to Vienna just before his death in 1911. Attempting to show the source of the composer's creative inspiration, director Ken Russell succeeds in linking a personality to a body of music, though there is an excess of Jewish stereotyping and references to the proto-Nazi tendencies of the period. A-IV (PG)

Mahogany (1975) Talented Diana Ross is wasted in a story about a black woman's rise from sales clerk in Chicago to famous model and fashion designer in Rome where she becomes disillusioned and returns to Chicago and the arms of her rejected lover (Billy Dee Williams). Directed by Berry Gordy, this Cinderella variation starts well enough but soon becomes mired in soap opera histrionics and sexual stereotyping. A-III (PG)

Maid in Sweden (1971) Swedish production about 17-year-old country girl (Christina Lindberg) who, on an innocent visit to her big sister in Stockholm, undergoes a prolonged bout of sexual awakening and initiation, thanks to the tutorial efforts of the sister and her boy-friends. Directed by Floch Johnson, the movie is little more than a vehicle for some grossly offensive nudity and simulated sex. O (R)

Maid to Order (1987) Spoiled Beverly Hills heiress (Ally Sheedy) learns a lesson in humility and caring when forced to work as a maid for a zany, garish couple (Dick Shawn and Valerie Perrine). Director Amy Jones sets the appropriate tone of

fantasy for this romantic fable which has a brief moment of comic nudity and some rough language. A-II (PG)

Maiden for a Prince, A (1967) Based on an historical incident, this bawdy Italian comedy in which the virility of a prince is put to an absurd test by his prospective in-laws satirizes Renaissance manners and morals. Some viewers may not find the subject particularly amusing or appropriate screen entertainment. A-IV (br)

Maids, The (1975) Screen version of the Jean Genet play about two maids (Glenda Jackson and Susannah York) who, whenever their mistress (Vivian Merchant) is absent, act out their hatred of her in little dramas of revolt which always climax in her murder. The last time they go into their act, one of them really dies, or so it seems. Directed by Christopher Miles, three talented actresses are wasted in a hopeless effort to find some meaning in a boring, repetitive drama that takes perverse pleasure in sadomasochistic cruelties. A-IV (PG)

Maidstone (1971) Novelist Norman Mailer made this movie by having a group of actors and non-actors improvise dialogue and action around a story of a movie director (Mailer) who decides to run for President. The result, unfortunately, is a tedious, self-conscious vanity production in which nothing much happens, unless one considers Rip Torn's violent on-screen fight with Mailer notable. Some graphic nudity and rough language. O (nr)

Main Chance (1966) British crime story in which a gambler outwits a group of international jewel smugglers and makes off with a fortune in diamonds. Director John Knight proves there is no honor among thieves rather smartly but tends to glamorize the amorality of the card-sharp hero. A-III (br)

Main Event, The (1979) Barbra Streisand, a high pressure perfume executive, finds that her accountant has absconded with her funds, leaving her but a single asset—the contract of a reluctant prizefighter, Ryan O'Neal. Attempting to recoup her losses, she forces him into the ring and their antagonism soon transmutes itself into true love. Erratic and not very funny comedy directed by Howard Zieff. Several sexually suggestive scenes. A-III (PG)

Maitresse (1976) French movie about a love affair between a country lout (Gerard Depardieu) and a city girl (Bulle Ogier), who works very hard at her chosen profession in which, clothed all in leather, she whips wealthy masochistic clients and provides whatever they request in brisk, businesslike fashion. Director Barbet Schroeder records these sessions with plodding, uncritical fidelity, showing far less interest in developing any credibility to the love affair. Tedious, ill-conceived movie with baldly explicit scenes of sadomasochism. O (R)

Make a Face (1971) Independent production about the lonely existence of a young woman (Karen Sperling who also produced and directed) near the border of schizophrenia, increasingly losing hold on what is real and what is fantasy. The more deeply troubled she becomes the more fragmented the movie and the more erratic and inexplicable are the events. An intriguing concept, it flounders in self-absorbed sexual fantasies and the limitations of low-budget filmmaking. A-IV (nr)

Making It (1971) Kristoffer Tabori plays a high school lothario whose aim is to make love with every female around. His irresponsible view of life

171

is made all the worse by the movie's portrayal of adults and life in general as thoroughly rotten, apparently justifying the contempt expressed by the boy's sexual vengeance. Director John Erman plays up the exploitative possibilities of the story at the expense of any moral relevance. Though there is nudity and coarseness, what offends most is the lack of any human values. O (R)

Making Love (1982) Predictable, uninspired triangle story about a husband (Michael Ontkean) who leaves his wife (Kate Jackson) for another man (Harry Hamlin). Under Arthur Hiller's flat direction, the romantic melodrama manages to work up no emotional power whatsoever, partly because homosexuality (a term that is never used and the word "gay" appears only once) is presented as nothing more than an acceptable variation of normal sexuality. This attempt to forestall moral implications and human consequences is as obviously fabricated as the rest of the movie. O (R)

Making Mr. Right (1987) Young professional woman giving up on romance finds true love in the arms of an android, made to resemble a real human being and for which she has been hired to program with the required social graces. Ann Magnuson and John Malkovich are the unlikely couple in director Susan Seidelman's social satire which has most of its focus on sexual matters. The movie manages to convey issues important to women but lacks a balanced approach to the relative importance of sex and love in a lasting relationship. Some crude language and sexual innuendo. A-III (PG-13)

Making the Grade (1984) Wretched little movie about an obnoxious rich kid who hires a tough city kid to go to prep school for him. Directed by Dorian Walker, it is crude, tasteless and sexually exploitative. O (R)

Malcolm (1986) A clever and affable story about a misunderstood young man (Colin Friels) who puts his mechanical abilities to work by teaming up with a pair of small-time felons. An Australian production directed by Nadia Tass and David Parker, it is an entertaining social comedy. Some harsh language and sexual references. A-III (PG-13)

Malcolm X (1972) Documentary based on Malcolm X's autobiography offers some selections from the black liberation leader's book (sensitively read by James Earl Jones) played against stock footage intended to sketch in Malcolm's early years. Its main substance, however, comes from newsreel interviews made after he had become a major public figure. Produced by Marvin Worth and Arnold Perl, the film suffers from the paucity of visual materials documenting Malcolm's life but at least the interviews let Malcolm speak for himself and viewers who wish to know more can read his extraordinary autobiography. A-II (PG)

Male of the Century (1976) French production directed by Claude Berri in which he also stars as the jealous husband whose wife (Juliet Berto) is taken hostage in a bank holdup. The movie flounders between comic vulgarity and soap opera histrionics before a final lunge into a moralistic conclusion about learning to live with our human imperfections. Failure in Gallic wit and taste in dealing with sexual matters. A-III (nr)

Malizia (1974) Italian sex comedy about a pretty young girl from the provinces (Laura Antonelli) who becomes the housemaid for an all-male household in Palermo, where all from widowed father to

a brat in kneepants make eyes at her. Directed by Salvatore Samperi, the movie relies upon comic inversion so that by the conclusion it is clear that the seemingly sweet young thing is the dominant figure who has been doing the seducing. Graphic sexual initiation of an adolescent. O (R)

Maltese Bippy (1969) Feeble horror comedy in which Dan Rowan and Dick Martin are victims of a conspiracy to steal a priceless gem hidden somewhere in their decaying Victorian mansion near a cemetery with walking corpses. Director Norman Panama seldom achieves anything more than an isolated funny line or sight gag. Mild sexual innuendo. A-II (G)

Maltese Falcon, The (1941) Classic crime melodrama adapted from the Dashiell Hammett novel by director John Huston is skillfully constructed around the search for a priceless statue by gumshoe Sam Spade (Humphrey Bogart) after his partner is murdered for it. Mary Astor, Sidney Greenstreet and Peter Lorre shine in support of Bogart as the tough-minded detective who solves the case with a mix of logic, charm and muscle instead of mindless violence. A-II (br)

Mame (1974) Lucille Ball stars as the flamboyant Auntie Mame in director Gene Saks' overblown movie version of the hit Broadway musical. Though the fun of the original is still there, it is obscured by an overly lavish and slow-paced production that robs the material of any spontaneity. Mediocre entertainment at best. A-II (PG)

Man, The (1972) Intelligent adaptation of mushy Irving Wallace novel scores as a melodrama about a black man thrust into the White House by a freak accident. The story concerns no real political issues but it is absorbing to watch the character of the new President (James Earl Jones in a fine performance) develop from figurehead to forceful chief executive. Rod Sterling gets credit for wresting a credible screenplay from the Wallace original and Joseph Sargent directs with a sure sense of popular entertainment. A-II (PG)

Man, a Woman and a Bank, A (1979) Routine bank heist movie about an engineer (Donald Sutherland) and an old friend (Paul Mazursky) who join forces to rig the workings of the bank's computer and the photographer (Brooke Adams in a bright performance) who is on to them. Directed by Noel Black, the predictable plot moves at a sluggish pace with little to recommend it save some picturesque views of Vancouver and Macao. Acceptance of casual sex and frequent rough language. A-III (PG)

Man and a Woman, A (1967) The soap opera sudsiness of this tender, optimistic love story about a widowed auto test-driver (Jean-Louis Trintignant) and a widowed script girl (Anouk Aimee) is enhanced by the lush cinematic style of director Claude Lelouch and a haunting musical background. In a graphic sexual encounter, virtue triumphs in effect, but rather slowly for the sensibilities of some viewers. A-III (br)

Man and a Woman: 20 Years Later, A (1986) Director Claude Lelouch's sequel has none of the charm and appeal of the original. Instead, he has made a glossy-looking movie about filmmaking that has its clever moments but lacks any humanity in its characters. Permissive attitude toward sexual affairs. A-III (PG)

Man and Boy (1972) Western about a black ex-cavalry man (Bill Cosby) who struggles to maintain his homestead in spite of racial tensions after the Civil War. Most of the picture, however, deals with the odyssey of father and young son trying to recover a stolen horse. Directed by E.W. Swackhamer, the racial dimension is handled quite well and the story has a certain gritty honesty but the plot has some gaping holes and foggy motivations, especially in a climactic shootout. Some salty dialogue may be inappropriate for pre-teens. A-II (G)

Man Called Adam, A (1966) Muddled and melodramatic story of a jazz musician (Sammy Davis Jr.) struggling against his own personal problems and racial prejudice is unfortunately not helped by director Leo Penn's heavy-handed treatment of mature themes. Some sexual innuendo. A-III (br)

Man Called Dagger, A (1967) Low-budget spy story about an agent (Jan Murray) who thwarts a scheme by neo-Nazis to conquer the world. Ineptly directed by Richard Rush, it is excessively violent and sexually suggestive. O (br)

Man Called Flintstone, The (1966) Big screen version of the Hanna-Barbera television cartoon series about the Flintstone family in which Fred's resemblance to a secret agent results in his being sent to Paris on a spy mission. Harmless slapstick fun though some adults may find it a bore. A-I (br)

Man Called Horse, A (1970) Richard Harris plays a wealthy Englishman who is captured by Sioux Indians and, after undergoing a painful and humiliating captivity, wins the respect of his captors and is ultimately accepted as a member of the tribe. Director Elliot Silverstein succeeds to a large extent in attempting to portray Native Americans as something more than Hollywood stereotypes. In doing this, however, the dramatization includes some nudity and a number of scenes of torture, scalping and painful rites of initiation. A-IV (PG)

Man Called Sledge, A (1971) Routine caper movie with James Garner playing the title character, a hard-bitten, semi-respectable outlaw who'd rather rob than kill, but who has been forced for economic reasons to do both. With sidekick Dennis Weaver, Garner and his gang set out to pull off a fantastic gold heist. As directed by Vic Morrow, however, the story heavily accents the violence, including a brutal rape, which occurs in a desecrated church. O (R)

Man Could Get Killed, A (1966) James Garner plays an innocent American banker who gets embroiled in one mysterious situation after another in this caper spoof featuring Melina Mercouri in an international smuggling ring. There is nothing new here but what gives the comedy some class is the stylish tongue-in-cheek direction under Ronald Neame and Cliff Owen. Some comic violence. A-II (br)

Man for All Seasons, A (1966) Engrossing drama of the last seven years in the life of Thomas More, Henry VIII's chancellor, who met a martyr's death rather than compromise his conscience during a period of religious turmoil. Standout performance by Paul Scofield in the title role, among a number of other notable performances from a uniformly fine cast. Adapted for the screen by Robert Bolt from his own stage play and masterfully directed by Fred Zinnemann, the movie achieves an authentic historical dimension that makes its events more accessible and thereby more universal. Profoundly entertaining. A-I (G)

Man Friday (1976) Defoe's story about two men's survival on a desert island is turned into a moralistic attack on the evils of civilization as Crusoe (Peter O'Toole) attempts to infect the noble savage Friday (Richard Roundtree) with such ignoble concepts as master and servant, personal property, competition, greed and sexual guilt. Despite some occasional humor, director Jack Gold cannot sustain credibility in the movie's sophomoric central thesis, let alone its bloody conclusion which turns the 19th-century adventure classic on its head. A-III (PG)

Man from O.R.G.Y., The (1970) Robert Walker Jr., super-sleuth from the Organization for the Rational Guidance of Youth (O.R.G.Y.), must uncover three lost ladies of easy virtue whose branded behinds prove them beneficiaries of their deceased madam's will. Directed by James Hill, the movie veers into a series of vicious murders and inane burlesque skits relying heavily on nudity and racial slurs. O (R)

Man from Snowy River, The (1983) Australian Western about a young man (Tom Burlinson) who tames a herd of wild horses and wins the love of a spirited young woman (Sigrid Thornton). Kirk Douglas is on hand in a dual role playing twin brothers. The scenery is impressive and so are the horses, but director George Miller fares less well with the humans in this moderately entertaining, but far from inspired movie. Some restrained violence. A-II (PG)

Man in the Glass Booth, The (1975) Screen version of Robert Shaw's play about a Jewish survivor of the Nazi death camps who becomes a wealthy New York businessman until arrested and put on trial in Israel as a Nazi war criminal. Edward Anhalt's script shifts the emphasis from the question of the man's true identity to his motivation in testifying about the irrational prejudice that caused the Holocaust. Though director Arthur Hiller fails to integrate all of the themes, including that of a Christ figure, and Maximilian Shell's performance in the title role is uneven, the movie's effort to evoke a more human response to the enormity of the Nazi crimes is of more than passing merit. Mature themes would be accessible to most older teenagers. A-III (PG)

Man in the Wilderness (1971) Richard Harris plays a frontiersman abandoned in hostile Indian country by a trapping expedition after being mauled by a bear. Recovering, he treks through the wilds seeking revenge on the expedition's leader (John Huston). Richard C. Sarafian's direction becomes tiresome in cutting back and forth between tracker, Indians and struggling expedition and the final confrontation is jarringly anti-climactic. The movie's rewards are in its photography of the great, rugged wilderness conveying nature's power and dignity, as well as several sights along the way, notably the trailside birth of an Indian baby, that have their own stunning, eerie beauty. Considerable violence. A-III (GP)

Man Is Not a Bird (1974) Excellent Yugoslavian drama about a middle-aged engineer whose work takes him to a small town for a couple of weeks where he passes the evenings in a brief affair that ends badly. Director Dusan Makavejev creates a picture of people mesmerized by the daily routine of their lives from which they escape only through momentary diversions. Though produced in a socialist country, its mood of quiet desperation could be mirrored in any industrialized country of the world. A-III (nr)

Man of Iron (1982) Polish production directed by Andrzej Wajda presents a powerful account of the confrontation between Solidarity labor union and Poland's Communist regime at the Gdansk shipyards which ended in Solidarity's victory in August 1980. Though the mix of real characters and documentary footage with a fictional story line isn't as smooth as it might be, the result is a dramatic and courageous movie in its own right, one that will have a continuing significance for those concerned about human rights. A-II (PG)

Man of La Mancha (1972)   Disappointing screen version of the Dale Wasserman musical about Cervantes transforming his Inquisition cell into the world of Don Quixote preserves enough of the music and lyrics to please most admirers of the original, but just barely. Peter O'Toole in the title role and Sophia Loren as Aldonza/Dulcinea are miscast. Even worse, director Arthur Hiller's tight, literal camera and endless pans work against the romantic poetry of the story and, by dwelling on its adventure aspects, misses the work's emphasis on the power of ideals and the artistic spirit. Mature themes. A-III (PG)

Man of the Year (1973)   Witless Italian sex farce about the misadventures of a poor Sicilian (Lando Buzzanca) with a genital deformity that makes him irresistible to women. Produced, written and directed by Marco Vicario, it's a low-budget one-joke movie that never rises above the level of adolescent sex fantasy. O (R)

Man on a Swing (1974)   The brutal murder of a young girl has the police baffled until a clairvoyant comes forward with some information about the crime that could only be known to the murderer. Good performances by Cliff Robertson as the dogged police chief and Joel Grey as the wildly erratic clairvoyant, but director Frank Perry's drama is full of holes, false clues and an abrupt ending that will satisfy only those interested in parapsychology and the fact that it is difficult to distinguish genuine mediums from fakers. A-III (PG)

Man on the Roof (1977)   Deceptively simple, straightforward crime thriller about the murder of a police inspector and the subsequent siege of the heavily armed killer who takes to a roof top and cuts down the policemen attempting his capture. Swedish production directed by Bo Widerberg, its attention to detail and urban environment give the sometimes melodramatic events an emotional impact that places it in a class far above the conventional thriller. Its dramatic credibility is helped also by the performances of a superior cast headed by Carl-Gustaf Lindstedt. Some scenes of graphic violence. A-III (R)

Man Who Fell to Earth, The (1976)   Arty science-fiction movie about a visitor from outer space (David Bowie) who has left his own drought-stricken planet in an effort to save his dying wife and child, but how is never quite clear. Director Nicholas Roeg, a former cameraman, prefers flashy visual effects rather than less picturesque exposition that would better advance the story line and develop characterization. Several scenes of nudity in a sexual context. O (R)

Man Who Had Power Over Women, The (1970) Rod Taylor stars as the London-based manager of a bratty rock star but he has grown sick of his lucrative job and a marriage that has soured. When he becomes romantically involved with the wife (Carol White) of his best friend, a happy ending is hard to contrive. As directed by John Kish, the well-acted, potentially interesting melodrama con-centrates on the slick and flashy rather than facing up to the moral questions, including abortion, that it raises. A-III (R)

Man Who Haunted Himself, The (1971)   Stuffy British executive Roger Moore has no difficulty getting back into the swing of things following a nasty auto accident, but he does develop a problem in trying to cope with a look-alike double who is out to smash Moore's career and marriage. Moore is quite good as the confused businessman but director Basil Dearden's psychological drama lacks tautness and relies upon too many plot contrivances. Adult situations. A-III (PG)

Man Who Loved Cat Dancing, The (1973) Sarah Miles, running away from her husband in the Old West, is picked up by Burt Reynolds' outlaw band. After being humiliated, menaced, brutalized and finally raped, she at last finds true love and the strength to kill her husband. Directed by Richard C. Sarafian, the movie never gets below the surface of its inept plot, so burdened is it with complications often bordering on the ridiculous. Long-drawn out scenes of sexual menace and the implication that rape has served to "liberate" this woman from her sexual fears constitute a male fantasy that should be put to rest. O (PG)

Man Who Loved Women, The (1977)   Trivial French production about a man (Charles Denner) whose single passion is his pursuit of women is little more than a loosely-tied collection of bland vignettes, which are seldom amusing and never moving. Directed by Francois Truffaut, it is a weak and shallow effort, especially because the activity of its title character is given no moral context whatsoever. Some gratuitous nudity. O (nr)

Man Who Loved Women, The (1983)   Burt Reynolds plays a famous sculptor whose insatiable pursuit of women is eventually and quite literally the death of him. The story is told in flashbacks by his psychiatrist (Julie Andrews), incessantly droning on with some of the most banal insights ever set to film. Directed by Blake Edwards, the limp comedy is a poor remake of a 1977 French movie. Some extremely crude sexual sequences. O (R)

Man Who Skied Down Everest, The (1976)   In 1970, Japanese skier Yuichiro Miura set out from Katmandu, Nepal, for Mt. Everest where his objective was not to make an ascent to the peak but to reach a ledge 400 yards short of the crest from which he would ski down to the valley that lay more than a mile below. What happened during this dangerous undertaking may be seen in a splendid Academy Award-winning documentary with a narration adapted from Miura's diary, giving Western viewers some insights into this feat as a quest in achieving harmony with nature. An exciting adventure documentary, filled with dazzling scenic beauty, it is absorbing fare for the entire family, including those unconcerned with the paradoxes of Eastern and Western philosophy. A-I (G)

Man Who Wasn't There, The (1983)   Gimmicky 3-D movie about a liquid that makes the drinker (Steve Guttenberg) invisible, free to explore a women's locker room among other things, while eluding various American and foreign agents. Amateurishly directed by Bruce Malmuth, the movie has little plot, humor or excitement. In 3-D, a bad movie simply gains another dimension of awfulness. Exploitative nudity. O (R)

Man Who Would Be King, The (1975)   Sean

Connery and Michael Caine star as highly imperfect heroes in a movie based on a Rudyard Kipling story about two British soldiers who pursue a dangerous dream of founding a kingdom of their own in the remote mountains of northern India. Director John Huston has fashioned a vigorous, romantic adventure saga tinged with realism and featuring some fine acting, including that of Christopher Plummer as Kipling who, one suspects, would have thoroughly enjoyed the movie version. Some violent action scenes. A-III (PG)

Man with Connections, The (1970) French anti-war comedy about an enterprising draftee (Guy Bedos) who wins the respect of his military superiors by claiming to be a personal friend of Brigitte Bardot, but even this fails to save him from being sent to the front where he serves more time in the stockade than in defending French imperialism. Director Claude Berri's lightly humorous, occasionally caustic and witty, account is too loosely plotted and nostalgically self-indulgent to be completely satisfying. A-III (R)

Man with One Red Shoe, The (1985) An innocent bystander (Tom Hanks), mistaken for an enemy agent by the CIA, goes through his daily routine blissfully unaware that he is in mortal danger from various and sundry agents who are following his every move. Directed by Stan Dragoti, this comedy is an innocuous remake of the stylish French farce, "The Tall Blond Man with One Black Shoe." Comic violence and a bit of sexual innuendo. A-II (PG)

Man with the Balloons (1968) Failed Italian story about a man (Marcello Mastroianni) who goes bonkers when his girl friend (Catherine Spaak) leaves him. Directed by Marco Ferrari, the story treatment exploits nudity. O (br)

Man with the Glass Eye, The (1972) Confused mystery yarn about a rash of murders decimating a gang of weird characters who use a vaudeville troupe as a cover for their dealings in white slavery and heroin smuggling. Badly-dubbed German import directed by Alfred Vohrer relies on grotesque characterizations in a story punctuated by sex and gore. A-III (PG)

Man with the Golden Gun, The (1974) Rather tired spy adventure with James Bond (Roger Moore) as the target for a million-dollar assassin (Christopher Lee) who uses golden bullets. Director Guy Hamilton offers the standard Bond mayhem, including a spectacular auto stunt, but the once brittle and bright double-entendres are now merely tasteless and smutty remarks. Maud Adams and Britt Ekland are the decoratively exploited females. A-III (PG)

Man with Two Brains, The (1983) Brilliant brain surgeon (Steve Martin) is married to a woman (Kathleen Turner) who has a beautiful body but loathes him, while the woman who loves him is a bodyless brain being kept alive by a mad scientist (David Warner). Guess what happens? Director Carl Reiner has a lot of good fun with such things as Warner's Frankenstein-style layout in a sleek condominium and a very tough Austrian test for drunk drivers, but the silliness does pall after a while. Some rather explicit sexual byplay and nudity. O (R)

Man, Woman and Child (1983) Sappy screen version of a soppy novel by Erich Segal about a perfect American couple (Martin Sheen and Blythe Danner) and their two perfect children, all living in perfect bliss until Sheen finds out he is the father

of a bastard son conceived during a weak moment while in France a decade earlier. The waif is brought to California where he turns out to be perfectly irresistible and all ends predictably. Director Dick Richards' slick and manipulative melodrama leaves a soapy aftertaste. Glossy depiction of the affair (in flashbacks). A-III (PG)

Manchurian Candidate, The (1962) Fine political spine-tingler with Laurence Harvey as Korean War POW transformed by Red Chinese hypnosis into a deadly instrument of assassination. Returned to the U.S. during the time of a Presidential campaign, his behavior toward wife and family is at times unaccountably strange and by the time an Army psychiatrist (Frank Sinatra in a solid acting performance) figures out why, a major manhunt and race with time are on. Director John Frankenheimer has fashioned a superior suspense movie with a growing intensity that adults and older teenagers may appreciate. A-III (br)

Mandabi (1970) From Senegal comes a small gem of a tale about a money order (which is what the title means) for a small amount of money sent from France by a hard-working young man to his uncle in Dakar whose attempts to cash it become an odyssey through the senseless byways of modern bureaucracy. Even when it despairs, the film is balanced by humor and belief in the eventual triumph of human righteousness. Very convincing performances by a non-professional cast in a very professionally made movie directed by Ousmane Sembene. A-II (nr)

Mandingo (1975) Old South plantation owner (James Mason) runs a "breeding farm" for black slaves, a business allowing his son (Perry King) to take his choice of black women when not off setting up fighting matches for his full-blooded Mandingo slave (Ken Norton) with whom his wife (Susan George) takes to sleeping out of pique at her husband's infidelity. Directed by Richard Fleischer, it's sordid melodramatic trash, forgettable save for its cynical box-office manipulation of racial tensions in sexual contexts. Violence, sadism, nudity and graphic sex. O (R)

Manhattan (1979) Successful TV comedy writer (Woody Allen), whose wife (Meryl Streep) has left him for another woman, is having an affair with a 17-year-old high school girl (Mariel Hemingway) but then gets involved with the lover (Diane Keaton) of his best friend (Michael Murphy). Greatly aided by romantic black-and-white photography and a lush Gershwin score, director Allen has made a small but clever bittersweet comedy about sexual relationships, often amusing, but just as often flat. Though the movie's moral vision puts a premium on being faithful and really caring about people, it seems largely to excuse the sexual weaknesses of its characters. A-IV (R)

Manhattan Project, The (1986) Over-long melodrama, loosely based on fact, about a teenager (Christopher Collet) who builds an atomic bomb at home to protest the construction of a nuclear plant near his home. A physicist from the lab (John Lithgow) tries to save the boy—and the New York area—from potential disaster. Failed social commentary, token teen romance and a single harsh expletive. A-II (PG-13)

Manhunter (1986) The twist in this crime thriller is in following an FBI agent (William Peterson) who uses both imagination and intuition to reconstruct the mind of a serial killer in order to track him down. Director Michael Mann emphasizes the psychological elements of detection rather than resorting to the more conventional means of guns and brawn. Glimpses of grisly photos of murder victims, a bedroom scene and some foul language. A-III (R)

Manitou, The (1978) A 500-year-old Indian medicine man comes back to life and wrecks all sorts of havoc in this inept and ludicrous horror movie starring Tony Curtis and Susan Strasberg. Director William Girdler's otherwise innocuous effort contains violence and nudity. O (PG)

Mannequin (1987) A stock boy (Andrew McCarthy) has his life changed when the mannequin he created comes to life (Kim Cattrall) and falls in love with him while helping to foil a villainous attempt to buy out the store for which he works. Michael Gottlieb directs a romantic fantasy in which Miss Cattrall, an older woman, seduces the younger, seemingly innocent youth. Characterizations stressing the physical aspects of the relationship, sexual references, crude jokes and poorly executed slapstick comedy. A-III (PG)

Manson (1973) Filmmaker Laurence Merrick's exploitative documentary supposedly examining the social ills behind the crimes committed by the hippie clan led by Charles Manson exposes little more than the director's own cynicism and the morbidity of its intended audience. Relentlessly foul language with occasional matching visuals only further emphasizes this work's moral vacuum. O (R)

Marathon Man (1976) Dustin Hoffman stars as an introspective student who finds himself involved with a terrifying fugitive Nazi (Laurence Olivier). Director John Schlesinger has made a shrewd, hollow and profoundly anti-human thriller, heavy on violence and exploiting the tragedy of the Holocaust. O (R)

March or Die (1977) Dick Richards directs a muddled action adventure epic starring Gene Hackman as a cynical major in the French Foreign Legion who, following action in World War I, is given the task of protecting an archaeological expedition in the Sahara led by Max Von Sydow. Among a cast including Catherine Deneuve, only Terence Hill manages to come out of this cliche-ridden melodrama with any amount of luster. Violence and brutal view of life. A-III (PG)

Marco (1974) Disappointing musical treatment of the Marco Polo success story has a number of amusing moments, supplied principally by the uncontrollable mugging of Zero Mostel as the naughty-but-nice Kubla Khan, and Cie Cie Win as his nice-but-naughty warrior-daughter. As the intrepid Marco, Desi Arnaz Jr.'s role demands little acting but lots of cheery grinning. Directed by Seymour Robbie, the funny bits and pieces cannot overcome the dull stretches in a drawn-out, generally slack production. Some risque byplay and mild double entendres. A-II (G)

Marco the Magnificent (1966) Disappointing adventure movie based on the adventures of Marco Polo (Horst Buchholz) in carrying a message from the pope to Kubla Khan in China. Directed by Denys De La Patelliere and Noel Howard, the plodding and episodic script is of less interest than the spectacle and beautiful photography. Some violence. A-II (br)

Margo (1971) Israeli production about a stodgy university professor (Oded Teomi) who is brought out of his shell by a country girl (Levanna Finkelstein) giving him the maternal care, zest for life

and simple pleasures that his swinging, pseudo-sophisticated wife cannot. Lacking wit and originality, director Menahem Golan's effort simply romanticizes adultery and divorce in sun-drenched Jerusalem with little rhyme and no reason. O (R)

Maria's Lovers (1985) World War II veteran (John Savage) returns from a prisoner-of-war camp to marry his childhood sweetheart (Nastassia Kinski) but when he can't consummate the marriage, she is courted by a host of suitors. In a ponderous slow-moving melodrama, director Andrei Konchalovsky generates far less emotion than needed to keep it from being a bore. Some too-graphic bedroom sequences. O (R)

Marie (1985) Following the true story of Marie Ragghianti, a divorced mother of three children and the first woman to head the Tennessee Board of Pardons and Paroles, the movie details her courage in refusing to cooperate in the graft and corruption of the governor who appointed her to office. Directed by Roger Donaldson, this inspiring film portrait owes much to a superb performance by Sissy Spacek in the title role. Several scenes of violence. A-II (PG-13)

Marjoe (1972) Documentary look behind the gaudy facade of the evangelical "business" in the Southwest, focusing on the spotted career of itinerant preacher Marjoe Gortner, a young man who began bigtime tent preaching at the age of four and who now, in his mid-twenties, wants to cash in his ministry and expose himself and his fellow evangelist-hustlers. When filmmakers Howard Smith and Sarah Kernochan get away from Marjoe's somewhat suspect self-confessions, they find a chilling system of religious exploitation based on a fundamentalist fear of God and viewers will have to decide for themselves how unbiased is their portrayal of the dark underside of that old time religion. A-III (PG)

Mark of the Devil (1972) Wretched little horror movie about a 16th-century witch hunter (Herbert Lom) and his young assistant (Udo Kier) who go from town to town searching out evidence of witchcraft. Director Michael Armstrong spends a good deal of time in the torture chamber demonstrating the uses of such instruments as tongue extractors, thumb screws, racks and spiked chairs, torturing not only a host of hapless actors but also the audience. Extreme violence, a few rapes and some nudity. O (R)

Marlowe (1969) James Garner stars as Raymond Chandler's hard-boiled detective Philip Marlowe in a complicated plot involving blackmail and ice-pick murders. Garner's Marlowe relies on whimsy but lacks the essential inner toughness of this school of private eye. Director Paul Bogart and cast (including William Daniels and Jackie Coogan) try hard but can't quite bring the movie off as a cohesive whole. Sensationalistic treatment with nudity in story's conclusion. O (PG)

Marnie (1964) Flawed but masterfully eccentric thriller stars Tippi Hedrin as a compulsive thief caught in the act by wise and worldly journalist Sean Connery. Instead of turning her in, he marries the disturbed girl and tries to discover the reasons for her irrational behavior. Director Alfred Hitchcock explores the theme of the redeeming power of love with some compassion but the treatment is adult. A-III (br)

Maroc 7 (1967) Agent Gene Barry tracks international jewel thief Cyd Charisse to Morocco where she plans her next robbery in director Gerry

O'Hara's dull and implausible crime story. Excessive sexual innuendo and some violence. O (br)

Marooned (1969) Space mission goes awry when three astronauts (Gene Hackman, Richard Crenna and James Franciscus) get stranded on a space station and ground control (headed by Gregory Peck) tries to get a rescue rocket ready in time to save them. Under the direction of John Sturges, what could have been a gripping adventure yarn bogs down in some fine space and electronic effects that detract interest from the human dimension of the plot and the moral questions raised by it, such as risking the rescue mission in an unproven craft. A-II (PG)

Marquise of O..., The (1976) French adaptation of a 19th-century novel by Heinrich von Kleist about a woman (Edith Clever) who is rescued from enemy soldiers by a seemingly virtuous count who takes advantage of her sedated sleep as he guards her through the night. Director Erich Rohmer has fun with the conventions of the time but does not betray Kleist's characters and their concerns. A-II (PG)

Marriage Came Tumbling Down, The (1968) The focus of this slight but beautifully tender little French movie is Michel Simon's performance as an aging, earthy, yet wise and loving grandfather who helps save his philandering grandson's marriage. Unfortunately, director Jacques Poitrenaud fails to give much substance to the young couple's roles so that their final reconciliation has small significance. However, the lovely countryside of Provence and Simon's sensitive and profoundly human characterization makes it well worth viewing. A-II (G)

Marriage of a Young Stockbroker, The (1971) Failed satire about a neophyte broker (Richard Benjamin) who is a failure in his attempts to control his compulsive voyeurism, which cause endless professional and marital problems, until his realization at movie's end that he need not be ruled by society's conventions. For all of its humorous digs at social conformity, director Lawrence Turman fails to elicit any sympathy for his alienated young man whose real problem is a complacent smugness that makes him and the movie a bore. Its treatment of women is consistently demeaning, for example, the sordid scene with a nymphomaniac should have been played for compassion instead of snickers. O (PG)

Marriage of Maria Braun, The (1979) German melodrama about a woman (Hanna Schygulla) whose husband returns from a Russian P.O.W. camp after World War II to discover she is having an affair with an American soldier, kills him and goes to prison. Vowing to have a fortune waiting when he gets out, she rises to be top executive at a textile firm through an affair with its owner. Directed by Rainer Werner Fassbinder, this hard-edged portrait of pragmatic amorality seems to be saying that postwar Germany, like Maria, lost its soul in the struggle for material prosperity. Some rough language and brief nudity. A-IV (R)

Married Couple, A (1970) Canadian documentary about the marital games that go on within a troubled Toronto household in which husband and wife act out their inner frustrations and conflicts for the benefit of a movie crew. Directed by Allan King, the film might serve a psychologist or marriage counselor as a point of departure for discussion purposes but in itself it lacks the coherence to justify the extremities of emotion, rough language and nudity it displays. A-IV (nr)

Marry Me, Marry Me (1969) French production about an amiable but aimless young man (Claude Berri) who is so uncertain about marrying his already pregnant sweetheart (Elizabeth Wiener) that he has a quick affair before going through with the ceremony. A fatuous epilogue suggests the hero's fears of marriage to have been unjustified. Also directed by Berri, the story is as aimless as its self-absorbed central character, but in the background are some interesting aspects of Jewish life, especially the wedding feast and a certain sense of sadness at the erosion of Jewish traditions in the affluent, socially permissive present. A-III (PG)

Martyr, The (1976) Israeli-German screen biography of a Polish physician and educator, Dr. Janusz Korczak, who in 1942 accompanied a group of wartime orphans to the Warsaw Ghetto and then to the extermination camp of Treblinka where they all perished together. Directed by Alexander Ford, it is a rather plodding and unimaginative dramatization, but the concluding scene of the children with Dr. Korczak (Leo Genn in a very credible performance) at their head, marching with dignity to the train that will take them to Treblinka, is heart-rending and unforgettable. A-II (nr)

Martyrs of Love (1969) Czechoslovakian movie offering three surrealistic episodes on the theme of frustrated desire focusing on the monotonous life of a junior clerk, the aristocratic dreams of a servant girl and a lonely man's need to feel part of a family. Directed by Jan Nemec, its serio-comic mixture of reality and fantasy is very effective but many will find its absurd logic and bizarre scenes pointless, if not unsettling. A-III (nr)

Mary, Queen of Scots (1971) Historical drama details the downfall of the Scottish queen (Vanessa Redgrave) in a 16th-century power struggle with Elizabeth of England (Glenda Jackson). Charles Jarrott directs the fascinating story of two strong women, both utterly egotistical but otherwise completely opposite personalities, slugging it out dramatically and politically in a contest of wits and wills. Besides a slice of history, the movie's value is to afford two accomplished actresses the opportunity to play against one another. A-II (GP)

M*A*S*H (1970) Anti-war comedy about a Mobile Army Surgical Hospital during the Korean War where a trio of skilled battle surgeons (Donald Sutherland, Elliott Gould and Tom Skerritt) maintain their sanity by engaging in crazy hijinks outside the operating room. Robert Altman directs Ring Lardner, Jr.'s episodic screenplay with an uneven mixture of comic styles, leaning heavily on irreverence and ridicule of authority figures. Good cast also includes Robert Duvall as a pious hypocrite and Sally Kellerman as the head nurse. Gory operating room sequences and sexually oriented humor. A-IV (PG)

Mask (1985) Sentimental, slow-moving story of a youth with a deformed face who makes a happy life for himself with the help of an understanding mother (Cher). Director Peter Bogdanovich offers a relatively benign view of the lifestyle of a motorcycle gang, involving drug abuse and sexual promiscuity. A-IV (PG-13)

Mass Appeal (1984) Screen version of Bill C. Davis' stage comedy about the pastor (Jack Lemmon) of an affluent suburban parish who is assigned to take an outspoken young seminary student (Zeljko Ivanek) under his wing. Davis' play is really about two characters much alike in everything but age who have suffered through unhappy childhoods and never established a good relationship with their families. For them the priesthood is a refuge from the harsh complexities of life. Since the inaccuracies about the Catholic Church (and there are many) are innocuous, this is for adults and adolescents. A-II (PG)

Massacre in Rome (1973)   On March 23, 1944, Italian partisans attacked a column of SS police troops marching through the center of Rome and killed 33 of them. Within 24 hours, 335 Italians were dead, executed in reprisal on the direct orders of Hitler. Director George Pan Cosmatos effectively sets up this specific moment in history and the motivations of the various characters involved, capably performed by a strong cast including Richard Burton, Marcello Mastrioanni and Leo McKern. The provocative re-creation, based on the book by Robert Katz, avoids the easy oversimplifications of most such movies to pose troubling issues of moral responsibility for war-time atrocities that deserve thoughtful consideration by its audience. A-III (PG)

Master Gunfighter, The (1975)   American gunslinger and samurai sword fighter (Tom Laughlin) marries into an aristocratic Spanish family in Old California but has to fight their son (Ron O'Neal) when he takes to stealing gold and killing Indians in order to pay the Yankee taxes on the family hacienda. Directed by Frank Laughlin, the result is a tedious, pretentious, badly acted but lushly produced Western whose theme of anti-violence is conveyed mostly through violence. A-III (PG)

Masters of the Universe (1987)   Live-action sci-fi fantasy based on the Mattel toy line and TV cartoon series about the ongoing conflict between heroic warrior He-Man (Dolph Lundgren) and power crazed Skeletor (Frank Langella). Gary Goddard directs using ample comic-book stylized violence in this purely escapist zapfest that might adversely affect the very young. A-II (PG)

Matchless (1968)   Steely-eyed Patrick O'Neal is an espionage agent of passing skill in this intermittently comic spy melodrama with an invisible man gimmick. He gets by with a little help from secret agent Ira Furstenburg and the stupidity of heavies Donald Pleasence and Henry Silva. Italian production directed by Alberto Lattuada has some violence, but its suggestive costuming and situations are excessive. O (br)

Matewan (1987)   Chris Cooper stars as a union organizer who comes to the coal fields of West Virginia after World War I to help the miners win a bitter, bloody strike. Written and directed by John Sayles, the movie is admirable in its idealistic picture of the workers' solidarity united against the company's reliance upon force. Some graphic violence and a verbal account of a sexual assault. A-III (PG-13)

Matilda (1978)   Elliott Gould plays a seedy promoter who discovers a down-at-the-heels kangaroo act and with the help of sportswriter Robert Mitchum steers the beast to a bout with the heavyweight champion of the world. Director Daniel Mann's mirthless, blindingly dumb comedy is an embarrassment to sit through. The realistic violence of the final boxing match is not the sort of thing most parents would want their younger children exposed to. A-II (PG)

Mattei Affair, The (1973)   Enrico Mattei, head of the state's oil cartel, was perhaps the most powerful man in Italy when he died under mysterious circumstances in a plane crash in 1962. In following his career and in examining the contradictory evidence about the crash, this Italian dramatization is as dynamic as Mattei himself, played by Gian Maria Volonte with the complete assurance of the self-confident man who relishes competition. Implicit throughout director Francesco Rosi's fast-moving, impressionistic re-creation are questions about the wider issues of social justice that are seldom raised in the ruthless battle to control the world's oil resources. Some scenes of stylized violence. A-III (R)

Matter of Days, A (1969)   French student activist studying in Prague, believing the Czech liberalization to be tainted with bourgeois materialism, returns to Paris during the May 1968 student riots. Though the Soviet invasion a few months after the completion of the movie proved her political views wrong-headed, the drama is of some interest for its picture of 1960's youth with their easy comradeship, their insatiable quest for new values and their inevitable sexual candor. A-IV (R)

Matter of Innocence, A (1967)   Failed British adaptation of a Noel Coward story about a young girl (Hayley Mills) being raised by her reprobate uncle (Trevor Howard). Guy Green's heavyhanded direction makes even more offensive scenes of her learning about sex, alcohol and larceny. O (br)

Matter of Time, A (1976)   Well-intentioned but hopelessly sentimental and disjointed treatment of the Cinderella theme defeats the best efforts of Liza Minnelli, Ingrid Bergman and Charles Boyer. Directed by Vincente Minnelli, the inept Italian production has some occasional rough language and a comically-meant attempted rape scene. A-III (PG)

Maurie (1973)   Fact-based dramatization of Cincinnati Royals basketball player Jack Twyman (Bo Svenson) who devoted himself to caring for teammate Maurice Stokes (Bernie Casey) after a 1957 head injury during a game resulted in total paralysis. The result is a saga of determination, love, and endless hours of pain from expensive treatments which gradually brought back his powers of speech and partial control of body movement. Though director Daniel Mann's movie is slow, it is never tedious in recounting without sentimentality but plenty of honest emotion the story of teammates who summoned the inner strength necessary to surmount a time of deep crisis. A-I (G)

Max Dugan Returns (1983)   A long-absent father (Jason Robards) turns up at the home of his daughter (Marsha Mason), an impoverished widow with a teenage son (Matthew Broderick). He has only six months to live, is remorseful and also has more than a half-million in cold cash of dubious origin neatly packed in one of his suitcases. Bland, contrived comedy written by Neil Simon and directed by Herbert Ross, it is mildly amusing thanks to the skill and personality of its performers. Some mild verbal vulgarities and a fuzzy moral stance towards stealing, but it's basically innocuous. A-II (PG)

Max Havelaar (1979)   Dutch adventure drama about a brave and exuberantly idealistic government official (Peter Faber) in mid-19th century Java who almost single-handedly takes on the entrenched exploiters of the native population until the authorities finally send him back to Holland. Director Fons Rademakers has succeeded admirably in his re-creation of a bygone and little-known era, with Faber giving a vital, wholly convincing performance as the anti-colonial hero. Engrossing and largely entertaining but with several instances of brutal violence. A-III (R)

Maxie (1985) A young couple (Glenn Close and Mandy Patinkin) rent a house that had once belonged to a promising Hollywood starlet named Maxie (Close in dual role). Seeing her second chance at stardom, Maxie's spirit inhabits the wife's body with comic results. Directed by Paul Aaron, the movie almost succeeds in reviving the madcap verve of the 1930's screwball comedies. Several restrained bedroom scenes. A-III (PG)

Maximum Overdrive (1986) Writer-director Stephen King's malevolent allegory about strange disturbances which turn every machine and truck in a small town into a murderous entity is preoccupied with the demonic. Virtually non-stop images of death and destruction, gore, violence and profanity. O (R)

Maya (1966) American boy (Jay North) discovers mystery in India when he visits his big-game hunter father (Clint Walker). John Berry directs the action adventure in a simple, fast-moving manner that emphasizes the sights and sounds of a fabled land. For the younger members of the family. A-I (br)

Mayerling (1968) Mushy, overlong, lavishly costumed tearjerker starring Catherine Deneuve and Omar Sharif in the story of the tragic royal romance between Austrian Crown Prince Rudolph and his young mistress which ends in double suicide in the royal lodge at Mayerling in 1889. British production directed by Terence Young has all the trappings of a good soap opera version of the life and leisure of the ruling class but comes up boring and emotionally empty. A-III (PG)

McCabe and Mrs. Miller (1971) Warren Beatty and Julie Christie star in a Western examining the reality of American frontier life in a story about a petty gambler who opens a brothel in a boom town and it becomes so successful that Eastern business interests decide to take it over. Director Robert Altman's effort has many interesting segments but fails to come together as a cohesive whole. Rough language and some graphic nudity in brothel scenes. O (R)

McCullochs, The (1975) Strong, self-made trucking magnate (Forrest Tucker) has built a successful career but at the expense of not spending enough time with his growing children and their problems. Produced, written, and directed by Max Baer, this sentimental chronicle of family life in the early 1950s offers no new insights into its characters or their times. Some macho brawling and boozing. A-III (PG)

McKenzie Break, The (1970) Absorbing though familiar World War II story manages to avoid most of the cliches inherent in prison camp pictures. Centered around two strong personalities (Brian Keith, a hard-boiled career officer sent to quell a riotous prison camp for Nazi officers, and Helmut Griem, an indomitable German officer fomenting trouble to cover up escape attempts), director Lamont Johnson's movie is nicely paced, with strong performances, a credible script and an attempt at characterization uncommon in this type of story. Tight, coherent and thoroughly intelligent contest of wills. Some violence. A-III (GP)

McMasters, The (1970) After the Civil War, black Union soldier Brock Peters returns to his former, aging employer Burl Ives who makes him co-owner of his ranch, an act of friendship which incites the bigotry of the neighboring ranchers led by ex-Confederate officer Jack Palance. To further complicate matters, the local down-trodden Indians help out with the ranch chores and give Peters a squaw (Nancy Kwan). The inevitable showdown is long and violent. A conventional Western ably directed by Alf Kjellin, what makes it noteworthy is its attempt to deal with a theme of interracial justice. A-III (PG)

McQ (1974) John Wayne stars as a Seattle policeman so determined to nail a notorious drug dealer that he turns in his badge and initiates justice on his own terms. Director John Sturges offers the usual brand of Wayne frontier justice updated to an urban setting. Violence and some sexual references. A-III (PG)

Me (1970) Quiet, unpretentious French drama about a 10-year-old boy (Michel Terrazon), an unwanted child shuttled from foster home to foster home, never fully trusted, loved or understood. By movie's end, though he has been returned to the institution, he has at last experienced affection and friendship from an aged grandmother who has taken the time to break through his defensive shell. Maurice Pialat's direction is restrained and unsentimental, while gently probing beneath the surface of events with a rare understanding of childhood and human nature in general. In distancing his subject matter he has re-created an all too real world of loneliness and hope, for the tender chords he strikes are at the heart of the human condition. A-II (nr)

Me, Natalie (1969) Patty Duke plays an unhappy but spunky teenage "ugly duckling" struggling to fend for herself in New York's Greenwich Village. Directed by Fred Coe, the movie either overstrains for laughs or settles for the cliches of sentimental melodrama, such as her affair with a married architect (James Farentino). Some entertaining moments but few serious insights. A-III (PG)

Mean Frank, Crazy Tony (1977) Mediocre Italian production about a deported American gang lord (Lee Van Cleef) who teams up with a bumbling, would-be gangster (Tony Lo Bianco) to knock over a really nasty mobster. Though director Michele Lupo treats the story in tongue-in-cheek fashion, there is still a great deal of graphic violence. O (R)

Mean Season, The (1985) A psychotic killer (Richard Jordan) stalks Miami and chats occasionally with the reporter (Kurt Russell) covering his crimes. A melodrama directed by Philip Borsos with ciphers for characters, it is of no more consequence than a ride on a roller coaster. Some bloody violence, premarital sex and brief nudity. A-III (R)

Mean Streets (1973) Robert De Niro and Harvey Keitel star in director Martin Scorsese's drama about small-time crime in New York's Little Italy. The drama has moments of power and effectiveness, mostly in its depiction of an authentic ethnic neighborhood, but it too often degenerates into a kind of bizarre freak show. Some intense violence, nudity and rough language. A-IV (R)

Meatballs (1979) Bill Murray cavorts as the director of a haplessly ill-organized summer camp. Canadian production ineptly directed by Ivan Reitman contains some relatively mild off-color jokes and sex-oriented pranks. A-III (PG)

Mechanic, The (1972) Twisted, ironic, somewhat depressing chiller about a cynical, cold-blooded Mafia hit man (Charles Bronson) who takes on an apprentice (Jan-Michael Vincent). Betrayal is in the wind, however, but from what direction isn't clear until the twist ending. Director Michael Winner has turned out a slick, suspenseful and not very pleasant crime movie. Several grisly murders. A-III (PG)

Medea (1971) Italian dramatization of the Medea myth, going beyond the confines of Euripides' tragedy by sketching in some of the background of a violent time and place. The focus, however, is on the title character and as performed by Maria Callas, the evil of this witch-goddess figure becomes increasingly palpable. Though some may fault the film for its departures from the classic tradition, few will deny the power of director Pier Paolo Pasolini's visualization of the ancient Greek world. A-III (nr)

Medicine Ball Caravan (1971) Documentary directed by Francois Reichenbach recording the travels of a musical troupe (B.B. King, Alice Cooper, Delaney and Bonnie, etc.) across the U.S. during the summer of 1970, promoting peace, love and music. Judging from the evidence on the screen, one would conclude that all counter-culturists know how to do is freak out, hassle with the fuzz and swim naked. Most of this is merely irritating, but viewers should know that Warner Brothers paid for both the tour and the movie which features many of their slower-selling recording artists, another example of the movie medium's potential as an instrument of commercial exploitation. A-IV (R)

Medium Cool (1969) Television news cameraman (Robert Forster) has no interest in the effect of the stories he covers until he falls in love with a young widow (Verna Bloom) whom he helps search for her runaway son in the midst of the violence and confusion of police-yippie confrontations during the 1968 Chicago Democratic Convention. Director Haskell Wexler's powerful movie intertwines staged drama and documentary footage in a convincing, seamless style that gives point to the work's probing into the ethics of news coverage. It is unfortunate that a bedroom romp with total nudity mars a significant attempt to question the role the media play in the violence of today's society. O (X/R)

Medusa Touch, The (1978) Richard Burton plays a man who can destroy others just by willing their death, a telekenetic power that psychiatrist Lee Remick discovers to her horror. Though the plot device is extremely implausible, director Jack Gold makes the most of it in turning out a well-acted, superior thriller. Some rather frightening violence and occasional anti-God rantings. A-III (PG)

Meetings with Remarkable Men (1979) Surface treatment of the formative years of Russian mystic G.I. Gurdjieff who before World War I discovered, hidden deep in the Asian hinterlands, an ancient monastic order in whose keeping were the secrets of the universe and the meaning of life. Directed by Peter Brooks, the natural spectacle of the rugged mountainous landscape of Afghanistan is more remarkable than any of the movie's portentous encounters or pretentious dialogue. A-III (G)

Megaforce (1982) Tongue-in-cheek adventure about an elite force put together by the nations of the free world to combat oppression. Directed by Hal Needham, it has a solid plot and there is a certain charm in its lack of pretension. Barry Bostwick carries off the hero's role with panache and just a touch of self-mockery, while Henry Silva, less burdened than he usually is as the heavy, gets a chance to lighten things up as a not-too-bad villain. Despite much cannon and rocket fire, there's not a drop of blood spilled or even an elbow dislocated during all the spectacular derring-do. Several mild double entendres. A-II (PG)

Melinda (1972) Black exploitation movie with Calvin Lockhart as a radio disk jockey whose casual acquaintance with Vonetta McGee pits him against Syndicate boss Paul Stevens because of an incriminating tape recording in her possession. Directed by Hugh A. Robertson, the muddled plot follows the formula of alternating violence with a smattering of soft core sex and climaxing in a bloody showdown with the crime kingpin. O (R)

Melody (1971) Unpretentious little movie about two London schoolboys (Mark Lester and Jack Wild) whose friendship is threatened when one of them develops a crush on 11-year-old Melody (Tracy Hyde). Puppy love leads to the announcement of their plans to marry, confounding parents and ending in a free-for-all at school between students and teachers. Sensitively directed by Waris Hussein, the engaging story of fantasy and romance presents a child's view of the adult world with much humor and gentle ironies that will appeal as much to parents as to pre-teens. A-II (G)

Melvin and Howard (1980) A supreme American loser and a supreme American winner forge a bond based upon mutual respect in this touching comedy about a gas station attendant (Paul LeMat) who discovers he is among the heirs of eccentric millionaire Howard Hughes (Jason Robards). Director Jonathan Demme's movie makes viewers feel a little better about this crazy, mixed-up but unique and quite wonderful country of ours. Some incidental nudity and some profanity. A-III (PG)

Memories of Underdevelopment (1973) Cuban production directed by Tomas Gutierrez Alea about the day-to-day recollections of an upper-middle class Cuban (Sergio Corrieri) who refused to join his family's flight from Castro by emigrating to Miami, but who also refuses to take part in a revolution that is distasteful to him personally and intellectually. Seen through the eyes of this alienated outsider are the changes taking place under the Marxist regime but the movie's relaxed, sometimes comic, presentation of revolutionary deficiencies helps give its picture of present Cuban life a sense of credibility instead of propaganda. A-III (nr)

Memory of Justice, The (1976) Documentary on the Nuremberg Trials of Nazi war criminals and whether they established a legal precedent for judging the wartime conduct of all nations. After an extensive examination of the Nuremberg process for trying crimes against humanity, producer-director Marcel Ophuls goes on to ask some uncomfortable questions about offenses committed by the Allies during the World War II and the Occupation, the conduct of the French military during the Algerian War and Americans during the Vietnam War. Ophuls brings patient intelligence and concern for human dignity to a four-and-a-half-hour demonstration of the difficulty but the necessity of establishing accountable standards of international conduct. Unflinching look at death camp atrocities and an unnecessary use of nudity. A-IV (PG)

Men (1986) Another round in the battle of the sexes is provided in this German production about a woman who, tired of her successful businessman husband, has an affair with a nonconformist musician. The husband moves in with his wife's lover and slowly transforms him into a hardworking ad agency executive, thereby saving his marriage. Director Doris Dorria's comedy of manners and morals concentrates more on the male cameraderie of the odd-couple relationship than on the wife's infidelity. Mild sexual innuendo. A-III (nr)

Menage (1986) French import about a couple who have their marriage turned inside out when a homosexual friend falls for the husband (Michel Blanc) who will do anything for his wife (Miou-Miou) who, it turns out, is infatuated with the friend (Gerard Depardieu). Director Bertrand Blier's gentle bedroom farce turns nasty as it depicts the treachery, deceit and brutality inevitable in the situation. Nudity, explicit sex and rough language. O (nr)

Mephisto (1982) Hungarian-German production directed by Istvan Szabo is an extremely interesting film about the temptation of power. A provincial German actor (Klaus Maria Brandauer) whose forte, ironically enough is playing the great tempter Mephisto, allows himself to be taken under the wing of a prominent member of the rising Nazi party and, when they come to power, becomes director of the Berlin National Theatre. The film lacks dramatic force, but it is nonetheless fascinating, especially Brandauer's brilliant performance as the good-hearted but feckless hero. Some rather graphic nudity. A-IV (R)

Mephisto Waltz, The (1971) Mediocre horror movie about a dying master pianist (Curt Jurgens) who befriends a young journalist (Alan Alda) because he needs a suitable body in which to continue his existence as a follower of Satan. Once this is established the suspense is over and the rest is a tiresome exercise in routine scenes of witchcraft rituals. Director Paul Wendkos works hard to create the reality of his occult world, but what was needed was a little subtlety and imaginative suggestion. Some violence. A-III (R)

Mercenary, The (1970) Loosely-plotted Italian spoof of spaghetti Westerns revolving around the waxing and waning fortunes of a taco-brained Mexican revolutionary (Tony Musante) and a stoic soldier-for-hire (Franco Nero) who is pitted against the sinister arch-villain of the piece (Jack Palance). Musante garners most of the laughs as the grinning fool of a would-be general leading an equally inept, rag-tag band of peasants. Directed by Sergio Corbucci, the frequently hilarious goings on should not be taken too seriously, especially all the shooting and bright red paint splattering everyone. Brief nudity. A-III (GP)

Merchant of Four Seasons, The (1973) German drama about a misfit whose whole life can be summed up as nothing but a series of rejections. His one chance of fitting into the system comes as a fruit peddler but his family's malice and his wife's infidelity destroy this spark of independence. Combining the artificiality of theatrical techniques with the actual reality of the streets, director Rainer Werner Fassbinder creates a depressing but challenging picture of the dehumanizing effects of modern society's materialistic values upon the individual. A-IV (nr)

Merry Christmas, Mr. Lawrence (1983) David Bowie and Tom Conti star in an English-Japanese production about the clash of cultures in a Japanese camp for British prisoners during World War II. At war's end, with the Japanese prisoners of the British, there is an indication that perhaps humanity can bridge such cultural chasms. The subject is almost a movie cliche and others have done it much better. Directed by Nagisa Oshima, the movie features much hard-edged samurai-code violence and an ambivalent attitude toward homosexuality. A-IV (R)

Merry Go Round (1976) Starring Senta Berger and Helmut Berger, this is an inane, tedious, badly-dubbed remake of the turn-of-the-century Schnitzler play about a series of sexual relationships coming full circle. O (R)

Merry Wives of Windsor, The (1966) Undistinguished British production of Otto Nocolai's opera based on Shakespeare's comedy about the buffoonish Falstaff (American bass Norman Foster) who is made sport of by two mischievous wives. Directed by George Tressler,it might be of interest to students of music but not drama. A-II (br)

Message, The (see: "Mohammad, Messenger of God")

Message from Space (1978) Mediocre Japanese production offering a pint-sized variation on the "Star Wars" theme with some plucky youngsters teaming up with an old-timer (Vic Morrow) to save the universe from intergalactic villains. Other familiar elements include a captive princess dressed in white, a cute little robot, two hotshot pilots and some bargain-basement mysticism. Directed by Kinji Fukasaku, the special effects are satisfactory, though the story line is cluttered and the comic relief not very amusing. A-II (PG)

Meteor (1979) Sean Connery and Natalie Wood star as scientists attempting to deflect a huge meteor heading for the earth and whose impact might bring on another Ice Age, among other calamities. Though ladened with disaster movie cliches, director Ronald Neame makes the premise into surprisingly good entertainment thanks to a good cast and several plot twists more sophisticated than is usual for this kind of movie. Some profanity. A-III (PG)

Michael and Helga (1969) Soporific German sex education movie uses impersonal diagrams and silly dramatizations to treat too many complicated biological, psychological and social aspects of its subject so that it tends to confuse more than enlighten viewers. Much too diffuse for parents to use in acquainting their offspring about the facts of life. A-IV (R)

Micki and Maude (1985) Broadcast journalist (Dudley Moore) marries his pregnant mistress (Any Irving) before divorcing his pregnant wife (Ann Reinking) because he loves them both. Director Blake Edwards comes up with a few funny moments but the sentimental treatment of the situation make the movie's attempts at farce unsatisfactory, if not dishonest. Sympathetic depiction of adultery. O (PG-13)

Midas Run (1969) British secret service officer (Fred Astaire) concocts an elaborate scheme to hijack a large gold shipment he is supposed to be guarding. Jumbled script and plodding direction by Alf Kjellin make the caper tiresome long before the end. Lengthy and over-drawn scene of lovemaking. O (PG)

Middle Age Crazy (1980) Successful contractor (Bruce Dern) with a gorgeous wife (Ann-Margret), a son who loves and admires him, a beautiful home and a host of friends but, in an oft told story, as he approaches 40, things start to fall apart for him. Directed by John Trent, it has fine performances from its principals and the familiar situation is treated with an unusual moral sense that makes it well worth seeing. Mature theme with some rough language and harsh satire. A-III (R)

Middle of the World, The (1975)   Swiss drama about a bright married engineer (Phillipe Leotard), chosen by party regulars to run for office, who pursues an indiscrete affair with a young waitress (Olimpia Carlisi) until she rejects his callous use of her. Directed by Alain Tanner, the movie proves a wise, humane parable about a comfortable, materialistic society that has lost its soul and sense of the dignity of the individual. It is somewhat ironic, however, that the narrative, in making a strong statement against the exploitation of women, is itself guilty of using an unnecessary amount of nudity in detailing the adulterous affair. O (nr)

Midnight Cowboy (1969)   A Texas bumpkin (Jon Voight) comes to New York City expecting to make his fortune as stud to what he believes are its endless supply of lonely women. In trying to cope with the reality of urban life, he relies on his friendship with another loser, a small-time con artist (Dustin Hoffman) crippled physically and emotionally with a hopeless dream of escaping to the sun. Director John Schlesinger treats with compassion this odyssey of two alienated outcasts blindly groping for some redemptive human fellowship in a society that values sex and money more than human beings. Some may find its realistic depiction of a sordid environment, with a graphic sexual encounter and a brutal outburst of violence, quite reprehensible. Others will find merit in its attempt to recognize the resilience of the human spirit and the dignity of the individual. Challenging fare, not for the casual viewer. A-IV (X/R)

Midnight Express (1978)   Wildly melodramatic movie directed by Alan Parker about the imprisonment of an American youth in a Turkish prison for narcotics smuggling wallows in bloody violence and cruelty, an indulgence hardly justified by its human rights plea. Further marred by sexual references and nudity. O (R)

Midnight Madness (1980)   Rival teams of college students compete in a dead-of-the-night treasure hunt in this slapdash effort at zany comedy written and directed by David Wechter and Michael Nankin. The laughs are few and the goings-on get tiresome. Some mild sexual innuendo in the dialogue. A-II (PG)

Midnight Man, The (1974)   Burt Lancaster plays a brutal ex-cop employed as security chief for a midwestern college campus with a bisexual counselor (Susan Clark), a sexpot student (Catherine Bache) who gets murdered and a corrupt sheriff (Harris Yulin). Director Roland Kibbee's confused plot is full of numbing twists and inconsistencies, leaving little justification for its violence and sexual references. O (R)

Midsummer Night's Dream, A (1967)   The New York City Ballet in its first feature-length presentation, conceived and choreographed by the company's artistic director, George Balanchine, with Suzanne Farrell as Titania, Edward Villella as Oberon and Arthur Mitchell as Puck. A treat for those who could not otherwise see this lavish, seldom-performed ballet with the music of Felix Mendelssohn. A-I (br)

Midsummer Night's Sex Comedy, A (1982) Woody Allen directs and stars in a slight little comedy of manners set in a Victorian house in rural New York at the turn of the century. Mia Farrow, Jose Ferrer and Mary Steenburgen are among the three couples who switch, or consider switching, partners in the course of a summer's day and night. There are few jokes, and just about all of them are about sex. Mature subject matter. A-III (PG)

Midway (1976)   Charlton Heston, Henry Fonda and Glenn Ford head an all-star cast in this occasionally effective re-creation of the most decisive naval battle of World War II. Unfortunately, director Jack Smight is unable to overcome the shallow fictional sub-plots that supposedly were meant to add human interest but which instead blunt the emotional potential of historical material capable of standing on its own. Wartime violence and some rough language. A-II (PG)

Mikado, The (l967)   Gilbert and Sullivan's timeless comic operetta about the son who defies his emperor father and wins his love, Yum-Yum, in a wonderful stage production of Japanese make-believe. Pleasant story, lovely costuming, wit, laughter and song by the D'Oyly Carte Opera Company adds up to excellent entertainment for everyone. A-I (br)

Mike's Murder (1984)   When Debra Winger's boyfriend, Mike (Mark Keyloun), is murdered, she investigates and learns about the drug trade and the seamy side of Los Angeles life. Winger has little to do in a listless melodrama, written and directed by James Bridges, that is as flat as its title. A-III (R)

Mikey and Nicky (1977)   Nicky (John Cassavetes) is a bookie who steals some money from his boss and, fearing he is marked for death, contacts the only man he can trust to help him, his boyhood friend Mikey (Peter Falk). The narrative consists of their odyssey through the course of one wild evening whose complications are, unfortunately, entirely predictable. Though the acting of the principals is excellent, especially in their interplay, director-writer Elaine May fails to offer enough substance to engage the viewer's emotions in any significant way. Somes violence, rough language and a frank treatment of sex. A-III (R)

Milestones (1975)   Fictional documentary about what happened to those involved in the protest movements of the 1960s whose failed efforts at changing the nature of the American politics and society led them inward, banding together in little groups for mutual support and survival. Interweaving the activities of some 50 characters may be confusing for those uninterested in political alienation, but filmmakers Robert Kramer and John Douglas have documented how a lost segment of a generation sees itself that has importance for future historians. Unconventional views, some nudity and a graphic birth sequence make this mature fare. A-IV (nr)

Milky Way, The (1969)   French production directed by Luis Bunuel about a pilgrimage made by two men to the shrine of St. James the Apostle in Spain, the road to which is known as "the Milky Way." It is an extraordinary journey of faith, ranging not only from place to place but from century to century as the pilgrims encounter advocates of past heresies and those who are true believers in orthodoxy. Bunuel provides a lively mixture of pious Christian traditions and superstitious beliefs through an episodic and absurdly humorous series of adventures that challenge the serious viewer with its ambiguous reflections on the relevance of religion in contemporary life. A-IV (PG)

Millhouse: A White Comedy (1971) Documentary on the life and career of Richard Millhouse Nixon begins with Nixon's 1962 "last" press conference and then returns to his origins and six political crises (including the famous 1956 "Checkers" speech), his role in the 1964 campaign and finally his election as President in 1968. Based solely on newsreel footage (and a few out-takes), the satiric intent of director Emile de Antonio's partisan selection of material can only amuse anti-Nixonites but will not convince his supporters of the shallowness and ineptness that de Antonio finds in the visual record. Lack of explanatory historical background limits its usefulness for young viewers. A-III (G)

Million Dollar Mystery (1987) Fluffy comedy adventure filled with car chases and demolition features an ensemble cast of new faces on a greedy search for four million dollars in hidden pay-off money. Director Richard Fleischer makes the most of the stark Southwest landscape shot exquisitely by Jack Cardiff as backdrop for the slapstick antics and dangerous stunts which form the substance of the movie. Some coarse language and sexual sight gags are brief and restrained. A-II (PG)

Mind of Mr. Soames, The (1970) Offbeat story about the education of a 30-year-old man (Terence Stamp) who, until a delicate brain operation restores consciousness, has been in a coma since birth. A compassionate physician (Robert Vaughn), realizing the man-child's need for tenderness and the simple pleasures of childhood, opposes the unyielding authoritarian rigors of the neurophysiological hospital staff in whose charge he has been placed. Though raising some provocative questions about the learning process and responsibility, director Alan Cooke's work is too episodic and diffuse to provide many insights in the matter. A-II (PG)

Mini-Skirt Mob, The (1968) Honeymooning couple (Ross Hagen and Sherry Jackson) are terrorized by motorcycle gang in a tawdry action film directed by Maury Dexter. Excessive sadistic violence and sexual innuendo. O (br)

Minnie and Moskowitz (1972) Improbable romance of a zany parking-lot attendant (Seymour Cassel) and a museum assistant (Gena Rowlands), carried on in shouting matches throughout Los Angeles. Minnie with her history of failed masochistic relationships and Moskowitz with his utter lack of direction are so unsuited for each other that the ending is sheer Hollywood romantic fantasy. Director John Cassavetes in characteristic improvisational style has made a wry, harshly shot but warmly acted contemporary version of the old saw about the attraction between opposites. Some rough language and sexual references. A-III (PG)

Minute to Pray, a Second to Die, A (1968) Routine Italian Western directed by Franco Giraldi about an outlaw hero (Alex Cord) who, fearing he has epilepsy, tries to go straight. Much standard violence. A-III (br)

Minx, The (1969) Sex exploitation movie about business executives planning a corporate merger during a stag weekend at a hunting lodge. Poorly staged and acted, it is punctuated with double crosses, orgies and voyeuristic fantasies. O (R)

Miracle of Love, The (1969) German sex education movie that confuses providing information about sex with prolonged demonstrations of sexual behavior and the depiction of erotic fantasies. Worthless. O (X)

Miracle of the White Stallions (1963) Disney drama about the World War II attempt to smuggle the Spanish Riding School's prize Lipizzan stallions out of Vienna before the city is occupied by the Russians. Directed by Arthur Hiller, the precision riding sequences show the great training of these famed horses, though their evacuation by military trucks is delayed somewhat by a bloodless battle sequence at the Czech border. Worthwhile family fare. A-I (br)

Mirage (1965) Gregory Peck plays an amnesia victim who is being stalked by a killer, Diane Baker is a woman out of his past, Walter Matthau is a private detective and, shrouded in the background, is a world peace organization. Directed by Edward Dmytryk, the ingredients of this suspense-filled puzzle may be familiar but their solution is intriguing and nicely integrated in the New York setting. A-II (br)

Mischief (1985) The class nerd (Doug McKeon) and a cool newcomer (Chris Nash) team up to pursue girls in a small-town high school in 1950's Ohio. Directed by Mel Damski, it's a sloppily executed affair in which all adults are depicted as semi-morons and its idea of humor is obscene language and boys peering up girl's dresses. Excessively graphic bedroom scene. O (R)

Mishima: A Life in Four Chapters (1985) Writer-director Paul Schrader attempts to do justice to the complex and flamboyant Japanese writer Yukio Mishima, who committed suicide by military ritual in 1970. The result is flat and listless, an illustrated slide lecture that doesn't come close to capturing the enigmatic Mishima. Brief nudity and violence. A-III (R)

Miss Mary (1986) British governess (Julie Christie) recalls the years she spent in Buenos Aires caring for the children of a wealthy family. The real interest of this Argentinian production, directed by Maria Luisa Bemberg, is its depiction of the politically confused and socially demoralized climate prior to the Peron dictatorship. Mature themes including several sexual encounters. A-III (R)

Missing (1982) Director Costa-Gavras in his first American movie presents a taut and powerful drama based upon an actual event, that of an American father's search for his son, a 31-year-old writer living with his wife in a Latin American country, who has disappeared in the midst of the brutal repression following a right-wing coup. Jack Lemmon and Sissy Spacek are outstanding as the concerned father and his daughter-in-law, with John Shea giving capable support as the missing man. Significant and absorbing work on a topical and important theme of human rights. General atmosphere of menace, a depiction of the aftermath of bloodshed and occasional profanity. A-II (PG)

Missing in Action (1984) Chuck Norris stars in a hokey, derivative movie directed by Joseph Vito about a commando operation mounted to rescue Americans still held prisoner in Vietnam. Gene Hackman did it better in "Uncommon Valor." Graphic wartime violence, rough language and Asian sterotyping. A-III (R)

183

Missing in Action 2: The Beginning (1985)   In a sequel with even more violence than its violent predecessor, this time around the blank-faced hero (Chuck Norris) is a prisoner of war in Vietnam a few years prior to the original. Directed by Lance Hool, this run-of-the-mill war movie overdoses on graphic depictions of brutality and sadism. O (R)

Mission, The (1986)   In the 1750s, the large and prosperous Jesuit Indian missions of South America were divided between Spain and Portugal. In retelling these events, Robert Bolt's screenplay focuses not on the religious but on the socio-political dimension of the colonial era and its injustices. The epic production is visually splendid, but Roland Joffe's direction is erratic and bogs down in contrasting a non-violent priest (Jermey Irons) and one (Robert De Niro) who leads the Indians against a colonial army. Although flawed, the work recalls a past that provides a context for current Latin American struggles. Violence and ethnographic nudity. A-III (PG)

Missionary, The (1982)   Writer-producer Michael Palin (of the Monty Python troupe) also stars as the Rev. Charles Fortescue, a missionary sent to the slums of London by his bishop (Denholm Elliot) to open up a home for fallen women, and with Lady Ames (Maggie Smith) as his patron, he has great success. Unfortunately, there is a rather snide quality to the comedy's religious and social criticism and there is one incredibly crude exchange between Mr. Fortescue and a tough prostitute. Some obscene language. O (R)

Mississippi Mermaid (1970)   Disappointing French melodrama about the mail-order bride (Catherine Deneuve) of a rich planter in the tropics (Jean-Paul Belmondo) who proves to be an imposter when she cleans out his bank account and disappears—but not for very long. A minor effort from director Francois Truffaut, it pays tribute to the old Hollywood action adventures while at the same time satirizing them with an incredibly absurd plot made worse by being badly dubbed into English. For Truffaut fans only. Brief nudity. A-III (GP)

Missouri Breaks, The (1976)   Jack Nicholson heads a band of rustlers and Marlon Brando is the ruthless killer hired to hunt them down. Director Arthur Penn's failed Western is full of loose ends and fey dialogue, an embarrassing muddlement that lumbers to a brutal conclusion for want of anything better to do. Excessive violence. O (PG)

Mister Buddwing (1966)   Forgettable melodrama about an amnesia victim (James Garner) whose career ambitions and marital woes are shown in flashbacks and dreams as his memory returns. Directed by Delbert Mann, the story is needlessly confusing in the use of three actresses in the role of his wife and the result doesn't add up to much. Mature sexual themes including abortion. A-III (br)

Misty (1961)   The story of some children who fall in love with a wild horse captured on an island off the Atlantic coast is tinged with history and a respect for nature. Produced by Robert B. Radnitz and directed by James B. Clark, the movie is beautifully done, the youngsters appealing and the result is superior family entertainment. A-I (br)

Misunderstood (1984)   Gene Hackman plays a widower who is slow to come to terms with his loss and make a new life for himself and his two young sons (Henry Thomas and Huckleberry Fox). Director Jerry Schatzberg's picture is pleasant

enough, with competent acting and exotic settings (Tunisia), but there are no dramatic sparks to speak of until a contrived tearjerker of an ending. Some vulgar language. A-II (PG)

Mitchell (1975)   Los Angeles police detective (Joe Don Baker) pursues two suave lawyers (Martin Balsam and John Saxon) mixed up in the heroin trade by using unorthodox methods that look suspiciously like police brutality. Directed by Andrew V. McLaglen, it's a fairly silly, slapped-together affair whose thin plot is nothing more than an excuse to string together a series of routine chases. Most, but not all, of the rough stuff is kept off-camera, substituting instead some sexual exploition scenes. O (R)

Mixed Company (1974)   Joseph Bologna and Barbara Harris star in a sentimental comedy drama about a couple who decide to augment their family, which already includes three children, with three more, each from a different race. Melville Shavelson directs a good-natured movie that carefully avoids any realistic situations of racial tension. Mildly entertaining, sometimes funny and touching, it seems like something made for television except for its strong language. A-III (PG)

Model Shop, The (1969)   French romantic drama about a brief encounter between an alienated Los Angeles dropout (Gary Lockwood) and an attractive model (Anouk Aimee) who takes him to bed, tells him her life story and he gives her money for her fare back to France. Though beautifully produced and mildly appealing, the movie lacks the charm and novelty of director Jacques Demy's earlier works and their unabashed romantic exuberance. A-III (PG)

Modern Problems (1981)   Chevy Chase plays an air traffic controller possessed of extrasensory powers which are put to no good use in a dreary, slipshod comedy that intersperses long boring stretches with only a few patches of fitful humor. Directed and co-written by Ken Shapiro, it has some vulgarity and incidental sexual byplay. A-III (PG)

Modern Romance (1981)   Obsessive and insecure film editor (Albert Brooks) has an on-again, off-again relationship with his girlfriend (Kathryn Harrold) but he can't break this recurring cycle of misery. Also written and directed by Brooks, it is a sometimes very funny movie, but suffers from a lack of structure and too much Brooks. Still, two hilarious sequences in the cutting room might make some viewers willing to forgive the movie's frequent slow stretches. Some brief semi-nudity, occasional rough language and a muddled view of sexual morality. A-III (R)

Modern Times (1936)   Written, produced and directed by Charles Chaplin, this insightful fable of man against machine features some of the great buffoons of the silent era and marks the last appearance of Chaplin's little tramp character. A model of comedic technique and refined slapstick humor, the movie deals with the consequences of industrialized society and the anxieties of Depression-era audiences as the little fellow dances his way through the hazards of a factory assembly line. For his final walk down the long empty road, Chaplin is accompanied by Paulette Goddard, who added an element of freshness to Chaplin's old-fashioned romance. A-I (G)

Modesty Blaise (1966)   Monica Vitti, Terence Stamp and Dirk Bogarde in a plot about a shipment of diamonds that is merely an excuse for a series of impossible adventures and characters that parody the cliches of popular culture. The opulent sets, costumes and gadgets are stylishly photographed and the dialogue and situations are outrageously exaggerated. Director Joseph Losey obviously enjoyed spoofing areas of the dark world that he has treated seriously so often before. A-III (br)

Mohammad, Messenger of God (1977)   Dramatic re-creation of the years from 610 A.D., when Mohammad was driven from Mecca for claiming to have received a new religion from the Angel Gabriel, to 630 when the victory of Islam was assured. The best feature of this religious epic directed by Moustapha Akkad is its sincerity in recounting the birth of Islam and some of the essential tenets of the Moslem religion. An international cast includes Anthony Quinn, Irene Papas and Michael Ansara. Some scenes of restrained violence. A-II (PG)

Molly Maguires, The (1970)   Fact-based and hard-hitting drama about the bloody upheavals in the Pennsylvania coal mining fields during the last part of the 19th century. The mine owners hire an undercover agent (Richard Harris) to ferret out the leaders (Sean Connery and Anthony Zerbe) of a secret band of miners (the Molly Maguires) who are using terrorist tactics to force better pay and working conditions from the owners. Director Martin Ritt has made a thoughtful movie about social justice and the futility of resorting to violence to correct injustices. Powerful entertainment. A-II (PG)

Moment by Moment (1978)   Middle-aged Beverly Hills housewife (Lily Tomlin) succumbs to the charms of a young drifter (John Travolta). Devoid of dramatic action, save for scenes of love-making punctuated by little spats of no consequence, writer-director Jane Wagner's movie has hardly a glimmer of wit, intelligence or credibility. Graphic and glossy depiction of adultery. O (R)

Mommie Dearest (1981)   Faye Dunaway plays Joan Crawford in this unpleasant screen version of the harsh biography written by her adopted daughter, Christina. Director Frank Perry alternates heavy doses of sensation and sentimentality without really getting at anything that might make its subject credible. Only occasionally does the episodic and overlong movie rise above the level of verge-of-hysteria soap opera. Some brief but graphic violence, rough language and vulgarity. A-III (PG)

Mona Lisa (1986)   Love-starved small-time tough (Bob Hoskins in a memorable performance) falls in love with the prostitute (Cathy Tyson) he chaffeurs around town, only to be victimized by his own blind trust and devotion. This British production's depiction of underworld violence, deception and betrayal leads nowhere. Brutal violence, brief nudity and some profanity. O (R)

Money Jungle, The (1968)   Routine detective melodrama about a private eye (John Ericson) who is hired to solve the mysterious murders of four geologists working aboard an off-shore oil rig. Intriguing but predictable plot competently directed by Francis D. Lyon. Violence. A-III (br)

Money, Money, Money (1973)   Amusing but overlong French comedy about a rag-tag band of con artists, petty thieves, bank robbers and other paunchy, middle-aged underworld types (among them, Lino Ventura, Jacques Brel and Charles Denner) adapt to changing times by turning to

kidnapping political figures and extorting high ramsoms from embarrassed governments. Directed by Claude Lelouch, the source of the comedy is how the inept misfits complement each other's foolishness and become so rich and successful that they themselves are kidnapped. The Gallic humor, including a Tahitian vacation among semi-clad native beauties, may escape some viewers. A-III (PG)

Money Pit, The (1986)   A young engaged couple (Tom Hanks and Shelley Long) buy a mansion and suffer humorous consequences when trying to fix it up. The strained comedy resorts to heavy doses of slapstick and the deteriorating condition of the house comes to mirror their increasingly exasperated relationship. Some sexually suggestive scenes are handled within the context of their successful efforts to build trust and strengthen commitment. A-II (PG)

Money Talks (1972)   Using the same formula as his popular "Candid Camera" TV show, director Allen Funt presents a series of trite sketches and allegedly spontaneous routines designed to show how ordinary people react to situations involving money. Among the offerings, one can watch men pluck, with varying degrees of hesitancy, a dollar bill taped to the backside of a sweet young thing, or listen to Funt interview his pretty three-year-old daughter, who openly exhibits a preference for being rich. At least she's candid about it. A-II (PG)

Monique (1970)   British exploitation movie about a French "au pair" girl (Sibylla Kay) hired to care for a young couple's boisterous children and instead seduces first the husband, then the wife and finally the trio wind up in bed together. Low-budget production directed by John Brown, it contains nudity in a sexual context. O (X/R)

Monitors, The (1969)   Failed satire about a police force of the future which relies on thought control to bring peace and order in a society beset by violence, brutality and rapaciousness. Directed by Jack Shea, a talented cast headed by Guy Stockwell, Susan Oliver and Keenan Wynn try desperately but fail to find anything humorous in a plot both tedious and inane. A-III (M)

Monkey Hustle, The (1977)   Black exploitation comedy about some supposedly loveable con artists who rally an inner-city neighborhood threatened by highway construction. Director Arthur Marks gets some good acting (Yaphet Kotto, Rosalind Cash, Kirk Calloway and Randy Brooks) but not much else. Some rough language and a frank treatment of sexual matters. A-III (PG)

Monkeys Go Home (1967)   Disney comedy in which ex-GI Dean Jones inherits an olive farm in France, retrains four Space Program astro-chimps to help out when a shortage of local olive pickers develops and outwits a conniving real estate man with the aid of a refreshing lass (Yvette Mimieux) and the village priest (Maurice Chevalier). Andrew V. McLaglen directs a slap-dash plot with monkey-shines galore that will appeal more to youngsters than their parents. A-I (br)

Monsieur Verdoux (1947)   Written, directed and produced by Charles Chaplin, the fact-based black comedy stars Chaplin in the title role as a French Bluebeard who marries women and then murders them for their money. Though his first serious role understandably disappointed audiences of its day, Chaplin as a performer was never better in the subtlety of gesture and expression. There is much sharp wit in the action but also some great slapstick, notably from Martha Raye who proves impervious to all murderous stratagems. Subtitled "A Comedy of Murder," the movie is a critical statement about the hypocrisy of society, neither cynical nor nihilistic, but attempts to punctuate a serious message with humor. A-III (nr)

Monsignor (1982) Christopher Reeve plays an American priest with a graduate degree in finance who rises in the church hierarchy when he gets the Vatican involved with the Mafia but who pauses on the ladder of success to have an affair with a Carmelite postulant (Genevieve Bujold). Directed by Frank Perry, its melodramatic account of an ambitious cleric is so simple-mindedly wrong-headed that it would be howlingly funny if it were not so grossly insulting to clergymen and institutional religion. Some gratuitous nudity. O (R)

Monster Squad, The (1987) Pre-teens foil Count Dracula's attempt to destroy an amulet bearing positive energy in this visually stunning mock horror flick from writer-director Fred Dekker. Lots of fun and frolic but explosively realistic demise of the monsters may chill the very young. A-II (PG-13)

Monster Zero (1970) Routine Japanese science fiction fantasy in which the title monster, Ghidrah, teamed with Godzilla and Rodan, attempt to conquer Earth for their masters on Planet X while Nick Adams leads a force of astronauts out to stop them. Directed by Inoshiro Honda, the movie's special effects will hold the attention of young viewers while grown-ups will chuckle at the anthropomorphic monsters. A-I (G)

Monte Walsh (1970) Once the Wild West was tamed, cowboys like Monte Walsh (Lee Marvin) found it hard to adapt to the demands of society. Jeanne Moreau and Jack Palance join Marvin in strong performances in a serio-comic study of ordinary cowpokes put out of work by a changing cattle industry that director William Fraker makes interesting despite a weak and aimless script with a hopelessly melodramatic climax. Some Hollywood heroics featuring fist fights and gun play. A-III (PG)

Monterey Pop (1969) Eye-staggering, ear-popping souvenir of the June 1967 Monterey music festival briefly captures the spirit of an age and a generation. The performers include The Mamas and the Papas, Jefferson Airplane, The Who, Janis Joplin, Jimi Hendrix and Ravi Shankar who closes the concert with his extraordinary sitar playing. Some sexually suggestive lyrics and gestures. A-III (nr)

Monty Python and the Holy Grail (1975) Departing from their BBC television format of unconnected skits, the Python comedy troupe zero in on the single subject of King Arthur and his dim-witted knights of the roundabout table. Directed by the Python's Terry Gilliam and Terry Jones, the episodic narrative strings together a series of gags, most of which are allowed to cross the threshold of boredom and then repeated to test one's patience further. Their brand of irreverent humor is an aquired taste, appealing to those who can find amusement in the concept of a feisty knight whose extremities are being lopped off one by one gamely urging a superior but reluctant opponent to fight on. Comic violence and sexual references. A-III (PG)

Monty Python's The Meaning of Life (1983) The Python troupe (John Cleese, Terry Gilliam, Eric Idle, Michael Palin and Terry Jones who also directed) breaks new ground, not in terms of satire, but of grossness for its own sake. There are indeed some very funny moments, but much of it is vile bile, the product of bright, well-bred but naughty boys who bear a lot of minor grudges, but lack the satiric ability to do a proper job on their targets. Graphic nudity and an attack on formal religion. O (R)

Moon Zero Two (1969) British science fiction yarn in which a woman (Catherine von Schell) enlists the aid of a space pilot (James Olson) to find her brother who is missing from his mining claim on the moon. Directed by Roy Ward Baker, the plot is that of a conventional claim-jumping Western with good special effects and little violence. A-II (G)

Moonlighting Mistress (1972) Wolfgang Becker directs an English-dubbed German exploitation movie about a husband who underestimates his wife's cleverness when he conspires with his mistress to murder her. O (R)

Moonraker (1979) British agent James Bond (Roger Moore) teams up with a CIA operative (Lois Chiles) to save the world from a deadly shower launched from outer space by a madman (Michael Lonsdale). Director Lewis Gilbert offers the usual Bond fare with the usual mix of stylized sex and violence. A-III (PG)

Moonshine War, The (1970) Internal revenue agent Patrick McGoohan and a murderous gang led by Richard Widmark go after poor country moonshiner Alan Alda who has inherited 150 barrels of perfect 'white lightning' from his dear departed dad. Director Richard Quine conveys a sense of Depression-era nostalgia but heavy-handedly injects farcial sex vignettes and a slapstick parody of mass killing to conclude a pointless plot. A- III (PG)

Moonstruck (1987) Good romantic comedy set in an Italian-American neighborhood in Brooklyn where a widow (Cher) accepts the proposal of a fastidious bachelor (Danny Aiello) but falls in love with his darkly emotional younger brother (Nicolas Cage). Director Norman Jewison concentrates more on the comedy of character than on incident and the result is pleasantly amusing, emotionally operatic and humanly uplifting. Several restrained scenes implying sex but the movie's moral perspective is implicit throughout. A-III (PG)

Moonwalk One (1973) Documentary recording man's first visit to the moon on Apollo II in 1969 is first-rate in explaining the technology of space flight, as well as imparting some of the wonderment and sense of history involved in this accomplishment. NASA-produced film, directed by Theo Kamecke, is a fine tribute to a scientific achievement that is truly awesome. A-I (G)

More (1969) Drug and sex melodrama about a German student's progressive addiction from marijuana to heroin to LSD and his fatal love affair with an attractive American woman. Director Barbet Schroeder never gets beyond a surface rendering of the descent into the world of addiction, using it mainly as a pretext to portray unnecessarily explicit scenes of sex and perversion. O (nr)

More American Graffiti (1979) Auto racing, Vietnam combat, peace demonstrations and Flower Children constitute the four facets of the sequel whose characters are now a few years older, have gone their seperate ways but have still kept in touch. The acting (Bo Hopkins, Ron Howard,

Candy Clark and Paul Le Mat) is quite good, but director B.W.L. Norton's effort seems simply to trade on late-1960s nostalgia without any of the wit and feeling of the original. Some rough language, the use of drugs and the shallow treatment of serious issues, such as the Vietnam conflict. A-III (PG)

More Dead Than Alive (1969) Standard Western about a notorious gunfighter (Clint Walker) who gives up his trade by becoming a sharpshooter in a travelling sideshow (run by Vincent Price) but is gunned down by the son of one of his former victims. Directed by Robert Sparr, the melodrama's anti-violence message is unconvincing, especially in view of its excessively gory visual effects. A-III (PG)

More Than a Miracle (1967) Uneven Italian-French romance set in the 17th century in which a Spanish prince (Omar Sharif) marries a Cinderella (Sophia Loren), with witches and saints helping matters along. The episodic story line with none-too-noble nobles and the all-too-common commoners, the bawdy earthiness of a few incidents and director Francesco Rosi's association of witchcraft with religion makes it all pretty hard to swallow. A-III (br)

Morgan! (1966) Young London non-conformist (David Warner), likeable but hard to understand, tries to win back his estranged wife (Vanessa Redgrave) but increasingly gets lost in his own fantasies, shown by scenes from old movies and camera effects. Director Karel Reisz has achieved a strange mixture of comedy and social comment, effectively brought off by the fine performances of the principals. A-III (br)

Morgan Stewart's Coming Home (1987) Jon Cryer is the wise son and Lynn Redgrave is the overly sophisticated, domineering mother and political power-broker who make a loving compromise when the family is duped by the father's unscruplous campaign manager in director Alan Smithee's comedy of manners and teen coming-of-age story. Two shower-room sight gags and some concluding rough language are brief and restrained comic asides in this movie which shows that patience and understanding help rebuild family ties. A-II (PG-13)

Morire Gratis (1969) Italian production about a sculptor (Franco Angeli) driving a load of narcotics from Rome to Paris and the woman he picks up along the way (Karen Blanguernon). Director Sandro Franchina prepares for the journey's inevitable tragic ending with a number of scenes of violence encountered along the way. Though it raises moral questions, it lacks depth and its perspective tends to be pessimistic. A-IV (nr)

Morning After, The (1986) A fading actress (Jane Fonda), prone to one-night stands and alcoholic blackouts, wakes up one morning in bed with a dead man. Director Sidney Lumet's thriller solves the murder mystery but it's a rather empty exercise in style without substance. Implied sex and some rough language. A-III (R)

Moscow on the Hudson (1984) Robin Williams stars as a jazz-playing Russian musician who falls in love with a department store salesclerk and finds a safe haven and the American Dream in New York City. Somewhat funny and vulnerable performance by Williams fails to save director Paul Mazursky's comic study of defection and exile in a movie that resorts to some nude bedroom scenes to heat up the action. O (R)

Moses (1976) Theatrical version of a European television mini-series on the Book of Exodus has serious shortcomings in its level of acting, especially Burt Lancaster's soporific performance as Moses, as well as in the script's plodding rationalizations of the appearance of the divine in human events. Directed by Gianfranco De Bosio, the dramatization is unconvincing, its secular interpretation of the Bible story lacks depth and its spectacle is low-budget and unimaginative. Some brief but graphic violence. A-III (PG)

Mosquito Coast, The (1986) Dissatisfied with the ills of modern civilization, an American intellectual (Harrison Ford) takes his family to a tropical wilderness but finds that life in this new Eden is no better than that which he fled. Adapted from Paul Theroux's novel and directed by Peter Weir, the movie's rather cynical outlook makes it less entertaining than thought-provoking fare. Mature themes. A-III (PG)

Mosquito Squadron (1970) World War II adventure with David McCallum leading a squadron of RAF fighter-bombers across the channel to destroy the Nazi center developing a super V-2 rocket and save one bomb to open up the POW-packed chateau next door. Director Boris Sagal handles the heroics as melodramatically as possible so that even the model planes used in re-creating the air battles seem to be overacting. A-I (G)

Most Beautiful Age, The (1970) Low-keyed Czechoslovakian drama about the generation gap in various levels of society, set in a sculpture studio where the inter-play between students, teachers, models and visitors occasion humorous, ironic, and even tragic observations on the human condition. Director Jaroslav Papousek has an eye for detail that lends substance and depth to the film and makes it a rewarding entertainment. Mature themes. A-III (nr)

Motel Hell (1980) Totally unappetizing horror movie with Rory Calhoun as a motel keeper whose sideline is selling smoked meat made out of humans whose vocal cords have been cut while being fattened before butchering. The grisly horror story is made all the more repugnant because director Kevin Connor apparently thinks it's a comedy. Excessively graphic violence and some nudity. O (R)

Mother (see: "The Toy Grabbers")

Mother and the Whore, The (1974) Provocative French drama about the self-deceptions of a pseudo-intellectual (Jean-Pierre Leaud) who, though kept by an older woman (Bernadette Lafont), gets involved with a young nurse (Francoise Lebrun) bent on marriage. The ambivalent, shifting relationships between the three are seen as basically dishonest, showing especially the man as a perpetual adolescent torn between the two aspects of the title. Director Jean Eustache has chosen a documentary approach to his material, filming in the less fashionable bistros and tenements frequented by his characters, using rough street language and explicit depiction of sexual relationships, challenging viewers about the contradictions of modern lifestyles. A-IV (nr)

Mother, Jugs & Speed (1976) Bill Cosby, Raquel Welch and Harvey Keitel respectively play the title characters in a failed comedy about a private ambulance service on the verge of bankruptcy and locked in a frantic rivalry with a competing service. Director Peter Yates stages some spectacular scenes of violent action but none

187

of it comes off as particularly amusing. Crude, tasteless and vulgar, especially in its sexual references. O (PG)

Mother Teresa (1986) Feature documentary by Ann and Jeanette Petrie on the life and work of a Catholic nun in India whose tireless efforts for the poorest of the poor have earned her the Nobel Peace Prize and recognition as a media star and secular saint. Inspirational portrait of a contemporary woman. A-I (nr)

Mother's Day (1980) Bloody shocker about a demented mother and her two cretinous sons who wreak all sorts of horrors on three young women. Poorly written and amateurishly directed by Charles Kaufman, it features excessively graphic violence and some nudity. O (PG)

Mountain Family Robinson (1979) After building a cabin on a mining claim in the Colorado Rockies, the family is informed that unless they mine their claim, they will lose their home. Though director John Cotter's simplistic plotting and saccharine characters are overly weighted, its vistas of nature and abundance of wildlife will satisfy young viewers. A-I (G)

Mountain Men, The (1980) Charlton Heston plays a trapper who has outlived his era with the decline of the fur trade and arrival of wagon trains of settlers in the Old West. Richard Lang's leaden direction of a cliched script centering on a Blackfoot warrior's attempt to revenge himself on the trapper for taking his squaw flounders in graphic violence, an extended rape scene and foul-mouthed profanity. O (R)

Mouse and His Child, A (1978) Animated feature about the adventures of a mechanical mouse and his son in the forbidding world outside of their toy store where their friends help them defeat their chief persecutor, a rat (voiced by Peter Ustinov), and gain self-winding status. Directed by Fred Wolf, the movie has its bright and clever moments, but is too often serious, if not downright somber, with many of the jokes and references not at all relevant for youngsters and too juvenile for adults. A-I (G)

Move (1970) Dim-witted comedy about a professional dog-walker and occasional porno pulp writer (Elliott Gould), in the midst of moving wife (Paula Prentiss), St. Bernard and their belongings to another apartment, dashes head-long from one unfunny non-crisis to another, including a casual dalliance with a model (Genevieve Waite). Directed by Stuart Rosenberg, the vulgar level of humor reaches rock bottom with a shot of Gould urinating in the kitchen sink to spite the landlord. Sexual references and nudity. O (R)

Movers and Shakers (1985) A limp satire on Hollywood movie making, written and produced by actor Charles Grodin (who also stars) and directed by William Asher. Some mild vulgarities and some tasteless humor. A-II (PG-13)

Movie, Movie (1978) Producer-director Stanley Donen has contributed a comic valentine to 1930s Hollywood movies by re-creating a modern version of the era's double features, pairing a black-and-white boxing melodrama and a musical in color, using virtually the same cast for both (George C. Scott, Trish Van Devere, Eli Wallach, Art Carney and others). The gentle parody captures well the innocent fantasies of a less sophisticated age, not to make fun of past movie conventions but to enjoy them in a more knowing way. Some ring violence and a sensuous nightclub dance. A-II (PG)

Moving Violations (1985) The feeble premise for director Neal Israel's failed comedy is the gathering together of some diverse types who must attend driving school to get back their licenses. Heavy emphasis on sexually oriented humor. O (PG-13)

Mr. Billion (1976) Poor Italian mechanic (Terence Hill) inherits the controlling interest in a vast American corporation, provided he can reach San Francisco by a certain day. Villainous Jackie Gleason hires Valerine Perrine to impede him, but, predictably enough, she switches sides. Pleasant and diverting, if more than slightly sappy, comedy directed by Jonathan Kaplan. Some limited violence. A-II (PG)

Mr. Klein (1977) French drama about a dealer in art objects (Alain Delon) who buys family heirlooms from Jews needing cash to escape the Nazi terror, but then he himself is mistaken for a Jew and handed over to the Germans, as were 13,000 others on what is known as Black Thursday, July 16, 1942. Directed with great sensitivity by Joseph Losey, it is exceptional in viewing the Holocaust as a universal experience, as meaningful to gentiles as to Jews. The nature of the theme, and some incidental nudity, make this a film for serious viewers. A-III (PG)

Mr. Love (1986) In this quirky British romance a timid gardener (Barry Jackson) who is caught in an unhappy 28-year marriage decides he must find love at least once before he dies. Director Roy Battersby's gentle satire implies that the self-indulgence of one's passions justifies infidelity. Romanticization of immoral behavior. O (PG-13)

Mr. Majestyk (1974) Charles Bronson stars as an embattled ex-convict determined to protect his farm from the inroads of mob-instigated labor problems. Director Richard Fleischer helps divert attention from an overly familiar story by making the most of the scenic Colorado hills and desert locations. Some violence and strong language. A-III (PG)

Mr. Mom (1983) When a father of three (Michael Keaton) loses his job, he takes over the household chores while his wife (Teri Garr) goes back to work. The comic complications of this role-reversal plot are mildly diverting with saccharine-coated problems and an old-fashioned happy ending sure to elicit groans from feminists. Director Stan Dragoti is helped greatly by the likeable leads in achieving a genial comedy whose sensibilities are of an earlier generation. The comedy toys with but firmly rejects several plot lines leading toward infidelity. A-II (PG)

Mr. Quilp (1975) Uninspired British musical version of Charles Dickens "The Old Curiosity Shop" about the villainous usurer, Quilp (Anthony Newley), the put-upon Little Nell and her improvident grandfather (David Warner). Directed by Michael Tuchner, it is a colorless, undistinguished effort which substitutes sweetness and light for Dicken's gritty melodrama. It may divert the very young but won't satisfy their older siblings and parents. A-I (G)

Mr. Ricco (1975) Routine police thriller about a San Francisco lawyer (Dean Martin) who gets his client off a murder rap but comes to regret it when he winds up in the middle between the authorities and a black activist cell. Directed by Paul Bogart, the movie has some suspense, occasionally clever dialogue and a good supporting cast, but there's nothing here that hasn't been seen before. A-III

(PG)
Mrs. Brown, You've Got a Lovely Daughter
(1968) Delightful British comedy in which some
working-class youths turn to performing professionally to support a racing greyhound, named
Mrs. Brown, whose puppy gets lost during an
unfortunate expedition to London. The plot, however, is only a nonsensical peg on which to hang a
number of pleasant songs by the teenage pop
singing group, Herman's Hermits, who here display some irresistible high spirits plus an off-beat
decency and good sense. A-I (br)
Mrs. Pollifax: Spy (1971) Rosalind Russell plays
a woman free of family commitments who satisfies
a life-long ambition to become a spy by joining the
CIA and winding up imprisoned with accomplice
Darren McGavin on an Albanian mountain top
from which she must effect a daring escape.
Director Leslie Martinson's adventure spoof is
laced with warm humor and clever situations and
features a winsome performance by its star in her
last screen appearance. A-II (G)
Mrs. Soffel (1985) Turn-of-the-century story of
a woman (Diane Keaton), married to a prison
warden (Edward Herrmann), who falls in love
with a condemned convict (Mel Gibson) and helps
him escape. Director Gillian Armstrong's powerful, well-acted movie balances sympathy for its
doomed principals with a clear-eyed depiction of
the devastation caused by the wife's betrayal of her
family and herself. Adultery, though clearly
depicted as wrong, is a major plot element. A-IV
(PG-13)
Muhair (1970) Argentinian sex melodrama with
Isabel Sarli as the object of passion and antagonism
between a father and son. Exploitative nudity. O
(nr)
Mumsy, Nanny, Sonny and Girly (1970) The
odd quartet of the title live in an out-of-the-way
Victorian mansion to which they lure unsuspecting
strangers to play "games" with them, which end in
their being murdered in one ghoulish way or
another. British horror movie directed by Freddie
Francis, it lacks any story development or suspense, fails to elicit sympathy for its looney protagonists and falls flat as comedy, though the dialogue is frequently unintentionally amusing. Violence. A-III (R)
Munster Go Home (1966) Big screen version of
a popular TV horror comedy series in which the
Munster family inherit a English manor but have
to eject the gang of counterfeiters occupying it.
Earl Bellamy directs the TV cast (Fred Gwynne,
Yvonne De Carlo, Al Lewis) with less attention to
the plot than the gags. Mildly entertaining but
mostly for the show's fans. A-I (br)
Muppet Movie, The (1979) After a chance
encounter with a Hollywood talent scout Dom
DeLuise, Kermit the Frog abandons his soggy
swamp for a movie career, taking the entire Muppet crew on a heart-warming cross-country jaunt
but it is Miss Piggy who saves the day by getting
Kermit his Hollywood audition. In their first
appearance on the big screen, Jim Henson's Muppet characters seem right at home and director
James Frawley's location filming gives them the
world as a stage. Charming and delightful entertainment for all. A-I (G)
Muppets Take Manhattan, The (1984) Kermit
and Miss Piggy emulate Mickey Rooney and Judy
Garland in this spoof of old-time Hollywood musicals. Under Frank Oz's direction, the third screen

outing of Jim Henson's Muppets offers some highly
entertaining musical numbers, much witty comedy
and a lot of fun. Highly recommended for family
viewing. A-I (G)
Murder by Death (1976) Eccentric criminolo-
gist (Truman Capote) invites five master detectives
and assistants (including David Niven, Maggie
Smith, Eileen Brennan and James Coco) to his
sinister mansion, intending to confound them with
a crime they cannot solve. Neil Simon's script owes
much to Agatha Christie's "Ten Little Indians,"
but its attempt to spoof whodunit movies is badly
wide of the mark. Director Robert Moore fails to
find much humor in the flimsy plot, multiple
inconsistencies and flat dialogue. Even the broad
performances of a capable cast don't help matters
much (Alec Guinness is wasted in a butler part).
Adult and frequently vulgar humor. A-III (PG)
Murder by Decree (1979) Sherlock Holmes
meets Jack the Ripper in this handsome, expensively mounted period piece in which Holmes
(Christopher Plummer) and Dr. Watson (James
Mason) trace a series of murders to a high person-
nage in Queen Victoria's England. Directed by
Bob Clark, a preposterous and incredibly untidy
plot is overcome by the fine acting of the principals
supported by such nonpareils as John Gielgud and
Anthony Quayle. Harmless but somewhat violent
and gory entertainment not meant for younger
viewers. A- III (PG)
Murder Czech Style (1968) Weak Czechoslovakian satire manifests a cynical view of marriage.
O (br)
Murder on the Orient Express (1974) Stylish
screen version of the Agatha Christie mystery with
Belgian detective Hercule Poirot (Albert Finney)
solving the murder of a man (Richard Widmark)
whom everyone on the train apparently had good
reason to kill. Set in the 1930s, director Sidney
Lumet emphasizes the elegance of the period, has
an enthusiastic all-star cast (Ingrid Bergman,
Wendy Hiller, Vanessa Redgrave, Lauen Bacall,
John Gielgud, et. al.) and is faithful to the original's
wit and verve. Exceptionally well-done escapist
entertainment for those who enjoy murder mysteries but the murder here is rather brutal and definitely not for pre-teens. A-II (PG)
Murderer's Row (1966) Dean Martin as Matt
Helm, the poor man's James Bond who specializes
less in espionage than in booze and broads. Its plot
about a kidnapped scientist is meant to be a spoof
of spy-spoof movies but offers little more than a
leer-filled bag of crude sexual innuendo and puerile naughtiness with Martin's lumbering characterization providing a paltry few unintentional guffaws. O (br)
Murders in the Rue Morgue (1971) Poor adaptation of the Poe story with a wooden performance
by Jason Robards matched by those of Christine
Kaufmann and Herbert Lom. Director Gordon
Hessler provides little tension in what was intended
as a horror story, though he keeps the make-up
artists and special effects department busy with a
plethora of acid murders, decapitations and dream
sequences. A-III (PG)
Murmur of the Heart (1971) French drama
about the sexual maturing of a precocious adolescent in an upper middle-class family whose comfortable materialism is more offensive than the
youth's unfortunate brothel initiation into sex or
the salvation-through-incest resolution of the story.
Directed by Louis Malle, the movie has some light

humor and fine performances but depicts the sexual and social antics of the disinterested father (Daniel Gelin), the disorganized mother (Lea Massari) and their three parasitic sons as both healthy and amusing. Bogus sense of values. O (nr)

Murph the Surf (see: "Live a Little, Steal a Lot")

Murphy's Law (1986) A ruthless felon (Carrie Snodgrass), determined to even the score with the men who sent her to prison, goes on a killing spree for which she frames a cop (Charles Bronson). J. Lee Thompson's direction succeeds only in exploiting vulgarity and violence for simplistic shock value. Profanity and nudity further mar the Bronson vehicle. O (R)

Murphy's Romance (1986) It isn't until movie's end that Sally Field in the role of a divorcee and James Garner as a widower twice her age realize that all their previous bickering means that they're in love, long after all but middle-aged romantics will have lost interest. Intruding into director Martin Ritt's mostly genial fantasy romance is some rough language and an inconsistent view of sexual morality. A-III (PG-13)

Murphy's War (1971) Offbeat drama about merchant seaman Peter O'Toole, sole survivor of a German submarine attack off South America near the end of World War II, who is picked up by barge owner Philippe Noiret and patched up by Quaker missionary Sian Phillips. O'Toole seeks to sink the U-boat by bombs from an ancient airplane, ramming it with the old barge and is still at it when the war ends. Director Peter Yates fails to make his implausible revenge tale exciting, let alone interesting. Some intense scenes of wartime violence. A-III (GP)

Music Lovers, The (1971) British production about the tormented life of 19th-century Russian composer Peter Ilyich Tchaikovsky (Richard Chamberlain) places too much stress on trying to link his music to his sexual disorientation and unconsummated marriage to a woman (Glenda Jackson) who, in a grisly set of sequences, goes quite mad. Directed by Ken Russell with characteristic visual extravagance and narrative weaknesses, the movie's Freudian approach is questionable but its interplay with realism and surrealism, objectivity and subjectivity, succeeds to a surprising degree. Mature themes and some nudity. A-IV (R)

Music Man, The (1961) Robert Preston stars as Professor Harold Hill in this rousing movie version of the Meredith Wilson musical. Fine family entertainment. A-I (br)

Mustang Country (1976) Joel McCrea plays an aging cowboy who is joined by a little Indian boy (Demetri Mina) in attempting to capture a wild horse while eluding a three-toed grizzly, the villain of the piece because he kills more than he eats. Directed by John Champion, the result is a predictable wildlife adventure movie for family viewers, but one that youngsters will especially enjoy. A-I (G)

Mutations, The (1974) Disagreeable British horror movie about a mad doctor (Donald Pleasence) whose attempt to create a new form of life that is both plant and animal requires experimental candidates that a sadistic freakshow owner (Tom Baker) helpfully supplies. Humorlessly directed by Jack Cardiff, the movie's collection of human mutants varies from the merely gruesome to the baldly disgusting, with a layer of coy nudity to add the final insult. O (R)

My American Cousin (1986) A Canadian pre-adolescent (Margaret Langrick) is lifted out of the boring doldrums of 1950's Vancouver when her teenaged American cousin (John Wildman) visits her staid and conventional family. Writer-director Sandy Wilson scores with a light and tender reminiscence of puppy love and awakening excitement with the world outside the home. Although there are some scenes of passionate cuddling, it is an essentially innocent treatment of youthful affection. A-II (PG)

My Bloody Valentine (1981) Low-budget Canadian exploitation movie about a demented coal miner who stalks his attractive young victims with a pick ax on Valentine's Day. Directed by George Mihalka, the absurd plot offers only violence and vast amounts of flowing blood. O (R)

My Bodyguard (1980) Young transfer student (Chris Makepeace), bullied by a neighborhood gang of toughs, hires a hulking, brooding classmate (Adam Baldwin) to act as his bodyguard. Some effective moments but it takes some uncertain turns before reaching a violent and far-fetched conclusion. Some sexual references and its simplistic solving of a problem by resorting to violence makes it dubious fare for young viewers. A-III (PG)

My Brilliant Career (1980) Bright Australian dramatization of a autobiographical novel about a young farm girl (Judy Davis in a dazzling performance) raised in poverty but determined to make a life of her own as a writer at the turn of the century. Gillian Armstrong directs a work that besides being very funny, very human, very touching and always entertaining, is a tribute to the human spirit and the artistic imagination. Exhilarating family fare. A-I (G)

My Demon Lover (1987) Scott Valentine is the youth with the Romanian curse that makes him turn into a beast whenever he thinks about sex. A noble act frees him into the arms of true love but director Charles Loventhal exploits sexual situations and bedroom scenes for one-joke humor about demonic violence. O (PG-13)

My Fair Lady (1964) Screen version of the Lerner and Loewe Broadway musical based on George Bernard Shaw's play, "Pygmalion," the story concerns Eliza Doolittle (Audrey Hepburn), a Covent Garden flower girl who longs for a better life and the egotistical bachelor Professor Henry Higgins (Rex Harrison) who bets a friend that he can transform Eliza's Cockney speech and manners so that she can pass for a lady at the upcoming Royal Ball. Predictably, it is not always the professor who gives the lessons. George Cukor's nimble direction, Cecil Beaton's stunning sets and costumes, the charming performances and the wonderful music add up to splendid family entertainment. A-I (G)

My Father, My Master (1977) Somber Italian production about a Sardinian youth, an illiterate shepherd until military service opens his eyes to a wider world, studies for a high school diploma and eventually obtains a degree in linguistics. Directed by Paolo and Vittorio Taviani, the emphasis is on the simple but backward life of rustic peasants where the family patriarch has total authority. The cruel beatings that the lad endured as a child and the dark and violent passions that permeate the culture in which he grew up make it a film for none but mature viewers. A-IV (nr)

My Favorite Year (1982) Peter O'Toole plays a

fading movie star who agrees to appear on a show in the early days of television comedy and a young gag writer (Mark Linn-Baker) is assigned to keep the drunken, womanizing actor in line. Director Richard Benjamin's comedy is bright and entertaining as long as talented, charming O'Toole is on screen, but when he's off, the picture quietly dies. Because the humor revolves around the hero's pursuit of women and the bottle, as well as some rather vulgar gags, it is not for younger viewers. A-III (PG)

My Friends (1976)   Italian comedy concerning the juvenile pranks of four middle-aged practical jokers for whom nothing is sacred except their own bond of camaraderie. Their idea of a good time, for example, is to go to the railroad station and slap the faces of people looking out the windows of departing trains. Directed by Mario Monicello, the movie's attitude towards people in general, and women in particular, is downright nasty, with nudity and vulgar language compounding the tastelessness. O (PG)

My Love Has Been Burning (1979)   Elegant Japanese production about a pioneer for women's rights in the 1890s. Kinuyo Tanaka plays the daughter of a wealthy family who through bitter personal experience of male domination of society becomes a dedicated feminist who founds a school for the education of women. Directed in 1949 by Kenji Mizoguchi, it is a feminist tract more than a credible drama, but one that has considerable historical interest in terms of the development of women's rights in Japan. A-II (nr)

My Lover, My Son (1970)   Failed British melodrama dealing with the sexual attraction a mother (Romy Schneider) develops for her understandably confused adolescent son (Dennis Waterman). Directed by John Newland, whose main object seems to be gaudiness, the screenplay all but drowns its principals in cheap melodramatic thrills, and neither the mother's ultimate comeuppance nor the son's more natural romance with a local girl can save the movie from deserved oblivion. O (R)

My Michael (1976)   Screen version of the Amos Oz novel, set in Israel during the 1950s, about a marriage that has withered because it never had a chance to grow. Understanding how the young couple's life together goes on unravelling in estrangement and alienation is possible only if seen as reflecting the embattled Israeli state, not at war but certainly not at peace, in their own land. While all the dimensions of this ambitious theme are not completely realized, director Don Wolman had made a challenging drama about the special complexities of Israeli life that is worth the attention of serious moviegoers. A-III (nr)

My Name Is Nobody (1974)   Henry Fonda and Terence Hill star in a lavish spoof of spaghetti Westerns, produced by Sergio Leone and directed by Tonino Valeria. Fonda is a laconic, aging marshal with the reputation of being the fastest gun in the West. Actually the sly, kinetic Hill is faster and saves the lawman from any number of mishaps on his last assignment before retirement. Though there are some charming comic bits, the movie's one-joke concept can only be characterized as a good-natured waste of time. A-II (PG)

My Night at Maud's (1970)   After resolving to marry a religiously devout student (Marie-Christine Barrault) he has never met, a 34-year-old engineer (Jean-Louis Trintignant) happens to meet a sensuous woman (Francoise Fabian) with whom

he spends the night in talking about everything from literature and mathematics to politics and religion. Intriguing French movie directed by Eric Rohmer, the intellectual talkathon focuses on the cerebral quest for life's meaning while indicating the difficulty of people to live up to the practical aspects of idealism and dogma, whether Christian or Marxist. The third in Rohmer's series of "Six Moral Tales," it has the ambiguity of real life and is a perfect discussion piece. A-III (GP)

My Old Man's Place (see: "Glory Boy")

My Secret Life (1971)   Canadian version of a book of Victorian pornography consists of a singularly dreary flood of sexual description vapidly read and illustrated with visuals that are numbing in their dullness. Directed by Leland R. Thomas, whatever its poetic aspirations, it is only a pretentious bore. Nudity in a sexual context. O (X)

My Side of the Mountain (1969)   Toronto youth journeys into the Quebec wilderness to prove that he can take care of himself, adapts quite easily to life in the forest and is befriended by a migrant folk singer (Theodore Bikel) who eventually rescues him during a snowstorm. Produced by Robert B. Radnitz and directed by James B. Clarke, its intriguing story has substance instead of cliches, in addition to magnificent photography capturing the beauty of its natural setting. Intelligent family fare whose spirit of adventure and youthful independence can be enjoyed by all. A-I (G)

My Sweet Charlie (1970)   Two fugitives—a frightened pregnant girl thrown out by her family (Patty Duke) and a black lawyer (Al Freeman Jr.) on the run for killing a white man in self defense—find themselves taking refuge in a vacant Southern beach house. The relationship has nothing to do with sex or sensationalism but with basic emotions of fear and prejudice that ultimately lead to honesty and recognition of each other as human beings. Director Lamont Johnson avoids melodramatic sentimentality, helped by sharp performances from his two principals and an intelligent script based on David Westheimer's novel. One of those rare made-for-television movies that earned subsequent distribution to movie theaters, it still has something relevant to say about ordinary people as well as social justice. A-II (G)

My Sweet Little Village (1987)   Czech director Jiri Menzel creates a gentle fable about fellowship and brotherhood in a tiny worker's commune. Imbedded in the narrative is a sly comment upon socialist ideals and an affirmation of the joys of a simple rural life. A-II (PG)

My Uncle Antoine (1972)   Canadian movie centering on a Christmas Eve during the 1940s when an adolescent gets his first glimpse of adulthood after he and his inebriated uncle lose a corpse they are transporting to the funeral parlor during a snowstorm and arrive home in the early morning to chance upon his aunt's act of infidelity. Directed by Claude Jutra, the film looks with clarity and compassion at the world of a small French-Canadian mining village and its vibrant community of characters seen in a montage of portraiture and vignette. Though rooted in a specific ethnic tradition, its perspective is universal enough to strike chords celebrating our common humanity. A-III (nr)

My Way (1974)   Muddled South African melodrama about the highly strained relations within the family of a success-driven building contractor (Joe Stewardson), a former marathon runner who demands success from his three sons, and the predictable conflicts and lapses that result. Directed by Emil Nofal, it is notable only for its complete absence of blacks, even in crowd scenes. Domestic violence. A-III (PG)

Myra Breckinridge (1970) Screen version of Gore Vidal's novel about a sex change operation turns satire into burlesque and, in trying to show how society has accepted the false values of Hollywood imagemaking, makes gross caricatures out of the notable (John Huston and Mae West) and less than notable (Rex Reed). Directed by Michael Sarne, the treatment is thoroughly distasteful and at times repulsive. Sexual innuendo, nudity, vulgar sight gags and rough language predominate. O (R)

Mysteries of the Organism (1971) The title refers to the fanciful theories of Wilhelm Reich, psychologist convicted of fraud in selling scientifically repudiated apparatus. Yugoslavian director Dusan Makavejev uses Reich as the central image in a movie devoted to contemporary sexual politics, and perhaps the only group that won't be offended by it are anarchists. Some of the bizarre sexual material is at best crude, and the result is less a commentary on the sexual confusion of the age than itself a product of it. O (nr)

Mysterious Island of Captain Nemo, The (1974) The famed Nautilus of Jules Verne has been dry-docked and is being used solely as a kind of plush houseboat by the mysterious Captain Nemo (Omar Sharif) who deters visitors by blasting them from afar with his robot ray guns. Curiously disjointed European co-production directed by Juan Antonio Bardem and Henri Colpi mixes a thin plot and some lovely scenery with a torrent of mushy dialogue and low-grade acting that results in less than enthralling children's fare. A-I (G)

Mystery of Thug Island, The (1966) Failed European adventure story ineptly directed by Nino Battiferri with Guy Madison fighting an outlaw cult operating under the direction of a pseudo-goddess in India. Stylized violence. A-II (br)

Mystery of Kaspar Hauser, The (1975) Compelling German drama about the discovery in the town square one morning in 1828 of a teenage boy capable of speaking but a few words, barely able to walk and apparently without any experience of human society. The mystery of his origins was never solved but he became an object of curiosity, exhibited in a sideshow and studied by scientists and philosophers until his equally mysterious murder in 1833. Director Werner Herzog is not interested in rational explanations of these fact-based events but in portraying the injustices committed against a totally innocent outsider by a complacent, self-satisfied society. A-III (nr)

N

Nada Gang, The (1974) French production about a small motley band of political extremists whose kidnapping of the American Ambassador leads authorities to use extreme counter-terrorist tactics, ultimately forcing the band's fanatic leader (Fabrio Testi) to conclude that violence from the left is as self-defeating as from the right. Directed by Claude Chabrol, the individual characterizations of a fine cast overcome stereotyped roles to involve viewers in the movie's obvious anti-terrorist message. Violent action and atmosphere. A-IV

(nr)
Nadine (1987) Warmhearted comedy romance about zany, fumbling couple (Kim Basinger and Jeff Bridges) whose marriage is reconciled after dangerously failed attempts to exploit profit from a set of highway plans. Writer-director Robert Benton's Southern gentility shows brightly through Basinger's frothy portrait of a 1950s working-class woman. A-II (PG)

Naked Among the Wolves (1967) Tender German movie about a little Jewish boy smuggled by a prisoner into a concentration camp where the child's survival becomes a symbol of the struggle between the inmates and their Nazi guards shortly before the camp's liberation by American troops. Directed by Frank Beyer, the movie has warmth, compassion and optimisim about the survival of the human spirit even in the most inhuman of circumstances. Restrained treatment of Nazi atrocities. A-II (br)

Naked Ape, The (1973) Failed screen version of the popular anthropology book by Desmond Morris uses live action segments and cartoon fantasies to illustrate the human evolution from the primate order, with emphasis on pair-mating. Adapted and directed by David Driver, it is a mish-mash of mindless shards seeking desperately to congeal into a whole, though Victoria Principal and Johnny Crawford are attractive as naked apes going bananas over each other. Inept treatment of an inert movie property relies on heavy-handed sexual humor. A- III (PG)

Naked Hearts (1970) French production about a group of aimless boys who band together for kicks and occasionally get into trouble, with the focus on one boy more sensitive, yet ultimately as irresponsible as his companions. French director Edouard Luntz captures a mood of loneliness and frustration, emphasized by harsh black-and-white photography of an alienating industrialized environment with its factory smoke stacks, seedy tenements and dirty streets. The reality of characters and situations requires a mature perspective. A-III (nr)

Naked Runner, The (1967) Frank Sinatra plays an American exile and ex-sharpshooter manipulated by British intelligence agents to kill an enemy agent in this suspenseful but wildly improbable yarn taken from the Francis Clifford novel. Director Sidney J. Furie is most concerned with the official ruthlessness that reduces people to instruments of power and, though the plot may be muddled, it is an interesting premise. Some violence. A-III (br)

Name of the Rose, The (1986) Darkly envisioned murder-mystery set in a medieval monastery features a Franciscan friar (Sean Connery) who uses logic to uncover the cause of a mysterious death among a Fellini-like assortment of grotesque and repulsive monks, all of whom appear to be either homocidal or homosexual. A freak show is all that emerges from this badly bungled adaptation of Umberto Eco's intriguing novel. Explicit sex scene, violence and burnings at the stake. O (R)

Namu, the Killer Whale (1966) Simple story of a fishing village set in an ocean cove where the local fishermen learn that killer whales are dangerous only if attacked. Directed by Laslo Benedek, it is wholesome children's fare and parents can enjoy the beautiful ocean setting, if not its pleasant but unremarkable tale. A-I (br)

Nana (1971) Swedish production directed by

Mac Ahlberg exploits Emile Zola's novel about a 19th-century French courtesan (Anna Gael) in a ridiculous updated movie version with excessively graphic sex and nudity. O (X)

Nanami (1969) Japanese story about two young people groping toward pure love despite their sordid environment starts well but their plight and aspirations are soon overpowered by arbitrary and confused melodrama and director Susumu Hani's lack of restraint in several sex scenes. O (nr)

Napoleon and Samantha (1972) Disney comedy about a young man (Michael Douglas) who gets involved with an orphaned little boy (Johnny Whitaker), his pet lion and his seven-year-old playmate (Jodie Foster). Among the problems are the burial of the boy's grandfather (Will Geer) and a menacing homicidal maniac. The movie could do without the latter but Geer's death is handled in a sensitive manner that provides a gentle lesson about the passage from life. Appealing performances from Geer and the children under the competent direction of Bernard McEveety make it an enjoyable family movie. A-I (G)

Nashville (1975) Robert Altman's ambitious backstage epic about the careers of the people who make the capital city of country music come alive is a consistently entertaining, at times enlightening, look at an uniquely American phenomenon. Unfortunately, in reaching for something more—an indictment of sorts of contemporary America—Altman lapses into a series of cliches regarding political elections, violence, Vietnam, etc. that are quite unworthy of his film at its best. Fine performances by Ronee Blakley, Henry Gibson, Lily Tomlin, Michael Murphy and many others in a large and talented cast. Some of the subject matter and its naturalistic treatment make this a movie not for casual viewers. A-IV (R)

Nashville Girl (see: "New Girl in Town")

Nasty Habits (1977) Clumsy screen version of "The Abbess of Crewe," Muriel Spark's satire paralleling the Watergate scandal with wiretapping in a Philadelphia convent. Directed by Michael Lindsay-Hogg, with Glenda Jackson as the autocratic abbess and Sandy Dennis as her kooky aide, the movie's jabs at institutional power vary from slapstick to long, talky sketches and occasional tastelessness. Though the film goes out of its way to insist that this order of nuns is not officially recognized, some may find the treatment of women religious and convent life offensive. A-IV (PG)

National Lampoon's Animal House (1978) After being expelled from college, the members of a rowdy fraternity get revenge on the school's administration and a rival fraternity by disrupting the homecoming parade. Directed by John Landis, the mindless, unfunny exercise in grossness tries to pass itself off as an anti-establishment comedy, despite reserving some of its most tasteless jibes for blacks and women. Exploitive sex and nudity. O (R)

National Lampoon's Class Reunion (1982) The 10th annual reunion of the class of '72 at Lizzie Borden High School is enlivened by a prowling homicidal maniac. Director Michael Miller's comedy is not even mildly funny in its reliance on extremely coarse humor and some nudity. O (R)

National Lampoon's European Vacation (1985) The family that cavorted their way across America on their first film vacation does so again, this time in Europe. Chevy Chase and Beverly

D'Angelo repeat their roles as the parents in a movie that is witless, vulgar, unfunny and in consistently bad taste. Nudity and sexually-oriented humor. O (PG-13)

National Lampoon's Vacation (1983) Chevy Chase stars in this comic saga of a family's misadventures driving from Chicago to a California amusement park. As in any trip there are moments of fun and humor and long stretches of dull, tedious travel. Directed by Harold Ramis, there is some tasteless humor involving a corpse, some sexual innuendo and brief nudity. A-III (R)

National Velvet (1945) Young English country girl (Elizabeth Taylor) and a disillusioned former jockey (Mickey Rooney) become friends, win a horse in a raffle and train it to run in the Grand National. Director Clarence Brown's picture of youthful determination is a winner and a perennial family classic. A-I (br)

Natural, The (1984) Screen version of the Bernard Malamud novel about a phenomenal baseball player (Robert Redford) is as much a fable about the temptations of worldly glory and the flesh as it is a red-blooded sports saga. Directed by Barry Levinson, it has a strong supporting cast (Robert Duvall, Glenn Close, Wilford Brimley) but muddles the story's underlying themes of self-deceit, evil and mortality. Promiscuity figures in the plot but is treated with restraint. A-III (PG)

Natural Enemies (1979) Successful magazine editor (Hal Holbrook) decides to shoot his wife (Louise Fletcher) and three teen-age children but his best friend (Jose Ferrer) tries desperately to argue him out of it. Written, produced and directed by Jeff Kanew, this story of marital breakdown is a cold and superficial exercise. Needlessly explicit brothel scene which includes partial nudity. O (R)

Navajo Joe (1967) Fed by the hatred of their half-breed leader, a gang of outlaws become compulsive Indian-killers until one heroic Indian (Burt Reynolds) outwits and destroys most of them when they try to rob a train. Routine sphagetti Western directed by Sergio Corbucci has an excess of wanton killings, brutality and sadism. O (br)

Nazarin (1968) Mexican story set in 1905 when a young priest comes into disfavor with his inflexible superiors, with the civil authorities and even with the poor when he tries to live a life of simplicity, poverty and charity among them. Director Luis Bunuel's 1958 production is not very optimistic about the possibility of idealism winning over the world but it is not critical of religion, only pious hypocrisy. A-III (br)

Nea (1978) When a rich and nasty 16-year-old girl (Ann Zacharias) writes a successful erotic novel, her lover-editor (Sammy Frey) claims credit and she exacts a cruel revenge. French director Nelly Kaplan evidently had social satire in mind, but the movie's exploitation of sex is more in evidence than any wit or insight. O (R)

Necromancy (1972) Pamela Franklin finds herself the latest candidate to play at witchcraft in a creepy little California village owned and completely dominated by Orson Welles, toy manufacturer and master of the occult. Written, produced and directed by Bert I. Gordon, it's not very scary but is slightly amusing in its ineptness and desperate attempts at plot twists and shocks. Innocuous save for some brief nudity and a nasty attack by rats. A-III (PG)

Ned Kelly (1970) Uneven but engrossing British

production about an Irish outlaw gang led by Kelly whose exploits in 1870s Australia grew in legend after betrayal by one of their own led to their capture and execution by the Crown. Mick Jagger in the tile role gives a successful portrayal as the embittered, hardened man-child outlaw. Tony Richardson's bold and sweeping direction, the beautifully muted color photography, and the bittersweet ballads about the now folk hero sung by Waylon Jennings (and composed by Shel Silverstein) are more than enough to recommend it. Some fairly graphic violence. A-III (PG)

Neighbors (1981) Director John G. Avildsen's screen version of Thomas Berger's black comedy about a staid suburbanite (John Belushi) who is driven crazy by a looney neighbor (Dan Aykroyd) is a muddled, dismal failure devoid of both laughs and insight. Senseless scene of seduction, much sexual innuendo and unusually crude language. O (R)

Nelson Affair, The (1973) Boudoir history of Admiral Lord Nelson's (Peter Finch) scandalous behavior with his beloved and presumably bewitching mistress Lady Emma Hamilton (Glenda Jackson in an eccentric performance). Scripted by Terence Rattigan and directed by James Cellan Jones, it is a literate if somewhat bland treatment of the stormy love affair. A-III (PG)

Neptune Factor, The (1973) Ben Gazzara heads the rescue submarine racing to recover the men trapped in an undersea research lab by a volcanic eruption in the North Atlantic. Canadian production directed by Daniel Petrie, the routine underwater adventure relies heavily on the special sub's scientific gadgetry and the exotic deep sea creatures which will engage the interest of younger viewers but adults may prefer staying on dry land. A-I (G)

Nest of Vipers (1979) Italian production about a callow piano student (Christian Borromeo) who has an affair with the mother (Senta Berger) of a fellow student and then abandons her for a beautiful young heiress (Ornella Muti). Director Tonino Cervi's story of jealousy and revenge is mired in graphically depicting the affairs as well as others including incest, lesbianism and homosexuality. O (R)

Network (1976) When a TV anchorman (Peter Finch) has a breakdown and rants and raves on camera, his ratings soar and an ambitious network executive (Faye Dunaway) centers a new program concept around him over the protests of a more humane executive (William Holden). Written by Paddy Chayefsky and directed by Sidney Lumet, the heavy-handed satire on the evils of television and its effects on the public misses as often as is on target. Needless subplot involves an adulterous affair with an explicit scene of lovemaking. O (R)

Nevada Smith (1966) Well-made Western about a youth (Steve McQueen) who, after his mother and father are tortured to death by three outlaws looking for gold, tracks them down, killing them one by one. Directed by Henry Hathaway, the revenge story is told in very violent fashion and there are some sexual references. A-III (br)

Never a Dull Moment (1968) Well-paced gangster spoof about a TV actor (Dick Van Dyke) who is mistaken for a killer and has to turn on all of his tough guy mannerisms while looking for a chance to escape a colorful mob of would-be art thieves (led by Edward G. Robinson). Though

there's nothing he can do to avoid the museum heist, it winds up a harmless caper in the pop art department. Jerry Paris directs a likable bit of light entertainment from the Disney Studio that will go down as easily with parents as with their children. A-I (G)

Never Cry Wolf (1983) Government naturalist (Charles Martin Smith), sent to the Canadian Arctic to determine if wolves are responsible for decimating the once abundant caribou herds, learns instead a lesson in survival and self-knowledge. Director Carrol Ballard's fact-based Disney drama allows the viewer to feel the wonder and excitement of the wilderness with insightful humor and stunning visuals. Some scenes of Smith eating mice and going naked in barren Arctic landsacpe. A-II (PG)

Never Give an Inch (see: "Sometimes a Great Notion")

Never Say Never Again (1983) Aging agent 007 (Sean Connery), shunted aside by a new chief, is called back to retrieve two nuclear warheads stolen by a charming and sinister villain (Klaus Maria Brandauer). Director Irvin Kershner's version of the Bond mystique goes overboard in treating violence as spectacle and promiscuity as hyperactive heroism. O (PG)

Never Too Late (1965) Uneven adaptation of the Broadway comedy about a couple who late in life have another child and the complications this causes in their lives. Under Bud Yorkin's direction, Paul Ford is practically the whole show as he tries in his hard-hearted but soft-headed way to cope with the situation. A-III (br)

NeverEnding Story, The (1984) German director Wolfgang Peterson's screen version of a popular fantasy novel about a schoolboy who escapes from class bullies by reading about (and then entering) a storybook world where his imagination runs wild and his courage is tested. Murky metaphysical references, vividly grotesque creatures and a concluding literary-inspired act of retribution offer more for adults than younger viewers, although there is enough fairy tale ambiance to hold their interest. A-I (PG)

New Angels, The (1966) Quasi-documentary with 9 vignettes showing the life of Italian young people attempts to make a serious social statement but its emphasis on the erotic details of sexual situations undermines the theme of director Ugo Gregorettti's effort. O (br)

New Centurions, The (1972) Screen version of Joseph Wambaugh's novel about a veteran police sergeant (George C. Scott) who schools a rookie cop (Stacy Keach) in handling Los Angeles street crime. Director Richard Fleischer's diffuse and episodic melodrama reduces characters and social issues to simple good-guy, bad-guy dramatics. Some bleary-eyed nightclub philosophizing comparing the collapse of law and order in Rome to present society (presumably symbolized by a topless dancer in the background) is the key to the movie's easy sympathies for the police taking the law into their own hands. Violent action and atmosphere. A-IV (R)

New Girl in Town (1977) Sympathetic account of the rise of a young woman (Monica Gayle) to stardom in the world of country western music. Under the direction of Gus Trikonis, however, the heroine spends a great deal of time taking off her clothes on camera, making doubtful the movie's sincerity of purpose. O (R)

New Land, The (1973) Sequel to "The Emigrants" continues its story of a Swedish family (Max von Sydow and Liv Ullmann) after they and a small band of farmers arrive in the Minnesota wilderness of the 1850s and set to work establishing homesteads, cultivating the land, raising their families and acclimatizing themselves to life in the New Land. Superbly directed by Jan Troell, the historical re-creation is an extraordinary achievement in conveying a sense of the pioneer spirit out of which our nation grew. A-II (PG)

New Leaf, A (1971) A slick, money-grubbing cad (Walter Matthau) courts and marries a wealthy spinster (Elaine May) whose passion is botany. She comes to love him dearly but undeservedly as he tries various schemes to kill her until an increasing glimmer of affection rises in his heart. Witty and fast-paced comedy, also written and directed by May, is frequently hilarious and often biting in its moral satire. A-III (G)

New Life Style, The (1970) Trashy German production about a conservative travel agent (Horst Tappet) who attends a business convention at the seashore and is soon having a whirl with a comely blonde (Renata Van Holt). Around them, swinging couples frolic freely and interchangeably according to their perverse preferences. Presented by Peter Savage, this burlesque is badly dubbed into English, further marring a bad experience. O (nr)

New York, New York (1977) Nostalgic musical romance about a 1940s showbiz couple (Liza Minnelli and Robert De Niro) who seek stardom and pay the price in an adulterous affair, drugs and alcohol abuse before achieving success. Directed by Martin Scorsese, the big budget musical is technically impressive but dramatically off key in its depiction of the trials and tribulations of marriage. A-III (PG)

Newman's Law (1974) George Peppard plays an incorruptible Los Angeles cop who, on the verge of arresting a drug ring, is framed on a drug charge, causing him to go off on his own to clear his record and knock off the villains to boot. Directed by Richard Heffron, the routine crime plot moves swiftly to its predictable bloody climax whose justification—taking the law into one's own hands—would be troubling if it were not here so unbelieveable. Some violence and rough language. A-III (PG)

Newsfront (1979) Australian production about the lives and careers of a veteran newsreel cameraman (Bill Hunter) and his assistant (Chris Haywood) from 1948 to 1956 when the nightly television news made the weekly newsreel redundant. Writer-director Philip Noyce pays more attention to the craft of the newsreel and its content during the era of its glory than to the private lives of its characters which receive rather soap opera treatment in marital problems and love affairs. Interesting re-creation but shallow human dimension. A-III (PG)

Next! (see: "The Next Victim")

Next Man, The (1976) Spoiled rich girl (Cornelia Sharpe) works as an assassin for a terrorist group, seducing and liquidating her victims in exotic corners of the world, but meets her match in a visionary Arab diplomat (Sean Connery). Director Richard C. Sarafian's mediocre, high gloss thriller offers little besides mindless violence, some gratuitous nudity and a brutal ending. O (R)

Next Stop, Greenwich Village (1976) Jewish youth (Lenny Baker) leaves his blue-collar Brooklyn neighborhood in 1953 to seek fame as an actor in Greenwich Village. His growth both on the stage and as a person is chronicled by director Paul Mazursky in a series of incidents that are often quite amusing and sometimes extremely touching. Though soft and sentimental in its portrayal of the young man and overly nostalgic about the era, the movie is positive in its assertions of values and sense of ethnic roots. One notable exception is its acceptance of abortion. A-IV (R)

Next Summer (1986) In a story about three generations and how each defines the nature of loving relationships, this French production features an impressive cast, including Claudia Cardinale, Jean-Louis Trintignant, Philippe Noiret and Fanny Ardant. Directed with charm and humor by Nadine Tintignant, each member of this family saga is shown grappling with the many facets of love, sex and marriage from the perspective of strengthening or weakening family ties. Adult theme. A-III (nr)

Next Victim, The (1971) Italian-Spanish co-production about a succession of young ladies who lose their lives to a savage razor-wielder whose real object is to terrorize one particularly fickle young lady (Edwige Fenech). Directed by Sergio Martino, the badly-dubbed terror mystery has an obvious twist ending, predictable suspense and abundant nudity. O (R)

Nice Girl Like Me, A (1969) Boring British melodrama about an unwed mother (Barbara Ferris) who conceives one child in Paris, another in Venice and acquires a third infant when it is dumped in her arms by a desperate Italian mother. Directed by Desmond Davis, there is a lot of lush photography of European cities and pastoral landscapes but the story lacks any social or moral perspective that might have given it some significance. A-III (PG)

Nicholas and Alexandra (1971) British epic offers the spectacle of glittering palaces, splendid pageantry and larger-than-life characters in ornate costumes but misses the historical context making understandable why this couple were the last of the Romanovs to rule Russia. Directed by Franklin J. Schaffner, the focus is on the domestic lives of the Tsar (Michael Jayston) and Tsarina (Janet Suzman), with occasional fragmentary scenes indicating the revolutionary events that were to sweep away the entire epoch. Grand-scale romance set against a turbulent but fuzzy background, with only Rasputin's rampant sexuality to give children pause, though all will wince at his brutal murder. A-II (PG)

Nickel Ride, The (1975) Aging, small-time operator (Jason Miller) gets into a tight spot trying to put together a deal for the crime syndicate and tries to avoid his inevitable fate. Though the narrative is somewhat muddled, director Richard Mulligan's treatment of the central issue of the man's survival is taut and powerfully done, with nicely nuanced characterizations and atmosphere of menace. Element of human compassion elevates it above standard crime movie. A-III (PG)

Nickelodeon (1977) Mildly humorous slapstick drama about the pioneer days of silent films stars Ryan O'Neal as young lawyer turned writer-director and Burt Reynolds as his star. Director Peter Bogdanovich's story has some amusing moments but is rather thin in dramatic developments, leaving the main focus on movie memorabilia. A-II (PG)

Night at the Bijou, A (see: "The Three Stooges Follies")

Night Call Nurses (1972) Sex comedy about nurses (Patricia T. Byrne, Alana Collins and Mittie Lawrence) who temper the needling they receive from psychotic doctors and patients by indulging in gratuitous sex relations with them. Directed by Jonathan Kaplan, it's exploitation drivel. O (R)

Night Caller (1975) Unsavory French production about a police inspector (Jean-Paul Belmondo) whose methods in trying to catch some bank robbers and a deranged serial murderer are both brutal and lack any sense of legal niceties. Director Henri Verneuil's disjointed crime thriller lacks any elements of tension or suspense. Violence, rough language and elements of sexual perversion. O (R)

Night Crossing (1982) Disney fact-based drama about two families (John Hurt, Jane Alexander, Beau Bridges and Glynnis O'Connor) who make their way to freedom from East Germany by way of a hot air balloon. While there are some moments of suspense and entertainment, director Delbert Mann doesn't deal adequately with the foreign setting, culture and people. Nevertheless, it provides the family audience with a harrowing reminder of the price of freedom. A-I (PG)

Night Digger, The (1971) British psychological thriller about an aging spinster (Patricia Neal), long dominated by a tyrannical adoptive mother, who falls in love with a psychotic killer twenty years her junior (Nicholas Clay). Good acting gives credibility to a rather preposterous situation, allowing director Alistair Reid the intriguing opportunity to probe into the darker corners of the human mind and soul. The result is a mixed bag, caught somewhere between a taut chiller and a human interest story. Some flashbacks indicating the killer's twisted sexuality and several grisly murders with oppressive sexual overtones. A-IV (R)

Night Evelyn Came Out of the Grave, The (1972) Italian production about an Englishman (Anthony Steffen) who is haunted by the ghost of his unfaithful wife and lapses into periods of insanity during which he becomes a sadistic libertine. Directed by Emilio P. Miraglia, the murder mystery is secondary to the sexual aspects which feature nudity. O (R)

Night Flight from Moscow (1973) Convoluted espionage story about a glowering Russian spy (Yul Brynner) who defects to the West and the CIA official (Henry Fonda) whose task is to determine whether the defector is an honest turncoat or a double agent. French production directed by Henri Verneuil has interesting details about counter-intelligence methods but the slow pace of the international yarn makes it a yawner. Some violence. A-III (PG)

Night Full of Rain, A (1978) The unhappy marriage of a rich American (Candice Bergen) and an Italian Communist journalist (Giancarlo Giannini) forms the basis for director Lina Wertmuller's story of their violent meeting and courtship told in flashbacks. Some nudity, sexual by-play and crudities. O (R)

Night Games (1980) Ludicrous and inept melodrama about a wife (Cindy Pickett), traumatized by a girlhood assault, who is cured of her frigidity by having sex with a stranger dressed in feathers. Listlessly directed by Roger Vadim, the acting is embarrassingly bad. Nudity and graphic sexuality abound. O (R)

Night in Heaven, A (1983) Married school teacher (Lesley Ann Warren) has an affar with a student (Christopher Atkins) who works as a male exotic dancer. Directed by John Avildsen, the crude effort emphasizes nudity and graphic sex while disparaging marital fidelity. O (R)

Night Moves (1975) Gene Hackman plays a Los Angeles private eye who traces a 16-year-old runaway to Florida living with her stepfather and his mistress who are both involved in a smuggling operation. Director Arthur Penn's muddled, badly acted detective melodrama features some brutal murders and resorts to sexual exploitation, especially of the girl, to keep things moving. O (R)

Night of Bloody Horror (1970) Gross horror movie about a mother who mummifies dead members of the family and her manic-depressive son suspected of three sensational murders. Producer-director Joy N. Houck Jr., while suggesting these may have been cases of accidental fratricide and paternal suicide, concentrates on explicit lovemaking, ax-wielding, and quarts of blood-letting. O (nr)

Night of Counting the Years, The (1975) Unusual Egyptian production about a poor village whose livelihood depends upon periodically selling archaeological treasures they have discovered in an unlooted royal tomb ingeniously hidden in the rocky heights above the Valley of the Kings on the Upper Nile. Writer-director Shadi Abdelsalam links the grandeur and beauty of the age of the pharaohs with the stark poverty of their black-robed descendents in a brilliantly photographed drama filled with many poetic and lyric passages evoking a sense of mystery appropriate to the land of the Sphinx. A-II (nr)

Night of Dark Shadows (1971) Spooky doings in a sequel to "House of Dark Shadows" center around Quentin (David Selby), the last of the Collins heirs who returns to the family mansion with his bride (Kate Jackson) and falls victim to reincarnations of his ancestors. Producer-director Dan Curtis dredges up a bushel of scary chestnuts for those who enjoy such things. Minimal gore but some sexual allusions suggest an adult perspective. A-III (GP)

Night of the Blood Monster (1972) British cut-rate costume melodrama with Christopher Lee as a lecherous witch hunter under James II. Lee gets his just desserts when William of Orange invades and wins the throne. Directed by Jess Franco, this is a talkie with a lot of posturing and little action. The sex and violence is mostly implied by using victims of rape and torture as background decoration. A-III (PG)

Night of the Comet (1984) Two teenage California Valley girls (Catherine Mary Stewart and Kelli Maroney) survive the passing of a comet which has reduced nearly everyone else to red dust. There are some bright moments in this tongue-in-cheek disaster thriller from director Thom Eberhardt, but silly zombie attacks and a benign view of one of the girl's promiscuity mars the movie's value as simple diversion. O (PG-13)

Night of the Executioners (see: "The Cop")

Night of the Following Day, The (1969) Failed crime melodrama in which four Americans (Marlon Brando, Richard Boone, Jess Hahn and Rita Moreno) concoct a scheme to kidnap a wealthy youth (Pamela Franklin) on her arrival in France. Directed by Hubert Cornfield, the plot is implausible and the characterizations are wildly unconvincing. Some violence, sex and graphic drug use. A-III (R)

Night of the Generals, The (1967) A detective story without much mystery but unusual because the suspects are World War II German Army generals (Donald Pleasence, Charles Gray and Peter O'Toole). Detective Omar Shariff plods along after his man with amiable determination but director Anatole Litvak's straight-forward narrative does not arouse much interest. Some brutal violence. A-III (br)

Night of the Grizzly, The (1966) Unpretentious Western directed by Joseph Pevney about a ranch family (Clint Walker and Marta Toren) who are trying to raise livestock on a range at the foot of the Rockies but their ranch draws an enormous grizzly bear who eludes every effort to trap him. Wholesome outdoor adventure fare for the family. A-I (br)

Night of the Juggler (1980) Psychotic (Cliff Gorman) kidnaps the teenage daughter of an ex-policeman (James Brolin) and the desperate father tracks down the killer himself, a chase that takes him into a very rough and sordid part of town. Director Robert Butler's moderately exciting thriller is marred by graphic violence, rough language and gratuitous nudity. O (R)

Night of the Lepus (1972) Zoologists Stuart Whitman and Janet Leigh, experimenting with hormones to reduce the rabbit population, accidentally produce a whole Arizona desert full of rabid cottontails as big as cattle who terrorize the countryside. Directed by William F. Claxton, the monster bunnies loom large on miniature sets, but not large enough to hide the inanities of the script. Still, this hare-raising tale delivers more chuckles than chills. A-II (PG)

Night of the Living Dead, The (1968) Low-budget horror movie whose plot centers on a group of strangers barricaded in a farmhouse while radiation-animated corpses who feed off the living try to storm in for their prey. Directed by George Romero, the unpolished look of the production (grainy black-and-white photography and use of local Pittsburgh residents) has a makeshift quality helping to sustain the dimension of nightmarish unreality. Every once in a while, there is some unconscious humor which nicely relieves the tension and helped earn its cult reputation. Several fleeting but graphic scenes of ghouls gnawing on various parts of the anatomy. A-III (nr)

Night of the Shooting Stars, The (1983) In the chaotic final days of World War II, some Italian peasants flee their villages and hide out in the woods, trying to avoid both retreating German soldiers and vengeful Fascists. Directed and written by Paolo and Vittorio Taviani, the narrative is seen through the perspective of a six-year-old girl who, years later, relates her impressions of war's absurdities to her young son. Visually stunning, often lyric essay on hope and human resilience. Brief, but intense violence. A-III (R)

Night of the Witches (1970) Failed horror movie about a venal preacher, a naive young man, and a cult of astrologers who kill people with bad horoscopes. Keith Erik Burt directs a tiresome exercise, relying solely upon sexual innuendo for energy. O (PG)

Night Patrol (1985) Stupid hijinks in the police department are the sole feature of this vulgar, sexually-exploitative clone of "Police Academy." O (R)

Night Porter, The (1974) Dirk Bogarde plays the porter in a Viennese hotel who resumes the sado-masochistic relationship he began years before with a woman inmate (Charlotte Rampling) of a concentration camp where he was a Nazi officer. Director Liliana Cavani claustrophobically dissects the terror and thrill of a renewed and sick lust that both know will ultimately destroy them. Though done with some artistic integrity, this exercise in abnormal psychology lacks dramatic coherence or human insight. Several explicit scenes of a sexual nature involving nudity and sadistic brutality. O (R)

Night Shift (1982) Night crew at the New York City morgue (Henry Winkler and Michael Keaton) turn the place into a call girl service. The situation allows for little but smirks and the few laughs are sight gags mainly about life in the big city. Under Ron Howard's heavy-handed direction, Winkler is overshadowed by Keaton's fine performance as a frenetic zany. Romanticizes prostitution and some brief nudity. O (R)

Night Stalker, The (1987) Demented tale about an alcoholic vice-squad detective duo solving the serial murders of hookers by a deranged killer. Nudity, profanity, violence and a tired plot unnerve even the most callous fan of crime melodrama. O (R)

Night the Lights Went Out in Georgia, The (1981) Dennis Quaid and Kristy McNichol play a brother and sister who dream of being big-time country-western singers in Nashville but face the predictable problems of earning a living in a small Georgia town. Director Ron Maxwell's attempt to cash in on the hit song of the title is mediocre at best. A-III (PG)

Night They Raided Minsky's, The (1968) Because this film celebrates the crude lustiness that characterized burlesque in the 1920s, some may find it an honest relief from the present era's over-glamorization of sex. As directed by William Friedkin, the movie's standout performance is by Norman Wisdom as a sad little comic, with Bert Lahr's last movie appearance adding some pathos and nostalgia to the proceedings. Unfortunately, however, the long-awaited "accident" that led to the first strip-tease gets most of the emphasis. O (PG)

Night Visitor, The (1971) A double murder disrupts a quiet Scandinavian countryside and the man under suspicion (Per Oscarsson) tells the police inspector (Trevor Howard) that the murders could only have been done by his brother-in-law (Max von Sydow) who resides in an escape-proof cell in a insane asylum. Directed by Laslo Benedek, this modern Gothic tale uses von Sydow's gymnastic skills and menacing presence to achieve a near perfect combination of thriller and mystery. Some violence. A-III (PG)

Night Watch (1973) Disappointing British murder melodrama revolves around whether Elizabeth Taylor is actually mad or only pretends to be in order to avenge herself on husband Lawrence Harvey for plotting to get her enormous wealth by doing away with her and marrying Billie Whitelaw. Under Brian Hutton's uncertain direction, Taylor's performance is a monotonous mixture of screechy emotional outbursts and frumphish attempts at feline sensuality, even as the muddled plot lurches towards its throat-slitting climax. A-III (PG)

Nightcomers, The (1972) Based on the Victorian characters in Henry James' supernatural story, "The Turn of the Screw," the movie ends where the original began and imagines the dark events transpiring between the groundskeeper (Marlon Brando) and his mistress (Stephanie Beacham) that leave two very troubled children for the new governess who arrives at the beginning of the James story. Director Michael Winner dramatizes literally the perverse tendencies and violent events (bizarre sado-masochistic games) which only lurked beneath the surface of the original James story. Climatic gore, nudity in a sexual context and a theme of evil in innocence. O (R)

Nighthawks (1981)   Intense thriller with Sylvester Stallone playing a New York City policeman assigned to an anti-terrorist unit whose mettle is tested by a clever and utterly ruthless German terrorist (Rutger Hauer). Director Bruce Malmuth fails to invest any human dimension to the violence and counter-violence that transpires, using the situation merely as the basis for exciting melodrama. Brutal violence and rough language. A-III (R)

Nightmare in Wax (1969)   Old-fashioned horror movie about a psychotic wax museum curator (Cameron Mitchell) who seeks vengeance on some old associates for having humiliated and disfigured him. Director Bud Townsend bridges the gaps in the story line with a little morbid humor, some mild horror and playful settings. A-II (M)

Nightmare on Elm Street, A (1984)   Freddie, a long-dead child murderer, haunts the dreams of some high students who also die from them. Directed by Wes Craven, the horror movie relies on graphic gore, sexual references and images of uncaring parents for the purpose of eliciting shock and irreverent humor. O (R)

Nightmare On Elm Street II: Freddy's Revenge, A (1985)   Foiled in the original, the slashing monster returns in this sequel, directed by Jack Sholder, to again take possession of a teenager so that he can do some further cutting up. More blood and gore mixed with sexual titillation aimed at teenagers. O (R)

Nightmare on Elm Street III, A (1987)   A group of youngsters are terrorized in their dreams by a restless, evil phantom who returns to avenge his death by fire at the hands of their parents. Classy special effects and tired plot directed by Chuck Russell depict blood and gore through sadistic violence with no other purpose but to shock. O (R)

Nightwing (1979)   An Indian deputy sheriff (Nick Mancuso), the deputy's girlfriend (Kathryn Harrold), and an obsessed scientist (David Warner) team up to track down and destroy a colony of ravenous, plague-bearing vampire bats. Director Arthur Hiller's modest thriller relies on an interesting mix of Indian mysticism and scientific facts but the action leads only to an anticlimax. Rather graphic violence and the use of drugs for religious purposes. A-III (PG)

Nijinsky (1980)   Biographical dramatization about legendary ballet dancer Vaslav Nijinsky (George de la Pena) and impresario Sergei Diaghilev (Alan Bates) places less emphasis upon ballet itself than upon their master-protege relationship and its homosexual dimension. Director Herbert Ross presents an elegant re-creation of pre-World War I Europe and the acting is of high order but some may find the pace of the drama far too languid and others will be uncomfortable with the frank, if non-explicit manner in which the homo-

sexual relationship is depicted. Graphic but brief scene of heterosexual lovemaking. A-IV (R)

9 1/2 Weeks (1986)   Director Adrian Lyne delivers a passionless expression of erotic fantasy in his sexually explicit depiction of a sado-masochistic love affair between an art gallery manager (Kim Basinger) and a financier (Mickey Rourke). Nudity and simulated sexual activity. O (R)

Nine Lives of Fritz the Cat, The (1974)   Based on R. Crumb's comic strip adventures of a funky feline whose primitive vulgarity and social irreverence some found refreshing, this inept animated version by Robert Taylor throws together a batch of disjointed and unimaginative episodes in a manner too literal and witless to be taken as satire. Its excesses of racial animosity and sexual exploitation go beyond questions of taste and tend to be socially destructive rather than purgative. O (R)

9.30.55 (see: "24 Hours of the Rebel")

9 to 5 (1980)   Dolly Parton, Jane Fonda and Lily Tomlin play a trio of harrassed and exploited secretaries who rise up in revolt against an autocratic boss (Dabney Coleman). Director Colin Higgins' promising satire becomes sheer silliness and then begins to drag fearfully. Some rough language, a scene of pot smoking and sexually oriented dream sequence in which the theme of male dominance is inverted. A-III (PG)

1918 (1985)   Mortality presses in upon ordinary happiness in a small Texas town as World War I is coming to an end in Europe and a killer flu epidemic rages at home. Written by Horton Foote and directed by Ken Harrison, it is an excellent movie that catches in wonderfully evocative fashion the terror and beauty of daily life. Though the setting is a vanished era, it nonetheless gives some rich insights into one's own life. There is nothing in it harmful to youngsters, but only children of a certain level of maturity will be able to appreciate it. A-I (nr)

1984 (1984)   Uninspired screen version of George Orwell's foreboding vision of a totalitarian state crushing the individual rights of its hapless citizens loses here both the original's passionate idealism and sense of immediacy. Director Michael Radford's drily somber work lacks the sense of human nobility that is the story's thematic core but it does offer a nuanced performance by Richard Burton as a Big Brother surrogate and John Hurt as the rewriter of history. Some violence and brief nudity. A-III (R)

1941 (1979)   Japanese submarine sighted off the coast of Southern California in the early days of World War II starts a panic with rumors of an invasion. Director Steven Spielberg wastes the comic talents of Dan Aykroyd and John Belushi in a vulgar, tedious, supremely unfunny comedy. Sexual connotations abound and there is some slapstick nudity. O (PG)

1900 (1977)   Sprawling, disjointed narrative spanning 70 years of Italian history seen through the eyes of two men born in 1901, one an aristocrat (Robert De Niro), the other a Marxist (Gerard Depardieu). Director Bernardo Bertolucci's view of history lacks dramatic force and the human frame of reference is chiefly sex and politics. Extravangant depiction of violence and exploitation of nudity. O (R)

90 Days (1986)   A young Canadian has three months in which to decide if he will marry the Korean woman he has sent for via a mail-order service. Director Giles Walker's small Canadian comedy explores the pitfalls of the male ego with charm and subtlety while showing that happiness and commitment can develope without premarital sex. A few harsh expletives and running gag about artificial insemination. A-III (nr)

99 and 44/100% Dead (1974) Silly, badly done gang-war movie starring Chuck Conners, Richard Harris, Edmond O'Brien and Bradford Dillman as various mobster types. Directed by John Frankenheimer, the movie fails to be either a serious crime melodrama or a comic-strip crime spoof, and consequently leaves the audience feeling uncomfortable about its realistic scenes of shoot-outs and sadistic brutality. A-III (PG)

99 Women (1969) Crude European exploitation movie, directed by Jess Franco, centers on the more sordid aspects of life in a women's prison and is merely an excuse to portray nudity and perversion. O (R)

92 in the Shade (1975) Peter Fonda and Warren Oates play fishing boat owners competing for the tourist trade in the Florida Keys. The only element that works in this failed comedy by writer-director Thomas McGuane is Fonda's madcap father (William Hickey) and goatish grandfather (Burgess Meredith who spends most of his time ogling Sylvia Miles). Some exploitative sexual elements. O (R)

Ninth Configuration, The (1980) Stacy Keach plays a government psychologist trying to determine if the inmates of an asylum housed in a Californian Gothic castle are really psychological casualties of the Vietnam War or fakes. Writer-director William Blatty attempts to explore more than the nature of mental illness by introducing such issues as the existence of God, but the drama gets mired down in the more graphic aspects of insanity and unorthodox therapy. Disturbing and provocative movie with suicide as a plot device, some extreme violence and rough language. A-IV (R)

No Blade of Grass (1970) Ecological disaster destroys all varieties of grasses and drives a London family to flee to their relative's farm in the north. Along the way the father (Nigel Davenport) kills anyone who stands in his way but when they finally arrive at the farm they are faced with the father's brother waving a machine gun against unwelcome guests. Unsubtle melodrama directed by Cornel Wilde bludgeons viewers with assorted violence, blood and gore, a motorcycle gang rape and a very realistic birth sequence. Cruelly cynical conception of the anarchy and inhumanity resulting from the spectre of doomsday. O (R)

No Deposit, No Return (1976) Disney movie with a better than average cast (David Niven, Herschel Bernardi and Darren McGavin) about two kids who stage their own kidnapping in order to join their mother in Hong Kong. Director Norman Tokar's plot is as old as O'Henry's "The Ransom of Red Chief," but that won't bother youngsters. A-I (G)

No Drums, No Bugles (1971) Small, unpretentious Civil War drama about a West Virginia farmer (Martin Sheen) who rather than take up arms, leaves his wife and child for a solitary three-year self-imposed confinement in the backwoods. The substance of the movie is taken up with his techniques for survival in the forest through the changing seasons and Sheen makes it an absorbing experience in a tour de force performance. Written, produced and directed by Clyde Ware, it is not a tract against the evils of war but a comment on the sacrifices that must be made by those who place themselves outside the accepted standards of the community. Some motivations are unclear and an ambiguous ending make it best suited for an adult audience, but it is certainly one that could be appreciated by older teenagers. A-III (G)

No Mercy (1986) Chicago cop (Richard Gere) avenges the murder of a fellow officer by using a beautiful Cajun (Kim Basinger) as the bait to smoke out and kill a crime boss of the Louisiana bayous. Director Richard Pearce's nasty, brutish thriller with implied sexual and explicit physical violence and excessive profanity. O (R)

No Small Affair (1984) When a 16-year-old boy (Jon Cryer) gives a boost to the career of a young singer (Demi Moore), she takes him to bed in gratitude. Director Jerry Schatzberg's limp romantic comedy is filled with unpleasant characters in an uninvolving plot. Endorses sexual promiscuity. O (R)

No Time for Breakfast (1978) French tearjerker about a witty, vivacious woman (Annie Girardot), senior physician at a Paris hospital, an ideal wife and extraordinary mother, who has an affair and developes a cancer which goes into remission when family ties are restored. Director Jean-Louis Bertucelli coats the fact-based story with melodramatic overtones. Casual acceptance of infidelity and a nude bathtub scene. O (nr)

No Way Out (1975) Predictable Italian crime melodrama about what happens to a decent, hard-working family man (Alain Delon) when he tries to retire from his job as a Mafia hit-man. Director Duccio Tessari's dreary, mediocre movie deals in the standard violence of the genre, though women are treated especially brutally and there is a gratuitous lesbian scene. O (R)

No Way Out (1987) Triangular power struggle forms when a high-ranking politico (Gene Hackman) and his chief counsel (Will Patton) try to cover up the accidental death of a party girl (Sean Young) unknowingly shared by his CIA liaison (Kevin Costner). Director Roger Donaldson deals with abuse of power but uses an indecorously erotic scene of lovemaking prior to his taut but fluid development of the betrayal theme. A-III (R)

No Way to Treat a Lady (1968) Rod Steiger plays a madman with a severe mother complex who changes disguises for five compulsive murders, while a likeable police detective (George Segal) tries to outwit him. Director Jack Smight provides an effective mixture of adult comedy, pyschodrama and an upbeat love story. A-III (br)

Nobody's Fool (1986) Abandoned by her boyfriend when she becomes pregnant, a teenager (Rosanna Arquette) is befriended by a local theater director (Eric Roberts) who helps her refocus her life after giving up her baby for adoption. Directed by Evelyn Purcell, the movie is more about building one's self-esteem and trust than about sexual relationships. Implied sexual encounter and brief scene of violence. A-II (PG-13)

Nomads (1986) A French anthropologist (Pierce Brosnan) is tormented by punkrocker demons who invade his Los Angeles home. After the evil spirits are transferred at his death to his doctor (Lesley-Anne Down), the malevolent punkrockers scare her out of California. Profanity, brief nudity and scenes of violence. O (R)

None but the Brave (1965) Frank Sinatra directs as well as stars in this anti-war movie set on an out-of-the-way Pacific island during World War II where the crew of a crashed American plane have to deal with a small Japanese outpost. The story's message of brotherhood is clearly stated but a bit too violently. A-II (br)

Norma Rae (1979)   Inspiring drama with Sally Field in the title role as an Alabama textile worker recruited by a tenacious labor organizer (Ron Liebman) to help rally her exploited co-workers into forming a union in the face of tough tactics by an unenlightened management. Director Martin Ritt's dramatic expose of social injustice gives viewers some people and a cause to cheer about. Absorbing, thoughtful entertainment. Some frank references to sexual misconduct. A-III (PG)

Norman Is That You? (1976)   Failed situation comedy about a father (Redd Foxx) who discovers that his son is a homosexual. Though the visual elements are restrained, director George Schlatter's movie stereotypes blacks, women and homosexuals, conveys a smug contempt for parental authority and affection and exploits a serious theme in a witless manner. O (PG)

Norseman, The (1978)   Viking chieftain (Lee Majors) leads his men to the shores of the New World to rescue his father (Mel Ferrer) held prisoner by the Indians. Director Charles B. Pierce's low-budget, low-IQ saga presents Indians as the treacherous, bloodthirsty stereotypes that one would have thought had passed from the screen forever. Generous amount of violence and bloodshed. A-III (PG)

North Avenue Irregulars, The (1979)   Standard Disney comedy about a minister (Edward Herrmann) who takes over a failing parish in a small town and, along with other revitalizing measures, mobilizes a predictablly zany collection of church women to put some illegal gamblers out of business. Director Bruce Bilson concludes the action with a car-crunching slapstick chase. Fair family fun, but less than appealing view of women. A-I (G)

North Country (1972)   Ron Hayes is a bush pilot who delivers mail-and-supplies to those rugged individualists who have chosen to live off the land in the lonely, lovely wilds of Alaska. Functioning as a filmmaker in his spare time, Hayes conceived and photographed this documentary view of the modern pioneer on America's last frontier. Its blending of scenery, rare wildlife and the people who live in the land of the Eskimo make an outdoor adventure that is unusually satsifying family fare. A-I (G)

North Dallas Forty (1979)   Nick Nolte and Mac Davis star as professional football players who love the game but not what commercialism has done to it. Nolte is excellent and director Ted Kotcheff's expose of the hypocrisy and violence of professional sports has some very effective moments, especially the effects of drug abuse, but its focus becomes obscured in promiscuous sex and the athletes' propensity for pranks. Some nudity and much rough language. O (R)

Norwood (1970)   Corny but entertaining Glen Campbell vehicle following his misadventures after military service as he innocently transports some stolen cars to New York, has a one night stand with a pretty hippie in Greenwich Village, meets Kim Darby on a bus and brings her back to his Southern home along with a midget and a performing rooster. Campbell's fans will enjoy the romp, though some may be put off by the salty

dialogue and tasteless but brief situations. A-III (G)

Nosferatu, the Vampire (1979)   Slow but stylish German version of the vampire legend, patterned on F.W. Murnau's 1922 classic film, relies upon mood and atmosphere to create an eerie sense of evil and terror rather than resorting to the cheap tricks and shock effects. Under Werner Herzog's direction, Klaus Kinski is suitably malevolent in the title role, with Isabelle Adjani and Bruno Ganz offering fine support. The overt sexual references and nightmarish quality of the visuals make it unsuitable for youngsters. A-III (PG)

Not on Your Life (1966)   Spanish-made black comedy about a good-natured Madrid undertaker (Nino Manfredi) who is persuaded to take the vacant post of state executioner. Directed by Luis Berlanga, the mostly genial movie satirizes government bureaucracy, human foibles and, quite grimly, capital punishment. A-III (br)

Nothing but a Man (1965)   Black railroad worker (Ivan Dixon) settled down in a southern town but he and his wife (Abbey Lincoln) are confronted by a hostile community that deprives him of one job after another. Directed by Michael Roemer and Robert Young, the movie is episodic and anything but slick, yet it has the ring of actuality found in a good documentary and its story has universal implications. Some violence and a few profanities. A-III (br)

Nothing by Chance (1975)   A group of pilots try to recapture the pre-war barnstorming days in which bi-planes toured rural America giving farmers and townspeople the opportunity of experiencing the pleasures of open-cockpit flight. Though it has some picturesque aerial photography, William Barnett's documentary will disappoint nostalgia and aviation buffs because of its concentration on the touring pilots and a pretentious narration written by Richard Bach. A-I (G)

Nothing in Common (1986)   A wonderfully witty and wise portrait of a young ad agency superstar (Tom Hanks) who must settle accounts with his divorcing parents (Jackie Gleason and Eva Marie Saint) before it's too late. Director Garry Marshall's serio-comic movie features warm and insightful performances by the three principals as they try to reconcile their differences. Some profanity and sexual scenes. A-III (PG)

Nothing Personal (1980)   Romantic screwball comedy about a militant college professor (Donald Sutherland) who goes to Washington to battle a giant corporation bent on the slaughter of baby seals. The insincere social commentary is overpowered by a seduction scene in which Suzanne Sommers as the helpful lawyer futher obscures Sutherland's motives. A-III (PG)

Now You See Him, Now You Don't (1972)   Although apple-cheeked college boy Kurt Russell doesn't know how he invented a chemical that makes people invisible, he does realize it will come in handy against gangster Cesar Romero. Robert Butler directed the carefully homogenized Disney production which, although morally unimpeachable, nonetheless continues the Disney tradition of setting ususally inane comedies in a safe, largely white, middle-class context whose values, if they exist at all, are purely material, bereft of any spiritual or even social dimension. A-I (G)

Nude Bomb, The (see: "The Return of Maxwell Smart")

Number One (1969)   Charlton Heston plays an

aging, once-great quarterback who after some humilitating failures on the field is emotionally torn over retiring. His inability to communicate with his career-oriented wife (Jessica Walter) leads to a one-night stand with a more than cooperative lady sports enthusiast. Director Tom Gries does as well as he can with a story that offers not enough football for the fans and not enough human interest for non-fans. A-III (PG)

Nun, The (1971) French dramatization of Diderot's 18th-century novel about a young girl (Anna Karina), forced by her mother into the convent, who in desperation escapes with a discontented priest and ultimately destroys herself. Although the narrative's exaggerations and stereotyped characters and situations may annoy or disturb some, director Jacques Rivette's main theme is the arbitrary exercise of power which in the historical context of this period is not without interest. Mature themes. A-IV (PG)

Nun at the Crossroads (1970) When a Belgian nun (Rosanna Schiaffino) becomes pregnant after being raped during a 1960s uprising in the Congo, her stern superiors in Brussels prefer that she leave the convent and so she brings up the child alone while engaging in missionary work as a laywoman. Italian-Spanish co-production directed by Julio Buchs with a heavy hand and little help from a generally unconvincing cast. Superficial melodrama. A-III (PG)

Nunzio (1978) Often moving story of a retarded young man (David Proval) whose loving mother (Morgana King) indulges his fantasies of being Superman while his tough truckdriver brother (James Andronica) tries to protect him from abuse in their ethnic Brooklyn neighborhood. Director Paul Williams' concentrates on character and setting, gradually building through incident and dialogue a convincing picture of the love that binds a family together. Unfortunately, a needlessly graphic rape scene, omitted from the original release, has been inserted subsequently. O (PG/R)

Nutcracker, The Motion Picture (1986) Tchaikovsky's fairy-tale ballet, a perennial Christmas favorite, has been given a darker interpretation as representing a young girl's sensual daydreams that are part of the fears and doubts of coming of age. Performed by the Pacific Northwest Ballet, the movie version's psychological implications will elude younger members of the family. A-II (PG/G appeal)

Nuts (1987) Barbra Streisand stars as a high-priced prostitute charged with manslaughter but whose competency to stand trial is at issue. Director Martin Ritt's highly contrived courtroom drama spends more time trying to manipulate the emotions of viewers than it does in trying to probe the issues facing women in a male-dominated society. Much sexually explicit language and references. A-IV (R)

O

O Lucky Man! (1973) British surreal allegory about a young innocent (Malcolm McDowell) whose attempts to succeed in a world he can't understand result in an absurd series of misadventures involving Ralph Richardson, Rachel Roberts, Arthur Lowe, and Mona Washbourne. The targets of director Lindsay Anderson's satiric jabs include corrupt officials, military xenophobia, medical

experimentation, sex clubs and a host of other aspects of irrational social activity. Some will find its narrative disjointed and senseless, while others will welcome its pro-human, pro-individual stance. It is quite discreet in handling sex and violence, using such scenes only to make a point. A-IV (R)

Oblomov (1981) Russian dramatization of Ivan Goncharov's 19th-century novel about an absentee landlord who has made sloth his life's work. Oleg Tabakov is excellent in the title as the lazy hero whose pampered upbringing leaves him ill-prepared for even the moderate rigors of adulthood as a member of a privileged class. Director Nikita Mikhalkov's puts too much effort into atmospheric effects and not enough into moving the overlong story forward. Still, the marvellous recreation of late 19th-century Russian life is engrossing and worth seeing. A-II (nr)

Oblong Box, The (1969) Weak British horror movie loosely based on an Edgar Allen Poe story in which a man (Alastair Williamson), horribly disfigured by an African spell, is kept locked up by his brother (Vincent Price) but when he breaks out, terrible things happen in the neighborhood. Directed by Gordon Hessler, the hazy narrative relies solely on visuals of blood and gore for effect, with little attempt at building suspense. A-III (M)

Obsession (1976) On a business trip to Italy, widower Cliff Robertson falls in love with Genevieve Bujold because she resembles his wife who, along with their daughter, had been killed in a kidnapping 15 years before. This sets up a plot reminiscent of Hitchcock's "Vertigo," but director Brian De Palma attempts to pump romance into Robertson's Italian affair and an absurd conclusion make the result a disappointing miscalculation. Some violence and a muted incest theme. A-III (PG)

Octopussy (1983) Superagent James Bond (Roger Moore) is once again on the trail of an international conspiracy, this time involving an East German circus, a maverick Soviet general, an Asian dealer in counterfeit gems and an Oriental ring of women. Like previous Bond outings, the plot is less important than director John Glen's tongue-in-cheek treatment of the unflappable, fantasy hero surrounded by curvaceous women, cartoon violence, mechanical gimmickery and exotic locales. The venerable formula succeeds only intermittently, partly because of heavy-handed double-entendres and sexual encounters. A-III (PG)

Odd Couple, The (1968) Two men separated from their wives and sharing an apartment discover what incompatibility is all about. One is obsessively neat (Jack Lemmon) and the other is a compulsive slob (Walter Matthau). The story is a nice twist on the adjustments people have to make in life as well as marriage and both principals take good advantage of the comic potential of teaming a disparate pair. Director Gene Sacs relies on Neil Simon's adaptation of his own stage play and the result is often hilarious comedy. Some sexual references. A-III (G)

Ode to Billy Joe (1976) Based on a popular Bobbie Gentry song about two Mississippi Delta teenagers (Robby Benton and Glynnis O'Connor) whose brief romance, in the long-ago summer of 1953, ends in tragedy when the boy throws himself off the Tallahatchie Bridge. Not even the considerable charm of the acting nor the beauty of the Delta setting can help director Max Baer overcome the thin, contrived plot and insufferably cute dialogue. A-III (R/PG)

Odessa File, The (1974) Screen version of the Frederick Forsyth thriller about a German journalist (Jon Voight) who seeks to track down a Nazi war criminal (Maximilian Schell) and comes into conflict with the dreaded Odessa, a secret Nazi organization bent on regaining power. Too heavy and slow moving to be a really effective melodrama, director Ronald Neame has made a run-of-the-mill entertainment with serious overtones. Some violence. A-III (PG)

Oedipus, the King (1968) Static British version of the Greek tragedy by Sophocles features Christopher Plummer and Lilli Palmer under the direction of Philip Saville. A-II (G)

Off Beat (1986) Judge Reinhold plays a loser who impersonates a New York police officer, foils a bank robbery and falls in love with a female cop (Meg Tilly) while rehearsing for a police dance benefit. A weak romantic comedy with a narrow range of emotions and an improbable story line. Brief nudity and some harsh language. A-III (PG)

Offence, The (1973) Veteran London police detective (Sean Connery), in interrogating a man picked up for the rape murder of a number of school girls, pummels the taunting suspect to death and his world crumbles. Director Sidney Lumet compassionately explores the man's psychological and spiritual disintegration through flashbacks and flashforwards, actual events and fragmentary memories of the detective's past experiences. Casual moviegoers may find it a difficult, distasteful experience, but it has value as a picture of the results of constant exposure to violence and sordid criminality that are a part of law enforcement. Challenging but thoughtful mature fare. A-III (R)

Officer and a Gentleman, An (1982) Bitter loner (Richard Gere) enters officer candidate school with the dream of becoming a Navy pilot but he and a buddy (David Keith) get involved with two local women (Debra Winger and Lisa Blount) who want to get married to escape their drab lives as factory workers. During the course of their gruelling training under a tough drill sergeant (Louis Gossett, Jr.), his buddy hangs himself in despair over his relationship and his career. Director Taylor Hackford's romance is old-fashioned enough to contrive a happy ending but not old-fashioned enough to avoid steamy sex scenes and rough language. O (R)

Official Story, The (1985) An upper-class Argentine wife (Norma Aleandro) whose wealthy husband is a friend of the powerful, begins to suspect that her adopted daughter might be the child of a mother victimized by the right-wing government's reign of terror five years before. The Argentinian production, directed and co-scripted by Luis Puenzo, is a extraordinary work that subordinates politics to human characterizations of anguish and nobility. Some brief violence and rough language. A-II (nr)

O Dad, Poor Dad, Mama's Hung You in the Closet and I'm Feeling So Sad (1966) Failed screen version of Arthur Kopit's play about an overpowering mother (Rosalind Russell) and her inhibited son (Robert Morse). Richard Quine's direction of the black comedy tends to be more offensive than funny and some of the tasteless treatment plays with the prurient. O (br)

Oh, Heavenly Dog (1980) A murdered detective (Chevy Chase) is reincarnated as a lovable mutt (Benji) whose mission is to solve the crime.

Jane Seymour provides some romantic interest. Director Joe Camp's canine movie is sometimes amusing, but slow paced, overly cute and, in general, pretty tepid stuff. Some double entendres and a significant amount of profane language. A-III (PG)

Oh! Calcutta! (1972) Poor quality videotaped stage performance of an erotic revue consisting of a series of vignettes intending to reflect both the sexual obsessions and hang-ups of society but its heavy reliance on nudity never gets much further than exhibitionism. O (nr)

Oh! What a Lovely War (1969) British musical version of World War I covers events from Sarajevo to America's entrance in the conflict as told in a series of sketches conveying the mood, motives and attitudes of the British government, military, clergy, common soldier and the folks at home. Directed by Richard Attenborough, with a large and talented British cast, the ambitious but largely successful work intermixes song and comedy with the ugly reality of the battlefield. Its anti-war perspective emphasizes the futility and waste of a war in which a generation of young men sacrificed their lives. A-II (G)

Oh, God! (1977) California supermarket manager (John Denver) becomes a middle-class Moses when chosen by God (George Burns) to tell the world that he is alive and well. As might be expected, no one believes him and complications arise. The gentle comedy, written and directed by Carl Reiner, has its heart in the right place and provides some effective moments, Burns and Denver both being very appealing performers. Reiner's idea of a non-sectarian God who denies original sin, pronounces morality to be entirely subjective and says that Jesus is his son only in the sense that God is the father of all presents a special problem for parents of young viewers who might not understand the fantasy nature of the comedy. Moreover, while sparing other religious groups, the movie makes a Billy Graham-style evangelist into a gross caricature. A-III (PG)

Oh, God! Book II (1980) George Burns returns as the Almighty, his comic timing as quasi-omnipotent as ever. This time he teams up with an 11-year-old schoolgirl whom he persuades to launch an ad campaign promoting him. Directed by Gilbert Cates, it is entertaining, if only mildly funny fare. Though there is less of the secular humanism that marred the original, the concept of Burns as God together with a bit of mild vulgarity may not suit all tastes. A-II (PG)

Oh, God! You Devil (1984) George Burns is back as the Divinity with an infinite number of one-liners. This time he gets to double as the devil and play poker for an errant soul. Director Paul Bogart fashions a comedy that is only mildly amusing and what humor there is comes from Burns. A few sexual references in the dialogue, but otherwise innocuous. A-II (PG)

Oklahoma! (1955) Screen version of the classic Rogers and Hammerstein musical is a stunning, delightful and surprisingly serious production. The period is one of relative innocence in the days when Oklahoma was getting ready to join the Union and everything was up-to-date in Kansas City. Shirley Jones is absolutely winsome as the fresh-as-milk farm girl, Gordon MacRae almost outsmarts himself as her cowpoke-beau Curley and Rod Steiger is malevolent as her would-be suitor Jud Fry. The plot is corny as all get-out, the music and dance numbers charming and memorable but the melodrama tends to be a touch too heavy. A-II (br)

Oklahoma Crude (1973) Turn-of-the-century man-hating oil prospector (Faye Dunaway) reluctantly accepts help from her ne'er-do-well father (John Mills) and a drifter (George C. Scott), in order to keep the big oil combine's enforcer (Jack Palance) from jumping her claim. Her wild-cat well, naturally, comes up a gusher as does her emotional turnabout toward reformed daddy and new-found friend. Directed by Stanley Kramer, there's plenty of old-fashioned action and melodrama here, making fairly solid entertainment for adults who don't mind some Oklahoma crude violence and language. A-III (PG)

Old Boyfriends (1979) Recently divorced woman in her 30's (Talia Shire) tries to make sense out of her life by hitting the road in her Firebird and looking up old boyfriends (Richard Jordan and John Belushi). A third, she discovers, has died in Vietnam and she quickly transfers her affections to his mentally disturbed younger brother (Keith Carradine). Directed by Joan Tewkesbury, the dreary story suffers from the same malaise that afflicts the heroine. Some rough language and adult situations. A-III (R)

Old Curiosity Shop, The (see: "Mr. Quilp")

Old Dracula (1976) Director Clive Donner's spoof of the classic horror tale portrays women as sex objects and becomes little more than a sex farce using brief nudity and crude sight gags for humor. Unfortunately, the presence of David Niven in the cast may arouse unwarranted expectations that the movie offers more than cheap thrills. O (PG)

Old Gun, The (1976) French World War II drama about a doctor (Philippe Noiret) who sends his wife and child to the countryside far from the fighting but on a visit finds that they have been killed in a massacre by a Nazi unit that becomes the target for his revenge. Director Robert Enrico's use of flashbacks recalling details of the doctor's marriage may be sentimental, but they are effective in conveying the outrage that motivates his vengeance. Strong images of wartime violence. A-III (R)

Old Yeller (1958) Dorothy McGuire, Fess Parker and Chuck Connors star in this Disney movie about a lovable mongrel that proves invaluable to a Texas family. A-I (G)

Oliver! (1968) Rousing British musical drawn from the Charles Dickens classic, "Oliver Twist," but bearing little resemblance to the original. Lionel Bart's adaptation borrows only the chief characters and turns them loose in what amounts to a colorful, swirling-stomping-singing Cockney street show. As Fagin, rubber-faced Ron Moody carries most of the burden as if it were light as a feather, with Mark Lester perfectly winning as Oliver, Jack Wild stealing scene after scene (along with handy wallets) and Harry Secombe as a bumbling Mr. Bumble. Under Carol Reed's direction, it all adds up to delightful fare for the entire family. A-I (G)

Oliver's Story (1979) Listless romantic melodrama, a sequel to "Love Story," takes up the life of widowed Oliver Barrett (Ryan O'Neal) whose father-in-law (Edward Binns) urges to start anew which he does by having an affair with a rich WASP (Candice Bergen). Director John Korty has difficulty fleshing out the characterizations of the two principals in their ambiguous affair which

ultimately becomes tiresome. A-III (PG)

Omega Man, The (1971) Post-nuclear holocaust movie about the apparently last healthy man on earth (Charlton Heston) wandering around downtown Los Angeles by day and by night trying to fend off bands of radiation-diseased ghouls. Directed by Boris Sagal, the situation becomes little more than a shallow, garden-variety romantic melodrama with the hero teaming up with some refugee kids hanging out in the hills and the only untainted woman around (Rosalind Cash) with whom he has some coyly ludicrous love scenes. A-III (PG)

Omen, The (1976) The American ambassador to Great Britain (Gregory Peck) finds himself the foster father of the anti-Christ in director Richard Donner's slick, expensively mounted but essentially trashy horror show. Though it refers to scripture and religious beliefs, its only interest in religion is in terms of its exploitation potential. Some intense violence. O (R)

On a Clear Day You Can See Forever (1970) Screen version of a Lerner-Lane musical about a Brooklyn coed (Barbra Streisand) who is cursed with ESP and memories of a past incarnation as a 19th-century coquette with whom her psychiatrist-teacher (Yves Montand) falls in love. Under Vincent Minnelli's direction, Streisand shines but the rest is glossy romantic fluff. Brief seduction scene. A-II (G)

On Any Sunday (1971) Written, produced, directed and narrated by Bruce Brown, this enthralling documentary on motorcycle racing may popularize this endurance sport in the same way that Brown's "The Endless Summer" glorified surfing. Filmed in five countries, the emphasis is on the action and the racers, including top professionals Mert Lawwill and Malcom Smith, as well as actor Steve McQueen. A-I (G)

On Golden Pond (1981) Warm movie about the bickering relationship of an aging couple (Katherine Hepburn and Henry Fonda) at the lakeside vacation home where they have spent their summers for four decades. Visiting is their divorced, middle-aged only child (Jane Fonda), forever at odds with her cantankerous father. Directed by Mark Rydell, the sentimental story revolves around Henry Fonda who gives a fine performance (his last), despite the shallow, caricature-like nature of the role. Too much of the humor leans upon the device of putting vulgarities in the mouth of either the old man or a 13-year-old boy spending a month with the aging couple. A-III (PG)

On Her Majesty's Secret Service (1969) This caper takes James Bond (George Lazenby) to the Swiss Alps where he uncovers an insidious plan to threaten the world with genetic extinction. Director Peter Hunt makes a conscious effort to outdo its predecessors in scope, excitement and visual effects, but only succeeds in presenting more of the same formula of fantasy sex and violence. A-III (PG)

On My Way to the Crusades I Met a Girl Who... (1969) Completely unfunny Italian comedy about an upstart knight (Tony Curtis), his enterprising bride (Monica Vitti) and a chastity belt, the device allegedly employed by departing crusaders to insure their wives faithfulness. Directed by Pasquale Feste Campanile, the tastelessness of the story calls for little more than one-dimensional lechery from its participants. O (R)

On the Edge (1986) Bruce Dern plays a long-distance runner who 20 years after being unjustly denied a chance at Olympic competition determines to prove his talent and integrity in the toughest race of his career. Filmed on location in the beautiful Mill Valley region of northern California, the movie is an impressionistic, somewhat rambling essay on the male jock mentality. Some partial nudity and brief profanity. A-II (PG-13)

On the Nickel (1980) Ralph Waite stars in this story (which he also wrote and directed) of the Los Angeles Skid Row, known as "The Nickel," a place where society's dropouts drown their despair in alcohol. While an admirable attempt to define the helplessness of these unfortunates, the movie is far too long, the action quite repetitive and the use of comic relief is unfortunate. Depiction of sordid environment is not too strong for older teenagers. A-III (R)

On the Right Track (1981) A small boy (Gary Coleman) who lives in a locker at Chicago's Union Station makes a living as a shoeshine boy with a psychic ability to pick winning horses. Directed by Lee Phillips, the cluttered plot of this thin comedy throws the whole burden upon the young actor, and some may find his charm not enough to sustain it. Adult romantic complications are inappropriate in a movie aimed at children. A-III (PG)

On the Yard (1979) Screen version of Malcolm Braly's prison novel centers on a wheeler-dealer (Thomas Waites) who rules over the other inmates until a determined rival inmate (John Heard) brings about his downfall. Subplots involve a prisoner desperate for parole (Mike Kellin) and the obsession of another (Joe Grifasi) to escape in a balloon he is secretly building. Raphael D. Silver's direction is too uncertain and his characterizations too sketchy to achieve anything more than a realistic depiction of the violent world of prison. A-III (R)

On Valentine's Day (1986) After shocking a small Southern town with their elopement, a young couple find reconciliation with their parents and friends. Horton Foote's contemplative little movie covers wide-ranging emotional ground in its exploration of small-town intimacies and the erosion of traditions through careful characterizations of one family. The semi-autobiographical narrative is propelled, albeit slowly, by a spirit of unbridled loyalty and devotion tinged with a sense of loss for pre-World War I ways of life. A brief but brutal suicide scene. A-II (PG)

Once Before I Die (1966) John Derek and Ursula Andress spend much of their time together in this attempt at a World War II thriller making love just out of range of the camera and the advancing Japanese tanks and artillery. Derek gets killed but Andress carries on, ultimately giving significance to the coy title by taking a young soldier into her arms one fateful night. Overblown and undernourished. O (br)

Once Bitten (1985) A vampire (ineptly played by Lauren Hutton) must find a teenage virgin male in order to preserve her youth. He in turn must lose his virginity to escape the curse of the undead. Lots of tasteless humor and mindless sexual innuendo. O (PG-13)

Once in Paris (1978) Frank D. Gilroy wrote, produced and directed this romance about the relationship between a screenwriter (Wayne Rodgers), an heiress (Gayle Hunnicut) and a chauffeur (Jack Lenoir). Filmed in Paris, the lame and languid story condones infidelity and adultery. O

(R/PG appeal)

Once Is Not Enough (see: "Jacqueline Susann's Once Is Not Enough")

Once Upon a Time in America (1984) Italian director Sergio Leone has attempted to make an American urban crime epic but his melodramatic tale of Jewish gangsters (Robert De Niro and James Woods) is dull and lifeless in spanning 30 years in the lives of characters impossible to be concerned about, not only because their actions are so brutal, but also because their motivations never rise above the most elemental. Excessive violence and a crude and brutalizing depiction of sex. O (R)

Once Upon a Time in the West (1969) Any movie with such a plainly mythic title can't be all bad and this one really isn't bad at all. Epic, stately spaghetti Western directed by Sergio Leone, its wispy plot concerns hired killer Henry Fonda's pursuit of outlaw Charles Bronson and widow Claudia Cardinale's land, but it contains a whole encyclopedia of Western cliches and stereotypes that are irresistible for Western buffs. Others may enjoy it as a knowing spoof but one that is overlong and featuring some rather intense violence. A-III (PG)

Once You Kiss a Stranger (1969) Failed thriller about a psychopathic young woman (Carol Lynley) who murders one golf pro in order to blackmail a competing pro (Paul Burke) into murdering her psychiatrist. Mindless script ineptly directed by Robert Sparr. A-III (M)

One and Only, The (1978) Henry Winkler plays a boorish college dropout in the 1950s who goes to New York to become a Broadway star but, to avoid starvation, becomes a wrestler and wins fame and fortune in the ring. Director Carl Reiner tries very hard for the proper blend of humor and nostalgia but his egotistical hero lacks the essential charm the role intended. The lightweight comedy has a heavy load of crude sexual and scatological references. A-III (PG)

One and Only Genuine Original Family Band, The (1968) Uneven Disney musical about a family (grampa, Walter Brennan, Janet Blair, Buddy Ebsen and eight kids) who emigrate from Nebraska to the Dakota territory just in time to get embroiled in partisan politics over Dakota's proposed statehood and the presidential race between Grover Cleveland and Benjamin Harrison. Behind its over-cute tendencies and over-sentimental songs by the Sherman brothers, the movie has some infectious high spirits, but director Michael O'Herlihy might have done a better job mining the genuine lode of Americana to be found in the book by Laura Van Nuys. A-I (G)

One Brief Summer (1972) Talky British soap opera about a middle-aged financier (Clifford Evans) who carries on a torrid romance with a 17-year-old girl (Felicity Gibson) vacationing on his estate. Director John Mackenzie photographs the boring affair in musty blue hues and glazes the superficial characterizations with bits of gratuitous nudity and kinky eroticism. O (R)

One Crazy Summer (1986) Absurdist comedy replete with tiresome bathroom humor, some profane gestures and vulgar sight gags has a group of high school grads saving the ancestral home of a streetwise girl (Demi Moore) from a ruthless developer and his son. Taking place on Nantucket Island, the movie is essentially pulp entertainment, vapid enough to cause goof-ball behavior in the young and immature. A-III (PG)

One Day in the Life of Ivan Denisovich (1971) British screen version of Russian novelist Alexander Solzhenitsyn's account, based on his own experience, of what daily life meant to a prisoner of a forced labor camp in the Soviet penal system. Directed by Casper Wrede, Tom Courtney excels in the title role, conveying the feeling of a prisoner trying to survive each day by keeping alive the hope of freedom.. A powerful indictment of Soviet oppression, it is filled with gloomy images of human suffering and hardship but it also details the little victories which lessened the pain of injustice. A-II (G)

One Flew Over the Cuckoo's Nest (1975) Screen version of the Ken Keasy novel about an abortive rebellion in a mental institution led by a drifter (Jack Nicholson) feigning mental illness to avoid being sent to a prison farm. Director Milos Forman's smooth, low-keyed movie about life in an asylum is filled with colorful, often amusing incidents and characterizations, but the central confrontation between the sane drifter and the repressed and repressing nurse (Louise Fletcher) is too contrived to evoke a strong emotional response. Some violence, very rough dialogue and an incident presenting loveless sexual intercourse as therapeutic. A-IV (R)

One from the Heart (1982) Teri Garr and Frederic Forrest fall out of love and back into it in this lavishly produced musical that seems more interested in its technical effects than in its story of a young couple's relationship. Directed by Francis Ford Coppola, the result is artificial and tedious. Some partial nudity, sexual byplay and profanity. A-III (R)

100 Rifles (1969) Arizona deputy (Jim Brown) tracks a bank robber (Burt Reynolds) into Mexico where ultimately he takes a leading part in an uprising by the Yaqui Indians against the central government. Director Tom Gries pulls out all the stops in orchestrating the horse opera's violence, ranging from fist fights to total massacre. Overemphasis on brutal action wastes potential of plot and characters. O (PG)

101 Dalmations (1961) Villainess Cruella Deville, one of Disney's more cunning evildoers, attempts to kidnap 101 Dalmation puppies but is foiled by two lovable children. The animated feature retains its original charm and vitality. A-I (G)

One Is a Lonely Number (1972) Intelligent soap opera about a housewife (Trish Van Devere), devastated by a bitter divorce from a philandering husband, who gets some inspiration and hope from a kindly old grocer (Melvyn Douglas). Director Mel Stuart's treatment vacillates between being simplistic and tough, harsh and sentimental, but there are some worthwhile insights along with all the superficialities. A-IV (PG)

One Little Indian (1973) Above average Disney adventure set in the Old West about a U.S. Calvary corporal (James Gardner) on the run from an unjust court martial, a white boy being raised by the Indians and a pretty widow lady (Vera Miles) who helps both of them. Directed by Bernard McEveety, what makes the movie of more than average interest is that the corporal's predicament is for disobeying orders by defending Indian women and children during a no-prisoner raid. What makes it fun is that his escape across the desert is by camel, a temperamental beast responsible for much of the film's comedy. A-I (G)

One Magic Christmas (1985) Failed Disney movie directed by Philip Borsos lets materialistic values predominate in a story starring Mary Steenburgen and Gary Basaraba supposedly learning about "the true spirit" of Christmas. A-II (G)

$1,000,000 Duck (1971) Disney situation comedy about a Peking duck who lays golden eggs but when its owners (Sandy Duncan and Dean Jones) try to turn them into cash, they get in trouble with the Treasury Department. Director Vincent McEveety offers standard animal antics and climactic chase sequence that will divert, if not delight pre-teens. A-I (G)

One More Saturday Night (1986) Director Dennis Klein overcomes a weak script and subject matter to provide an affectionate glance at the adaptability and resourcefulness of less-than-articulate teenagers (and some adults) who struggle during a typical weekend date night in contemporary suburbia. Some rough language and a brief instance of nudity in a sexual context are offset by honest and objective performances. A-III (R)

One More Time (1970) In a sequel to "Salt and Pepper," comedy duo Peter Lawford and Sammy Davis, Jr. chase about the English countryside in a contrived and irrelevant diamond smuggling plot that is terribly forced and unfunny. Directed by Jerry Lewis, the timing of all the gags is off, the plot predictable and the dialogue stupid. Some sexual innuendo. A-III (PG)

One More Train to Rob (1971) Slack Western with George Peppard as ex-con returned to take revenge on his partner (John Vernon) who double-crossed him by not only taking the gold but also his girlfriend (Diana Muldaur). Director Andrew V. McLaglen offers more cliches than action but its bawdy language and violent situations are not for youngsters. A-III (GP)

One Night at Dinner (1971) Italian production about a dramatist (Jean-Louis Trintignant) who decides to base his next play on the personal affairs of his seductive wife (Florinda Bolkan), his friend (Tony Musante) who is pursuing her and the bisexual stage star (Lino Capolicchio) on whose affections they both trade. Directed by Giuseppe Patroni Griffi, the movie tries to justify infidelity and promiscuity but offers only teasing eroticism. O (R)

One of Our Dinosaurs Is Missing (1975) Walt Disney romp set in London during the 1920s with a gang of nannies, headed by Helen Hayes, and a clutch of Oriental villains, led by Peter Ustinov, vying with each to recover a secret Chinese formula hidden in a dinosaur skeleton. Directed by Robert Stevenson, the slapstick affair will appeal to the very young but the Oriental stereotypes may not amuse adults. A-I (G)

One on One (1977) Robby Benson stars as a hotshot basketball player recruited by a college coach who tries to make him give up his scholarship when he doesn't measure up to expectations. Directed by Lamont Johnson, the cluttered story line makes only a token gesture towards exposing the corruption of college sports. Glossy, sympathetic depiction of a casual sexual relationship. O (PG)

One Sings, the Other Doesn't (1977) French production about the women's liberation movement centering on the developing relationship between two women (Therese Liotard and Valerie Mairesse) through identity crises, abortion and career changes. Director Agnes Varda has made a thesis film with considerable charm and appeal but little insight into its theme of the relativistic nature of sexual morality. O (nr)

One Spy Too Many (1966) Secret gas is stolen from an Army testing unit and agents Solo (Robert Vaughn) and Kuryakin (David McCallum) set off in pursuit of the thief (Rip Torn). Directed by Joseph Sargent, the third movie derived from the TV series, "The Man from U.N.C.L.E.," is one too many. Stylized violence. A-II (br)

1000 Convicts and a Woman (1971) When the trusty warden's lusty daughter (Alexandra Hay) comes home from school on holiday, all manner of havoc breaks loose on dad's normally quiet prison farm. The exploitation movie's ridiculous ineptness fails to mitigate the unsubtle titillation. O (R)

One Trick Pony (1980) Singer-composer Paul Simon stars as a band leader whose marriage is on the rocks and whose group is breaking up. An ambitious movie, directed by Robert M. Young and written by Simon, it is very knowing about the tensions in the popular music industry between those who run the business and those who provide the talent, but less sure about the personal problems of those involved. Several sexually explicit scenes, nudity and gross language. O (R)

One Woman or Two (1987) Ex-model (Sigourney Weaver) impersonates a patroness of the sciences (Dr. Ruth Westheimer) to escape a pesty ex-lover. Gerard Depardieu and Michael Aumont are the duped scientists who discover the remains of a 2-million-year-old woman as well as the deception. The conclusion of director Daniel Vigne's dizzy romantic comedy has brief nudity in a sexual context. A-III (PG-13)

Onion Field, The (1979) Two petty criminals (James Woods and Franklyn Seales) kidnap two policemen, brutally murdering one of them (Ted Danson), and the consequences nearly destroy the surviving officer (John Savage) in this somber, slow-moving but gripping movie version of Joseph Wambaugh's novel. Director Harold Becker conveys the grim reality of police work and the varied, intensely human character of those involved on both sides of the law. Violence, rough language and frank depiction of the seamy details of criminal life. A-IV (R)

Only Game in Town, The (1970) Two lonely people in Las Vegas, a mixed-up compulsive gambler (Warren Beatty) and a hefty chorus girl (Elizabeth Taylor), meet by chance, take up residence together and ultimately fall in love. Though overlong and lacking comic flair, director George Stevens' movie offers some interesting delineations of character and excursions into motive and meaning but never with any real depth or emotion. A-III (PG)

Only When I Larf (1968) Three con artists (Richard Attenborough, David Hemmings, and Alexandra Stewart) pull some neat capers on a variety of vicitms ranging from gullible New York stock speculators to army officers from an emerging African nation. For the most part Basil Deardon directs the international swindles with a light, witty touch, but in following the novel by Len Deighton, there are some slow moments with a love triangle and assorted jabs at contemporary social values. A-III (G)

Only When I Laugh (1981) Marsha Mason plays a successful actress who is a reformed alcoholic whom circumstances conspire to push to the brink once more. Contributing to her problems are her daughter (Kristy McNichol), a homosexual actor (James Coco) and a rich man's wife (Joan Hackett) who is pathologically afraid of growing old. Written by Neil Simon and directed by Glenn Jordan, it's a moderately entertaining blend of laughs and seriousness. Aside from some occasional foul language, the contrived plot is innocuous. A-II (R)

Open Season (1974) Grisly plot about three war buddies (Peter Fonda, John Phillip Law and Richard Lynch) who on their annual people-hunting trip kidnap a couple (Albert Mendoza and Cornelia Sharp) for a week of rape and mayhem before the father (William Holden) of a previous victim puts a revengeful stop to it. Directed by Peter Collinson, the exercise in sadism has nothing to redeem it. O (R)

Opening Night (1978) Director John Cassavetes explores the terrors of aging in the story of a popular stage actress facing her first role as an older woman, and the prospect of a future limited to character parts. Gena Rowlands' performance as a woman on the edge is universal in capturing the dread and fear of a person making the passage to a new stage in life. An exceptional supporting cast (Joan Blondell, Paul Stewart and Ben Gazarra) is pushed to the limits of their craft. Mature themes. A-III (nr)

Operation Kid Brother (1967) Inept spy spoof about an international scheme to hypnotize the world's great powers into surrendering most of their gold reserves to a gang of crooks. Neil Connery, Sean's younger brother, apparently was never told that he was acting in a take-off and hence he doesn't. A-II (br)

Operation Leontine (1973) In this zany French spoof of the crime genre, Francoise Rosay plays a feared former gang leader who emerges from retirement for one last caper and outwits and outguns all her gangster opponents. Directed by Michel Audiard, the stylish, well-acted movie adds up to little more than a collection of sight gags (some quite hilarious) and adult fantasies revolving around rival gang's double-crossing one another. A-III (M)

Operation S.N.A.F.U. (1974) Failed World War II comedy about some unwilling Allied soldiers (Jason Robards, Martin Landau and Peter Falk) sent into German-held Sicily to destroy artillery positions impeding a seaborne invasion. Filmed in Italy and Yugoslavia, director Nanni Loy's slapstick treatment of a cornball plot is rarely amusing. Some rough language and raunchy humor. A-III (nr)

Operation Thunderbolt (1978) Director Menahem Golan's dramatization of the heroic rescue by Israeli commandos of the Jewish hostages at Entebbe Airport perhaps errs on the side of being too scrupulous in avoiding the sensational. Thus there is considerable plodding and skimping on characterization, but the subject itself has enough excitement and heroism to make it an entertaining and quite moving viewing experience. A-II (PG)

Ophelia (1974) Modern version of "Hamlet" attempts to make the audience question its initial sympathy for the title character (Andre Jocelyn) and prepare it for an ending which Shakespeare never envisioned. Director Claude Chabrol turns the original into a study of destructive obsessions involving such themes as family tensions, middle-class materialism, the sense of the irreparable and emotional ambivalence. While not entirely successful, the adaptation has brilliance and imagination. A-II (nr)

Opium War, The (1978) Chinese production about the early 19th-century imperial commissioner sent from Peking to put a stop to the opium trade at the port of Canton but instead sets off a war between China and Great Britain. Director Chen Chun-li's highly romanticized and stylized dramatization gives only sketchy details of the conflict but is worth seeing for its spectacle and sheer novelty, if nothing else. A-II (nr)

Optimists, The (1973) Aged ex-vaudevillian (Peter Sellers), reduced to entertaining on the London streets with his scruffy little trained dog Bella, gradually develops a cherished friendship with two young slum children (played delightfully by Donna Mullande and John Chaffey). The British production, warmly directed by Anthony Simmons, has much to say about the world of children and the importance of the magical and the incongruous in their world. Meaningful family entertainment. A-I (PG)

Orca (1977) Shark-hunter Richard Harris decides to go after bigger game and, in attempting to catch a male killer whale, kills its mate, a pregnant female, thus incuring the wrath of the male. Charlotte Rampling is on hand as a whale specialist who seems to have a soft spot in her heart for big brutes of all sorts. Director Michael Anderson's seafaring adventure has some scenic beauty but its story is mediocre entertainment at best. Some rather graphic violence. A-III (PG)

Orchestra Rehearsal (1979) Italian production about an orchestra whose members are constantly being distracted by each other and the inane questions of a television crew. A union dispute leads to violence and ultimately choas. Director Federico Fellini's failed fable about the tension between authority and the individual becomes a disjointed series of gags and jabs at music, nationality, television, art, sports, sex and other perennial favorites. Minor work from a great director. A-III (R)

Ordinary People (1980) Donald Sutherland and Mary Tyler Moore give fine performances as confused and troubled parents trying to cope with the psychological aftershocks that result when the older of two sons dies in a boating accident and the surviving son (Timothy Hutton) attempts suicide. Directed by Robert Redford, the movie hints that the characters' complacent and wholly materialistic environment may have contributed to the family's instability, but these aspects remain underdeveloped. The problems are very real but the movie is strangely cool and distanced from them. Due to the heaviness of the theme and some instances of rough language, it is for mature viewers. A-III (R)

Organization, The (1971) Sidney Poitier in a third outing as Lt. Virgil Tibbs of the 1967 movie, "In the Heat of the Night," finds himself involved in a situation where the police are using extra-legal methods to apprehend a gang trafficking in heroin. Directed by Don Medford, the thriller concentrates on chase scenes without any attempt at characterization or addressing the moral and legal issues inherent in the plot. Physical and psychological violence. A-III (R)

Orpheus (1949) Startlingly designed, exquisitely photographed version of the classic myth about the relationship between love and death visualized with haunting beauty in this French movie directed by artist and poet Jean Cocteau. A-II (br)

Oscar, The (1966) One-dimensional story of the efforts of a psycopath (Stephen Boyd) to achieve Hollywood stardom has all the empty glitter of Tinsel Town but director Russell Rouse goes to excess in sexual suggestiveness. O (br)

Osterman Weekend, The (1983) Screen version of Robert Ludlum's espionage thriller about a television talk show host (Rutger Hauer) who is used by a CIA agent (John Hurt) in a ruse to discredit the head of intelligence (Burt Lancaster). Directed by Sam Peckinpah, the convoluted plot serves up a thoroughly distasteful stew of gratuitous violence and sex, with not a trace of human feeling. O (R)

Otello (1986) Franco Zeffirelli's lavish production of the Verdi opera, with Placido Domingo in the title role, emphasizes the visuals at the expense of the rather depressing libretto, based on Shakespeare's play about jealousy leading to murder and suicide. A-II (PG)

Othello (1966) British adaptation of Shakespeare's play with Laurence Olivier as the epileptic general whose jealousy and passion destroy him, abetted by Frank Finlay as Iago and Maggie Smith as Desdemona. Directed by Stuart Burge, it is a photographed performance in which simple stage backgrounds, stage movements and camera close-ups focus all attention on the lead actor and Shakespeare's language. A-II (br)

Other, The (1972) Sleepy Connecticut farm in the summer of 1935 is the setting for a tale of horror and suspense involving the possession of an innocent child by the evil spirit of his dead twin. Director Robert Mulligan gets the proper atmosphere but the story, based on the Thomas Tryon novel, gets so convoluted in the deaths of family members that it becomes a bit unbelievable and more than a touch too gruesome. A-III (PG)

Other Side of Midnight, The (1977) Screen version of Sidney Sheldon novel about a poor French girl (Marie-France Pisier), jilted and left pregnant by a romantic American World War II pilot (John Beck), who becomes the mistress of a Greek tycoon (Raf Vallone) and seeks revenge on the faithless American. Directed Charles Jarrott's vulgar, trashy melodrama features a great deal of nudity and explicit sex. O (R)

Other Side of the Mountain, The (1975) Good telling of fact-based story about young skier Jill Kinmont (Marilyn Hassett) who, completely paralyzed from the chest down after a 1956 fall in pre-Olympic competition, overcame her handicap to make a new life for herself as a grade-school teacher. Director Larry Peerce at times veers into sentimentality, but for the most refrains from tampering with the emotional power inherent in the story of an individual's achievement over cruel odds. Very appealing young cast also includes Belinda J. Montgomery and Beau Bridges. A-II (PG)

Other Side of the Mountain, Part II, The (1978) Sequel to the movie about paralyzed skier Jill Kinmont (Marilyn Hassett) takes up the events leading to her marriage to John Boothe (Timothy Bottoms). Though lacking the drama of the original, director Larry Peerce's movie is consistently entertaining and, at times, quite moving, chiefly because of Hassett's superb performance. Brief sequence involving premarital sex. A-III (PG)

Other Voices (1970) Documentary by David Sawyer and Robert Elfstrom details the confrontational "verbal shock" therapy used on mentally ill patients at the Delaware Valley Mental Foundation. Suicide prevention is a primary objective of the treatment but the movie's realistic observation of the private lives of these patients offers the lay audience little insight into the complexity of the social and moral problems of mental health care. A-IV (nr)

Otley (1969) Sardonic British satire about a drifter (Tom Courtenay) who muddles his way into the middle of an espionage caper, winds up being pursued by two rival spy organizations and falls for a temptress with ambiguous allegiances (Romy Schneider). Directed by Brian Clement, the story gets lost in its own intrigues but Courtenay holds it together with a likeable comic performance and some sharp comments on the times and people's lack of integrity. A-III (PG)

Our Latin Thing (1972) Latino music documentary filmed in and around New York City's Cheetah nightery, the Leon Gast production fills the screen with people enjoying the vibrant sounds of Johnny Pacheco, Willie Colon, El Conde and many other performers (there are no subtitles for the Spanish lyrics). Though partly a plug for the record company issuing works by these performing artists, it stands on its own as a lively, appealing musical celebration of life. A-II (nr)

Our Man Flint (1966) Spy spoof with James Coburn as an agent with an eye more for the ladies than the job in hand has been directed by Daniel Mann with a heavy emphasis on sexually suggestive situations and references. O (br)

Our Mother's House (1967) Disturbing British movie about seven children who, to avoid being sent to an orphanage, bury their deceased mother secretly and hold seances in which they continue to invoke her advice. When their long absent father (Dirk Bogarde) turns up and announces he is going to sell "our mother's house," the children deal forcefully with the situation. Director Jack Clayton effectively tells a rather chilling parable of the influence, for good or evil, excercised on children by their elders. A-III (br)

Our Time (1974) Set unconvincingly in 1955, this film coyly depicts the frantic sexual experimentation of two WASP school girls (Pamela Sue Martin and Betsy Slade), which for one leads to abortion and death. Directed by Peter Hyams, the tearjerker's contrast between the good girl who pays with her life for making a mistake and the more calculating, unscathed friend conveys a sour, half-hearted lesson in life. A-IV (PG)

Our Winning Season (1978) High school senior (Scott Jacoby) trains earnestly to win the mile run in the season's finale but in the interim the movie marks time with a string of less-than-compelling vignettes of school life. Director Joe Rubin's only attempt at deeper significance involves an affair between the hero's best friend and his sister before the friend goes off to die in Vietnam. Banal in every department. A-III (PG)

Out of Africa (1985) Slow-moving narrative and beautiful photography characterize this dramatization of storyteller Isek Dinesen's (Meryl Streep) years as a plantation owner in East Africa and her love affair with a hunter (Robert Redford). Produced and directed by Sydney Pollack, the movie celebrates the mystique of Africa rather than the muddled romance of its two main characters. Romanticized treatment of adultery. A-IV (PG)

Out of Bounds (1986) An Iowa farmboy (An-

thony Michael Hall) is hunted by drug peddlers, police and corrupt narcs when he picks up the wrong bag upon arriving in Los Angeles to visit his brother. Derivative script and melodramatic treatment. Profanity and needlessly extended violence and bloodshed. O (R)

Out of It (1969) Story of a shy adolescent (Barry Gordon) who is inept in dealing with girls has some funny and perceptive moments but not enough substance for a feature-length movie. Director Paul Williams makes things worse by pretentious and obtrusive camera techniques. A-III (PG)

Out of Sight (1966) Spies vie with rock music group in director Lennie Weinrib's innocuous entry for the youth market. A-II (br)

Out-of-Towners, The (1970) Midwestern couple (Jack Lemmon and Sandy Dennis) on a business trip to New York City try to cope with an hilarious series of mishaps, including a garbage strike, a snafu with hotel reservations, a rainy night in Central Park, a mugging to go with it, the siege of the Cuban U.N. embassy and a stolen car chase. Arthur Hiller's spirited direction of Neil Simon's script provides lots of fun at the expense of big-city life for family viewers. A-I (G)

Outback (1971) On his way from a backcountry one-room schoolhouse to Sydney for the Christmas holidays, a naive young teacher (Gary Bond) falls in with a depraved and besotted one-time doctor (Donald Pleasance) who insists on showing him some of the perverse ways he passes his time, the highlight of which is a drunken kangaroo hunt slaughtering the defenseless animals for amusement. Directed by Ted Kotcheff, this is a disturbing picture of life in Australia's outback which, unfortunately, provides little positive insight to justify its tasteless language and brutal visuals. A-IV (R)

Outfit, The (1974) Two born losers, an ex-con (Robert Duvall) and an ex-torpedo (Joe Don Baker), team up to take over the gang (headed by Robert Ryan), methodically mowing their way up the mob ranks and robbing syndicate operations for ready cash. An action-packed, B-grade, old-time gangster movie with plenty of violence, but under John Flynn's direction there is such a dreamlike 1950s nostalgia coating the entire proceedings, that none of it can be taken seriously. A-III (PG)

Outland (1981) It's high noon on a moon of Jupiter with Sean Connery playing a beleagured federal marshal involved in an old-fashioned Western shoot-out with a team of killers sent to stop his investigation of Peter Boyle's deadly mining operation. Written and directed by Peter Hyams, the sci-fi movie lacks energy and imagination but does have a sympathetic depiction of the friendship that grows between the marshal and space doctor Frances Sternhagen. Moderately entertaining but has scenes of intense violence. A-III (R)

Outlaw Blues (1977) Peter Fonda and Susan Saint James star in a comic chase adventure about a singer-songwriter on the run after being framed for a crime. Directed by Richard T. Heffron, it is an amiable and fairly entertaining movie but the romantic relationship between the principals is rich in sexual innuendo. A-III (PG)

Outlaw Josey Wales, The (1976) At the outbreak of the Civil War, Northern guerrillas slay the wife and young son of a Missouri farmer (Clint Eastwood who also directs), leaving him for dead. He settles the score by wreaking havoc as a Confederate guerrilla who befriends a strange assortment of colorful characters along the way. Graphic scene of attempted rape and lack of any moral perspective to balance the unremitting slaughter. O (PG)

Outrageous! (1977) Canadian production about a young mental patient (Hollis McLaren) who escapes and takes refuge with a homosexual hairdresser (Craig Russell) who helps her to cope with the demons of her schizophrenia and she, in turn, encourages him to embark upon a new career as a satiric female impersonator. Director Richard Benner's movie is alive with humor, vitality, and warmth thanks to some witty dialogue and two superb performances by the principals. Frank, thoroughly objective presentation of the homosexual subculture. A-IV (R)

Outrageous Fortune (1987) Arthur Hiller directs Bette Midler and Shelley Long as aspiring actresses who singlemindedly seek revenge when they learn that they have been betrayed by the same man with whom they have had affairs at the same time. Negative stereotyping of women, a casual attitude toward sex and rough language leave no room for genuine comedy. O (R)

Outside Man, The (1973) Jean-Louis Trintignant plays a hired killer brought to Los Angeles to knock off a mob biggie, but then finds himself being hunted by an equally faceless killer. Ann-Margret is cast as a friend-of-a-friend who gets dragged into the confusion by her pretty heels, and Roy Scheider plays the sadistic silent type on Trintignant's tail. Director Jacques Deray's intriguing melodrama of a stranger in a strange land is packed with sly comic touches and has restrained, but continuous tension and violence. A-III (PG)

Outsider, The (1980) Thriller about an Irish-American youth (Craig Wasson) who leaves his affluent Detroit family to fight in Belfast with the Provisional IRA. Blinded by the love of an Irish girl (Patricia Quinn), he is unaware that he is being used as a pawn in their dangerous game. Director Tony Luraschi gets excellent performances from a fine Irish and English cast. The movie shows the grimy details of life in war-torn Belfast and is a thoughtful commentary on the victimized people of Ulster and the injustices on both sides. A-III (R)

Outsiders, The (1983) Screen version of S.E. Hinton's novel about three youths (Matt Dillon, C. Thomas Howell and Ralph Macchio) growing up in Tulsa, Okla., during the 1960s. Director Francis Ford Coppola's fragile mood piece can't quite connect the youths' violent ways with their discussions of "Gone with the Wind" and Robert Frost's poetry. The violence in a fight between rival gangs is very pronounced. A-III (PG)

Over the Brooklyn Bridge (1984) Brooklyn luncheonette owner (Elliott Gould) yearns to open a restaurant in Manhattan but his rich uncle won't come across with the financing unless he gives up his WASP girl friend (Margaux Hemingway) and marries a nice Jewish girl (Carol Kane). Director Menahem Golan's failed ethnic comedy drama is embarrassingly bad on all counts. Much sexually oriented humor and some rough language. A-III (R)

Over the Top (1987) A truck driver (Sylvester Stallone) tries to win back the son he abandoned by showing off his physical prowess. Limp, unconvincing drama directed by Menahem Golan says little about the nature of father-son relationships and opts instead for the goofy contortions of an

arm-wrestling championship. Some midly vulgar language and momentary violence are evident. A-II (PG)

Overboard (1987) When a rich lady (Goldie Hawn) suffers amnesia, a rough carpenter (Kurt Russell) claims her as the mother of his four unruly children. Directed by Garry Marshall, the tasteless sex farce relies on the suggestiveness of a situation that makes light of adultery and uses vulgar language and references. O (PG)

Owl and the Pussycat, The (1970) Barbra Streisand plays a would-be model working as a part-time hooker and George Segal is a would-be writer working in a bookstore who, when both are kicked out of their apartments, find themselves the oddest of bedfellows. Director Herbert Ross undercuts the situation's potential for lighthearted comedy by giving it an overly realistic treatment, emphasizing its acceptance of casual sex. O (R)

Oxford Blues (1984) Director Robert Boris badly bungles this remake of "A Yank at Oxford" (1938) by making its hero (Rob Lowe) such a dislikable heel that most American viewers probably will cheer for the British when he takes on the upper-class establishment. Favorable attitude toward sexual promiscuity. O (PG-13)

P

Pacific Vibrations (1971) Producer-director John Severson's documentary presents a colorful and musically pulsating portrait of the West Coast surfer. His treatment, however, tries a bit too hard to deemphasize the joyousness of this obviously fun sport and tries to elevate it into something of sociological significance and ecological importance in the battle to save the California coastline. Some discussion of hedonistic lifestyles. A-II (G)

Pad and How to Use It, The (1966) Weak sex comedy adapted from a Peter Shaffer play about an inept young man (Brian Bedford) and his pursuit of a swinger (Julie Sommars). Directed by Brian G. Hutton, it makes extensive use of sexual innuendo. A-III (br)

Paddy (1970) Irish production about a supposedly likeable but totally irresponsible Dublin lad (Des Cave) who alternately services a middle-aged widow (Judy Cornwell), indulges in occasional orgies and fathers a child with a girl friend (Dearbhla Molloy) whom he abandons. Directed by Daniel Haller, the episodic movie wanders about aimlessly, uncertain of its theme, statement or sympathies in telling the story of an immature teenager. O (PG)

Pain in the A—, A (1975) French farce in which a professional assassin (Lino Ventura) checks into a hotel to carry out a job but the bungling attempts at suicide by the man in the next room (Jacques Brel) distract him with a series of frenetic mishaps. Director Edouard Molinaro keeps things moving at a good pace, with some fine comic moments, until the one-joke situation finally wears thin. Brief but graphic violence and a comically intended nude scene. A-III (PG)

Paint Your Wagon (1969) Screen adaptation of the Lerner and Loewe musical about two mining partners (Lee Marvin and Clint Eastwood) who "marry" the discarded second wife (Jean Seberg) of a pioneer Mormon, though monogamy triumphs in the end. Director Josh Logan's lavish production has plenty of lush scenery and swirling action to go with the lively songs and dances, but it's all pretty earthbound entertainment. Some frontier humor and ambiance are not for all tastes. A-III (M)

Painters Painting (1973) Documentary on the post-war rise and influence of New York as a center of the art world, it consists mainly of interviews with many of those who contributed to this development from de Kooning to Warhol as well as some prominent art dealers and collectors. Produced and directed by Emile De Antonio, it is a valuable resource for the history of contemporary American art. A-I (nr)

Palaces of a Queen (1967) Documentary tour of Buckingham Palace, St. James Palace, Windsor Castle, Kensington Palace and the Palace of Holyroodhouse in Edinburgh, showing the art treasures, architecture and furnishings of a royal way of life long past. Directed by Michael Ingrams and narrated by Sir Michael Redgrave, it is an agreeable way to renew a sense of history, though most youngsters will find it a long sit. A-I (br)

Pale Flower (1974) This 1964 Japanese gangster melodrama tells the story of a hit man (Ryo Ikebe) who gets out of prison, meets a beautiful but compulsive gambler, pulls another job and returns to jail. Director Masahiro Shinoda builds up the alienated ambiance of the Tokyo criminal underworld into an exotic but convincing picture of crime familiar the world over. A-III (nr)

Pale Rider (1985) Clint Eastwood plays a mysterious stranger who helps a group of embattled miners in their struggle with a brutal magnate determined to take over their claims. In all essentials a remake of "Shane" updated by resort to a little sex and a lot more violence. O (R)

Pancho Villa (1973) Telly Savalas plays the Mexican revolutionary as a blithering idiot who forces his advocates to watch home movies of his exploits when he is not abusing women or cynically executing opponents. Director Gene Martin occasionally interrupts the juvenile horseplay to stage some tiresome shootouts and a head-on train collision. There's more entertainment in Villa's encyclopedia entry. A-III (PG)

Panic in Needle Park, The (1971) Grim and harshly realistic love story about a wasted junkie (Al Pacino) struggling to survive in New York City's underworld of drugs and his doomed romance with the girl (Kitty Winn) he introduces to hard drugs and who then turns tricks to feed their habit. Directed by Jerry Schatzberg, the drama convincingly shows the horrors of drug addiction and its toll on human potential. Much brutality and foul language, with graphic depiction of heroin injections and occassional nudity. A-III (R/PG)

Paper Chase, The (1973) First-year Harvard law student Hart (Timothy Bottoms) quickly finds himself torn between the cool, cruel competitive life of the intellect, personified in distinguished law contracts professor Kingsfield (John Houseman who steals the show), and the warm, sensuous spontaneous life of the body, personified in Kingsfield's daughter (Lindsay Wagner). Director James Bridges conveys well the pressures of campus life, especially in Hart's study group with students whose varied personalities and weaknesses represent a cross section of humanity. Mature treatment although accessible for older teenagers. A-III (PG)

Paper Lion (1968) Alan Alda stars as journalist George Plimpton investigating the world of professional football by actually playing quarterback for the Detroit Lions. Directed by Alex March, it's a fairly interesting football movie for those who don't normally follow the sport. A-I (G)

Paper Moon (1973) Entertaining period comedy in which a bumbling con man (Ryan O'Neal) finds himself saddled with a 9-year-old girl (Tatum O'Neal) who proves to be more adept at his profession than he is. Directed by Peter Bogdanovich, there is occasional rough language and adult references. A-III (PG)

Paper Tiger (1976) David Niven plays a mildmannered school teacher tutoring the young son of a Japanese official (Toshiro Mifune) when terrorists strike and kidnap both of them. Although the film is sentimental and poorly directed by Ken Annakin, it conveys effectively the influence upon a youngster of an imaginative adult who proves heroic when put to the test. The movie's realistic treatment of terrorist violence may adversely affect its intended pre-teen audience. A-III (PG)

Papillon (1973) Steve McQueen and Dustin Hoffman star in this generally entertaining drama of one man's daring attempts to escape from Devil's Island, an inhumane penal system designed to break both body and spirit. Director Franklin Schaffner neatly balances adventure and spectacle with a vivid depiction of the horrors of prison life. Viewers may not appreciate some of the brutality and references to masturbation and homosexuality, yet such scenes are necessary to the factual description of the convict's world and are in no way sensationalized. A-III (PG)

Parades (1972) Muddled film-within-a-film story follows the making of a documentary about a pacifist soldier's suicide which triggers a riot and the massacre of protesting students outside a military stockade. Though well-intentioned, director Robert J. Siegel's dramatization is artifical and unconvincing while the issues it raises are treated inadequately. Some sadistic violence and coarse language. A-III (R)

Paradise (1982) Two teenagers (Phoebe Cates and Willie Aames) survive an attack on their caravan and find bliss in various lushly appointed oases in director Stuart Gillard's shoddy, trashy little movie that attempts to do the "Blue Lagoon" number with camels. Exploitative nudity and graphic sex. O (R)

Paradise Alley (1978) Sylvester Stallone (who also wrote and directed), stars as one of three tough brothers from the New York slums trying for big money in the wrestling ring in the 1940s. Rivalry between brothers and the machinations of a petty gangster (Kevin Conway) complicate matters. Though the movie has a few good moments, it never rises above the level of pulp melodrama and sometimes sinks to that of a cartoon. The violence of the wrestling sequences make this mature viewing fare. A-III (PG)

Paradise, Hawaiian Style (1966) Innocuous Elvis Presley vehicle directed by Michael Moore in another Hawaiian musical romance. A-I (br)

Parallax View, The (1974) Gripping thriller about an unorthodox reporter (Warren Beatty) whose investigation of a senator's assassination leads him to suspect that the murder was the work of a nationwide conspiracy. Though it's bit too contrived, director Alan Pakula keeps the action tense and taut until the sudden, smashing climax. The result is a first-rate suspense chiller that makes clever use of a number of political conspiracy theories without pretending to be a serious statement on the subject. Some violence and rough language. A-III (R)

Paranoia (1969) Italian-French import with Carroll Baker and Lou Castel in a cliched plot mixing rich, neurotic widow, lonely villa and masterful stranger in a tiresome ritual of sex and violence plot directed by Umberto Lenzi. O (R)

Parasite (1982) Robert Glaudini plays a scientist with nothing better to do than developing creatures that fasten onto people, propagate and burst out at odd moments through various sections of their victim's anatomy. Directed by Charles Band, it is a loathsome exercise in nausea. Excessively graphic sex and violence. O (R)

Pardon Mon Affaire (1977) French sex farce about a middle-aged man (Jean Rochefort) who is encouraged by his friends to seduce a beautiful model (Anny Duperey) and his infidelity leads to a comic expose in full view of television news cameras. Director Yves Robert has a difficult time striking the proper balance between the comic and the serious in a story devoted to an adulterous situation. O (PG)

Parent Trap, The (1961) Identical twins (Hayley Mills), raised separately by parents (Maureen O'Hara and Brian Keith) who split up shortly after their birth, only learn of the others existence at summer camp and they concoct an elaborate scheme to get Mom and Dad back together again. Typical sentimental Walt Disney family comedy, with parents having the IQ of domestic pets and no match for precocious youngsters. Still, it's genial and mostly heart-warming with good acting thrown in for good measure. A-I (br)

Paris Vu Par... (see: "Six in Paris")

Paris, Texas (1984) Father and son are reunited and then son and mother are reunited as dad rides off into the sunset. Directed by Wim Wenders, it is a pretentious and boring effort with a hero (Harry Dean Stanton) who at first won't talk and then won't stop talking. Some rough language. A-II (R)

Part 2, Sounder (1976) Tepid sequel continuing the story of a black family of sharecroppers in the rural Louisiana of the 1930s focuses on how the father (Harold Sylvester) rallies his neighbors to build a new school that will keep the teacher (Annazette Chase) from leaving for a better job in the North. Produced, as was the original, by Robert B. Radnitz and directed by William A. Graham, the plot is disappointingly predictable, but some fine acting, the beauty of the setting, and its earnest sense of humanity make it above average family entertainment. A-I (G)

Part II, Walking Tall (1975) Sequel, far more restrained and low key than its violent predecessor, picks up the story of Sheriff Buford Pusser as he searches for the criminals who killed his wife but, by sequel's end, the man responsible is still at liberty. Capably directed by Earl Bellamy, Svenson's characterization of the fighting sheriff is much more credible than the melodramatic script. A-III (PG)

Partner (1974) Heavy-handed Italian production about a schizophrenic drama teacher (Pierre Clementi) whose other personality is that of a violent revolutionary. Directed by Bernardo Bertolucci in the heat of the political upheavals of 1968, the drama tries to relate art to politics, making an unconvincing statement about revolution as a creative act. Suicide figures into the abstract plot line. A-III (nr)

Partners (1982) Ryan O'Neal and John Hurt star as detectives, one of them homosexual, who are assigned to pose as a homosexual couple in order to investigate a murder in a stupid comedy directed by James Burrows. O'Neal and Hurt struggle admirably with an underdeveloped script that turns homosexual and heterosexual characters alike into insulting stereotypes. Exploitative nudity. O (R)

Party, The (1968) Well-meaning, disaster-prone actor from India (Peter Sellers), instead of receiving a pink slip for his unwitting sabotage on a remake of "Gunga Din," gets an invitation to the producer's home for a pretentious Hollywood party that he turns into total chaos. Director Blake Edwards borrows liberally from the situations and sight gags of silent slapstick but in the thin, one-joke context of a hopeless bungler, the hilarity soon gives way to tedious repetitiousness, especially in a prolonged and tasetless bathroom sequence. A-III (br)

Passage, The (1979) World War II story about a fiendish Nazi (Malcolm McDowell) who pursues an escaping scientist (James Mason) and his family across the Pyrenees where they get help from a stalwart Basque guide (Anthony Quinn). Mediocre British production directed by J. Lee Thompson, it is filled to excess with sadistic violence and brutality. O (R)

Passage to India, A (1984) Screen version of the E.M. Forster classic about the inability of two diverse cultures to have any but perilous contact in the British-ruled India of the 1920s as seen in a story centering around a question of rape. Though painstakingly crafted by director David Lean and superbly acted by an outstanding cast (Judy Davis, Victor Banerjee, Dame Peggy Ashcroft, James Fox and Alec Guinness), the movie fails to dramatize convincingly the mysticism at the heart of its theme. Flawed but culturally rich entertainment. A-II (PG)

Passenger, The (1970) Polish production about two women who meet by accident on an ocean liner, triggering memories of their days in a concentration camp together: one a Nazi officer, the other a prisoner. Both stories are related subjectively in flashback and their differing perspectives become both fascinating and disturbing. Although director Andrej Munk died before the movie's completion, what he did accomplish are brilliant fragments in a compelling exploration of human motivation and justification. A-III (nr)

Passenger, The (1975) Empty Italian drama in which a TV journalist (Jack Nicholson), exasperated by an assignment in North Africa and acting on impulse, switches passport photos with a European who dies of a heart attack and finds that he has assumed the identity of an international gun runner. Director Michelangelo Antonioni has made a visually stunning work, yet its plot contrivances are more irritating than mysterious and its delving into the interior of its characters is without interest. A-III (PG)

Passion of Anna, The (1970) Swedish production about a human cipher (Max von Sydow), living hermit-like on a small island, who becomes friendly with a cynical architect (Erland Josephson), his wife (Bibi Andersson), and their close friend, Anna (Liv Ullmann). Eventually he and Anna share their loneliness and then part even more hopeless than when they first met. Director Ingmar Bergman's bleak vision of people unable to find salvation from existential despair questions

211

the meaning of life. A suicide and brief shots of mutilated animals combined with the moral ambiguity of the brief affair make this adult fare. A-III (R)

Passover Plot, The (1977) Dramatization of a book by biblical archaeologist Hugh J. Schonfield presents Jesus as a good and pious man who believed himself to be the Messiah but his plan to fake his death by Roman crucifixion failed, leaving his disciples to invent the story of his resurrection. Directed by Michael Campos, the movie is deeply flawed in narrative construction, acting and production values but many Christians will find its muddled attempt to demythologize the Gospels repugnant. O (PG)

Pat Garrett and Billy the Kid (1973) The story of Garret (James Coburn), in the hire of ruthless cattlemen, tracking down his old saddle mate Billy (Kris Kristofferson) is intended to show the slow passing of the Western frontier in the 1880s. The end result is a ponderous and depressing study of men whose time has past. It's a familiar theme for director Sam Peckinpah who, once again, cannot resist graphic depictions of blood-spattered killings and various characters' rough use of women. O (R)

Patch of Blue, A (1966) An honest look at racial relations in the story of a blind girl (Elizabeth Hartman), living in a dismal tenement, who is befriended by a gentle black man (Sidney Poitier). Love blooms, perhaps too dependent on the girl's blindness and despite the shrill opposition of her mother (Shelley Winters). The movie avoids the obvious cliches and scores some points for human values in an adult way. A-III (br)

Paternity (1981) Callous egomaniac (Burt Reynolds) decides he wants a son and interviews prospective surrogate mothers. Beverly D'Angelo, a musician working as a waitress, gets the job and foolishly falls in love with the boor. Directed by David Steinberg, the ill-conceived romantic plot results in a slack and listless comedy of sexual politics with a false female stereotype and some rough language. A-III (PG)

Patrick (1979) Tacky little thriller from Australia about a young man (Robert Thompson) who, while being kept alive on a support system, develops a "seventh sense" that enables him to perform all sorts of disgusting stunts when he becomes attached to a pretty nurse (Susan Penhaligon). Directed by Richard Franklin, it is a painful experience in every respect, with violence and a graphic depiction of some alleged medical techniques. A-III (PG)

Patti Rocks (1988) Boring, pretentious and ultimately repellent movie about a married clod (Chris Mulkey) who cajoles a friend (John Jenkins) into coming with him to help persuade his pregnant, out-of-town girlfriend to have an abortion. Directed ineptly by David Burton Morris, the movie consists of little more than an interminable car ride with two adolescent males talking dirty about sex and women, with the payoff being a romp in the girlfriend's bed. Unremittingly rough language and a simulation of sex. O (R)

Patton (1970) Long, detailed, absorbingly complex examination of the World War II leadership of General George S. Patton, one of the most controversial figures in U.S. military history. George C. Scott's memorable performance in the title role manages to convey a paradoxical, multifaceted character by skillfully blending his love of

the fray and his intense will to win with his deep-seated hatred of war itself. Director Franklin Schaffner's powerful dramatization makes use of violence and profanity within a creditable context. Neither a glorification of war nor an anti-war tract, the movie pays homage to the indomitable spirit of a man who could achieve his destiny, unfortunately, only in wartime. A-II (PG)

Paul and Michelle (1974) Noxious sequel to "Friends" returns to the perils of Paul (Sean Bury) who finds Michelle (Anicee Alvina) living with their young daughter and an understanding American (Keir Dullea). They fly off to Paris to resume their lives in a morass of sickly-sweet dialogue, carefully photographed nudity, Michelle's abortion of the American's baby and Paul's fat allowance being cut off by Daddy and they separate yet again. Directed by Lewis Gilbert, it is sheer exploitation without pretense of moral perspective. O (R)

Pauline at the Beach (1983) French comedy about six oddly assorted lovers and would-be-lovers who pursue and flee one another at a seaside resort in Brittany in late summer while talking endlessly about the nature of love. As with director Eric Rohmer's better movies, it is never dull, never less than diverting, but is satisfied with clever surfaces rather than underlying meaning. Extremely mature subject matter. A-IV (R)

Pawnbroker, The (1966) Holocaust survivor (Rod Steiger) runs a pawnshop in Harlem in a movie intermingling his experiences of oppression with those of the inhabitants of a black ghetto. Directed by Sidney Lumet, it is a powerful, effective parable on human solidarity and the pain of life. Adult treatment. A-III (br)

Payday (1973) Gritty study of second-rate Country-Western singer (Rip Torn) whose career has peaked without his even knowing it, and whose life is about to go right over the edge in a series of one-night stands, cheap motel rooms, good bourbon, popped uppers and downers and a ragged assortment of groupies and hangers-on. Director Daryl Duke's picture of the tormented, self-destructive anti-hero on a lonesome road with nothing at the end has the tragic sense of reality. Some rough language and brief nudity. A-IV (R)

Payment in Blood (1969) Dreary Italian Western set right after the Civil War when disbanded military freebooters (led by Guy Madison) terrorized the Southwest. Director E.G. Rowland's badly-staged violence and even worse acting is a tiresome bore. A-III (R)

Peace Killers, The (1971) Brutal motorcycle gang makes war on a commune of peaceful pot-smokers when one of the gang's women trades in her backseat on a cycle for a snug little sleeping bag at the commune. Directed by Douglas Schwartz, the resulting reprisals would make grown men blanch at scenes of utter brutality, torture, gang rape, and general mayhem. O (R)

Peach Thief (1969) Disappointing Bulgarian import tells a World War I story about a frustrated young wife (Nevena Kokanova) who has a fore-doomed affair with a Serbian prisoner-of-war (Rade Markovich). The meager and predictable story lacks individuality and human resonance. A-III (nr)

Pedestrian, The (1974) Demanding German drama about an aging industrialist (Gustav Rudolf Sellner) who is tortured by guilt and the fear that his secret crime as a Nazi officer responsible for an atrocity is about to be made public because of the digging and sifting into the incident by a German news magazine. Director Maximilian Schell questions what might be called a moral statute of limitations in his complex probing of personal and collective guilt. Strong subject not for casual moviegoers. A-III (PG)

Pee Wee's Big Adventure (1985) Comic personality Pee Wee Herman's search for his stolen bike takes him on a madcap chase from the Alamo in Texas to Hollywood. Directed by Tim Burton, the humor is puerile with occasional slapstick violence. A-II (PG)

Peggy Sue Got Married (1986) A middle-aged mom (Kathleen Turner), about to be divorced from her unfaithful husband (Nicolas Cage), relives her past when she faints at a class reunion and discovers that the person she was and has become are one and the same. Director Francis Ford Coppola carefully controls the sentimental romanticism inherent in this story showing the continuum of values through the course of an individual's life. Brief scene of lovemaking and some rough language. A-II (PG-13)

Pendulum (1969) George Peppard, Jean Seberg and Richard Kiley star in a fast-paced crime thriller about a dedicated cop (Peppard) who within the space of a few weeks finds himself on both sides of the issues surrounding civil rights of accused criminals. With strong performances and fine location photography of the nation's capital, director George Schaefer's work poses some tough questions about law enforcement and the justice system, providing enough material for viewers to draw their own conclusions. A-II (M)

Penitentiary (1980) A young black (Leon Issac Kennedy), wrongly convicted and set to prison, takes up boxing and battles his way to vindication. The mediocre melodrama, written and directed by Jamaa Fanaka, provides an excessively graphic depiction of the corruption, brutality and homosexuality pervading prison life. O (R)

Penitentiary II (1982) Young convict (Leon Isaac Kennedy) gains freedom and respectability by his boxing skills. Director Jamaa Fanaka's sequel, however, falls far short of the barely competent standards of the original. Repulsive, brutal mess with excessive violence. O (R)

Penitentiary III (1987) A boxer (Leon Isaac Kennedy) fights his way out of a prison dominated by a wealthy degenerate inmate (Tony Geary) but can't overcome the nightmarish plot absurdities and writer-director Jamaa Fanaka's near farcical excesses of violence and brutality. O (R)

Pennies from Heaven (1981) Comedian Steve Martin plays a straight role in this almost unqualified disaster. As an unsuccessful peddler of sheet music in the Depression era, Martin is beastly to women and takes refuge from harsh reality by imagining lavish Busby Berkley-style production numbers. Neither director Herbert Ross nor writer Dennis Potter seem to have any idea how to adapt the story and concept for a feature movie. Besides the amorality of the hero, the plot contains scenes dealing with prostitution and abortion. A-III (R)

Penthouse, The (1967) Failed adaptation of a play by C. Scott Forbes in which two psycopaths keep a man (Terence Morgan) and his mistress (Suzy Kendall) prisoner in their penthouse apartment, the woman in the bedroom and the man tied to a chair. Director Peter Collinson's attempt to make a statement about hypocrisy and disillusion-

ment fails because of its contrived and melodramatic treatment and becomes little more than a tiresome exercise in sadism. O (br)

People Next Door, The (1970) J.P. Miller's adaptation of his award-winning television play about a middle-class teenager (Deborah Winters) who grooves with the boys and trips on LSD to escape the reality of her hypocritical parents (Eli Wallach and Julie Harris). Drearily moralizing, one-dimensional melodrama contrasts parents who drink and hide their sexual indiscretions with youngsters who smoke dope and flaunt theirs. Director David Greene's treatment fosters false stereotypes, uses unnecessary nudity and fails to deal adequately with the serious problem of drug abuse in suburbia. O (R)

People of the Wind (1976) British documentary follows the annual trek of a nomadic tribe in southern Iran which each spring must bring their sheep and cattle from winter quarters to fresh grazing lands on a journey through perilous mountain terrain. Directed by Anthony Howarth, it is the record of a fiercely independent people who accept such dangers as the price of remaining free from the influences of the outside world. A-I (nr)

People That Time Forgot, The (1977) Rescue attempt on a prehistoric island brings viewers back to the same ice-bound fastness teeming with prehistoric monsters and cavemen depicted in "The Land That Time Forgot." Directed by Kevin Connor, the British production is lackluster, with tepid acting from Patrick Wayne and Doug McClure, but its silly special effects may amuse youngsters. A-II (PG)

Peppermint Soda (1979) French production about two sisters in 1963, one of whom is 15 and trying to cope with love, politics and anti-Semitism while her 13-year-old sister wants to follow her example but is not quite ready. Directed by Diane Kurys, the beautifully-made movie is about people in the midst of life, but many viewers may find the pace too leisurely for enjoyment. A-II (nr)

Perceval (1978) Stylized French production based on the medieval romance about the knight (Fabrice Luchini) who joins King Arthur's court, fails to claim the Holy Grail when he has the chance, and is punished for his ignorance. Directed by Erich Rohmer, the visuals beautifully evoke the world of the Middle Ages and its code of chivalry as well as the conflict in Christendom between the spiritual and temporal. A-II (nr)

Percy (1971) Witless British sex farce about a young man (Hywel Bennett) with a genital transplant that fascinates both the medical world and several young ladies who discover his new acquisition. Directed by Ralph Thomas, its snickering tone is even more offensive than such scenes as a nurse doing a striptease to test his convalescence. O (R)

Perfect (1985) Rolling Stone reporter becomes involved with an aerobics instructor while researching a story on health clubs. A muddied and pretentious movie that has nothing to say. Favorable view of promiscuity and one thoroughly distasteful sequence involving a male stripper. O (R)

Perfect Couple, A (1979) Middle-aged, browbeaten son of a wealthy, conservative Greek family (Paul Dooley) uses a computer dating service which matches him with an aspiring rock singer (Marta Heflin). They surmount all difficulties, proving that director Robert Altman has a heart

213

and the title is not ironically meant. The film does have some cheerful moments, and the acting is quite good, but the whole thing is so inconsequential that it often seems in danger of evaporating. A-III (PG)

Perfect Friday (1970) British caper movie tries to liven up the muddled plot revolving around bank teller Stanley Baker's clever bank robbery with an incoherently staccato narrative, false plot twists and shots of accomplice Ursula Andress undressed. Director Peter Hall's sense of timing and humor is as badly off the mark as the movie's sense of moral perspective. O (R)

Performance (1970) A hood (James Fox), on the run from the mob, takes refuge with a temporarily retired pop singer (Mick Jagger) awaiting the return of his inspiration in the company of several fans (Anita Pallenberg and Michele Breton). Bizarre British drama directed by Don Cammell and Nicholas Roeg is a pseudo-sophisticate's vision of evil with the kind of slick gimmickry that promises revelations but never rises above its shallow fascination with the perversities it supposedly explores. It's a morass of unrelieved violence, drug use, sex and grotesque immoralities. O (R)

Perils of Gwendoline, The (1985) Coy, flyblown adventure movie, by French director Just Jaeckin, about a trio of explorers in a land ruled by warrior women. Obviously meant to be satirical and sexy, it's merely distasteful and boring. O (R)

Perils of P.K., The (1986) Amateurish, lowbudget sex farce centering around a neurotic middle-aged woman recounting her sexual daydreams and memories to a psychiatrist. Vulgar sight gags and crude gestures, foul language and off-color sexual jokes. O (R)

Persecution and Assassination of Jean-Paul Marat As Performed by the Inmates of the Asylum of Charenton under the Direction of the Marquis De Sade, The (1967) The play by Peter Weiss examines the conflict between the political autocracy of the French revolutionary Marat and the social anarchy of De Sade. Peter Brooks directs the Royal Shakespeare Company in a screen version that is not so much a record of its staging and performances as it is a surprisingly good movie that never quite overcomes the weaknesses of its material. Complex, sometimes shocking, the drama's criticism of social, political and religious conventions will agitate some but give others a number of insights into the conflict between freedom and authority. A-IV (br)

Persona (1967) Swedish drama about an actress (Liv Ullmann) who suddenly cannot speak, fails to respond to psychiatric treatment and is sent to a seaside villa for a rest in the care of a talkative, sympathetic nurse (Bibi Andersson). There the two women seem to change roles and their personal identities become strangely intermingled. Directed by Ingmar Bergman, it is intensely personal, largely obscure and not a little disturbing. A-IV (br)

Personal Best (1982) Two female track stars (Mariel Hemingway and Patrice Donnelly) carry on a homosexual affair in a dull, unbelievably crude and relentlessly simpleminded movie written and directed by Robert Towne. Excessive nudity. O (R)

Personal Services (1987) Julie Walters plays a waitress turned brothel madam and given to arrogant bawdiness in this wry but imbalanced sex farce commenting on ruling class hypocrisy.

Director Terry Jones is only partially critical of sexual perversion and insists on romanticizing an immoral profession. Nudity and kinky sex are used as sources of humor. O (R)

Personals (1972) Sex exploitation director Armand Weston stages hardcore demonstrations to complement his interviews with people who advertise their appetites in sex-oriented publications. O (nr)

Pete "n' Tillie (1972) Awkward and at times grating serio-comedy in which Pete (Walter Matthau) meets Tillie (Carol Burnett) in sunny California, bed down, get married, raise a son only to lose him to leukemia, separate and finally re-unite. Director Martin Ritt proceeds with a wildly inappropriate mixture of sardonic humor, slapstick, stark tragedy, heavy melodrama and cheap soap operatics. Lapses in taste include an excessive amount of profanity and a shrill bit of blasphemy. A-IV (PG)

Pete Seeger...A Song and a Stone (1972) Documentary on one of the bedrock figures of American folk song shows him in performance and conversation about his music and its relation to such issues as ecology. The stone in the title represents the only weapon Seeger has ever carried, a little one he keeps in his banjo, symbolic of breaking Establishment windows. Seeger's songs and his little stone are at the core of this engaging and rewarding work directed by Robert Elfstrom. A-II (nr)

Pete's Dragon (1977) Pete, a young orphan (Sean Marshall), and Elliot, an amiable dragon, are befriended by a lighthouse keeper's daughter (Helen Reddy) in a small Maine fishing village at the turn of the century. Disney musical fantasy, directed by Don Chaffey, combines live-action with animation. The dragon's ability to become invisible is the chief source of humor in a slow-moving picture that also features Mickey Rooney, Red Buttons and Shelley Winters. A-I (G)

Peter Rabbit and Tales of Beatrix Potter (1971) British ballet production conjures up Beatrix Potter's delicate animal fables and through Frederick Ashton's choreography enables them to dance and pantomime their way into the hearts of story lovers. Director Reginald Mills frees the work from the stage by photographing it in a picturesque English countryside and patterns the costumes on the soft, cuddly textures and pale pastels of the famous Potter sketches. A beautiful way to introduce youngsters to the world of Peter Rabbit and the art of the ballet. A-I (G)

Petulia (1968) An affair between a discontented wife (Julie Christie) and a divorced doctor (George C. Scott) is ended when her husband (Richard Chamberlain) finds out and brutally beats her. In picturing a sick society, director Richard Lester follows the story's alienated characters as they check in and out of a San Francisco hospital where it is easier to mend broken bodies than damaged lives. The humor is dark but the effect is stunning. A-III (R)

Phantasm (1979) Dreadfully amateurish attempt to cross comedy with horror in a story about two brothers in a graveyard battle with brown-robed dwarfs and a fiendish undertaker on the lookout for bodies, dead or alive. Directed by Don Coscarelli, the movie employs excessive violence, gore and nudity. O (R)

Phantom of Terror, The (see: "The Bird with the Crystal Plumage")

Phantom Tollbooth (1970) Rather listless youngster (Butch Patrick) escapes through a tollbooth which appears in his bedroom into a world of fantasy where he meets an assortment of allegorical figures and learns the value of using time well and making the most of his schooling. Feature-length cartoon from director Chuck Jones makes playful, intelligent use of visual metaphors and clever word-turns that may motivate some youngsters' interest in reading and writing. A-I (G)

Phantom of Liberty, The (1974) French production freely shifts through a series of loosely connected vignettes beginning as a costume drama set in Toledo during the Napoleanic era returning to contemporary scenes of political, social and religious satire. Directed by Luis Bunuel, the narrative's general complexity, as well as its anticlerical references, casual nudity and mature sexual motifs, make this surrealistic work not for all audiences. A-IV (R)

Phantom of the Paradise (1974) Loosely based on "The Phantom of the Opera," the updated version is about an aspiring rock composer (William Finley) whose face is mutilated by a recording press and his rock cantata on the Faust legend is stolen by a ruthless music producer (Paul Williams) who wants it for the opening of his new house, the Paradise. The composer seeks revenge by terrorizing those working in the Paradise in an effort to have his one love (Jessica Harper) sing his cantata. Director Brian De Palma uses the almost surrealistic plot to concoct a unique combination of horror and comedy, avoiding excess while making some incisive comments about the state of modern music. A-III (PG)

Phar Lap (1984) Rousing, wholesome entertainment from Australia about a famous Depression-era racehorse who meets a tragic end. Though not especially dramatic, director Simon Wincer's work with Tom Burlinson, Martin Vaughan and Ron Liebman is nonetheless interesting family entertainment. A-I (PG)

Phase IV (1974) Sci-fi tale of the world being taken over by ants acting out of mass instinct. The photographic techniques somehow make the ants and their colony a much more believable world than that of the cast of human characters (Nigel Davenport, Michael Murphy and Lynne Frederick). Although artist-director Saul Bass's ending is a little muddled, getting there is half the fun. A-II (PG)

Phedre (1973) Marie Bell, the legendary actress of the Comedie Francaise, plays the tragic queen in Racine's 17th-century version of the Greek myth of Theseus, the prince torn between two loves. Director Pierre Jourdan has tried to do more than record a stage performance, yet the play is necessarily artificial and stage-bound. Though the English subtitles give only a suggestion of Racine's complicated romantic verse, the work is of interest to students of French culture and drama. A-II (PG)

Philadelphia Experiment, The (1984) Routine time-travel adventure with Michael Pare and Bobby Di Cicco playing World War II sailors projected into the present. Directed by Stewart Raffill, the result is innocuous and moderately entertaining. A-II (PG)

Photographer, The (1975) Demented photographer (Michael Callan), who hates his mother, murders his models while taking pictures of their death agonies, until murdered by a model who

hates her father. Pointless, absurd and relentlessly violent story. O (PG)

Phynx, The (1970) Intended as a satire of both foreign intrigue movies and popular music, director Lee H. Katzin's story about a group of rock musicians who are sent to Albania to rescue some American show people is merely dull and boring, save for the brief appearances of some famous performers of the past (Ruby Keeler, Dorothy Lamour, Busby Berkely, Leo Gorcey, Huntz Hall and many others). Some slapstick violence and sexual references. A-III (PG)

Piaf—The Early Years (1982) Disappointing dramatization of French singer Edith Piaf's life from her birth in 1915, through her formative years in the seedy underworld of criminals and prostitutes who helped her eke out a living as a street singer until her success as a top Paris entertainer in the 1930s. Director Guy Casaril has trouble maintaining interest in the muddled continuity of the narrative but Brigitte Ariel in the title role is moderately successful in overcoming this handicap. Rather romantic treatment of Piaf's affairs of the heart. A-III (PG)

Pickpocket (1969) Alienated youth turns to petty crime as a kind of lark but, not very good at it, is caught and sent to prison where he is visited by a young woman who cares for him and will be waiting when he is released. French production directed by Robert Bresson in 1956, the work has nothing to do with crime thrillers but is an austere look at a lost soul and his possible chance of redemption. Challenging but worthwhile fare for reflective viewers. A-II (nr)

Pickup Artist, The (1987) Unintelligent late-teen romance about an aggressive womanizer (Robert Downey) and promiscuous museum guide (Molly Ringwald) who take a tumble in the front seat, solve father Dennis Hopper's gambling debt to tough Harvey Keitel and find true love without much happiness or a solution to their bad habits. Director James Toback indulges in TV superficiality and tired stereotyping in this lazy tale which endorses gambling and recreational sex. A-III (PG-13)

Pickup on 101 (1972) College coed (Lesley Warren) heading toward a New Mexico commune and a rock guitarist (Martin Sheen) on his way to Los Angeles are brought together on the road by an old hobo (Jack Albertson) whose redemptive quality brings the young couple to transcend their own selfishness and learn that love means more than sex. Director John Florea has a script loaded with simplistic and pietistic preachments but at least it tries for something a bit more substantial than the ususal sentimental romance. A-III (PG)

Picnic at Hanging Rock (1979) On a sunny St. Valentine's day in 1900, a group of Australian schoolgirls go off on a picnic to a strange and foreboding place called Hanging Rock where three of the girls and one teacher disappear without a trace. Director Peter Weir's fact-based, never solved mystery creates an eerie, otherworldly atmosphere as the girls explore the ledges and recesses of the ancient rock formation. The somberness of the theme and an emphasis on suppressed sexuality make it mature fare. A-III (PG)

Picture Mommy Dead (1966) Suspense melodrama about a young heiress (Susan Gordon) who returns to the house where her mother had burned to death many years before and, in the company of her father and step-mother (Don Ameche and

Martha Hyer), strange things begin happening to her. Director Bert I. Gordon tries to do something with all the frights and hallucinations contained in the script but the result borders on the absurd. Stylized violence. A-III (br)

Piece of Pleasure, A (1976) French drama about a "liberated" husband (Paul Gegauff who also wrote the script) who pushes his less-educated wife (Danielle Gegauff) into a chaos of sexual experimentation with predictably tragic results. That people are capable of destroying themselves by their own self-deceptions may sound like a fairly banal theme, but director Claude Chabrol presents it as a harrowing truth, with a level of human involvement, yet distancing itself from their excesses. A-IV (R)

Piece of the Action, A (1977) Two smooth con men (Bill Cosby and Sidney Poitier) are blackmailed by a retired police detective (James Earl Jones) into working for a youth center devoted to educating ghetto youngsters and getting them jobs. Directed by Poitier, the comedy-melodrama quickly exhausts the situation and is only mildly entertaining. Strong language and a muddled sense of morality (the two criminals show no signs of remorse and Poitier lives in unwedded bliss). A-III (PG)

Pieces of Dreams (1970) A troubled, lonely pastor (Robert Forster), out of touch with his people and bored with the routine chores of parish life, leaves the priesthood and marries a divorced social worker (Lauren Hutton). Director Daniel Haller fails to get inside the personal world of his characters and their spiritual conflicts, leaving one with the impression that the priest's ultimate decision was motivated by little more than a tumble in the hay. A-IV (PG)

Pied Piper, The (1972) British production filmed in Germany by French director Jacques Demy results in a confused retelling of the medieval tale about the piper (folk singer Donovan) who comes to save the hamlet of Hamelin from the Black Plague by leading a parade of rodents down to the river to drown but unpaid returns to spirit the town's children away to a happier clime. It mixes childlike fantasy with such a cluttered picture of the people and artifacts of medieval life that its simple story line is often difficult to follow. A-II (G)

Pierrot le Fou (1969) Unconventional French melodrama about a man and a woman (Jean-Paul Belmondo and Anna Karina) whose relationship is based upon misunderstandings and boredom. Director Jean-Luc Godard's highly subjective, stream-of-consciousness lacks narrative coherence yet conveys the need people have for ideals in a world of absurdity. A-IV (nr)

Pigeons (1971) Trite and silly story about aimless urban youth, here a yuppie New York cab driver (Jordan Christopher) who falls for a cute neighbor (Jill O'Hara) but their romance withers on a trip to the suburbs to meet his neurotic folks. Directed by John Dexter, the story is overly familiar and the treatment overly cute. Some relatively innocuous nudity. A-III (R)

Ping Pong (1987) Young Chinese law clerk (Lucy Sheen) rediscovers her cultural roots and inadvertently reunites a fragmented family while executing the will of a wealthy Chinese businessman. British import from director Po Chih Leong deals affectionately with the social and cultural pressures that alienate westernized foreign nationals and erode their family ties. Charming but slow moving portrait. A-I (nr)

Pink Floyd (1974) The musical group of the title in a sophisticated, heavily electronic rock concert that their fans will appreciate, though others may be put off by the intensity of sound and artiness of image (most of it was filmed in an ampitheater amid the ruins of Pompeii. Directed by Alan Parker, it features Bob Geldof, Christine Hargreaves, James Laurenson, Eleanor David and Bob Hoskins. A-II (G)

Pink Jungle, The (1968) Amusing comedy-adventure with a twist ending in which a photographer (James Garner) and pretty model (Eva Renzi) helicopter into a Latin American jungle for a lipstick ad layout, are mistaken for spies and get involved with a flamboyant wheeler-dealer (George Kennedy) searching for a lost diamond mine. Directed by Delbert Mann, it's generally fast-paced and funny, if a trifle condescending toward that nameless Latin government, and Kennedy nearly steals the show. A-II (br)

Pink Narcissus (1971) The phallic fantasies of a young homosexual introvert assembled by an anonymous filmmaker who uses tumultuous music and no dialogue to accompany a hothouse montage of floating doilies and bizarre superimpositions. The lugubrious exercise incorporates indecent exposures of the anatomy. O (nr)

Pink Panther Strikes Again, The (1977) Peter Sellers returns as Inspector Clouseau, but the one-joke nature of his success through bungling has worn rather thin, especially the running gag of karate assaults by his Oriental servant. The plot revolves around the machinations of Clouseau's former superior (Herbert Lom) who, driven mad by the constant incompetence of his underling, has gotten control of a doomsday machine. Director Blake Edwards achieves some good comic bits but mainly relies on slapstick violence and sexually-derived humor. A-III (PG)

Pink Telephone, The (1977) French production about an American conglomerate (run by Michel Lonsdale) which tries to induce an aging French factory owner (Pierre Mondy) to sell out by setting him up with a call girl (Mireille Darc) with whom he falls in love. Director Edouard Molinaro and writer Francis Verber resist a pat sentimental and moralistic ending and concentrate on illustrating the lack of values operating in an amoral environment. Well-acted and directed, the movie's adult theme contains brief nudity and rough language. A-IV (R)

Pinocchio (1940) Among Walt Disney's best animated features is the story of a wooden-headed puppet who wants to be a real boy but keeps getting into trouble, most notably with the help of Honest John and an almost terminal trip to Pleasure Island. With Jiminy Cricket as his conscience, he escapes just in time to rescue the wood carver Geppetto from Monstro the Whale. Grand family entertainment. A-I (G)

Pipe Dreams (1976) Going to Alaska in an attempt to win back her estranged husband, a woman (Gladys Knight) gets involved in breaking up a teenage prostitution ring. The failed romantic melodrama is poorly directed and carelessly edited by Stephen Verona. Some violence, rough language and a scene of an attempted abortion. A-III (PG)

Pirate, The (1948) Gene Kelly and Judy Garland sing and dance to the tunes of Cole Porter in director Vincente Minnelli's energetic musical romance set in the swashbuckling days of piracy in Caribbean waters. Stylized violence. A-II (br)

Pirate Movie, The (1982) Incompetent movie musical revolves around contemporary characters (Kristy McNichol and Christopher Atkins) who find themselves in the world of Gilbert and Sullivan's "The Pirates of Penzance." Filmed in Australia by director Ken Annakin, the movie desperately tries to evoke laughter at any cost, relying mainly on pratfalls, vulgar language and crude double entendres, but nothing can save it from its own ineptitudes. A-III (PG)

Pirates (1986) Director Roman Polanski's obsessively detailed and ornamental portrait of the era when galleons feared ships flying the Jolly Roger features Walter Matthau as an irascible pirate captain determined to possess a solid gold throne. Unfortunately, the overblown action epic leaves little room to develope a somewhat whimsical plot. Vulgarity, brutality and disproportionate amounts of realistically-staged sea battles. A-III (PG)

Pirates of Penzance, The (1983) Screen adaptation of a New York stage version of the Gilbert and Sullivan operetta has a fine cast headed by George Rose, whose rendition of "A Modern Major General" is easily the best moment, Linda Ronstadt as Mabel and Kevin Kline as the Pirate King. Directed by Wilfred Leach, it is good family entertainment though some may find it much too stage-bound. A-I (G)

Pirosmani (1978) Russian import about an obscure Georgian painter whose work has grown in stature since his death in 1919. Director Georgy Shengelaya employs beautifully stark images to show how the artist's imagination was rooted in his rural environment and time period, one that is rather exotic because so unfamiliar. His kind of folk art appealed to the common people because of its traditional ethnic and religious themes and symbolism. A-II (nr)

Pixote (1982) Harrowing and poignant Brazilian drama about a gang of nomad boys in Rio and the terrible things they do to survive. Directed by Hector Babenco, this powerful movie is definitely not for the faint of heart or weak of stomach because it involves sordid violence and graphic sexuality. A-IV (nr)

Pizza Triangle, The (1970) Stylish Italian satire about a tragic love affair involving a Marxist bricklayer (Marcello Mastroianni) who leaves his wife for a cemetery flower peddler (Monica Vitti) and then becomes insanely jealous when she in turn falls in love with a pizza cook (Giancarlo Giannini). Director Ettore Scola is not interested in his hackneyed romantic plot except as a device supporting a pastiche of comic styles and sensibilities poking fun at movie cliches and stereotypes as well as Italian life and institutions. Some rough language. A-III (R)

Place Called Glory, A (1966) Undistinguished Western directed by Ralph Gideon with Lex Barker as a gunfighter who joins a pal in cleaning out a town full of bad men. Stylized violence. A-II (br)

Place Called Today, A (1972) The stakes are the mayor's office in a racially polarized New Jersey city, but the issues are buried in an onslaught of unrelenting violence and explicit nudity. Written and directed by Don Schain and starring his wife, Cheri Caffaro, there is no reason for others to share their voyeur-exhibitionist relationship. O (X)

Place for Lovers, A (1969) Lovely American (Faye Dunaway) initiates an affair with a romantic Italian (Marcello Mastroianni) who learns only after falling hopelessly in love that she is doomed by a fatal disease. Directed by Vittorio De Sica, the melodrama's amoral approach to love and life is handled in a heavy, pretentious manner. A-III (R)

Places in the Heart (1984) Sally Field plays a young widow struggling to keep her family together and her integrity intact after her husband's death in rural Texas during the Depression. Under Robert Benton's direction, Field's performance winningly conveys a character of strong faith and good will in the face of adversity. A-II (PG)

Plague of the Zombies, The (1966) Routine British horror movie directed by John Gilling about a man (Andre Morell) who can turn people into the walking dead. Restrained gore. A-II (br)

Planes, Trains and Automobiles (1987) Steve Martin plays a hapless traveler trying to get from New York to Chicago in time to have Thanksgiving with his family but, among other disasters and discomforts, planes are grounded, trains break down and even automobiles catch fire. Adding to the disagreeable experiences of the journey is fellow traveler John Candy in director John Hughes' comedy which, though uneven, does have its truly hilarious moments. Some very rough language and sexual references. A-III (R)

Planet of the Apes (1968) Charlton Heston plays the leader of a space expedition who lands his craft on an unnamed planet in the constellation of Orion where he discovers a civilization presided over by apes who are trying to domesticate a species of human beings. Director Franklin J. Schaffner's screen version of Pierre Boulle's novel is an entertaining allegorical warning to damage-prone mankind. Some violence and mature themes. A-III (G)

Plastic Dome of Norma Jean, The (1974) The media's inevitable victimization of the personalities that they create is the theme of this story about a young woman (Sharon Henesy) whose gift of clairvoyance is used to popularize an exceptionally undistinguished rock group. The script and direction by Juleen Compton prove simply inadequate to the ambitions of what proves to be a terribly flawed movie. Mature themes. A-III (nr)

Platoon (1986) The Vietnam War as experienced by a raw recruit (Charlie Sheen) is evoked with relentless realism in scenes of battle and brutality in writer-director Oliver Stone's haunting reminiscence of its horrors and inhumanity. Its excessive violence, unrelenting profanity and graphic depiction of representative atrocities are stomach-churning, but serve as a corrective to Rambo-style romanticizations of the war. A-IV (R)

Play Dirty (1969) British World War II story about a motley collection of criminals sent behind German lines in North Africa under the command of an inexperienced but decent officer (Michael Caine). Andre de Toth's direction emphasizes the ugly realities of survival in the desert but its anti-war message suffers from overkill and borders on a cynical destruction of all values. Strong graphic violence. A-III (PG)

Play It Again, Sam (1972) Woody Allen plays a balding, bespectacled loser who grooves on Humphrey Bogart movies (and even conjures Bogey up for on-the-spot advice in touchy situations). When his beautiful, brainy wife (Susan Anspach) walks out on him, his best friends (Diane Keaton and Tony Roberts) devote themselves to setting up blind dates (Jennifer Salt, Viva and Joy Bang). A very funny comedy directed by Herbert Ross, it's not a family film, but one most older teens and adults will thoroughly enjoy for some witty insights into the mating game. A-III (PG)

Play It As It Lays (1972) Failed exploration of contemporary womanhood and decadent movie industry folk based on the Joan Didion novel. Tuesday Weld is the unsuccessful actress, neglected wife and mother on a Hollywood odyssey into self-realization. Director Frank Perry envisions life as a crap game, but doesn't see beyond the superficial characters whose confusion he portrays. A suicide and marital problems are central to the plot. A-IV (R)

Play Misty for Me (1971) Slick disk jockey (Clint Eastwood) has a near-tragic romantic involvement with one of his fans, a severely disturbed woman (Jessica Walter) who is given to very dangerous fits of jealousy. Also directed by Eastwood, his performance is less wooden than usual though still lethargic and it is up to Walter to supply the spark, here of manic menace. Gripping but flawed psychodrama lacks any sense of the moral implications of the situation. Violence and gore with brief nudity. A-IV (R)

Players (1979) Ali MacGraw plays the contented, middle-aged mistress of magnate Maximilian Schell but she falls in love with young tennis hustler Dean-Paul Martin and has to choose between security and romance. Directed by Athony Harvey, the turgid melodrama deals in simplistic love-hate characterizations consistent with its muddled conclusion. Condones an illicit sexual relationship. O (PG)

Playing for Keeps (1986) A teenager elicits the help of friends to convert a dilapidated hotel his mom has inherited, foiling attempts by unscrupulous real estate agents to convert the site into a secret toxic waste dump. Predictable and simplistic in plot, the movie highlights matter-of-fact acceptance and depictions of casual sex relations between the kids. O (PG-13)

Playtime (1973) Monsieur Hulot (Jacques Tati) wanders through various vignettes with characteristic absent-mindedness, totally unsurprised by any absurdity that crosses his path. The 1967 French comedy is a loose-collection of anecdotes about the depersonalized steel-and-glass environments comprising the urban landscape, a Parisian maze which writer-producer-director Tati treats with the humor of the urban commonplace. A-I (nr)

Plaza Suite (1971) Walter Matthau plays the central character in each of three segments about successive occupants of the same suite in New York's famed Plaza Hotel. Directed by Arthur Hiller, derived from the Broadway play by Neil Simon, the lame comedy matches Matthau's penchant for mugging with Simon's middlebrow humor resulting in only a passing diversion. Mature themes. A-III (PG)

Plenty (1985) Impressionistic chronicle of the growing disillusionment and mental instability of an English woman (Meryl Streep), a heroine of the French Resistance, over the course of the two decades following World War II. Directed by Fred Schepisi, the sole bright spot in this cold, tedious, unfocused and intellectually muddled movie is John Gielgud's performance as a befuddled but honorable diplomat. Some fairly graphic bedroom scenes. A-IV (R)

Pocket Money (1972) Slight but frequently amusing contemporary Western about a down-on-his-luck cattleman (Paul Newman) who is sent south of the border to buy rodeo bulls for a shady entrepreneur (Strother Martin) but there he's betrayed by an old friend (Lee Marvin) and the man who hired him. Directed by Stuart Rosenberg, the lackluster buddy movie has some fine rodeo action and adult humor. A-III (PG)

Point Blank (1967) Double-crossed in a robbery by a friend who takes not only the loot and his wife but also leaves him for dead, tough guy Lee Marvin comes back to uncover an underworld connection which he destroys man by man until all responsible are dead. Director John Boorman's brutally violent and illogical crime thriller is handled with a technical virtuosity that is sometimes effective but frequently pretentious and overblown in its graphic depiction of violence. O (br)

Point of Terror (1971) Pop singer (Peter Carpenter) plays up to the lusting wife of the crippled owner of a record company but, when she refuses to marry him after he kills her spouse, he switches his affections to her comely daughter who has reaped the lioness' share of Daddy's inheritance. The sordid melodrama depends totally upon crude sensationalism for cheap thrills. O (R)

Police Academy (1984) Reluctant police recruit (Stephen Guttenberg) finds that law enforcement can be fun in this dismal, failed comedy directed by Hugh Wilson. It relies heavily on sexually oriented humor, some nudity and rough language to convey its crude message of social irresponsibility. O (R)

Police Academy 2: Their First Assignment (1985) Sequel directed by Jerry Paris is somewhat less vulgar than the original but vulgar enough, as well as altogether lackluster and unfunny. Sexually oriented humor. A-III (PG-13)

Police Academy 3: Back in Training (1986) Police recruits try to save the prestige of the training academy's aging director in a tasteless movie whose failed humor is derived chiefly through sadistic violence, lewd jokes and slapstick stunts. O (PG)

Police Academy 4 (1987) Limp plot and lame script with unfunny Keystone Cop slapstick antics by Steve Guttenberg, Bobcat Goldthwaite and company is featured in this edition which deals with the academy's post-graduate project involving a citizens action group. Tame in language and sexual references, director Jim Drake's movie emphasizes aerial and ballooning chase sequences. Mild-mannered but sophomoric entertainment. A-III (PG)

Police Call 9000 (see: "Detroit 9000")

Police Connection, The (see: "Badge 373")

Policeman, The (1972) Israeli import features Shay K. Ophir as a Jaffa policeman whose 20-year career is distinguished only by its lack of arrests. Learning that Ophir is about to be fired, some crooks stage a heist to save his job. Director Ephraim Kishon uses a number of sweet, light, and warm moments to celebrate human solidarity. A-II (nr)

Policewoman (1974) Sondra Currie and her squad of distaff detectives turn the underworld upside down by outdoing their brothers in blue. Director Lee Frost's mindless female crimestopper movie offers a variety of wild fights, hints of sadism, endless car chases, undeleted expletives and a sprinkling of coy nudity. O (R)

Poltergeist (1982) Suburban couple (Jobeth Williams and Craig T. Nelson) find their cosy existence disturbed when their five-year-old daughter gets trapped in the television screen and a parapsychologist (Beatrice Straight) is called in to retrieve her. Along the way to the burial grounds, producer Steven Spielberg and director Tobe Hooper treat viewers to some special effects violence and gore, teenage sexuality and a benign look at Mom and Dad smoking marijuana at bedtime. O (R/PG appeal)

Poltergeist II: The Other Side (1986) Angry spirits led by a demonic minister (Julian Beck) return to torment and terrorize the Freeling family just when they thought it was safe to leave grandma's house. The family has become more cynical, and the effects less frightening but more disgusting, in this sequel. The Vomit Creature sequence may be too gruesome for the very young in an otherwise mild-mannered Gothic tale. A-II (PG-13)

Polyester (1981) Saga relating the sorrows of Francine Fishpaw, an overweight suburban matron (played by female impersonator Divine) and the man (Tab Hunter) who seems to be the answer to her dreams. Baltimore writer-director John Waters often shows real satirical flair, but he too often tries to get laughs by appealing to the sadistic streak in an audience. Romantic homosexual aspect figures in the plot. O (R)

Poor Cow (1968) British story of life in London's slums where an impoverished, too-young mother (Carol White) drifts into degrading situations, even posing for lecherous amateur photographers while her husband (John Bindon) and lover (Terence Stamp) are in prison. Directed by Kenneth Loach, the stuff of social protest is certainly here, but artistic discipline is lacking in such matters as a gory scene of childbirth and several erotic sequences whose point is less dramatic than exploitative. O (br)

Popcorn (1969) Loud, cluttered documentary with pop music groups, such as the Vanilla Fudge, the Rolling Stones, the Bee Gees and a host of others, performing amid psychedelic lights and wildly fast editing. Some extremely fleeting nudity and a suggestive performance involving Jimi Hendrix make it inappropriate for youngsters. A-III (G)

Pope Joan (1972) Legendary tale of a 9th-century woman (Liv Ullmann) who disguised herself as a man and worked her way up to the papacy. Directed by Michael Anderson, the British production is both a dramatic clunker and an historical yawner which fails to convey any sense of the life and experience of Christianity in the early Middle Ages. Graphic rape scene and the suggestion of lesbianism in the convent. A-IV (PG)

Pope of Greenwich Village, The (1984) Two amateur hustlers (Mickey Rourke and Eric Roberts) run afoul of both the mob and corrupt police. Though it lacks dramatic power, director Stuart Rosenberg's movie presents a sensitive study of a streetwise collection of characters made interesting because of good acting and perceptive script. Some scenes of restrained sex and violence. A-III (R)

Popeye (1980) Disappointing attempt to bring Popeye and the Thimble Theater gang to the screen is clever and sometimes mildly amusing, but never very funny. Robin Williams works valiantly as the hero, but neither director Robert Altman nor writer Jules Feiffer have given him much to do. The songs and dances are leaden and witless. Some slightly naughty visuals and expletives dragged in for no good purpose. A-II (PG)

Popi (1969) Puerto Rican widower (Alan Arkin), struggling to give his sons something of a decent life amidst the slums of New York City, finds that he can't make it even with his three jobs as handyman, bus boy and hospital orderly. Director Arthur Hiller skirts sentimental melodrama and Arkin's comic lightness keeps viewers engaged in a potentially tragic story, the point of which is that there are no fantasy solutions to the hard realities of poverty. Some brutal aspects of slum life. A-II (G)

Porky's (1982) Sex-obsessed adolescents cavort at a Florida high school during the Eisenhower era. Director Bob Clark's extended dirty joke is made even more offensive by some ill-advised stabs at seriousness. Witlessly vulgar movie with much nudity, graphic sexuality and an almost non-stop flow of verbal obscenities. O (R)

Porky's II: The Next Day (1983) Sequel dishes up more of the same elaborate but boring hijinks of sex-crazed Florida high school boys, most of whom look old enough to play their teachers. Directed again by Bob Clark, it differs from the original only in having an even more muddled and disjointed story line. Excessive nudity and scabrous dialogue. O (R)

Porky's Revenge (1985) The old gang at Angel Beach High who now look old enough, if not bright enough, to be out of graduate school are at it again. This effort directed by James Komack, like the previous ones, is beneath contempt. Exploitative nudity and tedious, mindless vulgarity. O (R)

Portnoy's Complaint (1972) Sneering, caustic and self-defeating adaptation of the Philip Roth novel about the sexual fetishes and fixations of a Jewish youth (Richard Benjamin). Produced and directed by Ernest Lehman, its social satire is an extraordinarily repulsive mix of vulgar sight gags, crude bathroom humor, sexual escapades and profanity that add up to a demeaning stereotyped portrait of Jewish family life. O (R)

Portrait of the Artist As a Young Man, A (1979) Screen version of James Joyce's autobiographical novel about his aesthetic and philosophical development during his school and university years before departing for Paris. Director Joseph Strick's uninspired, talky drama has a number of good performances, the most memorable of which is John Gielgud as the Jesuit retreat master delivering the famous sermon on hell. The tension between religious faith and literary aspirations is at the heart of the adaptation and is treated in serious and mature fashion. A-IV (nr)

Poseidon Adventure, The (1972) Massive tidal wave overturns ocean liner, nearly killing everyone but leaving just enough survivors to exemplify every stereotype and cliche in this old-fashioned disaster movie. Gene Hackman plays a liberal minister leading his instant flock of Hollywood stars to the deepest part of the overturned hull where there is an air pocket and chance of escape. Ronald Neame directs the mushy but occasionally gripping yarn for those seeking escapist fare. Stylized violence, a few sexual references and some rough language. A-III (PG)

Posse (1975) Kirk Douglas plays a politically ambitious U.S. marshal in late 19th-century Texas who battles outlaws by means of his own well-trained, fantically loyal posse but runs into trouble when he brings in a popular train robber (Bruce Dern). Also directed by Douglas, the simplistic morality tale is heavy-handed in its use of violence and offensive in a needless bit of sexual exploitation. O (PG)

Possession of Joel Delaney, The (1972) Strained horror movie with some pretensions to social commentary tells the story of an affluent New York divorcee (Shirley MacLaine) and her brother (Michael Hordern), seemingly possessed by the malevolent soul of a dead Puerto Rican youth who had brutally murdered several women. The social dimension shows the cultural gulf between the Park Avenue rich and those living in Spanish Harlem. Director Waris Hussein resorts to shock tactics considerably lessening the intensity of his film's serious subject matter by punctuating action with beheaded nude bodies and a climax that is as berserk as poor Joel. A-IV (R)

Postman Always Rings Twice, The (1981) Failed screen version of James M. Cain's bleak, Depression-era tale of passion and retribution about an adulterous couple (Jessica Lange and Jack Nicholson) who conspire to kill the woman's husband. Directed by Bob Rafelson, the slow-moving, uninvolving movie devotes most of its energy to conveying in needless detail, the sadomasochistic sexual relationship between the two principals, neither of whom give very convincing performances. Excessively graphic display of sex. O (R)

Pound (1970) Absurdist social satire in which the actors assume the roles of dogs waiting in the city pound to be destroyed. These sad, lonely, unfulfilled social outcasts are potential elements for a meaningful exploration of one or another aspect of the human condition. Unfortunately, director Robert Downey's improvisational approach lacks any insight and the content consists of little else but gross crudities played simply for irreverent and tasteless humor in a style that is more asinine than canine. O (X)

Power (1986) Richard Gere stars as a public relations expert and power broker in this glamourized depiction of the media process which creates and manipulates the image of politicians. The drama asserts that television is the major influence in molding public opinion. The narrative is spotted with a profanity unnecessary for characterization. O (R)

Power, The (1967) As his colleagues die mysteriously, scientist George Hamilton has to discover which of those involved in his pain-resistance experiment is a superintelligent being. The thriller has an interesting premise, but suspense drains off through credibility gaps in the plot and Byron Haskin's slack direction. Benign attitude toward premarital sex. A-III (br)

Practice Makes Perfect (1980) Jean Rochefort plays a famous pianist, a conceited self-centered woman chaser, who gets a mild comeuppance when he tries to abandon his second wife (Nicole Garcia) and their three children by running off with the granddaughter (Catherine Le Prince) of an old flame (Danielle Darrieux). French sex farce directed by Philippe de Broca, it's all very light, very sentimental and passably droll for adults who enjoy such fare. A-III (nr)

Premonition, The (1976) Unconvincing thriller concerns a parapsychologist's attempt to find a missing child through the foster mother's psychic contact with the child's dead mother. Though it has some eerie moments and suggests some gory horrors, one doesn't have to be clairvoyant to perceive how badly director Robert Allen Schnitzer has missed the mark. A-III (PG)

President's Analyst, The (1968) James Coburn plays shrink to the Commander-in-Chief who develops a case of the jitters when the revelations that relieve the President's tensions also happen to be state secrets. But he also discovers that he is being pursued by agents and double-agents who alternately want him to keep the lid on or blow it off. Director Theodore J. Flicker's comedy has some adult humor. A-III (br)

Pretty Baby (1978) The story of a 12-year-old girl (Brooke Shields), born and raised in a house of prostitution, who eventually marries historical figure E.J. Bellocq (Keith Carradine), a photographer who first came to photograph her mother (Susan Sarandon). Director Louis Malle's listless, dubiously nostalgic tour of a bordello relies on extravagant nudity and the flagrant exploitation of a 12-year-old girl. O (R)

Pretty Maids All in a Row (1971) Failed sex farce stars Rock Hudson as a high school guidance counselor who cures the coeds' hang-ups by couch therapy, and solves sophomore John David Carson's perpetual erection by introducing him to teacher-sexpot Angie Dickinson. As some of the pretty coeds wind up as corpses, super-sleuth Telly Savalas questions the student counselor's methods. Directed by Roger Vadim, there is little comedy or mystery in a work whose sole purpose seems to be to exploit sex. O (R)

Pretty Poison (1968) Psychological terror movie about a mad youth running murderously amok is of routine interest, but director Noel Black has gotten subtle and chilling characterizations from Anthony Perkins as a crazed killer and Tuesday Weld as the perverse teenage nymph who inspires him. A-III (R)

Pretty in Pink (1986) Self-sufficient, self-assured teenager (Molly Ringwald) goes to the junior prom alone when let down by the boy who was to take her. Director John Hughes provides a positive portrayal of a teenager who maintains a wholesome sense of her own identity despite the peer pressures and scorn of some of her classmates. Sexual innuendo and harsh language. A-III (PG-13)

Prettykill (1987) Expensive New York call girl (Season Hubley) has her life threatened by a schizophrenic Southern charmer (Suzanne Snyder) she temporarily takes under her wing. Hubley's plight brings her closer to her long time boy friend, a police detective (David Birney). Director George Kaczender's failed psycho-thriller plays more like a distorted caricature of a romance. Some partial nudity and unwholesome mix of sex and bloody violence. O (R)

Prick Up Your Ears (1987) Harshly realistic depiction of the doomed love affair between British playwright Joe Orton (Gary Oldman) and collaborator Kenneth Halliwell (Alfred Molina). Uncompromising direction by Stephen Frears dwells too vividly on the details of sordid homosexual encounters and a concluding bloody murder and suicide scene. Vanessa Redgrave co-stars in the British production which has brief male nudity and vulgar language. O (R)

Priest and the Girl, The (1973) The story told by this 1966 Brazilian drama is of a young priest, overwhelmed by the poverty and injustice of the backward community to which he has been sent, blindly runs away in the company of a sensual young girl who looks to him for protection from her brutal guardian. Director Joaquim Pedro de Andrade's slow moving study of spiritual aridity is less concerned with his two central characters than in the barren lives of the people who inhabit a desolate part of the world. A-III (nr)

Priest's Wife, The (1971) Careless Italian romp stars Sophia Loren as a suicidal pop singer and Marcello Mastroianni as the priest who becomes the object of her attentions. What begins as a rather lighthearted spoof of the issue of priestly celibacy, ends up as a humorless and bitter indictment of church law. While the viewer is mercifully spared the visual aspects of the pair's sexual relationship, director Dino Risi's irreverent and occasionally tasteless humor is more an insult to one's intelligence than to one's religious convictions. A-IV (PG)

Prime Cut (1972) Tough slice of crime melodrama about a hired killer (Lee Marvin) sent to extol tribute from a double-crossing Kansas City gangster (Gene Hackman) who sells beef and women. As directed by Michael Ritchie, the fast-paced action becomes a senseless nightmare of white slavery, drugs and meatpacking treated with blood, gore, nudity and foul language. O (R)

Prime of Miss Jean Brodie, The (1969) Poignant screen version of Muriel Spark's novel about a lovable, eccentric school teacher (Maggie Smith in a grand performance) who just doesn't fit in with the faculty or administration at the conservative Edinburgh girls' school in the 1930s. She's demanding but her "gurrls" love her until one of them (Pamela Franklin) betrays her. Director Ronald Neame handles with great sensitivity the moral ambiguities of the teacher's odd personal traits as well as that of her precocious student who poses in the nude for the art teacher. A-III (PG)

Prince of Darkness (1987) Failed horror movie about the discovery by a priest (Donald Pleasence) that a secret vault in a Los Angeles church contains an ancient jar holding a cosmic force that if let loose will become the Son of Darkness. Directed self-indulgently by John Carpenter, the boring and pretentious movie talks itself to death but sprinkles in enough blood-and-gore scenes and vomiting zombies to offend moral sensibilities. O (R)

Prince of the City (1981) Treat Williams plays a New York City detective who, tormented by guilt, comes forward to cooperate with federal authorities investigating police corruption. Director Sidney Lumet succeeds in portraying the human complexity in this flawed but gripping drama that has some of the inexorable force of Greek tragedy. Williams is particularly fine among a strong cast giving many excellent performances. Though the violence is extremely restrained, a somber and difficult theme with much rough language. A-III (R)

Princess Yang Kwel Fel (1972) One of the most beautiful color movies ever made, this 1955 Japanese production retells a Chinese legend about a graceful princess who dies for her emperor and whose love lives on after death. Directed by Kenji Mizoguchi, the narrative is slow and measured but the interest lies less in its traditional story than in the beauty and grace of its presentation done with an artistry that is genuine and universal. A-II (nr)

Princess, The (see: "A Time in the Sun")

Prison Guard (1973) Surrealistic Czech drama about institutional dehumanization tells the story of a young prison guard in the 1920s whose experiences teach him that brutality is the best way to deal with prisoners. Having previously taken out his frustrations on his dog, the guard turns to beating the inmates when one of them runs off with his wife. Director Ivan Renc's characters are strange and disturbing inhabitants of a bleak terrain that corresponds to the barrenness of their lives. A-III (nr)

Prisoner of Second Avenue, The (1975) Uneven screen verison of Neil Simon's Broadway comedy about a middle-aged New Yorker (Jack Lemmon) who loses his job, gets mugged while his apartment is robbed and who endures all sorts of other urban traumas with the help of a sensible, down-to-earth wife (Anne Bancroft). Director Melvin Frank pumps up all the life possible in a script whose wisecracks are not necesarily witty and whose profanity impedes one's willingness to sympathize with the characters. A-III (PG)

Prisoner of Zenda (1979) Peter Sellers plays the dual role of the foppish King Rudolph of Ruritania and the stout-hearted Englishman who takes his place to foil a plot against the throne. Under Richard Quine's direction, the action and pageantry in gorgeous settings are treated realistically rather than as fantasy so that the result falls between two stools, being neither funny, nor romantic enough. A-II (PG)

Private Benjamin (1980) When her husband dies on their wedding night, the distraught bride (Goldie Hawn) joins the New Army as an impossibly inept recruit whom boot camp changes into a person able to look after herself, until she meets a rich, handsome French doctor. Some good laughs from old military jokes updated to the coed Army, with Eileen Brennan especially funny as a wacky martinet. Sexual morality is ridiculed in a number of scenes and there is brief nudity and some rough language. O (R)

Private Duty Nurses (1972) Doctors and patients concerned about such matters as racial discrimination, military service and water pollution in sunny Santa Monica devote equal time to gratuitous sexual pursuits with student nurses in waterbeds. Directed by George Armitage, the failed sex farce is devoid of wit, taste and interest. O (R)

Private Eyes (1981) Anemic little slapstick comedy stars Tim Conway and Don Knotts as a Sherlock Holmes-Dr. Watson duo solving a murder in a spooky old house. Director Lang Elliot serves up all the predictable comic cliches of the genre but none of them are very funny. Several mild vulgarisms. A-II (PG)

Private Function, A (1985) With rationing in effect at the end of World War II, an English couple (Michael Palin and Maggie Smith) steal the pig that local dignitaries are secretly fattening up for a banquet celebrating Princess Elizabeth's wedding. The English comedy, directed by Malcolm Mowbray, is slow-moving and leans heavily on vulgar humor some may find offensive. Restrained bedroom scene. A-III (R)

Private Lessons (1981) Housekeeper Sylvia Kristel gives the master's teenage son a hands-on course in sex. Directed by Alan Myerson, it's a failed little exploitation comedy with nudity and graphic sex. O (R)

Private Life of Sherlock Holmes, The (1970) Plodding spy melodrama without much mystery to it takes some extreme liberties with the Conan Doyle character by making the Victorian detective not only a cocaine addict but sexually ambiguous as well. Directed with a heavy hand by Billy Wilder, the lightweight case involves Holmes (Robert Stephens) and Dr. Watson (Colin Blakely) in the search for the missing husband of a mysterious woman (Genevieve Page), with some assistance from Holmes' brother, Mycroft (Christopher Lee). Lacking lightness and imagination, it will irritate Holmes' fans and disappoint others. Some sexual innuendo. A-III (GP)

Private Navy of Sgt. O'Farrell, The (1968) Unfunny World War II comedy set on a Pacific island where O'Farrell (Bob Hope) tries to raise morale on an Army-Navy base by importing some nurses who turn out to be all male except for Phyllis Diller. Director Frank Tashlin can't get much out of the situation except to parody some other films. A-II (G)

Private Parts (1973) Creepy, campy, sex-and-horror movie about a teenage girl who becomes a more or less willing victim to an assortment of sinister types inhabiting a creaky flea-bag hotel managed by her crazed aunt. Directed by Paul Bartel, nudity and cheap thrills abound. O (R)

Private School (1983) Self-described comedy is no more than a B-grade sexploitation movie, from the vulgar lyrics of the opening song to the closing scene where the graduating class simultaneously indulges in an obscene gesture to their headmistress. Directed by Noel Black, it consists of an unremitting stream of sexual scenes, jokes and dialogue. O (R)

Privates on Parade (1984) Uneven British satire about a motley collection of misfit soldiers who, under the flamboyant leadership of a homosexual director (Dennis Quilty), put on a variety show for troops fighting Communist guerrillas in 1948 Malaya and, thanks to invincible stupidity of their unit commander (John Cleese), become directly involved in the conflict. Director Michael Blakemore scores enough satiric hits to overcome its excess of double entendres, a bit of blasphemy, a brief bedroom scene involving nudity and its abundance of homosexual references. A-III (R)

Privilege (1967) Uneven British cautionary tale about the use of the mass media to manipulate and control public opinion, as seen in the case of a pop singing star (Paul Jones). Directed by Peter Watkins, there is more flash than substance, so that its unfocused indignation blunts its criticism and ultimately leaves viewers without a constructive point of view. A-IV (br)

Prizzi's Honor (1985) Middle-aged man (Jack Nicholson) falls in love with a beautiful and mysterious woman (Kathleen Turner) and she with him. It turns out they are both in the same line of work, but since that happens to be killing people, it makes for complications once they're married. Though this very black comedy is directed with great skill and flair by John Huston, its level of violence is extremely mature fare and not suited to everybody's taste. A-IV (R)

Prodigal, The (1983) Produced by the Rev. Billy Graham's organization, the movie is a modern retelling of the parable about the repentance of a man who squandered his inheritance but, despite some fine acting and good intentions, it doesn't quite come together as persuasive drama. Its shortcomings, however, do not keep it from being inspirational family entertainment. A-II (PG)

Producers, The (1967) Farce about an accountant (Gene Wilder) who gets involved with would-be producer (Zero Mostel) of a buoyant musical based on the life of Hitler. Some of the laughs are a little sick around the edges, but those who don't mind bawdy and blatant satire should survive the experience. Director Mel Brooks gets a brilliant comic performance from Mostel, well supported by Wilder. Matter of comic taste. O (br)

Professionals, The (1966) Four soldiers of fortune (Lee Marvin, Burt Lancaster, Woody Strode and Robert Ryan) are hired to rescue a woman (Claudia Cardinale) being held for ransom by a Mexican bandit (Jack Palance). What raises this above the level of the average action adventure movie is the stylish manner and steady pace of director Richard Brooks' homage to the special skills of a group. Some brutal violence, coarse language and several sensuous scenes. A-III (br)

Project X (1968) Futuristic, science-fiction reconstruction of the 22nd century, in which the quality of life has drastically changed but the ideological tensions between East and West have persisted. In the end, it turns out that the movie's pretensions and sometimes effective special effects are used for nothing more than a routine secret agents melodrama that might as well have taken place in the present. A-II (br)

Project X (1987) Unpleasant military monkey business is challenged by altruistic recruit with a social conscience (Matthew Broderick) in this story about lovable chimps used for flight simulation testing. His attempt to help them escape nearly causes a nuclear disaster. Director Jonathan Kaplan's lightweight tale of youthful idealism vs. duty is shareable family entertainment, though there is a touch of rough language. A-II (PG)

Projectionist, The (1971) Chuck McCann runs the projector in a New York movie theater and is given to lapsing into movie-based fantasies in which he becomes Capt. Flash, has conversations with Bogart, feasts in Babylon, shoots down Ming's space ship and cavorts with King Kong. Directed by Harry Hurwitz, its collection of movie nostalgia is somewhat self-indulgent but should delight the buffs and has enough off-beat comedy for the uninitiated to enjoy. Some brief sexual fantasies. A-III (GP)

Prologue (1970) Stilted, uneven, and technically inferior study of war dissenters during the riots at the Chicago Democratic Convention in 1968. Directed from a Canadian perspective by Robin Spry, the black-and-white semi-documentary pretentiously contrasts the brutality of the police with gentle lovemakers in a commune. Gratuitous nudity. O (br)

Prom Night (1980) Mad killer seeks revenge by stalking high school students on the night of the big dance and slashing their throats whenever they stray from the dance floor. Directed by Paul Lynch, the horror story is more dumb than nasty, but some of its grisly scenes are excessively graphic. O (R)

Promise Her Anything (1966) Mediocre romantic comedy about a recent widow (Leslie Caron), on the lookout for a new father for her young son, settles first on her boss (Robert Cummings) but then finds true love with a low-budget moviemaker (Warren Beatty). Director Arthur Hiller's predictable story offers little new in an old scenario. A-III (br)

Promise at Dawn (1970) French adaptation of

novelist Romain Gary's memoir of his boyhood days and aspirations living with his loving mother (Melina Mercouri) in the Leningrad of the 1920s. Directed by Jules Dassin, these poignant recollections become a buoyantly human portrait, rich in the cultural humor and solid values that stoke the human spirit's inexhaustible striving for identity and achievement. A scene dealing with the young man's sexual awakening and his mother's response require a mature perspective. A-III (GP)

Promise, The (1979) Silly tearjerker about a woman (Kathleen Quinlan), disfigured in an auto accident, who is separated from her lover (Stephen Collins) when his wealthy mother (Beatrice Straight) offers to pay for expensive plastic surgery, provided she never see her son again. Directed by Gilbert Cates, the sentimental, overwrought melodrama has a permissive attitude about premarital sex. A-III (PG)

Promised Lands (1974) Directed by Susan Sontag, this documentary about Israel at the time of the October War proves a poetic and moving meditation on the tragedy of a nation's struggle for existence in a land claimed by others. From its opening shots of the diverse cultural traditions that co-exist in Israel to its concluding episode of a soldier being treated for battle trauma, the film's images connect again and again with the precise detail or telling scene to express the bewildering complexity of the problems facing this beleaguered state. A-II (nr)

Promises in the Dark (1979) Counterpointing the decline of a 17-year-old terminal cancer patient (Kathleen Beller) with her doctor's (Marsha Mason) renewed interest in romance after the experience of bitter divorce, producer-director Jerome Hellman offers us a sentimental melodrama that contains scattered bits of insight. The movie does not go too deeply into the complex moral problems it raises, notably the cutting off of life-sustaining systems when life ceases to be viable. A-IV (PG)

Prophecy (1979) When a health department doctor (Robert Foxworth) takes his pregnant wife (Talia Shire) on an assignment checking the environmental effects of a paper mill in the Maine woods, they become the target of an exceptionally ill-tempered mutant. Everything about director John Frankenheimer's ecological shocker is so ludicrous and inept that it overwhelms the ecological message it's supposedly plugging. Some intense violence. A-III (PG)

Protector, The (1985) Two New York policemen (Jackie Chan and Danny Aiello) wreak havoc in Hong Kong where they have gone to break up a drug ring in a mindlessly violent movie written and directed by James Glickenhaus. Besides the violence there is some exploitative nudity. O (R)

Protocol (1984) Dizzy cocktail waitress (Goldie Hawn) becomes a national heroine when she thwarts the assassination of a visiting Arab leader which gives some nasty State Department types the idea of using her as a diplomatic pawn. Directed by Herbert Ross, it's a routine comedy vehicle for its star who would be better if the role was just a bit less lovable and cute. Sexually oriented humor, including depicting Arabs throughout as oversexed buffoons. A-II (PG)

Providence (1977) Uneven British drama about a 78-year-old novelist (John Gielgud) trying to come up with a story interweaving fantasies about his son (Dirk Bogarde), his son's wife (Ellen Bur-

styn), her friend (David Warner) and his son's imaginary mistress (Elaine Stritch). Director Alain Resnais fails to create any consistent emotional mood for scriptwriter David Mercer's indulgent jumping back and forth in time and space to indicate a failing imagination. Gielgud's character is not only foul-mouthed and lecherous, but is excessively graphic in his complaints about failing bodily functions set against unpleasant shots of his autopsy. O (R)

Prudence and the Pill (1968) Brittle British comedy with Deborah Kerr and David Niven dealing with the advent and repercussions of the contraceptive pill in a manner that overlooks the basic issues of premarital sex, adultery and divorce. When two households take to underhanded pill-swapping for various reasons, the final result is two marriages, two divorces and remarriages and babies under every cabbage leaf. Despite a few smiles, director Fielder Cook gets them by ignoring the emotional upheaval that such finagling would produce. O (R)

Psychic Killer (1976) Lightweight horror movie about a man (Jim Hutton) who projects mental powers to avenge his unjust incarceration in a mental institution. Director Raymond Danton uses parapsychology to explain the plot's series of gruesome murders but nothing can justify their bloody detail, the nudity or the movie's resolution in vigilante justice. O (PG)

Psycho II (1983) Norman Bates (Anthony Perkins) is declared sane and comes home after more than 20 years in a mental institution. This time poor Norman is the victim of a mother and daughter (Vera Miles and Meg Tilly) who are determined to push him over the edge again so that he has to be recommitted. Director Richard Franklin diminishes tensions by the broad in-joke quality of the whole enterprise but the conclusion is explicitly graphic in its bloody violence. O (R)

Psycho III (1986) Tony Perkins directs and stars in this intense, brutally sardonic drama in which Norman Bates once again goes over the edge providing the audience with a parade of gruesomely victimized women in various states of undress. Excessive mix of sex and violence. O (R)

Psychopath, The (1966) Mild British mystery thriller directed by Freddie Francis in which the investigation of four murders leads a London police inspection (Patrick Wymark) to the strange house of widow (Margaret Johnston) confined to a wheelchair. Stylized violence. A-II (br)

Psych-Out (1968) Cliched story of hippie life in San Francisco's Haight-Ashbury district with Susan Strasberg as a deaf teenage runaway and Dean Stockwell as a freaked-out guru. Director Richard Rush tries to balance his picture of the dropout lifestyle but conventional society is shown as responsible for such alienation. Confused treatment of violence, sex and drugs. A-III (br)

Psychout for Murder (1971) Rossano Brazzi plays the head of a wealthy but depraved Italian family and has a luscious offspring (Adrienne La Russa) whose heart, deep down inside, only belongs to Daddy. Directed by Edward Ross, its sordid story of revenge and incest has no redeeming elements. O (R)

Public Eye (1972) Witty British production about an insecure newlywed (Michael Jayston) who hires a private eye (Topol) to tail his capricious wife (Mia Farrow). Detective and wife flirt innocently after they discover a bond of attraction in their mutually unorthodox personalities. Director Carol Reed proves his adeptness at handling romantic comedy as he blends the sprightly performances of the three stars with a sumptuous tour of London. A-II (G)

Pufnstuf (1970)   Director Hollingsworth Morse's merry romp of song, dance and adventure features young Jack Wild as a human visitor to the magical land of Living Island, home of a dotty assortment of colorful stuffed animals overseen by their gentle dragon of a mayor, the Hon. H.R. Pufnstuf. Kids will enjoy the antics, although the flute-napping Witchiepoo (Billie Hayes) makes up in decibels what she lacks in scariness. Grown-ups might enjoy it too, especially those who like the idea of an absent-minded owl who sounds like Ed Wynn, a blind bat-messenger who keeps banging into walls, and a cheerful lion who does a pretty good turn at W.C. Fields. A-I (G)

Pulp (1972)   Michael Caine plays a hack author hired to ghost-write the memoirs of aging gangster-movie actor Mickey Rooney, but soon discovers himself in the middle of a murder caper not unlike the plots of any number of his own cheap novels. Though occasionally very funny, director Michael Hodges cannot sustain his spoof on old Hollywood crime movies as a coherent whole. Some mature references. A-III (PG)

Pumping Iron (1977)   Unassuming documentary about the world of body builders, singling out for major consideration Austrian-born Arnold Schwarzenegger, six-time winner of the "Mr. Olympia" title. Directed by George Butler and Robert Fiore, the film has some human touches that are entertaining and sometimes moving but its adulation of Schwarzenegger's limited view of life and his blunt advocacy of hedonism makes this questionable material for younger viewers. A-III (PG)

Pumping Iron II: The Women (1985)   Mostly boring documentary by George Butler and Charles Gaines (who also made the original) about women bodybuilders participating in Las Vegas competition. Snide approach to its subject leaves a bad taste. Some brief partial nudity and a general air of vulgarity. A-III (nr)

Punishment Park (1971)   Social drama imagines a kangaroo court of conservative Americans conducting the trials of an assortment of conscientious objectors, hippies and peaceniks in a tent on the edge of the Mojave Desert whose heat is part of the terrors awaiting those sentenced for punishment. Directed by Peter Watkins, the nearsighted political tract about repression and dissent is steeped in brutality and foul language which antagonize rather than inspire, provoke disdain rather than assent. A-IV (R)

Puppet on a Chain (1972)   British adaptation of the Alistair MacLean novel about Interpol agents (Sven-Bertil Taube and Barabara Parkins) assigned to uncover the Amsterdam drug connection. Directed by Geoffrey Reeve, the movie's high point is a speedboat chase through the canals of Amsterdam, but the rest of it goes from run-of-the-mill to dull. Some sadistic violence is not redeemed by its sophomoric preaching on the fate of a teenage drug addict who figures in the plot. A-III (PG)

Purple Hearts (1984)   Mediocre Vietnam War soap opera about the efforts of a Navy doctor (Ken Wahl) and nurse (Cheryl Ladd) to resolve all the obstacles that stand in the way of the inevitable clinch. Directed by Sidney J. Furie, the movie's sentiments are about as genuine as the contrived and improbable dialogue that passes here for the utterances of brave men under fire. Premarital sex figures in the theme and there is one restrained bedroom scene in addition to some very rough language. A-III (R)

Purple Rain (1984)   Rock star Prince's film debut features graphic sex, nudity, and an outrageous treatment of women that goes beyond anything demanded by plot considerations. O (R)

Purple Rose of Cairo, The (1985)   Woody Allen comedy about a Depression-era housewife (Mia Farrow), married to an insensitive brute (Danny Aiello), whose only solace is going to the movies. One day, while watching a romance, its handsome young hero (Jeff Daniels) steps out of the screen into the audience and tells her that he loves her. There are some good moments and some laughs, but the comedy is not especially inspired and its rather grim, realistic mood suggests pretensions to seriousness that the movie is incapable of supporting. A-II (PG)

Pursuit of D.B. Cooper, The (1981)   Slapdash chase-comedy inspired by a successful 1971 airplane hijacking and robbery, is such mediocre fare that even so capable an actor as Robert Duvall looks bad in his role of determined insurance investigator. Treat Williams fares even worse as the happy-go-lucky criminal who is less than endearing. Though director Roger Spottiswoode's movie plays on a cartoon level, its benign attitude toward crime and an amorous sequence are adult material. A-III (PG)

Pursuit of Happiness (1971)   Failed melodrama about a campus drop-out (Michael Sarrazin), who has turned his back on both his WASP background and synthetic college radicals, winds up in jail and in the end decides to escape to Canada with his girl friend (Barbara Hershey). Directed by Robert Mulligan, the manipulative plot loads the deck against society, making it to blame for the problems of its misguided, misunderstood young man. There are some real issues here but they are treated only superficially. Several silly nude scenes. A-IV (GP)

Pussycat, Pussycat, I Love You (1970)   Utterly dismissable sex farce about a writer (Ian McShane) who cheats on his wife (Anne Calder-Marshall) and her retaliation in kind. Written and directed by Rod Amateau, it is a totally inept production devoid of any but sophomoric humor. The theme involves adultery, with some nudity and tasteless sight gags. O (PG)

Putney Swope (1969)   Uneven satire in which blacks take over a Madison Avenue advertising agency and, despite their ban on alcohol, cigarette and war-toy advertising, their basic philosophy is as money-oriented as their white predecessors. Director Robert Downey's off-beat, irreverent humor uses a machine-gun barrage of complex irony and slapstick imagery, only some of which hit their intended targets. Very casual approach to sex, some scenes of extensive nudity and rough language. O (R)

Puzzle of a Downfall Child (1970)   Tired melodrama starring Faye Dunaway in the story of a fashion model's rise to the top where she leads a life of illusion and delusion. The tale has been told too many times and in too many better versions than this particularly hollow attempt by director Jerry Schatzberg. Some nudity and sexual references. A-III (R)

Pyx, The (1973)   Montreal hooker (Karen Black) falls to her death from a high rise, clutching a pyx (a container holding communion wafers) and wearing an inverted cross around her neck. Investigating her death, a detective (Christopher Plummer) uncovers a strange underworld where drugs, prostitution and religious perversion go hand in hand. Directed by Harvey Hart, the occult mystery's treatment of the diabolic makes a fairly intriguing horror fantasy, though its inversion of religious symbols is disturbing and at times repulsive. A-IV (R)

Q

Q (1982)   Failed horror movie about the feeding habits of a giant predatory bird, once an Aztec god but now reduced to living in a cramped nest in the peak of the Chrysler Building and grabbing a bite wherever she can. David Carradine, Candy Clark and Michael Moriarty are featured in this lackluster, ludicrous chiller produced and directed by Larry Cohen. Some disgusting violence, brief nudity and much foul language. O (R)

Quackser Fortune Has a Cousin in the Bronx (1970)   He also has an unusual profession collecting horse manure in the Dublin streets for sale to gardening ladies, an offbeat girl friend (Margot Kidder) and all of the bluff humor, warmth, rascality and pathos too often assigned to movie Irishmen. Fortunately, Quackser (so dubbed because of the duck sounds he made as a wee babe) is played by Gene Wilder, and without him, director Waris Hussein's movie would be just another charming but slight slice of Irish life. Some fairly graphic love scenes make it adult fare. A-III (R/PG)

Quadrophenia (1979)   British musical (whose title comes from "The Who" album that serves as the score) re-creates in gritty, vital fashion the world of the Mods and the Rockers, rival youth gangs of the 1960s who affected different versions of rebellion against the values of their working-class parents. Director Frank Roddam fails to offer any perspective on the characters and environment he has so skillfully evoked and the movie ends in an anarchistic, morally ambiguous scene. Graphic depiction of drug abuse and sexual promiscuity as well as rough language. A-IV (R)

Queen of Blood (1966)   Routine horror movie written and directed by Curtis Harrington features a futuristic gimmick and stars Basil Rathbone and John Saxon. A-I (br)

Queens, The (1967)   Italian movie with four stories directed by Mauro Bolognini, Mario Monicelli, Antonio Pietrangeli and Luciano Salce tends to be dehumanizing in its one-sidedly negative view of women (Monica Vitti, Claudia Cardinale, Raquel Welch and Capuchine). O (br)

Quest for Fire (1982)   Ludicrously serious prehistoric adventure tale about three warriors (Everett McGill, Ron Perlman and Nameer Eli-Kadi) whose search for fire when that of their clan has been extinguished by a marauding band of Neanderthals leads to a humanizing encounter with a more culturally advanced girl (Rae Dawn Chong) who helps them learn to laugh and even fall in love. Directed by Jean-Jacques Annaud who co-scripted with Gerard Brach, its attempts at authenticity are made even more ludicrous by brutal sex scenes, violent combat and other assorted caveman antics. O (R)

Quicksilver (1986)   Ill-conceived youth movie in which a young stockbroker (Kevin Bacon) has a run of bad luck, quits the market to become a bicycle courier and saves his new working-class friends from dope pushers, loan sharks and dead-end jobs. Directed by Tom Donnelly, it is a phony picture of a teenage hero demonstrating that immaturity and juvenile behavior can lead to success. A-III (PG)

Quiet Cool (1986)   When a gang of dope addicts brutally murder a peaceful family, they themselves are hunted down and killed in an extraordinarily violent and sadistic manner. The crude and bloody story encourages vigilantism. O (R)

Quiet Days in Clichy (1970)   Screen version of a Henry Miller novel about the dehumanized sexual adventures of two writers down and out in Paris. The result is human debasement, made all the worse by an irrelevant scatological music-lyric soundtrack supplied by Country Joe McDonald. O (nr)

Quiet Earth, The (1986)   New Zealand scientist (Bruno Lawrence) awakes one morning to discover that he is the last man alive after a U.S. celestial experiment goes haywire. Director Geoff Murphy's quaint science fiction mystery has some suspense and a warning against tampering with the laws of nature. Several scenes with nudity. A-III (nr)

Quiet Place in the Country, A (1970)   When a troubled abstract-expressionist artist (Franco Nero) is placed in an institution (a nice quiet place in the country) by his mistress (Vanessa Redgrave), his madness crystalizes into an object of tediousness rather than of possible interest. Director Elio Petri chooses to use tricky nude shots and violent erotic dreams to hold attention, but the movie crumbles as it goes all out for slick sensationalism. O (R)

Quiller Memorandum, The (1967)   Resurgence of Nazism in post-war Germany is the background for this spy story with George Segal, Max von Sydow, Senta Berger and Alec Guinness in a cameo. Director Michael Anderson gets some suspenseful moments in a convoluted thriller that is spun out beyond its limits. A-III (br)

Quintet (1979)   Director Robert Altman's failed futuristic fable about six citizens of an ice-bound, dying world engaged in a lethal cat and mouse game of survival that gives the movie its title. Paul Newman, Bibi Andersson, Fernando Rey, and Vittorio Gassman head the fur-swathed cast of an ambitious but hapless attempt to philosphize about the meaning of life. Graphic depiction of brutal killings. O (R)

R

Ra Expeditions, The (1972)   Documentary record of anthropologist Thor Heyerdahl's voyage from Africa to the Americas in a papyrus reed boat called the Ra, the name of an Egyptian god. Using a reed craft of early Mediterranean design, Heyerdahl set out to demonstrate that such a ship could stand the long voyage between hemispheres, and does on a second try. Produced and directed by Lennart Ehrenberg, the documentary enables a vicarious sharing of adventure on high seas. A-I (G)

Rabbit, Run (1971)   Failed screen version of John Updike's dark and brooding novel probing the shadowed corners of the mind of an irresponsible young man (James Caan) who persists in chasing illusions and women with equal fervor, resulting in a ruined marriage and shattered dreams. Director Jack Smight dissipates the novel's passionate intensity by concentrating on the surface level of the action. Graphic sexual depictions. O (R)

Rabbit Test (1978) Failed sex farce about the world's first pregnant man is comedienne Joan Rivers' debut as a director. Posing a feminist satire, the effort lacks the wit and satiric nuance that might have saved it from being ploddingly tasteless and offensive. Unfunny jokes about religious beliefs are scattered throughout this indelicate comedy. O (PG)

Rabid (1977) Canadian production about a young woman (porno star Marilyn Chambers) who undergoes plastic surgery only to find herself turned into a vampire who soon has a good portion of the population of Montreal going green in the face, frothing at the mouth and biting one another. Directed by David Cronenberg, it's a nauseating, gory piece of trash. O (R)

Race for Your Life, Charlie Brown (1977) Feature cartoon based on the Charles M. Schulz comic strip which tells of the adventures and perils that the Peanuts characters encounter while spending the summer at a wilderness camp out West. Though little of the subtlety of Schulz at his best is represented, the movie will entertain younger children. A-I (G)

Race with the Devil (1975) Businessmen (Warren Oates and Peter Fonda) on a vacation trip with their wives inadvertently come upon some Satanists at their rituals and then are pursued across Texas by the vengeful cultists. Directed by Jack Starrett, the silly horror movie has a bad script, a few scares and some bloodshed. A-III (PG)

Rachel, Rachel (1968) Joanne Woodward plays a painfully lonely and somewhat repressed woman teaching school in a small midwestern town and concerned about becoming a dowdy spinster. When an old school chum (James Olsen) visits, she falls hopelessly in love and has a brief, intense affair that ends harshly and with bitterness. Directed by Paul Newman, the story is poignant and terribly human with excellent performances. A-III (R)

Racing with the Moon (1984) Likable teenager (Sean Penn), finishing high school during World War II, falls for a winsome California beauty (Elizabeth McGovern) and both try to get money for a friend's abortion. Nostalgic romance from director Richard Benjamin captures the atmosphere and the mood of the period but concentrates too heavily on the sexual nature of youthful relationships. Some nudity and a benign view of premarital sex. O (R/PG appeal)

Rad (1986) Talia Shire stars in her own production of a story about a teenage bike enthusiast who overcomes an unscrupulous businessman's plot to keep him from winning a national championship race. Directed by Hal Needham, it is a pretentious and simplistic tale and its execution is graceless and unrewarding. Several obscene gestures by Ray Walston in a cameo role and some rough language by a little girl seem quite unnecessary. A-II (PG)

Radio Days (1987) Writer-director Woody Allen celebrates the positive impact of radio on the lives of a New York family which resembles his own in this nostalgic view of the 1940s. Two women (Dianne Wiest and Mia Farrow) who seek romance via different paths, provide an amiable leitmotif. However, the values of that era have

been lost and even the fond memories are fading. A-II (PG)

Radioactive Dreams (1986) Two youths leave their bomb shelters after 15 years to explore the post-nuclear world outside. Passing through a desolate and bleak landscape, they encounter a vile assortment of mutants and perverted road life. Many visual effects are used by director Albert Pyun simply to frame violence, brutality, nudity and profanity. O (R)

Rafferty and the Gold Dust Twins (1975) Bumbling Los Angeles driving-test examiner (Alan Arkin) is kidnapped by roving hippies (Sally Kellerman and Mackenzie Phillips) and forced at gunpoint to drive them to New Orleans. Directed by Dick Richards, everything about this predictable heart-tug road movie is bogus, including the realistic language and frequently sordid situations. O (R)

Raga (1971) American documentary provides an historical introduction to the musical heritage of India and Ravi Shankar's part in introducing it to Western audiences. Produced and directed by Howard Worth, the account is filled with insights about the individual and the cultural diffusion engendered by modern world communications. A-I (nr)

Rage (1972) After camping out with his boy one night, an Arizona sheep farmer (George C. Scott) wakes to the horror of finding his son and flock dying in convulsions. When he finally learns that a secret military test of nerve gas is responsible, he goes beserk and sets out to destroy those he considers responsible. The story of a decent man crushed by a technocracy unconcerned with the individual is told by Scott in his debut as a director in purely melodramatic terms with two-dimensional figures and plot contrivances. Yet it is close enough to reality to trouble any viewer's complacency, though its violent conclusion undercuts the meaning of what precedes these scenes of destruction. A-III (PG)

Raggedy Ann and Andy (1977) Feature-length musical cartoon inspired by the long-time childhood favorites is, unfortunately, distinguished more by the technical excellence of Richard Williams' animation than by any real creative verve or even sense of imagination. The songs are mostly forgettable and there is no story line of any significance to keep children's attention. A-I (G)

Raggedy Man (1981) A young divorcee (Sissy Spacek) in a small Texas town during the Second World War has a brief romance with a sailor passing through (Eric Roberts) and fends off the unwelcome attentions of two local louts who threaten her and her two boys. Director Jack Fisk fails badly in the attempt to mix childlike whimsey, light romance and Gothic terror. Some violence and premarital sex are central to the plot. A-III (PG)

Raging Bull (1980) Hard-edged, uncompromising portrait of former middleweight boxing champ, Jake La Motta (Robert De Niro in an outstanding performance) and his agonizing relationship with his second wife (Cathy Moriarity) and his brother (Joe Pesci). Director Martin Scorsese's stark black-and-white treatment conveys La Motta's often grim, violently hostile personality, which, the film suggests was born of sexual problems. Brutal fight scenes, a graphic bedroom sequence and rough language. A-III (R)

Ragman's Daughter, The (1974) British bittersweet romance between a young tough who steals out of need and his hopelessly middle-class girl friend who does it for kicks. Scripted by Alan Sillitoe and directed by Harold Becker, the predictable plot lacks energy and drive as well as credibility. A-III (nr)

Ragtime (1981) Loose, sporadically effective adaptation of the E.L. Doctorow patchwork novel about some representative Americans at the turn of the century. Notable among them are James Cagney as the police commissioner of New York City and a black piano player (Harold E. Rollins, Jr.) who turns into a revolutionary combating social injustice. Directed by Milos Forman, it succeeds as a lavish historical re-creation but gets low grades in the matter of credible characterization. An excessively extended sequence involving partial nudity and some rough language. A-IV (PG)

Raid on Rommel (1971) World War II adventure gasps along with Richard Burton's commandos as they fight Rommel's Afrika Korps across the Sahara and through Tobruk to an awaiting rescue unit, leaving a path of mayhem and devastation in their wake. Directed by Henry Hathaway, the action sequences are made up of stock footage and darkened sequences lifted from the 1966 "Tobruk." Ludicrous desert action histrionics. A-III (PG)

Raiders of the Lost Ark (1981) Tongue-in-cheek action melodrama about Indiana Jones, an archeologist-adventurer (Harrison Ford), and his feisty girlfriend (Karen Allen) who save the biblical Ark of the Covenant for the good old U.S.A. despite the worst efforts of a clutch of Nazi villains. Director Steven Spielberg's attempt to recapture the excitement of the old movie serials becomes tiresome and repetitious in its reliance upon constant action. Intense violence, gruesome special effects and a questionable use of something as sacred as the Ark as a source of destructive power. A-III (PG)

Railroad Man, The (1965) Series of misfortunes plague a working-class family in Italy after World War I. The sincerity of the characterizations more than outweigh the contrivances of the plot. Pietro Germi both directs and stars as the head of the family but it is a child actor (Eduardo Nevola) who will steal the affection of even the most cynical viewer. A-II (br)

Railway Children, The (1971) Three children (Jenny Agutter, Sally Thomsett and Gary Warren) and their mother (Dinah Sheridan) are forced to move from their comfy Victorian mansion to an austere cottage in the country along the railway tracks while they wait expectantly for their Daddy to be cleared of false charges. Directed by Lionel Jeffries, the entire production is colored with an instinctive, childlike innocence and loyalty providing viewers of all ages with a warming and reassuring conviction that even in the most adverse times hope and love can, indeed must, exist. A-I (G)

Rain for a Dusty Summer (1972) Humberto Almazan, a popular Mexican actor who retired from the screen at the age of 35 to become a missionary priest, returns to portray Father Miguel Pro, a Mexican priest whose ministry during a time of religious oppression in the 1920s made him a folk hero and, ultimately, a martyr. Unfortunately, Arthur Lubin's heavy-handed direction of an oversimplified, melodramatic script makes the religious theme appear absurd and prevents a talented cast (including Ernest Borgnine as the dictator)

from developing any but superficial characterizations, especially with the flat, expressionless dubbing of the mostly Spanish-speaking cast. Restrained violence. A-II (GP)

Rain People, The (1969) Shirley Knight plays a pregnant woman fleeing husband and home to come to terms with her womanhood and incomplete sense of fulfillment. Written and directed by Francis Ford Coppola, the movie's theme of flight from responsibility is treated with poetic intensity and subtle nuance. Some violence and sexual references. A-III (PG)

Rainbow Brite and the Star Stealer (1985) In her film debut, Rainbow Brite, the creation of toy manufacturers, must save the universe from destruction. Not strong on imagination or substance but lots of color and action designed to sell dolls to the toddler crowd. A- I (G)

Raise the Titanic! (1980) Failed action melodrama with Jason Robards and Richard Jordan in a story about attempts by American and Russian soldiers of fortune to recover rare minerals from the sunken luxury liner. Director Jerry Jameson's lackluster underwater adventure is unbelievably lethargic and muddleheaded. A-II (PG)

Raisin in the Sun, A (1961) Fine screen version of the Lorraine Hansberry play about a young black man in a Chicago slum (Sidney Poitier) whose ambitions for getting ahead in the world come into conflict with his mother (Claudia McNeil in a great performance). What keeps this story about the evils of segregation from being dated is that director Daniel Petrie and a very capable cast have focused their energies on human values rather than ready-made solutions. A-II (br)

Raising Arizona (1987) Nicolas Cage and Holly Hunter play a simple-minded childless couple who kidnap one of a set of quintuplets to raise as their own in this madcap comedy from the Coen brothers, Joel and Ethan. Stridently-effective parody of socially conscious drama has some vulgar and brutal moments played with deadpan intensity by Cage and a host of crude and profane heavies, perfectly restrained at the borderline of good taste. A-III (PG-13)

Rambo (see: "First Blood")

Rambo: First Blood Part II (1985) Rambo (Sylvester Stallone) is released from prison to undertake a secret mission to free Americans still being held in Vietnam and, after much slaughter, does so only to face the traitor who wanted the mission to fail. Playing shamelessly upon the fears and hopes of the relatives of MIA's, this comic-strip movie features excessive violence. O (R)

Ramparts of Clay (1971) French director Jean-Louis Bertucelli uses scenes of everyday life in a small Tunisian village at the edge of the Sahara to tell the story of a young woman (Leila Schenna) who can no longer accept the old patterns in which she has been raised. This is a beautiful work showing the dignity of a simple way of life, while conscious of the irreversible forces that will transform it. A-II (GP)

Ran (1985) Samurai version of Shakespeare's King Lear by director Akira Kurosawa is, unfortunately, little more than an opulently staged historical pageant, lacking pathos and tragic force. Many battle scenes but the violence is stylized. A-II (R)

Rancho Deluxe (1975) Jeff Bridges and Sam Waterson star as footloose and free-spirited modern rustlers finally apprehended by a bumbling Slim Pickens. Director Frank Perry's unfunny comedy is further undone by nudity and graphic sexuality. O (R)

Rape of Love (1979) Difficult French drama about an attractive, self-possessed and quite intelligent young nurse (Nathalie Nell) who is abducted by four men and brutally raped. Directed by Yannick Bellon, it is a serious attempt to deal with a detestable crime of violence and its consequences, not only for the victim, her fiance, family and friends, but also for the rapists and society as a whole. Despite its good intentions, however, the rape scene is unnecessarily graphic and extended. O (nr)

Rappin' (1985) A young ex-convict adept at rapping (the street art of fast talking) comes to the aid of the urban poor victimized by nasty landlords and the like. The actors, under Joel Silberg's direction, are personable but the flimsy story is nothing but a frame for a skill that's not likely to enthrall most viewers. A-II (PG)

Rascal (1969) A boy (Bill Mumy), a dog and a mischievous racoon spend a summer together in Small Town, U.S.A., in the innocent days just before World War I. Director Norman Tokar keeps the action lively (especially that of Rascal, the racoon) and the sentiment wholesome in this Disney production celebrating the virtues of rural America. A-I (G)

Rasputin (1966) Failed British dramatization of a sinister monk (Christopher Lee) in the Czar's court before the Russian Revolution. Directed by Don Sharp, the evil actions depicted are excessive in their visual detail. O (br)

Ratboy (1986) A boy whose facial deformity makes him look like a rodent becomes exploited for monetary gain. Directed by actress Sandra Locke (who also plays a leading role as one of those taking advantage of the boy), this version of the beauty-and-the beast fable lacks any convincing insight and relies upon conventional plot devices, including negative stereotyping of black Los Angelinos and people in the entertainment business. Liberal sprinklings of profanity. A-III (PG-13)

Raw Deal (1986) Fueled by pride and a promise, a small town sheriff (Arnold Schwarzenegger) massacres an entire crime syndicate in a bloody shoot-out providing a primitive brand of justice on the behalf of the slain son of his former FBI buddy (Darren McGavin). The excessive violence isn't justified by plot or characterization. O (R)

Razor in the Flesh (1974) Brazilian drama about a prostitute tormented by her pimp who in turn is taunted by a homosexual until the roles are reversed and attacker becomes victim and the story becomes a parable about the interchangeable roles of oppressor and oppressed. Directed by Braz Chediak, the movie is about characters living at the last extremities of humanity, vividly reacting with the desperation of those who can only hurt others and themselves because they have nothing left to hope for. As a reminder of our common human fraility, it cuts to the bone. A-IV (R)

Razor's Edge, The (1984) The path to salvation is hard in this ill-conceived and shallow remake of the 1946 version of the W. Somerset Maugham novel. Bill Murray plays a World War I veteran who travels in Europe to find the meaning of life and some measure of inner peace. Under the direction of John Byrum, Murray has difficulty displaying the emotion and sensitivity required by the role. Empty parable with some harsh language. A-III (PG-13)

Re-Animator (1985) In this abysmal effort, a zealous young scientist (Jeffrey Combs) develops a serum to raise the dead. Directed by Stuart Gordon, it's an abundantly gory affair made all the more revolting by its attempts at grisly humor. O (R rating surrendered by distributor and no longer applies)

Real Genius (1985) When a college science whiz (Val Kilmer) and his fellow students discover they have been tricked by their professor (William Atherton) into helping create a laser weapon for the military establishment, they revolt and destroy their work. Director Martha Coolidge is unable to get any laughs from this failed satire on higher education. Some vulgar language and sexual promiscuity A-III (PG)

Real Life (1979) Episodic comedy, written and directed by comedian Albert Brooks, in which he plays the role of a moviemaker who wants to capture on film the life of a real American family, a Phoenix veterinarian (Charles Grodin), his wife (Francis Lee McCain) and their two children. While frequently hilarious, with a touch of black humor, many of the jokes are adult in nature but probably not too strong for older teenagers. A-III (PG)

Rebellion in Patagonia (1977) When armed violence broke out in 1921 between the landowners and striking workers of Patagonia, Argentina's southernmost state, the government intervened by sending in troops to help the landowners crush the workers. Large-scale Argentinian re-creation directed by Hector Olivera has much colorful action with hard-riding gaucho bands pitted against columns of soldiers in vintage autos. There are, however, some strong scenes of violence illustrating the inequities of power and class. A-III (nr)

Reckless (1984) Pretentious, slow-moving account of star-crossed teenaged lovers (Aidan Quinn and Daryl Hannah) in a grimy, impoverished steel town treads numbingly familiar ground. Director James Foley has found no way to recharge the old formula nor has writer Chris Columbus discovered anything of significance. Aimed at a teenage audience, it has an abundance of nudity and graphic sex. O (R)

Reckoning, The (1970) Nicol Williamson gives a brilliant performance as a London businessman who drinks too much, drives too fast, uses and abuses women, ruins business rivals, and even commits murder to avenge his father's death back in the Liverpool slum where he grew up. It is a portrait of a ruthless, amoral fellow, and yet director Jack Gold's fast-moving action melodrama takes a reckoning not only of him but of a society that rewards his brand of cut-throat tactics in life as well as the business world. A disturbing movie not intended as escapist fare. A-IV (R)

Red Beard (1969) Japanese character study of a 19th-century doctor (Toshiro Mifune) who must be incredibly tough and unbending in running a clinic for the poor and yet tender and loving in his ministry to those who need his care. Director Akira Kurosawa's movie conveys the complexities of compassion in the person of this hard-headed, single-minded doctor made credible by Mifune's great performance. Realist depictions of the period's crude operating facilities. A-III (nr)

Red Dawn (1984) Director John Milius presents a preposterous and heavy-handed war movie with the premise that the United States has been invaded by Russian and Cuban troops. A group of teenage Rambo's (led by Patrick Swayze and C. Thomas Howell) take up guerrilla warfare to preserve the integrity of America. Because of its violence and its glorification of the macho rather than patriotism, it is not for immature viewers. A-III (PG-13)

Red Mantle, The (see: "Hagbard and Signe")

Red Psalm (1973) Hungarian import uses a 19th-century peasant revolt as a socialist hymn celebrating the collective power of the people in their continuing struggle against oppression. Director Miklos Jancso's lyric flow of images is choreographed to a symphony of folk song and the movie's poetic strength is rooted in its agrarian setting and Eastern European folk traditions. Some may be offended by the work's appropriation of religious symbolism in a revolutionary context. A-IV (nr)

Red Sky at Morning (1971) Mindless World War II coming-of-age story set in New Mexico where a callow youth (Richard Thomas) lusts after a plump schoolmate (Catherine Burns) while his boozy mother (Claire Bloom) needs help fending off amorous "uncles." Directed by James Goldstone, the plot's serious level is hindered by the melodramatic treatment, with moral insights getting lost in the shuffle. A-III (PG)

Red Sonja (1985) Plodding, lackluster sword-and-sorcery movie directed by Richard Fleischer and starring muscleman Arnold Schwarzenegger who helps out a woman warrior intent on vengeance. The only bright spots are bits of unintentional humor. Some violence. A-III (PG-13)

Red Sun (1972) The gimmick for this bloody European Western teams a hard-bitten cowboy (Charles Bronson) with an inscrutable samurai warrior (Toshiro Mifune) in order to track down an outlaw (Alain Delon) who double-crossed the cowboy and dishonored the samurai. Along for the ride is a superfluous prostitute (Ursula Andress). Granted the fantasy plot, director Terence Young treats the derring-do with too little whimsical flair and too much prosaic gore. A-III (GP)

Red Tent, The (1971) Ambitious Italian-Russian re-creation of the crash of an Italian dirigible over the North Pole in the spring of 1928. Under the command of General Umberto Nobile (Peter Finch), the crew pitches a red tent hoping to be spotted by rescuers while three of their members go in search of help. Directed by Mikhail K. Kalatozov, the classic adventure of man vs. nature aspires to epic height but blunders with a frame device of Nobile's tortured memories and feelings of failure. Gruelling picture of struggle for survival that has one of the leading characters (Sean Connery) committing suicide. A-III (G)

Red and the White, The (1969) Hungarian dramatization about the confused struggles between Communists and anti-Communists that broke out in Eastern Europe after the Russian Revolution. Director Miklos Jancso's picture of a violent era when a man's shirt was worth more than his life is set against the bleak but hauntingly beautiful Volga countryside. A-III (nr)

Red, White and Blue (1971) Taking as its pretext the 1971 Report of the Commission on Obscenity and Pornography, the exploitation documentary even gives the President's commissioners a minute or two of interview time before getting to explicit illustrations of the report's subject. O (X)

Reds (1981) Warren Beatty stars as John Reed, the radical American journalist who was in Russia during the 1917 Communist Revolution and whose sympathetic account of it, "Ten Days That Shook the World," made him famous. Also written and directed by Beatty, the movie re-creates on an epic scale Reed's involvement, political and romantic, in the turbulent events of those days until his death in 1920. The result is intelligent and appealing because the sheer spectacle of events is balanced by the personal level, especially his relationship with his wife (Diane Keaton). Benign view of adultery and radical politics, though the context is such that there is no question of blurring the moral perspective of a mature viewer. A-III (R/PG appeal)

Reed: Insurgent Mexico (1974) John Reed, the American newspaper correspondent who gained fame through his reports on the Russian Revolution, had previously covered Mexico in the revolutionary chaos of 1913-1914. Reconstructing this period is a Mexican movie following Reed's sojourn with various rebel units, his struggle to maintain his objectivity about events in the face of his inclinations to side with the oppressed, and his symbolic act of solidarity with the revolution that ends the movie. The result has the feeling of an historical document as well as a convincing character study of an idealist. A-II (nr)

Reefer Madness (1936) Reissue of a movie antique about the evils of marijuana has appeal today apparently because it is so easy to laugh at but also perhaps because it all seems so familiar. It underscores the point, however, that preachy exaggeration is the worst kind of propaganda. A-III (PG)

Reflection of Fear, A (1973) Failed Gothic horror movie about a disturbed young woman (Sandra Locke) who lives with her mother (Mary Ure) in a sinister mansion where a series of gruesome murders take place when her estranged father (Robert Shaw) pays a call. Directed by William Fraker, it has a good cast, moody atmosphere but muddled script with a ludicrous conclusion. Heavy-handed sexual implications. A-III (PG)

Reflections in a Golden Eye (1967) Screen version of the Carson McCullers' novel about the twisted relationships and abnormal inclinations of a homosexual Army officer (Marlon Brando). Directed by John Huston, the movie's treatment of its various characters communicates little insight or compassion. Exploitative nudity. O (br)

Reincarnate, The (1971) Creepy 8,000-year-old man (Jack Creley) convinces a reluctant young sculptor (Jay Reynolds) to give up his body when he explains that a mind transplant involves the deflowering of a young virgin. Wooden acting and leaden script detailing the intricacies and advantages of reincarnation result in occult balderdash, seasoned with some coy titillation. A-III (R/GP appeal)

Reincarnation of Peter Proud, The (1975) Young man (Michael Sarrazin) dreams of his own murder in a previous life and falls in love with the woman (Jennifer O'Neill) who was his daughter in that life. Director J. Lee Thompson's muddled story has frequent nudity and graphic sex scenes. O (R)

Reivers, The (1969) Screen version of William Faulkner's last novel about a 12-year-old boy (Mitch Vogel) from a small Southern town in 1905 who is introduced to some of the realities of the adult world when taken on a trip to Memphis by a devil-may-care cousin (Steve McQueen). Director

Mark Rydell has created a rich bit of Americana that owes as much to Mark Twain as to Faulkner, but its story of growth towards manhood may be perplexing for youngsters, especially a lengthy brothel sequence. A-III (M)

Relations (1971) The stale theme of this Danish exploitation import is the infatuation of a middle-aged businessman (Bjorn Puggard) for a scheming teenager (Gertie Jung) who gets his cash for her procurer-boyfriend (Paul Glargard). Director Hans Abramson prolongs the trio's restless relations to the point of senseless boredom. O (R)

Remember My Name (1979) Woman (Geraldine Chaplin), sent to prison for trying to kill her husband's mistress, returns to harrass her now ex-husband (Anthony Perkins) and his new wife (Berry Berenson), at first from a distance, but then moves in for closer encounters of various kinds. The melodrama is rather flat and listless, further dragged down by mannered performances and the uninspired direction of Alan Rudolph. Rough language and adult situations. A-III (R)

Reminiscences of a Journey to Lithuania (1974) Independent filmmaker Jonas Mekas' record of a visit to the land of his birth is as informal as a family album and as filled with warmth and affection. Mekas serves as an always enthusiastic guide to this celebration of his past through the present and his unpretentious pleasure at showing his family bonds will most likely stimulate remembrances of one's own immigrant roots. A-I (nr)

Remo Williams: The Adventure Begins (1985) A New York policeman (Fred Ward) who was apparently slain in an encounter with muggers has actually been given a new identity as a member of a secret organization dedicated to seeing that justice is done despite a defective legal system. Though amoral in concept, director Guy Hamilton's movie is so divorced from reality that it is for the most part inoffensive. Aside from a brutal opening scene, the violence is muted. A-III (PG-13)

Renaldo & Clara (1978) Singer Bob Dylan makes his debut as a movie director by taking footage from one of his concert tours and interspersing it with some absurd and awkward episodes acted out in improvisational style by himself, his wife and friends (Sam Shepard, Ronee Blakley, Joni Mitchell, Arlo Guthrie and Joan Baez). The result is a tedious, dismal exercise in self-indulgence. Although there is some rough language, like much of the other dialogue, it is almost unintelligible. A-III (R)

Replay (1978) When a young woman (Marie-Jose Nat) loses her memory in an auto crash, her loving husband (Victor Lanoux) seems overly solicitous in his efforts to help her regain her past. Director Michel Drach's psychological melodrama provides little more than some modest diversion, adult in theme, with infidelity figuring as a minor element in the plot. A-III (nr)

Report from China (1971) Japanese documentary filmed in 1966-67 during the flux of the Cultural Revolution shows the total faith of the Chinese leadership in the efficacy of ideology to solve their many economic and social ills as well as their willingness to sacrifice everything for the future. A-I (nr)

Report on the Party and the Guests, A (1968) A friendly outing in the woods is disrupted when some menacing strangers escort the group of picnickers to a lakeside party where they are commanded to enjoy themselves. When one escapes the party, his friends join in the deadly pursuit. Czechoslovakian director Jan Nemec's parable on freedom and force has a threatening atmosphere of restraint and absurdity that makes for some very unsettling viewing, which is the reason it was originally banned by Communist officials. A-III (br)

Report to the Commissioner (1975) Violent urban drama about a young detective (Michael Moriarity) and his baptism of fire as a member of a New York City undercover narcotics squad. Directed by Milton Katselas, the movie is partially successful in conveying its complex vision of a claustrophobic urban hell. Sordid backgrounds and incidents. A-III (PG)

Reptile, The (1966) Routine British horror movie directed by John Gilling about a woman who can turn herself into a snake. A-II (br)

Rescuers, The (1977) Two members of the International Rescue Aid Society of mice are selected to save an orphan girl in the clutches of the wicked Madame Medusa who is ensconced on her beached Mississippi sternwheeler in the dark Louisiana swamps. The action in this Disney animated feature directed by Wolfgang Reitherman is fast and, at times, perhaps too scary for tiny tots. For all others, however, it is consistently entertaining, helped along by an imaginative group of human and animal characters and several pleasant songs. A-I (G)

Restless Natives (1986) Lighthearted comedy features exquisite scenic backgrounds of the Scottish highlands in an implausible story about two youths (Joe Mullaney and Vincent Friell) who devise an outlandish scam to extort money from tourists in the hope of gaining financial security before they hit the ripe old age of 20. Their only potential problem is a vacationing CIA agent (Ned Beatty). Director Michael Hoffman concentrates on the relationship between the two friends rather than the flimsy plot and its twist ending. A-II (PG)

Resurrection (1980) Engrossing but flawed drama about a woman (Ellen Burstyn) who discovers that she has the power to heal people after barely surviving a tragic accident in which she loses her husband. The screenplay by Lewis John Carlino sets up a fascinating situation, but neither Carlino nor director Daniel Petrie is able to work it out in satisfactory fashion. The spiritual side of faith healing is dealt with in very unimaginative fashion showing the afterlife, for example, as being, quite literally, the light at the end of the tunnel. Theme and language require a mature perspective. A-III (PG)

Return from Witch Mountain (1978) The further adventures of the two castaway space children from "Escape to Witch Mountain" with Tony falling into the villainous hands of Christopher Lee and Bette Davis who are intent on using the boy's powers for personal gain. Tia, with the aid of the lovable kind of street gang that exists nowhere outside of Disney films, rescues him in the nick of time. The sequel, directed by John Hough, is a movie that younger children will enjoy. A-I (G)

Return of a Man Called Horse, The (1976) Sequel finds bored English nobleman (Richard Harris) back in South Dakota when his adopted Indian tribe needs a leader. After another gruesome purification ceremony consisting of mind-altering drugs and of having bones inserted into his chest, he leads his tribe to victory over their

230

enemies. Director Irvin Kershner delivers a serious film, entertaining and beautifully photographed but, its emphasis on violence makes this decidedly mature fare. A-III (PG)

Return of Count Yorga, The (1971) Though this time the gentlemanly ghoul (Robert Quarry) falls in love (his one weakness), most of his time is spent, however, preying upon a neighboring orphanage. The sequel is properly amusing and frightening, with director Bob Kelljan sprinkling the proceedings with enough blood, however, to warrant caution for young or squeamish viewers. A-II (GP)

Return of Martin Guerre, The (1983) Engrossing, fact-based French production about a 16th-century peasant who abandons his wife and disappears from his native village to reappear some eight years later, much improved in every way. Accepted by his wife and most of the villagers, a squabble over property a few years later provokes the accusation that he's an imposter, and a trial with tragic results ensues. Written by Jean-Claude Carriere and directed by Daniel Vigne, the movie is partly a mystery but most of all a love story that most adults will find intriguing entertainment. Brief nudity and sexual references. A-III (nr)

Return of Maxwell Smart, The (1980) TV's secret agent Maxwell Smart (Don Adams) is assigned to thwart a villain (Vittorio Gassman) who has developed a bomb capable of destroying all the clothing in the world. Director Clive Donner's woefully inept and dull comedy relies on sexual innuendo. A-III (PG)

Return of Sabata (1972) Frank Kramer (alias Gianfranco Parolini) directs this third installment in the spaghetti Western series spoofing spaghetti Westerns. This time the sooty-suited hero with the twitching nostrils (Lee Van Cleef) matches wits and weapons with the Irish boss of a cardboard Texas town whose citizens are being taxed to the tune of a million dollars. Sabata comes to the rescue and sneers at the audience as he rides away from his bordello beauty and a cast full of sloppily-dubbed characters. A-III (PG)

Return of the Jedi (1983) George Lucas' enjoyable third installment in the Star Wars saga, directed by Richard Marquand, brings back the heroes from the first two episodes to battle Darth Vader's Deathstar. Luke Skywalker (Mark Hamill) has a revealing confrontation with Vader; Princess Leia (Carrie Fisher) and Han Solo (Harrison Ford) finally get somewhere with their romance; Billy Dee Williams saves the day with his air support; and R2D2 and C3PO steal some major scenes. The violence and tension from some of the nasty characters (Jabba the Hutt is not only scary, but disgusting) may be too intense for the younger crowd. A-II (PG)

Return of the Living Dead (1985) Written and directed by Dan O'Bannon, this is yet another tedious variation on the horror movie theme of the dead coming to life and devouring the living. Nudity, violence and bloodly gore. O (R)

Return of the Pink Panther, The (1975) The Pink Panther, the sacred jewel of the Middle East kingdom of Lugash, has been stolen again and only Inspector Clouseau (Peter Sellers) can get it back again. Directed by Blake Edwards, the comedy is relatively innocent and, thanks to Sellers, has more then a few funny moments. Some slapstick violence. A-II (G)

Return of the Secaucus Seven, The (1980) Nothing much happens except a weekend of talking during a reunion of seven friends who, as college students on a 1960s protest march, once spent a night together in jail in Secaucus, N.J. Written and directed by John Sayles on a shoe-string budget, the movie won't satisfy everyone, but the dialogue is bright and some of the insights are clever. The frankness of the language, especially about sex, would rule out younger viewers. A-III (R)

Return of the Seven (1966) Director Burt Kennedy's shallow, violent sequel to John Sturges' 1960 "The Magnificent Seven," lacks original's flair and high-powered sense of adventure. Yul Brynner, Robert Fuller and Jordan Christopher are three of the deadly septet, leading a small parade back to a little Mexican town where one of their companions is being held prisoner. A-III (br)

Return of the Soldier, The (1985) Wealthy middle-aged man (Alan Bates) returns from World War I with a case of selective amnesia. Forgotten are the years with his spoiled, ill-tempered wife (Julie Christie); remembered instead is his first love, a working-class woman (Glenda Jackson) now grown quite dowdy and, like himself, married. Well-acted English production directed by Alan Bridges from the Rebecca West novel, but the period piece is very slight and its neat resolution is unsatisfying. A-III (nr)

Return of the Streetfighter, The (1975) Japanese karate action film the villain being the American heading the Mafia branch in the Far East. Minimal production values and excessive violence. O (R)

Return of the Tall Blond Man with the One Black Shoe, The (1976) French production in which Pierre Richard again stars as the concert violinist mistaken for a superspy and unaware that he is the object of assassination attempts. This time the action takes place in Rio de Janiero with the lovely Mireille Darc on hand as decoration but director Yves Robert's comic touch is not nearly as deft as it was in the original. Restrained violence. A-III (nr)

Return to Macon County (1975) Two young men (Nick Nolte and Don Johnson) bound for California in a souped-up car pick up a chunky girl who constantly smiles when she is not pointing a large pistol at people and sometimes even when she is. Director Richard Compton's thin, aimless youth movie dips into sexual exploitation for want of anything better to do. O (PG)

Return to Oz (1985) Grim, joyless sequel to the grand Judy Garland original that attempts to make up for its lack of warmth and imagination by substituting an abundance of special effects. The scariness of some of the latter are inappropriate for pre-teenagers. A-II (PG)

Reuben, Reuben (1983) Alcoholic, womanizing Scottish poet (Tom Conti) sponges his way through the New England campus circuit in director Robert Ellis Miller's uneven social satire which details the slow disintegration of a creative soul. The script is very literate and Conti's performance is exquiste but his several sexual conquests compound the movie's already muddled moral perspective. A-III (R)

Revenge of the Nerds (1984) Misfit college freshmen (Robert Carradine and Anthony Edwards) form a fraternity to protect themselves and fight the persecution of college jocks. The underdog heroes' attitude toward women is as reprehensible as that of their tormentors. Director Jeff Kanew's farce is full of vulgarities, much nudity and the romantic treatment of what is in effect rape. O (R)

Revenge of the Nerds II: Nerds in Paradise (1987) Director Joe Roth's silly sequel has the goofy Tri Lambdas seeking to retrieve their integrity at a fraternity conference in Fort Lauderdale. Reinforces false stereotypes of women, bad habits and vulgarity via peekaboo nudity, slapstick humor and crude sight gags in the cause of telling kids not to judge others on surface values. A-III (PG-13)

Revenge of the Ninja (1983) Japanese warrior (Sho Kosugi) comes to the United States where he makes short order of an illegal drug operation and battles old enemies. Directed by Sam Firstenberg, the action is mostly of the martial arts variety but a number of weapons are used in achieving an extremely bloody victory. Excessive violence and gore. O (R)

Revenge of the Pink Panther (1978) Peter Sellers romps again as the bumbling Inspector Clouseau who gains glory, inadvertently as usual, by breaking up an international drug ring headed by Robert Webber, thanks to some timely help from Webber's mistress, Dyan Cannon. Directed by Blake Edwards, the plot is cluttered and noticeably less scintillating than its predecessors. Some sexual innuendo. A-III (PG)

Revengers, The (1972) William Holden stars as a rancher who, after his family is slaughtered by renegade Indians, dedicates his life to avenging them and, with the help of a second-string wild bunch (including Ernest Borgnine and Woody Strode), he kills just about everyone who crosses his path until gentled by an Irish spinster (Susan Hayward). Directed by Daniel Mann, this violent and bloody Western has a totally unmotivated ending. A-III (PG)

Revolution (1968) Jack O'Connell's documentary presents a one-sided view of the hippie counterculture with an emphasis upon sex and nudity. O (br)

Revolution (1986) Director Hugh Hudson's epic treatment of the American Revolution is grand spectacle but lacks a credible human dimension. What it offers, instead, are underdeveloped characters (notably Al Pacino in the central role) and episodic plot contrivances. Violent battle scenes. A-II (PG)

Revolutionary, The (1970) College student (Jon Voight) moves from a radical student movement, to a socialist worker's organization, to a short-lived stint in the army and, finally, to an anarchists' bomb plot. The result is less the story of a young man's political radicalization than it is the meanderings of a social misfit. Paul Williams' low-keyed direction tends to level rather than highlight plot development and leaves too many significant questions unanswered. A-III (GP)

Reward, The (1965) On the arid, sun-drenched plains of Mexico, a small band of bounty hunters are destroyed by their greed and moral decay. Director Serge Bourguignon's story of death in the desert makes its point about life by turning the desperate journey of the last survivor (Max Von Sydow) to reach a lake into the quest for a moral oasis. A-II (br)

Rhinestone (1984) Embarrassingly bad romantic match-up in which Dolly Parton tries to make a country-western singer out of tough New York cabby Sylvester Stallone. Director Bob Clark's unfunny musical comedy exploits Parton's physical attributes and musical abilities but merely makes Stallone look silly. Vulgar dialogue and benign view of casual sex. A-III (PG)

Rich and Famous (1981) Screen version of the John Van Druten play about two very different women (Candice Bergen and Jacqueline Bisset), both writers, who preserve a friendship for more than two decades despite the strains caused by emulation and jealousy. Directed by George Cukor, the glossy soap opera pays more attention to its glamorous locations than to the human dimension of its story. The sole redeeming feature is good acting by the principals. General air of vapid amorality and two graphic sexual sequences. O (R)

Rich Kids (1979) Uneven melodrama about the effect of divorce on two adolescents (Trini Alvarado and Jeremy Levy) whose wealthy and adulterous parents (John Lithgow and Kathryn Walker) seem unconcerned about their offspring. The two teenagers spend a weekend together in an exotically appointed bachelor apartment. The situation leads to an angry, recriminatory adult confrontation, involving spouses current and former, lovers, friends, and one or two relatively innocent bystanders. Directed by Robert Young, the movie raises but doesn't probe too deeply into questions of parental responsibility and glosses over the sexual implications of the young people's weekend together. A-III (PG)

Richard (1972) Political spoof with little satirical bite blending newsreel footage with staged segments in order to trace Richard Nixon's journey from whipping cookie batter of an evening in Whittier, Calif. to fireside reminiscenes at the White House. Directed by Lorees Yerby and Harry Hurwitz, the resulting lampoon, more than anything else, provides proof that this is a free country. A-III (PG)

Richard Pryor Live on Sunset Strip (1982) Stand-up comic performance, with the usual obscenities and scatological references, though Pryor is in a mellower, more humane mood than in his previous performance movie. Under Joe Layton's direction, Pryor's humor and his perception of human nature are usually on target and often extremely funny, but his sexually oriented jokes and vulgar language may offend those unfamiliar with his style. A-IV (R)

Riddle of the Sands, The (1984) British melodrama about two chaps from Oxford who accidentally uncover German preparations for an invasion of England in 1901. Michael York and Simon MacCorkindale are fine as the stuffy pair who prove their mettle once the going gets tough, but they can't save a languid movie that lacks even a good villain. Director Tony Maylam succeeds best with the period atmosphere but its intrigue and derring-do are only mildly diverting. A-II (PG)

Ride Beyond Vengeance (1966) After a long absence, a buffalo hunter (Chuck Connors) returns home with a sizable sum of money and then revenges on the three who steal it from him. Directed by Bernard McEveety, it is a tough, almost cynical story of human greed and brutality. Much violence. A-III (br)

Ride a Wild Pony (1976) Colorful Disney adventure, set in the Australian Outback before World War I, in which a poor lad attempts to recover his pony after it has come into the possession of a spoiled cripple, the little daughter of the town's wealthiest family. It is up to the horse, in the satisfying conclusion, to decide for one child or the other. Better than average children's movie directed by Don Chaffey with some good touches of reality and a solid theme of human selflessness. A-I (G)

Rider on the Rain (1970) Intriguing French mystery thriller about a newlywed (Marlene Jobert) who kills her attacker and then is afraid to tell husband, friends, or the police. After she has disposed of the body, a stranger (Charles Bronson) begins to badger her about it and a neatly matched duel of wits ensues. Director Rene Clement has hit the mark with this suspenseful melodrama, with plenty of moody atmosphere and engaging characterizations. The tribulations of the heroine are not for the youngsters. A-III (GP)

Right On! (1971) Documentary of performances by a talented but angry rock group, The Original Last Poets (Gylan Kain, David Nelson, and Felipe Luciano), whose songs echo the pain and frustration of ghetto life and insist on racial pride as the means for redeeming the future. By filming the group in New York slums framed by the Manhattan skyline, director Herbert Danska finds the visual equivalent to their music. Some violent and vulgar lyrics, but motivated by a sense of hope rather than hopelessness. A-IV (nr)

Right Stuff, The (1983) Screen version of Tom Wolfe's book about the original seven astronauts aspires to be an American epic and is an extraordinary tribute to the first pioneers of the U.S. space program, notably Chuck Yeager (Sam Shepard), Alan Shepard (Scott Glenn) and John Glenn (Ed Harris). Director Philip Kaufman captures the gallant endeavor in a style that's at once respectful yet exhuberant, lavishly entertaining and very inspiring. Unfortunately, a scene about masturbation, intended as a bit of comic relief during a sequence of laboratory tests, is mature fare. A-III (R/PG appeal)

Ring of Bright Water (1969) London clerk (Bill Travers) leaves his computerized job to move to a small cottage in the Scottish highlands with an otter. Unpretentious British story directed by Jack Couffer proves intelligent, entertaining family fare. A-I (G)

Rings Around the World (1966) Compilation movie showing famous circus acts from various countries produced and directed by Gilbert Cates and narrated by Don Ameche. A-I (br)

Rio Lobo (1970) Stylish Western with John Wayne as a Civil War veteran pursuing two traitors for hijacking an army payroll, and not perturbed in the least by a small army of hired gunslingers nor a final thunderous shootout with an entire town taking part. Under Howard Hawks' deft direction, there is plenty of rough horseplay and tongue-in-cheek references to Wayne's overweight condition and old age in general. Violence, both physical and psychological, and some adult sexual references. A-III (G)

Riot (1968) Set within the grime and frustration of prison life is a realistic drama in which an inmate (James Brown), unwittingly caught up in fast-moving events, assumes leadership of a full scale revolt by the entire prison. Director Buzz Kulik's movie is by no means casual entertainment but it is very knowing about prison life and injustices. Several violent, bloody sequences bolster the dramatic action and the dialogue is a bit rough.

A-IV (R/GP)
Rise of Louis XIV, The (1970) French historical dramatization meticulously traces the gradual assumption of power by the Sun King, from the time he assumed the crown to his undercutting the noblity by enticing them to spend their lives in the frivolous splendors of the court at Versailles. Directed by Roberto Rossellini, the re-creation of the period is beautifully exquisite and painstakingly detailed but those uninterested in history may find the pace interminably slow. A-I (G)

Risky Business (1983) Enterprising young prostitute (Rebecca De Mornay) persuades a high school senior (Tom Cruise), while his affluent parents are away on vacation, to turn his plush Chicago home into a bordello for his classmates. Written and directed by Paul Brickman, it is much slicker than similar exploitation movies aimed at teenagers but it is appallingly crass in its celebration of promiscuity. Nudity and graphic sexuality as well as a benign view of deceit, manipulation and sexual indulgence. O (R)

Rita, Sue and Bob Too (1987) British sex farce posing as ribald social satire about two lower-class teenagers sexually exploited by a married man who in turn ruin his already failing marriage and then exploit him. Director Alan Clarke displays a callous hand in his graphic depiction of sex with minors, nudity and profanity. O (R)

Ritz, The (1976) Screen version of a mediocre Broadway comedy about an Italian-American businessman from Cleveland (Jack Weston) hiding out from a murderous brother-in-law (Jerry Stiller) in a homosexual bathhouse where he is pursued by an off-key Puerto Rican singer (Rita Moreno) who thinks he is a Hollywood producer. Directed by Richard Lester, it's an ugly, disagreeable attempt at farce. Ethnic stereotyping and some foul language O (R)

Rivals (1972) Clunker about an Oedipal 10-year-old brat (Scott Jacoby) who is so fatally jealous of his widowed mother (Joan Hackett) and her childish second husband (Robert Klein) that he makes a humiliating mess of trying to have sex with his dumb but nubile babysitter. Director Krishna Shah is hopelessly adrift in dealing with the esoteric lifestyles of Americans with too much money. Repugnant trash. O (R)

River, The (1984) Ernest but dull effort to dramatize the plight of the American farmer tells the story of a farm family (Mel Gibson and Sissy Spacek) who must battle nature, bill collectors and public indifference in their struggle to hold on to their land and livelihood. The characters simply do not come alive in an unfocused script directed by Mark Rydell. Some violent encounters and a restrained bedroom scene. A-II (PG-13)

River Niger, The (1976) Powerful drama about a black American's struggle to forge his own identity out of a tragic history of blacks as the eternally Displaced Persons of our nation. Though director Krishna Shah fails to overcome the stage origins of the work, this does lessen the value of its hopeful message about the choices facing our society, its moving portrait of closely-knit family life and the strong performances of James Earl Jones, Cicely Tyson and Glynn Turman. Mature themes. A-III R)

River's Edge (1987) The callous sex killing of a young high school girl is viewed by her apathetic peers as an occasion for protective support of her psychopathic boy friend who becomes the equally innocent victim of an adult psychotic (Dennis Hopper). Director Tim Hunter's picture of several troubled youths downplays emotional and spiritual issues in favor of sensationalistic profanity, nudity and permissive teen sex. O (R)

Riverrun (1970) When a sea-going father (John McLiam) visits the sheep farm where his daughter (Louise Ober) and her young man (Mark Jenkins) live, he is at first amused by their attempt to get back to nature and escape the dehumanization of city life, but when he learns that she is pregnant and not formally married, he is determined to take her away. Written and directed by John Korty, the contrivances of romantic melodrama are evident but the generational theme of value systems is handled sensitively and treated with honesty. A-III (R)

Road Movie (1974) Wildly exaggerated melodrama about two truck drivers (Robert Drivas and Barry Bostwick) whose friendship is shattered when they pick up a fuel-stop prostitute (Regina Baff) in a story that ends with the destruction of the truck and the death of one of them. Directed by Joseph Strick, whatever intentions the movie had as social commentary on the dangers of the road is undone by the movie's meanness of characters and their rough language. A-III (nr)

Road to Salina (1971) Dreadfully pretentious European production set in the middle of a baked salt flat where Lana Turner runs a gas station-cafe and mistakes Robert Walker for her runaway son. Her daughter (Mimsy Farmer) goes along with the situation by engaging in a sexual relationship that had originally sent the son packing. Directed by Georges Lautner, the muddled incest theme is conveyed with many arty scenes of graphic love-making. O (R)

Road Warrior, The (1982) Set in a post-nuclear wasteland, this Australian action thriller pits a surviving outpost of civilization clustered around a still functioning oil refinery against the barbarian horde who need gasoline for their motley assortment of vehicles. Max (Mel Gibson), a wandering loner, is chosen to deliver the gas through hostile lines. Except for director George Miller's stylish use of the setting, there is little in this blood-and-gore epic to occupy the mind. Excessive violence. O (R)

Roadie (1980) Failed spoof of rock music's subculture follows the misadventures of a country bumpkin (rock singer Meatloaf) who is convinced by a whacky groupie to become a "roadie" or general roustabout and handyman for a traveling rock group. Director Alan Rudolph offers few good sight gags and plenty of bad ones, with lots of ear-numbing music. Some jokes about sex and drugs. A-III (PG)

Robbery (1967) Fact-based British thriller about the hijacking of the Royal Mail train with three millions pounds in cash and the escape of the robbery's mastermind (Stanley Baker) from the police dragnet. Director Peter Yates builds a lot of excitement and suspense, with a refreshingly minimum amount of violence. A-II (br)

Robert et Robert (1980) Slight French comedy about two hapless and, apparently, hopeless bachelors (Jacques Villeret and Charles Denner) who meet while enlisting aid from a computerized matrimonial service and find themselves banding together against a hostile world. Directed by Claude Lelouch, the two principals are forced to fall back upon their quirks of character to keep the humor going. Mature theme and treatment. A-III (nr)

Robin Hood (1973) Disney feature cartoon offers a humorous version of the exploits of the English folk hero who robbed from the undeserving rich to give to the exploited poor. The cast consists of crisply drawn animals who lend themselves to such characterizations as Robin being a crafty fox and King John as an anemic lion. Older viewers will appreciate the classic Disney-style animation under the direction of Wolfgang Reitherman, while younger viewers enjoy the comic derring-do. A-I (G)

Robin and Marian (1976) Disappointing British addition to the Robin Hood legend set some 20 years after his youthful adventures in Sherwood Forest. Robin (Sean Connery) and his now melancholy men rescue Maid Marian (Audrey Hepburn) from a convent and the clutches of the dastardly Sheriff of Nottingham (Robert Shaw). Under Richard Lester's direction the performances are very good but the mood of the piece is confused, halfway between genuine romance and clumsy demythologizing. Some violence, crude humor and a sympathetically viewed suicide. A-III (PG)

Robinson Crusoe and the Tiger (1972) Amateurish Spanish version of the Daniel Defoe classic tale of shipwreck and survival with Crusoe played by Hugo Stiglitz who double-takes his way through various episodes of being chased by everything from sharks and panthers to bats and tigers. Directed by Rene Cardona Jr., its stagey camerawork and droning narration may put the small fry to sleep. A-I (G)

Robocop (1987) Futuristic urban crime drama about a good Detroit cop (Peter Weller) shot up by hoods and recycled into a robotized part-man, part-machine programmed to rid the streets of crime. Dutch director Paul Verhoeven doesn't spare any blood and gore in his relentlessly graphic depiction of violent law enforcement tactics used against equally violent criminals. Conveys a dangerous ends-justifies-the-means brand of justice. O (R)

Rocky (1976) Underdog Philadelphia club fighter, Rocky Balboa (Sylvester Stallone), has a shot at the heavyweight championship with the help of a tough old trainer (Burgess Meredith). Director John Avildsen concentrates on the gritty, back-street quality of life in the old neighborhood and the relationship that grows between Rocky and the introverted sister (Talia Shire) of his best friend. The bloody brutality of the boxing game is abundantly evident. A-III (PG)

Rocky II (1979) Writer-director Sylvester Stallone stars as the prizefighter unable to settle down with a new wife (Talia Shire), house and baby. Low on cash and brains, he accepts a rematch with Apollo Creed (Carl Weathers), the undefeated champ whom he almost beat in the first film. Though the sequel is formula entertainment with its theme of the victorious underdog, the movie clearly celebrates the violence of the ring, assigning value as much to the brutal sport as to its likeable hero's will and determination. A-III (PG)

Rocky III (1982) Apollo Creed (Carl Weathers) trains his former opponent (Sylvester Stallone) so that he can hold on to his title against a snarling and vicious challenger (Mr. T.). Also written and directed by Stallone, it may not be a knockout but it is good, solid entertainment. The carnage in the ring, though of briefer duration than previously, is still very intense. A-III (PG)

Rocky IV (1985) Sylvester Stallone gets back in the ring for the fight of his life against a Russian Olympic boxing machine (Dolph Lundgren). Stallone directs himself fighting to avenge the death of Apollo Creed (Carl Weathers) while regaining American honor. The sensitive may find the fight scenes too brutal. A-III (PG)

Roller Boogie (1980) Spoiled little rich girl (Linda Blair) flees parents and promising career as flutist for the joys of the roller skating rink. Director Mark L. Lester forgets the plot to focus on scenes of nubile youngsters in scanty costumes skating and dancing to disco rhythms. The boring exercise in coed velocity has little to offer its intended teenage audience. A-III (PG)

Rollerball (1975) The title refers to a brutal game invented by the rulers of a future society in order to keep their subjects docile by watching the violence of others. When one of the star players (James Caan) begins attracting his own followers, he is ordered to retire but instead leads a revolt. Directed by Norman Jewison, the movie has little to offer except the lavish violence of the game and then of the revolt, thereby exploiting what supposedly it intended to condemn. O (R)

Rollercoaster (1977) Slack thriller about an extortionist (Timothy Bottoms) who plants bombs on rollercoasters and the safety inspector (George Segal) who chases him across the country. Directed by James Goldstone, the movie's sole aim is visceral excitement unhindered by any larger concerns, including the risk entailed by putting such an idea into the public consciousness. Graphically depicted rollercoaster crash. A-III (PG)

Rolling Thunder (1977) When a returned Vietnam prisoner-of-war (William Devane) finds that his wife and son have been murdered during a robbery, he sets out to exact a bloody vengeance. Written by Paul Schrader and directed by John Flynn, the movie's mayhem and slaughter exploits the serious issue of the problems of returned prisoners-of-war. Its reverence for guns approaches fetishism. O (R)

Rollover (1981) Slick romantic melodrama about a bank president's widow (Jane Fonda) who uncovers fraud in the international monetary system after Arab finaciers decide not to redeposit (rollover) their huge sums in her bank and her boy friend (Kris Kristofferson) tries to save the day. Directed by Alan J. Pakula, the plot is so contrived that the proceedings are hard to take. Several restrained sex scenes and some rough language. A-III (R)

Romance of a Horsethief (1971) Folk tale set in a Polish village near the German border in 1904 where most of the peasants subsist by selling stolen horses to the Imperial German Cavalry. When the local Cossack commander (Yul Brynner) requisitions all horses and conscripts the young men for the Czar's war against Japan, some of the villagers (Eli Wallach, David Opatoshu and Lainie Kazan) turn the tables on the Russian officer. Director Abraham Polonsky tells the tale in lively farcical fashion but some indulgent nudity and rough verbal exchanges between wily Wallach and his mistress Kazan spoil what should have been a lighthearted adventure. O (GP)

Romancing the Stone (1984) Sedate novelist (Kathleen Turner) finds herself plunged into wild adventure when she goes to Colombia to ransom her kidnapped sister but a handsome American adventurer (Michael Douglas) turns up to save her at fairly regular intervals. Directed by Robert Zemeckis, the exotic romance strives hard for, but never achieves, a tongue-in-cheek style to take the realistic edge off the action and allow for laughs. Some graphic violence, rough language and partial nudity in a bedroom scene. A-III (PG)

Romantic Comedy (1983) Mediocre screen version of Bernard Slade's play about a successful Broadway playwriting team (Dudley Moore and Mary Steenburgen), whose professionalism takes a decade or so to ripen into romance. As directed by Arthur Hiller, the movie is not very romantic or comic, but the charm of the principals makes it a shade less unbearable. Though adultery figures in the plot, it is not condoned and the whole enterprise is rather innocuous. A-II (PG)

Romantic Englishwoman, The (1975) Starts out in a Central European spa and quickly goes from Baden-Baden to worse in a continental triangle involving Michael Caine, Helmut Berger and Glenda Jackson. Very British production directed by Joseph Losey attempts to be civilized and very arch, but aside from an occasional joke that comes off, it is a pretentious nothing. Sexual situations and some nudity. O (R)

Romeo and Juliet (1968) Director Franco Zeffirelli's somewhat free interpretation of Shakespeare's tragedy of young love offers much energetic action in a stylish production with teenaged Olivia Hussey and Leonard Whiting in the title roles. Brief nude scene. A-IV (G/PG)

Ronja, Robbersdaughter (1986) Swedish import directed by Tage Danielsson features two children reacting to the selfish insensitivity of their fueding families in a medieval forest setting. Exemplary for its insight and understanding about the feelings of children in relation to parental weaknesses, the movie has two brief scenes of nudity, treated innocently and humorously, in an otherwise delightfully entertaining feature for children. A-I (nr)

Room Service (1938) Groucho, Chico and Harpo Marx perform their antics with help of a young showgirl (Lucille Ball) in this madcap comedy about a wisecracking producer's need to get financing for a play so he can pay his hotel bill. Directed by William A. Seiter, the Marx Brothers' brand of irascible humor featured clever turns on words, old vaudevillian routines and non-violent slapstick as they mocked the conventions of manners (but not morals) of the times. A-I (br)

Room with a View (1986) Radiant romance set in Edwardian England depicts a love triangle resolved when the petulant heroine (Helena Bonham-Carter) chooses the good commoner over the wealthy toff. James Ivory directs from an adaptation of the E.M. Forster story of manners and self-determination. Scene of male nudity is a satiric comment on post-Victorian prudishness. A-III (nr)

Roommates (1971) Greenwich Village roommates (Dan Mason and Harvey Marks) with girl friends who come and go, seemingly available to either, spend a good deal of their time on the street, much of it waiting to cross at intersections. Written and directed by Jack Baran, the material is so thin, so shallow, so uninspired and banal that perhaps its deepest insight is realizing how long it takes a New York traffic light to change. Casual sex scenes. A-IV (R)

Roommates, The (1973) Five permissive college girls vacationing at a California resort become

235

romantically involved with various available males (ranging from a timid teenager to an implacable ex-husband), seemingly undeterred by the news of a perverted killer on the loose. Written and directed by Arthur Marks, the relationships are mere contrivances pandering to prurient taste. O (R)

Rooster Cogburn (1975) Two Hollywood institutions, John Wayne and Katharine Hepburn, spoof one another's on-screen, off-screen images in a Western set against some beautifully photographed Oregon locales. Directed by Stuart Millar, it's a self-indulgent exercise but, for all that, many will still find its stars most engaging performers, though youngsters likely will find it pretty tame fare. A-II (PG)

Rose for Everyone, A (1967) Italian production directed by Franco Rossi whose treatment tends to be complacent about its charitable but promiscuous heroine (Claudia Cardinale). O (br)

Rose, The (1979) Glossy romantic tragedy about a flamboyant, whiskey-swilling rock star of the late 1960s (Bette Midler), someone much like Janis Joplin. When she finds a man she really loves (Frederic Forrest), the blow of losing him shatters whatever stability she has left. Fine performance by Midler and the capable direction of Mark Rydell convey with some force how too much success can alienate one from all those values that give significance to life. Sympathetic depiction of illicit sexual relationships, drug and alcohol indulgence and some very rough language. A-IV (R)

Rosebud (1975) Failed, boring thriller about Middle East terrorists and their captives aboard a pleasure yacht. Directed by Otto Preminger, the movie is a plodding succession of seemingly endless sequences where each minor bit of action is talked to death in frequently redundent dialogue. Some violence. A-III (PG)

Roseland (1977) Three nostalgic stories set in the venerable Manhattan ballroom telling of a widow (Teresa Wright) whose dancing partner (Lou Jacobi) helps her forget her dead husband; a charming gigolo (Christopher Walken) who appeals to a dancing instructor (Helen Gallagher) and a recent divorcee (Geraldine Chaplin); and an elderly German woman (Lilia Skala) who dreams of winning a dance contest despite the shortcomings of her partner (David Thomas). Directed by James Ivory, the romantic movie provides a lightly diverting, affectionate look at human foibles. A-II (PG)

Rosemary's Baby (1968) Modern-day horror story about a young husband (John Cassavetes) who turns his wife (Mia Farrow), body and soul, over to the next-door neighbors, a coven of witches (led by Ruth Gordon and Sidney Blackmer) so she can become the mother of Satan Incarnate. Directed by Roman Polanski, the production values are topnotch and performances completely chilling, but the movie's inverted Christian elements denigrate religious beliefs. Brief nudity. O (R)

Rosie (1967) Wealthy widow (Rosalind Russell) alarms her heirs with her spending sprees and, to protect their inheritance, they have her committed to a high security rest home from which she is rescued by the loyal family lawyer (Brian Aherne). Directed by David Lowell Rich, the material may be predictable but the two veteran leads make it work. Some mature treatment. A-III (br)

Rough Cut (1980) Fluffy, implausible romantic comedy about a Scotland Yard inspector (David Niven) who blackmails a high society kleptomaniac (Lesley-Anne Down) to set up her jewel thief lover (Burt Reynolds) so he can be arrested. Directed by Donald Siegal, the film's pervasive amorality and sexual references make it adult fare. A-III (PG)

Round Midnight (1986) Musical tribute to the expatriate black American jazz musicians living and performing in 1959 Paris. Using tenor saxophonist Dexter Gordon as its central character much of the movie's charm and appeal stem from its careful weaving of original jazz performances into this celebration of the art, craft and personalities of the l950s. Some harsh language. A-II (R)

Round-Up, The (1969) Hungarian dramatization of the Austrian repression of those who took part in the Revolution of 1848 and became guerrillas after its failure. Director Miklos Jancso gets haunting black-and-white images of the prisoners' isolation and the pressures to betray others. Some physical but mostly psychological violence and brief nudity. A-IV (nr)

Roxanne (1987) Written and performed by Steve Martin, this contemporary version of Cyrano de Bergerac is an unfunny combination of slapstick, physical comedy and perfunctory sexual tease. Director Fred Schepisi offers only a vanity production for a remarkably untalented Daryl Hannah whose portrayal of young womanhood is caught between 1960s mindless love-child and a seductive Botticelli Venus. Slapstick violence, dumb jokes and casual acceptance of premarital sex defeat any sense of romantic idealism. A-III (PG)

Royal Flash (1975) Disappointing tongue-in-cheek adventure in which the English hero (Malcolm McDowell) incurs the wrath of Otto von Bismarck (Oliver Reed) and gets involved in the 19th-century maneuvering to unite the German states under the Prussian king. Directed by Richard Lester, the action drags and the humor is forced rather than intentive. Romantic situations and restrained violence. A-III (PG)

Royal Hunt of the Sun (1969) Disappointing screen version of Peter Shaffer's play about the clash of cultures when 16th-century Spanish adventurers under Pizarro (Robert Shaw) invaded the empire of the Incas ruled by Atahuallpa (Christopher Plummer). Directed by Irving Lerner, the narrative is little more than a series of encounters between the two principals who give highly mannered stage performances. A-III (G)

R.P.M. (1970) When Gary Lockwood and fellow foul-mouthed students take over the campus administration building, college president Anthony Quinn (hopelessly miscast) gets them to stop the agitation but a million-dollar computer has been damaged and the police intervene with brutal force. Erich Segal's script is a mishmash of easy problems and stereotyped solutions, ploddingly directed by Stanley Kramer. Unconvincing melodrama about student unrest, with much violence and sexual situations. A-IV (R)

Ruby (1977) Murdered gangster comes back to haunt his killers, all of whom work at a Florida drive-in owned by the dead man's mistress (Piper Laurie). Directed by Curtis Harrington, the absurd and slipshod horror movie tries to shock with excessively violent and crude visual effects. O (R)

Ruling Class, The (1972) Screen version of Peter Barnes' play satirizing the British upper classes in a story about the demented Earl of Gurney (Peter O'Toole in a madcap virtuoso performance) who, once he is cured of believing he is God, assumes the identity of Jack the Ripper. Directed by Peter Medak, the looney black comedy even has some hilarious song and dance numbers but the nonsense goes on much too long and becomes repetitive. Some may take the casebook condition of claiming to be the Deity as irreverent but religion is not at all under attack here. A-IV (PG)

Rumble Fish (1983) Failed screen version of a S.E. Hinton novel with Matt Dillon giving an overwrought Brando imitation as a teen-ager trying to live up to the bad reputation of his brother (Mickey Rourke) and drunken father (Dennis Hopper). Director Francis Ford Coppola's confusing portrait of a youth struggling to regain self-esteem is marred by gang-war violence, some nudity and brief but graphic sex. O (R)

Run After Me—Until I Catch You (1979) Soggy French farce about the owner of a canine beauty parlor (Annie Girardot) and her romance with a tax collector (Jean-Pierre Marielle). Director Robert Pouret makes a feeble attempt to show that middle-aged people can be as romantic, foolish and funny as any other age group. Adult situations. A-III (PG)

Run Before the Wind (1972) New York art director (Jean Yves) races a sailboat from San Francisco to Tokyo in a semi-documentary that captures the breathtaking ocean vistas and challenging duties of the 6000-mile contest. Written, produced and directed by Brud Talbot, the movie becomes exploitation fare by punctuating the voyage with a series of sexually graphic daydreams. O (R)

Run for Your Wife (1967) Weak comedy about an Italian's search for an American bride highlights promiscuous sex. O (br)

Run the Wild River (1971) Shooting the rapids in huge rubber pontoons is a rugged way to find adventure, the challenge here taking the form of a river in southern Mexico that had never been run before. The thrills are real enough, with boats bouncing off rocks and swirling in the foaming waters, but too much footage is devoted to travelogue excursions into the surrounding countryside to pad out a documentary short into a full-length feature. A-I (nr)

Run Wild, Run Free (1969) British story in which a mute country child (Mark Lester) is befriended by a retired Army officer (John Mills) who teaches him to train a falcon and tame a wild colt, with predictable but quite satisfying results. Directed by Richard C. Sarafian, the story has appeal for adults as well as children both for its human qualities and the delights of nature. A-I (G)

Runaway (1984) Silly science fiction vehicle for Tom Selleck who plays a futuristic cop on the runaway squad, a branch of the police force assigned to corralling robots that have run amok. Directed by Michael Crichton, its unintentionally funny high-tech mayhem provides passable entertainment for action fans. Some violence and brief nudity. A-III (PG-13)

Runaway Train (1985) Alaskan train, whose steely-black locomotive is hurtling out of control, carries two escaped convicts (Jon Voight and Eric Roberts) along with a napping railroad worker (Rebecca DeMornay). Directed by Andrei Koncha-

lovsky and based on a screenplay by Akira Kurosawa, something has been lost in the translation. Senseless plot, excessive violence and coarse language. O (R)

Runner Stumbles, The (1979) Fact-based story of a gifted but morose pastor (Dick Van Dyke) of a small-town parish in the 1920s who is accused of murdering a young nun (Kathleen Quinlan) to whom he had shown special attention. Director Stanley Kramer delicately tries to avoid the sensational but its superficial treatment of the Catholic context, sketchy characterizations and a bizarre climax add up to a disappointing muddle. Because it deals with the emotional involvement of a priest and nun under extremely melodramatic circumstances, it is mature viewing fare that some may find distasteful. A-IV (PG)

Running (1979) Aging marathon runner (Michael Douglas), who has a reputation for choking up in the clutch both in running and in life, resolves to vindicate himself and win back his estranged wife (Susan Anspach) by making it to the Olympics. Directed by Steven Hillard Stern, the grimly determined athlete featured in the foreground proves less compelling than the pageantry of Montreal's Olympics in the background. Some foul language. A-III (PG)

Running Scared (1986) Director Peter Hyams' rough-edged action comedy about veteran Chicago undercover cops (Billy Crystal and Gregory Hines) making their last drug bust before early retirement to the good life in Key West is waylaid by violence, harsh language, brief nudity and ethnic stereotyping. O (R)

Russian Adventure (1966) Picturesque Russian travelogue showing scenes of cities and countryside, the Bolshoi Ballet and the Moscow State Circus, but anyone hoping to learn more about what life in the Soviet Union is like will be disappointed. A-I (br)

Russian Roulette (1975) Mediocre Canadian melodrama about the attempted assassination of a Soviet leader visiting Vancouver in which a Mountie (George Segal) becomes the unwitting tool of both Russian and Canadian counter-intelligence. Directed by Lou Lombardo, the plot is too convoluted for its own good but it's diverting, especially the lovely location photography. Some violence. A-III (PG)

Russians Are Coming, the Russians Are Coming, The (1966) Inspired farce built around the accidental grounding of a Russian submarine off the coast of Cape Cod. Producer-director Norman Jewison ably handles a fine cast including Alan Arkin, Carl Reiner, Eva Marie Saint, Jonathan Winters and Paul Ford. The movie's satire can be appreciated at several levels and will be enjoyed by the whole family. A-I (br)

Rustler's Rhapsody (1985) Spoof of the singing cowboy movies, written and directed by Hugh Wilson and starring Tom Berenger, starts out promisingly enough but soon goes flat. A-II (PG)

Ruthless People (1986) Corrupt garment industry magnate (Danny DeVito) is delighted when his wife (Bette Midler) is kidnapped by a couple (Helen Slater and Judge Reinhold) he has wronged, but the three become friends and hatch a scheme to ruin the magnate. The hostility and profanity in this movie directed by Jim Abrahams, David Zucker and Jerry Zucker is excessive and the use of nudity in a sight gag in a movie produced by the Disney subsidiary Touchstone virtually defiles the memory of the man whose name is synonymous with family entertainment. O (R)

Ryan's Daughter (1970) Robert Mitchum is a rural Irish schoolteacher married to simmering Sarah Miles who develops a mad passion for British officer Christopher Jones. Huge, sweeping drama written by Robert Bolt and directed by David Lean is set along the ruggedly beautiful coast of Dingle during the explosive time of the 1916 Easter Rebellion. Caught in the middle between forces of political upheaval and old-fashioned lust is village pastor Trevor Howard. The performances of both Howard and Mitchum bring depth and breadth to match Lean's sprawling visualization of what is, on balance, a rather confused moral drama on a theme of adultery. Brief nudity. A-III (PG)

Ryder P.I. (1986) Inept, humorless parody of a TV detective show starring Bob Nelson relies on silliness and gross humor for a few laughs. Sexually derived vulgarities pervade the sophomoric narrative. A-III (PG-13)

S

Sabata (1970) Sharp-eyed marksman (Lee Van Cleef) wipes out a couple of hundred baddies in record time in this tongue-in-cheek Italian Western directed by Frank Kramer. Superficially little above the cartoon level of derring-do, what makes it fun is the skill with which its stunts are conceived and executed and the wry wit with which it regards its own shaggy story. Stylized violence. A-III (GP)

Sacco & Vanzetti (1971) European co-production about two Italian immigrants, cobbler Sacco (Riccardo Cucciolla) and fishmonger Vanzetti (Gian Maria Volonte), who were convicted of murder and, despite protests that this was a miscarriage of justice, executed in 1927 by the State of Massachusetts. Director Giuliano Montaldo centers not on the question of their guilt but on the judicial process in a trial tainted by prejudice and perjury because of the pair's anarchist views. The mostly courtroom dramatization is uneven, but much of it works extremely well. Accessible for most older teenagers. A-III (GP)

Sacrifice, The (1986) Swedish production in which a group of adults and one child pass through a night of confusion and fear, including portents of a nuclear-devastated landscape. Director Andrei Tarkovsky's murky religious allegory about an aging writer's bargaining with God to save others relies upon long silences, ritualized dialogue and beautiful but static photography. A very personal film about love and compassion, the effect is strangely cold and distant. A-III (PG)

Safe Place, A (1971) Tuesday Weld plays a New Yorker who spends most of her time in and around Central Park, remembering her past and fantasizing about the present, though no reason is ever indicated why this young woman is so tied to her childhood. Written and directed by Henry Jaglom, the movie has no substance beyond its self-conscious attempt to reflect the way a disoriented mind copes with the passage of time. A-III (GP)

Sailor Who Fell from Grace with the Sea, The (1976) Failed adaptation of Yukio Mishima's novel in which a sailor (Kris Kristofferson) decides to give up the sea and marry a wealthy widow (Sarah Miles) but a gang of schoolboys take drastic action to prevent him from betraying his manly career. Writer-director Lewis John Carlino has turned this into a glossy, sentimental love story ruined by a bunch of rotten kids. Ludicrous, excessive sex scenes. O (R)

Saint Jack (1979) Screen version of the Paul Theroux novel about an expatriate American (Ben Gazzara) who makes his way with flare and humor as a procurer in modern-day Singapore but balks at blackmailing a visiting U.S. Senator. Director Peter Bogdanovich's rather thin and slow-paced melodrama shows far too benign an attitude toward the hero's character and profession, and it also has one quite suggestive sequence. O (R)

Saint Joan (1957) Screen version of George Bernard Shaw's play about the French heroine (Jean Seberg) whose voices led her to take up arms for her king against the English who put her to death as a heretic. Adapted by Graham Greene and directed by Otto Preminger, the result is flat and static but Shaw's jabs at authority, secular and religious, emerge often enough to make it interesting. A-II (br)

Salesman (1969) Documentary showing the day-to-day life of four door-to-door Bible salesmen who work the Boston area and then start a campaign in Florida. It is not about the commercialization of religion or the tricks of the trade, though viewers will see a little bit of both. It is essentially about the effect of this trade upon these individuals and their relations with others. Directed by Albert and David Maysles, it is a rare picture of people seen through the perspective of their line of work. A-II (G)

Sallah (1965) Israeli comedy about an immigrant (Haym Topol) who defeats the many bureaucratic attempts to integrate him into his new community. Writer-director Ephraim Kishon comes up with a highly amusing satire that succeeds best with its outrageous sight gags. A-II (br)

Salo (1977) Italian sex fantasy directed by Pier Paolo Pásolini set in the Fascist state during the final days of World War II when four officials decide to finish their lives by perversely victimizing a group of boys and girls rounded up by their thuggish guards. O (nr)

Salt and Pepper (1968) Witless British espionage spoof about night-club owners (Sammy Davis Jr. and Peter Lawford) who get mixed up in a plot against the government. Directed by Richard Donner, the mostly unfunny proceedings depend largely on sexually oriented dialogue and situations. O (G)

Salut L'Artiste (1976) Charming French trifle directed by Yves Robert about a second-rate actor (Marcello Mastroianni) who thinks his Italian accent robs him of good roles and his mistress (Francoise Fabian) who knows his frailties only too well. Incidental nudity. A-IV (nr)

Salvador (1987) Out-of-work photojournalist (James Woods) takes his buddy (James Belushi) on a trek to Latin America for fun and games but finds instead the harsh realities of civil war and militarism's reckless disregard for the value of human life. Profuse profanity and extensive depiction of war atrocities make director Oliver Stone's political essay palatable only for the thick-skinned and tough-minded. A-IV (R)

Salzburg Connection, The (1972) Fitful screen version of a Helen MacInnes novel of international intrigue as various agents (Barry Newman, Karen Jensen and Klaus-Maria Brandauer) vie to find a chest containing the names of World War II Nazi collaborators hidden on the bottom of a sinister Alpine lake. Directed by Lee Katzin, aside from some sparkling but occasionally violent action sequences, the escapist adventure has little but the beautiful setting of Salzburg and the surrounding Austrian Alps to recommend it. A-III (PG)

Sam Whiskey (1969)   Angie Dickinson tries to protect the family name by seducing Burt Reynolds into retrieving some gold bars stolen by her dead husband and returning them to the U.S. Mint before the theft is discovered. Directed by Arnold Laven, the movie's sense of morality displays the same lightheadedness as that of the heroine. Some nudity. O (PG)

Sam's Son (1985)   Hollywood producer returns to his hometown for a premiere and recalls his loving father, who always had faith in him. Writer-director Michael Landon's first feature is very sentimental, unabashedly uplifting entertainment and succeeds in large part because of some good acting. A-II (PG)

Sambizanga (1973)   Effective Angolan-made drama about the colonial injustices that led to their struggle for independence from Portuguese rule, as seen in the story of a wife's search for her husband, taken by the police in a dawn raid on their village. Directed by Sarah Maldoror, it is a sophisticated study of simple people, oppressed but beginning to learn the possibility of alternatives. The enemy is presented as colonialism and not race (whites are among the revolutionaries and blacks among the police). A-II (nr)

Same Time, Next Year (1978)   Screen version of Bernard Slade's slick comedy of extramarital bliss in which an accountant from New Jersey (Alan Alda) meets a demure housewife (Ellen Burstyn) at a California seaside resort in 1951, and they begin an affair that continues for the next 26 years, limited to a single week-end each year. Directed by Robert Mulligan, there is a moderate amount of cleverness and amusing lines but, though the fantasy-level of the proceedings makes somewhat less offensive the condoning of this particular brand of adultery, there remains something intrinsically offensive about the premise of the movie. O (PG)

Sand Pebbles, The (1966)   Steve McQueen stars as a hardbitten member of the crew of an American gunboat assigned to Chinese waters in 1926 to protect U.S. commercial interests by its presence during a time of social and political unrest. Director Robert Wise manages to sustain interest and suspense almost to the end of this convoluted epic which is mostly a serious, sometimes grim study of the causes and effects of intervention by one country in the affairs of another. Some rather intense violence. A-III (M)

Sandakan 8 (1977)   Japanese movie about a feminist (Komaki Kurihara) researching the life of an old woman (Kinuyo Tanaka) who as a girl had been sold into prostitution at the beginning of the century. Director Kei Kumai has made a work of some cultural and historical value, gets superb performances but his feminist message is rather preachy and somewhat sentimental. Mature themes. A-III (R)

Sands of Iwo Jima (1949)   John Wayne gives a standout performance as a tough Marine sergeant leading his men against the Japanese in the Pacific. Director Allan Dwan's movie of men in battle is a fairly realistic portrayal of island warfare and the not-so-easy courage of those who fought it. A-II (br)

Sands of the Kalahari (1966)   British melodrama about the struggle for survival of the six survivors of a plane crash in the African desert, among them the usual assortment of good (Harry Andrews) and bad (Nigel Davenport), hard (Stanley Baker) and soft (Theodore Bikel) stereotypes. Directed by Cy Enfield, the lone woman passenger (Susanna York) is almost raped and the proceedings are grim, thirsty going. A-III (br)

Santa Claus: The Movie (1985)   The story of Santa Claus (David Huddleston) gets off to a good start but slows down to a crawl when a subplot about a disillusioned elf (Dudley Moore) and a wicked 20th-century toy maker (John Lithgow) is introduced. The beautiful cinematography of the North Pole and Santa's workshop is wasted on an ultimately silly and forgettable story. A-II (PG)

Santa Fe Satan (see: "Catch My Soul")

Sasquatch (1978)   Psuedo-documentary about a motley expedition's venture into the wilds of British Columbia in search of the legendary ape-like creature called Sasquatch by the Indians. The acting is atrocious and the general tone is one of tedium which some stock footage of wildlife and scenic views does little to alleviate. A-I (G)

Sasuke Against the Wind (1973)   Japanese samurai movie about warring feudal clans whose loyalties shift back and forth while ninja (samurai spies) sow dissension and mistrust among their enemies. Director Masahiro Shinoda portrays the ninja as figures of moral ambiguity, men in any period of history using violence and corruption for "higher" ends. The visually beautiful black-and-white action film has some strong violence serving to open up the question of moral values in a violent world. A-III (nr)

Satan's Brew (1977)   German movie directed by Rainer Werner Fassbinder in which an author suffering acute writer's block tries a number of desperate measures to break through, each of them involving cruel exploitation of one sort or another, sexual more often than not. Excess in sexual treatment. O (nr)

Satan's Sadists (1971)   Clean-cut ex-marine (Gary Kent) battles in his own merciless manner a gang of motorcycle maniacs (led by Russ Tamblyn) in order to save a mindless coed (Jackie Taylor). Directed by Al Adamson, the crude proceedings are excessively violent. O (R)

Saturday Morning (1971)   Dated documentary recording a group encounter session with 20 Southern California teenagers talking, at times quite crudely, among themselves about parents, sex and love. Directed by Kent Mackenzie, what emerges from their statements is general confusion and uncertainty about their identity and social roles. Perhaps useful for group discussion purposes but without some mature guide, it can only further confuse young viewers. A-III (R/GP appeal)

Saturday Night at the Baths (1975)   Low-budget movie about the initiation into homosexuality of a young pianist hired to play at a mecca for homosexuals in New York City. The quality of its inspiration and characterization is more sad than gay. O (R)

Saturday Night Fever (1978)   Brooklyn youth (John Travolta) works hard six days a week and escapes into the magic time of Saturday night at the local discotheque where he is the king of the dance floor and girls are readily available. The movie's dramatic tension comes from the youth's gradually becoming aware of the emptiness of his life. Directed by John Badham, this vivid portrayal of blue-collar youth at play is filled with coarse language and sexual references but it comes to grips with some fundamental and extremely painful moral and social problems. A-IV (R/PG)

Saturn 3 (1980)   Mediocre British science fiction movie with Kirk Douglas and Farrah Fawcett living in tranquility aboard a deep space station until psychotic Harvey Keitel drops in with a robot named Hector who kills people that disagree with him. Directed by Stanley Donen, there is a very violent finale and some nudity in a sexual context. O (R)

Savage! (1973)   American mercenary (James Iglehardt) brings along his carnival girl friends when he joins rebels in their struggle to overthrow sadistic military leaders in an obscure jungle country. Director Cirio H. Santiago exploits the women for casual sex and steers hundreds of puppet soldiers into bloody massacres. Terrible rubbish. O (R)

Savage, The (1952)   Interesting Western about a white boy raised as a Sioux Indian (Charlton Heston) whose loyalty to his tribe is tested when pioneers arrive to stake out a settlement. Directed by George Marshall, the story holds the viewer's attention, the backgrounds are authentic and the fighting is minimal. A-I (br)

Savage Is Loose, The (1974)   Soggy melodrama about a shipwrecked family stranded on a remote island where their young son grows to adolescence and his sexual longings lead him to taunt his father (George C. Scott) to mortal combat, with winner take all, meaning Mom (Trish Van Devere). Also produced and directed by Scott, the plodding narrative is dramatically unconvincing while its treatment of incest is exploitative and the story's resolution morally unsupportable. The movie could be severely disturbing to youngsters, particularly those wrestling with their own growing awareness of sexuality. O (R)

Savage Island (1985)   Director Edward Muller's story of women behind bars in the tropics is filled with violence and graphic sex. O (R)

Savage Messiah (1972)   Uneven British screen biography of Henri Gaudier-Brzeska (Scott Anthony), a young French painter who came to London in 1910, began his career in a great burst of energy and died at the age of 23 in the trenches of World War I. Director Ken Russell makes convincing the young artists's brother-sister relationship with an older woman (Dorothy Tutin) who inspires his love and artistic endeavors. In placing the figure in his times, however, Russell strays over the edge of taste in some scenes at the decadent Vortex Club and in depicting at great length the crass vulgarity of a naked society girl. O (R)

Savage Seven, The (1968)   Deadly motorcycle gang movie directed by Richard Rush makes no pretense that it is anything more than a vehicle for an exhibition of sadistic brutality and casual sex. O (br)

Savage Sisters (1974)   Philippine exploitation movie about a trio of women (Gloria Hendry, Cheri Caffaro and Rosanna Ortiz) who team to hunt down the villains who have stolen a million dollars intended to finance a revolution. Directed by Eddie Romero, the low-budget action movie limps along on excessive violence and soft-core sex. O (R)

Savage Streets (1984)   Director Danny Steinmann's crude and violent exploitation movie about teenage gangs and vengeance, with one of the ringleaders being Linda Blair. Sexual violence. O (R)

Savage Wild, The (1970)   George Eastman wrote, produced, directed and stars in a documentary providing a remarkably vivid portrait of the lives and habits of three Alaskan wolves which he caught as cubs and photographed over a period of two years before releasing them in the wilds. Young audiences will relate to the director's daughter who shares in the raising of the cubs, though they may be slightly alarmed at seeing the grown wolves hunting down and devouring a caribou. A-I (G)

Savages (1972)   Failed fable in which a primitive tribe is civilized in one day by the decaying remains of a higher culture and then that night falls back into barbarism. Director James Ivory tries an allegorical form and satiric style clearly foreign to his previous compassionate intercultural studies and the result is a hodge-podge of individual scenes that fail to mesh into a consistent whole. Some bizarre sexual scenes. O (nr)

Save the Children (1973)   Documentary directed by Stan Lathan records the vibrant performances at the 1972 PUSH (People United to Save Humanity) Expo's celebration of the black musical heritage from basic gospel through classic rhythm and blues to the soul sound and polished nightclub swinging. The final segment is in Rev. Jesse Jackson's church where he preaches the message of saving children and all sorts of other people in a way that has a compelling effect upon the congregation and, deservedly, the viewer. A-I (G)

Save the Tiger (1973)   Harried West Coast clothing executive (Jack Lemmon) goes through a personal and business crisis over a 36-hour period and discovers that there is nothing left to believe in. Directed by John G. Avildsen, the movie is not without interest or rewards, and it is especially good at conveying a sense of the American everyman caught in the pressure-cooker of gritty, everyday life. The problem is that the character has no other values than his material affluence and his fear of losing it evokes only pity rather than sympathy. A-III (R)

Say Hello to Yesterday (1971)   Through the course of a single sunny day, a British suburban matron (Jean Simmons) is encountered, pursued, and seduced by an obnoxious, devil-may-care youth (Leonard Whiting). Directed by Alvin Rakoff, the unwholesome story of a brief encounter offers implausible characters in a shallow plot about a superficial relationship whose inevitable denouement is a slightly ludicrous bedroom scene. O (PG)

Say One for Me (1959)   Artificial melodrama about a parish priest (Bing Crosby) in an off-Broadway church who sings a little and reforms a few show people (Robert Wagner, Debbie Reynolds and Ray Walston). Directed by Frank Tashlin, the proceedings are contrived and the sentiment is somewhat hollow. A-II (br)

Sayonara (1957)   Screen version of James Michener's novel about an Army officer (Marlon Brando) stationed in Japan who falls in love with a stage performer (Miko Taka), thereby complicating his life and future. Directed by Joshua Logan, it's an intelligent drama with good performances and exotic Japanese locales and customs. A-III (br)

Scalawag (1973) Middling pirate adventure based loosely on Robert Louis Stevenson stars peg-legged Kirk Douglas (who also directs) as he sails along the California coast robbing gold-laden merchantmen, as well as hobbling upon the hardscrabble coastal area where Mark Lester and his pretty sister are trying to maintain a faltering homestead. There's old-fashioned romance, double-crosses and a climactic fight deep inside a cave holding a fortune in gold doubloons. What's not old-fashioned is a clumsy rape attempt played for laughs. A-II (G)

Scalpel (1978) Plastic surgeon remakes the face of a beaten-up go-go dancer to resemble that of his runaway daughter in order to cash in on a five million dollar will left in his daughter's name. Directed by John Grissmer, the movie indulges in some gore, has a casual attitude toward the value of human life and uses nudity and titillating references to incest. O (PG)

Scalphunters, The (1968) Burt Lancaster stars as a frontier fur trapper determined to retrieve his winter's haul stolen by Indians, who in return have left him a runaway slave (Ossie Davis), a situation further complicated when white scalphunters take the furs from the Indians. Directed by Sidney Pollack, it is a well-researched Western that makes some points about racial relations but it chiefly shows what a fine actor Davis can be. A-II (br)

Scandal at Scourie (1953) Norman Corwin's story about a Protestant couple (Greer Garson and Walter Pidgeon) who adopt a Catholic orphan, an act which scandalizes their Canadian community. Directed by Jean Negulesco, the situation is interesting but the treatment is not very convincing. A-II (br)

Scandalous (1984) Television journalist (Robert Hays), working on an expose of an uncle-niece team of con artists (John Gielgud and Pamela Stephenson), suddenly finds himself accused of murdering his unloving but rich spouse. Director Rob Cohen's mishmash of a plot becomes a wasted effort for all concerned. Some adult humor. A-III (PG)

Scandalous John (1971) Irascible, unpredictable old man (Brian Keith), dreaming of the old days when he and the West were young and exciting, begins imagining himself a Western Don Quixote and the man (Alfonso Arua) hired to care for him becomes his jovial Sancho Panza as the two do battle against some land developers. Keith faultlessly treads the narrow line between comic madness and pathos in a thoroughly delightful Disney production directed by Robert Butler. A-I (G)

Scanners (1981) Repellent Canadian horror movie about the super-intelligent people of the title whose highly developed brains can cause such things as heads to explode when they put their minds to it. Directed by David Cronenberg, the flimsy plot about tracking down some deviant scanners is only an excuse for gory special effects of explicit violence. O (R)

Scarecrow (1973) Uneven buddy movie about two drifters (Gene Hackman and Al Pacino) who meet on a Western road, throw in together and decide to go back East to open a carwash. What follows is an odyssey of hitch-hiking and hopping freights from one tank town to another, and some of their encounters with American low lifes are quite gross. Directed by Jerry Schatzberg, the two principals give solid performances of the mismatched characters but the movie is more discour-aging than illuminating in its portrayal of the male bond. Tawdry details abound and among the sordid incidents are a brutal rape attempt, a savage prison beating and a brief but graphic encounter with a prostitute. O (R)

Scarecrow in a Garden of Cucumbers (1972) Amateurish musical comedy spoof about a star-struck Kansan (female impersonator Holly Woodlawn) who encounters the expected variety of vulgar New York City types in quest of Broadway fame. Film school graduate Robert J. Kaplan gets a failing grade for his purported direction. A-III (nr)

Scarface (1983) Repellent remake of Howard Hawk's 1932 gangster classic is set in present day Miami where a Cuban immigrant and hardened criminal (Al Pacino) makes it in no time from the bottom rung to the top in the drug rackets. Director Brian De Palma's ugly, turgid, foul-mouthed and violent movie owes little to the original and is classic only in the sense of its crude self-indulgence. Perversely excessive violence. O (X/R appeal)

Scars of Dracula (1971) Nearby villagers are unable to help three young people trapped in the castle lair of Dracula (Christopher Lee) but two of them survive after a bolt of lightening finally destroys the monster. British production directed by Roy Ward Baker is one of the less interesting of the Dracula movies. Though less frightening than tedious, its visualization of blood-lust makes it inappropriate for youngsters. A-III (R)

Scavenger Hunt (1980) Uninvolving plot about a rich eccentric (Vincent Price) whose will decrees that his fortune go to the heir that scores the most points in a scavenger hunt. Robert Morley, as his lawyer, manages to give the only dignified performance in this excruciatingly silly movie directed by Michael Schultz. A-II (PG)

Scavengers, The (1970) Demented, racist captain (Jonathan Bliss) spurs his mangy band of Confederates on to rape and murder as they commandeer a Civil War-torn Kentucky town to capture a Union gold shipment. Director R.L. Frost treats the gross killings and sexual abuse with repulsive intensity. O (R)

Scenes from a Marriage (1974) Episodic Swedish drama about a middle-aged couple (Liv Ullmann and Erland Josephson) who after ten years of a seemingly ideal marriage, get divorced when the husband falls in love with a younger woman. Seven years later, though married to different partners, they drift into an affair with each other, relatively happy in their new-found discovery of themselves. Written, produced and directed by Ingmar Bergman, the movie uses exterior moments in the couple's relationship to tellingly reveal the interior pain and loneliness that constitute the motivation for their actions. Some may object to its depiction of the intimate details of married life but, for many, it will hit the mark for honesty and truth in showing the frail attempts by which one individual reaches out to another. A-IV (PG)

Scent of a Woman, The (1976) Director Dino Risi's tedious, sentimental and often distasteful account of a blinded Italian army officer (Vittorio Gassman) who journeys from Turin to Naples to carry out a suicide pact with a fellow officer but is redeemed by the love of a young woman. Excessive nudity and graphic sex. O (R)

Schizoid (see: "A Lizard in a Woman's Skin")

School Girls, The (1972) German exploitation

movie directed by Ernst Hoffbauer offers dreary dramatizations of a so-called psychologist's case histories demonstrating the morality of various forms of sexual promiscuity. O (nr)

Schoolgirls Growing Up (1972) Sequel to the German exploitation piece in which director Ernst Hoffbauer offers fuller illustrations of female teen-agers' lunchtime confessions with even more gross graphics. O (nr)

Scorchy (1976) Narcotics agent Connie Stevens is ever eager to give her all in the fight against crime. Much sex, much mayhem, no intelligence. O (R)

Scorpio (1973) Good espionage thriller about a CIA agent (Burt Lancaster) who senses his number is up and tries to disappear with his wife and the money he has made selling classified information. Director Michael Winner fills in the plot, which has enough twists to satisfy spy buffs, with plenty of solid action and fast-paced excitement. The amoral world of espionage stories is very evident here and the cynicism of its characters is not for anyone who might take them seriously. A-III (PG)

Scott Joplin (1977) Screen biography of the gifted black ragtime composer (Billy Dee Williams) does not gloss over the less entertaining aspects of his career and grim death. Thanks to some good performances, the colorful backgrounds of the era and, above all, Joplin's music, it is an enjoyable, and at times, affecting movie in spite of the self-conscious direction of Jeremy Paul Kagan. A-II (PG)

Scratch Harry (1969) Although its plot had some potential for making valid comments on marriage and social values, it loses dramatic perspective on its amoral characters with the introduction of an extended lesbian sequence, a completely gratuitous love-making episode and sporadic nudity. O (R)

Scream and Scream Again (1970) British horror movie in which Vincent Price plays a mad doctor assembling living organs to create a master race. Director Gordon Hessler's thriller leaves little to the imagination by dwelling at length on violence, blood and gore. O (PG)

Scream, Blacula, Scream (1973) Sequel in which Blacula (William Marshall) rises from the dust to put the bite on the brothers and sisters of Los Angeles but he winds up on the wrong end of a voodoo pin-sticking spree when he tangles with sexy Pam Grier. Director Bob Kelljan's campy B-grade horror movie has fanged ghouls coming out of the woodwork at the eerie mansion where much of the action, including a gory climax, takes place. A-III (PG)

Scream of Terror, The (see: "Point of Terror")

Screwballs (1983) Mindless, unfunny comedy about five high school students and their pursuit of the one unattainable girl at their school. Director Rafal Zielinski's focus is totally on sex with excessive reliance upon nudity as a source of humor. O (R)

Scrooge (1970) British musical version of Dickens' "A Christmas Tale" concentrates on poor old misanthropic Scrooge (Albert Finney), a thoroughly craven humbug whose disagreeableness is never believable and hence all the more fun to watch. Directed by Ronald Neame, it is a light, intelligent, and very amusing effort which wisely concentrates on the plot, using song and dance sparingly but well. The acting by the ghosts (Alec Guinness, Edith Evans, and Kenneth More) is

especially imaginative and the mood of the film is closely tied to Ronald Searle's delightful caricatures appearing with the credits. It's a movie for those who still have enough of the child within them to be able to relax and enjoy an old-fashioned bit of make-believe. A-I (G)

Scuba (1973) Documentary follows six young diving enthusiasts in the Caribbean as they search the ocean floor for buried treasure, feed fish and visit the decaying hulks of ancient wrecks. Narrated by Lloyd Bridges and directed by Ambrose Gaines, there is some quite engaging underwater photography of sea life that provides an experience of nature's beauty. A-I (G)

Sea Gull, The (1968) Screen version of Chekhov's play about a dacha full of characters (Simone Signoret, Vanessa Redgrave, James Mason and David Warner) quietly destroying themselves and one another through lovelessness and infatuation for the wrong people. Director Sidney Lumet brings a fresh eye to the play's tensions and impending sense of tragedy but some will find it rather static and overlong. A-III (G)

Sea Gypsies, The (1978) Handome widower (Robert Logan), his two young daughters, a woman photographer (Mikki Jamison-Olsen) and a little black stowaway set off on a round-the-world sailing trip but the boat sinks off the coast of Alaska and the movie becomes a family-style Robinson Crusoe adventure. Needless to say, everyone cooperates to cope with the forbidding terrain and climate and the incursions of hostile animals. Writer-director Stewart Raffill has made a pleasant and unpretentious entertainment for the whole family. Very young children, however, might be frightened by skillfully-done scenes involving unfriendly animals. A-I (G)

Sea Hawk, The (1940) Errol Flynn established himself as the king of the swashbuckers in this lavish Warner Brothers adventure in which he starred as an English privateer eliminating the Spanish foe from the high seas during the reign of Queen Elizabeth I. Director Michael Curtiz contrasts schoolboy romance with ruthless ambition in the Flynn character who contests the villainous Henry Daniell. Swordplay and light comedy are supported by the rousing Erich Wolfgang Korngold music score. A-I (br)

Sea Pirate, The (1967) Mediocre Italian adventure movie about the crew of a corsair who turn to piracy when the French take all the booty, one half of which, according to the unwritten code of the high seas, belongs to the crew. Directed by Roy Rowland, its story of an outlaw hero (Gerald Barray) is leagues away from the Robin Hood legend but its swashbuckling violence is relatively innocuous. A-II (br)

Sea Wolves, The (1981) Fact-based World War II story about some overage, overweight British civilians in India who steal into the neutral harbor of Goa to destroy a German freighter. Director Andrew V. McLaglen focuses not on the gallantry of the amateur commandos but on the derring-do of two intelligence agents (Gregory Peck and Robert Moore) who prepare the way. Preposterous subplot involves a dalliance between Moore and a beautiful German spy (Barbara Kellerman). Some violence, vulgar language and incidental nudity. A-III (PG)

Seance on a Wet Afternoon (1964) Intelligent British mystery thriller about a neurotic medium (Kim Stanley), her weak but compassionate husband (Richard Attenborough) and the kidnapping of a small child. Director Bryan Forbes builds a stark, somber atmosphere as riveting as it is disquieting, in a work that has a lot of psychological tension but no cheap thrills. A-II (br)

Search, The (1948) American soldier (Montgomery Clift) stationed in Germany tries to find the relatives of a boy he has befriended while his mother is desperately searching for him. Director Fred Zinnemann's story of World War II's displaced persons is entirely credible in its treatment of their problems and genuinely moving in its respect for the human dignity of all involved. A-I (br)

Search for Solutions, The (1980) Extremely well-done inquiry into the scientific method of problem-solving is designed to stimulate the interest of youngsters. Director Michael Jackson and producer James C. Crimmins lead the viewer through an imaginative and thoughtful odyssey which is part dramatization, part newscast, part interview and part straight documentary. Very entertaining as well as informative. A-I (G)

Searchers, The (1956) Western classic about a Comanche raid on a Texas ranch in which the Indians take captive a young girl (Natalie Wood) whose uncle (John Wayne) stays on their trail for five years before the final showdown. Director John Ford's leisurely tour of Monument Valley provides the proper setting for a crackling good tale of pioneer life and characters, told with good humor, taut but spare action and a full command of the Western movie myth that he helped create. A-II (br)

Sebastian (1967) British satire about the rehumanization of a mathematical genius (Dirk Bogarde) who is so obsessed with his government work that he barely notices that all of his assistants are pretty young women, until the prettiest among them (Susannah York) ultimately manages to make him look up from his desk and try a little tenderness. Slightly marred by cliche visits to discotheque and LSD-type freakout, but has some genuinely witty dialogue and Bogarde's top-notch acting. A-III (br)

Second Gun, The (1973) Tedious documentary attempts to prove that Sen. Robert F. Kennedy was assassinated not by Sirhan B. Sirhan, the man convicted of the murder, but by a nearby security guard. Director Gerard Alcan raises some intriguing questions but hardly supplies enough convincing evidence and his argument requires some maturity to sort things out and place them in proper perspective. A-III (PG)

Second Hand Hearts (1981) Barbara Harris plays a widow with three children and Robert Blake is a self-described bum who marries her in a drunken stupor but awakes to face up to his responsibilities and they try to find happiness as a family. The comedy's heart, second hand or otherwise, is in the right place, but it suffers from an uncertainty of tone under Hal Ashby's direction. Some vulgarities and a homosexual encounter. A-III (PG)

Seconds (1966) Middle-aged banker fed up with his deadening routine pays a mysterious organization to provide a new identity but he finds his new life not what he expected. Directed by John Frankenheimer, it's intriguing mystery with a troubling ending. Sexually exploitive sequence. O (br)

Secret, The (1975) French thriller about a man (Jean-Louis Trintignant) who escapes from a psychiatric ward and is given refuge by a couple (Philippe Noiret and Marlene Jobert) after telling them that he is hiding from government agents ordered to kill him. Directed by Robert Enrico, the suspense and red herrings are handled rather clumsily but the skillful acting and characterizations keep one's attention to the chilling climax. Some violence and sexual implications. A-III (nr)

Secret Admirer (1985) A girl's anonymous love letters to a boy who is her best friend keep falling into the wrong hands, including those of their respective parents, making for all sorts of complications in this inept teenage comedy from director David Greenwalt. Benign view of teenage drinking and promiscuity, brief nudity and some harsh language. O (R)

Secret Agent Fireball (1966) Mediocre Italian spy melodrama directed by Martin Donan about an American agent (Richard Harrison) assigned to Europe to protect an international scientific project. Stylized violence. A-III (br)

Secret Agent Super Dragon (1966) Routine European-made spy melodrama directed by Calvin J. Padgett about a CIA agent (Ray Danton) who foils the plans of an underground group to control the world through a drug that turns people into human robots. Stylized violence and mild sexual innuendo. A-III (br)

Secret Ceremony (1968) Morbid, disquieting melodrama about the unhealthy relationship between a middle-aged prostitute (Elizabeth Taylor) and a retarded girl (Mia Farrow) who, though they need help, cannot help each other. Directed by Joseph Losey, the story has a heavy touch of madness, incest, suicide and sexual shenanigans introduced by Robert Mitchum's uninvited presence. A-IV (R)

Secret Life of an American Wife, The (1968) Failed satire in which a bored suburban housewife (Anne Jackson) tries to convince a movie star (Walter Matthau) that she's a high-priced call girl. Directed by George Axelrod, the situation is not only unfunny but its blatant toying with adultery is punctuated by tasteless sight gags and language. O (R)

Secret of Magic Island (1964) Real, not cartoon, domestic animals, employed with remarkable skill, are the only performers in this simple fairy tale which will be of special interest to animal lovers and the very young. A-I (br)

Secret of My Success, The (1987) Ambitious college-educated Kansas farmboy (Michael J. Fox) takes the sexual route to the top of the corporate ladder as a mailboy impersonating an executive in a madcap comedy about business ethics and the new American dream of instant achievement. Helen Slater is the love interest and Margaret Whitton plays the amorous woman who gets him to the top. Director Herbert Ross goes the bedroom humor route dependent upon sexual innuendo, negative stereotypes of women and acceptance of adultery. O (PG-13)

Secret of NIMH, The (1982) Uneven animated feature about a mother mouse who, anxious to save her family and home from a farmer's plow, seeks help from some rats with human intelligence gained inadvertently when they were subjected to various experiments at the National Institute for Mental Health (NIMH). Though director Don Bluth's graphics have the style and texture of the Walt Disney classics, unfortunately it lacks both a compelling story and a strong central character. It is on balance better than average family entertainment, with some scary moments for the very young. A-I (G)

Secret of Santa Vittoria, The (1969) Anthony Quinn and Anna Magnani star in an adaptation of Robert Crichton's comic novel about an Italian village hiding its prize wine from the Germans during World War II. Directed by Stanley Kramer, it's broad in style, but its characters are warm and the plot is entertaining. A-II (PG)

Secret of the Sword, The (1985) Animated feature starring He-Man, a hero who has progressed from toy to movie star. The plot has to do with He-Man's quest for his long-lost twin sister, She-Ra. Too unsubstantial to sustain a feature-length movie and the animation is entirely undistinctive. A-I (G)

Secret Policeman's Other Ball, The (1982) Filmed record of two London revues that the British Monty Python troupe did for Amnesty International. Some of the skits are very funny, but the rock interludes are undistinguished. Only for the most avid Python fans. Some sexually oriented humor and occasional rough language. A-III (R)

Secret Rites (1971) Italian psuedo-documentary collection of what it describes as "weird practices" from around the world. Others would call it a bizarre, vulgar and sensationalistic peep show, presented by director Ramiro Arango without pretext of cultural context or sociological significance. O (R)

Secret War of Harry Frigg, The (1968) Grinning Paul Newman fills the title role in this off-base Army comedy about a private who's only adept at escaping from the base stockade, a skill which gets him promoted to the rank of brigadier general in order to help spring a covey of fellow generals from an Italian POW camp. Directed by Jack Smight, it's an unfunny clunker in which even Newman looks bad. A-II (br)

Secret World, The (1969) Treehouse-centered world of an 11-year-old boy is the secret world of the title, but is not the central interest of this French movie. Instead it is the youth's random consideration of the realtionships between his uncle, his mistress and his wife. Between the uncle's mistress and the youngster grows an ambiguous friendship which turns out to be a modified mother-son relationship, sought by the boy who has lost his real mother in a car accident. A-III (PG)

Secretary, The (1972) Amateurish melodrama about a broker who encourages his wife's affair with his best friend while he enjoys the charms of his secretary and her pot-smoking friends. Written, produced and directed by William Diehl, Jr., it is blatantly sex-oriented entertainment. O (R)

Secrets (1979) Young couple (Jacqueline Bisset and Robert Powell) revitalize their sagging marriage with an afternoon of therapeutic adultery—she with a Swedish businessman, he with a woman executive. Trivial, low-budget movie directed by Philip Saville insults the intelligence while exploiting nudity and condoning adultery. O (R)

Seducers, The (1971) Italian exploitation movie about a group of unpleasant people on a yachting excursion who spend the entire movie seducing one another in various combinations. Director Ottavio Alessi makes the stultifying action even more unpleasant by filming it in bilious seaweed-green hues. Stay ashore. O (X/R)

Seduction, The (1982) Failed suspense thriller about a mentally disturbed young man (Andrew Stevens) who pursues and terrorizes a beautiful Los Angeles television newswoman (Morgan Fairchild). Directed by David Schmoeller, it's a deadly dull affair that exploits the subject with a great deal of nudity. O (R)

Seduction of Inga, The (1972) Swedish exploitation movie about a rural innocent (Marie Liljedahl) trying to cope with urban males. O (R)

Seduction of Joe Tynan, The (1979) Failed melodrama about the moral disintegration of an ambitious politician (Alan Alda) whose affair with a beautiful civil rights lawyer (Meryl Streep) almost destroys his marriage and career. Directed by Jerry Schatzberg, the story borders on soap opera despite some good acting. Though the adultery is presented as wrong, it is depicted quite vividly in some bedroom scenes and there is also vulgar and profane language. A-III (R)

Seduction of Mimi, The (1974) Italian satire about a Sicilian metal-worker (Giancarlo Giannini) who gets fired for voting against the bosses, works hard at a factory in Turin, is promoted back to his home town but, in seeking revenge for his wife's unfaithfulness, gets unwanted help from the Mafia and becomes trapped forever serving those he had originally opposed. Written and directed by Lina Wertmuller, the theme of the poor being exploited by the powerful is entirely serious but the treatment is in hilarious black comedy style. Some excesses in sexual treatment and language. O (R)

See No Evil (1971) Effective British thriller about a blind woman (Mia Farrow) who awakes to discover that everyone in the household has been slaughtered and panics when she realizes that the killer will return to recover some incriminating evidence. Though director Richard Fleischer doesn't play quite fair in his emotional manipulations, he achieves some high-intensity terror found in the best of Hitchcock. The violence is more implicit than explicit but its aura of psychological horror is not meant for youngsters to handle. A-III (GP)

Seems Like Old Times (1980) Offbeat romance about a liberal lawyer (Goldie Hawn) whose ex-husband (Chevy Chase) seeks her help when he becomes a fugitive mistakenly wanted for bank robbery, even though she is married to a stuffy district attorney (Charles Grodin). Predictable comedy, written by Neil Simon and directed by Jay Sandrich, is a guileless, innocent adult entertainment that succeeds in delivering a large number of laughs. Some bedroom pranks and occasional profanities. A-III (PG)

Seizure (1975) Turgid Canadian chiller about a horror writer-illustrator whose imaginings become real when a group of weekend visitors arrive at his eerie estate and a series of gruesome murders ensue, everything from knifings to head crushings. Directed by Oliver Stone, the ridiculous plot renders the contrived and clumsily handled violence relatively innocuous. A-III (PG)

Semi-Tough (1977) Burt Reynolds and Kris Kristofferson star in a comedy about pro football players and their playmates. Directed by Michael Ritchie, it has some genuinely funny moments but its satiric focus is unclear, often turning nasty and relying for humor on foul language and nudity. O (R)

Sender, The (1982) Horror clunker about a troubled amnesiac (Zeliko Ivanel) in the care of a pretty psychiatrist (Kathryn Harrold), given to wearing provocative clothing, who discovers that her patient has the deadly power to transmit his nightmares to other people. Directed by Roger Christian, this incoherent and violent movie contains gore, sexual innuendo and flirts with blasphemy. O (R)

Sense of Loss, A (1972) In his disturbing documentary about the violent strife in Northern Ireland, Marcel Ophuls examines the conflict by allowing its inhabitants, from all corners and levels, to speak for themselves. The result is a document that addresses with chilling directness a situation apparently beyond control of political forces and national aims and, indeed, very nearly beyond rational comprehension. A-II (nr)

Senso (1970) Set in the 19th century during the time of Garibaldi, this 1954 Italian melodrama relates the story of a passionately indiscreet countess (Alida Valli) and an unscrupulous lieutenant (Farley Granger). Directed by Luchino Visconti, the movie probes the relationship of personal and class attitudes, love and infidelity, evoking the ambivalences and decadence of a society in transition. A-III (nr)

Sensual Man, The (1977) Giancarlo Giannini is wasted in this muddled movie about the sexual misadventures of the lustful son of a noble Sicilian family. Writer-director Marco Vicario has taken Vitaliano Brancati's acclaimed novel, one of whose themes was the linking of sexual exploitation with the economic and social, and made a fatuous and tedious movie that itself exploits sex. O (R)

Sensuous Teenager, The (1972) French exploitation movie directed by Max Pecas with Sandra Jullien acting the role of an incontinent nymphomaniac in a softcore sex fantasy. O (R)

Sentinel, The (1977) Young couple (Christina Raines and Chris Sarandon) experiences terror and unnatural phenomena in a New York brownstone. Although director Michael Winner's horror movie purports to depict a struggle between good and evil, it deals in gross violence and nudity. O (R)

Separate Peace, A (1972) Faithful screen version of the novel by John Knowles, set in a New England prep school just before World War II, in which a shy and studious student (Parker Stevenson) leaves adolescence forever behind after inadvertently causing the death of his gregarious and athletic roommate (John Heyl). Directed by Larry Peerce, the film captures the spirit of the original in its ambiguous statement about the effect of the past in the formation of the mature adult. A-II (PG)

Serafino (1970) Earthy Italian comedy about the misadventures, mainly amorous, of a lustful but dense shepherd (Adriano Celentano) who is almost snared by his beautiful cousin (Ottavia Piccolo) but escapes marriage at the cost of his lean inheritance. Director Pietro Germi departs from his usual sophisticated brand of satire for a gritty, sweaty, extremely loud comedy with only modest results. Bawdy humor and coarse language. A-III (GP)

Serail (1976) Stylish French movie about a novelist who buys a chateau because he is intrigued by the odd behavior of its housekeeper (Leslie Caron), its owner (Marie-France Pisier) and its apparent ghost (Bulle Ogier). Written and directed by Eduardo de Gregorio, the mystery deepens until, at last, the mood shifts from suspense to horror. A sequence employs sexually explicit dialogue as unnecessary as it is offensive. O (R)

Sergeant, The (1968) Outwardly tough but inwardly unstable Army sergeant (Rod Steiger) gets into real trouble when a young recruit (John Phillip Law) comes into conflict with his latent-homosexual superior. Director John Flynn helps enhance Steiger's fine performance by carefully creating the bleak postwar Army environment with effective detail. Solid, finely wrought, adult drama. A-III (R)

Sergeant Rutledge (1960) Good Western in which a black trooper (Woody Strode) faces a court martial charged with murder and rape. Director John Ford tells the story in flashbacks as the court examines the evidence, with Strode coming across as a strong figure of considerable integrity. A-II (br)

Sergeant Ryker (1968) Korean War story of a soldier (Lee Marvin) accused of collaborating with the enemy but who insists he was following the orders of an officer now dead. Directed by Buzz Kulik, the courtroom drama raises a number of moral questions about responsibility in wartime. A-II (br)

Sergeant York (1941) Gary Cooper stars as a backcountry youth drafted into the Army in World War I who overcomes his pacifist convictions to become a sharpshooting hero. Director Howard Hawks has combined solid movie of Americana with a sensitive story of conscience. A-I (br)

Serial (1980) Cynical social satire about the effects of experimenting with hedonistic lifestyles and the narcissistic search for cures by a California couple (Martin Mull and Tuesday Weld) and their rebellious teenage daughter (Jennifer McAlister). Directed by Bill Persky, the movie lacks the intelligence and integrity to carry off the satire and settles instead for sexual orgies, nudity, rough language and easy stereotypes. O (R)

Serpent, The (see: "Night Flight from Moscow")

Serpent's Egg, The (1978) Director Ingmar Bergman's story of an American Jew (David Carradine) stranded in Berlin in 1923, with the German economy in total collapse and anti-Semitism on the rise is a dramatic muddlement which seems to be aiming at some sort of political commentary but failing badly. The somberness of its atmosphere and its vivid depictions of the squalor of the times make it decidedly mature fare. A-IV (R)

Serpico (1973) Screen version of the life and hard times of Frank Serpico (Al Pacino), the New York City patrolman whose disclosure of deep and insidious corruption within the police force went unheard until he told the press, after which a commission was set up to reform the department. Director Sidney Lumet's movie is gritty and uncompromising, convincingly realistic, yet engrossing in its human drama and tension. Its theme of corruption is unpleasantly graphic and some will find its implications frightening. A-IV (R)

Servant and Mistress (1978) French melodrama about a man (Victor Lanoux) who comes to claim his inheritance when his wealthy uncle dies but finds that the entire estate has been left to the maid (Andrea Ferreol). Seeking revenge, she gives him the option of leaving without a penny or staying on as her servant. Director Bruno Gantillon's well-acted but tedious parable on the misuse of power in human relations is seriously offensive in several scenes of sexuality. O (nr)

Seven Alone (1975) Disappointing re-creation of an historical incident that took place in 1843 when seven children, led by their 14-year-old brother (Stewart Peterson), traveled a good portion of the Oregon Trail on their own after losing their parents. Earl Bellamy's uncertain direction lacks the feel of pioneer realities and stereotypes the Indians. Take the children if there is nothing else to see, but don't expect a great deal. A-I (G)

Seven Beauties (1976) Italian tragicomedy about a petty crook (Giancarlo Giannini) in 1930s Naples who bungles a murder, gets drafted in World War II, deserts while being shipped to the Russian front, is interned in a concentration camp but survives having learned nothing. Director Lina Wertmuller's vision, though dark and stormy, is also permeated with a love for the beauty and richness of life. Some grisly violence and an earthy treatment of sex. A-IV (R)

Seven Brides for Seven Brothers (1954) Western musical about Oregon pioneers who, when their brother (Howard Keel) brings home a bride (Jane Powell), go out and kidnap some local belles. Directed by Stanley Donen, the zest of the music, dancing and story carry the movie in highly enjoyable fashion. A-II (br)

Seven Cities of Gold (1955) Plodding melodrama about Spanish conquistadores hunting for Indian gold with the good Padre Junipero Serra (Michael Rennie) trying to avert bloodshed. Directed by Robert D. Webb, it's a well-intentioned but shallow historical adventure. A-I (br)

Seven Days in May (1964) Top American general (Burt Lancaster) plots to take over the government to thwart the President (Frederic March) from signing a disarmament agreement with the Russians. Directed by John Frankenhiemer, the suspense thriller is credibly done and provides food for thought. A-II (br)

Seven Days to Noon (1950) Excellent British thriller about a deranged scientist (Barry Jones) who threatens to destroy London with an atomic bomb unless the world disarms. Directed by Roy and John Boulting, the plot is neatly worked out, the acting is first rate and the suspense has real point. A-I (br)

Seven Faces of Dr. Lao (1964) Diverting entertainment focusing on a traveling circus owned by the mysterious Dr. Lao (Tony Randall who also plays seven other roles) whose performances work strange effects on his audience in a town of the Old West. Director George Pal's fantasy has imaginative special effects and its story should intrigue youngsters and amuse adults. A-I (br)

Seven Golden Men (1969) Routine Italian heist movie about the intricate maneuvers used to get into a bank vault, steal the loot and then lose it in a series of double crosses. Director Marco Vacario's crime movie is not a spoof, though it does have some humor and some personable crooks (Philippe Leroy, Gastone Moschin, Jose Suarez and Rossana Podesta). A-II (G)

Seven Little Foys, The (1955) Dramatization of vaudeville comedian Eddie Foy (Bob Hope) who has problems raising his family of seven when his wife (Millie Vitale) dies. Directed by Michael Shavelson, the saga of a show business family has good acting, some humor and does not follow the usual sentimental formula. A-II (br)

Seven Minutes, The (1971) Numbingly sensationalistic rendering of Irving Wallace's novel about a California pornography trial has all the depth of a Hollywood press release and all the titillation of an arcade peep show. Director Russ Meyer's characters are uniformly stereotypes, the relevant issues are hopelessly obscured and there is some explicit sexual action. O (R/PG)

Seven Percent Solution, The (1976) Sigmund Freud (Nichol Williamson) meets Sherlock Holmes (Alan Arkin) in a stylish and mostly entertaining mystery directed by Herbert Ross. An incidental brothel scene and some frightening images that occur while Holmes is suffering from narcotic withdrawal symptoms are not for youngsters. A-III (PG)

Seven-Ups, The (1974) Action-packed but hackneyed story of a special police unit, headed by Roy Scheider, that gets in the middle of an elaborate gangland war. Directed by Phil D'Antoni, New York City is well used as the battleground where cop and criminal shoot it out, and where it is hard to tell the hunter from the hunted. Elaborate and intense car chases and an assortment of other special effects violence. A-III (PG)

1776 (1972) Entertaining screen version of the popular Broadway musical by Sherman Edwards and Peter Stone about the travails of the Continental Congress in forging the Declaration of Independence utilizes most of the original cast from William Daniels' John Adams to Howard Da Silva's Benjamin Franklin. Director Peter Hunt, who also directed the stage musical, relies on the original staging rather than trying for any big screen effects and it works well in mixing some light, diverting entertainment with some serious asides, such as slavery and marital loneliness. A-II (G)

Seventh Continent, The (1968) Czech-Yugoslav children's fantasy about a magical island which becomes the refuge for all the youngsters of the world who are ignored and forgotten by their busy parents, leaving the adult world behind in squabbles about how their children can be gotten back. Directed by Dustan Vukotic, it has a number of highly imaginative scenes and good special effects but tends to dwell too long on the tiresome adults. A-I (br)

Severed Head, A (1971) Failed British adaptation of the Iris Murdoch novel purports to be a sophisticated comedy of manners about the savagely civilized exercise of mixing and matching mates (among them, Lee Remick, Richard Attenborough, Claire Bloom and Clive Revill). Among all the soap opera forsaking of partners, director Dick Clement forsakes taste with some unnecessarily bare anatomy. A-IV (R)

Sex of Angels, The (1969) This Italian import, in which three affluent female delinquents trick a medical student onto a yachting trip and cause his death with drugs, is lurid trash. O (X)

Sex with a Smile (1976) Perhaps the least offensive element in this unfunny, soft-core, four-part Italian sex farce about four lusting men is that Marty Feldman, billed as the star, appears in only one segment. O (R)

Sextette (1979) Mae West plays a glamourous movie star whose wedding night with husband number six is interrupted by former husbands and the need to rescue a summit conference near shambles. Director Ken Hughes's farce is insufferably boring and, as might be expected, overflowing with an abundance of double entendres. A-III (PG)

Sgt. Pepper's Lonely Hearts Club Band (1978) Peter Frampton and the Bee Gees attempt to turn the Beatles' famous music album into a movie in which they play small-town musicians temporarily corrupted by becoming Los Angeles rock stars.

When they learn that baddies have despoiled their home town, they return to right all wrongs. Director Michael Schultz gets more the feel of an animated cartoon than a live-action and George Burns does some narration since the movie has no dialogue. Some suggestive gestures and lyrics as well as pot smoking and the use of cocaine. A-III (PG)

Shadow of a Doubt (1943) Young girl (Teresa Wright) begins to suspect that her favorite uncle (Joseph Cotton) is wanted for a series of murders. Director Alfred Hitchcock unfolds his usual dark doings in the commonplace setting of the solid citizens of small-town America with uncommonly rewarding results. A-II (br)

Shadow of the Hawk, The (1976) Terribly amateurish movie about an Indian medicine man (Chief Dan George) who wants his grandson (Jan-Michael Vincent), an IBM executive, to take over his practice and ward off the evil that threatens the tribe. Canadian production directed by George McCowan, the story is awfully far-fetched and not particularly scary. A-II (PG)

Shaft (1971) Director Gordon Parks adroitly uses New York City as the backdrop for what is really only a routine, if fast-paced and savvy, detective story involving a private eye (Richard Roundtree) and the police department in a power struggle between a black mobster (Moses Gunn) and the Mafia to control the drug, prostitution and numbers racket in Harlem. Some sharp and vicious violence, brief nudity and realistic street language. A-III (R)

Shaft in Africa (1973) John Shaft (Richard Roundtree) is taken out of Harlem by an African diplomat who requires his services to break up a contemporary slave ring being run by a depraved Arab (Frank Finlay). Directed by John Guillermin, the plot is merely a pretext for indulging in graphic violence, explicit nudity and extremely crude dialogue. O (R)

Shaft's Big Score (1972) When a big-time Harlem numbers operator dies, there is a scramble by black and white mobsters to take over the racket. Director Gordon Parks has turned his sequel into black exploitation, once again using Richard Roundtree as his hip private detective but this time smothering him in both easy (and often nude) women and gimmicky situations. Abundance of explicit violence and nudity. O (R)

Shaggy D.A., The (1977) Disney sequel has the now grownup hero (Dean Jones) a crusading district attorney candidate running against a crooked incumbent (Keenan Wynn) and severely inconvenienced by his sudden transformations. Directed by Robert Stevenson, the humor is very broad and the slapstick heavy-handed even by Disney standards. All but very young children will likely be bored much of the time. A-I (G)

Shaggy Dog, The (1959) Disney comedy directed by Charles Barton about a teenager whom a magic ring turns into a dog every now and then. The comic premise will appeal to youngsters, if not their parents. A-I (br)

Shake Hands with the Devil (1959) American student (Don Murray) in Ireland in the 1920s gets drawn into the struggle against British rule by a tough rebel leader (James Cagney). Director Michael Anderson is less interested in the issues of the conflict than the human casualties in this cycle of violence. A-II (br)

Shakespeare Wallah (1966) Director James Ivory's gentle study of the old and the new in modern India centers around an itinerant group of Shakespearean actors who find it difficult to bridge the gap between the old Anglo-Indian past and the changing values of the new India. One of the highlights is its ironic contrast between the romantic notions of a young English actress (Felicity Kendal) and the materialism of an Indian movie star to whom she is attracted. Many adults will find it an utterly disarming picture of a culture in transition. A-III (br)

Shakiest Gun in the West, The (1968) Western comedy in which Don Knotts stars as a dentist who bungles his way to becoming a hero. Directed by Alan Rafkin, it's a pint-sized version of Bob Hope's "Paleface," but not nearly as amusing. A-I (br)

Shalako (1968) Unconvincing Western about an aristocratic hunting expedition caught poaching on Apache land and rescued by a wily Indian fighter (Sean Connery). Director Edward Dmytryk handles the episodic action quite clumsily and the contrived love interest is ridiculous. Stylized violence. A-III (PG)

Shame (1969) Bleak Swedish drama about a couple (Liv Ullmann and Max Von Sydow) who escape a civil war by living on an island where they torment one another until the war drives them to a lifeboat drifting to sea. Director Ingmar Bergman's theme is the responsibility, personal and societal, for the kind of self-destruction imaged by civil war. Very intense, introspective movie but powerfully told and worth seeing. Violence. A-III (R)

Shameless Old Lady, The (1966) Gently satiric French story of an old lady (Sylvie), widowed in her seventies, who is clearsighted enough not to let her offspring take charge of her affairs but uses her small estate to enjoy the final months of her life. Directed by Rene Allio, it is an objective yet tender look at old age and the passive role assigned to it by social convention. A-II (br)

Shampoo (1975) Warren Beatty stars as a Beverly Hills hairdresser who becomes involved with his clients, especially Julie Christie, Goldie Hawn and Lee Grant. Directed by Hal Ashby, it is mindless fare as much devoid of humor as of humanity. Verbal obscenities and graphic depiction of sexual misbehavior. O (R)

Shamus (1973) Tough private eye from Brooklyn (Burt Reynolds) gets embroiled in a nasty little adventure involving diamond-heisting, gun-running, and double-crossing double-crossers. Directed by Buzz Kulik, the shallow plot's fast-paced action is done with some genial humor which helps diffuse numerous savage beatings and several restrained sex scenes. A-III (PG)

Shane (1953) Western classic about a gunfighter (Alan Ladd) who comes to the aid of a family of settlers (Van Heflin, Jean Arthur and Brandon De Wilde) in their battle against local ranchers. Directed by George Stevens, it's an epic tale of the conflict between cattlemen of the open range and homesteaders seeking farmland. Sylized violence. A-II (br)

Shanghai Killers, The (1973) Routine martial arts programmer from Hong Kong in which the warrior swords go snicker-snack and the studio crew throw rubber hands and arms and buckets of blood around with wild abandon, all in service of the usual senseless violence. O (R)

Shanghai Surprise (1986) Sean Penn and Madonna give woefully inadequate performances in a supposedly romantic adventure set in 1930's China involving a search for a lost shipment of opium intended for wounded soldiers in a mission hospital. Brutal violence, sex scenes and profanity. A-III (PG-13)

Shanks (1974) Odd but inept chiller starring French mime Marcel Marceau in the dual role of an ancient scientist and his deaf-mute assistant in a story-within-a-story involving an electronic device which can restore the dead to life. Directed by William Castle, the disjointed segments of the generally aimless and confused plot are introduced by title cards which don't help a bit. Some gruesome and violent visuals. A-III (PG)

Sharks' Treasure (1975) Not very exciting movie about diving for sunken treasure and a boat hijacking by murderous escaped convicts. Directed by Cornel Wilde (who also stars), it's routine adventure fare save for a homosexual reference in the plot. A-III (PG)

Sharky's Machine (1981) Burt Reynolds (who also directed) plays a tough and aggressive Atlanta detective demoted for overzealousness to the vice squad where he cracks down on prostitutes and drug dealers. Though the crime movie has some good moments (such as burly policeman Bernie Casey being a Zen devotee) and is consistently entertaining until its lackluster conclusion, the action includes a harrowing and far-fetched torture scene, some other graphic violence and very crude language. A-III (R)

She's Gotta Have It (1986) A serio-comic movie about a strong-willed, independent black woman (Tracy Camila Johns) who confounds three egocentric males. Director Spike Lee brings imagination and vitality to this low budget, black-and-white feature that offers some interesting characterizations with an accomplished all-black cast. Explicitly depicted sexual encounters, nudity and one scene of sexual brutality. O (R)

Sheba Baby (1975) Avenging black woman (Pam Grier) annihilates an army of hoods of various hues. Directed by William Girdler, it is a tasteless fantasy of sex and violence, though handled with some restraint. A-III (PG)

Sheena (1984) Comic book jungle drama about a female Tarzan named Sheena (Tanya Roberts) who runs through Africa scantily clad in animal skins, pursued by a romantic TV reporter (Ted Wass). Directed by John Guillermin, it is so bad that it provokes laughter in all the wrong places. Extensive nudity. O (PG)

Sheila Levine is Dead and Living in New York (1975) Failed screen version of Gail Parent's acerbically witty novel about a small-town girl (Jeannie Berlin) who escapes to New York in search of meaning and marriage, finds a doctor (Roy Scheider) and convinces him that country virtues are better than urban sophistication. Not only are the principals miscast, but director Sidney Furie is out of his element in working with a script that has the deadly mediocre level of TV situation comedy. A-III (PG)

Shinbone Alley (1971) Disappointing cartoon version of the Broadway musical based on Don Marquis' classic "archy and mehitabel" about the cockroach chronicler of the irrepressible alley cat whose spirit has transmigrated from Cleopatra. Directed by John D. Wilson, with the central characters voiced by Eddie Bracken and Carol Channing, the result simply lacks the elemental zest and witty irony of the Marquis original. A-I (G)

Shining, The (1980) Disappointing screen version of the Stephen King novel is a haunted house movie on a grand scale with Jack Nicholson as a writer who takes the job of winter caretaker of a hotel resort in the Colorado Rockies, accompanied by wife (Shelley Duvall) and young son (Danny Lloyd). Tormented and manipulated by the evil lurking in the massive hotel (the scene of a brutal axe murder), he is taken to the brink of madness and tries to kill his family. Director Stanley Kubrick's ponderous horror movie is predictable and slow-paced in building to its violent climax. Graphic violence, a needlessly extended erotic sequence and some rough language. O (R)

Shoah (1985) Death camp survivors, former Nazi officials and Poles living in the vicinity of the extermination sites are interviewed by producer-director Claude Lanzmann in this French documentary on the Holocaust. Although it does not show any photographs of Hitler's mass murder of European Jewry, the survivors' oral history of events is powerful and often shocking, all the more so because it personalizes the horror of the camps. Subtitled and more than nine hours in length, the work is a valuable educational resource on the Holocaust. A-II (nr)

Shock Troops (1968) French-Italian production about a group of French resistance fighters in World War II who raid a German prison to rescue 12 men sentenced to death but find that they have saved one man too many (Michel Piccoli) and suspect he may be a spy. Directed by Costa-Gavras, the story is much like other movies about the French Resistance, though its action scenes are almost documentary-like in effect. Wartime violence and brutality. A-III (R)

Shoes of the Fisherman, The (1968) Uneven screen version of the Morris L. West novel about a Russian bishop (Anthony Quinn) who becomes Pope and decides that the Vatican's wealth be given to the world's poor gets lost in a series of subplots. Directed by Michael Anderson, there is a lot of religious pageantry and international intrigue, but mainly conveyed on a superficial level. A-I (br)

Shogun Assassin (1980) Samurai swordsman wields his blade tirelessly in dispatching legions of assassins in this campy Americanized version of a Japanese martial arts movie directed by Kenji Jisumi. Narrated by a child, the action is a visual ballet of incessant violence and bloodshed. O (R)

Shoot (1976) Painfully well-intentioned diatribe directed by Harvey Hart against the cult of guns has a preposterous story of two groups of hunters who, because of an accidental shooting death, begin an armed war against each other. Much violence. A-III (R)

Shoot the Moon (1982) Successful Hollywood writer (Albert Finney) walks out on his wife (Diane Keaton) and four young daughters in director Alan Parker's account of sometimes savage marital strife. Though there are some effective touches, the movie withholds so much vital information about the principals that it becomes irritating and pretentious. Some intense violence and very rough language. A-III (R)

Shooting Party, The (1985) In the fall of 1913, some aristocrats gather at the estate of a nobleman (James Mason) to do a bit of shooting and carry on some romantic intrigues on the eve of the war that would end their world forever. Alan Bridges directs a thoughtful and entertaining film, if a bit slow-moving and predictable at times. Superbly acted but contains a rather explicit bedroom scene. A-IV (nr)

Shootist, The (1976) Uneven Western directed by Don Siegel in which a legendary gunfighter (John Wayne), told by a doctor (James Stewart) that he is dying of cancer, engages in a final shoot-out. The movie's glossing over of the hero's various moral failings makes it mature fare. A-III (PG)

Shootout (1971) Familiar revenge plot about a stoic ex-con (Gregory Peck) on his way to settle accounts with a double-crossing partner starts going astray when he is detained by a dependent widow (Pat Quinn) and a homeless waif (Dawn Lyn) who may be his daughter by a prostitute. Director Henry Hathaway leaves family audiences far behind with some sadistic violence, including a gang rape in a brothel and coarse language out of the mouth of a nine-year-old. Grim stuff. O (GP)

Shop on Main Street, The (1966) Czechoslovakian drama about the tragedy of life under a puppet Nazi regime is sensitively detailed in the unusual friendship that develops between a simple man (Josef Kroner) and an elderly Jewish widow (Ida Kaminska) over whose button shop he has been appointed "Aryan Controller." The high skill with which the situation is drawn by director Jan Kadar matches the movie's forceful condemnation of moral passivity in the face of inhumanity. A-III (br)

Short Circuit (1986) Number Five is a lovable robot who acquires human attributes after being struck by lightning and befriended by Ally Sheedy, an ill-tempered snack-wagon operator. Steve Guttenberg plays Number Five's inventor in this routine romance from director John Badham. Some suggestive comments and mild profanity are lost in the context of chase scenes. A-I (PG)

Short Eyes (1977) Screen version of Miguel Pinero's play about prison life tells the story of a man (Bruce Davison), accused of molesting a little girl, who is thrust into a volatile environment where the other prisoners subject him to systematic and brutal harassment as someone who is lower than them. Directed by Robert M. Young, the movie's strength is in the almost overpowering realism of its mood and setting and the compelling personalities of its characters. Although the rough language, the violence and the threatening atmosphere are thoroughly justified in content, the movie is not for everyone. A-IV (R)

Shout at the Devil (1976) Comedy about a boozy buccaneer (Lee Marvin) in World War I Southeast Africa who cons upright Britisher (Roger Moore)into a little elephant-tusk poaching on German territory suddenly turns nasty when Moore's wife is brutalized and his infant daughter burned to death by German forces. Directed by Michael Klinger, the movie has a blood-and-gore conclusion. A-III (PG)

Shout, The (1979) Intriguing psychological thriller about a mysterious stranger (Alan Bates) who threatens the husband (John Hurt) of a woman he wants to take (Susannah York) with the lethal power of a shout capable of killing everything within hearing distance, a mystical technique learned during a long stay among Australian aborigines. British production directed by Jerzy Skolimowski, it is beautifully photographed and performed but it cannot sustain its fragile premise.

Mature treatment. A-III (R)

Showdown (1973) Saddle-worn tale of two boyhood chums whose trails diverge but intertwine years later when one of them, an outlaw on the run (Dean Martin) seeks refuge from a one-time girl friend (Susan Clark), now the wife of the other, an upright sheriff (Rock Hudson). George Seaton directs the B-grade Western with deadly earnestness, relieved only by some foggy flashbacks of the pair's boyhood escapades and a few good action scenes. A-II (PG)

Shuttered Room, The (1967) British supsense thriller directed by David Greene about a couple (Carol Lynley and Gig Young) who journey to a New England island to take possession of the house where the wife grew up but find themselves harassed by the islanders and warned of a dire evil in the house. Excessive violence, a near rape and scenes with semi-nudity. O (br)

Sicilian, The (1987) Failed screen version of the Mario Puzo novel focuses on Salvatore Giuliano (Christopher Lambert), a historical figure whose rebellion against Sicily's Mafia, landowners and churchmen ended in 1950 with his murder. Directed by Michael Cimino, the movie is muddled and disjointed, with a narrative that is often ludicrous and lacking in a sense of the area's culture and history. Graphic violence, brief nudity and some rough language. A-IV (R)

Sicilian Clan, The (1970) Epic French heist tale is a duel of wits and guts between white-maned crime patriarch (Jean Gabin) and ambitious Paris hood (Alain Delon) over an impossibly complicated plane hi-jack of a fortune in jewels, with frustrated but persistent police inspector (Lino Ventura) keeping one step behind all the way. Directed by Henri Verneuil, the briskly-paced story of honor among thieves has a number of superior action sequences from an ingenious jail escape at the start to a grandly anti-climactic shoot-out. A-III (GP)

Sid and Nancy (1987) All the sordid details of physical and spiritual disintegration are celebrated in this harsh and excessively explicit portrait of the sadistic, self-destructive lives of British punk rock music star Sid Vicious and his American girlfriend, Nancy. Without care for the reasons behind Sid's tragic self-destruction, the film is masochistically exploitative. O (R)

Siddhartha (1973) Screen version of Hermann Hesse's novel about a Brahmin's son, Siddhartha (Shashi Kapoor), who rebels at his father's asceticism, rejects the message of various holymen, is disappointed with the pleasures of sex and the rewards of business, but finally discovers enlightenment in nature and the unity of life. Written, produced and directed by Conrad Rooks, the movie attempts to create a mystic experience, rendering the abstract and sometimes ponderous philosophizing of the text into the sheer beauty of poetic imagery, ably supplied by Sven Nykvist's camera. Some will find it an uplifting experience, while others will see only an album of pretty pictures. Restrained but erotic sex scene. A-III (R)

Sidecar Racers (1975) Young American (Ben Murphy), at loose ends in Australia, becomes involved in the hazardous sport of sidecar motorcycle racing. Directed by Earl Bellamy, it's an innocuous, mildly diverting action movie but some romantic complications are not for the youngsters. A-III (PG)

Sidewinder 1 (1977) Mediocre motorcycle racing movie directed by Earl Bellamy in which engineer Alex Cord develops a new cycle and goes into partnership with driver Michael Parks to refine it. An extramarital relationship makes it adult fare. A-III (PG)

Sign of the Virgin (1969) Failed Czechoslovakian comedy about a lonely soldier whose girl friend is smuggled onto the base by his comrades so they can spend the evening together in sick bay. Director Zbynek Brynych's attempts at humor are disappointingly clumsy as are several unnecessarily graphic scenes of the young couple. O (nr)

Silencers, The (1966) Shabby imitation spy spoof of James Bond spy adventure movies with Dean Martin playing Matt Helm, free-lance superspy who spends much of his time cracking heads and getting his own bent occasionally. When not thus engaged, he chases an assortment of comely female spies around the set. The comic level is uniformly low and so is the moral tone of the action. O (br)

Silent Movie (1976) Writer-director Mel Brooks stars as a washed-up director who gets the head of his studio (Sid Caesar) to let him make a silent comedy provided he can get Hollywood's biggest stars to participate. The result is sometimes funny, sometimes not, but it is harmless fun and less vulgar than other Brooks' comedies. Adult humor. A-III (PG)

Silent Night, Deadly Night (1984) Maniac dressed in a Santa Claus costume uses an axe to kill people. Dreadfully produced exploitative horror suggests that director Charles Sellier Jr. should think about another line of work. Excessive gory violence. O (R)

Silent Night, Evil Night (see: "Black Christmas")

Silent Partner, The (1979) Dull bank teller (Elliott Gould) keeps out a large cache of money for himself during a bank hold-up but the robber (Christopher Plummer) is a cunning sadist who doesn't like being made a fool of. What follows includes a brutal murder and a savage beating. Directed by Daryl Duke, the film is cleverly done and well acted, but the cheap, corrosive cynicism that permeates it, together with the sex and violence inserted to jolt the audience, is seriously offensive. O (R)

Silent Rage (1982) Small-town sheriff (martial-arts whiz Chuck Norris) confronts a seemingly indestructible superman fashioned by an irresponsible scientist. Directed by Michael Miller, it is an utterly inconsequential effort of deadening predictability. Considerable violence, though stylized, and some fleeting nudity. A-III (R)

Silent Running (1972) Above average tale of ecological disaster in the not-too-distant future where the commander (Bruce Dern) of a space ark refuses the order to destroy its precious cargo of plant life that can no longer grow on earth. Directed by Douglas Trumbull, the sci-fi effects are good and the story's theme of humanity's relationship to the environment is thoughtful. Unfortunately, the weak story line ends in the confusion of madness and restrained mayhem. A-II (GP/G)

Silkwood (1983) Fact-based story of Karen Silkwood (Meryl Streep), a worker in a plutonium processing factory who died in a 1974 auto accident, on her way to tell a reporter what she knew about unsafe conditions in the plant. The movie does not confront the question of whether this was indeed an accident or a murder committed to prevent her evidence from being revealed. Instead, director Mike Nichols has invested a great deal of labor and care in depicting something of Silkwood's independent lifestyle on the job and in relations to her roommate (Cher) and boy friend (Kurt Russell). The result is a nicely-crafted disappointment. A-III (R)

Silver Bears (1978) Michael Caine stars in this leaden-paced, largely unfunny comedy of international intrigue involving a hoax about a silver mine. Directed by Ivan Passer, it affects a sympathetic attitude towards adultery. O (PG)

Silver Bullet (1985) A small town is terrorized by a maniacal killer, coincidentally enough, only when the moon is full. When most of the members of a posse formed to track down the killer are annihilated, it is left to a 12-year-old handicapped boy to convince the town that the killer is a werewolf. Based on a Stephen King novella, director Daniel Attias takes liberties with Hollywood werewolf conventions that may offend hardcore Lon Chaney fans. Graphic violence with gory murder sequences as well as some vulgar language. O (R)

Silver Streak (1976) Gene Wilder and Jill Clayburgh battle a ruthless gang of killers aboard a transcontinental train, aided by Richard Pryor, whose comic talents give the movie a much needed lift when he appears halfway through. Directed by Arthur Hiller, it is moderately entertaining but has some unnecessary profanity and a rather crude love scene. A-III (PG)

Silverado (1985) Big, gaudy Western, as artificial as its title, in which two strangers meet on the road to Silverado and unite to fight evil and injustice. One problem, among the many that afflict the movie, is that director Lawrence Kasdan fails to make the bad guys seem very formidable competition. Nor can one find much to cheer about in the four lackluster heroes weighed down by a convoluted and contrived story line and a tone that wavers between spoof and dead seriousness. Some moderate violence. A-II (PG-13)

Simon (1980) Anemic satire about a mischievous group of scientists (headed by Austin Pendleton) who brainwash an eccentric philosophy teacher (Alan Arkin) into believing he is from outer space. Written and directed by Marshall Brickman, the acting is good but the laughs are few and far between. Some sexual innuendo and a feeble thrust at organized religion. A-III (PG)

Simon of the Desert (1969) Surrealistic Mexican fantasy about a hermit (Claudio Brook), who like his 5th-century namesake, Simeon Stylites, exiles himself to the top of a pillar in the wilderness living in prayer, doing penance, and working miracles, but constantly at war with himself, his followers and the devil (Silvia Pinal). Director Luis Bunuel's satiric foray into the sacred and the profane deals in paradox and the contradictions inherent in human nature. His ironic wit and uncomfortable insights will be appreciated most by those willing to reconcile the movie's ambiguities with their own beliefs. A-IV (nr)

Simon the Swiss (1971) French crime thriller about a petty crook (Jean-Louis Trintignant) who thinks he's pulled off the perfect crime when he kidnaps a bank clerk's small child and gets the bank to pay a fortune in ransom. Director Claude Lelouch's plot has all kinds of intricate turns and twists and the likable hero is anything but a Robin Hood. Intelligent entertainment with much psychological tension and some physical violence. A-III (G)

Simple Story, A (1980) Moody French portrait of a divorced woman (Romy Schneider) in middle age crisis and agonizing over whether to have an abortion or raise her child. Directed by Claude Sautet, the movie avoids sentimental melodramatics in favor of thoughtful, sensitive probing of life's moral priorities. A-III (nr)

Sin of Adam and Eve, The (1973) Writer-producer-director Michael Zachary's literal visualization of Genesis uses an off-screen narrator to add some sensual embellishments to the Biblical text while on-screen bare, healthy primates George Rivers and Candy Wilson explore an Eden which seems to have been culled from the Burpee Seed Catalogue. O (R)

Sinbad and the Eye of the Tiger (1977) Slow-paced bit of leaden whimsy follows a voyage of Sinbad (Patrick Wayne) to the polar regions to free a prince from a witch's spell. The acting is undistinguished, Sam Wanamaker's direction is haphazard and only a few special effects merit anything more than passing interest. A-II (G)

Sinful Davey (1969) Tongue-in-cheek adventure movie about an 18th-century Scottish laddie (John Hurt) who deserts the English army and embarks upon a career as a highwayman. Director John Huston relies upon an abundance of misadventures, escapes and turnabouts in a stylish action story done in fun. Some explicit romantic interludes. A-III (PG)

Singing Nun, The (1966) Hollywood's tribute to the joyful spirit of a young Dominican nun is colorful, sentimental and lively. Henry Koster's glossy direction is out of tune with the reality of a basically interior story about the difficulty of secular fame for a member of a religious community. Greer Garson as the mother superior turns in a well-balanced performance while Debbie Reynolds sings prettily and Agnes Moorehead provides comic relief. There is some pleasant amusement, a little uplift and the music of "Soeur Sourire" is well worth hearing. A-I (br)

Sisters (1973) Failed horror thriller about a Staten Island reporter (Jennifer Salt) who happens to observe a bloody murder in a neighboring apartment house occupied by a schizophrenic Siamese twin (Margot Kidder) and her mad doctor-husband (Bill Finley). Assisting her investigation is a bumbling, comic-relief detective (Charles Durning) Directed by Brian De Palma, the movie's mixture of mindless comedy and visceral gore presumes an audience willing to participate in such voyeuristic displays of violence. O (R)

Sitting Ducks (1980) Two bumbling con men (Michael Emil and Zach Norman) steal some mob gambling receipts and flee to Miami with two women who have been hired to bump them off. Amateurish sex farce directed by Henry Jaglom gets off to a good start but becomes progressively less amusing as it wears on. Demeaning treatment of sex and some rough language. O (R)

Sitting Target (1972) Atrocious British crime story about an escaped convict (Oliver Reed), his stashed loot and adulterous wife (Jill St. John). Directed by Douglas Hickox, the movie wallows in cruelty, sadism, gore, betrayal and self-destruction. O (R)

Six in Paris (1969) Light, colorful and entertaining compilation of short vignettes by six French directors (Jean-Luc Godard, Jean-Daniel Pollet,

Jean Rouch, Jean Douchet, Claude Chabrol and Eric Rohmer). Despite the assortment of stories and styles, they cohere nicely and leave viewers with a memorable experience of several interesting Parisian characters. Mature themes and treatment. A-III (nr)

Six Pack (1982) Kenny Rodgers plays a fading racecar driver who becomes the surrogate father of six needy orphans. Pretty soon he's back on top with the kids as his pit crew and he even decides to marry Erin Gray whom he favors with his presence every few months. Directed by Daniel Petrie, it's sheer, contrived mediocrity from start to finish. Foul language out of the mouths of babes and a benign attitude toward casual sex. A-III (PG)

Six-Pack Annie (1975) Young girl (Lindsay Bloom) becomes a prostitute in order to save her aunt's restaurant from foreclosure. Directed by Graydon F. David, the tedious, flat movie is as consistently vulgar as it is unfunny. O (R)

Six Weeks (1982) Congressional candidate (Dudley Moore) befriends a youngster dying of leukemia (Katherine Healy) who persuades her wealthy mother (Mary Tyler Moore) to back his campaign but when she succumbs to his charm, he reciprocates and his marriage is in jeopardy. Director Tony Bill's romance is outrageously sentimental, totally detached from both political and human realities and cloyingly smug in its hedonistic values. A-III (PG)

Sixteen Candles (1984) A girl (Molly Ringwald) is devastated when her family, in the throes of preparing for her older sister's marriage, forgets about her 16th birthday. Were that not enough, she is pursued by a skinny freshman (Anthony Michael Hall) while longing for a handsome, unattainable senior (Michael Schoeffling). Director John Hughes' old-fashioned comedy about the anguish of adolescence is updated, alas, by a dose of foul language, pervasive vulgarity, some shower room nudity and a benign view of casual sex. Some other not-so-bright spots include nasty stereotyping of Orientals and Italians and some National Lampoon-style laughs at the expense of a girl in a body brace. O (PG)

Skateboard (1978) Down-on-his-luck agent (Allen Garfield) extricates himself from the clutches of a loan shark by becoming a skateboard entrepreneur. Directed by George Gage, it is a very bad little movie hastily and cheaply slapped together to cash in on a fad, it is also offensive in its benign attitude towards teenage promiscuity and drinking. O (PG)

Skatetown, U.S.A. (1979) Ho-hum homage to the fad of disco roller skating pits nice young man against tough dude in competing for the big skating crown. Written, produced and directed by William Levey, the undernourished story line constantly halts for unfunny comic sketches (Ruth Buzzey and Flip Wilson), undistinguished songs and skating numbers. Frequently sleazy mood and abundance of marijuana consumption in the background, and sometimes the foreground, make it highly dubious fare for any but mature viewers. A-III (PG)

Skezag (1971) Well-intended but amateurish documentary about drug abuse goes on endlessly with New York addicts using street language describing the scene. In the last sequence, however, filmmakers Joel Freedman and Phil Messina revisit an addict who is now a walking dead man, hollow of soul and poisoned of body, conveying most effectively what had been missing so incessantly in the preceding footage. Those last few minutes say more than anyone needs to know about the white powder that destroys so many young Americans. A-IV (nr)

Ski Bum, The (1970) Failed screen version of a Romain Gary novel about a young drifter (Zalman King) hanging around a Colorado winter resort who becomes embroiled in a crooked business scheme, is roundly double-crossed and left emotionally shattered by the experience. Directed by Bruce Clark, the plot is episodic and underdeveloped, the characters are superficial and their motivations often enigmatic. A confused morality underpins the story. O (R)

Ski Fever (1969) Ski instructor (Martin Milner) at an Austrian ski lodge finds his contract requires him to socialize with the guests and, by the time of the movie's romantic fade-out, he has teamed up with one of them (Claudia Martin). Directed by Curt Siodmak, it's an inept story built around some footage of the Austrian Giant Slalom but not even ski enthusiasts will find it worth seeing. A-III (M)

Skidoo (1969) Retired thug (Jackie Gleason) is ordered by his old boss (Groucho Marx) to rub out a loquacious friend (Mickey Rooney) safely ensconced in prison. Directed by Otto Preminger, it is a mixture of inert comedy and ponderous satire, done in consistently bad taste with some lecherous dialogue and sexual shenanigans. O (M)

Skin Game (1971) In the pre-Civil War border states, a cunning con artist (James Garner) makes the rounds selling his slave (Lou Gossett) and then waiting with the cash for him to escape and proceed to the next con, until another crook (Susan Clark) adds a new dimension of confusion. Director Paul Bogart blends large doses of improbability with pinches of reality to keep the interracial swindle skimming along its superficial surface, only touching on the serious for comic effect. A-III (GP)

Skullduggery (1970) Witless, at times tasteless comedy about an anthropologist (Susan Clark) whose New Guinea expedition is led by their guide (Burt Reynolds) into uncharted territory where they discover a species of apes that manifest distinctly human qualities. Directed by Gordon Douglas, the question of whether the creatures are indeed human is kicked around in aimless fashion, matched by banal dialogue and half-dimensional characterizations. Reference to bestiality. A-III (PG)

Sky Bandits (1986) A British production set in World War I France tells the comic adventures of two bank robbers (Scotty McGinnis and Jeff Osterhage) who join the army to avoid prison and blunder their way through the war in a series of stolen airplanes. Directed by Zoran Perisic, the charm of this elegantly photographed movie derives from high-spirited performances and fanciful sets, props and special effects. A postbedroom scene and some very stylized wartime violence. A-II (PG)

Sky Riders (1976) Routine melodrama about the rescue of a family kidnapped by terrorists through the intervention of some daring hanggliding enthusiasts is distinguished only by some spectacular aerial photography. Directed by Douglas Hickox, the movie's violent elements include the terrorists' threatening of a small child. A-III (PG)

Skyjacked (1972) Effective thriller about an American airliner hijacked to Russia. Captain Charlton Heston keeps his planeload of problem characters under control on a flight chock full of dangerous situations, ending in a shootout at Moscow airport. John Guillermin directs with emphasis upon suspense rather than trying to develop characterization or the numerous subplots. Unpretentious escapist entertainment. A-II (PG)

Slams, The (1973) Super-bad, super-cool Jim Brown is in the penitentiary but has stashed away $1.5 million in Mafia drug money for his planned break-out to escape to the Caribbean with girl friend Judy Pace. Directed by Jonathan Kaplan, the brutal and sadistic action is as relentless and explicit as the prison language which consists largely of racial, sexual and just plain mean insults. O (R)

Slap, The (1976) Lightweight comedy drama, a sort of updated "Father of the Bride," in which such talented actors as Lino Ventura, Annie Giradot and Isabelle Adjani struggle gallantly with an aimless script more suited to American televison than a French feature. Sexual innuendo. A-III (PG)

Slap Shot (1977) Paul Newman stars as an aging player-coach who rejuvenates an inept bush-league hockey team by introducing the wonders of dirty playing to his charges. Directed by George Roy Hill, the playing is but one of the dirty elements in a crude, foul-mouthed comedy. Some nudity. O (R)

Slaughter (1972) Black exploitation story of an ex-Green Beret (Jim Brown) who pummels his way into an international conspiracy and becomes the unwilling employee of the U.S. Government. Directed by Jack Starrett, the production values are minimal, with the emphasis on the hero's biceps and his winning ways with knuckles and bullets. Excessively graphic violence and sex. O (R)

Slaughter Hotel (1973) The hotel in question is a country rest home where medieval weapons decorate the parlors and become the means by which a prowling psychopath viciously disposes of sexually frustrated women and their nurses. Dreadfully inept Italian production directed by Fernanado Di Leo with gross violence. O (R)

Slaughter's Big Rip-Off (1973) Big, bad Jim Brown mows his way through the Los Angeles branch of the Syndicate (headed by Ed McMahon) and plows through a number of willing female sex objects. Directed by Gordon Douglas, rip-off is the operative word in this cheap sex-and-violence exploitation job. O (R)

Slaughterhouse Five (1972) Uneven screen version of Kurt Vonnegut, Jr.'s time-tripping novel about the progress of a soldier (Michael Sacks) from POW chaplin's assistant, to witness at the 1945 firebombing of Dresden, to post-war participant in the American Way of Life and, at last, the captive of a Hollywood starlet (Valerie Perrine), the girl of his erotic dreams. Directed by George Roy Hill, the wildly seriocomic satire on American manners and mores is mostly on target and the acting is first-rate, though its hero's helplessness in dropping in and out of time tends to be confusing and, at times, incoherent. Marred by unnecessary nudity. A-IV (R)

Slave of Love, A (1978) Movie company in the Crimea grinds out melodramatic romances seemingly oblivious to the Bolshevik revolution sweeping across 1917 Russia. In the end, the company's empty-headed but beautiful star (Elena Solovei) joins her cameraman in smuggling out film of czarist atrocities in the area. Gorgeously photographed and engagingly acted, director Nikita Mikhalkov's nostalgic tribute to the silent movies and their age of innocence is an enjoyable experience in spite of perfunctory Soviet propaganda. A-III (nr)

Slaves (1969) Inept melodrama about a hard-working slave (Ossie Davis) unjustly sold to a bad master (Stephen Boyd) whose mistreatment drives him to foment a slave uprising. Director Herbert Biberman depends largely upon dialogue rather than visuals to convey the historical reality of the terrible injustices of slavery. It is an important subject and it is unfortunate that it has been done poorly. Several scenes with nudity. A-III (R)

Slayground (1984) The getaway car in a robbery crashes into a limousine, killing the young daughter of a millionaire who retaliates by hiring a professional hitman to track down the gang's leader (Peter Coyote), a sensitive fellow already badly upset by the tragic turn of events. British production directed by Terry Bedford is a run-of-the-mill chase movie with some pretentious literary overtones. Stylized violence. A-III (R)

Sleeper (1973) Typically wacky Woody Allen spoof on contemporary society's pop foibles in a plot casting Woody as a chap who goes into the hospital for routine surgery and wakes up 200 years from now in a world gone mad with people dependent upon electronic gadgets (most of which don't work). Without an identity, he becomes tapped to lead a revolution and soon finds that his new friends are often more dangerous than his intended enemies. The humor is rapid-fire, mainly of the one-liner and sight gag variety and his satirical targets include just about every institution or group on the scene. A-III (PG)

Sleeping Beauty (1959) This classic story of love conquering evil remains the late Walt Disney's last great achievement of storytelling in fully-detailed animation. Fine family entertainment. A-I (G)

Sleeping Car Murders, The (1966) French suspense thriller about a homicidal maniac. Directed by Costa-Gravas, it affects a benign attitude towards premarital sex and unnecessarily graphic treatment of several erotic sequences. O (br)

Slender Thread, The (1966) A telephone is the only means by which a psychology student (Sidney Poitier) can hope to save a woman (Anne Bancroft) who has taken an overdose of barbiturates. Director Sydney Pollack's story has an overabundance of contrivances, but the acting of the principals makes it all seem urgent and worth the emotional involvement. A-II (br)

Sleuth (1972) Stylish screen version of Anthony Shaffer's play about an urbane detective-story writer (Laurence Olivier) who invites his wife's lover (Michael Caine) to his mansion and the two engage in a game of wits which becomes progressively more deadly. Directed by Joseph Mankiewicz, the intricately plotted thriller is carried off by the tautly-balanced performqnces of the two principals but attentive viewers will see through the mystery early on. Some sharp tension and suspense make it mature fare. A-III (PG)

Slipper and the Rose, The (1976) Richard Chamberlain and Gemma Craven star in a pleasant and very entertaining British version of the Cinderella story as directed by Bryan Forbes. A-I (G)

Slither (1973) Offbeat comedy adventure about a dense ex-con (James Caan) and his equally bumbling partner (Peter Boyle) who wend their way across rural California in search of a hidden stash of embezzled cash. Directed by Howard Zieff, there's plenty of fun along the way as the inept pair try to figure out the secret of the loot's location, but the chuckles trail off badly with a twist ending. Some rough language. A-III (PG)

Slogan (1970) French story of a love affair between a married middle-aged director of television commercials (Serge Gainsbourg) and a mixed-up adolescent (Jane Birkin) might be taken as a parody of other glamorous but empty screen romances. Directed by Pierre Grimblat, this film's characters serve simply as cardboard contrivances for glossy photographic effects and for sensationalizing what should have been a rather painful moral dilemma. O (GP)

Slow Dancing in the Big City (1978) Tough, streetwise columnist for a New York newspaper (Paul Sorvino) falls in love with a beautiful Canadian dancer (Anne Ditchburn) who is making her debut at Lincoln Center but is afraid it might be her finale. Thanks to an appealing performance by Sorvino, the movie has a few good moments but, as directed by John G. Avildsen, its blatant sentimentality, its contrived plot and its shallow characterizations prevent it from being anything more than mediocre entertainment. A-II (PG)

Slugger's Wife, The (1985) Failed Neil Simon comedy about a baseball star (Michael O'Keefe) married to a rock singer (Rebecca DeMornay). Some sexually oriented scenes and a rather benign view of premarital sex. A-III (PG-13)

Small Change (1976) Episodic French serio-comedy about the natural innocence of childhood that protects youngsters from being overwhelmed by the harsher realities of life. Director Francois Truffaut offers adult viewers a chance to rediscover their own childhood as well as being more sympathetic to the needs of youngsters who depend upon them. Excellent movie for parents to share with their youngsters. A-II (PG)

Small Circle of Friends, A (1980) Radcliffe coed (Karen Allen) becomes the mistress of two Harvard students (Brad Davis and Jameson Parker) during the late 1960s campus anti-war activities. Director Rob Cohen's trio appear less committed to the protest movement than to indulging their selfish egos. Benign view of illicit sex and some graphic visuals of sexual activity. O (R)

Small Town in Texas, A (1976) Young convict (Timothy Bottoms) gets out of prison and returns home to find himself harrassed by the corrupt sheriff who framed him. Director Jack Starrett's mindlessly violent chase movie is of no interest. O (R)

Smashing Time (1968) English musical satire on London's Mod Scene which draws two country girls (Rita Tushingham and Lynn Redgrave) who become overnight successes, but disillusioned with fame, return home. Directed by Desmond Davis, the movie is an uncomfortable mixture of realism and stylization, superficial plot and slapstick treatment. A-III (br)

Smic Smac Smoc (1972) French romantic comedy about three Marseilles dock workers (Charles Gerard, Jean Collomb and Amidou), one of whom decides to marry the baker's maid (Catherine Allegret) and the other two host a wacky wedding-day celebration that lands all the revelers in the clink. Unpretentious little movie with plenty of charm and smiles, directed by Claude Lelouch with a few of his friends, including composer Francis Lai as a blind accordionist playing lush themes from earlier Lelouch movies. Some earthy dialogue. A-III (GP)

Smile (1975) Facile car salesman (Bruce Dern) is a judge in the American Miss beauty contest who, by its end, begins to realize that his philosophy of life has been as empty as that of the contest. Director Michael Ritchie's satire affects a snickering, superior attitude towards the people it pictures as crass and ludicrous and itself becomes nothing more than a peep show, lacking in a sense of humanity which might have redeemed its dabbling in voyeurism. Sexual situations. O (PG)

Smile Orange (1976) Comedy directed by Trevor Rhone set in Jamaica about a black waiter and his encounters with American tourists results in some satiric but good-natured thrusts at human nature whether black, white or brown. Its paper-thin story, however, grows increasingly silly and some exploitative nudity could easily have been done without. O (PG)

Smith (1969) Contemporary Western about a cattle rancher (Glenn Ford) who champions an Indian accused of murder. Unusually good Disney effort dealing with racial intolerance and the need for people of different cultures to get along together, though director Michael O'Herlihy's sentimental lack of realism mars the central trial sequences. Good family setting with warmly likeable characters. A-I (G)

Smokey and the Bandit (1977) Burt Reynolds, Sally Fields and Jackie Gleason star in this chase comedy about a daredevil trucker pursued by a state trooper. Director Hal Needham's action comedy has little humor and lots of elaborate but boring car crashes. Some rough language, many vulgarities and suggestion of premarital sex. A-III (PG)

Smokey and the Bandit II (1980) Burt Reynolds, Sally Field and Jackie Gleason do it again in a sequel which, like the original, is essentially a live-action version of a Road Runner cartoon. Directed by Hal Needham, this time the plot involves trucking a pregnant elephant over several state lines, with the usual car chases and crashes, an abundance of crude sexual references and vulgar language. A-III (PG)

Smokey and the Bandit, Part 3 (1983) Burt Reynolds makes but the briefest of appearances in this sequel about a trucker (Jerry Reed) racing the clock to transport a plastic replica of a shark on time in spite of being pursued by a loud-mouthed sheriff (Jackie Gleason). Director Dick Lowry's chase farce hits new lows in moral as well as entertainment terms. Demeaning sexual humor and foul language. O (PG)

Smoky (1966) Fess Parker stars in a nicely done family-type Western based on the Will James novel about a rancher and an outlaw mustang stallion. Directed by George Sherman, it affords plenty of outdoor action for all. A-I (br)

Smooth Talk (1986) Written and directed by Joyce Chopra, it is the story of a maturing teenage girl (Laura Dern) who places herself in a dangerous situation when a soft-spoken stranger (Treat Williams) talks her into accepting him as her first lover. The movie seems to accept this as a reasonable introduction to womanhood. O (PG-13)

Snoopy, Come Home (1972) Disappointing animated feature from the Peanuts gang of Charles M. Schulz uses a lot of aimless skits to pad out a saccharine story of Snoopy's visit to his original owner, a little girl who lies ailing in the hospital. Directed by Bill Melendez, the result lacks author Schulz's characteristic humor and intelligence in dealing with the little joys and anxieties of childhood. A-I (G)

Snow Job (1972) Failed caper movie involves ex-ski champion Jean-Claude Killy in the robbery of a posh ski resort high in the Italian Alps from which he skies down the impossible slope of an adjacent glacier in a heart-thumping display of skiing skills and thrills, some of which are pretty terrifying. Aside from that, director George Englund can't do much with a silly plot, shallow characterizations and the star's impressive lack of acting talent. A-III (G)

Snow White and the Seven Dwarfs (1937) Walt Disney's first feature-length fairy tale remains an amazingly fresh and inventive landmark in the history of movie animation. Sequences such as Snow White's flight from the terrifying Queen, the antics of the dwarfs and the forest animals racing to the rescue through a frightening storm retain their original vitality and impact. Disney's combination of sentiment, laughter, and excitement makes the movie an especially satisfying entertainment for every age. A-I (G)

Snowball Express (1972) Big-city accountant (Dean Jones) leaves his boring job to run a tumble-down Colorado ski resort hotel inherited from a distant relative and his enthusiasm is enjoyably infectious as he wins out over avalanches, bank foreclosures, burst water pipes and other impossible odds. Above average Disney comedy directed by Norman Tokar has some very funny moments, a fine supporting cast and a story that should hold the interest of the entire family. A-I (G)

So Fine (1981) Meek college professor (Ryan O'Neal) comes out of his shell to save his father's garment business by accidentally inventing jeans with transparent seats but gets into trouble through a reluctant affair with a gangster's wife (Mariangela Melato). Written and directed by Andrew Bergman, the vulgar and mostly unfunny comedy tries to get laughs from overt sexuality and obscene language. O (R)

S.O.B. (1981) Hollywood producer (Richard Mulligan) attempts to transform his multi-million dollar flop into a box office winner by persuading its star, who's also his wife (Julie Andrews), to forsake her wholesome screen image and bare her breasts on camera. Directed by Blake Edwards, the satiric comedy has some very funny moments, but they do not soften the movie's basically cynical outlook and amoral perspective which exploits its audience in the same way as the moviemakers it criticizes. Some sequences involving nudity. O (R)

Socrates (1971) Italian director Roberto Rossellini re-creates the life of the Greek philosopher drawing heavily on the works of Plato and other traditional sources for script and setting. In the title role, Jean Sylvere is quite acceptable and the drama of his trial and subsequent death becomes increasingly involving and poignant. However, so much philosophy reduced to English subtitles for 120 minutes becomes essentially a rapid reading exercise. A-I (nr)

Sol Madrid (1968) Routine crime melodrama directed by Brian G. Hutton in which an undercover agent (David McCallum) is sent to Mexico to break up a narcotics ring which he does by using a gangster's girl friend as bait. Some fairly heavy violence. A-III (br)

Solarbabies (1986)   Sci-fi escapist fantasy about a group of rebellious adolescents who escape from a state-run orphanage of the distant future and help save their planet from destruction. Silly plot but imaginative special effects from director Alan Johnson who doesn't help matters by trying to enliven the action with stylized violence. A-II (PG-13)

Soldier Blue (1970)   Based on the notorious 1864 Sand Creek Massacre of some 500 Cheyenne braves, women and children by the U.S. Cavalry, the account begins with a tedious romance between a soldier (Peter Strauss) and a former Indian captive (Candice Bergen) who, when she learns of the impending attack on the Indian village, tries to prevent the slaughter. Director Ralph Nelson's well-intentioned attempt to confront a military atrocity becomes itself a brutalizing experience by wallowing in graphic depictions of bloodshed and rape. Excessive, stomach-wrenching violence. O (R)

Soldier in Skirts (see: "Triple Echo")

Soldier of Orange (1979)   Dutch production about a wealthy, aristocratic young student (Rutger Hauer in a superb performance) who is caught up in the catastrophe of the Nazi invasion and becomes a hero of the Resistance. Directed by Paul Verhoeven, it is at its best as an old-fashioned war movie fortified with credibility and heightened emotions that are above the usual. Too often, however, it indulges in showy stunts that have a jarring effect and its depiction of sexuality is excessively graphic. O (R)

Soldier's Story, A (1984)   When a black sergeant (Adolph Caesar) is murdered at an Army camp in 1944, the investigating officer (Howard Rollins, Jr.) discovers that the victim was a ruthless tyrant who had been well hated by his men. Directed by Norman Jewison, this excellent movie looks at racial prejudice from a number of perspectives that make it unusually effective. Some violence and rough language. A-II (PG)

Soleil-O (1973)   Young accountant from a former French African colony (Robert Linesol) arrives in Paris looking for work but finds instead racism, ranging from the subtle to the blatant, becomes increasingly bewildered and finally ends on the brink of violent despair. Mauritanian production written and directed by Mel Hondo, the use of ironic humor and lively music keeps the plight of the black emigrant worker from becoming totally depressing. A-III (nr)

Some Call It Loving (1973)   Pretentious hot-house fantasy about a musician (Zalman King) who buys a Sleeping Beauty from a sideshow, wakes the sleeper (Tisa Farrow) and has her join him and his strange companions (Carol White and Veronica Anderson) in perverse games. Directed by James B. Harris, it's a glossy exercise in voyeurism and its leering attitude toward women and sex is degrading. O (R)

Some Girls Do (1971)   Bulldog Drummond (Richard Johnson) returns as an anemic James Bond imitation with a gaggle of gorgeous girls on a secret island hideout from which the baddies plan to rule the world with a super-destructive weapon. Lackluster British movie directed by Ralph Thomas goes one step further in reducing women

to objects by making them mechanical dummies activated by a convenient off/on switch behind the ear. A-III (G)

Some Kind of a Nut (1969)   When a bank teller (Dick Van Dyke) grows a beard, his boss takes it as a sign of non-conformity and orders him to shave it off. As fellow employees and associates choose sides in the course of the dispute, the hero rediscovers the sterling qualities of his about-to-be ex-wife (Angie Dickinson). Director Garson Kanin fails in his attempt at a whimsical examination of a man's search for integrity and individuality. A-III (PG)

Some Kind of Hero (1982)   Returned Vietnam prisoner of war (Richard Pryor) finds himself neck-deep in trouble when a high-priced prostitute (Margot Kidder) falls in love with him and he gets involved with organized crime. Ill-assorted mix of comedy and melodrama which director Michael Pressman is unable to organize into any semblance of unity. Some graphic sex, cheap thrills and low humor. O (R)

Some Kind of Wonderful (1987)   A confused teen-ager struggles against authority figures and shallow advice from parents and schoolmates in overcoming his insecurities while asserting his non-conformist aspirations. Director John Hughes' adolescent soap opera passively accepts teen sex as a natural outcome of rapid physical and underdeveloped emotional maturity as well as subtly undermining trust in the values of the adult world. A-III (PG-13)

Some of My Best Friends Are... (1971)   Mervyn Nelson's documentary on the patrons of a gay bar borders on exploitation of its subject through demeaning cliche and stereotype that contribute nothing of understanding nor insight into homosexuality and how it affects these men's lives. O (R)

Somebody Killed Her Husband (1978)   Innocuous bit of fluff in which a bumbling but charming clerk (Jeff Bridges) in Macy's toy department falls in love with a beautiful customer (Farrah Fawcett) who soon becomes a widow when somebody kills her husband. Directed by Lamont Johnson, it's a fairly entertaining mystery comedy except for its benign view of adultery. A-III (PG)

Someone Behind the Door (1971)   Plodding murder melodrama about a neurologist (Anthony Perkins) who plans to kill his wife's lover by using an escaped lunatic (Charles Bronson) but the plan goes badly awry. Directed by Nicolas Gessner, the dull and static movie contains a rape scene that is ludicrous despite its ferocity. A-III (GP)

Something Big (1971)   Failed Western spoof about an outlaw (Dean Martin) who abducts the wife (Honor Blackman) of a U.S.Cavalry officer (Brian Keith) in order to trade her for a Gatling gun so he can mow down an army of Mexican bandits and take their hoard of stolen treasure. Directed by Andrew V. McLaglen, the comedy consists of overacting and double entendre and the action is of the tired fantasy variety. A-III (GP)

Something for Everyone (1970)   Bleak comedy about an aspiring footman (Michael York), in the employ of an enchanting countess (Angela Lansbury), who decides that the swiftest path to noble rank is through the bedroom, with a few slayings along the way. Directed by Harold Prince, there are a few pleasant moments in this adult fairy tale, but not nearly enough for most tastes. Stylized sex and violence. A-IV (R)

Something Short of Paradise (1979)   On-again, off-again comedy romance between the manager of a New York art cinema (David Steinberg) and a journalist (Susan Sarandon) develops rather slowly, hampered by a needlessly complex flashback stucture. As directed by David Helpern, the result is only moderately entertaining. The nature of the relationship between the two lovers makes it adult fare. A-III (PG)

Something Wicked This Way Comes (1983) Disney adaptation of the Ray Bradbury story about a strange traveling carnival that disrupts life in a small Illinois town sometime in the 1920s. The evil carnival master (Jonathan Pryce) fulfills peoples's desires, but in a way that costs them dearly. When two adventurous boys (Vidal Peterson and Shawn Carson) tumble to the carnival master's secret, they become the special object of his malevolence. Jack Clayton directs all this with just the right blend of tension and human warmth but some of the special effects are definitely not for younger viewers. A-II (PG)

Something Wild (1986) Eccentric young woman (Melanie Griffith) seduces a corruptible yuppie (Jeff Daniels) into a kinky romance based on mutual deception but, when her husband (Ray Liotta) gets out of prison, the affair becomes deadly. Although indicating the moral bankruptcy of the central characters, director Jonathan Demme's emphasis on the sexual nature of their relationship results in just another male sex fantasy. Nudity in a sexual context, brutal violence and profanity. O (R)

Sometimes a Great Notion (1971) Muddled screen version of the Ken Kesey novel about a family of independent Oregon loggers whose reliance on rugged individualism makes them defy a strike action called by their fellow loggers and this has dire, far-reaching consequences. Directed by Paul Newman, who also stars as the family's leader, the story's action is effectively presented, notably the difficulty and dangers of logging, and is extremely well acted. However, the movie's sympathies about its larger theme of individualism versus society and changing conditions are ambiguous, if not confused, especially in its final, vulgar gesture of defiance. Heavy-going even for adults. A-IV (GP)

Somewhere in Time (1980) Young playwright (Christopher Reeve) wills himself back several generations into the past to meet the famous actress (Jane Seymour) with whose portrait he has fallen in love. Directed by Jeannot Szwarc, the sentimental romance and its lovely images (filmed on Mackinac Island) are for incurable romantics only. A-II (PG)

Son of Blob (1972) Once again the creeping crimson mass has fun overrunning Small Town U.S.A., sparing no one in its path until a fearless couple (Robert Walker, Jr. and Gwynne Gilford) remember the chilling device used by Steve McQueen to stop the blob in the original. Directed by Larry Hagman, the object this time is to glean smiles instead of screams from undemanding viewers who are helped by delightful cameos from the likes of Godfrey Cambridge and Shelley Berman. Fantasy violence. A-II (GP)

Song of Norway (1970) Huge, panoramic biographical portrait of composer Edvard Grieg (Toralv Maurstad), filmed in the natural splendor of his beautiful Norway. Part of the saga involves the two women in his life: the heiress who rejects his love and then tries to buy him back (Christina Schollin) and the patient admirer and singer of his

works whom he eventually marries (Florence Henderson). Written and directed by Andrew Stone, the result is a stunning musical postcard, but its personal drama does not measure up to its magnificent location photography. Still, it offers more than enough wholesome entertainment to satisfy most family viewers. A-I (G)

Song of the South (1946) James Baskett gives a winning performance as Uncle Remus, the wise old storyteller who helps a youngster (Bobby Driscoll) understand the ways of the world through folktales about Brer Rabbit and his friends. The Disney version of Joel Chandler Harris' tales from the mythic Old South is a warm and zestful mixture of animation and live action that most parents will enjoy as much as the youngsters. A-I (G)

Sophie's Choice (1982) Plodding screen version of William Styron's novel about a Polish survivor of Auschwitz (Meryl Streep) who in 1947 has found refuge in a garish pink boarding house in Brooklyn with her lover (Kevin Kline), an American Jew of mercurial temperament. A young, inexperienced Southern writer (Peter MacNichol) gets caught up in their lives, their lies and their secrets (including one that gives the story its title). Director Alan J. Pakula gets good performances and tries to keep the sluggish narrative moving but in the end it seems hardly worth the effort. Suicide figures in the plot and there is some brief nudity and rough language. A-III (R)

Sorcerer (1977) Four down-and-outers (Roy Scheider, Bruno Cremer, Francisco Rabal and Amidou) in a South American backwater seize the chance to drive trucks loaded with dynamite over some 200 miles of jungle road in order to put out a burning oil well. Director William Friedkin sketches in the background of each of the four, unlike the original 1953 French movie, "The Wages of Fear," upon which it is based, but in doing so diffuses the impact of the dangerous truck ride. Occasional violence and a scene showing the victims of the oil well explosion. A-III (PG)

Sorrow and the Pity, The (1972) Classic documentary directed by Marcel Ophuls examines France during the German Occupation and replaces the legend of popular resistance with the fact of complicity by large sections of society. Focusing on the town of Clermont-Ferrand, Ophuls uses it as a measure of the nation's collaboration with the Nazis. The object is not to judge the inhabitants of the village but to show how easy it is for people in crisis to accept tyranny and yet believe that they are free. A-II (PG)

Soul Man (1986) Youth from a wealthy family finds a way to pay for his Harvard Law School education by means of a minority student scholarship when he takes pills that blacken the color of his skin. This disappointing youth-oriented comedy fails to deliver any insightful social satire save some foul one-liners. Instead, it affirms the materialistic aspirations of young people, faces issues of racial prejudice only superficially and is accepting of promiscuous sex and false social values. O (PG-13)

Soul of Nigger Charley, The (1973) Lame sequel to "The Legend of Nigger Charley" finds the two ex-slaves (Fred Williamson and D'Urville Martin) up against some Confederate aristocrats who are trying to re-create the Old South in Mexico. Director Larry Spangler places the emphasis squarely on the action sequences with lots of special-effects bullet impacts. A-III (R)

Soul Soldier (1972) Low-budget story of the mostly-black 10th Cavalry of Fort Davis, Texas, and their heroism against the Indians on the Western frontier concentrates on foolishness at the fort rather than fortitude in the field. Directed by John Cardos, the shoddy production wastes a capable cast (Rafer Johnson, Lincoln Kilpatrick, Janee Michelle, Cesar Romero and Robert Dix) in sexual hijinks and violent heroics. O (R/GP)

Soul to Soul (1971) In celebration of its 14th year as an independent African nation, Ghana sponsored a music festival featuring a number of America's top black rock, jazz, and blues performers, including Wilson Pickett, Ike and Tina Turner, Roberta Flack, Santana and many others. Denis Sanders' fine documentary follows the performers to Ghana, conveys some of their reflections on their participation but mostly encapsulates the festival in a joyous musical entertainment that is universal in its appeal. A-I (G)

Sound of Music, The (1965) Particularly fine screen version of the Broadway musical about the formative years of the Trapp Family Singers combines an interesting story, a solid cast (headed by Julie Andrews and Christopher Plummer), lovely music and intelligent lyrics, colorful scenery and pleasant fantasy to entertain the mind and enliven the spirit. Directed by Robert Wise, it has held up over the years as thoroughly refreshing family entertainment. A-I (G)

Sounder (1972) Appealing story of a black family of Louisiana sharecroppers struggling to survive against natural and human odds during the early days of the Depression. When the father (Paul Winfield) is jailed for stealing food, his wife (Cicely Tyson) and three children (Kevin Hooks is the eldest) are left to crop the sugar cane on their own. The boy's subsequent odyssey to find the labor camp where his father is being held provides additional drama. Produced by Robert B. Radnitz and directed by Martin Ritt, it captures the humanity of the characters and a fine, distanced sense of its sleepy Southern locale. The movie earns a deep emotional response from its audience because its story and characters are believable. Not only a valid examination of the black experience in America, it is also a fine family experience. A-I (G)

Soup for One (1982) Nice young man (Saul Rubinek) wanders through New York's frenetic singles scene in search of the ideal wife in this sometimes bright but more often erratic and awkward romantic comedy written and directed by Jonathan Kaufer. Some of the jokes are more mean-spirited than genuinely satiric and its rather heavy dependence on nudity for comic relief makes this unsuitable entertainment. O (R)

Soupcon (1980) Celebrating their 25th wedding anniversary, a couple (Jean Carmet and Marie Dubois) declare to their surprised family that they are separating. Both discover in the end, that growing old together is perhaps better than chasing illusions of freedom. French production directed by Jean Charles Tacchella is a Gallic bit of whimsey with some nicely turned characterizations and a frank treatment of sex. A-III (nr)

Southern Comfort (1981) Louisiana National Guardsmen become lost in the bayous and run afoul of vengeful Cajuns, in this grim, somber, altogether pretentious melodrama directed by Walter Hill. Aside from some spectacular cinematography by Andrew Laszlo, it has little to recommend it, though Powers Boothe makes an effective screen debut as one of the hapless guardsmen. Violence and rough language. A-III (R)

Southern Star, The (1969) Fortune-hunter George Segal and girl friend Ursula Andress trek across Africa's jungles in pursuit of a diamond thief but are themselves pursued by a crook who wants both the prize diamond and the girl. Directed by Sidney Hayers, there's lots of cliched action done in tongue-in-cheek fashion, including Orson Welles as an effeminate outlaw, but there is no reason for its excessively graphic violence. O (PG)

Soylent Green (1973) Charlton Heston plays a New York City cop in the year 2022 when lack of food forces people to subsist on a mysterious substance called Soylent Green, the secret of which Heston discovers after the voluntary death of his assistant (Edward G. Robinson). For all its posturing about ecological and moral disaster, it's no more than a routine detective movie with a slick and shallow futuristic setting. A-III (PG)

Spacecamp (1986) Kate Capshaw portrays an astronaut who takes a team of teenagers through training exercises at the National Aeronautics and Space Administration's facility of the same name in Huntsville, Ala. The youngsters are put to the test of courage and determination when they are accidently launched into a space shuttle by an affectionate robot. Director Harry Winer offers a somewhat inspiring and informative promo for the space program that youngsters will find engaging. A-I (PG)

Spacehunter: Adventures In the Forbidden Zone (1983) Failed sci-fi fantasy about three 21st-century damsels in distress who are rescued from a perverted mutant by the driver of a futuristic junkmobile (Peter Strauss). Directed by Lamont Johnson, this 3-D adventure is only for those who are amused by stupidity and mediocrity. Mild violence. A-II (PG)

Sparkle (1976) Absurdly melodramatic story of a Harlem girl (Irene Cara) who gains success as a singer. In spite of Cara's strong performance, Sam O'Steen's direction cannot make credible the anti-climactic crime elements grafted onto the plot. Restrained depiction of drugs and sex. A-III (PG)

Spartacus (1960) Adventure epic traces the spectacular events that shook the Roman Empire during the great slave revolt of the first century B.C. Kirk Douglas is appropriately brave and sweaty in the title role of the gladiator who leads the revolt with Jean Simmons as the slave girl he loves. Director Stanley Kubrick gets scope and splendor in an historical re-creation that has some sense of history to it. A-III (br)

Spasmo (1976) Umberto Lenzi directs Suzy Kendall and Robert Hoffman in a murky Italian celebration of sex and bloodshed. O (nr)

Special Day, A (1977) The day of the title is that of Hitler's state visit to Rome which is used as the background and counterpoint to an encounter between a downtrodden wife (Sophia Loren) and an harassed homosexual (Marcello Mastroiani) who has been fired from the government radio station and faces even graver measures. Directed by Ettore Scola, the movie focuses not on the moral aspect of the wife's being unfaithful to her brutal husband but upon the human anguish of the two principals. A-IV (nr)

Special Delivery (1976) Failed comedy melodrama about a bank robber (Bo Svenson) and a kooky young woman (Cybill Shepherd) teaming up to recover some loot stashed in a mail box. Directed by Paul Wendkos, it is a jumble of many styles and plots, none of them very good. Some sexual innuendo. A-III (PG)

Special Section (1975) Story of injustices rendered by a special court instituted by France's Vichy government to satisfy the demands of their Nazi conquerors. Directed by Costa-Gavras, the movie is loosely episodic and lacking in characterization but excels in its re-creation of the period. As a result one can learn a little bit of history and be fairly entertained but moved hardly at all. A-II (PG)

Specialist, The (1975) Overwrought soap opera about rival lawyers (Adam West and John Anderson) in a small town who get involved in a case of entrapment and blackmail. Directed by Hikmet Avedis, it has a great deal of nudity, probably meant to take one's mind off a talky, determinedly simple-minded script. O (R)

Spectre of Edgar Allan Poe, The (1974) Inept low-budget horror movie about E.A. Poe (Robert Walker, Jr.) who delivers his deranged true-love Lenore (Mary Grover) into the hands of the mad Dr. Grimaldi (Cesar Romero) whose asylum is an authentically creepy Southern mansion. Written and directed by Mohy Quandour, the silly script is treated so seriously that it becomes unintentionally quite funny. A-II (PG)

Speedway (1968) Routine Elvis Presley musical in which he plays a stock-car racer involved with leading lady Nancy Sinatra and the Internal Revenue Service. Director Norman Taurog keeps the action adventure moving at a pedestrian pace. A-II (G)

Spetters (1981) Dutch import about three young men with little else on their minds but motorcycle racing, sex and idolizing race champ Rutger Hauer. Directed by Paul Verhoeven, the movie reflects the confused values of a segment of contemporary youth but adds nothing of significance to the subject. Some graphic nudity and sexually explicit scenes. O (R)

Sphinx, The (1981) Beautiful Egyptologist (Lesley-Anne Down) with pluck and luck, eludes hordes of Levantine villains and discovers a cache of ancient treasures stolen by grave robbers. The thoroughly muddled thriller, based on a novel by Robin Cook and directed by Franklin J. Schaffner, is so badly done that it will have viewers giggling halfway through and hooting in derision by the end. Some unnecessary violence. A-III (PG)

Spider's Stratagem, The (1973) Intriguing Italian mystery about a man (Giulio Brogi) returning to the town where 30 years earlier his father had been murdered by local Fascists and learns more than he wants to know about those responsible. Directed by Bernardo Bertolucci, the well-crafted movie is a satisfying mystery story, yet there is substance in its treatment of corruption in the Mussolini era. Mature theme. A-III (nr)

Spies Like Us (1985) Chevy Chase and Dan Aykroyd sink to the lowest common denominator in a vain attempt to get laughs in this mindless and meandering comedy about two incompetant federal agents who are chosen to be decoys in an international spy ring. Much coarse language and sexual innuendo with brief nudity in a sexual context. O (PG)

Spikes Gang, The (1974) Formula Western about a bank robber (Lee Marvin) who initiates a trio of wide-eyed youngsters (Gary Grimes, Ron

Howard and Charlie Martin Smith) into a life of crime and then betrays them. Directed by Richard Fleischer, the B-grade screenplay offers the usual violence and a distasteful scene involving religious articles. A-IV (PG)

Spinout (1966) Innocuous Elvis Presley vehicle directed by Norman Taurog in which the singer escapes the clutches of three women who want to marry him. Pre-teens may find it boring but not Presley fans. A-I (br)

Spirit of the Beehive, The (1976) Spanish movie set in 1940 deals with two children growing up in the aftermath of the Civil War. Directed by Victor Erice, it is one of those rare films that captures something of the secret world of childhood, with its strange notions and innocent rituals, yet also mirrors the adult world and its way of dealing with terrible realities. A-II (nr)

Spirits of the Dead (1969) Trilogy of short stories by Edgar Allen Poe as told by three European directors. Roger Vadim's medieval tale of a decadent heiress (Jane Fonda) who kills her cousin (Peter Fonda) is dull but Louis Malle's story of a corrupt man (Alain Delon) pursued by his righteous double overdoses on nudity and sadistic violence. In a class by itself is Federico Fellini's "Toby Dammit" about an alcoholic English actor (Terrence Stamp) who comes to Rome to star in a Western. It's a small gem, capturing the grotesquely surrealistic, grim and ironic humor of Poe's "Never Bet the Devil Your Head." O (R)

Spite Marriage (1929) Buster Keaton, the great stoic master of silent comedy, plays an actor married out of spite by a jilted actress (Dorothy Sebastian) whose affection he finally wins after overcoming all manner of surrealistic complications. Directed by Edward Sedgwick, Keaton makes the best out of a heavy-handed plot but his comic efforts seem forced and lack the easy air of spontaneity that marked his best work. A-I (br)

Splash (1984) Mediocre Disney romantic comedy about a mermaid (Daryl Hannah) who falls in love with a human (Tom Hanks). Directed by Ron Howard, the movie is modestly successful as escapist entertainment, with slapstick chase scenes and klutzy over-acting. Brief nudity and graphic sexual references in the dialogue. A-III (PG)

Split, The (1968) Inept crime movie directed by Gordon Fleming about a gang's robbery of a box-office during a big sporting event. Gratuitous brutality and graphic sexual treatment. O (R)

Split Image (1982) Bright young man (Michael O'Keefe) falls in love with a young girl (Karen Allen) and is entrapped by a religious cult (headed by Peter Fonda), but his desperate parents hire a seedy deprogrammer (James Woods) to win him back. Director Ted Kotcheff's flashy, melodramatic and highly superficial treatment of a serious social problem may serve some adolescents as a cautionary tale. Some rough language. A-III (R)

Spook Who Sat by the Door, The (1973) Black exploitation movie about a token black CIA agent (Lawrence Cook) who returns to his Chicago home where he raises and trains a street army intended first to turn the ghetto into a riot zone and then to take over the city, the state, the nation, the world! Directed by Ivan Dixon, it starts as wry comedy but turns vicious halfway through when it begins taking its message of violent revolution seriously. Dreary abundance of racial cliches and stereotypes. A-III (PG)

Sporting Club, The (1971) Failed version of

Thomas McGuane's novel about an exclusive club of Detroit's wealthiest citizens and their alienated offspring and servants who try to wreck it. Directed by Larry Peerce, the movie lacks the wit, imagination and sensitivity needed to suggest, rather than simply depict, the terrible heritage of sex and violence it supposedly is condemning. O (R)

Spot (see: "Dogpound Shuffle")

Spring Fever (1983) Undernourished story of a Florida tennis tournament for teenage girls stars Susan Anton and Jessica Walters as tennis mothers, with Carling Bassett the daughter struggling to be a champ. Innocuous little movie directed by Joseph L. Scanlan, a love affair figures in the plot. A-III (PG)

Spy In Your Eye (1966) Routine Italian spy caper directed by Vittorio Sala whose chief gimmick is a mini-camera placed by enemy agents in the glass eye of an American colonel (Dana Andrews) by which they monitor what the Americans are up to. Mild violence and derring-do. A-II (br)

Spy Who Came in from the Cold, The (1966) Sobering screen version of the John Le Carre novel about a shabby British spy (Richard Burton) whose cynicism grows as his assignment in Berlin becomes a maze of betrayals and counterbetrayals. Director Martin Ritt's spy movie is not an escapist adventure but one that demonstrates the loss of humanity on the part of those who treat people only as means of achieving their ends. A-III (br)

Spy Who Loved Me, The (1977) Roger Moore and Barbara Bach stars as James Bond and a beautiful Russian spy who find themselves united against the usual all-powerful villain bent upon a free enterprise conquest of the world and who employs a steel-toothed henchman named Jaws (Richard Kiel). Styled sex and violence. A-III (PG)

Spy with a Cold Nose, The (1967) Minor British spy spoof about the bumbling antics of some secret agents (Laurence Harvey and Lionel Jeffries). Daniel Petrie, the humor is mild and the plot slight. A-III (br)

S*P*Y*S (1974) Failed comedy with Elliott Gould and Donald Sutherland as inept CIA agents who, after fouling up a defection by murdering two Russian agents, are on the run as marked men sought by both sides. Blankly directed by Irvin Kershner, the comedy is low, witless and frequently tasteless. A-III (PG)

Square Dance (1987) Young girl with religious convictions (Winona Ryder) forsakes the custody of her cranky grandpa to live with her tragically flawed mother (Jane Alexander). She overcomes disillusionment with the adult world while expressing the inner strength and grace that propel her with loving enthusiasm toward womanhood. Sexual references and some rough dialogue do not dim the luster of director Dan Petrie's joyous affirmation of the beauty and wisdom of youthful innocence. A-II (PG-13)

Squeeze, The (1987) Struggling set designer and compulsive gambler (Michael Keaton) teams up with a process server (Rae Dawn Chong) to confound and foil a scam defrauding the New York lottery with a magnetic box he finds and then loses to corporate thugs. Mild-mannered comedy directed by Roger Young has little else save Keaton's charm which lessens the casual acceptance of his dangerously amoral behavior. Comic seduction

scene and some violence are adult fare. A-III (PG-13)

Squeeze Play (1981) Rival community softball teams, with husbands on one side and wives on the other, battle for the play-offs. Amateurish movie directed by Samuel Weil, it contains graphic sex, nudity and unrelieved profanity. O (R)

Squirm (1976) Low-budget horror movie directed by Jeff Lieberman about an invasion of killer worms that almost wipes out a small Southern town. Disgusting scenes of violence. O (R)

SSSSSSSS (1973) Unpretentious thriller about a rather nice but quite mad zoologist (Strother Martin) who is working on a serum to transform people into snakes because reptiles, being coldblooded, will not be affected when pollution shrouds earth from the sun. Director Bernard Kowalski capitalizes on Martin's fondly dotty performance rather than his experiments with deadly cobras. Viewers with a phobia for snakes should be warned away, but the less squeamish will find it an engaging, at times witty, entertainment. A-III (PG)

St. Elmo's Fire (1985) Seven friends cope with the world after graduating from Georgetown University. Director Joel Schumacher's cast of characters consists almost entirely of shallow, boring, self-absorbed individuals, and their mostly favorable view of sexual promiscuity is in keeping with the amoral atmosphere that pervades the movie. O (R)

St. Ives (1976) Formula detective mystery directed by J. Lee Thompson with Charles Bronson as a retired journalist who becomes a go-between in a scheme to recover some stolen papers has too many gaping holes in the plot for even this kind of light entertainment. Some incidental sex and violence. A-III (PG)

St. Valentine's Day Massacre, The (1967) Bloody re-creation of one of the more lurid episodes in American gangland history when Chicago's Al Capone (Jason Robards) wiped out some of his competitors. Directed by Roger Corman, the acting is overdone but, then, so too is the violence. A-III (br)

Stagecoach (1939) Inside the stage to Lordsburg is a microcosm of Western characters, including an outlaw (John Wayne), an outcast dance hall girl (Claire Trevor) and a drunken doctor (Thomas Mitchell), while outside the Apaches are on the warpath. Director John Ford's classic Western is a grand outdoor adventure, with spectacular stunt work, and a story that places its characters in the midst of the basic conflict between the freedom of the frontier and the constraints of civilization. A-II (br)

Stagecoach (1966) Poor remake of the Western classic about an oddly assorted group (Alex Cord, Bing Crosby, Van Heflin, Slim Pickens) crowded in a stagecoach under Indian attack. Directed by Gordon Douglas, there are some good action scenes to enliven the ride but the characterizations are embarrassingly bad. A-II (br)

Staircase (1969) The terrible loneliness of two homosexuals (Richard Burton and Rex Harrison) is the subject of Charles Dyer's adaptation of his own play told basically in a series of bickering arguments about their fears, vanity and lack of future. Directed by Stanley Donen, the earnest examination of each man's desperate dependence upon the other fails as entertainment and falls short as a truly insightful human document, partly because two expert actors are more intent on portraying homosexuals than creating two believable human beings. A-IV (R)

Stakeout (1987) Voyeurism turns into romance when a cop on surveillance (Richard Dreyfuss) falls for the target of his perusal, a escaped con's girl (Madeline Stowe). Director John Badham subverts mystery and in-depth characterization to depiction of a simple love affair. Some violence, brief nudity and a sex scene make this mature fare. A-III (R)

Stalking Moon, The (1968) Above average Western in which an Apache (Nathaniel Narcisco), feared for his cruelty, follows the trail of those who have taken his young son and leaves his own path of dead settlers while a former Army scout (Gregory Peck), who has the boy, waits on his ranch for the inevitable arrival of his menacing pursuer. Directed by Richard Mulligan, the Western has some physical violence but its cat-and-mouse story is plotted almost totally for its suspense potential which it achieves with some intelligence. A-I (G)

Stand By Me (1986) The power of this drama lies in the simple, profound truths four boys learn about themselves while on a journey through the backwoods of their rural hometown in the late 1950s. Director Rob Reiner's pre-teen coming-of-age picture carefully avoids excess while focusing upon simple tests of patience, courage, caring and the joys of male camarderie. Some harsh language, uncharacteristic of the times, and brief violence but it is an experience some parents might wish to share with their youngsters. A-III (R)

Stand Up and Be Counted (1972) Journalist Jacqueline Bisset is assigned to cover the Women's Liberation Movement in her home town and finds plenty of fodder within her own family. Idiotic comedy directed by Jackie Cooper not only belittles women in its contrived episodes involving shrill maidens and audacious matrons but also insults the viewer's intelligence by its parade of unsavory situations and its very explicit sexual banter. O (PG)

Stanley (1972) The title critter is a very agile rattlesnake used by a very disturbed Seminole Indian (Chris Robinson) to dispose of a lot of people who annoy him. Produced and directed by William Grefe, the script tosses serpents and victims together guilelessly to evoke clumsy guffaws more than sincere shudders. Some sexual insinuations and vulgar language. A-III (PG)

Star! (1968) Lovely, lively musical based on the life of British stage star Gertrude Lawrence who is portrayed as a very nice, very talented, very ambitious and very tough lady. In the role is Julie Andrews whose characterization and singing are excellent in director Robert Wise's brilliant re-creation of British life from World War I through World War II, giving the proceedings a perspective both interesting and illuminating. A-II (G)

Star Chamber, The (1983) When a judge (Michael Douglas), disillusioned by the legal technicalities that force him to free defendants he considers guilty, joins a secret group who execute those who have escaped the penalty of the law, he finally comes to realize they are no better than criminals. Director Peter Hyams' plodding, contrived and muddled story at least raises some questions about crime, law and vigilante justice. Some brutal violence and much profanity. A-III (R)

Star 80 (1983) Fact-based story of Dorothy Stratten, Playboy Playmate and budding movie star (Mariel Hemingway), who was murdered by her husband (Eric Roberts). Though director Bob Fosse is rather superficial in the characterizations and lets the playboy philosophy get off much too easily, the movie is grimly moral in its implications about the consequences of promiscuity. The nature of its theme and frequent nudity, though never in a genuinely erotic context, make it very mature fare. A-IV (R)

Star Is Born, A (1976) Third version of the durable classic about the incompatibility between career and marriage proves little more than a starring vehicle for Barbra Streisand as a rock music superstar going to the top of the charts as the career of her husband (Kris Kristofferson) is sinking into oblivion. Director Frank Pierson develops little depth to their relationship and the romantic interludes are silly (though they do provide some relief from the din of the Muzak rock score). Coarse language and vulgar characters. A-III (R)

Star Spangled Girl (1971) Mediocre adaptation of Neil Simon's Broadway comedy about the ideological clash between a little gal from Way Down South (Sandy Duncan) and a pair of radical Los Angeles underground newspapermen (Todd Susman and Tony Roberts). Directed by Jerry Paris, the only bright thing about the so-so comic romance is Duncan's cute performance. A-III (G)

Star Trek: The Motion Picture (1980) The familiar faces of TV's Starship Enterprise crew are back with William Shatner, now an admiral, and Leonard Nimoy as Spock, to do battle with an ominous alien adversary. Directed by Robert Wise, the heart of the movie is its spectacular special effects with the characters in a supporting role. Trekkies, nevertheless, will find it nostalgic entertainment but youngsters may find it a long sit. A-I (G)

Star Trek II: The Wrath of Khan (1982) Capt. Kirk (William Shatner), promoted to a desk job, makes it back to the helm of the Enterprise in time to confront a flamboyant villain (Ricardo Montalban). Director Nicholas Meyer's sequel attempts to be droll and lively but is only slightly more entertaining than its dull and ponderous predecessor. Torture sequence involving the insertion of parasites into the ears of victims is rather strong, but the action is otherwise innocuous. A-II (PG)

Star Trek III: The Search for Spock (1984) Considerably better than its two predecessors, the sequel involves the efforts of Admiral James Kirk (William Shatner) and his crew to return to the planet Genesis, resting place of Capt Spock (Leonard Nimoy), who gave his life to save the Enterprise in the last outing, on the chance that he might somehow be restored to life. Some heavy breathing Klingon pirates (led by Christopher Lloyd) try to prevent this, but all obstacles are surmounted for the grand climax on Vulcan (presided over by Judith Anderson). Harve Bennett's intelligent script and Nimoy's capable direction prove that it is possible to be both entertaining and civilized. A-II (PG)

Star Trek IV: The Voyage Home (1986) Admiral Kirk (William Shatner) and the Enterprise crew (the original cast members of the television series) return to 1986 San Francisco to retrieve two humpbacked whales that may be the key to saving Earth from alien destruction. Directed by Leonard Nimoy, its entertaining mix of sci-fi, ecological advocacy and satiric jabs at contemporary pop culture is charmingly visualized. Documentary footage of whales being slaughtered and a few coarse words bring home some of the realities of environmental waste. A-II (PG)

Star Wars (1977) Set in a galaxy other than our own, a desperate struggle takes place between evil usurpers of empire and a dedicated band of rebels (Carrie Fisher, Mark Hamill, Harrison Ford and Alec Guinness). Written and directed by George Lucas, the outcome never is in doubt because the movie's conventions are as old-fashioned as its story of good triumphing over evil. The special effects are stunning, the characters imaginative and the narrative intriguing. Much stylized violence. A-II (PG)

Starchaser (1985) Young Orin uses a magic sword to free his people from enslavement by a wicked despot. This animated 3-D movie is passable entertainment for juveniles except for an abundance of cartoon violence. A-II (PG)

Stardust (1975) Sequel to "That'll Be the Day," a British movie about a would-be rock star (David Essex), has him forming a Beatles-like group and becoming a superstar. Directed by Michael Apted, the result has a slickness and pace that are engaging, though it is a bit heavy in showing the corrupt consequnces brought about by sudden fame and fortune. A-III (R)

Stardust Memories (1980) Dry autobiographical parody from director Woody Allen focuses upon a writer-director (Allen) suffering from middle-class, middle-aged neuroses that come with success. The True Confession-style work is only fitfully funny, and its serious flights of fantasy stop far short of anything with depth. Satirical treatment of promiscuous relationships and frequent profanity. A-III (PG)

Starman (1984) Alien from another planet (Jeff Bridges) takes on the human form of the much-loved dead husband of a young widow (Karen Allen). Directed by John Carpenter, it does fairly well at creating the mood of a sci-fi fantasy and yet resorts to such scenes as the ever-popular car chase for excitement. Some violence and a restrained bedroom scene. A-II (PG)

Starship Invasions (1978) Inept, ludicrous, boring Canadian movie directed by Ed Hunt about good and bad flying saucers locked in a battle upon which the fate of Earth depends. Violence and tasteless depiction of experiments on human beings. A-III (PG)

Starstruck (1983) Australian musical comedy about the staging of a New Year's Eve show by a young woman (Jo Kennedy) and her cousin (Ross O'Donovan) to raise money to save the family's pub. Directed by Gillian Armstrong, it is good light entertainment but, unfortunately, because of its benign view of casual sex and brief nudity, it cannot be recommended for youngsters. A-III (PG)

Start the Revolution Without Me (1970) Fumbled period comedy about two sets of twins (Gene Wilder and Donald Sutherland), one pair aristocratic and the other of peasant stock, who get switched at birth and, years later, get mixed up again during the French Revolution when those raised as noble twins become confused with the cowardly peasant twins who are unwilling members of the revolting mob led by Jack McGowran. Though the situation is promising, Bud Yorkin's direction is remarkably dull, with heavy slapstick routines, inane dialogue and poorly staged attempt at spoofing the old swashbuckler movies. A-III (PG)

Starting Over (1979) Divorced man (Burt Reynolds) finds himself drawn to a nice, sensible, but rightly wary school teacher (Jill Clayburgh). The problem is that he is still strongly attached to his former wife (Candice Bergen) who now shows up wanting to give it another try. Directed by Alan J. Pakula, the movie is often very funny, largely due to Reynolds' engaging performance, but it grows repetitive and its humor doesn't blend easily with its more serious concerns. Occasional foul language and some sexual references. A-III (R)

State of Siege (1973) Fact-based political drama about an American official (Yves Montand) who in 1970 was kidnapped, accused of being a police specialist in torture and murdered by Uruguayan terrorists. Directed by Costa-Gavras, the movie accepts revolutionary change as necessary but demonstrates the futility of political terrorism, both by those who have power and those who want it. Excessively graphic scene of torture. A-IV (nr)

Statue, The (1971) Drearily unfunny one-line joke about the relative size of male organs, belonging in this case to a Nobel Prize-winner (David Niven) and the man who modeled for the lower portion of a large nude statue of the prize-winner. British production directed by Rod Amateau is an exercise in high-density witlessness. O (R)

Stavisky (1975) French production set in the Depression of the 1930s presents an emotionally engaging character study of the era's best known swindler, Serge Alexandre Stavisky (Jean-Paul Belmondo), whose destruction mirrors the collapse of capitalism and the rise of fascism. Directed by Alain Resnais, the powerful visuals and flawless narrative flow make it rewarding viewing, whatever the value of its historical insights about a past world. Mature themes. A-III (PG)

Stay As You Are (1980) A married man in his 50s (Marcello Mastroianni) falls in love with a teenage girl (Natassia Kinski), who he discovers may be his own daughter. Directed by Alberto Lattuada, the story goes nowhere and evaporates into a series of arty sequences that seem to come from a fashion magazine. Exploitation of the incest theme and extravagant nudity. O (nr)

Stay Away, Joe (1968) Poor Elvis Presley vehicle in which he plays a contemporary Indian who rides a lot of bucking bronchos, chases a lot of pretty girls and sings a lot of songs. He also gets in a number of fights trying to get a good deal from the government for his southwestern Indian tribe. Directed by Peter Tewksbury, besides the miscasting of Burgess Meredith, Joan Blondell and Katy Jurado, the Indian stereotypes are ludicrous. A-III (PG)

Stay Hungry (1976) Muddled story in which Jeff Bridges plays a youth hired by some crooks to dicker the owners of a Southern health spa out of their property but instead befriends its muscleman (Arnold Schwarzenegger) and his ex-girl friend (Sally Field). Directed by Bob Rafelson, the murky plot resorts to an unhealthy mix of sex and violence. O (R)

Staying Alive (1983) The disco king of "Saturday Night Fever" (John Travolta) goes from chorus boy to star with the help of the two women in his life (Cynthia Rhodes and Finola Hughes). Director Sylvester Stallone's sequel is a loud, vulgar bit of mediocre entertainment, that is not all moving and with no semblance of the bothersome demands of reality. Benign attitude toward casual sex. A-III

(PG)
Steagle, The (1971)   Uneven comic fantasy set during the 1962 Cuban missle crisis when a professor (Richard Benjamin) throws caution to the winds by flying off to Chicago for a tryst with his former girl friend's daughter, on to a Las Vegas romp with a couple of frisky stewardesses and a minister and then to Hollywood for a climactic movie shoot-out. Written and directed by Paul Sylbert, the movie lacks consistency in its attempts at comedy and satire, too often settling for much that is crudely vulgar and sexually exploitative. Some religious implications that are tasteless if not offensive. O (R)

Steele Justice (1987)   Martin Kove is a troubled and vengeful Vietnam veteran who blasts away a good portion of the Vietnamese underworld involved in drugs and extortion in director Robert Boris' tabloid depiction of ruthless crime met with equally violent and bloody retribution. Bloody ballistics, fiery pyrotechnics, lame acting and dialogue from ethnic stereotypes spell exploitation. O (R)

Steelyard Blues (1973)   Donald Sutherland, Jane Fonda, and Peter Boyle romp aimlessly in a lightweight, adolescent fantasy about three losers who dream of flying away in a reconditioned World War II bomber to find a land without jails. Directed by Alan Myerson, there are some occasional laughs to be had among the elaborate gags and frantic comedy conveying socio-political banalities about being free in today's restrictve society. Worth seeing for some momentary diversion but not worth a moment's thought. A-III (PG)

Stepfather, The (1987)   Chilling portrait of a psychopath (Terry O'Quinn) who slaughters his family, changes his identity and remarries only to be inspired once again to kill. Director Joseph Rubin touches upon the precarious nature of modern relationships and mutual trust but gets carried away with brutality, bloody murder and some brief nudity in this suspense thriller. O (R)

Stepford Wives, The (1975)   Katherine Ross stars in this failed thriller about suburban wives behaving like docile, mindless windup dolls. Directed by Bryan Forbes, the harder it tries to be frightening and sinister, the more laughable it becomes. Adult hokum because of language and some visuals. A-III (PG)

Stepmother, The (1972)   Pretentious story about the tenuous friendships and nebulous liaisons which cause much unhappiness for a devout, temperamental architect (Alejando Rey) and all those around him. Written, produced and directed by Hikmet L. Avedis, the movie indulges in the stale techniques of hazy flashbacks and freeze-frames while attempting to keep viewers awake by tossing in some perfunctory nudity and a few murders. O (R)

Steppenwolf (1974)   Max Von Sydow stars as Herman Hesse's alienated outsider whose life illustrates industrial society's need to reconcile the spiritual and physical through people's re-establishing contact between the body and the soul. Writer-director Fred Haines fails to establish the character as anything more than a poor social misfit in what proves to be little more than a pictorialization of Hesse's text. Questionable sexual sequence. A-IV (R)

Sterile Cuckoo, The (1969)   Off-beat look at college romance in which a coed (Liza Minelli) comes out of her alienated shell to pursue a naive freshman (Wendell Burton) and involves him in obligations and responsibilities beyond his ability or desire to assume. Director Alan J. Pakula has made a little film with small pretensions about young people's growth to self-awareness and responsible relationships. Some restrained sexual scenes. A-IV (R)

Stevie (1981)   British screen biography of English poet Stevie Smith (Glenda Jackson) the tough but sensitive spinster who lived just about all of her life in the same row house in a London suburb with her loving maiden aunt (Mona Washbourne). Based on Hugh Whitemore's play and directed by Robert Enders, the movie's warmly sympathetic portrayal of these two women is unusually intelligent and articulate. It also proves to be highly entertaining fare, thanks largely to their memorable, very human performances. A-II (PG)

Stewardesses, The (1970)   Stilted staging, slushy sound and indolent editing ground this plotless 3-D picture of a flock of mini-dressed airline hostesses who indulge in sexual adventures between flights. Excessive nudity. O (X/R)

Stick (1985)   Burt Reynolds, playing an ex-convict, runs into some nasty people in Miami, makes mincemeat of them and lives happily ever after. Director Reynolds' screen version of the Elmore Leonard novel turns the gritty original into a glossy and cartoonish star vehicle. Excessively graphic violence and amoral tone mark this vanity production. O (R)

Stigma (1972)   Cheap exploitational melodrama about a doctor (Philip M. Thomas) trying to track down the prime source of an epidemic of venereal disease among an island community in Massachusetts Bay. Written and directed by David E. Durston, relationships and revelations become ridiculously squalid, while dialogue and situations grow increasingly hysterical and explicit. Trash. O (R)

Stiletto (1969)   Cynical, fast-paced crime melodrama about a playboy (Alex Cord) who is called upon to repay a mobster for saving his life and finds himself hopelessly involved in the mob's criminal activities. Directed by Bernard Kowalski, the movie's overriding theme of brute force against force presents a pessimistic, unnerving view of life. Merciless violence and some nudity. O (R)

Still of the Night (1982)   New York psychiatrist (Roy Scheider) is irresistibly drawn to a mysterious woman (Meryl Streep) who may have murdered one of his patients and may make him her next victim. Director Robert Benton's attempt at Hitchcock-style suspence has no sense of emotion or reality and none of Hitchcock's stylish virtues. Murky plot and stylized violence are not for the youngsters. A-II (PG)

Sting, The (1973)   Robert Redford and Paul Newman team up as two Chicago con men who concoct an elaborate scheme involving a phony betting parlor to get revenge on New York gangster Robert Shaw while turning a handome profit. Director George Roy Hill's action comedy is solid entertainment, though some might find it more than a little contrived. The Depression era setting includes a house of prostitution. A-III (PG)

Sting II, The (1983)   Dreadfully inept sequel written by David S. Ward and directed by Jeremy Paul Kagan has Jackie Gleason and Mac Davis essay the roles originated by Newman and Redford. A movie to be avoided at all cost. Some sexually oriented humor. A-III (PG)

Stingray (1978)   Two callow youths buy a car,

unaware that it contains a large quantity of heroin and money, and are pursued by a murderous trio, led by a woman disguised as a nun. Richard Taylor directs the movie-long car chase interspersed with brawls and brutal killings of various sorts. Violence and low moral tone. O (PG)

Stir Crazy (1980)   Failed comedy about two losers from New York (Gene Wilder and Richard Pryor) who find themselves doing time in a Southwestern prison after being framed on a bank robbery charge. Bruce Jay Friedman's script directed by Sidney Poitier relies on vulgar jokes and crude sight gags that quickly wear thin. Lewd scene in a go-go bar and frequent profanity. O (R)

Stolen Kisses (1969)   French director Francois Truffaut carries on the story of young Antoine Doinel (Jean-Pierre Leaud) from "The Four Hundred Blows" (1959) who here takes faltering steps towards maturity in a series of jobs, gets involved with an older woman (Delphine Seyrig) but finally squares himself with his girl friend. His haphazard misadventures are told in a relaxed episodic manner and Truffaut ends with the implication that Antoine has finally grown up. Some sexual situations and brief nudity. A-IV (R)

Stone Boy, The (1984)   Thoughtful study of a rural family tragedy as bereaved parents (Robert Duvall and Glenn Close) try to come to terms with the death of their teenage son, accidentally shot by his younger brother (Jason Preston). The father's decision to let the boy work out his trauma on his own is a bit hard to take, but otherwise, director Chris Cain's fine, quiet movie is well worth seeing. Some relatively mild profanity used by the boy's grandfather in an attempt to jar his grandson out of his sense of isolation. A-II (PG)

Stone Killer, The (1973)   Sprawling crime epic about a tough cop (Charles Bronson) on the trail of a Sicilian mobster (Martin Balsam) who plans to use some Vietnam vets to assassinate the non-Sicilian gang that took over the New York underworld. Directed by Michael Winner, the film's core theme is the nearly interchangeable identities of police and criminal as they act out their respective vicious roles within a society pictured on the verge of collapse. Heavy violence. A-IV (R)

Stoolie, The (1974)   Seedy, smalltime hustler (nightclub comic Jackie Mason) is a police informer who takes the funds intended to set up a crook and flees to Miami where he finds true love (Marcia Jean Kurtz) just as the cops catch up with him. Directed by John Avildsen, the old-fashioned melodrama is long on romance and short on logic and credibility but does have good characterizations and gritty, realistic locales. A-III (PG)

Stop the World—I Want to Get Off (1966)   British musical about an average man (Tony Tanner) who marries his employer's daughter, has a couple of kids and a few affairs, winds up with a title and the realization that he has never loved anyone but himself. Director Philip Saville photographs the stage production rather than turning it into a movie. A-III (br)

Story of a Love Affair (1975)   Italian melodrama about a woman (Lucia Bose) who joins her former lover in causing the death of her jealous industrialist husband with tragic consequences. Made in 1950 by director Michelangelo Antonnioni, the chief interest in the work is its focus on the social disparity between the luxury-loving wife and her jobless husband making the conclusion inevitable. A-III (nr)

Story of a Teenager, The (1975)   A high school football star tries to make a home for his kid brother but their alcoholic father tragically interferes. The film is well-intended as a look at the pressures of adolescence, but its script is simply too melodramatic and its treatment woefully inadequate to the task. Some intense violence. A-III (PG)

Story of a Woman (1970)   Romantic tripe about a Swedish pianist studying in Rome (Bibi Andersson) who has an affair but when she discovers her lover (James Farentino) is already married, returns to Stockholm and marries an American (Robert Stack). Years later back in Rome, she must choose between her husband and child and her passion for her former lover. Directed by Leonardo Bercovici, this dull, boring effort has an excessively graphic bedroom scene. O (R)

Story of Adele H., The (1976)   French romance of a 19th-century woman (Isabelle Adjani), the daughter of Victor Hugo, who exhausted her health in pursuing a worthless cad around the world, was brought back to France and lived under constant care for another 40 years, keeping a journal devoted to her obsessive passion. Director Francois Truffaut's adaptation of the journal is done with a fine blend of detachment, compassion and respect for a woman who wasted her life in one sense and yet, in another, through the journal, turned it into a creative act. A-III (PG)

Story of Christiane F. (1982)   German drama about a 13-year-old girl (Natja Brunkhorst) who drifts into drug addiction because of the squalid environment in which she lives. Director Ulrich Edel's coldly clinical yet lurid account of the hell of drug abuse lacks a moral perspective adequate to the horrific events it matter-of-factly chronicles. Innumerable scenes of needles being thrust into arms and its depiction of sexual activity make this extremely mature fare. A-IV (nr)

Story of F, The (1971)   Compilation of excerpts from mostly faded stag movies whose fuzzy photography of mechanically-performed sex acts will leave viewers disgusted by the commercial shoddiness of Jim Babb's movie and its anti-censorship narration. O (nr)

Story of Sin (1976)   Walerian Borowczyk's screen version of Stefan Zeromski's novel about a hopeless love affair beautifully evokes its turn-of-the-century era but wallows in passionate despair and focuses on the erotic elements of the story. O (R)

Straight Time (1978)   Dustin Hoffman plays an ex-con who, when pressured by a cynical parole officer (Emmet Walsh), gives up on going straight and re-enters the criminal underworld. Directed by Ulu Grosbard, there is not enough in the script to involve the viewer with the characters, and while the fine acting and austere texture of the movie earn respect, one cannot really care about what happens to anybody in the story. The violence and rough language are part of the context but the gratuitous nudity is not. O (R)

Straight to Hell (1987)   Madcap spoof of a spaghetti Western, this farcical celebrity showcase from director Alex Cox mixes madness and mayhem with touches of sexual seduction and teasing to evoke a sense of the Theater of the Absurd. Cameo cast including Joe Strummer, Elvis Costello and Courtney Love are all bandits trying to survive in a zany town. Some violence and sexual sight gags are not for youngsters. A-III (R)

263

Strange Affair, The (1968) Failed British crime melodrama about corruption in the London police department in connection with a pornography ring. Directed by David Greene, the slow and contrived plot makes sensationalistic use of violence and nudity. O (R)

Strange Behavior (1981) Offbeat horror movie about the revenge of a mad scientist, set in the kind of small Midwestern town inextricably bound up with this genre. What makes it unusual is that the town was re-created rather well in New Zealand by director Michael Laughlin who got a few American actors (Michael Murphy and Louise Fletcher) to journey there. Unfortunately, the story piles on the gruesome details of violent deaths to a needlessly excessive degree. O (R)

Strange Brew (1983) The comic duo of Doug and Bob McKenzie (Dave Thomas and Rick Moranis who also directed) lampoon Canada mercilessly as a land of rubes and rustics in an intentionally incoherent plot about a brewery run by arch-villain Max von Sydow with Paul Dooley as his cowardly lackey. Chiefly serving as a vehicle for the McKenzie pair of spaced-out zanies, whose substance addiction happens to be beer, the comedy is a random collection of stale sight gags and boisterous stupidities that grow increasingly tiresome. Course language and a visual sexual reference. A-III (PG)

Strange Invaders (1983) Some less-than-cuddly E.T.'s descend upon Centreville, Ill., one night in the 1950s and stay on in human form for a quarter of a century wearing the same style clothes as when they first arrived, something quickly noted by a professor (Paul LeMat) who arrives there looking for his missing wife. The silly plot is somewhat engaging but director Michael Laughlin's handling of it is plodding and uninspired. Some messy special effects when the aliens strip off their human exteriors to reveal their true life forms. A-II (PG)

Strange Shadows in an Empty Room (1977) Director Martin Herbert's frantic exercise in mindless violence about a detective trying to find the murderer of his sister. The Italian production was filmed in Montreal with second-string American leads, and there is not another nice thing to say about it. Nudity, brutality and sheer nastiness. O (R)

Strange Vengeance of Rosalie, The (1972) Botched contemporary horror story about a traveling salesman (Ken Howard) who is tricked by a young girl (Bonnie Bedelia) into visiting her dead grandfather's hovel in a deserted Western wasteland and then breaks his leg to keep him there. Director Jack Starrett dissipates the terror of the situation with a subplot about a menacing motorcycle hood (Anthony Zerbe) who harasses the girl both for her grandfather's hidden gold and her body. A-III (R/PG)

Stranger, The (1968) Italian-French adaptation of the Albert Camus novel about the senseless murder of an Arab tough by a Frenchman (Marcello Mastroianni) and his subsequent trial and conviction of the crime. Directed by Luchino Visconti, it is a painstaking and often beautiful translation of the Nobel Prize Winner's object lesson in existential absurdity. A-IV (br)

Stranger and the Gunfighter, The (1976) Italian production directed by Anthony Dawson about a gunslinger (Lee Van Cleef) and a kung-fu master (Lo Lieh) who team up to find a lost fortune, clues to which are tatooed on four former mistresses of the deceased owner. Intended as a comic mixture of sex and violence, the result is offensive. O (PG)

Stranger in the House (see: "Black Christmas")

Stranger in Town, A (1967) Sadistic Italian Western directed by Vance Lewis in which a stranger in Mexico (Tony Anthony) makes a deal with a bandit gang to help steal a shipment of gold but when they take it all, he follows and picks them off one by one, until he has all the loot. Cynical treatment employs brutal, sadistic violence. O (R)

Stranger Is Watching, A (1982) Rapist-murderer (Rip Torn) kidnaps a young girl (Shawn Von Schreiber) and a television newswoman (Kate Mulgrew) and holds them prisoner beneath New York's Grand Central Station. Director Sean Cunningham's dull, plodding thriller is derived from a novel by Mary Higgins Clark. Because of violence, rough language and the sordid nature of the story, it is not for young viewers. A-III (R)

Stranger Returns, The (1968) Standard Italian Western directed by Vance Lewis in which a lone stranger (Tony Anthony) sees bandits rob a stagecoach and kill all its passengers, then follows them and exterminates the lot. Much cruelty and violence. A-III (R)

Straw Dogs (1971) Introverted American mathematician (Dustin Hoffman) takes his sabbatical in the small English village where his wife (Susan George) grew up, and in her boredom, she begins to flirt with her former admirers, leading ultimately to a brutalizing double rape. The movie ends in a bloodbath precipitated by the husband's refusal to let a mob invade his home to lynch an injured man who has taken refuge there. Director Sam Peckinpah benefits from some uncommonly good acting but the characters are contrived stereotypes who would be more at home in a Western movie than the English countryside. As with the rape scene, the attack on the house is particularly brutal and vicious, wallowing in an excess of violence that the plot supposedly condemns. O (R)

Strawberry Statement, The (1970) Phony screen version of James Kunen's novel purports to be about the radicalizing of a college student (Bruce Davison) who, drawn into participating in a campus sit-in by a pretty revolutionary (Kim Darby), winds up being gassed and bludgeoned when the police and national guard brutalize the protestors. Stuart Hagmann's gimmicky direction calls more attention to itself than to the social and political issues which the movie supposedly is addressing. Further clouding matters is the movie's emphasis on sex and the heavy-handed stylized violence of the riot sequence. O (R)

Streamers (1983) Screen version of David Rabe's play about barracks tension exploding into violence during the early days of the Vietnam War creates sympathy for its characters (Matthew Modine, Michael Wright and Mitchell Lichtenstein), though the presentation itself remains too stagebound. Directed by Robert Altman, the essential problem with the movie, as with the play, is the attempt to load melodrama with heavy philosophical significance. Admirable intentions but disappointing results. Some violence and rough language. A-III (R)

Street Fighter, The (1975) Japanese martial arts movie revolving around a missing oil heiress and a repulsive thug (Sonny Chiba) who undertakes her rescue. Superior special effects but excessively violent. O (X/R)

Street People (1976) Aimless, shamelessly derivative gangster movie directed by Maurizio Lucidi in which Roger Moore and Stacy Keach take on a cast of dubbed-in Italian heavies. Some nudity but most offensive is its mindless brutality. O (R)

Street Smart (1987) Magazine reporter (Christopher Reeve), trying to further his career, writes a fictional account of a pimp's daily activities, passes it off as a fact and becomes embroiled in a dilemma when his article is subpoened as evidence in the murder trial of a real pimp (Morgan Freeman). Harsh language, instances of brutality and brief nudity, acceptance of fornication and mindless revenge erode the value of director Jerry Schatzberg's few insightful moments. O (R)

Streets of Fire (1984) Listless, boring rock 'n' roll story about a brooding outsider of a hero (Michael Pare) who rescues a rock star (Diane Lane) from a gang of bikers with the help of a straight-shooting female sidekick (Amy Madigan). Written and directed by Walter Hill, it turns out to be another tedious, stylized celebration of the macho mystique. Violence and a homosexual dance sequence. A-III (R/PG)

Streets of Gold (1986) A Jewish emigre (Klaus Maria Brandauer) from the Soviet Union where he had once been an Olympic contender gets some measure of satisfaction from teaching two Brooklyn street kids the art of boxing so they can compete with a visiting Soviet boxing team. In a well-intentioned but predictable plot following the underdog formula, the movie weakly affirms believing in oneself and one's talents. Profanity and violence in and out of the ring by the principals provide no positive role models for youngsters. A-III (R)

Streetwalkin' (1985) A prostitute tries to escape from her pimp in this sordid little movie exploiting sex and violence while having pretensions as social commentary. O (R)

Stripes (1981) After bungling their way though basic military training, Bill Murray and his troop of losers create havoc in Czechoslovakia. Director Ivan Reitman's mediocre hit-or-miss comedy has only scattered laughs and an occasional serious bit at odds with the rest. Extravagant use of nudity, sexual promiscuity and rough language. O (R)

Stripper (1986) Pseudo-documentary on a strip tease competition is an exploitation movie about women who are paid to display their bodies to voyeurs. O (R)

Stroker Ace (1983) Race car driver (Burt Reynolds) wants to break his contract representing a fried chicken franchiser (Ned Beatty) and to seduce a principled young woman (Loni Anderson). Director Hal Needham's action comedy has plenty of racing sequences, including several crashes, and humor with a minimum of subtlety. Occasional strong language and one relatively mild bedroom scene but, all in all, it's fairly good escapist entertainment for mature viewers. A-III (PG)

Strongest Man in the World, The (1974) Two college students (Kurt Russell and Joe Flynn) accidentally concoct a formula that gives people unlimited strength. Plodding, poorly-scripted Disney comedy directed by Vincent McEveety. A-I (G)

Stroszek (1977) Slight German tale of three Berliners (a street musician, a hapless prostitute and their landlord) who go off to join the landlord's son in Wisconsin but their hope in the American dream proves to be an empty one. Writer-director Werner Herzog seems to just let things happen and the result is often little more than a home movie with artisic pretensions. Mature themes. A-III (nr)

Stuck on You (1984) A palimony suit serves as the peg on which to hang a series of vulgar, unfunny skits in this low-budget comedy directed by Michael Herz and Samuel Well. Much nudity. O (R)

Stud, The (1979) Directed by Quentin Masters and written by Jackie Collins, this embarrassingly sordid British production stars Joan Collins in a story detailing the rise and fall of a working-class youth (Oliver Tobias) whose only salable asset is his body. O (R)

Student Nurses, The (1970) Exploitation movie about a group of aging apprentice nurses and their sexual exploits: one has a torrid affair with a resident doctor, another gets pregnant and has an amateur abortion and one has sex with a dying teenager. Directed by Stephanie Rothman, its treatment of the sexual goings on is relatively anemic both visually and morally. O (R)

Stunt Man, The (1980) Fugitive from the police (Steve Railsback) is hidden by a manic movie director (Peter O'Toole) on condition that he do some dangerous stunts but he makes a mistake by falling for its star (Barbara Hershey). Directed by Richard Rush, the movie-within-a-movie plot starts well but soon becomes repetitious and drags considerably thereafter. Graphic depiction of sex with extensive nudity. O (R)

Subject Was Roses, The (1968) Fine drama about a Bronx Irish family's domestic crisis succeeds far beyond the limitations of its basically one-set story. Starring Patricia Neal and Jack Albertson as the parents, and Martin Sheen as their serviceman son, the movie probes the love and hate that alternately bind the three together and tear them apart. Adapted from Frank Gilroy's Broadway drama, the movie contains intimate touches of family life, its joys and its frustrations, and is masterful in its revelation of human nature, jealousy and love. Mature themes. A-III (G)

Submarine X-1 (1968) British World War II story directed by William Graham about the training of submarine crews for an experimental mini-sub under a harsh and disliked commander (James Caan). The underwater sequences with the miniature submarines will be enjoyed by youngsters and the only violence is the sinking of a German battleship. A-I (G)

Suburban Wives (1972) Lurid British sex melodrama about how bored housewives discover new ways to kill time and devise new means of supplementing the family income. Exploitative nudity. O (R)

Succubus (1969) Trashy German movie about a woman (Janine Reynaud) who does a sado-sexual nighclub act and finds it difficult to separate her stage fantasies from her private life. Director Jess Franco's effort is short on plot and characterization, and long only on erotic situations. O (R)

Such a Gorgeous Kid Like Me (1973) Lighthearted French farce about a sociologist (Claude Brasseur) whose research brings him to do a prison interview with a beautiful but amoral murderess (Bernadette Lafont). Enamoured, he eventually proves her innocence but she in turn frames him for her latest murder and becomes a media celebrity. Directed by Francois Truffaut, the comedy bubbles brightly, the plot's twists and turns are delightful and, best of all, it has a feeling for humanity that cloaks even the worst of its characters with an elemental dignity. Some strong language and sexual escapades. A-III (R)

Such Good Friends (1971) Director Otto Preminger has transformed Lois Gould's sly, satirical novel about the seamy underside of New York's cocktail party set into a souped-up sexual soap opera. The movie is a series of melodramatic tableaux that become progressively cheaper in their depiction of the harsh discoveries a youngish wife (Dyan Cannon) makes about her dying husband (Lawrence Luckinbill) and her own series of sexual adventures, past and present. O (R)

Sucker, The (1966) Funny French comedy directed by Gerard Oury in which a smuggler (Louis de Funes) hires a sucker (Bourvil) to drive him from Naples to Bourdeaux but when the booby learns that the car is loaded with drugs, gold and jewels, he outsmarts the crooks. Some sexual innuendo. A-III (br)

Sudden Death (1985) Female "Death Wish" variant in which a young woman (Denise Coward) buys a gun after being raped and goes hunting without a license. The woefully inept movie dangerously attempts to find an audience by suggesting vigilantism, yet its central interest is an exploitation of sex and violence. O (R)

Sudden Impact (1983) Dirty Harry (Clint Eastwood who also directs) is back, this time in picturesque Santa Cruz to halt a series of gruesome shootings that prove to be the work of a gang rape victim (Sondra Locke) exacting vengeance upon those who brutalized her. With the two having so much in common, the outcome is entirely predictable. Excessive violence and the espousal of an end-justifies-the-means outlook. O (R)

Sudden Terror (1971) Above average British thriller about a youngster (Mark Lester) living on a Mediterranean island who happens to see a policeman shoot the visiting president of an African nation. Afraid of going to the police and unable to convince his grandfather (Lionel Jeffries) that he is telling the truth, the boy is left to the mercy of the murderer in a violent chase criss-crossing the island. Director John Hough offers a mixture of suspense and sly British humor, with a decided Hitchcock flair. Series of violent murders and grisly auto smash-ups. A-III (GP)

Sudden Wealth of the Poor People of Kombach, The (1974) Fact-based German dramatization set in the early 19th century when a group of simple peasants rob a tax-collector but are quickly apprehended since they are the only ones buying goods in an area where everyone else is starving. Director Volker Schlondorff's excellent visual recreation foreshadows the violent struggles for social justice that break out in Europe a few decades later. A-III (nr)

Sugar Hill (1974) Ludicrous horror film about a black woman (Marki Bey) who uses voodoo to summon a horde of moss-covered, chrome-eyed zombies to hack to pieces the murderers of her husband. The hacking is bloody enough to be sure, but Paul Maslansky's direction, not to mention the dialogue, the make-up and the acting, is so inept that the entire effort comes off as something of a caricature. A-III (PG)

Sugarland Express, The (1974) Young wife (Goldie Hawn) breaks her small-time criminal hubby (William Atherton) out of a Texas jail, helps

him steal a state trooper's car and, with its cop (Michael Saks) as hostage, the unlikely trio pick up a mass following of local lawmen. With the news media reporting the caravan's every turn, public sentiment builds up enough to make the edgy wife-husband team into the stuff of legend, inevitably ending in tragedy. Director Steven Spielberg's fact-based story has the feel of real people with very real needs and flaws, achieved by unusually fine performances from the principals. Much tension and some heavy violence. A-III (PG)

Summer Lovers (1982) Given an Aegean holiday as a graduation present, a callow youth (Peter Gallagher) takes his girl friend (Daryl Hannah) to a picturesque Greek island where a French archaeologist (Valerie Quennessen) teaches them that threesomes have more fun than couples. Achieving the emotional level of a tourism poster, writer-director Randall Kleiser's movie is an experience in boredom of appeal only to desperate voyeurs. Excessive nudity. O (R)

Summer of '42 (1971) Sticky little romantic melodrama about three foul-mouthed teens who come of age during the first summer of World War II in a lush Cape Cod setting. Of the three, the focus is on the quiet-but-deep dreamer (Gary Grimes) and his interest in the fetching form of the grief-stricken war widow (Jennifer O'Neill) who invites him to share her bed. Director Robert Mulligan tries to balance all the nostalgia with a little honesty in depicting the limbo of loneliness and longing between adolescence and manhood but stumbles at the end. Mature theme. A-IV (R/PG)

Summer Paradise (1978) Swedish movie about four generations of a family who gather to spend the summer in a comfortable old house in beautiful natural surroundings becomes an intricate study of their relationships, lives, careers and values. Director Gunnel Lindblom uses her family setting to offer a sharp, passionate but non-doctrinaire critique of modern society, not least of its targets being abortion, mercy killing and the pill. Unnecessary use of nudity in a manner quite incidental to the movie's themes and development. A-IV (nr)

Summer Rental (1985) Innocuous little comedy, directed by Carl Reiner, about a family's Florida vacation simply doesn't have enough humorous material to be worth the effort. Some fairly vulgar sequences say little about family ties or vacationing. A-II (PG)

Summer School (1987) A gym teacher (Mark Harmon) becomes a reluctant remedial English instructor whose non-conformist tactics finally produce positive results with a group of impudent teen-agers forced to spend their summer in school. The deals which are struck between teacher and student in writer-director Carl Reiner's light comedy address social and sexual issues best viewed from a mature perspective to avoid false impressions. A-III (PG-13)

Summer Wishes, Winter Dreams (1973) Character study of a woman (Joanne Woodward) whose mother's death initiates a mid-life crisis which, despite her understanding husband (Martin Balsam), nearly sweeps her away. Woodward's moving performance reveals the private agony of a lonely, desperate woman who has allowed life to slip past her because of her refusal to deal with its realities but who tries to struggle for a new understanding of self and a renewed need for others. Gilbert Cates's sensitive direction shows an understanding for the subtleties of intimate relationships, their pain and love. A-III (PG)

Summerdog (1977) Mild little comedy about a family who fall in love with a dog that attaches itself to them on their summer vacation. The problem, happily overcome of course, is how to bring him home when their landlord does not allow pets. There is some lovely photography but it is a movie for younger and less demanding viewers. A-I (G)

Summertime (1955) Katharine Hepburn plays a spinster on a vacation in Venice who becomes enchanted with a handsome Italian (Rosanno Brazzi) but, when she learns he is married, cuts her vacation short and returns home, a sadder but wiser person. British production directed by David Lean is a classic romantic melodrama, faultlessly told with charming, bittersweet humor and the eye-filling, Renaissance splendor of the city of canals. A-III (br)

Summertime Killer (1973) Formula revenge tale about a young man (Christopher Mitchum) who kidnaps the daughter (Olivia Hussey) of a member of the gang that killed his father and then falls in love with her while being trailed to Lisbon by a crooked cop (Karl Malden). Director Antonio Isasi makes the most of motorcycle chases in the picturesque Portuguese countryside but has much less success with tracking a largely incoherent plot. Amoral characters and situations. A-III (PG)

Summertree (1971) Hollow melodrama about a talented guitarist (Michael Douglas) who, drafted before he can enroll in music school, disillusioned by the woman he loves (Brenda Vaccaro) and prevented by his parents (Jack Warden and Barbara Bel Geddes) from escaping to Canada, becomes another victim of the Vietnam era. Directed by Anthony Newley, the characters and their experiences don't add up and its unearned sentimentality trivializes a serious subject. Especially soft-headed is a nude love scene with ludicrous superimpositions of luxuriant vegetation. A-III (PG)

Sunburn (1979) Insurance investigator (Charles Grodin) hires a model (Farrah Fawcett) to act as his wife while in Acapulco on a murder-suicide case with a $5 million pay-out. Joined by a retired sleuth (Art Carney), the trio pull off the solution with lots of assistance from scenery, costumes and sneaky tactics. Directed by Richard C. Sarafian, it's simple escapist fare with well-intentioned bunglers bringing more cunning crooks to justice. A-II (PG)

Sunday, Bloody Sunday (1971) British stiff-upper-lip triangle between a successful middle-aged physician (Peter Finch), an attractive divorcee (Glenda Jackson) and a young, pleasant but uncommitted art designer (Murray Head) whose companionship and affections the two older people knowingly if regretfully share. Directed by John Schlesinger, the locale is contemporary London, peopled by middle-class ciphers who live in a world bereft of hope and spiritual freedom. Sensitive, nuanced portrayal of tortured relationships but morally ambiguous in its conclusion. Details of the homosexual relationship are restrained but central to the plot. A-IV (R)

Sunday in the Country (1976) Dull, predictable Canadian movie about a seemingly mild-mannered farmer (Ernest Borgnine) who takes the law into his own hands in brutal fashion. O (R)

Sunday in the Country, A (1985) Warm, insightful French movie about one day in the life of an old painter (Louis Ducreux). In his country home near Paris on a beautiful spring Sunday in 1912, the old man is visited by his dull son and his even duller wife with their three lively children, joined a little later by the artist's unmarried daughter who is his delight. Nothing happens out of the ordinary except that this marvellously discerning film creates a family context that is universal in showing the bafflements and complexities of human love and ambition. A small masterpiece directed by Bertrand Tavernier. A-I (G)

Sunday Lovers (1981) Failed omnibus movie about the amorous adventures of four middle-aged men in four different countries presented in separate episodes directed by Bryan Forbes, Edouard Molinaro, Dino Risi and Gene Wilder. The segments range from mediocre to dismal, with Wilder's being the worst. Prolonged nude love scene. O (R)

Sundowners, The (1960) Excellent story about the joys and hardships of an itinerant Australian sheepherder (Robert Mitchum) whose passion for the unencumbered life is in direct conflict with the yearnings of his wife (Deborah Kerr) to settle down. Directed by Fred Zinnemann, the movie's characters and its locale are finely evoked in a story that is part outdoors adventure and part domestic drama. A-II (br)

Sunflower (1970) Italian tearjerker about a newly married couple (Sophia Loren and Marcello Mastroianni) whose life is disrupted when he is sent to the Russian front during World War II. When he does not return, she journeys to Russia and finds him married and with a child. Eventually following her back to Milan, he learns she is now in love with someone else. Directed by Vittorio De Sica, the movie is not essentially concerned with such matters as marital commitment and fidelity, and younger adolescents are likely to misunderstand the moral ambiguities of the story's human complications. A-III (G)

Sunnyside (1979) A tough street fighter (Joey Travolta) wants to stop gang warfare and start a new life. Haphazardly directed by Timothy Galfas, the movie brutalizes viewers with incessant violence. O (R)

Sunshine Boys, The (1975) Good screen version of the Neil Simon comedy about an old vaudeville team (George Burns and Walter Matthau), long separated, who are brought together, despite their antagonism, for one last performance. Director Herbert Ross gets an excellent performance from Burns, and though Matthau overacts, there are enough laughs to provide an evening's entertainment. Some rough language. A-III (PG)

Super Cops, The (1974) Fact-based story about two New York City detectives, nicknamed Batman (Ron Liebman) and Robin (David Selby), whose turf is a Brooklyn ghetto and its liver-colored tenements, gaudy pimp-dope dealer hangouts and crime-ridden streets. As directed by Gordon Parks, there is an undeniable vigor in this fast-paced movie and great appeal in its two central figures and solid supporting cast. However, it goes to excess in its graphic violence, coarse street humor and relentlessly foul language. O (R/PG)

Super Stooges Versus the Wonder Women (1974) Inept Italian adventure fantasy about a band of Amazons who meet their match in a trio of super heroes. Director Al Bradley's low-grade sword-and-sandals action offers inane buffoonery, poorly staged battles and minor skirmishes, both military and romantic. A-III (PG)

Superargo and the Faceless Giants (1971) Mad doctor (Guy Madison) turns abducted athletes into bank-robbing robots until foiled by Superargo (Ken Wood), retired wrestler and masked mystic, indomitable in crimson bullet-proof costume, together with ray gun and supercar. Directed by Paul Maxwell, it's a throwback to the simple spills and thrills of the old Saturday matinee serials but lacks their corny charm. A-I (G)

Superbeast (1972) Shoestring Philippine horror movie about ape-like mutants resulting from the botched attempts of a mad doctor (Craig Littler) in reconditioning hardened criminals on his jungle river island outside Manila. Director George Schenck botches a plot derived from any number of older, better movies, with his only innovation being the use of some stock medical footage of a cadaver's dissection. A-III (R)

Superdad (1974) West Coast teenagers have their summer beach party fun interrupted by a dumb but well-meaning father (Bob Crane) who opposes his daughter's (Kathleen Cody) involvement with a directionless youth (Kurt Russell). Though intended as the usual lightweight Disney family fare, director Vincent McEveety's picture of family life and values is a tasteless mixture of middle-class affluence, alienation and artificiality. A-II (G)

Superfly (1972) Black exploitation movie about a tough, cool drug dealer (Ron O'Neal) who is planning one last deal so he can make a killing and get out but the police (all white) and a New York City commissioner want in. Directed by Gordon Parks Jr., the super antics of affluent criminals glamorize these fantasy characters as viable, attractive figures to be admired. Excessive violence and sex. O (R)

Superfly T.N.T. (1973) Middling sequel takes the ex-drug dealer (Ron O'Neal who also directed) from Harlem to Rome where he pitches in with his special brand of hustling know-how in order to help an emerging West African nation. The role has taken on some fairly human characteristics but, unfortunately, the change gets lost in the context of a static story offering little but glamorous location photography and mildly violent action. A-III (R)

Supergirl (1984) Superman's cousin (Helen Slater) does battle with a wicked witch, the fate of mankind depending upon the outcome. Faye Dunaway and Brenda Vaccaro are among the nasties in a wooden film directed by Jeannot Szwarc. Restrained attempted rape scene and some profanity. A-II (PG)

Superman (1978) The Man of Steel (Christopher Reeve) is brought to Earth from the dying planet Krypton, nurtured by the kindhearted Kents and becomes a reporter in Metropolis where he meets Lois Lane (Margot Kidder). As Superman, he encounters evil in the person of master criminal Lex Luthor (Gene Hackman) and his cronies (Ned Beatty and Valerie Perrine). Fun-filled comic book fantasy adventure directed by Richard Donner has some pyrotechnics that may be too intense for the very young. A-II (PG)

Superman II (1981) Exciting, romantic and often very funny sequel has three nasty villains from Krypton show up to wreak havoc just as Superman (Christopher Reeve) gives up his powers in order to make love to an ordinary mortal (Margot Kidder). Directed by Richard Lester, the special effects, especially the climatic battle between superhero and supervillains above the streets of New York, are very effective. Unfortunately, some of the violence is rather intense and the sympathetic portrayal of premarital sex between the principals makes it inappropriate for youngsters. A-III (PG)

Superman III (1983) Weak sequel which fails to mesh two plots, the first involving the return of Superman (Christopher Reeve) to Smallville for his high school reunion and the second concerning a ruthless tycoon (Robert Vaughn) disrupting the world economy with the aid of an incompetent dishwasher-turned-computer-wizard (Richard Pryor). Directed by Richard Lester, it's a muddled, unfocused effort that keeps promising to develop into something entertaining but never quite does. Realistic fight sequence and Superman's bad conduct while under the baleful influence of Kryptonite rule out younger viewers. A-II (PG)

Superman IV: The Quest for Peace (1987) The Man of Steel (Christopher Reeve) battles his evil clone created by Lex Luthor (Gene Hackman) in this even-tempered sequel which features an appearance by Mariel Hemingway as a romantic rival to Lois Lane (Margot Kidder). Director Sidney J. Furie stages a violent conflict which may be too intense for the very young. A-II (PG)

Support Your Local Gunfighter (1971) James Garner plays an ingenuous con man who tricks a small town divided by rival mine operators into believing that an innocuous rummy (Jack Elam) is a dangerous gunslinger. Under Burt Kennedy's direction, the amiable Western comedy meanders its way through predictable but amusing plot twists and cliches before reaching its long-overdue happy ending. A-II (G)

Support Your Local Sheriff (1969) Gentle, genuinely funny spoof of the Hollywood Western and its heroes. When a gold strike transforms a slow-moving pioneer settlement into a raucous, lawless boom town, the local folk hire quiet drifter James Garner as sheriff and he institutes a series of clever and non-lethal maneuvers aimed at ridding the town of crime and violence. Garner is past master at this kind of genial characterization and his performance combines neatly with Burt Kennedy's deft, off-beat direction to make a very solid comedy. Joan Hackett supplies the romantic interest and Walter Brennan, Jack Elam and Bruce Dern are excellent support. A-I (G)

Suppose They Gave a War and Nobody Came (1970) Witless, unfunny slapstick comedy about a skirmish that develops between U.S. military units and the paramilitary units of a town near an Army base somewhere in the Southwest. Viewers should receive Purple Hearts and director Hy Averback should be court-martialed. Most of the senseless violence is between machines with nary a drop of spilt blood. A-III (PG)

Surburban Wives (1972) Lurid British sex melodrama-farce about bored housewives supplementing the family income. Its sense of humor is either unintentional or inappropriate. O (R)

Sure Thing, The (1985) Two college freshmen (John Cusack and Daphne Zuniga) share a ride to California. He's got a date with a "sure thing" and she's going to join her fiance. What results is mildly amusing. Director Rob Reiner's movie is about romance instead of sex, a refreshing concept for a teenage movie, yet it accepts promiscuity as a way of life for most young people. A comically intended scene involving a sex act occuring in the background further lessens its suitability for youngsters. A-III (PG-13)

Surrender (1987) Old-fashioned romantic comedy updated for the sexually explicit 1980s with the story of a writer (Michael Caine) who believes all women to be greedy until he finds one (Sally Field) who does not seem interested in whether he has any money. Written and directed by Jerry Belson, it has some sharp satire on contemporary materialism and a few good sight gags but its matter-of-fact acceptance of extramarital relationships is objectionable. O (PG)

Survive (1976) Poorly-made, badly-dubbed Mexican movie about a plane crash in the Andes whose survivors are forced to eat the flesh of those who were killed in order to survive until rescued. Directed by Rene Cardona Jr, the moral issues involved in the situation are beyond the range of this cheap exploitation effort. A-III (R)

Survivors, The (1983) When a young executive (Robin Williams) and the manager of a gas station (Walter Matthau) thwart the holdup of a diner by a robber (Jerry Reed), they spend the rest of the movie trying to survive the crook's relentless pursuit. Director Michael Ritchie's social satire attempts a bit too much, especially in terms of a sagging American economy, but it is nonetheless an often hilarious, consistently entertaining movie. Some adult humor. A-III (R)

Suspect (1987) Good suspense story of murder and corruption in the nation's capital stars Cher as a public defender who proves her indigent client innocent, with some assistance from a juror (Dennis Quaid) who has a romantic interest in her. Directed by Peter Yates, the center of the movie is the character played extremely well by Cher who conveys the strength, intelligence, dedication and appeal of the role. Some graphic violence and a lot of moody tension and menace. A-III (R)

Suspiria (1977) Tasteless Italian horror movie directed by Dario Argento about an innocent ballet student who finds herself in an dance academy run by a coven of witches. Excessive blood and gore. O (R)

Swappers, The (1970) Pseudo-documentary about affluent middle-class marrieds in Britain who trade mates in sexual games supposedly to heal marital problems or at least provide a thrilling diversion from them. Patent sex exploitation. O (R)

Swarm, The (1978) Air Force General Richard Widmark and scientist Michael Caine try to stop the progress of billions of perturbed killer bees and save the lives of the usual collection of aged and aging actors who assemble for such disaster movies. Since Widmark and Caine spend most of the movie trying to outshout each other, the bees, not surprisingly, almost prevail. Director Irwin Allen's effort would be silly if it were not so inane. A-II (PG)

Swashbuckler (1976) Witless pirate movie directed by James Goldstone that, in a mistaken attempt to combine tongue-in-cheek action with straight melodrama, is so achingly bad that a competent cast (Robert Shaw, James Earl Jones, Peter Boyle) can do nothing to make it bearable. Some brief nudity. A-III (PG)

Sweden, Heaven and Hell (1969) Italian psuedo-documentary filmmaker Luigi Scattini journeys to Sweden to show all manner of excesses, sexual and otherwise, most of which are staged to sanctimonious moralization of the narrator. Sheer exploitation. O (X/R)

Swedish Fly Girls (see: "Christa")

Sweet Body of Deborah (1969) Shoddy Italian-French import about a young man (Jean Sorel) who concocts a scheme to murder his new wife (Carroll Baker) for her insurance money but she double-crosses him. Directed by Romolo Guerrieri, the inept melodrama offers generous portions of sex and nudity. O (R)

Sweet Charity (1969) Overblown screen version of Broadway musical about a dance-hall hostess (Shirley MacLaine) who gets the romantic runaround from a series of guys who try to break her heart of gold. But her spirit is buoyant and there is true love around the corner (John McMartin). Directed by Bob Fosse, it tries so hard it gets tiresome. A-II (G)

Sweet Dreams (1985) Moving and entertaining biography of country-western singer Patsy Cline (Jessica Lange) whose career was cut short in a 1963 plane crash. Director Karel Reisz concentrates on characterization rather than showbiz glitter and there is some fine acting, but the movie's episodic structure undercuts its dramatic impact. Some vulgar language and vividly displayed passion, loving as well as violent, mark the relationship between the heroine and her husband. A-III (PG-13)

Sweet Jesus, Preacher Man (1973) Low-budget black exploitation movie about a criminal (Roger E. Mosley) who poses as the new pastor of a small congregation (after incinerating the real clergyman) in order to double-cross a white racketeer. Director Henning Schellerup has a flair for confusing characters and situations in dimly lit scenes. Excessive violence, some explicit sex and rough language. O (R)

Sweet Liberty (1986) The lighthearted vehicle written and directed by Alan Alda is a disappointingly shallow view of the sexual and professional frustrations of an amiable historian (Alda) whose book is being made into a movie. The comic touches don't override the movie's celebration of permissive casual sex with several partners as an acceptable route to mutual trust and devotion. O (PG)

Sweet Light in a Dark Room (1966) Czechoslovakian drama set in Nazi-occupied Prague where a student makes an attempt to help a Jewish girl hide from the deportations. Director Jiri Weiss maintains a grim wartime atmosphere and his two young principals (Dana Smutna and Ivan Mistrik) are credible in a life-and-death situation. A-II (br)

Sweet Lorraine (1987) Young woman (Trini Alvarado) rediscovers family ties and a sense of belonging while working for her grandmother (Maureen Stapleton) during a summer at a resort hotel. Director Steve Gomer mixes nostalgia with delicate romance in a family story marred only by some harsh language in a kitchen scene. A-II (PG-13)

Sweet November (1968) Sappy romance about a woman (Sandy Dennis) who is in the habit of changing male roommates each month and November happens to be Anthony Newley's turn. The reason for living life in joyous monthly installments is because the woman is dying of the standard Hollywood non-disfiguring but incurable disease. Directed by Robert Ellis Miller, there is some gentle humor at work in the script but the basic theme of the movie is unacceptable, even though given mild treatment. O (br)

Sweet Revenge (1977) Stockard Channing

plays a tough teenage car thief and Sam Waterson is the good-natured lawyer who constantly comes to her rescue only to be rewarded with contempt for his efforts. Director Jerry Schatzberg attempts to carry off a kind of conversion of his heroine at the end of this run-of-the-mill comedy melodrama but its morality (she sets fire to a valuable car bought with stolen money) is highly ambiguous. A-III (PG)

Sweet Ride, The (1968) Trashy tangled tale having to do with the wasted lives and energies of a pack of Malibu beach bums (such as Tony Franciosa and Michael Sarrazin) and their assorted girlfriends (most notably, Jacqueline Bisset). Directed by Harvey Hart, its sexual misadventures are not redeemed by one character's sudden moral awakening. O (R)

Sweet Saviour (1971) Exploitation movie featuring Troy Donahue in a sick and revolting movie based transparently on the Charles Manson-Sharon Tate murder sensation. Written, produced and directed by Bob Roberts, it's a tawdry attempt to cash in on a notorious tragedy. O (X/R)

Sweet Sugar (1973) Exploitative women's prison-escape movie with Ella Edwards and Phyllis Davis as the black and white ring leaders. Directed by Michel Levesque in Costa Rica, the bargain basement proceedings are soured with the usual violence, lewd characters, nudity and dirty dialogue. O (R)

Sweet Sweetback's Baadasssss Song (1971) Melvin Van Peeples wrote, produced, directed and stars as Sweetback, a name derived from his sexual prowess, who brutally murders two brutal cops and becomes a fugitive from The Man. The result is a largely incoherent chase movie, utterly defeated by flashy camera effects, overly graphic sex and violence, extraordinarily rough language and degrading stereotypes, black and white. O (X/R)

Swept Away (by an Unusual Destiny in the Blue Sea of August) (1975) Italian satire about a spoiled rich woman (Mariangela Melato) marooned on a deserted island with proletarian brute (Giancarlo Giannini). Directed by Lina Wertmuller, the battle of the sexes between classes gets swept away in some extensive depictions of lovemaking. O (R)

Swimmer, The (1968) Adaptation of the John Cheever story about a middle-aged suburbanite (Burt Lancaster) who swims home through the pools of his affluent neigbors, a journey recalling his wasted life. Directed by Frank Perry, the swim is a long one and the recollections, especially of past affairs, lead to only a banal conclusion. A-III (PG)

Swimming Pool, The (1970) Static French plot revolves around a triangle (Romy Schnedier, Alain Delon and Maurice Ronet) with nubile Jane Birkin coolly observing and finally taking part in their sexual games. Placed in a glamorous resort setting, the inner sterility of these social parasites is conveyed with deadening dullness. Moral issues drown in waves of ennui. O (R/GP)

Swing Shift (1984) Young housewife (Goldie Hawn) takes a job in an aircraft factory after her husband (Ed Harris) enlists in the Navy at the start of World War II. Making friends with an independent young woman (Christine Lahti), she eventually falls into an affiar with a personable young man exempt from service (Kurt Russell). Directed by Jonathan Demme, the flawed but superbly acted and often quite moving movie recaptures the

hopes and fears, the aspirations and idealism of a now vanished era. Though sympathetic in its depiction of adulterous conduct, it clearly shows that adultery is harmful. Occasional rough language. A-III (PG)

Swinger, The (1966) Good girl (Ann-Margaret) poses as a bad girl in order to sell some of her stories to a sex magazine. Directed by George Sidney, it is a silly exercise in titillation. O (br)

Swingin' Pussycats, The (1972) German sex comedy about three sexually agile sisters who scamper insatiably about their spacious estate to romp with any visitor, nobleman or commoner. Directed by Alexis Neve, it's totally unamusing exploitation fare. O (R)

Swingin' Stewardesses, The (1972) Director Michael Thomas turns a standard European travelogue into soft-core pornography in a badly dubbed, ridiculously inept, thoroughly tedious exploitation movie. O (R)

Swiss Family Robinson (1960) Good Disney version of the classic adventure about a shipwrecked family (headed by John Mills and Dorothy McGuire) living in a tree house on a deserted island learning to survive offers an engrossing picture of family devotion and solidarity. Nicely directed by Ken Annakin, much of the fun for children will come from the delightful and inventive conveniences the family builds and their relationships with the island's wildlife including an elepant, turtle and ostrich. A-I (G)

Sword and the Stone, The (1963) Disney cartoon version of the Arthurian legend of a young squire who, with the help of a wizard, becomes the king of England by pulling a sword from a boulder. Directed by Wolfgang Reitherman and featuring the voices of Sebastian Cabot, Karl Swenson and Rickie Sorenson, the movie is pleasant viewing for children but offers little for older members of the family. A-I (br)

Sylvester (1985) The story of a girl and her horse. Good acting by Melissa Gilbert and Richard Farnsworth as a gruff but lovable trainer, but little else to recommend this cliched tale directed by Tim Hunter. Vulgar language, a graphic near-rape and implied premarital sex propel the narrative out of its romantic framework. A-III (PG)

Synanon (1965) Edmond O'Brien, Chuck Connors, Eartha Kitt and Richard Conte star in a movie about the work of Synanon House, a haven for the cure of drug addiction near Santa Monica, California. Directed by Richard Quine, the movie's problem lies in exploiting too many side stories to the detriment of making understandable the problems with which it deals. A-III (br)

T

Table for Five (1983) Failed tearjerker in which a divorced husband (Jon Voight) takes his three children on a Mediterranean cruise, during which his ex-wife (Millie Perkins) dies in an accident and the children's stepfather (Richard Crenna) starts showing up at ports of call demanding custody of the still unknowing children. Directed by David Seltzer, the sentimental hokem seems interminable. Shipboard romance with a lovely Frenchwoman (Marie-Christine Barrault) is adult fare. A-III (R)

Taipan (1986) Rambling epic soap opera leaves out the history, drama and details of the economic exploitation of China during the 1840s when British traders dominated the opium and tea trades, centering instead on the sexual exploitation of bare-breasted Chinese women. Based on James Clavell's best-seller about a Scotchman (Bryan Brown) who loses, then regains control of a lucrative Hong Kong trading post, the photography of actual Chinese locales is picturesque but Daryl Duke's direction is ponderous. Much nudity, sexual activity and brutality. O (R)

Take, The (1974) Billie Dee Williams stars as a cop who's tough on the mob but takes money from them on the side in a muddled detective thriller which tries to create a complex environment where cops and crooks are interchangeable and money makes the world go round. Unfortunately, director Robert Hartford-Davis never bothers to explain the two sides of Williams' character or what the action is really all about, especially why the mob is attacking Paloma, New Mexico. A-III (PG)

Take a Girl Like You (1970) British production about an innocent young teacher (Hayley Mills) being pursued by her landlord (John Bird) and fellow teacher (Oliver Reed), both nasty rather than romantic types. Directed by Jonathan Miller, the heavy-handed melodrama deals in the corrupting influence of swingers and their world of casual sex. O (R)

Take a Hard Ride (1975) Routine Western about a wrangler (Jim Brown), entrusted by his dying boss (Dana Andrews) to bring his widow the money from the sale of a herd, who forms an uncertain alliance with a devil-may-care gambler (Fred Williamson) as various villains pop out of the sagebrush on the way home. Directed by Anthony Dawson, it's bland and harmless save for a lot of unimaginative chases and gunfights. A-II (PG)

Take Down (1979) Small-town teacher (Edward Herrmann) becomes the reluctant coach of the high school's game but inept wrestling team and has to motivate the one youngster (Lorenzo Lamas) who could boost it to the championship. Though the plot is entirely predictable, director Keith Merrill gives it some heart and his handling of the young cast makes it fun. Wholesome teen entertainment. A-II (PG)

Take It All (1966) French-Canadian production directed by Claude Jutra about an immoral young man's sexual experiences is offensive in its suggestive treatment in spite of its superficial condemnation of the hero. O (br)

Take the Money and Run (1969) Woody Allen stars as the world's least dangerous criminal, botching bank jobs and terrorizing no one but himself. Also directed by Allen, it's an entertaining romp through many fields and styles of humor, one-line witticisms, subtle jokes and sight gags galore. Some sexual references and a few profanities. A-III (PG)

Taking of Pelham One Two Three, The (1974) New York City transit policeman (Walter Matthau) has to outwit a heavily armed band of desperate men (led by Robert Shaw) who have seized control of a subway train and are holding its passengers hostage for ransom. Director Joseph Sergent's rattling-good action movie keeps the mood claustrophobic, the suspense tightly wound and paced with just the right amount of comic relief. The cast is top-notch, all of whom hit the mark as New York types. The only distraction is its relentlessly crude language which, unlike the subway, never stops. A-III (R)

Taking Off (1971) Uneven satire on the genera-

tion gap in suburbia follows the frantic search of parents (Buck Henry and Lynn Carlin) for their teenaged daughter who they think has run away when, in fact, she has only gone to the big city for a rock musical audition. Directed by Milos Forman, the parents come off worse than the kids, partly because they're older and should know better. It is mostly a series of outrageous burlesques, some riotously funny, others merely outrageous or excessive, such as a strip poker scene and one with youngsters singing an Elizabethan-style ballad with obscene lyrics. A-IV (R)

Tales from the Crypt (1972) Touring a subterranean burial ground, five sightseers find themselves locked in with the crypt-keeper (Sir Ralph Richardson) who reveals to them the horrible fate that awaits each. Solid British horror movie has a good cast (Peter Cushing, Ian Hendry, Patrick Magee, Nigel Patrick and Joan Collins) and five fairly intriguing tales which Freddie Francis directs with some verve, a lot of polish and even restraint in the visuals. A-III (PG)

Tales from the Crypt, Part II (see: "The Vault of Horror")

Tales That Witness Madness (1973) Failed British terror movie with Donald Pleasance as a psychiatrist explaining four case histories (involving Kim Novak, Peter McEnery, Suzy Kendall, Georgia Brown and Joan Collins) which in the end boil down to a padded cell for the good doctor. Directed by Freddie Francis, neither the frights nor the occasional nudity are worthy of comment or the viewer's time. A-III (R)

Talk of the Town, The (1942) Schoolteacher (Jean Arthur) rents her house to a law professor (Ronald Colman) who discovers a suspected radical (Cary Grant) hiding in the attic. Director George Stevens' romantic comedy contrasts civic corruption with social duty as the teacher finds herself emotionally caught between the two men. A-II (br)

Tall Blond Man with One Black Shoe, The (1973) French comedy about a violinist (Pierre Richard) chosen to be the pawn between two factions struggling for control of a counter-espionage agency simply because he happens to be wearing an unmatched pair of shoes. Oblivious to all the assassination attempts surrounding his daily rounds, Richard is fine as are the comic efforts of Bernard Blier, Jean Rochefort, Jean Carmet and Mireille Darc. Directed by Yves Robert, it is a drolly amusing, frequently hilarious, comedy of errors carried off in high style. A-III (PG)

Tall Women, The (1967) Spanish Western directed by Sidney Pink about a wagon train of women facing hostile Indians on the wild frontier has excessive violence and sexual innuendo. O (br)

Tam Lin (1971) Domineering, aging millionairess (Ava Gardner), living on a sinister Scottish estate with a coven of coed decadents, keeps her current paramour (Ian McShane) in line by showing him a few grisly snapshots of what happened to past lovers whose attentions wandered. Hothouse melodrama is best summed up as a soggy misfire by novice director Roddy McDowall. A-III (GP)

Tamarind Seed, The (1974) Russian spy (Omar Sharif) falls in love with a secretary in the British Foreign Office (Julie Andrews) and their romance becomes hopelessly entangled in international intrigue. Directed by Blake Edwards, its fine cast and gorgeous location photography are wasted by a script that misses both as love story and as spy thriller. A-III (PG)

Taming of the Shrew, The (1967) Sparkling but noisy adaptation of the Shakespeare play with bravura performances by Elizabeth Taylor as the comely shrew and Richard Burton as the rowdy tamer. Director Franco Zeffirelli's inventive staging preserves the flavor of the original but never seems firmly in control of the action or the actors. Mature treatment. A-III (br)

Tank (1984) Career Army sergeant uses a Sherman tank to rescue his unjustly arrested son from a vicious southern sheriff (G.D. Spradlin) and then heads for the state line stirring the sympathy of the nation. Audience reaction to director Marvin Chomsky's movie is likely to be much less spectacular because after the breakout, the story becomes increasingly silly and unentertaining. Some violence and rough language. A-III (PG)

Taps (1981) Highminded teenage cadets take control of a military boarding school when they learn the authorities are going to close it. George C. Scott does his usual fine job as the officer who inspires the boys to make their stand and Timothy Hutton is good as the insurgent leader. Directed by Harold Becker, the rather implausible youth-in-revolt drama fails to make its story of courage and leadership very credible. Some violence and coarse language. A-II (PG)

Target (1985) A middle-aged father (Gene Hackman) gains the admiration of his son (Matt Dillon) when his wife (Gayle Hunnicutt) is kidnapped on a European trip, and dull old Dad, who has a secret CIA past, becomes transformed into a superagent as the two attempt to find Mom. Directed by Arthur Penn but so preposterous that it skirts parody in spots, it is, nonetheless, entertaining fantasy fare, especially for fathers weary of feeling like Rodney Dangerfield. A bit of rough language and some violence. A-II (R)

Targets (1968) Modest crime thriller concerning a psychopathic killer (Tim O'Kelly) on the loose with an arsenal of weapons and a retired movie actor (Boris Karloff) who confront each other in a drive-in movie theater. Written and directed by Peter Bogdanovich, the contrast between the horror of reality and that of fantasy don't quite come off, partly because Karloff in his few scenes steals the film. Some stylized violence but no insights. A-III (R/PG)

Tarzan and the Great River (1967) Tarzan (Mike Henry) journeys to the upper reaches of the Amazon to put a halt to some occult goings-on by a tribe of headhunting terrorists. Directed by Robert Day, it's an exciting enough adventure, if all-too-familiar for older members of the family. A-I (G)

Tarzan and the Jungle Boy (1968) Newspaperwoman comes looking for a youngster lost years before in the jungle and runs into a slew of obstacles, including some unfriendly natives (led by Rafter Johnson). Tarzan (Mike Henry) flexes his muscles and puts everything right in director Robert Day's routine adventure. A-I (G)

Tarzan and the Valley of Gold (1966) Standard jungle adventure directed by Robert Day with Tarzan (Mike Henry) getting involved with some spies. A-I (br)

Tarzan, the Ape Man (1981) Embarrassingly inept version of the jungle hero's adventures with Miles O'Keeffe in the title role, Bo Derek in various stages of undress and the ape in the cast the only character to emerge with any dignity from a debacle created by John Derek. O (R)

Tarzan's Deadly Silence (1970) The Ape Man (Ron Ely), despite being temporarily deafened by an explosion, saves a native tribe from the exploitation of a megalomaniac trying to set up a jungle empire. Directed by Robert L. Friend, it's the usual wilderness adventure, though fans may be disappointed that there is no Jane and no blood-curdling jungle call. Directed by Robert L. Friend. A-I (G)

Tarzan's Jungle Rebellion (1970) Archaeologist (Sam Jaffe) searching for a lost civilization, a native looking for a sacred statue to establish his rule over the jungle and a group simply after gold come up against the lord of the jungle (Ron Ely). Director William Whitney follows the formula without much conviction. A-I (G)

Taste the Black Earth (1971) Polish dramatization of the 1920 uprising against the Germans occupying the coal mining region of Silesia is shown through the eyes of a young lad who refuses to let his six older brothers go to battle without him. Written and directed by Kazimierz Kutz, the movie is less an historical narrative than a patriotic ballad told with great feeling, much visual poetry and emphasis on the absurdities of civilians pitted against soldiers. A-II (nr)

Taste the Blood of Dracula (1970) Disappointing British horror movie wastes its first half on a ridiculous club dabbling in sex and satanism while the remainder is routine-to-inferior vampire lore in which Dracula (Christopher Lee) has only one big scene. Directed by Peter Sasdy, it offers only some slack suspense and almost no psychological terror. A-III (PG)

Tattoo (1981) Bruce Dern plays a man obsessed with the mystique of tattooing who kidnaps model Maud Adams and proceeds to decorate her body with the fervor of a graffiti artist embroidering his own subway car, until the contrived plot suddenly turns perverted hero into expert lover. Directed by Bob Brooks, the dreary, pretentious story lacks any credible sense of logic. Some nudity and graphic sexuality. O (R)

Tattooed Swordswoman, The (1974) Japanese Yakuza (gangster) movie about an imprisoned woman's dream which after her release comes back to haunt her. Director Teyuo Ishii's effort has more of interest than the usual spectacular swordplay because it vividly incorporates elements of supernatural horror within its traditional revenge plot. A-III (nr)

Taxi Driver (1976) Disturbing portrait of a troubled New York cabby (Robert De Niro), apparently traumatized by service in Vietnam, lost in his macho fantasies and infatuated with a political worker (Cybill Shepherd) whose rejection triggers his suppressed rage into an orgy of killings. Director Martin Scorsese's excursion into urban alienation and irrational violence lacks a distancing objectivity and its attempts to shock are excessively graphic in scenes of bloodshed. O (R)

Teachers (1984) Nick Nolte stars as a harassed but effective and idealistic teacher in a zoo-like high school. Directed by Arthur Hiller, the crude, disjointed effort seems just another teenage exploitation movie. Rough language, nudity and a sympathetic view of abortion. O (R)

Tear in the Ocean, A (1973) The remnant of the Nazi onslaught of a peaceful Hassidic community in Poland joins the local resistance group operating from the country estate of an idealistic nobleman (Armand Abplanalp) but the ultimate result is tragedy, as the Poles themselves turn on their Jewish allies during the count's absence. Written, produced and directed by Henri Glaeser, the complex movie views the Holocaust from a variety of perspectives, challenging viewers with its questions rather than comforting them with facile answers. A-II (nr)

Teen Wolf (1985)   High school lad (Michael J. Fox) becomes a big man on campus when he discovers that he is a werewolf in this moderately funny teenage comedy. Directed by Rod Daniel, the movie is marred by jokes about alcohol and drugs as well as some vulgarity and sexually oriented humor. A-III (PG)

Teen Wolf Too (1987)   Mild sequel in which the younger brother (Jason Bateman) of the high school student who in the original "Teen Wolf" became a basketball star when he turned into a werewolf goes to college and becomes a boxing champ when he discovers his brother's condition runs in the family. Directed by Christopher Leitch, it is more tiresome than silly, except for the violence of its boxing scenes and a benign attitude towards casual sex. A-III (PG)

Teenage Mother (1973)   Sleazy movie about the social and sexual rivalries of a class of inane high school students and how they are corrupted by a health instructor. Directed by Jerry Gross, the movie's scenes of rape and seduction are restrained but not some documentary footage showing the ghastly details of a forceps delivery of a baby. O (GP)

Teenage Sex Report (1973)   German exploitation movie about the sexual fears of teenage girls narrated by a "doctor" and directed by Ernst Hofbauer. Ugh. O (R)

Telefon (1977)   Russian agent (Charles Bronson) is sent to the U.S. to eliminate a fanatical maverick comrade (Donald Pleasence) who is bent upon activating a long-discarded sabotage scheme. Mediocre thriller made more bearable by a lavish production, Don Siegel's smooth direction and Lee Remick's personable performance as an American double agent. Some graphic violence. A-III (PG)

Telephone Book, The (1971)   Squeaky-voiced Alice (Sarah Kennedy) falls in love with surly-voiced John Smith (Norman Rose) during his first obscene phone call to her. The parade of perverts and exhibitionists that follows in writer-director Nelson Lyon's sour enterprise is sheer sexual exploitation. O (X)

Tell Me a Riddle (1980)   Melvyn Douglas and Lila Kedrova play an elderly Jewish immigrant couple, at odds for decades, who are reconciled while visiting their granddaughter (Brooke Adams). Although the fine acting is at times quite moving, Lee Grant's direction of a script awkwardly updating the 1961 story by Tillie Olsen is often clumsy. Somber theme and an implied acceptance of abortion. A-III (PG)

Tell Me That You Love Me, Junie Moon (1970)   Screen version of Marjorie Kellogg's novel about a disfigured woman (Liza Minnelli), an epileptic (Ken Howard) and a paralyzed homosexual (Robert Moore) who band together to live on their own. Director Otto Preminger's treatment dredges up a dozen sicknesses and perversions with consistent shallowness and lack of understanding, winding up with a limp moral of love conquers all. A-IV (R/GP)

Tell Them Willie Boy Is Here (1969)   Reserva-

tion Indian (Robert Blake) at the turn of the century is caught between tribal tradition and the white man's law when he kills the father of his sweetheart (Katharine Ross). The clash of two cultures, the injustice of the dominant one and the human fallibility on both sides are themes left largely unexplored in director Abraham Polonsky's drama which spends more time on the abrasive relationship between the fair-minded sheriff (Robert Redford) and the frustrated reservation doctor (Susan Clark). The result is no more than an average Western chase movie with an unhappy ending. A-III (PG)

Tempest (1982)   Famous architect (John Cassevetes), beset with faddish mid-life crisis, flees wife (Gena Rowlands) and job to an idyllic Greek isle with his daughter (Molly Ringwald) and mistress (Susan Sarandon). Director Paul Mazursky's updating of Shakespeare's autumnal comedy is sometimes charming, certainly never dull, but fails to overcome the handicap of its boorish, unappealing hero. Some frank references to sexual matters, including adultery, and rough language. A-III (PG)

Tempter, The (1978)   Italian version of "The Exorcist" whose theme of demonic possession is crudely handled by director Alberto de Martino with improbable appearances by Mel Ferrer and Arthur Kennedy, nauseating special effects and heavy doses of brutal violence and dumb sex. O (R)

10 (1979)   Successful middle-aged composer (Dudley Moore) abandons his mature lover (Julie Andrews) to pursue a young beauty (Bo Derek), even though she happens to be on her honeymoon. Directed by Blake Edwards, the sometimes funny comedy tries to have it both ways by indulging the same male sex fantasies that supposedly it is satirizing. Frequent nudity, shaky morality and rough language. O (R)

Ten Commandments, The (1956)   Less an inspirational story based on biblical sources than a dramatic vehicle with a sense of history, the Cecil B. DeMille epic offers some spectacular recreations, excellent technical effects and good acting from a fine cast, including Charlton Heston as Moses, Yul Brynner, Anne Baxter, Edward G. Robinson and many other stars. A-I (G)

Ten Days' Wonder (1972)   Complex French suspense drama based on an Ellery Queen mystery about a man (Anthony Perkins) who suspects that he has committed murder during a recent mental blackout. Director Claude Chabrol is less interested in the fairly simple mystery than in exploring the relationship between the strange characters (including Orson Welles and Marlene Jobert) living on the man's country estate, the decadent atmosphere that pervades his household and the sense of impending disaster that mounts throughout the film (and it is a shocker). Mature theme. A-III (R/PG)

Ten from Your Show of Shows (1973)   Top comedy in some choice cuts from the classic Sid Caesar television show of the early 1950s, when Sid, Imogene Coca, Carl Reiner and Howie Morris had as much fun doing their wacky bits as viewers have ever since. For those looking for lots of laughs dished up with a heaping spoonful of plain old nostalgia, this is unsurpassed entertainment. A-I (G)

Ten Little Indians (1966)   Director George Pollack's routine remake of the classic Agatha Christie movie mystery, "And Then There Were None" (1945), has a good cast (Hugh O'Brian, Wilfrid Hyde-White, Stanley Holloway, Leo Genn and Dennis Price) and a still intriguing plot. Stylized violence. A-III (br)

Ten Little Indians (1975) Stylish version of the Agatha Christie mystery in which ten strangers (including Oliver Reed, Stephane Audran, Elke Sommer and Richard Attenborough) confess to past crimes before falling victim to swift punishment. Director Peter Collinson moves the action from a remote island to a byzantine hotel in the middle of a desert and introduces a variant ending written by Dudley Nichols. Restrained violence. A-II (PG)

10 Rillington Place (1971) Superior fact-based drama about a 1952 British murderer of six women (Richard Attenborough in a brilliant performance as a quite ordinary person about whom something is not quite right) who was apprehended only after the husband (John Hurt) of one of the victims had been hanged for his wife's murder. Directed by Richard Fleischer, the emphasis is on the death of an innocent man and the nonentity who was capable of such brutal crimes. In the end it leaves viewers pondering the human inadequacies of the judicial system. A-III (GP)

10:30 P.M. Summer (1966) Director Jules Dassin's depiction of the complete alienation of an individual (Melina Mercouri) presents a degrading view of life, with some grossly indecent visuals. O (br)

Ten to Midnight (1983) Retrograde thriller about a police sergeant (Charles Bronson) who, discharged for falsifying evidence against the man terrorizing his daughter (Lisa Eilbacher), sets out on his own to stop the handsome psycho (Andrew Stevens) who kills his victims while in the nude. Directed by J. Lee Thompson, the movie's treatment of violence, nudity and graphic sex is thoroughly objectionable. O (R)

Tenant, The (1976) Mediocre French thriller in which a meek clerk (Roman Polanski who also directed) rents a room in a rather sinister Paris apartment house, learns that the former occupant threw herself out of the window and, with increasing paranoia, comes to believe his own life is in danger. Some chilling and effective moments lead only to a disappointing anti-climax. Its theme of madness, depicted with some slashing knives and bouncing heads, are adult fare. A-III (R)

Tenchu! (1972) During the civil wars of the 1860s assassin bands of samurai roamed Japan eliminating political opponents and their followers. This film by Hideo Gosha traces the exploits of one such group and the trouble its leader (Tatsuya Nakadai) has in manipulating his most devoted cutthroat (Shintaro Katsu). The result is a lush production that is little more than a routine exercise in the futility of violence. A-III (nr)

Tender Mercies (1983) Down-on-his-luck country-western singer (Robert Duvall), whose drinking broke up his first marriage, meets and weds a young widow (Tess Harper) who runs a ramshackle motel with her young son (Allan Hubbard). Director Bruce Bereford gets feeling performances from his cast, most especially Duvall in one of his best roles, and treats in a refreshingly uncynical, matter-of-fact manner the widow's strong religious convictions and her quiet pride when she sees her son and husband baptized. A rare movie, tough and gentle, inspiring and immensely entertaining,

but the serious nature of the story is more appropriate for adults and older adolescents. A-II (PG)

Tender Moment, The (1971) Failed French romantic melodrama about a teenager (Renaud Verley) and an older woman (Nathalie Delon) who fall in love, have an affair and separate when the man the woman had been living with returns. Director Michel Boisrond's story is not one of lost innocence (the boy has been sleeping with a housemaid, even "lending" her to classmates) and his older paramour is presented as something of a nymphomaniac so that the result celebrates nothing but the sexual imperative. O (GP)

Tender Warrior, The (1972) Filmed in Georgia, this portrait of a modern Huck Finn provides fine matinee fare for the small fry. The boy (Charles Lee) keeps tabs on all the wild animals of his domain, who respond when he calls them by name. Directed by Stewart Raffill, the photography beautifully captures the swamplands teeming with wildlife as background for this simple story. A-I (G)

Tentacles (1977) Poor Italian imitation of the marine menace formula substitutes a giant octopus for rogue shark. John Huston, Shelley Winters and Henry Fonda are out-acted by several killer whales in a story that is more tedious than threatening. Director Oliver Hellman's specal effects are unconvincing, except for the grisly visuals of a bloody victim. Some needless profanity. A-III (PG)

Teorema (1969) Paradoxical Italian drama about the isolated world of a comfortable middle-class family which is transformed by sexual intimacy with a mysterious visitor (Terence Stamp). Director Pier Paolo Pasolini's theme is the corruption of material values but he approaches it in such coldly intellectual style that one is uninvolved in the events. Though the use of sex is symbolic and not graphically depicted, some viewers will reject its appropriateness as a plot premise. A-IV (nr)

Teresa the Thief (1979) Italian drama about a woman's tragic life (Monica Vitti) after being abandoned to the streets by an abusive father at age 11, made pregnant by a man who marries her just to escape military service and finally left to a life of prisons and mental institutions. Director Carlo Di Palma only partially achieves the intended blend of pathos and comedy, and the movie's graphic, slice-of-life naturalism is mature fare. A-III (nr)

Term of Trial (1963) Middle-aged schoolmaster (Laurence Olivier), happily married (to Simone Signoret), finds himself pursued by a schoolgirl (Sarah Miles) who works out a nasty trap for him, oblivious to its tragic consequences. Solid adult drama directed by Peter Glenville, with fine performances from all three principals. A-III (br)

Terminal Man, The (1974) George Segal plays a scientist given to violent seizures who has his brain hooked to a computer to control them but short circuits turn him into a menace for what appears to be most of Southern California. Director Mike Hodges' version of Michael Crichton's novel takes a ridiculous concept to extremes. Much hokey violence. A-III (PG)

Terminator, The (1984) Violent sci-fi movie in which a killing machine in the shape of a man (Arnold Schwarzenegger) comes back from the future to assassinate a young waitress destined otherwise to bear a son who will lead the humans to victory over android rule of a post-nuclear world.

James Cameron directs the action in taut, suspenseful fashion but its violence is overdone and a bedroom scene goes much further than necessary. O (R)

Terms of Endearment (1983)   Uneven comedy about a mother-daughter relationship, that of a wealthy, imperious Houston widow (Shirley MacLaine) and her only child (Debra Winger) who marries a man her mother detests. The mother herself becomes involved with the wrong sort of man, in the person of a lecherous, dissipated former astronaut (Jack Nicholson), a confrontation of opposites that is sometimes very funny. Though consistently amusing, there is something uncomfortable about the way in which director James L. Brooks invites laughter at his characters for three-quarters of the way and then demands empathy for them in the tearjerker conclusion. Some fairly graphic references to sexual activity and a benign attitude toward sex outside of marriage. A-III (PG)

Terror in the Wax Museum (1973)   Dotty John Carradine's wax dummies appear to come to life and re-enact their grisly crimes in turn-of-the-century London. Director Georg Fenady's plot is as creaky as the museum's backstairs, and the suspense is as phony as the dummies, but for undemanding horror fans it provides some lightweight diversion. A-II (PG)

Terrorists, The (1975)   A group of political terrorists seize a British ambassador in Scandinavia and demand the release of their comrades from a British prison, something which the country's head of security (Sean Connery) sets out to thwart. Directed by Caspar Wrede, the suspense and excitement are well maintained, though in a chilly, abstract manner, that makes the ironic ending arbitrary and disappointing. Some violence and much threatened violence. A-III (PG)

Terry Whitmore, for Example (1969)   Vietnam deserter Whitmore, a 21-year-old black Marine corporal from Memphis who was wounded and awarded the Bronze Star, explains his reasons for deserting the Corps in an oral history documentary filmed in Sweden by Bill Brodie. Viewers will have to determine how typical were his experiences and motivation but his account does not seem to have any political axe to grind. Explicit description of a sexual encounter. A-IV (nr)

Tess (1980)   British screen version of the Thomas Hardy novel about the young Wessex woman (Nastassia Kinski) whose life is irrevocably changed when her father discovers that the family are the impoverished descendants of a noble line. Directed by Roman Polanski, it is an always beautiful, at times powerful, drama whose somber theme of a woman doomed by class and circumstance is not for younger viewers. A-II (R)

Test of Love, A (1985)   A courageous teacher (Angela Punch McGregor) takes an institution to court to effect the release of a bright child suffering from cerebral palsy who has been diagnosed as severely retarded. Fine Australian production directed by Gil Brealey offers solid entertainment and is immensely inspiring. A-II (PG)

Testament (1983)   A family in a small American community attempts to cope with the aftermath of a nuclear war in this grim but extraordinary movie about a mother (Jane Alexander) who tries to make life go on for her three children after her husband (William Devane) perishes in the nuclear strike. The warmth and compassion she embodies vivifies and makes moving a story that otherwise might be unbearable. Director Lynne Littman spares the audience most of the more horrific results of nuclear disaster, but what it shows and what it implies are unsettling enough. The subject matter and a restrained bedroom scene are more suited for adults and older adolescents. A-II (PG)

Tex (1982)   Good Disney version of S.E. Hinton's story about two teenage brothers, one earnest and responsible (Jim Metzler), one amiable but somewhat feckless (Matt Dillon), who attempt to cope with life while living by themselves on a rundown ranch outside Tulsa. Though director Tim Hunter's plot is overloaded with incident and occasionally veers into extravagant melodrama, its virtues outweigh its flaws, making it entertaining and sometimes moving. Restrained scene of teenage sexual discovery and some jocular references to sex and drugs. A-II (PG)

Texas Across the River (1966)   Spanish nobleman (Alain Delon) has trouble adjusting to the ways of the Old West, in particular a peculiar cowboy (Dean Martin) and his Indian companion (Joey Bishop). Director Michael Gordon makes no pretense of plot but strings together a series of humorous mishaps spoofing Western conventions. Of little interest but mostly innocuous. A-I (br)

Texas Chainsaw Massacre, The (1974)   Fiendish butcher out in the Texas bush country carves up four or five (it is difficult to determine the sum from the scattered parts) outdoors adventurers and then goes on a wild rampage of slaughter with a chainsaw and other instruments of destruction, including a meat hook. Directed by Tobe Hooper, what is more dehumanizing than all the violence is that the treatment seems to regard it as amusing. O (R)

Texas Chainsaw Massacre, Part II, The (1986) Grotesque parody of the blood-and-gore genre of horror films features a leather-faced maniac twitching riotously in the air each time he approaches a new victim with his chainsaw. Making it even worse is director Tobe Hooper's vain attempt to distance the viewer from the movie's sadistic action through misconceived comic exaggeration. Gory violence, often in a sexual context. O (R)

Thank God, It's Friday (1978)   Youth exploitation movie about the problems that develop one Friday night at a disco, set against a blaring background of frenetic music. Directed by Robert Klane, it juggles a dozen or so stereotyped characters and, though the pace is lively, the comedy is tiresome and repetitious. Some failed jokes about sex and drugs. A-III (PG)

Thank You All Very Much (1969)   British melodrama in which a young woman (Sandy Dennis) living alone in London becomes pregnant as the result of her first and only sexual experience, decides against abortion and becomes an unwed mother. Director Waris Hussein does well in depicting the life of Londoners and is sensitive to the young woman's situation but the treatment is superficial and makes no attempt to understand the woman and her future. A-III (PG)

That Championship Season (1982)   Jason Miller directs his own adaptation of his prize-winning play about four middle-aged men (Bruce Dern, Paul Sorvino, Stacy Keach, and Martin Sheen) who gather with their former coach (Robert Mitchum) to celebrate the 24th anniversary of winning the state high school basketball championship. As the evening of drinking wears on, the guilty secrets of each come out, but before they do, most viewers will have lost interest. Some strong language. A-III (R)

That Cold Day in the Park (1969) Failed psychological melodrama in which a lonely spinster (Sandy Dennis) invites a drifter (Michael Burns) in out of the rain for a hot meal and goes to bizarre lengths trying to get him to share her bed. Director Robert Altman juxtaposes two unbelievable characters in a series of impossibly phoney situations that lead to no insights about social alienation but only to morbid, sexually explicit sensationalism. O (R)

That Darn Cat (1966) Disney live-action adventure comedy in which Hayley Mills gets FBI agent Dean Jones to follow the trail of a mischievous cat who is the only clue to the whereabouts of a kidnapped bank-teller. Robert Stevenson directs the antics but it is the cat who steals the show. Youngsters will love it and it's not too hard on the parents either. A-I (G)

That Man Bolt (1973) Fred Williamson stars as the super-smooth courier of valuables for well-heeled international clients but this trip he's double-crossed by his employers and he works out a nifty cross of his own. Directed by Henry Levin, it has plenty of action, often quite violent but relieved by whimsical staging, and there's some sexual innuendo. A-III (R)

That Man from Rio (1964) French production with Jean-Paul Belmondo and Francois Dorleac in an hilarious spoof of stereotype characters and stock situations that typify mystery adventure movies. Directed by Philippe de Broca with real Gallic flair, the comedy is first-class entertainment. A-II (br)

That Obscure Object of Desire (1977) Disappointing French production in which a wealthy middle-aged Parisian (Fernando Rey) falls hopelessly in love with a young Spanish woman (alternately played by Carole Bouquet and Angela Molina) who leads him a merry chase. Director Luis Bunuel's surrealistic treatment of the romantic situation makes shallow attempts at social commentary. Excessive use of nudity. O (R)

That Splendid November (1970) Failed Italian melodrama about the nymphomaniacal aunt (Gina Lollobridgida) and her determinedly incestuous nephew (Paolo Turco), both of whom are but one small part of a large Sicilian clan specializing in sexual pastimes. Directed by Mauro Bolognini, the result is an inept exercise in studied decadence and heavily erotic atmosphere. O (GP)

That Was Then, This Is Now (1985) From the work of novelist S.E. Hinton, the bard of misunderstood youth, comes a story of two boys (Craig Sheffer and Emilio Estevez) who hang out together wondering about the meaning of it all until one falls in love and gets a job while the other wallows yet deeper in self-pity. Directed by Christopher Cain, the movie is so dull and pretentious that it is painful to watch. Benign view of premarital sex. O (R)

That'll Be the Day (1975) British drama, based loosely on the formation of the Beatles rock group, tells the story of an young man (David Essex) who is helped to find some direction in his life by a casual friend (Ringo Starr in a non-musical role). Director Claude Whatham's movie is raw, often ragged, but full of feeling and compassion, and it will interest both rock fans and those who like unvarnished pictures of unwashed types. A-III (PG)

That's Dancing (1985) A film compilation of great moments in dancing from the film musicals of the 1930s to the recent past. Produced by Jack Haley, Jr., the movie is very entertaining but real fans will note some significant omissions and yearn for more extended selections. A-I (G)

That's Entertainment (1974) Singing, dancing historical survey of the best of the MGM musicals charms the eye and ear with romantic fantasy. Written, produced and directed by Jack Haley, Jr., the selection of excerpts from these musicals demonstrates effortlessly why their appeal endures from generation to generation. A-I (G)

That's Entertainment, Part 2 (1976) Fred Astaire and Gene Kelly (who also directs) serve as hosts for this anthology from Hollywood's musical past, though there are brief glimpses of such comedians as the Marx Brothers, Jimmy Durante, Laurel and Hardy, and Abbott and Costello as well as a sequence devoted to the films of Spencer Tracy and Katherine Hepburn. Highly enjoyable but not up to the original's consistent quality. A-I (G)

That's Life (1986) Fumbling, self-centered husband (Jack Lemmon), preoccupied with thoughts of old age and death, is insensitive to the needs of his wife (Julie Andrews) as she awaits the results of a cancer test. Director Blake Edwards uses sexual encounters as a source of comic relief in an exploration of family ties that has few genuine moments. His infidelity is treated as a symptom of an inner insecurity left unresolved and overshadowed by the image of a strong woman and mother who absorbs all family ills. Brief nudity. A-III (PG-13)

Theatre of Blood (1973) Gruesome British chiller has its genuinely amusing moments as a B-grade Shakespearean actor (Vincent Price) takes his revenge on the stuffy circle of London critics who thwarted his career. Each execution is conducted through a re-enactment of the murder scene from one of the Bard's tragedies in which the critic had lambasted Price's performance. Director Douglas Hickox stages the action with a distinct flair and the cast of British character actors is marvelous. The gore becomes a bit tacky at times but horror fans will find it has a touch of class. A-III (R)

There Was a Crooked Man (1970) Offbeat Western about a reform-minded warden (Henry Fonda) who rises to the moral challenge of a convict renegade (Kirk Douglas) to practice what he preaches about rehabilitation and trust. The twist ending has to do with a race to the death for a secret pile of Spanish gold. Directed by Joseph L. Mankiewicz, it's corny but effective, if occasionally violent and tasteless, as the two leads ham up a storm. A-III (R)

There's a Girl in My Soup (1970) Disappointing screen version of the popular London play about a sex-obsessed TV gourmet (Peter Sellers) whose freewheeling amorous affairs grind to a halt when he tries to introduce an uninhibited hippie (Goldie Hawn) into his more sumptuous world. Director Roy Boulting's farfetched, frequently tasteless humor, coupled with the compromising situations of a belabored script, thwart the comic talents of Sellers and Hawn. O (R)

Therese (1986) French dramatization is an impressionistic account of the religious idealism of a 19th-century woman from the age of 15 when she joined a cloistered convent of Catholic nuns to her death there 9 years later of tuberculosis. Director Alain Cavalier visualizes the harsh simplicity liberating the interior life of a religious community whose traditions may be more confusing than inspiring for contemporary viewers. A-III (nr)

Therese and Isabelle (1968) Director Radley Metzger's account of a lesbian love affair is sexually exploitative. O (br)

Thermidor (1971) Italian documentary about 19th-century European nationalism and the competition for Empire that resulted in the bloodbath of the First World War. Director Tinto Brass relies heavily on the narration to make all the wars and internal strife understandable but it's a complex period and casual viewers may find it a struggle. History teachers, however, might make good use of its dramatic visuals. A-II (nr)

They All Laughed (1981) Screwball comedy is aggressively unfunny as it follows the antics of four private detectives, some beautiful women and other odd assortments of New Yorkers (among whom are Audrey Hepburn, Ben Gazzara, John Ritter and Dorothy Stratten). Written and directed by Peter Bogdanovich, the plot is thin to the point of transparency. Illicit sexual relationships. A-III (PG)

They Call Her One Eye (1974) Scandinavian exploitation import about a woman (Christina Lindberg) forced into prostitution who finally takes a sadistic revenge on the vice ring who enslaved her as a prostitute. Absurd sex and violence. O (R)

They Call Me Mister Tibbs! (1970) Routine sequel to "In the Heat of the Night" finds its homicide specialist (Sidney Poitier) slithering through slimy red herrings to fish out the strangler of an overworked call girl. The bright spots in the plodding crime melodrama are with his wife (Barbara McNair), though he finds the growing pains of his son almost as troublesome as the murder case. Director Gordon Douglas provides plenty of slam-bang action, including the movie's opening sequence depicting a sadistic sex slaughter and clinical police work in more graphic terms than a lay audience might wish. A-IV (GP)

They Call Me Trinity (1971) Italian Western spoof stars the grinning Terence Hill as the grimiest, laziest, fastest outlaw gun on the frontier who is drawn into a conflict involving evil rancher Farley Granger and some pacifist Mormon farmers. He and his brother (Bud Spencer), posing as a lawman, radicalize the farmers and teach them a primitive form of martial arts in time for the climactic showdown. Directed by E.B. Clucher, the shooting and mayhem are comically genial rather than the usual cynical violence of the genre. A-III (G)

They Came from Within (1976) Canadian science fiction movie about parasites that take over the inhabitants of an apartment building. Directed by David Cronenberg, the amateurish effort is disgusting in its exploitation of gory violence, sex and nudity. O (R)

They Came to Rob Las Vegas (1969) Elke Sommer joins Gary Lockwood in pulling off a spectacular plan to hijack an armored car carrying the mob's casino loot as it speeds across the Nevada desert. European co-production directed by Antonio Isasi has an imaginative heist plot that only works sporadically because unsavory subplots with sex and violence keep getting in the way. A-III (R)

They Don't Wear Black Tie (1983) Fine Brazilian movie about how a wildcat strike disrupts the domestic life of a working-class family in Sao Paulo. Directed by Leon Hirszman, the essential drama is played out on the family level, leading to a tragic clash between the father who supports the strike and his son who believes people should go their own way. Not a very entertaining movie but one that provides some insights into the human reality behind the headlines of Latin American strife. Some nudity and rough language. A-IV (nr)

They Might Be Giants (1971) George C. Scott plays a demented New York judge who believes himself to be Sherlock Holmes and Joanne Woodward is a psychiatrist named Watson enlisted to bring him back to his senses. Between the promising opening scenes and the closing shot in front of a Central Park underpass where the principals bravely face the dread Dr. Moriarity, director Anthony Harvey has supplied too many slack spots and unconnected parts to justify the question of whether the judge or society are the more insane. A-III (G)

They Only Kill Their Masters (1972) James Garner gives a wry performance as a small-time peace officer who's dumb like a fox, involved in a nasty murder case that unpeels some of the respectable veneer on his little coastal town. Displaced divorcee Katharine Ross finds a place not only in bachelor Gardner's bed but on his list of murder suspects as well. Director James Goldstone can't decide whether to play it straight or go for laughs and winds up doing neither well. A-III (PG)

They Shoot Horses, Don't They? (1969) Marathon dances were a popular form of distraction from the desperate times of the Depression, the period re-created by director Sydney Pollack's movie with Jane Fonda, Michael Sarrazin, Red Buttons and Susannah York all staggering around under the cruel gaiety of Master of Ceremonies Gig Young, urging the exhausted contestants on to win the $1500 pot at the end of the musical rainbow. Sometimes depressing, not at all pleasant movie but it does have the grimy texture of an agonized era. A-III (PG)

Thief (1981) After a long prison term, a skilled safecracker (James Caan) wants to pull a couple of big jobs and retire on the proceeds but, when he deals with a mob leader (Robert Prosky), he discovers too late that there is no way out of mob connections. Written and directed by Michael Mann, the emotional depth in Caan's characterization places it far above the usual standard of crime movie, though the story may be too grim for some tastes. A lot of tension, some violence and rough language. A-III (R)

Thief of Hearts (1984) Slick, chrome-plated little melodrama about a burglar (Steven Bauer) who falls in love with a woman (Barbara Williams) whose intimate diaries were part of the loot he took from her house. Some serious possibilities of the story lose out to a blaring, obtrusive score and director Douglas Day Stewart's fondness for nudity and graphic sex. O (R)

Thief of Paris, The (1967) Fair French satire in which its 19th-century anti-hero (Jean-Paul Belmondo) recalls the motives and circumstances that caused his career as a thief. Directed by Louis Malle, the movie's slow pace is offset by some intelligent criticism of middle-class hypocrisy and some appropriate period costuming and sets. A-III

(br)
Thief Who Came to Dinner, The (1973) Pretentious heist movie about a computer engineer (Ryan O'Neal) who starts a new career robbing the safes of Houston's finest families and leaving behind a chessman as his trademark. On his trail is a dogged insurance investigator (Warren Oates) who knows but can't prove it. Listlessly directed by Bud Yorkin, the movie never catches fire and begins to irritate with its repetitious comments about society's hypocrisy. A-III (PG)

Thieves (1977) Often affecting and funny story of an upwardly mobile Mahattan couple (Charles Grodin and Marlo Thomas) whose impending divorce gets sidetracked by the heroine's wild-eyed cabby father (Irwin Corey) and other assorted characters, including the police. Directed by John Berry, the comedy is saved from being too-cute and self-conscious by some exceptionally good acting. Infidelity and abortion figure in the plot (though not favorably), and there is frequent use of blasphemous expletives. A-III (PG)

Thieves Like Us (1974) Set in the Deep South of the 1930s, the story concerns a trio of escaped convicts (Keith Carradine, Bert Remsen and John Schuck) who take to smalltime bank robbing. Director Robert Altman's backroads ballad with conventional bloody ending is long on sleepy Southern atmosphere and earthy humor but short on engaging characterizations (save Shelley Duvall's tender-waif performance) and narrative. A-III (R)

Thing, The (1982) Director John Carpenter's brutal, simple-minded remake of the classic 1951 horror movie in which a research group in Antarctica struggles with a protean monster from outer space features Kurt Russell, A. Wilford Brimley, Richard Dysart and Richard Masur. Excessive violence and appalling lack of respect for mangled human remains. O (R)

Thing with Two Heads, The (1972) Racial bigot (Ray Milland) awakens to find his pale head attached to the hulking black frame of a condemned convict (Rosie Grier) who, buying time to prove his innocence, has volunteered his body for the dying Milland. Director Lee Frost forsakes all hope of evoking horror and simply joins the cast in having some dumb fun. A-II (PG)

Things Are Tough All Over (1982) Inept comedy with Cheech Marin and Thomas Chong driving a money-laden car from Chicago to Las Vegas for two rich Arabs, whose roles they also take. Directed by Tom Avildsen, it has the usual problem of beating jokes into the ground, but happily, the emphasis on narcotics has been dropped this time, though there is still the customary foul language, coarse humor and a brief bit of nudity. O (R)

Things of Life (1970) Slow-moving French portrait of a middle-aged engineer (Michel Piccoli) torn between conflicting feelings toward his estranged wife, his mistress, and his own shaky dreams. Director Claude Sautet juggles together a convoluted tangle of flashes forward and backward, but the slickly confected pastry reveals a definite soap opera base. A-III (GP)

Think Dirty (1978) Bumbling, good-natured, happily married adman (Marty Feldman) is ordered to launch a lewd ad campaign selling porridge. Feldman, directing his own screenplay, is more interested in laughs than in sexual titillation, but the humor is often heavy-handed and

there is some nudity thrown in for bad measure. O (R)

36 Hours (1965) Neat suspense thriller about a fantastic plot by German intelligence to get information about the Allied invasion. Directed by George Seaton with Rod Taylor, Eva Marie Saint and James Garner, the gimmicks are entertaining and most viewers will excuse its melodramatic conclusion. A-II (br)

Thirty-Nine Steps, The (1980) Lackluster British version of John Buchan's classic espionage yarn, made famous by the Hitchcock movie, about the pursuit both by police and nasty spies of an innocent man (Robert Powell) who has seemingly stumbled onto the plans to start World War I. Directed by Don Sharp, the 1914 setting is fine, the acting is excellent but the brisk action is by now routine. Stylized violence. A-II (PG)

This Beast Must Die (see: "This Man Must Die")

This Happy Feeling (1958) Secretary Debbie Reynolds falls for new boss Curt Jurgens, an older actor, while John Saxon also pursues her. Romantic triangle from director Blake Edwards is typical 1950's fluff in which feelings of love caused all the complications and sex was relegated to being treated with coy allusions. A-II (br)

This Is Elvis (1981) Complete but somewhat superficial look at superstar Elvis Presley using a documentary format with candid shots, home footage, scenes from television appearances and dramatic action, all pointing to the image of a man being devoured by his fans. Best are the 38 Presley songs presented. Some sexual innuendo make the movie less suitable for youngsters. A-III (PG)

This Is Spinal Tap (1984) Mock documentary on the last, inglorious American tour of an aging English heavy metal group whose fame is long gone makes the grade as a subtle, sometimes very funny satire both on rock groups and on the documentaries made about them. The four principals (Rob Reiner as the director and Michael McKean, Christopher Guest and Harry Shearer as the not over-bright leaders of the group) also collaborated on the script. Reiner tripled as director. There is a great deal of crude language and many sexual references in the dialogue and lyrics, but these are essential to the satirical nature of the movie. A-II (R)

This Man Must Die (1970) Superior French suspense drama follows a father (Michel Duchaussoy) in tracking down the hit-and-run driver (Jean Yanne) who killed his son but he finds that retribution is not so simple. Director Claude Chabrol convincingly portrays the father's cold determination in seeking revenge but is more interested in the wider circle of guilt that this incurs. Some sexual situations. A-III (GP)

This Property Is Condemned (1966) Trashy soap opera about a young woman (Natalie Wood) in a small Southern railroad town during the Depression who falls in love with the man (Robert Redford) sent by the railroad company to fire most of its workers. Directed by Sydney Pollack, the movie is excessively suggestive in its treatment of sexual situations. O (br)

This Savage Land (1968) Pioneer Ohio widower (Barry Sullivan) brings his family to settle in Kansas after the Civil War but they are harrassed by Southern vigilantes in Vincent McEveety's rather pedestrian Western. Stylized violence. A-II (br)

This Special Friendship (1967) French story of

a homosexual attraction between two boys in a strict Catholic boarding school in the 1920s ends in tragedy. Directed by Jean Delannoy in sensitive and thoughtful fashion, it leaves the viewer to judge the nature of the relationship and the way in which the school authorities dealt with it. Mature fare. A-III (br)

This Time I'll Make You Rich (1975) Totally undistinguished formula kung-fu action adventure produced in Hong Kong by Joseph E. Levine. Restrained violence. A-III (PG)

Thomas Crown Affair, The (1968) Steve McQueen plays a wealthy, clever Bostonian who gets away with two perfect bank robberies before meeting his match in insurance investigator Faye Dunaway. The two engage in a totally amoral game of cat and mouse that ends in a love match, with the law left holding the bag. In director Norman Jewison's smoothly calculated, slickly executed work, it seems that crime pays quite well. O (R)

Thomasine and Bushrod (1974) Vonetta McGee and Max Julien play a black Bonnie and Clyde duo fighting racial oppression and injustice in the West of 1911. Though it has all the now-standard cliches of period cars, a redneck sheriff (George Murdock), bank robberies, news accounts and a bloody finale, director Gordon Parks Jr. fails to make the characters credible or the situations plausible. A-III (PG)

Thoroughly Modern Millie (1967) In a musical spoof of the Roaring Twenties, Julie Andrews and Mary Tyler Moore seek careers and romance in New York City with the help of handsome John Gavin and debonair James Fox. Director George Roy Hill's irreverent lark gets some good support from Bea Lillie and Carol Channing, some songs that characterize the period and a fast-moving script that has something for everybody. A-I (G)

Those Calloways (1965) Predictable Disney movie in which a backwoods family (Brian Keith, Vera Miles, Brandon De Wilde) tries to keep hunters from shooting the Canadian geese that migrate through their area. Directed by Norman Tokar, the outdoors sequences are fine, especially those of the wild geese. A-I (br)

Those Daring Young Men in Their Jaunty Jalopies (1969) The Monte Carlo Rally in the early part of the century served as an endurance test for cars, and in many respects this movie about the rally proves to be much the same kind of test for viewers. Director Ken Annakin has a large cast of comedians (best are Peter Cook and Dudley Moore) but the tired formula racing action is unfunny, though it does some tasteless off-color jokes. Vintage car fanciers might enjoy it. A-II (G)

Those Fantastic Flying Fools (1967) Phineas T. Barnum (Burl Ives), straight from bankruptcy in the U.S., arrives in Victorian England ready to construct the first rocket ship to the moon. Director Don Sharp can't do much with a script riddled with cliches but the obvious and predictable slapstick difficulties of building the rocket may prove diverting fun for the very young. A-I (br)

Those Lips, Those Eyes (1980) Sentimental look at summer theater in a 1951 Cleveland suburb where a college student (Thomas Hulce) takes a job as a prop man and gets so carried away with show business and one of the dancers (Glynnis O'Conner) that he wants to go to New York, much to the anguish of his father (Jerry Stiller). Directed by Michael Pressman, the nostalgia is unfortunately

marred by some explicit nudity in a bedroom scene, compounded by the movie's rather benign attitude toward casual sex. O (R)

Those Magnificent Men in Their Flying Machines (1965) Early vintage aircraft are the real stars and source of fun in this colorful comedy spectacular about a 1910 air race from England to France. Good musical score, tongue-in-cheek script and international cast including Alberto Sordi, Gert Frobe, Jean-Pierre Cassell, Terry Thomas and Red Skelton, are some of the reasons for the success of this entertainment package from director Ken Annakin. A-I (G)

Thousand Clowns, A (1966) Screen version of Herb Gardner's Broadway comedy about a cheerful eccentric (Jason Robards) who has withdrawn from society to live as he pleases until a social worker (Barbara Harris) perks his romantic interest and he must decide how to adjust to the demands of responsiblity. Producer-director Fred Coe retains the good-natured wit and feeling for people in its humorous digs at social conformity, though the closer it strives for contemporary relevance, the more it loses its shield of fantasy and romantic innocence. Mature treatment. A-III (br)

Three (1969) Three young people (Robie Porter, Sam Waterston, Charlotte Rampling) spend a summer touring Europe and come to know one another and themselves better. There's not much plot or action, but there's plenty of gorgeous scenery and some shallow characterizations intended to show the subtle development of human relationships and self-awareness. A-III (PG)

Three Amigos (1986) Steve Martin stars in and produces but doesn't dominate this pictorially grand but sometimes brutal Western parody about three silent screen actors playing silly caballeros in a Mexican village that mistakes them for hired gunmen. Chevy Chase and Martin Short supply the slapstick and wit for director John Landis whose interest seems rooted in the physical comedy and dangerous stunts. Stylized violence and some rough language. A-II (PG)

Three Brothers (1982) French-Italian drama in which three brothers whose lives have taken divergent paths return to their native village in Southern Italy when their mother dies. Director Francesco Rosi's warmly human study of family bonds has fine acting, especially Charles Vanel's awesome presence as their peasant father, and many touching moments, mostly in flashbacks. Despite its many virtues, the story fails to come together as a whole and the result is a disappointment. A-II (PG)

Three Bullets for a Long Gun (1972) Formula Italian Western plods the traditional trail with an unscrubbed hero (Beau Brummell) and his bungling sidekick (Keith G. Wat) who together outwit a horde of rapacious renegade soldiers. Director Peter Henkel has no fresh ideas to dress up the violence in this dreary, low-budget programmer. A-III (PG)

Three Caballeros, The (1945) Walt Disney's colorful celebration of our neighbors to the South follows Donald Duck's tuneful trip to Latin America. Among the animated characters that he meets are Jose Carioca and Panchito who teach him about their customs and culture. Informative as well as good fun. A-I (G)

Three Days of the Condor (1975) CIA agent (Robert Redford), on the run from assassins who may be fellow agents, happens on a woman (Faye

Dunaway) who lends him at first reluctant, then enthusiastic assistance. Directed by Sydney Pollack, it's a slickly done but shallow movie whose heroics are implausible and whose idealism is more than a little inconsistent. Some violence, occasional rough language and a love affair between the two principals. A-III (R)

Three for the Road (1987) Director B.W.L. Norton's teen comedy-romance disguised as rebellious youth road movie features Charlie Sheen as an aspiring politician who delivers a senator's troubled daughter (Kerri Green) to a prison-like school. Falling in love, he helps her to escape into the custody of her estranged mom (Sally Kellerman) who has a change of heart. Shows how idealistic dedication can lead to misplaced trust when duty and conscience conflict. Some rough language and midly permissive attitude toward teen romance. A-II (PG)

Three in the Attic (1969) Grade-B youth sex fantasy in which a three-timing college student (Christopher Jones) is abducted by the wronged trio (Yvette Mimieux, Judy Page and Maggie Thrett) and punished with having to indulge them incessantly in the sorority-house attic. Producer-director Richard Wilson rings the changes on a thoroughly tasteless situation. O (R)

Three in the Cellar (see: "Up in the Cellar")

Three into Two Won't Go (1969) British drama about a couple (Rod Steiger and Claire Bloom) whose marriage is in serious trouble because of the husband's habit of picking up women on his business trips. Directed by Peter Hall, the movie's dramatic potential in probing the problems of married life is, unfortunatelty, undermined by focus on the prurient antics of the husband's latest misadventure (Judy Geeson). O (R)

Three Lives (1971) Author Kate Millet's documentary consists of interviews with three women who, in a series of separate monologues, express the message of Women's Liberation and, among other things, the male influences in their lives. Its plain and simple technique adds rather than detracts from credibility of the three who seem to epitomize the personal commitment that Women's Lib requires of those who espouse it. Some strong language. A-III (nr)

Three Men and a Baby (1987) The carefree life of three bachelors (Tom Selleck, Steve Guttenburg and Ted Danson) changes when they become responsible for an infant girl fathered by one of them. Director Leonard Nimoy gets a few genuine laughs out of the situation but the entertainment level is pretty flat. Benign view of casual sex. A-III (PG)

Three Men and a Cradle (1986) French comedy in which three single, macho males confront their shallow emptiness when an unexpected visitor, a baby, changes their lifestyle and elicits feelings of tenderness and devotion. Writer-director Coline Serreau's film is uplifting, even inspirational, for male audiences in its demonstration that tenderness is an important aspect of manliness. A-II (PG-13)

Three Musketeers, The (1974) Satiric British version of the Dumas classic zestfully follows the shambling trail of the raw and foolish D'Artagnan (Michael York)in his quest to become one of the Musketeers (Oliver Reed, Richard Chamberlain and Frank Finlay). Directed by Richard Lester, it is an energetic swashbuckler in the grand style, offering an entertaining mix of romantic adventure and slapstick comedy, even if the frenetic humor sometimes wears a bit thin. Some restrained sexual innuendo. A-II (PG)

Three on a Couch (1966) Jerry Lewis directs himself in the story of an inventive fellow using his wits and several disguises (including that of a female) in order to win the heart of his psychiatrist fiancee (Janet Leigh) who keeps postponing the wedding date because she claims her patients need her more. Typical Lewis vehicle though with more than usual sexual innuendo. A-III (br)

Three Sisters, The (1969) Russian adaptation of the Chekhov play about a 19th-century family whose financial reverses keep them in a remote garrison town, each of them overwhelmed by the sense of frustrated desires and the ultimate hopelessness of their fate. Writer-director Sergei Samsonov is faithful to the original by centering the movie on characterization and mood rather than on dramatic plot. A-II (nr)

Three Stooges Follies, The (1974) Entertaining collection of World War II-vintage movie short subjects, headlining the Stooges' neanderthal variety of slapstick humor, an acquired taste perhaps best left uncultivated. On the other hand, this package of instant nostalgia includes a Buster Keaton short, a wartime serial with Batman and Robin fighting a Japanese spy ring and a rousing finale with Kate Smith singing a flag-waving medley of patriotic songs. All in glorious black-and-white. A-I (G)

Three the Hard Way (1974) Black exploitation movie about three superheroes (Jim Brown, Fred Williamson and Jim Kelly) who join in tracking down a villain plotting to put a serum in America's drinking water that will kill only blacks. Ineptly directed by Gordon Parks Jr., the movie's plot premise borders on the socially irresponsible. Some brutal as well as sadistic violence. O (R)

Three Tough Guys (1974) Hard-hitting priest (Lino Ventura) and a down-at-the-heels detective (Isaac Hayes) join forces in solving a bank robbery that has cost the one a parishioner and the other his job. The plot's trail of corpses is fairly routine but one can enjoy the fine performances of the two principals. Italian production directed by Duccio Tessari makes intelligent use of Chicago's architecture and lakefront, often making the background more interesting to watch than any of the fantasy violence that clutters the view. A-III (PG)

Three Warriors (1977) Native American (Lois Red Elk) returns to the reservation with her young son who learns about his people's customs and heritage from his grandfather, assisted by a lame horse and a good-natured forest ranger (Randy Quaid) who's chasing rustlers. In the context of credible acting, the beautiful cinematography of Bruce Surtees and the sensitive direction of Keith Merrill, it is a good family movie that parents can enjoy as much as their children. A-I (G)

3 Women (1977) Director Robert Altman explores the friendship between two single women (Shelley Duvall and Sissy Spacek), unskilled workers in a geriatric facility, and an unhappily married artist (Janice Rule) whose work on a grotesque mural keeps her on the periphery until the movie's bleak, simplistic resolution which brings the three together in a strong, sexless relationship. Though thoughtful in its character study of the women, promiscuity figures in the plot and camera's obsession with the exaggerated sexual characteristics of the mural's semi-human figures make it questionable fare. A-IV (PG)

Threesome (1970) Stale Danish exploitation movie about an innocent young woman's (Judy Brown) journey down some of the darker corridors of sexual corruption. Fashion designer setting, with copious and explicit sex scenes. O (nr)

Threshold (1983) Canadian drama about an American heart specialist (Donald Sutherland) and an eccentric but brilliant research biologist (Jeff Goldblum) who join forces to develop an artificial heart. Director Richard Pearce successfully avoids all the melodramatic cliches inherent in the situation and the result is a good, if not especially inspired movie. A-II (PG)

Thumb Tripping (1972) Two idealistic college students (Meg Foster and Michael Burns) waste their summer (and the viewer's time) hitchhiking East from Big Sur and meet bigots, thugs and perverts along the way. Directed by Quentin Martin, the treatment of the episodes is explicit in both visuals and language, but far more offensive is the movie's smug attitude toward its finally disillusioned youngsters. O (R)

Thunder Alley (1967) Suspended race car driver (Fabian) takes a job as stunt driver while trying to prove his innocence. Directed by Richard Rush, the routine action film is marred by scenes of casual sex. O (br)

Thunder and Lightning (1977) Mediocre chase thriller in which a hippie moonshiner and his girl (David Caradine and Kate Jackson) race across the Florida Everglades with tough Northeastern bootleggers in hot pursuit. Daring stunts, failed humor and lame dialogue dominate in a movie directed by Corey Allen. Gratuitious use of slap-stick violence and nudity. O (PG)

Thunderbirds Are Go (1967) British space fantasy uses animated puppets to tell the story of the Thunderbirds International Rescue unit who are on the job when sabotage wrecks a flight to Mars. Lots of action and noise as well as imaginative puppet work and special effects. Should engage the 7 to 13 crowd, and parents won't get too bored in the process. A-I (br)

Thunderbolt and Lightfoot (1974) Clint Eastwood and Jeff Bridges play a pair of bungling bank robbers teamed up with former gang members George Kennedy and Geoffrey Lewis. The character study of good and bad criminals is couched in amoral terms, with viewers expected to sympathize with the first two. Instead of settling for a solid, albeit fantasy-prone, action adventure, director Michael Cimino goes for cheap thrills with needless nudity and profanity, bringing it to a close with some downright ugly, savage deaths. O (R)

THX 1138 (1971) In a futuristic underground world, a minor technician named THX 1138 (Robert Duvall) rebels against its sterile, dehumanizing conditions and tries to escape through a maze of electronic devices and guard robots to the unknown outside world. Director George Lucas creates a terrifying technological future out of the materials of today but it is difficult to empathize with the story's dehumanized characters who have been stripped of all sensitivity and emotion. Though the movie is visually extraordinary and its story has substance, a rather explicit love scene and an extended sequence with a nude dancer limit its audience. A-IV (GP)

Tick...Tick...Tick... (1970) Using their newly acquired voting privileges, the blacks of a small Southern county elect one of their own (Jim Brown) as sheriff and, after some stereotyped black and white hostilities, a crisis unites both races behind their sheriff and the ending indicates a rosy future of racial harmony. Shallow treatment by director Ralph Nelson of a serious subject. A-III (G)

Ticket to Heaven (1981) Well-made Canadian movie about the efforts to rescue a young man (Nick Mancuso) who left his Toronto home and turned up in San Francisco, gaunt-cheeked and hollow-eyed, selling flowers on a street corner as a member of a religious cult. Directed by Ralph L. Thomas, the dramatization has unusual credibility and will be of special interest to teenagers and concerned parents. A-II (PG)

Tidal Wave (1975) Clumsy Americanized version of a Japanese disaster movie directed by Shiro Mariano is not only episodic and lacking any sense of pace but it is badly dubbed and cluttered with unconvincing inserts of Lorne Greene as a U.N. delegate. Though one gets bored of the same old shot of lava flowing into the sea, several scenes are too graphic for very young viewers. A-III (PG)

Tiger Makes Out, The (1967) Postman Eli Wallach decides one day to revolt against bureaucratic routine, kidnaps suburban housewife Anne Jackson and she undertakes to educate her captor. Directed by Arthur Hiller, the subsequent action tends to be overdone, but what is enjoyable are the excellent performances of the two principals. A-III (br)

Tightrope (1984) Clint Eastwood plays a New Orleans police detective searching for a sadistic killer whose aberrant sexual proclivities he fears he might share. Written and directed by Richard Tuggle, the movie embodies an interesting theme, but the execution of it falls short, even though Eastwood's performance is one of his best. The sex and violence loom much too large. O (R)

Tiko and the Shark (1966) Harmless, sometimes charming story of the romance between a Polynesian boy and girl, the lad's friendship with a shark and their role in the activities of an island fishing village. Directed by Falco Quilici, the movie's simple story and gorgeous photography should appeal to youngsters. A-I (br)

Till Marriage Do Us Part (1979) Italian sex comedy directed by Luigi Comencini deals with the many tribulations endured by a noble Sicilian lady (Laura Antonelli) who discovers on her wedding night that her husband is in fact her brother. Excessive nudity and graphic sexuality. O (R)

Time After Time (1979) H.G. Wells (Malcolm McDowell) uses a time machine to pursue Jack the Ripper (David Warner) to modern-day San Francisco where the author and a liberated woman executive (Mary Steenburgen) get involved in a duel of wits with the mad killer. Director Nicholas Meyer's romantic thriller is moderately entertaining, especially the satiric asides about modern technology, but it has some rather violent touches involving the Ripper's crimes, some profanity and implied premarital sex. A-III (PG)

Time Bandits (1981) Witty British comedy about a gang of greedy but good-hearted dwarfs who steal a map of creation from the Supreme Being (Ralph Richardson) and use it to bring an adventurous lad into a variety of historical epochs, meeting Napoleon (Ian Holm), Greek warrior Agamemnon (Sean Connery) and Robin Hood (John Cleese). Directed by Terry Gilliam, it is sometimes amusing and always intelligent, but its appeal for youngsters is spoiled by typical Monty Python vlulgarities and black humor, some of it violent. A-III (PG)

Time for Burning, A (1967) Extraordinary documentary of what happened when a pastor tried to get his all-white congregation to meet with nearby blacks. Produced by the Lutheran Film Associates and directed by William Jersey, it is a moving document of troubled times and the need for human understanding. A-I (br)

Time for Killing, A (see: "The Long Ride Home")

Time In the Sun, A (1969) Sensitive Swedish drama about a young journalist (Lars Passgard) who pursues and wins the woman (Grynet Molvig) of his dreams, despite the fact that she is fatally afflicted with Hodgkin's Disease. Director Ake Falck invests a good deal of human warmth in an unusual story of married life, human suffering and the healing power of love. Restrained lovemaking scene. A-III (R)

Time Lost and Time Remembered (1966) Unhappily married woman (Sarah Miles) returns to her home town in the West of Ireland to find the boy she loved now engaged to another. Director Desmond Davis evokes beautifully the Irish atmosphere and locale but the story is somewhat sentimentalized. Mature themes. A-III (br)

Time of Roses (1970) Tangled tale from Finland about a supposedly perfect society in 2012 whose government manipulates the news, unaware of a plot to expose its deceptive methods through a television documentary about a woman who died in 1976. Directed by Rista Jarva, the movie's intriguing and challenging themes are treated with a cerebral aloofness that leaves the viewer uninvolved and unmoved. A-III (nr)

Time to Sing, A (1968) Country musical comedy about a farm boy (Hank Williams Jr.) who becomes a singing star despite many obstacles in a cliched, sentimental but tuneful picture directed by Arthur Dreifuss. For those who enjoy the country music sound. A-I (br)

Timerider (1983) Motorcycle racer (Fred Ward) finds himself whisked back in time to the late 19th century where he gets mixed up with some lowlifes of various sorts. Directed by William Dear, it is a simple-minded attempt to combine science fiction and the Western with little result. Considerable, though restrained, sex and violence. A-III (PG)

Tin Drum, The (1980) German adaptation of Gunter Grass' satiric novel about a boy (David Bennent) who, in protest against the absurd world of adults, decides to stop growing on his third birthday and shows his anguish at events by beating on a tin drum. Directed by Volker Schlondorff, the work is a serious attempt to show the moral and political corruption of the 1930s that led to Germany's defeat in the cataclysm of World War II. Though it has moments of brilliance, it founders on trying to accomodate its vivid, often gross slice-of-life realism to some abrupt and arbitrary excursions into absurdity. Crudely graphic treatment of sex, especially in scenes with the 13-year-old Bennent. O (R)

Tin Men (1987) Danny DeVito and Richard Dreyfuss are 1960s aluminum siding salesman obsessed with getting even with each other over a car accident. Barbara Hershey plays DeVito's estranged wife who becomes fair game for the vindictive seduction by Dreyfuss in director Barry Levinson's wry and ribald comedy. Profanity and adultery are the sources of humor in this film. O

(R)

TNT Jackson (1975) Standard black exploitation movie directed by Cirio Santiago with Jeanne Bell as a martial arts addict. Excessive violence and nudity. O (R)

To Be Free (1973) Psychiatrist tries hypnotism as short-cut therapy for a sexually confused young woman, with obviously dire consequences for them both. Director Ned Bosnick's banal plot is treated with gimmicky camera techniques and a soft-core approach to sexual anomalies. O (R)

To Be or Not to Be (1983) Director Mel Brooks fails in his attempt to remake the 1942 Ernst Lubitsch black comedy about a Warsaw drama troupe who outwit the Nazis and save the Polish underground, with himself and Anne Bancroft in the roles created by Jack Benny and Carole Lombard. Unfortunately, Brooks has neither the sophisticated wit of Lubitsch nor Benny's subtlety and sense of timing. Instead his humor runs from crude slapstick to bad taste, trivializing the Nazis and there is nothing intrinsically amusing about the Gestapo, however klutzy, however roly-poly. A-II (PG)

To Commit a Murder (1969) French spy thriller in which an agent (Louis Jordan) either has to prevent a noted scientist from defecting to Red China or kill him and his accomplice (Edmond O'Brien). Directed by Edouard Molinaro, the formula plot is neatly packaged and moderately entertaining. Some violence. A-III (PG)

To Die in Madrid (1966) Excellent French documentary by Niclole Stephane and Frederic Rossif describes the bitter struggle that was the Spanish Civil War. Fine editing and a poetic commentary by Madeleine Chapsal help re-create the anguished emotions of 1936–39 and derive some significance from the tragic war. A-II (br)

To Die of Love (1972) Fact-based French drama about a teacher (Annie Girardot) who falls in love with a 17-year-old student (Bruno Pradal) and wants to marry him but, harassed by officals, she commits suicide. Directed by Andre Cayatte, the movie is more concerned with the impersonal bureaucratic system responsible for the tragedy than it is with the two main characters. Those viewing it as nothing more than a love story will find it romanticizing a relationship that the movie does not even try to make dramatically credible. A-IV (GP)

To Find a Man (1972) Self-centered Catholic girl (Pamela Martin) finds herself pregnant and returns home for the Christmas holidays to find an abortionist with some help from the boy next door (Darren O'Connor). The trouble with director Buzz Kulik's mediocre effort is its shallow treatment of adolescent values and acceptance of abortion as natural in a society where everything, including morality, is disposable. O (R/GP)

To Live and Die in L.A. (1985) Director William Friedkin attempts to make a Southern California version of the "French Connection" in this story of two Treasury agents (William Petersen and John Pankow) pursuing a vicious counterfeiter (Willem Dafoe). The result, however, has no more depth than an extended music video. Brutal and so amoral that it's hard to tell the good guys from the bad. O (R)

To Sir, with Love (1967) Sentimental British melodrama about an American (Sidney Poitier) in London who takes a teaching job and tries to turn his students from a Cockney slum into ladies and gentlemen. Poitier dominates the movie as well as the classroom. Directed by James Clavell, it offers some pat solutions for real problems, student transformations seem overswift, but the fine supporting cast show aspects of life, love and teenagers that American audiences will find familiar, despite the accent. A-II (br)

To Trap a Spy (1966) Movie version of the TV spy series, "The Man from U.N.C.L.E.," features Robert Vaughn going through his paces as a superagent with little help from the sets, the gimmicks or director Don Medford. Violence and sexual innuendo. A-III (br)

Tobruk (1967) World War II story about a British commando column (Rock Hudson, George Peppard, Nigel Green) disguised as a German convoy bringing Allied prisoners through the desert into the German base of Tobruk to destroy its oil stockpiles. Directed by Arthur Hiller, the straightforward action narrative alludes to the absurdity of war and has an interesting sub-plot dealing with anti-Semitism. It brings a measure of intelligence to the usual mindless war formula. Stylized violence. A-II (br)

Today We Kill ...Tomorrow We Die! (1971) Poor Italian Western about a rancher (Montgomery Ford) who recruits four gunslingers to wipe out the gang responsible for the rape-murder of his wife. Director Tonino Cervi's production values are laughable but the violence is not. A-III (GP)

Todd Killings, The (1971) Lurid fact-based melodrama about a perverse killer (Robert F. Lyons) who sexually assaulted and mutilated a number of teenage girls in Tucson, Ariz. Directed by Barry Shear, the movie dwells on the sensational aspects of the case and as a result is quite sordid in its details. O (R)

Together (1971) Pseudo-documentary promotes a summertime romp at the estate of a self-proclaimed pioneer in sexual guidance. Filmmakers Roger Murphy and Sean C. Cunningham encounter uninhibited and unclad couples who explicate and demonstrate their host's theories of tactile therapy. O (R)

Together Brothers (1974) Good action movie, filmed in steamy Galveston, Texas, with a cast largely of unknowns, it involves a black street gang tracking down the killer of a cop who treated them fairly. Director William A. Graham gets some extraordinarily sensitive character portrayals and conveys a feel for the ramshackle black ghettos of Galveston. Though there is a minimum of street language, the sudden, concluding violence is adult fare. A-III (PG)

Tokoloshe (1971) Uneven South African production about a winsome Bantu youngster (Saul Pelle) who escapes the curse of the evil spirit of the title through his mother's intervention and reaches safety in Johannesburg. Directed by Peter Prowse, the sequences in the city unfortunately lack the narrative interest and sense of conviction found in the earlier portions of the movie. A-I (G)

Tokyo Story (1972) Elderly couple on their first visit to the Tokyo homes of their children meet only disguised rejection except, ironically, for the kindness of their dead son's wife. When the mother dies shortly upon returning to their country village, it is only the widowed daughter-in-law who shows any real feeling of loss. Director Yasujiro Ozu's eloquent treatment of old age makes it a uniquely moving hymn to life. A-I (nr)

Tom Horn (1980) Frontier hero at the end of his career (Steve McQueen) is hired by a group of ranchers to stop some rustlers, a job he performs with such murderous zeal that they decide to get rid of him by framing him for murder. Though director William Wiard fails to provide much dramatic steam, McQueen's solid performance raises the material a notch above the standard Western. Some graphic violence. A-III (R)

Tom Sawyer (1973) Reader's Digest musical adaptation of the Mark Twain classic with Johnny Whitaker as Tom, Jeff East as Huck, Jodie Foster as Becky and Celeste Holm as Aunt Polly. Directed by Don Taylor, the movie is a quite diverting though undistinguished bit of nostalgia that, if it misses the wit and cultural perceptions of the orginal, succeeds nonetheless in being continually engaging. Young viewers will be delighted. A-I (G)

Tommy (1975) British adaptation of Peter Townshend's rock opera about a pinball wizard (Roger Daltrey) who becomes a religious guru and ends as a rejected mystic calling out for a new consciousness. Though the performances of Eric Clapton, Elton John and Tina Turner are excellent, director Ken Russell's treatment is ludicrously out of control, obscuring the sense of the opera by an undue emphasis on visual pyrotechnics that is not dramatic but destructive. Satiric jabs at religion are excessive if taken literally. A-IV (PG)

Tomorrow (1972) Winter watchman (Robert Duvall) for a backwoods Mississippi sawmill gives shelter to a pregnant woman (Olga Bellin) abandoned by her husband. As the winter passes, he falls in love with her, but she dies shortly after her child is born. Adapted from a William Faulkner story by Horton Foote and directed by Joseph Anthony, the material is sparse, even tedious, but the characters—the taciturn man of the land and the wornout woman—convey a genuine sense of the American rural ethic. A-II (PG)

Tonka the Comanche (1958) Director Lewis R. Foster's mildly entertaining Disney movie is set in the Old West where a young Indian (Sal Mineo) captures a wild stallion, loses him and then gets him back again. A-I (br)

Tony Rome (1967) Frank Sinatra stars as a Miami private eye who displays a nice sense of values and humor as his work takes him deeper and deeper into the corrupt layers of the resort town. Directed by Gordon Douglas, its sporadic gunplay and fist-fights are standard but some of the subject matter is sordid and some of the language is rough. A-III (br)

Too Late the Hero (1970) Routine World War II movie set on a small Pacific island in which an Allied patrol (Cliff Robertson and Michael Caine) makes its way to the far end of the island, blows up the Japanese radio transmitter and returns to home base. Director Robert Aldrich offers the usual amount of blood and violence in glossy color but all except hardened action buffs will find it disappointing. A-III (GP)

Tootsie (1982) Very funny movie in which an actor (Dustin Hoffman), desperate for a job, dresses up as a woman to get a part in a TV soap opera, but his success with the role makes his life very complicated, especially when he fall in love with his beautiful co-star (Jessica Lange). Directed by Sydney Pollack, the romantic comedy also shows much about being a woman in a man's world. Because of the sexual nature of much of the humor, it is adult fare. A-III (PG)

Top Gun (1986)   This high-energy celebration of the exploits of Navy aviation hot shots features Tom Cruise as a high-velocity American jet pilot whose bravado disguised as bravura wins the trust and admiration of his comrades, the affection of his female training consultant and audience commendation for patriotic hip-shooting heroism. The movie's correlation of sexual prowess with combat skills, profanity and brief nudity make it adult fare. A-III (PG)

Top of the Heap (1972)   Black policeman in Washington, D.C., (Christopher St. John who also wrote, produced and directed) works with racist, bribe-taking fellow officers and off the job his wife browbeats him, his daughter experiments with sex and drugs and even his boozy mistress mocks him with abandon. He proves as nasty as anyone else in a movie that goes out of its way to alienate viewers with needless, salacious nudity and an endless barrage of gutter epithets. O (R)

Top Secret (1984)   Creators of "Airplane" (Jim Abrahams, David Zucker and Jerry Zucker) have set out to parody movies of international intrigue. But this time they haven't gotten it right and most of the jokes misfire. Some sexually oriented humor. A-III (PG)

Topaz (1969)   Alfred Hitchcock's adaptation of the pulpy Leon Uris novel about high-powered espionage and counterspying in a variety of exotic locales. The dialogue is mostly banal and the action largely unconvincing, but there are occasional glimmers of the Hitchcock touch in subtle plot twists here and blind alleys there. Diverting if ultimately disappointing. Some physical and psychological violence and a lot of confusing intrigue. A-III (PG)

Topo Gigio (1966)   Delightful little movie about a small talking mouse who outwits a wicked magician to save his friends. Young children will love it and the puppet characterization is droll enough to please their parents. A-I (br)

Tora! Tora! Tora! (1970)   Huge, sprawling and occasionally unfocused wartime epic based on the events leading up to the surprise Japanese attack on Pearl Harbor. Director Richard Fleischer alternates American and Japanese points of view as the one side goes about its daily routines unsuspecting the deadly assault that the other side is preparing. The Japanese segments are the more interesting in showing less known aspects of a strategy that some realized would start an unwinnable war. A-I (G)

Torchlight (1985)   The destruction of a successful businessman and loving husband (Steve Railsback) by cocaine is a serious and important theme but director Tom Wright's treatment is so uninspired and at times ludicrous that the movie fails even as a cautionary tale. Explicit depiction of drug taking. A-III (R)

Torn Curtain (1966)   Slack Alfred Hitchcock suspense thriller about an American physicist (Paul Newman) who pretends to defect to East Germany in order to get some secret information. The predictable plot is further marred by a detailed treatment of a realistically brutal killing. O (br)

Torso (1975)   Low-budget European co-production is a heavy-breathing, sex-and-brutality melodrama directed by Sergio Martino and dubbed into a language at times reminiscent of idiomatic English. O (R)

Torture Dungeon (1970)   Bungled medieval tale about a duke's problems in ensuring an heir for his kingdom, preoccupied as he is in dispatching his peers of both sexes by prolonged torture or sudden death. Played apparently for laughs, the movie is far from funny in its own preoccupation with nudity and acts of swift, bloody violence. O (R)

Touch, The (1971)   Failed English-language production written and directed by Ingmar Bergman, the story is of a love triangle involving a busy, sensitive husband (Max von Sydow), his uncertain wife (Bibi Andersson) and her importunate, apparently unbalanced and unfeeling lover (Elliott Gould). Though it has flashes of Bergman's mastery in handling themes of alienation and searching, Gould is a classic case of miscasting and his performance makes the whole affair seem no more than campy soap opera. Ambiguous attitude towards adultery. A-IV (R)

Touch and Go (1975)   French World War II comedy about a French deserter (Michel Picoli), an inept British officer (Michael York) and the wife of the Swiss consul (Marlene Jobart) who find themselves fleeing for their lives from Nazis who are certain they are spies. Director Philippe de Broca's comedy is full of sight gags, absurd situations and broad humor that not everyone appreciates. His insistence upon the wartime vulnerability of his characters, however, makes the laughter at their ridiculous adventures somewhat uneasy. A-III (nr)

Touch and Go (1987)   Improbable romance of a star pro hockey player (Michael Keaton) and a down-and-out Hispanic single parent (Maria Conchita Alonzo) who meet when the hockey star drags her son, who helped mug him, home. Simplistic, forced characterizations with no understanding of parenthood, some foul language and a semi-nude bedroom scene type this as adult fare. A-III (R)

Touch Me (1971)   Four couples debase themselves in a mechanical marathon of hardcore theatrics with the encouragement of a "trained psychologist" who alleges that such explicit enactment of fantasies helps release people's human potentiam. Pseudo-documentary exploitation directed by Sam Weston. O (nr)

Touch of Class, A (1973)   London-based American executive (George Segal) and a British career woman (Glenda Jackson) meet, a love affair ensues and then the man's vacationing wife, kids, and in-laws return unexpectedly bringing all the inevitable and predicatable complications that follow. Director Melvin Frank's central problem is that his stars don't seem very comfortable as a romantic couple, a feeling many will share about a comedy whose theme is adultery. Frank tries to keep it light and witty but, after a tasteless bedroom scene, the froth goes flat and only a stale aftertaste remains. Some scatological epithets. A-III (PG)

Touchables, The (1968)   Dull British sex fantasy ineptly directed by Robert Freeman in which four teenage girls kidnap a rock star and force him to make love to them. O (R/PG)

Touched by Love (1980)   Fact-based story about a young nurse (Deborah Raffin) who takes it upon herself to bring a teenage victim of cerebral palsy (Diane Lane) out of her deep depression, partly through an extraordinary exchange of letters with Elvis Presley. Directed by Gus Trikonis, the acting is very credible and the story is told with just the right balance of emotion and sentimentality. Rare, immensely enjoyable family movie. A-I (PG)

Tough (1974)   Pre-teen (Dion Gosset) has problems with his parents, teachers and, finally, the police. Nothing unusual about this picture of the generation gap except that the family are middle-class blacks living in the suburbs and suffering the same problems as many of their white neighbors. Written, produced, and directed by Horace Jackson, regrettably the characterizations and plot situations are too thinly drawn for either credibility or insight, and the principals rarely rise above stereotypes. A-I (G)

Tough Guys (1986) Silly and somewhat crude comedy exploiting the seasoned acting talents of Burt Lancaster and Kirk Douglas who star as thieves released after 30 years in prison into a society neglectful and uncaring about its senior citizens. Bemused by the disordered world that confronts them, the proud oldtimers decide to pull off one more caper just to show that they can. Unseemly sexual encounter and much harsh language. A-III (PG)

Tout Va Bien (1973) Muddled French story of a factory strike, with a great deal of ideological debate from all sides. Director Jean-Luc Godard's return to the narrative form and the use of actors (Jane Fonda and Yves Montand) have little appeal except for those interested in political cinema. A-III (nr)

Tower of Screaming Virgins (1972) The teasing title delivers only a treacherous trio: an icy French queen and her haughty handmaidens who lure lovers to the castle and slay them in the wake of an evening's ecstasy. Swashbuckling Terry Torday foils their scheme while director Francois Legrand indulges the theme of incest in a bloody-awful French-German co-production. O (R)

Towering Inferno (1974) A 135-story office-residential tower goes up in smoke trapping hundreds of Hollywood extras and a score of past and present stars. Director John Gillermin's disaster movie is weak in plot and characterization, but stunningly realistic in its special effects of death and destruction. A-III (PG)

Town Called Hell, A (1971) Mexico in 1895 is the setting for a series of slaughters between revolutionary guerrillas (led by Robert Shaw) and government soldiers (led by Telly Savalas) who torture and execute various peasants and prisoners. Directed by Robert Parrish, the movie is unrelenting in its emphasis on violence and senseless punishment. O (R)

Town That Dreaded Sundown, The (1977) Tedious, solemn and embarrassingly inept fact-based movie, featuring Ben Johnson and Andrew Prine, about the summer-long rampage of a homicidal maniac in 1940's Texarkana, Arkansas. Directed by Charles B. Pierce, the movie's depiction of brutal atrocities is all the more disagreeable when the ending states that the killer was never apprehended. O (R)

Toy, The (1979) French comedy about the spoiled 10-year-old son of a tyrannical tycoon (Michel Bouquet) who, told he can have any toy he wants in a store owned by his father, points to a hapless writer in his father's employ. The writer (Pierre Richard) goes along with the joke, develops a warm relationship with the boy and helps bring about the father's comeuppance. Mild, innocuous entertainment. A-II (PG)

Toy, The (1982) Dreary adaptation of a mediocre French comedy about a poor journalist (Richard Pryor) so desperate for money that he lets a ruthless tycoon (Jackie Gleason) hire him to be the playmate of his spoiled, affection-starved son. Directed by Richard Donner, the talents of everyone in the movie are wasted in an embarrassingly failed comedy. Some comically intended scenes with sexual implications. A-III (PG)

Toy Grabbers, The (1971) Toy company head (Julie Newmar) wants the services of a talented toy maker (Wally Cox) and entrusts the task to her imbecilic son (Victor Buono) who uses a string of seductive beauties to secure a contract. From there writer-producer-director Don Joslyn veers into black comedy, adding crude touches that do little to compensate for all the nudity employed in this odious ode to motherhood. O (R/GP/R)

Toys Are Not for Children (1972) Marcia Forbes sleepwalks through her starring role as a young woman afflicted with an Electra complex, obsessively searching for dear old daddy. Though not quite soft-core pornography, there are enough visuals and coarse language to offend everyone. O (R)

Trackdown (1976) Vicious vigilante potboiler in which a Montana rancher (Robert Mitchum) comes to Los Angeles to wreak havoc among the scum who have brutalized his young runaway sister (Karen Lamm). Directed by Richard T. Heffron, the brutalization is dwelt upon with sickening detail that would be intolerable even in a movie dealing seriously with the social problems that this one cynically exploits. Excessive violence and sexual perversion, nudity and some racist attitudes. O (R)

Tracks (1979) Jumpy Army sergeant (Dennis Hopper), escorting home the body of a Vietnam comrade, finds himself drawn to a college girl (Taryn Power) but his problems seem to stem more from an unrequited love for mama than the horrors of Vietnam. Directed by Henry Jaglom, the soppy, self-indulgent movie is less ambiguous than it is pointless. Excessive nudity. O (R)

Trading Places (1983) Caustic streetwise con man (Eddie Murphy) switches roles with a wealthy snob in a brokerage firm (Dan Aykroyd) in a less than noble experiment concocted by the two billionaire brothers who own the firm. The elaborate game of greed provides some insight into aspects of prejudice, but director John Landis relies too often on nudity, vulgarity and profanity as sources of humor. O (R)

Traffic (1972) Fine French comedy from director Jacques Tati who returns in his comic character of Monsieur Hulot in a story following the series of mishaps that occur as he shepherds a station-wagon camper from Paris to Amsterdam for an automobile show. There is no need for dialogue (grunts and groans suffice) because the situations are as universal as the visual gags that develop from them. The comedy is relaxed, refreshing and even the habitually grouchy will get a few belly-laughs. A-I (G)

Tragedy of a Ridiculous Man (1982) Italian drama about a wealthy factory owner (Ugo Tognazzi) whose son is kidnapped by political terrorists. Directed by Bernardo Bertolucci, the movie's modest premise provided a chance to come to grips with the realities of contemporary terrorism, but instead it tries to make obscurity and ambiguity do duty for profundity. One is never quite sure what's going on, and neither is Bertolucci. Some wholly gratuitous nudity. O (PG)

Trail of the Pink Panther (1982) Collection of outtakes and reprises of earlier movies in the series

285

stitched together with some flat and uninspired new material using the gimmick of a TV reporter trying to find out what Inspector Clouseau was really like. It's a poor excuse for a movie, though if writer-director Blake Edwards only intended to show how much the late Peter Sellers is missed, he's succeeded admirably. Brief nudity and some sexually oriented humor. A-III (PG)

Train Robbers, The (1973) Good Western about a poor widow (Ann-Margret) who gets a tough hombre (John Wayne) and a couple of his pals (Ben Johnson and Rod Taylor) to go to Mexico to retrieve a fortune in stolen gold and bring it back past hordes of outlaws. Along the way there's plenty of entertaining action, slowed only by a few too many reflections on the old days. Director Burt Kennedy's witty dialogue and light touch keep this melodramatic tale moving at a fast and breezy clip. A-II (PG)

Traitor's Gate (1966) Uneven British thriller directed by Freddie Francis about an attempt to steal the crown jewels from the Tower of London has a complicated plot with some violence and a restrained striptease scene. A-III (br)

Traitors, The (1974) Argentinian drama paralleling the corruption of a Peronist union leader who sells out the workers with the growth of a revolutionary group determined to destroy him and the ruling class he has come to represent. The fictional story easily encompasses the realities of the country's social, economic and political history, and viewers may find it a helpful introduction to the complexities of Latin American political developments. A-III (nr)

Tramplers, The (1966) Leaden-paced Italian Western ineptly directed by Albert Band about a family feud which ultimately drives the father (Joseph Cotten) insane. Stylized violence. A-II (br)

Trans-Europ-Express (1968) Convoluted French movie-within-a-movie directed by Alain Robbe-Grillet about a drug smuggler (Jean-Louis Trintignant) and a prostitute (Marie-France Pisier) for whom he entertains sadistic as well as amorous feelings. Excessive in its treatment of sexual themes. O (br)

Transylvania 6-5000 (1985) Two bumbling reporters (Jeff Goldblum and Ed Begley, Jr.) for a tabloid magazine get hot on the trail of the Frankenstein monster and some of his friends. Director Rudy DeLuca works hard but there are few laughs, even for viewers in a very silly mood. Some mild sexually oriented jokes. A-II (PG)

Trash (1970) Apt title for director Andy Warhol's listless story of a heroin addict (Joe Dallesandro) whose habit has rendered him listless and impotent while his transvestite lover (Holly Woodlawn) has a passion for scrounging in garbage heaps. Total nudity, graphic drug use and gutter language. O (nr)

Traveling Executioner, The (1970) Clunker about an itinerant with an electric chair (Stacy Keach) who makes the rounds of Southern prisons in the 1920s until a beautiful murderess (Mariana Hill) seduces him into helping her escape, the plan misfires and he winds up being strapped into his device. Directed by Jack Smight, the unfunny black comedy suffers from Keach's grotesque performance and an excess of sexual scenes and references. O (R)

Travels with My Aunt (1972) Primly proper British accountant (Alec McCowen) is suddenly whisked off to Paris by his wildly eccentric aunt (Maggie Smith) and finds himself an accessory in drug smuggling and other illegal activities that he comes to find exhilarating. Smith is badly miscast and director George Cukor is given to mounting grandiose but leaden set pieces that turn Graham Greene's light comedy into a heavy fantasy that will strike some as vulgar farce. A-IV (PG)

T.R. Baskin (1971) Bright, ambitious woman from a small Ohio town (Candice Bergen) has a hard time adjusting to life in Chicago, especially creepy blind dates and swinging singles places. Among the men who disappoint her is a children's book editor (James Caan). By movie's end the audience will have lost interest in all the contrived nonsense that director Herbert Ross puts his confused heroine through. A-III (GP)

Treasure Island (1934) The classic Hollywood version of the Robert Louis Stevenson adventure saga, with Wallace Berry outstanding as Long John Silver and Jackie Cooper as the stout-hearted Jim Hawkins. Directed by Victor Fleming, it is still enjoyable family fare, though youngsters may be disappointed by its black-and-white photography. (Produced before there were ratings.)

Treasure Island (1950) The Disney version of the Stevenson classic stars Robert Newton as a scenery-chewing Long John Silver with little Bobby Driscoll as a suitably serious Jim Hawkins. Directed by Byron Haskin, the adventure gets fairly intense at times but the kids will love it. A-I (G)

Treasure Island (1972) Disappointing British screen version of the R.L. Stevenson classic, with Orson Welles garbling the role of Long John Silver. Director John Hough takes a rather uninspired literal approach to the high adventure of the novel, the characters are but cardboard caricatures and the cast simply read their lines against the pretty Spanish coast. Nonetheless, the little ones will still enjoy this classic tale of buried treasure. A-I (G)

Treasure of Matecumbe (1976) Routine Walt Disney adventure about two boys (Johnny Doran and Billy Attmore) and some buried treasure in the exotic Florida Keys. Directed by Vincent McEveety, the search goes on a bit too long but younger viewers should enjoy the locale and the Huck Finn hijinks. A-I (G)

Treasure of San Gennaro, The (1968) Italian heist spoof in which two American gangsters (Harry Guardino and Senta Berger) come to Naples to rob its cathederal of a fortune in jewels and enlist the help of a good-hearted, somewhat dim local crook (Nino Manfredi). During the course of the thoroughly wacky, bungled theft, director Dino Risi builds a consistently amusing, often hilarious satiric comedy on Neapolitan manners and mores. A-II (br)

Treasure of the Four Crowns, The (1983) Dreadful Spanish-made 3-D movie about a Mission Impossible attempt, led by Tony Anthony, to recover some crowns having mystical powers from the hands of the villainous head of a cult. Directed by Fernando Baldi with the emphasis upon things whizzing out at the viewer and murkily photographed, it achieves intense boredom and eyestrain. Some violence. A-II (PG)

Tree Grows in Brooklyn, A (1945) Screen version of the Betty Smith novel about a young girl (Peggy Ann Garner) growing up in a working-class Brooklyn neighborhood at the turn of the century. Director Elia Kazan sensitively tells of her troubled family's hand-to-mouth existence, with father

(James Dunn) mostly unemployed and often drunk, mother (Dorothy McGuire) holding the family together and the kids experiencing the various pains and joys of being young during hard times. Sensitive, evocative picture of family life. A-II (br)

Tree of Wooden Clogs, The (1979) Quiet, richly textured Italian dramatization of the lives of four peasant families living in a communal farmhouse as tenant farmers on a Lombardy estate at the end of the last century. Covering a period of some nine months, beginning with the fall harvest and ending with the spring planting, it depicts the everyday life of rural people who maintain their human dignity in spite of an oppressive system that exploits them. Written, photographed and directed by Ermanno Olmi, it is a striking portrait of a people in an era of social injustice. A-II (nr)

Trenchcoat (1983) Poor Disney comedy about a would-be mystery story writer (Margot Kidder) who runs into all sorts of nasty people during a vacation on Malta. The script is matched in ineptness only by the direction of Michael Tuchner which underscores everything that would have been better passed over as quickly as possible. Some moderate violence and a few mild vulgarities. A-II (PG)

Trial of Billy Jack, The (1974) Using the same mixture of violence and simple-minded idealism that marked the original "Billy Jack," co-writer-director-star Tom Laughlin's sequel offers as an alternative to contemporary injustices only a shallow romanticism that has little relevance to the real world. A-IV (PG)

Trial of the Catonsville Nine, The (1972) Screen version of Rev. Daniel Berrigan's play about the 1968 trial of nine Vietnam War protestors who readily admitted burning draft records in Catonsville, Maryland, using the trial as a forum to argue against the war's morality. Handsomely photographed by Haskell Wexler, the movie employs the same cast and director (Gordon Davidson) as the stage version. Producer Gregory Peck deserves credit for preserving on film this particular aspect of the peace movement. A-II (PG)

Tribute (1980) Screen version of the Bernard Slade play about a lecherous, incorrigibly nonserious but lovable press agent (Jack Lemmon) who, knowing he has but a short time to live, tries to make peace with his priggish son (Robby Benson) and remarried ex-wife (Lee Remick). Directed by Bob Clark, it is civilized entertainment but not nearly as moving or funny as it was meant to be. Brief nudity and some rough language. A-III (PG)

Trick Baby (1972) Gritty street movie about two Philadelphia con artists, one of whom is black (Mel Stewart) while the other (Kiel Martin) insists he was born black and only looks white. Together they are truly democratic in hustling everyone, regardless of race. Director Larry Yust makes an entertaining game of watching them keep one step ahead of the cops and the avenging mob, though its genial air of amorality, some nudity and rough language limit its audience considerably. A-IV (R)

Trilogy (1969) Theatrical adaptation of three television plays written by Truman Capote and directed by Frank Perry consists of "Miriam" about a retired nurse (Mildred Natwick); "Among the Paths to Eden" about an aging spinster (Maureen Stapleton); and "A Christmas Memory" about the elderly relative (Geraldine Page) of an orphaned boy (narrated by Capote). Creatively made and beautifully acted, the work reaffirms the delight to be found in ordinary lives and people when they are observed by a humane sensibility. Some intense scenes. A-II (G)

Trinity Is Still My Name (1972) Terence Hill repeats his role as the vagabond outlaw Trinity, as does Bud Spencer as his ornery, hulking brother. Director E.B. Clucher plays everything for laughs and the hijinks are refreshingly in good-humor. The fun is constant, no one gets killed and there's not even a shot fired. A few risque lines will zoom right over the heads of youngsters. A-II (G)

Trip, The (1967) Director Roger Corman's movie about the psychedelic experiences of LSD presents a one-sided, excitement-ladened view of the drug's effects. The result serves not to enlighten, but to expose impressionable viewers to the temptation of dangerous experimentation. Exploitative use of sexual imagery. O (br)

Trip to Bountiful, The (1986) Geraldine Page gives a memorable performance as a feisty old woman who can't stand living with her daughter-in-law and, when her son refuses to take her, sets off by herself to see her home town of Bountiful, Texas. On this journey to a place that is now a ghost town, the viewer comes to respect the indomitable spirit of a strong personality who refuses to give up in spite of waning physical strength. John Masterson directs Horton Foote's story with dignity and compassion, though some of the old woman's difficulties might be upsetting to the very young. A-II (PG)

Triple Cross (1967) Lengthy, fact-based World War II espionage movie is a vehicle for Christopher Plummer as Eddie Chapman, a safe-cracker and opportunist who worked both sides of the Channel as double agent for Germany and England. Director Terence Young's complicated plot tries too hard for effects that seem more often cynical than ironic. Restrained bedroom scenes. A-III (br)

Triple Echo (1973) Fetid British drama about a woman (Glenda Jackson) whose husband is in a World War II POW camp and an Army deserter (Brian Deacon) whom she dresses up as a woman and passes him off as her sister until a lecherous army sergeant (Oliver Reed) discovers the deception. Director Michael Apted's talented cast tries so hard to make this credible but can't overcome an overwhelming sense of disbelief. It all seems a rather pointless exercise in the by-ways of sexual ambivalence and self-identity. O (R)

Tristana (1970) Spanish production about an innocent young woman (Catherine Deneuve) who, after being seduced by her guardian (Fernando Rey), runs away with a painter only to return to torment her former guardian in his old age. Surrealist director Luis Bunuel is in top form in this story of an ironic reversal of roles that rests on such themes as middle-class materialism, anti-clericalism, human deformity and the dead hand of convention. Bunuel is a moralist rather than a realist and his sense of evil and dark humor are not for casual viewers. A-III (GP)

Trog (1970) Low-budget British monster movie in which the head of a research laboratory (Joan Crawford) subdues, studies, and educates a rather ludicrous ape-man that is eventually killed by the local townpeople because of fear and superstition. Director Freddie Francis treats the story as a serious, if heavy-handed, plea for human understanding but the result is only slow and melodramatic entertainment. A-II (GP)

Trojan Women, The (1971) Directed by Michael Cacoyannis, this adaptation of Euripides' tragedy about the shattering effect of war on society is faithful to the original and frequently flamboyant. In spite of the stately acting of Katharine Hepburn as Hecuba, the Trojan queen, and Irene Papas as Helen, the cause of the war, the result is of more interest to the student of ancient Greek drama than the casual moviegoer. A-III (GP)

Tron (1982) Disney high-tech sci-fi adventure in which three heroes (Jeff Bridges, Cindy Morgan and Bruce Boxleitner), on the trail of a greedy villain (David Warner), get caught in the workings of a computerized video game. Fortunately, director Steven Lisberger has treated the material with a certain amount of humor, but how much you enjoy it depends upon your enthusiasm for the special effects which are the movie's reason for being. Some violence and also the clear implication that the heroine has gone to bed with both of her heroic companions. A-III (PG)

Tropic of Cancer (1970) Screen version of Henry Miller's long-banned autobiographical novel about an impoverished expatriate writer (Rip Torn) and his chiefly sexual exploits in the Paris of the early 1930s. Directed by Joseph Strick, the movie's most serious failure is not its shallow characterization of the writer, nor its crude images and cruder language, but its overall disregard of women as no more than sex objects. O (X)

Tropical Ecstasy (1970) The theme of the prostitute redeemed by love provides a flimsy excuse for Argentina's Isabel Sarli to spend half the movie stripping and sitting in the shallow surf with a poor fisherman, played by Armando Bo, her real-life husband who also wrote, produced and directed this paltry exercise in exploitation. O (nr)

Trouble in Mind (1986) Unlikable crime melodrama directed by Alan Rudolph about a cynical ex-cop (Kris Kristofferson) who tries to help a young punk in trouble (Keith Carradine) but gets romantically involved with two women (Genevieve Bujold and Lori Singer). Excessive violence and sex scenes. O (R)

Trouble Man (1972) Slick black action movie about a supertough, supercool dude (Robert Hooks) who is being used by one black gambling ring to wipe out another but when he catches on, they all go down in a series of shoot-outs. Directed by Ivan Dixon, its violent action and constant rough language, despite coy restraint in several sex scenes, is for undemanding but hardy adults. A-III (R)

Trouble with Angels, The (1966) Episodic screen version of Jane Trahey's comic recollections of life in a Catholic girl's boarding school revolves around the finely balanced battle of wit and will between the girls and the nuns. Rosalind Russell is in top form as the mother superior who squelches the adolescent mischief concocted by Hayley Mills and June Harding. Save for a few mawkish scenes, director Ida Lupino has made the sentimental comedy seem amusingly fresh and enjoyable. A-I (br)

Trouble with Girls, The (1969) The Chautauqua show, a bit of Americana that was part carnival, part educational forum, serves as a the background for an Elvis Presley movie set in the 1920s. Peter Tewksbury has not helped matters much by directing the picture as if it were all high camp and the plot bogs down in some heavy dramatics about a local murder but, on the whole, it's a relaxed venture into nostalgia. A-III (G)

Truck Turner (1974) Los Angeles tracker of bail-jumpers (Isaac Hayes) is kept busy looking for pimps, prostitutes, dope dealers and other low types while trying to keep his feisty girlfriend (Annazette Chase) out of prison. Director Jonathan Kaplan's work is so relentlessly awful, in terms of both quality and its view of humanity, that its excessive violence is almost beside the point. O (R)

True Confessions (1981) Uneven screen version of John Gregory Dunne's novel about troubled brothers in late 1940's Los Angeles, the one (Robert De Niro) being a monsignor adept at political infighting and the other (Robert Duvall) a tough police sergeant intent on solving the murder of a prostitute. Director Ulu Grosbard uses the crime as the core of this interesting but only moderately effective melodrama intertwining religion, politics and crime. Because of its relentless concentration upon the seamy side of things (brothels, morgues and a pornographic film), some adults may find it unsuitable entertainment. A-IV (R)

True Grit (1969) Great, rousing Western based on the Charles Portis novel about a justice-minded little gal with true grit (Kim Darby) who, while trailing her father's killer, joins forces with Marshall "Rooster" Cogburn (John Wayne) and a Texas Ranger (Glen Campbell). Directed with gusto by Henry Hathaway, their adventures and scrapes with death are furious and action-packed, and the whole show is leavened nicely with earthy, very human touches and humor. Because there is some stylized violence, parents should accompany the young ones. A-I (G)

True Stories (1986) Director David Byrne presents a sociological vision of arcane Americana in this whimsical movie about the style, spirit and substance of small-town life in the Southwest. With Byrne himself serving as a somewhat sardonic on-screen commentator, the movie offers a series of documentary vignettes of more or less ordinary town activities. Driven by an eclectic musical score, the result is a wholesome and innocent post-modern version of "Our Town." A-II (PG)

Trygon Factor, The (1968) Muddled British mystery directed by Cyril Frankel in which a Scotland Yard inspector (Stewart Granger) traces a series of unsolved robberies to a bogus order of nuns. Violence. A-III (br)

Tsar to Lenin (1971) Documentary on the Russian Revolution presents rare footage of the royal family, the Bolshevik leaders, the complicated events of the February and October revolutions and the subsequent terrors of the Civil War. Valuable as this footage is, the movie is relatively unsophisticated in the use it makes of it. A-I (nr)

Tuff Turf (1985) WASP golden boy finds himself at inner-city high school and makes things even tougher for himself by going after the girl friend of a gang leader. Mindless youth exploitation movie directed by Fritz Kiersch with a blaring musical score and some scenes of despicable violence. O (R)

Tunnelvision (1976) Sick satire about television programming of the future features Howard Hesseman, Betty Thomas, Chevy Chase and Larraine Newman. Directed by Neal Israel and Brad Swirnoff, it offers a series of degrading, detestable and altogether unfunny vignettes. O

(R)

Turk 182 (1985) In rescuing a little girl from a burning building, an off-duty New York fireman (Robert Urich) is badly injured. When he's refused compensation, his young brother (Timothy Hutton) embarks on a campaign for justice by embarrasing the mayor with graffiti signed "Turk 182," his injured brother's nickname and badge number. A crude, noisy movie directed by Bob Clark with pretensions to folk epic grandeur. Sexual promiscuity. O (PG-13)

Turning Point, The (1977) Shirley MacLaine and Anne Bancroft star as one-time rival ballerinas who renew their feud when MacLaine's daughter (Leslie Browne) joins Bancroft's troupe. Directed by Herbert Ross, the old-fashioned sentimental melodrama is set against the glamorous world of ballet, with plenty of grand dance sequences. Brief nudity and a benign attitude toward illicit sex. A-III (PG)

Turtle Diary (1986) Adaptation of playwright Harold Pinter's story of an author (Glenda Jackson) and a bookseller (Ben Kingsley) who are brought together by their mutual aspiration to free three sea turtles from the London aquarium. Director John Irvin's delicate, contemplative narrative is a testament to gentle souls who set simple goals and celebrate small, private victories. Brief but intense scene of violence. A-II (PG)

Twelve Chairs, The (1970) Uneven comedy set in the Soviet Union of 1927 when a deposed nobleman (Ron Moody) learns that the family jewels were hidden in a confiscated dining room chair but his search is complicated by a suave con artist (Frank Langella) and a greedy priest (Dom DeLuise). Written and directed by Mel Brooks, the comedy depends upon old-fashioned mugging and slapstick spiked with some modern cynicism but by the end the farce turns to bathos and disappointment. A-III (GP/G appeal)

Twelve Chairs, The (1973) Soviet cinema is not known for its levity or wit and yet both are in evidence in this large-scale extravaganza in the picaresque adventures of a grasping ex-aristocrat (A. Gomiashvili) and a conniving proletarian (S. Filippov) who are forced to work together in searching for a fortune hidden in a chair seized during the Revolution. Directed by Leonid Gaidai, it is a good-humored and often hilarious picture of the flaws and strengths that made up life in the Soviet Union of the 1920s and the ending has considerably more bite than the boisterous 1970 Mel Brooks' version. A-II (nr)

25th Hour, The (1967) Well-intentioned European co-production showing how senseless coincidences and petty officials separate a Romanian peasant (Anthony Quinn) from his wife (Virna Lisi) during World War II. Their ultimate reunion as a beaten family of displaced persons demonstrates the devastating effects of war on the innocent. Director Henri Verneuil has a worthy theme but the plot contrivances are thin and the production is flat and plodding. A-II (br)

24-Hour Lover (1970) Heavy-handed German sex farce about a young wine salesman who dallies on his daily round of kitchens and parlors, until ultimately collapsing from sheer exhaustion. The movie just repeats one long tired joke without wit or style. O (R)

24 Hours of the Rebel (1977) Mediocre story about the effect the news of actor James Dean's death has upon a group of college students in a small Arkansas town who seem to find movies more real than their own lives. Written and directed by James Bridges, the movie fails to build much sympathy for its two principal characters (Richard Thomas and Deborah Benson) or explain why they are drawn so compulsively to Dean's screen persona. Several scenes of youthful sexual explorations and vulgar language. A-III (PG)

20,000 Leagues Under the Sea (1954) Marvelous Disney version of the classic Jules Verne sea yarn about a terrifying, red-eyed monster sinking whalers and other 19th-century vessels, a survivor of which (Kirk Douglas) is taken aboard the submarine "Nautilus" by the nefarious Captain Nemo (James Mason) wants to rule the high seas. Others aboard are a marine scientist (Paul Lukas) and his droll assistant (Peter Lorre). Directed by Richard Fleischer, the story is great fun for all ages and the special effects are really special. A-I (G)

Twice in a Lifetime (1985) This is a big, glossy valentine to adultery in which a 50-year-old steelworker (Gene Hackman) falls in love with a barmaid (Ann-Margret) and leaves his wife (Ellen Burstyn) and children. Directed by Bud Yorkin, the movie lacks authentic characters and motivation, relying instead upon a dense sentimental smokescreen in its attempts to justify the husband's wholly selfish actions. O (R)

Twilight People (1972) The title refers to the gruesome results of a mad doctor (Charles Macaulay) in trying to create a new breed of humans but his experiments have yielded only a bat man, a panther woman, a wolf girl and assorted other odd hybrids. Low-budget Philippine production directed by Eddie Romero, the childish story goes from the utterly unbelievable to the ludicrous, but its violent conclusion is not for the youngsters. A-III (PG)

Twilight Zone—The Movie (1983) Anthology movie, inspired by the popular 1960s television series, is made up of five separate episodes by four different directors, and only the one about an airline passenger (John Lithgow) who spots an odd-looking creature sitting on the wing, rises above mediocrity. Some frightening effects here and in three of the other four segments make it inappropriate fare for younger viewers. A-II (PG)

Twilight's Last Gleaming (1977) Burt Lancaster plays a cashiered Air Force general who seizes control of a nuclear missile launching site in an attempt to alter government policies. Director Robert Aldrich, not known for his subtlety, has made an extremely clumsy, if well-intentioned movie, whose ham-handed approach to a complex moral issue, as well as its extreme, if sporadic, violence and rough language make it questionable fare at best. O (R)

Twinkle, Twinkle, Killer Kane (see: "The Ninth Configuration")

Twins of Evil (1972) British horror movie about a 17th-century witch-hunter (Peter Cushing) whose voluptuous twin nieces catch the eye of a depraved devil worshipper (Damien Thomas) and soon one of them is drawn into his evil sphere but Cushing is unable to tell which is the witch. Directed by John Hough, it's an exercise in pumped-up suspense with more than usual reliance on graphic gore, nudity and a spot of kinky eroticism. O (R)

Twist and Shout (1986) Danish import about two teenagers experiencing the pains of growing up in the 1960s without any parental guidance to help them cope with their adolescent sexual desires and the tragic consequences that result. Nudity, sexual encounters and graphic depiction of abortion. O (R)

Twisted Nerve (1969) British psychological thriller about an unstable young man (Hywel Bennett) who gradually loses control of his faculties and becomes a homicidal maniac. Directed by Roy Boulting, the plot tries to integrate the effects of heredity and environment upon the youth but the sexual nature of the problems touched upon in the course of the movie make it adult fare. A-III (PG)

Twitch of the Death Nerve, The (1973) Sadistic Italian terror movie directed by Mario Bava starts with the strangling of a crippled countess and from there to non-stop slaughter of her husband, offspring, hirelings and neighbors. The horror is the sickening way in which the murders are perpetrated. Repugnant violence. O (R)

Two (1969) Danish exploitation sequel to "I, a Woman" makes no pretense at being anything but a cold exercise in senseless promiscuity, almost mechanical in its frequent exposure of Gio Petre's body. Director Mac Ahlberg adds insult to injury by tacking on an absurdly insincere moral ending. O (nr)

Two English Girls (1972) Director Francois Truffaut has made the perfect companion movie for his previous "Jules and Jim." The situation this time is neatly reversed, with the man (Jean-Pierre Leaud) in love with two sisters and unable to make a commitment to either. Some viewers will find the situation completely amoral, and often ridiculously romantic. But as a picture of life at the turn of the century, with its very formal etiquette, suppressed emotions and artifical manners, it couldn't be better. A-IV (nr)

Two for the Road (1967) Producer-director Stanley Donen's saga about a modern marriage on wheels that skids dangerously but doesn't quite crack up, teams Audrey Hepburn and Albert Finney as the troubled couple. By following the pair on their various jaunts through Europe, Donen provides both a fluid vehicle for narrative development as well as strikingly scenic backgrounds. A-III (br)

Two Gentlemen Sharing (1969) Failed British drama about a white Londoner (Robin Phillips) and an upwardly mobile black from the West Indies (Hal Frederick) who share a London mews apartment, have their separate problems and end with one discovering his homosexuality and the other returning to Jamaica. Director Ted Kotcheff's treatment lacks any subtlety, especially in several lovemaking scenes. A-III (R)

200 Motels (1971) Written, produced and directed by Frank Zappa, the title refers to the bleak digs occupied by touring groups such as Zappa's The Mothers of Invention during the course of an average year. It features, however, rough language and a smutty lyric, explained with glee by a pair of semi-nude groupies, as well as a raunchy cartoon sequence depicting the sleazy side of life. O (R)

Two Men of Karamoja (1974) Documentary account of seven months of conflict and change in Uganda's Kidepo Valley National Park as the British chief warden prepares to turn the preserve over to a native warden. Directed by Natalie and Eugene Jones, the movie examines not only the park's wildlife problems but its native population whose tribal structures are changing with the times. Much of this ethnograhpic material is best suited for adults and older adolescents. A-III (R/PG appeal)

Two Minute Warning (1976) Gathered in the Los Angeles Coliseum are an assortment of disaster veterans (Charlton Heston, John Cassavetes, Martin Balsam and David Jansen) and 100,000 extras when a sniper is spotted, the police move in and the arena is turned into a Roman forum of bloodshed and graphic violence. Directed by Larry Peerce, the mindless fantasy plays on fears and anxieties of random senseless violence in extreme fashion. O (R)

Two Mules for Sister Sara (1970) Prostitute masquerading as a nun (Shirley MacLaine) in order to help Mexican rebels is joined by a cowboy loner (Clint Eastwood) in undertaking the capture of a French garrison and they fall in love. Directed by Don Siegel, there are some good action sequences but the comic irreverences (a supposed nun smoking, drinking and cursing like a trooper), like the movie, are not to be taken seriously. A-III (PG)

Two of a Kind (1983) John Travolta and Olivia Newton-John have the misfortune to star in a dreadful movie about God's sending a quartet of angels to earth to try and reform two nasty people. Written and directed by John Herzfield, it is for the most part innocuous, except for some profanity. A-III (PG)

Two of Us, The (1968) Excellent French story of a little Jewish boy (Alain Cohen) who is hidden from the Nazis on a remote farm in Occupied France by an elderly anti-Semite (Michel Simon). Directed by Claude Berri, the movie is a very touching, gentle sort of comedy, told simply through an accumulation of incidents rather than a tightly-knit plot. Everyone can identify with and enjoy the warm, human relationship between the old man and the young lad. A-I (br)

Two or Three Things I Know About Her (1970) Director Jean-Luc Godard's paean to Paris (the "Her" of the title) follows the fragmentary story of a part-time prostitute (Marina Vlady) but Raoul Coutard's camera is focused on the ever-changing face of a modern city. Though the movie is heavily laced with philosophical asides and interruptions, it is often amusing, at times illuminating and always stunningly beautiful in its picture of a great city. A-III (nr)

Two People (1973) Trivial romantic claptrap about a Vietnam deserter (Peter Fonda) and a jaded divorcee (Lindsay Wagner) who meet in Marrakech, talk their way to Casablanca, make love in Paris and finally fly to New York where he is going to turn himself in. Directed by Robert Wise, the budding romance is totally unmotivated and certainly made no more credible by a ridiculously over-extended, semi-nude love scene. A-IV (R)

2001: A Space Odyssey (1968) Director Stanley Kubrick's epic, co-written with Arthur C. Clarke, is both science fiction and metaphysical poetry in an unconventional mixture of astounding images and music from the remembered past, the identifiable present and the projected future. The recurring image of a monolith symbolizes a superhuman existence as a 700-foot spacecraft carries astronauts (Keir Dullea and Gary Lockwood) and Hal, a talking computer, on a half-billion mile trip to Jupiter. Kubrick's preoccupation with the fate of humanity's relationship to the machine is fundamentally optimistic. For young people and imaginative adults but too long, deep and intense for little children. A-II (G)

2010 (1985)   Sequel to "2001: A Space Odyssey" in which Roy Scheider leads a joint American-Soviet probe of Jupiter to discover the fate of the spacecraft sent there in the original. Writer-director Peter Hyams overwhelms the story with spectacular special effects but young people especially should find it an engaging voyage into space. A-I (PG)

2000 Years Later (1969)   Weak satire in which an ancient Roman (John Abbott), sent by the god Mercury, fails to warn society of the consequences of its moral corruption. Bert Tenzer's low-budget, amateurish production, lacking any moral focus of its own, merely exaggerates and exploits the more obviously decadent elements of the day. O (R)

Two Weeks in September (1967)   Failed French romance directed by Serge Bourguignon in which a model (Brigitte Bardot), living with a man in Paris, accepts an assignment in London where she acquires a new lover and then can't decide which one she really wants. Suggestive treatment of illicit sex. O (br)

Two-Lane Blacktop (1971)   Introspective young man (folk-rock singer James Taylor) who lives on the road in his 1955 Chevy coupe races the owner of a Pontiac G.T.O. (Warren Oates) in a back roads tour across America. Director Monte Hillman's low-key approach does not romanticize his drifters of the road but along the way shows some of the reasons why they have opted out of the mainstream. Some realistic street language. A-III (R)

U

Ugly Dachshund, The (1966)   Disney comedy about a Great Dane puppy who gets mixed in with a litter of dachshunds but wins a place with the family of Dean Jones and Suzanne Pleshette. Directed by Norman Tokar, it is for dog lovers and small children. A-I (br)

Ugly Ones, The (1968)   Sordid Italian-Spanish Western directed by Eugenio Martin about a bounty hunter (Richard Wyler) on the trail of a depraved Mexican bandit (Tomas Milian). It revels in protracted scenes of violence and brutality. O (R)

Ulysses (1967)   Director Joseph Strick's adaptation of the James Joyce classic makes a static movie but it may be of interest to those who have studied the Irish author's work. Those unfamiliar with the novel are likely not only to find the movie incomprehensible but its verbal treatment of sexual and religious matters to be offensive. A-IV (br)

Ulzana's Raid (1972)   Tracking a band of raiding Apaches are a hardened scout (Burt Lancaster), his Indian sidekick (Jorge Luke) and a greenhorn officer fresh out of West Point (Bruce Davison), unsure of himself and his religious inhibitions about the brutal methods used to hunt and destroy the Indians. On the action level, director Robert Aldrich's Western works fairly well, but it raises moral questions of justice and retribution that require more than well-staged fight scenes and good location photography. The violent visuals of frontier savagery borders on the exploitative. A-IV (R)

Uncle, The (1966)   Warm British movie about the groping, confused efforts of a 7-year-old lad to cope with the mysteries of birth, death and growing up over the course of a summer. Directed by Desmond Davis, the movie is unusal in its realistic depiction of a wholesome childhood set within the context of happy family life. Though about the world of a child, young children may find some of its aspects perplexing. A-II (br)

Uncle Joe Shannon (1979)   Burt Young stars in his own screenplay about a trumpet player who hits the skids after the tragic death of his wife and young son but regains his self-esteem and starts on the road back when he becomes the unofficial guardian of a young boy. Directed by Joseph C. Hanwright, the result is mawkish melodrama chock-full of embarrassingly bad moments. A-II (PG)

Uncle Tom's Cabin (1977)   Sincere but woefully inept retelling of the famous Harriet Beecher Stowe classic, unfortunately contains some crass exploitation scenes. Though the main part of the movie was apparently made abroad, the American distributors seem to have clumsily inserted scenes of sex and brutality utterly at variance with the rest of the narrative. O (R)

Uncle Vanya (1972)   Brooding Soviet version of Anton Chekhov's play takes place in the claustrophobic rooms of a diplapidated manor where Vanya (Innokenty Smoktunovsky), the estate's caretaker despairs at his wasted life and the local doctor (Sergei Bondarchuk) is the only character who sees the absurd social injustices of his time. Writer-director Andrei Mikhalkov-Konchalovsky evokes the impoverished spirit of pre-revolutionary Russia by alternating scenes of one-tone sepia with those of muted color and the result will affect all who care about the depths of human feelings. A-II (nr)

Uncommon Valor (1983)   Wealthy Texas oil man (Robert Stack), whose son is a Vietnam War MIA, hires a Marine colonel (Gene Hackman) to rescue him and his comrades, among them the colonel's own son. Though it has a fairly literate script by Joe Gayton, director Ted Kotcheff does not do much to lift it above the level of routine action adventure. Violence and the heroic depiction of a native drug dealer who gives his all for the American cause. A-III (R)

Undefeated, The (1969)   Post-Civil War story in which a group of Confederate families (led by Rock Hudson) heading for asylum in Mexico under Emperor Maximilian join forces with a former Union officer (John Wayne) bringing a herd of horses south of the border as they fight off Mexican bandits and get embroiled in the Mexican Civil War. Directed by Andrew V. McLaglen, it's an unpretentious, old-fashioned cowboy movie that can be enjoyed by any who like Western action and adventure. A-I (G)

Under Fire (1983)   American photojournalist (Nick Nolte) covering the Sandinista revolution in Nicaragua loses his sense of detachment at seeing the brutality of the Somoza regime and agrees to fake a story suggested by his lover and fellow journalist (Joanna Cassidy). Directed by Ron Shelton and Clayton Frohman, the powerful and extremely entertaining film conveys the feel of guerrilla warfare, especially in an urban environment, with uncanny force. Violence and rough language. A-III (R)

Under Milk Wood (1973)   British dramatization of the Dylan Thomas poem-play, with Richard

Burton and Ryan Davies as the two narrators who pass through the little Welsh seacoast town of Llareggub and share the lives of its inhabitants with the viewer much as did the Stage Manager in "Our Town." Directed by Andrew Sinclair, its great compression of incidents involving some 60 actors in a fast-paced, impressionistic scenario does not lend itself to casual viewing. Several scenes of unabashed sensuality and earthiness. A-IV (R/PG)

Under the Cherry Moon (1986) Rock star Prince and his comic sidekick Jerome Benton try to resurrect the age of Valentino's sensual mystique in this shimmering black-and-white male fantasy about black American gigilos trying to strike it rich in the beautiful resort city of Nice, France. The movie's preoccupation with sex distorts the meaning of a loving relationship. A-III (PG-13)

Under the Rainbow (1981) Legendary off-screen drunken carousing by the diminutive actors playing Munchkins in "The Wizard of Oz" (1938) becomes the central premise of a dim comedy burdened by slapstick subplots involving a mad assassin and Axis spies, all in service of a predictable romance between a Secret Service agent (Chevy Chase) and a movie studio assistant (Carrie Fisher). Director Steve Rash lavishes his energies on re-creating the Depression era and evoking some measure of nostalgia but the movie's many sight gags fall embarrassingly flat. Coarse language, double entendres and bawdy situations as well as tasteless stereotyping of little people. A-III (PG)

Under the Volcano (1984) Screen version of the Malcolm Lowry novel about an alcoholic English diplomat serving in Mexico (Albert Finney) is an impressive work but fails to convey the inner drama that gave such tragic force to the original, despite Finney's powerful performance. Nevertheless, director John Huston's effort is well worth seeing, though its adult treatment includes a vicious, sordid scene in a brothel. A-III (R)

Undercovers Hero (1975) Peter Sellers plays six roles, ranging from a British intelligence agent to Adolf Hitler, in a sex farce about how World War II was really won in a Paris bordello run by Lila Kedrova. Directed by Roy Boulting, the thoroughly inane script works on the same low level of wit as the pun of the title. O (R)

Underground (1970) B-grade World War II movie about the abduction of a Nazi general by the French underground (led by Robert Goulet). Little attempt is made to advance sympathy for either side in a weak story with confusing flashbacks, lackluster action photography and elements of sex and torture. A-III (PG)

Underground (1976) Documentary about what happened to some of those who were radicalized by the failure of the protest movements of the 1960s. Directed by Emile de Antonio, Mary Lampson and Haskell Wexler, the film consists essentially of a group interview with five surviving members of the Weather Underground who went into hiding after the explosion of their New York bomb factory in 1970. A tragic part of American history. A-III (nr)

Undertaker and His Pals, The (1972) Sharing the bodies of the young ladies they slay, the pals serve choice cuts to customers in their luncheonette while the mortician dresses up the remains and gives trading stamps to the grieving family. Awful amateurish production coats its tongue-in-cheek gruesomeness with excessively graphic views of the murdered victims. O (R)

Une Femme Douce (1971) French drama about a woman (Dominique Sanda) who commits suicide and her husband (Guy Frangin) who tries to find out why. Director Robert Bresson's investigation is really into the emptiness of middle-class lives in which material objects consume people's entire interest to the detriment of interpersonal relationships. Sparse and demanding, it is a very interior film whose text is the ambiguous surface of reality. A-III (nr)

Unfaithfully Yours (1984) Symphony conductor (Dudley Moore) wrongly suspects his wife (Natassja Kinski) of being unfaithful and fantasizes revenge while on the podium. Director Howard Zieff's expensively mounted comedy is not anywhere near as funny as the 1948 Preston Sturges original. Though otherwise innocuous, it is marred by an ill-conceived shower scene and excessive bedroom sequence. O (PG)

Unholy Rollers, The (1972) The rise of a young roller skater (Claudia Jennings) into the big-time roller derby involves women slugging it out like animals in one small-town rink after another, shown with an excess of breast-bashing, groin-stomping visuals. Directed by Vernon Zimmerman, the movie's off-camera commentary is provided by a pair of ring-side announcers using tongue-in-cheek burlesque humor. O (R)

Unidentified Flying Oddball (1979) Good Disney comedy about an American space scientist (Dennis Dugan) and his look-alike robot who land in King Arthur's Court and save the monarch (Kenneth More) from being overthrown by Merlin (Ron Moody) and Sir Mordred (Jim Dale). Russ Mayberry directs the proceedings with proper charm and ingenuous good humor, leaving family audiences happier for the viewing. A-I (G)

Uninhibited, The (1968) Mediocre Spanish drama about a group of drop-outs from life trying to rekindle some sense of direction and responsibility. Directed by Juan Antonio Bardem, the movie's theme has merit but its amoral setting and treatment may offend some adult viewers. A-IV (br)

Unman, Wittering and Zigo (1971) Group of British schoolboys murder their teacher and threaten to do likewise to his replacement (David Hemmings) unless he goes along with their plans. Hemmings doesn't believe them at first, and by the time he does, no one else will. This juxtaposition of innocence and corruption is powerful material, but director John Mackenzie loses control of it early on in the film, making several scenes involving sex ludicrous and dramatically implausible. A-III (GP)

Unmarried Woman, An (1978) Jill Clayburgh stars as a reasonably happy wife who is forced to begin a new life when her husband (Michael Murphy) deserts her and their teenage daughter for a younger woman. Though it supposedly is about the trauma and suffering of a woman struggling to forge a new identity, writer-director Paul Mazursky's work is a bit too slick and sentimental to be very moving or very convincing. Extremely well-acted and relatively sincere effort contains some rough language, nudity and one needlessly graphic love-making scene. O (R)

Until September (1984) Young American in Paris (Karen Allen) becomes involved with a suave Frenchman quite capable of juggling a wife, two children and a mistress, but she wants to play for keeps. Director Richard Marquand's limp and uninventive romance falls back upon abundant nudity in a vain attempt to sustain interest. Benign view of adultery. O (R)

Up in Smoke (1978) Utterly mindless comedy about two California potheads (counterculture figures Cheech Marin and Tommy Chong) who travel to Tiajuana in search of some marijuana and subsequent pursuit by bumbling narcotics cop (Stacey Keach). Director Lou Adler's jokes, when not witless cliches about the pleasures of the drug culture, depend heavily on the titillating and the scatological. O (R)

Up in the Cellar (1970) Deprived of a college scholarship by a discerning computer, a youth (Wes Stern) seeks revenge on the college's pompous president (Larry Hagman) by seducing his wife, daughter, and black mistress-secretary. Though a number of director Ted Flicker's well-deserved jabs sting the college administration scene, the light touch never gets funny enough and the moral tone never gets high enough to save this slipshod attempt at adult entertainment. O (R)

Up the Academy (1980) Tedious, sophomoric romp set in a military academy ruled by a sadistic headmaster (Ron Leibman, who wisely had his name taken off the credits). Though director Robert Downey's visuals are restrained, the movie makes excessive use of sexual innuendo, rough language and all-around vulgarity. O (R)

Up the Creek (1984) Four college losers (Tim Matheson, Jennifer Runyon, Stephen Furst and Dan Monahan) battle military cadets and intense preppies to win a raft race in another exercise in brain-dead humor. Directed by Robert Butler, the movie contains abundant nudity and crude sexual humor. O (R)

Up the Down Staircase (1967) Screen version of Bel Kaufman's novel about a dedicated young teacher (Sandy Dennis) overwhelmed by school regulations, supply shortages, overcrowding, disciplinary problems and some misguided colleagues, but who manages to do some real teaching in spite of it all. Director Robert Mulligan's realistic drama about the problems of a big city high school is helped by some humor and a fine supporting cast. A-II (br)

Up the Junction (1968) Peter Collinson directs the British story of a rich woman (Suzy Kendall) seeking to find some sense of purpose in the slums of Battersea. It will impress some viewers as an honest essay in social realism while striking others as patronizing and banal. Casual moviegoers may find its coarse and vulgar language offensive. A-IV (br)

Up the MacGregors (1967) Forgettable Italian-Spanish Western directed by Dario Sabatello is routine Saturday matinee fare. Mild violence. A-II (br)

Up the Sandbox (1972) Seriocomic story of a somewhat mad Manhattan housewife (Barbra Streisand) who finds herself experiencing an acute identity crisis and creates a soaring fantasy life that enables her to escape a myriad of troubles and even transcend them. Directed by Irvin Kershner, the housewife's struggle for liberation is what makes the film, despite its cinematic flaws in some of the flights of fantasy (including an abortion clinic), engagingly healthy and at times quite wise. A-IV (R)

Up to His Ears (1966) Failed French adventure comedy directed by Philippe De Broca about a bored millionaire who is chased around exotic Oriental locales by hired killers. Sexual innuendo. A-III (br)

Uptight (1968) Updated version of "The Informer" (1936) replaces the IRA with a black revolutionary group, one of whom is wanted for murder and is betrayed for the reward by a former member of the group (Julian Mayfield). Directed by Jules Dassin, the movie has raw power and plenty of tension but oversimplifies the issues facing black Americans after Martin Luther King Jr.'s assassination. Mature themes. A-III (PG)

Uptown Saturday Night (1974) Sidney Poitier and Bill Cosby play a couple of would-be sharpies who get caught in the middle of a Harlem gang war when they try to enlist the services of gangster Harry Belafonte to get back the money stolen from them. Also directed by Poitier, it's a pleasantly entertaining, good-natured comedy with some good acting. A-III (PG)

Urban Cowboy (1980) John Travolta plays a rural Texan who comes to the big city of Houston to find work and becomes romantically involved with Debra Winger in a honky tonk saloon whose feature attraction is a mechanical broncho. Directed by James Bridges, it's a boring, embarrassingly adolescent movie celebrating the masculine virtues of hard drinking, fighting and wenching. O (PG)

Used Cars (1980) Nasty supposed comedy about rival car dealers with Kurt Russell, Jack Warden, Deborah Harmon and Andrew Duncan. Directed by Robert Zemeckis, there is nothing funny about the totally amoral and tasteless story which also employs nudity and rough language. O (R)

Utamaro and His Five Women (1972) Encapsulating the vision of an 18th-century Japanese artist, known especially for his prints of beautiful women, director Kenji Mizoguchi's movie succeeds admirably is showing an artist's view of his world. It is a paean to a vital classicism, both in subject and technique, idealizing a society in which people worked and lived in a harmony unknown in modern times. A-III (nr)

V

Vagabond (1986) French director Agnes Varda offers a somber, flawed observation of spiritual and moral decay as a young female drifter's last days are recounted by the people she's met on the road to self-effacement. As a vision of alienated youth, the movie depicts casual sex as symptomatic of spiritual disintegration with much more emotional ground to be explored. Simple yet profound, although a potentially confusing work. A-III (nr)

Valachi Papers, The (1972) Charles Bronson plays the role of Joe Valachi, the late Mafia informer whose revelations formed the book by Peter Maas upon which the movie is based. Director Terence Young has passed up the opportunity to provide a rare glimpse inside the workings of organized crime in order to produce one more straight action movie, filled with brutality and sudden violence. Several scenes of gangland inhumanity require a strong stomach. A-IV (R/PG)

Valdez Is Coming (1971) Tedious Western in which a Mexican-American deputy (Burt Lancaster) tries to collect some money for an Indian widow from those who had mistakenly shot her husband and then goes after the rancher responsible. Directed by Edwin Sherin, the heavy-handed plot development contains much violence and smatterings of sex and near-nudity. A-III (GP)

Valentino (1977) British director Ken Russell's screen biography of Rudolph Valentino (Rudolf Nureyev) is a boring, overdone piece of pretentious trash having only the remotest connection with the famous movie star's life. Nudity and graphic sexuality. O (R)

Valerie and Her Week of Wonders (1974) Czechoslovakian fantasy in which a 13-year-old girl's daydreaming transforms her ordinary world into one filled with strange adventures, bizarre characters and the first vague stirrings of sexual awareness. Directed by Jaromil Jires, the setting is a picturesque village at the turn of the century, affording lush imagery, striking compositions, colorful costuming and ornamental detail that lend themselves easily to a surrealistic picture of a young adolescent's imagination. Literal-minded viewers may be confused by the movie's lack of narrative guideposts but the juxtaposition of religious and Freudian symbolism invites deeper psychological probing by those so inclined. A-IV (nr)

Valley Girl (1983) San Fernando Valley girl (Deborah Foreman) throws over her handsome but dumb Valley boy friend in favor of a punk rocker from Hollywood (Nicolas Cage), much to the consternation of her friends. Directed by Martha Coolige, this Romeo and Juliet variation makes some gestures in the direction of satire, but essentially is another teen exploitation movie, with graphic nudity and rough language. O (R)

Valley of Gwangi, The (1969) A group of riders from a Wild West show (headed by James Franciscus) go in search of a major attraction in a hidden Mexican valley where prehistoric monsters survive protected from the outside world by a band of mysterious gypsies. Director James O'Connolly has done a routine job in directing what is essentially a nonsensical exercise of the special effects department and one's imagination. A-I (G)

Valley of Mystery (1967) Airliner crash-lands in South American jungle among whose perils are a tribe of headhunters, but the pilot (Richard Egan) manages to keep the survivors alive until rescued by helicopters. Director Josef Leytes turns a routine adventure story into a slack melodrama of little interest. Stylized violence. A-II (br)

Valley of the Dolls (1967) Trashy melodrama based on a trashy novel about decadence in the world of show business and the deleterious effects of gulping pep and sleeping pills. Directed by Mark Robson, the insight is nil, most of the acting is embarrassingly bad and it elicits only pained disbelief at its amateurishness and a few laughs where none was intended. O (br)

Vampire Circus (1972) British horror movie in which a traveling troupe of gypsy vampires (Adrienne Corri and Anthony Corlan) visit a Serbian village to revive a dead count who had been killed there 15 years before. Director Robert Young tries to make up for the script's lack of wit and suspense with a fair sprinkling of incidental sex, but with little success. A-III (R/PG)

Vampire Lovers (1970) Minimal British horror movie about a female vampire with lesbian inclinations who ravages the young maidens of a peaceful little hamlet. Directed by Roy Ward Baker, the movie emphasizes blood and sex at the expense of more traditional horror elements. O (R)

Van, The (1977) Gawky youth (Stuart Getz) becomes a Don Juan when he buys a van in this shoddy low-budget sex-exploitation movie directed by Sam Grossman. O (R)

Vanishing Point (1971) Speed demon (Barry Newman) attempts to outrun the police of four states aided by a blind disc jockey (Cleavon Little) who monitors police frequencies. Directed by Richard C. Sarafian, the plot is aimless, marked by a number of hair-raising near crack-ups and some gratuitous nudity. O (GP)

Vanishing Wilderness (1974) Slow-moving, incoherent parade of unrelated wildlife scenes, directed by Arthur Dubs and Heinz Seilmann, with an obnoxiously cute narration by Rex Allen. It ranks low on the scale of well-made nature documentaries. A-I (G)

Vault of Horror, The (1973) Unimaginative British horror movie offers five tales, interwoven with vampires, voodoo, murder and torture, with a cast including Daniel Massey, Terry-Thomas, Glynis Johns and Curt Jurgens. Directed by Roy Ward Baker, there is too much emphasis on mutilation and blood for younger viewers, and not enough psychological terror to chill the hearts and imaginations of horror devotees. A-III (R/PG)

Velvet Vampire, The (1971) Low-budget horror about newlyweds (Michael Blodgett and Sherry Miles) who come for a weekend in a desert hotel whose hostess (Celeste Yarnall) is desperate for new blood. Director Stephanie Rothman requires hardly a stitch of clothing for the atrocious acting of all participants in this silly exercise. O (R)

Vengeance of Fu Manchu, The (1967) Master criminal Fu Manchu (Christopher Lee) sets out to murder all the world's chiefs of police and, through plastic surgery, replace them with his own men but is foiled by Scotland Yard's Nayland Smith (Douglas Wilmer). Directed by Jeremy Summers, the British production's weak story makes middling adventure entertainment. Stylized violence. A-II (br)

Vengeance of She, The (1968) Weak British adventure fantasy based on characters created by H. Rider Haggard in which an occult power compels a young woman (Olinka Berova) to journey to a hidden city in North Africa to become the lost queen of its ruler (John Richardson). Directed by Cliff Owen, the action is pedestrian and the plot mistakes silliness for imagination. Mild violence. A-II (G)

Venom (1982) Deadly snake cavorts about a household taken over by ruthless international terrorists in this mediocre and farfetched melodrama directed by Piers Haggard. A fine cast, including Klaus Kinski, Nicol Williamson, Oliver Reed, Sarah Miles and Sterling Hayden, is wasted in a mindless effort that features violence and some restrained sexual activity. A-III (R)

Venus in Furs (1970) European co-production about a beautiful woman who, after being raped, mutilated and murdered, returns from the dead seeking vegeance on her killers. Directed by Jess Franco, its below-standard production values complement its ludicrous sex-exploitation plot. O (R)

Verdict, The (1982) When a drunken wreck of a lawyer (Paul Newman) presses a medical malpractice suit against a Boston Catholic hospital represented by a powerful attorney (James Mason), he overcomes his personal problems by relying upon his heart instead of his mind during the extended court battle. Though director Sidney Lumet's script has a faulty perspective on church procedures, Newman's performance outweighs such defects. The sexual aspects of the story are done with the greatest restraint, but it does contain some foul language from one of its characters. A-II (R)

Veronique (1976) Warm, sensitive French movie follows a perceptive 13-year-old girl's not especially eventful summer. Director Claudine Ghuilmain fulfills her modest aims in showing the youngster's experiences and some misunderstandings in what is little more than a string of vignettes best appreciated by adult viewers. A-III (nr)

Vertigo (1958) Fine suspense thriller from Alfred Hitchcock in the tale of a retired detective (James Stewart) called back for a private investigation of a seemingly shady lady (Kim Novak). Naturally they fall in love and land in high danger. Jimmy gulps and stammers a lot, Kim just smolders and Hitch masterfully pulls the strings. A-II (PG)

Very Curious Girl, A (1970) French social satire about the revenge a young gypsy (Bernadette Lafont) takes on the people of a small village who have exploited her and her mother. Director Claude Makovski has elicited strong and convincing performances from a cast mainly of villagers and peasants in creating a strange atmosphere of a primitive morality based on ignorance, simplicity and superstition. A-IV (R)

Very Happy Alexander (1969) Elegant French comedy about middle-age rebellion in which a brow-beaten husband (Philippe Noiret) scandalizes his neighbors by leading a life of lazy indolence after the death of his finger-snapping wife. He finds a soul-mate in a shiftless woman (Marlene Jobert) but when she snaps her fingers, he leaves her at the altar. Directed by Yves Robert, it is essentially a bucolic poem in which Noiret's warm, human performance makes convincing the urge to return to the unregimented life of Eden. A-II (nr)

Very Natural Thing, A (1974) Young man leaves the monastic life, becomes a high school teacher and takes a male lover whose promiscuity eventually results in a break-up. Director Christopher Larkin's movie is a sincere and obviously deeply-felt effort to present the moral dilemmas of a homosexual relationship but it is painfully naive about film technique and embarrassingly romantic about its theme. Several nude scenes of male grapplings. O (R)

Vice Squad (1982) Prostitute (Season Hubley) is saved from from the clutches of a brutal pimp (Wings Hauser) by a stalwart policeman (Gary Hanson) in a loathsome, unremittingly brutal and squalid movie directed by Gary A. Sherman. O (R)

Victor/Victoria (1982) Unemployed singer (Julie Andrews) dresses up as a man in order to get a job as a female impersonator and soon is the toast of 1934 Paris. Helping her along the way is an aging homosexual (Robert Preston) and complicating her life is a Chicago nightclub owner (James Garner). Directed by Blake Edwards, the humor is fitful, more slapstick than witty, and the situation stretches itself thin long before movie's end. Benign attitude toward homosexuality, though given the farcical context, unlikely to blur the moral outlook of adults. A-IV (PG)

Victory (1981) World War II movie in which a soccer game between a crack German team and a group of Allied prisoners (including Michael Caine, Sylvester Stallone and Pele, the Brazilian soccer legend) is used to mask an escape from the packed Paris stadium where it is being played. Well directed by John Huston, it's a sports movie with some taut wartime suspense. Solid entertainment for the whole family. A-I (PG)

Videodrome (1983) Seedy operator of a sleazy television station (James Woods) gets hooked on the unrelenting sado-masochism of a program called Videodrome which is actually a sinister plot against humanity carried out by some villains steeped, like the movie itself, in ill-digested media theories of Marshall McLuhan. Written and directed by David Cronenberg, there are some hints of satire, but no hint of intelligence or perspective, and its imagination is as dull as it is perverse. Sado-masochistic sex and exceedingly gory violence. O (R)

View to a Kill, A (1985) In another 007 adventure for the perpetually adolescent, James Bond (Roger Moore) is pitted against a rather pallid villain (Christopher Walken) who wants to remove all competition for his new computer chip by inducing an earthquake that will obliterate Silicon Valley. Director John Glen's pulp action-adventure fantasy has excessive violence and a benign view of promiscuity. O (PG)

Vigilante (1983) Brutal variation on the theme of the good guys getting fed up and taking the law into their own hands features Robert Forster joining forces with some vigilantes after his family is attacked by degenerate punks. Directed by William Lustig, the proceedings are cynically exploitative and incredibly violent. O (R)

Viking Queen, The (1967) Generally inept, tawdry spear-and-sandal epic set in rustic Britain during the Roman occupation where a haughty overseer (Don Murray) of a defeated but proud Viking tribe falls in love with its queen (Carita). British production directed by Don Chaffey, the tale of carnage and intrigue lavishes the budget on bloody action and skimps on the costuming to near-nudity. O (br)

Villa Rides (1968) Buzz Kulik directs a dismissible, violent Western, starring Yul Brynner as the menacing Mexican revolutionary and Robert Mitchum as a tough American gun-runner. Kulik ignores the historical complexity of the period and emphasizes its violence, with men being lined up and slaughtered, ad nauseam. O (R)

Villain (1971) Nasty excursion into the lower depths of the British underworld in which a small-time homosexual hood (Richard Burton) carves up a stool pigeon, blackmails a lusty Member of Parliament and bungles a payroll heist, while on his case is a rumpled Scotland Yard detective (Nigel Davenport) who exacts his just desserts, but just barely. Directed by Michael Tuchner, the acting is very good, the plot only routine, but the overall tint of moral decay and degradation is suffocating. O (R)

Villain, The (1979) Kirk Douglas, Ann-Margret and Arnold Schwarzenegger toil through director Hal Needham's spoof of Western outlaws and other heavies to no avail. One is left with the impression of watching a live-action version of a Road-Runner cartoon for no apparent reason. Vulgar language and suggestive gowns. A-III (PG)

Vincent, Francois, Paul and the Others (1976) Disappointing French import deals with the crisis of middle age in a series of loosely strung-together sketches exhibiting little but the Gallic charm of such performers as Yves Montand, Michel Piccoli,

Serge Reggiani, and Stephane Audran. Directed by Claude Sautet, it is not much of a movie but, for those interested, the performances are worth observing. A-III (nr)

Violent Four, The (1968) Italian crime melodrama about a gang of ruthless bank-robbers (led by Gian Maria Volonte and Tomas Milian) who are so successful that the police call in troops to hunt them down. Directed by Carlo Lizzani, the clumsy and overlong narrative uses a forced semi-documentary style and suffers from tired images out of American gangster movies. Much violence. A-III (M)

Violets Are Blue (1986) Kevin Kline plays the big fish in a small pond who slips in and out of an extramarital relationship with his former sweetheart (Sissy Spacek) who has returned home on vacation after being away for 13 years. Infidelity is treated as an egocentricity, not a moral breakdown. The script tends also to celebrate characters without conscience as its anti-hero gets his old flame out of his system without any consequences. Director Jack Fisk's movie romanticizes adultery. O (PG-13)

Violette (1978) Fact-based French dramatization of a 1933 case in which a 14-year-old girl (Isabelle Hupert) decided that she would be happier as an orphan and poisoned her parents but her mother (Stephane Audran) survived to become her most vehement accuser. Whatever political, social or artistic implications this somber event may have remain obscure because director Claude Chabrol centers on the depiction of the heroine's promiscuity as the motivation for her callous crime. A-IV (R)

Virgin Soldiers (1970) Group of bumbling, ill-suited young British draftees (Hywel Bennett, Nigel Davenport and Jack Sheperd) in a 1951 Malayan transit camp are initiated into the arts of love and war. Directed by John Dexter, the central failure of the movie is its inability to decide whether or not to take itself seriously and the result is a curiously flat, not very amusing string of incidents. Some violence, bloodshed, a sequence with a Singapore prostitute and two sexual encounters. A-III (R)

Virgin Witch, The (1972) British potboiler about runaway sisters who hitchhike to London, meet the lesbian proprietress of a modeling agency and later become willing initiates in a coven of orgiastic witches. Director Ray Austin exploits everybody concerned, including the audience. O (R)

Virgin and the Gypsy, The (1970) British adaptation of the D.H. Lawrence story about two sisters who return from a French finishing school to their father's country rectory where one is content to settle down and the other (Joanna Shimkus) falls in love with a gypsy (Franco Nero). Directed by Christopher Miles, the re-creation of the 1925 English countryside is lovely to look at, though the dated romantic story doesn't quite fare as well. Brief nudity and a resolution some may mistake as an endorsement of promiscuity. A-IV (R)

Virility (1976) One more satire on Sicilian honor, this one about a father's frantic efforts to prove to the rumor mongers that his son is not a homosexual. There is nothing light or subtle about Paola Cavara's direction of the film's offensive material. O (R)

Viscount, The (1967) Failed European spy movie directed by Maurice Cloche features excessive brutality and sexual suggestiveness. O (br)

Vision Quest (1985) A gung-ho high school wrestler (Matthew Modine) is distracted from his goal of a state championship and a scholarship by a sultry young woman (Linda Fiorentino). What happens is, like its young hero, a bore in a movie directed by Harold Becker with a blaring soundtrack and rough language typical of such youth films. Though there is no nudity characters talk about sex and its desirability constantly, presenting a benign view of fornication. O (R)

Visions of Eight (1973) Eight different directors (Arthur Penn, Kon Ichikawa, Milos Forman, Claude Lelouch, John Schlesinger, Mai Zetterling, Michael Pfleghar and Juri Ozerov) offer eight different views of the 1972 Munich Olympics. Despite the inevitable unevenness, it is a rewarding experience affording viewer's a different, more personal perspective of a familiar sports competition. A-I (G)

Visit to a Chief's Son (1974) American anthropologist (Richard Mulligan) brings his teenage son (Philip Hodgdon) to Kenya on a trip studying and photographing the Masai tribes and their lives become enmeshed in those of the people they have come to visit. Directed by Lamont Johnson, this cross-cultural tale of how a father and his son achieve a healthy relationship in the picturesque African veldt is a good family experience, though some parents may not appreciate a brief skinny-dip in the wilds. A-II (G)

Visiting Hours (1982) Minimal Canadian effort at a horror movie with Lee Grant playing a woman terrorized by beefy maniac Michael Ironside. Directed by Jean Claude Lord, the stupid plot is frequently revolting and has not a single redeeming quality. O (R)

Visitors, The (1971) Two recent parolees from prison for rape and murder committed in Vietnam visit a third vet who testified against them at their trial, now living on a farm with his common-law wife, and after interminable tension, the final, inevitable scenes of rape and violence occur. Directed by Elia Kazan, the story's pessimism is as deep and dark as its moral perspective is shallow and glossy. O (R)

Viva Italia (1978) Bland anthology film featuring several stories done by directors Mario Monicelli, Dino Risi and Ettore Scola, with such stars as Vittorio Gassman, Alberto Sordi, and Ugo Tognazzi. Most of the incidents are comic, ranging from moderately amusing to boring and tasteless, with the serious vignettes faring not much better. Coarse language and humor. A-III (R)

Viva Knievel (1977) Flamboyant mortorcycle stuntman Evel Knievel gets the chance to play himself in a rather innocent and sentimental little melodrama which presents its folk hero as instrumental in reuniting a father and his young son as well as thwarting a gang of narcotics smugglers. Directed by Gordon Douglas, it is for the young and very undemanding. A-II (PG)

Viva la Muerte (1973) Written and directed by avant-garde playwright Fernando Arrabal, this is an impassioned, surrealistic expression of growing up during the Spanish Civil War. The movie's central experience (which is autobiographical) concerns a youngster's growing realization that his mother has betrayed his father into the hands of the local fascists. Some viewers will be repelled by its emotional ferocity and pervasive imagery of seduction, mutilation, degradation and sexual fantasies. O (nr)

Viva Max (1969)   Peter Ustinov plays a bumbling Mexican general who recaptures the Alamo with a hundred equally bumbling soldiers while Jonathan Winters as a National Guard general mainly battles the witless script. Director Jerry Paris simply misses the mark in trying to expand a single gag into a feature comedy. A-I (G)

Vixen (1969)   Sex exploitation movie directed by Russ Meyers alludes to such social issues as racial prejudice, the draft and politics as an excuse to offer graphic displays of adultery, lesbianism, incest and an attempted rape. O (X/R)

Vladimir and Rosa (1971)   Low budget, politically-committed French film dealing with the 1969 Chicago Conspiracy Trial as part of the process in changing the capitalistic system. Director Jean-Luc Godard's work possesses a coherence of style and content (and even some humor) but as political propaganda, it is preaching only to the already converted. A-IV (nr)

Voices (1979)   Young singer (Michael Ontkean) and a deaf girl (Amy Irving) who wants to be a dancer fall in love but the story is slight and the dialogue often ludicrous. A subplot involving the hero's raucous all-male family is so awkwardly handled by director Robert Markowitz that it is at best a distraction. Ambiguous view of pre-marital sex and a suggestive dance sequence. A-III (PG)

Volcano (1977)   Director Donald Brittain's documentary reconstructs the life of Malcom Lowry, author of "Under the Volcano," who died from an overdose of sleeping pills in 1957, relying upon interviews with family, friends and associates and by visiting places where he had lived in England, the United States, Mexico and Canada. The short passages read by Richard Burton from his novel are too few for one to gain any sense of the work's literary merit, but anyone interested in literature or in people will find it a fascinating experience of life on the edge. A-II (nr)

Volunteers (1985)   Supposedly madcap adventures of Peace Corps volunteers (John Candy and Tom Hanks) in the jungles of Thailand range from dull to vapid in a mindless comedy directed by Nicholas Meyer. Some nudity and vulgarity are the sole, albeit offensive, punctuations in a simplistic story about evading a gambling debt. O (R)

Von Richthofen and Brown (1971)   Director Roger Corman's anti-war extravaganza makes camera fodder out of the air aces of World War I (John Phillip Law and Don Stroud are the opposing aviators of the title). Though director Roger Corman's movie has stilted dialogue and wooden acting, it is saved by the excellence of its biplane footage. The planes dominate the screen, making an interesting contrast to more familiar scenes of modern warfare's carefully programmed annihilation of distant, dehumanized enemies. A-II (GP)

Von Ryan's Express (1965)   Fast-paced World War II action thriller focuses on some prisoners-of-war (with Frank Sinatra as their leader) who escape by train through the Italian Alps into Switzerland. Directed by Mark Robson, the movie has a fine international supporting cast and moments of high excitement, though some scenes are played too heavily for laughs and patriotism. A-I (br)

Voyage of Silence (1968)   Impressive French drama about the victimization of illegal Portuguese workers who slip across the border seeking work in France. Directed by Christian de Chalogne, it shows the aloofness of society and its institutions in the face of suffering and exploitation. An important work on social justice. A-II (br)

Voyage of the Damned (1977)   Fact-based story about a German ship carrying some 900 Jewish refugees on the eve of World War II but were denied entry by Cuba and the United States. Director Stuart Rosenberg has turned the tragedy into sluggish melodrama with a disjointed script and an all-star cast (including Faye Dunaway, Oskar Werner and Max Von Sydow). Frank treatment of a couple's marital problems. A-III (PG)

Voyage to Grand Tartarie (1978)   Failed French satire in which a young man (Jean-Luc Bideau), whose wife is the victim of a random killing, drops everything and embarks on a wild, eccentric journey through France beset with all sorts of social, political, spiritual and physical ills. Director Jean-Charles Tacchella's effort lacks both humor and perception as well as makes excessive use of nudity. O (nr)

Vulture, The (1966)   Low-budget, unimaginative science fiction movie written and directed by Lawrence Huntington with Akim Tamiroff in the cliched role of mad scientist. For undemanding viewers only. A-I (br)

W

W (1974)   Ridiculous B-grade suspense thriller in which Twiggy plods through her role as the nervous heroine being terrorized by her mad ex-husband (Dirk Benedict) who has escaped from prison after his conviction for her murder. Directed by Richard Quine, the senseless plot is only an excuse for putting a vulnerable young woman at the mercy of a maniacal sadist. Some feeble psychological and physical violence. A-III (PG)

Wacky World of Mother Goose (1968)   Animated fantasy in which Mother Goose (voice of Margaret Rutherford) leaves all her nursery rhyme characters to visit her sister on the moon but they are imprisoned by a wicked count and she has to come to the rescue. Very young children may enjoy all the movie's repetitions but parents will find it rather dull and unimaginative. A-I (br)

Waco (1966)   Routine Western directed by R.G. Springsteen in which a gunslinger (Howard Keel) is reformed by his former girl friend (Jane Russell) and her minister husband (Wendell Corey). Stylized violence. A-II (br)

Wait Until Dark (1967)   Audrey Hepburn stars as a recently blinded housewife who undergoes a harrowing trial when three men (Alan Arkin, Richard Crenna and Jack Weston) invade her apartment in search of a doll containing a cache of heroin. Director Terence Young's adaptation of Frederick Knott's hit play is scripted and edited with such intensity that even its slightly incredible elements pass in a taut suspense melodrama for all but the youngest members of the family. A-II (br)

Waiting for Caroline (1969)   Canadian version of the old story about the girl (Alexandra Stewart) who can't make up her mind which of her two lovers to marry and in the end gets neither. Writer-director Ron Kelly is more interested in social comment than making the characters interesting, let alone credible. Some nudity. O (nr)

Walk in the Shadow (1966)   Good British movie of rights in conflict when a father's religious beliefs cause him to refuse a blood transfusion for his daughter and her death results in his being put on trial. Director Basil Dearden builds the situation with precision and fairness to all concerned until, after the verdict, it reveals its own point of view. A-II (br)

Walk in the Spring Rain, A (1970) Happily married professor (Fritz Weaver) takes a sabbatical to write a book in the Great Smoky Mountains where his wife (Ingrid Bergman) finds herself falling in love with the kind, earthy handyman (Anthony Quinn). Directed by Guy Green, it's a slow-moving, old-fashioned sentimental melodrama that romantics will love and others dismiss as a tearjerker. A-III (PG)

Walk Proud (1979) Sensitive but inarticulate Chicano youth (Robby Benson), trapped in a morass of machismo and gang warfare in Los Angeles, tries to go straight when he falls in love with a dentist's daughter. Under Robert Collins' direction, Benson is just not credible as a Chicano, and he and his gang are a singularly elderly collection of teenagers. Some violence. A-III (PG)

Walk with Love and Death, A (1969) Failed medieval romance about two young lovers (Anjelica Huston and Assaf Dayan) caught in the midst of a peasant's war and doomed to death either by knight's sword or serf's cudgel. Directed by John Huston, the dark atmosphere of feudalism is convincing but little else is, especially the acting of its two young principals. Mature theme and treatment. A-III (PG)

Walk, Don't Run (1966) Cary Grant is the main attraction in this genial situation comedy about a rooming shortage during the Tokyo Olympics where he serves as matchmaker for room-mates Samantha Eggar and Jim Hutton. Director Charles Walters brings off the sight gags and zany dialogue in relaxed style. A-III (br)

Walkabout (1971) Australian story of a lovely teenager (Jenny Agutter) and her six-year-old brother (Lucien John) who, stranded deep in the wilderness after their father commits suicide, are rescued by a young aborigine (David Gumpilil) who leads them to eventual safety. Nicolas Roeg does better with his stunning location photography than he does with his heavy-handed direction of a movie that practically shouts out its theme of noble savagery. Extended nude swimming scene and the aborigine's suicide are questionable elements. A-IV (R/GP appeal)

Walker (1987) Mangled story of William Walker, the American adventurer who overthrew the Nicaraguan government in 1855 and set up his own corrupt regime until deposed two years later. The potential drama of these historical events is ignored by director Alex Cox who treats the events instead in an exaggerated style closer to slapstick than satire or surrealism. Muddled treatment of a past episode of contemporary political significance, much graphic violence and some sexual references. A-IV (R)

Walking Stick, The (1970) Young girl crippled with polio (Samantha Eggar) is courted and won by a persistent young artist (David Hemmings) who is obviously not as sincere in his affections as he appears. Director Eric Till proceeds with such a heavy hand that any subtleties are lost in a welter of dramatic close-ups and romantic bursts of color photography. A-III (PG)

Walking Tall (1973) Fact-based story of Tennessee sheriff Buford Pusser (Joe Don Baker) who walks tall and clubs freely in his campaign to close down rural vice in the county where he lives as well as root out the accomodating political corruption that allows the vice to flourish. Nice objectives but the means used to achieve them in director Phil Karlson's dramatization are ignoble, ugly and downright vicious. Super-violent rendering of a noxious vigilante message. O (R)

Walking Tall, Part II (see: "Part II, Walking Tall")

Walkover (1969) Polish drama directed by Jerzy Skolimowski carries on the story of "Identification Marks: None" whose young hero is now making a meager living as a boxer unable to get a factory job. Scheduled to fight a tough ring opponent, he flees town but returns to face the challenge, and presumably the challenge of life in a socialist state. Its theme of alienation and its episodic presentation serve to disorient the viewer but the work leads to a positive conclusion of self-awareness. A-II (nr)

Wall in Jerusalem, A (1972) Excellent documentary account of the birth of the state of Israel in 1948, and its struggle for survival ever since, limits itself chiefly to political history, detailing various major events and the leaders who participated in them. Director Frederic Rossif's compilation of archival footage makes a fascinating visual chronicle and Richard Burton's narration lets the images communicate the emotion while it understates the facts. A-I (nr)

Wall Street (1987) An earnest young stockbroker (Charlie Sheen) wants to make an honest million but a financial wheeler-dealer (Michael Douglas) teaches him that there are easier ways to make money than working for it. Directed by Oliver Stone, the cautionary tale does a creditable job in showing how part of the financial community has made greed a way of life but is somewhat unconvincing in its dramatization of the corruption of an innocent and his ultimate redemption. Several scenes depicting sexual activity and some very rough language. A-IV (R)

Wanda (1971) Low-budget but impressive portrait of a woman, a nobody wandering through life conditioned to being badly used by others, who meets an insecure petty thief (Michael Higgins) and the two go off together, leaving viewers hoping this relationship will turn out better than her other experiences. Directed by and starring Barbara Loden, the movie succeeds in making an unvarnished plea for understanding the needs of isolated, impoverished human beings. A-III (GP)

Wanda Nevada (1979) Laid-back gambler (Peter Fonda who also directs) wins an orphan (Brooke Shields) in a poker game and then goes hunting for gold with her in the Grand Canyon. Indian ghosts and a couple of flesh and blood villains complicate matters, but not enough to make things interesting. Some violence and the unresolved nature of the relationship between the two principals make this aimless movie adult fare. A-III (PG)

Wanderer, The (1969) French screen version of the Alain-Fournier novel about the romantic illusions of youth melting into the realities and responsibilities of adulthood in a story focusing on the one boy in the class who never quite matures and ultimately brings tragedy to those he loves most. Director Jean-Gabriel Albicocco has beautifully filmed the simple narrative, conveying well the glow of nostalgia of the adult narrator remembering the years of growing up. A-II (G)

Wanderers, The (1979) Screen version of the

novel by Richard Price about a group of Italian teenagers growing up in the Bronx in 1963 has a lot of vitality and some good acting (Ken Wahl, John Friedrich, Karen Allen). Philip Kaufman's direction, however, is too pretentious to stir any real emotional response in a movie that lacks a significant context. Violence, sexual references and foul language. O (R)

Wannsee Conference, The (1987) German dramatization of the meeting held on January 20, 1942, at which the final decision was made by the Nazi leadership to exterminate all European Jews. Directed by Heinz Schirk, it is an historical document filled with anti-Semitic statements but the brutish manner of the participants shows them clearly as racists. Mature theme and treatment. A-III (nr)

Wanted Dead or Alive (1987) Bounty hunter (Rutger Hauer) tracks down a ruthless international terrorist (Gene Simmons), but is then set up as bait, loses his best friend and his lover, resulting in his inflicting a terrible vengeance on those responsible. Its rough language, bloodshed and brutality are not redeemed by director Gary Sherman's eye-for-an-eye brand of justice. O (R)

War and Peace (1968) Massive Russian version of the Tolstoy novel, originally released in three parts, evokes both the feeling of an era (1805 Russia threatened by Napoleon's march east) and Tolstoy's vision of individuals and destiny. Directed by and starring Sergei Bondarchuk as the contemplative Pierre, the movie in its sweep and detail provides an absorbing visual rendition of a great classic. A-I (GP)

War Between Men and Women, The (1972) Caustic cartoonist with failing eyesight (Jack Lemmon) hates women, children and dogs, and naturally succumbs to the charms of a divorcee (Barbara Harris) who has three children and a terrier. Losing his sight completely, he is overtaken by a bout of self-pity that cuts him off from wife and children. Written and directed by Melville Shavelson, it tries to wring humor and pathos out of a human tragedy by using casual profanity, misanthropic wit and finally cloying sentimentality. A-III (PG)

War Between the Planets (1971) Italian sci-fi programmer about the choleric commander (Jack Stuart) of a space expedition whose mission is to destroy a gaseous asteroid that is causing tidal waves and other catastrophic destruction on Earth. Director Anthony Dawson tries to compensate for his undernourished script by using low-budget special effects but they don't hide the fact that this is a colossal clunker. A-I (G)

War Devils, The (1973) Routine Italian action movie with Guy Madison leading a squadron of U.S. paratroopers behind German lines in Tunisia but he turns the mission into a personal battle between himself and the German commander (Van Tenney). Director Bert Albertini serves up World War II according to the war-is-fun formula with a lot of special effects flourishes. A-III (PG)

War Game, The (1967) British docudrama about the effects of nuclear warfare on a civilian population features non-professionals in realistically simulated scenes. Produced, written and directed by Peter Watkins, the movie gets considerable shock value from its hypothetical events but in making the unthinkable appear possible, it raises important questions of public concern. A-III (br)

War Games (see: "Suppose They Gave a War and Nobody Came?")

War of the Gargantuas (1970) Below average Japanese monster movie about a scientist (Russ Tamblyn) whose experiments on a baby ape go awry and it and a companion grow large enough to crush the city of Tokyo. Director Inoshiro Honda relies on nature and the special effects crew to resolve the difficulty, while leaving a few cardboard buildings standing for a sequel. A-I (G)

War Wagon, The (1967) Familiar Western story stars John Wayne as a supertough hombre recently let out of jail and bent on avenging the dastardly deeds of Kirk Douglas, the gunman who framed him and took away his land. Director Burt Kennedy mixes some comedy with the rough, he-man action. A-II (br)

Warehouse (1974) Strange Japanese story of a blind sculptor who kidnaps a beautiful model and imprisons her in his hidden studio where she becomes as obsessed as he with tactile sensations, leading to tragedy for both. As an allegory on the consequences of enslavement to the senses, director Yasuzo Masumura's treatment will please neither hedonist nor puritan, but its technical virtuosity in creating the intensely physical world of a mad artist does have some interest. A-IV (nr)

WarGames (1983) Good teen suspense thriller about a high school computer-wizard (Matthew Broderick) who breaks into a government nuclear-strategy computer and starts playing a war game whose logical conclusion is nuclear Armageddon. Directed by John Badham, the story loses much of its momentum when the program's designer (John Wood) is tracked down and points out the just desserts of human folly just before the slack conclusion. A few vulgar expletives. A-II (PG)

Warlords of Atlantis (1978) Innocuous British adventure with two young scientists (Doug McClure and Peter Gilmore) who find themselves in the power of the rulers of an undersea kingdom where they encounter a beautiful and apparently ageless princess (Cyd Charisse). Directed by Kevin Connor, there's plenty of paper-mache monsters, wooden dialogue and leaden comic relief. A-II (PG)

Warm December, A (1973) Black doctor (Sidney Poitier) is racing motorcycles on a vacation in England when he runs across the gorgeous niece of an African ambassador (Ester Anderson), falls in love but then learns she is dying of sickle cell anemia. Also directed by Poitier, the romantic melodrama is laid on with a sledgehammer to the tune of "Love Story" and its entertainment appeal is limited to devotees of the TV soaps. A-III (PG)

Warning Shot (1966) Story begins interestingly as a social drama about a policeman (David Janssen) who kills a highly-regarded public figure. From there the movie turns into a routine detective thriller directed by Buzz Kulik with little suspense but more than a little violence. A-II (br)

Warning Sign (1985) An accident in a genetic engineering lab where biological warfare experiments are being carried on causes those inside to be transformed into crazed zombies save for a lone security guard (Kathleen Quinlan). Written and directed by Hal Barwood, it is a run-of-the-mill exercise in gory violence. O (R)

Warriors, The (1979) Screen version of Sol Yurick's novel about a youth gang trying to make their way back to their own neighborhood through a New York City in which every hand is turned against them. Directed by Walter Hill, the gang's sordid adventures are of even less interest than its one-dimensional characters and their stilted dialogue. Constant violence and glorification of vicious behavior. O (R)

Watched! (1974) Interesting independent production about a drug case prosecutor (Stacy Keach) who is set up by his own agents after he begins to have second thoughts about the legality of their surveillance methods. Written and directed by John Parsons, the movie suggests that bugging has become a way of life in America, with some well-executed scenes of extra-legal surveillance techniques. A-III (R)

Watcher in the Woods, The (1980) Mediocre Disney suspense thriller in which an American teenager (Lynn-Holly Johnson) staying in a gloomy English country house tries to solve the mystery of what happened to the teenage girl who disappeared from the house 30 years before. Directed by John Hough, the script and its mystery are rather banal but the movie does have its frightening moments. Though too scary for pre-teens, its primary appeal is to younger teenagers. A-II (PG)

Water (1986) This adult comedy is funnier on paper as Michael Caine stars as the frustrated governor of an underdeveloped island nation in the Caribbean. Prosperity and independence are achieved only after diuretic mineral water and oil are discovered at a defunct U.S. drilling rig. Ethnic jokes, TV sitcom-style humor and sexual innuendo predominate as "Water" oozes rather than bubbles. A-III (PG-13)

Waterhole No. 3 (1967) When the fastest con artist in the West (James Coburn) lifts a thief's wallet containing a map to a cache of stolen gold, he lights out for the loot with the robber in pursuit and the Army pursuing him. Directed by William Graham, the tone of the movie is coarse, bawdy and frequently just plain crude. O (br)

Waterloo (1971) Stately, grandiose set piece recreates Napoleon's return from exile on Elba to his final defeat at Waterloo. Director Sergei Bondarchuk reduces the two principal opponents, Napoleon (Rod Steiger) and Wellington (Christopher Plummer), to little more than historical caricatures speaking the famous epigrams attributed to them. Yet the movie comes alive in the broad, colorful sweep of action sequences showing an epic moment in European history. A-II (G)

Watermelon Man (1970) When a mindlessly bigoted white (Godfrey Cambridge) one night turns black, he undergoes the indignities and injustices of white America. Unfortunately, in dealing with all-too-familiar racial stereotypes (sexual, musical, commercial), director Melvin Van Peebles' satire is crude, embarrassing, and at times consciously offensive. Though terribly uneven, it at least attempts to deal with the festering ulcer of everyday racial prejudice. A-IV (R)

Watership Down (1978) British animated adaptation of Richard Adams' popular novel about a band of brave rabbits making a dangerous journey in search of a new home has been done with taste and intelligence under Martin Rosen's direction. Some of the voices belong to John Hurt, Ralph Richardson, Denholm Elliot and Harry Andrews, with Zero Mostel providing comic relief as a zany German seagull. Some scenes may be too intense for younger children. A-II (PG)

Wattstax (1973) Exciting documentary directed by Mel Stuart with rock, jazz, and general all-around soul performers (Issac Hayes, The Staple Singers, Bar-Kays), centering around the black experience and, in particular, the Los Angeles community of Watts. Giving it continuity is a funny but sad and, at times, raunchy commentary by Richard Pryor. A-III (R)

Way, Way Out! (1966) Jerry Lewis movie about a trip to the moon is preoccupied with sex in its dialogue, costuming and situations. O (br)

Way We Live Now, The (1970) Advertising agency director (Nicholas Pryor), separated from his wife, has long conversations with himself and imaginary famous visitors but his time is mostly given to stalking and bedding women. Written, produced, directed and photographed by Barry Brown, the incessant talk is pretentious and the long string of sexual adventures tedious but exploitative. O (R)

Way We Were, The (1973) Robert Redford and Barbra Streisand as ill-matched lovers in a serio-comic story sweeping from Ivy League idylls in the late 1930s into World War II and on to Hollywood in the post-war era of blacklisting. There is just too much material here for anyone to put into a coherent shape, and director Sydney Pollack succumbs to the temptation of trivializing the period and their events in favor of the sheer glamour of it all. It's slick and shallow but romantics may find it diverting. A-III (PG)

Way West, The (1967) Fairly good pioneer Western with Kirk Douglas as a harried wagon-master trying to get a wagon train of Western settlers through the mountains and past Indian perils. Director Andrew V. McLaglen gets rugged acting support from Richard Widmark and Robert Mitchum, with Lola Albright on hand for the boys to fight over. A-III (br)

W.C. Fields and Me (1976) Directed by Arthur Hiller, this story of the romance between the Hollywood comedian (Rod Steiger) and Carlotta Monti (Valerie Perrine) distorts the people and events of an era shamelessly and has a tone of leering vulgarity that destroys any pretense of serious intent. O (PG)

We All Loved Each Other So Much (1977) Warm and moving Italian comedy about three men (Vittorio Gassman, Nino Manfredi and Stefano Satta Flores) who love the same woman (Stefania Sandrelli) at one time or another, with varying degrees of intensity, over the course of three decades. Directed by Ettore Scola, it is a rare, wise and entertaining movie on the theme of love and friendship. A-II (PG)

We Will All Meet in Paradise (1978) Thin French comedy about the life and times of four overaged, overindulged, middle-class Dead End Kids (Jean Rochfort, Claude Brasseur, Guy Bedos, and Victor Lanoux) as they go through a round of sophomoric escapades. Directed by Yves Robert, the result is a tepid comedy of manners whose sole merit is the considerable charm of the performers. Adultery figures in the plot. A-III (PG)

Wedding, A (1978) Some 20 major characters, and perhaps twice as many minor ones, assemble for a satiric assault on the extravagance of a wedding in a family recently risen to affluence. With no central plot worth mentioning, director Robert Altman lets the action go in every direction at once, much of it revolving around the many skeletons in the family closet. The actors (among them, Lillian Gish, John Cromwell, Vittorio Gassman, Dina Merrill, Howard Duff, Carol Burnett and Paul Dooley) are better than the material in this extremely uneven effort that is further marred by sexual goings on and gratuitous nudity. O (R)

Wedding in Blood (1974) Disappointing French crime story about a couple (Stephane Audran and Michel Piccoli) who, drawn together by an almost incendiary passion, conspire to murder their spouses. Instead of trying to create a truly chilling horror movie out of this story of forbidden desire and desperate murder, director Claude Chabrol uses it to express his moralistic views on the middle class and their loss of values. A-III (PG)

Wedding in White (1973) Hard-edged but compassionate Canadian drama set in a small town during World War II tells the story of a father (Donald Pleasence) who, learning his teenage daughter (Carol Kane) is pregnant after an assault by a drunken soldier, persuades his best friend (Leo Phillips), a bachelor in his mid-fifties, to marry the girl, thereby saving the family reputation. Director William Fruet uses the situation to focus on the limited horizons and narrow attitudes of small-town life which proves just as much a closed society as the nearby prisoner-of-war camp where the father works. A-IV (R)

Wedding Night (1970) Irish movie about a young Catholic woman (Tessa Wyatt) whose fears of sex and pregnancy make her unable to consummate her marriage. Directed by Piers Haggard, the story is told in strong and pointed discussions of the contraceptive pill, morality, the medical profession and an uncomprehending husband. Thoughtful drama about a deeply emotional subject, but offers no positive solutions. A-IV (PG)

Wedding Party, The (1969) Unsure about marrying his fiancee (Jill Clayburgh), a prospective bridegroom (Charles Pfluger) tries a variety of ruses to call off the wedding. Directed by Cynthia Munroe, Brian De Palma and Wilford Leach, the low-budget black-and-white production tries all kinds of camera tricks but can't save its hodge-podge of comedy, satire and fantasy. A-III (nr)

Wednesday's Child (1972) British dramatization of the gradual psychic destruction of a young woman (Sandy Ratcliff) by her repressive working-class parents and by the behaviorist theories practiced on her in a government-run mental hospital. Written by David Mercer and directed by Kenneth Loach, the result is a plea for respect for the individuality of the person that is a powerfully moving, incontrovertible statement. A-III (nr)

Weekend (1968) Apocalyptic French vision of modern civilization's self-destruction is contructed out of a disjointed narrative of motorized mayhem, dehumanized people and mindless revolution. Directed by Jean-Luc Godard, the movie's attempts to shock and its static militant speeches become simplistic attacks on traditional morality and existing social values. O (nr)

Weekend Murders (1972) Routine Italian mystery movie in which the relatives (among them, Anna Moffo) of a deceased British earl gather at his plush estate to learn of their legacies, fall prey to grisly pranks, sexual dalliances and ultimately five murders. The real villain of the piece is director Michele Lupo, who indulges in acute camera angles, and wears out his zoom lens in a supreme display of technique over talent. A-III (R)

Weekend Pass (1984) Four sailors just out of boot camp hit Los Angeles on a weekend pass in this mediocre effort. Writer-director Lawrence Bassoff has put a variety of Los Angeles back-grounds to good use, but his script is thoroughly pedestrian. Although veering toward romantic wholesomeness, some graphic, utterly gratuitous nudity in an early cabaret sequence is highly offensive. O (R)

Weekend at Dunkirk (1966) French sergeant (Jean-Paul Belmondo), among the mass of troops trapped by the Germans in the Dunkirk pocket in June 1940, has to decide whether to try to escape with the British, desert and return home or stay and be captured. Directed by Henri Verneuil, the beaches of Dunkirk were a bitter French defeat and this movie is a grim picture of war without any of the usual movie heroics. A-III (br)

Weekend with the Babysitter (1970) Low-budget exploitation movie about a suburban husband's marijuana smoking with the family's teen-age sitter while his wife shoots heroin with cut-throat drug smugglers. Sexual activity predominates in a ludicrous script with amateur actors. O (R)

Weird Science (1985) Two high school nerds conjure up their idea of the perfect woman (Kelly LeBrock) on a computer and have all their dreams of popularity and wild adventure fulfilled. Essentially a one-joke affair, written with an excess of rough language and directed with too many sexual inferences by John Hughes, it's a vulgar, mediocre effort which does a hard sell of promiscuity to teenagers. O (PG-13)

Welcome Home, Soldier Boys (1972) Four Vietnam vets (Joe Don Baker, Alan Vint, Paul Koslo and Elliott Street) pull into the sleepy hamlet of Hope, New Mexico, gang-rape a girl, kill everyone in town and then burn it to the ground. Directed by Richard Compton, the gruesome and ultimately cynical movie contributes nothing to understanding the problems of Vietnam veterans. O (R)

Welcome to L.A. (1977) Listless and pretentious account of the amorous adventures of a young song writer (Keith Carradine) whose charm is such that women jostle and trample one another in a mad rush to enjoy his favor. Writer-director Alan Rudolph's unsurprising message is that sex without love is unrewarding and that Los Angeles has some sort of monopoly on self-deception. Gratuitous nudity. O (R)

Welcome to the Club (1971) Generally witless comedy about a naive Quaker morale officer (Brian Foley) who attempts to integrate a postwar Hiroshima officer's club, and comes off more as a fool than as a nice guy going through some sobering disillusionment. Directed by William Shenson, the result is rather depressing and, whatever its good intentions in trying to satirize both the military and bigotry, it contains considerable offensiveness, notably foul language. O (R)

West Side Story (1961) Rousing Broadway musical, with choreography by Jerome Robbins and music by Leonard Bernstein, is a contemporary, inner-city adaptation of the classic Romeo and Juliet theme, in which Richard Beymer and Natalie Wood play Tony and Maria, the star-crossed lovers set apart ethnically and by their opposing street gang backgrounds. Directed by Robert Wise, the movie captures the grit of life in the city's lower depths, with glimmers of hope and elements of tragedy in a delicate balance. In terms of energy and verve, its songs and the dance numbers are outstanding. Some of the social issues, relationships and street language, however, require a fairly mature sensibility on the part of the viewer. A-III (br)

Westworld (1973) James Brolin and Richard Benjamin vacation in a futuristic resort where, during the fun and games, a Western gunslinger robot (Yul Brynner) malfunctions, turns on the vacationers and starts to stalk them. Unfortunately, after about ten minutes, writer-director Michael Crichton has explored all the subtleties of the one-idea situation. Some ludicrous nonsense about "willing" female robots. A-III (PG)

Wetherby (1985) Vanessa Redgrave plays a schoolteacher in a small town who becomes the indirect victim of an act of violence that seems to be wholly unprovoked. But was it? This superbly acted but somewhat thin and contrived murder mystery, written and directed by playwright David Hare, explores the question of suicide in a careful, literate and sometimes compelling fashion. Good entertainment for mature viewers, although there is some violence and a few fairly restrained bedroom scenes. A-III (R)

Whales of August, The (1987) Two aged sisters (Bette Davis and Lillian Gish), sharing a cottage on an island off the coast of Maine, rely upon each other since one is blind but wealthy and the other is poor but kind. Director Lindsay Anderson's picture of old age and sibling rivalries is finely told through mood and characterization, and though sentimental, it is full of heart and small truths. Some incidental profanity. A-II (nr)

What? (1973) Innocent young woman (Sydne Rome) wanders into the house of an eccentric millionaire (Hugh Griffith) and is assaulted by various perverted characters, stripped of her identity as well as her clothes and spends the rest of the movie in various stages of undress. Director Roman Polanski apparently intended this bizarre Alice in Wonderland story to be amusing but its gross sexual activity and extensive nudity, as well as some violently scabrous language, make it anything but. O (X/R)

What a Way to Die (see: "Beyond Control")

What Am I Bid? (1967) The son of a country music star decides to forgo cattle auctioneering and launch his own singing career is the thin story line used to showcase some old and new talent in the world of country and western music. Written and directed by Gene Nash, it's pleasant if unimaginative entertainment. A-I (br)

What Became of Jack and Jill? (1972) Paul Nicholas and Vanessa Howard are the title characters who gruesomely plot the death of Jack's 78-year-old grandmother (Mona Washbourne) so they can enjoy London with the old lady's money. The moral of this rather improbable, mediocre little horror is offset by director Bill Blain's sleazy resort to a lot of ogling, pawing and some attic sex. O (GP)

What Did You Do in the War, Daddy? (1966) The combination of bosomy Italian girls and a local wine festival sidetrack a platoon of invading G.I.s' (Dick Shawn, Carroll O'Connor, James Coburn, Cameron Mitchell and Aldo Ray) who are supposed to be out after Nazi troops. Directed by Blake Edwards, vulgarity and dumb sight gags are the order of the day in a movie presumably showing that war isn't hellish at all but just a lot of off-color fun. O (br)

What Do You Say to a Naked Lady? (1970) Allen Funt employs the familiar hidden camera techniques of the TV show, except that here he focuses on nudity as a supposed source of humor. Unfortunately, the use of unsuspecting victims confronted with completely naked men and women walking out of office elevators or flagging down taxis shows no more maturity or insight than the silly pranks on the TV show. O (X/R)

What Next? (1970) Swedish exploitation movie about a prostitute, her incestuous relationship with her father, her blackmail of the man who killed him and her purification in a flaming finale which only adds to the repugnance of the proceedings. O (nr)

What's Good for the Goose (1970) Failed British movie in which a glum bank manager (Norman Wisdom) is introduced to the psychedelic world of free love, loud music and general aimlessness by an uninhibited hitchhiker (Sally Geeson) who is always ready to disrobe and jump into bed. Directed by Menahem Golan, the movie's attempt to pass this off as social comment fails to overcome the exploitative elements that predominate. O (R)

What's New Pussycat? (1965) Wacky plot about a demented psychiatrist (Peter Sellers) whose efforts to sort out his hectic life bring him into contact with an inordinate number of loony types (Peter O'Toole, Paula Prentiss, Capuchine, Woody Allen and Ursula Andress) running free and easy, in and around Paris. Directed by Clive Donner, the laughs in this attempt at screwball comedy are only intermittent and their taste level is abysmally low. O (br)

What's So Bad About Feeling Good (1968) Colorful tropical bird infects the rude, scowling citizens of New York City with a mysterious happiness virus and within hours everyone is smiling and polite to one another, including George Peppard and Mary Tyler Moore playing reformed hippies. But when New Yorkers also quit gambling, smoking and drinking, the government develops an antidote to protect their tax revenues. Produced and directed by George Seaton, it's an amusing little satire on urban life that some may find infectious. Romantic complications. A-III (br)

What's the Matter with Helen? (1971) Two mothers (Debbie Reynolds and Shelley Winters) with a troubled past start a dance school for children in 1930s Hollywood until poor Shelley goes bonkers and puts her entire rabbit warren to the knife. Director Curtis Harrington has a lot of fun with the gaudy period settings and fashions but mixes in a bit too much blood and gore for younger viewers, but they wouldn't appreciate Reynolds' tap dances and tangos anyway. A-III (GP)

What's Up Tiger Lily? (1966) Woody Allen's re-editing and dubbing of a Japanese spy movie is at times amusing, often self-conscious but mostly tiresome. Some smutty dialogue and visuals. O (br)

What's Up, Doc? (1972) Funny, stylish and entertaining comedy loosely strings two plots together, one involving a group of four identical valises, the other following a kooky student (Barbra Streisand) in her zany pursuit of an absent-minded college professor (Ryan O' Neal) who has come to San Francisco with his persistent fiancee (Madeline Kahn) to receive a research grant. Produced and directed by Peter Bogdanovich, this throwback to the Hollywood screwball comedies of the 1930s is great fun for family audiences. A-I (G)

Whatever Happened to Aunt Alice? (1969) Suspense thriller with Geraldine Page as a widow, left without any observable means of income, who combines murder and gardening as profitable pastimes in bilking a series of housekeepers out of their life savings. Routine chiller directed by Lee H. Katzin. A-II (PG)

When a Stranger Calls (1979) Homicidal maniac (Tony Beckley) stalks a babysitter (Carol Kane) in this plodding, mediocre thriller directed by Fred Walton. Some intense violence and the impending threat of violence are adult fare. A-III (R)

When Dinosaurs Ruled the Earth (1971) British production directed by Val Guest is a few cuts above the average prehistoric monster movie which, aside from some Hollywood bikinis on the cavewomen, has some authentic-looking overgrown reptiles, birds, and dinosaurs. It's an enjoyable movie for the youngsters, not too scary and colorful enough to hold their attention. A-I (G)

When Eight Bells Toll (1971) British adaptation of an Alistair MacLean novel about a Bond-type government agent (Anthony Hopkins) and his gentle partner (Corin Redgrave) who are dispatched to the Western Highland lochs to find out what lies behind the disappearance of several gold-carrying ships. Directed by Etienne Perier, the plot employs masterful twists and cross currents, but though handled with restraint, it is adult fare both in story and treatment. A-III (GP)

When Father Was Away on Business (1985) Yugoslavian production set in the time of Tito's break with the Soviet Union, has a plot following a philandering husband who is denounced by his mistress as a political deviant and ends up in a labor camp. This warm human comedy by director Emir Kusturica ends in the resolution of personal problems and political differences during a madcap wedding feast of family forgiveness. Some coarse language and partial nudity are treated with restraint. A-III (R)

When the Legends Die (1972) Above average Western in which a sharp rodeo hustler (Richard Widmark) takes in an 18-year-old Ute Indian (Frederic Forrest) and teaches him the tricks of the trade but the youth does not see the value in taking money from suckers and returns to the reservation, sadder but wiser. Produced and directed by Stuart Millar, the fine character study of the two principals is chiefly what is of interest here, and not its commonplace message. Implied sexual affair. A-III (PG)

When Time Ran Out (1980) Paul Newman, Jacqueline Bisset, Burgess Meredith, Ernest Borgnine and other unfortunates are trapped on a Pacific island when the local volcano lets go. Directed by James Goldstone, the disaster epic is so dreadful that it could put an end to the disaster epic once and for all, though it probably won't. A-II (PG)

When You Comin' Back, Red Ryder? (1979) A half-crazed Vietnam vet (Marjoe Gortner) and his hippie girl friend (Candy Clark) terrorize and humiliate five people (notably Lee Grant and Pat Hingle) in a roadside diner in a desolate region of New Mexico. Though there are some credible performances in this adaptation of Mark Medoff's play directed by Milton Katselas, its psychological as well as physical violence and frequent sexual crudities destroy whatever social comment may have been intended. O (R)

Where Angels Go...Trouble Follows! (1968) Weak sequel to "The Trouble with Angels" in which a liberal young nun (Stella Stevens) tries to update the convent boarding school headed by a traditionalist Mother Superior (Rosalind Russell) by leading a busload of nuns and their students to a peace rally. Directed by James Neilson, the old pros overcome the painfully contrived story and turn it into light, unsophisticated entertainment. A-I (G)

Where Does It Hurt? (1972) Failed comedy about a slick California hospital whose administrator (Peter Sellers) divides his time between fleecing unwitting patients and molesting the pretty females on the staff. Directed by Rod Amateau, the result is not only unfunny, but unrelentingly tasteless and offensive. O (R)

Where Eagles Dare (1969) A spy-counter-spy melodrama set in the Bavarian Alps during World War II pits Richard Burton, Clint Eastwood and Mary Ure against what must be half the German army ensconced in a castle literally inaccessible except by cable car. Brian Hutton directs the Alistair MacLean script which consists of an interminable, totally implausible series of killings, escapes and pyrotechnic displays. A-III (PG)

Where It's At (1969) Las Vegas casino owner (David Janssen) teaches his disinterested son (Robert Drivas) the tricks of exploiting the tourist trade but the lad beats his father at his own game, gains control of the casino and then hands it back, realizing it is his father's whole life but will never be his. Director Garson Kanin tries to gloss over a most implausible script by resorting to some sexual diversions. O (R)

Where the Boys Are '84 (1984) Four women college students (Lisa Hartman, Lorna Luft, Wendy Schaal and Lynn-Holly Johnson) go to Fort Lauderdale for the spring break and carry on like amateur hookers, but viewers are supposed to believe its very wholesome and therapeutic. Director Hy Averback's updating of a silly 1960 movie contains nudity, sexually oriented humor and an appalling moral outlook. O (R)

Where the Buffalo Roam (1980) Bill Murray portrays famed underground journalist Hunter S. Thompson, who seems to have derived much of his inspiration from drugs and alcohol. Director Art Linson tries to blend serious social concern with outrageous comedy but is only intermittently successful. Rough language and use of drugs. A-III (PG)

Where the Lilies Bloom (1974) Four sturdy Appalachian children keep the death of their widowed father a secret so the state won't take them away to an orphan's home and provide for themselves out of the profits of "wildcrafting" (collecting and preparing certain herbs and wild flowers prized for their medicinal qualities). The Robert B. Radnitz production directed by William A. Graham tells its story of youngsters learning to care for themselves in the adult world with warm humor and genuine sensitivity to the conditions of life for the rural poor. A rare and satisfying entertainment for the entire family. A-I (G)

Where Were You When the Lights Went Out? (1968) Typical Doris Day vehicle revolving around a woman's honor seemingly compromised but untarnished in the final reel. The only novelty here is that the story is placed in the context of the 1965 power failure that darkened New York City and director Hy Averback does get some good comic bits from Robert Morse and Terry Thomas who are caught up in the contrived circumstances of the plot during the Great Blackout. A-III (PG)

Where's Jack? (1969) British adventure story

set in 18th-century London about a locksmith's apprentice (Tommy Steele) turned thief and highwayman by necessity and a popular hero by virtue of his incredible escapes from prison. Director James Clavell carefully ensures that the cruelty and violence of the period do not overpower the human values of loyalty and comradeship that are at its heart. A-II (G)

Where's Poppa? (1970) New York lawyer (George Segal) tries to cope with his senile mother (Ruth Gordon) by hiring a nurse (Trish Van Devere) to care for her. Directed by Carl Reiner, the situation becomes a black-humored nightmare, with gags involving rape, muggings, nursing homes and other human ills, going beyond the line of tastelessness. O (R)

Which Way Is Up? (1977) A poor fruit-picker (Richard Pryor), suddenly finds himself the chosen tool of the powerful and in a position to be rewarded amply for his subservience. Directed by Michael Schultz and adapted from Lina Wertmuller's "The Seduction of Mimi" the serious nature of the comedy is fatally undercut by Pryor's too broad performance. Excessive reliance on foul language and sex to get laughs. O (R)

Which Way to the Front? (1970) Jerry Lewis directs as well as stars as a man who, when rejected by the army in World War II, forms his own little fighting force composed of similar rejects, defeats the Axis in Europe and proceeds to win the war in the Pacific. Some isolated skits are funny, but on the whole, the poor timing and dull material make the comic fantasy seem interminable. Fantasy violence. A-II (G)

Whiffs (1975) Elliott Gould plays a medically discharged Army private whose use as a chemical warfare guinea pig has, among other ill effects, left him impotent. Gould gets his revenge, and cures his malady, by using stolen Army gas to disable an entire town and clean out its banks. Director Ted Post does nothing to redeem a singularly unfunny and tasteless screenplay, many of whose failed jokes have to do with the hero's sexual incapacity. O (PG)

Whirlpool (1970) Danish exploitation import about a wealthy woman (Pia Anderson), her psychopathic nephew (Karl Lanchbury) and a young model (Vivian Neves) lured into a sex triangle that ends with her rape-murder. Director J.R. Larrath, inept at fashioning suspense or terror, suffocates his English-speaking cast in a cesspool of stupefying dialogue, sex and blood. O (X)

Whisperers, The (1967) Dame Edith Evans gives a brilliant performance as an impoverished old woman, beset by loneliness and physical infirmity, victimized and abandoned by an unfeeling husband and son, and finding her only comfort in the world of her imagination. Directed by Bryan Forbes, it is a compassionate examination of the struggles of old age and achieved without false sentimentality. A-II (br)

Whistle Blower, The (1987) Veteran spy Michael Caine finds a way to avenge the death of his son, a British intelligence agent, without jeopardizing his position in the international club of spy organizations. British director Simon Langton's murder mystery has a plot device concerning infidelity and a far more subtle, pulpy and pernicious political bite which may confuse youngsters and certainly annoy sophisticated adults. A-III (PG)

White Dawn, The (1974) Challenging fact-based story of three whalers (Warren Oates, Timothy Bottoms and Lou Gossett) marooned in the 1890s on Baffin Island, 700 miles below the North Pole, are taken in by local Eskimos but their initial warm relationship degenerates into mistrust and finally vengeance as the two alien cultures threaten each other. Directed by Philip Kaufman, the corrupting influence of civilization on the savage innocence of the natives is depicted in realistic, often grisly, detail and Eskimo sexual customs are treated without sensation or exploitation. A-III (R/PG)

White Lightning (1973) Routine country melodrama in which hard-driving Arkansas moonshiner (Burt Reynolds) is paroled from prison in order to get the goods on a county sheriff (Ned Beatty) who is not only taking graft but also murdered Reynolds' kid brother. Crisply directed by Joseph Sargent, the fragmented story of rough backwoods codes and justice is of less interest than the high-powered car chases that keep the dust swirling on those backcountry roads. Some romantic escapades. A-III (PG)

White Line Fever (1975) Young trucker Jan-Michael Vincent fights corruption in director Jonathan Kaplan's passably entertaining, though needlessly violent action movie. Benign attitude toward vigilantism. A-III (PG)

White Nights (1985) Excellent dance sequences highlight this movie about a dissident Vietnam veteran (Gregory Hines) and a Russian defector (Baryshnikov) who flee to freedom from behind the Iron Curtain. Director Taylor Hackford emphasizes the romantic complications between Isabella Rossellini and Hines in a test of commitment in the face of betrayal. A-II (PG-13)

White Sister (1973) Uneven Italian melodrama about the Mother Superior (Sophia Loren) of a hospital in northern Italy whose confrontations with one of the male staff (Adriano Celentano), a lusty malingerer and a communist to boot, leads inevitably to a rather idealized romance, very platonic but serious enough to make both parties come to mature decisions about their lives. Director Alberto Lattuada plays it broadly, offering some pithy comic moments in the best tradition of Italian social comedy, but not enough to overcome the story's underlying sentimentality. A-III (R)

Who Is Harry Kellerman and Why Is He Saying Those Terrible Things About Me? (1971) Wealthy composer-singer of pop hits (Dustin Hoffman) is a 40-year-old schizophrenic whose life is being pulled apart by personal and business problems and to top it all off, some guy named Harry Kellerman is calling all of his girl friends and saying "terrible things" about him. Directed by Ulu Grosbard, the confused psychodrama is too introverted, too slick and too specialized to appeal to a wide audience. Adult themes, brief nudity and some rough language. A-III (GP)

Who Is Killing the Great Chefs of Europe? (1978) Screen version of the novel by Nan and Ivan Lyons about an epicurean publisher (Robert Morley) of a gourmet magazine whose list of the world's best chefs are being murdered one by one in the manner of the preparation of their specialty. Ted Kotcheff's heavy-handed direction doesn't help a talented cast including Jacqueline Bisset, Jean-Pierre Cassel, Philippe Noiret, Jean Rochefort and George Segal. Some violent visuals and much tasteless humor. A-III (PG)

Who Killed Mary What's'ername? (1971) No one really much cares, except a rich diabetic, former boxing champ (Red Buttons) who sets out to track down the killer of a Greenwich Village hooker. Director Ernie Pintoff doesn't seem able to cope with the twisted plots and tangled lines of this rather sordid mystery story. A-III (GP)

Who Says I Can't Ride a Rainbow? (1971) Fact-based story of Barney Morovitz (Jack Klugman), founder of PONY foundation, a homemade zoo in a rundown section of New York's Greenwich Village, who has to frantically relocate his enterprise after Big Business encroaches upon his cherished patch of ground. Directed by Edward Mann, besides the sincere acting of all involved, its chief merit is that it cares about youngsters, especially kids of different races who grow up together on the cold concrete streets of a big city. A-I (G)

Who Slew Auntie Roo? (1972) The best aspect of this garden-variety horror movie is its integration of the familiar Hansel and Gretel story with the on-screen tale, set in the turn-of-the-century English countryside, in which orphaned Mark Lester and Chloe Franks have been taken in by Shelley Winters, who in Lester's eyes is trying to fatten them up. Though Ralph Richardson and Lionel Jeffries steal some colorful moments in bit parts, under Curtis Harrington's direction most of the picture is drab and slow-moving. Some scenes may be too intense for younger viewers. A-II (GP)

Who'll Stop the Rain? (1978) Hard-edged screen version of a Robert Stone novel about a Vietnam war correspondent (Michael Moriarty) who sends his wife (Tuesday Weld) two kilos of heroin, but things go awry and the wife assisted by an old Marine buddy (Nick Nolte) are off on an existential odyssey, trailed by ugly thugs and corrupt policemen. Director Karel Reisz explores an America as full of dope, death and depravity as the Vietnam which had generated the illicit cargo. Adult themes, drug use and strong language. A-III (R)

Who's Afraid of Virginia Woolfe? (1966) Director Mike Nichols' adaptation of the Edward Albee play amounts to a high-then-low-level encounter group session involving two college faculty couples who thrash out their bitterness and frustrations during a semi-drunken evening. The main event features Richard Burton and Elizabeth Taylor who are old veterans of marital bouts, while George Segal and Sandy Dennis are rank amateurs, and as the tension mounts and they begin going for each other's throats, verbally, the air turns rather blue. The very nature of the movie, with its rough language and unsavory slice of married life and human relationships needs an adult's perception for full comprehension and understanding. It is definitely not an entertainment for the casual viewer. A-IV (br)

Who's That Girl (1987) Dull and lifeless vanity production showcasing music idol Madonna as an ex-con trying to vindicate herself while ruining the marriage plans of her escort (Griffin Dunne). Director James Foley is unable to tone down the hard edge of the essentially irresponsible role model his star awkwardly creates in this failed action comedy of interest only to diehard fans. A-III (PG)

Who's That Knocking at My Door? (1969) Potentially interesting but unrealized attempt to show an Italian American youth's re-examination of his emotionally religious upbringing in relation to his sexual hang-ups. Director Martin Scorsese handles the subject with little depth or conviction and goes to extremes with a lengthy erotic montage. O (R)

Wholly Moses (1980) Boring Biblical comedy in which the brother-in-law of Moses (Dudley Moore) believes he is the one entrusted with a mission from God. Directed by Gary Weis, its attempts at humor can best be described as tiresome, mirthless, and witless. Occasional vulgar jokes and some incidental irreverence. A-III (PG)

Whose Life Is It, Anyway? (1981) Brilliant, witty sculptor (Richard Dreyfuss), paralyzed from an auto accident and dependent upon a dialysis machine and constant medication, retains a lawyer to force the hospital to release him, an action that will result in his speedy death. Directed by John Badham, the movie pits the patient's reasons for being allowed to die against his doctor's (John Cassavetes) determination to keep him alive at all costs. The treatment of the theme as well as a nude sequence make this questionable adult fare. A-IV (R)

Why (1972) Italian morality tale about a family vacation that turns into a nightmare when the father (Alberto Sordi) is arrested for an unspecified crime, shunted from prison to prison, until finally accused of murdering a man he's never even heard of. By the time the mistake is cleared up and he is released, he is a broken man. Director Nanni Loy allows nothing to be overstated, but omits none of the harrowing details that indict a society that permits such bureaucratic indifference and brutal prison conditions to exist. A-III (PG)

Why Anna? (see: "Diary of a Schizophrenic Girl")

Why Does Herr H. Run Amok? (1978) Tedious German melodrama about a hard-working, inoffensive husband who suddenly goes over the edge and murders his wife and children and some other people unfortunate enough to be within reach at the moment. Director Rainer Werner Fassbinder does not answer the question his title poses but simply records the events that end in such violent tragedy. A-III (nr)

Why Not! (1979) Thin French comedy directed by Coline Serreau deals with the lives and domestic habits of a cozy trio (Sami Frey, Mario Gonzales and Christine Murillo) whose sleeping arrangements are quite complicated. Though the focus is not exclusively on sex, and there is an occasional droll sequence, its use of nudity and benign attitude towards moral anarchy are offensive. O (nr)

Why Would I Lie? (1980) Social worker (Treat Williams), who's also a compulsive liar, adopts a young boy (Gabriel Swann) and then tries to reunite him with his ex-con mother (Lisa Eichhorn). Directed by Larry Peerce, the pointless plot contains vulgarity, profanity and a warm endorsement of promiscuity. O (PG)

Wicked Dreams of Paula Schultz, The (1968) Low burlesque about an East German woman decathalon champ (Elke Sommer) who tries to defect to the West rather than be sent to work in a tractor factory. Directed by George Marshall, the feeble attempts at humor resort to some very crudely contrived calendar-art shots and sequences, a lesbian joke and other misguided attempts at humor. O (br)

Wicked Lady (1983) Thoroughly inept remake of a 1945 British Restoration-era movie about a bored English noblewoman (Faye Dunaway) who turns to highway robbery for diversion. Under Michael Winner's aimless direction, not only does Dunaway give a poor performance but also cast adrift are Alan Bates, John Gielgud, Denholm Elliott and Prunella Scales. Abundant nudity and crass vulgarity. O (R)

Wicked, Wicked (1973) Clumsy thriller about the hunt for a psycho (Randolph Roberts) who murders blondes checking into an old seaside resort whose new singer (Tiffany Bolling) sports a blonde wig. Written, produced and directed by Richard L. Bare, the movie uses an ineffective split screen process. Restrained sex and violence. A-III (PG)

Wicker Man, The (1980) British melodrama in which a police sergeant (Edward Woodward) is called to a small island off the west coast of Scotland to investigate the disappearance of a child whom, he finds, has been made a human sacrifice in a pagan rite. Directed by Robin Hardy, the movie shows signs of intelligence and sophistication but its tragic ending is unprepared from what has gone before. Excessive nudity. O (R)

Widow Couderc, The (1974) Complex French melodrama set in the 1930s in which a killer (Alain Delon) hides out working on the farm of a widow (Simone Signoret) but life is so peaceful there that he begins thinking of it as home until someone in the small, inbred rural community calls the attention of the police to the outsider. Director Pierre Granier-Deferre's picture of country life contrasts human frailty with the beauty of the natural order, lust with love and death with life in a way which may discomfort some but evoke a sympathetic response in others. A-IV (nr)

Wifemistress (1979) Italian sex comedy in which a rich merchant (Marcello Mastroianni), implicated in a crime and forced into hiding in a building across the street from his home, observes the erotic as well as humanitarian activities of his formerly repressed wife (Laura Antonelli) who thinks he is dead. Directed by Marco Vicario, it is little more than a tepid and uninspired period comedy whose simplistic anti-religious views and frequent nudity are offensive. O (R)

Wilby Conspiracy, The (1975) Sidney Poitier and Michael Caine star in a political chase melodrama set against the background of apartheid South Africa but Nicol Williamson steals the show as a cooly fanatic policeman. Director Ralph Nelson's movie is taut and well acted but is marred by some unnecessary sexual hijinks and a violent conclusion that sets up a moral problem beyond its depth. O (PG)

Wild Angels, The (1966) Motorcycle gang movie with Peter Fonda and directed by Roger Corman is excessively violent and its theme of social protest is bogus. O (br)

Wild Bunch, The (1969) William Holden and Ernest Borgnine star in director Sam Peckinpah's violent and unglamorized account of the end of an outlaw band who had outlived the frontier era. Though its intentions are to show the ugly reality underlying the Western movie myth, the general viewer is apt to find the work's brutality and several sexual scenes quite excessive. A-IV (R)

Wild Child, The (1970) Exceptional French dramatization about a young boy who was found in 1798 living as an animal in a forest and the doctor who, rather than place him in an asylum, took him into his own home for more intense care. Director Francois Truffaut (who also plays the doctor) creates an austerity of image, settings and music

(Vivaldi) to mirror the child's alienation and gradual response to the doctor's openness. Most of all, the moving drama is an affirmation of the tireless efforts of educators to overcome environmental handicaps and an act of faith that humanity will survive in spite of itself. A-II (PG)

Wild Country, The (1971) Pittsburgh family (Steve Forrest, Vera Miles, Ron Howard and Clint Howard) arrives in the Wyoming territory of the 1880s full of hope and fervor of the early settlers but their farm is below expectations, their water supply jeopardized by cattlemen and a devastating cyclone nearly destroys their homestead. Above average Disney production directed by Robert Totten provides a wholesome, quality adventure story for solid family entertainment. A-I (G)

Wild Duck, The (1977) Pallid German adaptation of the Ibsen classic, Director Hans W. Geissendorfer unwisely "opens up" the play to the extent of showing Hedvig's cherished wild duck, but has made a much more critical mistake in casting a fat and clownish actor (Peter Kern) as the feckless but attractive Hjalmar. A-II (nr)

Wild Eye, The (1968) Italian story about a sleazy movie director (Philippe Leroy) who makes exploitation pseudo-documentaries by inventing what he thinks the public wants to believe is real. Director Paolo Cavara proceeds to demonstrate this sort of dishonesty by himself staging a number of sadomasochistic scenes. O (nr)

Wild Geese, The (1978) Richard Burton, assisted by Roger Moore, Richard Harris and Hardy Kruger, lead a mercenary army to Africa to rescue a democratic African leader (Winston Ntshona). Although director Andrew V. McLaglen has a talented cast, a literate script and some well photographed action sequences, the complexity of its racial and political context are beyond the movie's capability to treat responsibly. The graphic nature of its brutal violence and accompanying rough language are excessive. O (R)

Wild in the Sky (1972) Brandon de Wilde and two fellow draft-dodgers escape jail by commandeering a SAC bomber captained by Robert Lansing and try to make it to Cuba as General Keenan Wynn back at SAC headquarters issues insane orders to stop them. Directed by William T. Naud, this low-budget flying Ship of Fools tries to work both the hijack and anti-war angles but is consistent only in its cheap vulgarities and exploitation of serious themes. O (GP)

Wild in the Streets (1968) Young pop singer (Chris Jones) mobilizes America's youth, gets elected President and puts everyone over 30 into concentration camps. Director Barry Shear tries to satirize the youth culture of the 1960s while exploiting it as well but it is the kind of free-from-responsibility fantasy that is not good for adolescents. A-III (R/GP)

Wild Life, The (1984) Dreary sequel to "Fast Times At Ridgemont High" shows what happens to Eric Stoltz after he graduates and moves into a swinging singles apartment complex. Directed by Art Linson, the proceedings feature the same sort of benignly viewed sexual amorality which permeated the first movie. Nudity and rough language. O (R)

Wild Pack, The (1972) Produced, directed and written by Hall Bartlett from a novel by Jorge Amado, the movie follows the fates of a gang of homeless children in Bahia, Brazil, as they struggle to survive on the fringes and in the slums of an indifferent South American society. It unfortunately clutters its statement of revolutionary protest with a romantic subplot and a graphic rape sequence. O (nr)

Wild Party, The (1975)   Part musical, part study of late 1920s Hollywood decadence and part compassionate character study of a silent film comedian (James Coco) ruined by the coming of sound pictures. Directed by James Ivory, these diverse elements fail to fuse and the result is an aimless, repetitious and more than a little distasteful melodrama. Excessive sexual display. O (R)

Wild Racers, The (1968)   American race car driver (Fabian) gets a shot at the Grand Prix circuit and leaves behind a trail of a compliant women. Director Dan Haller intercuts stock racing footage with numerous suggestive situations in the story of a man who values machines more than human beings. O (br)

Wild Rovers (1971)   William Holden and Ryan O'Neal are quite effective in this flawed but engagingly bittersweet study of ordinary cowpokes who dream of owning a little ranchero down in Mexico, rob a Montana bank and head toward the distant border. Written and directed by Blake Edwards, the characterizations are its strong point, the plot rather shaky and slow-moving and the resolution is a downer. Some brutal violence and a gratuitous bordello scene. A-III (GP)

Wild Season (1968)   Belgian movie about the life of North Sea fishermen centers around a young boy who tries to prove to his father that he can be just as good a man as was the son lost at sea. Directed by Emil Nofal, the natural elements surpass the labored efforts of the actors but younger audiences will enjoy the outdoor adventure aspects of the story without much concern about character motivations. A-I (nr)

Wild Thing (1987)   Orphaned child (Rob Knepper) grows up essentially on his own in the bowels of a deserted inner-city hovel and one day avenges his parents' death at the hands of ruthless drug dealers while saving a young social worker (Kathleen Quinlan). Director Mac Reid uses the thematic razor's edge of revenge to mutilate scriptwriter John Sayles' childlike fable. Restrained violence and a scene of implied sex lessen the urban Tarzan yarn's suitability for youngsters. A-III (PG-13)

Wildcats (1986)   Goldie Hawn stars in this failed comedy about a woman coach of an inner-city high school football team. Excessive amounts of streetwise profanity, brief nudity and a scene involving simulated fornication make this vanity production by director Michael Ritchie off limits for its intended youthful audience. O (R)

Wilderness Family, Part 2, The (see: "The Further Adventures of the Wilderness Family")

Wilderness Journey (1972)   In the Far North, a 12-year-old Eskimo lad (Tony Tucker Williams) embarks on a courageous canoe journey to find his father (Richard Stitt), a hunting-party guide whose assistance is needed back home. The boy's adventure is made suspenseful and engrossing by Chuck D. Keen's superlative photography of the region and its wildlife and by the reverent narration explaining the tradition of the boy's ancestors. Directed by Ford Beebe, whose career in films dates back to 1914, the movie is splendid family entertainment. A-I (G)

Will Penny (1968)   Fine Western about an aging, illiterate but still capable cowhand (Charlton Hes-

ton) who after the fall roundup spends the winter looking after the cattle in the hills where he becomes the protector of a lost pioneer woman (Joan Hackett) and her son. Director Tom Gries has achieved a realistic portrait of a cowboy whose code of morality reflects the rigors of frontier life, the shortage of marriageable women and the rudimentary nature of early Western justice. A-III (br)

Will the Real Norman Mailer Please Stand Up? (1970)   Low-budget documentary gives a rather interesting and fairly objective account of the life and times of popular author Norman Mailer, centering on his views and activities related to the anti-Vietnam movement. Unfortunately, the result provides little more than a superficial understanding of this enigmatic public figure and the rather amateurish production further detracts from its value. A-III (nr)

Willard (1971)   Horror fantasy about a psychotic young man (Bruce Davidson) who, after the death of his mother (Elsa Lanchester), trains an army of rats to exact revenge for the injustices heaped upon him and his family by a businessman (Ernest Borgnine), but alas, he trains the little beasties all too well. Tighter editing and pacing might have given director Daniel Mann a first-class horror movie but, as it is, animal trainer Moe Di Sesso runs away with the prize for his direction of the rats. A-II (GP)

Willie & Phil (1980)   Writer-director Paul Mazursky's tale of a three-sided friendship begins with the 1970 meeting of Willie (Michael Ontkean) and Phil (Ray Sharkey) as they come out of a screening of Truffaut's triangle movie, "Jules and Jim," the inspiration for Mazursky's work. The trio is completed a few days later when they meet free-spirited Jeannette (Margot Kidder) and the movie follows their shifting relationships over the entire decade of the 1970s. Mazursky has created three charming characters and places their quest for meaning and fulfillment within the context of the ethnic, moral and religious traditions each represents. However, the nature and treatment of the theme makes this strictly mature viewing. A-III (R)

Willie Dynamite (1974)   Big city's most successful pimp (Roscoe Orman) vies with a reformed-hooker-turned-social-worker (Diana Sands) over the girls he tries to keep on the street while she tries to get them off. Directed by Gilbert Moses, it is a lifeless, aimless and meaningless attempt to blend outright black exploitation material with a sober examination of the psychology of the pimp and his women. The result is largely a waste of time. O (R)

Willy Wonka and the Chocolate Factory (1971)   Screen version of Roald Dahl's children's story about a candy manufacturer (Gene Wilder) who conducts an electrifying tour of his factory for the five lucky children who learn that greed and selfishness can be their own reward. Even the punishments, occasionally a bit gruesome for younger children, are in good fun. Director Mel Stuart manages to avoid the cloying sentimentality of similar children's movies, though it's never quite as magical as one would have hoped. A-I (G)

Wind and the Lion, The (1975)   Writer-director John Milius takes some liberties with the 1904 incident in which Teddy Roosevelt (Brian Keith) thundered against a Moroccan brigand (Sean Connery) for kidnapping an American citizen (Candice Bergen). The historical facts are more interesting than this artificial romance, bogus adventure movie that glamorizes weapons and their use. Violence. A-III (PG)

Wind from the East (1972) French director Jean-Luc Godard's first directly political work, this 1969 effort fails both as a movie and as Maoist propaganda. Basically a film of ideas, its dialectical progress fitfully winds down to a final call for total revolution, but it is unlikely to persuade viewers to accept its convictions. A-IV (nr)

Windows (1980) Failed thriller about a psychotic, homicidal lesbian (Elizabeth Ashley) who cherishes an unholy and, at times, quite noisy passion for a mousy friend (Talia Shire). Director Gordon Willis leaves his actresses to their own devices in the heavy-breathing and crying department while he devotes his energies to getting some exquisite views of the Manhattan skyline and landmarks. A brutal scene involving sexual assault is needlessly graphic. O (R)

Windwalker (1981) A dying Cheyenne patriarch (Trevor Howard) yearns to see once again the son who was kidnapped by hostile Crows when he was an infant. Aside from the miscasting of Howard, director Keith Merrill has created an extremely authentic picture of Indian life told in an unusually absorbing story. Because of the violence and conflict essential to the plot, it is not suited to very young children, but for older ones, the dignity with which it portrays Indians and their culture recommends it highly. A-II (PG)

Windy City (1984) Written and directed by Armyan Bernstein, this story of young men growing up on the North Side of Chicago with their dreams unrealized has some good acting (John Shea, Kate Capshaw, Josh Mostel and Jim Borrelli) but can't overcome the handicaps of banal dialogue and sketchy characterizations. Considerable violence and gore. A-III (R)

Wings (1927) Silent screen epic about two young men (Buddy Rogers and Richard Allen), in love with the same girl (Jobyna Ralston), who wind up in the same flying squadron during World War I where their rivalry turns to friendship until one of them is accidentally killed by the other. Clara Bow is the girl-next-door who follows Rogers to France as a nurse. Directed by William Wellman, it's a classic adventure film with a refreshing sense of innocence unembarrassed by any doubts about the justice of the actions of the principals. A-II (br)

Winners, The (see: "My Way")

Winning (1969) Paul Newman is ruggedly impressive as a race-car driver whose obsession with the track leads his neglected wife (Joanne Woodward) to dally with his chief competitor (Robert Wagner). Directed by James Goldstone, the movie is as slick and quick as the race cars that provide its action thrills, and its message boils down to the fact that sometimes winning is really losing. A-III (PG)

Winter Kills (1979) Failed screen version of Richard Condon's novel about the brother (Jeff Bridges) of an assassinated U.S. President who years later discovers that the actual assassin was not the man accused but another who was the agent of a vast and intricate conspiracy. Directed by William Richert, nothing makes much sense in this ill-conceived and badly executed melodrama which exploits memories of a tragic moment in American history. Some scenes of graphic sex. O (R)

Winter Soldier (1972) During the winter of 1971, 200 men calling themselves Vietnam Veterans Against the War, sat before members of the press in Detroit and ruefully related their military experiences. The Pentagon refuted none of their testimony which found its way into the Congressional Record. Eighteen anonymous friends of the veterans preserved the recollections of some of these men in a documentary which eminently deserves to be seen as part of the record of a very troubled time in the history of our nation. A-III (nr)

Winter Wind (1970) Hungarian director Miklos Jancso relates an incident about a Croatian anarchist in the 1930s who is considered a hero by his followers but only after they have destroyed him. The film is not for casual viewers but those interested in foreign films or European politics will find it worth seeing. A-III (nr)

Wisdom (1986) Ridiculous teenage Bonnie-and-Clyde team (Emilio Estevez and Demi Moore) show their defiance of adult authority and social injustice by destroying mortgage records. The vanity production, written and directed by Estevez, centers on an unhealthy preoccupation with guns and violence along with profanity and casual sex. O (R)

Wise Blood (1980) Screen version of Flannery O'Connor's novel about a God-haunted young man (Brad Dourif) who on his way to Taulkinham, Tenn., to preach a new religion, meets such bizarre characters as a failed preacher pretending he is blind (Harry Dean Stanton), his mildly depraved daughter (Amy Wright) and a jovial evangelist (Ned Beatty). Director John Huston has made a powerful and provocative movie whose spiritual implications are as compelling as its artistic excellence. The incidental violence and moral complexity are more appropriate for adult viewers. A-III (PG)

Wise Guys (1986) Brian De Palma's brash and audacious parody of the gangster film relies too heavily upon profanity and violence as source of humor. Although Danny De Vito and Joe Piscopo create frantically likable but bungling small-time hoods, their stereotyped characterizations, along with others in the film, are likely to give offense to some Italian and Jewish viewers. O (R)

Wish You Were Here (1987) British director David Leland's sensitive, bittersweet evocation of a youngster's coming of age in a 1950s English coastal town focuses upon her sexual initation, disappointments with her father and encounters with the male-dominated working class society of the period. The sexually explicit but emotionally accurate portrait of a young woman's discovery of self-worth and meaning has brief nudity and some vulgar language. A-III (R)

Wishing Machine, The (1970) Czechoslovakian children's story about two boys whose visit to an industrial fair leads them to imagine they can make a trip to the moon. Written and directed by Josef Pinkava, the movie (dubbed into English) has imaginative visuals and a pleasant story that small children will enjoy because it is, from beginning to end, entirely made for them. A-I (G)

Witchboard (1987) This horror tale demonstrates the bloody consequences of using a Quija board alone. Tawny Kitaen jousts with an evil spirit and manages to get her former boyfriend killed and her current lover nearly dismembered in a story of the supernatural that presents all its gory excesses and vulgarities in broad daylight. O (R)

Witchcraft '70 (1970)   Self-described as a serious documentary study of contemporary witchcraft throughout the world, it is anything but a documentary, though it does flit from place to place, seeking out what, apparently, is the main ingredient for any occult ceremony, namely that the participants be as naked as possible. Few will be bewitched, many will be bothered, and almost all will be bewildered. O (X/R)

Witchmaker, The (1971)   Psychology professor (Alvy Moore) stupidly leads his students into the Louisiana swamplands to investigate a series of occult-oriented murders where they succumb to spells cast by a maniacal fiend (John Lodge) who drains his victims' blood for use in satanic orgies. Written, produced and directed by William O. Brown, the feeble horror concoction keeps the camera at a distance from the mayhem. A-III (M/R)

With Six You Get Egg Roll (1968)   Doris Day plays a widow in coveralls with three sons and Brian Keith is a widower with one daughter who try to keep their courtship a secret from the children and then get them to all act in harmony as part of the new family. Director Howard Morris is not only stuck with a contrived and saccharine situation, with four over-cute children, but the movie gags on attempts at slapstick humor. The result is the kind of entertainment film that gives family pictures a bad name. A-II (G)

Without a Stitch (1970)   To cure the frigidity of a young girl who is introduced to a life of sex and perversion, she is taught that anything is permissible as long as it does not hurt anybody. What is particularly insidious about this exploitation movie is that it not only portrays and exploits nudity and immorality, but makes a clear effort to win its viewers to accept a similar mode of thinking and living. O (R)

Without a Trace (1983)   Fact-based story of a six-year-old boy who is kidnapped on the way to school in New York City and his mother (Kate Nelligan) who convinces a police detective (Judd Hirsch) to stay on the case even when it looks as if there is no hope. Thanks largely to the performances of Hirsh and Nelligan, there are some good moments, but for the rest director Stanley Jaffe's effort remains a flat and uninspired story, sorely lacking any real dramatic development and with a ludicrous sentimental ending. Some strong language. A-II (PG)

Without Apparent Motive (1972)   Tough, ruthless detective (Jean-Louis Trintignant) must flush out a madman who has been going about the picturesque city of Nice popping off one victim after another with his sniper's rifle. Nearly every encounter in director Philippe Labro's movie has sex simmering just below the surface and, as the story builds towards climax and resolution, twisted sexual relations not surprisingly provide all the keys. A-III (PG)

Witness (1985)   Tough Philadelphia police detective (Harrison Ford) hides out among the Amish to protect his life and that of a young boy who witnessed a murder committed by a corrupt fellow detective. He and the boy's widowed mother (Kelly McGillis) are drawn to each other despite their different worlds. Director Peter Weir gets excellent performances in a good romantic melodrama that also offers some relatively thoughtful reflections on violence and non-violence. Some graphic violence and brief nudity are handled as restrained but essential plot devices. A-IV (R)

Wiz, The (1978)   Diana Ross stars as Dorothy, the girl who flies over the rainbow in a black musical version of "The Wizard of Oz." Chasing Toto into a snowstorm in Harlem, she winds up on the yellow brick road with the Scarecrow (Michael Jackson), the Tinman (Nipsey Russell) and the Cowardly Lion (Ted Ross) on their way to meet the Wiz (Richard Pryor). Directed by Sidney Lumet, it has lavishly staged musical numbers, opulent costumes and colorful settings, but is overlong and its humor seems addressed more to adults and teenagers than younger viewers. A-II (G)

Wizard of Oz, The (1939)   Dorothy rides her tornado to the magic land over the rainbow in the classic that launched Judy Garland's career and has given generations of families prime entertainment again and again. A-I (G)

Wizards (1977)   Animated feature starts with a thermonuclear destruction of human life on earth, then jumps to the far distant future in which mutants inhabit radioactive lands and elves and fairies live in the uncontaminated area where are born twin wizards who battle for the future of the planet. It is animator Ralph Bakshi's most polished effort with bold, imaginative graphics and effective integration of live action footage. A number of violent visuals. A-III (PG)

Wolfen (1981)   Murky thriller in which a hard-boiled, nearly burnt-out detective (Albert Finney) investigating three brutal murders links them to some menacing wolflike creatures seen roaming the streets of New York. Directed by Michael Wadleigh with some spectacular camera effects, the story suggests that these preternatural creatures are punishment for the sins of a rapacious society, but its sense of moral indignation doesn't justify the violence and graphic depiction of blood and gore. A-III (R)

Woman Next Door, The (1981)   Weak French romantic melodrama about a happily married couple who move next door to another happily married couple but, as it happens, the wife who has just moved in (Fanny Ardant) and the husband next door (Gerald Depardieu) had had a stormy love affair seven years before and soon the two are off and running again. Director Francois Truffaut handles this material with his usual adroitness, but to little purpose in a story that proves banal and unmoving, with some questionable amorous sequences. A-IV (R)

Woman Times Seven (1967)   Italian potpourri of comedy, farce and pathos is directed by Vittorio De Sica with Shirley MacLaine as the heroine of each episode. It is needlessly marred by one tasteless and provocative sequence. O (br)

Woman at Her Window, A (1978)   Slack French 1930s political drama in which an Austrian woman (Romy Schneider) tries to help a Communist fugitive (Victor Lanoux) escape the secret police in Athens by involving her husband (Umberto Orsini) and a wealthy friend (Philippe Noiret). Director Pierre Granier-Deferre's narrative is needlessly complex and muddled, though it has compelling acting and some philosophical depth. Several scenes of police brutality. A-III (nr)

Woman in Red, The (1984)   Gene Wilder directs and also stars as a philandering advertising manager who pursues a beautiful model (Kelly Le Brock) while keeping his wife (Judith Ivy) in the dark. It is an ill-conceived and clumsily-executed attempt to recast a French farce about adultery

("Pardon Mon Affaire") in an American mold. Nudity and a benign attitude toward illicit sex. O (PG-13)

Woman of the Ganges (1974) French writer Marguerite Duras' story of a man at a resort during its winter off-season where he meets, or perhaps imagines that he meets, the woman of the title whom he had loved in India long ago. Also directed by Duras, the highly verbal movie takes place not on the screen, but in the mind of the beholder willing to plumb its blend of time, memory and illusion. A-III (nr)

Woman Under the Influence, A (1974) The woman of the title (Gena Rowlands) is a mother of three small children in the middle of a nervous breakdown while her husband (Peter Falk), a rough, callous but loving man, is totally unable to cope with the situation. Directed by John Cassavetes in his characteristic improvisational style, the result is full of the small realities and individual details that make up ordinary human experience but it is short on the sort of heightened drama one expects from a conventional movie narrative. A-III (R)

Woman's Decision, A (1977) Sensitive, extremely well-acted Polish triangle story whose heroine (Maya Komorowska) is married to a wonderful husband (Piotr Franczewski), has an affectionate son and a modern apartment in Warsaw but finds herself wanting to give it all up for the company of a footloose man (Marek Piwowski). Directed by Krzystof Zanussi, it is a perceptive study of the interior struggle each of the characters undergoes during the course of the narrative. A-III (nr)

Women (1978) Sensitive Hungarian character study of an unlikely and slowly developing friendship between the wife of a successful engineer (Marina Vlady) and a factory worker (Lili Monori) whose husband is an alcoholic. The melodramatic plot and its soap opera problems simply provide the background against which director Marta Meszaros explores the human needs that draw these two women together despite their differences in character, education and social position. Mature themes. A-III (nr)

Women in Cages (1971) Philippine exploitation movie directed by Gerry De Leon about a group of women prisoners who use their sadistic lesbian matron as a hostage to escape into the jungle where they fall prey to bounty hunters and flesh-peddlers. Heavy-duty debasement. O (R)

Women in Cellblock 7 (1977) Inanely plotted, badly acted and atrociously dubbed Italian exploitation movie about a woman who goes to prison to get evidence to save her father. Abundant nudity. O (R)

Women in Love (1970) British adaptation of the D.H. Lawrence novel about the gradual involvement of two couples, one (Alan Bates and Glenda Jackson) having a rather healthy though incomplete relationship while the other (Oliver Reed and Jennie Linden) tragically ends in suicide. Directed by Ken Russell, the acting is first-rate, the photography almost too beautiful and the treatment of the convoluted relationships remains on the superficial level of the physical. Lengthy naked wrestling match between the men is more symbolic than erotic. O (R)

Women in Revolt (1972) Three women from different social levels (female impersonators Candy Darling, Holly Woodlawn and Jackie Cur-tis) get caught up in the Women's Liberation Movement. Typical of the poor film quality and sexual explicitness of Andy Warhol's efforts in the past, it makes men, women and sex look ridiculous, ugly and perverted. O (nr)

Won Ton Ton, the Dog Who Saved Hollywood (1976) Director Michael Winner's wretchedly thrown-together slapstick comedy about a wonder dog of the old silent movie era is made all the more tasteless by seeing performers one once admired in a series of painfully inane cameos. It is definitely not for young viewers. O (PG)

Wonderful Crook, The (1977) Off-beat French comedy about a good-natured, but inept young man (Gerald Depardieu) who, in order to pay the employee's wages of his family's furniture business, undertakes a series of holdups and falls in love with one of his victims (Marlene Jobert). Neither his wife (Dominique Labourier) nor his employees suspect his double life until the police arrive to arrest him. Directed by Claude Goretta, the movie details in a warmly humorous manner the complications that can arise from a simplistic notion of "doing good." Brief nudity and vulgar language. A-III (nr)

Woodstock (1970) Documentary about the landmark musical event that brought together a half million young people to hear a parade of such talented performers as Richie Havens, Joan Baez, Country Joe and the Fish, The Who, Sha-na-na, Arlo Guthrie, Crosby Stills and Nash, Joe Cocker and so on. Directed by Michael Wadleigh, it is dazzling in image and sound but as a record of this particular music festival, it concentrates on the positive themes of love and peace, giving scant attention to the drugs and commercialism that for many marred the event. Brief nudity and some rough language and lyrics. A-IV (R)

Work Is a Four Letter Word (1968) British comedy about a man (David Warner) who grows mushrooms that have a narcotic effect. Directed by Peter Hall, its premise is better than the results. A-III (br)

World According to Garp, The (1982) Uneven screen version of John Irving's novel about a fragile writer (Robin Williams) overwhelmed by catastrophes, bizarre events and his indomitable mother (Glenn Close). Under George Roy Hill's direction, Williams by going all out to turn the character into a lovable schnook makes his problems seem even crueler and more arbitrary than they might have been. Some nudity and graphic sexual references. A-III (R)

World of Buckminster Fuller, The (1974) Educational documentary directed by Robert Snyder provides a coherent outline of Fuller's basic concepts as well as a personal portrait of a humanist who put his scientific knowlege to the task of considering the present under the aspects of the future rather than from the conventional wisdom of the past. A-I (nr)

World of Hans Christian Andersen, The (1971) Feature-length cartoon about the childhood of young Hans and where he got some of the ideas for his highly imaginative fairy tales. The animation is colorful and creative, though stylistically comparable to Saturday morning TV shows. It provides a wonderful world of fantasy to absorb the small fry at a matinee. A-I (G)

World of Henry Orient, The (1964) Peter Sellers stars in a wacky comedy about a fair-to-middling concert pianist whose pursuit of extra-curricular love (Paula Prentiss) is foiled by the unwitting but persistent efforts of two teenage girls who just may be his only fans in all the world. Directed by George Roy Hill, the acting is very good, the comedy nicely paced and the romantic element only in the background. A-II (br)

World of Susie Wong, The (1961)   Exotic but unappetizing tale of the rough life and times of a Hong Kong lady of the night, toned down from Paul Osborn's play in the Hollywood version starring Nancy Kwan as Susie and William Holden as her American love interest. Directed by Richard Quine, its plush production of a sentimental romance may have some interest for hardy adults, but not for youngsters or those with reservations about a drama which unfolds, for the most part, in a seamy brothel. O (br)

World Without Sun (1964)   Documentary made by oceanaut Jacques-Yves Cousteau details the human conquest of underwater space. It is an opportunity to see and experience an incredibly beautiful part of creation, till now hidden from human eyes. A-I (br)

World's Greatest Athlete, The (1973)   Frustrated coach (John Amos) vacationing in Africa discovers a Tarzan-like jungle youth (Jan-Michael Vincent) and brings him to his sunny California campus where he starts making a shambles of the record books. Directed by Robert Scheerer, it is the Disney studio's special-effects men who save the day for sports as well as for parents who with their children will have to take the yawns along with the laughs in this matinee special. A-I (G)

World's Greatest Lover, The (1977)   Failed comedy written and directed by Gene Wilder who also stars as a hapless oaf who goes to Hollywood in the 1920s hoping to win a studio-sponsored world's greatest lover contest. The direction is inept, the writing shows no vestige of wit or originality and Wilder's performance is loud, vulgar and supremely unfunny. Boring but its low level of humor is not for young viewers. A-III (PG)

Woyzeck (1979)   Stark German adaptation of Georg Buchner's 19th-century play about a much-abused soldier (Klaus Kinski) in a small garrison town who goes mad and brutally murders the woman (Eva Mattes) he has been too poor to marry. Directed by Werner Herzog, the story of a man's alienation and descent into irrationality is powerfully acted and its dark mood unrelieved. A-III (nr)

WR—Mysteries of the Organism (see: "Mysteries of the Organism")

Wraith, The (1986)   A brutally murdered teenager (Charlie Sheen) returns as an avenging angel to race to their deaths the depraved auto gang that had killed him. A deadly supernatural demolition derby filmed on the picturesque highways of Arizona sells violence, vengeance and a few sexual inferences with foul language to a youth market already overburdened with negative role models. A-III (PG-13)

Wrath of God, The (1972)   Hard-drinking, gun-toting renegade priest (Robert Mitchum) joins forces with two other fugitive misfits to erase a fanatical madman-rancher in Central America during the revolutionary 1920s. Directed by Ralph Nelson, the result is downright painful in some sections, embarrassing and simply ludicrous in others. Some heavy violence. A-IV (PG)

Wrecking Crew, The (1968)   The only funny aspect of this limp spy spoof is watching Dean

Martin lumber through it as super-agent Matt Helm entrusted to guard a gold shipment from Denmark to London, giving rise to jokes about Danish pastries (one of whom is Elke Sommer). Directed by Phil Karlson, the level of crude sexual humor is beneath adolescent interest. O (PG)

Wrong Box, The (1966)   British black comedy revolves around the bumbling attempts of someone to kill off members of a family in order to obtain a large inheritance. Directed by Bryan Forbes, the script is not very sharp but the acting of John Mills, Ralph Richardson, Michael Caine and Peter Sellers is first rate. The most hilarious performance, a classic of its kind, belongs to Wilfred Lawson as the old family retainer. A-II (br)

Wrong Is Right (1982)   Failed black comedy in which Sean Connery plays a television news commentator who finds himself in the middle of a struggle between an American President (George Grizzard), his political rival (Leslie Nielsen), Arab terrorists and assorted villains to gain possession of two suitcases containing nuclear bombs. Writer-director Richard Brooks tries to satirize amorality in high places but the humor is flat and the story terribly jumbled. Graphic violence. A-III (R)

Wrong Move, The (1978)   Tedious, empty German drama in which a moody would-be writer (Rudiger Vogler), who doesn't like people and has no interest in politics, takes a rambling journey through West Germany. Written by Peter Hanke and directed by Wim Wenders, the random incidents and various characters met along the way occasion little interest for the young man and less for the viewer. Mature themes. A-III (nr)

WUSA (1970)   Confused political melodrama about the right-wing owner (Pat Hingle) of a New Orleans radio station, its liberal disc jockey (Paul Newman), his waitress girl friend (Joanne Woodward) and a manic social worker (Tony Perkins). Director Stuart Rosenberg toys with ill-formed notions of political polarization and reduces them to cliches in a nearly incoherent plot. A-III (PG)

Wuthering Heights (1970)   Good British version of the Emily Bronte romantic classic of tragic love on the moors stars Anna Calder-Marshall as Cathy and Timothy Dalton as Heathcliff. Director Robert Fuest has made a conscious effort to enable young viewers to identify with the doomed pair but in doing so, he has softened the rough edges of the characters and the malevolent nature of their relationship. Good cast and fine creation of mood and period. A-II (G)

W.W. and the Dixie Dancekings (1975)   Burt Reynolds plays a professional con man who takes in hand a hapless group of country musicians. Director John G. Avildsen's comedy is often hilarious and is marked by fine acting. One scene at a drive-in is adult fare. A-III (PG)

X

X, Y & Zee (1972)   Shrill British sex melodrama involving a self-destructive, affluent, childless couple (Elizabeth Taylor and Michael Caine) and an attractive widow (Susannah York) with whom the husband falls in love and the wife tries to seduce in order to thwart the interest of her errant spouse. Directed by Brian G. Hutton, the perverse triangle is a vulgar, one-dimensional affair with brief nudity and considerable abusive language. O (R/PG)

Xala (1975)   Black African satire, filmed in Senegal, about a prosperous businessman who takes a third wife but, unable to consummate the marriage, is convinced someone has cursed him with a spell of impotence and spends all his money seeking the help of witch doctors. Director Ousmane Sembene's metaphor of impotence is vividly applied to the neo-colonialist values of the African middle class that is the movie's main target. A-III (nr)

Xanadu (1980) Olivia Newton-John sings her way through her role as a materialized Greek muse who inspires a middle-aged musician (Gene Kelly) and a young artist (Michiel Beck) to become partners in a nightclub. Directed by Robert Greenwald, the movie offers little but special effects, optical devices and a few vulgar dance numbers in what is essentially an illustrated sound-track album. A-II (PG)

Y

Yakuza, The (1975) Robert Mitchum plays an American back in Japan, where he had served in the Occupation, to help get back a friend's kidnapped daughter (Keiko Kishi) by having a top gangster (Ken Takadura) repay the favor he owes the American. Though Mitchum is able to rise above the inane story with some dignity, director Sydney Pollack's Japanese gangster movie (which is what the title means) proves silly as well as repugnant in its exotic brutality and simple-minded concept of manhood. A-III (R)

Yanks (1979) Overlong but beautifully photographed re-creation of a worn and ravaged England during World War II offers the thin story of two English women (Vanessa Redgrave and Lisa Eichhorn) and two American soldiers (William Devane and Richard Gere) told in terms of parallel romances. Directed by John Schlesinger, the story suffers from a slow-moving pace and lack of focus which leaves it without much dramatic force. Adultery figures in the plot, with some profane language and some bedroom scenes. A-III (R)

Year of Living Dangerously, The (1983) Muddled story of an Australian correspondent (Mel Gibson) who arrives in 1965 Indonesia, a country on the verge of revolution, comes to rely on the information provided by an Asian cameraman (Linda Hunt in a male role) and engages in a torrid love affair with a British intelligence agent (Sigourney Weaver). Director Peter Weir re-creates the place and chaotic period very effectively but characterizations are sketchy and the action lacks coherence. Though it has compassion for the poor and oppressed, the sexual relationship makes it mature fare. A-III (PG)

Year of the Dragon (1985) A police captain and Vietnam veteran (Mickey Rourke) wages war against a dapper but ruthlessly deadly Chinatown gang lord (John Lone). Directed by Michael Cimino, and written by Oliver Stone, the film is muddled almost to the point of incoherence by extreme amounts of profanity and violence while being pointedly racist and sexist. O (R)

Year of the Quiet Sun, A (1985) An American soldier (Scott Wilson) and a Polish widow (Maja Komorowska) fall in love despite their lack of a common language in Russian-occupied Poland in the grim days following World War II. Under the masterful direction of Krzysztof Zanussi, the Polish production probes into the tragic complications

arising from a relationship foundering over cultural differences. Sensitive treatment of serious matters. A-II (PG)

Year of the Woman (1973) Pretentious documentary on the politicization of women's rights adds, unfortunately, little enlightment about the subject. It suffers not only from missed opportunities to demonstrate systematic injustice, but from the misuse of interviews with articulate individuals, edited mainly to serve the needs of filmmaker Sandra Hochman. A-IV (nr)

Yearling, The (1946) A young boy's attachment to an orphaned fawn relieves the loneliness of his harsh life in the Florida wilderness in this family classic starring Gregory Peck and Jane Wyman as the parents and Claude Jarman Jr. as the boy. Director Clarence Brown's version of the Marjorie Kinnon Rawlings' story is both a genuine portrait of rural America and a sincere celebration of family life. A-I (G)

Years of Lightning, Day of Drums (1966) Celebratory documentary about the promise of President Kennedy's years in office as seen from the perspective of his tragic assassination and burial. It recalls vividly the feeling of personal loss experienced by people around the world during that terrible November in 1963. A-I (br)

Yellow Submarine (1968) Wonderful animated feature for young and old, with music from the Beatles' Sgt. Pepper album, follows the adventures of John, George, Paul and Ringo to the never-neverworld of Pepperland where they find that the Blue Meanies are overrunning its lovely terrain. Director George Dunning's animation is a wonder, the music a delight and, of course, Sgt. Pepper and his Lonelyhearts Club Marching Band get their peaceful land back at the end, and those Blue Meanies are not all that mean. A-I (G)

Yellowbeard (1983) Several of the Monty Python troupe join forces with Cheech and Chong, Susannah York, James Mason, Peter Boyle, Madeline Kahn, and the late Marty Feldman in this leaden, stultifyingly unfunny pirate spoof directed by Mel Damski. Brief nudity and an abundance of coarse jokes. A-III (PG)

Yentl (1983) Barbra Streisand musical in which she stars in the title role as an intelligent Jewish woman living in Eastern Europe at the turn of the century who dresses as a man in order to study in a yeshiva (male religious school) and finds herself attracted to a student (Mandy Patinkin) already engaged to be married. When the engagement is called off, Yentl is persuaded to become the bridegroom instead, but all is resolved when she leaves handsome student and his beloved by emigrating to America and less restrictive educational prerequisites. Streisand, who also produced, directed and co-authored the script, is on center stage for almost the entire length of the movie, a bit much for all but her most avid fans. Yentl's mock marriage to another woman makes the movie inappropriate for young viewers. A-III (PG)

Yes, Giorgio (1982) Operatic tenor Luciano Pavarotti makes his film debut as a great opera star who, despite his wife in Italy, has a love affair with a beautiful American doctor (Kathryn Harrold) during a tour of the U.S. Pavarotti's singing would be enough to recommend it except that director Franklin J. Schaffner's supremely silly movie takes a benign attitude toward the adulterous affair, which is not just incidental, but the main focus of the plot throughout. O (PG)

Yo Yo (1967) French comedy about a millionaire's son (Pierre Etaix) who, after his father is ruined in the Depression, becomes a renowned clown, makes a fortune in the novelty business but ultimately rejects the grand yet lonely style of life in which he had been raised. Also directed by Etaix, the episodic tale is told mainly through sight gags and visual humor that bears comparison with the antics of Keaton, Chaplin and Lloyd. A-II (br)

Yog—Monster from Space (1971) Japanese monster moviemaker Ishiro Honda has picked the farthest recesses of his brain to create an elephantine octopus with a mitre-shaped head. The sight of this super squid might thrill moppets, but older kids may yawn and yearn for more imaginative stuff, and they are right. A-I (G)

You Are What You Eat (1968) Pseudo-documentary about the youth counter-culture of the 1960s presents a montage of disjointed scenes of the so-called love generation engaged in various sexual activites, pot smoking, rock song gatherings and street happenings, sprinkled with scenes of the cult heroes of the period. Directed by Barry Feinstein, it tries to be outrageous but is mostly tasteless and vulgar. Some exploitative nudity. O (br)

You Can't Steal Love (see: "Live a Little, Steal a Lot")

You Can't Win 'Em All (1970) Tony Curtis and Charles Bronson cavort through post-World War I Turkey as a pair of roguish mercenaries, periodically betraying each other for the least whiff of beauty or booty. Director Peter Collison's tired, formula adventure features Turkey's matinee idol, Fikret Hakan, but the real star of this turkey is a beautiful old steam-engine, lovingly photographed against picturesque Turkish locations. A-II (PG)

You Light Up My Life (1977) Young singer-composer (Didi Conn) breaks away from the smothering influence of her comedian father and comes to New York determined to rely on no one but herself. Director Joseph Brooks' neatly packaged bit of nothing fails to hold its thin story line together despite Conn's good performance. An incident of premarital sex is presented as a moral lapse which the heroine immediately regrets. A-II (PG)

You Only Live Twice (1967) Sean Connery in his fifth appearance as James Bond goes through the motions of tracking down some mission space capsules amidst oriental intrigue in Japan and finally bests his arch foe Blofeld (Donald Pleasence). The agent 007 formula of impersonal sex and violence has worn thin with the result that director Lewis Gilbert's Bond movie is just another mediocre spy thriller. A-III (GP)

You Only Love Once (1969) Unpretentious French romance depicting the loving relationship of a couple (Karen Blanguernon and Frederic de Pasquale) from first fancy to marriage, parenthood, estrangement and reconciliation. Directed by Dirk Sanders, it is a gay, moody, colorful expression of the simple things in real life, often having the effect of a lilting visual ballet, and is well worth seeing for its vision of the constancy of love. A-II (G)

You'll Like My Mother (1972) When her husband is killed in Vietnam, the pregnant widow (Patty Duke) visits her mother-in-law but is met with unaccountable hostility, is troubled by a menacing man lurking in the shadows and gradually realizes she is being kept a prisoner in the creaky old mansion. Directed by Lamont Johnson, the twisting plot of this tight little mystery thriller offers a goodly number of chills and shocks. A-III (PG)

You're a Big Boy Now (1967) Wacky comedy about young man (Peter Kaster) who, in trying to make the transition from adolescence to independence from overbearing father (Rip Torn) and clinging mother (Geraldine Page), gets his own apartment and becomes infatuated with an actress (Elizabeth Hartman). Directed by Francis Ford Coppola, its exaggerated comic style does not always succeed, especially with some of the erotic elements. A-IV (br)

You're Lying (1973) Powerful Swedish semi-documentary indictment of the inadequacies and outright injustices existing in a penal system that prides itself on being the best in the world. Directed by Vilgot Sjoman, it demonstrates the contradictions between official policy and the actual practice of using prisons to effect social rehabilitation as well as society's indifference to how its prisons actually operate. Excessively explicit treatment of sexual matters. O (nr)

You've Got to Walk It Like You Talk It or You'll Lose That Beat (1971) Director Peter Locke's low-budget story of a confused young man in search of himself (Zalman King) is a witless attempt to satirize the Establishment but all that emerges is a stupefying amount of visual and verbal crudity. O (nr)

Young Americans (1967) Semi-documentary on a national tour of teenage singers presenting a program of show tunes, spirituals, folk songs and traditional melodies. Written and directed by Alex Grasshoff, the material is blended into a pleasant story of the personal interaction between the talented young musicians and the reaction of audiences to the troupe's humor and enthusiasm. A-I (br)

Young Billy Young (1969) Standard Western about the new marshall (Robert Mitchum) of a lawless town who takes the job in order to avenge the killing of his son while befriending a wild youth (Robert Walker) who reminds him of his dead boy. Directed by Burt Kennedy, the story is entirely predictable and the relationship between the older man and the youth is never explored with any depth. Some rather bloody shoot-outs. A-II (G)

Young Couple, A (1971) Familiar French tale of a young couple (Anna Gael and Alain Libolt) who marry, enjoy a rich party-going life but separate when the self-centered wife and the husband cannot reconcile their different visions of life. Directed by Rene Gainville, it is a well-made but somewhat fleeting portrait of early married life and the consequences of infidelity. A-III (nr)

Young Doctors in Love (1982) Stupid spoof of doctor movies and soap operas intermixes sketches and sight gags with a narrative line about the adventures of first-year interns. Directed by Gary Marshall, there are a few good laughs along the way, but excessive vulgarity sours the humor. Some nudity. O (R)

Young Frankenstein (1974) Director Mel Brooks' spoof of the venerable horror classic stars Gene Wilder as an American doctor who inherits the family's Transylvanian estate, with Peter Boyle as the monster whose prodigious sexual appetite provides the one-liner for the movie. Bright spots are Marty Feldman whose pop-eyes are upstaged by his shifting hump and Cloris Leachman as the housekeeper whose name causes horses to whinny. Though generally amusing, with some clever bits and occasionally hilarious moments, it features much vulgarity, verbal and otherwise. A-IV (PG)

Young Girls of Rochefort, The (1967) French musical romance in which false values are nicely ribbed, star-crossed lovers are united and everyday dreams come true when a fair comes to town and two local girls (Catherine Deneuve and Francoise Dorleac) join in the fun. Directed by Jacques Demy, the production has some simple charm but suffers from a static setting, lack of continuity and a surfeit of non-professional singing. A-II (br)

Young Runaways, The (1968) Contrived story of three teenagers who flee abusive home situations and find their fate on their own even worse. Director Arthur Dreifuss treats a significant social subject in a superficial manner, leaving viewers with no clear insight into the reasons or solutions of the problem. Mature themes. A-III (R)

Young Sherlock Holmes (1985) A series of fatal accidents in Victorian London baffle the police but not a student named Sherlock Holmes (Nicolas Rowe) and his school chum John Watson (Alan Cox). Directed by Barry Levinson, Chris Columbus' script gives a convincing account of Holmes' early school days that is entirely in keeping with the character of the master sleuth found in the pages of Arthur Conan Doyle's classic stories. The special effects are spectacular, but never gory or overdone, though some nightmare sequences may frighten young children. A-II (PG-13)

Young Winston (1972) British dramatization of Churchill's memoir, "My Early Life," retells uncritically his own version of his formative years from war correspondent in the Boer War to Parliament, with Simon Ward in the title role. Directed by Richard Attenborough, it excells as a panorama of life in the Empire before World War I, through a succession of tableaux of balls and battles, of parliamentary debates and family discourses. Although not a perfect film, it is a film of idealism and very enjoyable on a number of levels. A-II (PG)

Young World (1966) French movie about the sexual excesses of contemporary youth indulges in needlessly detailed erotic treatment. O (br)

Youngblood (1978) Black youth (Bryan O'Dell) joins a street gang for self-protection and, when the gang takes on the local drug organization, he finds himself on a collision course with his older brother. It is an excessively violent movie whose morality is as muddled as its story line. O (R)

Youngblood (1986) Rob Lowe stars as the young and talented amateur hockey player who must come to terms with the violence of his sport and his determination to be a winner. When turning the other cheek doesn't work, he learns how to be tough but still proves he can outclass the brutes. Nevertheless he can't resist a final display of macho combat to satisfy his critics. Brutality, an explicit nude sex scene and ambivalent values ruin a simple tale about sports ethics for youngsters. O (R)

Your Three Minutes Are Up (1973) Unemployed swinger (Ron Liebman) initiates his younger, hardworking buddy (Beau Bridges) into a series of con games that at first seem easy and fun but they threaten the young man's approaching marriage (to Janet Margolin) and in the end events take an ugly turn. Director Douglas Schwartz introduces some heavy-handed and explicit sex scenes which only compound the problem of its murky underlying morality. O (R)

Your Turn, My Turn (1979) Unpleasant French comedy romance stars Marlene Jobert as the mother of an 8-year-old boy who meets Philip Leotard, the father of a 9-year-old girl, and though encumbered by their perceptive chilen, they begin an adulterous affair. Directed by Francoise Leterrier, the movie's Gallic view of life is not especially amusing despite its frothy treatment. Benign attitude towards adultery. O (nr)

Yours, Mine and Ours (1968) Fact-based story of a Navy widower (Henry Fonda) and a Navy widow (Lucille Ball) who fall in love, get married and merge their 18 children into one big, happy family. Director Melville Shavelson's comedy has predictable but genuinely funny complications such as interrupted honeymoon, identity crises, bathroom lineups, troop-movement planning and buying but it also keeps in touch with human reality. Underneath it all is a gently moving story of love the way it is. Admittedly directed toward popular appeal, it is humorous enough for sophisticated tastes as well. Truly a family picture. A-I (br)

Z

Z (1969) When a leftist minister (Yves Montand) in the Greek government is assassinated, the investigating magistrate (Jean-Louis Trintignant) tries to untangle the shadowy affair in order to find those responsible. The French dramatization directed by Costa-Gavras is a taut political thriller that goes beyond Greek politics and party labels because it is interested in justice and critical of any system of government that justifies criminal acts and violence in attaining its objectives. A-II (PG)

Zabriskie Point (1970) Taking its title from a promontory that overlooks Death Valley, director Michelangelo Antonioni's first movie about America is critical of its ill-treatment of youth and its self-cannibalism through violence and material excess, topped off in an explosive finale. Yet, because the message is expressed largely via cliches, all that it underscores is that perhaps middle-aged filmmakers should avoid making youth-oriented movies about other cultures. Some excessive sexual scenes. O (R)

Zachariah (1971) Director George Englund updates the Western with rock music, hippie garb, the search for identity and a plea for peace, all laced together with self-parody and an incurable romanticism. The two heroes (Don Johnson and John Rubenstein) show the audience that peace, love and friendship are possible in a world of violence, hate and mistrust. Hokey as it sounds, the movie works if given a chance, and its overriding values and goals cannot be dismissed too lightly. A-III (GP)

Zandy's Bride (1974) Gene Hackman plays a rough and tough Western rancher circa 1870 who is finally mellowed by Liv Ullmann, his mail order bride from Minnesota. Though the narrative is disappointingly little more than a disorganized series of scenes between two extreme character types, director Jan Troell re-creates the frontier era with authority, gets excellent performances from his principals and conveys some insights into human relations. Adult material, including a rape. A-III (PG)

Zardoz (1974) British science fiction fantasy set

in 2293 when technology has given the power of eternal life to a single enclave of humans whose paradise is penetrated and ultimately destroyed by a barbarian (Sean Connery) from the Outlands. Director John Boorman's vision of the shapelessness of things to come needs a road map simply to follow the plot and sort out its intended parables. Some violence, confused religious references and brief nudity. A-III (R)

Zatoichi: The Blind Swordsman (see: "Zatoichi's Conspiracy")

Zatoichi Meets Yojimbo (1972) Japanese movie hero Zatoichi (Shintaro Katsu) is a blind masseur whose skill with a stick sword makes him invulnerable to the gangs of cut-throats and samurai bands which inhabit the medieval milieu of his films. Director Kihachi Okamoto pits Zatoichi against Toshiro Mifune's classical characterization of the samurai professional turned free agent in an action fantasy about a violent world where death is only as real as the special effects man can make it. A-III (nr)

Zatoichi's Conspiracy (1974) Director Kimiyoshi Yasuda is back with another adventure of Zatoichi (Shintaro Katsu), the blind, flabby, masseur whose exploits with a cane-sword make him the terror of criminals and equal to a samurai squad. Zatoichi is visiting his home town just as it is taken over by a vicious crook in league with the corrupt bailiff of the district. There is the final showdown in a crescendo of special effects. A-III (PG)

Zelig (1983) Director Woody Allen spoofs the American obsession with celebrity in this comedy about an obscure clerk (also Allen) in the 1920s who wants so desperately to fit in that he develops a malady transforming him physically and mentally into a person quite like whomever he happens to be with. A mildly amusing comedy in which the camerawork of Gordon Willis weaves the Zelig saga into actual historical footage, making for some good sight gags. A-II (PG)

Zeppelin (1971) While the Kaiser's dirigibles bomb London from heights out of range of early biplanes, British intelligence decides to slip a spy into the Zeppelin works where he learns of a secret mission that will destroy British morale decisively. In an old-fashioned plot of wartime adventure, a good cast (Michael York, Marius Goring, Elke Sommer and Alexandra Stewart) are pleasantly relaxed as they go through their paces. Director Etienne Perrier has laced his action with humor, suspense and some quite good special-effects work. A-I (G)

Zero Population Growth (1972) In some brave new world of the future, joy has gone out of life because childbirth has been made punishable by death, though Oliver Reed and Geraldine Chaplin risk all to procreate. Directed by Michael Campus, the movie pretends to be an indictment of 20th-century decadence but is simply a rather plodding exercise whose outcome is ridiculously anticlimactic. Adult theme. A-III (PG)

Zig Zag (1970) George Kennedy plays a man dying of a brain tumor who sets himself up to be convicted of an unsolved crime and arranges through a lawyer (Eli Wallach) that his wife (Anne Jackson) receive the reward offered by the insurance company. Directed by Richard Colla, the story's plot complications become a jumble of events and the incredibly contrived ending makes it not worth the effort. A-II (GP)

Zig Zag (1976) Catherine Deneuve and Bernadette Lafont play slightly talented show girls eager to get ahead, in an erratic French movie directed by Laszlo Szabo, which attempts to tell a tragicomic story against the background of a seedy entertainment world. Graphic sexual depiction. O (R)

Zita (1968) Evocative but flawed French movie of a young girl (Joanna Shimkus) trying to accept the trauma of her beloved aunt's impending death. Though beautifully directed by Robert Enrico, the story is susceptible to the interpretation that maturity is achieved through casual sex. O (M)

Zorro, The Gay Blade (1981) George Hamilton plays the son of Zorro, the legendary righter of wrongs and champion of oppressed peasants in Old California, with a twin brother (Hamilton again) who is a foppish homosexual. Directed by Peter Medak, the one-joke comedy has a lackluster plot, slow pacing and the smiles are few and far between. Occasional mild vulgarity and the homosexual aspect is amiably farcical. A-II (PG)

Z.P.G. (see: "Zero Population Growth")

Appendix

A CHOICE COLLECTION OF FAMILY MOVIES

Not all movies listed below will suit all tastes but there is enough variety to leave no one unsatisfied. Please check the capsule review to determine a movie's suitability for your own family.

SOMETHING FOR EVERYBODY

Adventure

Across the Great Divide
Adventures of the Wilderness Family, The
Africa—Texas Style
Arabian Adventure
Around the World in 80 Days
Batman
Boy Ten Feet Tall, A
Flight of the Doves
Further Adventures of the Wilderness Family
Life and Times of Grizzly Adams, The
Lost Horizon
Maya
Mountain Family Robinson
Night of the Grizzly, The
Sea Gypsies, The
Treasure Island
Wilderness Journey

Animals

Benji
Black Beauty
Black Stallion, The
Black Stallion Returns, The
Born Free
Brighty of the Grand Canyon
Brother of the Wind
Challenge to Be Free
Christian the Lion
Danny
Digby, the Biggest Dog in the World
Elephant Called Slowly, An
For the Love of Benji
Gentle Giant
George!
It's Showtime
Living Free
Magic of Lassie, The
Namu, the Killer Whale
National Velvet
Phar Lap
Ring of Bright Water
Summerdog
Tender Warrior, The

Fantasy

Adventures of Mark Twain, The
Alice of Wonderland in Paris
Blue Bird, The
Captain Nemo and the Underwater City
Charlotte's Web
Dark Crystal, The
Daydreamer, The
Dr. Who and the Daleks
E.T. The Extra-Terrestrial
Fantastic Voyage
Flight of the Navigator
Golden Voyage of Sinbad
Gulliver's Travels Beyond the Moon
Heidi's Song

Jack Frost
Labyrinth
Last Unicorn, The
Mouse and His Child, A
NeverEnding Story, The
Peter Rabbit and Tales of Beatrix Potter
Phantom Tollbooth, The
Pufnstuff
Secret of NIMH, The
Seven Faces of Dr. Lao
Willy Wonka and the Chocolate Factory
World of Hans Christian Anderson, The
Yellow Submarine

Drama

All Things Bright and Beautiful
And There Came a Man
Angel in My Pocket
Battlestar Galactica
Baxter!
Beau Geste
Beford Incident, The
Ben Hur
Big Hand for a Little Lady, A
Boy of Two Worlds
Boy Who Could Fly, The
Boys of Paul Street, The
Chariots of Fire
Cromwell
80 Steps to Jonah
84 Charing Cross Road
Enter Laughing
Fish Hawk
Friendly Persuasion
Gambit
Great Escape, The
Hand in Hand
Joni
Lollipop
Man for All Seasons, A
Maurie
1918

Drama (Continued)

Paper Lion
Railway Children, The
Run Wild, Run Free
Singing Nun, The
Star Trek
Touched by Love
True Grit
Two of Us, The
Victory
Who Says I Can't Ride a Rainbow!
Yearling, The
Yours, Mine, and Ours

Comedy

Bon Voyage, Charlie Brown (and Don't Come Back)
Boy Named Charlie Brown, A
Follow That Bird
Great Muppet Caper, The
Great Race, The
Hello Down There
Man Called Flintstone, The
Mrs. Brown, You've Got a Lovely Daughter
Munster Go Home
Muppet Movie, The
Muppets Take Manhattan, The
Optimists, The
Out-of-Towners, The
Race for Your Life, Charlie Brown, A
Russians Are Coming, the Russians Are Coming, The
Snoopy Come Home
Ten from Your Show of Shows
Those Magnificent Men in Their Flying Machines
Topo Gigio
Trouble with Angels, The
What's Up, Doc?

Musicals

Annie
Boy Friend, The

Chitty Chitty Bang Bang
Doctor Dolittle
Fiddler on the Roof
Finian's Rainbow
Godspell
Goodbye, Mr. Chips
Half a Sixpence
Hello Dolly!
Little Prince, The
Music Man, The
My Fair Lady
Oklahoma!
Oliver!
Scrooge
Sound of Music, The
That's Entertainment
Thoroughly Modern Millie

Religious

Bible, The
Gospel According to St. Matthew, The
Gospel Road
Greatest Story Ever Told, The
Ten Commandments

FOR TEENS AND GROWNUPS TOO

Adventure

Baby: Secret of the Lost Legend
Barbarosa
Crossed Swords
Gray Lady Down
High Wind in Jamaica
Jeremiah Johnson
Scalphunters, The
Shane
Where's Jack?
Will Penny
Windwalker

Fantasy

Close Encounters of the Third Kind
Cocoon
D.A.R.Y.L.
Day of the Dolphin, The
Empire Strikes Back, The
Explorers, The
Fahrenheit 451
Final Countdown
Goonies, The
Hellstrom Chronicle, The
Last Starfighter, The
Legend
Lord of the Rings
Peggy Sue Got Married
Phase IV
Purple Rose of Cairo, The
Return of the Jedi
Silent Running
Star Wars
2001: A Space Odyssey
War Games
Watership Down

Musicals

Camelot
Funny Girl
How to Succeed in Business without Really Trying
Oh! What a Lovely War
1776
Star!
Wiz, The

Humor

Christmas Story, A
Cloak and Dagger
Crocodile Dundee
Ferris Bueller's Day Off
Flim-Flam Man, The
Gods Must Be Crazy, The

Gregory's Girl
Heaven Can Wait
Hero at Large
Hot Millions
How I Won the War
Local Hero
Movie, Movie
Mr. Mom
Popeye
Popi
Radio Days
This Is Spinal Tap
World of Henry Orient, The
Zelig

Drama

Baby Blue Marine
Bang the Drum Slowly
Breaking Away
Capricorn One
Chosen, The
Christmas Tree, The
Coal Miner's Daughter
Conrack
Country
Cross and the Switchblade
Desert Bloom
Dogpound Shuffle
Dreamchild
Dresser, The
Echoes of a Summer
El Super
Escape Artist, The
Fool Killer, The
Great Santini, The
Guess Who's Coming to Dinner
Gypsy Girl
Heartland
Hide in Plain Sight
Junior Bonner
Karate Kid
Karate Kid Part II

Drama (Continued)

Lucas
Manhattan Project, The
Marie
Melody
Mind of Mr. Soames, The
My American Cousin
My Sweet Charlie
Natural, The
Other Side of the Mountain, The
Places in the Heart
Prodigal, The
Separate Peace, A
Stone Boy, The
Taps
Tender Mercies
Test of Love, A
To Sir, with Love
Tree Grows in Brooklyn, A
Trip to Bountiful, The
Up the Down Staircase
Verdict, The
Wait until Dark
Whisperers, The
White Nights
Young Sherlock Holmes

Social Issues

Ballad of Gregorio Cortez, The
Barren Lives
Boat Is Full, The
China Syndrome, The
Fail Safe
Hazel's People
Hell in the Pacific
Killing Fields, The
Missing
Official Story, The
Seven Days in May
Seven Days to Noon
Testament

Trial of the Catonsville Nine, The
Walk in the Sahdow
Without a Trace
Z

Historical

Ballad of a Soldier
Brother Sun, Sister Moon
Darwin Adventure, The
Emigrants, The
Gandhi
Give 'Em Hell, Harry
Gone with the Wind
Henry VIII and His Six Wives
Hoa-Binh
Joe Hill
Lawrence of Arabia
Mohammed, Messenger of God
Molly Maguires, The
New Land, The
Nicholas and Alexandra
Patton
Scott Joplin
Waterloo
Young Winston

Literature

Bostonians, The
Daisy Miller
Doctor Zhivago
Doll's House, A
Europeans, The
Far from the Madding Crowd
Heart Is a Lonely Hunter, The
Islands in the Stream
Julia
Kidnapped
Lord Jim
One Day in the Life of Ivan Denisovich
Passage to India, A
Raisin in the Sun

Literature (Continued)

Saint Joan
Tess
Three Musketeers, The
Tomorrow
War and Peace
Wuthering Heights

WALT DISNEY PRODUCTIONS

Absent-Minded Professor, The
Adventures of Bullwhip Griffin, The
Alice in Wonderland
Amy
Apple Dumpling Gang, The
Apple Dumpling Gang Rides Again, The
Aristocats, The

Bambi
Barefoot Executive, The
Bears and I, The
Bedknobs and Broomsticks
Biscuit Eater, The
Black Cauldron, The
Black Hole, The
Blackbeard's Ghost
Beatniks

Candleshoe
Castaway Cowboy, The
Cat from Outer Space, The
Charley and the Angel
Charlie, The Lonesome Cougar
Cinderella
Computer Wore Tennis Shoes, The

Devil and Max Devlin, The
Don't Look Now
Dumbo

Emil and the Detectives
Escape to Witch Mountain

Fantasia
Fighting Prince of Donegal, The
Follow Me, Boys!
Fox and the Hound, The
Freaky Friday

Gnome-Mobile, The
Great Mouse Detective
Greyfriars Bobby
Gus

Happiest Millionaire
Herbie Goes Bananas
Herbie Goes to Monte Carlo
Herbie Rides Again
Horse in the Gray Flannel Suit, The
Hot Lead and Cold Feet

Incredible Journey, The
Island at the Top of the World, The

Journey of Natty Gann, The
Jungle Book, The

King of the Grizzlies

Lady and the Tramp, The
Last Flight of Noah's Ark, The
Love Bug, The
Lt. Robin Crusoe, U.S.N.

Monkeys Go Home

Napoleon and Samatha
Never a Dull Moment
Never Cry Wolf
Night Crossing
No Deposit, No Return
North Avenue Irregulars, The
Now You See Him, Now You Don't

Old Yeller
One and Only Genuine Original Family Band, The
101 Dalmations
One Little Indian
One Magic Christmas
$1,000,000 Duck
One of Our Dinosaurs Is Missing

Walt Disney Productions (Continued)

Parent Trap, The
Pete's Dragon
Pinocchio

Rascal
Rescuers, The
Return from Witch Mountain
Ride a Wild Pony
Robin Hood

Scandalous John
Shaggy D.A., The
Shaggy Dog, The
Sleeping Beauty
Smith
Snow White and the Seven Dwarfs
Snowball Express
Something Wicked This Way Comes
Song of the South
Superdad
Swiss Family Robinson

Tex
That Darn Cat
Those Calloways
Three Cabelleros
Tonka the Comanche
Trenchcoat
Tron
20,000 Leagues Under the Sea

Ugly Dachshund, The
Unidentified Flying Oddball

Watcher in the Woods, The
Wild Country, The
World's Greatest Athlete, The

ROBERT B. RADNITZ PRODUCTIONS

And Now Miguel
Birch Interval
Dog of Flanders, A

Cross Creek
Hero Ain't Nothin' but a Sandwich, A
Island of the Blue Dolphins
Little Ark, The
Misty
My Side of the Mountain
Part 2, Sounder
Sounder
Where the Lilies Bloom

DOCUMENTARIES

Nature

African Elephant, The
American Wilderness
Animals Are Beautiful People
Blue Water, White Death
Cougar Country
Cry of the Wild
Glacier Fox, The
High, Wild and Free
North Country
Savage Wild
Scuba
World Without Sun

Culture & the Arts

Arthur Rubenstein—Love of Life
Bolshoi Ballet 67
Children of Theatre Street, The
Chronicle of Anna Magdelena Bach, The
Clowns, The
Don Quixote
Edvard Munch
Evening with the Royal Ballet, An
First Position
Hamlet
Homage to Chagall
I Am a Dancer

Culture & the Arts (Continued)

King Lear
La Boheme
Midsummer Night's Dream, A
Mikado, The
Nutcracker, The Motion Picture
Otello
Othello
Pirates of Penzance
Raga
Sea Gull, The
Uncle Vanya

People

Ben-Gurion Remembers
Film Portrait
Finest Hours, The
Holy Outlaw, The
I.F. Stone's Weekly
Idi Amin Dada
Malcolm X
Mother Theresa
Reminiscences of a Journey to Lithuania
Salesman
World of Buckminster Fuller, The
Years of Lightning, Day of Drums

Events

Battle of Britain
Battle of Algiers, The
Deadly Fathoms
Gizmo
Guns of August, The
Harlan County, U.S.A.
In the Year of the Pig
People of the Wind
Ra Expeditions, The
Report from China
Search for Solutions
Sense of Loss, A

Shoah
Sorrow and the Pity, The
Time for Burning, A
To Die in Madrid
Tsar to Lenin
Wall in Jerusalem, A

Pop Music Performances

Concert for Bangladesh
Don't Look Back
Elvis: That's the Way It Is
Johnny Cash: The Man, His World, His Music
Keep on Rockin'
Let It Be
Let the Good Times Roll
Our Latin Thing
Pink Floyd
Save the Children
Soul to Soul
Young Americans

Sports

Black Rodeo
Goal!
Visions of Eight